Writers'
& Artists'
YEARBOOK
2016

Other Writers & Artists titles include

Writers' & Artists' Companions
Series Editors: Carole Angier and Sally Cline
Each title is full of expert advice and tips from bestselling authors.

Crime and Thriller Writing by Michelle Spring and Laurie R. King
Life Writing by Sally Cline and Carole Angier
Literary Non-fiction by Sally Cline and Midge Gillies
Writing Children's Fiction by Yvonne Coppard and Linda Newbery
Writing Historical Fiction by Celia Brayfield and Duncan Sprott
Writing Short Stories by Courttia Newland and Tania Hershman
Novel Writing by Romesh Gunesekera and A.L. Kennedy
Playwriting by Fraser Grace and Clare Bayley

NEW in August 2015

Children's Writers' & Artists' Yearbook 2016

'Take the great advice that's in this *Yearbook*'
David Almond

'Whenever people ask me about how to get their work for children published . . . the first words to come out of my mouth are always: *Children's Writers' & Artists' Yearbook*'
Michael Rosen

You can buy copies from your local bookseller or online at www.writersandartists.co.uk/shop

Writers' & Artists' YEARBOOK 2016

ONE HUNDRED AND NINTH EDITION

THE ESSENTIAL GUIDE TO THE MEDIA AND PUBLISHING INDUSTRIES
The perfect companion for writers of fiction and non-fiction, poets, playwrights, journalists, and commercial artists

B L O O M S B U R Y
LONDON • OXFORD • NEW YORK • NEW DELHI • SYDNEY

Bloomsbury Publishing
An imprint of Bloomsbury Publishing Plc

50 Bedford Square
London
WC1B 3DP
UK

1385 Broadway
New York
NY 10018
USA

www.bloomsbury.com

BLOOMSBURY and the Diana logo are trademarks of Bloomsbury Publishing Plc

British Library Cataloguing-in-Publication Data
A catalogue record for this book is available from the British Library.

ISBN: PB: 978-1-4729-0707-3

2 4 6 8 10 9 7 5 3 1

Typeset by QPM from David Lewis XML Associates Ltd
Printed and bound in Great Britain by CPI Group (UK) Ltd, Croydon CR0 4YY

To find out more about our authors and books visit www.bloomsbury.com. Here you will find extracts, author interviews, details of forthcoming events and the option to sign up for our newsletters.

***Writers' & Artists'* team**
Editor Alysoun Owen
Articles Editor Virginia Klein
Listings Editors Lisa Carden, Rebecca Collins, Lauren Simpson
Editorial assistance Sophia Blackwell (poetry)
Database Manager Martin Dowling
Production Controller Ben Chisnall

A note from the Editor

The Editor welcomes readers to this edition of the *Writers' & Artists' Yearbook.*

One of the great pleasures of editing the *Yearbook* is deciding which writers and experts to invite to share their creative insight and knowledge. This year we have added more new articles than ever before. Together, the articles cover a wide spectrum of styles and genres: poetry – Julia Copus on *Becoming a published poet* (page 325), fiction – Alison Weir on *Writing historical fiction* (page 295) and non-fiction – Rose Prince on *Writing about food* (page 313). But, how do you become a good and a successful writer? How do you get your novel, poem, short story, article or playscript noticed by an editor or an agent? The answer is simple: READ. At least that's the advice that recurs throughout this book. 'Read, read, read ... and read attentively', advises Susan Hill (see *The only book you will ever need*, page 268); Sara Wheeler agrees: '... read all the time' (see *Being a travel writer*, page 317).

As well as being devourers of other people's words, writers are encouraged to WRITE and to practice their art. Ben Schott is 'amazed by the number of would-be writers who aren't always writing', and puts perfecting one's craft at the top of his list (see *On writing: essential advice for writers*, page 265). Self-published author Mel Sherratt concurs: 'Write, write, write,' (see *Being a self-published author*, page 589), while Danny Hahn stresses that a literary translator must be both 'an uncommonly close, sensitive and wise reader' *and* 'a fantastically accomplished and versatile writer' (see *Literary translation*, page 302). Lauren Simpson in *Editing your work* (page 629) recommends striving for editorial excellence and writers are encouraged by Judith Heneghan to make full use of literary events (see *Festivals for writers*, page 481).

We have articles on writing *for* the theatre and writing *about* the theatre. Mike Poulton felt he could produce better translations of classic plays than those he was hearing on stage. In *Bringing new life to classic plays* (see page 367) he advises others on how it can be done. Mark Fisher describes the life and art of the critic in *Writing about theatre: reviews, interviews and more* (page 375).

In our annual round-up of the book market, there is good news from both Tom Tivnan in *News, views and trends in book publishing* (page 128) and Philip Jones in *Electronic publishing* (page 573). Nick Spalding celebrates the range of publishing options open to authors (see *Notes from a hybrid author*, page 593). Illustrators looking for new avenues for their work should consult *Graphic novels: how to get published* (page 252) and *Getting your greeting cards published* (page 463).

Rachel Joyce, writer of this year's *Foreword* (page xi), exhorts you to take yourself seriously as a writer, so that others – readers, and the agents and publishers listed in this book – might do likewise. Good luck.

Alysoun Owen
Editor

All articles, listings and other material in this *Yearbook* are reviewed and updated every year in consultation with the bodies, organisations, companies and individuals that we select for inclusion. To the best of our knowledge the websites, emails and other contact details are correct at the time of going to press.

Dedication

This edition of the *Yearbook* is dedicated to the memory of that great writer Terry Pratchett, who died in March 2015. For many years we have included an article from him on being a successful fantasy author. The advice he gives is a reminder of what writing – at its best and most enjoyable, for both writers and readers – can be.

'Genres are – fantasy perhaps most of all – a big bulging pantry of plots, conceits, races, character types, myths, devices and directions, most of them hallowed by history. You're allowed to borrow, as many will have done before you; if this were not the case there would only ever have been one book about a time machine. [...] They're all just ingredients. What matters is how you bake the cake: every decent author should have their own recipe and the best find new things to add to the mix.'

More than a book

Writers & Artists online

The *Writers' & Artists' Yearbook* is a highly regarded resource within the publishing and wider media industries. In response to the changing world of publishing and to the needs of writers and would-be writers, Writers & Artists also provides online support and information.

The Writers & Artists **website** (www.writersandartists.co.uk) provides up-to-the-minute writing advice, blogs, competitions and the chance to share work with other writers. Our **editorial services** offer guidance from experienced agents and editors on all stages in the development of a manuscript – from proposal, through the various editing phases, up to submission to an agent. To receive our regular **newsletter**, you can sign up at www.writersandartists.co.uk/register.

Our **listings service** can be accessed at www.writersandartists.co.uk/listings. In addition to all the listings in this edition of the *Yearbook*, subscribers are able to search hundreds of listings only available online, including those for *Newspapers and magazines overseas*, a range of *Literary agents* for non-English speaking countries, *Editorial, literary and production services, Government offices and agencies, Picture agencies and libraries*, and a much longer list of *Self-publishing providers* (see page 613).

The Writers & Artists **self-publishing comparison site** (www.selfpubcompare.com) is aimed at writers who are interested in self-publishing their book but are not sure how to get started. It provides an instant, independent set of results to meet each writer's specific self-publishing requirements.

Short story competition

The annual *Writers' & Artists' Yearbook* Short Story Competition offers published and aspiring writers the chance to win a cash prize of £500 and a place on an Arvon residential writing course. In addition, the winner's story will be published on the Writers & Artists website.

To enter the competition, submit a short story (for adults) of no more than 2,000 words, on the theme of 'Ageing' by 15 February 2016 to competition@bloomsbury.com. For full details, terms and conditions, and to find out more about how to submit your entry, visit www.writersandartists.co.uk/competitions.

You might like to read *Writing short stories* on page 241 and *Flash fiction* on page 248 of this *Yearbook*.

ARVON runs three historic writing houses in the UK, where published writers lead week-long residential courses. Covering a diverse range of genres, from poetry and fiction to screenwriting and comedy, Arvon courses have provided inspiration to thousands of people at all stages of their writing lives. You can find out more and book a course online at www.arvon.org.

Contents

Praise for the *Yearbook*

'The best bit of help I can give is to buy a copy of the latest edition of the *Writers' & Artists' Yearbook.*'
Susan Hill

'The one-and-only, indispensable guide to the world of writing.'
William Boyd

'A must for established and aspiring authors.'
The Society of Authors

'Every writer can remember her first copy of the *Writers' & Artists' Yearbook.*'
Rose Tremain

'When you're looking to get published, it's your Bible.'
Patrick Ness

'Everything you need to know about the business of being a writer.'
Lawrence Norfolk

'The wealth of information . . . is staggering.'
The Times

'The definitive resource.'
Writing Magazine

'Packed with tips and professional insight.'
The Association of Illustrators

'As an aspiring author, the best thing you can buy is the *Writers' & Artists' Yearbook* . . . It's the key if you want to get published.'
Samantha Shannon

Foreword

Rachel Joyce is the author of the *Sunday Times* and international bestsellers *The Unlikely Pilgrimage of Harold Fry* (Doubleday 2012), *Perfect* (Doubleday 2013) and *The Love Song of Miss Queenie Hennessy* (Doubleday 2014). *The Unlikely Pilgrimage of Harold Fry* was shortlisted for the Commonwealth Book Prize and longlisted for the Man Booker Prize and has been translated into 34 languages. Rachel was awarded the Specsavers National Book Awards 'New Writer of the Year' in December 2012 and shortlisted for the 'Writer of the Year' 2014. She is also the author of the short story, *A Faraway Smell of Lemon* and the forthcoming short story collection, *A Snow Garden & Other Stories* (Doubleday 2015), as well as a new novel for 2016, *The Music Shop*. Rachel moved to writing after a 20-year career in theatre and television, performing leading roles for the RSC, the Royal National Theatre, the Royal Court, and Cheek by Jowl. She has written over 20 original afternoon plays for BBC Radio 4 and major adaptations for the *Classic Series*, *Woman's Hour*, plus a TV drama adaptation. See more at www.rachel-joyce.co.uk.

When I was 14, I finished my first novel. *Sisters* was short, I admit – possibly no more than 500 words. It was written in couplet form and was autobiographical. During the course of this tale, the older sister (*me*) did everything to save her two younger sisters (*mine*) from unhappiness, general uncleanliness and also TB (we had just made a family visit to Haworth). For lots of reasons, it was important for me to tell that story. But here is the thing – as soon as I finished my book, I wanted more. Even then. I wanted it *published*. I tell you this in a light-hearted way but you have to understand that, when I wrote it, it was not light-hearted. That story was a part of me. It marked who I was – and I wanted people to know that.

I find it hard to explain why it isn't enough for me to write a story and keep it to myself; why I must take it into the world; why I need … *what*? What is it I need? The approval of others? The affirmation? The challenge? The sharing? More and more, I feel that writing is about saying, 'This is how the world seems to me' – followed by a question mark. Writing is a deeply solitary process but it is also, I think, the most generous piece of reaching out. I write in order to understand.

But back to *Sisters*. I didn't mention to anyone I had written a book. I didn't dare. I was a quiet child. I wanted people to know who I was, but I didn't seem to be very good at showing it, at least not in a day-to-day way. I decided to give myself a pseudonym as a writer: Mary Thorntons. *Mary* because I thought it sounded intellectual and *Thorntons* because I made a mistake (I misremembered Thornfield from *Jane Eyre*). I had a hunch Mary Thorntons sounded altogether more writerly than Rachel Joyce.

So I had my BOOK. I had my WRITER'S NAME. What next? I went to my local library in West Norwood because that was where we always went for information. I headed for the reference section (I knew it well) and, with a beating heart, I found a heavy manual called the *Writers' & Artists' Yearbook*. We are talking 1976. I sat alone, where no one could see me, and I opened it.

All I can tell you is that it was like discovering a friend – someone who took my writing seriously and who had practical knowledge in spadefuls. It provided a bridge between my story and the professional world of publishing. I couldn't believe that everything I needed to know was in one book. I wrote down the names and addresses of publishers who were interested in rhyming books (there weren't many). I noted the word count they expected (short) and the kind of accompanying letter. I also discovered that it was important to include my name and address (Mary Thorntons, West Norwood).

Now, 40 years later, I have done at last what I wasn't able or ready to achieve when I was 14. Over the years, I have written in different media: short stories and novels, for radio and television. And here too is a new edition of the *Writers' & Artists' Yearbook* – the 109th to be exact. The book you are holding will give you all the up-to-date information it offered me when I was 14, but it also offers far more. Along with clear detailing of all the contacts you can possibly need, it now provides advice from many well-respected voices in the publishing industry about editing, how to pitch your book, writing for the theatre, copyright law, finance, how to attract the attention of an agent, self-publishing (to name just a few of the topics). If you take your writing at all seriously, and that part of you that wants your writing not only to be finished but to find its place in the world, then … well done, you have come to the right place. There may be a lot of information to be found if you trawl the internet, but here it is all under one roof. Think of yourself as being in the best writers' Christmas market. It is all here.

People ask me sometimes for my advice to a new writer. I say the obvious things: 'Keep going' and 'Don't let go until you really believe you have scraped right down to the bare bones of the truth'. But it might be better to say, 'Take yourself seriously'. If you don't take yourself seriously as a writer then how can you expect anyone else to? Nurture the part of yourself that needs to write. Listen to how it works, what it needs, its ups and downs. Don't think of it as short term. It is a part of you, in the same way that your thoughts are part of you and so is your blood. And when your writing is done, be practical. Know your stuff about the world you are entering. Know where to place what you have done.

Read this book very carefully. Treasure it. Keep it beside you. It is your friend.

Rachel Joyce

Newspapers and magazines
Getting started

Of the titles included in the newspapers and magazines section of this *Yearbook*, almost all offer opportunities to the writer. Many publications do not appear in the lists because the market they offer for the freelance writer is either too small or too specialised, or both. To help writers get started, we offer some guidelines for consideration before submitting material.

Study the market

• The importance of studying the market cannot be overemphasised. It is an editor's job to know what readers want, and to see that they get it. Thus, freelance contributions must be tailored to fit a specific market; subject, theme, treatment, length, etc must meet the editor's requirements. This is discussed further in *Writing for newspapers* on page 3, *Writing for magazines* on page 8 and *Writing features for newspapers and magazines* on page 13.
• Magazine editors complain about the unsuitability of many submissions, so before sending an article or feature, always carefully study the editorial requirements of the magazine – not only for the subjects dealt with but for the approach, treatment, style and length. These comments will be obvious to the practised writer but the beginner can be spared much disappointment by consulting copies of magazines and studying their target market in depth.
• For additional information on markets, see the UK & Ireland volume of *Willings Press Guide*, which is usually available at local reference libraries.

Check with the editor first

• Before submitting material to any newspaper or magazine it is advisable to first contact the relevant editor. The listings beginning on page 16 give the names of editors for each section of the national newspapers. A quick telephone call or email to a magazine will establish the name of the relevant commissioning editor.
• Most newspapers and magazines expect copy to be sent by email.
• Editors who accept postal submissions expect them to be well presented: neatly typed, double spaced, with good margins, on A4 paper is the standard to aim at. Always enclose an sae (stamped addressed envelope) for the return of unsuitable material.
• It is not advisable to send illustrations 'on spec'; check with the editor first. For a list of publications that accept cartoons see page 762.

Explore the overseas market

• For newspapers and magazines outside the UK, visit www.writersandartists.co.uk/listings. For fuller listings, refer to the *Willings Press Guide* Volume for World News Media.
• Some overseas magazine titles have little space for freelance contributions but many of them will consider outstanding work.
• It is worth considering using an agent to syndicate material written for the overseas market. Most agents operate on an international basis and are more aware of current market requirements. Listings for *Syndicates, news and press agencies* start on page 96.

Understand how newspapers and syndicates work

• The larger newspapers and magazines buy many of their stories, and the smaller papers buy general articles, through well-known syndicates. Another avenue for writers is to send printed copies of their stories published at home to an agent for syndication overseas.

• For the supply of news, most of the larger UK and overseas newspapers depend on their own staff and press agencies. The most important overseas newspapers have permanent representatives in the UK who keep them supplied, not only with news of special interest to the country concerned, but also with regular summaries of British news and with articles on events of particular importance. While many overseas newspapers and magazines have a London office, it is usual for freelance contributions to be submitted to the headquarters' editorial office overseas. Listings of *National newspapers UK and Ireland* start on page 16.

Payment

• The *Yearbook* has always aimed to obtain and publish the rates of payment offered for contributions by newspapers and magazines. Many publications, however, are reluctant to state a standard rate, since the value of a contribution may be dependent not upon length but upon the standing of the writer or the information supplied. Many other periodicals prefer to state 'by negotiation' or 'by arrangement', rather than giving precise payment information.

See also...

- *Writing for newspapers,* page 3
- *Writing for magazines,* page 8
- *Writing features for newspapers and magazines,* page 13
- *Regional newspapers UK and Ireland,* page 24

Writing for newspapers

There are still many opportunities for working as a freelance journalist. Kate Mead gives guidance on newspaper writing style, how to promote yourself, finding and pitching stories, and how to survive and thrive in this competitive field.

Over the last few years, the newspaper industry has made the headlines for all the wrong reasons. Post Leveson and with staff cuts and more and more readers going online to read their news, the glory days of Fleet Street have been well and truly consigned to the archives. However, the appetite for news has not diminished and as pressures grow to deliver more to a digitally fluent readership, good freelancers with great ideas are needed more than ever.

The news formula

Writing for newspapers can be quite formulaic and may not suit creative wordsmiths. In press, the story is everything so how you word your article often comes second to the who, what, where, when, why and how in your telling. A trick is to assume that the reader of your well-crafted article will only read the first three lines before moving on. Although slightly disheartening, it is a good assumption to make because the most important facts should be imparted at the top of the story with as much punch and brevity as possible. And if compelling enough, they will read on. This is known in the trade as the 'inverted pyramid' model where the most important details are at the top, more detail about the earlier facts come next, then a good emotive, relevant quote and finally general, background information. Though quite old, the format still exists today for two good reasons. Firstly, your reader can leave the story at any point and still understand it even without the detail and secondly, the less important information can be 'cut from the bottom' by sub-editors.

There are slight variations to this style depending on whether you are writing a news story, feature or analysis. For instance, a feature may start with a quote or anecdotal observation to create atmosphere and the crux of the story is dropped to the third line. And analytical pieces that run alongside a story depart from traditional news-writing altogether. For example, note the different writing styles taken from the *Evening Standard* on 7 and 8 July 2005:

> STUNNED and bloodied survivors today gave graphic accounts of how Tube trains and a bus were blown apart by this morning's explosions.
> *News lead by Jonathan Prynn, Ed Harris and Oliver Finegold, 7 July 2005*

> FOR the 900 Londoners packed inside the Piccadilly line Tube train at morning rush hour, Thursday 7 July began as a normal summer's day.
>
> The train pulled into King's Cross at 8.54am, disgorging commuters and pausing to take on new ones, and then continued on its way towards Russell Square and the West End.
>
> But a few seconds later, without warning, at 8.56am there was a blinding flash followed by an ear-splitting bang as a massive explosion ripped apart the front carriages of the Tube.
> *Feature by David Cohen, 8 July 2005*

Bear in mind that editors and subs will tinker with your copy to fit in with the house style – that is their job after all – so it is best not to get too precious about your wording. But to avoid your article being completely rewritten, familiarise yourself with their style. Some broadsheet newspapers helpfully have their stylebook online.

Starting out

An accredited course by the National Council for the Training of Journalists (NCTJ, www.nctj.com) is the most recognised in the trade. The NCTJ also offers a number of one-day courses for freelancers. The National Union of Journalists (NUJ, www.nuj.org.uk) also provides affordable and comprehensive courses for freelancers, both members and non-members, who are either launching their career or need to brush up their skills. It is a tough call to start out as a freelancer and many journalists opt to work for a newspaper or agency first before going it alone. However, there are freelancers that join the industry from a different work background, such as law or finance, and the specialist knowledge can be invaluable to editors. But equally, it is wise to avoid being too 'niche' when you start out; best to have a broad appeal first to help you get established.

If you have no experience or cuttings to show, it may be difficult to convince editors that you are up to the job. Think about offering yourself for an internship or if you have some experience, apply for paid shifts on news desks. Shifts can be offered to you on a freelance basis and are usually at unsociable hours when staff numbers are at a minimum. It can be a thankless task but meet it with enthusiasm and file some clean, accurate and swift copy and you could make some vital contacts for future pitches.

Setting up and nurturing good relationships with the people who commission your work is essential. When approaching someone new, try to introduce yourself by asking him or her out for a coffee or asking to have a chat on the telephone – but make sure they are not on deadline. Then follow this up with an email about yourself giving them a few lines about pitches you are going to send them. This will help them look out for your email in the future – but make sure you don't leave it too long. Out of sight is very much out of mind in the freelance world.

Once commissioned for the first time, it is vital that you deliver what you offer otherwise your relationship with the editor will suffer. Make sure you have already got the green light from your interviewees and secure any access you need before you pitch it. Honesty is the best policy; offering a picture feature on Area 51 when you have sent one email to the Pentagon is foolish. Similarly, if an editor likes your proposal but asks you for a bit extra or a different angle, agree to research it further but don't promise them the moon on a stick. They are reasonable people and will understand that in the world of news you cannot always predict the outcome. But their patience will wear a little thin if you hand them a story that is a million miles from what you promised.

Promote yourself

In this field, you can't afford to sit and wait for the phone to ring but you can certainly promote yourself to make that more likely to happen. A blog can go further than a CV as it not only showcases your work, knowledge and skills but it also allows you to publish work that was never commissioned. If an editor researching a particular topic finds your article online, it would make sense to commission you. After all, you have proven that you've already done the groundwork.

It is also a good way for people to get in touch with you with potential stories. If they find you have written a similar story to their own, they are more likely to trust you with theirs. There are also online directories that can promote you to contributors and editors alike. One that I particularly like for its affordability and hit rate is the freelance journalist directory(www.journalism.co.uk/freelance-journalist-directory/s41). Another very good site to promote your work is clippings.me. This free website is an online portfolio that allows you to put all your work – links, jpgs, PDFs, video and audio – in one place. And remember to publicise your links with a simple email signature or a link on your Twitter and Facebook accounts.

Finding a story

With the internet full of micro news sites breaking new stories by the minute, it can often seem harder than ever today to find an exclusive or unique story to sell. But don't underestimate your own knowledge and that of the people in your social circles. An inquisitive mind and a gregarious attitude can help you find plenty of stories to pursue; it is just a question of recognising the potential. Every story is 'local' so your own experiences can be a great starting point. With a questioning mind and an appetite for news, your world, no matter how small it may feel, is your oyster.

But equally, information on the web gives you no excuse to stick to your own back yard. Twitter and Facebook can be great for spotting the trends but make sure you go off the beaten track too. If your story crosses continents there can be great forums online to help you share ideas with foreign journalists. For investigative journalists, the International Consortium of Investigative Journalists (ICIJ, www.icij.org) encourages cross-border collaboration and Europe's i-scoop (http://i-scoop.org/scoop) is a great example of how the internet can facilitate good international journalism partnerships. And helpmeinvestigate.com is a good way to connect with people interested in investigating similar issues.

Do your research thoroughly. There is nothing more embarrassing than pitching a great feature idea to a commissioning editor when she published a similar one only six months prior. And keep in mind the bigger picture. Offer a photograph package to your editors; it can help sell your copy and increase your fee too. And if you have found some video footage to go with the story or indeed filmed it yourself, that's even better for their website. It can't hurt to send them your copy with a note of potential follow-ups you could do – you never know, it could lead to another commission in the same week. Utilise the advantage you have of being a freelancer – you can offer the editor something that newspaper staff can't. You have the freedom to explore the stories that interest you and the time to do a good job – and if you do that, you can be guaranteed that more work will come your way.

The source of a story

Forging a good relationship with the people who give you information is essential. As a freelancer you are a business and your reputation precedes you. If you misquote someone or fail to protect their interests, word will spread and you might find it difficult to convince other people of your integrity. Furthermore, you never know when you will need them again in the future. But most importantly, if you create a relationship of trust with them you are less likely to be ripped off. If your source agrees to talk to you and only you, you cannot be gazumped by another freelancer, or indeed allow an editor to hand the job to one of his staffers. It rarely happens but when it does, it hurts your confidence and your bank balance.

In a similar vein, if you are reporting an event or investigating something in the public domain, timing is everything. Have the story in the bag before singing about it, whether that be forming a loyal relationship with a source or covering an event to its completion. That way, it is you and only you that has the story and editors can take it or leave it but they can't steal it.

Pitch perfect

Pitches are tough for even the most seasoned freelancer. They can be intimidating, unpleasant and uncomfortable. But like a medical procedure, vital. Sometimes it can feel like a minefield, so it is best approached as if you are going into battle.

First, know your editor. Are you aiming for the main news pages or looking at the supplements? Is it a feature or a lead story? On a news desk, there is almost no good time to call, especially on a daily, as editors are always busy. So make sure you know the right person to ring beforehand. National newspapers tend to have specific editors for crime, environment, health and politics. Make sure you speak to the right person or you may experience the wrath of a grumpy journalist.

Second, timing is everything. Find out the deadline of the relevant newspaper section you are pitching to. Features and supplements work independently to the news desk so you need to time your pitch long before their deadline and ideally shortly before their conference, where they feed ideas to their managing editors. Bear in mind that editors will have hundreds of emails a day but a voice at the end of the telephone is more memorable, but just make sure you are remembered for the right reason by getting your timing right.

Third, know your strategy. Some people prefer to pitch an idea before doing any work on it at all. I find this risky as you might be commissioned for something you can't deliver. A safer option is to do your interviews and research and write a 'memo' ready to send to your editor with a catchy headline at the top and two or three pull-out quotes to give a flavour of what you have. This helps you to give a confident pitch and you have something to send immediately by email. Sometimes editors will ask for the full article on the agreement that if they publish it you will be paid. This is a conundrum for many freelancers as there is a risk that you put in all the work with no return. However, the risk might be worth taking to help forge a new relationship with an editor. When you become a regular contributor to a newspaper, you are in a stronger position to refuse.

Finally, be brave and go in fighting! Be confident about your story – if you don't believe in it, nobody else will. Calculate a realistic fee based on how much work you put in, where it is likely to be placed and how much space it is likely to fill. Don't be fobbed off that there is no budget for freelancers – if the story is strong enough, the newspaper will pay for it.

Perks and pitfalls

Working from home has its advantages and disadvantages. While you may be grateful to miss a daily commute, having a home office means there is no escape from work. An advantage of being in a newsroom is that you can thrash out ideas with colleagues.

Networking with other freelancers can therefore be a lifeline especially when times are hard so signing up to an online freelance forum or going to events and meet-ups can help relieve the self-employed blues. Remember you are also on your own when things go wrong so it is wise to have some union support. The NUJ and the British Association of Journalists (BAJ, www.bajunion.org.uk) both offer legal benefits and insurance.

Choosing a career as a freelance journalist is by no means the easy option and should come with a health warning. It requires an unlimited resource of tenacity, imagination and hope and can be exhausting. But the reward of a varied and exciting work life means that many veteran freelancers wouldn't dream of returning to 'employment'. These are precarious times for the industry so the real advantage of freelancing is independence – make it your business to adapt with the times and you could be helping to set the news agenda of the future.

Useful contacts

BAJ – British Association of Journalists
website www.bajunion.org.uk
See page 498

Freelance journalist directory
website www.journalism.co.uk/freelance-journalist-directory/s41

ICIJ – International Consortium of Investigative Journalists
website www.icij.org

NCTJ – National Council for the Training of Journalists
website www.nctj.com
See page 516

NUJ – National Union of Journalists
website www.nuj.org.uk
See page 517

Kate Mead was news editor at the Kentish Times Newspaper Group before embarking on her freelance career specialising in crime reporting, investigative journalism and human interest features. She has worked on a freelance basis for the *Sunday Mirror*, *Evening Standard* and Press Association and has had her work commissioned by the *Observer*, *Daily Telegraph*, *Independent*, *Private Eye* and the *Daily Mirror* among others. Read her blog at investik8.wordpress.com.

See also...

- *Getting started*, page 1
- *Writing for magazines*, page 8
- *Writing features for newspapers and magazines*, page 13
- *Regional newspapers UK and Ireland*, page 24
- *Syndicates, news and press agencies*, page 96
- *Copyright questions*, page 667
- *UK copyright law*, page 672
- *The laws of Privacy, Confidentiality and Data Protection*, page 691
- *Defamation*, page 696

Writing for magazines

Hero Brown gives some tips on how to break into the competitive world of writing for magazines.

Ask magazine journalists what it was like working in the Eighties and early Nineties and they'll tell you a tale of fabulous fees and eager commissioning editors. These days, with economic hard times still bruising the UK and magazine advertising revenues badly affected, the climate has changed. Only the leanest, most street-smart of magazines survive. Editors commission more features in-house, they're more diligent at using up their back catalogue of purchased features, and they think more carefully about the features they commission.

What does this mean for journalists trying to write for magazines? Simply that it's tougher now to get your break into the industry. But don't despair. Bright journalists with great ideas are always in demand, so if you're up for the fight, read on.

The Three Commandments

Whether you're writing for magazines, newspapers or online, there are three cardinal rules that you must never forget (or beware the consequences with an irate editor). Not very creative rules, I grant you, and yes, they sound so simple... but you'd be surprised how often journalists fail at this basic hurdle. Make life easy for yourself and ingratiate yourself to the features desk by doing the following:

• **Write to length.** The editor and designer have worked out how many pages of the magazine your feature will take up and given you a word count accordingly – let's say 1,000 words. If you've enjoyed crafting your feature so much that you can't bear to cut back your 2,000-word masterpiece, what you are actually handing over is a feature two magazine pages longer than the one asked of you. Quite an assumption! You've also given the features editor a whole lot of extra work and hassle too, because halving your copy (yes, it will happen!) is not so much an edit but a rewrite as the feature will have to be chopped up and stuck together again, and your beautifully wrought Titian might end up looking like a chipped mosaic.

• **Spell-check your copy.** Spell-checking is just what it says on the tin. But if you don't do it (and scan your grammar while you're at it) it looks lazy and unprofessional.

• **File on time**. This is vital: print-runs don't wait for the muse to hit you. If you file late, the editorial team falls behind, and the sub-editor works late into the night... Not a good idea if you want to be recommissioned.

Work out your strengths

There are so many magazines published in the UK that deciding who to contact for work can feel overwhelming. Rather than panicking and flitting between dozens of potential magazines, take some time to think about what you really want. Which magazines do you like best, and why? What subjects are you most interested in, or knowledgeable about (not necessarily the same thing)? And what are your own writing strengths? If you're good at putting people at ease, perhaps you'll be talented at finding and interviewing case studies. If you're meticulous about detail and like to get under the skin of a story, perhaps investigative features are your strength. If you have great contacts in the fashion industry, then style journalism is a potential place to start.

Let's assume that you've worked out the type of features you'd like to write and the publication that best fits your interest and outlook. Now it's time to research. Buy the magazine regularly and look strategically at the types of articles that appear – generally, there's a format that will be repeated in each issue. For example, women's glossies broadly tend to include a celebrity interview, features on health, beauty, something news-led, an emotional case-study feature and perhaps a first-person viewpoint. Work out why a certain feature exists, and then pitch for that slot. Read rival magazines too – it's no good pitching an idea that was in another publication the previous month.

Work out the lead times for magazines – often they work two months ahead, so any ideas you pitch will have to be at least that far in advance or they won't be relevant. Stay up to date with news, search the internet, view potential stories from unusual angles. If an idea has already been written, look at it from the reverse; see if there's a different spin you can put on it to make it more relevant or fresh.

Pitching your idea

As in other industries, experience is important in journalism, and brilliant as you undoubtedly are, you're unlikely to get the *Vogue* cover story at your first stab (or your second!). If you haven't been published before, or only a little, you need patience, perseverance and some tenacity. There are some simple ways to help yourself to reach your goal. Before you pitch your idea, do yourself a favour and find out who edits the magazine section you want to write for. Trust me when I say it's very irritating for busy editors to be asked by writers who they should send their ideas to. If you can't be bothered to research that, an editor will wonder what else you can't be bothered to research properly.

When you pitch the idea, you can telephone, email or, if you're being super gung-ho, text (good luck with that one!). Personally, I'd be wary of cold-calling your feature proposal. If you catch an editor on a bad day he or she might not give you a decent chance to explain your idea. Perhaps the safer route is to send a brief synopsis of your idea via email. A couple of paragraphs is ample, but make sure you include evidence of why the idea is new, different, worth publishing – it shows you've already taken time to research the feature, and instils confidence. Use a headline and strapline to 'sell' the synopsis – it's a great way of getting an editor to visualise the piece in the magazine.

Once you've emailed your idea, try to be patient. The desire to check your email hourly to see if you've had a response will leave you slumped and disconsolate within days (I know, I used to do it myself). The reality is that, unlike newspapers with their fast turnarounds, magazines often only have features meetings weekly or even fortnightly so it's unlikely you'll hear back immediately. Simply check the relevant editor has received your proposal once you've emailed it, ask when the next features meeting will be held and then if you can't stand the wait, call afterwards to hear the verdict.

Common sense

If you've been researching a great idea, the last thing you want to happen is for it to be stolen from you. However, it's counter-productive to be too coy about your ideas. From the editor's point of view, it's impossible to commission an idea that's padlocked in a lead box. For the writer, the danger is that refusing to divulge your idea properly leaves you sounding paranoid or pretentious, and therefore more trouble than you're worth. If you respect the publication, the odds are you'll also be able to respect its editors, but if you still feel uncomfortable about handing over the crown jewels, perhaps do some research on the journalists you best trust before getting in touch. Don't forget that you will have an email record and timeline of your correspondence as a protection against someone taking your idea.

Close, but no cigar

Be prepared that if you're pitching an idea to a magazine but have no published work to date, it's possible (though by no means inevitable) that you won't be commissioned straight away. Assuming you have piqued the editor's interest, one of two things may happen. Firstly, if the idea is of interest, you may be offered a fee for the idea. This means you'll get paid an agreed amount, but the editor will get someone more experienced to write it. If you have lots of ideas, this can be a good way to make money and work your way into an editor's little black book.

The other option is that you may be asked to write the feature 'on spec'. In other words, the editor likes your idea but wants you to write and submit the feature before deciding if it's well written enough to go in the magazine. You are perfectly within your rights to politely decline and take your feature to other publications – the editor will understand fully. If other editors offer the same response, you can either see it as a shameful affront on your journalistic integrity, or you can shake your brain into action and see it for what it is – an opportunity.

If you're starting out, you need to show confidence in your own ability and take every chance you can find to get published. Even if the feature doesn't quite hit the mark, you'll get free advice on how to improve and perhaps another shot with the same editor. If you agree to write on spec, it's worth asking at this early stage what the fee would be if your feature is accepted. This will allow you to work out whether you want to do the work involved, and also gives you peace of mind that you have a written agreement (an email confirmation is fine) that you will be paid, should your feature be published.

If you do happen to be commissioned in full from the beginning, make sure you have a contract. This is sent from the magazine, stating your name, address, feature you're writing, fee that you're being paid and deadline. Usually you just sign it, send it back to the magazine and keep a copy.

Make yourself indispensable

Work experience, though usually embarked upon for love not money, is an excellent way of giving yourself a head start in journalism, and magazines always seem to find room for an extra pair of hands to help at the coal face. Competition is fierce, so you need to work your contacts, beautify your CV and make a compelling argument for why it should be you rather than the 300 other journalists who deserve an internship.

If you make it into the building, well done, you're halfway to your goal. Next, make sure you're super-nice at all times, never balk at making tea, grit your teeth through any casual condescension, and trust me, eventually you'll be given the chance to write something. Even if it's 150 words in the news section, suddenly you're a published journalist and your prospects immediately perk up. Editors can see you have staying power, persistence and potential. Hopefully you've also made some useful contacts, not just at your magazine but at the magazine next door, and the ones above and below your floor.

Get connected

If you've had a couple of commissions, fantastic. Now's the time to set yourself up on LinkedIn (www.linkedin.com) and make formal connections with the editors you've dealt with. A whole swathe of magazine editors will be able to see the publications you've written for, and what sort of person you're like to deal with. Gorkana (www.gorkana.com) is another great resource for journalists. There's a whole section on magazine jobs, permanent and freelance, from glossies to weeklies, style to sports, plus a massive PR directory if you need help with specific stories. Just register for regular updates.

You'll need an online presence too. The days of lugging around a plastic file of yellowing clippings is long gone. If you're already published, set up a simple website to showcase your work. It will look slight at first, but it only takes a few good commissions to look more beefy.

Blogging

Blogging is another simple but effective way to showcase your writing. A couple of years ago I started a blog called Muddy Stilettos – 'the urban guide to the countryside' around Buckinghamshire/Oxfordshire where I live. It's become a whopping big advert for my writing and I've won a lot of commissions off the back of it. So again, be strategic. Think about the publications you want to write for and tune your blog accordingly to make it a must-read. Find out about writing with SEO (search engine optimisation), tagging and social media in mind. If you end up writing for online magazines, these are all skills that will help you get commissioned or taken on permanently.

Negotiating fees

Unless you're a big name journalist, too much foot-stomping about money will just result in a weary sigh from your editor who will probably remind you of your relative inexperience. Feature fees are often worked out on word count – generally it's around £300 per 1,000, but it entirely depends on the publication and the editor involved. Sometimes it's a flat fee for a certain feature slot and there's no getting around it. Of course, there's nothing to stop you asking nicely for an extra £50 or £100 if you think the fee is too low – your editor may well respect you for it. If there's some travel involved, that can be a legitimate way to bolster the money.

As you become more established, you may feel more comfortable negotiating a higher rate. It's entirely a personal decision and you'll sense when you've pushed it as far as you can. If you really feel you've been taken for a ride, you can get in touch with the National Union of Journalists to find out the minimum freelance rates you can expect. However, if you talk to other journalists, most will regale you with stories of early work written for little money, just for the experience. In a sense, the experience is the fee and it really is valuable in its own right.

Diversify or specialise?

Many journalists enjoy researching and writing about lots of different subjects, and find the idea of being a specialist – for example, a health or interiors journalist – limiting. But there are definite benefits of focusing on a single area in journalism. Namely, if you become the expert, you are in demand. And if you're in demand, your rates are substantially higher. Eventually, you may be able to move into different media if you so wish, such as television and radio, and at that point, ironically, you may well be able to diversify into other areas. It may seem premature to be thinking about this if you're only just getting to the point of being published, but it's worth considering now in terms of pitching ideas and gaining contacts in the right areas. If you're not sure, and want to go with the flow, that's OK too.

If you're still not having any luck...

Ask for help. A good editor will take a minute out of their day to explain to you exactly what they need and why you are not offering the right story. He or she may suggest other publications that better suit your style of writing – maybe they see a quality in you that you can't yet see yourself. Don't lose confidence but keep an open mind, and whatever you do, keep writing, keep pitching ideas, keep networking. With talent and a sprinkle of luck, that magical magazine commission will arrive in the end.

Hero Brown is a former magazine editor at the *Independent on Sunday* and deputy editor of *Red* magazine. She now freelances for *Marie Claire, Red*, the *Observer* and the *Sunday Telegraph* among others. Read her blog at www.muddystilettos.co.uk.

See also...

- *Writing for newspapers*, page 3
- *Writing features for newspapers and magazines*, page 13
- *Marketing yourself online*, page 602
- *Copyright questions*, page 667
- *UK copyright law*, page 672
- *The laws of Privacy, Confidentiality and Data Protection*, page 691
- *Defamation*, page 696

Writing features for newspapers and magazines

Merope Mills outlines a route to success for prospective feature writers to follow.

Newspapers and magazines are experiencing their most profound change in a century. Every title – be it broadsheet, tabloid or glossy magazine – is finding its way in these increasingly digital times. It's a revolution that is both frightening and exciting in equal measure. ABC figures are largely in decline but online 'unique users' are, mostly, on the up. Feature writers these days can reach enormous audiences from around the world, but finances at many titles have never been tighter. For several years now, budgets have been cut, staff numbers slashed and freelancers' contracts have been terminated. But just when you think it's all doom and gloom for print, there are unexpected success stories – such as the launch of the *Independent's* sister title *i*; the launch of the free magazines *Stylist* and *ShortList*, and the huge popularity of the now free *Evening Standard*.

No one could accurately predict what shape the industry will take a few years from now, but one thing is for sure: every title needs great writers, ideas and well-written content. But be it for the print or online arm of its operation, making the right approach, especially if you are unknown to an editor, is more essential than ever.

Starting out

If you're new to writing, the best thing you can do is play to your strengths. Do your friends tell you your emails make them fall off their chairs laughing? Then maybe a humorous column beckons. Do you have specialist knowledge? A green-fingered writer might be able to spot a gap in the market in a gardening title, for example. When starting out in journalism, it is often best to stick to factual journalism that you can write about entertainingly. Most comment and analysis columnists these days are personalities who already carry authority – novelists, television celebrities or journalists who have built up a reputation across many years. If you're at the start of your career, your opinion (though extremely valid) will count for very little unless it's backed up by something solid. The majority of newspaper and magazine freelancers are feature writers as news reporters tend to be on staff.

The internet

As a freelance writer, the internet is your friend. A newspaper or magazine has a finite number of pages and therefore a limited number of people that can write for it. Its online equivalent, on the other hand, can accommodate many more voices. If you have a niche subject and a valid angle on a story and the newspaper or magazine editor can't accommodate you in print, they may be able to include your piece online.

If you already have your own blog, so much the better. In the newspaper industry, it used to be traditional for writers to work their way up the ladder through local papers. Today, the talent seems increasingly to come from the internet. Its advantages are plain: a writer with a blog has a stash of readily available, easily accessible cuttings that clearly establish their identity. Better still for an editor, if it's a good blog it may even have built up its own raft of followers who would keenly follow the blogger if they were to shift to print.

The rise of Twitter presents endless opportunities for the freelance writer. The trick is learning how to exploit it. The master at this, in my opinion, is the freelance writer Sali Hughes – who appears regularly in womens' magazines such as *Red* and *Grazia*, as well as writing comment pieces for the *Guardian*. When I found her on Twitter she seemed smart and funny, so I became one of her many thousands of followers. Eventually, off the back of that digital relationship, I hired her for the beauty column in *Weekend*. She told me that Twitter is invaluable to her freelance career: one of her editors will see something she's tweeted and then ask her to write a longer feature on the subject. She is also comfortable having conversations with her readers – both on Twitter and 'below the line' (with people who comment on her column). Embracing new technology and fostering a community of fans in this way is a fantastic example of how to make social media work for you.

Ideas

Good ideas are the essence of a good journalist. But you must avoid the obvious. Don't write to a magazine or newspaper editor suggesting an interview with Madonna – it's likely they've already had that idea and probably aren't casting around for writers. If you're just starting out, think laterally. Look in the less obvious sections or supplements for columns that an editor might struggle to fill. In a travel magazine or newspaper travel section, for example, you probably won't be able to bag a 2,000-word commission on a Maldives beach holiday, but there may be a small regular section on B&Bs or budget holidays around the UK that grander, established writers probably won't be pitching for. Don't be shy of writing about yourself and your own experiences. Again, the rise of the internet means that newspapers and magazines increasingly see the value of readers' stories and contributions. Look for those 'first person' slots and think if you've got a good personal story that would suit. From tiny acorns like that, whole careers can grow. Once you've established contact and written something, however small, bigger things may well flourish.

Respond quickly to time-sensitive ideas that are the lifeblood of newspaper features and weekly magazines, and if there is something in the news or something trending on Twitter that you think you can spin a feature out of – act fast. When something is big news or goes viral and you have an idea, get in quick – before someone beats you to it.

Contacting the publication

Whether you are published or unpublished, the most important thing is to write a convincing email or letter. Keep your idea succinct – no more than two paragraphs. (Think of it like the newspaper or magazine's standfirst. On publication, they have to sell the idea to the readers in a few brief sentences – so you should be able to do the same.) If you've written before, include a few links to your most relevant work. Lots of people tell me they write for the *Guardian*, but all too often I find myself searching the archive for their byline, never to find it. It's so much easier to point to your work within your pitch.

It sounds obvious, but make sure your idea is right for the publication you're contacting. Don't blanket-email every title you can think of with the same idea, hoping that somewhere it will stick. It's good for an editor to know that you're familiar with their product and that you're suggesting an idea specifically for their section and readership. I get way too many ideas that are a completely wrong fit for the *Guardian*. It's a waste of everybody's time.

Above all, the most important thing you can do is *read* the publication you're pitching to, before getting in contact.

It's a writer's instinct to send things to the editor of the publication, but there's often someone else who will consider your idea quicker and give you an answer. Perhaps it's the deputy editor, the commissioning editor or the features editor. If it's a more specific idea – to do with fashion, health or food, for example – find out who is in charge of that area and contact them. Make a call first to see who the best person to receive your pitch is, if you're not sure. Always address them by name. If you can't be bothered to write a personal email, it doesn't suggest you're likely to be a thorough journalist.

Style

Again, read the publication, and writers you particularly admire. They might be owned by the same company – Murdoch's News International – but there's a world of difference between writing for the *Sun* and *The Times*. They might both deal in celebrity and fashion, but *Grazia* and *Vogue* have completely different styles and sections. You must adapt to the publication, and think about whether the way you've written a piece is suitable.

There is no formula to writing features you can follow for every publication, but it is common to start a piece with some 'colour'. This means beginning a piece by focusing on one anecdote or one particular person's story or quote before broadening it out to explain why their tale matters and what it represents. By the third or fourth paragraph there should really be an explanation of what trend/event/issue your piece is about. The body of any feature should have enough case studies (usually at least three people) to back up the facts and opinions that make the thrust of the piece.

Money

You've had an idea accepted – now what? The first thing to do is agree a fee. Most commonly you will be offered the publication's lineage fee (a standard rate, paid by the word). This can vary widely, so make sure you're happy with this before you start. The National Union of Journalists (www.nuj.org.uk) offers a guide to freelance rates that is worth checking. Also make it clear if you will be submitting expenses receipts and give a rough estimate of what these might be, so your editor can budget for them. Establish who owns copyright beforehand, in case you want to sell second rights to another publication. Having said that, most titles have a syndication service and are more likely to be able to place it elsewhere for you, taking a cut if they do. This is worth investigation.

Deadlines and editing

Don't miss a deadline – even if you are sure that the piece won't be printed imminently. You probably aren't familiar with the title's production schedule and deadlines are usually there for a reason, so don't ignore them. It's also better to be open to your editor's thoughts and rewriting suggestions. Their job is to make the piece better, not worse, so it's in everyone's best interest not to be a prima donna about your copy. If you're not sure of the reason for the changes, just ask.

Breaking into the industry isn't easy, but writing for newspapers and magazines can have many rewards – from meeting interesting people, to seeing your name in print for the first time, to receiving a cheque for your first published piece of work. All you need is a nice style, some good ideas and a little bit of luck!

Merope Mills is Executive Editor of the *Guardian* and Editor of the Saturday *Guardian* . She was formerly editor of the *Guardian*'s *Weekend* magazine.

National newspapers UK and Ireland

Daily Express

Northern & Shell Building, 10 Lower Thames Street, London EC3R 6EN
tel 020-8612 7000
email news.desk@express.co.uk
website www.express.co.uk
Editor Hugh Whittow
Daily Mon–Fri 55p, Sat 85p
Supplements **Daily Express Saturday**

Exclusive news; striking photos. Leader page articles (600 words); facts preferred to opinions. Payment: according to value.

Deputy Editor Michael Booker
Diary Editor Jack Teague
Environment Editor John Ingham
Fashion & Beauty Editor Mernie Gilmore
Features Editor Fergus Kelly
News Editor Geoff Maynard
Online Editor Emily Fox
Political Editor Macer Hall
Sports Editor Duncan Wright
Travel Editor Jane Memmler
Women's Editor Mernie Gilmore

Daily Express Saturday Magazine

Editor Graham Bailey
Free with paper

Daily Mail

Northcliffe House, 2 Derry Street, London W8 5TT
tel 020-7938 6000
email news@dailymail.co.uk
website www.dailymail.co.uk
Editor Paul Dacre
Daily Mon–Fri 60p, Sat 90p
Supplements **Weekend**

Founded 1896.

City Editor Alex Brummer
Commissioning Features Editor Laura Freeman
Diary Editor Sebastian Shakespeare
Education Correspondent Laura Clark
Features Editor Leaf Kalfayan
Foreign Editor Anthony Harwood
Health Editor Justine Hancock
Business & Property Correspondent Louise Eccles
Literary Editor Sandra Parsons
Moneymail Editor James Coney
News Editor Ben Taylor
Picture Editor Craig Gunn
Political Editor James Chapman
US Showbiz Editor Sara Nathan
Head of Sport Lee Clayton
Travel Editor Mark Palmer

Daily Mirror

1 Canada Square, Canary Wharf, London E14 5AP
tel 020-7293 3000
email mirrornews@mirror.co.uk
website www.mirror.co.uk
Editor Lloyd Embley
Daily Mon–Fri 55p, Sat 70p
Supplements **The Ticket, We Love TV**

Top payment for exclusive news and news pictures. Freelance articles used, and ideas bought: send synopsis only. Unusual pictures and those giving a new angle on the news are welcomed; also cartoons. Founded 1903.

Business Editor Graham Hiscott
Executive Features Editor Shiraz Lalani
Health Correspondent Editor Andrew Gregory
News Editor Barry Rabbetts
Picture Editor Ben Jones
Political Editor Jason Beattie
Sports Editor Dominic Hart
US Editor Chris Bucktin

Daily Record

1 Central Quay, Glasgow G3 8DA
tel 0141 309 3000
email reporters@dailyrecord.co.uk
London office 1 Canada Square, Canary Wharf, London E14 5AP
tel 020-7293 3000
website www.dailyrecord.co.uk
Daily Mon–Fri 50p, Sat 70p
Supplements **Saturday, Seven Days, Living, TV Record, Road Record, Recruitment Record, The Brief, The Winner**

Topical articles, from 300–700 words; exclusive stories of Scottish interest and exclusive colour photos.

Editor Murray Foot
Assistant Editor Gordon Robertson
Features Editor Melanie Harvey
News Editor Kevin Mansi
Sports Editor Austin Barrett

Saturday

Free with paper
Lifestyle magazine and entertainment guide. Reviews, travel features, shopping, personalities. Payment: by arrangement. Illustrations: colour.

Daily Star

Express Newspapers, Northern & Shell Building, 10 Lower Thames Street, London EC3R 6EN
tel 020-8612 7000
email news@dailystar.co.uk
website www.dailystar.co.uk
Editor Dawn Neesom
Daily Mon–Fri 40p, Sat 60p
Supplements **Hot TV, Seriously Football**

Hard news exclusives, commanding substantial payment. Major interviews with big-star personalities; short features; series based on people rather than things; picture features. Payment: by negotiation. Illustrations: line, half-tone. Founded 1978.

Music Editor Kim Carr
Deputy Sports Editor Andy Rose
Deputy Editor (news) John McJannet

Daily Star Sunday

Express Newspapers,
The Northern and Shell Building,
10 Lower Thames Street, London EC3R 6EN
tel 020-8612 7424
website www.dailystar.co.uk/sunday
Editor Peter Carbery
Sun £1
Supplements **OK! Extra**

Opportunities for freelancers.

Daily Telegraph

111 Buckingham Palace Road, London SW1W 0DT
tel 020-7931 2000
email dtnews@telegraph.co.uk
website www.telegraph.co.uk
Editor Chris Evans
Daily Mon–Fri £1.40, Sat £2
Supplements **Gardening, Motoring, Property, Review, Sport, Telegraph Magazine, Travel, Weekend, Your Money**

Articles on a wide range of subjects of topical interest considered. Preliminary letter and synopsis required. Length: 700–1,000 words. Payment: by arrangement. Founded 1855.

Deputy Editor Allister Heath
Executive Editor Ben Clissitt
Arts Editor-in-Chief Sarah Crompton
Deputy Director of Content Robert Winnet
Director of Lifestyle Jane Bruton
Weekend Editor Ian Macgregor
Assistant City Editor Jonathan Sibun
Head of Technology Matt Warman
Education Editor Graeme Paton
Environment Editor Geoffrey Lean
Fashion Editor Lisa Armstrong
Acting Features Editor Paul Clements
Health Editor Laura Donnelly
Executive Foreign Editor Con Coughlin
Executive Political Editor James Kirkup
TV and Radio Editor Serena Davies

Telegraph Online

email dtnews@telegraph.co.uk
website www.telegraph.co.uk
Daily Free to internet subscribers

Based on the *Daily Telegraph*. Founded 1994.

Telegraph Magazine

Editor Michele Lavery
Free with Sat paper

Short profiles (about 1,600 words); articles of topical interest. Preliminary study of the magazine essential. Illustrations: all types. Payment: by arrangement. Founded 1964.

Financial Times

1 Southwark Bridge, London SE1 9HL
tel 020-7873 3000
email ean@ft.com
website www.ft.com
Editor Lionel Barber
Daily Mon–Fri £2.50, Sat £3
Supplements **Companies & Markets, FTfm, FT Reports, FT Executive Appointments, FT Weekend Magazine, House and Home, FT Money, How To Spend It, FT Wealth, Life & Arts**

One of the world's leading business news organisations, the FT provides premium and essential news, commentary and analysis. More people than ever are readers and subscribers to FT content. The FT aims to make its authoritative, award-winning and independent journalism available to readers anytime, anywhere and on whichever device they may choose.

Deputy Editor John Thornhill
FT.com Managing Editor Robert Shrimsley
News Editor Alec Russell
FT Weekend Editor Caroline Daniel
Business Editor Sarah Gordon
Comment & Analysis Editor Fred Studemann
Associate Editor Michael Skapinker
Economics Editor Chris Giles
Political Editor George Parker
Financial and Assistant Editor Patrick Jenkins
International Affairs Editor David Gardner
Management Editor Andrew Hill
Lex Editor Stuart Kirk
Alphaville Editor Paul Murphy
Foreign and Assistant Editor Roula Khalaf
World News Editor Ben Hall
US Managing Editor Gillian Tett
Executive Newspaper Editor Hugh Carnegy
Asia Editor David Pilling
World Trade Editor Shawn Donnan

The Guardian

King's Place, 90 York Way, London N1 9GU
tel 020-3353 2000
email national@theguardian.com
website www.theguardian.com
Editor Katherine Viner
Daily Mon–Fri £1.60, Sat £2.50
Supplements **Sport, G2, Film & Music supplement, The Guide, Weekend, Review, Money, Work, Travel, Family, Cook**

Few articles are taken from outside contributors except on its feature and specialist pages. Illustrations: news and features photos. Payment: apply for rates. Founded 1821.

Business Editor Fiona Walsh
Commentisfree Editor Natalie Hanman

Deputy Editors David Shariatmadari
Comment Desk Editor Philip Oltemann
Economics Editor Larry Elliott
Education Editor Alice Woolley
Fashion Editor Jess Cartner-Morley
Network Editor Clare Margetson
Head of Media Jane Martinson
Head of Culture Caspar Llewellyn Smith
The Guide Editor Paul MacInnes
Defence & Intelligence Correspondent Ewan MacAskill
National News Dan Sabbagh
Literary Editor Claire Armitstead
*Head of Technology*Jemima Kiss
Head of Politics Patrick Wintour
Head of Society, Health, Education Patrick Butler
Review Editor Lisa Allardice
Society Editor Alison Benjamin
Head of Sport Ian Prior
Music Editor Michael Hann
Head of Travel Andy Pietrasik

theguardian.com/uk
website www.theguardian.com/uk
Director of Digital Strategy Wolfgang Blau

Weekend
Editor Melissa Denes, *Commissioning Editor* Abigail Radnor
Free with Sat paper
Features on world affairs, major profiles, food and drink, home life, the arts, travel and leisure. Also good reportage on social and political subjects. Illustrations: b&w photos and line, cartoons. Payment: apply for rates.

Herald

Herald & Times Group, 200 Renfield Street, Glasgow G2 3QB
tel 0141 302 7000
email news@theherald.co.uk
English office 58 Church Street, Weybridge, Surrey KT13 8DP
tel (01932) 821212
website www.heraldscotland.com
Editor Magnus Llewellin
Daily Mon–Fri £1, Sat £1.30

Articles up to 1,000 words. Founded 1783.
Arts Editor Keith Bruce
Business Editor Ian McConnell
Diary Editor Ken Smith
Senior Features Writer Barry Didcock
Digital Editor Calum MacDonald
News Editor Ian Marland
Deputy Sports Editor James Morgan

Independent

Northcliffe House, 2 Derry Street, London W8 5HF
tel 020-7005 2000
email newseditor@independent.co.uk
website www.independent.co.uk
Editor Amol Rajan
Daily Mon–Fri £1.40, Sat £1.80
Supplements **Monday Sport, Saturday Sport, Radar, Traveller, The Independent Magazine**

Occasional freelance contributions; preliminary letter advisable. Payment: by arrangement. Founded 1986.
Arts Editor David Lister
Editor of i Oliver Duff
City Editor Jim Armitage
Comment Editor Simon O'Hagan
Education Editor Richard Garner
Features Editor Rebecca Armstrong
Foreign Editor David Wastell
Deputy Editor Dan Gledhill
Literary Editor Arifa Akbar
Assistant Editor & Media Editor Ian Burrell
Head of Pictures Sophie Batterbury
Political Editor Andrew Grice
Sports Editor Simon Rice
Head of Travel Ben Ross

Independent Magazine
email magazine@independent.co.uk
Free with Sat paper
Profiles and illustrated articles of topical interest; all material commissioned. Preliminary study of the magazine essential. Length: 500–3,000 words. Illustrations: cartoons; commissioned colour and b&w photos. Payment: by arrangement. Founded 1988.

Independent on Sunday

2 Derry Street, London W8 5HF
tel 020-7005 2000
website www.independent.co.uk
Editor Lisa Markwell
Sun £2.20
Supplements **Sport, The New Review, Arts & Books**

News, features and articles. Illustrated, including cartoons. Payment: by negotiation. Founded 1990.
Arts Editor Hugh Montgomery
Deputy Editor James Hanning
Literary Editor Katy Guest
Head of Pictures Sophie Batterbury
Political Editor Jane Merrick
Sports Editor Matt Tench

New Review
tel 020-7005 2000
Editor Mike Higgins

Free with paper
Original features of general interest with potential for photographic illustration. Material mostly commissioned. Length: 1,000–5,000 words. Illustrations: transparencies. Payment varies.

Irish Examiner

Linn Dubh, Assumption Road, Blackpool, Cork, Republic of Ireland
tel +353 (0)21 4272722 (newsroom)

email news@examiner.ie
website www.irishexaminer.com
Editor Tim Vaughan
Daily Mon–Fri €2, Sat €2.20

Features. Material mostly commissioned. Length: 1,000 words. Payment: by arrangement. Founded 1841.

Executive Editor (news and digital) Dolan O'Hagan
Features Editor Vickie Maye
Picture Editor Jim Coughlan
Sports & Deputy Editor Tony Leen

Irish Independent

27–32 Talbot Street, Dublin 1, Republic of Ireland
tel +353 (0)1 7055333
email info@independent.ie
website www.independent.ie
Editor Fionnan Sheahan
Daily Mon–Sat €1.90, Sat €2.30

Special articles on topical or general subjects. Length: 700–1,000 words. Payment: editor's estimate of value.

Business Editor Maeve Dineen
Education Editor Katherine Donnelly
Weekend Review Editor Frank Coughlan
News Editor Kevin Doyle
Executive Editor (sport) Dave Courtney
Motoring Editor Eddie Cunningham
Health Correspondent Eilish O'Regan
Security Editor Tom Brady
Technology Editor Adrian Weckler
Associate Editor Dearbhail McDonald

The Irish Times

The Irish Times Building, PO Box 74,
24–28 Tara Street, Dublin 2, Republic of Ireland
tel +353 (0)1 6758000
email newsdesk@irishtimes.com
website www.irishtimes.com
Editor Kevin O'Sullivan
Daily Mon–Fri €2, Sat, €2.50
Supplements **The Irish Times Magazine (Sat), Health + Family (Tue), Business (Daily), The Ticket (Fri), Go Travel (Sat), Sport (Mon, Wed, Sat)**

Mainly staff-written. Specialist contributions (800–2,000 words) by commission on basis of ideas submitted. Payment: at editor's valuation. Illustrations: photos and line drawings.

Deputy Editor Denis Staunton
Business Editor John McManus
Arts Editor Laurence Mackin
Acting Education Editor Deirdre Falvey
Foreign Editor Chris Dooley
Features Editor Conor Goodman
Foreign Policy Editor Patrick Smyth
News Editor Roddy O'Sullivan
Picture Editor Frank Miller
Political News Editor Arthur Bessley
Picture Editor David Sleator or Frank Miller
Communities Editor David Labanyi
Home Page Editor Paddy Logue
Sports Editor Malachy Logan

The Irish Times on the Web

website www.irishtimes.com
Digital Development Editor Hugh Linehan
Breaking News Editor David Labayani
Online Sports Editor Noel O'Reilly

Mail on Sunday

Northcliffe House, 2 Derry Street, London W8 5TT
tel 020-7938 6000
email news@mailonsunday.co.uk
website www.mailonsunday.co.uk
Editor Geordie Greig
Sun £1.50
Supplements **You, EVENT**

Articles. Payment: by arrangement. Illustrations: line, half-tone; cartoons. Founded 1982.

Arts Editor Dominic Connolly
City Editor Simon Watkins
Books Editor Marilyn Warnick
Deputy Features Editor Nicholas Pyke
Literary Editor Susanna Gross
News Editor David Dillon
Picture Editor tbc
Political Editor Simon Walters
Sports Editor Alison Kervin

Financial Mail on Sunday

tel 020-7938 6984
Part of main paper
City, industry, business, and personal finance. News stories up to 1,500 words. Payment: by arrangement. Full colour illustrations and photography commissioned.

EVENT

Editor Gordon Thomson
Free with paper
Fresh and exclusive take on celebrity, film, music, TV and radio, books, theatre, comedy, food, technology and cars. Founded 2013.

You

Editor Sue Peart, *Deputy Editor* Catherine Fenton
Free with paper
Women's interest features. Length: 500–2,500 words. Payment: by arrangement. Illustrations: full colour and b&w drawings commissioned; also colour photos.

Morning Star

(formerly Daily Worker)
People's Press Printing Society Ltd,
William Rust House, 52 Beachey Road,
London E3 2NS
tel 020-8510 0815
email reception@peoples-press.com
website www.morningstaronline.co.uk
Editor Richard Bagley

Daily Mon–Sat £1

Newspaper for the labour movement. Articles of general interest. Illustrations: photos, cartoons, drawings. Founded 1930.

Arts & Media Editor Cliff Cocker
News Editor Adrian Roberts
Political Editor John Haylett
Sports Editor Greg Leedham
Features Editor Ros Sitwell

Observer

Kings Place, 90 York Way, London N1 9GU
tel 020-3353 2000
email news@observer.co.uk
website http://observer.theguardian.com/
Editor John Mulholland
Sun £2.90
Supplements **The Observer Magazine, The New Review, Sport, Observer Food Monthly, Observer Tech Monthly, The New York Times International Weekly**

Some articles and illustrations commissioned. Payment: by arrangement. Founded 1791.

Economics Editor Heather Stewart
Consumer Affairs Correspondent Lisa Bachelor
Assistant Editor (comment) Robert Yates
Fashion Editor Jo Jones
Assistant Editor (national & international news) Julian Coman
News Editor Lucy Rock
Books Editor Lisa O'Kelly
Oberver Food Monthly Editor Allan Jenkins
Observer Tech Monthly Deputy Editor Ian Tucker
Picture Editor Greg Whitmore
Political Editor Toby Helm
Readers' Editor Stephen Pritchard
Sports Editor Matthew Hancock
The New Review Editor Jane Ferguson

Observer Magazine

tel 020-3353 2000
email magazine@observer.co.uk
Editor Ruaridh Nicoll
Free with paper

Commissioned features. Length: 2,000–3,000 words. Illustrations: first-class colour and b&w photos. Payment: NUJ rates; see website for details.

Observer Online

website http://observer.theguardian.com/

People

(formerly Sunday People)
1 Canada Square, Canary Wharf, London E14 5AP
tel 020-7293 3601
email mirrornews@mirror.co.uk
website www.mirror.co.uk
Sun £1.20
Supplements **Take it Easy**

Exclusive news and feature stories needed. Investigative and campaigning issues. Features and human interest stories as speciality. Strong sports following. Payment: rates high, even for tips that lead to published news stories.

Executive Editor Hanna Tavner
Political Editor Nigel Nelson
Sports Editor James Brown

Take it Easy

Editor Samantha Cope
Free with paper

Scotland on Sunday

Orchard Brae House, 30 Queensferry Road, Edinburgh EH4 2HS
tel 0131 620 8620
email reception@scotsman.com
website www.scotsman.com
Sun £1.70

Features on all subjects, not necessarily Scottish. Payment: varies. Founded 1988.

Editor Ian Stewart
Deputy Editor Kenny Farquharson
Sports Editor Graham Bean

Spectrum Magazine

Editor Alison Gray
Free with paper

Scotsman

Barclay House, 108 Holyrood Road, Edinburgh EH8 8AS
tel 0131 620 8620
email reception@scotsman.com
website www.scotsman.com
Editor Ian Stewart
Daily Mon–Fri £1, Sat £1.30
Supplements **Saturday Magazine, Critique, Property, Motoring, Recruitment**

Considers articles on political, economic and general themes which add substantially to current information. Prepared to commission topical and controversial series from proved authorities. Length: 800–1,000 words. Illustrations: outstanding news pictures, cartoons. Payment: by arrangement. Founded 1817.

Arts Editor Roger Cox
Deputy Business Editor Scott Reid
Home Affairs Correspondent Chris Marshall
Foreign Editor Rob Corbidge
ScottishGroup Political Editor Tom Peterkin
Sports Editor Colin Leslie

Scottish Sun

News International Newspapers, Scotland, 6th Floor, Guildhall, 57 Queen Street, Glasgow G1 3EN
tel 0141 420 5200
email exclusive@the-sun.co.uk
website www.thescottishsun.co.uk
Editor Gordon Smart
Daily Mon–Fri 40p, Sat–Sun 50p
Supplements **Fabulous**

Scottish edition of the *Sun*. Illustrations: transparencies, colour and b&w prints, colour cartoons. Payment: by arrangement. Founded 1985.

Sun

The News Building, 1 London Bridge Street, London SE1 9GF
tel 020-7782 4100
email exclusive@the-sun.co.uk
website www.thesun.co.uk
Editor David Dinsmore
Daily Mon–Fri 40p, Sat 60p, Sun 70p
Supplements **Cashflow, TV Magazine**

Takes freelance material, including cartoons. Payment: by negotiation. Founded 1969.

Deputy Editor Simon Cosyns
Business Editor Simon English
Deputy Head of Content Sean Hamilton
Head of Features Kara Dolman
Health & Science Editor Emma Little
Political Editor Tom Newton Dunn
Head of Showbiz Dan Wootton
Online Sports Editor Jim Munro
Travel Editor Lisa Minot

Sun on Sunday

3 Thomas More Square, London E98 1XY
tel 020-778 24100
email exclusive@the-sun.co.uk
website www.thesun.co.uk
Editor Victoria Newton
Sun 60p
Supplements **Fabulous**

Takes freelance material. Founded 2012 replacing the *News of the World*.

Sunday Business Post

Hambleden House, 19/26 Pembroke Street Lower, Republic of Ireland
tel +353 (0)1 6026000
email sbpost@iol.ie
website www.businesspost.ie
Editor Ian Kehoe
Sun €2.70

Features on financial, economic and political topics; also lifestyle, media and science articles. Illustrations: colour and b&w photos, graphics, cartoons. Payment: by negotiation. Founded 1989.

Editor of Sunday Business Post magazine Fiona Ness
Acting News Editor Catherine O'Mahony
News Editor Catherine O'Mahony
Political & Deputy Editor Pat Leahy
Political Correspondent Michael Brennan
Managing Editor Gillian Nelis
Books & Arts Editor Nadine O'Regan
Fashion Editor Lisa Brady

Sunday Express

Northern & Shell Building, 10 Lower Thames Street, London EC4R 6EN
tel 020-8612 7000
email sundaynews@express.co.uk
website www.express.co.uk/news/sunday
Editor Martin Townsend
Sun £1.35
Supplements **'S' Sunday Express, Property, Review, Sport, Travel, Financial**

Exclusive news stories, photos, personality profiles and features of controversial or lively interest. Length: 800–1,000 words. Payment: top rates. Founded 1918.

Features Editor Amy Packer
Deputy Editor Stephen Rigley
Political Editor Caroline Wheeler
Sports Editor Scott Wilson
City Editor Geoff Ho
Education Editor Hilary Douglas
Arts & Entertainment Editor Clair Woodward
Literary & Music Editor Charlotte Heathcote

'S' Sunday Express

tel 020-8612 7257
Editor Margaret Hussey
Free with paper

Sunday Herald

200 Renfield Street, Glasgow G2 3QB
tel 0141 302 7000
email news@sundayherald.com
website www.heraldscotland.com
Editor Richard Walker
Sun £1.50
Supplements **Sport, Sunday Herald Magazine**

News and stories about Scotland, the UK and the world. Opportunities for freelancers with quality contacts. Founded 1999.

Group Arts Editor Alan Morrison
Business Editor Colin Donald
Features Editor Garry Scott
Foreign Editor David Pratt
Investigations Editor Paul Hutcheon
News Editor Neil Mackay
Scottish Political Editor Tom Gordon
Sports Editor Jonathan Jobson
Opinion Editor Susan Flockhart

Sunday Independent

27–32 Talbot Street, Dublin 1, Republic of Ireland
tel +353 (0)1 7055333
email info@independent.ie
website www.independent.ie
Editor Cormac Bourke
Sun €2.70

Special articles. Length: according to subject. Illustrations: topical or general interest, cartoons. Payment: at editor's valuation.

Business Editor Nick Webb
Deputy Editor Willie Kealy
Deputy Editor Jody Corcoran
Life Magazine Editor Brendan O'Connor
Sports Editor John Greene

Sunday Mail

1 Central Quay, Glasgow G3 8DA
tel 0141 309 3000
email reporters@sundaymail.co.uk
London office 1 Canada Square, Canary Wharf, London E14 5AP
website www.dailyrecord.co.uk
Editor Jim Wilson
Sun £1.30
Supplements **Entertainment, Fun on Sunday, Jobsplus!, 7-Days, Right at Home**

Exclusive stories and pictures of national and Scottish interest; also cartoons. Payment: above average.
Health Editor Dr Gareth Smith
Deputy Editor Brendan McGinty
Head of Images Andrew Hosie
Political Editor Mark Aitken
Sports Editor George Cheyne

Sunday Mirror

1 Canada Square, Canary Wharf, London E14 5AP
tel 020-7293 3000
email scoops@sundaymirror.co.uk
website www.mirror.co.uk
Editor Alison Phillips
Sun £1.10
Supplements **Notebook, Holidays & Getaways**

Concentrates on human interest news features, social documentaries, dramatic news and feature photos. Ideas, as well as articles, bought. Payment: high, especially for exclusives. Founded 1963.
Features Editor Caroline Waterston
Picture Editor Mark Moylan
Sports Editor David Walker

Sunday Post

D.C. Thomson & Co. Ltd, 144 Port Dundas Road, Glasgow G4 0HZ
tel 0141 332 9933
email mail@sundaypost.com
Postal address 80, Kingsway East, Dundee DD4 8SL
tel (01382) 223131
website www.sundaypost.com
Editor Donald Martin
Sun £1.50
Supplements **Travel & Homes, TV & Entertainment**

Human interest, topical, domestic and humorous articles, and exclusive news. Payment: on acceptance.

iN10 magazine

tel (01382) 223131
Editor Dawn Donaghey
Monthly Free with paper

General interest articles. Length: 1,000–2,000 words. Illustrations: colour transparencies. Payment: varies. Founded 1988.

Sunday Telegraph

111 Buckingham Palace Road, London SW1W 0DT
tel 020-7931 2000
email stnews@telegraph.co.uk
website www.telegraph.co.uk
Editor Ian MacGregor
Sun £2
Supplements **Business Reporter, Life, Money, Seven, Sport, Stella, Discover**

Occasional freelance material accepted.
Group Business Editor James Quinn
Comment Editor Will Heaven
Group City Diary Editorr Anna White
Economics Columnist Liam Halligan
Assistant Foreign Editor Bonnie Malkin
Group Head of Books Gaby Wood
London Editor Andrew Gilligan
Picture Editor Mike Spillard
Seven Editor Ross Jones
Group Head of Travel Charles Starmer-Smith

Stella

tel 020-7931 2000
email stella@telegraph.co.uk
Editor Michele Lavery (acting)
Free with paper

All material is commissioned. Founded 1995.

The Sunday Times

The News Building, 1 London Bridge Street, London SE1 9GF
tel 020-7782 5000
email newsdesk@sunday-times.co.uk
website www.thesundaytimes.co.uk
Editor Martin Ivens
Sun £2.50
Supplements **Appointments, Business, Culture, Driving, Home, Money, News Review, Sport, Style, The Sunday Times Magazine, Travel**

Special articles by authoritative writers on politics, literature, art, drama, music, finance, science and topical matters. Payment: top rate for exclusive features. Founded 1822.
Deputy Managing Editor Kathleen Herron
Editorial Director Eleanor Mills
Culture Editor Helen Hawkins
Economics Editor David Smith
Literary Editor Andrew Holgate
Political Editor Tim Shipman
Social Affiars Editor Nick Hellen
Sports Editor Alex Butler
Deputy Travel Editor Martin Hemming

The Sunday Times Magazine

tel 020-7782 5000
Editor Sarah Baxter
Free with paper

Articles and pictures. Illustrations: colour and b&w photos. Payment: by negotiation.

The Times

3 Thomas More Square, London E98 1XY
tel 020-7782 5000

email home.news@thetimes.co.uk
website www.thetimes.co.uk
Editor John Witherow
Daily Mon–Fri £1.20, Sat £1.50
Supplements **Books, Bricks & Mortar, Crème, Football Handbook, The Game, The Knowledge, Money, Times 2, Times Law, The Times Magazine, Times Sport, Travel, Arts and Entertainment, Fashion, Saturday Review, Technology Review, Weekend**

Outside contributions considered from experts in subjects of current interest and writers who can make first-hand experience or reflection come readably alive. Phone appropriate section editor. Length: up to 1,200 words. Founded 1785.

Executive Editor Roger Alton
Deputy Editor Emma Tucker
Associate Editor Danny Finkelstein
Education Editor Greg Hurst
Fashion Editor Laura Craik
Foreign Editor Roland Watson
Health Editor Chris Smyth
Business Editor Richard Fletcher
Head of Digital at The Times & Sunday Times Alan Hunter
Literary Editor Robbie Millen
Media Editor tbc
Political Editor Francis Elliott
Property Editor Anne Ashworth
Science Editor Tom Whipple
Sports Editor Tim Hallissey
Travel Editor Jane Knight

The Times Magazine

Editor Louise France
Free with Sat paper
Features. Illustrated.

Wales on Sunday

6 Park Street, Cardiff CF10 1XR
tel 029-2024 3602
email newsdesk@walesonline.co.uk
website www.walesonline.co.uk
Editor tbc
Sun £1
Supplements **Life on Sunday, Sport on Sunday**

National Sunday newspaper of Wales offering comprehensive news, features and entertainment coverage at the weekend, with a particular focus on events in Wales. Accepts general interest articles, preferably with a Welsh connection. Founded 1989.

Political Editor David Williamson
Head of Sport Paul Abbandonato

Regional newspapers UK and Ireland

Regional newspapers are listed in alphabetical order under region. Some will accept and pay for letters to the editor, brief fillers and gossip paragraphs, as well as puzzles and quizzes.

BELFAST

Belfast Telegraph

124–144 Royal Avenue, Belfast BT1 1EB
tel 028-9026 4000
email editor@belfasttelegraph.co.uk
email newseditor@belfasttelegraph.co.uk
website www.belfasttelegraph.co.uk
Editor Mike Gilson
Group Managing Editor Paul Connolly
Daily Mon–Sat 80p

An Independent News & Media publication. Any material relating to Northern Ireland. Payment: by negotiation. Founded 1870.

Irish News

113–117 Donegall Street, Belfast BT1 2GE
tel 028-9032 2226
website www.irishnews.com
Editor Noel Doran
Daily Mon–Sat 70p

Founded 1855.

News Letter

Ground Floor, Metro Building,
6–9 Donegall Square South, Belfast BT1 5JA
tel 028-9089 7700
email slnews@sundaylife.co.uk
website www.belfasttelegraph.co.uk/sunday-life
Editor Rankin Armstrong
Daily 95p

Pro-Union. Founded 1737.

Sunday Life

124–144 Royal Avenue, Belfast BT1 1EB
tel 028-9026 4000
email sinews@sundaylife.co.uk
website www.sundaylife.co.uk
Editor Martin Breen
Sun £1.50

Items of interest to Northern Ireland Sunday tabloid readers. Payment: by arrangement. Illustrations: colour and b&w pictures and graphics. Founded 1988.

CHANNEL ISLANDS

Guernsey Press and Star

PO Box 57, Braye Road, Vale, Guernsey GY1 3BW
tel (01481) 240240
website www.thisisguernsey.com/guernsey-press
Editor Shaun Green
Daily Mon–Sat 60p

News and feature articles. Length: 500–700 words. Illustrations: colour and b&w photos. Payment: by negotiation. Founded 1897.

Jersey Evening Post

PO Box 582, Five Oaks, St Saviour, Jersey JE4 8XQ
tel (01534) 611611
email news@jerseyeveningpost.com
website www.thisisjersey.com
Editor Chris Bright
Daily Mon–Sat 50p

News and features with a Channel Islands angle. Length: 1,000 words (articles/features), 300 words (news). Illustrations: colour and b&w. Payment: £110 per 1,000 words. Founded 1890.

CORK

Evening Echo (Cork)

Evening Echo Publications Ltd, City Quarter, Lapps Quay, Cork, Republic of Ireland
tel +353 (0)21 4272722
email news@eecho.ie
website www.eveningecho.ie
Editor Maurice Gubbins
Daily Mon–Sat €1.50

Articles, features and news for the area. Illustrations: colour prints.

DUBLIN

Herald

Independent House, 27–32 Talbot Street, Dublin 1, Republic of Ireland
tel +353 (0)1 7055722
email hnews@independent.ie
website www.herald.ie
Editor Stephen Rae
Daily Mon–Sat €1.20

Articles. Payment: by arrangement. Illustrations: line, half-tone, cartoons.

EAST ANGLIA

Cambridge News

Winship Road, Milton, Cambs. CB24 6PP
tel (01223) 434437

email newsdesk@cambridge-news.co.uk
website www.cambridge-news.co.uk
Editor Paul Brackley
Daily Mon–Fri 60p, Sat 60p

The voice of the Cambridge region – news, views and sport. Illustrations: colour prints, b&w and colour graphics. Payment: by negotiation. Founded 1888.

East Anglian Daily Times

30 Lower Brook Street, Ipswich, Suffolk IP4 1AN
tel (01473) 230023
website www.eadt.co.uk
Editor Terry Hunt
Daily Mon–Fri 70p, Sat £1.20

Features of East Anglian interest, preferably with pictures. Length: 500 words. Illustrations: colour, b&w. Payment: negotiable. Illustrations: NUJ rates. Founded 1874.

Eastern Daily Press

Prospect House, Rouen Road, Norwich NR1 1RE
tel (01603) 628311
London office House of Commons Press Gallery, House of Commons, London SW1A 0AA
tel 020-7219 3384
website www.edp24.co.uk
Editor Nigel Pickover
Daily Mon–Fri 80p, Sat £1.60

Limited market for articles of East Anglian interest not exceeding 900 words. Founded 1870.

Ipswich Star

Archant Regional, Press House,
30 Lower Brook Street, Ipswich, Suffolk IP4 1AN
tel (01473) 230023
website www.ipswichstar.co.uk
Editor Terry Hunt
Mon–Fri 60p

Founded 1885.

Norwich Evening News

Prospect House, Rouen Road, Norwich NR1 1RE
tel (01603) 628311
website www.eveningnews24.co.uk
Editor Nigel Pickover
Daily Mon–Sat 60p

Interested in local news-based features. Length: up to 500 words. Payment: NUJ or agreed rates. Founded 1882.

EAST MIDLANDS

Burton Mail

Burton Daily Mail Ltd, 65–68 High Street, Burton on Trent DE14 1LE
tel (01283) 512345
email editorial@burtonmail.co.uk
website www.burtonmail.co.uk
Editor Kevin Booth
Daily Mon Sat 40p

Features, news and articles of interest to Burton and south Derbyshire readers. Length: 400–500 words. Illustrations: colour and b&w. Payment: by negotiation. Founded 1898.

Chronicle & Echo, Northampton

Northamptonshire Newspapers Ltd, Upper Mounts, Northampton NN1 3HR
tel (01604) 467000
email editor@northantsnews.co.uk
website www.northamptonchron.co.uk
Editor David Summers
Daily Thurs £1.30

Articles, features and news – mostly commissioned – of interest to the Northampton area. Length: varies. Payment: by negotiation. Founded 1931.

Derby Telegraph

Northcliffe House, Meadow Road, Derby DE1 2BH
tel (01332) 291111
website www.derbytelegraph.co.uk
Editor Neil White
Daily Mon–Sat 50p

Articles and news of local interest. Payment: by negotiation.

Leicester Mercury

St George Street, Leicester LE1 9FQ
tel 0116 251 2512
website www.leicestermercury.co.uk
Editor-in-Chief Richard Bettsworth
Daily Mon–Fri 60p, Sat 70p

Occasional articles, features and news; submit ideas to editor first. Length/payment: by negotiation. Founded 1874.

Nottingham Post

3rd Floor, City Gate, Tollhouse Hill, Nottingham NG1 5FS
tel 0115 948 2000
email newsdesk@nottinghampostgroup.co.uk
website www.nottinghampost.com
Editor Mike Sassi
Daily Mon–Sat 60p

Material on local issues considered. Founded 1878.

Peterborough Evening Telegraph

Telegraph House, 57 Priesgate, Peterborough PE1 1JW
tel (01733) 555111
email news@peterboroughtoday.co.uk
website www.peterboroughtoday.co.uk
Editor Mark Edwards
Daily Mon–Sat 45p

LONDON

Evening Standard
Evening Standard Ltd, 2 Derry Street,
London W8 5TT
tel 020-3367 7000
website www.standard.co.uk
Editor Sarah Sands
Daily Mon–Fri Free

Founded 1827.

ES Magazine
Executive Editor Andrew Barker
Weekly Free with paper on Fri

Feature ideas, exclusively about London. Payment: by negotiation. Illustrations: all types.

Homes and Property
Editor Janice Morley
Weekly Free with paper on Wed

UK property. Payment: by negotiation.

NORTH

Berwick Advertiser
90 Marygate, Berwick-upon-Tweed,
Northumberland TD15 1BW
tel (01289) 306677
email advertisernews@tweeddalepress.co.uk
website www.berwick-advertiser.co.uk
Editor Stuart Laundy
Daily Mon–Fri 80p

Articles, features and news.

Carlisle News and Star
CN Group, Newspaper House, Dalston Road,
Carlisle CA2 5UA
tel (01228) 612600
website www.newsandstar.co.uk
Editor David Helliwell
Daily Mon–Sat 60p

Darlington and Stockton Times
Darlington DL1 1NF
tel (01325) 381313
email newsdesk@nne.co.uk
website www.darlingtonandstocktontimes.co.uk
Editor Malcolm Warne
Weekly Fri £1

Founded 1847.

Durham Times
PO Box 14 Priestgate Darlington,
Co. Durham DL1 1NF
tel (0191) 384 4600
email durhamtimes@nne.co.uk
website www.durhamtimes.co.uk
Editor Tom Kearney
Weekly £1

Evening Chronicle
ncjMedia Ltd, Groat Market,
Newcastle upon Tyne NE1 1ED
tel 0191 201 6446
email ec.news@ncjmedia.co.uk
website www.chroniclelive.co.uk
Editor Darren Thwaites
Daily Mon–Sat 60p

News, photos and features covering almost every subject of interest to readers in Tyne & Wear, Northumberland and Durham. Payment: by prior arrangement.

Gazette
Gazette Media Company Ltd,
105–111 Borough Road, Middlesbrough TS1 3AZ
tel (01642) 245401
email news@gazettemedia.co.uk
website www.gazettelive.co.uk
Editor Chris Styles
Daily Mon–Sat 60p

News and topical and lifestyle features. Length: 600–800 words. Illustrations: line, half-tone, colour, graphics, cartoons. Payment: £75 per 1,000 words; scale rate or by agreement for illustrations. Founded 1869.

Hartlepool Mail
Northeast Press Ltd, New Clarence House,
Wesley Square, Hartlepool TS24 8BX
tel (01429) 239333
email mail.news@northeast-press.co.uk
website www.hartlepoolmail.co.uk
website www.peterleestar.co.uk
Editor Joy Yates
Daily Mon–Sat 65p

Features of local interest. Length: 500 words. Illustrations: colour, b&w photos, line. Payment: by negotiation. Founded 1877.

Journal
Groat Market, Newcastle upon Tyne NE1 1ED
tel 0191 201 6446
email jnl.newsdesk@ncjmedia.co.uk
website www.thejournal.co.uk
Editor tba
Daily Mon–Fri 70p, Sat £1.20

News, sport items and features of topical interest considered. Payment: by arrangement.

North-West Evening Mail
Newspaper House, Abbey Road, Barrow-in-Furness,
Cumbria LA14 5QS
tel (01229) 840100
email news.em@nwemail.co.uk
website www.nwemail.co.uk
Editor Jonathan Lee
Daily Mon–Fri 60p, Sat 70p

Articles, features and news. Length: 500 words.

Illustrations: colour photos and occasional artwork. Covering the whole of South Cumbria. Founded 1898.

Northern Echo

Priestgate, Darlington, Co. Durham DL1 1NF
tel (01325) 381313
website www.thenorthernecho.co.uk
Editor Peter Barron
Daily Mon–Fri 70p, Sat 90p

Articles of interest to North-East and North Yorkshire; all material commissioned. Preliminary study of newspaper advisable. Length: 800–1,000 words. Illustrations: line, half-tone, colour – mostly commissioned. Payment: by negotiation. Founded 1870.

The Shields Gazette

Chapter Row, South Shields, Tyne & Wear NE33 1BL
tel 0191 427 4800
website www.shieldsgazette.com
Editor Joy Yates
Daily Mon–Sat 70p

The Sunday Sun

Groat Market, Newcastle upon Tyne NE1 1ED
tel 0191 201 6201
email scoop.sundaysun@ncjmedia.co.uk
website www.sundaysun.co.uk
Editor Matt McKenzie
Sun £1

Key requirements: Looking for topical and human interest articles on current problems. Particularly welcomed are special features of family appeal and news stories of special interest to the North of England. Length: 200–700 words. Payment: normal lineage rates, or by arrangement. Illustrations: photos. Founded 1919.

Sunderland Echo

Echo House, Pennywell, Sunderland,
Tyne & Wear SR4 9ER
tel 0191 501 5800
email echo.news@northeast-press.co.uk
website www.sunderlandecho.com
Editor John Szymanski
Daily Mon–Sat 70p

Local news, features and articles. Length: 500 words. Illustrations: colour and b&w photos, line, cartoons. Payment: by negotiation. Founded 1875.

NORTH WEST

Blackpool Gazette

Blackpool Gazette and Herald Ltd, Avroe House, Avroe Crescent, Blackpool Business Park,
Squires Gate, Blackpool FY4 2DP
tel (01253) 400888
email editorial@blackpoolgazette.co.uk
website www.blackpoolgazette.co.uk
Editor John Rhodes
Daily Mon–Sat 45p

Local news and articles of general interest, with photos if appropriate. Length: varies. Payment: on merit. Founded 1929.

Bolton News

The Wellsprings, Civic Centre, Victoria Square,
Bolton, Lancs. BL1 1AR
tel (01204) 522345
email newsdesk@nqw.co.uk
website www.theboltonnews.co.uk
Editor-in-Chief Ian Savage
Daily Mon–Sat 65p

Founded 1867.

Chester Chronicle

Maple House, Park West, Sealand Road,
Chester CH1 4RN
tel (01244) 340151
email newsroom@cheshirenews.co.uk
website www.chesterchronicle.co.uk
Editor Michael Green
Weekly Thurs 85p

Local news and features. Founded 1775.

Lancashire Evening Post

Oliver's Place, Preston PR2 9ZA
tel (01772) 254841
email lep.newsdesk@lep.co.uk
website www.lep.co.uk
Editor Gillian Gray
Daily Mon–Sat 70p

Topical articles on all subjects. Area of interest: Wigan to Lake District, Lancs., and coast. Length: 600–900 words. Illustrations: colour and b&w photos, cartoons. Payment: by arrangement.

Lancashire Telegraph

Newspaper House, 1 High Street, Blackburn,
Lancs. BB1 1HT
tel (01254) 678678
email lt_editorial@nqnw.co.uk
website www.lancashiretelegraph.co.uk
Editor Kevin Young
Daily Mon–Sat 65p

Will consider general news items from East Lancashire. Payment: by arrangement. Founded 1886.

Liverpool Echo

PO Box 48, Old Hall Street, Liverpool L69 3EB
tel 0151 227 2000
website www.liverpoolecho.co.uk
Editor Alastair Machray
Daily Mon–Fri 65p, Sat £1

Articles of up to 600–800 words of local or topical

interest; also cartoons. Payment: according to merit; special rates for exceptional material. Connected with, but independent of, the *Liverpool Post*. Articles not interchangeable.

Manchester Evening News

Mitchell Henry House, Hollinwood Avenue, Chadderton OL9 8EF
tel 0161 832 7200 (editorial)
email newsdesk@men-news.co.uk
website www.manchestereveningnews.co.uk
Editor Rob Irvine
Daily Mon–Sat 65p

Feature articles of up to 1,000 words, topical or general interest and illustrated where appropriate, should be addressed to the Features Editor. Payment: on acceptance.

Oldham Chronicle

PO Box 47, 172 Union Street, Oldham, Lancs. OL1 1EQ
tel 0161 633 2121
email news@oldham-chronicle.co.uk
website www.oldham-chronicle.co.uk
Editor David Whaley
Daily Mon–Fri 65p

News and features on current topics and local history. Length: 1,000 words. Illustrations: colour and b&w photos and line. Payment: £20–£25 per 1,000 words; £16.32–£21.90 for illustrations. Founded 1854.

SCOTLAND

Courier

D.C. Thomson & Co. Ltd, 80 Kingsway East, Dundee DD4 8SL
tel (01382) 223131
London office 185 Fleet Street, London EC4A 2HS
tel 020-7400 1030
website www.thecourier.co.uk
Editor Richard Neville
Daily Mon–Sat 70p
Supplements **House & Home, magazine**

Founded 1801 and 1816.

Dundee Evening Telegraph and Post

80 Kingsway East, Dundee DD4 8SL
tel (01382) 223131
email newsdesk@eveningtelegraph.co.uk
London office 185 Fleet Street, London EC4A 2HS
tel 020-7400 1030
website www.eveningtelegraph.co.uk
Daily Mon–Fri 50p

Evening Express (Aberdeen)

Aberdeen Journals Ltd, PO Box 43, Lang Stracht, Mastrick, Aberdeen AB15 6DF
tel (01224) 344150
email ee.news@ajl.co.uk
website www.eveningexpress.co.uk
Editor Alan McCabe
Daily Mon–Sat 55p

Lively evening paper. Illustrations: colour and b&w. Payment: by arrangement.

Evening News (Edinburgh)

Barclay House, 108 Holyrood Road, Edinburgh EH8 8AS
tel 0131 620 8620
email news_en@edinburghnews.com
website www.edinburghnews.scotsman.com
Editor Frank O'Donnell
Daily Mon–Sat 70p

Features on current affairs, preferably in relation to the circulation area. Women's talking points; local historical articles; subjects of general interest; health, beauty and fashion.

Glasgow Evening Times

200 Renfield Street, Glasgow G2 3QB
tel 0141 302 7000
website www.eveningtimes.co.uk
Editor Tony Carlin
Daily Mon–Sat 60p

Founded 1876.

Greenock Telegraph

2 Crawfurd Street, Greenock PA15 1LH
(01475) 726511
email editorial@greenocktelegraph.co.uk
website www.greenocktelegraph.co.uk
Editor Brian Hossack
Daily Mon–Fri 40p

News and features from the area in and around Greenock. Founded 1857.

Inverness Courier

New Century House, Stadium Road, Inverness IV1 1FG
tel (01463) 233059
email editorial@inverness-courier.co.uk
website www.inverness-courier.co.uk
Editor Robert Taylor
Tue 70p, Fri 90p

Articles of Highland interest only. Unsolicited material accepted. Illustrations: colour and b&w photos. Payment: by arrangement. Founded 1817.

Paisley Daily Express

Scottish and Universal Newspapers Ltd, 14 New Street, Paisley, Renfrewshire PA1 1YA
tel 0141 887 7911
website www.dailyrecord.co.uk/all-about/paisley
Editor Gordon Bury
Daily Mon–Sat 45p

Articles of Paisley interest only. Considers unsolicited material.

Press and Journal
Lang Stracht, Aberdeen AB15 6DF
tel (01224) 343311
email pj.newsdesk@ajl.co.uk
website www.pressandjournal.co.uk
Editor Damian Bates
Daily Mon–Fri 70p, Sat 80p

Contributions of Scottish interest. Payment: by arrangement. Illustrations: half-tone. Founded 1747.

SOUTH EAST

The Argus
Argus House, Crowhurst Road, Hollingbury, Brighton BN1 8AR
tel (01273) 544544
email editor@theargus.co.uk
website www.theargus.co.uk
Group Editor Michael Beard
Daily Mon–Fri 65p, Sat 85p

Established 1880.

Banbury Guardian
7 North Bar, Banbury, Oxon OX16 0TQ
tel (01295) 227758
email editorial@banburyguardian.co.uk
website www.banburyguardian.co.uk
Editor Jason Gibbins
Daily Mon–Sat 90p

Local news and features. Founded 1838.

Echo
Newspaper House, Chester Hall Lane, Basildon, Essex SS14 3BL
tel (01268) 522792
email echonews@nqe.com
website www.echo-news.co.uk
Editor Chris Hatton
Daily Mon–Fri 65p

Mostly staff-written. Only interested in local material. Payment: by arrangement. Founded 1969.

Essex Chronicle
Kestrel House, Hedgerows Business Park, Chelmsford Business Park, Chelmsford CM2 5PF
tel (01245) 602 700
email advertising@essexchronicle.co.uk
website www.essexchronicle.co.uk/news
Editor Paul Dent-Jones
Weekly Thurs 80p

Local news and features for Essex. Founded 1764.

Hampshire Chronicle
5 Upper Brook St, Winchester, Hants SO23 8AL
tel (01962) 861860
email news@hampshirechronicle.co.uk
website www.hampshirechronicle.co.uk
Editor Keith Redbourn
Weekly Thurs £1

Founded 1772.

Isle of Wight County Press
Brannon House, 123 Pyle Street, Newport, Isle of Wight PO30 1ST
tel (01983) 535007
email editor@iwcp.co.uk
website www.iwcp.co.uk
Editor Alan Marriott
Weekly Fri 75p

Articles and news of local interest. Founded 1884.

Kent and Sussex Courier
Courier House, 80–84 Calverley Road, Tunbridge Wells, Kent TN1 2UN
tel (01892) 239042
email editor@courier.co.uk
website www.courier.co.uk
Editor Roger Kasper
Weekly Fri 80p

Local news, articles and features. Founded 1872.

Medway Messenger
Medway House, Ginsbury Close, Sir Thomas Longley Road, Medway City Estate, Strood, Kent ME2 4DU
tel (01634) 227800
website www.kentonline.co.uk
Editor Bob Bounds
Mon 65p, Fri £1.10

Emphasis on news and sport from the Medway Towns. Illustrations: line, half-tone.

The News, Portsmouth
100 Lakeside, North Harbour, Portsmouth PO6 3EN
tel 023-9266 4488
email newsdesk@thenews.co.uk
website www.portsmouth.co.uk
Editor Mark Waldron
Daily Mon–Fri 70p, Sat 85p

Articles of relevance to South-East Hampshire and West Sussex. Payment: by arrangement. Founded 1877.

Oxford Mail
Newspaper House, Osney Mead, Oxford OX2 0EJ
tel (01865) 425262
email newsdesk@nqo.com
website www.oxfordmail.co.uk
Editor Simon O'Neill
Daily 65p

Oxford Times
Newsquest Oxfordshire & Wiltshire, Osney Mead, Oxford OX2 0EJ
tel (01865) 425262
website www.oxfordtimes.co.uk
Editor Simon O'Neill

Weekly Thurs £1.30p
Supplements **Oxford Limited Edition, In Business**

Local weekly newspaper for Oxford. Founded 1862.

Reading Chronicle

50/56 Portman Road Reading Berks RG30 1BA
tel (0118) 955 3333
email news@readingchronicle.co.uk
website www.readingchronicle.co.uk
Editor Lesley Potter
Weekly Thurs 70p

Southern Daily Echo

Newspaper House, Test Lane, Redbridge, Southampton SO16 9JX
tel 023-8042 4777
email newsdesk@dailyecho.co.uk
website www.dailyecho.co.uk
Editor Ian Murray
Daily 65p

News, articles, features, sport. Length: varies. Illustrations: line, half-tone, colour, cartoons. Payment: NUJ rates. Founded 1888.

Swindon Advertiser

100 Victoria Road, Old Town, Swindon SN1 3BE
tel (01793) 528144
email newsdesk@swindonadvertiser.co.uk
website www.swindonadvertiser.co.uk
Editor Gary Lawrence
Daily Mon–Sat 65p

News and information relating to Swindon and Wiltshire only. Considers unsolicited material. Founded 1854.

SOUTH WEST

Cornish Guardian

High Water House, City Wharf, Malpas Road, Truro TR1 1QH
tel (01872) 271451
email cgedit@c-dm.co.uk
website www.cornishguardian.co.uk
Editor Zena O'Rourke
Weekly Wed £1.10

Items of interest for Cornwall. Founded 1901.

Cornishman

First floor, 13/14 Market Place, Chapel Street, Penzance TR18 2JB
tel (01736) 335512
email Newsdesk@cornishman.co.uk
website www.thisiscornwall.co.uk
Editor Jacqui Walls
Weekly Thurs £1.10

Local news and features. Founded 1878.

Daily Echo

Richmond Hill, Bournemouth BH2 6HH
tel (01202) 554601
email newsdesk@bournemouthecho.co.uk
website www.bournemouthecho.co.uk
Editor Tony Granville
Daily Mon–Fri 65p, Sat 85p

Founded 1900.

Dorset Echo

Fleet House, Hampshire Road, Weymouth, Dorset DT4 9XD
tel (01305) 830930
email newsdesk@dorsetecho.co.uk
website www.dorsetecho.co.uk
Editor Toby Granville
Daily Mon–Fri 50p, Sat 55p

News and occasional features (1,000–2,000 words). Illustrations: b&w photos. Payment: by negotiation. Founded 1921.

Express & Echo

Express & Echo News & Media, Heron Road, Sowton, Exeter EX2 7NF
tel (01392) 442211
website www.exeterexpressandecho.co.uk
Editor Jon-Paul Hedge
Weekly Thurs £1

Features and news of local interest. Length: 500–800 words (features), up to 400 words (news). Illustrations: colour. Payment: lineage rates; illustrations: by negotiation. Founded 1904.

Gloucester Citizen

6–8 The Oxebode, Gloucester GL1 2RZ
tel (01452) 420621
website www.thisisgloucestershire.co.uk
Editor Jenny Eastwood
Daily Mon–Fri 40p, Sat 45p

Local news and features for Gloucester and its districts. Length: 1,000 words (articles/features), 300 words (news). Illustrations: colour. Payment: by negotiation.

Gloucestershire Echo

Third Floor, St James's House, St James's Square, Cheltenham, Glos. GL50 3PR
tel (01242) 278000
email echo.news@glosmedia.co.uk
website www.thisisgloucestershire.co.uk
Editor Matt Holmes
Daily Mon–Fri 70p, Sat 80p

Specialist articles with Gloucestershire connections; no fiction. Founded 1873.

Herald

The Plymouth Herald, 3rd Floor, Studio 5–11, Millbay Road, Plymouth PL1 3LF
tel (01752) 765500
email news@plymouthherald.co.uk
website www.plymouthherald.co.uk
Editor Paul Burton

Daily Mon–Sat 45p

Local news, articles and features. Will consider unsolicited material. Welcomes ideas for articles and features. Illustrations: colour and b&w prints.

Herald Express

Harmsworth House, Barton Hill Road, Torquay, Devon TQ2 8JN
tel (01803) 676767
website www.torquayheraldexpress.co.uk
Editor Jim Parker
Weekly Thurs £1

Hereford Times

Holmer Road, Hereford HR4 9UJ
tel (01432) 845873
email news@herefordtimes.com
website www.herefordtimes.com
Editor Clive Joyce
Weekly Thurs £1.20

Local news, sports and features. Founded 1832.

Post

Temple Way, Bristol BS2 0BU
tel 0117 934 3000
website www.bristolpost.co.uk
Editor Mike Norton
Daily Mon–Thurs 60p, Fri 70p

Takes freelance news and articles. Payment: by arrangement. Founded 1932.

Sunday Independent

The Sunday Independent Newspapers Ltd, Webbs House, Tindle Suite, Liskeard, Cornwall PL14 6AH
tel (01579) 342174
email newsdesk@sundayindependent.co.uk
website www.sundayindependent.co.uk
Editor John Collings
Sun £1

Sport and news features on West Country topics; features/articles with a nostalgic theme; short, quirky news briefs (must be original). Length: 600 words (features/articles), 300 words (news). Illustrations: colour, b&w. Payment: by arrangement. Founded 1808.

Western Daily Press

Bristol Evening Post and Press Ltd, Temple Way, Bristol BS99 7HD
tel 0117 934 3000
website www.westerndailypress.co.uk
Editor Ian Mean
Daily Mon–Fri 75p, Sat £1.50

National, international or West Country topics for features or news items, from established journalists, with or without illustrations. Payment: by negotiation. Founded 1858.

Western Morning News

Western Morning News, 3rd Floor, Studio 5–11, Plymouth PL1 3LF
tel (01752) 765500
website www.westernmorningnews.co.uk
Editor Bill Martin
Daily Mon–Fri 55p, Sat 85p

Articles plus illustrations considered on West Country subjects. Founded 1860.

WALES

Cambrian News

7 Science Park, Aberystwyth, Ceredigion SY23 3AH
tel (01970) 615000
email edit@cambrian-news.co.uk
website www.cambrian-news.co.uk
Editor Beverly Thomas
Weekly Wed 80p for the Aberystwyth, South and Machynlleth & Llanidloes editions; Thurs 70p for the Meirionnydd and Arfon & Dwyfor editions

Wales' biggest-selling weekly newspaper. Payment for freelance articles and pictures by arrangement. Founded 1860.

Daily Post

Vale Road, Llandudno Junction, Conwy LL31 9SL
(01492) 574452
email welshnews@dailypost.co.uk
website www.dailypost.co.uk
Editor Linda Roberts
Daily Mon–Sat 60p

Leader

NWN Media Ltd, Mold Business Park, Wrexham Road, Mold, Flintshire CH7 1XY
tel (01352) 707707
website www.leaderlive.co.uk
Editor Barrie Jones
Mon–Fri 55p

South Wales Argus

South Wales Argus, Cardiff Road, Maesglas, Newport, Gwent NP20 3QN
tel (01633) 810000
email newsdesk@gwent-wales.co.uk
website www.southwalesargus.co.uk
Editor Kevin Ward
Daily Mon–Sat 65p

News and features of relevance to Gwent. Length: 500–600 words (features); 350 words (news). Illustrations: colour prints and transparencies. Payment: £30 (features), £20 (news) per item; £20–£25 (photos). Founded 1892.

South Wales Echo

6 Park Street, Cardiff CF10 1XR
tel (02920) 223333
email echo.newsdesk@walesonline.co.uk
website www.walesonline.co.uk
Editor Tim Gordon

Daily Mon–Fri 55p, Sat 75p

Evening paper: news, sport, features, showbiz, news features, personality interviews. Length: up to 700 words. Illustrations: photos, cartoons. Payment: by negotiation. Founded 1884.

South Wales Evening Post

South Wales Evening Post, Urban Village,
High Street, Swansea SA1 1NW
tel (01792) 510000
email postnews@swwmedia.co.uk
website www.southwales-eveningpost.co.uk
Editor Jonathan Roberts
Daily 48p

Western Mail

6 Park Street, Cardiff CF10 1XR
tel 029-2022 3333
website www.walesonline.co.uk
Editor Alan Edmunds
Daily Mon–Fri 70p, Sat Free

Articles of political, industrial, literary or general and Welsh interest are considered. Illustrations: topical general news and feature pictures, cartoons. Payment: according to value; special fees for exclusive news. Founded 1869.

WEST MIDLANDS

Birmingham Mail

BPM Media (Midlands), 6th Floor, Fort Dunlop,
Fort Parkway, Birmingham B24 9FF
tel 0121 234 5536
London office 1 Canada Square, Canary Wharf,
London E14 5AP
tel 020-7293 3000
email newsdesk@birminghammail.co.uk
website www.birminghammail.co.uk
Editor David Brookes
Daily Mon–Sat 55p

Features of topical Midland interest considered. Length: 400–800 words. Payment: by arrangement. Founded 1870.

Birmingham Post

6th Floor, Fort Dunlop, Fort Parkway,
Birmingham B24 9FF
tel 0121 234 5000
London office 22nd Floor, 1 Canada Square, Canary Wharf, London E14 5AP
tel 020-7293 3455
website www.birminghampost.co.uk
Editor Stacey Barnfield
Weekly £1.70

Authoritative and well-written articles of industrial, political or general interest are considered, especially if they have relevance to the Midlands. Length: up to 1,000 words. Payment: by arrangement.

Coventry Telegraph

Thomas Yeoman House, Leicester Row,
Coventry CV1 4LY
tel 024-7663 3633
email news@coventrytelegraph.net
website www.coventrytelegraph.net
Editor Keith Perry
Daily Mon–Fri 60p, Sat 70p

Topical, illustrated articles with a Coventry or Warwickshire interest. Length: up to 600 words. Payment: by arrangement.

Express & Star

51–53 Queen Street, Wolverhampton WV1 1ES
tel (01902) 313131
email newsdesk@expressandstar.co.uk
website www.expressandstar.com
Editor Keith Harrison
Daily Mon–Sat 55p, Sat 70p

Founded 1874.

Sentinel

Staffordshire Sentinel News & Media Ltd,
Sentinel House, Etruria, Stoke-on-Trent ST1 5SS
tel (01782) 864100
email newsdesk@thesentinel.co.uk
website www.stokesentinel.co.uk
Editor Martin Tideswell
Daily Mon–Sat 45p

Articles and features of topical interest to the north Staffordshire/south Cheshire area. Illustrations: colour and b&w. Payment: by arrangement. Founded 1873.

Shropshire Star

Waterloo Road, Ketley, Telford TF1 5HU
tel (01952) 242424
website www.shropshirestar.co.uk
Editor Martin Wright
Daily Mon–Fri 50p, Sat 60p

Daily paper: news and features. No unsolicited material; write to Features Editor with outline of ideas. Payment: by arrangement. Founded 1964.

Sunday Mercury

6th Floor, Fort Dunlop, Fort Parkway,
Birmingham B24 9FF
tel 0121 234 5493
website www.birminghammail.co.uk
Executive Editor Paul Cole
Sun £1.20

News specials or features of Midland interest. Illustrations: colour, b&w, cartoons. Payment: special rates for special matter.

Worcester News

Berrows House, Hylton Road, Worcester WR2 5JX
tel (01905) 748200

website www.worcesternews.co.uk
Editor Peter John
Daily Mon–Sat 65p

Local and national news, sport and features. Will consider unsolicited material. Welcomes ideas for articles and features. Length: 800 words (features), 300 words (news). Payment: by negotiation. Illustrations: colour jpg files.

YORKSHIRE/HUMBERSIDE

Grimsby Telegraph

80 Cleethorpe Road, Grimsby,
North East Lincs. DN31 3EH
tel (01472) 360360
email newsdesk@grimsbytelegraph.co.uk
website www.thisisgrimsby.co.uk
Editor Michelle Lalor
Daily Mon–Sat 45p

Considers general interest articles. Illustrations: line, half-tone, colour, cartoons. Payment: by arrangement. Founded 1897.

Halifax Courier

PO Box 19, King Cross Street, Halifax HX1 2SF
tel (01422) 260200
email editor@halifaxcourier.co.uk
website www.halifaxcourier.co.uk
Editor John Kenealy
Fri £1.10

Huddersfield Daily Examiner

Pennine Business Park, Longbow Close,
Bradley Road, Huddersfield HD2 1GQ
tel (01484) 430000
email editorial@examiner.co.uk
website www.examiner.co.uk
Editor Roy Wright
Daily Examiner 65p, Weekend Examiner 80p

No contributions required at present. Founded 1851.

Hull Daily Mail

Blundell's Corner, Beverley Road, Hull HU3 1XS
tel (01482) 327111
website www.hulldailymail.co.uk
Editor Neil Hodgkinson
Daily Mon–Sat 50p

Lincolnshire Echo

Ground Floor, Witham Wharf,
Brayford Wharf East Lincoln LN5 7HY
tel (01522) 820000
website www.lincolnshireecho.co.uk
Editor Mel West
Weekly Thurs £1.10

Press

Newsquest York, PO Box 29, 76–86 Walmgate,
York YO1 9YN
tel (01904) 567131
email newsdesk@thepress.co.uk
website www.yorkpress.co.uk
Managing Editor Perry Austin-Clarke
Daily Mon–Sat 60p

Articles of North and East Yorkshire interest. Length: 500–1,000 words. Payment: by arrangement. Illustrations: line, half-tone. Founded 1882.

Scarborough News

Newchase Court, Hopper Hill Road,
Scarborough Y011 3YS
tel (01723) 383817
website www.thescarboroughnews.co.uk
Editor Ed Asquith
Weekly £1,20
Entertainment Sue Wilkinson
News Ed Asquith

Scunthorpe Telegraph

4–5 Park Square, Scunthorpe,
North Lincolnshire DN15 6JH
tel (01724) 273273
email newsdesk@scunthorpetelegraph.co.uk
website www.scunthorpetelegraph.co.uk
Editor David Atkin
Weekly Thurs £1

Local news and features. Founded 1937.

Sheffield Star

York Street, Sheffield S1 1PU
tel 0114 276 7676
website www.thestar.co.uk
Editor James Mitchinson
Daily Mon–Sat 65p

Well-written articles of local character. Length: about 500 words. Payment: by negotiation. Illustrations: topical photos, line drawings, graphics, cartoons. Founded 1887.

Telegraph & Argus

Hall Ings, Bradford BD1 1JR
tel (01274) 729511
email newsdesk@telegraphandargus.co.uk
website www.thetelegraphandargus.co.uk
Editor Perry Austin-Clarke
Daily Mon–Sat 60p

Daily paper: news, articles and features relevant to or about the people of West Yorkshire. Length: up to 1,000 words. Illustrations: line, half-tone, colour. Payment: features from £15; line from £5, b&w and colour photos by negotiation. Founded 1868.

Yorkshire Evening Post

No 1 Leeds, 26 Whitehall Road, Leeds LS1 1BE
tel 0113 238 8917
website www.yorkshireeveningpost.co.uk
Editor Jeremy Clifford
Daily Mon–Sat 45p

News stories and feature articles. Illustrations: colour and b&w, cartoons. Payment: by negotiation. Founded 1890.

Yorkshire Post

No 1 Leeds, 26 Whitehall Road, Leeds LS12 1BE
tel 0113 243 2701
London office 292 Vauxhall Bridge Road, London SW1V 1AE
tel 020-7963 7646
website www.yorkshirepost.co.uk
Editor Jeremy Clifford
Daily Mon–Fri 80p, Sat £1.70
Supplements **Yorkshire Post Magazine**

Authoritative and well-written articles on topical subjects of general, literary or industrial interests. Founded 1754.

Magazines UK and Ireland

Listings for regional newspapers start on page 24 and listings for national newspapers start on page 16. For quick reference, magazines are listed by subject area starting on page 729.

Accountancy

145 London Road, Kingston-upon-Thames, Surrey KT2 6SR
tel 020-8247 1379
email accountancynews@wolterskluwer.co.uk
website www.accountancylive.com
Editor Sara White
Monthly £85 p.a. (magazine only) £99 p.a. (Accountancy Live)

Articles on accounting, taxation, audit, financial, legal and other subjects likely to be of professional interest to accountants in practice or industry, and to top management generally. All feature ideas to be submitted by email in the form of a brief, bullet-pointed synopsis. Founded 1889.

Accountancy Age

Incisive Media, Haymarket House, 28–29 Haymarket, London SW1Y 4RX
tel 020-484 9700
email news@accountancyage.com
website www.accountancyage.com
Editor Kevin Reed
Weekly £95 + VAT p.a.

Articles of accounting, financial and business interest. Illustrations: colour photos; freelance assignments commissioned. Payment: by arrangement. Founded 1969.

Accounting & Business

Association of Chartered Certified Accountants, 29 Lincoln's Inn Fields, London WC2A 3EE
tel 020-7059 5000
email info@accaglobal.com
website www.accaglobal.com
Editor-in-Chief Jo Malvern
10 p.a. £10, £85 p.a.

Journal of the Association of Chartered Certified Accountants. Features accountancy, finance and business topics of relevance to accountants and finance directors. Length: 1,100 words. Illustrated. Founded 1998.

Acumen Literary Journal

6 The Mount, Higher Furzeham, Brixham, South Devon TQ5 8QY
tel (01803) 851098
email patriciaoxley6@gmail.com
website www.acumen-poetry.co.uk
Editor Patricia Oxley
3 p.a. (Jan/May/Sept) £5.50, £15.50 p.a.

Poetry, literary and critical articles, reviews, literary memoirs, etc. Send sae with submissions; online submissions also accepted (see website for guidelines). Payment: small. Founded 1985.

Aeroplane Monthly

Kelsey Publishing Group, Cudham, Kent TN16 3AG
tel (01959) 541444
website www.aeroplanemonthly.com
Editor Ben Dunnell
Monthly £4.30

Articles and photos relating to historical aviation. Length: up to 3,000 words. Illustrations: line, half-tone, colour, cartoons. Payment: £60 per 1,000 words, payable on publication; photos £10–£40; colour £80 per page. Founded 1973.

Aesthetica Magazine

PO Box 371, York YO23 1WL
tel (01904) 629137
email info@aestheticamagazine.com
website www.aestheticamagazine.com
Editor Cherie Federico
Bi-monthly £4.25

International art and culture magazine featuring articles on visual arts, film, performance and music. For freelance opportunities, contact the editor. Founded 2002.

Africa Confidential

Asempa Ltd, 73 Farringdon Road, London EC1M 3JQ
tel 020-7831 3511
email editorial@africa-confidential.com
website www.africa-confidential.com
Managing Editor Clare Tauben
Fortnightly £842 p.a. (print), £723 p.a. (online only)

News and analysis of political and economic developments in Africa. Unsolicited contributions welcomed, but must be exclusive and not published elsewhere. Length: 1,200-word features, 500-word pointers. Payment: from £300 per 1,000 words. No illustrations. Founded 1960.

Africa: St Patrick's Missions

St Patrick's, Kiltegan, Co. Wicklow, Republic of Ireland
tel +353 (0)59 6473600
email africa@spms.ie
website www.spms.org
Editor Rev. Tim Redmond

9 p.a. £10 p.a. (€15)

Articles of missionary and topical religious interest. Length: up to 1,000 words. Illustrations: colour.

African Business

IC Publications Ltd, 7 Coldbath Square,
London EC1R 4LQ
tel 020-7841 3210
email editorial@africasia.com
website www.africasia.com
Editor Anver Versi
Monthly £3, £40 p.a.

Articles on business, economic and financial topics of interest to businessmen, ministers and officials concerned with African affairs. Length: 1,000–1,400 words; shorter coverage 500 words. Illustrations: line, half-tone, cartoons. Payment: £90–£100 per 1,000 words; £1 per column cm for illustrations. Founded 1978.

Agenda

The Wheelwrights, Fletching Street, Mayfield,
East Sussex TN20 6TL
tel/fax (01435) 873703
email editor@agendapoetry.co.uk
website www.agendapoetry.co.uk
Editor Patricia McCarthy
Quarterly £28 p.a. (£35 libraries and institutions); £22 OAPs/students

Poetry and criticism. Study the journal and visit the website for submission details before submitting via email (submissions@agendapoetry.co.uk). Young poets and artists aged 16–38 are invited to submit work for the online publication *Broadsheet.*

AIR International

Key Publishing Ltd, PO Box 100, Stamford,
Lincs. PE9 1XQ
tel (01780) 755131
email airint@keypublishing.com
website www.airinternational.com
Editor Mark Ayton
Monthly £4.60

Technical articles on aircraft; features on topical aviation subjects – civil and military. Length: up to 3,000 words. Illustrations: colour transparencies/ prints, b&w prints/line drawings. Payment: £50 per 1,000 words or by negotiation; £20 colour, £10 b&w. Founded 1971.

All Out Cricket

TriNorth Ltd, Unit 3.40, 1–3 Brixton Road,
London SW9 6DE
tel 020-3176 0187
email comments@alloutcricket.com
website www.alloutcricket.com
Editor Phil Walker
12 p.a. £4.25

Humour, insight, expert commentary, interviews, photography and lifestyle. Email editor with ideas first. Payment by negotiation. Founded 2004.

Amateur Gardening

Time Inc. (UK), Westover House, West Quay Road,
Poole, Dorset BH15 1JG
tel (01202) 440840
email amateurgardening@timeinc.com
website www.amateurgardening.com
Editor Tim Rumball
Weekly £1.99

No longer accepts any form of unsolicited material. Founded 1884.

Amateur Photographer

(incorporating Photo Technique)
Time Inc. (UK), The Blue Fin Building,
110 Southwark Street, London SE1 0SU
tel 020-3148 5000
email amateurphotographer@timeinc.com
website www.amateurphotographer.co.uk
Editor Nigel Atherton
Weekly £2.99

Unsolicited editorial submissions are not encouraged. Founded 1884.

Amateur Stage Magazine

3Fold Media, 3rd Floor, 207 Regent Street,
London W1B 3HH
tel 020-7622 6670
email editor@amateurstagemagazine.co.uk
website www.amateurstagemagazine.co.uk
Editor Julian Cound
Monthly £32 p.a.

Articles on all aspects of amateur theatre, preferably practical and factual. Length: 600–2,000 words. Illustrations: photos, line drawings. Payment: none. Founded 1947.

Ambit

Staithe House, Main Road, Brancaster Staithe,
Norfolk PE31 8BP
tel 07503 633601
email info@ambitmagazine.co.uk
website www.ambitmagazine.co.uk
Editor Briony Bax
Quarterly £29.99 p.a. (UK)

Literary magazine. Publishes poetry, fiction, flash fiction and art in a full-colour quarterly magazine. Accepts submissions via online portal (see website for details): two submissions windows per year, 1 February to 1 April and 1 September to 1 November. Work sent outside these windows will not be accepted. Contributors may send up to five poems in one document or a story of up to 5,000 words; flash fiction no more than 1,000 words. Payment: see website. Founded 1959 by Dr Martin Bax.

Android Magazine

Imagine Publishing Ltd, Richmond House,
33 Richmond Hill, Bournemouth BH2 6EZ

tel (01202) 586200
email enquiries@imagine-publishing.co.uk
website www.littlegreenrobot.co.uk
Editor-in-Chief Nick Roberts
Monthly £4.99

Magazine focused solely on the Android operating system for phones and tablet PCs. Includes features, tips, tutorials and tweaking information, as well as app and hardware reviews. Unsolicited material not accepted but pitches are welcome via email.

Angler's Mail

Time Inc. (UK), The Blue Fin Building,
110 Southwark Street, London SE1 0SU
tel 020-3148 4159
email anglersmail@timeinc.com
website www.anglersmail.com
Editor Tim Knight
Weekly £1.90

News items about coarse fishing. Payment: by agreement.

Angling Times

Bauer Media, Media House,
Peterborough Business Park, Lynchwood,
Peterborough PE2 6EA
tel (01733) 395097
email steve.fitzpatrick@bauermedia.co.uk
website www.gofishing.co.uk/Angling-Times
Editor Steve Fitzpatrick
Weekly £86 p.a.

Articles, pictures, news stories, on all forms of angling. Illustrations: line, half-tone, colour. Payment: by arrangement. Founded 1953.

Apollo

22 Old Queen Street, London SW1H 9HP
tel 020-7961 0150
email editorial@apollomag.com
website www.apollo-magazine.com
Editor Thomas Marks
Monthly £5.95

Scholarly and topical articles of c. 2,000–3,000 words on art, architecture, ceramics, photography, furniture, armour, glass, sculpture and any subject connected with art and collecting. Interviews with collectors. Exhibition and book reviews, articles on current developments in museums and art galleries, regular columns on the art market and contemporary art. Payment: by arrangement. Illustrations: colour. Founded 1925.

Arc

c/o New Scientist, Lacon House,
84 Theobald's Road, London WC1X 8NS
tel 020-7611 1205
email simon.ings@arcfinity.org
website www.arcfinity.org
Editor Simon Ings
Bi-monthly £4.99 (ebook), £20 (hardback)

Journal of the future from the makers of *New Scientist*. Speculative short stories, features and essays. Material mostly commissioned. Length and payment: £500 for features between 2,000 and 3,000 words; £250 for essays between 1,000 and 1,500 words, and £1,500 for fiction between 5,000 and 10,000 words. Founded 2012.

The Architects' Journal

EMAP, Telephone House, 69–77 Paul Street,
London EC2A 4NW
tel 020-3033 2741
website www.architectsjournal.co.uk
Acting Editor Rory Olcayto
Weekly £5

Articles (mainly technical) on architecture, planning and building, accepted only with prior agreement of synopsis. Illustrations: photos and drawings. Payment: by arrangement. Founded 1895.

Architectural Design

John Wiley & Sons, 25 John Street,
London WC1N 2BS
tel 020-8326 3800
email architecturaldesign@wiley.com
website www.architectural-design-magazine.com
Editor Helen Castle
6 double issues p.a. £124 p.a. (print)

International architectural publication comprising an extensively illustrated thematic profile and magazine back section, *AD Plus*. Uncommissioned articles not accepted. Illustrations: drawings and photos, line (colour preferred). Payment: by arrangement. Founded 1930.

The Architectural Review

EMAP, Telephone House, 69–77 Paul Street,
London EC2A 4NW
tel 020-3033 2741
email areditorial@emap.com
website www.architectural-review.com
Editor Catherine Slessor
Monthly £10.99

Articles on architecture and the allied arts (urbanism, design, theory, history, technology). Writers must be thoroughly qualified. Length: up to 3,000 words. Payment: by arrangement. Illustrations: photos, drawings, etc. Founded 1896.

Architecture Today

161 Rosebery Avenue, London EC1R 4QX
tel 020-7837 0143
email editorial@architecturetoday.co.uk
website www.architecturetoday.co.uk
Editor Chris Foges
10 p.a. £45 p.a.

Mostly commissioned articles and features on today's European architecture. Length: 200–800 words.

Illustrations: colour. Payment: by negotiation. Founded 1989.

Art Business Today

Unit 2, Wye House, 6 Enterprise Way, London SW18 1FZ
tel 020-7381 6616
email info@fineart.co.uk
website www.artbusinesstoday.co.uk
Managing Editor Annabelle Ruston
5 p.a. £6.50

Distributed to the fine art and framing industry. Covers essential information on new products and technology, market trends and business analysis. Length: 800–1,600 words. Illustrations: colour photos, cartoons. Payment: by arrangement. Founded 1905.

Art Monthly

4th Floor, 28 Charing Cross Road, London WC2H 0DB
tel 020-7240 0389
email info@artmonthly.co.uk
website www.artmonthly.co.uk
Editor Patricia Bickers
10 p.a. £4.80, £48 p.a.

Features on modern and contemporary visual artists and art history, art theory and art-related issues; exhibition and book reviews. All material commissioned. Length: 750–1,500 words. Illustrations: b&w photos. Payment: features £100–£200; none for photos. Founded 1976.

The Art Newspaper

70 South Lambeth Road, London SW8 1RL
tel 020-3416 9000
email londonoffice@theartnewspaper.com
website www.theartnewspaper.com
Editor Jane Morris
11 p.a. £8.50

International coverage of visual art, news, politics, law, exhibitions with some feature pages. Length: 200–1,000 words. Illustrations: b&w photos. Payment: £350+ per 1,000 words. Founded 1990.

Art Quarterly

The Art Fund, 2 Granary Square, London N1C 4BH
tel 020-7225 4800
email info@artfund.org
website www.artfund.org
Interim Editor Claire Wrathall
Quarterly Free to members

Magazine of the Art Fund. Features on current events in the art world and coverage of the Art Fund's campaigns and grant-giving activities.

ArtReview & ArtReview Asia

1 Honduras Street, London EC1Y 0TH
tel 020-7490 8138
email office@artreview.com
website www.artreview.com
Editor Mark Rappolt
ArtReview Monthly £36 p.a. (print), £27 p.a. (iPad edition); ArtReviewAsia 3 p.a. £26 p.a. (print and online)

Modern and contemporary art and style features and reviews. Proposals welcome. Payment: from £350 per 1,000 words. Illustrations: colour. Founded 1949.

The Artist

The Artists' Publishing Co. Ltd, Caxton House, 63–65 High Street, Tenterden, Kent TN30 6BD
tel (01580) 763673
email info@tapc.co.uk
website www.painters-online.co.uk
Editor Sally Bulgin
13 p.a. (issues published every four weeks) £3.99

Practical, instructional articles on painting for all amateur and professional artists. Payment: by arrangement. Illustrations: line, half-tone, colour. Founded 1931.

Artists & Illustrators

Jubilee House, 2 Jubilee Place, London SW3 3TQ
tel 020-7349 3700
email info@artistsandillustrators.co.uk
website www.artistsandillustrators.co.uk
Editor Steve Pill
Monthly £4.20

Practical and inspirational articles for amateur and professional artists. Length: 500–1,500 words. Illustrations: hi-res digital images, hand-drawn illustrations. Payment: variable. Founded 1986.

Astronomy Now

Pole Star Publications, PO Box 175, Tonbridge, Kent TN10 4ZY
tel (01732) 446110
email editorial2015@astronomynow.com
website www.astronomynow.com
Editor Keith Cooper
Monthly £4.50

Specialises in translating exciting astronomy research into articles for the lay reader. Also covers amateur astronomy with equipment reviews and observing notes. Send sae for writers' guidelines. Length: 1,000–2,000 words. Payment: 15p per word; from £10 per photo. Founded 1987.

Athletics Weekly

PO Box 614, Farnham, Surrey GU9 1GR
tel (01733) 808550
email jason.henderson@athleticsweekly.com
website www.athleticsweekly.com
Editor Jason Henderson
Weekly £2.75

News and features on track and field athletics, road running, cross country, fell and race walking.

Material mostly commissioned. Length: 300–1,500 words. Illustrations: colour and b&w action and head/shoulder photos, line. Payment: varies. Founded 1945.

Attitude

Attitude Media, 33 Peartree Street, London EC1V 3AG
tel 020-7608 6363
email attitude@attitude.co.uk
website www.attitude.co.uk
Editor Matthew Todd
13 p.a. £4.85

Men's style magazine aimed primarily, but not exclusively, at gay men. Covers style/fashion, interviews, reviews, celebrities, humour. Illustrations: colour transparencies, b&w prints. Payment: £150 per 1,000 words; £100 per full-page illustration. Founded 1994.

The Author

84 Drayton Gardens, London SW10 9SB
tel 020-7373 6642
website www.societyofauthors.org/author
Editor James McConnachie
Quarterly £12

Organ of the Society of Authors. Commissioned articles from 1,000–2,000 words on any subject connected with the legal, commercial or technical side of authorship. Little scope for the freelance writer: preliminary letter advisable. Illustrations: line, occasional cartoons. Payment: by arrangement. Founded 1890.

Auto Express

Dennis Publishing Ltd, 30 Cleveland Street, London W1T 4JD
tel 020-7907 6000
email editorial@autoexpress.co.uk
website www.autoexpress.co.uk
Editor-in-Chief Steve Fowler
Weekly £2.80

News stories, and general interest features about drivers as well as cars. Illustrations: colour photos. Payment: features £350 per 1,000 words; photos, varies. Founded 1988.

Aviation News

Key Publishing, PO Box 100, Stamford PE9 1XQ
tel (01780) 755131
email dino.carrara@aviation-news.co.uk
website www.aviation-news.co.uk
Editor Dino Carrara
Monthly £4.40

Covers all aspects of aviation. Many articles commissioned. Payment: by arrangement.

BackTrack

Pendragon Publishing, PO Box 3, Easingwold, York YO61 3YS
tel/fax (01347) 824397
email pendragonpublishing@btinternet.com
website www.pendragonpublishing.co.uk
Editor Michael Blakemore
Monthly £4.40

British railway history from 1820s to 1980s. Welcomes ideas from writers and photographers. Articles must be well researched, authoritative and accompanied by illustrations. Length: 3,000–5,000 words (main features), 500–3,000 words (articles). Illustrations: colour and b&w. Payment: £30 per 1,000 words, £18.50 colour, £10 b&w. Founded 1986.

Banipal

1 Gough Square, London EC4A 3DE
tel 020-7832 1350
email editor@banipal.co.uk
website www.banipal.co.uk
Editor Samuel Shimon
4 p.a. £21 p.a. (print only, new subscribers; £19 p.a. for renewals), £18 p.a. (digital)

Showcases contemporary Arab authors in English translation. Welcomes inquiries from authors and translators; see website for full submission guidelines.

The Banker

FT Business, 1 Southwark Bridge, London SE1 9HL
tel 020-7873 3000
email brian.caplen@ft.com
website www.thebanker.com
Editor-in-Chief Brian Caplen
Monthly £695 p.a.

Global coverage of retail banking, corporate banking, banking technology, transactions services, investment banking and capital markets, regulation and top 1,000 bank listings.

Baptist Times

129 Broadway, Didcot, Oxon OX11 8RT
tel (01235) 517677
email editor@baptisttimes.co.uk
website www.baptisttimes.co.uk
Editor Paul Hobson
Website only.

Religious or social affairs, news, features and reviews. Founded 1855.

BBC Good Food

Immediate Media Co. Ltd, Vineyard House, 44 Brook Green, London W6 7BT
email enquiries@bbcgoodfoodmagazine.com
website www.bbcgoodfood.com
Editor Gillian Carter
Monthly £3.99

Inspiration for everyday, weekend and seasonal cooking for cooks of all levels. Features recipes from many BBC TV chefs as well as other leading food writers, along with an extensive range of hints, tips and features.

BBC Sky at Night Magazine

Immediate Media Co. Ltd, Fairfax House, Bristol BS1 3BN
tel 0117 314 8758
email chris.bramley@immediate.co.uk
website www.skyatnightmagazine.com
Editor Chris Bramley
Monthly £4.99

Offers a mix of practical observing tips and information, space science features and equipment information to both experienced astronomers and those new to the subject. Founded 2005.

Bella

H. Bauer Publishing, Academic House, 24–28 Oval Road, London NW1 7DT
tel 020-7241 8000
website www.bellamagazine.co.uk
Editor Julia Davis
Weekly 92p

Women's magazine with celebrity interviews, exclusive photos, real-life stories, high-street fashion, diet advice, health, food and travel. Payment: by arrangement. Founded 1987.

Benn's Media

Cision UK Ltd, Longbow House, 20 Chiswell Street, London EC1Y 4TW
tel 020-7251 7259
email info.uk@cision.com
website www.cision.com
Editor Laura Warrick
1 p.a. £495 two-volume set; £275 one volume

Reference guide to the world's news media in two volumes. Covers newspapers, broadcast stations and news agencies as well as business and consumer periodicals for UK and Ireland.

Best

Hearst Magazines UK, 33 Broadwick Street, London W1F 0DQ
tel 020-7339 4500
email jackie.hatton@hearst.co.uk
website www.bestdaily.co.uk
Editor Jackie Hatton
Weekly 92p

Short stories. No other uncommissioned work accepted, but always willing to look at ideas/outlines. Length: 1,000 words for short stories, variable for other work. Payment: by agreement. Founded 1987.

The Big Issue

43 Bath Street, Glasgow G2 1HW
tel 0141 352 7260
email editorial@thebigissue.com
website www.bigissue.com
Editor Paul McNamee
Weekly £2.50

Features, current affairs, reviews, interviews – of general interest and on social issues. Length: 1,000 words (features). No short stories or poetry. Illustrations: colour and b&w photos and line. Payment: £160 per 1,000 words. Founded 1991.

Bike

Bauer Consumer Media, Media House, Lynchwood, Peterborough PE2 6EA
tel (01733) 468181
email bike@bauermedia.com
website www.bikemagazine.co.uk
Editor Hugo Wilson
Monthly £4.10

Motorcycle magazine. Interested in articles, features, news. Length: articles/features 1,000–3,000 words. Illustrations: colour and b&w photos. Payment: £140 per 1,000 words; photos per size/position. Founded 1971.

Bird Watching

Bauer Consumer Media, Media House, Lynchwood, Peterborough PE2 6EA
tel (01733) 468201
email birdwatching@bauermedia.co.uk
website www.birdwatching.co.uk
Editor Matthew Merritt
Monthly £4.50

Broad range of bird-related features and photography, particularly looking at bird behaviour, bird news, reviews and UK birdwatching sites. Limited amount of overseas features. Emphasis on providing accurate information in entertaining ways. Send synopsis first. Length: up to 1,200 words. Illustrations: emailed jpgs and photo images on CD, bird identification artwork. Payment: by negotiation. Founded 1986.

Birdwatch

Warners Group Publications, The Chocolate Factory, 5 Clarendon Road, London N22 6XJ
tel 020-8881 0550
website www.birdwatch.co.uk
Managing Editor Dominic Mitchell
Monthly £4.10

Topical articles on all aspects of British and Irish birds and birding, including conservation, identification, sites and habitats and equipment, as well as overseas destinations. Length: 700–1,500 words. Illustrations: hi-res jpgs (300 dpi at 1,500 pixels min. width) of wild British and European birds considered; submit on CD/DVD or full size via email or file-sharing site. Artwork by negotiation. Payment: £50 per 1,000 words; colour: photos £15–£40, cover £75, line by negotiation; b&w: photos £10, line £10–£40. Founded 1991.

Black Beauty & Hair

Hawker Publications, 2nd Floor, Culvert House, Culvert Road, London SW11 5DH

tel 020-7720 2108
email info@blackbeautyandhair.com
website www.blackbeautyandhair.com
Editor Irene Shelley
Bi-monthly £2.99

Beauty and style articles relating specifically to the black woman; celebrity features. True-life stories and salon features. Length: approx. 1,000 words. Illustrations: colour and b&w photos. Payment: £100 per 1,000 words; photos £25–£75. Founded 1982.

Black Static

TTA Press, 5 Martins Lane, Witcham, Ely, Cambs. CB6 2LB
website www.ttapress.com
Editor Andy Cox
Bi-monthly £4.99

New horror and dark fantasy stories. Also features interviews with, and profiles of, authors and film-makers. Send sae with all submissions. Considers unsolicited material and welcomes ideas for articles and features. Length: 3,000–4,000 words (articles and features), short stories unrestricted. Illustrations: send samples and portfolios. Payment: by arrangement. Founded 1994.

BMA News

British Medical Association, BMA House, Tavistock Square, London WC1H 9JP
tel 020-7383 6122
email news@bma.org.uk
website www.bma.org.uk/news-views-analysis
Editor Caroline Winter-Jones
£120 p.a.

News and analysis. Length: 700–1,000 words (features), 100–300 words (news). Illustrations: any colour and b&w artwork. Payment: by negotiation. Founded 1966.

The Book Collector

(incorporating Bibliographical Notes and Queries)
22 Clarendon Road, London W11 3AB
tel 020-7792 3492
email editor@thebookcollector.co.uk
website www.thebookcollector.co.uk
Editorial Board Nicolas Barker (Editor), P. Cleaver, A. Edwards, J. Fergusson, T. Hofmann, S. Lane, D. McKitterick, J. Winterkorn
Quarterly £55 p.a. (UK), €85 (Europe), US$115 (RoW; airmail)

Articles, biographical and bibliographical, on the collection and study of printed books and MSS. Payment: for reviews only. Founded 1952.

Books Ireland

Unit 9, 78 Furze Road, Dublin 8, Republic of Ireland
tel +353 (0)1 2947860
email una@wordwellbooks.com
website www.wordwellbooks.com
Editor Tony Canavan
Bi-monthly €5.95, €35 p.a. (€45 p.a. to UK mainland)

Reviews of Irish-interest and Irish-author books, as well as articles of interest to librarians, booksellers and readers. Length: 800–1,400 words. Founded 1976.

The Bookseller

Ground Floor, Crowne House, 56–58 Southwark Street, London SE1 1UN
tel 020-3358 0365
email felicity.wood@thebookseller.co.uk
website www.thebookseller.com
Editor Philip Jones,
Features Editor Tom Tivnan
Weekly £4.95

Journal of the UK publishing, bookselling trade and libraries. While outside contributions are welcomed, most of the journal's contents are commissioned. Length: about 1,000–1,500 words. Payment: by arrangement. Founded 1858.

Bowls International

Key Publishing Ltd, PO Box 100, Stamford, Lincs. PE9 1XQ
tel 07791 696718
email sian.honnor@keypublishing.com
website www.bowlsinternational.com
Editor Sian Honnor
Monthly £28 p.a.

Sport and news items and features; occasional, bowls oriented short stories. Illustrations: colour transparencies, b&w photos, occasional line, cartoons. Payment: sport/news approx. 25p per line, features approx. £50 per page; colour £25, b&w £10. Founded 1981.

British Birds

4 Harlequin Gardens, St Leonards-on-Sea TN37 7PF
tel (01424) 755155
email editor@britishbirds.co.uk
website www.britishbirds.co.uk
Editor Dr Roger Riddington
Monthly £53 p.a. (£60 p.a. overseas)

Publishes major papers on identification, behaviour, conservation, distribution, ecology, movements, status and taxonomy with official reports on: rare breeding birds, scarce migrants and rare birds in Britain. Payment: token. Founded 1907.

British Chess Magazine

Albany House, Shute End, Wokingham, Berks. RG40 1BJ
email editor@britishchessmagazine.co.uk
website www.britishchessmagazine.co.uk
Co-editors James Pratt, IM Shaun Talburt
Monthly £4.20, £45 p.a., £57 p.a. (Europe), £68 (RoW)

Authoritative reports and commentary on the UK and overseas chess world. Payment: by arrangement. Founded 1881.

British Deaf News

British Deaf Association, 3rd Floor,
356 Holloway Road, London N7 6PA
tel 020-7697 4140
email bdn@bda.org.uk
email membership@bda.org.uk (membership enquiries)
website www.bda.org.uk/British_Deaf_News
Editor Anna Tsekouras
Monthly £10 p.a. (online subscription), from £30 p.a. (print)

Includes interviews, exclusives, campaigns, profiles and special features. Founded 1872.

The British Journal of Photography

Apptitude Media, 5–25 Scrutton Street,
London EC2A 4HJ
tel 020-8123 6873
email bjp.editor@bjphoto.co.uk
website www.bjp-online.com
Editor Simon Bainbridge
Monthly £7.99

Focus on all aspects of professional photography: articles on fine art, commercial, fashion, social and press, alongside technical reviews of the latest software and equipment. Founded 1854.

British Journalism Review

SAGE Publications, 1 Oliver's Yard, 55 City Road,
London EC1Y 1SP
tel 020-7324 8500
email editor@bjr.org.uk
website www.bjr.org.uk
Editor Kim Fletcher
Quarterly £44 p.a. for individuals (print only; institutional rates also available)

Comment/criticism/review of matters published by, or of interest to, the media. Length: 1,500–3,000 words. Illustrations: b&w photos. Payment: by arrangement. Founded 1989.

British Medical Journal

BMJ Publishing Group, BMA House,
Tavistock Square, London WC1H 9JR
tel 020-7387 4410
email fgodlee@bmj.com
website www.bmj.com/thebmj
Editor Dr Fiona Godlee
Weekly Free to members of BMA; for subscription details see website

Medical and related articles. Payment: by arrangement. Founded 1840.

British Philatelic Bulletin

Royal Mail, Tallents House, 21 South Gyle Crescent,
Edinburgh EH12 9PB
email bulletin.enquiries@royalmail.co.uk
website www.royalmail.com/stamps
Editor William Doherty
Monthly £12.95 p.a.

Articles on any aspect of British philately – stamps, postmarks, postal history; also stamp collecting in general. Length: up to 1,500 words (articles); 250 words (news). Payment: £75 per 1,000 words. Illustrations: colour. Founded 1963.

Broadcast

Media Business Insight Ltd, 101 Finsbury Pavement,
London EC2A 1RS
tel 020-3033 4267
email chris.curtis@broadcastnow.co.uk
website www.broadcastnow.co.uk
Editor Chris Curtis
Weekly From £245 p.a.

For people working or interested in the UK and international broadcast industry. News, features, analysis and opinions. Covers the latest developments in programming, commissioning, digital, technology and post-production. Illustrations: colour, b&w, line, cartoons.

Building

UBM Information Ltd, 3rd Floor,
245 Blackfriars Road, London SE1 9UY
tel 020-7560 4000
email building@ubm.com
website www.building.co.uk
Editor Sarah Richardson
Weekly £4.25

Covers all aspects of the construction industry from architecture to development to social housing, industrial and manufacturing aspects of the building industry. Will consider articles on architecture at home and abroad; also news and photos. Payment: by arrangement. Founded 1842.

Building Design

UBM EMEA Built Environment,
240 Blackfriars Road, London SE1 8BF
tel 020-7921 5000
email buildingdesign@ubm.com
website www.bdonline.co.uk
Editor Thomas Lane

Daily online newspaper and magazine plus monthly digital edition. News and features on all aspects of architecture and urban design. All material commissioned. Length: up to 1,500 words. Illustrations: colour and b&w photos, line, cartoons. Payment: £150 per 1,000 words; illustrations by negotiation. Founded 1970.

Bunbury Magazine

5 Chester Street, Bury, Lancs. BL9 6EU
tel 07446 025630
email submissions@bunburymagazine.com
website www.bunburymagazine.com
Directors and Editors Christopher Moriarty, Keri-Ann Edwards

Online arts and literature magazine committed to providing a platform to both grass-roots and established writers and artists. Submissions welcomed on a variety of subjects, from poetry to artwork, flash fiction to graphic stories, life writing to photography, but please see website for full guidelines. Also offers editorial services and a regular writers' group, Do the Write Thing. Founded 2013.

The Burlington Magazine

14–16 Duke's Road, London WC1H 9SZ
tel 020-7388 8157
email editorial@burlington.org.uk
website www.burlington.org.uk
Editor Richard Shone
Monthly £16.60

Deals with the history and criticism of art; book and exhibition reviews; illustrated monthly Calendar section. Potential contributors must have special knowledge of the subjects treated; MSS compiled from works of reference are unacceptable. Length: 500–5,000 words. Payment: up to £150. Illustrations: colour images. Founded 1903.

Buses

Key Publishing Ltd, Foundry Road, Stamford, Lincs. PE9 2PP
tel (01780) 484630
Editor Alan Millar, PO Box 14644, Leven KY9 1WX
tel (01333) 340637
email buseseditor@btconnect.com
website www.busesmag.com
Monthly £4.40

Articles of interest to both road passenger transport operators and bus enthusiasts. Preliminary enquiry essential. Illustrations: digital, colour transparencies, half-tone, line maps. Payment: on application. Founded 1949.

Business Traveller

Panacea Publishing, 5th Floor, Warwick House, 25 Buckingham Palace Road, London SW1W 0PP
tel 020-7821 2700
email enquiries@panaceapublishing.co.uk
website www.businesstraveller.com
Editor-in-Chief Tom Otley
10 p.a. £42.95 p.a. (print), £27.49 (digital)

Articles, features and news on consumer travel aimed at individual frequent international business travellers. Submit ideas with recent clippings and a CV. Length: varies. Illustrations: colour for destinations features; send lists to Deborah Miller, Picture Editor. Payment: on application. Founded 1976.

Cambridge Magazine

Cambridge Newspapers Ltd, Winship Road, Milton, Cambridge CB24 6PP
tel (01223) 434419
email alice.ryan@cambridge-news.co.uk
Head of Magazines Alice Ryan
Monthly Split free and paid-for (cover price £3.95)

Features-led magazine on Cambridge, focusing on arts and culture, people and places, homes and gardens, food and drink, fashion and beauty, gears and gadgets. Created in 2013 following the merging of the *Cambridgeshire Journal* and *Style* magazines.

Campaign

Haymarket Business Publications Ltd, 174 Hammersmith Road, London W6 7JP
tel 020-8943 5000
email maisie.mccabe@haymarket.com
website www.campaignlive.co.uk
Editor-in-Chief Claire Beale
Weekly £3.70

News and articles covering the whole of the mass communications field, particularly advertising in all its forms, marketing and the media. Features should not exceed 2,000 words. News items also welcome. Press day, Wednesday. Payment: by arrangement.

Candis

Newhall Publications Ltd, Newhall Lane, Hoylake, Wirral CH47 4BQ
tel 0151 632 3232
email fiction@candis.co.uk
website www.candis.co.uk
Editor Flic Everett
Monthly £3.50 Subscription only

Commissions one 2,500 word short story each month by a well-known published author. Unsolicited material is no longer received and will be returned unread. Writers willing to share a personal life story or experience for real lives feature may send a synopsis to editor@candis.co.uk. Also covers health, news, celebrity interviews, family issues, fashion and beauty.

Car

Bauer Consumer Media, 3rd Floor, Media House, Lynchwood, Peterborough PE2 6EA
tel (01733) 468379
email car@bauermedia.co.uk
website www.carmagazine.co.uk
Editor Phil McNamara
Monthly £4.50

Top-grade journalistic features on car driving, car people and cars. Length: 1,000–2,500 words. Payment: minimum £350 per 1,000 words. Illustrations: b&w and colour photos to professional standards. Founded 1962.

Car Mechanics

Bauer Media Group, Media House, Lynchwood, Peterborough Business Park, Peterborough PE2 6EA
tel (01733) 468000
email carmechanics@bauermedia.co.uk
website www.carmechanicsmag.co.uk

Editor Martyn Knowles
Monthly £4

Practical articles on maintaining, repairing and uprating modern cars for DIY plus the motor trade. Always interested in finding new talent for our rather specialised market, but study a recent copy before submitting ideas or features. Email outlining feature recommended. Payment: by arrangement. Illustrations: line drawings, colour prints, digital images. Supply package of text and pictures. Founded 1958.

Caravan Magazine

Warners Group Publications, The Maltings, Bourne, Lincs. PE10 9PH
tel (01778) 391000
email johns@warnersgroup.co.uk
website www.caravanmagazine.co.uk
Managing Editor John Sootheran
Monthly £3.95

Lively articles based on real experience of touring caravanning, especially if well illustrated by photos provided by the author or from regional Tourist Boards, attractions etc. Payment: by arrangement. Founded 1933.

Carousel – The Guide to Children's Books

Saturn Business Centre, 54–76 Bissell Street, Birmingham B5 7HP
tel 0121 622 7458
email carousel.guide@virgin.net
website www.carouselguide.co.uk
Editor David Blanch
3 p.a. £4.95

Reviews of fiction, non-fiction and poetry books for children, plus in-depth articles; profiles of authors and illustrators. Length: 1,200 words (articles); 150 words (reviews). Illustrations: colour and b&w. Payment: by arrangement. Founded 1995.

Cat World

PO Box 2258, Pulborough RH20 9BA
tel (01903) 884988
email support@ashdown.co.uk
website www.catworld.co.uk
Editor Jill Mundy
Monthly £3.25

Bright, lively articles on any aspect of cat ownership. Articles on breeds of cats and veterinary articles by acknowledged experts only. No unsolicited fiction. All submissions by email or on disk. Illustrations: colour prints, tiffs. Payment: by arrangement. Founded 1981.

The Caterer

Travel Weekly Group Ltd, 52 Grosvenor Gardens, London, SW1W 0AU
tel 020-7881 4808
email info@caterer.com
website www.thecaterer.com
Editor Amanda Afiya
Weekly £3.70

Multimedia brand for the UK hospitality industry. In print and online, offers content, job news and a digital platform for hotel, restaurant, food service and pub and bar operators across the country. Article length: up to 1,500 words. Illustrations: line, half-tone, colour. Payment: by arrangement. Founded 1878.

The Catholic Herald

Herald House, Lambs Passage, Bunhill Row, London EC1Y 8TQ
tel 020-77448 3602
email editorial@catholicherald.co.uk
website www.catholicherald.co.uk
Editor Luke Coppen
Weekly £2

Independent newspaper covering national and international affairs from a Catholic/Christian viewpoint as well as church news. Length: articles 800–1,200 words. Illustrations: photos of Catholic and Christian interest. Payment: by arrangement.

Catholic Pictorial

36 Henry Street, Liverpool L1 5BS
tel 0151 522 1007
email p.heneghan@rcaol.co.uk
website www.catholicpic.co.uk
Editor Peter Heneghan
Monthly Free

News and photo features (maximum 800 words plus illustration) on Merseyside, regional and national Catholic interest only; also cartoons. Has a strongly social editorial and is a trenchant tabloid. Payment: by arrangement. Founded 1961.

Catholic Times

The Universe Media Group Ltd,
30 St Mary's Parsonage, Manchester M3 2WJ
email kevin.flaherty@thecatholicuniverse.com
website www.thecatholicuniverse.com
Editor Kevin Flaherty
Weekly £1.30

News (400 words) and news features (800 words) of Catholic interest. Illustrations: colour and b&w photos. Payment: £30–£80; photos £50. Relaunched 1993.

The Catholic Universe

The Universe Media Group Ltd,
30 St Mary's Parsonage, Manchester M3 2WJ
tel 0161 214 1249
email joseph.kelly@thecatholicuniverse.com
website www.thecatholicuniverse.com
Editor Joe Kelly
Weekly £1.30

Catholic Sunday newspaper. News stories, features and photos on all aspects of Catholic life required; also cartoons. Send sae with MSS. Payment: by arrangement. Founded 1860.

Central and Eastern European London Review

161 Fordwych Road, London NW2 3NG
tel 07983 918170
email ceel.org@gmail.com
website www.ceel.org.uk
Editor Robin Ashenden

Online magazine. Voluntary contributions sought on any aspect of Central and Eastern European life in the capital. Book/film reviewers especially welcome. Submissions: via email. Founded 2014.

Ceramic Review

63 Great Russell Street, London WC1B 3BF
tel 020-7183 5583
email editorial@ceramicreview.com
website www.ceramicreview.com
Editor Sue Herdman
6 p.a. £6.30, £36 p.a., £32 p.a. for Craft Potters Association members

High-quality international magazine containing critical features, reviews and practical information on all forms of ceramics and clay art. Welcomes article proposals: critical, profile, technical, historical or experiential, as well as looking at the role of ceramics within contemporary culture. Feature articles run from 800 to 1,400 words and must include large, high-resolution images. Payment is offered at current rates on publication.

Chat

Time Inc. (UK), The Blue Fin Building, 110 Southwark Street, London SE1 0SU
tel 020-3148 5000
email chat_magazine@timeinc.com
website www.chatmagazine.co.uk
Editor Gilly Sinclair
Weekly 90p

Tabloid weekly for women. Includes reader's letters, tips and true-life features. Payment: by arrangement. Founded 1985.

Church of England Newspaper

Religious Intelligence Ltd, 14 Great College Street, London SW1P 3RX
tel 020-7878 1001
email cen@churchnewspaper.com
website www.churchnewspaper.com
Editor Colin Blakely
Weekly £70 p.a.

Anglican news and articles relating the Christian faith to everyday life. Evangelical basis; almost exclusively commissioned articles. Study of paper desirable. Length: up to 1,000 words. Illustrations: photos, line drawings, cartoons. Payment: c. £40 per 1,000 words; photos £22, line by arrangement. Founded 1828.

Church Times

108–114 Golden Lane, London EC1Y 0TG
tel 020-7776 1060
email news@churchtimes.co.uk
website www.churchtimes.co.uk
Editor Paul Handley
Weekly £1.95

Articles on religious topics are considered. No verse or fiction. Length: up to 1,000 words. Illustrations: news photos, sent promptly. Payment: £100 per 1,000 words. Negotiated rates for illustrations. Founded 1863.

Classic Boat Magazine

The Chelsea Magazine Co., Jubilee House, 2 Jubilee Place, London SW3 3TQ
tel 020-7349 3755
email Dan.Houston@chelseamagazines.com
website www.classicboat.co.uk
Editor Dan Houston
Monthly £4.75

Cruising and technical features, restorations, events, new boat reviews, practical, maritime history; news. Study of magazine essential: read three to four back issues and send for contributors' guidelines. Length: 500–2,000 words. Illustrations: colour and b&w photos; line drawings of hulls. Payment: £75–£100 per published page. Founded 1987.

Classic Cars

Bauer Consumer Media, Media House, Lynchwood, Peterborough Business Park, Peterborough PE2 6EA
tel (01733) 468000
email classic.cars@bauermedia.co.uk
website www.classiccarsmagazine.co.uk
Editor Phil Bell
Monthly £4.50 (print), £3.99 (iPad and Android platforms)

Specialist articles on older cars and related events. Length: from 150–4,000 words (subject to prior contract). Photography: classic car event photography on spec; feature photography on commission basis. Payment: by negotiation. Founded 1973.

Classic Rock

Prospect Business Centre, 3 Stanley Boulevard, Blantyre G72 0BN
email media@teamrock.com
website www.classicrockmagazine.com
13 p.a. £5.50

Focuses on hard rock, heavy metal and the older generation of 'Rockers'. Features the real stories behind rock legends with in-depth profiles, interviews, news overviews, tour dates, retrospective articles and reviews.

Classical Music

Rhinegold Publishing Ltd, 20 Rugby Street, London WC1N 3QZ

tel 020-7333 1729
email classical.music@rhinegold.co.uk
website www.classicalmusicmagazine.org
Editor Kimon Daltas
Fortnightly £4.95

News, opinion, features on the classical music business. All material commissioned. Illustrations: colour photos and line; colour covers. Payment: minimum £120 per 1,000 words. Founded 1976.

Climb Magazine

Greenshires Publishing, 160–164 Barkby Road, Leicester LE16 8FZ
tel 0116 2022600
email climbmagazine@gmail.com
website www.climbmagazine.com
Editor David Pickford
12 p.a. £4.35

Climbing magazine covering mainly British rock climbing. Features all aspects of climbing worldwide from bouldering to mountaineering. Contact Editor to discuss requirements. Founded 1987.

Climber

Warner Group Publications, The Maltings, West Street, Bourne, Lincs. PE10 9PH
tel (01778) 391000
email climbercomments@warnersgroup.co.uk
website www.climber.co.uk
Editor David Simmonite
Monthly £3.99

Articles on all aspects of rock climbing/mountaineering in Great Britain and abroad, and on related subjects. Study of magazine essential. Length: 1,500–2,000 words. Illustrations: colour transparencies. Payment: according to merit. Founded 1962.

Closer

Bauer Consumer Media, Endeavour House, 189 Shaftesbury Avenue, London WC2H 8JG
tel 020-7437 9011
email closer@closermag.co.uk
website www.closeronline.co.uk
Editor Lisa Burrow
Weekly £1.50

Women's entertainment magazine with true-life stories and celebrity articles, letters, listings and reviews. Payment by negotiation.

Coin News

Token Publishing Ltd, Orchard House, Duchy Road, Heathpark, Honiton, Devon EX14 1YD
tel (01404) 46972
email info@tokenpublishing.com
website www.tokenpublishing.com
Editor John W. Mussell
Monthly £4

Articles of high standard on coins, tokens, paper money. Send text in digital form. Length: up to 2,000 words. Payment: by arrangement. Founded 1964.

Commercial Motor

9 Sutton Court Road, Sutton, Surrey SM1 4SZ
tel 020-8652 3500
website www.commercialmotor.com
Editor Will Shiers
Weekly £2.90

Technical and road transport articles only. Length: up to 1,500 words. Payment: varies. Illustrations: drawings and photos. Founded 1905.

Community Care

Reed Business Information Ltd, Quadrant House, The Quadrant, Sutton, Surrey SM2 5AS
tel 020-8652 3500
email comcare.adults@rbi.co.uk
website www.communitycare.co.uk
Content Director Ruth Smith
Weekly

Online magazine site with articles, features and news covering the Social Services sector.

Company

Hearst Magazines UK, National Magazines House, 72 Broadwick Street, London W1V 2BP
tel 020-7439 5000
email company.mail@hearst.co.uk
website www.company.co.uk
Editor Victoria White
Daily

Online magazine. Articles on a wide variety of subjects, relevant to young, independent women. Most articles are commissioned. Payment: usual magazine rate. Illustrated. Founded 1978.

Computer Arts

Future Publishing Ltd, Quay House, The Ambury, Bath BA1 1UA
tel (01225) 442244
email hello@computerarts.co.uk
website www.computerarts.co.uk
Editor Nick Carson
Monthly £6

Magazine for digital artists and designers with in-depth tutorials together with tips for web design, typography, 3D, animation, motion graphics and multimedia. Also reviews the latest hardware and software releases and includes interviews with leading figures in the global design world.

Computer Weekly

1st Floor, 3–4 Little Portland Street, London W1W 7JB
tel 020-7186 1400
email cw-news@computerweekly.com
website www.computerweekly.com
Editor Bryan Glick

Weekly Free to registered subscribers

Feature articles on IT-related topics for business/ industry users. Length: 1,200 words. Illustrations: colour photos. Payment: £250 per 1,000 words. Founded 1966.

Computeractive

Dennis Publishing, 30 Cleveland Street, London W1T 4JD
tel 020-7907 6000
website www.computeractive.co.uk
Editor Daniel Booth
Fortnightly £1.99

Computing magazine offering plain-English advice for PCs, tablets, phones and the Internet, as well as product reviews and technology news.

Condé Nast Traveller

Condé Nast Publications Ltd, Vogue House, Hanover Square, London W1S 1JU
tel 020-7499 9080
email editorcntraveller@condenast.co.uk
website www.cntraveller.com
Editor Melinda Stevens
Monthly £4.10

Lavishly photographed articles on all aspects of travel, featuring exotic destinations and those close to home. Specialist pieces include food and wine, motoring, health, foreign correspondents, travel news, hotels. Illustrations: colour. Payment: by arrangement. Founded 1997.

Cook Vegetarian

Aceville Publications, 25 Phoenix Court, Hawkins Road, Colchester CO2 8JY
tel (01206) 508627
email fae@cookveg.co.uk
website www.cookveg.co.uk
Contact Fae Gilfillan
Monthly £3.99

Aimed at fans of meat-free cookery. Features recipes from a variety of cuisines and for diverse dietary requirements.

Cosmopolitan

Hearst Magazines UK, National Magazines House, 72 Broadwick Street, London W1F 9EP
tel 020-7439 5000
website www.cosmopolitan.co.uk
Editor-in-Chief Louise Court
Monthly £3.80

Articles. Commissioned material only. Payment: by arrangement. Illustrated. Founded 1972.

Cotswold Life

Archant House, Oriel Road, Cheltenham, Glos. GL50 1BB
tel (01242) 216050
email info@cotswoldlife.co.uk
website www.cotswoldlife.co.uk
Editor Mike Lowe, *Deputy Editor* Candia McKormack
Monthly £3.99

Articles on the Cotswolds, including places of interest, high-profile personalities, local events, arts, history, interiors, fashion and food. Founded 1967.

Country Homes and Interiors

Time Inc. (UK), The Blue Fin Building, 110 Southwark Street, London SE1 0SU
tel 020-3148 5000
email countryhomes@timeinc.com
website www.housetohome.co.uk/countryhomesandinteriors
Editor Rhoda Parry
Monthly £4.10

Articles on country homes and gardens, interiors, food, lifestyle. Payment: from £250 per 1,000 words. Founded 1986.

Country Life

Time Inc. (UK), The Blue Fin Building, 110 Southwark Street, London SE1 0SU
tel 020-3148 4444
website www.countrylife.co.uk
Editor Mark Hedges, *Deputy Editor* Rupert Uloth
Weekly £3.20

Illustrated journal chiefly concerned with British country life, social history, architecture and the fine arts, natural history, agriculture, gardening and sport. Length: about 1,000 or 1,300 words (articles). Illustrations: mainly colour photos. Payment: according to merit. Founded 1897.

Country Living

Hearst Magazines UK, National Magazines House, 72 Broadwick Street, London W1F 9EP
tel 020-7439 5000
email features@countryliving.com
website www.countryliving.co.uk
Editor Susy Smith
Monthly £4.10

Up-market home-interest magazine with a country lifestyle theme, covering interiors, gardens, crafts, food, wildlife, rural and green issues. Do not send unsolicited material or valuable transparencies. Illustrations: line, half-tone, colour. Payment: by arrangement. Founded 1985.

Country Smallholding

Archant Regional Ltd, Fair Oak Close, Exeter Airport Business Park, Clyst Honiton, Exeter EX5 2UL
tel (01392) 888481
email editorial.csh@archant.co.uk
website www.countrysmallholding.com
Editor Simon McEwan
Monthly £3.95

The magazine for smallholders. Practical, how-to articles and seasonal features on organic gardening, small-scale poultry and livestock keeping, country crafts, cookery and general subjects of interest to smallholders and others. Approach the Editor in writing or by phone or email with ideas. Length: up to 1,200 words. Payment: on application. Founded 1975 as *Practical Self-Sufficiency*.

Country Walking

Bauer Consumer Media, Media House, Lynchwood, Peterborough Business Park, Peterborough PE2 6EA
tel (01733) 468205
website www.LFTO.com
Editor Mark Sutcliffe
13 p.a. £4.20

Features. Length: 1,000 words on average. Illustrations: digital images. Payment: by arrangement. Founded 1987.

The Countryman

Country Publications Ltd, The Water Mill, Broughton Hall, Skipton, North Yorkshire BD23 3AG
tel (01756) 701381
email editorial@thecountryman.co.uk
website www.countrymanmagazine.co.uk
Editor Mark Whitley
Monthly £3.70

Features rural life, wildlife and natural history, country people, traditions, crafts, covering whole of UK. Positive view of countryside and rural issues. Non-political, and no bloodsports. Unusual or quirky topics welcomed. Copy must be well written and accurate, for well-informed readership who are generally 40+ with strong affection for countryside. Articles between 600-1,000 words. Illustrations: good-quality digital images, or b&w/colour photos. Study magazine before submitting ideas. Send detailed outline first. Payment: by agreement. Founded 1927.

craft&design Magazine

PO Box 5, Driffield, East Yorksshire YO25 8JD
tel (01377) 255213
email info@craftanddesign.net
website www.craftanddesign.net
Editor Angie Boyer
Bi-monthly £6.95, £39.50 p.a. (or £37.50 by Direct Debit) for UK subscribers

Features and news on designer makers and other areas of the craft industry. Aims to promote quality craftsmanship. Welcomes ideas for articles and features. Length: 1,000 words (articles and features). Payment £120 per 1,000 words. Illustrations: hi-res digital images. See website for all editorial copy dates. Founded 1983.

Crafts Magazine

44A Pentonville Road, London N1 9BY
tel 020-7806 2538
email editorial@craftscouncil.org.uk
website www.craftsmagazine.org.uk
Editor Grant Gibson
Bi-monthly £6.20

Magazine for contemporary craft, published by the Crafts Council. Specialist features, craft news and reviews, archive articles from the magazine's 35-year history and contributors from iconic institutions such as the V&A, Royal College of Art and Central St Martins. Submissions for review should include pictures and applicants should be mindful of the lead times associated with a bi-monthly schedule.

Criminal Law & Justice Weekly (incorporating Justice of the Peace)

LexisNexis, 30 Faringdon Street, London EC4A 4HH
tel 020-7400 2828
email diana.rose@lexisnexis.co.uk
website www.criminallawandjustice.co.uk
Consulting Editor John Cooper QC, *Magazine Editor* Diana Rose
Weekly Online subscription £99 p.a. including weekly pdf

Delivers information and acts as a resource for the criminal law professional and those working within the courts. Articles on criminal and local government law and associated subjects including family law, criminology, medico-legal matters, penology, police and probation. Length: 700 words for comment pieces; 1,700 words for features. Founded 1837.

Critical Quarterly

Newbury, Crediton, Devon EX17 5HA
tel (01359) 242375
email cs-journals@wiley.com
website http://onlinelibrary.wiley.com/journal/10.1111/(ISSN)1467-8705
Editor Colin MacCabe
Quarterly £36 p.a.

Fiction, poems, literary criticism. Length: 2,000–5,000 words. Study magazine before submitting MSS. Payment: by arrangement. Founded 1959.

Crystal Magazine

3 Bowness Avenue, Prenton, Birkenhead CH43 0SD
tel 0151 608 9736
email christinecrystal@hotmail.com
website www.christinecrystal.blogspot.com
Editor Christine Carr
Bi-monthly £18 p.a. (UK), £20 p.a. (overseas)

Poems, stories (true and fiction), articles. £10 to writer of most popular piece. Also includes Wordsmithing, a humorous and informative look into the world of writers and writing; readers' letters; subscribers' news; Crystal Companions, an opportunity for Crystallites (subscribers) to get in touch; competitions. Founded 2001.

Cumbria Magazine

Country Publications Ltd, The Water Mill, Broughton Hall, Skipton, North Yorkshire BD23 3AG

tel (01756) 701381
email editorial@cumbriamagazine.co.uk
website www.cumbriamagazine.co.uk
Features Editor Kevin Hopkinson
Monthly £2.90

Articles of genuine rural interest concerning the Lake District and surrounding areas, as well its people. Short length preferred. Illustrations: first-class photos. Payment: £70 per 1,000 words. Pictures extra. Founded 1951.

Custom Car

Kelsey Publishing Ltd, Cudham Tithe Barn, Berry's Hill, Cudham, Kent TN16 3AG
tel (01959) 541444
email cc.ed@kelseypb.co.uk
website www.customcarmag.co.uk
Editor David Biggadyke
Monthly £4.25

Hot rods, customs and drag racing. Length: by arrangement. Payment: by arrangement. Founded 1970.

Custom PC

Dennis Publishing Ltd, 30 Cleveland Street, London W1T 4JD
tel 020-7907 6000
website www.custompc.co.uk
Editor Ben Hardwidge
Monthly £5.99

Magazine covering performance PC hardware, technology and games with full-page and DPS single product reviews, group tests, and practical and technical features.

Cycle Sport

Time Inc. (UK), Leon House, 233 High Street, Croydon CR9 1HZ
tel 020-8726 8462
email cyclesport@timeinc.com
website www.cyclingweekly.co.uk/publication/cycle-sport
Editor Robert Garbutt
Monthly £4.95

Articles and features on European professional racing. Specially commissions most material but will consider unsolicited material. Welcomes ideas for articles and features. Length: 1,500–2,500 words. Illustrations: transparencies, colour and b&w artwork and cartoons, digital images. Payment: £120 per 1,000 words; £50–£150 illustrations. Founded 1991.

Cycling Weekly

Time Inc. (UK), Leon House, 233 High Street, Croydon CR9 1HZ
tel 020-8726 8453
email cycling@timeinc.com
website www.cyclingweekly.co.uk
Editor Robert Garbutt
Weekly £2.99

Racing and technical articles. Illustrations: topical photos with a cycling interest considered; cartoons. Length: not exceeding 2,000 words. Payment: by arrangement. Founded 1891.

Cyphers

3 Selskar Terrace, Ranelagh, Dublin 6, Republic of Ireland
tel +353 (0)1 4978866
website www.cyphers.ie
Editors Leland Bardwell, Eiléan Ní Chuilleanáin, Macdara Woods
€21/£25/$42 for 3 issues

Poems, fiction, translations. Payment: €35 to 50 per page. Submissions cannot be returned unless accompanied by postage (Irish stamps or International Reply Coupons.) Founded 1975.

Dalesman

Country Publications Limited, The Water Mill, Broughton Hall, Skipton, North Yorkshire BD23 3AG
tel (01756) 701381
email editorial@dalesman.co.uk
website www.dalesman.co.uk
Editor Adrian Braddy
Monthly £2.90

Articles and stories of genuine interest concerning Yorkshire (1,000 to 1,200 words). Payment: £70 per 1,000 words plus extra for useable photos/illustrations. Founded 1939.

Dance Today

The Dancing Times Ltd, 45–47 Clerkenwell Green, London EC1R 0EB
tel 020-7250 3006
email dancetoday@dance-today.co.uk
website www.dance-today.co.uk
Editor Nicola Rayner
Monthly £2.50

Ballroom, popular and social dancing from every aspect, ranging from competition reports to dance holiday features, health and fitness articles, and musical reviews. Well-informed freelance articles are used, but only after preliminary arrangements. Payment: by arrangement. Illustrations: action photos preferred, colour only. Founded 1956.

Dancing Times

The Dancing Times Ltd, 45–47 Clerkenwell Green, London EC1R 0EB
tel 020-7250 3006
email dt@dancing-times.co.uk
website www.dancing-times.co.uk
Editor Jonathan Gray
Monthly £3.50

Ballet, contemporary dance and all forms of stage dancing from general, historical, critical and technical angles. Well-informed freelance articles used occasionally, but only after preliminary arrangements. Payment: by arrangement. Illustrations: occasional line, action photos preferred; colour welcome. Founded 1910.

Dare

16 Connaught Place, London W2 2ES
tel 020-7420 7000
website www.therivergroup.co.uk
Editor Sarah Jane Biggs
Free

Superdrug magazine. Predominently features aspirational yet affordable beauty and fashion.

Darts World

MB Graphics, 25 Orlestone View, Ham Street, Ashford, Kent TN26 2LB
tel (01233) 733558
website www.dartsworld.com
Editor Michael Beeken
Monthly £2.95

Articles and stories with darts theme. Illustrations: half-tone, cartoons. Payment: £40–£50 per 1,000 words; illustrations by arrangement. Founded 1972.

The Dawntreader

24 Forest Houses, Cookworthy Moor, Halwill, Beaworthy, Devon EX21 5UU
email dawnidp@indigodreams.co.uk
website www.indigodreams.co.uk
Editor Dawn Bauling
Quarterly £4.25, £16 p.a.

Poetry, short stories and articles up to 1,000 words encompassing themes of the mystic, myth, legend, landscape, nature and love. New writers welcome. Lively feedback pages. No payment. Sae essential. Founded 2007.

Decanter

Time Inc. (UK), The Blue Fin Building, 110 Southwark Street, London SE1 0SU
tel 020-3148 4488
email editor@decanter.com
website www.decanter.com
Publishing Director Sarah Kemp
Monthly £4.40

Articles and features on wines, wine travel and food-related topics. Welcomes ideas for articles and features. Length: 1,000–1,800 words. Illustrations: colour. Payment: £250 per 1,000 words. Founded 1975.

delicious.

Axe & Bottle Court, 3rd Floor, 70 Newcomen Street, London SE1 1YT
tel 020-7803 4115
email readers@deliciousmagazine.co.uk
website www.deliciousmagazine.co.uk
Editor Karen Barnes
Monthly £4.10

Articles on food, recipes, preparation, trends, chefs, wine and ingredients. Founded 2003.

Derbyshire Life and Countryside

Archant Life, 61 Friargate, Derby DE1 1DJ
tel (01332) 227850
email joy.hales@derbyshirelife.co.uk
website www.derbyshirelife.co.uk
Editor Joy Hales
Monthly £3.15

Articles, preferably illustrated, about Derbyshire life, people, places and history. Length: up to 800 words. Some short stories set in Derbyshire accepted; no verse. Payment: according to nature and quality of contribution. Illustrations: photos of Derbyshire subjects. Founded 1931.

Descent

Wild Places Publishing, PO Box 100, Abergavenny NP7 9WY
tel (01873) 737707
email descent@wildplaces.co.uk
website www.wildplaces.co.uk
Editor Chris Howes
Bi-monthly £5.25

Articles, features and news on all aspects of cave and mine sport exploration (coalmines, active mining or showcaves are not included). Submissions must match magazine style. Length: up to 2,000 words (articles/features), up to 1,000 words (news). Illustrations: colour. Payment: on consideration of material based on area filled. Founded 1969.

Devon Life

Archant South West, Newbery House, Fair Oak Close, Exeter Airport Business Park, Clyst Honiton, Exeter, Devon EX5 2UL
tel (01392) 888423
email andy.cooper@archant.co.uk
website www.devonlife.co.uk
Editor Andy Cooper
Monthly £3.85

Articles on all aspects of Devon, including inspiring people, fascinating places, beautiful walks, local events, arts, history and food. Some articles online, plus a lively community of Devon bloggers. Unsolicited ideas welcome: 'ideal' articles comprise a main section of 650–700 words alongside two sections of associated facts/points of interest on the subject material. Founded 1963.

Diabetes Balance

Diabetes UK, 10 Parkway, London NW1 7AA
tel 020-7424 1000
email balance@diabetes.org.uk
website www.diabetes.org.uk
Editor Angela Coffey

Bi-monthly membership magazine

Articles on diabetes and related health and lifestyle issues. Length: 1,000–1,500 words. Payment: by arrangement. Illustrations: colour. Founded 1935.

The Dickensian

The Dickens Fellowship,
The Charles Dickens Museum, 48 Doughty Street, London WC1N 2LX
email M.Y.Andrews@kent.ac.uk
website www.dickensfellowship.org/dickensian
Editor Prof. Malcolm Andrews, School of English, Rutherford College, University of Kent, Canterbury, Kent CT2 7NX
3 p.a. £19 p.a. £25 p.a. institutions (reduced rate for Dickens Fellowship members)

Welcomes articles on all aspects of Dickens's life, works and character. Payment: none. Send contributions as both hard copy (enclose sae if return required) and email attachment to the Editor. Editorial correspondence may also be sent to the Editor. See website for house-style conventions.

Digital Camera

Future Publishing Ltd, Quay House, The Ambury, Bath BA1 1UA
tel (01225) 442244
website www.digitalcameraworld.com
Editor Benedict Brain
Monthly £4.99

Practical guide to creating better photographs. Each issue contains inspirational images, expert techniques and essential tips for capturing great images and on how to perfect them on a computer. Also includes reviews of the latest cameras, accessories and software.

Director

116 Pall Mall, London SW1Y 5ED
tel 020-7766 8950
email director-ed@iod.com
website www.director.co.uk
Editor Lysanne Currie
Monthly Free to Institute of Directors members; £34 p.a. for UK non-members (print)

Authoritative business-related articles. Send synopsis of proposed article and examples of printed work. Length: 500–2,000 words. Payment: by arrangement. Illustrations: colour. Founded 1947.

Disability Now

(published by Scope)
6 Market Road, London N7 9PW
tel 020-7619 7323 *minicom* 020-7619 7332
email editor@disabilitynow.org.uk
website www.disabilitynow.org.uk
Commissioning Editor Ian Macrae
Online free

Website for, about and by disabled people. Pitches are welcome from disabled journalists, writers or people who feel they have something to say about disabled life in Britain today. Content comes directly from the lives, experiences, views, opinions and concerns of disabled people. In addition to text content, we are also interested in receiving ideas from disabled people who can produce video content.

Diva

Millivres Prowler Ltd, Spectrum House, Unit M, 32–34 Gordon House Road, London NW5 1LP
tel 020-7424 7400
email edit@divamag.co.uk
website www.divamag.co.uk
Editor Jane Czyzselska
Monthly £3.99

Lesbian and bisexual women's lifestyle and culture: articles and features. Length: 200–2,000 words. Illustrations: colour. Payment: £15 per 100 words; variable per photo; variable per illustration. Founded 1994.

Diver

8 Mount Mews, High Street, Hampton, Middlesex TW12 2SH
tel 020-8941 8152
email enquiries@divermag.co.uk
website www.divernet.com
Publisher and Editor-in-Chief Nigel Eaton, *Editor* Steve Weinman
Monthly £4.40

Articles on sub-aqua diving and related developments. Length: 1,500–2,000 words. Illustrations: colour. Payment: by arrangement. Founded 1953.

DIY Week

15a London Road, Maidstone, Kent ME16 8LY
tel (01622) 687031
email fgarcia@datateam.net
website www.diyweek.net
Editor Fiona Garcia
Fortnightly £116 p.a. (UK), £148 p.a. (overseas)

Product and city news, promotions and special features on recent developments in DIY houseware and garden retailing. Payment: by arrangement. Founded 1874.

Dogs Today

The Old Print House, 62 High Street, Chobham, Surrey GU24 8AA
tel (01276) 858880
email enquiries@dogstodaymagazine.co.uk
website www.dogstodaymagazine.co.uk
Publisher Beverley Cuddy
Monthly £3.99

Study of magazine essential before submitting ideas. Interested in human interest dog stories, celebrity interviews, holiday features and anything unusual –

all must be entertaining and informative and accompanied by illustrations. Length: 800–1,200 words. Illustrations: colour, preferably digital. Payment: negotiable. Founded 1990.

The Dolls' House Magazine

Guild of Master Craftsman Publications Ltd,
86 High Street, Lewes, East Sussex BN7 1XN
tel (01273) 488005
website www.thegmcgroup.com
website www.craftsinstitute.com
Monthly £4.25

Dorset Life – The Dorset Magazine

7 The Leanne, Sandford Lane, Wareham,
Dorset BH20 4DY
tel (01929) 551264
email editor@dorsetlife.co.uk
website www.dorsetlife.co.uk
Editor Joël Lacey
Monthly £2.99

Articles (c. 1,200 words), photos (colour) and line drawings with a specifically Dorset theme. Payment: by arrangement. Founded 1967.

Drapers

EMAP, Telephone House, 69–77 Paul Street,
London EC2A 4NQ
tel 020-3033 2770
email eric.musgrave@emap.com
website www.drapersonline.com
Editorial Director Eric Musgrave
Weekly £5.79

Business editorial aimed at fashion retailers, large and small, and all who supply them. Payment: by negotiation. Illustrations: colour and b&w photos. Founded 1887.

Dream Catcher

Stairwell Books, 161 Lowther Street, York YO31 7LZ
tel (01904) 733767
email rose@stairwellbooks.com
website www.dreamcatchermagazine.co.uk
Editor John Gilham
Twice yearly £8 or £15 for two issues

International literary and arts journal. Welcomes poetry, short stories (optimum length of 2,000 words), artwork, interviews and reviews. Each issue features a selected artist whose work is reproduced on the cover and inside. *Dream Catcher* promotes reading and workshops across the UK. Founded 1996 by Paul Sutherland.

The Dublin Review

PO Box 7948, Dublin 1, Republic of Ireland
tel/fax +353 (0)1 6788627
email enquiry@thedublinreview.com
website www.thedublinreview.com
Editor Brendan Barrington
Quarterly €11.50

Essays, memoir, reportage and fiction for the intelligent general reader. Payment: by arrangement. Founded 2000.

Early Music

c/o Faculty of Music, University of Cambridge,
11 West Road, Cambridge CB3 9DP
tel (01223) 335178
email earlymusic@oxfordjournals.org
website http://em.oxfordjournals.org
Editor Francis Knights
Quarterly £64 p.a.

Lively, informative and scholarly articles on aspects of medieval, renaissance, baroque and classical music. Payment: £20 per 1,000 words. Illustrations: line, half-tone, colour. Founded 1973.

East Lothian Life

1 Beveridge Row, Belhaven, Dunbar,
East Lothian EH42 1TP
tel (01368) 863593
website www.eastlothianlife.co.uk
Editor Pauline Jaffray
Quarterly £3

Articles and features with an East Lothian slant. Length: up to 1,000 words. Illustrations: b&w photos, line. Payment: negotiable. Founded 1989.

Eastern Art Report

EAPGROUP International Media,
Eastern Art Publishing Group, PO Box 13666,
London SW14 8WF
tel 020-8392 1122
email ear@eapgroup.com
website www.easternartreport.net
Publisher/Editor-in-Chief Sajid Rizvi
Bi-monthly £6, £30 p.a. (individual), £60 p.a. (institutions)

Original, well-researched articles on all aspects of the visual and performing arts, cinema and digital media – Asian and diasporic, Buddhist, Islamic, Judaic, Indian, Chinese and Japanese; reviews. Length of articles: min. 1,500 words. Illustrations: colour or b&w, high-resolution digital format. No responsibility accepted for unsolicited material. Payment: by arrangement. Founded 1989.

eat in

H. Bauer Ltd, 24–28 Oval Road, London NW1 7DT
email cookeryed@eatinmagazine.co.uk
website www.eatinmagazine.co.uk
Editor-in-Chief Margaret Nicholls
Monthly £2.50

Cookery magazine featuring a range of food ideas and recipes, from seasonal meals to family and cost-conscious favourites. Readers can register to join the magazine's online community and submit tips and recipes for publication (www.eatinmagazine.co.uk/user/register).

Supported using public funding by
ARTS COUNCIL ENGLAND

'editing for writers who care about readers'
aesop
www.copyedit.co.uk
1970–2016
Based in Oxford, established for just over forty years, All Editorial Services Online for Publishers & Writers, is the home of professional editorial services in the UK
Among many other editorial services, AESOP offers: copyediting, proofreading, indexing, research, rewrites, ghostwrites, novelisation, thesis and dissertation editing for any kind of text destined for paper/electronic publication
contact: martin noble mart@copyedit.co.uk
aesop 28 Abberbury Road, Oxford OX4 4ES 01865 429563

FABER ACADEMY
CREATIVE WRITING
COURSES
WITH CHARACTER
VISIT FABERACADEMY.CO.UK
OR CALL US ON 0207 927 3827
ff

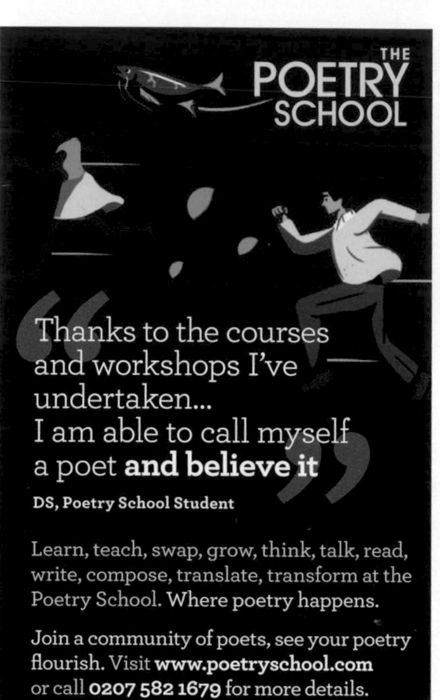
THE
POETRY
SCHOOL
Thanks to the courses and workshops I've undertaken... I am able to call myself a poet and believe it
DS, Poetry School Student
Learn, teach, swap, grow, think, talk, read, write, compose, translate, transform at the Poetry School. Where poetry happens.
Join a community of poets, see your poetry flourish. Visit www.poetryschool.com or call 0207 582 1679 for more details.

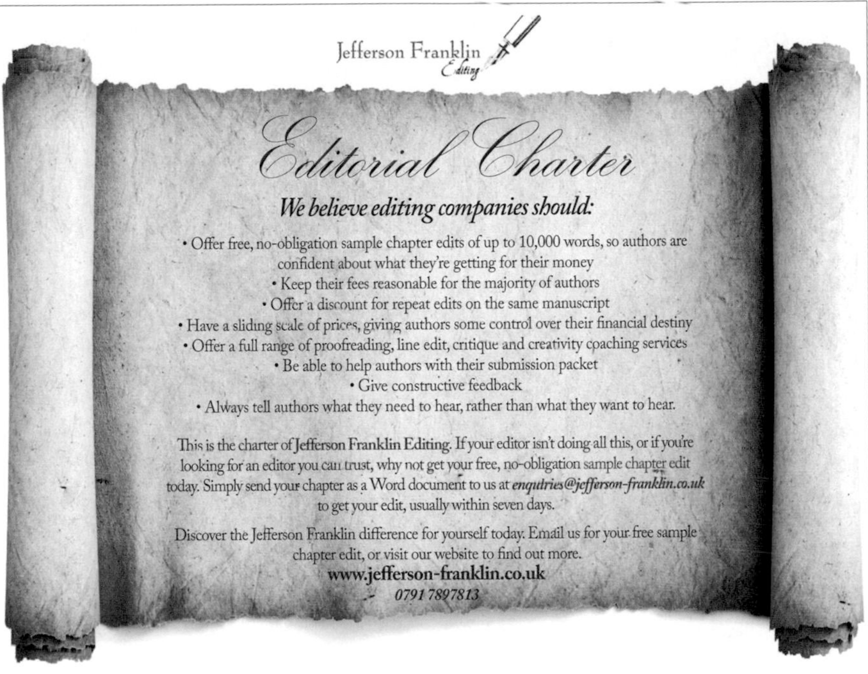
Jefferson Franklin
Editing
Editorial Charter
We believe editing companies should:
• Offer free, no-obligation sample chapter edits of up to 10,000 words, so authors are confident about what they're getting for their money
• Keep their fees reasonable for the majority of authors
• Offer a discount for repeat edits on the same manuscript
• Have a sliding scale of prices, giving authors some control over their financial destiny
• Offer a full range of proofreading, line edit, critique and creativity coaching services
• Be able to help authors with their submission packet
• Give constructive feedback
• Always tell authors what they need to hear, rather than what they want to hear.
This is the charter of Jefferson Franklin Editing. If your editor isn't doing all this, or if you're looking for an editor you can trust, why not get your free, no-obligation sample chapter edit today. Simply send your chapter as a Word document to us at enquiries@jefferson-franklin.co.uk to get your edit, usually within seven days.
Discover the Jefferson Franklin difference for yourself today. Email us for your free sample chapter edit, or visit our website to find out more.
www.jefferson-franklin.co.uk
0791 7897813

Economica
STICERD, London School of Economics,
Houghton Street, London WC2A 2AE
tel 020-7955 7855
website http://onlinelibrary.wiley.com/journal/10.1111/(ISSN)1468-0335
Editors Prof. F. Cowell, Prof. G. Benigno, Prof. L. Edlund
Quarterly From £48 p.a. (subscription rates on application)

Learned journal covering the fields of economics, economic history and statistics. Payment: none. Founded 1921; New series 1934.

The Economist
25 St James's Street, London SW1A 1HG
tel 020-7830 7000
website www.economist.com
Editor Zanny Minton Beddoes
Weekly £5

Articles staff-written. Founded 1843.

Edinburgh Review
22a Buccleugh Place, Edinburgh EH8 9LN
tel 0131 651 1415
email edinburgh.review@ed.ac.uk
website www.edinburgh-review.com
Editor Alan Gillis
3 p.a. £7.99

Submissions by post only: fiction, poetry and clearly written articles on literary and cultural themes. Payment: by arrangement. Founded 1969.

Electrical Review
SJP Business Media Ltd, 6 Laurence Pountney Hill, London EC4R 0BL
tel 020-7933 8999
email elinorem@electricalreview.co.uk
website www.electricalreview.co.uk
Editor Elinore Mackay
Monthly Free (restricted qualification; see website for details) or £201 p.a. (print and digital subscription)

Technical and business articles on electrical and control engineering; outside contributions considered. Electrical news welcomed. Illustrations: photos and drawings, cartoons. Payment: according to merit. Founded 1872.

ELLE (UK)
72 Broadwick Street, London W1F 9EP
tel 020-7150 7000
website www.elleuk.com
Editor Lorraine Candy
Monthly £4

Commissioned material only. Payment: by arrangement. Illustrations: colour. Founded 1985.

Embroidery
The Embroiderers' Guild, 1 King's Road,
Walton-on-Thames, Surrey KT12 2RA
mobile 07742 601501
email embroidery@embroiderersguild.com
website www.embroiderersguild.com/embroidery
Editor Joanne Hall
6 p.a. £4.99, £29.49 p.a.

News and illustrated features on all aspects of embroidery in contemporary design, fashion, illustration, interiors, art, general textiles and world embroidery. Features on internationally renowned makers, artists and designers working with textiles, stitch and embroidery. News covering exhibitions, books, interiors and products, plus event listings, book and exhibition reviews and opportunities. Length of articles accepted: exhibition reviews, 500 words; book reviews, 250 words; profile features, 1,000 words. Published six times a year: January, March, May, July, September and November. Founded 1932.

Empire
Endeavour House, 189 Shaftesbury Avenue,
London WC2H 8JG
tel 020-7295 6700
website www.empireonline.com
Editor-in-Chief Morgan Rees
Monthly £3.99

Guide to film on all its platforms: articles, features, news. Length: various. Illustrations: colour and b&w photos. Payment: approx. £300 per 1,000 words; varies for illustrations. Founded 1989.

Energy Engineering
Media Culture, Office 46, Pure Offices, Plato Close,
Leamington Spa, Warks. CV34 6WE
tel (01926) 671338
email info@energyengineering.co.uk
website www.energyengineering.net.co.uk
Managing Editor Steve Welch
6 p.a. £65 p.a.

Features and news for those engaged in technology, manufacturing and management. Contributions considered on all aspects of engineering. Illustrations: colour. Founded 1866.

The Engineer
Centaur Communications Ltd, 79 Wells Street,
London W1T 3QN
tel 020-7970 4437
email jon.excell@centaur.co.uk
website www.theengineer.co.uk
Editor Jon Excell
Fortnightly £3.70

Features and news on innovation and technology, including profiles, analysis. Length: up to 800 words (news), 1,000 words (features). Illustrations: colour transparencies or prints, artwork, line diagrams, graphs. Payment: by negotiation. Founded 1856.

Engineering in Miniature
TEE Publishing Ltd, The Fosse, Fosse Way,
Radford Semele, Leamington Spa, Warks. CV31 1XN

tel (01926) 614101
email info@engineeringinminiature.co.uk
website www.engineeringinminiature.co.uk
Managing Editor C.L. Deith
Monthly £3.50

Articles containing descriptions and information on all aspects of model engineering. Articles welcome but technical articles preferred. Payment dependent on pages published. Founded 1979.

The English Garden

Archant House, Oriel Road, Cheltenham, Glos. GL50 1BB
tel (01242) 211080
email theenglishgarden@archant.co.uk
website www.theenglishgarden.co.uk
Editor Stephanie Mahon
13 times p.a. £3.99

Features on gardens in the UK and Ireland, plants, practical gardening advice and garden design. Length: 700 words. Illustrations: colour photos and artwork. Payment: variable. Founded 1997.

Envoi

Meirion House, Glan yr afon, Tanygrisiau, Blaenau Ffestiniog, Gwynedd LL41 3SU
tel (01766) 832112
email info@cinnamonpress.com
website www.cinnamonpress.com
Editor Jan Fortune
3 p.a. £5.50

New poetry, including sequences, collaborative works and translations; reviews; articles on modern poets and poetic style. Sample copy: £5. Payment: complimentary copy. Founded 1957.

EQY (Equestrian Year)

Fettes Park, 496 Ferry Road, Edinburgh EH5 2DL
tel 0131 551 1000
email rbath@scottishfield.co.uk
website www.scottishfield.co.uk
Editor Richard Bath
Annual £5

Scottish equestrianism, all disciplines. Length of article accepted: 1,200 words. Founded 2015.

Erotic Review (eZine)

ER Magazine, 31 Sinclair Road, London W14 0NS
email editorial@ermagazine.org
website www.eroticreviewmagazine.com
Editor Jamie Maclean
Online

Sophisticated erotic lifestyle and fiction eZine for sensualists and libertines. Commissions features: 500-2,500 words; short fiction: 1,000–5,000 words. Illustrations and cartoons. Payment details can be obtained on request. Founded 1995.

Esquire

Hearst Magazines UK, National Magazines House, 72 Broadwick Street, London W1F 9EP
tel 020-7439 5601
website www.esquire.co.uk
Editor-in-Chief Alex Bilmes
Monthly £4.25

Quality men's general interest magazine – articles, features. No unsolicited material or short stories. Length: various. Illustrations: colour and b&w photos, line. Payment: by arrangement. Founded 1991.

Essentials

Time Inc. (UK), The Blue Fin Building, 110 Southwark Street, London SE1 0SU
tel 020-3148 7219
email essentials_feedback@timeinc.com
website www.essentialsmagazine.com
Editor Sarah Gooding
Monthly £2.99

Features, fashion, health, beauty, cookery, travel, consumer. Illustrations: colour. Payment: by negotiation. Founded 1988.

Essex Life

Press House, 30 Lower Brook Street, Ipswich IP4 IAN
tel 07834 101686
email julian.read@archant.co.uk
website www.essexlifemag.co.uk
Editor Julian Read
Monthly £3.95

No unsolicited material. Founded 1952.

Eventing

Time Inc. (UK), The Blue Fin Building, 110 Southwark Street, London SE1 0SU
tel 020-3148 4545
email sarah.jenkins@timeinc.com
website www.horseandhound.co.uk/publication/eventing-magazine
Content Director Sarah Jenkins
Monthly £4.10

News, special reports, gossip, profiles, topical features, event reports (from grassroots level to four-star in the UK and abroad), opinion pieces and 'Through the Keyhole' features – all connected to the sport of horse trials. Mostly commissioned, but all ideas welcome. Length: up to 1,500 words. Illustrations: colour, mostly commissioned. Payment: by arrangement. Founded 1984.

Evergreen

The Lypiatts, Lansdown Road, Cheltenham, Glos. GL50 2JA
tel (01242) 225780
email editor@evergreenmagazine.co.uk
website www.evergreenmagazine.co.uk
Editor Stephen Garnett
Quarterly £16 p.a.

Articles about Great Britain's heritage, culture, countryside, people and places. Length 250–2,000 words. Illustrations: digital; colour transparencies accepted only when accompanying articles. Payment: £15 per 1,000 words, £4 poems (12–24 lines). Founded 1985.

Everyday Practical Electronics

Wimborne Publishing Ltd, 113 Lynwood Drive, Merley, Wimborne, Dorset BH21 1UU
tel (01202) 880299
email editorial@wimborne.co.uk
website www.epemag.com
Editor Matt Pulzer
Monthly £4.40

Constructional and theoretical articles aimed at the student and hobbyist. Founded 1971.

Executive PA

21 Godliman Street, London EC4V 5BD
tel 020-7236 1118
email Cora@executivepa.com
website www.executivepa.com
Editor Cora Lydon
Bi-monthly £53 p.a.

Business to business for working senior secretaries and PAs. Length: 600–1,200 words. Illustrations: colour. Payment: £196 per 1,200 words. Founded 1991.

Families First

(formerly Home & Family)
The Mothers' Union, Mary Sumner House, 24 Tufton Street, London SW1P 3RB
tel 020-7222 5533
email familiesfirst@themothersunion.org
website http://muenterprises.org/familiesfirst
Editor Tola Fisher
Bi-monthly £2.75

Short articles on parenting, marriage, family life, Christian faith, fair trade and community life. Payment: from £80 per 1,000 words. Illustrations: colour photos and occasionally illustrations. Few unsolicited articles are accepted. Enclose sae. Founded 1954.

Family Law journal

Jordan Publishing Ltd, 21 St Thomas Street, Bristol BS1 6JS
tel (0117) 923 0600
email editor@familylaw.co.uk
website www.jordanpublishing.co.uk
website www.familylaw.co.uk
Editor Elizabeth Walsh
Monthly £315 p.a.

Practitioner journal, aimed at helping family law professionals keep abreast of latest developments in the field and their impact. Each issue includes news on legislative change, case reports, articles and news items. Length between 2,000 and 3,000 words, no illustrations. Founded 1971.

Family Tree

61 Great Whyte, Ramsey, Huntingdon, Cambs. PE26 1HJ
tel (01487) 814050
email editorial@family-tree.co.uk
website www.family-tree.co.uk
Editor Helen Tovey
Every 4 weeks £4.99, £48 p.a. Digital issues also available.

Features on family history and related topics. Payment: by arrangement. Founded 1984.

Farmers Weekly

Reed Business Information, Quadrant House, The Quadrant, Sutton, Surrey SM2 5AS
tel 020-8652 4911
email farmers.weekly@rbi.co.uk
website www.fwi.co.uk
Editor Karl Schneider
Weekly £3.10

Articles on agriculture from freelance contributors will be accepted subject to negotiation. Founded 1934.

Feminist Review

Palgrave Macmillan, The Stables, The Macmillan Campus, 4 Crinan Street, London N1 9XW
tel (01256) 329242
website www.feminist-review.com
Edited by a Collective
3 p.a. £48

Aims to unite research and theory with political practice and contribute to the development of both as well as the exploration and articulation of the socio-economic realities of women's lives. Welcomes contributions from the spectrum of contemporary feminist debate. Empirical work – both qualitative and quantitative – is particularly welcome. In addition, each issue contains some papers which are themed around a specific debate. Founded 1979.

FHM (For Him Magazine)

Bauer Media Group, Endeavour House, 189 Shaftesbury Avenue, London WC2H 8JG
tel 020-7295 8534
email joe.barnes@fhm.com
website www.fhm.com
Editor Joe Barnes
Monthly £3.99

Features, fashion, grooming, travel (adventure) and men's interests. Length: 1,200–2,000 words. Illustrations: colour and b&w photos, line and colour artwork. Payment: by negotiation. Founded 1987.

The Field

Time Inc. (UK), The Blue Fin Building, 110 Southwark Street, London SE1 0SU
tel 020-3148 4772

email thefield@timeinc.com
website www.thefield.co.uk
Editor Jonathan Young
Monthly £4.40

Specific, topical and informed features on the British countryside and country pursuits, including natural history, field sports, gardening and rural conservation. Overseas subjects considered but opportunities for such articles are limited. No fiction or children's material. Articles of 800–2,000 words by outside contributors considered; also topical 'shorts' of 200–300 words on all countryside matters. Illustrations: colour photos of a high standard. Payment: on merit. Founded 1853.

Financial Adviser

Financial Times Business, 1 Southwark Bridge, London SE1 9HL
tel 020-7775 3000
email hal.austin@ft.com
website www.ftadviser.com
Editor Ashley Wassall
Weekly £118.80 p.a.

Topical personal finance news and features. Length: variable. Payment: by arrangement. Founded 1987.

FIRE

Ground Floor, Rayford House, Hove BN3 5HX
tel (01273) 434943
email andrew.lynch@pavpub.com
website www.fire-magazine.com
Managing Editor Andrew Lynch
Monthly £84 p.a.

Articles on firefighting and fire prevention from acknowledged experts only. Length: 600 words. No unsolicited contributions. Illustrations: dramatic firefighting or fire brigade rescue colour photos. Also *Fire International*. Payment: by arrangement. Founded 1908.

Fishing News

INTRAFISH, Nexus Place, 25 Farringdon Street, London EC4A 4AB
tel 020-7029 5712
email editor@fishingnews.co.uk
website www.fishingnews.co.uk
Editor Cormac Burke
Weekly £2.99

News and features on all aspects of the commercial fishing industry. Length: up to 1,000 words (features), up to 500 words (news). Illustrations: colour and b&w photos. Payment: negotiable. Founded 1913.

Flash: The International Short-Short Story Magazine

Department of English, University of Chester, Parkgate Road, Chester CH1 4BJ
tel (01244) 513 152
email flash.magazine@chester.ac.uk
website www.chester.ac.uk/flash.magazine
Editors Dr Peter Blair, Dr Ashley Chantler
Biannual £5, £9 p.a.

Quality stories of up to 360 words (title included); see website for submission guidelines. Suggestions for reviews and articles considered. Payment: complimentary copy. Founded 2008.

Flora International

Wimborne Publishing, 113 Lynwood Drive, Merley, Wimborne, Dorset BH21 1UU
tel (01202) 880299
email editorial@wimborne.co.uk
website www.flora-magazine.co.uk
Editor Nina Tucknott
Bi-monthly £3.70

Magazine for flower arranging and floristry; also features flower-related crafts and flower arrangers' gardens. Unsolicited enquiries and suggestions welcome on any of these subjects. Send brief synopsis together with sample illustrations attached. Illustrations: transparencies, colour prints or high-res files on CD or email. Payment: £60 per 1,000 words, £10–£20 illustrations. Founded 1974.

Fly Fishing & Fly Tying

Rolling River Publications, The Locus Centre, The Square, Aberfeldy, Perthshire PH15 2DD
tel (01887) 829868
email MarkB.ffft@btinternet.com
website www.flyfishing-and-flytying.co.uk
Editor Mark Bowler
12 p.a. £3.50

Fly-fishing and fly-tying articles, fishery features, limited short stories, fishing travel. Length: 800–2,000 words. Illustrations: colour photos. Payment: by arrangement. Founded 1990.

Fortean Times

Dennis Publishing Ltd, 30 Cleveland Street, London W1T 3JD
tel 020-7907 6235
email drsutton@forteantimes.com
website www.forteantimes.com
Editor David Sutton
13 p.a. £4.25

Journal of strange phenomena, experiences, related subjects and philosophies. Includes articles, features, news, reviews. Length: 500–5,000 words; longer by arrangement. Illustrations: colour photos, line and tone art, cartoons. Payment: by negotiation. Founded 1973.

FourFourTwo

Haymarket, Teddington Studios, Broom Road, Teddington, Middlesex TW11 9BE
tel 020-8267 5848
email contact@fourfourtwo.com
website www.fourfourtwo.magazine.co.uk

Editor Gary Parkinson
Monthly £4.75

Football magazine with interviews, in-depth features, issues pieces, odd and witty material. Length: 2,000–3,000 (features), 100–1,500 words (Up Front pieces). Illustrations: colour transparencies and artwork, b&w prints. Payment: £200 per 1,000 words. Founded 1994.

France

Archant House, Oriel Road, Cheltenham, Glos. GL50 1BB
tel (01242) 216050
email editorial@francemag.com
website www.completefrance.com
Editor Carolyn Boyd
Monthly £3.99

Informed quality features and articles on the real France, ranging from cuisine to culture to holidays exploring hidden France. Length: 800–2,000 words. Payment: £100 per 1,000 words; £50 per page/pro rata for illustrations. Founded 1989.

Freelance Market News

8–10 Dutton Street, Manchester M3 ILE
tel 0161 819 9919
email fmn@writersbureau.com
website www.freelancemarketnews.com
Editor Angela Cox
11 p.a. £29 p.a.

Information on UK and overseas publications with editorial content, submission requirements and contact details. News of editorial requirements for writers. Features on the craft of writing, competitions, letters page. Founded 1968.

The Friend

173 Euston Road, London NW1 2BJ
tel 020-7663 1010
email editorial@thefriend.org
website www.thefriend.org
Editor Ian Kirk-Smith
Weekly £79 p.a. (paper + online), £59 p.a. (online only)

Material of interest to Quakers and like-minded people; political, social, economic, environmental or devotional, considered from outside contributors. Length: up to 1,200 words. Illustrations: b&w or colour prints, b&w line drawings and cartoons by email preferred. Payment: not usually but will negotiate a small fee with professional writers. Founded 1843.

Frieze

1 Montclare Street, London E2 7EU
tel 020-3372 6111
email editors@frieze.com
website www.frieze.com
8 p.a. £8

Magazine of European contemporary art and cultu[re] including essays, reviews, columns and listings. Frie[ze] Art Fair is held every October in Regent's Park, London, featuring over 150 of the most exciting contemporary art galleries in the world. Founded 1991.

The Furrow

St Patrick's College, Maynooth, Co. Kildare, Republic of Ireland
tel +353 (0)1 7083741
email furrow.office@may.ie
website www.thefurrow.ie
Editor Rev. Ronan Drury
Monthly €3.50

Religious, pastoral, theological and social articles. Length: up to 3,500 words. Payment: average €20 per page (450 words). Illustrations: line, half-tone. Founded 1950.

Galleries

Barrington Publications, Riverside Studios, Crisp Road, London W6 9RL
tel 020-8237 1180
email ed@galleries.co.uk
website www.galleries.co.uk
Editor Andrew Aitken
Monthly £28 p.a.

Art listings and editorial magazine describing current exhibitions and stock of commercial and public art galleries, galleries for hire and art services.

GamesMaster

Future Publishing Ltd, Quay House, The Ambury, Bath BA1 1UA
tel (01225) 442244
email gamesmaster@futurenet.co.uk
Editor Joel Gregory
Every 4 weeks £4.99

The UK's longest running video games magazine, covering the biggest and best games across all formats.

Garden Answers

Bauer Media Group, Media House, Lynchwood, Peterborough Business Park, Peterborough PE2 6EA
tel (01733) 468000
email gardenanswers@bauermedia.co.uk
website www.gardenanswersmagazine.co.uk
Editor Liz Potter
Monthly £3.75

Some commissioned features and articles on all aspects of gardening. Reader garden photo and interview packages considered. Study of magazine essential. Approach by email with examples of published work. Length: approx. 750 words. Illustrations: digital images and artwork. Payment: by negotiation. Founded 1982.

Garden News

Bauer Media Group, Media House, Lynchwood, Peterborough Business Park, Peterborough PE2 6EA

(01733) 468000
email gn.letters@bauermedia.co.uk
website www.gardennewsmagazine.co.uk
Editor Clare Foggett
Weekly £1.99

Up-to-date information on everything to do with plants, growing and gardening. Payment: by negotiation. Founded 1958.

Gay Times – GT

Spectrum House, 32–34 Gordon House Road, London NW5 1LP
tel 020-7424 7400
email edit@gaytimes.co.uk
website www.gaytimes.co.uk
Editor Darren Scott
13 p.a. £39 p.a.

Celebrity, gay lifestyle, health, parenting, music, film, technology, current affairs, opinion, culture, art, style, grooming, features and interviews. Length: up to 2,000 words. Payment: by arrangement. Founded 1984.

Geographical

3.20 QWest, 1100 Great West Road, London TW8 0GP
tel 020-8332 8434
email magazine@geographical.co.uk
website www.geographical.co.uk
Editor Geordie Torr
Monthly £4.50

Magazine of the Royal Geographical Society (with the Institute of British Geographers). Covers culture, wildlife, environment, science and travel. Illustrations: top-quality hi-res digital files, vintage material. Payment: by negotiation. Founded 1935.

The Geographical Journal

Royal Geographical Society (with the Institute of British Geographers), 1 Kensington Gore, London SW7 2AR
tel 020-7591 3026
email journals@rgs.org
website www.rgs.org/GJ
Editor Keith Richards
4 p.a. £273 p.a. print and online, £227 print or online only

Papers range across the entire subject of geography, with particular reference to public debates, policy-oriented agendas and notions of 'relevance'. Illustrations: photos, maps, diagrams. Founded 1893.

Gibbons Stamp Monthly

Stanley Gibbons Ltd, 7 Parkside, Ringwood, Hants BH24 3SH
tel (01425) 472363
email dshepherd@stanleygibbons.co.uk
website www.stanleygibbons.co.uk
Editor Dean Shepherd
Monthly £3.85

Articles on philatelic topics. Contact the Editor first. Length: 500–2,500 words. Payment: by arrangement, £60 or more per 1,000 words. Illustrations: photos, line, stamps or covers.

Glamour

6–8 Old Bond Street, London W1S 4PH
tel 020-7499 9080
email glamoureditorialmagazine@condenast.co.uk
website www.glamourmagazine.com
Editor Jo Elvin
Monthly £2

Lifestyle magazine containing fashion, beauty, real-life features and celebrity news aimed at women aged 18–34. Feature ideas welcome; approach with brief outline. Length: 500–800 words. Payment: by arrangement. Founded 2001.

Golf Monthly

Time Inc. (UK), The Blue Fin Building, 110 Southwark Street, London SE1 0SU
tel 020-3148 5000
email golfmonthly@timeinc.com
website www.golf-monthly.co.uk
Editor Michael Harris
Monthly £4.40

Original articles on golf considered (not reports), golf clinics, handy hints. Illustrations: half-tone, colour, cartoons. Payment: by arrangement. Founded 1911.

Golf World

Bauer Media Group, Media House, Lynchwood, Peterborough Business Park, Peterborough PE2 6EA
tel (01733) 468000
email nick.jwright@bauermedia.co.uk
website www.golf-world.co.uk
Editor Nick Wright
Every four weeks £4.40

Expert golf instructional articles, 500–3,000 words; general interest articles, personality features 500–3,000 words. No fiction. No unsolicited material. Payment: by negotiation. Illustrations: line, half-tone, colour, cartoons. Founded 1962.

The Good Book Guide

Editorial Office 33 Whitebeam Close, Colden Common, Winchester SO21 1AJ
tel (01962) 712507
email fiona@thegoodbookguide.com
Customer Services 41A All Hallows Road, Bispham, Blackpool, Lancs. FY2 0AS
tel 0121 314 3539
email enquiries@thegoodbookguide.com
website www.thegoodbookguide.com
Managing Director Graham Holmes, *Editorial Director* Fiona Lafferty
10 p.a. Subscription only. Annual subscription rates start at £24 (digital only); see website for full list.

Review journal with independent reviews recommending and selling the best books published in the UK. Founded 1977.

Good Housekeeping

Hearst Magazines UK, National Magazines House, 72 Broadwick Street, London W1F 9EP
tel 020-7439 5500 (cookery school enquiries)
email goodh.mail@hearst.co.uk
website www.goodhousekeeping.co.uk
Editorial Director Lindsay Nicholson
Monthly £3.99

Articles on topics of interest to intelligent women. No unsolicited features or stories accepted. Homes, fashion, beauty and food covered by staff writers. Payment: magazine standards. Illustrations: commissioned. Founded 1922.

Governance & Compliance

Institute of Chartered Secretaries and Administrators, Saffron House, 6–10 Kirby Street, London EC1N 8TS
tel 020-7580 4741
email ajones@icsaglobal.com
website www.icsa.org.uk/products-and-services/governance-and-compliance
Supervising Editor Alexandra Jones
Monthly £90 p.a. (free to members)

Published by the Institute of Chartered Secretaries and Administrators. Offers news, views and practical advice on the latest developments in governance and compliance.

GQ

Condé Nast Publications, Vogue House, Hanover Square, London W1S 1JU
tel 020-7499 9080
website www.gq-magazine.co.uk
Editor Dylan Jones
Monthly £3.99

Style, fashion and general interest magazine for men. Illustrations: b&w and colour photos, line drawings, cartoons. Payment: by arrangement. Founded 1988.

Granta

12 Addison Avenue, London W11 4QR
tel 020-7605 1360
website www.granta.com
Editor Sigrid Rausing
Quarterly £12.99, £32 p.a.

Original literary fiction, non-fiction, memoir, reportage and photography. Study magazine before submitting work. No academic essays or reviews. Note that submissions are accepted only only via online submissions system (https://granta.submittable.com/submit). Length: determined by content. Illustrations: photos and original artwork. Payment: by arrangement. Founded 1889; reconceived 1979.

Grazia

Bauer Consumer Media, Endeavour House, 189 Shaftesbury Avenue, London WC2H 8JG
tel 020-7437 9011
email graziadaily@graziamagazine.co.uk
website www.graziadaily.co.uk
Editor-in-Chief Jane Bruton
Weekly £2

Women's magazine with the latest trends, gossip, fashion and news in bite-size pieces.

Greetings Today

(formerly Greetings Magazine)
Lema Publishing, 1 Churchgates, The Wilderness, Berkhamstead, Herts. HP4 2AZ
tel (01442) 289930
website www.greetingstoday.co.uk
Editor Tracey Bearton
Monthly Controlled circulation

Trade magazine with articles, features and news related to the greetings card industry.Mainly written in-house; some material taken from outside. Length: varies. Illustrations: line, colour and b&w photos. Payment: by arrangement.

The Grocer

William Reed Publishing Ltd, Broadfield Park, Crawley, West Sussex RH11 9RT
tel (01293) 613400
website www.thegrocer.co.uk
Editor Adam Leyland
Weekly £3.20

Trade journal: articles, news or illustrations of general interest to the grocery and provision trades. Payment: by arrangement. Founded 1861.

Grow Your Own

25 Phoenix Court, Hawkins Road, Colchester CO2 8JY
tel (01206) 505979
email lucy.chamberlain@aceville.co.uk
website www.growfruitandveg.co.uk
Editor Lucy Chamberlain
Monthly £4.99

Magazine for kitchen gardeners of all levels of expertise. Will consider unsolicited material. Welcomes ideas for articles and features. Length: 1,000 words (articles), 1,500 words (features) 200 words (news). Illustrations: transparencies, colour prints and digital images. Payment: varies.

Guiding Magazine

17–19 Buckingham Palace Road, London SW1W 0PT
tel 020-7834 6242
email guiding@girlguiding.org.uk
website www.girlguiding.org.uk
Editor Jane Yettram
Quarterly

Official magazine of Girlguiding. Articles of interest to women of all ages, with special emphasis on youth work and the Guide Movement. Illustrations: line, half-tone, colour. Payment: £300 per 1,000 words.

Please contact editor with proposal in the first instance.

Guitarist

Future Publishing Ltd, Quay House, The Ambury, Bath BA1 1UA
tel (01225) 442244
website www.musicradar.com/guitarist
Editor Jamie Dickson
13 p.a. £5.75

Aims to improve readers' knowledge of the instrument, help them make the right buying choices and assist them in becoming a better player. Ideas for articles welcome. Founded 1984.

Gutter

49–53 Virginia Street, Glasgow G1 1TS
email info@guttermag.co.uk
website www.guttermag.co.uk
Managing Editor Henry Bell, *Editors* Adrian Searle, Colin Begg, *Reviews Editor* Katie Hastie
Biannual £6.99 One- and two-year subscriptions available

Award-winning print journal for fiction and poetry from writers born or living in Scotland. Invites submissions of up to 3,000 words of fiction or 120 lines of poetry, and seeks provocative work that challenges, reimagines or undermines the individual or collective status quo. See website for more information. Payment: a free two-year subscription to Gutter (worth £22). No longer offering editorial review.

H&E naturist

Hawk Editorial Ltd, PO Box 545, Hull HU9 9JF
tel (01482) 342000
email editor@henaturist.net
website www.henaturist.net
Editor Sam Hawcroft
Monthly £3.95

Articles on naturist travel, clubs, beaches and naturist lifestyle experiences from the UK, Europe and the world. Length: 800–1,200 words. Illustrations: prints and digital images featuring naturists in natural settings; also cartoons, humorous fillers and features with naturist themes. Payment: by negotiation but guidelines for contributors and basic payment rates available on request.

Harper's Bazaar

Hearst Magazines UK, 72 Broadwick Street, London W1F 9EP
tel 020-7439 5000
website www.harpersbazaar.co.uk
Editor-in-Chief Justine Picardie
Monthly £4.30

Features, fashion, beauty, art, theatre, films, travel, interior decoration – some commissioned. Founded 1929.

Health Club Management

Leisure Media Company Ltd, Portmill House, Portmill Lane, Hitchin, Herts. SG5 1DJ
tel (01462) 431385
email healthclub@leisuremedia.com
website www.healthclubmanagement.co.uk
Editor Kate Cracknell
11 issues per year £45 p.a. (UK; UK student rate £22), £57 (Europe), £80 (RoW)

Europe's leading publication for the health and fitness industry, covering the latest news, interviews, new openings and trends across the public and private health and fitness sectors. Magazine is available both digitally and as a printed copy. *Health Club Management Handbook*, an annual reference book for buyers and decision-makers in the health and fitness sector, is also available. Founded 1995.

Healthy

The River Group, 1 Neal Street, London WC2H 9QL
tel 020-7420 6502
email healthy@riverltd.co.uk
website www.healthy-magazine.co.uk
Editor Ellie Hughes
8 p.a. £15.90 p.a.

Holland & Barrett magazine. Health and nutrition information, features, tips, news and recipes, all from a holistic health angle. Ideas from freelancers welcome, with a view to commissioning. It does not do product reviews, will not mention products not available in Holland & Barrett and cannot cite any brand names in the copy. Email ideas in first instance. Payment by negotiation. Founded 1996.

Heat

Bauer Consumer Media, Endeavour House, 189 Shaftesbury Avenue, London WC2H 8JG
tel 020-7437 9011
email heatEd@heatmag.com
website www.heatworld.com
Editor Jeremy Mark
Weekly £1.65

Features and news on celebrities. Founded 1999.

Hello!

Wellington House, 69–71 Upper Ground, London SE1 9PQ
tel 020-7667 8700
website www.hellomagazine.com
Editor Rosie Nixon
Weekly £2

News-based features – showbusiness, celebrity, royalty; exclusive interviews. Payment: by arrangement. Illustrated. Founded 1988.

Hi-Fi News

MyTime Media Ltd, Enterprise House, Enterprise Way, Edenbridge, Kent TN8 6HF
tel 0844 8488822

email info@myhobbystore.co.uk
website www.hifinews.com
Editor Paul Miller
Monthly £4.50

Articles on all aspects of high-quality sound recording and reproduction; also extensive record review section and supporting musical feature articles. Audio matter is essentially technical, but should be presented in a manner suitable for music lovers interested in the nature of sound. Length: 2,000–3,000 words. Illustrations: line, half-tone. Payment: by arrangement. Founded 1956.

High Life

Cedar Communications Ltd, 85 Strand, London WC2R 0DW
tel 020-7550 8000
email high.life@cedarcom.co.uk
website www.cedarcom.co.uk
Editor Kerry Smith
Monthly Free £37 p.a.

Inflight consumer magazine for British Airways passengers. Articles on entertainment, travel, fashion, business, sport and lifestyle. Founded 1973.

History Today

2nd Floor, Staple Inn, London WC1V 7QH
tel 020-3219 7810
email admin@historytoday.com
website www.historytoday.com
Editor Paul Lay
Monthly £5.20

History in the widest sense – political, economic, social, biography, relating past to present; world history as well as British. Length: 3,500 words (articles); 600–1,200 words (news/views). Illustrations: prints and original photos. Do not send original material until publication is agreed. Accepts freelance contributions dealing with genuinely new historical and archaelogical research. Payment: by arrangement. Send sae for return of MS. Founded 1951.

Homes & Gardens

Time Inc. (UK), The Blue Fin Building, 110 Southwark Street, London SE1 0SU
tel 020-3148 5000
email HomesAndGardens@timeinc.com
website www.housetohome.co.uk/homesandgardens
Editor-in-Chief Deborah Barker
Monthly £4.30

Articles on home interest or design, particularly well-designed British interiors (snapshots should be submitted). Length: 900–1,000 words (articles). Illustrations: all types. Payment: generous, but exceptional work required; varies. Founded 1919.

Horse & Hound

Time Inc. (UK), 9th Floor, The Blue Fin Building, 110 Southwark Street, London SE1 0SU
tel 020-3148 4562
email sarah_jenkins@timeinc.com
website www.horseandhound.co.uk
Content Director Sarah Jenkins
Weekly £2.99

Special articles, news items, photos, on all matters appertaining to equestrian sports. Payment: by negotiation.

Horse & Rider

DJ Murphy Publishers Ltd, Marlborough House, Headley Road, Grayshott, Surrey GU26 6LG
tel (01428) 601020
email editor@djmurphy.co.uk
website www.horseandrideruk.com
Editor Louise Kittle
Monthly £3.99

Sophisticated magazine covering all forms of equestrian activity at home and abroad. Good writing and technical accuracy essential. Length: 1,500–2,000 words. Illustrations: photos and drawings, the latter usually commissioned. Payment: by arrangement. Founded 1959.

Hortus

Bryan's Ground, Stapleton, Nr Presteigne, Herefordshire LD8 2LP
tel (01544) 260001
email all@hortus.co.uk
website www.hortus.co.uk
Editor David Wheeler
Quarterly £40 p.a.(UK), £48 p.a. (Europe), £53 p.a. (RoW)

Articles on decorative horticulture: plants, gardens, history, design, literature, people; book reviews. Length: 1,500–5,000 words, longer by arrangement. Illustrations: line, half-tone and wood-engravings. Payment: by arrangement. Founded 1987.

Hot Press

13 Trinity Street, Dublin 2, Republic of Ireland
tel +353 (0)1 2411500
email info@hotpress.ie
website www.hotpress.com
Editor Niall Stokes
Fortnightly €3.50

High-quality, investigative stories, or punchily written offbeat pieces, of interest to 16–39 year-olds, including politics, music, sport, sex, religion – whatever's happening on the street. Length: varies. Illustrations: colour with some b&w. Payment: by negotiation. Founded 1977.

House & Garden

Vogue House, 1 Hanover Square, London W1S 1JU
tel 020-7499 9080
email houseandgarden@condenast.co.uk
website www.houseandgarden.co.uk
Editor Hatta Byng

Monthly £4.20

Articles (always commissioned), on subjects relating to domestic architecture, interior decorating, furnishing, gardens and gardening, exhibitions, travel, food and wine.

House Beautiful

Hearst Magazines UK, National Magazines House, 72 Broadwick Street, London W1F 9EP
tel 020-7439 5000
email julia.goodwin@natmags.co.uk
website www.housebeautiful.com
Editor Julia Goodwin
Monthly £3.70

Specialist features for the homes of today. Unsolicited manuscripts are not accepted. Illustrated. Founded 1989.

Housebuilder

27 Broadwall, London SE1 9PL
tel 020-7960 1630
email info@house-builder.co.uk
website www.house-builder.co.uk
Publishing Director Ben Roskrow
10 p.a. £93 p.a.

Official Journal of the Home Builders Federation published in association with the National House-Building Council. Technical articles on design, construction and equipment of dwellings, estate planning and development, and technical aspects of house-building, aimed at those engaged in house and flat construction and the development of housing estates. Preliminary letter advisable. Length: articles from 500 words, preferably with illustrations. Payment: by arrangement. Illustrations: photos, plans, construction details, cartoons.

The Huffington Post UK

email HuffPostUK@huffingtonpost.com
website www.huffingtonpost.co.uk
Editor-in-Chief Stephen Hull

Online news and commentary magazine, covering topics such as politics, sport, business, technology and entertainment. To submit an idea for a blog post, email the blog team direct (UKBlogTeam@Huffingtonpost.com).

ICIS Chemical Business

Reed Business Information, Quadrant House, The Quadrant, Sutton, Surrey SM2 5AS
tel 020-8652 3500
email icbeditorial@icis.com
website www.icischemicalbusiness.com
Global Editor Joseph Chang
Weekly £546.70 p.a. (print, digital and tablet access)

Articles and features concerning business, markets and investments in the chemical industry. Length: 1,000–2,000 words; news items up to 400 words. Payment: £150–£200 per 1,000 words.

Icon Magazine

Media 10, Crown House, 151 High Road, Loughton, Essex IG10 4LF
tel 020-3235 5200
email icon@icon-magazine.co.uk
website www.iconeye.com
Editor Christopher Turner
Monthly £5

Articles on new buildings, interiors, innovative design and designers. Payment by negotiation. Founded 2003.

Ideal Home

Time Inc. (UK), The Blue Fin Building, 110 Southwark Street, London SE1 0SU
tel 020-3148 5000
email ideal_home@timeinc.com
website www.housetohome.co.uk/idealhomemagazine
Editorial Director Isobel McKenzie-Price
Monthly £3.65

Lifestyle magazine, articles usually commissioned. Contributors advised to study editorial content before submitting material. Payment: according to material. Illustrations: usually commissioned. Founded 1920.

IHS Jane's Defence Weekly

Sentinel House, 163 Brighton Road, Coulsdon, Surrey CR5 2YH
tel 020-3253 2100
website https://janes.ihs.com
Editor Peter Felstead
Weekly £325 p.a. (print), £1,395 p.a. (online), £325 p.a. (digital)

International defence news; military equipment; budget analysis, industry, military technology, business, political, defence market intelligence. Payment: minimum £200 per 1,000 words used. Illustrations: colour. Founded 1984.

Improve Your Coarse Fishing

Bauer Media Group, Media House, Lynchwood, Peterborough PE2 6EA
tel (01733) 395134
email james.furness@bauermedia.co.uk
website www.gofishing.co.uk
Editor James Furness
Monthly £3.50

Articles on technique and equipment, the best venues, news and features. Ideas welcome by email. Founded 1991.

InStyle

Time Inc. (UK), The Blue Fin Building, 110 Southwark Street, London SE1 0SU
tel 020-3148 5000
email contact@instyleuk.com
website www.instyle.co.uk
Editor Charlotte Moore

Monthly £3.99

Fashion, beauty and celebrity lifestyle magazine for style-conscious women aged 25–44. Rarely accepts unsolicited material. Founded 2001.

Index on Censorship

92–94 Tooley Street, London SE1 2TH
tel 020-7260 2660
email info@indexoncensorship.org
website www.indexoncensorship.org
Chief Executive Jodie Ginsberg
Quarterly £32 p.a. (print)

Articles up to 3,000 words dealing with all aspects of free speech and political censorship. Illustrations: b&w, cartoons. Payment: £75 per 1,000 words. Founded 1972.

Ink Sweat and Tears

website www.inksweatandtears.com
Editor Helen Ivory

Poetry and prose webzine. Accepts submissions of up to 750 words (see website for full information) and also offers an online feedback service on poems; costs range from £20 for a single poem of 30 lines maximum to £150 for up to 400 lines of poetry (excluding titles).

Inside Soap

Hearst Magazines UK, 33 Broadwick Street, London W1F 0DQ
tel 020-7339 4588
email editor@insidesoap.co.uk
website www.insidesoap.co.uk
Editor Steven Murphy
Weekly £1.66

Gossip and celebrity interviews with soap and popular TV characters on terrestrial and satellite channels. Submit ideas by email in first instance. Payment by negotiation.

Inspire Magazine

CPO, Garcia Estate, Canterbury Road, Worthing, West Sussex BN13 1BW
tel (01903) 264556
email russbravo@cpo.org.uk
website www.inspiremagazine.org.uk
Editor Russ Bravo
8 p.a. Free/donation; available in churches

Magazine with 'good news' stories of Christian faith in action and personal testimonies. Length: 400–700 words (features). Freelance articles used rarely. Payment: up to £85.

Insurance Age

Incisive Media, 32–34 Broadwick Street, London W1A 2HG
tel 020-7316 9653
email emmanuel.kenning@incisivemedia.com
website www.insuranceage.com
Editor Emmanuel Kenning
Monthly £5

News and features on general insurance and the broker market, personal, commercial, health and Lloyd's of London. Payment: by negotiation. Founded 1979.

InterMedia

Highland House, 165 Broadway, London SW19 1NE
email jgrimshaw@iicom.org
website www.iicom.org
Projects Executive Joanne Grimshaw
Bi-monthly £175 p.a.

International journal concerned with policies, events, trends and research in the field of communications, broadcasting, telecommunications and associated issues, particularly cultural and social. Founded 1970.

International Affairs

The Royal Institute of International Affairs, Chatham House, 10 St James's Square, London SW1Y 4LE
tel 020-7957 5728
email adorman@chathamhouse.org
website www.chathamhouse.org/publications/ia
Editor Andrew Dorman
6 issues p.a. £82 p.a. individuals, £545 p.a. institutions

Peer-reviewed academic articles on international affairs; up to 50 books reviewed in each issue. Unsolicited articles welcome; preliminary letter advisable. Article length: max. 8,000 words. Illustrations: none. Payment: by arrangement. Founded 1922.

Interzone

TTA Press, 5 Martins Lane, Ely, Cambs. CB6 2LB
website www.ttapress.com
Editor Andy Cox
Bi-monthly £4.99

Science fiction and fantasy short stories, articles, interviews and reviews. Read magazine before submitting. Length: 2,000–6,000 words. Illustrations: colour. Payment: by arrangement. Founded 1982.

Investors Chronicle

Number One, Southwark Bridge, London SE1 9HL
tel 020-7873 3000
email ic.cs@ft.com
website www.investorschronicle.co.uk
Editor John Hughman
Weekly £4.50

Journal covering investment and personal finance. Occasional outside contributions for features are accepted. Payment: by negotiation.

Ireland's Own

Channing House, Upper Rowe Street, Wexford, Republic of Ireland
tel +353 (0)53 9140140

email info@irelandsown.ie
website www.irelandsown.ie
Editor Sean Nolan, *Assistant Editor* Shea Tomkins
€1.60

Short stories: non-experimental, traditional with an Irish orientation (1,800–2,000 words); articles of interest to Irish readers at home and abroad (750–900 words); general and literary articles (750–900 words). Monthly special bumper editions, each devoted to a particular seasonal topic. Suggestions for new features considered. Payment: varies according to quality and length. Founded 1902.

Irish Arts Review

15 Harcourt Terrace, Dublin 2, Republic of Ireland
tel +353 (0)1 6766711
email editorial@irishartsreview.com
website www.irishartsreview.com
Editor John Mulcahy
Quarterly €10

Magazine committed to promoting Irish art and heritage around the world with reviews of Irish painting, design, heritage, sculpture, architecture, photography and decorative arts.

Irish Farmers Journal

Irish Farm Centre, Bluebell, Dublin 12, Republic of Ireland
tel +353 (0)1 4199530
email edit@farmersjournal.ie
website www.farmersjournal.ie
Editor Justin McCarthy
Weekly €2.80

Readable, technical articles on any aspect of farming. Length: 700–1,000 words. Payment: £100–£150 per article. Illustrated. Founded 1948.

Irish Journal of Medical Science

Royal Academy of Medicine in Ireland, Setanta House, 2nd Floor, Setanta Place, Dublin 2, Republic of Ireland
tel +353 (0)1 6334820
email helenmoore@rcpi.ie
website http://www.springer.com/medicine/internal/journal/11845
Send material to Prof. James Jones
Quarterly €42, €156 p.a. (Ireland and EU), €192 p.a. (non-EU)

Official Organ of the Royal Academy of Medicine in Ireland. Original contributions in medicine, surgery, midwifery, public health, etc; reviews of professional books, reports of medical societies, etc. Illustrations: line, half-tone, colour.

Irish Medical Times

24–26 Upper Ormond Quay, Dublin 7, Republic of Ireland
tel +353 (0)1 8176300
email editor@imt.ie
website www.imt.ie
Editor Dara Gantly
Weekly €298 p.a. (Ireland), €434 p.a. (UK, Europe and RoW)

Medical articles. Length: 850–1,000 words. Payment: £100 per 1,000 words.

Irish Pages: A Journal of Contemporary Writing

129 Ormeau Road, Belfast BT7 1SH
tel 028-9043 4800
email editor@irishpages.org
website www.irishpages.org
Editor Chris Agee
Biannual £16/€26 p.a.

Poetry, short fiction, essays, creative non-fiction, memoir, essay reviews, nature writing, translated work, literary journalism, and other autobiographical, historical and scientific writing of literary distinction. Publishes in equal measure writing from Ireland and abroad. Accepts unsolicited submissions by post only. Payment: pays only for certain commissions and occasional serial rights. Founded 2002.

The Irish Post

Suite A, 1 Lindsey Street, London EC1A 9HP
tel 020-8900 4159
email editor@irishpost.co.uk
website www.irishpost.co.uk
Editor Siobhán Breatnach
Weekly (Wed) £1.30

Coverage of all political, social and sporting events relevant to the Irish community in Britain. Also contains a guide to Irish entertainment in Britain.

Irish Printer

Old Stone Building, Blackhall Green, Blackhall Place, Dublin 7, Republic of Ireland
tel +353 (0)1 4322271
website www.irishprinter.ie
Editor Maev Martin
Monthly €100.83 p.a.

Technical articles and news of interest to the printing industry. Length: 800–1,000 words. Illustrations: colour and b&w photos. Payment: €140 per 1,000 words; photos €30. Founded 1974.

Irish Tatler

Harmonia Ltd, Rosemount House, Dundrum Road, Dublin 14, Republic of Ireland
tel +353 (0)1 2405300
email jcollins@harmonia.ie
website www.irishtatler.com
Editor Jessie Collins
Monthly €34.80 p.a.

General interest women's magazine: fashion, beauty, interiors, cookery, current affairs, reportage and celebrity interviews. Length: 2,000–4,000 words. In association with ivenus.com. Payment: by arrangement.

jamie

19–21 Nile Street, London N1 7LL
tel 020-3375 5601
email contact@jamiemagazine.com
website www.jamiemagazine.com
Editor Andy Harris
Monthly £3.99

Seasonal recipes, tips, hints and features from a range of contributors, including Editor at Large, TV chef and restaurateur Jamie Oliver.

Jewish Chronicle

25 Furnival Street, London EC4A 1JT
tel 020-7415 1500
email editorial@thejc.com
website www.thejc.com
Editor Stephen Pollard
Weekly £1.90

Authentic and exclusive news stories and articles of Jewish interest from 500–1,500 words are considered. Includes a lively arts and leisure section and regular travel pages. Payment: by arrangement. Illustrations: of Jewish interest, either topical or feature. Founded 1841.

The Jewish Quarterly

28 St Albans Lane, London NW11 7QE
email editor@jewishquarterly.org
website www.jewishquarterly.org
4 p.a. £26 p.a. (print), £19.99 (digital)

Articles of Jewish interest, literature, history, music, politics, poetry, book reviews, fiction. Illustrations: colour. Founded 1953.

Jewish Telegraph

Telegraph House, 11 Park Hill, Bury Old Road, Prestwich, Manchester M25 0HH
tel 0161 740 9321
email manchester@jewishtelegraph.com
The Galehouse Business Centre, Chapel Allerton, Leeds LS7 4RF
tel 0113 295 6000
email leeds@jewishtelegraph.com
tel 0151 475 6666
email liverpool@jewishtelegraph.com
May Terrace, Giffnock, Glasgow G46 6LD
tel 0141 621 4422
email glasgow@jewishtelegraph.com
website www.jewishtelegraph.com
Editor Paul Harris
Weekly Manchester 60p, Leeds 55p, Liverpool 35p, Glasgow 60p

Non-fiction articles of Jewish interest, especially humour. Exclusive Jewish news stories and pictures, international, national and local. Length: 1,000–1,500 words. Payment: by arrangement. Illustrations: line, half-tone, cartoons. Founded 1950.

Kent Life

Archant Kent, Kent House, 81 Station Road, Ashford, Kent TN23 1PP
tel 07809 551221
email sarah.sturt@kent-life.co.uk
website www.kent-life.co.uk
Editor Sarah Sturt
Monthly £3.25

Local lifestyle magazine, celebrating the best of county life. Features local people, entertainment, Kent towns, walks, history and heritage. Welcomes ideas for articles and features, length: 1,000 words (articles/features). Illustrations: hi-res jpgs. Payment: contact editor. Founded 1962.

Kerrang!

Bauer Media Group, Endeavour House, Shaftesbury Avenue, London WC2H 8JG
tel 020-7182 8406
website www.kerrang.com
Editor-in-Chief Phil Alexander
Weekly £2.20

News, reviews and interviews; music with attitude. All material commissioned. Illustrations: colour. Payment: by arrangement. Founded 1981.

Kids Alive! (The Young Soldier)

The Salvation Army, 101 Newington Causeway, London SE1 6BN
tel 020-7367 4911
email kidsalive@salvationarmy.org.uk
website www.salvationarmy.org.uk/kidsalive
Editor Justin Reeves, *Deputy Editor* Cara Macfarlane
Weekly 50p (£39 p.a.)

Children's magazine: pictures, scripts and artwork for cartoon strips, puzzles, etc; Christian-based with emphasis on education and lifestyle issues. Payment: by arrangement. Illustrations: half-tone, line and 4-colour line, cartoons. Founded 1881.

Kitchen Garden

Mortons Media Group Ltd, Media Centre, Morton Way, Horncastle, Lincs. LN9 6JR
tel (01507) 529396
email sott@mortons.co.uk
website www.kitchengarden.co.uk
Editor Steve Ott
Monthly £4.99

Magazine for people with a passion for growing their own vegetables, fruit and herbs. Includes practical tips and inspirational ideas. Specially commissions most material. Welcomes ideas for articles and features. Length: 700–2,000 (articles/features). Illustrations: colour transparencies, jpgs, prints and artwork; all commissioned. Payment: varies. Founded 1997.

The Lady

39–40 Bedford Street, London WC2E 9ER
tel 020-7379 4717
email editors@lady.co.uk
website www.lady.co.uk

Editor Matt Warren
Weekly £2.50

Features, interviews, comment, columns, arts and book reviews, fashion, beauty, interiors, cookery, health, travel and pets. Plus classified ads, holiday cottages and pages of puzzles. No unsolicited manuscripts; brief pitches by email. Founded 1885.

The Lancet

125 London Wall, London EC2Y 5AS
tel 020-7424 4922
email editorial@lancet.com
website www.thelancet.com
Editor Dr Richard Horton
Weekly £5

Research papers, review articles, editorials, correspondence and commentaries on international medicine, medical research and policy. Material may be submitted directly through a dedicated online system. Founded 1823.

The Lawyer

79 Wells Street, London W1T 3QN
tel 020-7970 4000
email editorial@thelawyer.com
website www.thelawyer.com
Editor Catrin Griffiths
Weekly £3.95

News, articles, features and views relevant to the legal profession. Length: 600–900 words. Illustrations: as agreed. Payment: £125–£150 per 1,000 words. Founded 1987.

Legal Week

Incisive Business Media Ltd, Haymarket House, 28–29 Haymarket, London SW1Y 4RX
tel 020-7484 9700
email charlotte.edmond@incisivemedia.com
website www.legalweek.com
Editor Georgina Stanley
Weekly £300 p.a. (digital only), £375 (print and digital)

News and features aimed at business lawyers. Length: 750–1,000 words (features), 300 words (news). Payment: £200 upwards (features), £75–£100 (news). Considers unsolicited material and welcomes ideas for articles and features. Founded 1999.

Leisure Painter

Caxton House, 63–65 High Street, Tenterden, Kent TN30 6BD
tel (01580) 763315
email ingrid@tapc.co.uk
website www.painters-online.co.uk
Editor Ingrid Lyon
Every four weeks £3.99

Instructional articles on painting and fine art. Payment: £75 per 1,000 words. Illustrations: line, half-tone, colour, original artwork. Founded 1967.

LGC (Local Government Chronicle)

EMAP, Telephone House, 69–77 Paul Street, London EC2A 4NW
tel 020-3033 2787
email lgcnews@emap.com
website www.lgcplus.com
Editor Nick Golding
Weekly £196 p.a.

Aimed at senior managers in local government. Covers politics, management issues, social services, education, regeneration, industrial relations and personnel, plus public sector finance and Scottish and Welsh local government. Length: 1,000 words (features). Illustrations: b&w and colour, cartoons. Payment: by arrangement. Founded 1855.

Life and Work: The Magazine of the Church of Scotland

121 George Street, Edinburgh EH2 4YN
tel 0131 225 5722
email magazine@lifeandwork.org
website www.lifeandwork.org
Editor Lynne McNeil
Monthly £2.20

Articles not exceeding 1,200 words and news; occasional stories and poetry. Study the magazine and contact the Editor first. Payment: by arrangement. Illustrations: photos and colour illustrations.

Lincolnshire Life

County House, 9 Checkpoint Court, Sadler Road, Lincoln LN6 3PW
tel (01522) 527127
email editorial@lincolnshirelife.co.uk
website www.lincolnshirelife.co.uk
Editor Caroline Bingham
Monthly £3

Articles and news of county interest. Approach in writing. Length: up to 1,500 words. Illustrations: colour photos and line drawings. Payment: varies. Founded 1961.

The Linguist

The Chartered Institute of Linguists, Dunstan House, 14a St Cross Street, London EC1N 8XA
tel 020-7940 3100
email linguist.editor@ciol.org.uk
website www.ciol.org.uk
Editor Miranda Moore
Bi-monthly Free online or subscriptions available

Articles of interest to professional linguists in translating, interpreting and teaching fields. Articles usually contributed, but payment by arrangement. Most contributors have special knowledge of the subjects with which they deal. Length: 800–2,000 words.

Literary Review

44 Lexington Street, London W1F 0LW
tel 020-7437 9392
email editorial@literaryreview.co.uk
website www.literaryreview.co.uk
Editor Nancy Sladek
Monthly £3.95 (double issue December/January)

Reviews, articles of cultural interest, interviews and profiles. Material mostly commissioned. Length: articles and reviews 800–1,500 words. Illustrations: line and b&w photos. Payment: £25 per article; none for illustrations. Founded 1979.

Litro

1–5 Cremer Street, Studio 9.1, London E2 8HD
tel 020-3371 9971
email editor@litro.co.uk
website www.litro.co.uk
Editor-in-Chief Eric Akoto

Monthly £3 per single issue or £50 p.a. for All Access subscription

Literary magazine featuring fiction, non-fiction, reviews, articles of cultural interest, interviews, profiles and a monthly short story competition. Length: short stories, 2,500 words; articles and reviews, 800–1,500 words. Illustrations: line and b&w photos. Founded 2006.

Little White Lies

TCOLondon, 71a Leonard Street, London EC2A 4QS
tel 020-7729 3675
email hello@tcolondon.com
website www.littlewhitelies.co.uk
Editor David Jenkins
Bi-monthly £6

Independent movie magazine that features cutting-edge writing, illustration and photography to get under the skin of cinema. Also explores the worlds of music, art, politics and pop culture as part of its mission to reshape the debate across the movie landscape. Length: various. Illustrations and photography. Payment: varies for illustration, articles and reviews. Found 2005.

Living France Magazine

Archant Life, Archant House, Oriel Road, Cheltenham, Glos. GL50 1BB
tel (01242) 216050
email editorial@livingfrance.com
website www.livingfrance.com
Editor Eve Middleton
13 p.a. £3.99

Articles on travel, property and aspects of living in France, from having a baby to setting up utilities. Interviews with expats also featured. Founded 1990.

The London Magazine: A Review of Literature and the Arts

Administration 11 Queen's Gate, London SW7 5EL
email admin@thelondonmagazine.org
website www.thelondonmagazine.org
Editor Steven O'Brien
Bi-monthly £6.95

Poems, stories (2,000–5,000 words), memoirs, critical articles, features on art, photography, theatre, music, architecture, etc. Sae essential (three IRCs from abroad). Submissions by email accepted. No payment offered. First published in 1732.

London Review of Books

28 Little Russell Street, London WC1A 2HN
tel 020-7209 1101
email edit@lrb.co.uk
website www.lrb.co.uk
Editor Mary-Kay Wilmers
Fortnightly £3.75

Features, essays, poems. Payment: by arrangement.

Lothian Life

4/8 Downfield Place, Edinburgh EH11 2EW
tel 07905 614402
email office@lothianlife.co.uk
website www.lothianlife.co.uk
Editor Anne Hamilton
Online publication only

Articles, profiles, etc with a Lothians angle. Length: 500–2,000 words. Payment terms can be found on the website. Founded 1995.

Management Today

Teddington Studios, Broom Road, Teddington, Middx. TW11 9BE
tel 020-8267 5462
email mtsupport@haymarket.com
website www.managementtoday.co.uk
Editor Matthew Gwyther
Monthly £4.90

Company profiles and analysis – columns from 1,000 words, features up to 3,000 words. Payment: £350 per 1,000 words. Illustrations: always commissioned. Founded 1966.

Marie Claire

Time Inc. (UK), The Blue Fin Building, 110 Southwark Street, London SE1 0SU
tel 020-3148 7513
email marieclaire@timeinc.com
website www.marieclaire.co.uk
Editor-in-Chief Trish Halpin
Monthly £3.99

Feature articles of interest to today's woman; plus fashion, beauty, health, food, drink and travel. Commissioned material only. Payment: by negotiation. Illustrated in colour. Founded 1988.

Market Newsletter

Bureau of Freelance Photographers, Vision House, PO Box 474, Hatfield AL10 1FY
tel (01707) 651450
email mail@thebfp.com
website www.thebfp.com

Editor John Tracy
Monthly £54 p.a. UK (£75 overseas); free to members of BFP

Current information on markets and editorial requirements of interest to writers and photographers. Founded 1965.

Marketing Week

Centaur Communications, 50 Poland Street, London W1F 7AX
tel 020-7970 4000
email mw.editorial@centaur.co.uk
website www.marketingweek.co.uk
Editor Russell Parsons
Weekly £3.95

Aimed at marketing management. Accepts occasional features and analysis. Length: 1,000–2,000 words. Payment: £250 per 1,000 words. Founded 1978.

Mayfair

Paul Raymond Publications, 23 Lyon Road, Hersham, Surrey KT12 3PU
tel 020-8873 4406
email mayfair@paulraymond.com
website www.paulraymond.xxx
Editor Matt Berry
Monthly £5.20

High-quality glamour photography; explicit sex stories (no erotic fiction); male interest features – sport, humour, entertainment, hedonism. Proposals welcome. Payment: by arrangement. Founded 1965.

MBUK (Mountain Biking UK)

Immediate Media Co., Tower House, Fairfax Street, Bristol BS1 3BN
tel 0117 927 9009
email danny.walter@immediate.co.uk
website http://magazine.bikeradar.com/category/mountain-biking-uk
Editor-in-Chief Danny Walter
Every 4 weeks £49.49 p.a. (print), £27.99 p.a. (digital)

Magazine for mountain bike enthusiasts with features, reviews, news and world and domestic racing coverage.

Medal News

Token Publishing Ltd, Orchard House, Duchy Road, Heathpark, Honiton, Devon EX14 1YD
tel (01404) 46972
email info@tokenpublishing.com
website www.tokenpublishing.com
Editor John Mussell
10 p.a. £3.85

Well-researched articles on military history with a bias towards medals. Send text in digital form. Length: up to 2,000 words. Illustrations: if possible. Payment: by arrangement; none for illustrations. Founded 1989.

Media Week

Haymarket Publishing Ltd, 174 Hammersmith Road, London W6 7JP
tel 020-8267 4055
website www.mediaweek.co.uk
Editor Arif Durrani
No subscription charge

Online B2B magazine covering news, analysis, features and interviews on the UK media industry. Readership: 100,000 unique users per month. Founded 1985.

Men Only

Paul Raymond Publications, 23 Lyon Road, Hersham, Surrey KT12 3PU
tel 020-8873 4406
email menonly@paulraymond.com
website www.paulraymond.com
Editor Matt Berry
Monthly £4.30

High-quality glamour photography; explicit sex stories (no erotic fiction); male interest features – sport, humour, entertainment, hedonism. Proposals welcome. Payment: by arrangement. Founded 1971.

Men's Health

Hearst Magazines UK, 33 Broadwick Street, London W1F 0DQ
tel 020-7339 4400
email contact@menshealth.co.uk
website www.menshealth.co.uk
Editor Toby Wiseman
10 p.a. £3.99

Active pursuits, grooming, fitness, fashion, sex, career and general men's interest issues. Length 1,000–4,000 words. Ideas welcome. No unsolicited MSS. Payment: by arrangement. Founded 1994.

Methodist Recorder

122 Golden Lane, London EC1Y 0TL
tel 020-7251 8414
email editorial@methodistrecorder.co.uk
website www.methodistrecorder.co.uk
Editor Moira Sleight
Weekly £2.60

Methodist newspaper; ecumenically involved. Limited opportunities for freelance contributors. Preliminary contact advised. Founded 1861.

Military Modelling

PO Box 6018, Leighton Buzzard LU7 2RS
tel/fax (01689) 869849
email kelvin.barber@mytimemedia.com
website www.militarymodelling.com
Editor Kelvin Barber
Monthly £4.60

Articles on military modelling. Length: up to 2,000 words. Payment: by arrangement. Illustrations: line, half-tone, colour.

Mixmag

Mixmag Media, 90–92 Pentonville Road, London N1 9HS

tel 020-7078 8400
email mixmag@mixmag.net
website www.mixmag.net
Editor Nick DeCosemo
Monthly £4.95

Dance music and clubbing magazine. No unsolicited material. Payment: £200 per 1,000 words. Illustrations: colour and b&w. Founded 1983.

Model Boats

MyTimeMedia Ltd, PO Box 718, Orpington, Kent BR6 1AP
tel 0844 412 2262
email editor@modelboats.co.uk
website www.modelboats.co.uk
Editor Paul Freshney
Monthly £4.50

Founded 1964.

Model Engineer

MyTimeMedia Ltd, Enterprise House, Enterprise Way, Edenbridge, Kent TN8 6HF
tel 0844 4122262
email diane.carney@mytimemedia.com
website www.model-engineer.co.uk
Editor Diane Carney
Fortnightly £3.40

Detailed description of the construction of models, small workshop equipment, machine tools and small electrical and mechanical devices; articles on small power engineering, mechanics, electricity, workshop methods, clocks and experiments. Payment: up to £50 per page. Illustrations: line, half-tone, colour. Founded 1898.

Modern Language Review

Salisbury House, Station Road, Cambridge CB1 2LA
email mail@mhra.org.uk
website www.mhra.org.uk
Quarterly $55 p.a. (individual), $127 p.a. (e-only), $180 p.a. (institutions)

Articles and reviews of a scholarly or specialist character on English, Romance, Germanic and Slavonic languages, literatures and cultures. Payment: none, but electronic offprints are given. Founded 1905.

Mojo

Bauer Media Group, Endeavour House, 189 Shaftesbury Avenue, London WC2H 8JG
tel 020-7208 3443
email mojo@bauermedia.co.uk
website www.mojo4music.com
Editor-in-Chief Phil Alexander
Monthly £4.99

Serious rock music magazine: interviews, news and reviews of books, live shows and albums. Length: up to 10,000 words. Illustrations: colour and b&w photos, colour caricatures. Payment: £250 per 1,000 words; £200–£400 illustrations. Founded 1993.

Moneywise

Standon House, 21 Mansell Street, London E1 8AA
tel 020-7680 3600
website www.moneywise.co.uk
Editor Mark King
Monthly £3.95

Financial and consumer interest features, articles and news stories. No unsolicited MSS. Length: 1,500–2,000 words. Illustrations: willing to see designers, illustrators and photographers for fresh new ideas. Payment: by arrangement. Founded 1990.

The Moth

Drummullen, Cavan, Co. Cavan, Republic of Ireland
tel +353 (0)4 94362677
email editor@themothmagazine.com
website www.themothmagazine.com
Editor Rebecca O'Connor
Quarterly €5, €20 p.a., €40 institutions, libraries and schools

Arts and literature magazine featuring original poetry, short fiction, interviews and full-colour artwork. Submissions welcome, although potential contributors should familiarise themselves with the magazine first. Send no more than six poems and two short stories (max. 2,500 words) by email or post (with sae). Annual Ballymaloe International Poetry Prize (with €13,000 worth of prizes) and Moth Short Story Prize (€4,000 plus). Founded 2010.

Mother & Baby

Bauer Media Group, Endeavour House, 189 Shaftesbury Avenue, London WC2H 8JG
tel 020-7347 1869
website www.motherandbaby.co.uk
Editor-in-Chief Claire Irvin
Monthly £3.99

Features and practical information including pregnancy and birth and babycare advice. Expert attribution plus real-life stories. Length: 1,000–1,500 words (commissioned work only). Payment: by negotiation. Illustrated. Founded 1956.

Motor Boat and Yachting

Time Inc. (UK), The Blue Fin Building, 110 Southwark Street, London SE1 0SU
tel 020-3148 4651
email mby@timeinc.com
website www.mby.com
Editor Hugo Andreae
Monthly £4.50

General interest as well as specialist motor boating material welcomed. Features up to 2,000 words considered on all sea-going aspects. Payment: varies. Illustrations: high-resolution photos. Founded 1904.

Motor Cycle News

Bauer Media Group, Media House, Peterborough Business Park, Lynchwood, Peterborough PE2 6EA

tel 0845 601 1356
email mcn@motorcyclenews.com
website www.motorcyclenews.com
Editor Andy Calton
Weekly £2.20

Features (up to 1,000 words), photos and news stories of interest to motorcyclists. Founded 1955.

Motorcaravan Motorhome Monthly (MMM)

Warners Group Publications, West Street, Bourne, Lincs. PE10 9PH
tel (01778) 391154
email danielattwood@warnersgroup.co.uk
website www.outandaboutlive.co.uk
Managing Editor Daniel Attwood
Every four weeks £4.20

Articles including motorcaravan travel, owner reports and DIY. Length: up to 2,500 words. Payment: by arrangement. Illustrations: line, half-tone, colour prints and transparencies, high-quality digital. Founded 1966 as *Motor Caravan and Camping*.

Mslexia

PO Box 656, Newcastle upon Tyne NE99 1PZ
tel 0191 204 8860
email postbag@mslexia.co.uk
website www.mslexia.co.uk
Editorial Director Debbie Taylor
Quarterly £6.95

Magazine for women writers which combines features and advice about writing with new fiction and poetry by women. Considers unsolicited material. Length: up to 2,200 words (short stories), or up to four poems of no more than 40 lines each, in any style, which must relate to current themes (or adhere to poetry or short story competition rules). Also accepts submissions for other areas of the magazine, including Pen Portrait, Monologue, etc., variously themed and unthemed. Articles/features by negotiation. Illustrations: by commission only; email submissions welcome. Payment: by negotiation. Founded 1998.

Muscle & Fitness

Weider Publishing, 10 Windsor Court, Clarence Drive, Harrogate, North Yorkshire HG1 2PE
tel (01423) 504516
website www.muscle-fitness.co.uk
Editor John Plummer
Monthly £4.20

A guide to muscle development and general health and fitness. Founded 1988.

Music Teacher

Rhinegold House, 20 Rugby Street, London WC1N 3QZ
tel 07785 613145
email music.teacher@rhinegold.co.uk
website www.rhinegold.co.uk
Editor Thomas Lydon
Monthly £4.95

Information and articles for both school and private instrumental teachers, including reviews of books, music, software, CD-Roms and other music-education resources. Articles and illustrations must both have a teaching, as well as a musical, interest. Length: articles 600–1,700 words. Payment: £120 per 1,000 words. Founded 1908.

Music Week

Suncourt House, 18-26 Essex Road, London N1 8LN
tel 020-7226 7246
email musicweeksupport@intentmedia.co.uk
website www.musicweek.com
Editor Tom Pakinkis
Weekly £5.50

News and features on all aspects of producing, manufacturing, marketing and retailing music. Payment: by negotiation. Founded 1959.

Musical Opinion

1 Exford Road, London SE12 9HD
tel 020-8857 1582
email musicalopinion@hotmail.co.uk
website www.musicalopinion.com
Editor Robert Matthew-Walker
Bi-monthly £28 p.a.

Suggestions for contributions of musical interest, scholastic, educational, anniversaries and ethnic. DVD, CD, opera, festival, book, music reviews. Illustrations: colour photos. Founded 1877.

Musical Times

7 Brunswick Mews, Hove, East Sussex BN3 1HD
email mted@gotadsl.co.uk
website http://themusicaltimes.blogspot.co.uk
Editor Antony Bye
4 p.a. £10

Musical articles, reviews, 500–6,000 words. All material commissioned; no unsolicited material. Illustrations: music. Founded 1844.

My Weekly

D.C. Thomson & Co. Ltd, 80 Kingsway East, Dundee DD4 8SL
tel (01382) 223131
email myweekly@dcthomson.co.uk
website www.myweekly.co.uk
Editor-in-Chief Sally Hampton, *Assistant Editor (Features)* Sally Rodger, *Health Editor* Karen Byrom, *Celebrity Editor* Susan Anderson
Weekly 99p

Modern women's magazine aimed at 50+ age group. No unsolicited MSS considered. Send ideas or pitches to relevant department editor. Payment by negotiation. Illustrations: colour. Founded 1910.

The National Trust Magazine

The National Trust, Heelis, Kemble Drive, Swindon SN2 2NA
tel (01793) 817716
email magazine@nationaltrust.org.uk
website www.nationaltrust.org.uk
Editor Sally Palmer
3 p.a. £3.95 Free to members

Lifestyle title with focus on the National Trust, encompassing interiors, gardens, food, UK travel, wildlife, environment, topical features and celebrity content. No unsolicited articles. Length: 1,000 words (features), 200 words (news). Illustrations: colour transparencies and artwork. Payment: by arrangement; picture library rates. Founded 1932.

Nature

Macmillan Magazines Ltd, The Macmillan Building, 4 Crinan Street, London N1 9XW
tel 020-7833 4000 4640
email nature@nature.com
website www.nature.com/nature
Editor-in-Chief Philip Campbell
Weekly £135 p.a.

Devoted to scientific matters and to their bearing upon public affairs. All contributors of articles have specialised knowledge of the subjects with which they deal. Illustrations: line, half-tone. Founded 1869.

.net

Future Publishing Ltd, Quay House, The Ambury, Bath BA1 1UA
tel (01225) 442244
website www.netmag.co.uk
Editor Oliver Lindberg
Monthly £59.99 p.a. (print), £44.99 p.a. (digital), £71.99 p.a. (print and digital bundle)

Articles, features and news on the internet. Length: 1,000–3,000 words. Payment: negotiable. Illustrations: colour. Founded 1994.

New Humanist

The Rationalist Association, Merchants House, 5–7 Southwark Street, London SE1 1RQ
tel 020-3117 0630
email editor@newhumanist.org.uk
website https://newhumanist.org.uk
Editor Daniel Trilling
Bi-monthly £4.95

Articles on current affairs, philosophy, science, literature, religion and humanism. Length: 500–1,500 words. Illustrations: colour photos. Payment: nominal. Founded 1885.

New Internationalist

The Old Music Hall, 106–108 Cowley Road, Oxford OX4 1JE
tel (01865) 403345
email ni@newint.org
website www.newint.org
Editors Vanessa Baird, Chris Brazier, Hazel Healy, Dinyar Godrej, Jo Lateu
Monthly £4.45

World issues, ranging from food to feminism to peace; one subject examined each month. Length: up to 2,000 words. Illustrations: line, half-tone, colour, cartoons. Payment: £230 per 1,000 words. Founded 1973.

New Law Journal

LexisNexis Butterworths, Lexis House, 30 Farringdon Street, London EC4A 4HH
tel 020-7400 2580
email newlaw.journal@lexisnexis.co.uk
website www.newlawjournal.co.uk
Editor Jan Miller
48 p.a. £8, £346 p.a.

Articles and news on all aspects of civil litigation and dispute resolution. Length: up to 1,800 words. Payment: by arrangement.

New Musical Express (NME)

(incorporating Melody Maker)
Time Inc. (UK), The Blue Fin Building, 110 Southwark Street, London SE1 0SU
tel 020-3148 5000
email karen.walter@timeinc.com
website www.nme.com
Editor Mike Williams
Weekly £2.50

The latest music news, the best new bands, world exclusive features and new album reviews every week. Length: by arrangement. Preliminary letter or phone call desirable. Payment: by arrangement. Illustrations: action photos with strong news angle of recording personalities, cartoons. Founded 1952.

New Scientist

Lacon House, 84 Theobalds Road, London WC1X 8NS
tel 020-7611 1200
email news@newscientist.com
website www.newscientist.com
Editor-in-Chief Jeremy Webb
Weekly £3.90

Authoritative articles of topical importance on all aspects of science and technology. Potential contributors should study recent copies of the magazine and initially send only a 200-word synopsis of their idea. Does not publish non-peer-reviewed theories, poems or crosswords. Payment: varies but average £300 per 1,000 words. Illustrations: all styles, cartoons; contact art dept.

New Statesman

(formerly New Statesman & Society)
7th Floor, John Carpenter House, 7 Carmelite Street, London EC4Y 0AN
tel 020-7936 6400

email editorial@newstatesman.co.uk
website www.newstatesman.co.uk
Editor Jason Cowley
Weekly £3.95

Interested in news, reportage and analysis of current political and social issues at home and overseas, plus book reviews, general articles and coverage of the arts, environment and science seen from the perspective of the British Left but written in a stylish, witty and unpredictable way. Length: strictly according to the value of the piece. Illustrations: commissioned for specific articles, although artists' samples considered for future reference; occasional cartoons. Payment: by agreement. Founded 1913.

New Welsh Review

PO Box 170, Aberystwyth, Ceredigion SY23 1WZ
tel (01970) 628410
email submissions@newwelshreview.com
website www.newwelshreview.com
Editor Gwen Davis
Quarterly £7.99 (single edition, print), £3.99 (single edition, ePub)

Literary – critical articles, creative non-fiction, short stories, poems, book reviews and profiles. Especially, but not exclusively, concerned with Welsh writing in English. Length: up to 3,000 words (articles). Send by email or hard copy with a sae for return of material. Decisions within 3 months of submission. Illustrations: colour. Payment: £68 per 1,000 words (articles); £28 per poem, £100 per short story, £47 per review. Founded 1988.

newbooks magazine

1 Vicarage Lane, Stubbington, Hants PO14 2JU
tel (01329) 311419
email guy.pringle@newbooksmag.com
website www.nudge-book.com
Publisher Guy Pringle
3 p.a. £17.50 p.a. (UK)

The magazine for readers and reading groups. Includes extracts from new books, articles and features about and by authors, how the book trade works and how books reach publication and find a readership. A sample magazine is available for £5 from the website (strictly UK only). Free copies of featured books in each issue may be claimed as long as post and packing costs are covered.

Now

Time Inc. (UK), The Blue Fin Building, 110 Southwark Street, London SE1 0SU
tel 020-3148 5000
email nowletters@timeinc.com
website www.nowmagazine.co.uk
Editor Sally Eyden
Weekly £1.55

Celebrity gossip, news, fashion, beauty and lifestyle features. Most articles are commissioned or are written by in-house writers. Founded 1996.

Nursery World

MA Education, St Jude's Church, Dulwich Road, London SE24 0PB
tel 020-8501 6693
email news.nw@markallengroup.com
website www.nurseryworld.co.uk
Editor Liz Roberts
Weekly £2.95

For all grades of primary school, nursery and child-care staff, nannies, foster parents and all concerned with the care of expectant mothers, babies and young children. Authoritative and informative articles, 800 or 1,300 words, and photos, on all aspects of child welfare and early education, from 0–8 years, in the UK. Practical ideas, policy news and career advice. No short stories. Payment: by arrangement. Illustrations: line, half-tone, colour.

Nursing Times

EMAP, Telephone House, 69–77 Paul Street, London EC2A 4NQ
tel 020-7728 5000
email nursingtimes@emap.com
website www.nursingtimes.net
Editor Jenni Middleton
Weekly £2.90

Articles of clinical interest, nursing education and nursing policy. Illustrated articles not longer than 2,000 words. Press day: Friday. Illustrations: photos, line. Payment: NUJ rates; by arrangement for illustrations. Founded 1905.

OK!

Northern & Shell Building, 10 Lower Thames Street, London EC3R 6EN
tel 0871 434 1010
website www.ok.co.uk/home
Editor Kirsty Tyler
Weekly £2

Exclusive celebrity interviews and photographs. Submit ideas in writing. Length: 1,000 words. Illustrations: colour. Payment: £150–£250,000 per feature. Founded 1993.

The Oldie

65 Newman Street, London W1T 3EG
tel 020-7436 8801
email editorial@theoldie.co.uk
website www.theoldie.co.uk
Editor Alexander Chancellor
Monthly £3.95

General interest magazine reflecting attitudes of older people but aimed at a wider audience. Features (600–1,000 words) on all subjects, as well as articles for specific sections. Be familiar with the magazine prior to submitting work. See website for further guidelines. Enclose sae for reply/return of MSS. No poetry. Illustrations: welcomes b&w and colour cartoons. Payment: approx. £100–£150 per 1,000 words; £100 for cartoons. Founded 1992.

Olive

Immediate Media Co. Ltd, Vineyard House,
44 Brook Green, London W6 7BT
tel 020-7150 5000
website www.olivemagazine.com
Editor Christine Hayes
Monthly £3.90

Upmarket food magazine which aims to encourage readers to cook, eat and explore. Each edition includes a range of recipes for both everyday and weekend cooking, as well as information on techiques, trends and tips.

Opera

36 Black Lion Lane, London W6 9BE
tel 020-8563 8893
email editor@opera.co.uk
website www.opera.co.uk
Editor John Allison
13 p.a. £5.60

Reviews of opera from the UK and around the world, including profiles of opera's greatest performers and a comprehensive calendar of productions and events. Length: up to 2,000 words. Payment: by arrangement. Illustrations: photos.

Opera Now

Rhinegold House, 20 Rugby Street,
London WC1N 3QZ
tel 020-7333 1729
email opera.now@rhinegold.co.uk
website www.rhinegold.co.uk
Editor Ashutosh Khandekar
Monthly £4.95

Articles, news, reviews on opera. All material commissioned only. Length: 150–1,500 words. Illustrations: colour and b&w photos, line, cartoons. Payment: £120 per 1,000 words. Founded 1989.

Our Dogs

Northwood House, Greenwood Business Centre,
Regent Road, Salford M5 4QH
tel 0844 504 9001
email editorial@ourdogs.co.uk
website www.ourdogs.co.uk
Editor Alison Smith
Weekly £2.25

Articles and news on the breeding and showing of pedigree dogs. Illustrations: b&w photos. Payment: by negotiation; £10 per photo. Founded 1895.

Park Home & Holiday Caravan

Kelsey Publishing Ltd, Cudham Tithe Barn,
Berry's Hill, Cudham, Kent, TN16 3AG
tel (01959) 543530
email phhc.ed@kelsey.co.uk
website www.parkhomemagazine.co.uk
Editor Alex Melvin
12 p.a. £2.95

Informative articles on residential mobile homes (park homes) and holiday static caravans – personal experience articles, site features, news items. No preliminary letter. Payment: by arrangement. Illustrations: line, half-tone, colour transparencies, digital images, cartoons. Founded 1960.

PC Advisor

IDG Communications Ltd, 101 Euston Road,
London NW1 2RA
tel 020-7756 2800
email jim_martin@idg.co.uk
website www.pcadvisor.co.uk
Editor Jim Martin
Monthly CD edition £4.99, DVD edition £5.99

Aimed at PC-proficient individuals who are looking for IT solutions that will enhance their productivity at work and at home. Includes information on the latest hardware and software and advice on how to use PCs to maximum effect. Features are commissioned; unsolicited material may be considered. Length: 1,500–3,000 words (features). Illustrations: colour artwork. Payment: dependent on feature type. Founded 1995.

PC Pro

Dennis Publishing Ltd, 30 Cleveland Street,
London W1T 4JD
tel 020-7907 6000
email news@pcpro.co.uk
website www.pcpro.co.uk
Editor-in-Chief Tim Danton
Monthly £5.99 (DVD edition), £4.99 (CD edition)

In-depth industry comment and news, reviews and tests, aimed at IT professionals and enthusiasts. Email feature pitches to editor@pcpro.co.uk. Founded 1994.

Peace News

5 Caledonian Road, London N1 9DY
tel 020-7278 3344
email editorial@peacenews.info
website www.peacenews.info
Editors Milan Rai, Emily Johns
6 p.a. £2

Political articles based on nonviolence in every aspect of human life. Illustrations: line, half-tone. No payment. Founded 1936.

Pensions World

LexisNexis, Quadrant House, The Quadrant, Sutton,
Surrey SM2 5AS
tel 0845 370 1234
email stephanie.hawthorne@lexisnexis.co.uk
website www.pensionsworld.co.uk
Editor Stephanie Hawthorne
Monthly £150 p.a.

Specialist articles on pensions, investment and law. No unsolicited articles; all material is commissioned. Length: 1,400 words. Payment: by negotiation. Founded 1972.

People Management

Haymarket Network, Teddington Studios,
Broom Road, Teddington TW11 9BE
tel 020-8267 5013
email PMeditorial@haymarket.co.uk
website www.peoplemanagement.co.uk
Editor Robert Jeffrey
Monthly £105 p.a. (UK)

Magazine of the Chartered Institute of Personnel and Development. News items and feature articles on recruitment and selection, training and development; pay and performance management; industrial psychology; employee relations; employment law; working practices and new practical ideas in personnel management in industry and commerce. Length: up to 2,500 words. Payment: by arrangement. Illustrations: contact art editor.

People's Friend

D.C. Thomson & Co. Ltd, 80 Kingsway East,
Dundee DD4 8SL
tel (01382) 223131
email peoplesfriend@dcthomson.co.uk
website www.thepeoplesfriend.co.uk
Send material to The Editor, Angela Gilchrist
Weekly £1.05

Fiction magazine for women of all ages. Serials (60,000–70,000 words) and complete stories (1,000–4,000 words) of strong romantic and emotional appeal. Considers stories for children. Includes knitting and cookery. No preliminary letter required. Illustrations: colour. Payment: on acceptance. Founded 1869.

People's Friend Pocket Novel

D.C. Thomson & Co. Ltd, 80 Kingsway East,
Dundee DD4 8SL
tel (01382) 223131
email tsteel@dcthomson.co.uk
website www.thepeoplesfriend.co.uk
Editor Tracey Steel
2 per month £2.99

40,000-word family and romantic stories aimed at 30+ age group. Payment: by arrangement. No illustrations.

Period Living

Centaur Special Interest Media,
2 Sugar Brook Court, Aston Road, Bromsgrove,
Worcs. B60 3EX
tel (01527) 834400
email period.living@centaur.co.uk
website www.periodliving.co.uk
Editor Rachel Watson
Monthly £3.99

Articles and features on decoration, furnishings, renovation of period homes; gardens, crafts, decorating in a period style. Illustrated. Payment: varies, according to work required. Founded 1990.

The Photographer

The Coach House, The Firs, High Street,
Whitchurch, Bucks HP22 4SJ
tel (01296) 642020
email editor@bipp.com
website www.bipp.com
Editor Jonathan Briggs
Quarterly £20 p.a. (UK residents), £40 p.a. (EU residents), £50 (RoW); free to all members of British Institute of Professional Photography

Journal of the British Institute of Professional Photography. Authoritative reviews, news, views and high-quality photographs.

Pick Me Up

Time Inc. (UK), The Blue Fin Building,
110 Southwark Street, London SE1 0SU
tel 020-3148 5000
email pickmeup@timeinc.com
website www.pickmeupmagazine.co.uk
Editor Gilly Sinclair
Weekly 68p

Upbeat women's magazine containing real-life stories and puzzles.

Picture Postcard Monthly

15 Debdale Lane, Keyworth, Nottingham NG12 5HT
tel 0115 937 4079
email reflections@postcardcollecting.co.uk
website www.postcardcollecting.co.uk
Editor Brian Lund
Monthly £36 p.a. (UK)

Articles, news and features for collectors of old or modern picture postcards. Length: 500–2,000 words. Illustrations: colour and b&w. Payment: £27 per 1,000 words; £1 per print. Founded 1978.

Planet: The Welsh Internationalist

PO Box 44, Aberystwyth, Ceredigion SY23 3ZZ
tel (01970) 611255
email planet.enquiries@planetmagazine.org.uk
website www.planetmagazine.org.uk
Editor Emily Trahair
Quarterly £6.75

Articles on culture, society, Welsh current affairs and international politics, as well as short fiction, poetry, photo essays and review articles. Article length: 1,500–2,500 words. Payment: £50 per 1,000 words. Submissions by post or email. For articles, email enquiry in first instance. Founded 1970.

PN Review

(formerly Poetry Nation)
Carcanet Press Ltd, 4th Floor, Alliance House,
30 Cross Street, Manchester M2 7AQ
tel 0161 834 8730
email info@carcanet.co.uk
website www.pnreview.co.uk
Editor Michael Schmidt

6 p.a. £6.99

Poems, essays, reviews, translations. Submissions by post only. Payment: by arrangement. Founded 1973.

Poetry Ireland Review/Éigse Éireann

32 Kildare Street, Dublin 2, Republic of Ireland
tel +353 (0)1 6789815
email publications@poetryireland.ie
website www.poetryireland.ie
Editor Vona Groarke
Quarterly €9.99; €50 p.a. (UK & Ireland)

Poetry. Features and articles by arrangement. Payment: €40 per contribution; €75 reviews. Founded 1981.

Poetry London

The Albany, Douglas Way, London SE8 4AG
tel 020-8691 7260
email admin@poetrylondon.co.uk
website www.poetrylondon.co.uk
Editors Ahren Warner and Martha Kapos (poetry), Tim Dooley (books)
3 p.a. £9, £25 p.a.

Poems of the highest standard, articles/reviews on any aspect of modern poetry. Comprehensive listings of poetry events and resources. Contributors must be knowledgeable about contemporary poetry. Payment: £20 minimum. Founded 1988.

Poetry Review

22 Betterton Street, London WC2H 9BX
tel 020-7420 9883
email poetryreview@poetrysociety.org.uk
website www.poetrysociety.org.uk
Editor Maurice O'Riordan
Quarterly From £35 p.a. for individuals

Poems, features and reviews. Send no more than six poems with sae. Preliminary study of magazine essential. Payment: £50+ per poem.

Poetry Wales

57 Nolton Street, Bridgend CF31 3AE
tel (01656) 663018
email info@poetrywales.co.uk
website www.poetrywales.co.uk
Editor Nia Davies
Quarterly £6.50

Poetry, criticism and commentary from Wales and around the world. Payment: by arrangement. Founded 1965.

The Police Journal: Theory, Practice and Principles

SAGE Publications, 1 Oliver's Yard, 55 City Road, London EC1Y 1SP
tel 020-7324 8500
website http://www.uk.sagepub.com/journals
Editor Professor Colin Rogers
Quarterly From £314 p.a. for individual print subscriptions, see website for further details

Articles of technical or professional interest to the Police Service throughout the world. Payment: none. Illustrations: line drawings. Founded 1928.

The Political Quarterly

Wiley-Blackwell, 9600 Garsington Road, Oxford OX4 2DQ
tel (01865) 776868
website www.politicalquarterly.org.uk
Editors Deborah Mabbett, Tony Wright MP
4 p.a. £272 p.a. print and online subscription (institution); £27 p.a. print and online subscription (individual)

Topical aspects of national and international politics and public administration; takes a progressive, but not a party, point of view. See website for submissions information.Length: average 5,000 words. Payment: about £125 per article. Founded 1930.

Post

Incisive Media, Haymarket House, 28–29 Haymarket, London SW1Y 4RX
tel 020-7484 9700
email postmag@incisivemedia.com
website www.postonline.co.uk
Editor Stephanie Denton
Weekly £8.60, £499 p.a.

Commissioned specialist articles on topics of interest to insurance professionals; news. Illustrations: colour photos and illustrations, colour and b&w cartoons and line drawings. Payment: £200 per 1,000 words; photos £30–£120, cartoons/line by negotiation. Founded 1840.

Poultry World

Reed Business Information, Quadrant House, The Quadrant, Sutton, Surrey SM2 5AS
tel 020-8652 4921
email poultry.world@rbi.co.uk
website www.fwi.co.uk/poultry
Editor Philip Clarke
Monthly £3.60

Articles on poultry breeding, production, marketing and packaging. News of international poultry interest. Payment: by arrangement. Illustrations: photos, line.

PR Week

22 Bute Gardens, London W6 7HN
tel 020-8267 4370
email john.harrington@haymarket.com
website www.prweek.com
Editor-in-Chief Danny Rogers
45 issues p.a. £3.80

News and features on public relations. Length: approx. 800–3,000 words. Payment: £250 per 1,000 words. Illustrations: colour and b&w. Founded 1984.

Practical Boat Owner

Westover House, West Quay Road, Poole,
Dorset BH15 1JG
tel (01202) 440820
email pbo@timeinc.com
website www.pbo.co.uk
Editor David Pugh
Monthly £4.30

Yachting magazine. Hints, tips and practical articles for cruising skippers. Send synopsis first. Payment: by negotiation. Illustrations: photos or drawings. Founded 1967.

Practical Caravan

Haymarket Consumer Media, Teddington Studios, Teddington Lock, Broom Road,
Teddington TW11 9BE
tel 020-8267 5629
email practical.caravan@haymarket.com
website www.practicalcaravan.com
Group Editor Rob Ganley
Every four weeks £4.20

Caravan-related travelogues, caravan site reviews; travel writing for existing regular series; technical and DIY matters. Illustrations: colour. Payment negotiable. Founded 1967.

Practical Fishkeeping

Bauer Media Group, Media House, Lynchwood, Peterborough Business Park, Peterborough PE2 6EA
tel (01733) 468000
website www.practicalfishkeeping.co.uk
Editor Karen Youngs
13 p.a. £4.20

Practical fishkeeping in tropical and coldwater aquaria and ponds. Heavy emphasis on inspiration and involvement. Good colour photography always needed, and used. No verse or humour, no personal biographical accounts of fishkeeping unless practical. Payment: by worth. Founded 1966.

Practical Photography

Bauer Media Group, Media House, Lynchwood, Peterborough PE2 6EA
tel (01733) 468000
website www.photoanswers.co.uk
Editor Ben Hawkins
13 issues p.a. £4.99

Aimed at photographic enthusiasts of all levels who want to improve their skills, try new techniques and learn from the experts. Excellent potential for freelance pictures: must be technically and pictorially superior and have some relevance to photographic technique. Ideas for features are welcome but must be considered, original and relevant. Send brief of idea in first instance. Rates are negotiable but are typically £60 per page pro rata for images and £120 per 1,000 words. Founded 1959.

Practical Wireless

PW Publishing Ltd, Tayfield House, 38 Poole Road, Bournemouth, BH4 9DW
tel 0845 803 1979
email don@pwpublishing.ltd.uk
website www.pwpublishingltd.uk
Editor Don Field
Monthly £3.99

Articles on the practical and theoretical aspects of amateur radio and communications. Constructional projects. Telephone or email for advice and essential PW author's guide. Illustrations: in b&w and colour; photos, line drawings and wash half-tone for offset litho. Payment: by arrangement. Founded 1932.

The Practising Midwife

66 Siward Road, Bromley BR2 9JZ
tel 020-8313 9617
website www.thepractisingmidwife.com
Editor Anna Byrom, *Managing Editor* Laura Yeates
Monthly £65 p.a. (UK individual), £50 p.a. (UK student), £75 (Europe). Other rates available; see website for full list.

Disseminates research-based material to a wide professional audience. Research and review papers, viewpoints and news items pertaining to midwifery, maternity care, women's health and neonatal health with both a national and an international perspective. All articles submitted are anonymously reviewed by external acknowledged experts. Length: 1,000–1,500 words (articles) or 2,000 words (research articles). Illustrations: colour transparencies and artwork; hi-res jpgs or pdfs. Payment: by arrangement. Founded 1991.

The Practitioner

Practitioner Medical Publishing Ltd,
10 Fernthorpe Road, London SW16 6DR
tel 020-8677 3508
email editor@thepractitioner.co.uk
website www.thepractitioner.co.uk
Editor Corinne Short
Monthly £85 p.a. (UK print), £85 (digital, individuals)

Articles on advances in medicine of interest to GPs and vocational registrars, and others in the medical profession. Founded 1868.

Press Gazette

John Carpenter House, John Carpenter Street, London EC4Y 0AN
tel 020-7936 6433
email pged@pressgazette.co.uk
website www.pressgazette.co.uk
Editor Dominic Ponsford
Weekly Online only

News and features of interest to journalists and others working in the media. Length: 1,200 words (features), 300 words (news). Payment: approx. £230 (features), news stories negotiable. Founded 1965.

Pride

1 Garratt Lane, London SW18 4AQ
tel 020-8714 467

email editor@pridemagazine.com
website www.pridemagazine.com
Publisher C. J. Cushnie
Monthly £3

Lifestyle magazine incorporating fashion and beauty, travel, food and entertaining articles for the woman of colour. Length: 1,000–3,000 words. Illustrations: colour photos and drawings. Payment: £100 per 1,000 words. Founded 1991; relaunched 1997.

Prima

Hearst Magazines UK, National Magazines House, 72 Broadwick Street, London W1F 9EP
tel 020-7439 5000
email prima@hearst.co.uk
website www.allaboutyou.com/prima
Editor Gaby Huddart
Monthly £3.10

Articles on fashion, home, crafts, health and beauty, cookery; features. Founded 1986.

Prima Baby & Pregnancy

Immediate Media Co. Ltd, Vineyard House, 44 Brook Green, London 7BT
tel 020-7150 5000
website www.madeformums.com
Editor Kelly Beswick
Monthly £2.99

Magazine covering all aspects of parenting, from pregnancy and childbirth through to baby, toddler and pre-schooler; plus health, lifestyle, crafts, food and fashion. Length: up to 1,000 words. Payment: by arrangement. Founded 1994.

Private Eye

6 Carlisle Street, London W1D 3BN
tel 020-7437 4017
email strobes@private-eye.co.uk
website www.private-eye.co.uk
Editor Ian Hislop
Fortnightly £1.80

Satire. News and current affairs. Payment: by arrangement. Illustrations and cartoons: colour or b&w. Founded 1961.

Professional Photographer

Archant House, Oriel Road, Cheltenham GL50 1BB
tel (01242) 216050
website www.professionalphotographer.co.uk
Group Editor Adam Scorey
Monthly £4.20

Features and interviews covering all aspects of professional photography. Gear tests by professional photographers. Length: 1,000–2,000 words. Illustrations: colour and b&w digital files. Payment: typically £200. Founded 1961.

Prole

15 Maes-y-Dre, Abergele, Conwy LL22 7HW
email admin@prolebooks.co.uk
website www.prolebooks.co.uk
Editors Brett Evans and Phil Robertson
3 p.a. (April/August/December) £6.70 (UK inc P&P), £18.60 p.a. (UK inc p&p)

Submissions of poetry, short fiction and creative non-fiction (7,500 words max) and photographic cover art welcome (please see our website for submission guidelines). Annual poetry and prose competitions. Payment: profit share. Founded: 2010.

Prospect Magazine

5th Floor, 23 Savile Row, London W1S 2ET
tel 020-7255 1281
email editorial@prospect-magazine.co.uk
website www.prospectmagazine.co.uk
Editor Bronwen Maddox
Monthly £4.95

Political and cultural monthly magazine. Essays, features, special reports, reviews, short stories, opinions/analysis. Length: 3,000–6,000 words (essays, special reports, short stories), 1,000 words (opinions). Illustrations: colour and b&w. Payment: by negotiation. Founded 1995.

Psychologies

Kelsey Publishing Group, Cudham Tithe Barn, Berry's Hill, Cudham, Kent TN16 3AG
tel (01959) 541444
email editor@psychologies.co.uk
website www.psychologies.co.uk
Editor Suzy Greaves
Monthly £3.80

Women's magazine with a focus on 'what we're like, not just what we look like'; features cover relationships, family and parenting, personality, behaviour, health, wellbeing, beauty, society and social trends, travel, spirituality and sex. Welcomes new ideas by email which fit into one of these areas, and suggestions should offer a combination of psychological insight and practical advice.

Pulse

140 London Wall, London EC2Y 5DN
tel 020-7214 0500
email feedback@pulsetoday.co.uk
website www.pulsetoday.co.uk
Editor Nigel Praities
Weekly Free on request

Articles and photos of direct interest to GPs. Purely clinical material can only be accepted from medically qualified authors. Length: 600–1,200 words. Payment: £150 average. Illustrations: b&w and colour photos. Founded 1959.

Q Magazine

Bauer Media Group, Endeavour House, 189 Shaftesbury Avenue, London WC2H 8JG
tel 020-7437 9011
email qmail@qthemusic.com
website www.q4music.com

Editor-in-Chief Phil Alexander
Monthly £4.20

Glossy music guide. All material commissioned. Length: 1,200–2,500 words. Illustrations: colour and b&w photos. Payment: £350 per 1,000 words; illustrations by arrangement. Founded 1986.

RA Magazine

Royal Academy of Arts, Burlington House, Piccadilly, London W1J 0BD
tel 020-7300 5820
website www.ramagazine.org.uk
Editor Sam Phillips
Quarterly £4.95 (£20 p.a.)

Visual arts and culture articles relating to the Royal Academy of Arts and the wider British and international arts scene. Length:150–1,800 words. Illustrations: consult the Editor. Payment: average £250 per 1,000 words; illustrations by negotiation. Founded 1983.

Racing Post

Floor 23, 1 Canada Square, Canary Wharf, London E14 5AP
tel (01635) 246505
email editor@racingpost.co.uk
website www.racingpost.com
Editor Bruce Millington
Mon–Fri £2.20, Weekender edition (Wednesday to Sunday) £3

News on horseracing, greyhound racing and sports betting. Founded 1986.

Radio Times

Immediate Media Co. Ltd, Vineyard House, 44 Brook Green, London W6 7BT
tel 020-7150 5429
email feedback@radiotimes.com
website www.radiotimes.com
Editor Ben Preston
Weekly £1.80

Articles that preview the week's programmes on British TV and radio. All articles are specially commissioned – ideas and synopses are welcomed but not unsolicited MSS. Length: 600–2,500 words. Payment: by arrangement. Illustrations: mostly in colour; photos, graphic designs or drawings.

RAIL

Bauer Media Group, Lynchwood, Peterborough Business Park, Peterborough PE2 6EA
tel (01733) 468000
email rail@bauermedia.co.uk
website www.railmagazine.com
Managing Editor Nigel Harris
Fortnightly £3.60

News and in-depth features on current UK railway operations. Length: 2,000–3,000 words (features), 250–400 words (news). Illustrations: colour and b&w photos and artwork. Payment: £75 per 1,000 words; £15–£40 per photo except cover (£100). Founded 1981.

Railway Gazette International

DVV Media UK Ltd, NINE, Sutton Court Road, Sutton, Surrey SM1 4SZ
tel 020-8652 5200
email editor@railwaygazette.com
website www.railwaygazette.com
Editor Chris Jackson
Monthly £105 p.a.

Deals with management, engineering, operation and finance of railway, metro and light rail transport worldwide. Articles of business interest on these subjects are considered and paid for if accepted. No 'enthusiast'-oriented articles. Phone or email to discuss proposals. Illustrated articles, of 1,000–2,000 words, are preferred.

The Railway Magazine

Media Centre, Morton Way, Horncastle, Lincs. LN9 6JR
tel (01507) 529589
email railway@mortons.co.uk
website www.railwaymagazine.co.uk
Editor Nick Pigott
Monthly £4.25

Illustrated magazine dealing with all railway subjects; no fiction or verse. Articles from 1,500–2,000 words accompanied by photos. Preliminary letter desirable. Payment: by arrangement. Illustrations: digital; black and white and colour transparencies. Founded 1897.

Reach Poetry

Indigo Dreams Publishing Ltd, 24 Forest Houses, Cookworthy Moor, Halwill, Beaworthy, Devon EX21 5UU
email publishing@indigodreams.co.uk
website www.indigodreams.co.uk
Editor Ronnie Goodyer
Monthly £4.25, £48 p.a.

Unpublished and original poetry. Submit up to three poems for consideration by post (include sae for reply) or email. New poets encouraged. Features lively subscribers' letters and votes pages. No payment; £50 prize money each issue. The editors have been awarded the Ted Slade Award for Services to Poetry 2015. Founded 1998.

Reader's Digest

PO Box 7853, Ringwood BH24 9FH
tel 0845 601 2711
email info@readersdigest.co.uk
website www.readersdigest.co.uk
Editor-in-Chief Tom Browne
Monthly £3.79

Original anecdotes, short stories, letters to the editor and jokes may be submitted online for consideration.

Real People

Hearst Magazines UK, National Magazines House, 72 Broadwick Street, London W1F 9EP
tel 020-7339 4570
email samm.taylor@hearst.co.uk
website www.realpeoplemag.co.uk
Editor Samm Taylor
Weekly 67p

Magazine for women with real-life tales of ordinary people coping with extraordinary events, plus puzzles section.

Reality

Redemptorist Communications, 75 Orwell Road, Rathgar, Dublin 6, Republic of Ireland
tel +353 (0)1 4922488
email info@redcoms.org
website www.redcoms.org
Editor Fr. Gerry Moloney CSSR
Monthly €2

Illustrated magazine for Christian living. Illustrated articles on all aspects of modern life, including family, youth, religion, leisure. Length: 1,000–1,500 words. Payment: by arrangement; average £50 per 1,000 words. Founded 1936.

Record Collector

The Perfume Factory, Room 101, Diamond Publishing, 140 Wales Farm Road, London W3 6UG
tel 020-8752 8172
email ian.mccann@metropolis.co.uk
website www.recordcollectormag.com
Editor-in-Chief Ian McCann
Monthly £4.20

Covers all areas of music, with the focus on collectable releases and the reissues market. Specially commissions most material but will consider unsolicited material. Welcomes ideas for articles and features. Length: 2,000 words for articles/features; 200 words for news. Illustrations: transparencies, colour and b&w prints, scans of rare records; all commissioned. Payment: negotiable. Founded 1980.

Red

Hearst Magazines UK, National Magazines House, 72 Broadwick Street, London, W1F 9EP
tel 020-7150 7600
email red@redmagazine.co.uk
website www.redonline.co.uk
Editor-in-Chief Sarah Bailey, *Send material to* Sarah Tomczak, Features Director
Monthly £4.20

High-quality articles on topics of interest to women aged 25–45: humour, memoirs, interviews and well-researched investigative features. Approach with ideas in writing in first instance. Length: 900 words upwards. Illustrations: transparencies. Payment: NUJ rates minimum. Founded 1998.

Red Pepper

44–48 Shepherdess Walk, London N1 7JP
email office@redpepper.org.uk
website www.redpepper.org.uk
Co-editors Michael Calderbank, James O'Nions, Emma Hughes, Hilary Wainwright, Michelle Zellers
Bi-monthly £3.95

Independent radical magazine: news and features on politics, culture and everyday life of interest to the left and greens. Material mostly commissioned. Length: news/news features 200–800 words, other features 800–2,000 words. Illustrations: photos, graphics. Payment: for investigations, otherwise only exceptionally. Founded 1994.

Reform

(published by United Reformed Church)
86 Tavistock Place, London WC1H 9RT
tel 020-7916 8630
email reform@urc.org.uk
website www.reform-magazine.co.uk
Editor Stephen Tomkins
10 issues p.a. £3, £25 p.a.

Articles of religious or social comment. Illustrations: graphic artists/illustrators. Payment: by arrangement. Founded 1972.

Report

ATL, 7 Northumberland Street, London WC2N 5RD
tel 020-7930 6441
email report@atl.org.uk
website www.atl.org.uk/report
Editors Alex Tomlin, Charlotte Tamvakis
9 p.a. £2.50, £15.50 p.a., £27 p.a. overseas, free to members

The magazine from the Association of Teachers and Lecturers (ATL). Features, articles, comment, news about nursery, primary, secondary and further education. Payment: minimum £120 per 1,000 words.

Restaurant Magazine

William Reed Business Media, Broadfield Park, Crawley RH11 9RT
tel (01293) 613400
email editorial@restaurantmagazine.co.uk
website www.bighospitality.co.uk
Editor Stefan Chomka
Monthly £4.50

Articles, features and news on the restaurant trade. Specially commissions most material. Welcomes ideas for articles and features. Illustrations: colour transparencies, prints and artwork. Payment: variable. Founded 2001.

Resurgence & Ecologist

The Resurgence Trust, Fort House, Hartland, Bideford, Devon EX39 6EE
tel (01237) 441293
email editorial@resurgence.org
website www.theecologist.org

Editor-in-Chief Satish Kumar
6 p.a. £4.95

Interested in environment and social justice investigations and features, green living advice and ideas, grassroots activism projects, artist profiles and reviews. Proposal first in most cases. Payment: various. See website for further guidance.

Retail Week

EMAP, Telephone House, 69–77 Paul Street, London EC2A 4NW
tel 020-3033 2741
website www.retail-week.com
Editor-in-Chief Chris Brook-Carter
Weekly £6.99

Features and news stories on all aspects of retail management. Length: up to 1,400 words. Illustrations: colour photos. Payment: by arrangement. Founded 1988.

The Rialto

PO Box 309, Aylsham, Norwich NR11 6LN
email info@therialto.co.uk
website www.therialto.co.uk
Editor Michael Mackmin
3 p.a. £8.50 per issue, £24 p.a. for UK subscriptions; for overseas subscriptions, please consult the website

68pp A4 magazine, mainly poetry but with occasional prose pieces. Prose is commissioned, poetry submissions are very welcome. For poets and poetry. Submit up to 6 poems; sae essential. Payment: by arrangement. Founded 1984.

Right Start

PO Box 481, Fleet, Hants GU51 9FA
tel 07867 574590
email lynette@rightstartmagazine.co.uk
website www.rightstartmagazine.co.uk
Editor Lynette Lowthian
Bi-monthly £10.90 p.a.

Features on all aspects of preschool and infant education, child health and behaviour. No unsolicited MSS. Length: 800–1,500 words. Illustrations: colour photos, line. Payment: varies. Founded 1989.

Royal National Institute of Blind People (RNIB)

105 Judd Street, London WC1H 9NE
tel 020-7388 1266 0845 758 5691
email shop@rnib.org.uk
website www.rnib.org.uk
Head of Content, Digital & Reading Services Clive Gardiner

The Royal National Institute of Blind People publishes a variety of titles in a range of formats (including audio, email, braille and Daisy) for adults and young people.

Rugby World

Time Inc. (UK), 7th Floor, The Blue Fin Building, 110 Southwark Street, London SE1 0SU
tel 020-3148 4708
email rugbyworld@timeinc.com
website www.rugbyworld.com
Editor Owain Jones
Monthly £4.40

Features and exclusive news stories on rugby. Length: approx. 1,200 words. Illustrations: colour photos, cartoons. Payment: £120. Founded 1960.

Runner's World

Hearst Rodale Ltd, 33 Broadwick Street, London W1F 0DG
tel 020-7339 4400
website www.runnersworld.co.uk
Editor Andy Dixon
Monthly £4.50

Articles on running, health and fitness, and nutrition. Payment: by arrangement. Founded 1979.

Running Fitness

Kelsey Publishing Group, PO Box 978, Peterborough PE1 9FL
tel (01959) 530530
email natasha.shiels@kelsey.co.uk
website www.runningfitnessmag.co.uk
Editor Natasha Shiels
Monthly £2.99

Practical articles on all aspects of running lifestyle, especially road running training and events, and advice on health, fitness and injury. Illustrations: colour photos, cartoons. Payment: by negotiation. Founded 1985.

RUSI Journal

Whitehall, London SW1A 2ET
tel 020-7747 2600
email publications@rusi.org
website www.rusi.org
Editor Emma De Angelis
Bi-monthly; available as part of RUSI membership (from £100 p.a.; concessions available) or a subscription in conjunction with RUSI Whitehall Papers.

Journal of the Royal United Services Institute for Defence and Security Studies. Articles on international security, military science, defence technology and procurement, and military history; also book reviews and correspondence. Length: 3,000–3,500 words. Illustrations: colour photos, maps and diagrams.

Safety in Education Journal

Royal Society for the Prevention of Accidents, 28 Calthorpe Road, Edgbaston, Birmingham B15 1RP
tel 0121 248 2000
email acoleman@rospa.com
website www.rospa.com
Acting Editor Andy Coleman
3 p.a. £13 p.a. + VAT for members of Safety

Education Department (£15 p.a. + VAT for non members)

Articles on every aspect of good practice in health and safety management in schools and colleges and safety education including safety of teachers and pupils in school, and the teaching of road, home, water, leisure and personal safety by means of established subjects on the school curriculum. All ages. Published in electronic form only. Founded as *Child Safety* 1937; became *Safety Training* 1940; *Safety Education* 1966.

Saga Magazine

Saga Publishing Ltd, The Saga Building, Enbrook Park, Sandgate, Folkestone, Kent CT20 3SE
tel (01303) 771523
email editor@saga.co.uk
website www.saga.co.uk/magazine
Editor Katy Bravery
Monthly From £18.95 p.a.

General interest magazine aimed at the intelligent, literate 50+ reader. Wide range of articles from human interest, real-life stories, intriguing overseas interest (not travel), some natural history, celebrity interviews, photographic book extracts – alls. Articles mostly commissioned or written in-house, but genuine exclusives welcome. Illustrations: colour, digital media; mainly commissioned but top-quality photo feature suggestions sometimes accepted. Payment: competitive rate, by negotiation. Founded 1984.

Sainsbury's Magazine

Seven, 3–7 Herbal Hill, London EC1R 5EJ
tel 020-7775 7775
email feedback@sainsburysmagazine.co.uk
website www.sainsburysmagazine.co.uk
Editor-in-Chief Helena Lang
Monthly £1.80

Features: general, food and drink, health, beauty, homes; all material commissioned. Length: up to 1,500 words. Illustrations: colour and b&w photos and line illustrations. Payment: varies. Founded 1993.

Sarasvati

24 Forest Houses, Cookworthy Moor, Halwill, Beaworthy, Devon EX21 5UU
email dawnidp@indigodreams.co.uk
website www.indigodreams.co.uk
Editor Dawn Bauling
Quarterly £4.25, £16 for 4 issues

International poetry and short story magazine. New writers/poets encouraged. Lively feedback pages. Several pages given to each subscriber. Prose length: 1,000 words or under. Founded 2008.

The School Librarian

1 Pine Court, Kembrey Park, Swindon SN2 8AD
tel (01793) 530166
email sleditor@sla.org.uk
website www.sla.org.uk
Editor Steve Hird
Quarterly £85 p.a.

Official journal of the School Library Association. Articles on school library management, use and skills, and on authors and illustrators, literacy, publishing. Reviews of books, CD-Roms, websites and other library resources from preschool to adult. Length: 1,800–3,000 words (articles). Payment: by arrangement. Founded 1937.

Scientific Computing World

Unit 9, Clifton Court, Cambridge, CB1 7BN
tel (01223) 275464
email editor.scw@europascience.com
website www.scientific-computing.com
Editor-in-Chief Dr Tom Wilkie
6 p.a. Free to qualifying subscribers, other subscription rates apply (see website)

Features on hardware and software developments for the scientific community, plus news articles and reviews. Length: 800–2,000 words. Illustrations: colour transparencies, photos, electronic graphics. Payment: by negotiation. Founded 1994.

Scots Heritage

Fettes Park, 496 Ferry Road, Edinburgh EH5 2DL
tel 0131 551 1000
email rbath@scottishfield.co.uk
website www.scotsheritagemagazine.co.uk
Editor Richard Bath
Quarterly £2.95

Scottish history, clans and culture magazine. Length of article accepted: 1,200 words. Founded 1995.

The Scots Magazine

D.C. Thomson & Co. Ltd, 80 Kingsway East, Dundee DD4 8SL
tel (01382) 223131
email mail@scotsmagazine.com
website www.scotsmagazine.com
Monthly From £22 p.a.

Articles on all subjects of Scottish interest, but authors must also be Scottish. Illustrations: colour and b&w photos. Articles paid on acceptance: unsolicited material considered. Preliminary enquiries advised. Founded 1739.

The Scottish Farmer

Newsquest, 200 Renfield Street, Glasgow G2 3QB
tel 0141 302 7732
email alasdair.fletcher@thescottishfarmer.co.uk
website www.thescottishfarmer.co.uk
Editor Alasdair Fletcher
Weekly £119 p.a.

Articles on agricultural subjects. Length: 1,000–1,500 words. Payment: £80 per 1,000 words. Illustrations: line, half-tone, colour. Founded 1893.

Scottish Field

Fettes Park, 496 Ferry Road, Edinburgh EH5 2DL
tel 0131 551 1000
email rbath@scottishfield.co.uk
website www.scottishfield.co.uk
Editor Richard Bath
Monthly £3.95

Scottish lifestyle magazine: interiors, food, travel, wildlife, heritage, general lifestyle. Length of article accepted: 1,200 words. Founded 1903.

Scottish Home and Country

42 Heriot Row, Edinburgh EH3 6ES
tel 0131 225 1724
email magazine@swri.demon.co.uk
website www.swri.org.uk
Editor Liz Ferguson
Monthly £1.30

Articles on crafts, cookery, travel, personal experience, rural interest, women's interest, health, books. Length: up to 1,000 words, preferably illustrated. Illustrations: hi-res jpg/tif files, prints, cartoons and drawings. Payment: by arrangement. Founded 1924.

Scottish Memories

Celebrate Scotland, Warners Group Publications, 5th Floor, 31–32 Park Row, Leeds LS1 5JD
tel 0113 200 2929
email matthewh@warnersgroup.co.uk
website www.scottish-memories.co.uk
Editor Matthew Hill
Monthly £3.60

Scotland's premier nostalgia magazine. Features on living history from the 1940s to 1980s; wartime stories also considered if Scottish connection. Length: 600–1,800 words. Illustrations: required. Founded 1993.

Screen International

MBI Ltd, 101 Finsbury Pavement, London EC2A 1RS
tel 020-3033 4295
email matt.mueller@screendaily.com
website www.screendaily.com
Editor Matt Mueller
Monthly £19.95 per month for both print and digital access

International news and features on the international film business. No unsolicited material. Length: variable. Payment: by arrangement.

Sea Angler

Bauer Media Group, Media House, Lynchwood, Peterborough Business Park, Peterborough PE2 6EA
tel (01733) 395147
website www.gofishing.co.uk/Sea-Angler
Editor Cliff Brown
Monthly £3.45

Topical articles on all aspects of sea-fishing around the British Isles. Payment: by arrangement. Illustrations: colour. Founded 1972.

Sea Breezes

Media House, Cronkbourne, Tromode, Douglas, Isle of Man IM4 4SB
tel (01624) 696573
website www.seabreezes.co.im
Editor Hamish Ross
Monthly £49.80 p.a.

Factual articles on ships and the sea past and present, preferably illustrated. Length: up to 4,000 words. Illustrations: line, half-tone, colour. Payment: by arrangement. Founded 1919.

SelfBuild & Design

151 Station Street, Burton on Trent, Staffs. DE14 1BG
tel (01584) 841417
email ross.stokes@sbdonline.co.uk
website www.selfbuildanddesign.com
Editor Ross Stokes
Monthly £4.50

Articles on house construction for individual builders. Welcomes ideas for articles. Payment: £100–£200 per 1,000 words. Illustrations: colour prints, transparencies and digital.

The Sewing Directory

11a Tedders Close, Hemyock, Cullompton, Devon, EX15 3XD
tel (01823) 680588
email julie@thesewingdirectory.co.uk
website www.thesewingdirectory.co.uk
Content Editor Julie Briggs

Online directory of UK sewing business – sewing courses, fabric shops and sewing groups. Plus free sewing projects and technique guides. Payment: £40 per article/project. Founded 2010.

Sewing World

Traplet Publications Ltd, Willow End Park, Blackmore Park Road, Welland WR13 6NN
tel (01684) 588500
email sw@traplet.co.uk
website www.sewingworldmagazine.com
Monthly £5.99

Contemporary sewing magazine for sewing machine enthusiasts. Features, in-depth techniques and step-by-step projects including garments, quilts, home accessories, bags, small makes etc. Length: 1,000–1,500 words (articles). Illustrations: high-resolution colour. Payment: dependent on complexity of project/article. Founded 1995.

SFX Magazine

Future Publishing Ltd, Quay House, The Ambury, Bath, BA1 1UA
tel (01225) 442244
email sfx@futurenet.com
website www.gamesradar.com/sfx

Editor Richard Edwards
Every 4 weeks (13 p.a.) £4.99

Sci-fi and fantasy magazine covering TV, films, DVDs, books, comics, games and collectables. Founded 1995.

Ships Monthly

Kelsey Publishing Group, Cudham Tithe Barn, Berry's Hill, Cudham, Kent TN16 3AG
tel (01959) 541444
email ships.monthly@btinternet.com
website www.shipsmonthly.com
Editor Nicholas Leach
Monthly £4.25

Illustrated articles of shipping interest – both mercantile and naval, preferably of 20th and 21st century ships. Well-researched, factual material only. No short stories or poetry. 'Notes for contributors' available. Mainly commissioned material; preliminary letter essential, with sae. Payment: by arrangement. Illustrations: half-tone and line, colour transparencies, prints and digital images on CD with thumbprint contact sheet. Founded 1966.

Shooting Times and Country Magazine

Time Inc. (UK), The Blue Fin Building, 110 Southwark Street, London SE1 0SU
tel 020-3148 4741
email shootingtimes@timeinc.com
website www.shootingtimes.co.uk
Editor Alastair Balmain
Weekly £2.40

Articles on fieldsports, especially shooting, and on related natural history and countryside topics. Unsolicited MSS not encouraged. Length: up to 2,000 words. Payment: by arrangement. Illustrations: photos, drawings, colour transparencies. Founded 1882.

The Shropshire Magazine

Shropshire Newspapers, Ketley, Telford TF1 5HU
tel (01952) 241455
website www.shropshiremagazine.com
Editor Neil Thomas
Monthly £27 p.a.

Articles on topics related to Shropshire, including countryside, history, characters, legends, education, food; also home and garden features. Length: up to 1,500 words. Illustrations: colour. Founded 1950.

Sight and Sound

BFI, 21 Stephen Street, London W1T 1LN
tel 020-7255 1444
website www.bfi.org.uk/sightandsound
Editor Nick James
Monthly £4.50

Topical and critical articles on world cinema; reviews of every film theatrically released in the UK; book reviews; DVD reviews; festival reports. Length: 1,000–5,000 words. Payment: by arrangement. Illustrations: relevant photos, cartoons. Founded 1932.

Ski + Board

The Ski Club of Great Britain, The White House, 57–63 Church Road, London SW19 5SB
tel 020-8410 2000
email ben.clatworthy@skiclub.co.uk
website www.skiclub.co.uk
Deputy Editor Ben Clatworthy
Monthly in winter (Oct–Jan) £4.10

Articles, features, news, true-life stories, ski tips, equipment reviews, resort reports – all in connection with skiing and snowboarding. Please pitch during the first two weeks of the month. Payment: up to £180 per 1,000 words; £20–£150 per photo/illustration. Founded as *Ski Survey* 1972.

The Skier and Snowboarder Magazine

The Lodge, West Heath, Ashgrove Road, Sevenoaks TN13 1ST
tel 07768 670158
email frank.baldwin@skierandsnowboarder.co.uk
website www.skierandsnowboarder.co.uk
Editor Frank Baldwin
5 p.a. Free

Ski features, based around a good story. Length: 800–1,000 words. Illustrations: colour action ski photos. Payment: by negotiation. Founded 1984.

Slightly Foxed

53 Hoxton Square, London N1 6PB
tel 020-7549 2121
email all@foxedquarterly.com
website www.foxedquarterly.com
Publisher/Co-editor Gail Pirkis
Quarterly Single issue £10 (UK), £12 (Europe), £13 (RoW). Annual subscription: UK £40 p.a. (UK), £48 (Europe), £52 (Rest of WoW)

Independent-minded magazine of book reviews. Each issue contains 96pp of recommendations for books of lasting interest, old and new, both fiction and non-fiction – books that have inspired, amused, and sometimes even changed the lives of the people who write about them. Unsolicited submissions are welcome; see website for guidelines.

Slimming World Magazine

Clover Nook Road, Alfreton, Derbyshire DE55 4SW
tel (01773) 546071
email editorial@slimmingworld.com
website www.slimmingworld.com/magazine/latest-issue.aspx
Editor Elise Wells
7 p.a. £2.75 (£1.95 group members)

Magazine about healthy eating, fitness and feeling good with real-life stories of how Slimming World members have changed their lives, recipes and menu plans, health advice, beauty and fitness tips, features, competitions and fashion.

Smallholder

3 Falmouth Business Park, Bickland Water Road, Falmouth, Cornwall TR11 4SZ
tel (01326) 213340
email editor@smallholder.co.uk
website www.smallholder.co.uk
Editor Elizabeth Perry
13 p.a. £3.95

Articles of relevance to small farmers about livestock and crops, organics, conservation, poultry, equipment. Items relating to the countryside considered. Email for guidelines. Send for specimen copy. Length: single-page article 700 words; double-page spread 1,200–1,400 words with pictures. Payment: by negotiation; more for commissions and technical livestock articles.

Snooker Scene

Hayley Green Court, 130 Hagley Road, Halesowen, West Midlands B63 1DY
tel 0121 585 9188
email info@snookerscene.com
website www.snookerscene.co.uk
Editor Clive Everton
Monthly £3.20, £30 p.a. (print)

News and articles about the snooker and billiards scene for readers with more than a casual interest in the games. Payment: by arrangement. Illustrations: photos. Founded 1971.

Solicitors' Journal

Wilmington Publishing and Information Ltd, 6–14 Underwood Street, London N1 7JQ
tel 020-7490 0049
email editorial@solicitorsjournal.co.uk
website www.solicitorsjournal.com
Managing Editor Laura Clenshaw
Weekly (48 p.a) £350 p.a. (print and online)

Objective provider of current affairs to the legal industry, featuring a range of views on current issues. Covers case law updates, legal news, and comments from industry experts. Length of articles accepted: 500–2,000. Payment: none. Founded 1856.

The Songwriter

International Songwriters Association, PO Box 46, Limerick City, Republic of Ireland
tel +353 (0)61 228837
email jliddane@songwriter.iol.ie
website www.songwriter.co.uk
Editor James D. Liddane
Quarterly

Articles on songwriting and interviews with songwriters, music publishers and recording company executives. Length: 1,000–10,000 words. Payment: by arrangement. Illustrations: photos. Founded 1967.

Songwriting and Composing

Ebrel House, 2a Penlee Close, Praa Sands, Penzance, Cornwall TR20 9SR
tel (01736) 762826
email songmag@aol.com
website www.songwriters-guild.co.uk
Editor Roderick Jones
Quarterly Free to members

Magazine of the Guild of International Songwriters and Composers. Short stories, articles, letters relating to songwriting, publishing, recording and the music industry. Payment: negotiable upon content £25–£60. Illustrations: line, half-tone. Founded 1986.

Spear's Magazine

John Carpenter House, John Carpenter Street, London EC4Y 0AN
tel 020-7936 6445
email emily.rookwood@spearwms.com
website www.spearsmagazine.com
Editor-in-Chief William Cash, *Editor* Josh Spero, *Managing Editor* Emily Rookwood
Bi-monthly £100 p.a.

Guide to wealth management, business and culture. Topics covered include wealth management, the law, art, philanthropy, luxury, food and wine and global affairs. Readership includes ultra-high-net-worths, private bankers, top lawyers, philanthropists etc. Standard length of articles 850–1,300 words (features). Colour and b&w illustrations. Payment: 40p per word; £150+ for illustrations. Founded 2003.

Speciality Food

Aceville Publications, 21–23 Hawkins Road, Colchester CO1 8JY
email ross@aceville.com
website www.specialityfoodmagazine.com
Editor Ross Gilfillan
Bi-monthly £3.25

Trade magazine aimed at fine food retailers. Features a mix of news, comment and links to producers.

The Spectator

22 Old Queen Street, London SW1H 9HP
tel 020-7961 0200
email editor@spectator.co.uk
website www.spectator.co.uk
Editor Fraser Nelson
Weekly £4

Articles on current affairs, politics, the arts; book reviews. Illustrations: colour and b&w, cartoons. Payment: on merit. Founded 1828.

The Squash Player

460 Bath Road, Longford, Middlesex UB7 0EB
tel 020-8597 0181
email info1@squashplayer.co.uk
website www.squashplayer.co.uk
Editor Ian McKenzie

Bi-monthly £24 p.a.

Covers all aspects of playing squash. All features are commissioned – discuss ideas with the Editor. Length: 1,000–1,500 words. Illustrations: unusual photos (e.g. celebrities), cartoons. Payment: £75 per 1,000 words; £25–£40 for illustrations. Founded 1971.

Staffordshire Life Magazine

Sentinel House, Bethesda Street, Hanley, Stoke-on-Trent, ST1 3GN
tel (01785) 864100
email louise.elliott@thesentinel.co.uk
website www.staffordshirelife.co.uk
Editor Louise Elliott
12 p.a. £2.95

County magazine for Staffordshire. Historical articles; features on county personalities. No short stories. Contact the Editor in first instance. Length: 500–800 words. Illustrations: colour transparencies and prints. Founded 1948; relaunched 1980.

The Stage

Stage House, 47 Bermondsey Street, London SE1 3XT
tel 020-7403 1818
email editor@thestage.co.uk
website www.thestage.co.uk
Print Editor Alistair Smith
Weekly £2

Original and interesting articles on professional stage and broadcasting topics may be sent for the Editor's consideration. Length: 500–900 words. Payment: £100 per 1,000 words. Founded 1880.

Stamp Magazine

MyTimeMedia, Enterprise House, Enterprise Way, Edenbridge, Kent TN8 6HF
tel 0844 848 88 22
website www.stampmagazine.co.uk
Editor Guy Thomas
Monthly £3.95

Informative articles and exclusive news items on stamp collecting and postal history. Preliminary letter. Payment: by arrangement. Illustrations: line, half-tone, colour. Founded 1934.

Stand Magazine

School of English, University of Leeds, Leeds LS2 9JT
tel 0113 233 4794
email stand@leeds.ac.uk
website www.standmagazine.org
Managing Editor Jon Glover
Quarterly £7.50 plus p&p, £25 p.a.

Poetry, short stories, translations, literary criticism. Send sae/IRCs for return. Founded 1952.

The Strad

Newsquest Specialist Media, 2nd Floor, 30 Cannon Street, London EC4M 6YJ
tel 020-7618 3095
email thestrad@thestrad.com
website www.thestrad.com
Editor Chloe Cutts
12 p.a. plus occasional supplements. £5.20

Features, news and reviews for stringed instrument players, teachers, makers and enthusiasts – both professional and amateur. Specially commissions most material but will consider unsolicited material. Welcomes ideas for articles and features. Length: 1,000–2,000 (articles/features), 100–150 (news). Payment: £150–£300 (articles/features), varies for news. Illustrations: transparencies, colour and b&w prints and artwork, colour cartoons; some commissioned. Founded 1890.

Stuff

Haymarket Ltd, Teddington Studios, Broom Road, Teddington, Middlesex TW11 9BE
tel 020-8267 5052
email stuff@haymarket.com
website www.stuff.tv
Magazine Editor Will Dunn, *Stuff.tv Editor* Marc McLaren
Monthly £4.60

Articles on technology, games, films, lifestyle, news and reviews. Payment by negotiation. Founded 1996.

Style at Home

Time Inc. (UK), The Blue Fin Building, 110 Southwark Street, London SE1 0SU
email styleathome@timeinc.com
website www.housetohome.co.uk/styleathome
Editor Jennifer Morgan
Monthly £1.99

Interiors magazine aimed at woman interested in updating, styling and decorating their home. With an emphasis on achievable, affordable home make-overs, the magazine has regular articles showing transformed rooms as well as step-by-step projects, shopping ideas and a recipe section for keen cooks.

Suffolk Norfolk Life

Today Magazines Ltd, The Publishing House, Station Road, Framlingham, Suffolk IP13 9EE
tel (01728) 622030
email editor@suffolknorfolklife.com
website www.suffolknorfolklife.com
Editor Kevin Davis
Monthly £2.50

Articles relevant to Suffolk and Norfolk – current topics plus historical items, art, leisure, etc. Considers unsolicited material and welcomes ideas for articles and features. Send via email. Length: 900–1,500 words. Illustrations: transparencies, digital colour and b&w prints, b&w artwork and cartoons. Payment: £60–£80 per article. Founded 1989.

Surrey Life

c/o PO Box 412, Reigate, Surrey RH2 2DJ
tel (01903) 703730

email editor@surreylife.co.uk
website www.surreylife.co.uk
Editor Caroline Harrap
Monthly £3.25

Articles on Surrey, including places of interest, high-profile personalities, local events, arts, history, food, homes, gardens and more. Founded 1970.

Swimming Times Magazine

Swimming Times Ltd, SportPark, Pavilion 3, 3 Oakwood Drive, Loughborough, Leics. LE11 3QF
tel (01509) 640230
email swimmingtimes@swimming.org
website www.swimming.org/swimmingtimes
Editor Peter Hassall
Monthly £3.20 plus p&p

Official journal of the Amateur Swimming Association and the Institute of Swimming. Reports of major events and championships; news and features on all aspects of swimming including synchronised swimming, diving and water polo, etc; accompanying photos where appropriate; short fiction with a swimming theme. Unsolicited material welcome. Length: 800–1,500 words. Payment: by arrangement. Founded 1923.

The Tablet

1 King Street Cloisters, Clifton Walk, London W6 0GY
tel 020-8748 8484
email thetablet@thetablet.co.uk
website www.thetablet.co.uk
Editor Catherine Pepinster
Weekly £2.95

Catholic weekly: religion, philosophy, politics, society, books and arts. International coverage. Freelance work commissioned: do not send unsolicited material. Length: various. Illustrations: cartoons and photos. Payment: by arrangement. Founded 1840.

Take a Break

H. Bauer Publishing Ltd, Academic House, 24–28 Oval Road, London NW1 7DT
tel 020-7241 8000
email tab.features@bauer.co.uk
website www.takeabreak.co.uk
Features Editor Julia Sidwell
Weekly 90p

Lively, tabloid women's weekly. True-life features, health and beauty, family; lots of puzzles. Payment: by arrangement. Illustrated. Founded 1990.

Take a Break's Take a Puzzle

H. Bauer Publishing, Academic House, 24–28 Oval Road, London NW1 7DT
email take.puzzle@bauer.co.uk
website www.puzzlemagazines.co.uk/takeapuzzle
Editor Babetta Mann
Monthly £2.10

Puzzles. Fresh ideas always welcome. Illustrations: colour transparencies and b&w prints and artwork. Work supplied on Mac-compatible disk preferred. Payment: from £25 per puzzle, £30–£90 for picture puzzles and for illustrations not an integral part of a puzzle. Founded 1991.

TATE ETC

Tate, Millbank, London SW1P 4RG
tel 020-7887 8724
email tateetc@tate.org.uk
website www.tate.org.uk/tateetc
Editor Simon Grant
3 p.a. £15 p.a. (UK)

Independent visual arts magazine: features, interviews, previews and opinion pieces. Length: up to 3,000 words but always commissioned. Illustrations: colour and b&w photos. Payment: negotiable.

Tatler

Vogue House, Hanover Square, London W1S 1JU
tel 020-7499 9080
website www.tatler.co.uk
Editor Kate Reardon
Monthly £4.30

Smart society magazine favouring sharp articles, profiles, fashion and the arts. Illustrations: colour, b&w, but all commissioned. Founded 1709.

Taxation

Quadrant House, The Quadrant, Sutton SM2 5AS
tel 020-8212 1949
email taxation@lexisnexis.co.uk
website www.taxation.co.uk
Editor Richard Curtis
49 issues p.a £364 p.a.

Updating and advice concerning UK tax law and practice for accountants and tax experts. All articles written by professionals. Length: 2,000 words (articles). Payment £150 per 1,000 words. Founded 1927.

The Teacher

National Union of Teachers, Hamilton House, Mabledon Place, London WC1H 9BD
tel 020-7380 4708
email teacher@nut.org.uk
website www.teachers.org.uk/teacher-online
Editor Tash Shifrin
6 p.a. Free to NUT members

Articles, features and news of interest to all those involved in the teaching profession. Email outline in the first instance. Length: 650 words (single page), 1,200-1,300 (double page). Payment: NUJ rates to NUJ members. Founded 1872.

Television

RTS, Kildare House, 3 Dorsett Rise, London EC4Y 8EH

tel 020-7822 2810
email publications@rts.org.uk
website www.rts.org.uk
Editor Steve Clarke
Monthly

Articles on the technical aspects of domestic TV and video equipment, especially servicing, long-distance TV, constructional projects, satellite TV, video recording, teletext and viewdata, test equipment, monitors. Payment: by arrangement. Illustrations: photos and line drawings for litho. Founded 1950.

Tempo

Cambridge University Press,
The Edinburgh Building, Shaftesbury Road,
Cambridge CB2 8RU
email tempoeditor@cambridge.org
Editors Bob Gilmore, Juliet Fraser
Quarterly From £27/$45 p.a.; other rates apply (see website for details)

Authoritative articles on contemporary music. Length: 2,000–4,000 words. Payment: by arrangement. Illustrations: music type, occasional photographic or musical supplements.

The TES

26 Red Lion Square, Holborn WC1R 4HQ
tel 020-3194 3000
email newsdesk@tes.co.uk
email features@tes.co.uk
website www.tes.co.uk
Editor Ann Mroz
Weekly £36.75 p.a. (print)

Education newspaper. Articles on education written with special knowledge or experience; news items; books, arts and equipment reviews. Check with the news or picture editor before submitting material. Outlines of feature ideas should be emailed. Illustrations: suitable photos and drawings of educational interest, cartoons. Payment: standard rates, or by arrangement.

TES Magazine

Weekly Free with TES

Magazine for teachers focusing on their lives, inside and outside the classroom, investigating the key issues of the day and highlighting good practice. Length: 800 words max.

The TESS

tel 07825 033445
email scoted@tess.co.uk
website www.tes.co.uk/scotland
Senior Reporter Henry Hepburn
Weekly £1.95

Education newspaper. Articles on education, preferably 800–1,000 words, written with special knowledge or experience. News items about Scottish educational affairs. Illustrations: line, half-tone. Payment: by arrangement. Founded 1965.

TGO (The Great Outdoors) Magazine

30 Cannon Street, London EC4M 6YJ
tel 0141 302 7736
email emily.rodway@tgomagazine.co.uk
website www.tgomagazine.co.uk
Editor Emily Rodway
13 p.a. £4.45

Articles on walking or lightweight camping in specific areas, mainly in the UK, preferably illustrated with photography. Length: 700–2,000 words. Payment: by arrangement. Illustrations: colour. Apply for guidelines. Founded 1978.

that's life!

H. Bauer Publishing Ltd, Academic House,
24–28 Oval Road, London NW1 7DT
tel 020-7241 8000
email stories@thatslife.co.uk
website www.thatslife.co.uk
Editor Sophie Hearsey
Weekly 74p

Dramatic true-life stories about women. Length: average 1,000 words. Illustrations: colour photos and cartoons. Payment: up to £1,000. Founded 1995.

Third Way

108–114 Golden Lane, London EC1Y 0TG
tel 020-7776 1071
email editor@thirdway.org.uk
website www.thirdwaymagazine.co.uk
Editor Simon Jones
10 p.a. £38 p.a.

Aims to present biblical perspectives on the political, social and cultural issues of the day. Payment: by arrangement on publication. Email submissions preferred. Founded 1977.

This England

The Lypiatts, Lansdown Road, Cheltenham,
Glos. GL50 2JA
tel (01242) 225780
email editor@thisengland.co.uk
website www.thisengland.co.uk
Editor Stephen Garnett
Quarterly £4.75

Articles about England's traditions, customs and places of interest. Regular features on towns, villages, the English countryside, notable men and women, and readers' recollections. Length 250–2,000 words. Illustrations: digital; colour transparencies accepted only when accompanying articles. Payment: £25 per 1,000 words, £10 poems (12–24 lines). Founded 1968.

Time Out London

Time Out Group Ltd, 4th Floor,
125 Shaftesbury Avenue, London, WC2H 8AD
tel 020-7813 3000
email hello@timeout.com
website www.timeout.com

Editor Caroline McGinn
Weekly Free

Listings magazine for London covering all areas of the arts, plus articles of consumer and news interest. Illustrations: colour and b&w. Payment by negotiation. Founded 1968.

The Times Educational Supplement – see The TES

The Times Educational Supplement Scotland – see The TESS

Times Higher Education

26 Red Lion Square, London WC1R 4HQ
tel 020-3194 3000
email john.gill@tesglobal.com
website www.timeshighereducation.co.uk
Editor John Gill
Weekly £2.90

Articles on higher education written with special knowledge or experience, or articles dealing with academic topics. Also news items. Illustrations: suitable photos and drawings of educational interest. Payment: by arrangement. Founded 1971.

TLS (The Times Literary Supplement)

1 London Bridge Street, London SE1 9GF
tel 020-7782 4985
email queries@the-tls.co.uk
website www.the-tls.co.uk
Editor Peter Stothard
Weekly £3

Will consider poems for publication, literary discoveries and articles on literary and cultural affairs. Payment: by arrangement.

Today's Golfer

Bauer Media Group, Media House, Lynchwood, Peterborough Business Park, Peterborough PE2 6EA
tel (01733) 468000
email chris.jones@bauermedia.co.uk
website www.todaysgolfer.co.uk
Editor Chris Jones, *Managing Director Sport* Patrick Horton
Every 4 weeks £4.50, £58.50 p.a.

Specialist features and articles on golf instruction, equipment and courses. Founded 1988.

Top Santé Health & Beauty

Bauer Media Group, Endeavour House, 189 Shaftesbury Avenue, London WC2H 8JG
tel 020-7520 6592
website www.topsante.co.uk
Editor Jane Druker
Monthly £3.20

Articles, features and news on all aspects of health and beauty. Ideas welcome. No unsolicited features. Payment: illustrations by arrangement. Founded 1993.

Total Film

Future Publishing Ltd, 1–10 Praed Mews, London W2 1QY
tel 020-7042 4831
email jane.crowther@futurenet.com
website www.gamesradar.com/totalfilm
Acting Editor Rosie Fletcher
Monthly £3.99, £37.99 p.a.

Movie magazine covering all aspects of film. Email ideas before submitting material. Length: 400 words (news items); 1,000 words (funny features). Payment: 20p per word. Founded 1996.

Total Off-Road

Repton House G11, Bretby Business Park, Burton on Trent, Staffs. DE15 0YZ
tel (01283) 553243
email alan.kidd@assignment-media.co.uk
website www.toronline.co.uk
Editor Alan Kidd
Monthly £3.99

Features on off-roading: competitions, modified vehicles, overseas events. Length 1,200–3,000 words. Payment: £100 per 1,000 words. Illustrations: colour and b&w prints, transparencies and digital images. keen to hear from photographers attending UK/overseas off-road events. Preliminary email strongly advised.

Total Politics

Dods, 21 Dartmouth Street, London SW1H 9BP
tel 020-7593 5500
email david.singleton@dods.co.uk
website www.totalpolitics.com
Editor David Singleton
Monthly £3.99

Magazine for politicians and people interested in politics. Looking for relevant articles and features. Length: up to 2,200 words. Illustrations: colour and b&w photos and bespoke artwork. Payment: negotiable. Founded 2008.

Trail

Bauer Consumer Media, Media House, Peterborough Business Park, Peterborough PE2 6RA
tel (01733) 468363
email trail@bauermedia.co.uk
website www.livefortheoutdoors.com
Editor Simon Ingram
Monthly £3.99

Outdoor activity magazine focusing mainly on high level walking with some scrambling and climbing. Some opportunities for freelancers. Good ideas welcome.

Trout & Salmon

Bauer Media Group, Media House, Lynchwood, Peterborough PE2 6EA

tel (01733) 468000
email troutandsalmon@bauermedia.co.uk
website www.gofishing.co.uk/trout-and-salmon
Editor Andrew Flitcroft
13 p.a. £3.40, £44.20 p.a.

Articles of good quality with strong trout or salmon angling interest. Length: 400–2,000 words, accompanied if possible by good quality colour prints. Payment: by arrangement. Illustrations: line, colour transparencies and prints, cartoons. Founded 1955.

Truck & Driver

Road Transport Media Ltd, 9 Sutton Court Road, Sutton, Surrey SM1 4SZ
tel 020-8912 2141
email colin.barnett@roadtransport.com
website www.truckanddriver.co.uk
Editor Colin Barnett
Monthly £3.60

News, articles on trucks, personalities and features of interest to truck drivers. Words (on disk or electronically) and picture packages preferred. Preferred featyre length: 500–2,500 words. Illustrations: colour transparencies, digital and artwork, cartoons. Payment: negotiable. Founded 1984.

Trucking

Kelsey Media, Cudham Tithe Barn, Berrys Hill, Cudham, Kent TN16 3AG
tel (01733) 347559
email trucking.ed@kelsey.co.uk
website www.truckingmag.co.uk
Editor Andy Stewart
Monthly £3.50

For truck drivers, owner–drivers and operators: news, articles, features and technical advice. Length: 750–2,500 words. Illustrations: mostly 35mm digital. Payment: by negotiation. Founded 1983.

TV Times Magazine

Time Inc. (UK), The Blue Fin Building, 110 Southwark Street, London SE1 0SU
tel 020-3148 5615
email tvtimes@timeinc.com
website www.tvtimes.co.uk
Editor Ian Abbott
Weekly £1.40

Features with an affinity to ITV, BBC1, BBC2, Channels 4 and 5, satellite and radio personalities and TV generally. Length: by arrangement. Photographs: commissioned only. Payment: by arrangement.

25 Beautiful Homes

Time Inc. (UK), The Blue Fin Building, 110 Southwark Street, London SE1 0SU
email 25beautifulhomes@timeinc.com
website www.housetohome.co.uk/25beautifulhomes
Editor-in-Chief Deborah Barker
Monthly £4.10

Interiors magazine aiming to inspire affluent readers in their love for their homes. Each edition shows a selection of properties in the UK and Europe that have been renovated or built to a high standard. The magazine also features a selection of best buys in decorative accessories to help make beautiful homes achievable.

U magazine

Rosemount House, Dundrum Road, Dublin 14, Republic of Ireland
tel +353 (0)1 2405300
website www.harmonia.ie
Editor Jennifer Stevens
Fortnightly €44.20 p.a.

Fashion and beauty magazine for 18–25-year-old Irish women, with celebrity interviews, talent profiles, real-life stories, sex and relationship features, plus regular pages on the club scene, movies, music and film. Also travel, interiors, health, food, horoscopes. Material mostly commissioned. Payment: varies. Founded 1978.

Ulster Business

Greer Publications, 5B Edgewater Business Park, Edgewater Road, Belfast Harbour Estate, Belfast BT3 9JQ
tel 028-9078 3200
email davidelliott@greerpublications.com
website www.ulsterbusiness.com
Editor David Elliot
Monthly £2.30

Feature-based magazine with general business-related editorial for management level and above. Specially commissions most material but will consider unsolicited material. Welcomes ideas for articles and features. Length: 800 words (articles), 1,500 words (features). Payment: £60–£80 (articles), £120 (features). No illustrations required. Founded 1987.

Ulster Grocer

Greer Publications, 5B Edgewater Business Park, Belfast Harbour Estate, Belfast BT3 9JQ
tel 028-9078 3200
email alysonmagee@greerpublications.com
website www.ulstergrocer.com
Editor Alyson Magee
Monthly ABC controlled circulation

Northern Ireland retail food industry, wholesale, and supplier magazine. Founded 1972.

Under 5

Pre-school Learning Alliance, The Fitzpatrick Building, 188 York Way, London N7 9AD
tel 020-7697 2500
email editor.u5@pre-school.org.uk
website www.pre-school.org.uk

Editor Shannon Hawthorne
10 p.a. £38 p.a. (non-members)

Articles on the role of adults, especially parents/preschool workers, in young children's learning and development, including children from all cultures and those with special needs. Length: 600–1,200 words. Founded 1962.

Vanity Fair

The Condé Nast Publications Ltd, Vogue House, Hanover Square, London W1S 1JU
tel 020-7499 9080
website www.vanityfair.com
Editor-in-Chief Graydon Carter
Monthly £4.70

Media, glamour and politics for grown-up readers. No unsolicited material. Payment: by arrangement. Illustrated.

The Vegan

The Vegan Society, Donald Watson House, 21 Hylton Street, Birmingham B18 6HJ
tel 0121 523 1730
email editor@vegansociety.com
website www.vegansociety.com
Editor Various
Quarterly £3, £12 p.a.

Articles on health, nutrition, cookery, vegan lifestyles, land use, climate change, animal rights. Length: approx. 1,000 words. Payment: contributions are voluntary. Illustrations: photos, cartoons, line drawings – foods, animals, livestock systems, crops, people, events; colour for cover. Founded 1944.

VEGAN Life

Prime Impact, The Old School, Colchester Road, Wakes Colne, Colchester, Essex CO6 2BY
tel (01787) 224040
email chris@primeimpact.co.uk
website www.veganlifemag.com
Editor Chris Moore
Monthly £3.95

Lifestyle magazine covering all things vegan. Interested in vegan news; recipes; food and drink; celebrities, athletes, and artists; compassion pieces and animal rescue stories; restaurant reviews and vegan chefs; travel and leisure; health and nutrition; and in-depth features on the food industry, animal agriculture and exploitation, vegan advocacy etc. Length: generally 1,000–2,000 words, but flexible according to value of the article/feature. Images: writers and contributors should try and source their own large, high-quality images wherever possible. Payment: all contributions are voluntary. Writers credited for the pieces and bylines offered on request.

Vegetarian Living

Select Publisher Services Ltd, PO Box 6337, Bournemouth BH1 9EH
tel (01202) 586848
email paul@vegmag.co.uk
website www.vegetarianliving.co.uk
Editor Paul Morgan
Monthly £3.95

Aimed at people who want to be inspired by vegetarian cooking – whether they're vegetarian, vegan or simply want to eat more healthily. Articles on high-profile chefs, food writers and celebrities; eco/green living and community schemes/projects. Welcomes ideas for articles and features.

Viz

Dennis Publishing Ltd, 30 Cleveland Street, London W1T 4JD
tel 020-7907 6000
email viz@viz.co.uk
website www.viz.co.uk
Publisher Russell Blackman
10 p.a. £3.20

Cartoons, spoof tabloid articles, spoof advertisements. Illustrations: half-tone, line, cartoons. Payment: £300 per page (cartoons). Founded 1979.

Vogue

Vogue House, 1 Hanover Square, London W1S 1JU
tel 020-7499 9080
email vogue.com.editor@condenast.co.uk
website www.vogue.co.uk
Editor Alexandra Shulman
Monthly £3.99

Fashion, beauty, health, decorating, art, theatre, films, literature, music, travel, food and wine. Length: articles from 1,000 words. Illustrated.

The Voice

GV Media Group, Unit 235, Elephant and Castle Shopping Centre, London SE1 6TE
tel 020-7510 0340
email newsdesk@gvmedia.co.uk
website www.voice-online.co.uk
Editor George Ruddock
Weekly £1

Weekly newspaper for black Britons. Includes news, features, arts, sport and a comprehensive jobs and business section. Illustrations: colour and b&w photos. Open to ideas for news and features on sports, business, community events and the arts. Founded 1982.

Waitrose Kitchen

John Brown, 136–142 Bramley Road, London W10 6SR
tel 020-7565 3000
email waitrosekitchen@waitrose.co.uk
Editor William Sitwell
Monthly £1.20 (free to MyWaitrose members)

In-house magazine of the Waitrose Group. Features seasonal recipes, menu ideas and interviews.

walk

The Ramblers' Association, 2nd Floor,
Camelford House, 87–90 Albert Embankment,
London SE1 7TW
tel 020-7339 8540
email matthew.jones@ramblers.org.uk
website www.walkmag.co.uk
Editor Matthew Jones
Quarterly £3.60 Free to members

Magazine of the Ramblers' Association. Articles on walking, access to countryside and related issues. Material mostly commissioned. Length: up to 1,500 words. Illustrations: colour photos, preferably high quality, digitally supplied. Payment: by agreement. Founded 1935.

Wallpaper

IPC Media Ltd, The Blue Fin Building,
110 Southwark Street, London SE1 0SU
tel 020-3148 5000
email contact@wallpaper.com
website www.wallpaper.com
Editor-in-Chief Tony Chambers
12 p.a. £4.99

Interiors, architecture, fashion, entertainment and travel. Payment: by arrangement. Founded 1996.

Wanderlust

PO Box 1832, Windsor SL4 1YT
tel (01753) 620426
email editorial@wanderlust.co.uk
website www.wanderlust.co.uk
Editor Phoebe Smith
8 p.a. £3.99

Features on independent, adventure and special-interest travel. Visit www.wanderlust.co.uk/about for contributor guidelines. Length: up to 2,500 words. Illustrations: high-quality colour slides or digital. Payment: by arrangement. Founded 1993.

The War Cry

The Salvation Army, 101 Newington Causeway,
London SE1 6BN
tel 020-7367 4900
email warcry@salvationarmy.org.uk
website www.salvationarmy.org.uk/uki/WarCry
Editor Major Nigel Bovey
Weekly £38 p.a.

Voluntary contributions: Human interest stories of personal Christian faith. Founded 1879.

The Warwick Review

Department of English, University of Warwick,
Coventry CV4 7AL
email m.w.hulse@warwick.ac.uk
website www2.warwick.ac.uk/fac/arts/english/writingprog/warwickreview
Editor Michael Hulse
Quarterly £25 p.a.

Fiction, poetry, reviews, essays, interviews, symposia. Material mostly commissioned. Length: by agreement. Illustrations: none. Payment: by length – £25 minimum for poems, £50 minimum for prose. Founded 2007.

Wasafiri

The Open University in London,
1-11 Hawley Crescent, London NW1 8NP
email wasafiri@open.ac.uk
website www.wasafiri.org
Editor Susheila Nasta
4 p.a. £51 p.a. (print only), £51 (online only), £61 p.a. (print and online)

International contemporary literature. Accepts submissions for fiction, poetry, articles and interviews; see website for details. Founded 1984.

Waterways World

Waterways World Ltd, 151 Station Street,
Burton-on-Trent DE14 1BG
tel (01283) 742950
email robert.cowling@wwonline.co.uk
website www.waterwaysworld.com
Editor Bobby Cowling
Monthly £3.99

Feature articles on all aspects of inland waterways in Britain and abroad, including historical material; factual and technical articles preferred. No short stories or poetry. See website for notes for potential contributors (under the Writing for WW section). Payment: £70 per page (including illustrations). Illustrations: digital, colour transparencies or prints, line. Founded 1972.

The Week

30 Cleveland Street, London W1T 4JD
tel 020-7907 6000
email editorialadmin@theweek.co.uk
website www.theweek.co.uk
Editor-in-Chief Jeremy O'Grady, *Editor* Caroline Law
Weekly £3.10, £99.95 p.a. (print only), £109.95 p.a. (print + iPad editions), £94.99 p.a. (digital edition only)

Magazine that distils the best from the British and foreign press into 44pp, including news, art, science, business, property and leisure. Founded 1995.

The Weekly News

D.C. Thomson & Co. Ltd, 80 Kingsway East,
Dundee DD4 8SL
tel (01382) 575850
email weeklynews@dcthomson.co.uk
Weekly £1.20

Real-life dramas of around 500 words told in the first person. General interest fiction. Payment: on acceptance.

Weight Watchers Magazine

The River Group, 1 Neal Street, London WC2H 9QL
tel 020-7306 0304

email wwmagazine@riverltd.co.uk
Editorial Director Mary Frances
12 p.a. £2.75, £2 for members

Features: health, beauty, news; food-orientated articles; success stories: weight-loss, motivation, wellbeing. All material commissioned. Length: up to 3pp. Illustrations: colour photos and cartoons. Payment: by arrangement.

What Car?

Haymarket Motoring Magazines Ltd, Teddington Studios, Broom Road, Teddington, Middlesex TW11 9BE
tel 020-8267 5688
email editorial@whatcar.com
website www.whatcar.com
Editor Jim Holder
Monthly £4.99

Road tests, buying guide, consumer stories and used car features. No unsolicited material. Illustrations: colour and b&w photos, line drawings. Payment: by negotiation. Founded 1973.

What's on TV

Time Inc. (UK), 6th Floor, The Blue Fin Building, 110 Southwark Street, London SE1 0SU
tel 020-3148 5000
email wotv_enquiries@timeinc.com
website www.whatsontv.co.uk
Editor Colin Tough
Weekly 56p

Features on TV programmes and personalities. All material commissioned. Length: up to 250 words. Illustrations: colour and b&w photos. Payment: by agreement. Founded 1991.

WI Life

(formerly WI Home & Country)
104 New King's Road, London SW6 4LY
tel 020-7731 5777
email wilife@nfwi.org.uk
website www.thewi.org.uk/wie-and-wi-life
Editor Kaye McIntosh
8 p.a. as part of the WI subscription

Journal of the National Federation of Women's Institutes for England and Wales. Publishes material related to the Federation's and members' activities with articles of interest to members, mainly written in-house and by WI members. Illustrations: colour photos and artwork. Payment: by arrangement.

Willings Press Guide

Cision UK Ltd, Longbow House, 20 Chiswell Street, London EC1Y 4TW
tel (020) 251 7259
email info.uk@cision.com
website www.cision.com
1 p.a. £495 2-volume set; £295 1 volume

Two-volume reference guide to news media worldwide. Volume 1 covers UK and Ireland newspapers, news agencies, radio and television stations, and business/consumer periodicals and blogs. Volume 2 provides and overview of news media worldwide (excluding UK and Ireland).

The Wolf

email editor@wolfmagazine.co.uk
website www.wolfmagazine.co.uk
Editor James Byrne
Quarterly £5 (print, inc. p&p), £3 (digital), £15 p.a. (inc. p&p)

Independent poetry magazine. Also features interviews with leading contemporary poets, translations and critical prose. Welcomes submissions from writers and artists but see website for full guidelines before submitting any work. Founded 2002.

Woman

Time Inc. (UK), The Blue Fin Building, 110 Southwark Street, London SE1 0SU
tel 020-3148 5000
email woman@timeinc.com
website www.womanmagazine.co.uk
Editor-in-Chief Karen Livermore
Weekly 99p

News, celebrity and real-life features, of no more than 1,000 words. Particular interest in celebrity and diet exclusives. Payment: by negotiation. Digital images only. Read magazine prior to submission. Fiction not published. Founded 1937.

Woman Alive

(formerly Christian Woman)
Christian Publishing and Outreach, Garcia Estate, Canterbury Road, Worthing, West Sussex BN13 1BW
tel (01903) 604352
email womanalive@cpo.org.uk
website www.womanalive.co.uk
Editor Jackie Harris
Monthly £2.95

Aimed at women aged 25 upwards. Celebrity interviews, topical features, Christian issues, profiles of women in interesting occupations, Christian testimonies and real-life stories, fashion, beauty, travel, health, crafts. All feature articles should be illustrated. Length: 700–1,800 words. Payment £75–£130. Founded 1982.

woman&home

Time Inc. (UK), The Blue Fin Building, 110 Southwark Street, London SE1 0SU
tel 020-3148 5000
email woman&home@timeinc.com
website www.womanandhome.com
Editorial Director Sue James
Monthly £4.10

Centres on the personal and home interests of the

lively minded mature, modern woman. Articles dealing with fashion, beauty, leisure pursuits, gardening, home style; features on topical issues, people and places. Fiction: complete stories from 3,000–4,500 words in length. Illustrations: commissioned colour photos and sketches. Non-commissioned work is not accepted and cannot be returned. Founded 1926.

woman&home Feel Good Food

Time Inc. (UK), The Blue Fin Building,
110 Southwark Street, London SE1 0SU
tel 020-3148 5000
email woman&home@timeinc.com
website www.womanandhome.com
Editorial Director Sue James, *Editor* Jane Curran
6 p.a. £3.99

Seasonal food magazine from woman&home. Features a range of recipes, from family suppers to dishes for entertaining, all with an emphasis on cooking with ingredients when they are at their best. Also includes recipes from celebrity chefs, gourmet getaways and information on suppliers and producers.

Woman's Own

Time Inc. (UK), The Blue Fin Building,
110 Southwark Street, London SE1 0SU
tel 020-3148 5000
email womansown@timeinc.com
Editor Catherine Westwood
Weekly 99p

Modern women's magazine aimed at the 35–50 age group. No unsolicited features. Address work to relevant department editor. Payment: by arrangement.

Woman's Way

Harmonia Ltd, Rosemount House, Dundrum Road, Dublin 14, Republic of Ireland
tel +353 (0)1 2405300
email atoner@harmonia.ie
website www.womansway.ie
Editor Áine Toner
Weekly €1.49

Human interest, personality interviews, features on fashion, beauty, celebrities and investigations. Founded 1963.

Woman's Weekly

Time Inc. (UK), The Blue Fin Building,
110 Southwark Street, London SE1 0SU
tel 020-3148 5000
email womansweeklypostbag@timeinc.com
website www.womansweekly.com
Editor Diane Kenwood
Weekly 94p

Lively, family-interest magazine. Includes one three- or four-part fiction serial, averaging 3,500 words each instalment, of general emotional interest, and several short stories of 1,000–2,000 words of general emotional interest. Stories up to 7,000 words considered for Fiction Special. Celebrity and strong human interest features, health, finance and consumer features, plus beauty, diet and travel; also inspirational and entertaining personal stories. Payment: by arrangement. Illustrations: full colour fiction illustrations, small sketches and photos. Founded 1911.

Woman's Weekly Fiction Special

Time Inc. UK, The Blue Fin Building,
110 Southwark Street, London SE1 0SU
tel 020-3148 5000
Editor Gaynor Davies
20 issues p.a. £1.95

Minimum 20 stories each issue of 1,000–7,000 words of varied emotional interest, including romance, humour and mystery. Payment: by arrangement. Illustrations: full colour. Founded 1998.

The Woodworker

MyTime Media Ltd, Enterprise House,
Enterprise Way, Edenbridge, Kent TN8 6HF
tel 0844 848 8822
website www.getwoodworking.com
Editor Mark Cass
Monthly £3.75

For the craft and professional woodworker. Practical illustrated articles on cabinet work, carpentry, polishing, wood turning, wood carving, rural crafts, craft history, antique and period furniture; also wooden toys and models, musical instruments; timber procurement, conditioning, seasoning; tools, machinery and equipment reviews. Payment: by arrangement. Illustrations: line drawings and digital photos. Founded 1901.

World Fishing & Aquaculture

The Old Mill, Lower Quay, Fareham PO16 0RA
tel (01329) 825335
email editor@worldfishing.net
website www.worldfishing.net
Editor Carly Wills
11 issues p.a. £130 p.a.

International journal of commercial fishing. Technical and management emphasis on catching, processing and marketing of fish and related products; fishery operations and vessels covered worldwide. Length: 500–1,500 words. Payment: by arrangement. Illustrations: photos and diagrams for litho reproduction. Founded 1952.

The World of Interiors

The Condé Nast Publications Ltd, Vogue House,
1 Hanover Square, London W1S 1JU
tel 020-7499 9080
website www.worldofinteriors.co.uk
Contact Aliette Boshier

Monthly £4.99

All material commissioned: send synopsis/visual reference for article ideas. Length: 1,000–1,500 words. Illustrations: colour photos. Payment: £500 per 1,000 words; photos £125 per page. Founded 1981.

World Soccer

Time Inc. (UK), The Blue Fin Building,
110 Southwark Street, London SE1 0SU
tel 020-3148 5000
email worldsoccer@timeinc.com
website www.worldsoccer.com
Editor Gavin Hamilton
Monthly £4.30

Articles, features, news concerning football, its personalities and worldwide development. Length: 600–2,000 words. Payment: by arrangement. Founded 1960.

The World Today

Chatham House, 10 St James's Square,
London SW1Y 4LE
tel 020-7957 5712
email wt@chathamhouse.org.uk
website www.theworldtoday.org
Editor Alan Philps, *Assistant Editor* Agnes Frimston
Monthly £38 p.a. (£137 p.a. institutions, £30 p.a. students)

Analysis of international issues and current events by journalists, diplomats, politicians and academics. Length: 1,000–1,800 words. Payment: nominal. Founded 1945.

Writing Magazine

Warners Group Publications, 5th Floor,
31–32 Park Row, Leeds LS1 5JD
tel 0113 200 2929
email jonathant@warnersgroup.co.uk
website www.writers-online.co.uk
Editor Jonathan Telfer
Monthly £3.85, £39.90 p.a. (by Direct Debit; £45 p.a. otherwise. Includes *Writers' News*.)

Articles on all aspects of writing. Length: 800–2,000 words. Payment: by arrangement. Founded 1992. *Writers' News* (now part of *Writing Magazine*) features news competitions and market information. Length: up to 350 words. Payment: by arrangement. Founded 1989.

Yachting Monthly

Time Inc. (UK), The Blue Fin Building,
110 Southwark Street, London SE1 0SU
tel 020-3148 5000
email yachting.monthly@timeinc.com
website www.yachtingmonthly.com
Editor Kieran Flatt
Monthly £4.50

Articles on all aspects of seamanship, navigation, the handling of sailing craft, and their design, construction and equipment. Well-written narrative accounts of cruises in yachts. Length: up to 1,500 words. Illustrations: colour transparencies and prints, cartoons. Payment: quoted on acceptance. Founded 1906.

Yachting World

Time Inc. (UK), The Blue Fin Building,
110 Southwark Street, London SE1 0SU
tel 020-3148 4846
email yachting.world@timeinc.com
website www.yachtingworld.com
Editor Elaine Bunting
Monthly £4.60

Practical articles of an original nature, dealing with sailing and boats. Length: 1,500–2,000 words. Payment: varies. Illustrations: digital files, drawings, cartoons. Founded 1894.

Yachts and Yachting

The Chelsea Magazine Company, Jubilee House,
2 Jubilee Place, London SW3 3TQ
email Georgie.Corlett-Pitt@chelseamagazines.com
website www.yachtsandyachting.com
Editor Georgie Corlett-Pitt
Monthly £4.30

Technical sailing and related lifestyle articles. Payment: by arrangement. Illustrations: line, half-tone, colour. Founded 1947.

Yoga & Healthy Living

101 Matilda House, London E1W 1LF
tel 020-7480 5456
email janesill@aol.com
website www.yogaandhealthyliving.com
Editor Jane Sill
Monthly Online

Payment: by arrangement. Continuation of *Yoga & Health*. Founded 1983.

Yorkshire Life

PO Box 163, Ripon HG4 9AG
tel (01765) 692586
website www.yorkshirelife.co.uk
Editor Esther Leach
Monthly £2.99

Articles on Yorkshire, including places of interest, high-profile personalities, local events, arts, history and food. Unsolicited ideas welcome. Founded 1946.

You & Your Wedding

Immediate Media Co. Ltd, Vineyard House,
44 Brook Green, London W6 7BT
tel 020-7150 5376
website www.youandyourwedding.co.uk
Editor Maxine Briggs
Bi-monthly £4.99

Articles, features and news covering all aspects of planning a wedding. Submit ideas by email. Illustrations: colour. Payment: negotiable.

Your Cat Magazine

BPG Media, 1–6 Buckminster Yard, Buckminster, Grantham, Lincs. NG33 5SB
tel (01780) 766199
email editorial@yourcat.co.uk
website www.yourcat.co.uk
Editor Chloë Hukin
Monthly £3.35

Practical advice on the care of cats and kittens, general interest items and news on cats, and true-life tales and fiction (commission only). Length: 800–1,500 words (articles), 200–300 words (news), up to 1,000 words (short stories). Illustrations: hi-res digital, colour transparencies and prints. Founded 1994.

Your Dog Magazine

BPG Media, 1–6 Buckminster Yard, Buckminster, Grantham, Lincs. NG33 5SB
tel (01476) 859830
email editorial@yourdog.co.uk
website www.yourdog.co.uk
Editor Sarah Wright
Monthly £3.70

Articles and information of interest to dog lovers; features on all aspects of pet dogs. Length: approx. 1,500 words. Payment: £140 per 1,000 words. Founded 1994.

Your Horse

Bauer Media Group, Media House, Lynchwood, Peterborough PE2 6EA
tel (01733) 395055
email imogen.johnson@bauermedia.co.uk
website www.yourhorse.co.uk
Editor Imogen Johnson
13 issues p.a. £3.99

Practical horse care, riding advice and inspiration for riders and owners. Send feature ideas with examples of previous published writing. Specially commissions most material. Welcomes ideas for articles and features. Length: 1,500 words. Payment: £140 per 1,000 words. Founded 1983.

Yours

Bauer Consumer Media, Media House, Peterborough Business Park, Peterborough PE2 6EA
tel (01733) 468000
email yours@bauermedia.co.uk
website www.yours.co.uk
Editor Sharon Red
Fortnightly £1.49

Features and news about and/or of interest to the over-50s age group, including nostalgia and short stories. Study of magazine essential; approach in writing in the first instance. Length: articles up to 300 words, short stories up to 1,200 words. Payment: at the Editor's discretion or by agreement. Founded 1973.

Zoo

Bauer Consumer Media, Endeavour House, 189 Shaftesbury Avenue, London, WC2H 8JG
tel 020-7295 5000
email info@zootoday.co.uk
website www.zootoday.co.uk
Editor Damian McSorley
Weekly £1.99

Weekly entertainment magazine for young men with news, sport, girls, features, jokes and reviews. Founded 2004.

Syndicates, news and press agencies

Before submitting material, you are strongly advised to make preliminary enquiries and to ascertain terms of work. Strictly speaking, syndication is the selling and reselling of previously published work although some news and press agencies handle original material.

Academic File Information Services

Academic File International Syndication Services, EAPGROUP International Media, PO Box 13666, London SW14 8WF
tel 020-8392 1122
email afis@eapgroup.com
website www.eapgroup.com
Commissioning Editor Sajid Rizvi

Feature and photo syndication with special reference to the developing world and immigrant communities in the West. Founded 1985.

Advance Features

Stubbs Wood Cottage, Hammerwood, East Grinstead, West Sussex RH19 3QE
tel (01342) 850480
email advancefeatures@aol.com
website www.advancefeatures.uk.com
Managing Editor Peter Norman

Crosswords: daily, weekly and theme; general puzzles. Daily and weekly cartoons for the regional, national and overseas press (not single cartoons).

AFP (Agence France-Presse)

Floor 15, 200 Aldersgate, Aldersgate Street, London EC1A 4HD
tel 020-776 2740
email london.economics@afp.com
website www.afp.com

Major news agency with journalists in 150 countries across five geographical zones.

Neil Bradley Puzzles

Linden House, 73 Upper Marehay, Ripley, Derbyshire DE5 8JF
tel (01773) 741500
email bradcart@aol.com
Director Neil Bradley

Supplies visual puzzles to national and regional press; emphasis placed on variety and topicality with work based on current media listings. Daily single frame and strip cartoons. Founded 1981.

Brainwarp

23 Chatsworth Avenue, Culcheth, Warrington, Cheshire WA3 4LD
tel (01925) 765878
email sarah@brainwarp.com
website www.brainwarp.com
Contacts Trixie Roberts, Tony Roberts, Sarah Simmons

Writes and supplies original crosswords, brainteasers, wordsearches, quizzes and word games to editors for the printed page. Does not accept work from external sources. Standard fees for syndicated puzzles. Customised work negotiable. Founded 1987.

Bulls Presstjänst AB

Fabrikörvägen 8, Box 1228, 13128 Nacka Strand, Sweden
tel +46 8-55520600
website www.bullspress.com

Market newspapers, magazines, weeklies and advertising agencies in Sweden, Denmark, Norway, Finland, Iceland, Poland, The Baltic States, Germany, Austria and German-speaking Switzerland.

Syndicates human interest picture stories; topical and well-illustrated background articles and series; photographic features dealing with science, people, personalities, glamour; genre pictures for advertising; condensations and serialisations of bestselling fiction and non-fiction; cartoons, comic strips, film and TV rights, merchandising and newspaper graphics online.

Bulls Pressedienst GmbH
Eysseneckstrasse 50, D-60322 Frankfurt am Main, Germany
tel +49 (0)69 959 270 *fax* +49 (0)69 959 27222
email bhesse@bullspress.de

Bulls Pressetjeneste A/S
Hammersborg Torg 3, N-0179 Oslo, Norway
tel +47 2298 2660 *fax* +47 2220 4978
email info@bulls.no

Bulls Pressetjeneste
Roarsvej 2, DK–2000 Frederiksberg, Denmark
tel +45 3538 9099 *fax* +45 3538 2516
email kjartan@bulls.dk

Bulls Press
Arabiankantu 12, FIN–00560, Helsinki, Finland
tel +358 9-6129650 *fax* +358 9-656092
email sales@bullspress.fi

Bulls Press SP. z o.o.
17 Rejtana str. 24, 02–516 Warsaw, Poland
tel +48 22-646 8019 *fax* +48 22-845 9011
email office@bulls.com.pl

Bulls Press
Tornimäe 7–091, EE–10145 Tallinn, Estonia
tel +372 669 6737 *fax* +372 660 1313
email pilt@bulls.ee

Cartoons & Wordgames

341 Stockport Road, Mossley, Ashton-under-Lyne OL5 0RS
tel (01457) 834883

email email@wordgames.co.uk
website www.wordgames.co.uk
Managing Editor Tom Williams

Daily and weekly crosswords and variety puzzles. UK and worldwide. Founded 1980.

Celebritext Ltd

PO Box 63628, London SW9 1BA
tel 020-8123 1730
email info@celebritext.com
website www.celebritext.com
Contact Lee Howard

Specialises in film, TV and music celebrity interviews. Commission: 50%. Founded 2000.

Europa-Press

Fabrikörvägen 8, Box 1228, 13128 Nacka Strand, Sweden
tel +46 8-52210300
email richard@europapress.se
website www.europapress.se
Director Richard Steinsvik

Market: newspapers, magazines, weeklies and websites in Sweden, Denmark, Norway, Finland, and the Baltic states. Syndicates high-quality features of international appeal such as topical articles, photo features – b&w and colour, women's features, short stories, serial novels, non-fiction stories and serials with strong human interest, comic strips.

Europress Features (UK)

18 St Chad's Road, Didsbury,
Nr Manchester M20 4WH
tel 0161 445 2945
email lauenbergandpartners@yahoo.com

Representation of newspapers and magazines in Europe, Australia, United States. Syndication of top-flight features with exclusive illustrations – human interest stories – showbusiness personalities. 30–35% commission on sales of material successfully accepted; 40% on exclusive illustrations.

FAMOUS*

13 Harwood Road, London SW6 4QP
tel 020-7731 9333
email info@famous.uk.com
website www.famous.uk.com

Celebrity picture and feature agency. Supplies showbiz content to newspapers, magazines, websites, TV stations, mobile phone companies, books and advertisers worldwide. Represents celebrity journalists and photographers from Los Angeles, New York, Europe and Australia, syndicating their copy around the globe. Open to new material. Terms: 50%. Founded 1990.

Foresight News

Centaur Media Plc, Profile Group, 79 Wells Street, London W1T 3QN
tel 020-7970 4299
email info@foresightnews.co.uk
website www.foresightnews.com
Editor and Associate Publisher Nicole Wilkins

Offers a vast, fully searchable database featuring thousands of forthcoming events and news from across the UK and around the world, spanning a variety of sectors including politics, business, crime and home affairs, health, entertainment and sport.

Graphic Syndication

4 Reyntiens View, Odiham, Hants RG29 1AF
tel (01256) 703004
email flantoons@btinternet.com
Manager M. Flanagan

Cartoon strips and single frames supplied to newspapers and magazines in Britain and overseas. Terms: 50%. Founded 1981.

Guardian Syndication

Kings Place, 90 York Way, London N1 9GU
tel 020-3353 2539
email permissions.syndication@guardian.co.uk
website www.syndication.guardian.co.uk
Contact Helen Wilson

International syndication services of news and features from the *Guardian* and the *Observer*. Unable to syndicate content which hasn't been published in its own titles.

Hayters Teamwork

Hamilton House, Mabledon Place,
London WC1H 9BB
tel 020-7554 8555
email sport@hayters.com
website www.hayters.com
Chief Executive Gerry Cox, *Managing Director* Nick Callow

Sports news, features and data supplied to all branches of the media. Commission: negotiable according to merit. Part of Info Strada. Founded 1955.

Headliners

Rich Mix, 35–47 Bethnal Green Road,
London E1 6LA
tel 020-7749 9360
email enquiries@headliners.org
website www.headliners.org
Director Fiona Wyton

Offers young people aged 8–18 the opportunity to write on issues of importance to them, for newspapers, radio and TV. Founded 1995.

Independent Radio News (IRN)

Academic House, 24-28 Oval Road,
London NW1 7DJ
tel 020-3227 4044
email news@irn.co.uk
website www.irn.co.uk
Managing Director Tim Molloy

National and international news.

Knight Features Ltd

20 Crescent Grove, London SW4 7AH
tel 020-7622 1467
email info@knightfeatures.co.uk
website www.knightfeatures.com
Directors Peter Knight, Gaby Martin, Andrew Knight, Sam Ferris

Agent in the UK and Republic of Ireland for Universal Uclick, Creators Syndicate and comic classics including Dilbert, Peanuts and Garfield. Worldwide selling of puzzles, strip cartoons, crosswords, horoscopes and serialisations for print and digital media. Founded 1985.

London at Large Ltd

Canal Studios, 3–5 Dunston Road, London E8 4EH
tel 020-7275 7667
email info@londonatlarge.com
website www.londonatlarge.com
Editor Chris Parkinson

Forward planner serving the media: lists press contacts for parties, celebrities, launches, premieres, music, film, video and book releases. Founded 1985.

Maharaja Features Pvt. Ltd (1969)

5/226 Sion Road East, Sion, Bombay 400 022, India
tel +91 22-24097951
email mahafeat@gmail.com
Editor Mrs R. Ravi, *Managing Editor* K.R.N. Swamy

Syndicates feature and pictorial material of interest to Asian readers to newspapers and magazines in India, UK and elsewhere. Specialises in well-researched articles on India by eminent authorities for publication in prestigious journals throughout the world. Also topical features. Length: 1,000–1,500 words. Illustrations: b&w prints, colour transparencies, digital photographs.

National Association of Press Agencies (NAPA)

Suite 308, Queens Dock Business Centre, 67–83 Norfolk Street, Liverpool L1 0BG
tel 0870 240 0311
email enquiries@napa.org.uk
website www.napa.org.uk
Chairman Jon Harris
Membership £250 p.a.

A network of independent, established and experienced press agencies serving newspapers, magazines, TV and radio networks. Founded 1983.

New Blitz Literary, Editorial & TV Agency

Via di Panico 67, 00186 Rome, Italy
postal address CP 30047–00193, Rome 47, Italy
tel +39 06-4883268
email blitzgacs@inwind.it
Manager Giovanni A.S. Congiu

Syndicates worldwide: cartoons, comic strips, humorous books with drawings, feature and pictorial material, topical, environment, travel. Average rates of commission 60/40%, monthly report of sales, payment 60 days after the date of sale.

The Press Association

292 Vauxhall Bridge Road, London SW1V 1AE
tel 0870 120 3200
website www.pressassociation.co.uk
Chief Executive Clive Marshall, *Managing Director* Tony Watson

National news agency for the UK and Ireland. As a multimedia content provider across web, mobile, broadcast and print channels, the PA provides clients with feeds of text, data, photos and video. Services comprise live coverage of news, sport and entertainment as well as bespoke content marketing solutions for non-media clients. Founded 1868.

The Puzzle House

Ivy Cottage, Battlesea Green, Stradbroke, Suffolk IP21 5NE
tel (01379) 384656
email enquiry@the-puzzle-house.co.uk
website www.the-puzzle-house.co.uk
Partners Roy Preston & Sue Preston

Supply original crosswords, quizzes and puzzles of all types. Commissions taken on any topic, with all age ranges catered for. Wide selection of puzzles available for one-off usage. Founded 1988.

Rann Communication

120 Molesworth Street, North Adelaide SA 5006 Australia
postal address GPO Box 958, Adelaide, SA 5000, Australia
tel +61 (0)8 8211 7771
website www.rann.com.au
Managing Director Chris Rann

Full range of professional PR, press releases, special newsletters, commercial and political intelligence, media monitoring. Welcomes approaches from organisations requiring PR representation or press release distribution. Founded 1982.

Sirius Media Services

Suite 3, Stowmarket Business Centre, Needham Road, Stowmarket, Suffolk IP14 2AH
tel (01449) 678878
email info@siriusmedia.co.uk
website www.siriusmedia.co.uk

Crosswords, puzzles and quizzes.

Solo Syndication Ltd

Northcliffe House, 2 Derry Street, London W8 5TT
tel 020-7566 0360
website www.solosyndication.co.uk
Managing Director William Gardiner

Worldwide syndication of newspaper features, photos, cartoons, strips and book serialisations. Represents the international syndication of Associated Newspapers (*Daily Mail*, *Mail on Sunday*, *Mail Online*, *Metro*) and Universal Universal Uclick and Creators Syndicate in Africa and the Middle East.

The Telegraph – Content Licensing & Syndication

Telegraph Media Group,
111 Buckingham Palace Road, London SW1W 0DT
tel 020-7931 1010
email syndication@telegraph.co.uk
website www.telegraph.co.uk/syndication

News, features, photography & graphics, video, worldwide distribution and representation. Content licensing packages available for print or online use.

Visual Humour

5 Greymouth Close, Stockton-on-Tees TS18 5LF
tel (01642) 581847
email peterdodsworth@btclick.com
website www.businesscartoonshop.com
Contact Peter Dodsworth

Daily and weekly humorous cartoon strips; also single panel cartoon features (not gag cartoons) for possible syndication in the UK and abroad. Picture puzzles also considered. Submit photocopy samples only initially, with sae. Founded 1984.

WENN

4a Tileyard Studios, Tileyard Road, London N7 9AH
tel 020-7607 2757
email enquiries@wenn.com
website www.wenn.com

Provides the world's media with up-to-the-minute entertainment news and photos. Offices in Los Angeles, New York and Las Vegas. (Formerly World Entertainment News Network.)

Wessex News, Features and Photos Agency

Little Mead, Lower Green, Inkpen, Berks. RG17 9DW
tel (01488) 668308
email news@britishnews.co.uk
website www.britishnews.co.uk
Editor Jim Hardy

Freelance press agency with a network of writers and photographers across the UK. Providing real-life new stories and features for the national and international newspapers and magazines. Founded 1981.

Books

How to get published

The combined wisdom of the writers of the articles in the *Yearbook* provide some of the most up-to-date and best practical advice you will need to negotiate your way through the two main routes to publication. Whether you opt for the traditional route via an agent or the self-publishing model, there are key things it would be useful to consider before you begin.

There is more competition to get published than ever before. Hundreds of would-be books appear in the inboxes of publishers and literary agents every week, and both publishers and literary agents acknowledge that potential authors have to be really dedicated (and perhaps very lucky) to get their work published. That is one of the reasons so many writers are turning to self-publishing. So how can you give yourself the best chance of success whichever route you take?

1. Know your market

• Be confident that there is a readership for your book. Explore the intended market so you are sure that your publishing idea is both commercially viable and desirable to the reading public, agent or publisher.

• Know your competition and review the latest publishing trends: look in bookshops, at ebook stores, at online book sites, take an interest in publishing stories in the media and, above all, *read*. See *News, views and trends in book publishing* on page 128.

2. Agent, publisher or do-it-yourself?

• First decide if you want to try and get signed by a literary agent and be published by a traditional publisher. Self-publishing in both print and electronically has never been easier, quicker or cheaper.

• If you opt for the agent/publisher route, decide whether you prefer to approach an agent or to submit your material direct to a publisher. Many publishers, particularly of fiction, will only consider material submitted through a literary agent. See *How literary agencies work* on page 389, *How to get an agent* on page 392, *Being an agent in a digital age* on page 398, *How to attract the attention of a literary agent* on page 407 and *Understanding publishing agreements* on page 114 for some of the pros and cons of each approach. Whether you choose to approach an agent or a publisher, your work will be subjected to rigorous commercial assessment – see *Getting hooked out of the slush pile* on page 394 and *Letter to an unsolicited author* on page 404.

• For information about self-publishing in print and electronically, consult *Self-publishing for beginners* on page 582, *What do self-publishing providers offer?* on page 586, *Marketing, publicising and selling self-published books* on page 597 and *The Alliance of Independent Authors* on page 491.

3. Choose the right publisher, agent or self-publishing provider

• Study the entries in this *Yearbook*, examine publishers' lists and their websites, and look in the relevant sections in libraries and bookshops for the names of publishers which might be interested in your material.

• A list of literary agents starts on page 411.

• Listings of publishers' names and addresses start on page 148. A list of *Publishers of fiction*, by genre, is on page 737 and a list of *Publishers of non-fiction* starts on page 741.

• The list of *Children's book publishers and packagers* on page 756 includes publishers of poetry for children and teenage fiction. A list of *Literary agents for children's books* is on page 760. See also the *Children's Writers' & Artists' Yearbook 2016* (Bloomsbury 2015) for in-depth coverage of writing and publishing for the children's and young adult markets.

• Publishers which consider poetry for adults are listed on page 759.

• The electronic book market continues to grow. See *Electronic publishing* on page 573, *What do self-publishing providers offer?* on page 586, *News, views and trends in book publishing* on page 128 and *Print on demand* on page 135.

• Authors should not pay publishers for the publication of their work. There are many companies that can help you self-publish your book, for a fee; see *What do self-publishing providers offer?* on page 586. Make sure you know what it is the company will actually do and agree any fees in advance. See *Self-publishing for beginners* on page 582 and *Vanity publishing* on page 145.

4. Prepare your material well

• Presentation is important. No editor will read a handwritten manuscript. If your material is submitted in the most appropriate format an agent or publisher will be more inclined to give attention to it.

• Numerous manuscripts are rejected because of poor writing style or structure. A critique by an experienced editorial professional can help to iron out these weaknesses.

• It is understandable that writers, in their eagerness to get their work published as soon as possible, will send their manuscript in a raw state. Do not send your manuscript to a literary agent or publisher until it is *ready* to be seen. Wait until you are confident that your work is as good as it can be. Have as your mantra: edit, review, revise and then edit again. See *Letter to an unsolicited author* on page 404 and *Editing your work* on page 629.

5. Approach a publisher or literary agent in the way they prefer

• Submit your work to the right person within the publishing company or literary agency. Look at the listings in this *Yearbook* for more details. Most agents will expect to see a synopsis (see *Writing a synopsis* on page 104) and up to three sample chapters or the complete manuscript. Most publishers' and literary agents' websites give guidance on how to submit material, and should make clear if they accept unsolicited scripts by email or only by post.

• Never send your only copy of the manuscript. Whilst reasonable care will be taken of material in the possession of a publisher or agent, responsibility cannot be accepted if material is lost or damaged.

• Always include an sae with enough postage for the return of your material if sent by post, though most submissions tend now to be electronic and many agents have a specific 'submissions' email or button on their websites.

6. Write a convincing cover letter or email

• Compose your preliminary letter or email with care. It will be your first contact with an agent or publisher and needs to make them take notice of your book.

• When submitting a manuscript to a publisher, it is a good idea to let them know that you know (and admire!) what they already publish. You can then make your case about where your submission will fit in their list. Show them that you mean business and have researched the marketplace. See *The publishing process* on page 109.

• What is the USP (unique selling point) of the material you are submitting? You may have an original authorial 'voice', or you may have come up with an amazingly brilliant idea for a series. If, after checking out the marketplace, you think you have something truly original to offer, then believe in yourself and be convincing when you offer it around.

7. Network

• Writing can be a lonely business – don't work in a vacuum. Talk to others who write in the same genre or share a similar readership. You can meet them at literature festivals, conferences and book or writers' groups. Consider doing a course – see *Open evening* on page 638 and *Creative writing courses* on page 655.

• Go to a festival and be inspired! There are many literature festivals held throughout the year at which authors appear (see *Festivals for writers, artists and readers* on page 563 and *Festivals for writers* on page 481).

• Join one of the numerous online communities, book review and manuscript share sites; see *Book blogs* on page 610.

Publishers' contracts

Following a publishing company's firm interest in a MS, a publisher's contract is drawn up between the author and the publisher (see *Understanding publishing agreements* on page 114). If the author is not entirely happy with the contract presented to them or wishes to take advice, he/she could ask their literary agent, the Society of Authors (see page 485) or the Writers' Guild of Great Britain (see page 487) to check the contract on their behalf – providing the author has an agent and/or is a member of those organisations. Or you can seek advice from a solicitor. Before consulting a solicitor, make sure that they are familiar with publishing agreements and can give informed advice. Many local firms have little or no experience of such work and their opinion can often be of limited value meaning that the cost may outweigh any possible gains.

8. Don't give up!

• Agents receive hundreds of manuscripts every week. For an agent and publisher, there are many factors that have to be taken into consideration when evaluating these submissions, the most important of which is: 'Will it sell?' See *The publishing process* on page 109.

• Be prepared to wait for a decision on your work. Editors and agents are very busy people so be patient when waiting for a response. Don't pester them too soon.

• Publishing is big business and it is ever more competitive. Even after an editor has read your work, there are many other people involved before a manuscript is acquired for publication. People from the sales, marketing, publicity, rights and other departments all have to be convinced that the book is right for their list and will sell.

• The harsh reality of submitting a manuscript to a publisher or literary agent is that you have to be prepared for rejection. But many successful authors have received such rejections from a publisher at some time so you are in good company.

• For advice from established writers on how they first got into print see the articles under 'Inspirational writers' that start on page 241.

• Have patience and persevere. If the conventional route doesn't produce the results you were hoping for, consider the self-publishing route as a viable alternative.

Good luck!

Writing a synopsis

When publishers and literary agents ask for a synopsis to be submitted, writers often misunderstand what is required. Rebecca Swift provides clarification.

The dictionary definition of 'synopsis' (derived from the Ancient Greek meaning) is 'a brief description of the contents of something'. The purpose of a synopsis is to inform a literary agent or publisher of the type of book you are writing/have written in a concise, appealing fashion, conveying that you are in command of your subject matter. If you want your manuscript to be given serious consideration, a good synopsis is a crucial part of your submission.

This *Writers' & Artists' Yearbook* will inform you that most publishing houses no longer accept direct submissions but those that do (usually the smaller houses) will most often ask for a cover letter, synopsis and sample chapters rather than a whole work in the first instance. The same applies to literary agents. To put it simply, the sample chapters are to show how you write, and the synopsis is to tell the reader what happens when they have finished reading them. This will help inform the publisher/literary agent whether they think it is worth their while to read more. Then, if they want to read more, they will ask you.

So, the bottom line is this – if you want to have your manuscript read in its entirety you must invest time in getting your cover letter and book synopsis right. I know from my experiences at The Literary Consultancy (TLC) that many writers can get disconcerted and nervous by having to produce a synopsis and there are usually two reasons why.

First, a writer might have an unwieldy story that they themselves are not 100% convinced by, or a non-fiction project that they do not really know enough about. If this is so, summarising can be difficult because the thinking through and planning of the project has not been thorough in the first place.

In this instance, I would urge the writer to question why this process is so difficult. If it is because the story is insufficiently clear, persuasive or gripping, then more work needs to be done to get the manuscript into the kind of shape that would persuade an agent or editor to consider it further.

Second, a writer might genuinely be able to write a good book but not be experienced in the art of summarising a work in an effective manner. A few might even consider the act of doing so demeaning. If this is the case, I would urge you to think not of yourself, but of the reader, and treat the project as a literary exercise which you should try to enjoy: a challenge and opportunity to show your work off in its essential form. It might help to refer to book blurbs, or plot summaries in reference books such as *The Oxford Companion to English Literature*, or online, for example on Wikipedia.

In addition to letting a professional reader know what happens in your manuscript, the synopsis will also let them know at a glance if you have thought about how your work fits into the market. This is critical in non-fiction, less so with fiction, although with fiction awareness of what genre you have written in is vital. Also, if what you are writing coincides with any major anniversaries, for example, or might have a marketing 'hook' of any other kind, this is important to mention if not within the synopsis itself, then within a cover letter (see below).

Fiction synopses

A fiction synopsis should comprise a brief summary followed by a more detailed synopsis. But before writing either of these, you must clarify which genre your work fits into.

The most important thing to realise about fiction in respect of how you present it to representatives of the publishing industry is that it breaks down into different types, or genres. For those who think that the obsession with genres is a modern phenomenon, the lines from Polonius' famous speech in *Hamlet* might serve to prove the opposite. He describes the actors who have come to court as 'The best actors in the world . . . for tragedy, comedy, history, pastoral, pastoral-comical, historical-pastoral, scene individable, or poem unlimited'. Some of these dramatic forms are familiar and others not. There are always more genres being invented or cross-fertilised. It can be difficult to keep up!

The most popular genres today are, broadly speaking: crime, thriller, psychological thriller, detective, sci-fi, horror, comic, chick lit, lad's lit, historical, saga, literary, graphic, experimental, erotic, fantasy, romantic, women's commercial fiction and literary–commercial crossover – or, as it's becoming more widely coined, 'lit lite'.

Classifying your novel within a genre can be a challenge. This is largely because when most people start to write a novel they do so without having studied the genre they are writing for. Although when you start to write you may feel free to explore, practise and experiment without thinking in terms of the defining limits of a genre, by the time you come to submitting your work to be published it is very important to know which genre your work fits into. In all art forms there are rule breakers, but almost inevitably – as in the cases of Picasso, Virginia Woolf and, more recently, the US writer Michael Cunningham – even the greatest 'artists' have studied the traditional forms/genres before taking any risks.

A good starting point is to read books you consider similar to the one you are writing that are already published, and note how they are classified on the back cover. By reading, and sometimes studying literature and writing through other routes, you will also learn the possibilities and limits offered by your chosen genre. The bad news is, if you don't clarify what kind of book you have written, the chances are it will reflect in the text. If you don't clearly inform the agent or editor what your book is about and which category it falls into, it may all too quickly be labelled as a work which 'falls between two stools', is impossible to market and so doesn't get considered any further.

Writing a brief summary

Having made it your top priority to identify what type of novel you have written, you can make a start on your all-important synopsis. All good synopses should begin with a brief summary of 30–75 words, the sort of thing which appears on a book's back cover. For example, had you written *Pride and Prejudice* today:

> *Pride and Prejudice* is a contemporary, literary romance about a woman who falls in love with a man she thinks she hates.

Or,

> *Pride and Prejudice*, a contemporary, literary novel, tells the story of Elizabeth Bennet, a proud, intelligent woman, one of five sisters, whose mother is committed to marrying her children off as a matter of urgency. Elizabeth meets Darcy, owner of a grand estate, but considers him overly proud, arrogant and undesirable. In time, she learns that he is not all that he appears to be, and revises her prejudice, before they fall deeply in love.

Both these examples, one short, one longer, serve to whet the appetite for more detail to follow.

An example of an ostensibly weak synopsis, which rambles and fails to emphasise the most important points quickly enough, might be:

> Set at some point in the 19th century, five sisters are looking for husbands. Or is Mary, really? Anyway, their mother is a real fusspot and annoys everybody. Outside their house there are lots of fields and it is sometimes raining. The girls' father is gentle and kind, with grey hair but not good at standing up to his wife always. Mr Bingley is an important character who is very handsome, but is he as handsome as Mr Darcy? It is hard to tell!

Hopefully you can see the clear differences between the two.

Writing a detailed synopsis

Following the brief summary should be a more detailed synopsis of 350–450 words. Literary agents do not want a detailed chapter-by-chapter breakdown (if they do, they'll ask for one) as reading them can be tiresome and difficult to follow. The main aim of the longer synopsis is to give a detailed overview which clearly and concisely conveys how the story flows and unfolds, and (very importantly) what is interesting about it. The longer synopsis should also reconfirm when the story is set (i.e. is it contemporary or historical?); the setting or background (e.g. is it Thatcher's government in its last throes or are we in a quiet Devonshire village where nothing ever happens, but there is a sense of impending doom?); inform the reader about the central character (i.e. what is interesting about them and what happens on their journey), as well as giving brief reference to other characters that are directly pivotal to the plot. The longer synopsis should also highlight the dramatic turning points and tell the reader of any other salient information which will help convey what kind of work it is, how well imagined the characters are and how well thought through and alluring the plot is.

Cover letter

Alongside the synopsis should also be an excellent, economically written and confident sounding cover letter. This should simply address a well-researched literary agent by name (never put a generic 'Dear Sir/Madam').

In this you should say that you are enclosing a novel called 'X', which is a thriller/literary/coming-of-age/horror novel (identify genre). It does not matter if this is repeated on the synopsis page. You may also wish to refer to writers you feel you are similar to, although do be careful not to have misplaced arrogance in this. You might say, 'I write in the genre of John Grisham because he is a writer I read and hugely admire' or you might say, 'This is a novel in which *To Kill a Mockingbird* meets *Crash*' or 'Harper Lee meets J.G. Ballard' – but do be sure that you have the talent to match claims like these. Otherwise, let the agent decide and they will help market you to the publisher, and the publisher will then help market you to the public. If you admire an agent for a particular reason, for example because they publish a hero or heroine of yours, let them know.

Biographical note

If you have something interesting to say about yourself, such as that you have won a writing competition or have been published before in relevant publications, do include this briefly in the cover letter. It is for you to judge what is of particular interest about you, and how much to say, but you should also provide a fuller biographical note which sits well at the bottom of the synopsis page. As a guide, this should be 50–200 words. If you have been published, provide a summarised list of publications here. If you have not, or are trying to hide a career you think has gone off track and want to appear fresh, keep it brief and mention what you do, your age and anything that makes you sound interesting. If your career is related to your subject matter, then do say this. For example, 'I worked as a miner for 20 years' if your book is set in a mining community. Avoid listing technical publications as evidence of writing ability if you are submitting fiction. There is an enormous difference between writing technically and writing fiction, and if you don't seem to know this it is not impressive. This is different for non-fiction. As a rule, err on the side of brevity if necessary. If the reader loves your work they will be in touch to find out more about you. For help with learning how to self-market, read *Marketing Your Book: An Author's Guide* by Alison Baverstock (Bloomsbury 2007, 2nd edn).

It should be noted that if the work is literary, there may be less emphasis on plot and more on the quality of the prose. Due to current climates and publishing trends, this is a difficult time to publish literary fiction without strong plots, although things undoubtedly will change.

Non-fiction synopses

A synopsis for a work of non-fiction performs a different function. The consideration of whether a non-fiction book has a potential market is generally more straightforward than for new fiction. In the case of non-fiction you should certainly have carefully researched your market before submission and ideally list the competitors in the field, outlining why your project is different and why you are the writer best positioned to write the book you have. Further, you should be able to list any marketing opportunities your book may have, such as anniversary tie-ins, identifiable or even guaranteed readers – students, for example – if you teach a course and so on.

A literary agent is often prepared to sell a non-fiction work on synopsis and chapters only. This is an extreme rarity in the case of fiction. This is because it is easier for people to see if there is a gap in the market that can be filled by a non-fiction project, before the work is finished.

You may not need an agent for particular, more niche types of non-fiction book. In these cases publishers may well be prepared to take a direct submission from you. Again, this is because in the area of self-help or business books for example, the publisher of a list will know clearly what its gaps are. The list may have a standard format and you should certainly research this. Contact editors of specialised lists to find out if they have space for your idea, and so that they can let you know exactly how they like work to be presented before forming the project in your mind.

I think it best in general for the non-fiction writer to prepare two different types of proposal. The first would form an initial pitch and the second the follow-up proposal if the editor or literary agent asks to see more. Both documents need to be thoroughly persuasive as these may go directly towards securing a book deal.

Pitching for non-fiction

This should be no more than one or two pages. Include a brief summary (e.g. '*Flying High* is a book about the history of aeronautics' or '*My Name was Glory* is the biography of

Amanda Flemming, maid to Queen Gertrude and unknown holder of the Secret Chalice') and a description of the book content, with an argument for why it should be published now and why you are qualified to write it. Ideally, you should also include an overview of other work in the field and argue why yours fills an important gap. In addition, you should include a chapter breakdown, giving a provisional title for each chapter with a brief summary (30–75 words, as a guide only) of the contents of each chapter to show how the book is structured throughout. Here also, spell out any ideas you have about how the book might be marketed. As non-fiction markets are more specific than fiction markets, it is useful for the author to let the agent or editor know what hooks there might be to help sell copies. As I have said, if you are lucky enough to have any guaranteed markets, such as students on a course you teach, do of course inform the industry of this.

If you can, estimate a word count for the work. For some pre-formatted non-fiction titles, there will be a word length you will be expected to hit anyway. You will discover this as you research.

A more in-depth synopsis with sample chapter should include the initial pitch, but with any added material you can muster in terms of promoting your position as author or the book's market chances. Most importantly, in this second, longer pitch you need to show that you can write the book. Provide more in-depth chapter breakdowns (100–150 words each) and 5,000–10,000 words of polished, irresistibly clear and well-written text to show that you are capable of executing your intentions in a winning manner. Write the introduction and the opening chapter, if possible, to really show you mean business. Those two together would usually add up to 5,000–10,000 words.

Conclusion

Whilst it is worth spending time ensuring you have a good, short, confident cover letter and synopsis, it is important to stress that there is nothing as important to an editor than the quality of your writing and your ability to sustain the interest of a reader in the main body of the text. A synopsis is not a magic wand that will influence the real standard of a work. I have seen perfectly polished synopses followed by poor writing. The net result of this is that one feels excited, only to be let down, which is off-putting in itself. If you have the skill to write a gripping synopsis, use your energies wisely in advance of submitting to make sure that the book itself is as good as it can be. Focus, particularly, on fine-tuning the opening 50 pages. Your synopsis and summary should generally serve as a flag to indicate to the reader at what point the extract begins and a guide to the story beyond it. If the agent or publisher likes what they see well enough to ask for more . . . well done! Oh and good luck.

Rebecca Swift worked as an editor at Virago Press and writer, before co-founding The Literary Consultancy (www.literaryconsultancy.co.uk) with Hannah Griffiths in 1996. She has edited two books for Chatto & Windus, published poetry in *Staple*, *Vintage New Writing* and *Virago New Poets*, written an opera libretto, *Spirit Child*, and *Poetic Lives: Dickinson* (Hesperus Press 2011).

See also...

- *How to get an agent*, page 392
- *Letter to an unsolicited author*, page 404
- *The publishing process*, page 109

The publishing process

To someone who has never worked in publishing, seeing a typescript transformed into a book can seem almost magical. In reality the process is fairly straightforward, but there is real magic in the way that different departments work together to give each book the best possible chance of success. Bill Swainson explains the process.

Let's imagine a medium-sized publishing house that's big enough to have a fairly clear division of roles. I will describe the different stages of a book's journey as it metamorphoses from a typescript or digital file into a brand new book on a bookshop's shelves and/or an ebook in an e-tailer's catalogue.

Acquiring a book

Every publishing company acquires its books from similar sources, from literary agents, publishers in other countries, direct commissions from editors to authors and, very occasionally, from unsolicited proposals taken from what is known unceremoniously as the 'slush pile'. The in-house selection process goes something like this:

• The commissioning editor finds a book from among his or her regular weekly reading and makes a case for taking it on at an 'acquisitions meeting', which is attended by all the other departments directly involved in publishing the book, including sales, marketing, publicity and rights.

• Lively discussions follow and final decisions are determined from a mixture of commercial good sense (estimated sales figures, likely production costs and the author's track record) and taste – and the preferences of every company and every editor are different.

Getting the word out

Shortly after a book has been acquired, the commissioning editor will draft an 'advance information' (AI) sheet. This is the earliest attempt to harness the excitement that led to the book being signed, and it contains all the basic information needed by the rest of the company, including the title, ISBN, format, extent (number of pages), price, rights holder, sales points, quotes about previous books, short blurb and biographical note. It is the first of many pieces of 'copy' that will be written about the book, and will be used as the template for all the others, such as a catalogue entry, jacket blurb or press release.

A structural edit

As soon as the text arrives in the editorial department, it receives a 'structural edit'. In the case of a novel, this involves the commissioning editor looking at everything from the book's structure and narrative pacing to characterisation and general style. In the case of non-fiction, it also means considering whether illustrations, appendices, bibliography, notes and an index are needed.

Copy-editing

Next comes the copy-editing. This is designed to catch all the errors and inconsistencies in the text, from spelling and punctuation to facts, figures and tics of style. Most publishing houses now do this work on screen.

Once the copy-edit is finished, the author will be asked to review and approve the copy-edited text and answer any queries that may have arisen; and this is also the author's last chance to make significant changes. When the editor, copy-editor and author are happy that the marked-up typescript is in the best possible shape, it is sent to the production department for design and typesetting.

Design and typesetting

Long before they receive the typescript, designers will have got to work on the book's cover or jacket. It's crucial to get this right, if only because most (if not all) buying decisions are made before the book is printed. Up until that time, the cover is the book – it influences the trade buyers and, ultimately, it's one of the most important factors in encouraging customers to pick up the book and pay for it at the till.

Your editors will brief the production team on how they'd like your text typeset, which includes choosing a typeface. The production department will draft a 'type specification' or 'spec'. This may be created specifically for an individual book or a series spec will be used to give the latest volume the same look and feel as its predecessors.

The typescript is then usually despatched to an out-of-house typesetter to be turned into page proofs. Shortly before printing, the production manager (working with the commissioning editor and the designer) will choose the binding materials and any embellishments, such as headband, coloured or printed endpapers, or marker ribbon.

Ironing out the glitches

When the book has been typeset, the proofs normally shuttle back and forth in three stages.

• First proofs are read by the author and a proofreader. This is the last chance an author gets to make amendments.

• Second proofs, or 'revises', are checked against the collated first proofs and any last-minute queries are attended to. If an index is needed, it is compiled at this stage.

• The changes to the 'revises' result in third proofs which, in a perfect world, are checked against the second proofs and passed for press. Once in a while this actually happens!

• Ebooks also benefit from these processes, plus special ones for electronic text to enable the words to be reflowed in different fonts and sizes according to the reader's preference and the capability of their e-reader. The process is known in-house as 'qa' (quality assurance) and it involves checking the electronic file against the print version for any errors that may have crept in during the conversion process. However, in the future this process may become redundant as XML setting, which does not require conversion for ebook, takes over.

Going to press

Most publishing companies use only a few printers, with whom they are used to negotiating. A key role of the production department is to buy print at a rate that allows each tightly budgeted book to make money and – just as importantly – to manage the supply of reprints so that the publisher's warehouse is never short of stock. The initial print run (based on advance sales, track record and current state of the market) will be decided at a 'print-fix' meeting and the order placed with the printer. In the case of the ebook, distribution to various e-tailers is the equivalent.

Sales

'Selling in' in the home market (Britain and Ireland) is increasingly done by key account managers working with the chain buyers, as well as by a team of area managers or sales representatives. The reps visit bookshops in their designated area and try to achieve the sales targets set for each book. The number of copies sold pre-publication is known as the subscription sale, or 'sub'.

Selling books effectively to bookshops, supermarkets, other retailers and internet stores takes time and careful planning. The British and Irish book trade has developed in such a way that the sales cycle has extended to cover the best part of a year.

Many sales are also made in-house by phone and email, and via the internet. Most publishers have their own websites and provide customers with the opportunity to buy their books either directly or from another bookselling website.

Export sales are achieved using teams of international agents and reps run from the in-house export sales department. Here format, discount, royalty rates, shipping, and exchange rates are the key components. The margins are much tighter and it requires a lot of skill and chutzpah to generate significant sales and then to maintain a successful international presence.

Just like print sales, ebook sales come through a mixture of marketing, publicity, word of mouth and online promotion.

Marketing

The marketing department works alongside both the sales and publicity teams. It creates materials that help to sell the book – catalogues, 'blads' (literally 'book layout and design' – illustrated sales material), 'samplers' (booklets containing tantalising extracts), posters, and book proofs (bound reading proofs). Much of this work is now done through websites and social media, creating electronic extracts, and digital assets to promote the book and encourage pre-order.

The marketing department continues to create materials to sell the book on publication to the reader – building advertising campaigns across all types of media – the more imaginative often the better. The more traditional campaigns include London Underground or national rail poster advertising, press print advertising, digital advertising across various websites and promoted social media activity. This advertising activity, along with reviews and other publicity, entices customers into the shops to buy a particular book. It is at this stage especially that the marketing department will work very closely with the publicity department.

It also organises the company sales conferences at which the new season's publishing is presented for the first time to the sales reps and overseas agents. The run-up to the sales conference and the event itself is an exciting time and stimulates many of the best ideas on how to sell the new books.

Publicity

The publicity department works with the author and the media on 'free' publicity with the emphasis on the 'sell through'. This covers reviews, features, author interviews, bookshop readings and signings, festival appearances, book tours and radio and television interviews, and so on.

For each author and their book, the publicity department devises a campaign that will play to the book's or the author's strengths. For instance, best use will be made of written features or radio interviews for authors who are shy in public, just as full advantage will be made of public appearances for those authors who thrive on the thrill of showmanship.

In short, the publicist's careful work (which like much of publishing is a mixture of inspiration, enthusiasm, efficient planning and flexibility) is designed to get the best results for each individual author and title.

The rights department

It is the aim of this department to make the best use of all the rights that were acquired when the contract was first negotiated between publisher and author or the author's agent.

While literary agents are understandably keen to handle foreign and serial rights, many publishing houses have well-developed rights departments with good contacts and are also well placed to sell the rights of a book. Selling rights is very varied and includes anything from dealing with requests for film or television rights, the sale of translation rights to other countries, or serial rights to a newspaper, to smaller permission requests to reprint a poem or an extract. All are opportunities to promote the book and earn additional income for author and publisher, and at the time of first publication the rights, sales, marketing and publicity departments all work closely together.

Book fairs are key venues for the sale of foreign rights. At the Frankfurt Book Fair in October and at the London Book Fair in April, publishers and agents from all participating countries meet to form a rights 'bazaar'. Here, editors have the opportunity to hear about and sometimes even buy new books from publishing houses all over the world.

Paperbacks

Typically paperbacks are published a year after the original hardback publication (if there *is* a hardback). Paperback publishing is a key part of publishing today, and efforts are made to identify and broaden the likely market (readership) for a book, making sure that the cover and presentation will appeal to a wide audience. It's important to be creative and to position an author's books in the marketplace where they can be best seen, bought and read.

Accounts

Every successful business needs a good finance department. Most publishing houses split the work into two areas – purchase ledger and royalties. Purchase ledger deals with all incoming invoices associated with the company's business. The royalties department deals exclusively with author advances (payable on acquisition, and on delivery or publication of a book) and with keeping account of the different royalty percentages payable on book sales, serial deals, film rights, permissions, etc. This is done so that both author and agent can see that an accurate record has been kept against the happy day when the book earns back its advance (the point at which the royalties earned equal the advance paid) and the author starts earning additional income.

A special business

Publishing is a business, and commercial considerations will be apparent in every department; but it is a very special kind of business that frequently breaks many of the accepted rules and often seems to make no sense at all – just think of the hundreds of different lines, formats, price points and discounts! It shouldn't work – but somehow, miraculously, it does – as long as it is able to keep up with the pace of change.

Bill Swainson has worked for small, medium and large publishers since 1976 and was most recently a Senior Commissioning Editor at Bloomsbury Publishing Plc, where he edited non-fiction and fiction, including in translation.

See also...

- *Understanding publishing agreements*, page 114
- *How literary agencies work*, page 389
- *Electronic publishing*, page 573
- *Editing your work*, page 629

Understanding publishing agreements

Publishers usually require authors or their agents to sign a written legal contract when they decide to publish a book. Gillian Haggart Davies demystifies some of the clauses in such agreements.

Publishing agreements are contracts and are governed by contract law, the defining feature of which is that it treats parties to the contract as being of equal standing. To put this in context, in other areas the law deems that there is a 'weaker party' who needs to be protected, for example in employment and discrimination law a person with disabilities or a pregnant employee is deemed 'weaker' than the employer organisation. But this is not so with publishing agreements, albeit that we all know the reality of the situation is that the author/writer is the one (usually) who wants a publishing deal and the publisher, in certain circumstances, can take it or leave it so can dictate the terms.

If you have a literary agent, she or he should handle all these issues for you; and if you are a member of the Writers' Guild (see page 487), the National Union of Journalists (NUJ, page 517) or the Society of Authors (see page 485), they will help review the details of a contract. The main resource for lawyers in this field is *Clark's Publishing Agreements* (ed. Lynette Owen; Bloomsbury Professional 2013, 9th edn) which costs a hefty £142. It sets out standard form contracts for various kinds of publications. The contract for 'General book–author–publisher' has 35 clauses, some of which are 'legal nuts and bolts' and need not concern us too much – they are there to ensure the contract operates properly and can be enforced (e.g. 'Arbitration', 'Interpretation', 'Entire Agreement', '*force majeure*', 'Notices'). According to *Clark's*, 'The contract should empower both author and publisher with the confidence that each party will do its job to mutual advantage', and that a simple structure underlies all publishing contracts:

> 'The author owns the copyright in their work. In return for various payments, he/she licenses to the publisher, primarily exclusively, the right principally as readable text (printed book and ebook) to create multiple copies of that book and the further right to license others to exploit it in both readable text and other forms. The author writes; the publisher invests; from sales of copies of the book that they create together and the licensing of rights in it, the author earns royalties and other earnings, and the publisher makes its profit. It is as simple – and as complicated – as that.'

You may also want to refer to the Publishers Association Code of Practice on Author Contracts (www.publishers.org.uk) to see what the publishing industry suggested standards are and consult *The Media and Business Contracts Handbook* by Deborah Fosbrook and Adrian C. Laing (Bloomsbury Professional 2014, 5th edn).

So, there is a basic structure, and some clauses are 'more fundamental' than others. We do have judicial precedent suggesting that at the very least a publishing contract, to be accepted by the courts as such, must have terms dealing with royalties (or fees), print run and form of publication (e.g. hardback, paperback, etc). It can be a contract with those three things alone, and even if it is an implied or a verbal agreement, and as such can be enforced (in that case successfully by an author against the publisher.

What follows are some of the other more significant clauses which will be key for writers. Whatever kind of contract you see, remember that in principle you can add, delete and amend any of the clauses in it. In practical terms, it will depend on how much clout you or your agent have as to whether your publisher will be happy to negotiate or not and, perhaps to a certain extent, on the time available.

Rights

Rights are multiple and sub-divisible. You can license them outright or in part (e.g. sound recording not images, script not film, illustrations not text, English translation not other languages), and do so for a set period of time or forever (i.e. the duration of the copyright). You can choose the territory. You can grant exclusive or non-exclusive rights. *Clark's* lists 23 varieties of rights but that is not necessarily exhaustive.

It is key that you license and do not *assign* your rights as assignation is almost impossible to reverse. If you must assign copyright, note that you would have a small chance of legal protection because the publisher may owe you 'fiduciary duties', i.e. be obliged to look after your best interests; but this would be very difficult and costly to enforce and the best advice would always be to *never* assign rights.

Most publishers will want 'all rights' and 'world rights', but you or your agent may want to negotiate to retain certain rights. Consider whether the publisher would consult you before transferring their rights to a third party: they should. Would the publisher act on your behalf if someone else is in breach of your copyright? Would the publisher protect your work to the best possible extent? For example, if the work is posted online, would it be tagged for permissions information to enable anyone who wants to reuse it to find you or the publisher in order to ask permission? Subsidiary rights include, for example, anthology rights.

Serial rights are generally offered as 'first' and 'second'. First serial rights are often retained by authors and refer to the right to publish elsewhere (e.g. in a magazine feature in advance of a book's publication). Second serial rights can belong to a different party and are often controlled by the publisher. They concern rights to reprint after publication.

There have been calls for less slicing up of the copyright cake into so many individual rights, with the industry increasingly accepting the need to take a '360-degree' approach to intellectual property. However, this is a work in progress.

All of the above relates to the 'economic copyright' rights, but authors have moral rights too; see the PA Code of Practice on Author Contracts and the government's IPO website (www.ipo.gov.uk).

Delivery, acceptance and approval

The publisher will want to make sure it is not committing itself to publishing work which is not what it commissioned or not as expected and should of course be able to reject work which is poor, or which it considers to be factually incorrect or libellous, or unlawfully copied from someone else. But what can you do if a publisher wants to reject your work for another reason, perhaps because the market or competition has changed since you were commissioned? The Society of Authors in the past used to advise writers to not sign 'acceptance' clauses for this type of reason, arguing that publishers should fully assess the work by asking for a synopsis and specimen chapters, rather than letting an author complete the work, submit it and have it rejected. You may be powerless to remove such a clause but it is something to be aware of.

Timing of publication may also be important. For example, if you are writing a law book and the publisher fails to send it to press within a reasonable time, the book may well be so out of date as to be useless, and consequently your reputation would suffer as well as sales. You won't want to revise it without payment of a further fee. Another example may be that the publisher has budgetary reasons for the timing of publication or may want to link, for example, a sports book with an event such as the opening of the Commonwealth Games. These types of situations may be covered in a clause about 'Date of publication' or 'Publisher's responsibility to publish'.

Think about the details as well. What are you agreeing to deliver? For example, with some textbooks you may also be agreeing to deliver pictures as well as text, but is it clear who clears copyright permissions for the pictures? And who pays for it? The publisher may give you a budget to do this work or may just expect it to have been done, and if so, and if you have not done it, that could jeopardise the whole enterprise because it can be not only an expensive but potentially very lengthy process.

Some contracts may also require you to be around for editing queries within a certain time-period – failing which the publisher will bring someone else in to edit. Would you be happy with that? Is that a term in the contract? This also touches moral rights. Are you agreeing to future updates of the book within the fee?

Remember to check the termination clause ('break clause') too. No one is thinking about a relationship breaking down when a deal is being signed, but the reality is that things can go wrong and one party may want to get out. Publishing relationships tend to be personal and so in reality, if one party wants to go, the other party should probably think about letting this happen.

If a publisher decides to shelve publication of your book, the publisher might be in breach of contract; but in practice, it would be very difficult for an author in that situation to get an order from the court compelling the publisher to honour the contract and publish – especially if the book hasn't been edited yet. The author would have to claim for damages, and probably for payment of advances as yet unclaimed (subject to the contract terms), and possibly for loss of earnings for future editions if this pivots around cancellation of a first edition. But this is all about power and reputation and the lesser-known or unknown author may struggle to win such a fight and, more so, to be able to afford to go into battle in the first place. However, there is some hope if you are looking for it – in *Malcolm* v. *OUP* [1994] EMLR 17 Court of Appeal, around £17,500 was awarded against the publisher in favour of the disappointed author (although the court costs could easily be around the same again for such an author).

Outside the law of contract, any author who considers they have been wrongfully treated may also look to other areas of the law to support their case (for damage to goodwill and reputation under copyright moral rights; defamation; passing off, etc).

Alternatively, a publisher may have to enforce its rights and publish despite an author wishing to back out (say, to go with another publisher). The publisher will be legally entitled to do so depending on what the author signed up to, so be mindful of how long you are agreeing to tie yourself into a deal and how soon you can get out of it, if it is possible to do so. Ultimately, if authors break their side of the deal they will probably have to pay back any advances, and potentially damages too (although the courts do say that the damages sum claimed must be reasonably quantifiable by the party claiming loss: a difficult point to prove if the book wasn't even written, never mind marketed, etc). Again, it is about reputation and clout: when Penguin took legal action against Elizabeth Wurtzel for failure to deliver a follow-up to *Prozac Nation* (and for return of a $33,000 advance), and the case 'settled amicably', hefty sums of money were involved, albeit that the publisher is not prepared to disclose the final sum agreed.

Warranties and indemnities

With warranties and indemnities you 'warrant' to the publisher that you have done certain things like fact-checking, copyright clearance, checking there are no libellous or blasphemous or plagiarised statements and promise to 'indemnify' them against any losses they may suffer as a result of anything like that happening after publication. Indeed, careful publishers may want a lawyer to read your text (depending on what it is) to check for these things before publication. Is there a clause saying if this happens the publisher will bill you the author for the 'legalling'? I have seen some lawyer–authors strike warranties and indemnities out. In practice, you need to consider whether you would be in a financial position to indemnify a publisher against its loss – most individuals wouldn't be, especially against libel actions. (Remember, you cannot defame the dead but you can defame a business entity, so beware when writing blogs.) However, you may be confident that no issues will arise (famous last words); or you may be happy that you are 'decree proof' (no point suing you, you have no money); or you may have professional indemnity or another kind of insurance. Insurance is something authors should consider especially if they are writing on particular subjects (e.g. writing about medical dosages) or are of a certain profile.

Exclusion clauses and limitations of liability

The publisher may wish to exclude liability for certain eventualities. For example it may wish to exclude liability for any damage the author might suffer to her name because of the publication (loss of reputation), or might suffer 'loss of opportunity' (say if the contract is exclusive to one publisher and prevents him from taking the content off elsewhere). Note, however, that some contractual exclusions of liability – or purported exclusions – may fail (i.e. be legally unenforceable). For example, this may be the case if a publisher tried to prevent an author from including parody or satire in her work, fearing it may cause offence to some other author. Such a clause would technically now be unenforceable (in copyright terms anyway) because parody and satire is 'allowed' as a defence to breach of copyright. That said, in practice, the subject of the parody could have other civil law remedies against the publisher and/or author. The late Ronnie Barker hated Ben Elton's *Not the Nine O'Clock News* pastiche entitled 'The Two Ninnies', but Ronnie Barker would probably have never thought that this was a copyright issue; it was insult and injury to his reputation and goodwill that mattered to him in that kind of instance. In which case, the separate legal issues of libel and passing-off would arise. A publisher could also seek to avoid liability for those issues by including an exclusion clause in a publishing contract.

Royalty advances and payment

An 'advance' is an advance on royalties which will be earned on book sales. This is different from a flat fee that is paid for a commission. Obviously, royalties are a very good thing if sales are to be significant, but they are perhaps less useful to authors whose markets are small, such as academic or specialised areas, or for children's authors who receive lower royalty rates (say 5% of the book's published price rather than the 10% a writer of fiction for adults might receive), albeit perhaps dealing with bigger volumes. Some novelists receive huge advances that are never recouped by the publisher; the writers will receive royalty statements reporting a deficit but most publishers do not expect that deficit to be repaid. Clarifying what would happen about an unrecouped advance is therefore crucial. (Keep royalty statements for tax reasons: declare royalties as 'income' not 'other expenses'; losses/ unrecouped advances are 'expenses' for income tax.)

If you are to receive royalties only, or an advance on royalties, it is important that someone is actually going to market the book. The clause 'Production and promotion responsibility' refers to this.

If the royalties payable to you are expressed as a percentage of estimated receipts (what the publisher actually earns from the sale of your book) rather than as a percentage of the book's published price, you will want to ask the publisher what they estimate receipts to be. However, the publisher may wish that information to be confidential.

Date of payment

As an author, when do you want to be paid? Probably on receipt by the publisher of your typescript at the latest, if not on commission – depending on the job and your status. You do not want to be paid 'on publication' because for reasons beyond your control the book may never be published, for example due to the publisher going bust.

When does a publisher want to pay? Possibly not on receipt of the typescript because there is still the copy-editing, typesetting and printing to carry out.

Payment in three stages is pretty standard – on signature; on delivery of the typescript; and on the day of first UK publication. Four stages are also possible: as with three but with the third stage broken down into publication of hardback and of paperback editions.

The contract

As with most things in life, it is best to avoid contention, adversity and dispute where possible. Bear in mind that most publishers will be using a precedent form, i.e. a pro forma document. This may be historical or inherited from another part of the publishing group or a subsidiary/parent group and edited for your particular publication, so do not be surprised if it needs tweaking or renegotiating on issues which are important to you. Be firm and be understanding. The contract is possibly not the author's preferred focus, and it might also be a chore for the publisher.

Note too that you may have legal rights and remedies from areas of the law which are external to the contract, i.e. some things that are not explicitly written down in a contract may be enforceable by you under equity, breach of confidence, etc. The Contracts (Rights of Third Parties) Act 1999 might be interpreted by lawyers to mean that if an author tells the publisher to 'pay my royalties to my friend', the friend gets the legal right to sue the publisher under the contract if this does not happen.

Publishing agreements are a minefield but if you can think about what is most important for you, your publication and its markets, whilst also being aware of some of the issues noted above, you will at least be off to a good start.

Gillian Haggart Davies MA (Hons), LLB is the author of *Copyright Law for Artists, Designers and Photographers* (A&C Black 2010) and *Copyright Law for Writers, Editors and Publishers* (A&C Black 2011).

Promoting and selling your book

Book authors today – whether traditionally published or self-published – are increasingly involved in publicising their work. Mainstream publishers have their own staff to market, publicise and sell their books, but authors are often invited or even required to contribute to this process. Katie Bond outlines the main ways that authors can promote their books.

Newspapers are full of discouraging stories about how publishers only want to take on novels by glamorous young things or football manager memoirs or comedians' autobiographies. Let's quash that immediately: publishers want to publish the best books they can find in a wide variety of genres and sell the socks off them. But the days of the author scribbling in an attic loftily above the demands of commerce are long gone. Forget J.D. Salinger. In the UK over 150,000 new books are published each year and successful authors strike a balance between the solitary art of writing and the business side of joining the publishing industry, being part of the writing community and engaging with readers and potential readers online and in person. You can start by signing up to the free daily emails from the *Bookseller* (www.thebookseller.com) and from Book2Book (www.booktrade.info), which both give you the headlines of what's happening in the book industry and a good overview of the market and breaking stories. Publishers like 'promotable authors' as they can increase sales, and this article outlines the run-up to publication. My aim is to suggest how all authors – whether they are with a mainstream publisher or are self-published – can give their book a push.

Word-of-mouth sales

Personal recommendation is the number one factor in influencing a purchase according to every book-buying survey. The most powerful sales tool in publishing is word of mouth and this begins in-house. A commissioning editor can entice everyone in the company to read a book so that a hundred people are talking about it – every mention is a potential sale. *The Kite Runner* by Khaled Hosseini was a slow-burn book that took two years to become an international bestseller and reading group favourite. Such was the passion of its editor, Arzu Tahsin, for this novel that everyone at Bloomsbury read it and was 100% behind the book. Everyone played a part in its success by recommending the book to friends. If an author is aware of this, every person you meet – at your publishing house (whether they're in the accounts department, on reception or the Sales Director), in bookshops and libraries, or indeed anywhere in your professional capacity as 'an author' – becomes a VIP. I will never forget William Boyd – the first author I spoke to in my first job as a publicity assistant – asking and remembering my name and chatting to me when he called to speak to my boss. Having read and loved his books at university, I would have walked over hot coals to make sure that *The Blue Afternoon* was a success and any request of his was instantly top of my list. Geographical distance from your publisher may mean that you don't get the chance to visit them often but do try to meet as many people in different departments as possible, go to book launches and readings, keep an eye on your publisher's website and social media feeds and find out if your local sales rep would like to meet up for coffee when they're next on your patch.

Social media

Social media is the magic new ingredient in the publishing mix which empowers authors, publishers and readers to befriend and follow each other, promote books and hugely augment word-of-mouth recommendation and reach. Twitter keeps you up to date with the latest books news and enables you to join communities and conversations about books worldwide. It's fun, free and horribly addictive. Riot Communications (@RiotComms) recommends splitting your social media content three ways – a third about your books, a third personal and a third of general interest. Don't just broadcast on and on like the dinner party bore, but initiate and join in conversations. Short and snappy is vital, funny is ideal and positive will get more pick-up. The literary maestros of Twitter are Neil Gaiman (@neilhimself) and Margaret Atwood (@MargaretAtwood). Also look at how Georgina Moore at Headline (@publicitybooks) and Sam Eades (@SamEades) at Pan Macmillan create a buzz about the books they're promoting. Whether it's Facebook friends, Twitter followers, Pinterest pins, YouTube, Vine Videos or a lively blog, ask your publisher for social media tips, find a channel you enjoy and dedicate an hour a day to it.

Marketing and publicity

Marketing is an umbrella term that includes all the work a publisher does to promote or sell a book. Traditionally, 'marketing' is categorised as anything paid for (catalogues, advertising, posters and bookshop promotions) and 'publicity' (media coverage and author events at bookshops and festivals) is free. Social media has blurred this distinction and a good marketing and publicity duo can pull off a dazzling online campaign with virtually no marketing budget. There will be a person in both marketing and publicity departments assigned to your book and creating good relationships with both of them is crucial. Ask your editor to let you know who they are and contact them as early as possible to meet up and decide on a marketing and publicity plan.

The sell-in

The sales process begins 6–9 months prior to publication when the sales team use the marketing and publicity plans to begin selling books to the head offices of the major book chains – from Waterstones to Tesco, Amazon and the wholesalers who supply independent bookshops. Closer to publication, local sales reps also sell books to individual bookshops in their areas although the front-of-store promotions ('Read of the Week', '2 for 3', 'Book of the Month', etc) will be decided at head office level. The 'sell-in' is the process of persuading the bookshops to stock a particular book. The marketing department produces sell-in materials including six-monthly catalogues promoting the publisher's spring and autumn lists, and AIs (advance information sheets), bound proofs and glossy brochures on individual books. The initial print run for a book is based on the sell-in figures of advance orders placed for it. The speed at which a book can be reprinted (except highly illustrated and special format books) minimises the clash between publisher caution and author optimism and prevents lost sales if the initial print run sells out quickly.

The sell-out

This is the magic moment when a customer decides to buy a book. Marketing and publicity are geared towards boosting the sell-out in myriad ways from advertising, media and social media coverage to book jacket design and bookseller recommendation. A survey reported in the *Bookseller* revealed, 'The consumer needs at least five positive mentions of a product as well as easy availability before he will buy'. In a crowded marketplace, clear signposting is essential to enable the book to reach its target readership.

The book jacket and author photograph

'Never judge a book by its cover' is an outdated maxim. This is the most important marketing tool of all and can make or break a publication. Even if an old family portrait inspired your book, don't insist on having it on the cover if it isn't an eye-catching image. Conversely, do research what books in your genre look like to get a feel for the market, ransack old photograph albums, magazines and art galleries for images that you love and that you think are right for your book, and liaise closely with your editor who will brief the design team. For the author photograph, definitely allow yourself a little vanity – really good colour and black-and-white portraits are a must for publicity purposes and you want to look your absolute best.

Owning the digital space

Every author needs a web presence – whether it's a website, Facebook page or Tumblr blog. This is your own shop front/soap box to showcase your books, post all your latest news and create a community for your readers. For the wow factor check out www.worldofwalliams.com, www.jacquelinewilson.co.uk, www.thehungergames.co.uk and www.johnlecarre.com. Also have a look at www.jonmcgregor.com, one of my favourite author websites because I can hear Jon's voice in the copy and it showcases everything he believes in without creating an unmanageable workload of maintenance. Debut novelist Samantha Shannon is also working the digital space brilliantly. She combines her blog 'A Book from the Beginning' http://samantha-shannon.blogspot.co.uk with *The Bone Season* Facebook community www.facebook.com/TheBoneSeason and a Tumblr site http://sshannonauthor.tumblr.com. Talk to your marketer about what they think will work best for you and (budget permitting) get techie input on design and SEO (search engine optimisation); but most important of all keep it authentic, true to your books and simple enough that you can update it regularly and easily.

Publicity

Book publicity is incredibly varied and widespread from reviews to features, discussions to news stories, public appearances at bookshops, libraries and literary festivals to local stock signings and books for competition prizes. As a rough guide, a publicist starts work on book tours and long-lead magazine features 6–9 months ahead of publication. Finished copies of a book are printed approximately 4–6 weeks prior to publication and this period is the key time for confirming the media coverage. The publication date is the peg for the media, so coverage becomes increasingly unlikely months or even weeks after the publication date unless the book has taken off in a major way and its success becomes the story.

How authors can help

There is a limited amount that an author can do to help sales and marketing directly beyond being very nice to booksellers and librarians, providing details of any specialist sales outlets prior to publication and (gently, not forcefully) offering to sign copies of your book in bookshops after publication (having first checked anonymously that the bookshop does have copies in stock). If a bookshop doesn't have your book in stock, let your publisher know rather than complaining to the bookshop directly.

Authors can best focus their energies on social media and publicity where their input is vital. A publicist will be working on anything from 2–10 books in any one month so their time is limited. You need to give your publicist as much information as possible about you and your book and any potential publicity angles (see below). Together you can then agree the timescale of the publicity campaign, achievable and optimistic goals, how publicity will best sell your book and discuss any potential pitfalls. Be honest with your publicist and tell them the full story even if you decide not to talk about it to the media. Your publicist can advise you on how much of your private life to mine for publicity and how to maximise your control over the coverage. First-time novelist Clare Allan chose to write newspaper articles about how her ten years as a patient in mental hospitals had informed her novel *Poppy Shakespeare*, rather than be interviewed. Trust your instincts and don't let journalists pressurise you. Jon McGregor was longlisted for the Man Booker Prize for his first novel *If Nobody Speaks of Remarkable Things*. A *Guardian* journalist and photographer went to interview him in Nottingham and on discovering that he'd washed up dishes in a local restaurant to support himself whilst writing the book, tried to persuade him to be photographed at the kitchen sink. Jon declined. It was a wise decision as otherwise this picture would have haunted him for years.

Pre-publication checklist for the 'dream author'

If your book is being published by a mainstream publisher, your publicist is your primary contact for sales/marketing/publicity so the information below should be given to them to help plan the campaign.

- Make contact with the marketer, publicist and local sales rep at your publisher.
- Fill in the publisher's author questionnaire and write a 500–1,000-word piece about how you came to write your book and what's new and different about it.
- Make contact with your local bookshop, library, writers' groups, reading groups and literature festival and let them know that your book is being published.
- Research specialist sales outlets (e.g. wool shops for a book about knitting, football club fanzines for a book about football, or maritime museums for a novel about Nelson).
- Give the sales team any relevant information to drive sales regionally (e.g. if you're Welsh/Scottish/Irish or you lived in Cornwall for 20 years and have a huge network of family and friends there though you've recently moved to Derby).
- Make a list of any possible media angles relating either to you or the book.
- Make a list of any media contacts, both local and national.
- Research any anniversaries, exhibitions, television series or films that tie in with your book or the themes of your book and could create media hooks.
- If you're writing non-fiction, list what's new and newsworthy in your book (e.g. new source material or new angle). Differentiate your book from others on the same subject and list the other books in the same field.
- As you know your book best, suggest 500–2,000-word extracts that might work as stand-alone newspaper pieces.
- Write a description of your book in approximately 100–300 words (think book jacket copy style).
- If you think you could write newspaper articles, write paragraph pitches of ideas with potential word lengths. (Think of specific newspapers when you're doing this and be ruthless. Ask yourself if the feature is *really* relevant for the *Daily Mail's* Femail pages/*The Times'* Comment pages/the *Observer's Food Monthly* supplement.)
- Write a list of the contemporary authors you admire and particularly any authors whose work is similar to yours as their readers might enjoy your book.
- Look at your publisher's website and see if there is additional material you can provide – on your book or a review of another book or article/feature.
- If the idea of standing up in front of people and talking about your book makes you feel queasy, ask your publisher for media and presentation training (budget permitting of

course). Alternatively, go to other author events to see what works and what doesn't. (Shorter is *always* better and enlist the help of an honest friend for feedback.)

• Plan, prepare and practice your author event (from choosing the right passage for a reading from the book – one that is dramatic, self-contained, character-introducing, with the all-important want-to-read-on factor – to interacting with the audience). If you are nervous, write out your talk and repeat it aloud in front of the mirror at home.

• Listen or watch every television or radio programme before you go on it and always know the presenter's name.

Above all, charm, good manners and hard-working professionalism are the staple of the 'dream author' and will open promotional doors time and time again. Joanna Trollope, *doyenne* of the book tour, says: 'I think the advice I'd give to a first-time author is that *all* publicity (with some reservations, obviously, about the tabloids), however seemingly small, is worth doing because the whole process is really joining up the dots in a dot-to-dot picture (which *might* even turn out to be a little golden goose) and that whatever you do, do it with the best grace possible because no one in your professional life will ever forget that you were a treat to deal with.' Finally, when your friends and family tell you how much they love your book, ask them for a favour: a rave review on Amazon, Goodreads, Twitter or Facebook never goes amiss.

Katie Bond was Marketing and Publicity Director at Bloomsbury from 1999 to 2014 and handled PR for many bestselling authors including J.K. Rowling, Khaled Hosseini, Margaret Atwood and Donna Tartt. She won the first British Book Award's Publicity Nibbie for her campaign for Susanna Clarke's *Jonathan Strange and Mr Norrell*. Follow her on Twitter @KatieBond1.

See also...

- *Helping to market your book*, page 124
- *Marketing, publicising and selling self-published books*, page 597
- *Marketing yourself online*, page 602
- *Managing your online reputation*, page 607
- *Book blogs*, page 610

Helping to market your book

Alison Baverstock offers guidance on how authors can help to enhance their publisher's efforts to sell their book. The information in this article is also relevant to self-publishers.

Having a book accepted for publication is immensely satisfying – all the more so if in the process you have amassed a thick pile of rejection letters spanning several years. At this stage, some authors decide that, having committed themselves to work with a professional publishing house, this is the end of their involvement in the process. They will move on thankfully to write their next book.

Once you have delivered your manuscript and it has been accepted for publication, a publisher should handle all aspects of your book's subsequent development, from copy-editing and production to promotion and distribution. But there is a sound pragmatism in remaining vigilant. When it comes to the marketing of your book, there is a huge amount that you can do to help it sell.

The challenging marketplace

Each year in the UK alone, over 150,000 books get published or come out in new editions. All compete for the attention of the same review editors, the same stock buyers in bookshops, the vast number of titles available online and the largely static number of regular book-buying members of the general public. It follows that anything an author can do to help 'position' the book, to make it sound different, or just more interesting than those it competes with, will be a huge advantage.

The marketing of books is not usually an area of high spending and there are many reasons why. Books are relatively cheap (a paperback novel costs about the same as a cinema ticket, and much less than a round of drinks, an ebook even less), the publishers' profit margins are low, booksellers claim a percentage of the purchase price as discount (35–40%) and supermarkets and online selling facilities claim more, and books sell in relatively small quantities (a mass market novel selling 15,000 copies may be considered a 'bestseller' – compare that with the sales figures for computer games). Your publisher will probably try to make maximum use of (free) publicity to stimulate demand using low-cost marketing techniques. They are far more likely to arrange for the insertion of a simple leaflet as a loose insert in a relevant publication, organise a specific mailing to members of a relevant society, or organise social media marketing than to book television or billboard advertising. Your assistance in helping them reach the market could be invaluable – and indeed your willingness to participate in marketing may have played a big part in their deciding to commission you in the first place.

Examine your resources

Think in detail about what resources you have at your disposal that would help your book to sell, and then tell your publisher. Most publishers send you a publicity form about six months before publication, to obtain details of your book and to find out how you feel it can best be marketed. Whilst the publisher will probably not be able to fulfil all your ambitions (mass market advertising is not possible for every title), they will be particularly interested in your contacts. For example, were you at school with someone who is now a features writer on *The Times*? Even if you have not spoken since, they may still remember your name. Do your children attend the same school as a contact on your local paper? Do you belong to a society or professional organisation that produces a newsletter for members, organises a conference or regular dining club? How many friends do you have on Facebook, followers on Twitter, or email contacts? All these communication channels provide opportunities for both your publisher and you to send information on your book to potential purchasers and sources of publicity. If you work together on managing a social media campaign the message can be spread very quickly.

There are probably other things you could do too. Can you arrange for an editorial mention of your book in a society journal (which will carry more weight than an advertisement) or organise for your publisher to take advertising space at a reduced rate? Remember that the less it costs your publishing house to reach each potential customer, the more of the market they will be able to cover out of their planned budgetary spend.

Offer a peg to your publisher

In trying to stimulate demand for a book, publishers try to achieve publicity (or coverage in the media) at the time of publication. The most usual way of getting this is for the in-house publicist to send a press release about you and your book to journalists in the hope that they will be sufficiently interested to write about you or, even better, decide to interview you.

Your publisher will need 'pegs' on which to hang stories about you and your book, and it is helpful if you volunteer these rather than waiting to be asked. So, think back over your career and life in general. What is interesting about you? Are there any stories that arise out of the research for the book; incidents that give a flavour of the book and you as a writer?

Try to look at your life as others might see it; events or capabilities you take for granted might greatly interest other people. For example, novelist Catherine Jones (Kate Lace) is married to a former soldier, and moved house 15 times in 20 years. In that time she produced three children and had appointments with over 40 different classroom teachers. She speaks about her life in a very matter of fact way, but when she wrote her first novel, *Army Wives* (Piatkus), the media were quite fascinated by a world about which they clearly knew nothing. They found military jargon particularly compelling, and this proved a wonderful (and headline-producing) peg on which to promote her book.

Make yourself available

For a mass-market title, any publicity that can be achieved needs to be orchestrated at the time of publication. By this time the publisher will hopefully have persuaded booksellers to stock the book and copies will be in the shops. If the publicity is successful, but peaks before the books are available to buy, this prime opportunity has been missed. If there is no publicity on publication, and no consequent demand, the bookseller has the right to return the books to the publisher and receive a credit note. And in these circumstances it will be *extremely* difficult to persuade them to restock the title having been let down once.

Timing is therefore crucial, so make yourself available at the time of publication (this is not the time to take your well-earned break). Remember too that, unless you are a very big star, each newspaper or programme approached will consider its own requirements exclusively, and will not be interested in your own personal schedule. Not all journalists work every day, and even if they do they like to decide on their own priorities. If you ask for an interview to be rescheduled, it may be dropped completely.

Don't assume that only coverage in the national media is worth having as local radio and newspapers can reach a very wide audience and be particularly effective in prompting sales. You may be able to extend the amount of time and space you get by suggesting a competition or reader/listener offer. Local journalists usually have a much friendlier approach than those who work on the nationals, so if you are a novice to the publicity process this can be a much easier start – and an opportunity to build your confidence.

Contributing text for marketing

At several stages in the production process your publisher may request your input. You may be asked to provide text for the book jacket or for an author profile, to check information that will be included in the publisher's annual catalogue, or to provide biographical information for their website.

Think carefully about the words you have been asked for, who will read them and in what circumstances, and then craft what you write accordingly. For example, the text on a fiction book jacket (or 'blurb') should not retell the story or give away the plot; rather it should send signals that convey atmosphere, whet the appetite of the reader and show what kind of book they can expect. A non-fiction blurb should establish what the book will do for the reader and your qualifications for writing it. Potential buyers are likely to be reading the blurb in a hurry, perhaps whilst standing in a bookshop being jostled by other shoppers, so it is best to keep it brief.

A third party recommendation of your book will help enormously as this provides objective proof of what it is like and how useful it is. When books have come out as hardbacks, extracts from review coverage can be useful on the paperback edition. (Every author should keep a rigorous record of their review coverage, copies of which your publisher should send you. Things do sometimes go missing or get lost, and you are far more likely to remember the good ones, given that you are looking after a much smaller number of books than your publisher.) For previously unpublished authors, a relevant quotation is very helpful instead. Do you know anyone established in the appropriate field who could provide an endorsement for what you have written? It doesn't have to be from anyone famous, just someone relevant. For example, a children's book endorsed as a gripping read by a ten-year-old, or an educational text endorsed by a student who had just passed her exams could both be effective. Look too for reviews online that you can quote in support of your work; feedback from real readers many of whom take considerable pains to craft their contribution.

If you are asked to write website copy, be sure to look at the relevant site before you draft something. Think about the context in which your material will be seen and read (by whom, how often and for how long) and use this information as the basis for writing.

Marketing after publication

Although most of the effort in marketing your book will inevitably occur in the weeks leading up to publication (because next month's schedule will bring forward further titles that need the marketing department's attention), there is a great deal of opportunity to carry on selling your book afterwards.

Your activity on social media, whether to originate or back up your publishers' efforts will be particularly appreciated. Ensure your online addresses are available in every blurb you write about yourself, so that you can be found online. If you have a blog, write around the subject of your book (don't say so much though that there is no need to buy the publication). If you don't have a blog, find out if you can 'guest blog' on someone else's site – or even organise a 'blog tour', whereby you provide guest blogs for a series of sites within a short period of time (most owners will insist you say something different on every site). Chat on Twitter but remember that the most engaging contributions are those that offer interesting information or anecdotes rather than repeatedly exhorting the market to buy. Social media requires a light touch.

If you are asked to speak at a conference or run a training course, ask if your book can be included in the package available to delegates, either as part of the overall price or at a reduced rate. Ask the publisher for simple flyers (leaflets) on your book which you can hand out on suitable occasions. Then ask the organisers to put a copy inside the delegate pack, on every seat, or in a pile at the back of the hall (or preferably all three!). Similarly, you could consider running a competition through a local newspaper or giving a talk in a bookshop or school.

Give your publisher the details of speaking engagements or conferences at which they could usefully mount a display of all their titles (your own included). Even though they published your book, you cannot reasonably expect them to be specialists in every specific field you know intimately, so give them *all* the details they need. For a conference this would include the full title (not just the initials you refer to it by), the organiser's address and contact numbers (not the chairperson's address to which you should send associated papers), the precise dates and times, and any deadlines (e.g. stand bookings placed before a certain date may be cheaper). Finally, try to plan ahead rather than passing on key details at the last minute (this is one of publishers' most common complaints about authors).

When authors get together they will often moan about their publishers, and complain how little has been done for their title. But if that energy is channelled into helping promote the books, and working together, everyone benefits.

Dr Alison Baverstock is Associate Professor of Publishing at Kingston University, where she founded the MA in Publishing. A former publisher, and winner of the Pandora Prize for Services to Publishing, she has has written widely about publishing and writing. Her books include *Marketing Your Book: An Author's Guide* (Bloomsbury 2007, 2nd edn), *Is There a Book in You?* (Bloomsbury 2006), *The Naked Author: A Guide to Self-publishing* (Bloomsbury 2011) and, most recently, the fifth edition of *How to Market Books* (Routledge 2015). Her website is www.alisonbaverstock.com and you can follow her on Twitter @alisonbav.

See also...

- *Promoting and selling your book*, page 119
- *Marketing, publicising and selling self-published books*, page 597
- *Marketing yourself online*, page 602
- *Managing your online reputation*, page 607
- *Book blogs*, page 610

News, views and trends in book publishing

In his round-up of recent book industry news and trends, Tom Tivnan presents a heartening picture of renewed confidence and increasing sales, as print books and bookshops find a firm footing again after the digital shake-up and print sales of children's books hit a new high. Nevertheless, the trade continues to face challenging issues ahead.

Since the double whammy of the recession and digital disruption hit the British book trade in 2008, the trend in the industry has been of declining fortunes: book sales collapsing, bricks-and-mortar bookshops shuttering in record numbers and venerable publishing houses being snapped up by big conglomerates – a sorry state of affairs which may have led anyone who has read these annual book trade reviews in the last few editions of the *Writers' & Artists' Yearbook* to descend into despair.

Yet something happened last year. The ongoing slump in physical sales levelled off, with UK book buyers forking out £1.399bn in 2014 on print books according to industry monitor Nielsen BookScan. Yes, this was the seventh consecutive year of a slump in the market, but marginally so – it was just 1.2% down on 2013, a triumph of sorts – given that the market had lost over a fifth of its value since 2007 (a massive £400m drop). Add the approximately £375m in ebook sales to 2014's haul and the total overall UK market – print and digital combined – was £1.774bn, up 4% year-on-year. Into 2015, the rise continues, with first quarter revenues up 4% in print alone – 7% if ebooks are included.

The trade is back in the black, but it's not just the numbers. When walking the halls of big industry gatherings such as the London and Frankfurt book fairs or the Booksellers Association's annual conference, there is a palpable sense of rediscovered confidence. Publishers have springs in their steps; there is a buoyancy amongst booksellers. After a long malaise, the British book trade has its mojo back.

Chain reactions

The reasons for the trade's rebounding fortunes are many and complex. For bookshops, there may be something in the Nietzschean line: 'Whatever doesn't kill you makes you stronger'. Much to the delight of publishers, Waterstones is back, reasserting itself as the nation's top bricks-and-mortar book chain. It is four years since Russian oligarch Alexander Mamut bought the struggling chain from HMV and installed James Daunt as managing director. It was a business, Daunt said at the time, that 'had fallen off a cliff', with annual losses approaching £25m on sales of around £400m.

A series of painful restructures, reductions in stockholding (but actually increasing the range or number of titles the company holds) and changes to the chain's infrastructure have paid dividends. In accounts to the end of April 2015, the company is projected to break even – an incredible turnaround for a business that five years ago was considered by many analysts to be on its last legs.

Perhaps most importantly, Daunt has instilled a culture of bookselling led by expertise from the shopfloor. One of the consequences of this is that Waterstones is back to 'making' books. Take one of the biggest recent breakouts: *The Miniaturist* by Jessie Burton. This debut novel was published in summer 2014 with much hype, having been snapped up for a huge advance by Picador in the UK and sold in over 30 territories by Burton's young superstar agent, Juliet Mushens of the Agency Group (this is the stuff of debut novelists' dreams). *The Miniaturist* sold well but not spectacularly upon publication – until Waterstones championed it, eventually making it the their Book of the Year. It then zoomed to the stratosphere, hitting number one in the overall chart and becoming the biggest selling debut of 2014, with print sales over £2m.

Venerable chain Blackwell's (est. 1879) had also been in the doldrums for many a year, the ailing business largely propped up by the largesse of octogenarian multimillionaire owner Toby Blackwell. Blackwell's faith in the family firm (Toby is the grandson of founder Benjamin Henry Blackwell) and handing the keys of the business over to well-respected CEO David Prescott has paid off, with the chain chalking up a profit of £600,000 in 2014 on sales of £54.2m – its first time in the black in eight years. As with Waterstones, the road to solvency has been difficult, with a number of restructures and reorganisations.

The splashiest event of the bookselling calendar in 2014 undoubtedly was the move of Foyles' flagship Charing Cross Road London branch a couple of doors down to a new home at the former site of Central St Martins art school. A bookshop launch could hardly be starrier: Hilary Mantel cut the ribbon, and departments in the shop were formally opened by a luminary from each field – Jarvis Cocker for music, Grayson Perry for art, P.D. James for crime fiction, and so on.

But aside from the opening-night glitz, something very serious was going on, with lessons which can be applied to many a bookseller. The original Foyles shop had been in place since 1903, and though to its last day it remained a bibliophile and tourist mecca, its higgledy-piggledy nature made it unfit for purpose as a late 20th-century bookshop, let alone a 21st-century one. When envisioning what to do with the new space, Foyles consulted far and wide with booksellers, publishers, agents and the general public, about what would make the 'bookshop of the future'. There are whiz-bang digital innovations – for example when you log in to the shop's wi-fi, you can search whether a book is in stock and be directed to the shelves via an interactive map. Yet the core of the new Foyles is not necessarily digital but conceptual: it uses multi-purpose spaces and has the facility to move all the fixtures. The idea is that the space can't be static; to be as fresh and exciting in 2115 as it is in 2015, the physical bookshop has to be able to expand and contract to the needs of future customers.

The kids are all right

Yet, strangely, one of the reasons that the confidence is back is because of the slowdown of ebook sales. Determining exact ebook revenue is quite difficult as there is no overall monitor for their sales as there is for print books. Yet my magazine, the *Bookseller*, has been compiling a monthly ebook ranking since 2013, with data supplied by publishers, and has been canvassing publishers for overall year-end digital figures since 2009.

From 2009 to 2011, the industry saw massive triple-digit percentage rises year-on-year in ebook sales. Yet things have since quietened down: a 95% rise in 2012, 40% in 2013, and 13% in 2014. This, it should certainly be emphasised, is growth; if the print market had a 13% jump in sales last year, it would be sung from the rooftops. But if you were at a publishing digital conference in 2009 or 2010 (and there were many digital conferences then), you would have invariably encountered some smug digitalist predicting that by 2020 ebooks would control a majority of the market. Digital currently makes up about 20% of sales in revenue and 30% of copies sold of the entire market (being less expensive, ebooks do not generate as much cash per unit sold as print). At current growth curves, even a 50/50 'e' and 'p' split seems highly unlikely by the end of the decade. The bottom line: print is here to stay.

What the ebook slowdown has meant is that the industry has essentially sorted out which books work best in which formats. Broadly, digital is strongest in fiction (particularly in genres such as crime, romance, science fiction and fantasy), while print works best in non-fiction and children's – particularly in children's. Print sales for children's books have been surging in the last few years, but recently hit another level. In 2014, more money was made from the kids' market than in any time in British publishing history. Just over £336.5m worth of children's books were sold in 2014, a rise of 9.1% year-on-year. For the first time since book charts have been compiled, the children's market outsold adult fiction (£321.3m). The trend has continued into 2015, with overall children's sales up 14.7% in the first quarter.

Children's books and authors were the talking points of 2014; of the top ten bestselling books overall, seven of them were from the children's sector. There were a number of breakout years by American young adult (YA) authors all helped by film adaptations. The pack was led by John Green whose *The Fault in Our Stars* (Penguin 2012) was by far the bestselling book of the year, children's or adult (its two editions took in £4.6m), and who is responsible, for good or ill, for spearheading the 'sick lit' YA trend (*The Fault in Our Stars* is about young love in a cancer ward). Green's compatriots Veronica Roth [*Divergent* (HarperCollins 2011); £4m in overall sales], James Dashner [*The Maze Runner* (Delacorte Press 2009); £1.8m] and Gayle Forman [*If I Stay* (Dutton Books 2009); £1m] also broke through with help from Hollywood. Flying the flag for Britain was David Walliams who is arguably now more famous for his children's books than for his TV work. Walliams' *Awful Auntie* (HarperCollins 2014) was the second bestselling book of the year, and all told he churned out £9.1m, to become the second bestselling author of the year. *The Gruffalo* (Macmillan 1999) creator Julia Donaldson was once again the UK's top author, selling a whopping £12.7m through the tills. By doing so, Donaldson became the only author to sell over £10m in five consecutive years since accurate records began. Even J.K. Rowling only managed that feat four times in a row (from 2000–03).

Two other huge children's trends in 2014 mined previously untapped areas. Four of the top eight bestselling books last year were Egmont's tie-ins with Minecraft™, the hugely popular video game (around 60 million players worldwide). The official Minecraft books combined to sell £10.3m through the tills, an eye-popping number made all the more interesting given that Minecraft's main constituency is boys aged about 8–15, a demographic that is notoriously resistant to books. Another children's trend was the massive sales of YouTube vloggers Alfie Deyes and Zoe 'Zoella' Sugg. If you are over 18 you may not have even heard of them, but the young love them – Deyes' and Sugg's subscribers to their YouTube channels number in the millions (the two are also dating, which adds to the appeal). Both have parlayed their online success into bestsellerdom: Deyes' *The Pointless Book* (Blink 2014) was the number one paperback non-fiction title for 14 weeks in 2015, Sugg's YA novel *Girl Online* (Penguin 2014) hit the overall number one, breaking a record for the biggest-selling first week debut novel in history.

Because of Deyes' and Sugg's runaway hits, other publishers have piled in, signing up other YouTubers ('me too' publishing is a long tradition of the trade). For example, Louise Pentland, who has 1.8m subscribers to her fashion-themed 'Sprinkle of Glitter' YouTube channel, has two books slated for 2015 – a diary with Faber and a lifestyle guide with Simon & Schuster. Yet the interesting thing about the Minecraft and YouTubers trends is what it says about so-called 'digital natives'. There has been much hand-wringing in the trade that the generation growing up in the digital world will forsake reading due to all manner of distractions on their devices and the internet. Yet study after study has shown that reading levels are holding up and, intriguingly, under-20-year-olds seem to prefer to read in print. The numbers for Minecraft and the YouTubers back this up: overwhelming print sales, even though the content's original iteration was digital.

Amazon versus the rest of the world

A review of the year in the book trade would hardly be complete without Amazon getting into a bare-knuckle bust-up with some part of the trade. The feud of 2014 was a long-running dispute in the USA with Hachette, the French media conglomerate which owns publishers such as Little, Brown and Hodder & Stoughton. Hachette was renegotiating its contract in America with Amazon and it refused to give the online bookseller the right to set ebook prices. Amazon's response was to remove the 'Buy' button from a good portion of Hachette titles – both physical and digital – on its website.

The dispute lasted almost six months and was a reputational and financial hit for both companies. Amazon perhaps suffered slightly more on the reputation side, particularly after a 1,000-strong group of heavyweight writers called Authors United (members included Stephen King, Donna Tartt, Salman Rushdie and John Grisham) put a full-page advert in the *New York Times* decrying Amazon's tactics. The background is that this was the first round of contract renegotiations after the Big Five publishers (Hachette, Penguin Random House, Macmillan, HarperCollins and Simon & Schuster) all settled their ebook price-fixing antitrust suit taken up against them and Apple by the US government. All eyes were on Hachette *v* Amazon, as the outcome would perhaps determine the way all publishers interacted with the e-tailer in the future, not just in America, but across the globe.

When the stalemate ended, it was seen as a narrow win for the publisher. The outcome was that Hachette would indeed be able to set its own ebook prices, but Amazon would be able to 'incentivise' Hachette to bring prices down.

The newest battleground between Amazon and the trade is less contentious but no less intriguing: its 'all you can eat' subscription service, Kindle Unlimited. This 'Netflix for ebooks' model has actually been around for a few years (the American company Scribd has been doing it since 2010) but, until Amazon launched its own service in late 2014, subscription was not seen as particularly viable. Not that Amazon's lift-off was without its hitches – Kindle Unlimited had 600,000 titles at launch, the bulk of them by self-published authors who had not realised they had signed up to be on the service. Few traditional publishers have put their content on subscription services yet. But resistance seems to be easing; HarperCollins, for example, has made a lot of its backlist available on Scribd. This worries authors and agents, who say the complicated structure of payment (services base royalties on what percentage of a book the customer reads) means that it will be almost impossible to determine if a writer is being paid the appropriate amount.

Let us not over-egg the industry's new confidence. It is still very challenging for the trade with major concerns in the coming months. Independent publishers are worried about the ongoing 'conglomeratisation' of the industry in which acquisitions and mergers such as the Penguin Random House marriage and Hachette picking up former indies Constable & Robinson and Quercus, will mean the bigger players will have the spending power to hoover up the bulk of the writing talent. There are vast, troubling issues which have to be tackled at a governmental level, which will see the industry lobbying lawmakers in Westminster and Brussels like never before: rising business rates (a key issue for booksellers), library cuts, copyright protection and VAT on ebooks (the 20% sales tax has been imposed on ebooks by the EU since 1 January 2015). There will be tough times ahead – yet after a year like 2014, there is the sense the trade can handle it.

Tom Tivnan is features and insight editor of the *Bookseller*, and also its international editor. He wrote the text for *Tattooed by the Family Business* (Pavilion 2010). Previously a freelance writer, his work has appeared in the *Glasgow Herald*, the *Independent*, the *Daily Telegraph* and *Harper's Bazaar*. He has also worked as a bookseller for Blackwell's in the UK and Barnes & Noble in the USA.

See also...

- *Electronic publishing*, page 573

FAQs about ISBNs

The Nielsen ISBN Agency for UK & Ireland receives a large number of enquiries about the ISBN system. The most frequently asked questions are answered here.

What is an ISBN?

Contact details

Nielsen ISBN Agency for UK and Ireland
3rd Floor, Midas House, 62 Goldsworth Road, Woking GU21 6LQ
tel (01483) 712215
email isbn.agency@nielsen.com
website www.isbn.nielsenbook.co.uk

An ISBN (International Standard Book Number) is a product identifier used by publishers, booksellers and libraries for ordering, listing and stock control purposes. It enables them to identify a specific edition of a specific title in a specific format from a particular publisher. The digits are always divided into five parts, separated by spaces or hyphens. The five parts can be of varying length and are as follows:

- Prefix element – distinguishes the ISBN from other types of product identifier which are used for non-book trade products; three-digit number that is made available by GS1 (Global Standards – required for barcodes). Prefixes that have already been made available by GS1 are 978 and 979, but there may be a further prefix allocation made in the future as required to ensure the continued capacity of the ISBN system.
- Group Identifier – identifies a national, geographic or language grouping of publishers. It tells you which of these groupings the publisher belongs to (not the language of the book).
- Publisher Identifier – identifies a specific publisher or imprint.
- Title Number – identifies a specific edition of a specific title in a specific format.
- Check Digit – this is always and only the final digit which mathematically validates the rest of the number.

Since January 2007 all ISBNs are 13 digits long. The older ten-digit format can be converted to the 13-digit format by adding the 978 EAN (European Article Number, i.e. a 'barcode') prefix and recalculating the check digit.

Do all books need to have an ISBN?

There is no legal requirement for an ISBN in the UK and Ireland and it conveys no form of legal or copyright protection. It is a product identifier.

What can be gained from using an ISBN?

If you wish to sell your publication through major bookselling chains, independent bookshops or internet booksellers, they will require it to have an ISBN to assist their internal processing and ordering systems. The ISBN also provides access to bibliographic databases such as Nielsen Book's bibliographic database and Discovery Services (Nielsen BookData), which are organised using ISBNs as references. These databases are used by the book trade – publishers, booksellers and libraries – for internal purposes, to provide information for customers and to source and order titles. ISBNs are also used by Nielsen Book's Commerce Services (Nielsen BookNet TeleOrdering and Nielsen PubEasy) and Research Services (Nielsen BookScan and Books & Consumers) to monitor book sales. The ISBN therefore provides access to additional marketing opportunities which assist the sales and measurement of books (including ebooks and other digital products).

Where can I get an ISBN?

ISBN prefixes are assigned to publishers in the country where they are based by the national agency for that country. The UK and Republic of Ireland Agency is run by Nielsen. The Agency introduces new publishers to the system, assigns prefixes to new and existing publishers and deals with any queries or problems in using the system. The Nielsen ISBN Agency for UK & Ireland was the first ISBN agency in the world and has been instrumental in the set up and maintenance of the ISBN. Publishers based elsewhere will not be able to get numbers from the UK Agency but may contact them for details of the relevant agency in their market.

Who is eligible for ISBNs?

Any organisation or individual who is publishing a qualifying product for general sale or distribution to the market is eligible (see below, 'Which products do not qualify for ISBNs?' and *Self-publishing for beginners* on page 582).

What is a publisher?

The publisher is generally the person or body which takes the financial risk in making a product available. For example, if a product went on sale and sold no copies at all, the publisher is usually the person or body which loses money. If you get paid anyway, you are likely to be a designer, printer, author or consultant of some kind.

How long does it take to get an ISBN?

In the UK and Ireland the 'Standard' service time is 10 working days, the 'Fast Track' service is three working days, and the 'Super Fast Track' service is the same day for applications received before 1pm.

How much does it cost to get an ISBN?

In the UK and Ireland there is a registration fee which is payable by all new publishers. The fees for ISBNs are subject to review so applicants should check with the Agency. A publisher prefix unique to you will be provided and allows for ten ISBNs. Larger allocations are available where appropriate.

ISBNs are only available in blocks. The smallest block is 10 numbers. It is not possible to obtain a single ISBN.

Which products do not qualify for ISBNs?

Calendars and diaries (unless they contain additional text or images such that they are not purely for time-management purposes); greetings cards, videos for entertainment; documentaries on video/CD-Rom; computer games; computer application programs; items which are available to a restricted group of people, e.g. a history of a golf club which is only for sale to members or an educational course book only available to those registered as students on the course.

Can I turn my ISBN into a barcode?

Since ISBNs changed to 13 digits in 2007 it has been possible (with the appropriate software) to use the same number to generate a barcode. Information about barcoding for books is available on the Book Industry Communication website (www.bic.org.uk).

What is an ISSN?

An International Standard Serial Number is the numbering system for journals, magazines, periodicals, newspapers and newsletters. It is administered by the British Library, *tel* (01937) 546959.

Print on demand

David Taylor explains how print on demand is keeping books alive.

What is 'print on demand'?

Ever since mankind first started committing words to a physical form of delivery, whether on wood, stone, papyrus, illuminated text or moveable type, the method of supplying these for sale has largely followed a similar pattern: produce first and then sell. Of course, the risk in this is that the publisher can overproduce or underproduce. Overproduction means that the publisher has cash tied up in books that are waiting to be sold. Underproduction means that the publisher has run out and sales are being missed because the book is not available to buy.

If you walk around any publisher's distribution centre you will see huge quantities of printed books that are awaiting sale, representing large amounts of cash tied up in physical inventory. This is often referred to as 'speculative inventory' because the publisher has printed the books in anticipation of selling them. One of the hardest decisions that a publisher has to make is how many copies of a title to print upon publication; equally hard is how many to reprint if the initial print run is sold. Get these wrong and it can cost the publisher dearly and, in some extreme cases, prove mortal to the business.

For others in the supply chain, this model is also deeply flawed. The author whose title sells well can fall into the limbo of 'out of stock' pending a reprint decision by the publisher. The bookseller, who has orders for a title but cannot supply them, also loses sales and disappoints customers. In some cases, those orders are of the moment and when that moment passes, so does the sale. Last but by no means least, the book buyer is frustrated as they are unable to buy the book that they wish to read.

The supply model is also famously inefficient, characterised as it is by large amounts of speculative stock being printed, transported, stored in warehouses, transported again, returned from the bookseller if it does not sell and, in many cases, being pulped. Not only is this commercially inefficient, it is also environmentally costly, involving large amounts of energy being used to print and transport books that may end their life as landfill.

In the mid 1990s, developments in the then emerging field of digital printing started to hold out the possibility that this traditional 'print first then sell' model might be changed to a more commercially attractive 'sell first and then print' model. Such a supply model was premised upon a number of things coming together.

- First, the technology of digital printing advanced to the stage where simple text-based books could be produced to a standard that was acceptable to publishers in terms of quality.
- Second, the speed of digital presses advanced so that a book could be produced upon the receipt of an order and supplied back to the customer within an acceptable timeframe.
- Third, models started to emerge which married these digital printing capabilities to wholesaling and book distribution networks such that books could be stored digitally, offered for sale to the market with orders being fulfilled on a 'print-on-demand' (POD) basis from a virtual warehouse rather than a physical warehouse full of speculative inventory. This hybrid model requires a highly sophisticated IT infrastructure to allow the swift routing and batching of orders to digital print engines so that genuine single copy orders can be produced 'on demand'.

The first mover in developing this model was the US book wholesaler Ingram Book Group which, in 1997, installed a digital print line in one of their giant book wholesaling warehouses and offered a service to US publishers called Lightning Print. This service presented to publishers the option of allowing Ingram to hold their titles in a digital format, offer them for sale via Ingram's vast network of bookselling customers and then print the title when it was ordered. In addition, the publisher could order copies for their own purposes.

Eighteen years on, Lightning Source, which operates as the POD service for what has now become Ingram Content Group, has operations in the USA, the UK, Australia, a joint venture with Hachette in France, a research and training facility in Germany and agreements with POD vendors in Brazil, Russia, Poland, South Korea and Germany. Lightning Source print millions of books from a digital library of millions of titles from tens of thousands of publishers. The average print run per order is less than two copies.

POD service companies

Digital printing technology has developed at a staggering pace and the quality of digitally printed titles is now almost indistinguishable from titles printed using offset machines. The new generation of ink jet digital print engines are now established in the market and have taken the quality of digitally printed books to the next level, especially for full-colour titles. Speed of production has also improved at amazing rates. For example, Lightning Source now produces books on demand for Ingram customers within four hours of receiving the order, thereby allowing orders to be shipped within 24 hours to the bookseller. Ingram also recently acquired some robotic technology, taking the POD model to a true status of virtual wholesaler. Ingram's fourth American POD facility opened in California in late 2014 and deploys this next generation of capability.

The number and types of players in the POD market continues to expand. In the UK, Antony Rowe established a POD operation in partnership with the UK's biggest book wholesaler, Gardners, in early 2000. Antony Rowe's POD facility supplies orders on demand for Gardner's bookselling customers using a very similar model to that of Ingram and Lightning Source in the USA. Other UK printers have been scrambling to enter the fast-growing POD space with significant investments being made in digital printing equipment. Rather ironically, the arrival of the ebook is fuelling the growth of POD as publishers move more titles into shorter print runs or opt to operate from a virtual stock position as they attempt to cope with the shift from 'p' to 'e'. The last thing a publisher wants is a warehouse full of titles that are increasingly selling in an 'e' format. Publishers are increasingly moving to a 'p' and 'e' model of supply and using POD to offer a print alternative as well as an 'e' version.

In Germany, the book wholesaler Libri has a POD operation, Books on Demand, which also offers a self-publishing service to authors (see *Self-publishing for beginners* on page 582). Lightning Source and Antony Rowe deal only with publishers. Books on Demand have recently extended their offer into both France and the Netherlands and have an arrangement with Ingram so that their self-published authors can use the Lightning Source network to get their titles into North America, the UK and Australia. In the French market, the joint venture between Lightning Source and Hachette Livre and the arrival of the genuine single copy POD model has fuelled the growth of French self-publishing businesses which previously lacked this supply model.

In the Australian market, the arrival of Lightning Source in mid-2011 has had a dramatic impact on Australian self-publishing companies. Now that they have a POD model in their market, they are actively growing their title base and are able to offer Australian authors easy access to a global selling network in addition to local services. One of the most significant moves in this area was the purchase in 2005 by Amazon of a small US POD business called Booksurge. Like Libri's Books on Demand model, Amazon also offers a self-publishing service to authors and is actively leveraging its dominance of the internet bookselling market to develop innovative packages for authors via this model and their CreateSpace brand. The consensus within the book trade appears to be that Amazon sees POD as a very important part of the way in which they manage their supply chain and as a key opportunity to improve service levels to their customers. Amazon is now also a publisher in the traditional sense of the word and is using its own POD service to support the availability of many of these titles within their supply chain. In the wider world, traditional publishing and self-publishing seem to be moving ever closer together as witnessed by the rather surprising purchase in 2012 by Penguin of Author Solutions, which was at the time probably the largest self-publishing company in the market.

Elsewhere in the world, there are emerging POD supply models in an increasing number of countries including South America, India, China, Japan and Europe. Ingram is actively building supply partnerships with many of these organisations via its Global Connect programme, thereby offering publishers and authors an increasingly global option to make their books available on demand to their readers.

As digital print technology has improved, many traditional book printers have tried to enter this market and offer POD. However, without significant investment in the IT infrastructure needed to deliver single copy production at scale and speed and without allying that capability to an established book distribution or wholesaling network, many of these offers are effectively ultra short-run printing offers and cannot replicate the genuine POD supply model of a single copy printed when an order is received. Increasingly, as well, that supply model needs to be built on a global scale to offer authors and publishers the maximum exposure for their titles.

What POD means for authors

POD is impacting aspiring and published authors in different ways. The existence of POD has led to a whole set of new publishing models. Removing the need to carry speculative inventory has reduced the barriers to entry for organisations which want to enter the publishing space. For example, in the US market, Ingram's Lightning Source supply model has enabled a large number of self-publishing companies to flourish and to offer aspiring authors a wide range of services to get their work into print. These companies will typically use a POD service to do the physical printing and distribution of a title, and also use them to list the titles for sale via book wholesalers like Amazon and Gardners, internet booksellers like Amazon, and physical bookshop chains such as Barnes & Noble and Waterstones. Authors may also have the opportunity to order copies of their own titles. They would also offer the aspiring author a set of support services covering editorial, marketing, design, etc. See *Self-publishing providers* on page 613. In addition, Ingram recently launched its IngramSpark platform, specifically designed to allow smaller publishers and self-publishers access to its global supply chain for both POD and ebooks sale and supply.

No longer does an author wanting to self-publish have to commit upfront to buying thousands of copies of his or her title. The previously mentioned self-publishing organisations are large, sophisticated and have many tens of thousands of authors whose books are available for sale in mainstream book reselling outlets. In addition, traditional publishers who have historically been a little snooty about self-published books now view them in a slightly different light, perhaps as a less risky way of testing the market with new authors who are willing to pay for the privilege of being published. They trawl self-published titles for potential: there have been several well-publicised cases of authors who started out by self-publishing before being picked up by one of the established publishing houses (e.g. *Fifty Shades of Grey*).

The published author

The POD picture for the published author is a little more mixed. There is no doubt that traditional publishers are engaging more than ever before with the benefits that POD brings. The ability to reduce speculative inventory or get out of it completely, to ensure that sales are not missed, to reduce the risk of getting a reprint decision wrong, and even to bring titles back to life from the out-of-print graveyard, are all very attractive financial propositions. For the author who has a book already published, POD means sales are not missed and therefore royalties are forthcoming. Many books can languish in 'reprint under consideration' limbo for years: POD removes that category and ensures that books are available for sale. Probably the thorniest issue is around the decision to put a book out of print and here most author contracts have simply not caught up with the new technologies. Some contracts still require that the publisher has to keep physical inventory of a title to show that it is in print, yet many millions of books are in print and there is no physical inventory held anywhere. An author may therefore find their title being put out of print because of such a clause even though the publisher is willing to keep it in print but does not want to keep speculative inventory before an order is received.

The flip side of this, of course, is that a publisher might use POD to retain the rights to the title by printing a small amount of inventory when really the best thing for the author might be to allow the title to go out of print and get the rights back. There have been many cases where rights have reverted to the author who has then either set himself up as an independent publishing company or utilised the services of one of the self-publishing companies mentioned earlier. There have also been examples of literary agents using POD to offer a new publishing service to authors who may have the rights as the title has gone out of print at their original publisher.

In conclusion, the advice for both aspiring authors and published authors is to do your homework. For an aspiring author, look carefully at the various self-publishing organisations out there and do your sums. Are you better off using them or do you want to set up your own publishing company? For published authors, take a long hard look at how your contract defines 'out of print'. The old definition was typically based on 'no physical copies in existence': POD has made that irrelevant and your contract should reflect these new realities if you are to take full advantage of them.

And finally, here is one of the most delicious ironies of this whole model. The death of the physical book has been predicted many times now that we live in a digital age. POD has digital technology at its core and yet it is giving life to one of the oldest products on the planet: the paper book. POD is set to be at the heart of the way in which paper books are published, printed and distributed for many years to come. Without this new model, there would be far fewer books available to buy and read and I, for one, think that the world would be a duller place for that.

David Taylor has worked in the book trade since 1983 and spent most of his time in bookselling. He has worked at Ingram Content Group since 2003 and is currently Senior Vice President, Content Acquisition International, Ingram Content Group and Group Managing Director, Lightning Source UK Ltd. He is also a Director of Lightning Source Australia and President of Lightning Source France.

See also...

- *News, views and trends in book publishing,* page 128
- *Electronic publishing,* page 573

Public Lending Right

Under the PLR system, payment is made from public funds to authors (writers, translators, illustrators and some editors/compilers) whose books are lent out from public libraries. Payment is made once a year, and the amount authors receive is proportionate to the number of times that their books were borrowed during the previous year (July to June).

How the system works

From the applications received, the PLR office compiles a computerised register of authors and books. A representative sample of book issues is recorded, consisting of all loans from selected public libraries. This is then multiplied in proportion to total library lending to produce, for each book, an estimate of its total annual loans throughout the country. Each year the computer compares the register with the estimated loans to discover how many loans are credited to each registered book for the calculation of PLR payments. This is done using the ISBN printed in the book (see below).

Parliament allocates a sum each year (£6.6 million for 2014/15) for PLR. This fund pays the administrative costs of PLR and reimburses local authorities for recording loans in the sample libraries (see below). The remaining money is then divided by the total registered loan figure in order to work out how much can be paid for each estimated loan of a registered book.

Since July 2014 the UK PLR legislation has been extended to include public library loans of audiobooks ('talking books') and ebooks downloaded to library premises for taking away as loans ('on-site' ebook loans).

Further information

Public Lending Right
PLR Office, Richard House, Sorbonne Close, Stockton-on-Tees TS17 6DA
tel (01642) 604699
websites www.bl.uk/plr, www.plr.uk.com, www.plrinternational.com
Contact Head of PLR

The UK PLR scheme is administered by the British Library from its offices in Stockton-on-Tees (the 'PLR office'). The UK PLR office also provides registration for the Irish PLR scheme on behalf of the Irish Public Lending Remuneration office.

Application forms, information and publications are all obtainable from the PLR Office. See website for further information on eligibility for PLR, loans statistics and forthcoming developments.

British Library Advisory Committee for Public Lending Right
Advises the British Library Board and Head of PLR on the operation and future development of the PLR scheme.

Limits on payments

If all the registered interests in an author's books score so few loans that they would earn less than £1 in a year, no payment is due. However, if the books of one registered author score so high that the author's PLR earnings for the year would exceed £6,600, then only £6,600 is paid. (No author can earn more than £6,600 in PLR in any one year.) Money that is not paid out because of these limits belongs to the fund and increases the amounts paid that year to other authors.

The sample

Because it would be expensive and impracticable to attempt to collect loans data from every library authority in the UK, a statistical sampling method is employed instead. The sample represents only public lending libraries – academic, school, private and commercial libraries are not included. Only books which are loaned from public libraries can earn PLR; consultations of books on library premises are excluded.

The sample consists of the entire loans records for a year from libraries in more than 40 public library authorities spread through England, Scotland, Wales and Northern Ireland. Sample loans represent around 20% of the national total. All the computerised sampling points in an authority contribute loans data ('multi-site' sampling). The aim is to increase the sample without any significant increase in costs. In order to counteract sampling error, libraries in the sample change every three to four years. Loans are totalled every 12 months for the period 1 July–30 June.

An author's entitlement to PLR depends on the loans accrued by his or her books in the sample. This figure is averaged up to produce first regional and then finally national estimated loans.

ISBNs

The PLR system uses ISBNs (International Standard Book Numbers) to identify books lent and correlate loans with entries on the PLR Register so that payments can be made. ISBNs are required for all registrations. Different editions (e.g.first, second, hardback, paperback, large print) of the same book have different ISBNs. See *FAQs about ISBNs* on page 133.

Authorship

In the PLR system the author of a printed book or ebook is the writer, illustrator, translator, compiler, editor or reviser. Authors must be named on the book's title page, or be able to prove authorship by some other means (e.g. receipt of royalties). The ownership of copyright has no bearing on PLR eligibility. Narrators, producers and abridgers are also eligible to apply for PLR shares in audiobooks.

Co-authorship/illustrators. In the PLR system the authors of a book are those writers, translators, editors, compilers and illustrators as defined above. Authors must apply for

Summary of the 32nd year's results

Registration: authors. When registration closed for the 32nd year (30 June 2014) there were 54,839 authors and assignees.

Eligible loans. Of the 247 million estimated loans from UK libraries, 108 million belong to books on the PLR register. The loans credited to registered books – 44% of all library borrowings – qualify for payment. The remaining 56% of loans relate to books that are ineligible for various reasons, to books written by dead or foreign authors, and to books that have simply not been applied for.

Money and payments. PLR's administrative costs are deducted from the fund allocated to the British Library Board annually by Parliament. Operating the scheme this year cost £622,000, representing some 9.3% of the PLR fund. The Rate per Loan for 2014/15 was 6.66 pence. The amount distributed to authors was just over £6 million. Total government funding for 2014/15 was £6.66 million.

The numbers of authors in various payment categories are as follows:

*281	payments at	£5,000–6,600
359	payments between	£2,500–4,999.99
809	payments between	£1,000–2,499.99
879	payments between	£500–999.99
3,336	payments between	£100–499.99
16,387	payments between	£1–99.99
22,051	TOTAL	

* Includes 190 authors whose book loans reached the maximum threshold

registration before their books can earn PLR and this can be done via the PLR website. There is no restriction on the number of authors who can register shares in any one book as long as they satisfy the eligibility criteria.

Writers and/or illustrators. At least one must be eligible and they must jointly agree what share of PLR each will take based on contribution. This agreement is necessary even if one or two are ineligible or do not wish to register for PLR. The eligible authors will receive the share(s) specified in the application.

Translators. Translators may apply, without reference to other authors, for a 30% fixed share (to be divided equally between joint translators).

Editors and compilers. An editor or compiler may apply, either with others or without reference to them, to register a 20% share. An editor must have written at least 10% of the book's content or more than ten pages of text in addition to normal editorial work and be named on the title page. Alternatively, editors may register 20% if they have a royalty agreement with the publisher. The share of joint editors/compilers is 20% in total to be divided equally. An application from an editor or compiler to register a greater percentage share must be accompanied by supporting documentary evidence of actual contribution.

Audiobooks. PLR shares in audiobooks are fixed by the UK scheme and may not be varied. *Writers* may register a fixed 60% share in an audiobook, providing that it has not been abridged or translated. In cases where the writer has made an additional contribution (e.g. as narrator), he/she may claim both shares. *Narrators* may register a fixed 20% PLR share in an audiobook. *Producers* may register a fixed 20% share in an audiobook. *Abridgers*

Most borrowed authors

Children's authors

1 Daisy Meadows
2 Julia Donaldson
3 Francesca Simon
4 Adam Blade
5 Jacqueline Wilson
6 Roald Dahl
7 Mick Inkpen
8 Fiona Watt
9 Michael Morpurgo
10 Enid Blyton
11 Jeanne Willis
12 Terry Deary
13 Eric Hill
14 Lucy Cousins
15 Ian Whybrow
16 Lauren Child
17 Tony Ross
18 Roderick Hunt
19 Jeff Kinney
20 Giles Andreae

Authors of adult fiction

1 James Patterson
2 M.C. Beaton
3 Nora Roberts
4 Lee Child
5 David Baldacci
6 Anna Jacobs
7 Danielle Steel
8 Clive Cussler
9 Harlan Coben
10 Ian Rankin
11 Katie Flynn
12 John Grisham
13 J.D. Robb
14 Michael Connelly
15 Debbie Macomber
16 Peter Robinson
17 Alexander McCall Smith
18 Susan Lewis
19 Jo Nesbo
20 Rosie Goodwin

These two lists are of the most borrowed authors in UK public libraries. They are based on PLR sample loans in the period July 2013–June 2014. They include all writers, both registered and unregistered, but not illustrators where the book has a separate writer. Writing names are used; pseudonyms have not been combined.

(in cases where the writer's original text has been abridged prior to recording as an audiobook) qualify for 12% (20% of the writer's share). *Translators* (in cases where the writer's original text has been translated from another language) qualify for 18% (30% of the writer's share). If there is more than one writer, narrator, etc the appropriate shares should be divided equally. If more than one contribution has been made, e.g. writer and narrator, more than one fixed share may be applied for.

Dead or missing co-authors. Where it is impossible to agree shares with a co-author because that person is dead or untraceable, then the surviving co-author or co-authors may submit an application but must name the co-author and provide supporting evidence as to why that co-author has not agreed shares. The living co-author(s) will then be able to register a share in the book which reflects individual contribution. Providing permission is granted, the PLR Office can help to put co-authors (including illustrators) in touch with each other. Help is also available from publishers, writers' organisations and the Association of Illustrators.

Life and death. First applications may not be made by the estate of a deceased author. However, if an author registers during their lifetime the PLR in their books can be transferred to a new owner and continues for up to 70 years after the date of their death. The new owner can apply to register new titles if first published one year before, or up to ten years after, the date of the author's death. New editions of existing registered titles can also be registered posthumously.

Residential qualifications. PLR is open to authors living in the European Economic Area (i.e. EU member states plus Norway, Liechtenstein and Iceland). A resident in these countries (for PLR purposes) must have their only or principal home there.

Eligible books

In the PLR system each edition of a book is registered and treated as a separate book. A book is eligible for PLR registration provided that:

- it has an eligible author (or co-author);
- it is printed and bound (paperbacks counting as bound);
- it has already been published;
- copies of it have been put on sale, i.e. it is not a free handout;
- the authorship is personal, i.e. not a company or association, and the book is not crown copyright;
- it has an ISBN;
- it is not wholly or mainly a musical score;
- it is not a newspaper, magazine, journal or periodical.

Audiobooks. An audiobook is defined as an 'authored text' or 'a work recorded as a sound recording and consisting mainly of spoken words'. Applications can therefore only be accepted to register audiobooks which meet these requirements and are the equivalent of a printed book. Music, dramatisations and live recordings do not qualify for registration. To qualify for UK PLR in an audiobook contributors should be named on the case in which the audiobook is held; OR be able to refer to a contract with the publisher; OR be named within the audiobook recording.

Ebooks. Only ebooks downloaded to fixed terminals in library premises and then taken away on loan on portable devices to be read elsewhere qualify for PLR payment. As far as PLR is aware, no public libraries in the UK currently provide on-site ebook lending facilities and public library ebook loans in the UK are made to 'remote' off-site locations (e.g. people's homes). Remote ebook loans are covered by copyright licensing arrangements and a change in copyright legislation would be required for 'remote' loans to be included in the UK PLR scheme. The government is committed to looking at the feasibility of such a change in copyright law. Due to these current restrictions, PLR is recommending that ebooks are NOT registered for PLR at present.

Statements and payment

Authors with an online account may view their statement online. Registered authors who do not have an online account receive a statement posted to their address if a payment is due.

Sampling arrangements

To help minimise the unfairness that arises inevitably from a sampling system, the scheme specifies the eight regions within which authorities and sampling points have to be designated and includes libraries of varying size. Part of the sample drops out by rotation each year to allow fresh libraries to be included. The following library authorities have been designated for the year beginning 1 July 2014 (all are multi-site authorities). This list is based on the nine government regions for England plus Northern Ireland, Scotland and Wales.

- East – Essex, Southend-on-Sea and Thurrock, Norfolk
- London – Hillingdon, Southwark, Sutton, Triborough Libraries (Hammersmith and Fulham, Kensington and Chelsea, Westminster)
- North East – Gateshead, Middlesbrough, South Tyneside
- North West & Merseyside – Blackpool, Knowsley, Manchester, Salford, Warrington
- South East – East Sussex, Hampshire, Portsmouth
- South West – LibrariesWest (Bath & North East Somerset, Bristol, North Somerset, Somerset, South Gloucestershire)
- West Midlands – Telford and Wrekin
- Yorkshire & The Humber – North Yorkshire
- Northern Ireland – The Northern Ireland Library Authority
- Scotland – Edinburgh, Highland, Midlothian, North Lanarkshire
- Wales – Ceredigion, Vale of Glamorgan, Wrexham.

Participating local authorities are reimbursed on an actual cost basis for additional expenditure incurred in providing loans data to the PLR Office. The extra PLR work mostly consists of modifications to computer programs to accumulate loans data in the local authority computer and to transmit the data to the PLR Office at Stockton-on-Tees.

Reciprocal arrangements

Reciprocal PLR arrangements now exist with the German, Dutch, Austrian and other European PLR schemes. Authors can apply for overseas PLR for most of these countries through the Authors' Licensing and Collecting Society (see page 687). The exception to this rule is Ireland. Authors should now register for Irish PLR through the UK PLR Office. Further information on PLR schemes internationally and recent developments within the EC towards wider recognition of PLR is available from the PLR Office or on the international PLR website.

Vanity publishing

Mainstream publishers invest their own money in the publishing process. In contrast, vanity publishers require an up-front payment from the author to produce a book. Johnathon Clifford highlights the perils of vanity publishing.

My research into vanity publishing began in 1990 when a 12-year-old girl wrote to me stating she had found a publisher willing to publish her work. I telephoned the 'publisher' under the guise of an aspiring author, and this call was all it took for them to agree to publish my work. Their offer was 100 copies of a 38-page book for a fee of £1,900, with no need for them to see my poetry first.

Definition of vanity publishing

'Vanity publishing, also self-styled (often inaccurately) as "subsidy", "joint-venture", "shared-responsibility" or even "self" publishing, is a service whereby authors are charged to have their work published. Vanity publishers generally offer to publish a book for a specific fee, or offer to include short stories, poems or other literary or artistic material in an anthology, which the authors are then invited to buy.'

– Advertising Standards Authority definition of vanity publishing, 1997

Since then, I have written *Vanity Press & The Proper Poetry Publishers* (1991), a book based on feedback I received from vanity publishers, assisted the Advertising Standards Authority, and collaborated in making television and radio programmes. In 1999, I was invited to the House of Lords to talk about the problem of vanity publishing and the need for a change in the law to stop 'rogue traders' in the publishing world. However, it was not until 2008 that the law was suitably changed to enable the authorities to better curb the excesses of rogue vanity publishers, should they wish.

The perils of vanity publishing

'Vanity publisher' is a phrase I coined in the early 1960s when two American companies were advertising widely in the British press offering to publish poems for a payment of £9 and £12 per poem, respectively. Since then the term has extended its meaning to 'any company that charges a client to publish a book'.

Mainstream publishers invest in the marketing and promotion of a book and make their profit from its sales. In contrast, vanity publishers make their money from up-front charges. One of the main drawbacks of being published by a vanity publisher is its lack of credibility within the industry. The majority of booksellers and library suppliers are loath to handle vanity books and few reviewers are willing to consider a book published in this way. The Business Unit Director of one of the UK's biggest booksellers wrote in 1996: 'We do not buy from vanity publishers except in exceptional circumstances. Their books are, with one or two exceptions, badly produced, over-priced, have poor, uncompetitive jackets and usually have no marketing support.'

I have an extensive collection of documentation passed to me from authors who have approached one of the 100-plus vanity publishers operating in the UK. It consists of vanity publishers' initial promotional letters, subsequent written promises, the contracts and letters of complaint from the author, and the vanity publishers' response to those complaints. In recent years, court judgements have found that some vanity publishers are guilty of 'gross misrepresentation of the services they offer' and, as a result, some have been successfully sued and others forced into 'voluntary' liquidation – often only to swiftly reappear under different names.

How vanity publishers operate

Mainstream publishers never advertise for authors and almost never charge a client, whether known or unknown. Vanity publishers place advertisements wherever they possibly can inviting authors to submit manuscripts. Almost without exception, when authors submit work the vanity publisher will reply that they would like to publish the book but that, as an unknown, the author will have to pay towards the cost. Vanity publishers may tell the author they are very selective in the authors they accept and praise the work, but this is false flattery. I have not been able to find one person during the last 22 years who has been turned down by a vanity publisher – however poorly written their book is. The vanity publisher may state that this is the way many famous authors in the past set out, but this is untrue. Some famous, well-respected authors *have* self-published but none of the 'famous authors' they quote started their writing career by paying a vanity publisher. The BBC programme *Southern Eye* reported that many authors had been sent exactly the same 'glowing report', whatever the subject or quality of their book.

Vanity publishers have charged aspiring authors anything from £1,800 up to (in one recorded instance) £20,000 for publishing their book. Many authors have borrowed thousands of pounds on the strength of promised 'returning royalties', as authors are often led to believe that sales through the vanity publisher's marketing department will recoup their outlay.

In December 1997, *Private Eye* ran an article about three authors, one of whom had paid £2,400 and the other two £1,800 each to a vanity publisher, on the basis that their books would command a 'high level of royalties'. These royalties amounted to £16.35, £21.28 and £47.30 respectively. When the authors complained they each received a threatening letter from the vanity publisher's solicitor. The same company's business practices were featured on the BBC programme *Watchdog* in November 2002.

Some vanity publishers ask their clients to pay a 'subvention', the *Collins English Dictionary* definition of which is 'a grant, aid, or subsidy, as from a government', and therefore it is a meaningless term when used in the context of vanity publishing. However the request for payment is worded, it is the author who will bear the full cost of publishing their book. Not a share of, or a subsidy towards, but the whole cost and a healthy profit margin on top.

Few vanity publishers quote for a specific number of copies, leaving the author with little idea what they are paying for. Vanity publishers may simply keep manuscripts 'on file' and only print on demand, making it difficult to deliver copies quickly enough to the outlets which *do* order them. Other companies propose that once book sales have reached a certain 'target' figure, the client's outlay will be refunded. The number of copies required to be sold is always well in excess of a realistic target.

Some companies claim that part of the service they offer is to send copies of books they 'publish' to Nielsen Books, the Copyright Receipt Office and the British Library. In fact, this is a legal requirement for all UK publishers. Other companies claim a 'special' relationship which enables them to supply information on your book to particular outlets on the internet. But Amazon does not support this: 'Books are listed on Amazon.co.uk's website in a number of ways – we take feeds from BookData and Nielsen (who automatically update these details on our website) as well as from several wholesalers'.

Authors using a vanity publisher should be aware that once they have made the final payment, that the vanity publisher doesn't need to sell a single copy of their book.

Self-publishing — another form of vanity publishing?

One way for an author to see their book in print is to self-publish but, since that became more acceptable, some vanity publishers try to pass themselves off as self-publishers. For a book to be genuinely self-published, a name designated by the author as his or her publishing house must appear on the copyright page of the book as 'publisher' and the book's ISBN number must be registered by the ISBN Agency to that author as publisher.

All the copies of a self-published book are the property of the author to dispose of as they wish. If an author does not want to be involved with the sale and distribution of their book, this can be indicated by ensuring that when details of a book are sent to the ISBN Agency before publication they include a section on the form for 'Distributor (if different from Publisher)'.

On the title page of every book there is a paragraph which, in essence, states 'All rights are reserved. No part of this book can be stored on a retrieval system or transmitted in any form or by whatever means without the prior permission in writing from the *publisher*', i.e. not 'the author' who may have been led to believe that their book is '*self*-published'.

Any company which publishes books under its own name or imprint cannot, by definition, claim to help authors to self-publish. If the name of the company, not the author, appears in the book as that of the publisher, not only can the author not claim to have self-published their book, but they have lost all control over it. If, after the initial publication, someone should wish to produce large type copies (for the poorly-sighted), take up film or television rights, reprint the book under their own imprint, or to publish a copy in translation, there are (in some cases very lucrative) fees to be discussed and paid. But it is legally 'to the publisher' that such application must be made and it is legally 'the publisher' not the author who will benefit. *True* self-publishing gives authors much greater control over the production and dissemination of their books.

'But what does it matter?', I hear some of you ask. Where the honest publisher is concerned, not a great deal perhaps; but there have always been so many 'out there' whose intention is to relieve the unwary of their money, and they are aided in their intent by being able to refer to themselves in terms that are misleading.

Johnathon Clifford may be contacted via his website, www.vanitypublishing.info, which was archived by the British Museum Library in 2009. There you will find a free Advice Pack designed to protect aspiring authors.

Book publishers UK and Ireland

*Member of the Publishers Association or Publishing Scotland
†Member of the Irish Book Publishers' Association

AA Publishing

AA Media Ltd, Fanum House, Basing View, Basingstoke, Hants RG21 4EA
tel (01256) 491524
email aapublish@theaa.com
website www.theAA.com
Directors David Watchus (head of AA Media), Ryan Hennessey (production), Helen Brocklehurst (editorial), Steve Wing (mapping & digital services), Steve Dyos (sales & marketing)

Atlases, maps, leisure interests, travel including *Essential Guides*, *Spiral Guides*, *City Packs* and *Key Guides*. Founded 1979.

Abacus – see Little, Brown Book Group

Absolute Classics – see Oberon Books

Absolute Press – see Bloomsbury Publishing Plc

Academic Press – see Elsevier Ltd

Acorn Editions – see James Clarke & Co. Ltd

Addison-Wesley – see Pearson UK

Adlard Coles Nautical – see Bloomsbury Publishing Plc

Airlife Publishing – see The Crowood Press

Akasha Publishing Ltd

145–157 St John Street, London EC1V 4PW
tel 07939 927281
email info@akashapublishing.co.uk
website www.akashapublishing.co.uk
Director Segun Magbagbeola

Trade (fiction and non-fiction), African and Caribbean interest, fantasy/sci-fi, spirituality, metaphysical, Mind, Body & Spirit, ancient and classical history, alternative history, mythology, children's, Nuwaubian books, biographies and autobiographies. Founded 2012.

Philip Allan – see Hodder Education

Ian Allan Publishing Ltd

Riverdene Business Park, Molesey Road, Hersham, Surrey KT12 4RG
tel (01932) 266600
email marketing@ianallanpublishing.co.uk
website www.ianallanpublishing.com
Publisher Nick Grant, *Sales Manager* Nigel Passmore, *Director of Publishing* Kevin Robertson

An established independent publishers for railway, modelling and road transport enthusiasts, catering for almost every transport specialism. Also produces an eclectic range of social and military history titles for the general market. Transport: railways, shipping, road transport and modelling; naval, military and social history; reference books. Founded 1942.

Ian Allan Publishing (imprint)

Transport: maritime, road transport and modelling; naval, military and social history; reference books.

Oxford Publishing Company (imprint)

Transport: railways. Contact details as Ian Allan Publishing Ltd above.

Lewis Masonic (imprint)

tel (01986) 895433
email philippa.faulks@lewismasonic.co.uk
General Manager Martin Faulks

Freemasonary.

George Allen & Unwin Publishers – see HarperCollins Publishers

J.A. Allen

Clerkenwell House, 45–47 Clerkenwell Green, London EC1R 0HT
tel 020-7251 2661
email allen@halebooks.com
website www.allenbooks.co.uk
Publisher Lesley Gowers

Horse care and equestrianism including breeding, racing, polo, jumping, eventing, dressage, management, carriage driving, breeds, horse industry training, veterinary and farriery. Books usually commissioned but willing to consider any serious, specialist MSS on the horse and related subjects. Imprint of Robert Hale Ltd (page 170). Founded 1926.

Allen Lane – see Penguin Random House UK

Allison & Busby Ltd

12 Fitzroy Mews, London W1T 6DW
tel 020-7580 1080
email susie@allisonandbusby.com
website www.allisonandbusby.com
Publishing Director Susie Dunlop, *Sales & Digital Manager* Lesley Crooks

Fiction, general non-fiction, young adult and preschool. No unsolicited MSS. Founded 1967.

Allyn & Bacon – see Pearson UK

Alma Books

Hogarth House, 32–34 Paradise Road, Richmond, Surrey TW9 1SE
tel 020-8940 6917
website www.almabooks.co.uk
Directors Alessandro Gallenzi, Elisabetta Minervini

Contemporary literary fiction, non-fiction, classics, poetry, drama. Around 40% English-language originals, 60% translations. No unsolicited MSS by email. Founded 2005.

Alma Classics

Hogarth House, 32–34 Paradise Road, Richmond, Surrey TW9 1SE
tel 020-8940 6917
email agallenzi@almabooks.com
website www.almaclassics.com
Managing Director Alessandro Gallenzi

European classics, including novels, plays and poetry; art, literary, music and social criticism, biography and autobiography, essays, humanities and social sciences. No unsolicited MSS. Inquiry letters must include a sae. Series include: *Overture Opera Guides*, *Calder Collection*. Founded 2005.

The Alpha Press – see Sussex Academic Press

Amberley Publishing

The Hill, Stroud, Glos. GL5 4EP
tel (01453) 847800
email info@amberley-books.com
website www.amberley-books.com
Chief Executive Alan Mabley, *Publishing Director* Jonathan Jackson, *Sales Director* Nick Hayward, *Finance Manager* Carole Parnell

General history and local interest; specialisations include transport (railways, canals, maritime), industry, sport, biography and military history. Founded 2008.

Amgueddfa Cymru – National Museum Wales

Cathays Park, Cardiff CF10 3NP
tel 029-2057 3248
email books@museumwales.ac.uk
website www.museumwales.ac.uk
Head of Publishing Mari Gordon

Books based on the collections and research of Amgueddfa Cymru for adults, schools and children, in both Welsh and English.

Ammonite Press – AE Publications Ltd

166 High Street, Lewes, East Sussex BN7 1XU
tel (01273) 477374
email richard.wiles@ammonitepress.com
website www.ammonitepress.com
Joint Managing Directors Jennifer Phillips, Jonathan Phillips, *Managing Editor* Richard Wiles, *Publisher* Jonathan Bailey

Publishes authoritative books on practical photography, written by professional photographers, with a shared emphasis on both photographic technique and equipment. Also publishes stylish gift and coffee-table books on the subjects of social history, music, sport, fashion and politics. Founded 2008.

Andersen Press Ltd

20 Vauxhall Bridge Road, London SW1V 2SA
tel 020-7840 8703 (editorial), 020-7840 8701 (general)
email anderseneditorial@randomhouse.co.uk
website www.andersenpress.co.uk
Managing Director Mark Hendle, *Publisher* Klaus Flugge, *Directors* Philip Durrance, Joëlle Flugge, Rona Selby (editorial picture books), Charlie Sheppard (editorial fiction), Sarah Pakenham (rights)

Children's books: picture books, fiction for 5–8 and 9–12 years and young adult fiction. Will consider unsolicited MSS. Include sae and allow 3 months for response. For novels, send 3 sample chapters and a synopsis only. No poetry or short stories. Do not send MSS via email. Founded 1976.

The Angels' Share – see Neil Wilson Publishing Ltd

Anness Publishing

108 Great Russell Street, London WC1B 3NA *Head office* Blaby Road, Wigston, Leicester LE8 4SE
tel 0116 275 9086
email info@anness.com
website www.annesspublishing.com
Managing Director Paul Anness, *Publisher* Joanna Lorenz

Practical illustrated books on lifestyle, cookery, crafts, reference, gardening, health and children's non-fiction. Founded 1988.

Lorenz Books (hardback imprint)

Aquamarine (hardback imprint)

Southwater (paperback imprint)

Hermes House (promotional imprint)

Practical Pictures (image licensing)
website www.practicalpictures.com

Armadillo (children's imprint)

Anova Children's Books – see Pavilion Children's Books

Antique Collectors' Club Ltd

Sandy Lane, Old Martlesham, Woodbridge, Suffolk IP12 4SD

tel (01394) 389950
email info@antique-acc.com
website www.antiquecollectorsclub.com
Managing Director Diana Steel

World renowned publisher and distributor of definitive books on antiques, fashion, gardening, design and architecture. Founded 1966.

Appletree Press Ltd†

164 Malone Road, Belfast BT9 5LL
tel 028-9024 3074
email reception@appletree.ie
website www.appletree.ie
Director John Murphy

Gift books, guidebooks, history, Irish interest, Scottish interest, photography, sport, travel. Founded 1974.

Aquamarine – see Anness Publishing

Arc Publications

Nanholme Mill, Shaw Wood Road, Todmorden, Lancs. OL14 6DA
tel (01706) 812338
email arc.publications@btconnect.com
website www.arcpublications.co.uk
Directors Tony Ward (founder & managing editor), Angela Jarman (publisher & editor of Arc Music); *Editors* James Byrne (international), Jean Boase-Beier (translation), John W. Clarke (UK & Ireland), Ben Styles (digital editor)

Specialises in contemporary poetry and neglected work from the past: poetry from the UK and Ireland; world poetry in English; and bilingual translations from smaller languages (individual poets and anthologies). Imprints: Arc Publications and Arc Music. Refer to website for current publication list/catalogue and submissions policy. Email editors at: editorarcuk@btinternet.com. No unsolicited MSS. Founded 1969.

Architectural Press – see Elsevier Ltd

Arcturus – see W. Foulsham & Co. Ltd

Arden Shakespeare – see Bloomsbury Publishing Plc

Arena Publishing

6 Southgate Green, Bury St. Edmunds IP33 2BL
tel (01284) 754123
email arenabooks@tiscali.co.uk
website www.arenabooks.co.uk
Director James Farrell

Publishers of quality fiction, travel, history and current affairs, also of specialised social science, politics, philosophy and academic dissertations suitable for transcribing into book format. Special interest in publishing books analysing the debt-fuelled financial crisis from a non-party standpoint. New authors welcome. IPG member.

The Armchair Traveller *at the* bookHaus Ltd

70 Cadogan Place, London SW1X 9AH
tel 020-7838 9055
email info@hauspublishing.com
website www.thearmchairtraveller.com
Publisher Barbara Schwepcke

Publishes travel literature, the *Literary Traveller* series and the Armchair Traveller's *Histories* series.

Arrow Books Ltd – see Penguin Random House UK

Ashgate Publishing Ltd

Wey Court East, Union Road, Farnham GU9 9PT
tel (01252) 736600
email ashgate.online@ashgate.com
website www.ashgate.com
Chairman Nigel Farrow, *Managing Director & Humanities Publishing Director* Rachel Lynch
Humanities Ann Donahue (literary studies, 19th–20th centuries), Erika Gaffney (literary studies to 18th century; visual studies), Heidi Bishop (music), Sarah Lloyd (theology & religious studies), Thomas Gray (history), John Smedley (Publishing Director, Variorum imprint; history)
Social Sciences Alison Kirk (law), Guy Loft (aviation), Kirstin Howgate (international relations; politics), Val Rose (human geography; planning & design), Neil Jordan (sociology), Dymphna Evans (Publisher, reference and LIM)

Publishes a wide range of academic research in the social sciences and humanities, professional practice publications in the management of business and public services, and illustrated books on art, architecture and design. Founded 1967.

Gower (imprint)

website www.gowerpub.com
Publishing Director & Commissioning Editor Jonathan Norman

Business, management and training.

Lund Humphries (imprint)

website www.lundhumphries.com
Managing Director Lucy Clarke

Art and architectural history.

Variorum (imprint)

Publishing Director John Smedley

History.

Ashmolean Museum Publications

Beaumont Street, Oxford OX1 2PH
tel (01865) 288070
email dec.mccarthy@ashmus.ox.ac.uk
website www.ashmolean.org
Contact Declan McCarthy

Fine and applied art of Europe and Asia, archaeology, history, numismatics. No unsolicited MSS. Photographic archive. Museum founded 1683.

Atlantic Books

Ormond House, 26–27 Boswell Street, London WC1N 3JZ
tel 020-7269 1610
email enquiries@atlantic-books.co.uk
Ceo & Publisher Will Atkinson

Literary fiction, thrillers, history, current affairs, politics, reference, biography and memoir. Strictly no unsolicited submissions or proposals. In 2009 Atlantic Books entered a partnership with Australian publisher Allen & Unwin. Founded 2000.

Atlantic Europe Publishing Co. Ltd

The Barn, Bottom Farm, Bottom Lane, Henley-on-Thames, Oxon RG8 0NR
tel (01491) 684028
email info@atlanticeurope.com
website www.atlanticeurope.com
website www.curriculumvisions.com
Director Dr B.J. Knapp

Children's primary school class books: science, geography, technology, mathematics, history, religious education. No MSS accepted by post; submit by email only, no attachments. Founded 1990.

Atom – see Hachette UK

Atrium – see Cork University Press

Attic Press – see Cork University Press

Aureus Publishing Ltd

Castle Court, Castle-upon-Alun, St Bride's Major, Vale of Glamorgan CF32 0TN
tel (01656) 880033
email info@aureus.co.uk
website www.aureus.co.uk
Director Meuryn Hughes

Rock and pop, autobiography, biography, sport; also music. Founded 1993.

Aurora Metro

67 Grove Avenue, Twickenham TW1 4HX
tel 020-3261 0000
email info@aurorametro.com
website www.aurorametro.com
Managing Director Cheryl Robson

Adult fiction, young adult fiction, biography, drama (including plays for young people), non-fiction, theatre, cookery and translation. Submissions: send synopsis and 3 chapters as hard copy to: Neil Gregory, Submissions Editor, at address above. Biennial Competition for women novelists: The Virginia Prize For Fiction. New imprint: Supernova Books publishes non-fiction titles on the arts, culture and biography.

Authentic Media Ltd

52 Presley Way, Milton Keynes MK8 0ES
tel (01908) 268500
email info@authenticmedia.co.uk
website www.authenticmedia.co.uk
Publisher Malcolm Down

Biblical studies, Christian theology, ethics, history, mission, commentaries. Imprints: Paternoster, Authentic.

Avon – see HarperCollins Publishers

Award Publications Ltd

The Old Riding School, The Welbeck Estate, Worksop, Notts. S80 3LR
tel (01909) 478170
email info@awardpublications.co.uk

Children's books: full-colour picture story books; early learning, information and activity books. No unsolicited material. Founded 1972.

Bernard Babani (publishing) Ltd

The Grampians, Shepherds Bush Road, London W6 7NF
tel 020-7603 2581/7296
email enquiries@babanibooks.com
website www.babanibooks.com
Director M.H. Babani

Practical handbooks on radio, electronics and computing. Founded 1942.

Bailliere Tindall – see Elsevier (Clinical Solutions)

Duncan Baird Publishers – see Watkins Media Limited

Bantam – see Penguin Random House UK

Bantam Press – see Penguin Random House UK

Barefoot Books Ltd

294 Banbury Road, Oxford OX2 7ED
tel (01865) 3111000
email help@barefootbooks.com
website www.barefootbooks.co.uk
Owner, Co-founder & Ceo Nancy Traversy, *Co-founder & Editor-in-Chief* Tessa Strickland, *Group Operations Director* Karen Janson

Children's picture books, apps and audiobooks: myth, legend, fairytale, cross-cultural stories. See website for submission guidelines. Founded 1993.

Barrington Stoke

18 Walker Street, Edinburgh EH3 7LP
tel 0131 225 4113
email info@barringtonstoke.co.uk
website www.barringtonstoke.co.uk
Chairman Ben Thomson, *Managing Director* Mairi Kidd

Short fiction and non-fiction, specially adapted and presented for reluctant, struggling and dyslexic readers, aged 9–12 and 13+, with reading ages of 6–8. Short fiction (15,000 words) for adults with a reading age of 8. No picture books, no unsolicited submissions. Founded 1998.

Batsford – see Pavilion Books

BBC Books – see Penguin Random House UK

BBC Children's Books – see Penguin Random House UK

Belair – see Folens Publishers

Bell & Hyman Ltd – see HarperCollins Publishers

Bennion Kearny Ltd

6 Woodside, Churnet View Road, Oakamoor, Staffs ST10 3AE
tel (01538) 703591
email info@BennionKearny.com
website www.BennionKearny.com
Publisher James Lumsden-Cook, *Marketing* Adam Walters

Specialises in non-fiction, with an emphasis on sport, travel and business. Founded 2008.

Berg Publishers – see Bloomsbury Publishing Plc

Berlitz Publishing – see Insight Guides/Berlitz Publishing

BFI Publishing

Palgrave Macmillan, The Macmillan Building, 4 Crinan Street, London N1 9XW
tel 020-7833 4000
email bfipublishing@palgrave.com
website www.palgrave.com/bfi
Head of Publishing Rebecca Barden

Film, TV and media studies; general, academic and educational resources on moving image culture. Founded 1982.

BIOS Scientific Publishers – see Taylor & Francis Group

Birlinn Ltd

West Newington House, 10 Newington Road, Edinburgh EH9 1QS
tel 0131 668 4371
email info@birlinn.co.uk
website www.birlinn.co.uk
Directors Hugh Andrew, Neville Moir, Jan Rutherford, Andrew Simmons, Laura Poynton, Joanne Macleod

Scottish history, local interest/history, Scottish humour, guides, military, adventure, history, archaeology, sport, general non-fiction. Founded 1992.

Polygon (imprint)
New international and Scottish fiction, poetry, short stories, popular Scottish and international general interest. No unsolicited poetry accepted.

John Donald (imprint)
Scottish academic titles.

Mercat Press (imprint)
Walking guides.

BC Books (imprint)
Children's books, fiction and non-fiction.

Arena Sport (imprint)
Sports Books.

Birnbaum – see HarperCollins Publishers

A&C Black – see Bloomsbury Publishing Plc

Black Ace Books

PO Box 7547, Perth PH2 1AU
tel (01821) 642822
website www.blackacebooks.com
Publisher Hunter Steele, *Art, Publicity & Sales Director* Boo Wood

Fiction, Scottish and general; new editions of outstanding recent fiction. Some biography, history, psychology and philosophy. No submissions without first visiting website for latest list details and requirements. Imprints: Black Ace Books, Black Ace Paperbacks. Founded 1991.

Black & White Publishing Ltd*

29 Ocean Drive, Edinburgh EH6 6JL
tel 0131 625 4500
email mail@blackandwhitepublishing.com
website www.blackandwhitepublishing.com
Directors Campbell Brown (managing), Alison McBride

Non-fiction: humour, biography, crime, sport, cookery, general. Fiction: women's fiction, contemporary, psychological thrillers, crime, young adult (15+). Also publisher of *The Broons* and *Oor Wullie* books. Founded 1999.

Black Dog Publishing London UK

10A Acton Street, London WC1X 9NG
tel 020-7713 5097
email editorial@blackdogonline.com
website www.blackdogonline.com

Contemporary art, architecture, design, photography.

Black Lace – see Virgin Books (imprint, in partnership with Virgin Group), page 191

Black Swan – see Penguin Random House UK

Blackline Press

15 Lister Road, Ipswich IP1 5EQ
email info@blacklinepress.com
website www.blacklinepress.com
Proprietor Matt Smith

Specialises in football titles. Established 2009.

Blackstaff Press Ltd†

4D Weavers Court, Linfield Road, Belfast BT12 5GH
tel 028-9034-7510
email info@blackstaffpress.com
website www.blackstaffpress.com
Managing Editor Patsy Horton

Local interest titles, particularly memoir, history and humour. See website for submission guidelines before sending material. Founded 1971.

Blackstone Press Ltd – see Oxford University Press

Blackwater Press – see Folens Publishers

John Blake Publishing Ltd

(incorporating Metro Books, Blake Publishing, Dino Books, Independent Music Press, Max Crime and Smith Gryphon Ltd)
3 Bramber Court, 2 Bramber Road,
London W14 9PB
tel 020-7381 0666
email words@blake.co.uk
website www.johnblakepublishing.co.uk
Publisher John Blake, *Managing Director* Rosie Virgo

Popular non-fiction, including biographies, true crime, food and drink, humour, health and lifestyle. Imprints include Dino Books and Music Press Books. No unsolicited fiction. Founded 1991.

Blink Publishing

107–109 The Plaza, 535 Kings Road, Chelsea,
London SW10 0SZ
tel 020-3770-8888
email info@blinkpublishing.co.uk
email submissions@blinkpublishing.co.uk
website www.blinkpublishing.co.uk
Directors Perminder Mann (managing), Lisa Hoare (commercial), Clare Tillyer (acquisitions & rights), Emily Thomas (publisher/Blink Reality)

BLINK is an imprint focussed on the world of commercial, illustrated and non-illustrated adult non-fiction. With an emphasis on official, authorised authors and popular subjects, also, where relevant, books feature augmented reality technology. Their new imprint BLINK REALITY publishes in hardback and paperback, the focus is memoirs and real-life subjects for a wide commercial audience.

Bloodaxe Books Ltd

Eastburn, South Park, Hexham,
Northumberland NE46 1BS
tel (01434) 611581
email editor@bloodaxebooks.com
website www.bloodaxebooks.com
Directors Neil Astley, Simon Thirsk

Poetry. Check submissions guide on webside and send sample of up to a dozen poems with sae only if the submission fits the publisher's guidelines. No email submissions or correspondence. No disks. Founded 1978.

Bloomsbury Publishing Plc*

50 Bedford Square, London WC1B 3DP
tel 020-7631 5600
website www.bloomsbury.com
Founder & Chief Executive Nigel Newton, *Executive Director* Richard Charkin, *Group Finance Director* Wendy Pallot, *Non-executive Chairman* Sir Anthony Salz, *Non-executive Directors* Ian Cormack, Jill Jones, Stephen Page, *Group Company Secretary* Michael Daykin
Media enquiries Publicity Director, *tel* 020-7631 5670, *email* publicity@bloomsbury.com

A leading independent publicly-quoted publishing house with 4 worldwide publishing divisions: Bloomsbury Adult, Bloomsbury Children's & Educational, Bloomsbury Academic & Professional and Bloomsbury Information. It operates through offices in the UK, the USA (see page 221), India and Australia (see page 210). No unsolicited MSS unless specified below. The Bloomsbury Group includes the following: Absolute Press, Berg Publishers, The Continuum International Publishing Group Plc, Fairchild Books, Hart Publishing. Founded 1986.

Bloomsbury Adult Division

Managing Director Richard Charkin, *Group Editor-in-Chief* Alexandra Pringle, *Special Interest Publishing Director* Janet Murphy, *Publishing Director USA* George Gibson

Worldwide publisher for fiction authors including Margaret Atwood, Nadine Gordimer, William Boyd, Richard Ford, Niall Williams, Stephen Kelman, Colum McCann and Ann Patchett. Non-fiction categories include biography/memoir (Elizabeth Gilbert and Patti Smith), politics, science, history (William Dalrymple, Kate Summerscale, Frank Dikötter), philosophy and religion (A.C. Grayling) and cookery (Paul Hollywood, Hugh Fearnley-Whittingstall, Heston Blumenthal and Tom Kerridge), as well as reference books such as *Who's Who, Wisden Cricketers' Almanack* and *Reeds Nautical Almanac*. Market leaders in natural history, military and naval history, nautical and sports and fitness publishing, current affairs and religious titles. Fiction and non-fiction titles published out of the USA include *Salvage the Bones* by Jesmyn Ward and *Pearl of China* by Anchee Min. Market leaders in natural history, nautical and sports and fitness publishing, current affairs and religious titles.

Absolute Press

Publisher Jon Croft, *Editorial Director* Meg Avent
Specialist food imprint of Bloomsbury Publishing Plc.

General list: cookery, food-related topics, wine, lifestyle. No unsolicited MSS. Founded 1979.

Bloomsbury Children's & Educational Division
Managing Director Emma Hopkin, *Publishing Director & Editor-in-Chief* Rebecca McNally, *Education Publishing Director* Jayne Parsons
Editorial Directors Emma Blackburn (illustrated publishing), Ellen Holgate (fiction), Helen Diamond (educational resources), Saskia Gwinn (non-fiction)

Children's. Bloomsbury Children's Books is a global publisher for children of all ages up to 16 years including titles such as the *Harry Potter* novels by J.K. Rowling, *Holes* by Louis Sachar and *The Graveyard Book* by Neil Gaiman. Recent highlights include *Throne of Glass* by Sarah J Maas; *The Wall* by William Sutcliffe; shortlisted for the Carnegie Medal; and *Lion in my Cornflakes* by Michelle Robinson and Jim Field, which won the inaugrual Sainsbury's Picture Book award. No unsolicited MSS; send a synopsis with 3 chapters. Bloomsbury Spark e-first list launched 2013: www.bloomsburyspark.com.

Educational. Publishes around 80 titles per year for readers 4–14 years including non-fiction, poetry and fiction. Publishes around 100 titles per year for teachers and practitioners in the areas of early years, music, teachers' resources and professional development. Recent fiction and poetry successes include, *Stars in Jars* by Chrissie Gittins, Tom and Tony Bradman's *My Brother's Keeper* and Terry Deary's *World War II Tales*. Recent non-fiction highlights include *My Silly Book of Side-splitting Stuff* by Andy Seed, winner of Blue Peter's Best Book with Facts award, *Steve Jobs* by Karen Blumenthaland publishing with the National Archive. Recent education titles include: *100 Ideas for Secondary Teachers: Outstanding Lessons* by Ross Morrison McGill; *Let's Do Spelling* by by Andrew Brodie and *Continuous Provision The Skills* by Alistair Bryce-Clegg.

Bloomsbury Academic & Professional Division
website www.bloomsburyprofessional.com
website www.bloomsburyacademic.com
Managing Director Jonathan Glasspool. *Publishing contacts*: Martin Casimir (Managing Director, Bloomsbury Professional: law, tax & accountancy); Kathryn Earle (Head of Visual Arts Publishing); Jenny Ridout (drama, media & theatre studies); David Barker (education); David Avital (literary studies); Gurdeep Mattu (linguistics); Dominic Mattos (theology & biblical studies); Liza Thompson/ Colleen Coalter (philosophy); Lalle Pursglove (religious studies); Katie Gallof (media studies); Ally-Jane Grossan (sound studies); Emily Drewe (history); Alice Philips (classics & archaeology); Anna Wright (fashion); Rebecca Barden (design); Jennifer Schmidt (food studies/anthropology); Sinead Moloney (law).
Publishes over 1,500 academic and professional titles, textbooks and print and digital reference works. Typical customers include students, scholars, schools, universities/other higher education establishments and professional firms. Active imprints include Bloomsbury Academic, Bloomsbury Professional, Arden Shakespeare, Fairchild Books, Methuen Drama, T&T Clark and Hart Publishing. Historic imprints include Berg Publishers, Bristol Classical Press, Continuum, AVA.

Berg Publishers
Non-fiction, reference (subjects include fashion studies, design studies, food studies, cultural studies, visual culture, social anthropology, film studies), poetry and music. Founded 1983.

The Continuum International Publishing Group Ltd
Serious non-fiction, academic and professional, including scholarly monographs and educational texts and reference works in education, film, history, linguistics, literary studies, media studies, music, philosophy, politics; biblical studies, religious studies and theology. Imprints: Burns & Oates, Continuum, Network Continuum, T&T Clark International, Thoemmes Press, Mowbray.

Fairchild Books, incorporating AVA Publishing
Editorial Manager Georgia Kennedy
Subjects include fashion, interior design, graphic design, architecture, photography, film and animation, branding, marketing and advertising, product design.

Hart Publishing
16C Worcester Place, Oxford OX1 2JW
tel (01865) 517530
email mail@hartpub.co.uk
website www.hartpub.co.uk
Publisher Sinéad Moloney
Legal academic texts for law students, scholars and practitioners. Will consider unsolicited MSS. Submission guidelines on the website. Books, ebooks and journals on all aspects of law (UK domestic, European and International). Founded in 1996.

Bloomsbury Information Division
website www.qfinance.com
Managing Director Kathy Rooney *Key contacts* Vafa Payman (international business development), Anna Fleming (project delivery)
Publishes approx. 50 titles annually in business, finance, management, language, crosswords, reference and dictionaries. Also develops major digital knowledge hubs with external business partners including the German research organization, the IZA (Institute for the Future of Labor, http://wol.iza.org). The division provides management and publishing services to external partners such as Lloyds Bank, Roland Berger, Ernst & Young and the Qatar Foundation (www.bqfp.com.qa and www.qscience.com).

Blue Guides Ltd
Winchester House, Dean Gate Avenue,
Taunton TA1 2UH

tel 020-8144 3509
email editorial@blueguides.com
website www.blueguides.com

Blue Guides and *Blue Guide Travel Companions*. Detailed guide books with a focus on history, art and architecture for the independent traveller.

BMJ Books – see John Wiley & Sons Ltd

Bodleian Library Publishing
Osney One Building, Osney Mead, Oxford OX2 0EW
tel (01865) 283850
email publishing@bodleian.ox.ac.uk
website www.bodleianshop.co.uk
Head of Publishing Samuel Fanous

The Bodleian Library is the main library of the University of Oxford. The publishing programme creates gift, trade and scholarly books on a wide range of subjects drawn from or related to the Library's rich collection of rare books, manuscripts, maps, postcards and other ephemer.

The Bodley Head – see Penguin Random House UK

Bodley Head Children's Books – see Penguin Random House UK

Bookouture
23 Sussex Road, Uxbridge UB10 8PN
email pitch@bookouture.com
website www.bookouture.com
Managing Director & Publisher Oliver Rhodes, *Publishing Director* Claire Bord, *Senior Commissioning Editor* Keshini Naidoo

Bookouture is a digital imprint offering expertise, flexibility and great royalties (45% of net receipts on ebooks). Focuses on a small number of books. Founded 2012.

Booth-Clibborn Editions
Studio 83, 235 Earls Court Road, London SW5 9FE
tel 020-7565 0688
email info@booth-clibborn.com
website www.booth-clibborn.com

Illustrated books on art, popular culture, graphic design, photography. Founded 1974.

Bounty – see Octopus Publishing Group

Bowker
ProQuest/Dialog/Bowker, 3 Dorset Rise 5th Floor, London EC4Y 8E
tel 020-7832 1700
email sales@bowker.co.uk
website www.bowker.co.uk
Managing Director Doug McMillan

Publishes bibliographic information and management solutions designed to help publishers, booksellers and libraries better serve their customers. Creates products and services that make books easier for people to discover, evaluate, order and experience. Also generates research and resources for publishers, helping them understand and meet the interests of readers worldwide. Bowker, an affiliated business of ProQuest and the official ISBN agency for the United States has its headquarters in New Providence, New Jersey, with additional operations in the UK and Australia.

Boxtree – see Pan Macmillan

Marion Boyars Publishers Ltd
26 Parke Road, London SW13 9NG
email catheryn@marionboyars.com
website www.marionboyars.co.uk
Director Catheryn Kilgarriff

Literary fiction, film, cultural studies, jazz, cookery. Not currently accepting submissions. Founded 1975.

Boydell & Brewer Ltd
PO Box 9, Woodbridge, Suffolk IP12 3DF
tel (01394) 610600
email editorial@boydell.co.uk
website www.boydellandbrewer.com

Medieval studies, early modern and modern history, maritime history, literature, archaeology, art history, music, Hispanic studies. No unsolicited MSS. See website for submission guidelines. Founded 1969.

James Currey (imprint)
website www.jamescurrey.com

Academic studies of Africa and developing economies.

Bradt Travel Guides Ltd
IDC House, The Vale, Chalfont St Peter, Bucks. SL9 9RZ
tel (01753) 893444
email info@bradtguides.com
website www.bradtguides.com
Publishing Director Adrian Phillips

Travel and wildlife guides with emphasis on unusual destinations and ethical/positive travel. Founded 1973.

Brasseys Military – see Pavilion Books

Nicholas Brealey Publishing
3–5 Spafield Street, London EC1R 4QB
tel 020-7239 0360
email rights@nicholasbrealey.com
website www.nicholasbrealey.com
Managing Director Nicholas Brealey

Publishes subjects related to coaching, crossing cultures and the big ideas in business. Also popular psychology, science and philosophy, and includes an expanding travel writing/adventure list. Founded 1992 in London; also has offices in Boston.

Breedon Books Publishing Co. Ltd – see DB Publishing

Brilliant Publications*
Unit 10, Sparrow Hall Farm, Edlesborough, Dunstable LU6 2ES
tel (01525) 222292
email info@brilliantpublications.co.uk
website www.brilliantpublications.co.uk
Managing Director Priscilla Hannaford

Practical resource books for teachers and others concerned with the education of children 0–13 years. All areas of the curriculum published, but specialises in modern foreign languages, art and design, developing thinking skills and PSHE. Some series of books for reluctant readers, aimed at children 7–11 years. No children's picture books, non-fiction books or one-off fiction books. See Manuscript Guidelines on website before sending proposal. Founded 1993.

Bristol Classical Press – see Bloomsbury Publishing Plc

The British Library (Publications)
Publishing Office, The British Library, 96 Euston Road, London NW1 2DB
tel 020-7412 7535
email publishing_editorial@bl.uk
website www.bl.uk
Managers David Way (publishing), Lara Speicher (editorial)

Book arts, bibliography, music, maps, oriental, manuscript studies, history, literature, facsimiles, audio and multimedia. Founded 1979.

The British Museum Press*
38 Russell Square, London WC1B 3QQ
tel 020-7323 1234
email publicity@britishmuseum.co.uk
website www.britishmuseum.org/publicity
Director of Publishing Rosemary Bradley

Award-winning illustrated books for general readers, families, academics and students, inspired by the famous collections of the British Museum. Titles range across the fine and decorative arts, history, archaeology and world cultures. Division of The British Museum Company Ltd. Founded 1973.

Brockhampton Press – see Caxton Publishing Group

Andrew Brodie – see Bloomsbury Publishing Plc

Brown, Son & Ferguson, Ltd*
Unit 1, 426 Drumoyne Road, Glasgow G51 4DA
tel 0141 429 1234 (24 hours)
email info@skipper.co.uk
website www.skipper.co.uk
Editorial Director Richard B.P. Brown

Nautical books, plays. Founded 1860.

Bryntirion Press
(formerly Evangelical Press of Wales)
Bryntirion, Bridgend CF31 4DX
tel (01656) 655886
email office@emw.org.uk
website www.emw.org.uk
Publications Officer Shâron Barnes

Theology and religion (in English and Welsh). Founded 1955.

Burns & Oates – see Bloomsbury Publishing Plc

Business Plus – see Headline Publishing Group

Buster Books – see Michael O'Mara Books Ltd

Butterworth-Heinemann – see Elsevier Ltd

Butterworths – see LexisNexis

Calmann & King Ltd – see Laurence King Publishing Ltd

Cambridge University Press*
University Printing House, Shaftesbury Road, Cambridge CB2 8BS
tel (01223) 358331
email information@cambridge.org
website www.cambridge.org
Chief Executive Peter Phillips; *Managing Directors* Mandy Hill (academic), Michael Peluse (English Language Teaching), Hanri Pieterse (Cambridge Education)

Anthropology and archaeology, art history, astronomy, biological sciences, classical studies, computer science, dictionaries, earth sciences, economics, engineering, history, language and literature, law, mathematics, medical sciences, music, philosophy, physical sciences, politics, psychology, reference, technology, social sciences, theology, religion. English language teaching, educational (primary, secondary, tertiary), e-learning products, journals (humanities, social sciences, science, technical and medical). The Bible and Prayer Book. Founded 1534.

Campbell Books – see Pan Macmillan

Canongate Books Ltd*
14 High Street, Edinburgh EH1 1TE
tel 0131 557 5111
email info@canongate.co.uk
website www.canongate.net
Contacts Jamie Byng (publisher), Kate Gibb (finance), Caroline Gorham (production), Jenny Todd (associate publisher), Francis Bickmore (editorial), Andrea Joyce (associate rights)

Adult general non-fiction and fiction: literary fiction, translated fiction, memoir, politics, popular science, humour, travel, popular culture, history and biography. The independent audio publisher CSA WORD was acquired by Canongate in 2010, with audio now published under the Canongate label. Founded 1973.

Canopus Publishing Ltd

15 Nelson Parade, Bedminster, Bristol BS3 4HY
tel 07970 153217
email robin@canopusbooks.com
website www.canopusbooks.com
Director Robin Rees, *Art Director*, Jamie Symonds, *Editor* Sarah Tremlett

Packager and publisher in astronomy and aerospace. Founded 1999.

Canterbury Press – see Hymns Ancient and Modern Ltd

Jonathan Cape – see Penguin Random House UK

Jonathan Cape Children's Books – see Penguin Random House UK

Capuchin Classics – see Stacey International

Carcanet Press Ltd

4th Floor, Alliance House, 30 Cross Street, Manchester M2 7AQ
tel 0161 834 8730
email info@carcanet.co.uk
website www.carcanet.co.uk
Director Michael Schmidt

Poetry, *Fyfield* series, Oxford Poets, translations. Founded 1969.

Carlton Publishing Group

20 Mortimer Street, London W1T 3JW
tel 020-7612 0400
email enquiries@carltonbooks.co.uk
website www.carltonbooks.co.uk
Chairman Jonathan Goodman, *Editorial Director* Piers Murray Hill, *Publisher* Lisa Edwards

No unsolicited MSS; synopses and ideas welcome, but no fiction or poetry. Imprints: Carlton Books, André Deutsch, Goodman, Goodman Fiell, Prion. Founded 1992.

Goodman Fiell (imprint)

Stylish, intelligent books covering product and graphic design, architecture, fashion and culture.

Carlton Books (imprint)

Sport, music, history, puzzles, lifestyle, fashion, art, photography, popular culture, crime, science.

André Deutsch (imprint)

Autobiography, biography, military history, history, current affairs.

Goodman (imprint)

High-end illustrated books on popular culture and the arts.

Prion Books (imprint)

Humour, nostalgia.

Cassell Illustrated – see Octopus Publishing Group

Cassell Reference – see Weidenfeld & Nicolson

Caterpillar Books – see Little Tiger Group

Catholic Truth Society

40–46 Harleyford Road, London SE11 5AY
tel 020-7640 0042
email info@cts-online.org.uk
website www.cts-online.org.uk
Chairman Rt Rev. Paul Hendricks, *General Secretary* Fergal Martin LLB, LLM

General books of Roman Catholic and Christian interest, liturgical books, missals, Bibles, prayer books, children's books and booklets of doctrinal, historical, devotional or social interest. MSS of 11,000–15,000 words with up to 6 illustrations considered for publication as booklets. Founded 1868.

Caxton Publishing Group

20 Bloomsbury Street, London WC1B 3JH
tel 020-7636 7171
website www.caxtonpublishing.com
Director Finbarr McCabe

Reprints, promotional books, remainders. Imprints: Caxton Editions, Brockhampton Press, Knight Paperbacks.

Cengage Learning*

Cheriton House, Andover SP10 5BE
tel (01264) 332424
email emea.editorial@cengage.com
website www.cengage.co.uk

Actively commissioning texts for further education and higher education courses in the following disciplines: IT, computer science and computer applications; accounting, finance and economics; marketing; international business; human resource management; operations management; strategic management; organisational behaviour; business information systems; quantitative methods; psychology; hairdressing and beauty therapy; childcare; catering and hospitality; motor vehicle maintenance. Submit proposal either by email or by post.

Century – see Penguin Random House UK

The Chalford Press – see The History Press Ltd

Chambers Harrap Publishers Ltd – see Hodder Education

Chapman Publishing
4 Broughton Place, Edinburgh EH1 3RX
tel 0131 557 2207
email chapman-pub@blueyonder.co.uk
website www.chapman-pub.co.uk
Editor Joy Hendry

Poetry and drama: *Chapman New Writing Series*. Also the *Chapman Wild Women Series*. Founded 1986.

Paul Chapman Publishing – see SAGE Publications Ltd

Chartered Institute of Personnel and Development
CIPD Publishing, 151 The Broadway, London SW19 1JQ
tel 020-8612 6200
email publish@cipd.co.uk
website www.cipd.co.uk/bookstore
Head of Publishing Samantha Whittaker

People management, training and development.

Chatto & Windus – see Penguin Random House UK

Chicken House
2 Palmer Street, Frome, Somerset BA11 1DS
tel (01373) 454488
email chickenhouse@doublecluck.com
website www.doublecluck.com
Managing Director & Publisher Barry Cunningham, *Deputy Managing Director* Rachel Hickman

Fiction for ages 7+ and young adult. No unsolicited MSS. See website for details of *The Times*/Chicken House Children's Fiction Competition. Part of Scholastic Inc.

Child's Play (International) Ltd
Ashworth Road, Bridgemead, Swindon, Wilts. SN5 7YD
tel (01793) 616286
email office@childs-play.com
website www.childs-play.com
Chairman Adriana Twinn, *Publisher* Neil Burden

Children's educational books: board, picture, activity and play books; fiction and non-fiction. Founded 1972.

Christian Education*
(incorporating RE Today Services and International Bible Reading Association)
1020 Bristol Road, Selly Oak, Birmingham B29 6LB
tel 0121 472 4242
email anstice.hughes@christianeducation.org.uk
website www.christianeducation.org.uk
website www.retoday.org.uk

Publications and services for teachers and other professionals in religious education including *REtoday* magazine, curriculum booklets and classroom resources. Also publishes Bible reading materials.

Chrysalis Books Group – now Pavilion Books

Churchill Livingstone – see Elsevier (Clinical Solutions)

Churchwarden Publications Ltd
PO Box 420, Warminster, Wilts. BA12 9XB
tel (01985) 840189
email enquiries@churchwardenbooks.co.uk
Directors J.N.G. Stidolph, S.A. Stidolph

Publisher of *The Churchwarden's Yearbook*. Care and administration of churches and parishes.

Cicerone Press
2 Police Square, Milnthorpe, Cumbria LA7 7PY
tel (01539) 562069
email info@cicerone.co.uk
website www.cicerone.co.uk
Managing Director Jonathan Williams

Guidebooks: walking, trekking, mountaineering, climbing, cycling in Britain, Europe and worldwide.

Cico Books – see Ryland Peters & Small

Cisco Press – see Pearson UK

T&T Clark International – see Bloomsbury Publishing Plc

James Clarke & Co. Ltd
PO Box 60, Cambridge CB1 2NT
tel (01223) 350865
email publishing@lutterworth.com
website www.lutterworth.com
Managing Director Adrian Brink

The company started by publishing the religious magazine *Christian World*. Now publishes academic, scholarly and reference works, specialising in theology, history, literature and related subjects. Its publications include two series, the *Library of Theological Translations* and the *Library of Ecclesiastical History*. Publishes books and ebooks on: theology, philosophy, history and biography, biblical studies, literary criticism. Academic and reference books: dictionaries and encyclopaedias. Founded 1859.

The Lutterworth Press (subsidiary)
Books and ebooks on: history and biography, literature and criticism, science, philosophy, music, sport, art and art history, educational titles, biblical studies, theology, mission, religious studies,

collecting, academic and reference books. Imprints: Acorn Editions, Patrick Hardy Books.

Classical Comics

PO Box 16310, Birmingham B30 9EL
tel 0845 812 3000
email info@classicalcomics.com
website www.classicalcomics.com
Managing Director Gary Bryant

Graphic novel adaptations of classical literature.

Cló Iar-Chonnachta Teo.†

Indreabhán, Co. Galway, Republic of Ireland
tel +353 (0)91 593307
email eolas@cic.ie
website www.cic.ie
Director Micheál Ó Conghaile, *General Manager* Deirdre O'Toole

Irish-language – novels, short stories, plays, poetry, songs, history; CDs (writers reading from their works in Irish and English). Promotes the translation of contemporary Irish fiction and poetry into other languages. Founded 1985.

Co & Bear Productions

63 Edith Grove, London SW10 0LB
tel 020-7351 5545
email info@cobear.co.uk
website www.scriptumeditions.co.uk
Publisher Beatrice Vincenzini

High-quality illustrated books on lifestyle, photography, art. Imprints: Scriptum Editions, Cartago. Founded 1996.

Collins & Brown – see Pavilion Books

Collins Languages/COBUILD – see HarperCollins Publishers

Collins Gem – see HarperCollins Publishers

Collins Geo – see HarperCollins Publishers

Colourpoint Creative Limited

Colourpoint House, Jubilee Business Park, 21 Jubilee Road, Newtownards, Co. Down BT23 4YH
tel 028-9182 6339
email sales@colourpoint.co.uk
website www.colourpoint.co.uk
Publisher Malcolm Johnston, *Head of Educational Publishing* Wesley Johnston, *Marketing* Jacky Hawkes

Irish, Ulster-Scots and general interest including local history; transport (covering the whole of the British Isles), buses, road and railways; educational textbooks and resources. Short queries by email. Full submission in writing including details of proposal, sample chapter/section, qualification/experience in the topic, full contact details and return postage. Imprints: Colourpoint Educational, Plover Fiction. Founded 1993.

The Columba Press†

55A Spruce Avenue, Stillorgan Industrial Park, Blackrock, Co. Dublin, Republic of Ireland
tel +353 (0)1 2942556
email info@columba.ie
website www.columba.ie
Publisher & Managing Director Fearghal O Boyle

Religion (Roman Catholic and Anglican) including pastoral handbooks, spirituality, theology, liturgy and prayer; counselling and self-help. Founded 1985.

Connections Book Publishing Ltd

St Chad's House, 148 King's Cross Road, London WC1X 9DH
tel 020-7837 1968
email info@connections-publishing.com
website www.connections-publishing.com
Directors Nick Eddison, Ian Jackson, David Owen

Illustrated non-fiction books, kits and gift titles: broad, popular list including MBS, health, self-help, puzzles and relationships. Imprint: BOOKINABOX (gifts). Founded 1993.

Conran Octopus – see Octopus Publishing Group

Constable & Robinson Ltd – see Little, Brown Book Group

The Continuum International Publishing Group Plc – see Bloomsbury Publishing Plc

Conway – see Pavilion Books

Cork University Press†

Youngline Industrial Estate, Pouladuff Road, Togher, Cork, Republic of Ireland
tel +353 (0)21 4902980
website www.corkuniversitypress.com
Publications Director Mike Collins

Irish literature, history, cultural studies, landscape studies, medieval studies, English literature, musicology, poetry, translations. Founded 1925.

Attic Press and Atrium (imprints)

email corkuniversitypress@ucc.ie

Books by and about women in the areas of social and political comment, women's studies. Cookery, biography and Irish cultural studies (trade).

Council for British Archaeology

Beatrice de Cardi House, 66 Bootham, York YO30 7BZ
tel (01904) 671417
email info@archaeologyuk.org
website www.archaeologyuk.org
Director Mike Heyworth

British archaeology – academic; practical handbooks; general interest archaeology. *British Archaeology* magazine. Founded 1944.

Country Books

(incorporating Ashridge Press)
Courtyard Cottage, Little Longstone, Bakewell, Derbyshire DE45 1NN
tel (01629) 640670
email dickrichardson@country-books.co.uk
website www.countrybooks.biz
website www.sussexbooks.co.uk

Local history (new and facsimile reprints), family history, autobiography, general non-fiction, novels, customs and folklore. Books for the National Trust, Chatsworth House, Peak District NPA, Derbyshire County Council. Established 1995.

Countryside Books

2 Highfield Avenue, Newbury, Berks. RG14 5DS
tel (01635) 43816
website www.countrysidebooks.co.uk
Partners Nicholas Battle, Suzanne Battle

Publishes books of local or regional interest, usually on a county basis: walking, outdoor activities, also heritage, aviation, railways and architecture.

CRC Press – see Taylor & Francis Group

Creme de la Crime – see Severn House Publishers

Crescent Moon Publishing

PO Box 393, Maidstone, Kent ME14 5XU
tel (01622) 729593
email cresmopub@yahoo.co.uk
website www.crmoon.com
Director Jeremy Robinson *Editors* C. Hughes, B.D. Barnacle

Literature, poetry, arts, cultural studies, media, cinema, feminism. Submit sample chapters or 6 poems plus sae, not complete MSS. Founded 1988.

Cressrelles Publishing Co. Ltd

10 Station Road Industrial Estate, Colwall, Malvern, Herefordshire WR13 6RN
tel (01684) 540154
email simon@cressrelles.co.uk
website www.cressrelles.co.uk
Directors Leslie Smith, Simon Smith

General publishing. Founded 1973.

J. Garnet Miller (imprint)

Plays and theatre textbooks.

Kenyon-Deane (imprint)

Plays and drama textbooks for amateur dramatic societies. Plays for women.

New Playwrights' Network (imprint)

Plays for amateur dramatic societies.

Crown House Publishing Ltd

Crown Buildings, Bancyfelin, Carmarthen SA33 5ND
tel (01267) 211345
email books@crownhouse.co.uk
website www.crownhouse.co.uk
Chairman Martin Roberts, *Directors* David Bowman (managing), Glenys Roberts, Karen Bowman, Caroline Lenton, Cathy Heritage

IPA 2013 and 2014 Education Publisher of the Year with a large range of classroom resources and materials for professional teacher development. Also publish books on health and wellbeing, NLP, hypnosis, counselling, psychotherapy and coaching. Founded 1998.

Independent Thinking Press

Crown Buildings, Bancyfelin, Carmarthen SA33 5ND
tel (01267) 211345
email Caroline@independentthinkingpress.com
website www.independentthinkingpress.com

Publishes the thoughts and ideas of some of the UK's leading educational innovators including world-class speakers, award-winning teachers, outstanding school leaders and classroom revolutionaries.

The Crowood Press

The Stable Block, Ramsbury, Marlborough, Wilts. SN8 2HR
tel (01672) 520320
email enquiries@crowood.com
website www.crowood.com
Directors John Dennis (chairman), Ken Hathaway (managing)

Sport, motoring, aviation, military, martial arts, walking, fishing, country sports, farming, natural history, gardening, DIY, crafts, railways, model-making, dogs, equestrian and theatre. Founded 1982.

Airlife Publishing (imprint)

Aviation, technical and general, military, military history.

Benjamin Cummings – see Pearson UK

James Currey – see Boydell & Brewer Ltd

Terence Dalton Ltd

Arbons House, 47 Water Street, Lavenham, Sudbury, Suffolk CO10 9RN
tel (01787) 249290
Director T.A.J. Dalton

Non-fiction.

Darton, Longman & Todd Ltd

1 Spencer Court, 140–142 Wandsworth High St, London SW18 4JJ
tel 020-8875 0155
email willp@darton-longman-todd.co.uk
website www.darton-longman-todd.co.uk
Editorial Director David Moloney

Spirituality, prayer and meditation; books for the heart, mind and soul; self-help and personal growth;

biography; political, enviromental and social issues. Founded 1959.

DB Publishing
(an imprint of JMD Media Ltd)
29 Clarence Rd, Nottingham NG9 5HY
tel (017914) 647382
email steve.caron@dbpublishing.co.uk
website www.dbpublishing.co.uk
Directors Steve Caron (managing), Jane Caron (finance)

Primarily: football, sport, local history, heritage. Now considering all topics including fiction. Unsolicited MSS welcome. Preliminary letter essential. Founded 2009.

Giles de la Mare Publishers Ltd
PO Box 25351, London NW5 1ZT
tel 020-7485 2533
email gilesdelamare@dial.pipex.com
website www.gilesdelamare.co.uk
Chairman Giles de la Mare

Non-fiction: art, architecture, biography, history, music, travel. Telephone before submitting MSS. Founded 1995.

Dean – see Egmont UK Ltd

Dedalus Ltd
24 St Judith's Lane, Sawtry, Cambs. PE28 5XE
tel (01487) 832382
email info@dedalusbooks.com
website www.dedalusbooks.com
Chairman Margaret Jull Costa, *Publisher* Eric Lane, *Editorial* Timonthy Lane

Original fiction in English and in translation; Dedalus European Classics, Dedalus concept books. Founded 1983.

Richard Dennis Publications
The New Chapel, Shepton Beauchamp, Ilminster, Somerset TA19 0JT
tel (01460) 240044
email books@richarddennispublications.com
website www.richarddennispublications.com

Books for collectors specialising in ceramics, glass, illustration, sculpture and facsimile editions of early catalogues.

André Deutsch – see Carlton Publishing Group

diehard
91–93 Main Street, Callander FK17 8BQ
tel (01877) 339449
Director Sally Evans (editorial)

Scottish poetry. Founded 1993.

Digital Press – see Elsevier Ltd

Dino Books
3 Bramber Court, 2 Bramber Road, London W14 9PB
tel 020-7381 0666
email words@blake.co.uk
website www.dinobooks.co.uk

Popular children's non-fiction.

Discovery Walking Guides Ltd
10 Tennyson Close, Northampton NN15 7HJ
tel (01604) 244869
email ask.discovery@ntlworld.com
website www.dwgwalking.co.uk
website www.walking.demon.co.uk
Chairman Rosamund C. Brawn

Publishes 'Walk!' walking guidebooks to UK and European destinations; 'Tour & Trail Super-Durable' large-scale maps for outdoor adventures; 'Bus & Touring' maps; and 'Drive' touring maps. Premium content provider to 3G phone/tablet gps apps for Digital Mapping and Hiking Adventures. 2014 sees DWG launch their new digital range of Tour & Trail Custom Maps, including OSlike Custom Maps UK mapping, and their new digital guide book series combining book, maps and gps navigation in one Digital Adventure package. Publishing in conventional book/map format along with digital platforms. Welcomes project proposals from technologically (gps) proficient walking writers. Founded 1994.

John Donald – see Birlinn Ltd

Dorling Kindersley – see Penguin Random House UK

Doubleday Children's Books – see Penguin Random House UK

Doubleday (UK) – see Penguin Random House UK

The Dovecote Press Ltd
Stanbridge, Wimborne Minster, Dorset BH21 4JD
tel (01258) 840549
email online@dovecotepress.com
website www.dovecotepress.com
Editorial Director David Burnett

Books of local interest: natural history, architecture, history. Founded 1974.

Dref Wen
28 Church Road, Whitchurch, Cardiff CF14 2EA
tel 029-2061 7860
website www.drefwen.com
Directors Roger Boore, Anne Boore, Gwilym Boore, Alun Boore, Rhys Boore

Welsh language publisher. Original Welsh language novels for children and adult learners. Original, adaptations and translations of foreign and English language full-colour picture story books for children. Educational material for primary/secondary school children in Wales and England. Founded 1970.

University College Dublin Press[†]

H103 Humanities Institute, Belfield, Dublin 4, Republic of Ireland
tel +353 (0)1 7164680,
email ucdpress@ucd.ie
website www.ucdpress.ie
Executive Editor Noelle Moran

Humanities: Irish studies, history and politics, literary studies, social sciences, sociology. More recently expanded to include music and food science. Founded 1995.

Gerald Duckworth & Co. Ltd

30 Calvin Street, London E1 6NW
tel 020-7490 7300
email info@duckworth-publishers.co.uk
website www.ducknet.co.uk
Director Peter Mayer (publisher),

General trade publishers. Non-fiction: popular science, history, humour, arts, social science, biography, current affairs, humanities, social sciences, language, Mind, Body & Spirit, sport, travel & travel writing. Fiction: crime, thriller, historical, literary, general. Imprints: Duckworth, Duckworth Overlook, Nonesuch Press, Ardis. No unsolicited MSS. Founded 1898.

Dunedin Academic Press*

Hudson House, 8 Albany Street, Edinburgh EH1 3QB
tel 0131 473 2397
email mail@dunedinacademicpress.co.uk
website www.dunedinacademicpress.co.uk
Director Anthony Kinahan

Earth and environmental sciences, public health and social sciences (esp. children issues), history. See website for submission guidelines. Founded 2000.

Dynasty Press

36 Ravensdon Street, London SE11 4AR
tel 020-8675 3435
email admin@dynastypress.co.uk
website www.dynastypress.co.uk
Contact Roger Day

A boutique publishing house specialising in works connected to royalty, dynasties and people of influence. Committed to the freedom of the press to allow authentic voices and important stories to be made available to the public. Usually publishes titles which reveal and analyse the lives of those placed in the upper echelons of society. Founded 2008.

Earthscan

Dunston House, 14A St Cross Street, London EC1N 8XA
tel 020-7841 1930
email earthinfo@earthscan.co.uk
website www.earthscan.co.uk
Managing Director Jonathan Sinclair Wilson

Publishes under the Routledge imprint for Taylor & Francis Group (page 203). Academic and professional: sustainable development, climate and energy, natural resource management, cities and built environment, business and economics, design and technology.

Ebury Press – see Penguin Random House UK

Eden – see Penguin Random House UK

Edinburgh University Press*

The Tun – Holyrood Road, 12 Jackson's Entry, Edinburgh EH8 8PJ
tel 0131 650 4218
email editorial@eup.ac.uk
website www.euppublishing.com
Chairman Ivon Asquith, *Chief Executive* Timothy Wright, *Head of Editorial* Nicola Ramsey, *Head of Journals* Sarah Edwards, *Head of Sales & Marketing* Anna Glazier

Academic publishers of scholarly books and journals: film, media and cultural studies, Islamic and Middle Eastern studies, history, law, linguistics, literary studies, philosophy, politics, Scottish studies, American studies, religious studies, classical and ancient history. Trade: literature and culture, Scottish history and politics.

The Educational Company of Ireland

Ballymount Road, Walkinstown, Dublin 12, Republic of Ireland
tel +353 (0)1 4500611
email info@edco.ie
website www.edco.ie
Executive Directors Martina Harford (Chief Executive), Robert McLoughlin

Educational MSS on all subjects in English or Irish language. Trading unit of Smurfit Kappa Group – Ireland. Founded 1910.

Educational Explorers (Publishers)

Unit 5, Feidr Castell Business Park, Fishguard SA65 9BB
tel (01348) 874890
website www.cuisenaire.co.uk
Directors M.J. Hollyfield, D.M. Gattegno

Educational. Recent successes include: mathematics: *Numbers in Colour with Cuisenaire Rods*; languages: *The Silent Way*; literacy, reading: *Words in Colour*; educational films. No unsolicited material. Founded 1962.

Egmont UK Ltd*

The Yellow Building, 1 Nicholas Road, London W11 4AN
email info@egmont.co.uk
website www.egmont.co.uk

The UK's largest specialist children's publisher, publishing books from babies to teens, inspiring children to read. Publishes award-winning books, magazines, ebooks and apps each year. Egmont has a growing portfolio of digital publishing which includes: the first Flips books for Nintendo DS, apps for iPhone and iPad, ebooks and enhanced ebooks and online virtual worlds. Egmont UK is part of the Egmont Group and owned by the Egmont Foundation, a charitable trust dedicated to supporting children and young people. It is Scandinavia's leading media group and Europe's largest children's publisher telling stories through books, magazines, film, TV, music, games and mobile in 30 countries throughout the world. Founded 1878.

Egmont Press

email childrensreader@euk.egmont.com

Picture book and gift (ages 0+), fiction (ages 5+). Authors include Michael Morpurgo, Enid Blyton, Andy Stanton, Michael Grant, Lemony Snicket, Kristina Stephenson, Giles Andreae, Jan Fearnley and Lydia Monks. Submission details: visit website to see current policy.

Egmont Publishing Group

email charcterpr@euk.egmont.com

Egmont Publishing Group is the UK's leading licensed character publisher of books and magazines for children from birth to teen. Books portfolio includes Thomas the Tank Engine, Mr Men, Fireman Sam, Ben 10, Bob the Builder, Baby Jake and Everything's Rosie and covers a wide range of formats from storybooks, annuals and novelty books to colouring, activity and sticker books. Magazines portfolio includes *Thomas & Friends*, *Disney Princess*, *Toy Story*, *Barbie*, *Ben 10*, *Tinker Bell*, *Fireman Sam*, *We Love Pop* and girls' pre-teen magazine *Go Girl* and boys' lifestyle title *Toxic*.

Eland Publishing Ltd

61 Exmouth Market, London EC1R 4QL
tel 020-7833 0762
email info@travelbooks.co.uk
website www.travelbooks.co.uk
Directors Rose Baring, John Hatt, Barnaby Rogerson

Has a backlist of 125 titles in the areas of classic travel literature. No unsolicited MSS. Please email in first instance. Founded 1982.

Element – see Harper Thorsons, imprint of HarperCollins Publishers

11:9 – see Neil Wilson Publishing Ltd

Edward Elgar Publishing Ltd

The Lypiatts, 15 Lansdown Road, Cheltenham, Glos. GL50 2JA
tel (01242) 226934
email info@e-elgar.co.uk
website www.e-elgar.com
Managing Director Tim Williams

Economics, business, law, public and social policy. Founded 1986.

Elliott & Thompson

27 John Street, London WC1N 2BX
tel 020-7831 5013
email pippa@eandtbooks.com
website www.eandtbooks.com
Chairman Lorne Forsyth, *Director* Olivia Bays, *Publisher* Jennie Condell, *Senior Editor* Pippa Crane

History, biography, music, popular science, gift, sport, business, economics and adult fiction. Founded 2009.

Elsevier Ltd*

The Boulevard, Langford Lane, Kidlington, Oxford OX5 1GB
tel (01865) 843000
website www.elsevier.com
Ceo Ron Mobed

Academic and professional reference books; scientific, technical and medical books, journals, CD-Roms and magazines. No unsolicited MSS, but synopses and project proposals welcome. Imprints: Academic Press, Architectural Press, Bailliere Tindall, Butterworth-Heinemann, Churchill Livingstone, Digital Press, Elsevier, Elsevier Advanced Technology, Focal Press, Gulf Professional Press, JAI, Made Simple Books, Morgan Kauffman, Mosby, Newnes, North-Holland, Pergamon, Saunders. Division of Reed Elsevier, Amsterdam.

The Emma Press Ltd

118 Bathurst Road, Winnersh, Wokingham, Berks RG41 5JF
email queries@theemmapress.com
website http://theemmapress.com
Directors Emma Wright (publishing), Rachel Piercey (editorial)

Themed poetry anthologies, single-author poetry pamphlets and prose pamphlets, including short stories, essays, guides and recipes. Does not consider unsolicited MSS but runs bi-monthly open calls for submissions of poetry for anthologies and annual calls for poetry and prose pamphlets. Check website for details. Established 2012.

Encyclopaedia Britannica (UK) Ltd

2nd Floor, Unity Wharf, 13 Mill Street, London SE1 2BH
tel 020-7500 7800
email enquiries@britannica.co.uk
website www.britannica.co.uk
Managing Director Ian Grant, *VP of Operations* Jane Helps

Enitharmon

10 Bury Place, London WC1A 2JL
tel 020-7430 0844
email info@enitharmon.co.uk
website www.enitharmon.co.uk
Directors Stephen Stuart-Smith, Isabel Brittain

Imprints: Enitharmon Press: poetry, including fine editions. Some literary criticism, fiction, translations. Enitharmon Editions: Artists' books, prints. No unsolicited MSS. No freelance editors or proofreaders required. Founded 1967.

Lawrence Erlbaum Associates – see Taylor & Francis Group

Euromonitor International plc
60–61 Britton Street, London EC1M 5UX
tel 020-7251 8024
email info@euromonitor.com
website www.euromonitor.com
Directors T.J. Fenwick (managing), R.N. Senior (chairman)

Business and commercial reference, marketing information, European and International Surveys, directories. Founded 1972.

Europa Publications Ltd – see Taylor & Francis Group

Evangelical Press of Wales – see Bryntirion Press

Everyman – see The Orion Publishing Group Ltd

Everyman's Library
50 Albemarle Street, London W1S 4BD
tel 020-7493 4361
email books@everyman.uk.com
email guides@everyman.uk.com
website www.everymanslibrary.co.uk
Publisher David Campbell

Everyman's Library (clothbound reprints of the classics); *Everyman Pocket Classics*; *Everyman's Library Children's Classics*; *Everyman's Library Pocket Poets*; *Everyman Guides*; P. G. Wodehouse. No unsolicited submissions. Imprint of Alfred A. Knopf.

University of Exeter Press
Reed Hall, Streatham Drive, Exeter EX4 4QR
tel (01392) 263066
email uep@exeter.ac.uk
website www.exeterpress.co.uk
Publisher Simon Baker, Franca Driessen (sales, marketing, distribution)

Academic and scholarly books on European literature, film history, performance studies, local history (Exeter and the South West). Imprints include: University of Exeter Press, Bristol Phoenix Press, The Exeter Press. Distributor in the UK, Europe and the Middle East for US academic presses, including American Schools of Oriental Research, Centre for International Governance Innovation, Eliot Werner Publications, Kelsey Museum Publications, Lockwood Press, Yale Egyptological Insitute. Founded 1958.

Helen Exley®
16 Chalk Hill, Watford, Herts. WD19 4BG
tel (01923) 474480
website www.helenexleygiftbooks.com
Directors Dalton Exley, Helen Exley (editorial), Lincoln Exley, Richard Exley

Popular colour gift books for an international market. No unsolicited MSS. Founded 1976.

Eye Books
29 Barrow St., Much Wenlock, Shropshire TF13 6EN
tel 020-3239 3027
email dan@eye-books.com
website www.eye-books.com
Publisher Dan Hiscocks

Eye Books specialises in inspirational travel stories which aims to show that extraordinary things are done by ordinary people. Founded 1996.

F&W Media International Ltd
Brunel House, Ford Close, Newton Abbot, Devon TQ12 4PU
tel (01626) 323200
website www.fwmedia.co.uk
Managing Director James Woollam

A community-focused, creator of content (for books, ebooks and digital downloads) and marketer of products and services for hobbyists and enthusiasts including crafts, hobbies, art techniques, writing books, gardening, natural history, equestrian, DIY, military history, photography. Founded 1960.

F100 Group
34–42 Cleveland Street, London W1T 4LB
tel 020-7323 0323
email info@f100.com
website www.f100.com
Chairman Vitek Tracz

Life science publishing, electronic publishing and internet communities.

Faber and Faber Ltd*
Bloomsbury House, 74–77 Great Russell Street, London WC1B 3DA
tel 020-7927 3800
website www.faber.co.uk
Publisher & Chief Executive Stephen Page, *Finance Director* Mary Cannam, *Publishers* Hannah Griffiths (paperbacks, crime, fiction), Julian Loose (arts, non-fiction), Leah Thaxton (children's), *Faber Social Creative Director* Lee Brackstone, *Communications Director* Rachel Alexander, *Sales & Services Director* Charlotte Robertson, *Consumer Marketing Director* Matt Haslum, *Faber Press Director* Henry Volans, *Publishing Services Director* Nigel Marsh, *Rights Director* Lisa Baker, *Head of Faber Academy* Ian Ellard, *Faber Factory Director* Simon Blacklock, *Faber Factory Plus International Sales Manager* Anne Bowman

High-quality general fiction and non-fiction, children's fiction and non-fiction, drama, film, music, poetry. Unsolicited submissions accepted for poetry only. For information on poetry submission procedures, ring 020-7927 3800, or consult the website. No unsolicited MSS.

Fabian Society

61 Petty France, London SW1H 9EU
tel 020-7227 4900
email info@fabians.org.uk
website www.fabians.org.uk
General Secretary Andrew Harrop

Current affairs, political thought, economics, education, environment, foreign affairs, social policy. Also controls NCLC Publishing Society Ltd. Founded 1884.

Fairchild Books – see Bloomsbury Publishing Plc

CJ Fallon

Ground Floor, Block B, Liffey Valley Office Campus, Dublin 22, Republic of Ireland
tel +353 (0)1 6166400
email editorial@cjfallon.ie
website www.cjfallon.ie
Executive Directors Brian Gilsenan (managing), John Bodley (financial)

Educational textbooks. Founded 1927.

Featherstone Education – see Bloomsbury Publishing Plc

David Fickling Books

31 Beaumont Street, Oxford OX1 2NP
tel (01865) 339000
website www.davidficklingbooks.co.uk
Publisher David Fickling

Picture books, fiction for 5–8 and 9–12 years, young adult fiction and poetry. Will consider unsolicited MSS (first 3 chapters only); include covering letter and sae and allow 3 months for response. If possible, find an agent first. Founded 2000.

Fig Tree – see Penguin Random House UK

Findhorn Press Ltd

Delft Cottage, Dyke, Forres, Scotland IV36 2TF
tel (01309) 690582
email info@findhornpress.com
website www.findhornpress.com

Mind, Body & Spirit and healing. Founded 1971.

Fineleaf Editions

Moss Cottage Studio, Ross-on-Wye HR9 5TB
tel 07951 939688
email fineleafeditions@mac.com
website www.fineleaf.co.uk
Editor Philip Gray

Landscape, nature, social history, language, photography and fine art titles – in hardback, paperback and ebook formats. Founded in 2005.

First and Best in Education

Earlstrees Court, Earlstrees Road, Corby, Northants NN17 4HH
tel (01536) 399011
email sales@firstandbest.co.uk
website www.shop.firstandbest.co.uk
Contact Anne Cockburn (editor)

Education-related books (no fiction, no primary). Currently actively looking for new ideas for educational books. Email submissions to anne@firstandbest.co.uk. Founded 1992.

Fisherton Press

150 South Birkbeck Road, London E11 4JH
email general@fishertonpress.co.uk
website www.fishertonpress.co.uk
Director Ellie Levenson

A small independent publisher producing picture books for children under 7 that adults also like reading. Interested in receiving ideas and MSS from authors and portfolios and book ideas from illustrators.

Fitzrovia Press Ltd

10 Grafton Mews, London W1T 5JG
tel 020-7380 0749
email info@fitzroviapress.co.uk
email pratima@fitzroviapress.co.uk
website www.fitzroviapress.co.uk
Publisher Richard Prime, *Marketing Director* Pratima Patel

Fiction and non-fiction: Hinduism and creative writing grounded in Eastern philosophy that explores spirituality in the West. Submit outline plus sample chapter; no complete MSS. Founded 2008.

Five Star – see Serpent's Tail (imprint), page 194

Flame Tree Publishing

6 Melbray Mews, Fulham, London SW6 3NS
tel 020-7751 9650
email info@flametreepublishing.com
website www.flametreepublishing.com
Ceo/Publisher Nick Wells, *Managing Director* Francis Bodiam

Culture, cookery and lifestyle. Part of Flame Tree Publishing Ltd. Currently not accepting unsolicited MSS. Founded 1992.

Fleming Publications

9/2 Fleming House, 134 Renfrew Street, Glasgow G3 6ST
tel (0141) 3281935
email info@flemingpublications.com
website www.flemingpublications.com
Managing Editor Etta Dunn

Fiction, non-fiction, poetry, history, biography, photography and self-help.

Floris Books*

15 Harrison Gardens, Edinburgh EH11 1SH
tel 0131 337 2372
email floris@florisbooks.co.uk
website www.florisbooks.co.uk
Commissioning Editors Sally Polson, Eleanor Collins

Religion, science, philosophy, holistic health, organics, Mind, Body & Spirit, Celtic studies, crafts, parenting; children's books: board, picture books, activity books. Founded 1978.

Kelpies (imprint)

Contemporary Scottish fiction – picture books (for 3–6 years), young readers series (for 6–8 years) and novels (for 8–15 years). See website for submission details. Annual Kelpies Prize, see website.

Flyleaf Press

4 Spencer Villas, Glenageary, Co. Dublin, Republic of Ireland
tel +353 (0)1 2854658
email books@flyleaf.ie
website www.flyleaf.ie
Managing Editor James Ryan

Irish family history. Founded 1988.

Focal Press – see Elsevier Ltd

Folens Publishers

Hibernian Industrial Estate, off Greenhills Road, Tallaght, Dublin 24, Republic of Ireland
tel +353 (0)1 4137200
website www.folens.ie
Chairman Dirk Folens, *Managing Director* John O'Connor

Educational (primary, secondary, comprehensive, technical, in English and Irish). Founded 1956.

Blackwater Press (imprint)

General non-fiction, Irish interest. Founded 1993.

Fonthill Media Ltd

10 Hythe Bridge Street, Oxford OX1 2EW
tel (01865) 248856
email office@fonthillmedia.com
website www.fonthillmedia.com
Publisher & Ceo Alan Sutton

General history. Specialisations include biography, military history, aviation history, naval and maritime history, regional and local and history, transport (railway, canal, road) history, social history, sports history, ancient history and archaeology. Also publishes widely in the USA with American regional, local, military and transport history under the imprints of Fonthill, America Through Time and American History House. Founded 2011.

Footprint Handbooks

6 Riverside Court, Lower Bristol Road, Bath BA2 3DZ
tel (01225) 469141
email contactus@footprintbooks.com
website www.footprinttravelguides.com
Director Patrick Dawson

Travel guides.

W. Foulsham & Co. Ltd

The Old Barrel Store, Brewery Courtyard, Draymans Lane, Marlow, Bucks SL7 2FF
tel (01753) 526769
Managing Director B.A.R. Belasco, *Editorial Director* W. Hobson

Life issues. General know-how, cookery, health and alternative therapies, hobbies and games, gardening, sport, travel guides, DIY, collectibles, popular New Age. Imprints: Foulsham, Quantum. Founded *c.*1800.

Quantum (imprint)

Mind, Body & Spirit, popular philosophy and practical psychology.

Four Courts Press†

7 Malpas Street, Dublin 8, Republic of Ireland
tel +353 (0)1 4534668
email info@fourcourtspress.ie
website www.fourcourtspress.ie
Senior Editor Martin Fanning, *Marketing & Sales Manager* Anthony Tierney

Academic books in the humanities, especially history, Celtic and medieval studies, art, theology. Founded 1970.

Fourth Estate – see HarperCollins Publishers

Free Association Books

1 Angel Cottages, Milespit Hill, London NW7 1RD
email aosolomons@gmail.com
website www.freeassociationpublishing.com
Director Trevor E. Brown, *Publishing Director* Alice Solomons *Marketing Manager* Lisa Findley

Social sciences, psychoanalysis, psychotherapy, counselling, cultural studies, social welfare, addiction studies, child and adolescent studies. No poetry or fiction. Founded 1984.

Free Press – see Simon & Schuster UK Ltd

Samuel French Ltd*

52 Fitzroy Street, London W1T 5JR
tel 020-7387 9373, 020-7255 4300
email theatre@samuelfrench-london.co.uk
website www.samuelfrench-london.co.uk
Directors Nate Collins (chairman, USA), David Webster (operations)

Publishers of plays and agents for the collection of royalties. Will consider full-length plays only if have been performed professionally. One-act scripts, if received a production of some kind, should be submitted in full. Scripts not returned without a sae. Founded 1830.

The Friday Project – see HarperCollins Publishers

Frontinus Ltd

4 The Links, Cambridge Road, Newmarket CB8 0TG
tel (01638) 663456
email info@frontinus.org.uk
website http://pandhp.com
Directors Anthony Haynes, Karen Haynes

Publishes 6 titles a year in academic and professional non-fiction. No unsolicited MSS. Founded 2006.

Frontline – see Pen & Sword Books Ltd

FT Prentice Hall – see Pearson UK

David Fulton – see Taylor & Francis Group

Gaia Books – see Octopus Publishing Group

The Gallery Press

Loughcrew, Oldcastle, Co Meath, Republic of Ireland
tel +353 (0)49 8541779
email gallery@indigo.ie
website www.gallerypress.com
Editor/Publisher Peter Fallon

Poetry and drama – by Irish authors only at this time. Founded 1970.

Galley Beggar Press

email info@galleybeggar.co.uk
website www.galleybeggar.co.uk
Co-directors Eloise Millar, Sam Jordison

Independent publisher based in Norwich. Looks for authors whose writing shows great ambition and literary merit in their chosen genre. Original publishers of Eimear McBride's *A Girl is a Half-formed Thing* – winner of the Baileys Women's Prize for Fiction 2014. When submitting a MS authors must provide proof that they have read another book that Galley Beggar Press has published. Prefers completed MS; email as PDF or Word document. One submission per author. Considers a wide range of genres including fiction, non-fiction, quality sci-fi, novels and short stories. No poetry or children's. See website for detailed submission guidelines. Founded 2011.

Gallic Books

59 Ebury St, London SW1W 0NZ
tel 020-7259 9336
email info@gallicbooks.com
website www.gallicbooks.com
Managing Director Jane Aitken, *Editorial Director* Pilar Webb

French writing in translation. Only accepts submissions from French publishers or from agents representing French authors. Founded 2007. Imprint: Aardvark Bureau.

Garland Science – see Taylor & Francis Group

J. Garnet Miller – see Cressrelles Publishing Co. Ltd

Garnet Publishing Ltd*

8 Southern Court, South Street, Reading RG1 4QS
tel (01189) 597847
email info@garnetpublishing.co.uk
website www.garnetpublishing.co.uk
Managing Director Nadia Khayat

Art, architecture, photography, fiction, religious studies, travel and general, mainly on the Middle East and Islam. Accepts unsolicited material only if relevant to Islam and the Middle East. Founded 1991.

Ithaca Press (imprint)

A leading publisher of academic books devoted to Middle Eastern studies.

Geddes & Grosset

(an imprint of The Gresham Publishing Company Ltd)
Academy Park, Gower Street (Building 4000), Glasgow G51 1PR
tel 0141 375 1998
email info@geddesandgrosset.co.uk
website www.geddesandgrosset.com
Publishers Ron Grosset, Liz Small

Mass market reference *Word Power* – English language learning and health and well-being. Associated imprint: Waverley Books. Founded 1988.

Gibson Square

tel 020-7096 1100
email info@gibsonsquare.com
website www.gibsonsquare.com
Publisher Martin Rynja

Non-fiction: female interest, general non-fiction, biography, current affairs, philosophy, politics, cultural criticism, psychology, history, travel, art history, some fiction. Books should have the potential to engage the author in a debate; see website for guidelines or email to receive an automated response. Authors include Helena Frith Powell, Alexander Litvinenko, Melanie Phillips, Bernard-Henri Lévy, Diana Mitford, Lady Mosley, Anthony Grayling, John McCain. Founded 2001.

Gill & Macmillan†

Hume Avenue, Park West, Dublin 12, Republic of Ireland
tel +353 (0)1 5009500
email sales@gillmacmillan.ie
website www.gillmacmillan.ie

Founder and Chairman Michael Gill, *Managing Director* Dermot O'Dwyer

A leading independent publisher and distributor in Dublin. Its origins date back to 1856 when MHGill & Son, whose portfolio included printing and bookselling, was founded. In partnership with the Macmillan Group in London, Gill & Macmillan was founded 1968. Now fully owned by the Gill family following the buyout of the Macmillan interest in 2013.

Gill & Macmillan Books Division
website www.gillmacmillanbooks.ie
Irish interest non-fiction: biography, cookery, history, current affairs, Mind, Body & Spirit, giftbooks and children, reference, lifestyle. Publisher of established authors and champion of new voices.

Gill & Macmillan Primary Division
website www.gillandmacmillan.ie/primary
Textbooks, resources and digital content for Irish primary classrooms. Includes the English language programme Fireworks: www.fireworks.ie; the Maths programme Cracking Maths: www.crackingmaths.ie; and the phonics programme: www.phonics.ie.

Gill & Macmillan Secondary Division
website www.gillmacmillan.ie/secondary
Publishes print and digital texts, including online resources for the Junior and Leaving Certificate second-level curricular market. Product range includes the market leader in revision guides, *Less Stress, More Success* www.moresuccess.ie, and the online testing resource, www.etest.ie.

Gill & Macmillan Distribution Division
website www.gillmacmillan.ie/distribution
Ireland's largest distributor of books for publishers. Servicing over 50 publishers on a wide range of services, including physical distribution, sales representation, ONIX distribution and sales reporting.

The Gingko Library
70 Cadogan Place, London SW1X 9AH
tel 020-7838 9055
email barbara@thegingkolibrary.com
website www.gingkolibrary.com
Publisher Barbara Schwepcke

A library of thought and scholarship focusing on the Middle East and North Africa.

Ginn – see Pearson UK

GL Assessment*
9th Floor East, 389 Chiswick High Road, London W4 4AL
tel 020-8996 3333
email information@gl-assessment.co.uk
website www.gl-assessment.co.uk
Group Education Director Andrew Thraves

Testing and assessment services for education and health care, including literacy, numeracy, thinking skills, ability, learning support and online testing. Founded 1981.

Godsfield Press – see Octopus Publishing Group

The Goldsmith Press Ltd
Newbridge, Co. Kildare, Republic of Ireland
tel +353 (0)45 433613
email viv1@iol.ie
website www.gerardmanleyhopkins.org
Directors V. Abbott, D. Egan, *Secretary* B. Ennis

Literature, art, Irish interest, poetry. Unsolicited MSS not returned. Founded 1972.

Gollancz – see The Orion Publishing Group Ltd

Gomer Press
Llandysul, Ceredigion SA44 4JL
tel (01559) 363090
email gwasg@gomer.co.uk
website www.gomer.co.uk
website www.pontbooks.co.uk
Managing Director Jonathan Lewis, *Editors* Elinor Wyn Reynolds (adult, Welsh), Ceri Wyn Jones (adult, English), Sioned Lleinau (children's, Welsh), Cathryn Gwynn (children's, English)

History, travel, photography, biography, art, poetry and fiction of relevance to Welsh culture, in English and in Welsh. Picture books, novels, stories, poetry and teaching resources for children. Preliminary enquiry essential. Imprint: Pont Books (English books for children). Founded 1892.

Goss & Crested China Club
62 Murray Road, Horndean, Waterlooville PO8 9JL
tel 023-9259 7440
email info@gosschinaclub.co.uk
website www.gosschinaclub.co.uk
Managing Director Lynda J. Pine

Crested heraldic china, antique porcelain. Milestone Publications – publishing and bookselling division of Goss & Crested China Club. Mail Order only. Founded 1967.

Government Supplies Agency
Publications Division, Office of Public Works, 52 St Stephen's Green, Dublin 2, Republic of Ireland
tel +353 (0)1 6476834

Irish government publications.

Gower – see Ashgate Publishing Ltd

Granta Books
12 Addison Avenue, London W11 4QR
tel 020-7605 1360
website www.grantabooks.com
Publisher Sigrid Rausing, *Editorial Directors* Laura

Barber, Bella Lacey, *Commissioning Editors* Max Porter, Anne Meadows, *Rights Director* Angela Rose, *Publicity Director* Pru Rowlandson, *Production Director* Sarah Wasley, Sales, *Marketing & Digital Director* Iain Chapple, *Finance Manager* Morgan Graver

Literary fiction, memoir, nature writing, cultural criticism and travel. No submissions except via a reputable literary agent. An imprint of Granta Publications. Founded 1982.

Green Print – see Merlin Press Ltd

Gresham Books Ltd

The Carriage House, Ningwood Manor, Ningwood, Isle of Wight PO30 4NJ
tel (01983) 761389
email info@gresham-books.co.uk
website www.gresham-books.co.uk
Managing Director Nicholas Oulton

Hymn books, prayer books, service books, school histories and Companions.

Grub Street Publishing

4 Rainham Close, London SW11 6SS
tel 020-7924 3966, 020-7738 1008
email post@grubstreet.co.uk
website www.grubstreet.co.uk
Principals John B. Davies, Anne Dolamore

Adult non-fiction: military, aviation history, cookery. Founded 1992.

Guild of Master Craftsman Publications Ltd

166 High Street, Lewes, East Sussex BN7 1XU
tel (01273) 477374
email jonathanb@thegmcgroup.com
website www.gmcbooks.com
Joint Managing Directors Jennifer Phillips, Jonathan Phillips, *Managing Editor* Jonathan Bailey

GMC Publications is a diverse publisher of leisure and hobby project books, with a focus on all types of woodworking; from carving and turning to routing. Craft subjects include needlecraft, paper crafts and jewellery-making. The books are aimed at craftspeople of all skill levels. Founded 1979.

Button Books (imprint)

website www.buttonbooks.co.uk

A new imprint of GMC Publications publishing children's books and producing stationery for children aged 5 years and under.

Guinness World Records

3rd Floor, 184–192 Drummond Street, London NW1 3HP
tel 020-7891 4567
website www.guinnessworldrecords.com

Guinness World Records, *GWR Gamer's Edition*, TV and brand licensing, records processing. No unsolicited MSS. A Jim Pattison Group company. Founded 1954.

Gulf Professional Press – see Elsevier Ltd

Hachette Children's Group*

Carmelite House, 50 Victoria Embankment, London EC4Y 0DZ
website www.hachettechildrens.co.uk
Ceo Hilary Murray Hill

Children's non-fiction, reference, information, gift, fiction, picture, novelty and audiobooks. Unsolicited material is not considered other than by referral or recommendation. Formed by combining Watts Publishing with Hodder Children's Books in 2005. Part of Hachette UK (see page 169).

Hodder Children's Books (imprint)

Publishing Director Anne McNeil

Fiction, picture books, novelty, general non-fiction and audiobooks.

Orchard Books (imprint)

Publishing Director Megan Larkin

Fiction, picture and novelty books.

Little, Brown Books for Young Readers (imprint)

Publishing Director Karen Ball

Fiction, novelty, general non-fiction and audiobooks.

Franklin Watts (imprint)

Publishing Director Rachel Cooke

Non-fiction and information books.

Wayland (imprint)

Editorial Director Debbie Foy

Non-fiction and information books.

Orion Children's Books (imprint)

Publishing Director Fiona Kennedy

Fiction, picture books, novelty, general non-fiction and audiobooks.

Hachette UK*

Carmelite House, 50 Victoria Embankment, London EC4Y 0DZ
tel 020-7873 6000
website www.hachette.co.uk
Chief Executive Tim Hely Hutchinson, *Directors* Jamie Hodder Williams (Ceo, Hodder & Stoughton, Headline, John Murray Press, Quercus), Chris Emerson (Coo), Jane Morpeth (managing, Headline), Marlene Johnson (managing, Hachette Children's), David Young (Deputy Ceo, Hachette UK/Ceo, Orion), Malcolm Edwards (managing, Orion), Alison Goff (Ceo, Octopus), Ursula Mackenzie (Chairman, Little, Brown Book Group), Pierre de Cacqueray (finance), Richard Kitson (commercial/Chairman, Hachette Australia and Hachette New Zealand), Dominic Mahony (group HR), Michael Pietsch (Ceo, Hachette Book Group USA), Clare Harington (group

communications), Diane Spivey (group contracts), Hilary Murray Hill (Ceo, Hachette Children's Group), David Shelley (Ceo, Little, Brown Book Group), Lis Tribe (managing, Hodder Education)

Part of Hachette Livre SA since 2004. Hachette UK group companies: Hachette Children's Books (page 169), Headline Publishing Group (page 172), Hodder Education Group (page 173), Hodder & Stoughton (page 173), John Murray Press (page 182), Little, Brown Book Group (page 178), Octopus Publishing Group (page 184), Orion Publishing Group (page 185), Quercus Publishing Plc (page 195), Hachette Ireland, Hachette Australia (page 211), Hachette New Zealand (page 216), Hachette Book Publishing India Private Ltd.

Halban Publishers

22 Golden Square, London W1F 9JW
tel 020-7437 9300
email books@halbanpublishers.com
website www.halbanpublishers.com
Directors Martine Halban, Peter Halban

General fiction and non-fiction; history and biography; Jewish subjects and Middle East. No unsolicited MSS considered; preliminary letter or email essential. Founded 1986.

Haldane Mason Ltd

PO Box 34196, London NW10 3YB
tel 020-8459 2131
email info@haldanemason.com
website www.haldanemason.com
Directors Sydney Francis, Ron Samuel

Illustrated non-fiction books and box sets, mainly for children. No unsolicited material. Imprints: Haldane Mason (adult), Red Kite Books (children's). Founded 1995.

Robert Hale Ltd

Clerkenwell House, 45–47 Clerkenwell Green, London EC1R 0HT
tel 020-7251 2661
email enquire@halebooks.com
website www.halebooks.com
Directors Gill Jackson (managing & editorial), John Hale (chairman), Robert Hale (production)

Adult general non-fiction and fiction. Founded 1936.

Halsgrove Publishing

Halsgrove House, Ryelands Business Park, Bagley Road, Wellington, Somerset TA21 9PZ
tel (01823) 653777
email sales@halsgrove.com
website www.halsgrove.com
Managing Director Julian Davidson, *Publisher* Simon Butler

Regional books for local-interest readers in the UK. Also illustrated books on individual artists. Founded 1986.

Hamish Hamilton – see Penguin Random House UK

Hamlyn – see Octopus Publishing Group

Patrick Hardy Books – see James Clarke & Co. Ltd

Harlequin (UK) Ltd*

Eton House, 18–24 Paradise Road, Richmond, Surrey TW9 1SR
tel 020-8288 2800
website www.millsandboon.co.uk
Directors Tim Cooper (managing), Stuart Barber (finance), Angela Barnatt (production & operations), Donna Hillyer (editorial), Jackie McGee (human resources)

Founded 1908.

Mills & Boon Historical™ (imprint)
Senior Editor L. Fildew
Historical romance fiction.

Mills & Boon Medical™ (imprint)
Senior Editor S. Hodgson
Contemporary romance fiction.

Mills & Boon Cherish™ (imprint)
Senior Editor Bryony Green
Commercial literary fiction.

Mira Books® (imprint)
Editorial Director Donna Condon
Women's fiction.

Mills & Boon Modern Romance™ (imprint)
Senior Editor Joanne Grant

HarperCollins Entertainment – see HarperCollins Publishers

HarperCollins Publishers*

77–85 Fulham Palace Road, London W6 8JB
tel 020-8741 7070
also at Westerhill Road, Bishopbriggs, Glasgow G64 2QT
tel 0141 772 3200
website www.harpercollins.co.uk
Ceo Charlie Redmaybe

All fiction and trade non-fiction must be submitted through an agent, or unsolicited MSS may be submitted through the online writing community at www.authonomy.com. Owned by News Corporation. Founded 1819.

Harper NonFiction (division and imprint)
Publisher Carol Tonkinson
Autobiographies, entertainment, cookery, lifestyle and sport.

Avon
website www.avon-books.co.uk
Associate Publisher Caroline Ridding
Women's commercial fiction and crime.

HarperFiction
Publisher Kate Elton

General, historical fiction, crime and thrillers, women's fiction.

Voyager (imprint)
Publishing Director Jane Johnson

Fantasy/sci-fi.

Blue Door (imprint)
Publisher Patrick Janson-Smith

Commercial literary fiction and non-fiction.

The Borough Press (imprint)
Publisher Katie Espiner

Literary fiction.

HarperImpulse (imprint)
Publisher Kimberley Young

Digital first-romance fiction.

HarperCollins (imprint)
Publishing Director David Brawn

Agatha Christie, J.R.R. Tolkien, C.S. Lewis.

HarperTrue (imprint)
Publisher Carole Tonkinson

Digital-first imprint with focus on short, real-life stories.

HarperCollins Audio (imprint)
Director of Audio Jo Forshaw

See page 234.

Harper Thorsons (imprint)
Publisher Carole Tonkinson

Heatlh, personal development, spirituality and inspirational memoir.

HarperCollins Children's Books
website www.harpercollinschildrensbooks.co.uk
Publisher Ann-Janine Murtagh

Quality picture books for under 7s; fiction for 6+ years to young adult; graphic novels; TV/film tie-ins; properties.

Fourth Estate (imprint)
Publishing Director/Publisher Nick Pearson

Fiction, literary fiction, current affairs, popular science, biography, humour, travel.

The Friday Project
email info@thefridayproject.co.uk
website www.thefridayproject.co.uk
Publisher Scott Pack

Books developed from popular websites with publishing initiatives that embrace new digital technology. Imprints: Friday Books, Friday Fiction, Friday Food, Friday Children's, Friday Instants.

William Collins (imprint)
Publishing Director Arabella Pike, *Associate Publisher* Myles Archibald (natural history)

Collins Learning (division)
Managing Director Colin Hughes

Collins Language (division and imprint)
Publishing Director Elaine Higgleton (editorial)

Bilingual and English dictionaries, English dictionaries for foreign learners.

Collins Education (imprint)
Managing Director Colin Hughes

Books, CD-Roms and online material for UK primary and secondary schools and colleges.

Collins Geo (imprint)
Managing Director and Deputy Managing Director Collins Learning Sheena Barclay

Maps, atlases, street plans and leisure guides.

HarperTrue – see HarperCollins Publishers

Hart Publishing – see Bloomsbury Publishing Plc

Harvill Secker – see Penguin Random House UK

Haus Publishing Ltd

70 Cadogan Place, London SW1X 9AH
tel 020-7838 9055
email info@hauspublishing.com
website www.hauspublishing.com
Publisher Barbara Schwepcke

Publishes history, literary fiction, translated fiction, biography. Founded 2003.

Hawthorn Press

1 Lansdown Lane, Stroud, Glos. GL5 1BJ
tel (01453) 757040
email info@hawthornpress.com
website www.hawthornpress.com
Directors Martin Large

Publishes books for a creative, peaceful and sustainable world. Series include Early Years, Steiner/Waldorf Education, Crafts, Personal Development, Art and Science, Storytelling. Founded 1981.

Hay House Publishers

2nd Floor, Astley House, 33 Notting Hil Gate, London W11 3JQ
tel 020-3675 2450
email info@hayhouse.co.uk
website www.hayhouse.co.uk
Managing Director & Publisher Michelle Pilley, *International Sales & Operations Director* Diane Hill, *Communications Director* Jo Burgess, *Commissioning Editor* Amy Kiberd

Publishers of Mind, Body & Spirit; self-help; personal development; health and inspirational fiction. Head office in San Diego, California. Founded 1984; in UK 2003.

Haynes Publishing

Sparkford, Yeovil, Somerset BA22 7JJ
tel (01963) 440635
website www.haynes.co.uk
Directors J.H. Haynes (founder director), J. Haynes (chairman), Jeremy Yates-Round (managing & sales), G.R. Cook, J. Bunkum

Practical Manuals for the home; car, motorcycle, motorsport and leisure activities. Plus other practical books on home DIY and computing. Email: lmcintyre@haynes.co.uk, srendle@haynes.co.uk, jfalconer@haynes.co.uk.

Haynes Book Division (imprint)

email mhughes@haynes.co.uk
Editorial Director Mark Hughes

Colour manuals on transport, military, aviation, home, leisure and general interest.

Haynes Motor Trade Division (imprint)

email jaustin@haynes.co.uk
Editorial Director Matthew Minter

Car and motorcycle service and repair manuals and technical data books.

Head of Zeus

Clerkenwell House, 45–47 Clerkenwell Green, London EC1R 0HT
tel 020-7253 5557
email hello@headofzeus.com
website www.headofzeus.com
Chairman Anthony Cheetham, *Ceo* Amanda Ridout, *Fiction Publisher* Laura Palmer, *Non-fiction Publishers* Richard Milbank, Neil Belton, *Digital Publisher* Nicolas Cheetham, *Sales Director* Dan Groenewald

General and literary fiction, genre fiction and non-fiction. UK and Commonwealth distributers for MysteriousPress.com, one of the world's largest digital crime fiction lists. Founded 2012.

Headland Publications

Editorial office Tŷ Coch, Galltegfa, Llanfwrog, Ruthin, Denbighshire LL15 2AR
and 38 York Avenue, West Kirby, Wirral CH48 3JF
tel 0151 625 9128
email headlandpublications@hotmail.co.uk
website www.headlandpublications.co.uk
Editor Gladys Mary Coles

Poetry, anthologies of poetry and prose. No unsolicited MSS. Founded 1970.

Headline Publishing Group

Carmelite House, 50 Victoria Embankment, London EC4Y 0DZ
tel 020-7873 6000
email enquiries@headline.co.uk
website www.headline.co.uk
website www.hachettelivreuk.co.uk
Managing Director Jane Morpeth, *Publishing Director, Fiction* Mari Evans, *Publishing Director, Tinder Press* Imogen Taylor, *Publishing Director, Non-fiction* Jonathan Taylor

Commercial and literary fiction (hardback, paperback and ebook) and popular non-fiction including autobiography, biography, food and wine, gardening, history, popular science, sport, TV tie-ins. Publishes under Headline, Headline Review, Tinder Press, Headline Eternal. Part of Hachette UK (see page 169).

William Heinemann – see Penguin Random House UK

Heinemann – see Pearson UK

Christopher Helm – see Bloomsbury Publishing Plc

The Herbert Press – see Bloomsbury Publishing Plc

Hermes House – see Anness Publishing

Nick Hern Books Ltd

The Glasshouse, 49A Goldhawk Road, London W12 8QP
tel 020-8749 4953
email info@nickhernbooks.co.uk
website www.nickhernbooks.co.uk
Publisher Nick Hern, *Managing Director* Matt Applewhite

Theatre and performing arts books, professionally produced plays, performing rights. Initial letter required. Founded 1988.

Hesperus Press Ltd

28 Mortimer Street, London W1W 7RD
tel 020-4360 869
email info@hesperuspress.com
website www.hesperuspress.com

Under three imprints, Hesperus Press publishes over 300 books by many of the greatest figures in worldwide literary history, as well as contemporary and debut authors worth discovering. Hesperus Classics introduces forgotten books to new generations, Hesperus Nova showcases quality contemporary literature and Hesperus Minor rediscovers well-loved children's books from the past. Founded 2002.

Hippo – see Scholastic Ltd

Hippopotamus Press

22 Whitewell Road, Frome, Somerset BA11 4EL
tel (01373) 466653
email rjhippopress@aol.com
Editors Roland John, Anna Martin

Poetry, essays, criticism. Submissions from new writers welcome. Founded 1974.

Historical™ – see Harlequin (UK) Ltd

The History Press Ltd

The Mill, Brimscombe Port, Stroud, Glos. GL5 2QG
tel (01453) 883300
website www.thehistorypress.co.uk
Vice Chairman Stuart Biles, *Managing Director* Tim Davies, *Finance Director* Gareth Swain, *Strategic Development Director* Laura Perehinec, *Publishers* Sophie Bradshaw (general history & gift), Michael Leventhal (military & transport), Jamie Kinnear (local history), Susan Swalwell (Pitkin), *Rights* Anette Fuhrmeister

Tumbleweed (imprint)

Giftbooks.

The History Press (imprint)

Military history; aviation, maritime and railway transport history, local history; general history and biography.

Phillimore (imprint)

British local history and genealogy.

Pitkin (imprint)

History, heritage, leisure, travel.

Hodder & Stoughton

338 Euston Road, London NW1 3BH
tel 020-7873 6000
website www.hodder.co.uk
website www.hachettelivreuk.co.uk
Ceo Jamie Hodder Williams, *Managing Director* Carolyn Mays, *Deputy Managing Director* Lisa Highton, *Publishing Director* Carole Welch, *Non-fiction Director* Rowena Webb, *Non-fiction Publisher* Rupert Lancaster

Commercial and literary fiction; biography, autobiography, history, humour, Mind, Body & Spirit, travel, lifestyle and cookery and other general interest non-fiction; audio. No unsolicited MSS or synopses. Publishes under Hodder & Stoughton, Sceptre, Mobius. Part of Hachette UK (see page 169).

Hodder Children's Books – see Hachette Children's Group

Hodder Education

338 Euston Road, London NW1 3BH
tel 020-7873 6000
website www.hoddereducation.co.uk
website www.galorepark.co.uk
website www.risingstars-uk.com
website www.hachette.co.uk
Directors Lis Tribe (managing), Alex Jones (finance), Andrea Carr (Rising Stars, managing), Robert Sulley (international), Steve Connolly (digital & FE publishing), Paul Cherry (core subjects & Philip Allan) Jim Belben (humanities & social sciences), Alyssum Ross (business operations) , Janice Holdcroft (UK sales & development), Victoria Goodall (marketing), John Mitchell (Hodder Gibson)

School and College publishing. Part of Hachette UK (see page 169).

Hodder Faith

338 Euston Road, London NW1 3BH
tel 020-7873 6000
email faitheditorialenquiries@hodder.co.uk
website www.hodderfaith.com
Managing Director Jamie Hodder-Williams, *Director of Publishing* Ian Metcalfe

Bibles, Christian books, biography/memoir. Publishes New International Version (NIV) of the Bible, Today's New International Version (TNIV) of the Bible, New International Reader's Version (NIrV) of the Bible. Part of Hachette UK (see page 169).

Hodder Gibson*

2A Christie Street, Paisley PA1 1NB
tel 0141 848 1609
email hoddergibson@hodder.co.uk
website www.hoddergibson.co.uk
Managing Director John Mitchell

Secondary educational books specifically for Scotland. No unsolicited MSS. Part of Hachette UK (see page 169).

Hodder Headline Ltd – see Hachette UK

Hodder Wayland – see Hachette UK

Honno Ltd (Welsh Women's Press)

Honno, Unit 14, Creative Units,
Aberystwyth Arts Centre, Penglais Campus,
Aberystwyth, Ceredigion SY23 3GL
tel (01970) 623150
email post@honno.co.uk
website www.honno.co.uk
Editor Caroline Oakley

Literature written by women in Wales or women with a Welsh connection. All subjects considered – fiction, non-fiction, autobiographies. No poetry or works for children considered. Honno is a community co-operative. Founded 1986.

Hopscotch

(a division of MA Education)
St Jude's Church, Dulwich Road, London SE24 0PB
tel 020-7501 6736
email sales@hopscotchbooks.com
website www.hopscotchbooks.com
Associate Publisher Angela Morano-Shaw

Teaching resources for primary school teachers. Founded 1997.

Practical Pre-School Books

Early years teacher resources.

House of Lochar

Isle of Colonsay, Argyll PA61 7YR
tel (01951) 200323
email sales@houseoflochar.com
website www.houseoflochar.com
Managing Director Georgina Hobhouse, *Editorial Director* Kevin Byrne

Scottish history, transport, Scottish literature. Founded 1995.

How To Books Ltd – see Little, Brown Book Group

John Hunt Publishing Ltd

Laurel House, Station Approach, Alresford, Hants SO24 9JH
email office1@jhpbooks.net
website www.johnhuntpublishing.com
Director John Hunt

Global spirituality and Mind, Body & Spirit, history, religion and philosophy. See website for submission procedure. Imprint include: 6th Books for parapsychology, Axis Mundi Books for esoteric thought and practice, Ayni Books for complementary health, Dodona Books for divination, Moon Books for paganism and shamanism, O Books for broader spirituality, Earth Books for books on the environment, Iff Books for philosophy and popular science, Soul Rocks Books for alternative spirituality, Sassy Books for badass girls, Psyche Books for mind and self, Roundfire Books for fiction, Perfect Edge Books for literary fiction, Cosmic Egg Books for fantasy, Top Hat Books for historical fiction, Our Street Books for children, Lodestone Books for young adults, Liberalis Books for education, Compass Books for new writers, Changemakers Books for transformation, Christian Alternative for liberal Christianity, Business Books, Gaming Books and Zero Books for society, politics and culture. Founded 1989.

Hutchinson – see Penguin Random House UK

Hutchinson Children's Books – see Penguin Random House UK

Hymns Ancient and Modern Ltd*

Third Floor, Invicta House, 108–114 Golden Lane, London EC1Y 0TG
tel 020-776 7551
website www.hymnsam.co.uk
Publishing Director Christine Smith

Theological books with special emphasis on text and reference books and contemporary theology for both students and clergy. Founded 1929.

Saint Andrew Press

Publisher of the Church of Scotland.

Church House Publishing

Publisher of the Church of England – church resources, stationery and Common Worship.

Canterbury Press (imprint)

Norwich Books and Music, 13A Hellesdon Park Road, Norwich NR6 5DR
tel/fax (01603) 785925
website www.canterburypress.co.uk

Hymnals, popular religious writing, spirituality and liturgy.

SCM Press (imprint)

website www.scmpress.co.uk

Academic theology.

Icon Books Ltd

The Omnibus Business Centre, 39–41 North Road, London N7 9DP
tel 020-7697 9695
email info@iconbooks.com
website www.iconbooks.com
Directors Peter Pugh (chairman), Philip Cotterell (managing), Duncan Heath (editorial), Andrew Furlow (sales & marketing), Henry Lord (publicity)

Popular, intelligent non-fiction: Introducing series, literature, history, philosophy, politics, psychology, sociology, cultural studies, science, current affairs, computers, women, anthropology, humour, music, cinema, linguistics, economics. Submission details: will consider unsolicited MSS (adult non-fiction only). Founded 1991.

ICSA Publishing

Saffron House, 6–10 Kirby Street, London EC1N 8EQ
tel 020-7612 7020
email publishing@icsa.org.uk
website www.icsa.org.uk/bookshop
Managing Director Susan Richards

Publishing company of the Institute of Chartered Secretaries and Administrators, specialising in information solutions for legal and regulatory compliance. Founded 1981.

Igloo Books Ltd

Cottage Farm, Mears Ashby Road, Sywell, Northants NN6 0BJ
tel (01604) 741116
email editorial@igloobooks.com
website www.igloobooks.com

Children's books: licensed books, novelty, board, picture, activity, audio, education, ebooks and apps. Adult books: cookery, lifestyle, gift, trivia and non-fiction. Not currently accepting submissions. Founded 2005.

Impress Books Ltd

Innovation Centre, Rennes Drive, University of Exeter, Devon EX4 4RN
tel (01392) 262301
email enquiries@impress-books.co.uk
website www.impress-books.co.uk
Contacts Richard Willis, Colin Morgan

Provides quality thought-provoking titles for the enquiring general reader. Established 2004.

Imprint Academic

PO Box 200, Exeter, Devon EX5 5HY
tel (01392) 851550
email graham@imprint.co.uk
website www.imprint-academic.com
Publisher Keith Sutherland, *Managing Editor* Graham Horswell

Books and journals in politics, philosophy and psychology for both academic and general readers. Book series include *St Andrews Studies in Philosophy and Public Affairs. British Idealist Studies, Societas* (essays in political and cultural criticism), and the *Library of Scottish Philosophy*. Unsolicited MSS, synopses and ideas welcome by email to the Managing Editor or with return postage only. Founded 1980.

In Pinn – see Neil Wilson Publishing Ltd

Indepenpress Publishing Ltd

25 Eastern Place, Brighton BN2 1GJ
tel (01273) 272758
email info@penpress.co.uk
website www.indepenpress.co.uk
Directors Lynn Ashman (managing), Grace Rafael (production)

Literary fiction, general fiction, children's fiction, selected non-fiction. Members of the Independent Publishers Guild and Booksellers Association. Founded 1996.

Indepenpress (imprint)

Traditional publishing.

Pen Press (imprint)

Self-publishing, POD, Partnership.

Pink Press (imprint)

Gay and lesbian fiction.

Indigo Dreams Publishing Ltd

24 Forest Houses, Cookworthy Moor, Halwill, Beaworthy, Devon EX21 5UU
email publishing@indigodreams.co.uk
website www.indigodreams.co.uk
Editors Ronnie Goodyer, Dawn Bauling

Winners of Ted Slade Award for Services to Poetry 2015. Publishes approx. 50 titles per year. Main subject areas: (poetry) anthologies, collections, pamphlets, three magazines. New and experienced writers welcome. Also non-fiction.

Dorcas Imprints (imprint)

Editor Ronnie Goodyer, *Editor* Dawn Bauling
Publishes for niche markets or self-publishing projects.

Tamar Books (imprint)

Editor Ronnie Goodyer
Non-fiction subject matter relating to south west England.

Infinite Ideas

36 St Giles, Oxford OX1 3LD
tel (01865) 514888
email info@infideas.com
website www.infideas.com/publishing.asp
Managing Director Richard Burton

Lifestyle, *52 Brilliant Ideas* series (health, fitness, relationships; leisure and lifestyle; sports, hobbies and games; careers, finance and personal development), business books. *Infinite Success* series (re-interpreted personal development and business classics); *Feel Good Factory* series (lifestyle), *Wine* series (Classic Wine Library). Submit business book proposals directly to richard@infideas.com. Founded 2003.

Insight Guides/Berlitz Publishing

1st Floor West, Magdalen House, 136–148 Tooley Street, London SE1 2TU
tel 020-7403 0284
website www.insightguides.com
website www.berlitzpublishing.com
Consumer & Digital Marketing Executive Rebecca Lovell

Travel, language and related multimedia. Founded 1970.

Institute of Public Administration†

Vergemount Hall, Clonskeagh, Dublin 6, Republic of Ireland
tel +353 (0)1 2403600
email rboyle@ipa.ie
website www.ipa.ie
Publisher Richard Boyle

Government, economics, politics, law, public management, health, education, social policy and administrative history. Founded 1957.

Inter-Varsity Press

Norton Street, Nottingham NG7 3HR
tel 0115 978 1054
email ivp@ivpbooks.com
website www.thinkivp.com
Ceo B. Wilson

IVP is a charitable literature ministry, supporting the mission and ministry of the local church. Imprint: Apollos (Contact P. Duce via ivp@ivpbooks.com).

Irish Academic Press Ltd†

8 Chapel Lane, Sallins, Co. Kildare, Republic of Ireland
tel +353 (0)45 895562
email info@iap.ie
website www.iap.ie

General and academic pulishing with a focus on modern Irish history, politics, literature, culture and arts. Imprints: Irish Academic Press, founded 1974: Merrion Press, founded 2012.

Ithaca Press – see Garnet Publishing Ltd

IWM (Imperial War Museums)
Lambeth Road, London SE1 6HZ
tel 020-7416 5000
email publishing@iwm.org.uk
website www.iwm.org.uk

IWM tells the stories of people who have lived, fought and died in conflicts involving Britain and the Commonwealth since 1914. Drawing on the IWM's unique collections, publishes a large range of books linked to their exhibitions and archives. Books are produced both in-house and in partnership with other publishers.

Jacaranda Books Art Music Ltd
5 Achilles Road, West Hampstead,
London NW6 1DZ
020-7609 0891
email office@jacarandabooksartmusic.co.uk
website www.jacarandabooksartmusic.co.uk
Founder & Publisher Valerie Brandes, *Digital, Communications & Acquisitions* Jazzmine Breary

Independent publisher of literary and genre adult fiction, and non-fiction, including high-quality illustrated books. Titles and authors cross linguistic, racial, gender and cultural boundaries, highlighting issues affecting ethnic minorities, women, and young people. Publishes diverse writing with a focus on Africa, the Caribbean and the Diaspora. Authors include Stephen Thompson, Irenosen Okojie, Frances Mensah Williams, Fiston Mwanza Mujila, Obinna Udenwe, Pede Hollist and Jessie De Boer. Accepts unsolicited MSS – please consult the website for further information. Founded 2012.

JAI – see Elsevier Ltd

Jane's – see HarperCollins Publishers

Jane's Information Group
163 Brighton Road, Coulsdon, Surrey CR5 2YH
tel 020-8700 3700
website www.janes.com
Group Publishing Director Sean Howe

Professional business-to-business publishers in hardcopy and electronic multimedia: military, aviation, naval, defence, reference, police, geo-political. Consumer books in association with HarperCollins Publishers.

Jarrold Publishing – see The History Press Ltd

Joffe Books
Unit 3, 7A Plough Yard, London EC2A 3LP
email jasper@joffebooks.com
website www.joffebooks.com
Publisher Jasper Joffe

Independent publisher of digital and print fiction. Aceepts submissions from authors and agents, please see website for guidelines. Best-selling authors include T.J. Brearton, Taylor Adams and Emma Bennet. Focuses on high-quality thrillers, detective, and romance fiction. Founded 2012.

Jordan Publishing Ltd
21 St Thomas Street, Bristol BS1 6JS
tel 0117 918 1492
email sales@jordanpublishing.co.uk
website www.jordanpublishing.co.uk
Ceo Will Ricketts

Jordan Publishing Limited is the largest independent legal publisher in the UK. Produces practical information, online and in print, for practising lawyers and other professionals. Publishes textbooks, looseleafs, journals, court reference works and news services and also supplies software to law firms in the form of digital service PracticePlus – which combines step-by-step workflows, practice notes, automated court forms and links to core reference works. The company works with partners in key areas, such as the APIL series of guides, and also publishes around 40 new books and editions annually across a wide range of practice areas.

Michael Joseph – see Penguin Random House UK

Kenilworth Press – see Quiller Publishing Ltd

Kenyon-Deane – see Cressrelles Publishing Co. Ltd

Laurence King Publishing Ltd*
(formerly Calmann & King Ltd)
361–373 City Road, London EC1V 1LR
tel 020-7841 6900
email enquiries@laurenceking.com
website www.laurenceking.com
Directors Laurence King (managing), Nicholas Perren (chairman), Mark Scott (sales), Joanne Lightfoot (editorial), Philip Cooper (editorial), Maria Treacy-Lord (financial)

Illustrated books on design, contemporary architecture, art, interiors and fashion for the professional, student and general market. Founded 1976.

Kingfisher – see Pan Macmillan

Kingscourt – see McGraw-Hill Education

Jessica Kingsley Publishers*
73 Collier Street, London N1 9BE
tel 020-7833 2307
email hello@jkp.com
website www.jkp.com
Managing Director Jessica Kingsley

Psychology, psychiatry, arts therapies, social work, special needs (especially autism spectrum), education, law, practical theology and a small children's list focusing on books for children with special needs. Founded 1987.

Kluwer Law International

Zuidpoolsingel 2, 2408 ZE Alphen aan den Rijn, The Netherlands
tel +35 172-641-552
email sales@kluwerlaw.com
website www.kluwerlaw.com
Publisher Simon Bellamy

International law.

Charles Knight – see LexisNexis

Knight Paperbacks – see Caxton Publishing Group

Kogan Page Ltd*

120 Pentonville Road, London N1 9JN
tel 020-7278 0433
website www.koganpage.com
Chairman Phillip Kogan, *Directors* Helen Kogan (managing), Martin Klopstock (production), Mark Briars (financial), John Sadler (sales), Matthew Smith (editorial)

Training, business and management, human resource management, transport and distribution, marketing, sales, advertising and PR, finance and accounting, directories, small business, careers and vocational, personal finance, international business. Founded 1967.

Kube Publishing Ltd

(formerly the Islamic Foundation)
Markfield Conference Centre, Ratby Lane, Markfield, Leics. LE67 9SY
tel (01530) 249230
email info@kubepublishing.com
website www.kubepublishing.com
Managing Director Haris Ahmad

Books on Islam for adults and children.

Kudos Books – see Top That! Publishing plc

Kyle Books

192–198 Vauxhall Bridge Road London SW1V 1DX
tel 020-7692 7215
email general.enquiries@kylebooks.com
website www.kylebooks.com
Publisher & Managing Director Kyle Cathie, *Sales & Marketing Director* Julia Barder

Health, beauty, food and drink, gardening, reference, style, design, Mind, Body & Spirit. Founded 1990.

Peter Lang Ltd

52 St Giles, Oxford OX1 3LU
tel (01865) 514160
email oxford@peterlang.com
website www.peterlang.com
Directors Antonio Albalá de Rivas (Ceo, Peter Lang Publishing Group), Lucy Melville (managing/publishing), *Commissioning Editors* Hannah Godfrey, Christabel Scaife, Laurel Plapp

Part of the international Peter Lang Group, the company publishes across the humanities and social sciences, producing monographs, selected papers, conference proceedings and festschriften. Has a number of well-established series. Also publishes a small number of titles for the UK Trade as Peter Lang Oxford. Welcomes submissions from prospective authors. Founded 2006.

Lawrence & Wishart Ltd

99A Wallis Road, London E9 5LN
tel 020-8533 2506
email lw@lwbooks.co.uk
website www.lwbooks.co.uk
Managing Editor Sally Davison

Cultural studies, current affairs, history, socialism and Marxism, political philosophy, politics, popular culture.

Legend Business Ltd

The Old Fire Station, 140 Tabernacle Street, London EC2A 4SD
tel 020-7300 7370
email info@legend-paperbooks.co.uk
website www.legendtimesgroup.com
Managing Director Tom Chalmers, *Managing Director & Editor* Jonathan Reuvid, *Head of Publicity & Marketing* Lucy Chamberlain, *Sales Manager* Lottie Chase

A business book publisher with a wide-ranging and interactive list of business titles. Legend Business is also the publisher of the annual 'Investor's Guide to the United Kingdom'. Submissions can be sent to Tom Chalmers at submissions@legend-paperbooks.co.uk. Founded 2010.

Legend Press Ltd

The Old Fire Station, 140 Tabernacle Street, London EC2A 4SD
tel 020-7300 7370
email info@legend-paperbooks.co.uk
website www.legendtimesgroup.com
Managing Director Tom Chalmers, *Commissioning Editor* Lauren Parsons, *Head of Publicity & Marketing* Lucy Chamberlain, *Sales Manager* Lottie Chase

Legend Press is focused predominantly on publishing mainstream literary and commercial fiction. Submissions can be sent to submissions@legend-paperbooks.co.uk. Founded 2005.

Lewis Mason – see Ian Allan Publishing Ltd

LexisNexis

(formerly LexisNexis Butterworths)
Halsbury House, 35 Chancery Lane, London WC2A 1EL

tel 020-7400 2500
email customer.services@lexisnexis.co.uk
website www.lexisnexis.co.uk

Division of Reed Elsevier (UK) Ltd. Founded 1974.

Butterworths (imprint)

Legal and tax and accountancy books, journals, looseleaf and electronic services.

Charles Knight (imprint)

Looseleaf legal works and periodicals on local government law, construction law and technical subjects.

Tolley (imprint)

Law, taxation, accountancy, business.

The Lilliput Press Ltd†

62–63 Sitric Road, Arbour Hill, Dublin 7, Republic of Ireland
tel +353 (0)1 6711647
email info@lilliputpress.ie
website www.lilliputpress.ie
Managing Director Antony T. Farrell

General and Irish literature: essays, memoir, biography/autobiography, fiction, criticism; Irish history; philosophy; Joycean contemporary culture; nature and environment. Founded 1984.

Frances Lincoln Ltd

4 Torriano Mews, Torriano Avenue, London NW5 2RZ
tel 020-7284 4009
email reception@frances-lincoln.com
website www.frances-lincoln.com
Directors David Graham (managing), Maurice Lyon (editorial, children's books), Jon Rippon (finance), Gail Lynch (sales), Andrew Dunn (editorial, adult books)

Illustrated, international co-editions: gardening, architecture, environment, interiors, photography, art, walking and climbing, design and landscape, gift, children's books. Founded 1977.

Lion Hudson plc

Wilkinson House, Jordan Hill Road, Oxford OX2 8DR
tel (01865) 302750
email info@lionhudson.com
website www.lionhudson.com
Managing Director Nick Jones

Books for children and adults. Subject areas include Christian spirituality, reference, biography, history, contemporary issues and inspiration. Also specialises in children's bibles and prayer collections, as well as picture stories and illustrated non-fiction. Adult submissions: by email or hardcopy with return postage if return required. Children's submissions: hardcopy only with return postage if return required. Founded 1971 as Lion Publishing; merged with Angus Hudson Ltd in 2003.

Lion Books (imprint)

Christian books for general readers: information and reference, history, spirituality and prayer, issues, self-help.

Lion Children's Books (imprint)

Picture stories, illustrated non-fiction and information books on the Christian faith. Also specialises in children's Bibles and prayer collections.

Candle Books (imprint)

Children's Bibles and prayer collections, activity and novelty books, and other resources for Christian families and churches.

Monarch Books

Christian books: biography, issues of faith and society, humour, church resources.

Little, Brown Book Group

50 Victoria Embankment, London EC4Y 0DZ
tel 020-3122 6000
email info@littlebrown.co.uk
website www.littlebrown.co.uk
Chairman Ursula Mackenzie, *Ceo* David Shelley, *Coo* Ben Groves-Raines, *Directors* Emily-Jane Taylor (finance), Robert Manser (group sales), Charlie King (marketing)

Hardback and paperback fiction and general non-fiction. No unsolicited MSS. Part of Hachette UK (see page 169). Founded 1988.

Abacus (division)

Managing Director Richard Beswick

Trade paperbacks.

Atom (division)

website www.atombooks.co.uk

Teen fiction with a fantastical edge.

Corsair (division)

Publisher James Gurbutt

Pioneers of literary fiction from groundbreaking debuts to established authors. An imprint of @littlebrownuk.

Hachette Digital (division)

Publisher Sarah Shrubb; *Head of Digital & Online Sales* Ben Goddard

CDs, downloads and ebooks. See page 234.

Little, Brown (division)

Managing Director Richard Beswick, *Publishing Director* Clare Smith

General books: politics, biography, crime fiction, general fiction.

Orbit (division)

website www.orbitbooks.com
Publisher Tim Holman

Sci-fi and fantasy.

Piatkus Constable & Robinson (division)
website www.piatkus.co.uk
Publishing Director Tim Whiting (non-fiction)
Fiction and general non-fiction.

Sphere (division)
website www.twbookjuice.co.uk
Publisher (fiction) Catherine Burke, *Publishing Director (non-fiction)* Adam Strange
Hardbacks and paperbacks: original fiction and non-fiction.

Virago (division)
website www.virago.co.uk
Publisher Lennie Goodings, *Associate Publisher* Ursula Doyle
Women's literary fiction and non-fiction.

Little Black Dress – see Headline Publishing Group

Little Books Ltd
63 Warwick Square, London SW1V 2AL
tel/fax 020-7792 7929
email info@maxpress.co.uk
website www.littebooks.net
Contact Helen Nelson

History, biography, fiction and gift books. No unsolicited MSS. Founded 2001.

Little Tiger Group
1 The Coda Centre, 189 Munster Road, London SW6 6AW
tel 020-7385 6333
website www.littletiger.co.uk
Ceo Monty Bhatia

Children's picture books, novelty books, board books, pop-up books and activity books for preschool age to 7 years, and fiction for 6–12 years. See imprint websites for submissions guidelines. Imprints: Caterpillar Books (novelty), Little Tiger Press (picture books), Stripes (fiction). Founded 1987.

Little Tiger Press – see Little Tiger Group

Liverpool University Press
4 Cambridge Street, Liverpool L69 7ZU
tel 0151 794 2233
email lup@liv.ac.uk
website www.liverpooluniversitypress.co.uk

Liverpool University Press (LUP) is the UK's third oldest university press, with a distinguished history of publishing exceptional research since 1899, including the work of Nobel prize winners. LUP has rapidly expanded in recent years and now publishes approximately 70 books a year and 25 journals, specialising in literature, modern languages, history and visual culture. Shortlisted IPG Academic and Professional Publisher of the Year 2012, 2013, 2014, 2015.

Logaston Press
Little Logaston, Logaston, Woonton, Almeley, Herefordshire HR3 6QH
tel (01544) 327344
email logastonpress@btinternet.com
website www.logastonpress.co.uk
Proprietors Andy Johnson, Karen Johnson

History, social history, archaeology and guides to rural West Midlands and Mid and South Wales. Welcomes submission of ideas: send synopsis first. Founded 1985.

Lonely Planet
BBC Media Centre, 1 Wood Lane, London W12 7TQ
tel 020-8433 1333
email go@lonelyplanet.co.uk
website www.lonelyplanet.com
Founders Tony Wheeler, Maureen Wheeler, Owned by NC2 Media, *USA. Chief Operating Officer* Daniel Houghton, *Chief Technology Officer* Gus Balbontin; *Chief Financial Officer* Theo Sathananthan, *Head of Content* David Carroll, *Digital Editorial Director* Tom Hall, *Managing Destination Editor* Noirin Hegarty

A leading travel content provider in digital and print. Over the past 40 years Lonely Planet has printed over 120 million books in 12 different languages including country and regional guidebooks, city guides, pocket citybreak guides. Discover country guides, phrasebooks, walking guides, cycling guides, diving and snorkelling guides, pictorial books, healthy travel guides, wildlife guides, travel photography. London office established 1991.

Longman – see Pearson UK

Lorenz Books – see Anness Publishing

Luath Press Ltd
543/2 Castlehill, The Royal Mile, Edinburgh EH1 2ND
tel 0131 225 4326
email gavin.macdougall@luath.co.uk
website www.luath.co.uk
Director Gavin MacDougall

Committed to publishing well-written books worth reading. Publishes modern fiction, history, travel guides, art, poetry, politics and more. Over 300 titles in print. Award-winning and shortlisted titles include Ann Kelley's *The Bower Bird* and Robert Alan Jamieson's *Da Happie Laand*. UK distributor HarperCollins. Founded 1981.

Lund Humphries – see Ashgate Publishing Ltd

The Lutterworth Press
PO Box 60, Cambridge CB1 2NT
tel (01223) 350865
email publishing@lutterworth.com
website www.lutterworth.com
Managing Director Adrian Brink

A long-established independent British publishing house trading since the late 18th century. Originally founded as the Religious Tract Society, publishing activity was origianlly related to the areas of religion and children's literature. Published The Boy's Own Paper and the Girl's Own Paper. Soon added educational and adult non-fiction. Books and ebooks on: history and biography, literature and criticism, science, philosophy, music, sport, art and art history, educational titles, biblical studies, theology, mission, religious studies, collecting. Imprints: Acorn Editions, Patrick Hardy Books.

McGraw-Hill Education*

McGraw-Hill House, Shoppenhangers Road, Maidenhead, Berks. SL6 2QL
tel (01628) 502500
email emea_queries@mcgraw-hill.com
website www.mcgraw-hill.co.uk/schools
Managing Director (EMEA) Jill Jones *Managing Director (MEA/EE)* Thanos Blintzios, *Sales & Marketing Director (MEA)* Lefteris Souris, *Divisional Director (Higher Education Europe/South Africa)* Alice Duijser, *Divisional Director (Professional/Medical/ Open University Press)* Jim Voute, *Senior Sales & Market Manager (UK, North/Central Europe & South Africa Schools)* Katie Donnison, *Director (Warehouse & Inventory Management)* Stuart Thompson, *Credit Manager* Nirmal Noteha, *Vice President Human Resources (International)* Ruth Brotherton

Higher education: business, economics, computing, maths, humanities, social sciences, world languages. Professional: business, computing, science, technical, medical, general reference.

Kingscourt (imprint)
website www.kingscourt.co.uk
Primary and secondary education.

Open University Press (imprint)
email enquiries@openup.co.uk
website www.openup.co.uk
Social sciences.

Osborne (imprint)
Science, engineering, maths, computer science.

Macmillan Heinemann English Language Teaching – see Pan Macmillan

Macmillan Publishers Ltd – see Pan Macmillan

Made Simple Books – see Elsevier Ltd

Magi Publications – see Little Tiger Group

Management Books 2000 Ltd

36 Western Road, Oxford OX1 4LG
tel (01865) 600738
website www.mb2000.com
Directors N. Dale-Harris, R. Hartman

Practical books for working managers and business professionals: management, business and lifeskills, and sponsored titles. Unsolicited MSS, synopses and ideas for books welcome.

Manchester University Press

Altrincham Street, Manchester M1 7JA
tel 0161 275 2310
email mup@manchester.ac.uk
website www.manchesteruniversitypress.co.uk
Chief Executive Frances Pinter, *Editorial Director* Emma Brennan, *Director of Sales & Marketing* Simon Bell

Works of academic scholarship: social sciences, literary criticism, cultural studies, media studies, art history, design, architecture, history, politics, economics, international law, modern-language texts. Textbooks and monographs. Founded 1904.

Mandrake of Oxford

PO Box 250, Oxford OX1 1AP
tel (01865) 243671
email mandrake@mandrake.uk.net
website www.mandrake.uk.net
Directors Mogg Morgan, Kim Morgan

Art, biography, classic crime studies, fiction, Indology, magic, witchcraft, philosophy, religion. Query letters only. Founded 1986.

Mango Publishing

PO Box 13378, London SE27 OZN
tel 020-8480 7771
email info@mangoprint.com
website www.mangoprint.com

Poetry, fiction and non-fiction from the wider Caribbean region, the UK, the USA and Canada. Also translations of works not originally written in English. Founded 1995.

Manson Publishing Ltd

73 Corringham Road, London NW11 7DL
tel 020-8905 5150
email manson@mansonpublishing.com
website www.mansonpublishing.com
Managing Director Michael Manson

The company specialises in highly illustrated books and ebooks for professionals and students in medicine, veterinary medicine, plant science and earth science. Founded 1992.

Mantra Lingua Ltd

Global House, 303 Ballards Lane, London N12 8NP
tel 020-8445 5123
email info@mantralingua.com
website www.mantralingua.com
website www.discoverypen.co.uk
Managing Directors R. Dutta, M. Chatterji

Publishes picture books and educational resources. The unique talking pen technology enables any book to be sound activated. All resources are or can be narrated in multiple languages and educational posters for schools and museums have audio visual features to compact information. The company is looking for illustrators, authors, translators and audio narrators who are keen on the communications space. Founded in 2002. Divisions other than Education: Museums and Heritage, www.discoverypen.co.uk. The talking pen technology is being used by many museums of various sizes. The company is looking for illustrators and trail writers, tel: 0845 600 1361. Birding: www.birdvoice.net. The talking pen technology is used to help bird watchers double their bird recognition skills. The company is looking for specialist audio recordings of birds, frogs and other animals from around the world, tel: 0845 600 1361.

Marino Books – see The Mercier Press

Kevin Mayhew Ltd

Buxhall, Stowmarket, Suffolk IP14 3BW
tel (01449) 737978
email info@kevinmayhew.com
website www.kevinmayhew.com
Directors Kevin Mayhew, Barbara Mayhew

Christianity: prayer and spirituality, pastoral care, preaching, liturgy worship, children's, youth work, drama, instant art, eduational. Music: hymns, organ and choral, contemporary worship, piano and instrumental, tutors. Greetings cards: images, spiritual texts, birthdays, Christian events, musicians, general occasions. Contact Manuscript Submissions Dept before sending MSS/synopses. Founded 1976.

Medical™ – see Harlequin (UK) Ltd

Mentor Books†

43 Furze Road, Sandyford Industrial Estate, Dublin 18, Republic of Ireland
tel +353 (0)1 2952112
email admin@mentorbooks.ie
website www.mentorbooks.ie
Managing Director Daniel McCarthy, *Editor* Treasa O'Mahony

General: non-fiction, humour, biographies, politics, crime, history, guidebooks. Educational (secondary): languages, history, geography, business, maths, sciences. No unsolicited MSS. Founded 1980.

Mercat Press – see Birlinn Ltd

The Mercier Press†

Unit 3, Oak House, Riverview Business Park, Blackrock, Cork, Republic of Ireland
tel +353 (0)21 4614700
email info@mercierpress.ie
website www.mercierpress.ie
Directors J.F. Spillane (chairman), M.P. Feehan (managing), D. Crowley ACMA

Irish literature, folklore, history, politics, humour, academic, current affairs, health, mind and spirit, general non-fiction, children's. Founded 1944.

Merlin Press Ltd

99B Wallis Road, London E9 5LN
tel 020-8533 5800
email info@merlinpress.co.uk
website www.merlinpress.co.uk
Managing Director Anthony Zurbrugg

Radical history and social studies. Letters/synopses only.

Green Print (imprint)

Green politics and the environment.

Merrell Publishers Ltd

70 Cowcross Street, London EC1M 6EJ
tel 020-7928 8880
email mail@merrellpublishers.com
website www.merrellpublishers.com
Publisher Hugh Merrell, *Head of Editorial* Claire Chandler, *Head of Sales & Marketing* Helen Moss

High-quality illustrated books on all aspects of visual culture, including art, architecture, fashion photography and design. Unsolicited proposals welcomed but must be accompanied by return postage.

Methuen Drama – see Bloomsbury Publishing Plc

Methuen & Co Ltd

9 Allington Road, Newick, Lewes BN8 4NA
tel (01825) 721411
email editorial@methuen.co.uk
35 Hospital Fields Road, York YO10 4DZ
tel (01904) 624730
website www.methuen.co.uk
Managing Director Peter Tummons, *Editor* Naomi Tummons, *Sales* Peter Newsom

Literary fiction and non-fiction: biography, autobiography, travel, history, sport, humour, film, performing arts. No unsolicited MSS.

Politico's Publishing (imprint)

Politics, current affairs, political biography and autobiography.

Metro Books – see John Blake Publishing Ltd

Michelin Maps and Guides

Hannay House, 39 Clarendon Road, Watford, Herts. WD17 1JA
tel (01923) 205240
email travelpubsales@uk.michelin.com
website www.michelin.co.uk/travel
Commercial Director Ian Murray

Tourist guides, maps and atlases, hotel and restaurant guides.

Midland Publishing – see Ian Allan Publishing Ltd

Miller's – see Octopus Publishing Group

Mills & Boon Romance™ – see Harlequin (UK) Ltd

Milo Books Ltd

14 Ash Grove, Wrea Green, Preston, Lancs PR4 2N
tel (01772) 672900
email info@milobooks.com
website www.milobooks.com
Publisher Peter Walsh

True crime, sport, current affairs. Founded 1997.

Mira Books® – see Harlequin (UK) Ltd

Mitchell Beazley – see Octopus Publishing Group

Mobius – see Hodder & Stoughton

Modern Extra™ – see Harlequin (UK) Ltd

Modern Romance™ – see Harlequin (UK) Ltd

Monarch Books – see Lion Hudson plc

Morgan Kauffman – see Elsevier Ltd

Morrigan Book Company

Killala, Co. Mayo, Republic of Ireland
tel +353 (0)96 32555
email morriganbooks@gmail.com
Publishers Gerry Kennedy, Hilary Kennedy

Non-fiction: general Irish interest, biography, history, local history, folklore and mythology. Founded 1979.

Mosby – see Elsevier (Clinical Solutions)

Murdoch Books

Erico House, 6th Floor North,
93–99 Upper Richmond Road, London SW15 2TG
tel 020-8785 5995
email info@murdochbooks.co.uk
website www.murdochbooks.co.uk

Non-fiction: homes and interiors, gardening, cookery, craft, DIY. Owned by Australian publisher Allen & Unwin Pty Ltd.

John Murray Press

338 Euston Road, London NW1 3BH
tel 020-7873 6000
website www.johnmurray.co.uk
website www.hodder.co.uk
Managing Director Roland Philipps, *Publishing Director (fiction)* Eleanor Birne, *Publisher (non-fiction)* Georgina Laycock, *Editorial Director (fiction & non-fiction)* Mark Richards

Quality literary fiction and non-fiction: business, travel, history, entertainment, reference, biography and memoir, real-life stories. No unsolicited MSS without preliminary letter. Part of Hachette UK (see page 169).

Myriad Editions

59 Lansdowne Place, Brighton BN3 1FL
tel (01273) 720000
email info@myriadeditions.com
website www.myriadeditions.com
Directors Bob Benewick, Judith Mackay, Candida Lacey (managing director & publisher), Corinne Pearlman (creative director & graphics editor), Victoria Blunden (senior fiction editor), Holly Ainley (fiction editor)

Independent publisher of original literary fiction and graphic novels, and producer of the acclaimed 'state of the world' infographic atlases. Founded 1993.

National Trust – see Pavilion Books

Natural History Museum Publishing

Cromwell Road, London SW7 5BD
tel 020-7942 5336
email publishing@nhm.ac.uk
website www.nhm.ac.uk/publishing
Head of Publishing Colin Ziegler

Natural sciences, entomology, botany, geology, mineralogy, palaeontology, zoology, history of natural history. Founded 1881.

Nelson Thornes Ltd

– acquired by Oxford University Press

New Beacon Books

76 Stroud Green Road, London N4 3EN
tel 020-7272 4889
email newbeaconbooks@btconnect.com
website www.newbeaconbooks.co.uk
Directors Sarah White, Michael La Rose, Janice Durham

Small specialist publishers: general non-fiction, fiction, poetry, critical writings, concerning the Caribbean, Africa, African–America and Black Britain. No unsolicited MSS. Founded 1966.

New Cavendish Books

3 Denbigh Road, London W11 2SJ
tel 020-7229 6765
email sales@newcavendishbooks.co.uk
website www.newcavendishbooks.co.uk

Specialist books for the collector, art reference, Thai guidebooks. Founded 1973.

River Books (associate imprint)
The art and architecture of Southeast Asia.

New Holland Publishers (UK) Ltd

The Chandlery Unit 009,
50 Westminster Bridge Road, London SE1 7QY
tel 020-7953 7565
email enquiries@nhpub.co.uk
website www.newhollandpublishers.com
Managing Director Fiona Schultz

Illustrated non-fiction books on natural history, sports and hobbies, animals and pets, travel pictorial, travel maps and guides, reference, gardening, health and fitness, practical art, DIY, food and drink, outdoor pursuits, craft, humour, gift books. New proposals accepted (send CV and synopsis and sample chapters in first instance; sae essential).

New Island Books†

16 Priory Office Park, Stillorgan, Co. Dublin, Republic of Ireland
tel +353 (0)1 2784225
email info@newisland.ie
email editor@newisland.ie
website www.newisland.ie
Director Edwin Higel, *Editors* Dan Bolger (commissioning), Justin Corfield

Fiction, poetry, drama, humour, biography, current affairs. Submissions by email to editor@newisland.ie. Send the first 3 chapters as a Word document, plus a short synopsis, and include details of any previous publications. Founded 1992.

New Playwrights' Network

10 Station Road Industrial Estate, Colwall, Nr Malvern, Herefordshire WR13 6RN
tel (01684) 540154
email simon@cressrelles.co.uk
website www.cressrelles.co.uk
Publishing Director Leslie Smith

General plays for the amateur, one-act and full length.

New Rider – see Pearson UK

New Theatre Publications/The Playwrights' Co-operative

2 Hereford Close, Woolston, Warrington, Cheshire WA1 4HR
tel 0845 331 3516, (01925) 485605
email info@plays4theatre.com
website www.plays4theatre.com
Director Alison Hornby

Plays for the professional and amateur stage. Submissions encouraged. Founded 1987.

Newnes – see Elsevier Ltd

Nexus – see Virgin Books (imprint, in partnership with Virgin Group), page 191

Nia – see The X Press

Nightingale Press

7 Green Park Station, Green Park Road, Bath BA1 1JB
tel (01225) 478444
email sales@manning-partnership.co.uk
website www.manning-partnership.co.uk
Directors Garry Manning (managing), Roger Hibbert (sales)

Humour, gift. Owned by the Manning Partnership Ltd. Founded 1997.

Nonsuch Publishing Ltd – see The History Press Ltd

North-Holland – see Elsevier Ltd

Northcote House Publishers Ltd

The Paddocks, Brentor Road, Mary Tavy, Devon PL19 9PY
tel (01822) 810066
email northcotehouse@gmail.com
website www.writersandtheirwork.co.uk
Directors B.R.W. Hulme, A.V. Hulme (secretary), Sarah Piper (sales & marketing)

Education and education management, educational dance and drama, literary criticism (*Writers and their Work*). Founded 1985.

W.W. Norton & Company

Castle House, 75–76 Wells Street, London W1T 3QT
tel 020-7323 1579
email office@wwnorton.co.uk
website www.wwnorton.co.uk
Managing Director Edward Crutchley

English and American literature, economics, music, psychology, science. Founded 1980.

NWP – see Neil Wilson Publishing Ltd

Oak Tree Press†

19 Rutland Street, Cork, Republic of Ireland
tel +353 (0)21 4313855
email info@oaktreepress.com
website www.SuccessStore.com
Directors Brian O'Kane, Rita O'Kane

Business management, enterprise, accountancy and finance, law. Special emphasis on titles for small business owner/managers. Founded 1991.

Nubooks (imprint)
Ebooks.

Oberon Books

521 Caledonian Road, London N7 9RH
tel 020-7607 3637
email info@oberonbooks.com
website www.oberonbooks.com

Managing Director Charles Glanville, *Publisher* James Hogan, *Associate Publisher & Senior Editor* Andrew Walby

New and classic play texts, programme texts and general theatre and performing arts books. Founded 1986.

The O'Brien Press Ltd†

12 Terenure Road East, Rathgar, Dublin 6, Republic of Ireland
tel +353 (0)1 4923333
email books@obrien.ie
website www.obrien.ie
Directors Michael O'Brien, Ide ní Laoghaire, Ivan O'Brien, Mary Webb

Ireland's leading independent book publisher. Adult non-fiction: biography, politics, history, true crime, sport, humour, reference. Adult fiction, crime (Brandon). Children: fiction for all ages; illustrated fiction for ages 3+, 5+, 6+, 8+ years, novels (10+ and young adult) – contemporary, historical, fantasy. No poetry or academic. Unsolicited MSS (sample chapters only), synopses and ideas for books welcome by post only, and will not be returned (no unsolicited adult fiction MSS). Founded 1974.

The Octagon Press Ltd

78 York Street, London W1H 1DP
tel 020-7193 6456
email admin@octagonpress.com
website www.octagonpress.com
Director Anna Murphy

Travel, biography, literature, folklore, psychology, philosophy, with the focus on East–West studies. Welcomes single page book proposals via email. Unsolicited MSS not accepted. Founded 1960.

Octopus Publishing Group

Carmelite House, 50 Victoria Embankment, London EC4Y 0DZ
tel 020-3122 6000
email info@octopusbooks.co.uk
email publisher@octopusbooks.co.uk (submissions)
website www.octopusbooks.co.uk
Chief Executive Alison Goff, *Deputy Ceo & Group Sales & Marketing Director* Andrew Welham

Part of Hachette UK (see page 169).

Bounty (imprint)

email bountybooksinfo-bp@bountybooks.co.uk
Publisher Samantha Warrington

Promotional/bargain division of Octopus Publishing Group.

Cassell Illustrated (imprint)

Illustrated books for the international market specialising in popular culture.

Conran Octopus (imprint)

Quality illustrated books, particularly lifestyle, cookery, gardening.

Gaia Books (imprint)

The environment, natural living, health and the mind.

Godsfield Press (imprint)

email publisher@godsfieldpress.com

Mind, Body & Spirit with an emphasis on practical application.

Hamlyn (imprint)

Practical non-fiction, particularly cookery, health and diet, home and garden, sport, puzzles and reference.

Ilex Press (imprint)

email info@octopusbooks.co.uk

Illustrated books on art, design, digital photography and popular culture.

Miller's (imprint)

Antiques and collectables.

Mitchell Beazley (imprint)

Quality illustrated books, particularly cookery, wine, gardening and the natural world.

Philip's (imprint)

email publisher@philips-maps.co.uk

Atlases, maps, astronomy, globes.

Spruce (imprint)

Illustrated books for the international market, specialising in cookery, gift and humour.

Ticktock (imprint)

Publishes illustrated non-fiction books primarily for children 5–8 years.

The Oleander Press

16 Orchard Street, Cambridge CB1 1JT
tel (01638) 500784
website www.oleanderpress.com
Managing Director Dr Jane Doyle

Travel, language, Libya, Arabia and Middle East, Cambridgeshire, history, reference, classics. MSS welcome with sae for reply. Founded 1960.

Michael O'Mara Books Ltd

16 Lion Yard, Tremadoc Road, London SW4 7NQ
tel 020-7720 8643
email enquiries@mombooks.com
website www.mombooks.com
Chairman Michael O'Mara, *Managing Director* Lesley O'Mara, *Senior Editorial Director* Louise Dixon, *Editorial Director* Hugh Barker

General non-fiction: biography, humour, history. See website for submission guidelines. Imprint: Buster Books (activity, novelty, fiction and non-fiction for children and young adults). Founded 1985.

Omnibus Press/Music Sales Ltd

14–15 Berners Street, London W1T 3LJ
tel 020-7612 7400

email music@musicsales.co.uk
website www.omnibuspress.com
Chief Editor Chris Charlesworth

Rock music biographies, books about music. Founded 1976.

On Stream Publications Ltd
Currabaha, Cloghroe, Blarney, Co. Cork, Republic of Ireland
tel +353 (0)21 4385798
email info@onstream.ie
website www.onstream.ie
Owner Rosalind Crowley

Cookery, wine, travel, human interest non-fiction, local history, academic and practical books. Founded 1986.

Oneworld Publications
10 Bloomsbury Street, London WC1B 3SR
tel 020-7307 8900
email info@oneworld-publications.com
website www.oneworld-publications.com
Director Juliet Mabey (publisher)

Fiction and general non-fiction: current affairs, politics, history, Middle East, business, popular science, philosophy, psychology, green issues, world religions and Islamic studies; literary fiction, plus fiction that sits at the intersection of the literary and commercial, showcasing strong voices and great stories; young adult to children's fiction, and upmarket crime/suspense novels, as well as fiction in translation. No unsolicited MSS; email or send proposal via website. Founded 1986.

Onlywomen Press Ltd
40 St Lawrence Terrace, London W10 5ST
tel 020-8354 0796
email onlywomenpress@btconnect.com
website www.onlywomenpress.com
Managing Director Lilian Mohin

Lesbian feminist fiction, non-fiction and books for children. Founded 1974.

Open Gate Press*
(incorporating Centaur Press, founded 1954)
51 Achilles Road, London NW6 1DZ
tel 020-7431 4391
email books@opengatepress.co.uk
website www.opengatepress.co.uk
Directors Jeannie Cohen, Elisabeth Petersdorff, Sandra Lovell

Psychoanalysis, philosophy, social sciences, religion, animal welfare, the environment. Founded 1988.

Open University Press – see McGraw-Hill Education

Orbit – see Little, Brown Book Group

Orchard Books – see Hachette Children's Group

The Orion Publishing Group Ltd
Orion House, 5 Upper St Martin's Lane, London WC2H 9EA
tel 020-7240 3444
website www.orionbooks.co.uk
Directors Arnaud Nourry (chairman), Peter Roche (chief executive), Malcolm Edwards (deputy chief executive)

No unsolicited MSS; approach in writing in first instance. Part of Hachette UK (see page 169). Founded 1992.

Orion Fiction (division)
Managing Director Jon Wood

Trade and mass market fiction and non-fiction under Everyman, Orion and Phoenix imprints.

General Division
Directors Lisa Milton (managing), John Wood (fiction publishing)

Hardback fiction (popular fiction in all categories), non-fiction and audio.

Gollancz (imprint)
Contact Simon Spanton

Sci-fi and fantasy.

Orion Children's Books (division)
Publisher Fiona Kennedy

Fiction for younger and older readers, picture books.

Weidenfeld & Nicolson
See page 207.

Osborne – see McGraw-Hill Education

Oshun – see Penguin Random House (Pty) Ltd

Osprey Publishing Ltd
Kemp House, Chawley Park, Cumnor Hill, Oxford OX2 9PH
tel (01865) 727022
email info@ospreypublishing.com
website www.ospreypublishing.com

The leading publisher of illustrated military history, founded in 1968 and acquired by Bloomsbury Publishing Plc in 2014. Over 1,600 titles in print on a wide range of military history subjects from ancient times to the modern day.

Oversteps Books Ltd
6 Halwell House, South Pool, Nr Kingsbridge, Devon TQ7 2RX
tel (01548) 531969
email alwynmarriage@overstepsbooks.com
website www.overstepsbooks.com
Director/Managing Editor Dr Alwyn Marriage

Poetry. Email 6 poems that have been published, giving details of the magazines in which they appeared, the dates or issue numbers and the email addresses of the editors. Founded 1992.

Peter Owen Publishers

81 Ridge Road, London N8 9NP
tel 020-8350 1775
email aowen@peterowen.com
website www.peterowen.com
Directors Peter L. Owen (managing), Antonia Owen (editorial), Nick Kent (sales & marketing)

Backlist includes 10 Nobel Prize winners. Arts, belles lettres, biography and memoir, literary fiction, general non-fiction, history, theatre and entertainment. Do not send fiction without first emailing the Editorial Department even if an established novelist. No mass-market genre fiction, short stories or poetry; first novels almost never published. Founded 1951.

Oxford Publishing Company – see Ian Allan Publishing Ltd

Oxford University Press*

Great Clarendon Street, Oxford OX2 6DP
tel (01865) 556767
email enquiry@oup.com
website www.oup.com
Ceo Nigel Portwood, *Group Finance Director* Giles Spackman, *Global Academic Business Managing Director* Tim Barton, *Managing Director, Oxford Education* Kate Harris, *ELT Division Managing Director* Peter Marshall, *Human Resources Director* Paul Lomas, *Academic Sales Director* Alastair Lewis

Archaeology, architecture, art, belles lettres, bibles, bibliography, children's books (fiction, non-fiction, picture), commerce, current affairs, dictionaries, drama, economics, educational (foundation, primary, secondary, technical, university), encyclopedias, ELT, electronic publishing, essays, foreign language learning, general history, hymn and service books, journals, law, medical, music, oriental, philosophy, political economy, prayer books, reference, science, sociology, theology and religion; educational software; *Grove Dictionaries of Music & Art*. Trade paperbacks published under the imprint of Oxford Paperbacks. Founded 1478.

Palgrave Macmillan – see Pan Macmillan

Pan Macmillan*

20 New Wharf Road, London N1 9RR
tel 020-7014 6000
website www.panmacmillan.com
Managing Director Anthony Forbes Watson, *Creative Director* Geoff Duffield, *Publishers* Jeremy Trevathan (adult publisher), Robin Harvie (non-fiction), Paul Baggaley (Picador), Carole Tonkinson (Bluebird)

Novels, literary, crime, thrillers, romance, sci-fi, fantasy and horror. Autobiography, biography, business, gift books, health and beauty, history, humour, natural history, travel, philosophy, politics, world affairs, theatre, film, gardening, cookery, popular reference. Publishes under Macmillan, Tor, Pan, Picador, Sidgwick & Jackson, Boxtree, Bluebird, Macmillan Audio, Macmillan New Writing. No unsolicited MSS except through Macmillan New Writing. Founded 1843.

Bluebird (imprint)

Publisher Carole Tonkinson

Pan Macmillan's wellness and lifestyle imprint, publishing the very latest in diet, popular psychology, self-help as well as career and business, parenting and inspirational memoir.

Macmillan (imprint)

Adult Books Publisher Jeremy Trevathan, *Picador Publisher* Paul Baggaley, *Non-fiction Publisher* Robin Harvie, *Bluebird Publisher* Carole Tonkinson, *Editorial Directors* Georgina Morley (non-fiction), Kate Harvey

Hardback commercial fiction including genre fiction, romantic, crime and thrillers. Hardback serious and general non-fiction including autobiography, biography, economics, history, military history, philosophy, politics and world affairs, popular reference titles.

Mantle (imprint)

Publisher Maria Rejt

Tor (imprint)

Sci-fi, fantasy and thrillers published in hardback and paperback.

Pan (imprint)

Paperback imprint for Macmillan and Sidgwick & Jackson imprints. Founded 1947.

Picador (imprint)

Publisher Paul Baggaley, *Editorial Director* Kate Harvey

Literary international fiction, non-fiction and poetry published in hardback and paperback. Founded 1972.

Sidgwick & Jackson (imprint)

Publisher Robin Harvie, *Editorial Director* Ingrid Connell

Hardback popular non-fiction including celebrity and show business to music and sport. Founded 1908.

Macmillan New Writing (imprint)

website www.macmillannewwriting.com

Founded as a way of finding talented new writers who might otherwise go undiscovered. Publishes full-length novels by authors who have not previously published a novel. All genres considered and all submissions are assessed but MSS must be complete. No advance but the author pays nothing and receives a royalty of 20% on net sales. Send the complete novel by email via the website. Founded 2006.

Boxtree (imprint)

Publisher Robin Harvie

Brand and media tie-in titles, including TV, film,

music and internet, plus entertainment licences, pop culture, humour in hardback and paperback.

Macmillan Digital Audio (imprint)
Digital & Communications Director Sara Lloyd
Audio imprint for the entire Pan Macmillan list. See page 235.

Campbell Books (preschool imprint)
Editorial Director Stephanie Barton
Early learning, pop-up, novelty, board books for the preschool market. 0–6: picture books, activity and novelty (*publishers* Stephanie Barton & Suzanne Carnell), 6+ : fiction, non fiction, poetry (*publisher* Venetia Gosling).

Kingfisher (imprint)
tel 020-7014 6000
Publisher Belinda Rasmussen
Non-fiction: imprint of Macmillan Children's Books.

Macmillan Science and Education
The Macmillan Campus, 4 Crinan Street, London N1 9XW
tel 020-7833 4000
website http://se.macmillan.com
Ceo Science and Education Annette Thomas, *Ceo Education* S.J. Allen, *Ceo Science and Scholarly* S.C. Inchcoombe, *Director* D.J.G. Knight

Palgrave Macmillan (division)
website www.palgrave.com
Chairman Dominic Knight
Monographs and journals in academic and professional subjects. Publishes in both hard copy and electronic formats.

Macmillan Education Ltd (division)
email info@macmillan.com
website www.macmillaneducation.com
Chief Executive Simon Allen, *Managing Director* Helen Melia (Europe & Middle East), *Publishing Directors* Alison Hubert (Africa, Caribbean, Middle East, Asia), Kate Melliss (Spain), Sharon Jervis (Latin America), Sue Bale (dictionaries), Angela Lilley (international ELT)
ELT titles and school and college textbooks and materials in all subjects for the international education market in both book and electronic formats.

Pandora Press – see Rivers Oram Press

Paper Tiger – see Pavilion Books

Paperbooks Publishing Ltd

The Old Fire Station, 140 Tabernacle Street, London EC2A 4SD
tel 020-7300 7370
email info@legend-paperbooks.co.uk
website www.legendtimesgroup.com
Managing Director Tom Chalmers, *Commissioning Editor* Lauren Parsons, *Head of Publicity & Marketing* Lucy Chamberlaiin, *Sales Manager* Lottie Chase

Paperbooks is a recently relaunched non-fiction publisher, focusing on creating unique and creative books in a variety of genres. (Paperbooks started life as a fiction publisher, with titles still available under this name.) Submissions can be sent to submissions@legend-paperbooks.co.uk.

Pavilion Books

1 Gower Street, London WC1E 6HD
tel 020-74621500
email reception@pavilionbooks.com
website www.pavilionbooks.com
Chief Executive Polly Powell

Founded 2013; formerly Anova Books Group.

Batsford (imprint)
Publisher Tina Persaud
Chess, art techniques, film, fashion and costume, textile art, design, embroidery, heritage.

Collins & Brown (imprint)
Publisher Katie Cowan
Lifestyle and interiors, cookery, gardening, photography, pet care, health and beauty, hobbies and crafts, including *Good Housekeeping* branded books.

Conway (inc. Brasseys Military, Putnam Aeronautical)
Publisher John Lee
History and highly illustrated reference books on naval and maritime, aviation and military subjects, exploration, hobbies.

National Trust Books (imprint)
Senior Commissioning Editor Peter Taylor
Heritage, gardens, cookery.

Pavilion (imprint)
Editorial Director Fiona Holman
Cookery, gardening, travel, wine, photography, art, popular culture, gift.

Portico (imprint)
Publisher Katie Cowan
Humour, popular culture, quirky reference, sport.

Robson Books (imprint)
General non-fiction, biography, music, humour, sport.

Salamander (imprint)
Packager of made-to-order books on cookery, crafts, military, natural history, music, gardening, hobbies, transport, sports, popular reference.

Pavilion Children's Books

1 Gower Street, London WC1E 6HD
tel 020-7462 1500
website www.pavilionbooks.com
Commissioning Editor Katie Deane

Children's books: from baby and picture books to illustrated classics and fiction. Part of Pavilion Books Company Ltd. Submissions via an agent only.

Pavilion Publishing and Media Ltd

(Part of OLM Group)
Rayford House, School Road, Hove BN3 5HX
tel (01273) 434943
email info@pavpub.com
website www.pavpub.com
Ceo, OLM Group Peter O'Hara, *Managing Editor* Kerry Boettcher

Health and social care training resources, books and assessment tools in a variety of fields including learning disability, mental health, vulnerable adults, housing, drugs and alcohol, staff development, children, young and older people, and forensic services, aimed at front line workers, professionals and academics. Also, English language teaching books and resources aimed at newly-qualified and experienced teachers and teacher trainers in the ELT field. Founded 1987.

Peachpit Press – see Pearson UK

Pearson UK*

Edinburgh Gate, Harlow, Essex CM20 2JE
tel 0845 313 6666
website www.pearsoned.co.uk
President Rod Bristow

Allyn & Bacon (imprint)
Higher education, humanities, social sciences.

BBC Active (imprint)
Learning resources for children and adults.

Cisco Press (imprint)
Cisco-systems authorised publisher. Material for networking students and professionals.

Benjamin Cummings (imprint)
Higher education, science.

FT Prentice Hall (imprint)
Business for higher education and professional.

Harcourt (imprint)
Educational resources for teachers and learners at primary, secondary and vocational level. Provides a range of published resources, teachers' support, and pupil and student material in all core subjects for all ages. Imprints: Ginn, Heinemann, Payne-Gallway, Raintree, Rigby.

Longman (imprint)
Education for higher education, schools, ELT.

New Riders (imprint)
Graphics and design.

Peachpit Press (imprint)
Internet and general computing.

Penguin Longman (imprint)
ELT.

Prentice Hall (imprint)
Academic and reference textbooks.

QUE Publishing (imprint)
Computing.

SAMS Publishing (imprint)
Professional computing.

Wharton (imprint)
Business.

York Notes (imprint)
Literature guides for students.

Pen & Sword Books Ltd

47 Church Street, Barnsley, South Yorkshire S70 2AS
tel (01226) 734555/734222
email editorialoffice@pen-and-sword.co.uk
website www.pen-and-sword.co.uk
Managing Director Charles Hewitt, *Publishing Manager* Henry Wilson, *Commissioning Editors* Jamie Wilson, Phil Sidnell, Rupert Harding, Jen Newby, Eloise Hansen, Michael Leventhal, Julian Mannering, Rob Gardiner

Military history, aviation history, naval and maritime, general history, local history, family history, transport, social history, archaeology. Imprints: Leo Cooper, Frontline Books, Pen & Sword Military Classics, Pen & Sword Aviation, Pen & Sword Naval & Maritime, Remember When, Seaforth, Pen & Sword Digital, Claymore, Wharncliffe Transport, and Pen & Sword Discovery, Pen & Sword Social History, Pen & Sword Archaeology.

Frontline (imprint)
Military history.

Wharncliffe (imprint)
Local history.

Penguin Longman – see Pearson UK

Penguin Random House UK*

20 Vauxhall Bridge Road, London SW1V 2SA
tel 020-7840 8400
website www.penguin.co.uk
Ceo, Penguin Random House UK Tom Weldon, *Deputy Ceo* Ian Hudson, *Chairman* Gail Rebuck, *Directors* Mark Gardiner (finance), Graham Sim (creative), Brian Davies (overseas operations), Richard Cable (managing, Vintage Publishing), Rebecca Smart (managing, Ebury Publishing), Susan Sandon (managing, Cornerstone), Garry Prior (deputy group sales), Mark Williams (managing, distribution)

Penguin Random House UK comprises 8 publishing companies and more than 45 imprints. The company is part of the global Penguin Random House company which was formed in 2013 following the merger of Penguin and Random House.

80 Strand, London WC2R 0RL
tel 020-7010 3000
Managing Director, PRH Children's Francesca Dow, *Managing Director, Michael Joseph* Lousie Moore, *Managing Director, Penguin General* Joanna Prior, *Managing Director, Penguin Press* Stefan McGrath, *Group Sales Director* Mike Symons

61–63 Uxbridge Road, London, W5 5SA
tel 020-8579 2652
Mananing Director, Transworld Publishers Larry Finlay

Penguin General Books (literary division)
Managing Director Joanna Prior
No unsolicited MSS or synopses.

Viking (imprint)
Publishing Director Venetia Butterfield, *Editorial Director* Eleo Gordon, *Publishers* Mary Mount, Joel Rickett, Daniel Crewe
Fiction and general non-fiction for adults. Founded 1925.

Portfolio (imprint)
Publishing Director Joel Rickett, *Editor* Zoe Bohm
Business. Launched 2010.

Hamish Hamilton (imprint)
Publishing Director Simon Prosser
Fiction, belles lettres, biography and memoirs, current affairs, history, literature, politics, travel. No unsolicited MSS or synopses.

Fig Tree (imprint)
Publishing Director Juliet Annan
Fiction and general non-fiction. No unsolicited MSS or synopses.

Penguin Ireland (imprint)
Irish Book Publishers' Association, 25 St Stephen's Green, Dublin 2, Republic of Ireland
tel +353 (0)1 6617695
email info@penguin.ie
website www.penguin.ie
Managing Director Michael McLoughlin, *Publishing Director* Patricia Deevy, *Editor* Brendan Barrington, *Editor* Claire Pelly, *Children's Editor* Claire Hennessy
Fiction and non-fiction, mainly of Irish origin, but published to travel beyond the Irish market. Unsolicited MSS accepted.

Michael Joseph (commercial division)
Managing Director Louise Moore, *Editors* Louise Moore (general fiction for women, celebrity non-fiction), Maxine Hitchcock (general fiction for women, crime fiction, general fiction), Jessica Leeke (general fiction), Kimberley Atkins (general fiction for women), Rowland White (crime, thriller & adventure fiction, commercial non-fiction, popular culture & military), Emad Akhtar (crime, thriller, science fiction & fantasy), Alex Clarke (commercial fiction & commercial non-fiction), Daniel Bunyard (commercial non-fiction, popular culture & military), Fenella Bates (commercial non-fiction, popular culture & health), Lindsey Evans (cookery)

Penguin Press (division)
Managing Director Stefan McGrath, *Publishing Directors* Stuart Proffitt (Allen Lane), Simon Winder (Allen Lane), Helen Conford (Allen Lane & Particular Books), *Editorial Directors* Thomas Penn (Allen Lane), Alexis Kirschbaum (Allen Lane)
Serious adult non-fiction, reference, specialist and classics. No unsolicited MSS or synopses. Imprints: Allen Lane, Particular Books, Pelican, Penguin Classics.

Penguin Digital
tel 020-7840 8400 (Dan Franklin)
email Dfranklin2@penguinrandomhouse.co.uk
tel 020-7840 8400 (Videl Bar-Kar)
email vbar-kar@penguinrandomhouse.co.uk
Digital Publisher Dan Franklin, *Audio Publisher* Videl Bar-Kar

DK (division)
website www.dk.com
Ceo John Duhigg
Illustrated non-fiction for adults and children: gardening, health, medical, travel, food and drink, history, natural history, photography, reference, pregnancy and childcare, film and TV.

BradyGames & Prima Games (division)
Publisher Mike Degler
Computer games strategy guides and collectors' editions.

Travel (division)
website www.traveldk.com
website www.roughguides.com
Publisher Georgina Dee
Travel guides, illustrated travel books, phrasebooks and digital products. Includes *Rough Guides* and *DK Eyewitness Travel*.

Cornerstone (company)
Managing Director Susan Sandon, *Director of Publicity & Media Relations* Charlotte Bush
No unsolicited MSS accepted.

Arrow Books Ltd (imprint)
tel 020-7840 8414
Publisher Selena Walker, *Publishing Director* Jenny Geras
Paperback fiction and non-fiction.

Century (imprint)
tel 020-7840 8569
Publisher Selena Walker, *Publishing Director* Ben Dunn

Fiction, biography, autobiography, general non-fiction, true crime, humour.

Hutchinson (imprint)
tel 020-7840 8733
Publisher Jason Arthur, *Publishing Director* Jocasta Hamilton
Fiction: literary and women's fiction, adventure, crime, thrillers. Non-fiction: biography, memoirs, general history, politics, travel, current affairs.

Preface Publishing (imprint)
tel 020-7840 8892
Publisher Trevor Dolby
Commercial fiction and non-fiction.

Random House Books (imprint)
tel 020-7840 8451
Publishing Director Nigel Wilcockson
Non-fiction: social and cultural history, current affairs, popular culture, reference, business and economics.

William Heinemann (imprint)
tel 020-7840 8400
Publisher Jason Arthur
Fiction and general non-fiction: crime, thrillers, literary fiction, translations, history, biography, science.

Windmill Books (imprint)
tel 020-7840 8414
website www.windmill-books.co.uk
Publishing Director Laura Deacon
B-format paperback fiction and non-fiction.

Vintage (company)
Managing Director Richard Cable, *Deputy Managing Director* Faye Brewster, *Publishing Director, Vintage* Rachel Cugnoni, *Publicity Director* Christian Lewis, *Marketing Director* Roger Bratchell
Quality fiction and non-fiction. Predominantly in paperback. No unsolicited MSS.

The Bodley Head (imprint)
tel 020-7840 8514
Publishing Director Stuart Williams, *Editorial Director* Will Hammond
Non-fiction: history, current affairs, politics, science, biography, economics.

Jonathan Cape (imprint)
tel 020-7840 8608
Publishing Director Dan Franklin, *Deputy Publishing Director* Robin Robertson, *Editorial Director* Alex Bowler
Biography and memoirs, current affairs, drama, fiction, history, poetry, travel, politics, graphic novels, photography.

Chatto & Windus (imprint)
tel 020-7840 8745
Publishing Director Clara Farmer, *Deputy Publishing Director* Becky Hardie, *Editorial Director* Poppy Hampson
Belles lettres, biography and memoirs, current affairs, fiction, history, poetry, politics, philosophy, translations, travel. No unsolicited MSS.

Harvill Secker (imprint)
tel 020-7840 8893
Publishing Director Liz Foley, *Deputy Publishing Director* Michal Shavit
English literature and world literature in translation. Non-fiction (history, current affairs, literary essays, music). No unsolicited MSS.

Pimlico (imprint)
tel 020-7840 8836
Publishing Director Rachel Cugnoni
History, biography, literature. Exclusively in paperback. No unsolicited MSS.

Square Peg (imprint)
tel 020-7840 8894
Publishing Director Rosemary Davidson, *Editorial Director* Rowan Yapp
Eclectic, idiosyncratic and commercial non-fiction including humour, illustrated and gift books, food, nature, memoir, travel, parenting. Unsolicited MSS with sae.

Yellow Jersey Press (imprint)
tel 020-7840 8407
Editorial Director Matthew Phillips
Sport and leisure activities. No unsolicited MSS.

BBC Books (imprint)
tel 020-7840 8400
Publishing Director Paul Sowerbutts
TV and radio tie-ins and books linked to BBC brands and personalities.

Ebury Publishing (company)
website www.eburypublishing.co.uk
Managing Director Rebecca Smart, *Publisher/Deputy Managing Director* Jake Lingwood, *Director of Publicity & Media Relations* Sarah Bennie, *Marketing Director* Diana Riley

Ebury Press Fiction (imprint)
tel 020-7840 8400
Publishing Director Gillian Green
Commercial fiction, crime, thriller, romance, sci-fi, fantasy. Imprints: Del Rey, Rouge.

Ebury Press (imprint)
tel 020-7840 8400
Deputy Publisher Andrew Goodfellow
General commercial non-fiction, autobiography, memoir, popular history, sport, travel writing, popular science, humour, film/TV tie-ins, music, popular reference, cookery, lifestyle.

Ebury Enterprises
tel 020-7840 8400
Publishing Director Carey Smith
Gift books, branded and bespoke books.

Rider (imprint)
tel 020-7840 8400
Publishing Director Judith Kendra
Inspirational titles across the spectrum of psychology, philosophy, international affairs, biography, current affairs, history, travel and spirituality.

Time Out (imprint, in partnership with Time Out Group)
tel 020-7840 8798
Senior Publishing Brand Manager Luthfa Begum
Travel, film, reference and lifestyle published in a unique partnership with *Time Out* Guides.

Vermilion (imprint)
tel 020-7840 8400
Publishing Director Susanna Abbott
Personal development, health, diet, relationships, parenting.

Virgin Books (imprint, in partnership with Virgin Group)
tel 020-7840 8400
Deputy Publisher Ed Faulkner
Business and smart thinking, health and popular culture: entertainment, showbiz, arts, film and TV, music, humour, biography and autobiography, popular reference, true crime, sport, travel, memoir, environment. Imprints: Black Lace, Nexus, WH Allen.

Penguin Random House Children's Division UK (company)
80 Strand, London WC2R 0RL
tel 020-7010 3000
61–63 Uxbridge Road, London W5 5SA
tel 020-8231 6800
website www.penguin.co.uk
website www.kidsatrandomhouse.co.uk
Managing Director Francesca Dow, *Publisher* Annie Eaton (fiction), *Publisher* Amanda Punter (fiction), *Publisher* Juliet Matthews (media & entertainment), *Editorial Director* Alice Blacker (picture books), *Commissioning Editor* Andrea MacDonald (picture books), *Head of Licensing & Consumer Products* Susan Bolsover, *New Business Manager* Rich Haines (licensing & consumer products), *Art Director* Anna Bilson.
Children's paperback and hardback books: wide range of picture books, board books, gift books and novelties; fiction; non-fiction, popular culture, digital and audio. Pre-school illustrated developmental books for 0–6 years; licensed brands; children's classic publishing and merchandising properties. No unsolicited MSS or original artwork or text. Imprints: Ladybird, Puffin, Penguin, Bantam Press, Bodley Head Children's Books, Jonathan Cape Children's Books, Corgi Children's Books, Doubleday Children's Books, Hutchinson Children's Books, Red Fox Children's Books.

Tamarind Books (imprint)
tel 020-8231 6800
email info@tamarindbooks.co.uk
website www.tamarindbooks.co.uk
Deputy Publisher Sue Buswell
Multicultural children's picture books and posters. All books give a high positive profile to black children. Unsolicited material welcome with return postage. Founded 1987.

Razorbill (imprint)
Publisher Amanda Punter
Commercial teen fiction. Launched 2010.

BBC, Ladybird, Warne
Category Publisher, Warne Nicole Pearson, *Editorial Director, Ladybird* Heather Crossley, *Publisher, Media & Entertainment* Juliet Matthews, *Publishing Director, Media & Entertainment* Eric Huang, *Art Director, Media & Entertainment* Kirstie Billingham, *Creative Director* Ronnie Fairweather
Specialises in preschool illustrated developmental books for 0–6 years, non-fiction 0–8 years; licensed brands; children's classic publishing and merchandising properties. No unsolicited MSS.

Transworld Publishers (company)
Publisher Bill Scott-Kerr, *Publishing Director* Doug Young (general non-fiction)
No unsolicited MSS accepted.

Bantam Press (imprint)
Publishing Director Sally Gaminara
Fiction and general non-fiction: cookery, business, crime, health and diet, history, humour, military, music, paranormal, self-help, science, travel and adventure, biography, autobiography.

Black Swan (imprint)
Publisher Bill Scott-Kerr
Paperback quality fiction and non-fiction.

Doubleday (UK) (imprint)
Publishing Director Marianne Velmans
Literary fiction and non-fiction.

Eden (imprint) and Expert (imprint)
Publishing Director Susanna Wadeson
General non-fiction and fiction.

Transworld Crime & Thrillers (imprint)
Publishing Director Sarah Adams

Transworld Women's Fiction (imprint)
Editorial Director Harriet Bourton

Transworld Ireland (imprint)
Publisher Eoin McHugh

Percy Publishing
9 Warners Close, Woodford, Essex IG8 0TF
tel 020-8504 2570
email enquiries@percy-publishing.com
website www.percy-publishing.com
Director Clifford Marker; *Editors* Cherry Burroughs, Mike Harrington

Publisher of fiction of any genre. Imprint: Puppy Print for Children's fiction. Founded 2012.

Pergamon – see page 223

Persephone Books

59 Lamb's Conduit Street, London WC1N 3NB
tel 020-7242 9292
email info@persephonebooks.co.uk
website www.persephonebooks.co.uk
Managing Director Nicola Beauman

Reprints of forgotten classics by 20th-century women writers with prefaces by contemporary writers. Founded 1999.

Phaidon Press Ltd

Regent's Wharf, All Saints Street, London N1 9PA
tel 020-7843 1000
email enquiries@phaidon.com
website www.phaidon.com
Managing Director James Booth-Clibborn, *Publishers* Emilia Terragni, Deborah Aaronson

Visual arts, lifestyle and culture.

Philip's – see Octopus Publishing Group

Phillimore & Co. Ltd – see The History Press Ltd

Phoenix – see The Orion Publishing Group Ltd

Phoenix Yard Books

Phoenix Yard, 65 King's Cross Road, London WC1X 9LW
tel 020-7239 4968
email hello@phoenixyardbooks.com
website www.phoenixyardbooks.com

Picturebooks, fiction and children's colouring books. We no longer accept unsolicited MSS.

Piatkus – see Little, Brown Book Group

Pica Press – see Bloomsbury Publishing Plc

Picador – see Pan Macmillan

Piccadilly Press

5 Castle Road, London NW1 8PR
tel 020-7267 4492
email books@piccadillypress.co.uk
website www.piccadillypress.co.uk
Managing Director & Publisher Brenda Gardner

Early picture books, parental advice trade paperbacks, trade paperback children's fiction, young adult non-fiction and young adult fiction. Founded 1983.

Pimlico – see Penguin Random House UK

Pink Press – see Indepenpress Publishing Ltd

Pitkin Publishing Ltd – see The History Press Ltd

The Playwrights Publishing Company

70 Nottingham Road, Burton Joyce, Notts. NG14 5AL
email playwrightspublishingco@yahoo.com
website www.playwrightspublishing.com
Proprietors Liz Breeze, Tony Breeze

One-act and full-length drama published on the internet. Serious work and comedies, for mixed cast, all women or schools. Reading fee unless professionally produced or unwaged; sae required. Founded 1990.

Plexus Publishing Ltd

The Studio, Hillgate Place, 18–20 Balham Hill, London SW12 9ER
tel 020-8673 9230
email plexus@plexusuk.demon.co.uk
website www.plexusbooks.com
Editoiral Director Sandra Wake

Film, music, biography, popular culture, fashion, gift. Imprint: Eel Pie. Founded 1973.

Pluto Press

345 Archway Road, London N6 5AA
tel 020-8348 2724
email pluto@plutobooks.com
website www.plutobooks.com
Managing Director Anne Beech, *Sales Director* Simon Liebesny, *Marketing Managing Manager* Emily Orford, *Publicity Manager* Jon Wheatley

Politics, anthropology, development, media, cultural, economics, history, Irish studies, Black studies, Islamic studies, Middle East, international relations.

Point – see Scholastic Ltd

Policy Press

University of Bristol, 1–9 Old Park Hill, Clifton, Bristol BS2 8BB
tel 0117 954 5940
email pp-info@bristol.ac.uk
website www.policypress.co.uk
Director Alison Shaw, *Assistant Director* Julia Mortimer

Social science, specialising in social and public policy, criminology, social work and social welfare. Founded 1996.

Policy Studies Institute (PSI)

50 Hanson Street, London W1W 6UP
tel 020-7911 7500
email admin@policystudiesinstitute.org.uk

Economic, cultural, social and environmental policy, political institutions, social sciences.

Politico's Publishing – see Methuen & Co Ltd

Polity Press
65 Bridge Street, Cambridge CB2 1UR
tel (01223) 324315
website www.politybooks.com

Social and political theory, politics, sociology, history, media and cultural studies, philosophy, literary theory, feminism, human geography, anthropology. Founded 1983.

Polygon – see Birlinn Ltd

Pont Books – see Gomer Press

Poolbeg Press Ltd†
123 Grange Hill, Baldoyle, Dublin 13, Republic of Ireland
tel +353 (0)1 8063825
email info@poolbeg.com
website www.poolbeg.com
Directors Kieran Devlin (managing), Paula Campbell (publisher)

Popular fiction, non-fiction, current affairs. Imprint: Poolbeg. Founded 1976.

Portfolio – see Penguin Random House UK

Portico – see Pavilion Books

Portland Press Ltd*
Charles Darwin House, 12 Roger Street, London WC1N 2JL
tel 020-7685 2410
email editorial@portlandpress.com
website www.portlandpress.com
Directors Caroline Black (managing), John Misselbrook (finance)

Biochemistry and molecular life science books for graduate, postgraduate and research students. Illustrated science books for children: *Making Sense of Science* series. Founded 1990.

Portobello Books
12 Addison Avenue, London W11 4QR
tel 020-7605 1380
email mail@portobellobooks.com
website www.portobellobooks.com
Publisher Sigrid Rausing, *Editorial Directors* Laura Barber, Bella Lacey, *Senior Editor* Max Porter, *Editor* Anne Meadows, *Rights Director* Angela Rose, *Publicity Director* Pru Rowlandson, *Production Director* Sarah Wasley, *Sales, Marketing & Digital Director* Iain Chapple, *Finance Manager* Morgan Graver

Current affairs, polemic, cultural criticism, history, memoir, travel, fiction in translation. No submissions except via a reputable literary agent. An imprint of Granta Publications. Founded 2005.

T & AD Poyser – see Bloomsbury Publishing Plc

Preface Publishing – see Penguin Random House UK

Prestel Publishing Ltd
14–17 Wells Street, London W1T 3PD
tel 020-7323 5004
email editorial@prestel-uk.co.uk
website www.prestel.com
Managing Director Andrew Hansen, *Commissioning Editor* Ali Gitlow

Art, architecture, photography, design, travel, cultural history and ethnography. Headquarters in Munich with offices in New York and London. Founded 1924.

Princeton University Press – Europe
6 Oxford Street, Woodstock, Oxon OX20 1TR
tel (01993) 814500
email admin@pupress.co.uk
website www.press.princeton.edu
Publisher for Social Sciences Sarah Caro, *Editor for Humanities* Ben Tate, *Execuitve Editor for Physical and Earth Sciences* Ingrid Gnerlich

Academic publishing for the social sciences, humanties and sciences. The European office of Princeton University Press, founded in 1999.

Prion Books – see Carlton Publishing Group

Priory Press Ltd
The Priory, Abbots Way, Abbotswood, Ballsalla, Isle of Man IM9 3EQ
tel (01624) 824688
email lm@manx.net
website www.priory-press.co.uk
Directors Linda Mann (submissions editor), Timothy Mann (finance)

Small independent press. Publishing good quality holiday fiction, crime, supernatural, black comedy and short stories. All submissions by email in the first instance. Royalties paid annually 10–20%. Founded 2006.

Profile Books Ltd*
3 Holford Yard, Bevin Way, London WC1X 9HD
tel 020-7841 6300
email info@profilebooks.com
website www.profilebooks.com
Managing Director Andrew Franklin, *Publisher* Mike Jones

General non-fiction: history, biography, current affairs, popular science, politics, business, management, humour. Also publishers of *The Economist* books. No unsolicited MSS. Founded 1996.

Tindal Street Press (imprint)
email info@profilebooks.com
Literary fiction in English. No unsolicited MSS. Founded 1998.

Serpent's Tail (imprint)
email info@serpentstail.com
website www.serpentstail.com
Publisher Hannah Westland

Fiction and non-fiction; literary and non-mainstream work, and work in translation. No unsolicited MSS. Founded 1986.

Clerkenwell Press (imprint)
email info@clerkenwellpress.co.uk
Publisher Geoffrey Mulligan

Literary fiction in English and translation. No unsolicited MSS. Founded 2011.

Psychology Press*

27 Church Road, Hove, East Sussex BN3 2FA
tel 020-7017 6000
website www.psypress.com

Psychology textbooks and monographs. Imprint of Taylor and Francis Group, an informa business.

Psychology Press (imprint)
website www.psypress.com

Routledge (imprint)
website www.routledgementalhealth.com

Puffin – see Penguin Random House UK

Pulp Press – see Indepenpress Publishing Ltd

Pure Indigo Ltd

Publishing Department, 17 The Herons, Cottenham, Cambridge CB24 8XX
tel 07714 201555
email ashley.martin@pureindigo.co.uk
website www.pureindigo.co.uk/publishing
Commissioning Editor Ashley Martin

Pure Indigo Publishing develops innovative junior series fiction. All titles are available in both print and digital formats and are distributed internationally with select partners. The company also develops software products that complement the product range. The junior series fiction titles are developed in-house and on occassion authors and illustrators are commissioned to complete project-based work. If you would like to be considered for commissions then please visit the website. Not currently accepting submissions.

Pushkin Press*

71–75 Shelton Street, London WC2H 9JQ
tel 020-7470 8830
email books@pushkinpress.com
website www.pushkinpress.com
Publisher Adam Freudenheim, *Associate Publisher* Stephanie Seegmuller

Having first rediscovered European classics of the 20th century, Pushkin now publishes novels, essays, memoirs, children's books and everything from timeless classics to the urgent and contemporary. Imprints: Pushkin Press, Pushkin Children's Books, ONE. Founded 1997.

Putnam Aeronautical – see Pavilion Books

Quadrille Publishing

5th Floor, Alhambra House,
27–31 Charing Cross Road, London WC2H 0LS
tel 020-7839 7117
email enquiries@quadrille.co.uk
website www.quadrille.co.uk
Directors Alison Cathie (managing), Sarah Lavelle (editorial), Helen Lewis (art), Vincent Smith (production)

Illustrated non-fiction: cookery, food and drink, gift and humour, craft, health and beauty, gardening, interiors, Mind, Body & Spirit. Founded 1994.

Quantum – see W. Foulsham & Co. Ltd

The Quarto Group, Inc.

The Old Brewery, 6 Blundell Street, London N7 9BH
tel 020-7700 9000
email info@quarto.com
website www.quarto.com
Chairman Timothy Chadwick, *Ceo* Marcus Leaver, *Chief Financial Officer* Mick Mousley, *Director, Quarto International Co-editions Group* David Breuer, *President & Ceo, Quarto Publishing Group USA* Ken Fund, *Managing Director, Quarto Publishing Group UK* David Inman

The Quarto Group is a leading global illustrated book publisher and distribution group. It is composed of 3 publishing divisions: Quarto International Co-editions Group; Quarto Publishing Group USA; and Quarto Publishing Group UK; plus Books & Gifts Direct (a direct seller of books and gifts in Australia and New Zealand) and Regent Publishing Services, a specialist print services company based in Hong Kong. Quarto International Co-editions Group creates illustrated books that are licensed and printed for third party publishers for publication under their own imprints in over 30 languages around the world. The division includes: Quarto Publishing, Quarto Children's Books, words & pictures, Qu:id, Quintessence, Quintet Publishing, QED, RotoVision, Marshall Editions, Marshall Editions Children's Books, Small World Creations, Fine Wine Editions, Apple Press, Global Book Publishing, Iqon Editions Ltd., Ivy Press and Quantum Publishing. Book categories: practical art and crafts, graphic arts, lifestyle, reference, food and drink, gardening, popular culture.

Quarto Publishing Group UK

74–77 White Lion Street, London N1 9PF
tel 020-7284 9300

Aurum Press (imprint)
website www.aurumpress.co.uk

General adult non-fiction, illustrated and non-illustrated: history, sport, entertainment, biography, autobiography, military.

Frances Lincoln (imprint)
website www.franceslincoln.com
Illustrated, international co-editions: gardening, architecture, environment, interiors, photography, art, walking and climbing, design and landscape, gift.

Jacqui Small (imprint)
website www.jacquismallpub.om
Publisher Jacqui Small
Illustrated, international co-editions: interiors, food and drink, lifestyle, craft.

QUE Publishing – see Pearson UK

Quercus Publishing Plc
55 Baker Street, 7th Floor, South Block, London WIU 8EW
tel 020-7291 7200
email enquiries@quercusbooks.co.uk
website www.quercusbooks.co.uk
Directors Mike McGrath (executive director group sales), Wayne Davies (executive director digital), David North (executive director & publisher), Paul Lenton (finance director), Jon Riley (editor-in-chief), Roisin Heycock (children's publishing), Caroline Proud (sales director), Ron Beard (key accounts), David Murphy (key accounts), Lucy Ramsey (publicity), Daniel Bouquet (rights & co-editions)
Fiction and non-fiction. Acquired by Hodder & Stoughton in 2014 (page 173). Founded 2005.

Maclehose Press (imprint)
Publisher Christopher Maclehose

Jo Fletcher Books (imprint)
Publisher Jo Fletcher

Heron Books (imprint)
Publisher Susan Watt

Quest – see Top That! Publishing plc

Quiller Publishing Ltd
Wykey House, Wykey, Shrewsbury SY4 1JA
tel (01939) 261616
email info@quillerbooks.com
website www.quillerpublishing.com
Managing Director Andrew Johnston

Excellent Press (imprint)
All country subjects and general sports including fishing, shooting, cookery, natural history, gardening, gift books.

Kenilworth Press (imprint)
Equestrian (riding, training, dressage, eventing, show jumping, driving, polo). Publisher of BHS official publications.

Quiller Press (imprint)
Specialises in all country and country sports subjects, including fishing, shooting, cookery, humour and all field sports.

The Sportsman's Press (imprint)
All country subjects and general sports including fishing, fencing, shooting, equestrian and gunmaking; wildlife art.

Swan Hill Press (imprint)
Country and field sports activities, including fishing, cookery, shooting, falconry, equestrian, gundog training, natural history, humour.

Radcliffe Publishing Ltd
2nd Floor, 5 Thomas More Square, London E1W 1WY
tel (01235) 277177
email contact.us@radcliffepublishing.com
website www.radcliffepublishing.com
Directors Sharlene Tilley (managing), Jonathan McKenna (editorial), Will Fabert (financial)
Primary care, child health, palliative care, nursing, pharmacy, dentistry, counselling, healthcare organisation and management examination revision aids. A division of Electric World. Founded 1987.

Ragged Bears Ltd
79 Acreman St., Sherborne, Dorset DT9 3PH
tel (01935) 816933
email books@ragged-bears.co.uk
website www.ragged-bears.co.uk
Managing Director Pamela Shirley
Preschool picture and novelty books, first chapter books to young teen fiction. Emailed submissions preferred but if posted send sae. Do not send original artwork. Imprint: Ragged Bears. Founded 1994.

Raintree – see Pearson UK

Ransom Publishing Ltd
Unit 7, Brocklands Farm. West Meon GU32 1JN
tel (01730) 829091
email ransom@ransom.co.uk
website www.ransom.co.uk
Directors Jenny Ertle (managing), Steve Rickard (creative)
Teen fiction, reading programmes and books for children and adults who are reluctant and struggling readers. Range covers high interest age/low reading age titles, quick reads, reading schemes and titles for young able readers. Series include *Reading Stars*, *The Outer Reaches*, *Shades 2.0*, *Boffin Boy*, *PIG* and *Dark Man*. Email for submission guidelines. Founded 1995.

RBI Search
(formerly Reed Business Information)
Windsor Court, East Grinstead House, Wood Street, East Grinstead, West Sussex RH19 1XA
tel (01342) 326972
email info@rbi.co.uk
website www.reedbusiness.com
Managing Director Jane Burgess

Online information specialists including leading search engines such as kellysearch.com and bankersalmanac.com covering industrial, financial, travel and media sectors, including gazetteers.com, hotelsearch and Kemps. Part of Reed Elsevier plc. Founded 1983.

Reaktion Books

33 Great Sutton Street, London EC1V 0DX
tel 020-7253 1071
email info@reaktionbooks.co.uk
website www.reaktionbooks.co.uk
Publisher Michael R. Leaman

Art history, design, architecture, critical biography, history, cultural studies, film studies, animal studies, modern music history, food history, natural history, Asian studies, popular science, sports history, travel writing, photography. Founded 1985.

Red Dress Ink™ – see Harlequin (UK) Ltd

Red Rattle Books

23 Thornfield Road, Thornton, Liverpool L23 9XY
tel 07505 700515
email editorred@rattlebooks.co.uk
website www.redrattlebooks.co.uk
Editor Howard Jackson, *Manager* Angela Keith, *Media* Amy Jackson

An independent, family-run publishing company. Produces and promotes 4–6 books each year. Specialises in crime and horror. Accepts submissions from young writers and unpublished authors. Full MS or samples can be submitted at editor@redrattlebooks.co.uk. Titles accepted for publication are published in paperback and Kindle editions. Fees for MS are negotiated with authors or their agents. If MS not accepted, explanation given as to why not suitable and future advice offered. Founded 2012.

Thomas Reed – see Bloomsbury Publishing Plc

Reed Books – now Octopus Publishing Group

William Reed Directories

Broadfield Park, Crawley, West Sussex RH11 9RT
tel (01293) 613400
email directories@william-reed.co.uk
website www.william-reed.co.uk
Director Charles Reed

Publishers of leading business-to-business directories and reports, including *The Retail and Shopping Centre Directory* and *The Grocer Directory of Manufacturers and Suppliers*.

Reed Educational and Professional Publishing Ltd – see Harcourt (imprint)

Reeds Nautical Almanac – see Bloomsbury Publishing Plc

Revenge Ink

Unit 13, Newby Road, Hazel Grove, Stockport, Cheshire SK7 5DA
email amita@revengeink.com
website www.revengeink.com
Editor Gopal Mukerjee (with Amita Mukerjee)
Director Amita Mukerjee

Founded by siblings Gopal and Amita Mukerjee, the company publishes adult fiction (all kinds) and prefers unsolicited, first-time novelists or established writers seeking a new outlet for edgier material. Considers poetry if presented in an original, creative manner. Currently publishes approx. 7 titles a year. Does not publish children's fiction or non-fiction titles such as cookbooks, gardens and how-to books. The company is aiming to create a non-fiction imprint for new research in philosophy, history, critical theory and political analysis. Submission guidelines can be found on the website. By email, preferably, send short sample and query first. Founded 2007.

Rider – see Penguin Random House UK

Rigby – see Pearson UK

Rising Stars*

PO Box 105, Rochester, Kent ME2 4BE
tel 0800 091 1602
email info@risingstars-uk.com
website www.risingstars-uk.com

Educational publisher of books and software for primary school age children. Titles are linked to the National Curriculum Key Stages, QCA Schemes of Work, National Numeracy Framework or National Literacy Strategy. Approach by email with ideas for publishing.

River Books – see New Cavendish Books

Rivers Oram Press

144 Hemingford Road, London N1 1DE
tel 020-7607 0823
email ro@riversoram.com
website www.riversoram.com
Directors Elizabeth Rivers Fidlon (managing), Anthony Harris

Non-ficton: social and political science, current affairs, social history, gender studies, sexual politics, cultural studies. Founded 1991.

Pandora Press (imprint)

Feminist press. General non-fiction: biography, arts, media, health, current affairs, reference and sexual politics.

Roar Publishing – see Little Tiger Group

Robson Books – see Pavilion Books

Books

George Ronald

3 Rosecroft Lane, Oaklands, Welwyn, Herts. AL6 0UB
tel (01438) 716062
email sales@grbooks.com
website www.grbooks.com
Managers E. Leith, M. Hofman

Religion, specialising in the Bahá'í Faith. Founded 1939.

RotoVision

Sheridan House, 112–116A Western Road, Hove, East Sussex BN3 1DD
tel (01273) 727268
email sales@rotovision.com
website www.rotovision.com

Illustrated books on design, photography and the performing arts. Part of the Quarto Group.

Rough Guides – see Penguin Random House UK

Roundhouse Group

Unit B, 18 Marine Gardens, Brighton BN2 1AH
tel (01273) 603717
email sales@roundhousegroup.co.uk
website www.roundhousegroup.co.uk
Publisher Alan T. Goodworth

Non-fiction adult and children's books. No unsolicited MSS. Founded 1991.

Route

PO Box 167, Pontefract, West Yorkshire WF8 4WW
tel (01977) 797695
email info@route-online.com
website www.route-online.com
Contact Ian Daley, Isabel Galan

Contemporary fiction, cultural non-fiction and memoir, with a strong interest in music books. Unsolicited MSS discouraged, book proposals in first instance.

Routledge-Cavendish – see Taylor & Francis Group

Routledge – see Psychology Press

RoutledgeCurzon – see Taylor & Francis Group

RoutledgeFalmer – see Taylor & Francis Group

Rowman & Littlefield International*

Unit A Whitacre Mews, 26-34 Stannary Street, London SE11 4AB
01752 202360
email info@rowmaninternational.com
website www.rowmaninternational.com
Chief Executive Oliver Gadsby, *Editorial Director*, Sarah Campbell

A new independent academic publisher in philosophy, politics and international relations, cultural studies and economics, with a particular focus on the interdisciplinary nature of these subject areas.

Royal Collection Trust Publications

Stable Yard House, St James's Palace, London SW1A 1JR
tel 020-7024 5645
website www.royalcollection.org.uk
Commercial Publisher Jacky Colliss Harvey, *Academic Publisher* Kate Owen, *Content Manager* Elizabeth Simpson, *Publishing Assistant* David Tibbs

Subjects from within the Royal Collection. Founded 1993.

Royal National Institute of Blind People (RNIB)

PO Box 173, Peterborough, Cambs. PE2 6WS
tel 0303 1239999
email shop@rnib.org.uk
website www.rnib.org.uk

Magazines, catalogues and books for blind and partially sighted people, to support daily living, leisure, learning and employment reading needs. Produced in braille, audio, large/legible print and email. Founded 1868.

Ryland Peters & Small

20–21 Jockey's Fields, London WC1R 4BW
tel 020-7025 2200
email info@rps.co.uk
website www.rylandpeters.com
Directors David Peters (managing), Cindy Richards (publishing), Julia Charles (editorial), Leslie Harrington (art), Denise Lie (rights), Danny Parnes (UK & export sales)

High-quality illustrated books on food and drink, home and garden, babies and children, gift books. Founded 1995.

Cico Books (imprint)

tel 020-7025 2280
email mail@cicobooks.co.uk
website www.cicobooks.co.uk
Publisher Cindy Richards

Lifestyle and interiors, crafts and Mind, Body & Spirit. Founded 1999.

Saffron Books

PO Box 13666, London SW14 8WF
020-8392 1122
email saffronbooks@eapgroup.com
website www.saffronbooks.com
Founding Publisher & Editor-in-Chief Sajid Rizvi

Art criticism, history, African and Asian architecture, African and Asian art and archaeology, Central Asian studies, Korean linguistics and new fiction. Imprint: Saffron Books, Yeti Books (for children). Founded 1989.

SAGE Publications Ltd*

1 Oliver's Yard, 55 City Road, London EC1Y 1SP
tel 020-7324 8500
email info@sagepub.co.uk
website www.uk.sagepub.com

Founded 50 years ago, SAGE is an independent company that publishes journals, books and library products for the educational, scholarly and professional markets.

St. David's Press

PO Box 733, Cardiff CF14 7ZY
tel 029-2021 8187
email post@st-davids-press.com
website www.st-davids-press.com

Sports and popular culture including: rugby, football, cricket, boxing and walking. Founded 2002.

St Pauls

St Pauls Publishing, 187 Battersea Bridge Road, London SW11 3AS
tel/fax 020-7978 4300
email editorial@stpaulspublishing.com
website www.stpaulspublishing.com

Theology, ethics, spirituality, biography, education, general books of Roman Catholic and Christian interest. Founded 1948.

Salamander – see Pavilion Books

Salariya Book Company Ltd

Book House, 25 Marlborough Place, Brighton BN1 1UB
tel (01273) 603306
email salariya@salariya.com
website www.salariya.com
Managing Director David Salariya

Children's art, picture books, fiction and non-fiction. Imprints: Book House, Scribblers, Scribo. Founded 1989.

Salt Publishing

12 Norwich Road, Cromer, Norfolk NR27 0AX
tel (01263) 511011
email sales@saltpublishing.com
website www.saltpublishing.com
Publishing Director Christopher Hamilton-Emery, Jennifer Hamilton-Emery

Multi-award-winning indie publisher. Home of the Best British anthologies and the Modern Dreams fiction movement. Fiction and the Best British annual anthologies. Founded 1999.

SAMS Publishing – see Pearson UK

Sandstone Press Ltd

Dochcarty Road, Dingwall, Scotland IV15 9UG
tel (01349) 865484
email info@sandstonepress.com
website www.sandstonepress.com
Directors Robert Davidson (managing), Iain Gordon (financial), Moira Forsyth (editorial), Eilidh Smith (marketing & publicity), Sue Foot (administration)

Fiction, non-fiction and ebooks.

Saunders – see Elsevier (Clinical Solutions)

Sawday's

Merchants House, Wapping Road, Bristol BS1 4RW
tel (0117) 204 7810
email specialplaces@sawdays.co.uk
website www.sawdays.co.uk
Founder Alastair Sawday, *Managing Director* Tom Sawday

Independent travel. Founded 1994.

S.B. Publications

14 Bishopstone Road, Seaford, East Sussex BN25 2UB
tel (01323) 893498
email sbpublications@tiscali.co.uk
website www.sbpublications.co.uk
Proprietor Lindsay Woods

Local history, local themes (e.g. walking books, guides), specific themes. Founded 1987.

Scala Arts & Heritage Publishers Ltd

10 Lion Yard, Tremadoc Road, London SW4 7NQ
tel 020-7808 1550
email jmckinley@scalapublishers.com
website www.scalapublishers.com
Managing Director Jenny McKinley

Publishers of high-quality books and ebooks for museums, galleries, cathedrals and heritage sites both for on-site sale and in the general book trade. Clients include: The Royal Collection, The National Gallery, The Metropolitan Museum of Art, Westminster Abbey and other large and small institutions in the UK, Europe and abroad. Founded 1992.

Sceptre – see Hodder & Stoughton

Schofield & Sims Ltd

Dogley Mill, Fenay Bridge, Huddersfield HD8 0NQ
tel (01484) 607080
email post@schofieldandsims.co.uk
website www.schofieldandsims.co.uk
Chairman C.N. Platts

Educational: nursery, infants, primary; posters. Founded 1901.

Scholastic Ltd*

Euston House, 24 Eversholt Street, London NW1 1DB
tel 020-7756 7756
website www.scholastic.co.uk
Chairman M.R. Robinson, *Co-Group Managing Directors* Catherine Bell, Steve Thompson

Children's fiction, non-fiction and picture books, education resources for primary schools. Owned by Scholastic Inc. Founded 1964.

Scholastic Children's Books (division)
Euston House, 24 Eversholt Street, London NW1 1DB
tel 020-7756 7761
email submissions@scholastic.co.uk
website www.scholastic.co.uk
UK Publisher Miriam Farbey, *Editorial Director (non-fiction)* Elizabeth Scoggins, *Publisher (fiction & picture books)* Samantha Smith, *Editorial Director (picture, novelty, gift books)* Pauliina Malinen-Teodoro, i Antonia Pelari

Activity books, novelty books, picture books, fiction for 5–12 years, teenage fiction, series fiction and film/TV tie-ins. Imprints: Scholastic, Alison Green Books, Marion Lloyd Books, Klutz. No unsolicited MSS. Unsolicited illustrations are accepted, but do not send any original artwork as it will not be returned.

The Chicken House
See page 158.

Scholastic Educational Resources (division)
Book End, Range Road, Witney, Oxon OX29 0YD
tel (01993) 893456
Managing Director Gordon Knowles

Professional books, classroom materials and online resources for primary teachers.

Scholastic Book Fairs (division)
See page 240.

Science Museum Group
Exhibition Road, London SW7 2DD
tel 0870 870 4771
website www.sciencemuseum.org.uk

Science, engineering and technology, museum guides.

SCM Press – see Hymns Ancient and Modern Ltd

Scripture Union
207–209 Queensway, Bletchley, Milton Keynes, Bucks. MK2 2EB
tel (01908) 856000
email info@scriptureunion.org.uk
website www.scriptureunion.org.uk
Director of Ministry Development (Publishing) Terry Clutterham

Christian books and Bible reading materials for people of all ages; educational and worship resources for churches; children's fiction and non-fiction; adult non-fiction. Founded 1867.

Search Press Ltd
Wellwood, North Farm Road, Tunbridge Wells, Kent TN2 3DR
tel (01892) 510850
email searchpress@searchpress.com
website www.searchpress.com
Directors Martin de la Bédoyère (managing), Caroline de la Bédoyère (rights), Rosalind Dace (editorial)

Arts, crafts, leisure. Founded 1970.

SelfMadeHero
139 Pancras Road, London NW1 1UN
020-7383 5157
email info@selfmadehero.com
website www.selfmadehero.com
Managing Director & Publisher Emma Hayley, *Sales & Marketing Manager* Sam Humphrey, *Press Officer* Paul Smith, *Assistant & Digital Content Manager* Guillaume Rat

The UK's leading independent publisher of graphic novels and visual narratives. The list of award-winning fiction and non-fiction graphic novels spans literary fiction, biography, classic adaptation, sci-fi, horror, crime and humour. Founded 2007.

Seren
57 Nolton Street, Bridgend CF31 3AE
tel (01656) 663018
email seren@serenbooks.com
website www.serenbooks.com
Publisher Mick Felton

Poetry, fiction, literary criticism, biography, art – mostly with relevance to Wales. Founded 1981.

Severn House Publishers
Salatin House, 19 Cedar Road, Sutton, Surrey SM2 5DA
tel 020-8770 3930
email sales@severnhouse.com
website www.severnhouse.com
Chairman Edwin Buckhalter, *Publisher* Kate Lyall Grant

Hardback, paperback, ebook and large print adult fiction for the library market: mysteries, thrillers, detective, horror, romance. No unsolicited MSS; submissions via literary agents. Imprints: Crème de la Crime. Founded 1974..

Shearsman Books
50 Westons Hill Drive, Emersons Green, Bristol BS16 7DF
tel 0117 957 2957
email editor@shearsman.com
website www.shearsman.com
Contact Tony Frazer

Contemporary poetry in English and in translation.

Sheldon Press – see Society for Promoting Christian Knowledge

Sheldrake Press
188 Cavendish Road, London SW12 0DA
tel 020-8675 1767

email enquiries@sheldrakepress.co.uk
website www.sheldrakepress.co.uk
Publisher J.S. Rigge

History, travel, architecture, cookery, music; humour; stationery. Founded 1979.

Shepheard-Walwyn (Publishers) Ltd

107 Parkway House, Sheen Lane, London SW14 8LS
tel 020-8241 5927
email books@shepheard-walwyn.co.uk
website www.shepheard-walwyn.co.uk
website www.ethicaleconomics.org.uk
Director A.R.A. Werner

Independent publishing company established in 1971. History, biography, political economy, perennial philosophy; illustrated gift books; Scottish interest.

Shire Publications

Kemp House, Chawley Park, Cumnor Hill, Oxford OX2 9PH
tel (01865) 811332
email info@shirebooks.co.uk
website www.shirebooks.co.uk

Acquired by Bloomsbury Publishing Plc in 2014. Non-fiction publisher of history, heritage and nostalgia. Also provides publishing services to organisations such as museums, schools, universities and charities.

Short Books Ltd

Unit 316, ScreenWorks, 22 Highbury Grove, London N5 2EF
tel 020-7833 9429
email info@shortbooks.co.uk
website www.shortbooks.co.uk
Editorial Directors Rebecca Nicolson, Aurea Carpenter

Non-fiction and fiction. No unsolicited MSS. Founded 2000.

Sidgwick & Jackson – see Pan Macmillan

Sigma Press

Stobart House, Pontyclerc, Penybanc Road, Ammanford, Carmarthenshire SA18 3HP
tel (01269) 593100
email info@sigmapress.co.uk
website www.sigmapress.co.uk
Directors Nigel Evans, Jane Evans

Leisure: country walking, cycling, regional heritage, ecology, folklore; biographies. Founded 1979.

Silhouette® – see Harlequin (UK) Ltd

Simon & Schuster UK Ltd*

222 Gray's Inn Road, London WC1X 8HB
tel 020-7316 1900
email enquiries@simonandschuster.co.uk
website www.simonandschuster.co.uk
Directors Ian Chapman (Ceo), Suzanne Baboneau (managing), Jo Dickinson (publishing, editorial), Iain MacGregor (publishing, non-fiction), Ian Marshall (sport), Lara Hancock (children's picture books), Meg Wang (licensed character list)

Adult non-fiction (history, biography, current affairs, science, political, popular culture, sports books and memoirs). Adult fiction (mass-market, literary fiction, historical fiction, commercial women's fiction, general fiction). Bespoke and illustrated titles. Children's and young adult fiction, picture books, novelty, pop-up and licensed character. Founded 1986.

Simon & Schuster Audioworks
Fiction, non-fiction and business.

Singing Dragon

73 Collier Street, London N1 9BE
tel 020-7833 2307
email hello@singingdragon.com
website www.singingdragon.com
Director Jessica Kingsley

An imprint of Jessica Kingsley Publishers. Authoritative books on complementary and alternative health, Tai Chi, Qigong and ancient wisdom traditions for health, wellbeing and professional and personal development. Submission details on website. Founded 2008.

Siri Scientific Press

Arrow Mill, Queensway, Castleton, Rochdale OL11 2YW
tel 07770 796913
email books@siriscientificpress.co.uk
website www.siriscientificpress.co.uk
Publishing Consultant David Penney

Publisher of specialist natural history books including academic monographs, compiled edited volumes, photographic atlases, field guides and more general works. Specialise in works on entomology, arachnology and palaeontology, but will also consider other topics. Happy to hear directly from potential new authors. Founded 2008.

Smith Gryphon Ltd – see John Blake Publishing Ltd

Colin Smythe Ltd*

38 Mill Lane, Gerrards Cross, Bucks. SL9 8BA
tel (01753) 886000
website www.colinsmythe.co.uk
Directors Colin Smythe (managing & editorial), Leslie Hayward, Ann Saddlemyer

Irish biography, phaleristics, heraldry, Irish literature and literary criticism, Irish history. Other imprints: Dolmen Press, Van Duren Publishers. Founded 1966.

Snowbooks Ltd

website www.snowbooks.com
Directors Emma Barnes (managing), Rob Jones, *Publisher* Anna Torborg

Genre fiction: steampunk, fantasy, sci-fi and horror. General non-fiction. See website for submission guidelines. No postal submissions or calls please. Founded 2004.

Society for Promoting Christian Knowledge

36 Causton Street, London SW1P 4ST
tel 020-7592 3900
email spck@spck.org.uk
website www.spckpublishing.co.uk
Director of Publishing Joanna Moriarty

Founded 1698.

Sheldon Press (imprint)

Popular medicine, health, self-help, psychology.

SPCK (imprint)

Theology and academic, liturgy, prayer, spirituality, biblical studies, educational resources, mission, gospel and culture.

Society of Genealogists Enterprises Ltd

14 Charterhouse Buildings, Goswell Road, London EC1M 7BA
tel 020-7251 8799
email sales@sog.org.uk
website www.sog.org.uk
Chief Executive June Perrin

Local and family history books, software and magazines plus extensive library facilities.

Somerville Press Ltd

Dromore, Bantry, Co. Cork, Republic of Ireland
tel +353 (0)28 32873
email somervillepress@eircom.net
website www.somervillepress.com
Directors Andrew Russell, Jane Russell

Irish interest: fiction and non-fiction. Founded 2008.

South Street Press – see Garnet Publishing Ltd

Southwater – see Anness Publishing

Souvenir Press Ltd

43 Great Russell Street, London WC1B 3PD
tel 020-7580 9307/8
email souvenirpress@souvenirpress.co.uk
Managing Director Ernest Hecht

Archaeology, biography and memoirs, educational (secondary, technical), general, humour, practical handbooks, psychiatry, psychology, sociology, sports, games and hobbies, travel, supernatural, parapsychology, illustrated books. No unsolicited fiction or children's books; initial enquiry by letter essential for non-fiction. Founded 1951.

SPCK – see Society for Promoting Christian Knowledge

Speechmark Publishing Ltd

2nd Floor, 5 Thomas More Square, London E1W 1WY
tel (01908) 277177
email info@speechmark.net
website www.speechmark.net
Directors Sharlene Tilley (managing), Jonathan McKenna (editorial), Will Fawbert (financial)

Education, health, social care. A division of Electric World. Founded 1990.

Spellmount Ltd – see The History Press Ltd

Sphere – see Little, Brown Book Group

Spon – see Taylor & Francis Group

SportBooks Ltd

9 St Aubyns Place, York YO24 1EQ
tel (01904) 613475
email info@sportsbooks.ltd.uk
website www.sportsbooks.ltd.uk
Directors Randall Northam, Veronica Northam

Sport. Imprints: SportsBooks, BMM. Founded 1995.

The Sportsman's Press – see Quiller Publishing Ltd

Springer-Verlag London Ltd*

236 Gray's Inn Road, Floor 6, London WC1X 8HB
tel 020-3192 2000
website www.springer.com
General Manager Beverley Ford

Medicine, computing, engineering, mathematics, chemistry, biosciences. Founded 1972.

Spruce – see Octopus Publishing Group

Stacey International

128 Kensington Church Street, London W8 4BH
tel 020-7221 7166
email info@stacey-international.co.uk
website www.stacey-international.co.uk
Chairman Tom Stacey, *Managing Director* Struan Simpson, *Finance Director* Stephen Hill

Topical issues for *Independent Minds* series, encyclopaedic books on regions and countries, Islamic and Arab subjects, world affairs, children's books, art, travel, belles lettres, biography. Imprints: Capuchin Classics, Gorilla Guides. Founded 1974.

Capuchin Classics (imprint)

email info@capuchin-classics.co.uk
website www.capuchin-classics.co.uk
Contact Emma Howard
Enduring literary fiction, mostly 19th and 20th century. Founded 2008.

Stainer & Bell Ltd

PO Box 110, Victoria House, 23 Gruneisen Road, London N3 1DZ

Books

tel 020-8343 3303
email post@stainer.co.uk
website www.stainer.co.uk
Directors Keith Wakefield (joint managing), Carol Wakefield (joint managing & secretary), Amanda Aknai, Antony Kearns, Andrew Pratt, Nicholas Williams

Books on music, religious communication. Founded 1907.

Stellium Ltd

22 Second Avenue, Camels Head, Plymouth PL2 2EQ
tel (01752) 367300
email stelliumpub@gmail.com
website www.stelliumpub.com
Contacts Sasha Fenton, Jan Budkowski

Fiction, digital and self-publishing services. Founded 2013.

Stenlake Publishing Ltd

54–58 Mill Square, Catrine Ayrshire KA5 6RD
tel (01290) 552233
email sales@stenlake.co.uk
website www.stenlake.co.uk
Managing Director Richard Stenlake

Local history, Scottish language and literature especially Robert Burns, studio pottery, bee keeping, railways, transport, aviation, canals and mining covering Wales, Scotland, England, Northern Ireland, Isle of Man, Republic of Ireland and Zambia. Founded 1987.

Alloway Publishing (imprint)

website www.allowaypublishing.co.uk

Stonewood Press

97 Benefield Road, Oundle, Peterborough PE8 4EU
tel 0845 4564 838
email stonewoodpress@gmail.com
website www.stonewoodpress.co.uk
Publisher & Production Editor Martin Parker

Stonewood Press is an independent publisher dedicated to promoting new writing with an emphasis on contemporary short stories and poetry. Stonewood aims to publish challenging and high-quality writing in English without the pressures associated with mainstream publishing. Submission details on website. Founded in 2011.

Stripes – see Little Tiger Group

Summersdale Publishers Ltd

46 West Street, Chichester, West Sussex PO19 1RP
tel (01243) 771107
email submissions@summersdale.com
website www.summersdale.com
Editorial Director Claire Plimmer

Popular non-fiction, humour and gift books, travel writing and health and wellbeing. See website for guidelines. Founded 1990.

Sunflower Books

PO Box 36160, London SW7 3WS
tel/fax 020-7589 2377
email mail@sunflowerbooks.co.uk
website www.sunflowerbooks.co.uk
Director P.A. Underwood

Travel guidebooks.

Sussex Academic Press

PO Box 139, Eastbourne, East Sussex BN24 9BP
tel (01323) 479220
email edit@sussex-academic.com
website www.sussex-academic.com
Editorial Director Anthony Grahame

Founded 1994.

The Alpha Press (imprint)

International relations, Middle Eastern studies, cultural studies, theatre, philosophy, literary criticism, biography, history with a special emphasis on Spanish history, first nations studies, Latin American studies, theology and religion, Jewish and Israel studies (history, Holocaust, culture, biography), Asian studies, art history.

Sutton Publishing – see The History Press Ltd

Swan Hill Press – see Quiller Publishing Ltd

Sweet & Maxwell

100 Avenue Road, London NW3 3PF
tel 020-7393 7000
website www.sweetandmaxwell.co.uk
Directors Peter Lake (managing), Rob Martin (federated search strategy), Chris Elvin (customer operations), David Larson (finance), Dick Greener (legal affairs), Hilary Lambert (commercial), Terri Hawksworth (sales & marketing), Natasha Ruffet (human resources)

Law. Part of Thomson Reuters Ltd. Founded 1799; incorporated 1889.

Sweet Cherry Publishing*

Unit E, Vulcan Business Complex, Vulcan Road, Leicester LE5 3EB
tel 0116 212 9780
email info@sweetcherrypublishing.com
website www.sweetcherrypublishing.com
Director Mr A. Thadha

Children's series fiction specialist. Children's picture books, novelty books, gift books, board books, educational books and series fiction for all ages. Also welcomes young adult novels especially trilogies or series fiction. Likes to publish a set of books as a box set or in a slipcase. See website for submission guidelines. Founded 2011.

Tamarind Books – see Penguin Random House UK

Tango Books Ltd

PO Box 32595, London W4 5YD
tel 020-8996 9970
email info@tangobooks.co.uk
website www.tangobooks.co.uk
Directors Sheri Safran, David Fielder

Children's fiction and non-fiction novelty books, including pop-up, touch-and-feel and cloth books. Maximum 500 words. Submissions with sae or by email. No poetry or picture books.

Tarquin Publications

Suite 74, 17 Holywell Hill, St Albans AL1 1DT
tel (01727) 833866
email info@tarquinbooks.com
website www.tarquinbooks.com
Director Andrew Griffin

Mathematics and mathematical models, puzzles, codes and logic; paper cutting, paper engineering and pop-up books for intelligent children. No unsolicited MSS; send suggestion or synopsis in first instance. Founded 1970.

Taschen UK Ltd

5th Floor, 1 Heathcock Court, 415 Strand, London WC2R 0NS
tel 020-7845 8585
email contact-uk@taschen.com
website www.taschen.com

Publishers of art, anthropology and aphrodisia. Founded 1980.

Tate Enterprises Ltd

The Lodge, Millbank, London SW1P 4RG
tel 020-7887 8869
email submissions@tate.org.uk
website www.tate.org.uk/publishing
Tate Publishing Director Roger Thorp, *Publishing & Commercial Director* John Stachiewicz, *Merchandise Director* Rosey Blackmore, *Sales & Rights Director*, Fiona MacDonald, *Executive Editor* Jacky Klein, *Images Manager* Clive Coward, *Head of Production* Bill Jones

Publishers for Tate in London, Liverpool and St Ives. Exhibition catalogues, art books, children's books and merchandise. Also product development, picture library and licensing.

I.B.Tauris & Co. Ltd*

6 Salem Road, London W2 4BU
tel 020-7243 1225
website www.ibtauris.com
Chairman/Publisher Iradj Bagherzade, *Managing Director* Jonathan McDonnell

History, biography, politics, international relations, current affairs, Middle East, religion, cultural and media studies, film, art, archaeology, travel guides. Founded 1983.

Tauris Parke Paperbacks (imprint)

Non-fiction trade paperbacks: biography, history, travel.

Taylor & Francis Group*

2 and 4 Park Square, Milton Park, Abingdon, Oxon OX14 4RN
tel 020-7017 6000
email info@tandf.co.uk
website www.tandf.co.uk
website www.informa.com
Managing Director, Taylor & Francis Books Jeremy North

Academic and reference books.

Routledge (imprint)

website www.routledge.com
Addiction, anthropology, archaeology, Asian studies, business, classical studies, counselling, criminology, development and environment, dictionaries, economics, education, geography, health, history, Japanese studies, library science, language, linguistics, literary criticism, media and culture, nursing, performance studies, philosophy, politics, psychiatry, psychology, reference, social administration, social studies/sociology, women's studies, law. Directories, international relations, reference, yearbooks.

Garland Science (imprint)

website www.garlandscience.com
Bioscience textbooks and scholarly works.

Psychology Press

See page 194.

Spon (imprint)

website www.sponpress.com
Architecture, civil engineering, construction, leisure and recreation management, sports science.

CRC Press (imprint)

website www.crcpress.com
Science: physics, mathematics, chemistry, electronics, natural history, pharmacology and drug metabolism, toxicology, technology, history of science, ergonomics, production engineering, remote sensing, geographic information systems, engineering.

Teach Yourself – see Hodder Education

Tech-it-Forward

email forward@press-alt.com
website www.press-alt.com

Tech-it-Forward is an independent publishing house researching publishing in the field of tech-education. The company aims to publish distinctive, innovative and original titles beyond the curriculum. Imprint: Tif. Members of JISC TechDis & Load 2 Learn. Founded 2014.

The Templar Company Ltd

The Granary, North Street, Dorking, Surrey RH4 1DN

Books

tel (01306) 876361
email info@templarco.co.uk
email submissions@templarco.co.uk (submissions)
website www.templarco.co.uk
Directors Mike McGrath (managing), Amanda Wood (creative), Helen Bowe (sales & marketing)

Publisher and packager of high-quality illustrated children's books, including novelty books, picture books, pop-up books, board books, fiction, non-fiction and gift titles. Send submissions via email.

Tempus – see The History Press Ltd

Thames & Hudson Ltd*

181A High Holborn, London WC1V 7QX
tel 020-7845 5000
email sales@thameshudson.co.uk
website www.thamesandhudson.com
Directors T. Evans (Chairman), S. Reisz-Neurath (Deputy Chairman), R. Grisebach (Ceo), S. Thompson (publishing) L. Dietrich (international editorial), C. Ferguson (operations), C. Frederking (group sales), N. Palfreyman (production), C. Ridler (editorial), J. Honer (Head of Editorial), S. Forster (finance)

Illustrated non-fiction for an international audience of adults and children, specialising in art and art history, photography, design, travel, history, archaeology, architecture, fashion and contemporary media.

Think Books

Think Publishing Ltd, The Pall Mall Deposit, 124–128 Barlby Road, London W10 6BL
tel 020-8962 3020
website www.thinkpublishing.co.uk
Chairman Ian McAuliffe, *Chief Executive* Tilly Boulter

Specialises in books on the outdoors, gardening and wildlife. Publishes with the Wildlife Trusts, the Royal Horticultural Society and the Campaign to Protect Rural England and others. Founded 2005.

Thoemmes Press – see Bloomsbury Publishing Plc

Thomson Reuters – Round Hall

43 Fitzwilliam Place, Dublin 2, Republic of Ireland
tel +353 (0)1 6625301
website www.roundhall.ie
Director Catherine Dolan

Law. Part of Thomson Reuters.

Three Hares Publishing

4 Winton Avenue, London N11 2AT
tel 020-8245 2606
email hello@threeharespress.com
website www.threeharespublishing.com
Publisher Yasmin Standen

Looking for submissions and will consider fiction/non-fiction, novels, children's books, short stories. No picture books. Published a number of established authors and first-time authors. Interested in discovering new talent. Visit website for submission guidelines, online submissions only via website. Founded 2014.

Tide Mill Press – see Top That! Publishing plc

Time Out – see Penguin Random House UK

Time Warner – see Little, Brown Book Group

Times Books – see HarperCollins Publishers

Tindal Street Press – see Profile Books Ltd

Titan Books

144 Southwark Street, London SE1 0UP
tel 020-7620 0200
website www.titanbooks.com
Publisher & Managing Director Nick Landau, *Editorial Director* Katy Wild

Graphic novels, including *Simpsons* and *Batman*, featuring comic-strip material; film/TV tie-ins and cinema reference books. No fiction or children's proposals, no email submissions and no unsolicited material without preliminary letter. Email or send large sae for current author guidelines. Division of Titan Publishing Group Ltd. Founded 1981.

Tolley – see LexisNexis

Top That! Publishing plc

Marine House, Tide Mill Way, Woodbridge, Suffolk IP12 1AP
tel (01394) 386651
email customerservice@topthatpublishing.com
website www.topthatpublishing.com
Chairman Barrie Henderson, *Directors* David Henderson (managing), Simon Couchman (creative), Stuart Buck (production), Ian Peacock (financial), Daniel Graham (editorial), Steve Munnings (sales)

Children's activity books, novelty books, picture books, reference, character, gift books, early learning books, apps and digital animations. Imprint: Top That Publishing. Founded 1999.

Tor – see Pan Macmillan

Torque – see The History Press Ltd

Trentham Books

(imprint of the Institute of Education Press)
20 Bedford Way, London WC1H 0AL
tel 020-7911 5383 (production), or 020-7911-5563 (editorial)
email trenthambooks@ioe.ac.uk

Education (including specialist fields – multi-ethnic issues, equal opportunities, bullying, design and technology, early years), social policy, sociology of education, European education, women's studies. Does not publish books for use by parents or children, or fiction, biography, reminiscences and poetry.

Troika Books

Well House, Green Lane, Ardleigh, Colchester, Essex CO7 7PD
tel (01206) 233333
email martin-west@btconnect.com
website www.troikabooks.com
Publisher Martin West, *Rights* Petula Chaplin, *Publicity & Marketing* Andrea Reece, *Editor* Jess West

Publishes children's books from picture books through to young adult. Including early readers, fiction for 7–9 years, poetry. Founded 2012.

Troubador Publishing Ltd

9 Priory Business Park, Wistow Road, Kibworth, Leics. LE8 0RX
tel 0116 279 2299
email books@troubador.co.uk
website www.troubador.co.uk
Directors Jeremy Thompson (managing), Jane Rowland (operations)

Fiction and non-fiction with specialist lists in Italian studies, social justice and non-fiction. Self-publishing imprint: Matador. Founded 1996.

TSO (The Stationery Office)

St Crispins, Duke Street, Norwich NR3 1PD
tel (01603) 696876
email sales@tso.co.uk
website www.tso.co.uk

Publishing and information management services: business, directories, pharmaceutical, professional, reference, *Learning to Drive*.

Two Rivers Press Ltd

7 Denmark Road, Reading, Berks. RG1 5PA
tel 0118 987 1452
email tworiverspress@gmail.com
website www.tworiverspress.com
Managing Publisher Sally Mortimore, *Sales* Barbara Morris, *Poetry Editor* Peter Robinson, *Local Interest Editor* Adam Sowan, *Design & Illustration* Nadja Guggi, Sally Castle, Martin Andrews, *Marketing & Website* Karen Mosman

Champions the town and region's heritage and culture by publishing individually designed, carefully produced poetry, art and local interest books. Founded 1994.

Ulric Publishing

PO Box 55, Church Stretton, Shrops. SY6 6WR
tel (01694) 781354
email enquiries@ulricpublishing.com
website www.ulricpublishing.com
Directors Ulric Woodhams, Elizabeth Oakes

Non-fiction military and motoring history. Licensing and publishing services. No unsolicited MSS. P.O. Box for letters and billing only. Founded 1992.

Ulverscroft Group Ltd

The Green, Bradgate Road, Anstey, Leicester LE7 7FU
tel 0116 236 4325
email m.merrill@ulverscroft.co.uk
website www.ulverscroft.co.uk
Sales Manager Mark Merrill

Offers a wide variety of large print titles in hardback and paperback formats as well as abridged and unabridged audio books, many of which are written by the world's favourite authors and includes award-winning titles. Founded 1964.

Unicorn Press Ltd

66 Charlotte Street, London W1T 4QE
tel 07836 633377
email ian@unicornpress.org
website www.unicornpress.org
Directors Lord Ian Strathcarron, Hugh Tempest-Radford, Lucy Duckworth, Simon Perks

Cultural history, art reference, art history, architecture, artists' monographs, artists' biographies, gallery and museum catalogues, mediation. Imprints include: Unicorn Press (arts and cultural history), Universe Press (memoires) and Unity Press (mediation). Founded 1985.

Merlin Unwin Books Ltd

Palmers House, 7 Corve Street, Ludlow, Shrops. SY8 1DB
tel (01584) 877456
email books@merlinunwin.co.uk
website www.merlinunwin.co.uk
Chairman Merlin Unwin, *Managing Director* Karen McCall

Countryside books. Founded 1990.

Usborne Publishing Ltd

Usborne House, 83–85 Saffron Hill, London EC1N 8RT
tel 020-7430 2800
email mail@usborne.co.uk
website www.usborne.com
Directors Peter Usborne, Jenny Tyler (editorial), Robert Jones, Andrea Parsons

Children's books: reference, practical, craft, natural history, science, languages, history, geography, preschool, fiction. Founded 1973.

Vallentine Mitchell

Middlesex House, 29/45 High Street, Edgware, Middlesex HA8 7UU
tel 020-8952 9526
email info@vmbooks.com (general)
email editor@vmbooks.com (submissions)
website www.vmbooks.com

Directors Stewart Cass (managing), A.E. Cass, H.J. Osen, C.V. Callman

Jewish history, Judaism, Holocaust studies, Jewish culture, Jewish biography, Middle Eastern studies.

Variorum – see Ashgate Publishing Ltd

Veritas Publications†

Veritas House, 7–8 Lower Abbey Street, Dublin 1, Republic of Ireland
tel +353 (0)1 8788177
email publications@veritas.ie
website www.veritas.ie

Liturgical and Church resources, religious school books for primary and post-primary levels, biographies, academic studies, and general books on religious, moral and social issues.

Vermilion – see Penguin Random House UK

Verso Ltd

6 Meard Street, London W1V 3HR
tel 020-7437 3546
email enquiries@verso.co.uk
website www.verso.com
Directors Jacob Stevens (managing), Rowan Wilson (sales & marketing), Robin Blackburn, Tariq Ali

Current affairs, politics, sociology, economics, history, philosophy, cultural studies. Founded 1970.

Viking – see Penguin Random House UK

Vintage – see Penguin Random House UK

Virago – see Little, Brown Book Group

Virgin Books – see Penguin Random House UK

Virtue Books Ltd

Edward House, Tenter Street, Rotherham S60 1LB
tel (01709) 365005
email info@virtue.co.uk
website www.virtue.co.uk
Directors Peter E. Russum, Margaret H. Russum

Books for the professional chef: catering and drink.

The Vital Spark – see Neil Wilson Publishing Ltd

Voyager – see HarperCollins Publishers

University of Wales Press

10 Columbus Walk, Brigantine Place, Cardiff CF10 4UP
tel 029-2049 6899
email enquiries@press.wales.ac.uk
website www.uwp.co.uk
Director Helgard Krause

Academic, educational and professional publisher (Welsh and English). Specialises in the humanities and social sciences across a broad range of subjects: European studies, political philosophy, literature, history, Celtic studies and Welsh studies. Founded in 1922.

Walker Books for Young Readers, USA – see Bloomsbury Publishing Plc

Walker Books Ltd*

87 Vauxhall Walk, London SE11 5HJ
tel 020-7793 0909
website www.walker.co.uk
Directors Karen Lotz, Ian Mablin (non-executive), Roger Alexander (non-executive), Helen McAleer, Sarah Foster, Angela Van Den Belt, Ed Ripley, Jane Winterbotham, Alan Lee, John Mendelson, Hilary Berkman, James Cunningham

Children's: activity books, novelty books, picture books, fiction for 5–8 and 9–12 years, young adult fiction, series fiction, film/TV tie-ins, plays, poetry, digital and audio. Imprints: Walker Books and Walker Entertainment. Founded 1980.

Wallflower Press

4 Eastern Terrace Mews, Brighton BN2 1EP
email info@wallflowerpress.co.uk
website www.wallflowerpress.co.uk
Editorial Director Yoram Allon

Cinema and the moving image, including TV, animation, documentary and artists' film and video – both academic and popular. Contact by email in first instance. Founded 1999.

Ward Lock Educational Co. Ltd

BIC Ling Kee House, 1 Christopher Road, East Grinstead, West Sussex RH19 3BT
tel (01342) 318980
email wle@lingkee.com
website www.wardlockeducational.com
Directors Au Bak Ling (chairman, Hong Kong), Au King Kwok (Hong Kong), Au Wai Kwok (Hong Kong), Albert Kw Au (Hong Kong), *Company Secretary* Eileen Parsons

Primary and secondary pupil materials, Kent Mathematics Project: *KMP BASIC* and *KMP Main* series covering Reception to GCSE, *Reading Workshops*, *Take Part* series and *Take Part* starters, teachers' books, music books, *Target* series for the National Curriculum: *Target Science* and *Target Geography*, religious education. Founded 1952.

Warne – see Penguin Random House UK

Warner/Chappell Plays Ltd – see Josef Weinberger Plays Ltd

Watkins Media Limited

(a member of the Osprey Group)
359 Goswell Road London EC1V 7JL

tel 020-3468 0102
website watkinspublishing.com
website www.nourishbooks.com
website www.angryrobotbooks.com
website www.repeaterbooks.com
Owner Etan Ilfeld, *Publisher, Watkins* Jo Lal, *Publisher, Nourish* Grace Cheetham, *Marketing Director* Vicky Hartley, *Head of Design* Georgina Hewitt, *UK Sales Manager* Sian Jones *Vice President, US Sales & Marketing* John Tintera, *Angry Robot Managing Director* Marc Gascoigne, *Repeater Publisher* Tariq Goddard

Health and wellbeing, food and drink (Nourish); Mind, Body & Spirit (Watkins); sci-fi, fantasy (Angry Robot); politics, current affairs, fiction (Repeater).

Franklin Watts – see Hachette Children's Group

The Watts Publishing Group Ltd – see Hachette Children's Group

Waverley Books*

(an imprint of The Gresham Publishing Company Ltd)
Academy Park, Gower Street (Building 4000), Glasgow G51 1PR
tel 0141 375 1998
email info@waverley-books.co.uk
website www.waverley-books.co.uk
Publishers Ron Grosset, Liz Small

Books for the general trade and Scottish interest books. Associated imprint: Geddes & Grosset.

Wayland – see Hachette Children's Group

Weidenfeld & Nicolson

(part of the Orion Publishing Group Ltd)
Orion House, 5 Upper St Martin's Lane, London WC2H 9EA
tel 020-7240 3444
Managing Director Lisa Milton, *Publisher* Alan Samson, *Publishing Director, fiction* Kirsty Dunseath

Biography and autobiography, current affairs, history, travel, fiction, literary fiction, military history and militaria.

Weidenfeld & Nicolson Illustrated

Quality illustrated non-fiction: gardening, cookery, wine, art and design, health and lifestyle, history, popular culture, archaeology, British heritage, literature, fashion, architecture, natural history, sport and adventure.

Josef Weinberger Plays Ltd

12–14 Mortimer Street, London W1T 3JJ
tel 020-7580 2827
email general.info@jwmail.co.uk
website www.josef-weinberger.com

Stage plays only, in both acting and trade editions. Preliminary letter essential.

Welsh Academic Press

PO Box 733, Cardiff CF14 7ZY
tel 029-2021 8187
email post@welsh-academic-press.com
website www.welsh-academic-press.com

Political studies, medieval Welsh and Celtic studies, Scandinavian and Baltic studies, education, history, employment and industrial relations. Founded 1994.

Wharncliffe – see Pen & Sword Books Ltd

Whittet Books Ltd

1 St John's Lane, Stansted, Essex CM24 8JU
tel (01279) 815871
email mail@whittetbooks.com
website www.whittetbooks.com
Director George J. Papa, *Publisher* Shirley Greenall

Natural history, wildlife, countryside, poultry, livestock, horses, donkeys. Publishing proposals considered for the above lists. Please send outline, preferably by email. Founded 1976.

John Wiley & Sons Ltd*

The Atrium, Southern Gate, Chichester, West Sussex PO19 8SQ
tel (01243) 779777
email customer@wiley.co.uk
9600 Garsington Road, Oxford OX4 2DQ
tel (01865) 776868
website www.wiley.com

Wiley's core businesses publish scientific, technical, medical, and scholarly journals, encyclopedias, books, and online products and services; professional/trade books, subscription products, training materials, and online applications and websites; and educational materials for undergraduate and graduate students and lifelong learners. Global headquarters in Hoboken, New Jersey, with operations in the USA, Europe, Asia, Canada and Australia.

Neil Wilson Publishing Ltd*

226 Kings Street, Castle Douglas DG7 1DS
tel 01556 504119
email info@nwp.co.uk
website www.nwp.co.uk
Managing Director Neil Wilson

Leading independent publisher with a wide range of print and ebooks covering a broad range of interests. Submissions by email only. Include covering letter, author CV, synopsis and sample chapter.

The Angels' Share (imprint)

website www.angelshare.co.uk
Whisky-related matters (leisure, reference, history, memoir); food, cookery, beer.

11:9 (imprint)

website www.11-9.co.uk
Scottish Arts Council/National Lottery-funded

project to bring new Scottish fiction writing to the marketplace. Not commissioning at present.

In Pinn (imprint)
website www.theinpinn.co.uk
The outdoors: travel, hillwalking, climbing, mountain memoir.

NWP (imprint)
Scottish interest subjects including history, biography, true crime, culture, reference, traditional and popular music.

The Vital Spark (imprint)
website www.vitalspark.co.uk
Scottish humour.

Philip Wilson Publishers Ltd

6 Salem Road, London W2 4BU
tel 020-7243 1225
email pwilson@philip-wilson.co.uk
website www.philip-wilson.co.uk
Managing Director Jonathan McDonnell, *Publisher* Philip Wilson

Fine and applied art, architecture, photography, collecting, museums. A subsidiary of I.B.Tauris & Co Ltd. Founded 1975.

Windmill Books – see Penguin Random House UK

John Wisden and Co. Ltd – see Bloomsbury Publishing Plc

Wizard – see Icon Books Ltd

WLR Media & Entertainment

6–14 Underwood Street, London N1 7JQ
website www.wilmington.com
Managing Director Polly Augherinos

Publications: *Hollis PR Annual*, *Hollis Sponsorship Newsletter*, *Hollis Europe* and *The Knowledge*.

Wolters Kluwer (UK) Ltd*

(formerly Croner.CCH Group Ltd)
145 London Road, Kingston-upon-Thames, Surrey KT2 6SR
tel 0844 561 8166
email croner@wolterskluwer.co.uk
email cch@wolterskluwer.co.uk
website www.croner.co.uk
website www.cch.co.uk
website www.wolterskluwer.co.uk

Human resources, health and safety, tax and accountancy, education and healthcare, manufacturing and construction. Looseleaf, consultancy and online information services. Founded 1948.

The Women's Press

27 Goodge Street, London W1T 2LD
tel 020-7636 3992
email info@quartetbooks.co.uk
website www.quartetbooks.co.uk

Books by women in the areas of literary and crime fiction, biography and autobiography, health, culture, politics, handbooks, literary criticism, psychology and self-help, the arts. No email submissions; see website for guidelines. Founded 1978.

Wooden Books

Signature, 20 Castlegate, York YO1 9RP *or* Central Books, 99 Wallis Road, London E9 5LN
email info@woodenbooks.com
website www.woodenbooks.com
Directors John Martineau (managing), Anthony Brandt (secretary), Michael Glickman (overseas)

Magic, mathematics, ancient sciences, esoteric. Quality b&w illustrators may submit samples. Founded 1996.

Woodhead Publishing Ltd

80 High Street, Sawston, Cambridge CB22 3HJ
tel (01223) 499140
email wp@woodheadpublishing.com
website www.woodheadpublishing.com
Managing Director Martin Woodhead

Engineering, materials, welding, textiles, commodities, food science and technology, environmental science, mathematics, information and knowledge management (Chandos Publishing imprint). Founded 1989.

Wordsworth Editions Ltd

8B East Street, Ware, Herts. SG12 9HJ
tel (01920) 465167
email enquiries@wordsworth-editions.com
website www.wordsworth-editions.com
Managing Director Helen Trayler

Reprints of classic books: literary; children's classics; poetry; reference; Special Editions; mystery and supernatural. Because the company specialises in out-of-copyright titles, it is not able to consider new material for publication. Founded 1987.

The X Press

PO Box 25694, London N17 6FP
tel 020-8801 2100
email vibes@xpress.co.uk
website www.xpress.co.uk
Editorial Director Dotun Adebayo, *Marketing Director* Steve Pope

Black interest popular novels, particularly reflecting contemporary ethnic experiences. *Black Classics* series: reprints of classic novels by black writers. Founded 1992.

Nia (imprint)
Literary black fiction.

Y Lolfa Cyf

Talybont, Ceredigion SY24 5HE
tel (01970) 832304

email ylolfa@ylolfa.com
website www.ylolfa.com
Director Garmon Gruffudd, *Editor* Lefi Gruffudd

Welsh-language books; Welsh-language tutors; Welsh and Celtic interest books in English. Popular biographies and sports books in English. Founded 1967.

Yale University Press London

47 Bedford Square, London WC1B 3DP
tel 020-7079 4900
website www.yalebooks.co.uk
Managing Director Robert Baldock, *Sales/Sales & Marketing Director* Noel Murphy, *Publishers* Gillian Malpass (art history), Sally Salvesen (architecture & decorative arts), Heather McCallum (trade books), *Head of Rights* Anne Bihan

Art, architecture, history, economics, political science, religion, history of science, biography, current affairs and music. Founded 1961.

Yellow Jersey Press – see Penguin Random House UK

York Notes – see Pearson UK

Zambezi Publishing Ltd

22 Second Avenue, Camels Head, Plymouth PL2 2EQ
tel (01752) 367300
email info@zampub.com
website www.zampub.com
Contact Sasha Fenton, Jan Budkowski

Mind, Body & Spirit. Founded 1998 – **see also Stellium Ltd**

Zed Books Ltd

7 Cynthia Street, London N1 9JF
tel 020-7837 4014 (general)
email info@zedbooks.net
website www.zedbooks.co.uk
Commissioning Editors Ken Barlow, Kim Walker, Kika Sroka-Miller

Social sciences on international issues; gender and sexuality studies, politics, economics, development, international relations, environmental, sociology and social policy studies; area studies (Africa, Asia, Latin America and the Middle East). Founded 1976.

ZigZag Education

Unit 3, Greenway Business Centre, Doncaster Road, Bristol BS10 5PY
tel 0117 950 3199
email submissions@publishmenow.co.uk
website www.zigzageducation.co.uk
website www.publishmenow.co.uk
Development Director John-Lloyd Hagger, *Strategy Director* Mike Stephens

Teaching resources for UK secondary schools: English, maths, ICT, geography, history, science, business studies, politics. Founded 1998.

Book publishers overseas

Listings are given for book publishers in Australia (below), Canada (page 213), New Zealand (page 216), South Africa (page 217) and the USA (page 219).

AUSTRALIA

**Member of the Australian Publishers Association*

Access Press

PO Box 2300, Geraldton
tel +61 (0)408 943299
Managing Editor Jenny Walsh

Australiana, biography, non-fiction. Commissioned works and privately financed books published and distributed. Founded 1974.

ACER Press

19 Prospect Hill Road, Private Bag 55, Camberwell, Victoria 3124
tel +61 (0)3 9277 5555
email info@acer.edu.au
website www.acer.edu.au
General Manager/Publisher Ben Dawe

Publisher of the Australian Council for Educational Research. Produces a range of books and assessments including professional resources for teachers, psychologists and special needs professionals.

Allen & Unwin Pty Ltd*

83 Alexander Street, Crows Nest, NSW 2065
postal address PO Box 8500, St Leonards, NSW 1590
tel +61 (0)2 8425 0100
email info@allenandunwin.com
website www.allenandunwin.com
Chairman Patrick Gallaghe, *Executive Director* Paul Donovan, *Ceo* Robert Gorman, *Finance Director* David Martin, *Group Publishing Director* Sue Hines, *Publishing Director* Tom Gilliatt

General trade, including fiction and children's books, academic, especially social science and history. Founded 1990.

Michelle Anderson Publishing Pty Ltd*

PO Box 6032, Chapel Street North, South Yarra 3141
tel +61 (0)3 9826 9028
email mapubl@bigpond.net.au
website www.michelleandersonpublishing.com
Director Michelle Anderson

General health and mind/body. Founded 2004.

Bloomsbury Publishing PTY Limited

(Sydney office of Bloomsbury Publishing)
Level 4, 387 George St, Sydney, NSW 2000
tel +61 (0)2 8820 4900
email au@bloomsbury.com
website www.bloomsbury.com
Managing Director Kate Cubitt

Supports the worldwide publishing activities of Bloomsbury Publishing: caters for the Australia and New Zealand territories. See Bloomsbury Adult, Bloomsbury Children's & Educational, Bloomsbury Academic & Professional and Bloomsbury Information on page 153.

Cambridge University Press*

(Australian Branch)
477 Williamstown Road, Private Bag 31, Port Melbourne, Victoria 3207
tel +61 (0)3 8671 1400
email educationpublishing@cambridge.edu.au
website www.cambridge.edu.au
Chief Executive Stephen Bourne

Academic, educational, reference, English as a second language.

Cengage Learning Australia*

Level 7, 80 Dorcas Street, South Melbourne, Victoria 3205
tel +61 (0)3 9685 4111
website www.cengage.com.au

Educational books.

Dominie Pty Ltd

Drama (Plays & Musicals), 8 Cross Street, Brookvale, NSW 2100
tel +61 (0)2 9938 8686
email dominie@dominie.com.au
website www.dominie.com.au/drama

Australian representatives of publishers of plays and agents for the collection of royalties for Hanbury Plays, The Society of Authors, Nick Hern Books, Pioneer Drama, IT&M and Dominie Musicals.

EA Books

Engineers Media, PO Box 588, Crows Nest, NSW 2065
tel +61 (0)2 9438 5355
email eabooks@engineersmedia.com.au
website www.eabooks.com.au
Managing Editor Dietrich Georg

Publishing company of the Institution of Engineers Australia.

Elsevier Australia*

Tower 1, Level 12, 475 Victoria Avenue, Chatswood NSW 2067
tel +61 (0)2 9422 8500
email customerserviceau@elsevier.com
website www.elsevier.com.au
Managing Director Rob Kolkman

Science, medical and technical books. Imprints: Academic Press, Butterworth-Heinemann, Churchill Livingstone, Endeavour, Excerpta Medica, Focal Press, The Lancet, MacLennan and Petty, MD Consult, Morgan Kauffman, Mosby, Saunders, Science Direct, Syngress. Established 1972.

Hachette Australia Pty Ltd*

Level 17, 207 Kent Street, Sydney, NSW 2000
tel +61 (0)2 8248 0800
email auspub@hachette.com.au
website www.hachette.com.au
Directors Richard Kitson (Ceo), Louise Sherwin-Stark, David Cocking, Fiona Hazard, Justin Ractliffe, Phill Knight (ADS)

General, children's. Accepts MSS via website: www.hachette.com.au/manuscriptsubmissions

HarperCollins Publishers (Australia) Pty Ltd Group*

postal address PO Box A565, Sydney South, NSW 1235
tel +61 (0)2 9952 5000
website www.harpercollins.com.au
Publishing Director Shona Martyn

Literary fiction and non-fiction, popular fiction, children's, reference, biography, autobiography, current affairs, sport, lifestyle, health/self-help, humour, true crime, travel, Australiana, history, business, gift, religion. Now accepting unsolicited submissions online through *The Wednesday Post*. Visit www.wednesdaypost.com.au for more details.

Kangaroo Press – see Simon & Schuster (Australia) Pty Ltd

Lantern – see Penguin Australia Pty Ltd

Lawbook Co.

Level 5, 100 Harris Street, Pyrmont, NSW 2009
tel +61 (0)2 8587 7980
website www.thomsonreuters.com.au
Ceo Tony Kinnear

Law. Part of Thomson Legal.

LexisNexis Butterworths Australia*

Tower 2, 475–495 Victoria Avenue, Chatswood, NSW 2067
tel +61 (0)2 9422 2174

postal address Level 9, Locked Bag 2222, Chatswood Delivery Centre, Chatswood, NSW 2067
website www.lexisnexis.com.au
Publishing Director James Broadfoot

Accounting, business, legal, tax and commercial.

Lonely Planet*

90 Maribyrnong Street, Footscray, Victoria 3011
email go@lonelyplanet.co.uk
postal address Locked Bag 1, Footscray, Victoria 3011
tel +61 (0)3 8379 8000
website www.lonelyplanet.com
Ceo Daniel Houghto

A travel media company, Lonely Planet is the largest travel publisher in the world with 500 titles, content published in 13 languages, and products in over 150 countries. The company's ecosystem also includes mobile apps, magazines, an ebook portfolio, a website and a dedicated traveller community. Offices in US, Australia, the UK, India and China. Founded in 1973.

McGraw-Hill Education*

Level 2, The Everglade Building, 82 Waterloo Road, North Ryde NSW 2113
postal address Private Bag 2233, Business Centre, North Ryde, NSW 1670
tel +61 (0)2 9900 1800
website www.mcgraw-hill.com.au/
Publishing Director Nicole Meehan, *Managing Director* Cindy Jones

Educational publisher: higher education, primary education and professional (including medical, general and reference). Division of the McGraw-Hill Companies. Founded 1964.

Melbourne University Publishing*

187 Grattan Street, Carlton, Victoria 3053
tel +61 (0)3 9342 0300
email mup-info@unimelb.edu.au
website www.mup.com.au
Ceo/Publisher Louise Adler

Academic, scholastic and cultural; educational textbooks and books of reference. Imprints: Miegunyah Press, Victory Books. Founded 1922.

Pan Macmillan Australia Pty Ltd*

Level 25, 1 Market Street, Sydney, NSW 2000
tel +61 (0)2 9285 9100
email pansyd@macmillan.com.au
website www.panmacmillan.com.au
Directors Cate Paterson (publishing), Katie Crawford (sales), Tracey Cheetham (publicity & marketing)

Commercial and literary fiction; children's fiction, non-fiction and character products; non-fiction; sport.

Penguin Australia Pty Ltd*

707 Collins Street, Melbourne, Victoria 3008
tel +61 (0)3 9811 2400
postal address PO Box 23360, Melbourne, VIC 8012
website www.penguin.com.au
Ceo Gabrielle Coyne, *Publishing Directors* Ben Ball, Julie Gibbs, Laura Harris

Fiction, general non-fiction, current affairs, sociology, economics, environmental, travel guides, anthropology, politics, children's, health, cookery, gardening, pictorial and general books relating to Australia. Imprints: Penguin Books, Lantern, Viking. Part of Penguin Random House. Founded 1946.

Penguin Random House Australia Pty Ltd*

Level 3, 100 Pacific Highway, North Sydney, NSW 2060

tel +61 (0)2 9954 9966
email random@randomhouse.com.au
website www.randomhouse.com.au
Ceo Gabrielle Coyne, *Publishing Director* Nikki Christer, *Director of Marketing, Publicity & Digital ANZ* Sally Bateman, *Head of Publicity & Marketing* Karen Reid

General fiction and non-fiction; children's, illustrated. MSS submissions – for Random House and Transworld Publishing, unsolicited non-fiction accepted, unbound in hard copy addressed to Submissions Editor. Fiction submissions are only accepted from previously published authors, or authors represented by an agent or accompanied by a report from an accredited assessment service. Imprints: Arrow, Avon, Ballantine, Bantam, Black Swan, Broadway, Century, Chatto & Windus, Corgi, Crown, Dell, Doubleday, Ebury, Fodor, Heinemann, Hutchinson, Jonathan Cape, Knopf, Mammoth UK, Minerva, Pantheon, Pavilion, Pimlico, Random House, Red Fox, Rider, Vermilion, Vintage, Virgin. Subsidiary of Bertelsmann AG. Part of Penguin Random House.

University of Queensland Press*

PO Box 6042, St Lucia, Queensland 4067
tel +61 (0)7 3365 7244
email uqp@uqp.uq.edu.au
website www.uqp.com.au
Ceo Greg Bain

Non-fiction and academic in the fields of Australian history, Australian biography, Australian politics and current affairs, Australian social and cultural issues, and Australian indigenous issues. Australian fiction (adult, young adult and children's). Via agents only. Founded 1948.

Scholastic Australia Pty Ltd*

76–80 Railway Crescent, Lisarow, Gostord, NSW 2250
tel +61 (0)2 4328 3555
website www.scholastic.com.au
Publisher Andrew Berkhut

Children's fiction and non-fiction. Founded 1968.

Simon & Schuster (Australia) Pty Ltd*

office Suite 19A, Level 1, Building C, 450 Miller Street, Cammeray, NSW 2062
postal PO Box 448, Cammeray, NSW 2062
tel +61 (0)2 9983 6600
email cservice@simonandschuster.com.au
website www.simonandschuster.com.au
Managing Director Lou Johnson

Part of the CBS Corporation and is dedicated to producing an extensive range of books, in all formats. Publishes and distributes a wide variety of books in Australia and New Zealand across a broad range of fiction, non-fiction and children's categories. Imprint include: Atria, Free Press, Gallery, Howard, Pocket, Scribner, Simon & Schuster and Touchstone. Local authors include Ian Thorpe, Mark Tedeschi QC, Jenn J McLeod, Posie Graeme-Evans, Anita Heiss, Karen Davis, Anna Romer, Ted Prior, Kate Belle, Su Dharmapala, Johanna Nicholls, Mike Jones and Alan Gold. Authors published under the international imprints include: Hilary Clinton, Jackie Collins, Lynda LaPlante, Philippa Gregory, Martin Cruz Smith, Tom Rob Smith, Rhonda Byrne, Bob Woodward, Lisa Genova, Alice Hoffman, Vince Flynn, Nicholson Baker, Anita Diamant and Delia Ephron. Also acts as the local sales and distribution partner for 4 Ingredients, Watkins Books, Kyle Books and Pantera Press. Founded 1987.

Spinifex Press*

504 Queensberry Street, North Melbourne, Victoria 3051
postal address PO Box 212, North Melbourne, Victoria 3051
tel +61 (0)3 9329 6088
website www.spinifexpress.com.au
Managing Director Susan Hawthorne

Feminism and women's studies, art, astronomy, occult, education, gay and lesbian, health and nutrition, technology, travel, ebooks. No unsolicited MSS. Founded 1991.

UNSW Press*

University of New South Wales, UNSW Sydney, NSW 2052
tel +61 (0)2 9664 0900
email publishing@unswpress.com.au
website www.unswpress.com.au
Managing Director Kathy Bail, *Publisher* Phillipa McGuinness

Academic and general non-fiction. Politics, history, society and culture, popular science, environmental studies, Aboriginal studies. Includes imprints UNSW Press, New South and Choice. Founded 1962.

UWA Publishing*

UWA Publishing, University of Western Australia, M419, 35 Stirling Highway, Crawley 6009, Western Australia
tel +61 (0)8 6488 3670
email admin-uwap@uwa.edu.au
website www.uwap.uwa.edu.au
Director Terri-ann White

Fiction, general non-fiction, natural history, contemporary issues. Founded 1935.

Viking – see Penguin Australia Pty Ltd

John Wiley & Sons Australia, Ltd*

42 McDougall Street, Milton, Queensland 4064
tel +61 (0)7 3859 9755
website www.wiley.com.au

Educational, technical, atlases, professional, reference, trade journals. Imprints: John Wiley & Sons,

Jacaranda, Wrightbooks, Wiley-Blackwell, Frommer's, Jossey-Bass. Founded 1954.

Wiley-Blackwell Publishing*

Level 2, 155 Cremorne Street, Cremorne, Victoria 3121
tel +61 (0)3 9274 3100
email melbourne@wiley.com
website www.blackwellpublishing.com
Publishing Director Mark Robertson

Medical, healthcare, life, physical, earth sciences, professional.

CANADA

**Member of the Canadian Publishers' Council*

†Member of the Association of Canadian Publishers

Annick Press Ltd†

15 Patricia Avenue, Toronto, Ontario M2M 1H9
tel +1 416-221-4802
email annickpress@annickpress.com
website www.annickpress.com
Owner/Director Rick Wilks, *Associate Publisher* Colleen MacMillan, *Creative Director* Sheryl Shapiro, *Office Manager* Elaine Burns

Preschool to young adult fiction and non-fiction. Founded 1975.

Boardwalk Books – see Dundurn Press

Butterworths Canada Ltd – see LexisNexis Canada Inc.

Castle Street Mysteries – see Dundurn Press

The Charlton Press

PO Box 820, Station Willowdale B, North York, Ontario M2K 2R1
tel +1 416-488-1418
email chpress@charltonpress.com
website www.charltonpress.com
President W.K. Cross

Collectibles, Numismatics, Sportscard price catalogues. Founded 1952.

Douglas & McIntyre (2013) Ltd†

PO Box 219, Madeira Park, BC V0N 2H0
tel +1 604-254-7191
email info@douglas-mcintyre.com
website www.douglas-mcintyre.com
Publisher Howard White

General list: Canadian biography, art and architecture, natural history, history, native studies, Canadian fiction. Unsolicited MSS accepted. Founded 1971.

Dundurn Press†

3 Church Street, Suite 500, Toronto, Ontario M5E 1M2
tel +1 416-214-5544
email kmcmullin@dundurn.com
website www.dundurn.com
Publisher Kirk Howard

Canadian history, fiction, non-fiction and young adult fiction, mystery fiction, popular non-fiction, theatre, drama, translations. Founded 1972.

ECW Press Ltd†

2120 Queen Street E, Suite 200, Toronto, Ontario M4E 1E2
tel +1 416-694-3348
email info@ecwpress.com
website www.ecwpress.com
Publishers David Caron, Jack David

Popular culture, TV and film, sports, humour, general trade books, biographies, popular science, guidebooks. Founded 1979.

Fitzhenry & Whiteside Ltd

195 Allstate Parkway, Markham, Ontario L3R 4T8
tel +1 800-387-9776
email godwit@fitzhenry.ca
website www.fitzhenry.ca
Publisher Sharon Fitzhenry

Trade, educational, children's books. Founded 1966.

Gold Eagle Books – see Harlequin Enterprises Ltd

Harlequin Enterprises Ltd*

PO Box 615, Fort Erie, Ontario L2A 5X3
tel +1 888-432-4879
email customer_ecare@harlequin.ca
website www.eharlequin.com
Publisher/Ceo Donna Hayes

Fiction for women, romance, inspirational fiction, African–American fiction, action adventure, mystery. Non-fiction for women. Founded 1949.

Harlequin Books (imprint)

Contemporary and historical romance fiction in series.

Silhouette Books (imprint)

Contemporary romance fiction in series.

Steeple Hill (imprint)

Director, Global Single Titles Editorial Margaret O'Neill Marbury

Contemporary inspirational romantic fiction in series.

Luna Books (imprint)

Romantic fantasy.

HQN Books (imprint)

Romantic single title fiction, contemporary and historical.

Mira Books (imprint)

Fiction for women, contemporary and historical dramas, family sagas, romantic suspense and relationship novels.

Gold Eagle Books (imprint)
Series action adventure fiction.

Worldwide Mystery (imprint)
General Manager, Kimani Press Glenda Howard
Contemporary mystery fiction. Reprints only.

Kimani Press (imprint)
Contemporary romance fiction in series.

Spice (imprint)
Executive Editor Deborah Brody (non-fiction)
Women's erotic fiction.

HarperCollins Publishers Ltd*
2 Bloor Street East, 20th Floor, Toronto, Ontario M4W 1A8
tel +1 416-975-9334
email hccanada@harpercollins.com
website www.harpercollins.ca
President David Kent

Literary fiction and non-fiction, history, politics, biography, spiritual and children's books. Founded 1989.

Hounslow Press – see Dundurn Press

HQN Books – see Harlequin Enterprises Ltd

Kids Can Press Ltd†
25 Dockside Drive, Toronto, Ontario M54 0B5
tel +1 416-479-7000
email customerservice@kidscan.com
website www.kidscanpress.com/canada
Editorial Director Yvette Ghione

Juvenile/young adult books. Founded 1973.

Kimani Press – see Harlequin Enterprises Ltd

Knopf Canada – see Random House of Canada Ltd

LexisNexis Canada Inc.*
123 Commerce Valley Drive East, Suite 700, Markham, Ontario L3T 7W8
tel +1 905-479-2665
email info@lexisnexis.ca
website www.lexisnexis.ca

Law and accountancy. Division of Reed Elsevier plc.

Lone Pine Publishing
231–96 Street, Edmonton, Alberta T6N 1G3
tel +1 780-433-9333
email info@lonepinepublishing.com
website www.lonepinepublishing.com
President Grant Kennedy, *General Manager* Shane Kennedy

Natural history, outdoor recreation and wildlife guidebooks, self-help, gardening, popular history. Founded 1980.

Luna Books – see Harlequin Enterprises Ltd

McClelland & Stewart Ltd
1 Toronto Street, Suit 300, Toronto, Ontario M5C 2V6
tel +1 416-598-1114
email editorial@mcclelland.com
website www.mcclelland.com
President & Publisher Douglas Pepper

A division of Random House of, Canada Ltd, a Penguin Random House company. Founded 1906.

McGill-Queen's University Press†
1010 Sherbrooke Street West, Suite 1720, Montreal, Quebec H3A 2R7
tel +1 514-398-3750
email mqup@mcgill.ca
Queen's University, 144 Barrie Street, Kingston, Ontario K7L 3J9
tel +1 613-533-2155
email kingstonmqup@queensu.ca
website www.mqup.mcgill.ca

Academic, non-fiction, poetry. Founded 1969.

McGraw-Hill Ryerson Ltd*
300 Water Street, Whitby, Ontario L1N 9B6
tel +1 905-430-5000
website www.mheducation.ca/
President & Ceo David Swail

Educational and trade books.

Mira Books – see Harlequin Enterprises Ltd

Nelson Education*
1120 Birchmount Road, Scarborough, Ontario M1K 5G4
tel +1 416-752-9448
website www.nelson.com
President Greg Nordal, *Senior Vice President & Market Director, School Division* Chris Besse, *Senior Vice President, Media & Production Services* Susan Cline, *Senior Vice President, People & Engagement* Marlene Nyilassy

Educational publishing: school (K–12), college and university, career education, measurement and guidance, professional and reference, ESL titles. Division of Thomson Canada Ltd. Founded 1914.

NeWest Press†
201 8540, 109 Street, Edmonton, AB T6G 1E6
tel +1 780-432-9427
email info@newestpress.com
website www.newestpress.com
Directors Doug Barbour (President), Don Kerr (Vice-President)

Fiction, drama, poetry and non-fiction. Founded 1977.

Oberon Press

205–145 Spruce Street, Ottawa, Ontario K1R 6P1
tel +1 613-238-3275
email oberon@sympatico.ca
website www.oberonpress.ca

General fiction, short stories, poetry, some biographies, art and children's. Only publishes Canadian writers.

Oxford University Press, Canada

8 Sampson Mews, Suite 204, Don Mills, Ontario M3C 0H5
tel +1 416-441-2941
website www.oup.com
President David Stover

Educational and academic.

Pearson Canada*

(formerly Prentice Hall Canada and Addison-Wesley Canada)
26 Prince Andrew Place, Toronto, Ontario M3C 2T8
tel +1 416-447-5101
website www.pearsoned.ca
President Dan Lee

Academic, technical, educational, children's and adult, trade.

Penguin Random House Canada Ltd*

320 Front Street, Suite 1400, Toronto, Ontario M5V 3B6
tel +1 416-364-4449
website www.penguinrandomhouse.ca
Ceo R. Bradley Martin

Literary fiction, Commercial fiction, memoir, non-fiction (history, business, current events, sports), Adult and Children's. No unsolicited MSS; submissions via an agent only. Imprints: Anchor Canada, Allen Lane Canada, Appetite by Random House, Bond Street Books, Doubleday Canada, Emblem, Fenn, Hamish Hamilton Canada, Knopf Canada, McClelland & Stewart, Penguin Canada, Portfolio Canada, Puffin Canada, Random House Canada, Razorbill Canada, Seal Books, Signal, Tundra Books, Viking Canada, Vintage Canada. Subsidiary of Penguin Random House. Formed on I July 2013 as part of the worldwide merger of Penguin and Random House.

Pippin Publishing Corporation

PO Box 242, Don Mills, Ontario M3C 2S2
tel +1 416-510-2918
email jld@pippinpub.com
website www.pippinpub.com
President/Editorial Director Jonathan Lovat Dickson

ESL/EFL, teacher reference, adult basic education, school texts (all subjects), general trade (non-fiction).

Red Dress Ink – see Harlequin Enterprises Ltd

Ronsdale Press†

3350 West 21st Avenue, Vancouver, BC V6S 1G7
tel +1 604-738-4688
email ronsdale@shaw.ca
website www.ronsdalepress.com
Director Ronald B. Hatch

Ronsdale is a Canadian publisher based in Vancouver, BC, with some 250 books in print. Founded 1988.

Sandcastle Books – see Dundurn Press

Silhouette Books – see Harlequin Enterprises Ltd

Simon & Pierre Publishing – see Dundurn Press

Spice – see Harlequin Enterprises Ltd

Steeple Hill – see Harlequin Enterprises Ltd

Thompson Educational Publishing†

20 Ripley Avenue, Toronto, Ontario M6S 3N9
tel +1 416-766-2763
email info@thompsonbooks.com
website www.thompsonbooks.com
President Keith Thompson, *Vice-President* Faye Thompson

Social sciences. Founded 1989.

University of Toronto Press†

10 St Mary Street, Suite 700, Toronto, Ontario M4Y 2W8
tel +1 416-978-2239
email publishing@utpress.utoronto.ca
website www.utpress.utoronto.ca
President John Yates, *Vice President Scholarly Publishing* Lynn Fisher

Founded 1901.

Tundra Books

(a division of Random House of Canada Ltd, a Penguin Random House company)
320 Front Street West, Toronto, ON
tel +1 416-364-4449
email tundra@mcclelland.com
website www.penuinrandomhouse.ca
Editorial Director Tara Walker

Publisher of high-quality children's picture books and novels, renowned for its innovations. Publishes books for children to teens. Imprints: Jordan Fenn, Publisher of Fenn/Tundra (sport-themed children's books). Founded 1967.

Worldwide Mystery – see Harlequin Enterprises Ltd

NEW ZEALAND

**Member of the Publishers Association of New Zealand (PANZ)*

Auckland University Press*
University of Auckland, Private Bag 92019, Auckland 1142
tel +64 (0)9 373 7528
email press@auckland.ac.nz
website www.press.auckland.ac.nz
Director Sam Elworthy

Archaeology, architecture, art, biography, business, health, New Zealand history, Maori and Pacific studies, poetry, politics and law, science and natural history, social sciences. Founded 1966.

David Bateman Ltd*
30 Tarndale Grove, Albany, Auckland 0632
tel +64 (0)9 415 7664
email bateman@bateman.co.nz
website www.batemanpublishing.co.nz
Directors Janet Bateman, Paul Bateman, Paul Parkinson

General trade non-fiction publisher focusing on craft, natural history, gardening, health, sport, cookery, history, travel, motoring, maritime history, business, art, lifestyle for the international market. Founded 1979.

Bush Press Communications Ltd
postal address PO Box 33029, Takapuna, Auckland 0740
office 41 Hauraki Road, Takapuna 0622
tel +64 (0)9 486 2667
email bush.press@clear.net.nz
website www.bushpress.com
Governing Director/Publisher Gordon Ell

NZ natural and historic heritage. Books on behalf of institutions, family and local histories. Founded 1979.

The Caxton Press*
PO Box 25088, 113 Victoria Street, Christchurch 8144
tel +64 (0)3 366 8516
email peter@caxton.co.nz
website www.caxton.co.nz
Director Peter Watson

Local history, tourist pictorial, Celtic spirituality, parent guides, book designers and printers. Founded 1935.

Cengage Learning New Zealand*
Unit 4B, Rosedale Office Park, 331 Rosedale Road, Albany, North Shore 0632
postal address PO Box 33376, Takapuna, North Shore 0740
tel +64 (0)9 415 6850
General Manager, Higher Education Alex Chamoun

Educational books.

Dunmore Press Ltd*
P.O. Box 28387, Auckland 1541
tel +64 (0)9 521 3121
email books@dunmore.co.nz
website www.dunmore.co.nz
Director Sharmian Firth

Education secondary/tertiary texts and other, NZ society, history, health, economics, politics, general non-fiction. Founded 1970.

Edify Ltd*
PO Box 36502, Northcote, Auckland 0748
tel +64 (0)9 972 9428
email gethelp@edify.co.nz
website www.edify.co.nz
Ceo Adrian Keane

Edify is a publishing, sales and marketing business providing its partners with opportunities for their products and solutions in the New Zealand educational market. Exclusive representatives of Pearson and the New Zealand based educational publisher, Sunshine Books.

Hachette New Zealand Ltd*
PO Box 3255, Shortland Street, Auckland 1140
tel +64 (0)9 379 1480
email contact@hachette.co.nz
website www.hachette.co.nz
Melanee Winder

Sport, cooking, travel, general.

Halcyon Publishing Ltd
PO Box 360, Shortland Street, Auckland 1140
tel +64 (0)9 489 5337
email info@halcyonpublishing.co.nz
website www.halcyonpublishing.com
Managing Director/Publisher Graham Gurr

Hunting, shooting, fishing, outdoor interests. Founded 1982.

HarperCollins Publishers (New Zealand) Ltd*
Unit D, 63 Apollo Drive, Rosedale, Auckland 0632
tel +64 (0)9 443 9400
email publicity@harpercollins.co.nz
postal address PO Box 1, Shortland Street, Auckland
website www.harpercollins.co.nz

General literature, non-fiction, reference, children's. HarperCollins New Zealand does not accept proposals or MSS for consideration for publishing, except via the Wednesday Post portal on its website.

Learning Media Ltd*
Level 4, Willeston House, 22–28 Willeston Street, Te Aro, Wellington 6021
tel +64 (0)4 472 5522
email info@learningmedia.co.nz
PO Box 3293, Wellington 6140

An award-winning publisher, designer and developer of books, educational resources and interactive programmes for New Zealand and international markets. Texts published in English, Maori and five Pacific languages. Founded 1993.

LexisNexis NZ Ltd

181 Wakefield Street, Wellington 6011
tel +64 (0)4 385 1479
email customer.service@lexisnexis.co.nz
postal address PO Box 472, Wellington 6140
website www.lexisnexis.co.nz
Publisher John Henton

Law, business, academic.

McGraw-Hill Book Company New Zealand Ltd*

Level 8, 56–60 Cawley Street, Ellerslie, Auckland
postal address Private Bag 11904, Ellerslie, Auckland 1005
tel +64 (0)9 526 6200
website www.mcgraw-hill.com.au

Educational publisher: higher education, primary and secondary education (grades K–12) and professional (including medical, general and reference). Division of the McGraw-Hill Companies. Founded 1974.

New Zealand Council for Educational Research

Box 3237, Education House, 178–182 Willis Street, Wellington 6011
tel +64 (0)4 384 7939
email info@nzcer.org.nz
website www.nzcer.org.nz
Director Robyn Baker, *Publisher* David Ellis

Education, including educational policy and institutions, early childhood education, educational achievement tests, Maori education, curriculum and assessment. Founded 1934.

Otago University Press*

University of Otago, PO Box 56, Dunedin 9054
tel +64 (0)3 479 8807
email university.press@otago.ac.nz
website www.otago.ac.nz/press
Publisher Rachel Scott

New Zealand and Pacific history, social and cultural studies, as well as a wide range of scholarly to general books. Also publishes New Zealand's longest-running literary journal, Landfall. Founded 1958.

Penguin Random House New Zealand Ltd*

Private Bag 102902, Rosedale, North Shore, Auckland 0745
tel +64 (0)9 442 7400
email publishing@penguinrandomhouse.co.nz
website www.penguinrandomhouse.co.nz
Publishing Director Debra Millar, *Managing Director* Margaret Thompson

Adult and children's fiction and non-fiction. Imprints: Penguin, Vintage, Black Swan, Godwit, Viking, Puffin Books. Part of Penguin Random House. Founded 1973.

RSVP Publishing Company*

PO Box 47166, Ponsonby, Auckland 1144
tel/fax +64 (0)9 372 8480
email rsvppub@iconz.co.nz
website www.rsvp-publishing.co.nz
Managing Director/Publisher Stephen Ron Picard, *Sales & Marketing Director* Chris Palmer

Fiction, metaphysical, children's. Founded 1990.

Victoria University Press*

Victoria University of Wellington, PO Box 600, Wellington 6140
tel +64 (0)4 463 6580
email victoria-press@vuw.ac.nz
website www.victoria.ac.nz/vup
Publisher Fergus Barrowman, *Editor* Kyleigh Hodgson

Academic, scholarly books on NZ history, sociology, law; Maori language; fiction, plays, poetry. Founded 1974.

Viking Sevenseas NZ Ltd

201A Rosetta Road, Raumati 5032
tel +64 (0)4 902 8240
email vikings@paradise.net.nz
Managing Director M.B. Riley

Natural history books on New Zealand only.

SOUTH AFRICA

**Member of the Publishers' Association of South Africa*

Ad Donker – see Jonathan Ball Publishers (Pty) Ltd

Jonathan Ball Publishers (Pty) Ltd*

PO Box 33977, Jeppestown 2043
tel +27 (0)11 601 8000
email services@jonathanball.co.za
website www.jonathanball.co.za
postal address PO Box 33977, Jeppestown 2043
Publishing Director Jeremy Boraine

Founded 1977.

Ad Donker (imprint)

Africana, literature, history, academic.

Jonathan Ball (imprint)

General publications, current affairs, politics, business history, business, reference.

Delta Books (imprint)

General South African trade non-fiction.

Sunbird Publishers (imprint)

Illustrated wildlife, tourism, maps, travel.

Cambridge University Press*

(African Branch)
Lower Ground Floor, Nautica Building,
The Water Club, Beach Road, Granger Bay,
Cape Town 8005
tel +27 (0)21) 412 7800
email capetown@cambridge.org
website www.cambridge.org/africa
Publishing Director Johan Traut

Distance learning materials and textbooks for sub-Sahara African countries, as well as primary reading materials in 28 local African languages.

Delta Books – see Jonathan Ball Publishers (Pty) Ltd

Galago Publishing (Pty) Ltd

PO Box 1645, Alberton 1450
tel +27 (0)11 824 2029
email lemur@mweb.co.za
website www.galago.co.za
Managing Director Fran Stiff, *Publisher* Peter Stiff

Southern African interest: military, political, hunting. Founded 1981.

Jacklin Enterprises (Pty) Ltd

PO Box 521, Parklands 2121
tel +27 (0)11 265 4200
Managing Director M.A.C. Jacklin

Children's fiction and non-fiction; Afrikaans large print books. Subjects include aviation, natural history, romance, general science, technology and transportation. Imprints: Mike Jacklin, Kennis Onbeperk, Daan Retief.

Juta & Company Ltd*

1st Floor, Sunclare Building, 21 Dreyer Street,
Claremont 7708
tel +27 (0)21 659 2300
email cserv@juta.co.za
website www.juta.co.za
Ceo Lynne du Toit

Academic, learning, health, law and electronic. Founded 1853.

University of KwaZulu-Natal Press*

Private Bag X01, Scottsville, KwaZulu-Natal 3209
tel +27 (0)33 260 5226
email books@ukzn.ac.za
website www.ukznpress.co.za
Publisher Debra Primo

Southern African social, political, economic and military history, gender, natural sciences, African fiction and literature, genealogy, education, biography. Founded 1948.

Macmillan Education South Africa

2nd Floor, The Piazza, 34 Whiteley Road,
Melrose Arch 2116
tel +27 (0)11 731 3300
postal Private Bag X19, Northlands 2116
website www.macmillan.co.za
Managing Director Mandla Balisa

Educational titles for the RSA market.

NB Publishers (Pty) Ltd*

PO Box 879, Cape Town 8000
tel +27 (0)21 406 3033
email nb@nb.co.za
website www.nb.co.za
Director Eloise Wessels, *Director* Musa Shezi

General: Afrikaans fiction, politics, children's and youth literature in all the country's languages, non-fiction. Imprints: Tafelberg, Human & Rousseau, Queillerie, Pharos, Kwela, Best Books and Lux Verbi. Founded 1950.

New Africa Books (Pty) Ltd

1st Floor, 6 Spin Street, Cape Town 7700
tel +27 (0) 21 467 5860
email info@newafricabooks.co.za
postal address PO Box 46962, Glosderry 7702
website www.newafricabooks.co.za
Publishers Phakamani Dadlana, Brian Wafawarowa

General books, textbooks, literary works, contemporary issues, children and young adult. Formed as a result of the merger of David Philip Publishers (founded 1971), Spearhead Press (founded 2000) and New Africa Educational Publishing.

David Philip (imprint)

Academic, history, social sciences, politics, biography, reference, education.

Spearhead (imprint)

Current affairs, also business, self-improvement, health, natural history, travel.

Oxford University Press, Southern Africa*

Vasco Boulevard, N1 City, Goodwood,
Cape Town 7460
tel +27 (0)21 596 2300
email steve.cilliers@oup.com
email oxford.za@oup.com
postal address PO Box 12119, N1 City,
Cape Town 7463
website www.oxford.co.za
Managing Director Steve Cilliers

Pan Macmillan South Africa*

Private Bag X19, Northlands, Johannesburg 2116
tel +27 (0)11 731 3440
website www.panmacmillan.co.za
Managing Director Terry Morris

Imprints: Ravan Press, Picador Africa, Giraffe Books.

Pearson Marang (Pty) Ltd*

PO Box 396, Cnr Forest Drive and Logan Way,
Pinelands, 7405, Cape Town 8000

tel +27 (0)21 532 6000
email pearsonza.enquiries@pearson.com
website www.pearson.co.za
Learning Resources Director: Grades 8–12 Jacques Zakarian

Educational and general publishers. Heinemann and Maskew Miller Longman are part of Pearson.

Penguin Random House (Pty) Ltd*

Wembley Square, First Floor, Solan Road, Gardens, Cape Town 8001
PO Box 1144, Cape Town 8000
tel +27 (0)21 460 5400
email queries@randomstruik.co.za
website www.randomstruik.co.za
website www.penguinbooks.co.za
Managing Director Steve Connolly

Imprints: Penguin Random House, Struik Lifestyle, Struik Nature, Struik Travel & Heritage, Zebra Press, Penguin Fiction, Umuzi. Genres include general illustrated non-fiction; lifestyle; natural history; South African politics; sport; business; memoirs; contemporary fiction; literary fiction. Part of Penguin Random House. Founded 1962.

Oshun (imprint)

Fiction.

Zebra Press (imprint)

Life guides, memoirs and lighthearted entertainment for women.

Shuter and Shooter Publishers (Pty) Ltd*

110 CB Downes Road, Pietermaritzburg, KwaZulu-Natal 3201
tel +27 (0)33 846 8700
email sales@shuters.com
postal address PO Box 61, Mkondeni, KwaZulu-Natal 3212
website www.shuters.com
Chief Execute Officer P.B. Chetty

Core curriculum-based textbooks for use at foundation, intermediate, senior and further education phases. Supplementary readers in various languages; dictionaries; reading development kits, charts. Literature titles in English, isiXhosa, Sesotho, Sepedi, Setswana, Tshivenda, Xitsonga, Ndebele, isiZulu and Siswati. Founded 1925.

Sunbird Publishers – see Jonathan Ball Publishers (Pty) Ltd

Two Dogs

PO Box 53557, Kenilworth 7745
tel +27 (0)21 671 3440
email info@burntmedia.co.za
website www.burnetmedia.co.za
Publishing Manager Tim Richman

Innovative and irreverent non-fiction focusing on contemporary and lifestyle issues for the South African market. Various local bestsellers, some titles with international appeal. Send proposals by email. Imprint of Burnet Media, which also publishes the Mercury imprint. Founded 2006.

Unisa Press*

University of South Africa, PO Box 392, Unisa, Mackleneuk, Pretoria 0003
tel +27 (0)12 429 3316
email unisa-press@unisa.ac.za
website www.unisa.ac.za/press/
Director Elizabeth le Roux

Theology and all academic disciplines. Publishers of University of South Africa. Imprint: UNISA. Founded 1957.

Van Schaik Publishers*

PO Box 12681, Hatfield, Pretoria 0028
tel +27 (0)12 342 2765
email vanschaik@vanschaiknet.com
website www.vanschaiknet.com
Ceo Leanne Martini

Texts for the tertiary and private FET markets in South Africa. Founded 1915.

Wits University Press*

Private Bag 3, Wits 2050
tel +27 (0)11 717 8700/1
email veronica.klipp@wits.ac.za
postal address PO Wits, Johannesburg 2050
website www.witspress.co.za
Publisher Veronica Klipp

Wits University Press is committed to publishing well-researched, innovative books for academic and general readers. The areas of focus include art and heritage, popular science, history and politics, biography, literary studies, women's writing and select textbooks.

Zebra Press – see Penguin Random House (Pty) Ltd

USA

**Member of the Association of American Publishers Inc.*

Abbeville Press, Inc.

137 Varick Street, New York, NY 10013
tel +1 212-366-5585
website www.abbeville.com
Publisher/President Robert Abrams

Fine art and illustrated books. Founded 1977.

ABC-CLIO

130 Cremona Drive, Ste C,, Santa Barbara, CA 93117
tel +1 805-968-1911
website www.abc-clio.com

Academic resources for secondary and middle schools, colleges and universities, libraries and professionals (librarians, media specialists, teachers). Founded 1955.

Abingdon Press

2222 Rosa L. Parks Blvd., PO Box 280988, Nashville TN 37228
tel +1 800-251-3320
website www.abingdonpress.com
President & Publisher Neil Alexander, *Chief Content Officer & Book Editor* Brian K. Milford, *Chief Ministry Officer* Justin Coleman

General interest, professional, academic and reference, non-fiction and fiction, youth and children's non-fiction and VBS; primarily directed to the religious market. Imprint of United Methodist Publishing House with tradition of crossing denominational boundaries.

Harry N. Abrams Inc.

115 West 18th Street, New York, NY 10011
tel +1 212-206-7715
email abrams@abramsbooks.com
website www.abramsbooks.com
Ceo/President Michael Jacobs

Art and architecture, photography, natural sciences, performing arts, children's books. No fiction. Founded 1949.

Ace – see Penguin Random House

Akashic Books Ltd

232 Third St., Suite A115, Brooklyn, NY 11215
tel +1 718-643-9193
email info@akashicbooks.com
website www.akashicbooks.com
Contacts Johnny Temple (publisher), Johanna Ingalls (managing editor), Ibrahim Ahmad (senior editor), Aaron Petrovich (production manager), Susannah Lawrence (director of publicity & social media) and Katie Martinez (editorial & publicity assistant).

A Brooklyn-based independent company dedicated to publishing urban literary fiction and political non-fiction by authors who are either ignored by the mainstream, or who have no interest in working within the ever-consolidating ranks of the major corporate publishers.

The University of Alabama Press

Box 870380, Tuscaloosa, AL 35487-0380
tel +1 205-348-5180
website www.uapress.ua.edu
Director Curtis L. Clark

American and Southern history, African–American studies, religion, rhetoric and communication, Judaic studies, literary criticism, anthropology and archaeology. Founded 1945.

Amistad – see HarperCollins Publishers

Applause Theatre and Cinema Book Publishers

19 West 21st Street, Suite 201, New York, NY 10010
tel +1 212-575-9265
email info@applausepub.com
website www.applausepub.com
Publisher Michael Messina

Performing arts. Founded 1980.

Arcade Publishing

11th Floor, 307 West 37th Street, New York, NY 10038
tel +1 212-643-6816
website www.arcadepub.com
Executive Editor Cal Barksdale

General trade, including adult hardback and paperbacks. No unsolicited MSS. Founded 1988. Imprint of Skyhorse Publishing since 2010.

ArcheBooks Publishing Inc.

6081 Silver King Boulevard, Suite 903, Cape Coral, FL 33914
tel +1 239-542-7595 (toll free)
email info@archebooks.com
website www.archebooks.com
Publisher Robert E. Gelinas

Fiction and non-fiction (history and true crime). Send submissions via a literary agent. Founded 2003.

The University of Arkansas Press

McIlroy House, McIlroy Avenue, Fayetteville, AR 72701
tel +1 800-626-0090
email uapress@uark.edu
website www.uapress.com
Director Lawrence J. Malley

History, humanities, literary criticism, Middle Eastern studies, African–American studies, poetry. Founded 1980.

Atlantic Monthly Press – see Grove/Atlantic Inc.

Avery – see Penguin Random House

Avon – see HarperCollins Publishers

Back Bay Books – see Little, Brown & Company

Baker's Plays

7611 Sunset Boulevard, Hollywood, CA 90046
tel +1 323-876-0579
email info@bakersplays.com
website www.bakersplays.com
UK Agent Samuel French Ltd

Plays and books on the theatre. Also agents for plays. Division of Samuel French Inc. Founded 1845.

Ballantine Books – see Penguin Random House

Bantam Books – see Penguin Random House

Barron's Educational Series Inc.

250 Wireless Boulevard, Hauppauge, NY 11788
tel +1 800-645-3476
email barrons@barronseduc.com
website www.barronseduc.com
Chairman/Ceo Manuel H. Barron, *President/Publisher* Ellen Sibley

Test preparation, juvenile, cookbooks, Mind, Body & Spirit, crafts, business, pets, gardening, family and health, art, study guides, school guides. Founded 1941.

Beacon Press

25 Beacon Street, Boston, MA 02108
tel +1 617-742-2110
website www.beacon.org
Director Helene Atwan

General non-fiction in fields of religion, ethics, philosophy, current affairs, gender studies, environmental concerns, African–American studies, anthropology and women's studies, nature. Founded 1854.

Bella Books

PO Box 10543, Tallahessee, FL 32302
tel +1 800-729-4992
website www.bellabooks.com

Lesbian fiction: mystery, romance, sci-fi. Founded 1973.

Berkley Books – see Penguin Random House

Bloomsbury Publishing USA

(New York office of Bloomsbury Publishing)
1385 Broadway, New York, NY 10018
tel +1 212-419-5300
email ChildrensPublicityUSA@bloomsbury.com
website www.bloomsburyusa.com
Publishing Director George Gibson, *Other Contacts* Cindy Loh (children's), Kevin Ohe (academic), Priscilla McGeehon (Fairchild), Bill Sarr (chief financial officer)

Supports the worldwide publishing activities of Bloomsbury Publishing Plc: caters for the US market. See Bloomsbury Adult, Bloomsbury Children's & Educational, Bloomsbury Academic & Professional, Bloomsbury Information on page 153.

R.R. Bowker*

630 Central Avenue, New Providence, NJ 07974
tel +1 908-286-1090
website www.bowker.com
President & Ceo Annie M. Callanan

Bibliographies and reference tools for the book trade and literary and library worlds, available in hardcopy, on microfiche, online and CD-Rom. Reference books for music, art, business, the computer industry, cable industry and information industry. Division of Cambridge Information Group.

Boyds Mills Press

815 Church Street, Honesdale, PA 18431
website www.boydsmillspress.com

Fiction, non-fiction, and poetry trade books for children and young adults. Founded 1991.

Burford Books

Burford Books, Inc., 101 E State St., #301, Ithaca, NY 14850
tel +1 607 319 4373
email pburford@burfordbooks.com
website www.burfordbooks.com
President Peter Burford

Outdoor activities: golf, sports, fitness, nature, travel. Founded 1997.

Cambridge University Press*

32 Avenue of the Americas, New York, NY 10013
tel +1 212-924-3900
email newyork@cambridge.org
website www.cambridge.org/us

Academic and professional; Cambridge Learning (ELT, primary and secondary education).

Candlewick Press

99 Dover Street, Somerville, MA 02144
tel +1 617-661-3330
email bigbear@candlewick.com
website www.candlewick.com
President/Publisher Karen Lotz, *Creative Director/Associate Publisher* Chris Paul, *Executive Editorial Director/Associate Publisher* Liz Bicknell, *Editorial Director* Mary Lee Donovan

Books for babies through teens: board books, picture books, novels, non-fiction, novelty books. Submit material through a literary agent. Subsidiary of Walker Books Ltd, UK. Founded 1991.

Candlewick Entertainment

Group Editorial Director Joan Powers, *Group Art Director* Kristen Nobles
Media-related children's books, including TV and movie tie-in titles.

Cannongate US – see Grove/Atlantic Inc.

Center Street

Hachette Book Group USA, 12 Cadillac Drive, Suite 480 Brentwood, TN 37027
email centerstreetpub@hbgusa.com
website www.hachettebookgroup.com

Books with traditional values for readers in the US heartland. Division of Hachette Book Group. Founded 2005.

University of Chicago Press*

1427 East 60th Street, Chicago, IL 60637
tel +1 773-702-7700
website www.press.uchicago.edu

Scholarly books and monographs (humanities, social sciences and sciences); general trade books; reference books; and 50 scholarly journals.

Chronicle Books*

680 Second Street, San Francisco, CA 94107
tel +1 415-537-4200
email frontdesk@chroniclebooks.com
website www.chroniclebooks.com
website www.chroniclekids.com
Chairman & Ceo Nion McEvoy, *Publisher* Christine Carswell

Publishes award-winning, innovative books. Recognized as one of the 50 best small companies to work for in the U.S. Publishing list includes illustrated books and gift products in design, art, architecture, photography, food, lifestyle, pop culture and children's titles. Founded 1967.

Coffee House Press

79 13th Avenue NE, Suite 110, Minneapolis, MN 55413
tel +1 612-338-0125
website www.coffeehousepress.org
Publisher Chris Fischbach

Literary fiction, essays and poetry; collectors' editions. Founded 1984.

Collins – see HarperCollins Publishers

Columbia University Press*

61 West 62nd Street, New York, NY 10023
tel +1 212-459-0600
email jc373@columbia.edu
email es3387@columbia.edu
website www.cup.columbia.edu
President & Director Jennifer Crewe, *Editorial Director* Eric Schwartz

Scholarly, general interest, and professional books and upper-level textbooks in the humanities, social sciences, and earth and life sciences; reference works in print and electronic formats. Subjects include animal studies, Asian studies, conservation and environmental science, criminology, ecology, evolutionary studies, film, finance and economics, gender studies, history, international relations, journalism, literary and cultural studies, media studies, Middle Eastern studies, neuroscience, paleontology, philosophy, political philosophy, political science, religion, sociology, social work. Publishes poetry, fiction and drama in translation from Asian languages only. Founded 1893.

For MSS submission information see http://cup.columbia.edu/manuscript-submissions

Concordia Publishing House

3558 South Jefferson Avenue, St Louis, MO 63118
tel +1 314-268-1000
website www.cph.org
Publisher & Executive Director of Editorial Paul T. McCain

Religious books, Lutheran perspective. Few freelance MSS accepted; query first. Founded 1869.

Contemporary Books

130 East Randolph Street, Suite 400, Chicago, IL 60601
tel +1 800-621-1918
website www.mhcontemporary.com

Non-fiction. Imprints: Contemporary Books, Lowell House, Passport Books, VGM Career Books. Division of the McGraw-Hill companies.

The Continuum International Publishing Group Inc. – see Bloomsbury Publishing Plc

Cooper Square Publishing

4501 Forbes Boulevard, Suite 200, Lanham, Maryland 20706
tel +1 301-459-3366
website www.nbnbooks.com

Part of the Rowman & Littlefield Publishing Group. Founded 1949.

Northland Publishing (imprint)

website www.northlandbooks.com

American Southwest themes including home design, cooking and travel. Founded 1958.

Luna Rising (imprint)

website www.northlandbooks.com

Northland Publishing's bilingual (Spanish–English) imprint.

NorthWord Books for Young Readers (imprint)

11571 K–Tel Drive, Minnetonka, MN 55343
tel +1 800-462-6420
email rrinehart@rowman.com
website www.nbnbooks.com

Picture books and non-fiction nature and wildlife books in interactive and fun-to-read formats. Not accepting MSS at present. Founded 1989.

Rising Moon (imprint)

email editorial@northlandbooks.com
website www.northlandbooks.com

Illustrated, entertaining and thought-provoking picture books for children, including Spanish–English bilingual titles. Founded 1998.

Two-Can Publishing (imprint)

website www.northlandbooks.com

Non-fiction books and multimedia products for children 2–12 years to entertain and educate. Not accepting MSS at present.

Cornell University Press

(including ILR Press and Comstock Publishing Associates)

Sage House, 512 East State Street, Ithaca, NY 14850
tel +1 607-277-2338
email cupressinfo@cornell.edu
website www.cornellpress.cornell.edu
Director John G. Ackerman

Scholarly books. Founded 1869.

The Countryman Press

PO Box 748, Woodstock, VT 05091
tel ++1 802-457-4826
email countrymanpress@wwnorton.com
website www.countrymanpress.com
Editorial Director Ann Triestman

Cooking and lifestyle, outdoor recreation guides for anglers, hikers, cyclists, canoeists and kayakers, US travel guides, New England non-fiction, how-to books, country living books, books on nature and the environment, classic reprints and general non-fiction. No unsolicited MSS. Division of W.W. Norton & Co. Inc. Founded 1973.

Crown Publishing Group – see Penguin Random House

DAW Books Inc.

375 Hudson Street, 3rd Floor, New York, NY 10014
tel +1 212-366-2096
email daw@us.penguingroup.com
website www.dawbooks.com
Publishers Elizabeth R. Wollheim, Sheila E. Gilbert

Sci-fi, fantasy, horror and paranormal: originals and reprints. Imprints: DAW/Fantasy, DAW/Fiction, DAW/Science Fiction. Founded 1971.

Delacorte – see Penguin Random House

Dial Books for Young Readers – see Penguin Random House

Tom Doherty Associates, LLC

175 5th Avenue, New York, NY 10010
tel +1 212-388-0100
email enquiries@tor.com
website www.tor.com/

Fiction: general, historical, western, suspense, mystery, horror, science fiction, fantasy, humour, juvenile, classics (English language); non-fiction: adult and juvenile. Imprints: Tor, Forge, Orb, Starscope, Tor Teen. Founded 1980.

Dover Publications Inc.

31 East 2nd Street, Mineola, NY 11501
tel +1 516-294-7000
website www.doverpublications.com

Art, architecture, antiques, crafts, juvenile, food, history, folklore, literary classics, mystery, language, music, mathematics and science, nature, design and ready-to-use art. Founded 1941.

Dutton – see Penguin Random House

Dutton Children's Books – see Penguin Random House

Elsevier (Clinical Solutions)*

1600 John F. Kennedy Boulevard, Philadelphia, PA, 19103-2398
tel +1 215-239-3900
website www.elsevierhealth.com
website www.elsevier.com/clinical-solutions
Ceo Jay Katzen

Medical books, journals and electrical healthcare solutions. No unsolicited MSS but synopses and project proposals welcome. Imprints: Bailliere Tindall, Churchill Livingstone, Elsevier, Mosby, Pergamon, Saunders.

Faber and Faber, Inc. – see Farrar, Straus and Giroux, LLC

Facts On File Inc.

Infobase Publishing, 132 West 31st Street, New York, NY 10001
tel +1 800-322-8755
website www.factsonfile.com
Editorial Director Laurie E. Likoff

General reference books and services for colleges, libraries, schools and general public. Founded 1940.

Family Tree – see Writer's Digest Books

Farrar, Straus and Giroux, LLC

18th West 18th Street, New York, NY 10011
tel +1 212-741-6900
website www.fsgbooks.com
website www.fsgoriginals.com
President/Publisher Jonathan Galassi

Hill and Wang (imprint)

Publisher Ileen Smith

General non-fiction, history, public affairs, graphic novels. Founded 1956.

North Point Press (imprint)

Literary non-fiction, with an emphasis on natural history, ecology, yoga, food writing and cultural criticism.

Faber and Faber, Inc.

18 West 18th Street, New York, NY 10011
tel +1 212-741-6900
website www.fsgbooks.com
Publisher Mitzi Angel

Fiction, general non-fiction, drama, poetry, film, music.

Fodor's Travel Publications – see Penguin Random House

Fonthill Media LLC

12 Sires Street, Charleston, SC 29403
tel +1 843-203-3432

60 Thoreau Street #204, Concord, MA 01742-2411
tel +1 843-203-3432/978-341-8104
email info@fonthillmedia.com
website www.fonthillmedia.com
Publisher & President (Charleston SC Office) Alan Sutton, *Publisher (Concord MA Office)* Heather Martino

General history. Specialisations include biography, military history, aviation history, naval and maritime history, regional and local and history, transport history, social history, sports history, ancient history and archaeology. US imprints: Fonthill, America Through Time and American History House. Founded 2012.

Samuel French Inc.

235 Park Avenue South, Fifth Floor, New York, NY 10003
tel +1 212 206 8990
email info@samuelfrench.com
website www.samuelfrench.com

Play publishers and authors' representatives (dramatic).

Getty Publications*

1200 Getty Center Drive, Suite 500, Los Angeles, CA 90049
tel +1 310-440-6536
email booknews@getty.edu
website www.getty.edu

Art, art history, architecture, classical art and archaeology, conservation. Founded 1983.

David R. Godine, Publisher Inc.

15 Court Square, Suite 320, Boston, MA 02108
tel +1 617-451-9600
website www.godine.com
President David R. Godine

Fiction, photography, poetry, art, biography, children's, essays, history, typography, architecture, nature and gardening, music, cooking, words and writing and mysteries. No unsolicited MSS. Founded 1970.

Grand Central Publishing

(previously Warner Books Inc.)
237 Park Avenue, New York, NY 10017
tel +1 212-364-0600
email grandcentralpublishing@hbgusa.com
website www.hachettebookgroupusa.com

Fiction and non-fiction. Imprints: Aspect, Business Plus (business), Forever (romance), Vision (blockbuster fiction), Wellness Central (health and wellbeing), 5 Spot (women's fiction and non-fiction), Twelve, Springboard Press. Division of Hachette Book Group USA. Founded 1970.

Grosset & Dunlap – see Penguin Random House

Grove/Atlantic Inc.*

154 West 14th Street 12 Floor, New York, NY 10011
tel +1 212-614-7850
website www.groveatlantic.com
Publisher Morgan Entrekin

Fiction, biography, autobiography, history, current affairs, social science, belles lettres, natural history. No unsolicited MSS. Imprints: Atlantic Monthly Press, Black Cat, Mysterious Press, Grove Press. Founded 1952.

Hachette Book Group USA*

1290 Avenue of the Americas, New York, NY 10019
tel +1 212-364-1100
website www.hachettebookgroup.com

Divisions: Center Street (see page 221), Grand Central Publishing (see page 224); Hachette Audio; Hachette Nashville; Hyperion; Little, Brown and Company; Little, Brown and Company Books for Young Readers; Orbit. Imprints: Grand Central: Business Plus, Forever, Forever Yours, Grand Central Life & Style, Twelve, Vision. Hachette Nashville: Center Street, FaithWords, Jericho Books. Little, Brown and Company: Back Bay Books, Mulholland Books. Little, Brown Books for Young Readers: LB Kids, Poppy Orbit: Orbit, Redhook, Yen Press (see page 233).

Orbit (imprint)

website www.orbitbooks.net

Sci-fi and fantasy.

Harcourt Trade Publishers

215 Park Avenue South, New York, NY 10003
tel +1 212-592-1034
website www.hmhbooks.com
President/Publisher Dan Farley, *Editorial Director* Liz Van Doren

Fiction and non-fiction (history and biography) for readers of all ages. Part of the Houghton Mifflin Harcourt Book Group.

HarperCollins Publishers*

10 East 53rd Street, New York, NY 10022
tel +1 212-207-7000
website www.harpercollins.com
President/Ceo Brian Murray

Fiction, history, biography, poetry, science, travel, cookbooks, juvenile, educational, business, technical and religious. No unsolicited material; all submissions must come through a literary agent. Founded 1817.

HarperCollins General Books Group (division)

President/Publisher Michael Morrison

Imprints: Amistad, Avon, Avon A, Avon Inspire, Avon Red, Caedmon, Collins, Collins Business, Collins Design, Collins Living, Ecco, Eos, Harper Mass Market, Harper Paperbacks, Harper Perennial,

Harper Perennial Modern Classics, HarperAudio, HarperCollins, HarperCollins e-Books, HarperEntertainment, HarperLuxe, HarperOne, William Morrow, Morrow Cookbooks, Rayo.

HarperInformation (division)

Imprints: Access, HarperBusiness, HarperResource, William Morrow Cookbooks.

HarperSanFrancisco (division)

Imprint: HarperSanFrancisco.

HarperCollins Children's Books (division)

1350 Avenue of the Americas, New York, NY 10019
tel +1 212-261-6500
website www.harperchildrens.com
President/Publisher Susan Katz

Children's classic literature. Imprints: Amistad Press, Julie Andrews Collection, Joanna Cotler Books, Eos, Laura Geringer Books, Greenwillow Books, HarperChildren's Audio, HarperCollins Children's Books, HarperEntertainment, HarperTeen, HarperTrophy, Rayo, Katherine Tegen Books.

Harvard University Press*

79 Garden Street, Cambridge, MA 02138
tel +1 617-495-2600
email contact_hup@harvard.edu
website www.hup.harvard.edu
Director William P. Sisler, *Editor-in-Chief* Susan Boehmer

History, philosophy, literary criticism, politics, economics, sociology, music, science, classics, social sciences, behavioural sciences, law.

Hill and Wang – see Farrar, Straus and Giroux, LLC

Hippocrene Books Inc.

171 Madison Avenue, New York, NY 10016
tel +1 718-454-2366
email info@hippocrenebooks.com
website www.hippocrenebooks.com
President/Editorial Director George Blagowidow

International cookbooks, foreign language dictionaries, travel, military history, Polonia, general trade. Founded 1971.

Holiday House Inc.

425 Madison Avenue, New York, NY 10017
tel +1 212-688-0085
email info@holidayhouse.com
website www.holidayhouse.com
Vice President/Editor-in-Chief Mary Cash

General children's books. Send entire MS. Only responds to projects of interest. Founded 1935.

Henry Holt and Company LLC

175 Fifth Avenue, New York, NY 10010
tel +1 646-307-5238
website www.henryholt.com
Publisher Stephen Rubin

History, sports, politics, biography, memoir, novels. Imprints: Henry Holt, Metropolitan Books, Times Books, Holt Paperbacks. Founded 1866.

The Johns Hopkins University Press*

2715 North Charles Street, Baltimore, MD 21218–4319
tel +1 410-516-6900
email tcl@press.jhu.edu
website www.press.jhu.edu

History, literary criticism, classics, politics, environmental studies, biology, medical genetics, consumer health, religion, physics, astronomy, mathematics, education. Founded 1878.

Houghton Mifflin Harcourt*

222 Berkeley Street, Boston, MA 02116
tel +1 617-351-5000
website www.hmhco.com

Educational content and solutions for K-12 teachers and students of all ages; also reference, and fiction and non-fiction for adults and young readers. Founded 1832.

Hyperion

114 Fifth Avenue, New York, NY 10011
tel +1 800-242-7737
website www.hyperionbooks.com
President Robert Miller, *Vice-President/Publisher* Ellen Archer

General fiction and non-fiction, children's books. Division of Buena Vista Publishing, formerly Disney Book Publishing Inc. Founded 1990.

University of Illinois Press*

1325 South Oak Street, Champaign, IL 61820
tel +1 217-333-0950
email uipress@uillinois.edu
website www.press.illinois.edu
Editor-in-Chief Laurie Matheson

American studies (history, music, literature, religion), working-class and ethnic studies, communications, regional studies, architecture, philosophy, women's studies, film, classics. Founded 1918.

Indiana University Press

601 North Morton Street, Bloomington, IN 47404–3797
tel +1 812-855-8817
email iupress@indiana.edu
website www.indiana.edu/~iupress
Director Janet Rabinowitch

Specialises in the humanities and social sciences: African, African–American, Asian, cultural, Jewish and Holocaust, Middle East, Russian and East European, and women's and gender studies;

anthropology, film, history, bioethics, music, paleontology, philanthropy, philosophy and religion. Imprint: Quarry Books (regional publishing). Founded 1950.

International Marine Publishing

PO Box 235, Thomaston, ME 04861
tel +1 207-354-4014
website www.internationalmarine.com
website www.raggedmountainpress.com
Editorial Director Molly Mulhern

Imprints: International Marine (boats, boating and sailing); Ragged Mountain Press (sport, adventure/travel, natural history). A McGraw-Hill company.

University Press of Kansas

2502 Westbrooke Circle, Lawrence, KS 66045–4444
tel +1 785-864-4154
email upress@ku.edu
website www.kansaspress.ku.edu
Director Charles T. Myers, *Editor-in-Chief* Michael Briggs, *Senior Editor* Fred Woodward

American history (political, social, cultural, environmental), military history, American political thought, American presidency studies, law and constitutional history, political science. Founded 1946.

Knopf Doubleday Publishing Group – see Penguin Random House

Krause Publications

700 East State Street, Iola, WI 54990–0001
tel +1 800-258-0929
website www.krausebooks.com
Publisher Dianne Wheeler

Antiques and collectibles: coins, stamps, automobiles, toys, trains, firearms, comics, records; sewing, ceramics, outdoors, hunting. Imprint of F&W Publications Inc.

Little, Brown & Company

1271 Avenue of the Americas, New York, NY 10020
tel +1 212-522-8700
email publicity@littlebrown.com
website www.hachettebookgroup.com

General literature, fiction, non-fiction, biography, history, trade paperbacks, children's. Founded 1837.

Back Bay Books (imprint)

Fiction and non-fiction. Founded 1993.

Little, Brown Books for Young Readers

website www.lb-kids.com
website www.lb-teens.com
Publisher Megan Tingley, *Creative Director* Gail Doobinin

Picture books, board books, chapter books, novelty books and general non-fiction and novels for middle-grade and young adult readers.

Llewellyn Worldwide

2143 Wooddale Drive, Woodbury, MN 55125
tel +1 651-291-1970
email publicity@llewellyn.com
website www.llewellyn.com
Publisher Bill Krause

For over a century Llewellyn Worldwide Ltd. has been a publisher of New Age and Mind, Body & Spirit books, including self-help, holistic health, astrology, tarot, paranormal and alternative spirituality titles. Founded 1901.

The Lyons Press

246 Goose Lane, Guilford, CT 06437
tel +1 203-458-4500
website www.lyonspress.com
website www.globepequot.com
Associate Publisher Janice Goldklang

Fishing, hunting, sports, health and fitness, outdoor skills, animals/pets, horses, games, history/current affairs, military history, nature, games, reference and non-fiction. An imprint of Globe Pequot Press. Founded 1978.

McGraw-Hill Professional*

2 Penn Plaza, 12th Floor, New York, NY 10121
tel +1 212-904-2000
website www.mhprofessional.com
website www.mgeducation.com

McGraw-Hill Business

Management, investing, leadership, personal finance.

McGraw-Hill Consumer

Non-fiction: from health, self-help and parenting, to sports, outdoor and boating books. Publishing partnerships include Harvard Medical School and Standard & Poor's.

McGraw-Hill Education

Test-prep, study guides, language instruction, dictionaries.

McGraw-Hill Medical

Harrison's and reference for practitioners and medical students.

McGraw-Hill Technical

Science, engineering, computing, construction references.

Macmillan Publishers Inc.

175 Fifth Avenue, New York, NY 10010
tel +1 646-307-5151
email press.inquiries@macmillanusa.com
website http://us.macmillan.com

Imprints: Bedford/St Martins; Farrar, Straus & Giroux; Farrar, Straus & Giroux BYR; Feiwel & Friends; 01 First Second; Henry Holt and Company; Henry Holt BYR; Macmillan Audio; Picador; Square

Fish; St Martin's Press; Tor/Forge (see Tom Doherty Associates, LLC on page 223); W.H. Freeman; and Worth.

McPherson & Company

PO Box 1126, Kingston, NY 12402
tel +1 845-331-5807
email bmcphersonco@gmail.com
website www.mcphersonco.com
Publisher Bruce R. McPherson

Literary fiction; non-fiction: art criticism, writings by artists, film-making; occasional general titles (e.g. anthropology). No poetry. No unsolicited MSS; query first. Distributed in UK by Central Books, London. Imprints: Documentext, Treacle Press, Saroff Books. Founded 1974.

The University of Massachusetts Press

671 North Pleasant Street, Amherst, MA 01003
tel +1 413-545-2217
email info@umpress.umass.edu
website www.umass.edu/umpress
Director Mary Dougherty, *Senior Editor* Brian Halley

Scholarly books and works of general interest: American studies and history, black and ethnic studies, women's studies, cultural criticism, architecture and environmental design, literary criticism, poetry, fiction, philosophy, political science, sociology, books of regional interest. Founded 1964.

The University of Michigan Press

839 Greene Street, Ann Arbor, MI 48104–3209
tel +1 734-764-4388
email um.press@umich.edu
website www.press.umich.edu/
Director Philip Pochoda

Scholarly and general interest works in literary and cultural theory, classics, history, theatre, women's studies, political science, law, American history, American studies, anthropology, economics, jazz; textbooks in English as a second language; regional trade titles. Founded 1930.

Microsoft Press

One Microsoft Way, Redmond, WA 98052–6399
tel +1 425-882-8080
email 4bkideas@microsoft.com
website www.microsoft.com/learning/books/
Publisher Ben Ryan

Computer books. Division of Microsoft Corp. Founded 1983.

Milkweed Editions

1011 Washington Avenue South, Suite 300, Minneapolis, MN 55415
tel +1 612-332-3192
email editor@milkweed.org
website www.milkweed.org
Publisher Daniel Slager

Fiction, poetry, essays, the natural world, children's novels (8–14 years). Founded 1979.

University of Missouri Press

2910 LeMone Boulevard, Columbia, MO 65201
tel +1 573-882-7641
email upress@missouri.edu
website www.press.umsystem.edu
Editor-in-Chief Clair Wilcox

American and European history, African–American studies, American, British and Latin American literary criticism, journalism, political philosophy, regional studies. Founded 1958.

The MIT Press*

One Rogers Street, Cambridge, MA 02142–1493
tel +1 617-253-5646
website www.mitpress.mit.edu
Director Ellen Faran

Architecture, art and design, cognitive sciences, neuroscience, linguistics, computer science and artificial intelligence, economics and finance, philosophy, environment and ecology, new media, information science. Founded 1961.

The Monacelli Press – see Penguin Random House

Morehouse Publishing Co.

PO Box 1321, Harrisburg, PA 17105
tel +1 717-541-8130
email morehouse@morehousegroup.com
website www.morehousepublishing.org
Executive Editor Nancy Fitzgerald

Religious books, spirituality. Imprint of Church Publishing Inc.

William Morrow – see HarperCollins Publishers

Thomas Nelson Publisher

PO Box 141000, Nashville, TN 37214
tel +1 800-251-4000
email publicity@thomasnelson.com
website www.thomasnelson.com
Ceo Mark Schoenwald

Acquired by HarperCollins in 2012. Bibles, religious, non-fiction and fiction general trade books for adults and children. Founded 1798.

University of New Mexico Press

1717 Roma NE, MSC05 3185, Albuquerque, NM 87131-0001
tel +1 505-277-3495
email unmpress@unm.edu
website www.unmpress.com
Director John Byram, *Editor-in-Chief* Clark Whitehorn, *EDP Manager* Luther Wilson, *Managing Editor* Maya Allen-Gallegos

Western history, anthropology and archaeology, Latin American studies, photography, multicultural literature, fiction, poetry. Founded 1929.

The University of North Carolina Press*

116 South Boundary Street, Chapel Hill, NC 27514
tel +1 919-966-3561
website www.uncpress.unc.edu
Editor-in-Chief David Perry

American history, American studies, Southern studies, European history, women's studies, Latin American studies, political science, anthropology and folklore, classics, regional trade. Founded 1922.

North Light Books – see Writer's Digest Books

North Point Press – see Farrar, Straus and Giroux, LLC

Northland Publishing – see Cooper Square Publishing

NorthWord Books for Young Readers – see Cooper Square Publishing

W.W. Norton & Company Inc.*

500 Fifth Avenue, New York, NY 10110
tel +1 212-354-5500
website www.wwnorton.com
Vice President & Editor-in-Chief John Glusman

Literary fiction and narrative non-fiction, history, politics, science, biography, music and memoir.

University of Oklahoma Press

2800 Venture Drive, Norman, OK 73069–8216
tel +1 405-325-2000
website www.oupress.com
Director B. Byron Price, *Editor-in-Chief* Charles E. Rankin

American West, American Indians, classics, political science. Founded 1928.

Orbit – see Hachette Book Group USA

The Overlook Press

141 Wooster Street #4B, New York, NY 10012
tel +1 212-673-2210
website www.overlookpress.com
President & Publisher Peter Mayer

Non-fiction, fiction, children's books (*Freddy the Pig* series). Imprints: Ardis Publishing, Duckworth. Founded 1971.

Oxford University Press*

198 Madison Avenue, New York, NY 10016
tel +1 212-726-6000
website www.oup.com/us
President Niko Pfund

Academic and Trade, Bibles, English Language Teaching, English as a Second Language, higher education, law, medicine, music, journals, online, reference.

Paragon House Publishers

3600 Labore Road, Suite 1, St. Paul, Minnesota, MN 55110–4144
tel +1 651-644-3087
email paragon@ParagonHouse.com
website www.ParagonHouse.com
President Gordon L. Anderson

Textbooks and general interest in philosophy, religion, political economy and non-fiction.

Pelican Publishing Company

1000 Burmaster Street, Gretna, LA 70053
tel +1 504-368-1175
email editorial@pelicanpub.com
website www.pelicanpub.com
Publisher/President Kathleen Calhoun Nettleton

Art and architecture, cookbooks, biography, history, business, children's, motivational, political science, social commentary, holiday. Founded 1926.

Penguin Random House*

1745 Broadway New York, NY 10019
tel +1 212-782-9000
website http://global.penguinrandomhouse.com
Ceo Markus Dohle

With nearly 250 independent imprints and brands on 5 continents, more than 15,000 new titles and close to 800 million print, audio and ebooks sold annually, Penguin Random House is the world's leading trade book publisher. The company, which employs about 12,500 people globally, was formed on July 1, 2013 by Bertelsmann and Pearson, who own 53 percent and 47 percent, respectively. Like its predecessor companies, Penguin Random House is committed to publishing adult and children's fiction and non-fiction print editions, and is a pioneer in digital publishing. Its book brands include storied imprints such as Doubleday, Viking and Alfred A. Knopf (US); Ebury, Hamish Hamilton and Jonathan Cape (UK); Plaza & Janés and Alfaguara (Spain); and Sudamericana (Argentina); as well as the international imprint DK. Its publishing lists include more than 70 Nobel Prize laureates and hundreds of the world's most widely read authors. Penguin Random House champions the creative and entrepreneurial independence of its publishers, who work to maximize readership for its authors and to protect their intellectual property.

Crown Publishing Group

1745 Broadway, New York, NY 10019
tel +1 212-782-9000

website http://crownpublishing.com/
President & Publisher Maya Mavjee
The Crown Publishing Group originated in 1933 and is known today for the broad scope of its publishing program and its singular market responsiveness, qualities that are reflected in its selection of authors and books and in its efforts to market them. Provides a diverse program of imprints whose bestselling authors include President Barack Obama, First Lady Michelle Obama, George W. Bush, Gillian Flynn, Erik Larson, Rebecca Skloot, Ina Garten, Yotam Ottolenghi, Mindy Kaling, and Chip and Dan Heath. Imprints: Amphoto Books, Clarkson Potter, Crown Archetype, Crown Business, Crown Forum, Crown Publishers, Harmony Books, Hogarth, Image Books, Potter Craft, Potter Style, Ten Speed Press, Three Rivers Press, WaterBrook Multnomah and Watson-Guptill.

Knopf Doubleday Publishing Group
1745 Broadway, New York, NY 10019
tel +1 212-782-9000
website http://knopfdoubleday.com/
Chairman & Editor-in-Chief Sonny Mehta, *President* Tony Chirico
Alfred A. Knopf was founded in 1915 and has long been known as a publisher of distinguished hardback fiction and non-fiction. Its list of authors includes Cheryl Strayed, Toni Morrison, Cormac McCarthy, Alice Munro, Anne Rice, Anne Tyler, Sheryl Sandberg, Jane Smiley, Julia Child, Peter Carey, Kazuo Ishiguro, and Michael Ondaatje, as well as such classic writers as Thomas Mann, John Updike, Willa Cather, John Hersey and John Cheever. Imprints: Alfred A. Knopf, Anchor Books, Doubleday, Everyman's Library, Nan A. Talese, Pantheon Books, Schocken Books and Vintage Books.

Penguin Publishing Group
375 Hudson Street, New York, NY10014
tel +1 212-366-2000
website http://www.penguin.com/
President Madeline McIntosh
The Penguin Publishing Group is one of the leading US adult trade book publishers with a wide range of imprints and trademarks. The company possesses a list of bestselling, award-winning authors and a backlist of breadth, depth and quality, including Khaled Hosseini, Nora Roberts/J.D. Robb, Ken Follett, Tom Clancy, Sue Monk Kidd, James McBride, Elizabeth Gilbert, Sue Grafton, Junot Díaz, Geraldine Brooks, Jan Karon, Harlan Coben, Nathanial Philbrick, Thomas Pynchon, John Steinbeck, Arthur Miller, Clive Cussler, Michael Pollan, Eckhart Tolle, Ron Chernow, Kathryn Stockett, Nick Hornby and Liane Moriarty. Imprints: Ace, Avery, Berkley, Blue Rider Press, Celebra, Current, Dutton, InterMix, New American Library, Pamela Dorman Books, Penguin Press, Perigee, Plume, Portfolio, Putnam, Tarcher, Riverhead, Sentinel and Viking.

Random House Publishing Group
1745 Broadway, New York, NY 10019
tel +1 212-782-9000
website http://www.randomhousebooks.com
President & Publisher Gina Centrello
The Random House Publishing Group was formed upon the unification of the Random House Trade Group and the Ballantine Books Group in 2003. In 2008, the group added imprints from the Bantam Dell, Spiegel & Grau and Dial Press divisions, creating a creative powerhouse which publishes many of the best authors in both literary and commercial genres. Random House had its origins in 1925 when Bennett Cerf and Donald Klopfer, two New Yorkers in their mid-20s, acquired a line of classics and contemporary American works called The Modern Library from publisher Horace Liveright. Imprints: Ballantine Books, Bantam, Delacorte, Dell, Del Rey, The Dial Press, The Modern Library, One World, Presidio Press, Random House Trade Group, Random House Trade Paperbacks, Spectra, Spiegel & Grau, Triumph Books and Villard Books.

Penguin Young Readers
345 Hudson Street, New York, NY 10014
tel +1 212-366-2000
website www.penguin.com/children
President Don Weisberg
Penguin Young Readers Group is a leader in children's publishing with imprints that are home to many authors and artists including Laurie Halse Anderson, Jay Asher, Judy Blume, Jan Brett, Eric Carle, Harlan Coben, Ally Condie, Andrea Cremer, Roald Dahl, Tomie dePaola, Sarah Dessen, Anna Dewdney, Gayle Forman, Adam Gidwitz, John Green, John Grisham, Anthony Horowitz, Oliver Jeffers, Marie Lu, Mike Lupica, Richelle Mead, Brad Meltzer, Judy Schachner, Ruta Sepetys, Rick Yancey, as well as other popular authors and artists. Penguin Young Readers Group also incorporates perennial favorites such as *The Little Engine That Could*, *Madeline*, *Encyclopedia Brown*, *The Outsiders* and the *Nancy Drew and Hardy Boys* series. Imprints: Dial Books, Dutton, Grosset & Dunlap, Kathy Dawson Books, Nancy Paulsen Books, Philomel, Puffin, G. P. Putnam's Sons, Razorbill, Viking and Frederick Warne.

Random House Children's Books
1745 Broadway, New York, NY 10019
tel +1 212-782-9000
website www.randomhousekids.com
President & Publisher Barbara Marcus
Random House Children's Books is the world's largest English-language children's trade book publisher. Creating books for preschool children through young adult readers, in all formats from board books to activity books to picture books and novels, Random House Children's Books brings together award-winning authors and illustrators, world-famous franchise characters and multimillion-

copy series. Random House Children's Books publishes many of the world's bestselling and highly acclaimed authors and illustrators for young people today including Dr. Seuss, Marc Brown, Roald Dahl, Carl Hiaasen, Lauren Kate, Christopher Paolini, Philip Pullman, Leo Lionni, James Dashner, Brandon Sanderson, Louis Sachar, Richard Scarry, and Markus Zusak. The company is home to many series licenses and characters such as Babar, Barbie, the Berenstain Bears, Disney, Little Golden Books, Nickelodeon, Pat the Bunny, Sesame Workshop, Junie B. Jones and the Magic Tree House. Imprints: Alfred A. Knopf Books for Young Readers, Delacorte Press, Random House Books for Young Readers, Little Golden Books, Schwartz and Wade, Wendy Lamb Books, Ember, Bluefire, Dragonfly, Yearling Books, Laurel-Leaf, Princeton Review and Sylvan Learning.

University of Pennsylvania Press

3905 Spruce Street, Philadelphia, PA 19104–4112
tel +1 215-898-6261
email custserv@pobox.upenn.edu
website www.pennpress.org
Director Eric Halpern

American and European history, anthropology, art, architecture, business and economics, cultural studies, ancient studies, human rights, international relations, literature, Pennsylvania regional studies. Founded 1890.

Pennsylvania State University Press*

820 North University Drive, USB1, Suite C, University Park, PA 16802
tel +1 814-865-1329
email info@psupress.org
website www.psupress.org
Director Patrick Alexander

Art history, literary criticism, religious studies, philosophy, political science, sociology, history, Latin American studies and medieval studies. Founded 1956.

Perigee – see Penguin Random House

The Permanent Press

4170 Noyac Road, Sag Harbor, NY 11963
tel +1 631-725-1101
website www.thepermanentpress.com
Directors Martin Shepard, Judith Shepard

Literary fiction. Imprint: Second Chance Press. Founded 1978.

Philomel – see Penguin Random House

Plume – see Penguin Random House

Popular Woodworking – see Writer's Digest Books

Portfolio – see Penguin Random House

Potomac Books Inc.

22841 Quicksilver Drive, Dulles, VA 20166
tel +1 703-661-1548
email pbimail@presswarehouse.com
website www.potomacbooksinc.com
Publisher Samuel R. Dorrance

National and international affairs, history (military and diplomatic); reference, biography. Founded 1984.

Princeton University Press*

Princeton, NJ 08540
tel +1 609-258-4900
postal address 41 William Street, Princeton, NJ 08540
website www.press.princeton.edu
Director Peter J. Dougherty, *Editor-in-Chief* Brigitta van Rheinberg

Scholarly and scientific books on all subjects. Founded 1905.

Puffin Books – see Penguin Random House

Quarto Publishing Group USA

400 First Avenue North, Suite 400, Minneapolis, MN 55401
website www.quarto.com

Creates and publishes illustrated books in North America and sells co-editions of them internationally. The division comprises of 15 imprints; Book Sales, Cool Springs Press, Creative Publishing international, Fair Winds Press, Motorbooks, Quarry Books, QDS, Quiver, Race Point Publishing, Rock Point, Rockport Publishers, Voyageur Press, Walter Foster Publishing, Walter Foster, Jr. and Zenith Press. Subject categories include home improvement, gardening, practical arts and lrafts, Licensed children's books, transport, graphic arts, food and drink, sports, military history, Americana, health and body, lifestyle, pets and music. Details of the imprints can be found on the website. Founded 2004.

Rand McNally

PO Box 7600, Chicago, IL 60680
tel +1 847-329-8100
website www.randmcnally.com
President/Ceo Rob Apatoff

Maps, guides, atlases, educational publications, globes and children's geographical titles and atlases in print and electronic formats.

Rayo – see HarperCollins Publishers

Razorbill – see Penguin Random House

Rising Moon – see Cooper Square Publishing

Rizzoli International Publications Inc.

300 Park Avenue South, New York, NY 10010
tel +1 212-387-3400
email publicity@rizzoliusa.com
website www.rizzoliusa.com
Publisher Charles Miers

Art, architecture, photography, fashion, gardening, design, gift books, cookbooks. Founded 1976.

Rodale Book Group*

733 Third Avenue, New York, NY 10017
tel +1 212-573-0300
website www.rodale.com

General health, women's health, men's health, senior health, alternative health, fitness, healthy cooking, gardening, pets, spirituality/inspiration, trade health, biography, memoir, current affairs, science, parenting, organics, lifestyle, self-help, how-to, home arts. Founded 1932.

Routledge

711 Third Avenue, New York, NY 10017
tel +1 212-216-7800
website www.routledge.com
Vice President Sam Costanzo

Music, history, psychology and psychiatry, politics, business studies, philosophy, education, sociology, urban studies, religion, film, media, literary and cultural studies, reference, English language, linguistics, communication studies, journalism. Editorial office in the UK. Subsidiary of Taylor & Francis, LLC. Imprints: Routledge, Psychology Press, Focal Press. Founded 1834.

Rowman & Littlefield

4501 Forbes Blvd., Suite 200, Lanham, MD 20706
tel +1 301-459-3366
email customercare@rowman.com
website www.rowman.com
President & Ceo James E. Lyons

Rowman & Littlefield is an independent publisher specialising in academic publishing in the humanities and social sciences, government and official data and educational publishing.

Running Press Book Publishers

2300 Chestnut Street, Suite 200, Philadelphia, PA 19103
tel +1 215-567-5080
email perseus.promos@perseusbooks.com
website www.perseusbooksgroup.com/runningpress
Publisher Chris Navratil, *Directors* Frances Soo Ping Chow (design), Jennifer Kasius (editorial), Allison Devlin (marketing)

General non-fiction, TV, film, humor, history, children's fiction and non-fiction, food and wine, pop culture, lifestyle, illustrated gift books. Imprints: Running Press, Running Press Miniature Editions, Running Press Kids, Courage Books. Member of the Perseus Books Group. Founded 1972.

Rutgers University Press

106 Somerset Street, Third Floor, New Brunswick, NJ 08901
tel +1 800-848-6224
website www.rutgerspress.rutgers.edu
Director Marlie Wasserman, *Editor-in-Chief* Leslie Mitchner

Women's studies, anthropology, film and media studies, sociology, public health, cultural studies, clinical health, medicine, history of medicine, Asian–American studies, African–American studies, American studies, regional titles. Founded 1936.

St Martin's Press Inc.

175 Fifth Avenue, New York, NY 10010
tel +1 212-677-7456
website www.stmartins.com

Trade, reference, college. No unsolicited MSS. Imprints: St. Martin's Press, Griffin, Minotaur, Thomas Dunne Books. Founded 1952.

Scholastic Inc.*

557 Broadway, New York, NY 10012
tel +1 212-343-6100
email news@scholastic.com
website www.scholastic.com

Scholastic is the world's largest publisher and distributor of children's books and a leader in education technology and children's media. Founded: 1920. Divisions: Scholastic Trade Publishing, Scholastic Reading Club, Scholastic Book Fairs, Scholastic Education, Scholastic International, Media, Licensing and Advertising. Imprints include: Arthur A. Levine Books, Cartwheel Books, Chicken House, David Fickling Books, Graphix™, Orchard Books, Point™, PUSH, Scholastic en español, Scholastic Licensed Publishing, Scholastic Nonfiction, Scholastic Paperbacks, Scholastic Press, Scholastic Reference™, and The Blue Sky Press® are imprints of the Scholastic Trade Book Publishing division. In addition, Scholastic Trade Books includes Klutz®, a highly innovative publisher and creator of "books plus" for children.

Sentinel – see Penguin Random House

Sheridan House Inc.

15200 NBN Way, Blue Ridge Summit, PA 17214
tel +1 800-462-6420
email customercare@nbnbooks.com
website www.rowman.com
President James E. Lyons

Sailing, nautical, travel. Founded 1940.

Simon & Schuster Children's Publishing Division*

1230 Avenue of the Americas, New York, NY 10020
tel +1 212-698-7200
website www.simonsayskids.com
President & Publisher Jon Anderson, *Vice-President & Publishers* Valerie Garfield, Justin Chanda, Mara Anastas

Preschool to young adult, fiction and non-fiction, trade, library and mass market. Imprints: Aladdin

Paperbacks, Atheneum Books for Young Readers, Libros para niños, Little Simon, Margaret K. McElderry Books, Simon & Schuster Books for Young Readers, Simon Pulse, Simon Spotlight. Division of Simon & Schuster, Inc. Founded 1924.

Simon & Schuster, Inc.*

1230 Avenue of the Americas, New York, NY 10020
tel +1 212-698-7000
website www.simonandschuster.com
President & Ceo, Simon & Schuster Carolyn K. Reidy

General fiction and non-fiction. No unsolicited MSS. Imprints: 37 Ink, Aladdin, Atria Books, Atheneum Books for Young Readers, Beyond Words, Enliven, Free Press, Gallery Books, Howard Books, Jeter Publishing, Little Simon, Margaret K. McElderry, MTV® Books, North Star Way, Pocket Books, Pocket Star, Scout Press, Scribner, Simon & Schuster, Simon & Schuster Books for Young Readers, Simon Pulse, Simon Spotlight, Star Trek®, Strebor Books, Threshold Editions, Touchstone, Washington Square Press VHI® Books. Founded 1924.

Soho Press Inc.

853 Broadway, New York, NY 10003
tel +1 212-260-1900
email soho@sohopress.com
website www.sohopress.com
Publisher Bronwen Hruska

Literary fiction, commercial fiction, mystery, memoir. Founded 1986.

Stackpole Books

5067 Ritter Road, Mechanicsburg, PA 17055
tel +1 717-796-0411
email sales@stackpolebooks.com
website www.stackpolebooks.com
Publisher Judith Schnell

Nature, outdoor sports, crafts and hobbies, history, military history, regional and travel. Founded 1935.

Stanford University Press*

1450 Page Mill Road, Palo Alto, CA 94304–1124
tel +1 650-723-9434
email information@www.sup.org
website www.sup.org

Scholarly (humanities and social sciences), professional (business, economics and management science), high-level textbooks. Founded 1925.

Ten Speed Press

1745 Broadway, 10th Floor, New York, NY 10019
tel +1 510-559-1600
website http://crownpublishing.com/imprint/ten-speed-press/
President Phil Wood, *Publisher* Lorena Jones

Career/business, cooking, practical non-fiction, health, women's interest, self-help, children's. Imprints: Celestial Arts, Crossing Press, Tricycle Press. Founded 1971.

University of Tennessee Press*

110 Conference Center Building, Knoxville, TN 37996
tel +1 865-974-3321
website www.utpress.org
Director Jennifer Siler

American studies: African–American studies, Appalachian studies, history, religion, literature, historical archaeology, folklore, vernacular architecture, material culture. Founded 1940.

University of Texas Press*

PO Box 7819, Austin, TX 78713–7819
tel +1 512-471-7233
email info@utpress.utexas.edu
website www.utexaspress.com
Director David Hamrick, *Assistant Director & Editor-in-Chief* Theresa May

A book and journal publisher – a focal point where the life experiences, insights and specialised knowledge of writers converge to be disseminated in both print and digital format. Has published more than 3,000 books over 6 decades. Under the direction of David Hamrick, the Press produces approx. 100 new books and 11 journals each year. Founded 1950.

Tor Books – see Tom Doherty Associates, LLC

Tuttle Publishing/Periplus Editions

Airport Business Park, 364 Innovation Drive, North Clarendon, VT 05759
tel +1 802-773-8930
email info@tuttlepublishing.com
website www.peripluspublishinggroup.com
Ceo Eric Oey, *Publishing Director* Ed Walters

Asian art, culture, cooking, gardening, Eastern philosophy, martial arts, health. Founded 1948.

Two-Can – see Cooper Square Publishing

Viking Children's Books – see Penguin Random House

Viking Press – see Penguin Random House

Walker & Co.

175 Fifth Avenue, New York, NY 10010
tel +1 212-674-5151
website www.walkerbooks.com
website www.bloomsburykids.com
Publishers Emily Easton (children's), George Gibson (adult)

General. Walker Books and Walker Books for Young Readers are imprints of Bloomsbury Publishing Plc (page 153).

University of Washington Press

4333 Brooklyn Avenue NE, Seattle, WA 98105
Postal address Box 359570, Seattle, WA 981945
tel +1 206-543-4050

website www.washington.edu/uwpress
Director Nicole Mitchell

American studies, anthropology, Asian–American studies studies, Asian studies, art and art history, critical race studies, environmental studies, Jewish studies, music, regional studies, including history and culture of the Pacific Northwest and Alaska, Native and indeigenous studies, Scandinavian studies. Founded 1909.

WaterBrook Multnomah Publishing Group

12265 Oracle Blvd, Suite 200, Colorado Springs, CO 80921
tel +1 719-590-4999
email info@waterbrookmultnomah.com
website www.waterbrookmultnomah.com
Vice President & Publisher Alexander Field

Fiction and non-fiction with a Christian perspective. No unsolicited MSS. Subsidiary of Random House Inc. Founded 1996.

Watson-Guptill Publications

c/o Random House, 1745 Broadway, New York, NY 10019
tel +1 212-782-9000, +1 212 572 6066
website www.watsonguptill.com
website www.randomhouse.com/crown/watsonguptill

Art, crafts, how-to, comic/cartooning, photography, performing arts, architecture and interior design, graphic design, music, entertainment, writing, reference, children's. Imprints: Amphoto Books, Back Stage Books, Billboard Books, Watson-Guptill, Whitney Library of Design. Founded 1937.

Westminster John Knox Press

100 Witherspoon Street, Louisville, KY 40202–1396
tel +1 502-569-8400
website www.wjkbooks.com

Scholarly reference and general books with a religious/spiritual angle. Division of Presbyterian Publishing Corp.

John Wiley & Sons Inc.*

111 River Street, Hoboken, NJ 07030
tel +1 201-748-6000
email info@wiley.com
website www.wiley.com
President/Ceo William J. Pesce

Specialises in scientific, technical, medical and scholarly journals; encyclopedias, books and online products and services; professional/trade books, subscription products, training materials and online applications and websites; and educational materials for undergraduate and graduate students and lifelong learners. Founded 1807.

Workman Publishing Company*

225 Varick Street, New York, NY 10014
tel +1 212-254-5900
email info@workman.com
website www.workman.com
Editor-in-Chief Susan Bolotin

Popular non-fiction: business, cooking, gardening, gift books, health, how-to, humour, parenting, sport, travel. Founded 1968.

Writer's Digest Books

10151 Carver Road, Suite 200, Cincinnati, OH 45242
tel +1 513-531-2690
email writersdigest@fwmedia.com
website www.writersdigest.com

Market directories, books and magazine for writers, photographers and songwriters. Imprint of F&W Media Inc. Founded 1920.

Family Tree (imprint)

Genealogy.

North Light Books (imprint)

Fine art, decorative art, crafts, graphic arts instruction books.

Popular Woodworking (imprint)

How-to in home building, remodelling, woodworking, home organisation.

Yale University Press*

PO Box 209040, New Haven, CT 06520-9040
tel +1 203-432-0960
website www.yale.edu/yup
Editorial Director Christopher Rogers

Scholarly, trade books and art books.

Yen Press

Hachette Book Group, 237 Park Avenue, New York, NY 10017
email yenpress@hbgusa.com
website www.yenpress.com

Graphic novels and manga in all formats for all ages. Currently not seeking original project pitches from writers who are not already working with an illustrator. For submission guidelines see under Contact on website. Division of Hachette Book Group. Founded 2006.

Audio publishers

Many of the audio publishers listed below are also publishers of print books.

Abbey Home Media Group Ltd

435–437 Edgware Road, London W2 1TH
tel 020-7563 3910
email info@abbeyhomemedia.com
website www.abbeyhomemedia.com
Chairman Ian Miles, *Directors* Anne Miles, Dan Harriss, Emma Evans

Activity books, board books, novelty books, picture books, non-fiction, reference books and CDs. Advocates learning through interactive play. Age groups: preschool, 5 to 10 years.

Barefoot Books Ltd

294 Banbury Road, Oxford OX2 7ED
tel (01865) 311100
email help@barefootbooks.co.uk
website www.barefootbooks.co.uk
Owner, Co-founder and Ceo Nancy Traversy, *Co-founder and Editor-in-Chief* Tessa Strickland

Narrative unabridged audiobooks, spoken and sung. Founded 1993.

Canongate Audio Books

Eardley House, 4 Uxbridge Street, London W8 7SY
tel 020-7467 0840
website www.canongate.tv
Audio Director Jamie Byng

Classic literature including the works of Jane Austen, Charles Dickens, D.H. Lawrence and P.G. Wodehouse; also current literary authors. Publishes approx. 25 titles per year and has 150 titles available, including many short stories. Founded 1991 as CSA Word; acquired by Canongate in 2010.

Cló Iar-Chonnachta Teo

Indreabhán, Conamara, Co. Galway, Republic of Ireland
tel +353 (0)91 593307
email eolas@cic.ie
website www.cic.ie
Ceo Micheál Ó Conghaile, *General Manager* Deirdre O'Toole

Irish-language novels, short stories, plays, poetry, songs; CDs (writers reading from their works), bilingual books. Promotes the translation of contemporary Irish poetry and fiction into other languages. Founded 1985.

Creative Content Ltd

Roxburghe House, 273–287 Regent Street, London W1B 2HA
tel 07771 766838
email ali@creativecontentdigital.com
website www.creativecontentdigital.com
Publisher Ali Muirden, *Editorial Director* Lorelei King

Publishes audio digital downloads, on-demand CDs and ebooks in the business, language improvement, self-improvement, lifestyle and crime fiction genres. Founded 2008.

Hachette Audio

100 Victoria Embankment, London EC4Y 0DY
tel 020-7911 8056 (publicity)
email olivia.hutchings@littlebrown.co.uk
tel 020-7911 8171 (editorial)
email sarah.shrubb@littlebrown.co.uk (editorial)
Audio Publisher Sarah Shrubb

Audiobook list focus on unabridged titles from Little, Brown's bestselling authors such as Iain Banks, J.K. Rowling, Sarah Waters, Donna Tartt and Mark Billingham, as well as classics such as Joseph Heller's *Catch-22*, John Steinbeck's *Of Mice and Men* and Hans Fallada's *Alone in Berlin*. Publishes approx. 100 audiobooks per year. Founded 2003.

HarperAudio

77–85 Fulham Palace Road, London W6 8JB
tel 020-8741 7070
website www.harpercollins.co.uk
Director of Audio Jo Forshaw

Publishers of a wide range of genres including fiction, non-fiction, biography and crime and thriller. An imprint of HarperCollins. Founded 1990.

Hodder & Stoughton Audiobooks

338 Euston Road, London NW1 3BH
tel 020-7873 6000
website www.hodder.co.uk
Publisher Dominic Gribben

Publishes fiction and non-fiction from within the Hodder group as well as commissioning independent titles. Hodder is the UK publishing home of authors such as Stephen King, John Grisham, Elizabeth George, Alan Titchmarsh, Jean Auel, Jeffery Deaver, Jodi Picoult, Peter Robinson, George R. R. Martin, Miranda Hart, Chris Ryan, Michael Kane, David Mitchell and Alex Ferguson.

Isis/Soundings

Isis Publishing Ltd, 7 Centremead, Osney Mead, Oxford OX2 0ES
tel (01865) 250333
website www.isis-publishing.co.uk
Chief Executive Robert Thirlby

Complete and unabridged audiobooks: fiction, non-fiction, autobiography, biography, crime, thrillers, family sagas, mysteries, health, poetry, humour; large print books.

Library Magna Books Ltd
Magna House, Long Preston, Skipton,
North Yorkshire BD23 4ND
tel (01729) 840225
website www.ulverscroft.co.uk
Managing Director Robert Thirlby

Audiobooks and large print books. Founded 1973.

Macmillan Digital Audio
20 New Wharf Road, London N1 9RR
tel 020-7014 6000
email audiobooks@macmillan.co.uk
website www.panmacmillan.com
Digital & Communications Director Sara Lloyd, *Audio Publishing Manager* Rebecca Lloyd

Adult fiction, non-fiction and autobiography, and children's. Established 1995.

Naxos AudioBooks
5 Wyllyotts Place, Potters Bar, Herts. EN6 2JD
tel (01707) 653326
email info@naxosaudiobooks.com
website www.naxosaudiobooks.com
Managing Director Anthony Anderson

Classic literature, modern fiction, non-fiction, drama and poetry on CD. Also junior classics and classical music. Founded 1994.

The Orion Publishing Group Ltd
5 Upper St Martin's Lane, London WC2H 9EA
tel 020-7240 3444
email salesinformation@orionbooks.co.uk
website www.orionbooks.co.uk
Audio Publisher Pandora White

Adult fiction and non-fiction. Founded 1998.

Penguin Audiobooks
20 Vauxhall Bridge Road, London SW1V 2SA
tel 020-7840 8400
email vbar-kar@penguinrandomhouse.co.uk
website www.penguin.co.uk/shop/audio
Audio Publisher, Penguin Digital Videl Bar-Kar

Includes classic and contemporary fiction and non-fiction, autobiography, poetry, drama and, in Puffin Audiobooks, contemporary and classic literature for younger listeners. Authors include Nick Hornby, Claire Tomalin, Zadie Smith, Gervase Phinn, Michael Lewis, Dick Francis and Nicci French. Readings are by talented and recognisable actors. Now part of Penguin Random House UK. Founded 1993.

Random House Audio Books
20 Vauxhall Bridge Road, London SW1V 2SA
tel 020-7840 8400
email audioeditorial@randomhouse.co.uk
website www.randomhouse.co.uk/audio
Group Director, Consumer and Digital Development Hannah Telfer

Authors include Jo Nesbø, Lee Child, Kathy Reichs, Andy McNab, Robert Harris, Jack Dee, James Patterson, Ruth Rendell, Karin Slaughter, Ian McEwan and Sebastian Faulks. Approx. 500 titles available. Now part of Penguin Random House UK. Founded 1991.

Simon & Schuster Audio
Simon & Schuster UK, 1st Floor,
222 Gray's Inn Road, London WC1X 8HB
tel 020-7316 1900
email enquiries@simonandschuster.co.uk
website www.simonandschuster.co.uk/audio
Publishing Director Suzanne Baboneau

Fiction and non-fiction audiobooks. Fiction authors include Jackie Collins, Lynda La Plante and Tom Rob Smith. Non-fiction authors include Stephen Covey, Rhonda Byrne, Anthony Robbins and Spencer Johnson. Founded 1997.

SmartPass Ltd
15 Park Road, Rottingdean, Brighton BN2 7HL
tel (01273) 306203
email info@smartpass.co.uk
website www.smartpass.co.uk
website www.spaudiobooks.com
website www.shakespeareappreciated.com
Managing Director Phil Viner, *Creative Director* Jools Viner

SmartPass audio education resources present unabridged plays, poetry and dramatisations of novels as guided full-cast dramas for individual study and classroom use. Shakespeare Appreciated: full-cast unabridged plays with an explanatory commentary. SPAudiobooks: full-cast unabridged dramas of classic and cult texts.

Ulverscroft Group Ltd
The Green, Bradgate Road, Anstey, Leicester LE7 7FU
tel 0116 236 4325
email m.merrill@ulverscroft.co.uk
website www.ulverscroft.co.uk
Sales Manager Mark Merrill

Offers a wide variety of large print titles in hardback and paperback formats as well as abridged and unabridged audio books, many of which are written by the world's favourite authors and includes award-winning titles. Founded 1964.

Book packagers

Many modern illustrated books are created by book packagers, whose particular skills are in the areas of book design and graphic content. In-house desk editors and art editors match up the expertise of specialist writers, artists and photographers who usually work on a freelance basis.

Aladdin Books Ltd

2–3 Fitzroy Mews, London W1T 6DF
tel 020-7383 2084
email sales@aladdinbooks.co.uk
website www.aladdinbooks.co.uk
Directors Charles Nicholas, Bibby Whittaker

Full design and book packaging facility specialising in children's non-fiction and reference. Founded 1980.

Amber Books Ltd

74–77 White Lion Street, London N1 9PF
tel 020-7520 7600
email enquiries@amberbooks.co.uk
website www.amberbooks.co.uk
Managing Director Stasz Gnych, *Rights Director* Sara McKie, *Publishing Manager* Charles Catton, *Head of Production* Peter Thompson, *Design Manager* Mark Batley, *Picture Manager* Terry Forshaw

Book packager and publisher creating illustrated non-fiction books, ebooks and apps for adults and children. Subjects include military technology, military history, survival and family reference. Works include multi-volume sets for schools and libraries, encyclopedias and highly illustrated reference series. Military titles published under Amber imprint. Children's titles created under Tiptoe Books imprint. Opportunities for freelancers. Founded 1989.

Nicola Baxter Ltd

16 Cathedral Street, Norwich NR1 1LX
tel (01508) 766585, 07778 285555
email nb@nicolabaxter.co.uk
website www.nicolabaxter.co.uk
Director Nicola Baxter

Full packaging service for children's books in both traditional and digital formats. Happy to take projects from concept to finished work or supply bespoke authorial, editorial, design, project management, or commissioning services. Produces both fiction and non-fiction titles in a wide range of formats, for babies to young adults and experienced in novelty books and licensed publishing. Founded 1990.

Bender Richardson White

PO Box 266, Uxbridge, Middlesex UB9 5NX
tel (01895) 832444
email brw@brw.co.uk
website www.brw.co.uk
Directors Lionel Bender (editorial), Kim Richardson (sales & production), Ben White (design)

Specialises in children's and young people's natural history, science and family information. Opportunities for freelancers. Founded 1990.

The Book Guild Ltd

The Werks, 45 Church Road, Hove BN3 2BE
tel (01273) 720900
email info@bookguild.co.uk
website www.bookguild.co.uk
Directors Carol Biss (managing), Janet Wrench (production)

Publishing fiction and non-fiction. Offers a range of publishing options: a comprehensive package for authors incorporating editorial, design, production, marketing, publicity, distribution and sales; editorial and production only for authors requiring private editions; or a complete service for companies and organisations requiring books for internal or promotional purposes – from brief to finished book. Write for submission details. Founded 1982.

Breslich & Foss Ltd

2A Union Court, 20–22 Union Road, London SW4 6JP
tel 020-7819 3990
email sales@breslichfoss.co.uk
website www.breslichfoss.co.uk
Directors Paula G. Breslich, K.B. Dunning

Books produced from MSS to bound copy stage from in-house ideas. Specialising in crafts. Founded 1978.

John Brown Group – Children's Division

136–142 Bramley Road, London W10 6SR
tel 020-7565 3000
email andrew.hirsch@johnbrownmedia.com
website www.johnbrownmedia.com
Ceo Andrew Hirsch (operations), Sara Lynn (creative)

Creative development and packaging of children's products including books, magazines, teachers' resource packs, partworks, CDs and websites.

Cambridge Publishing Management Ltd

Burr Elm Court, Main Street, Caldecote, Cambs. CB23 7NU
tel (01954) 214000
email j.dobbyne@cambridgepm.co.uk
website www.cambridgepm.co.uk
Managing Director Jackie Dobbyne, *Editorial Manager* Ed Robinson

Independent publishing services company that specialises in the complete project management of both printed and digitally published content. Works with publishers, non-publishers (corporate clients, public sector organisations and charities) and self-publishers. Subject expertise includes education, English as a Foreign language, English Language Teaching, Modern Foreign Language, academic, professional and illustrated reference. Can handle high-volume series and multi-component courses for major publishers. Also offers a personal service to independent companies and individuals. Provides all elements of the editorial, design and production process from developing content to providing print-ready files to printers. Offers a cost-effective route to publication. All core activities are conducted in-house. Founded 1999.

Carroll & Brown Ltd

20 Lonsdale Road, London NW6 6RD
tel 020-7372 0900
email mail@carrollandbrown.co.uk
website www.carrollandbrown.co.uk
Managing Director Amy Carroll

Publishers and packagers of health, parenting, pregnancy and lifestyle titles. Opportunities for freelancers. Founded 1989.

Chase My Snail

19 Darnell House, Royal Hill, London SE10 8SU
tel 0785 267 5689
email headsnail@chasemysnail.com
website www.chasemysnail.com
Publishing Director Daniel Ford

Produces top-quality books, especially non-fiction sports, fitness and travel publications, for the co-edition market. Handles writing, editing, proofing and design to take the book through from concept to final files.

Creative Plus Publishing Ltd

2nd Floor, 151 High Street, Billericay, Essex CM12 9AB
tel (01277) 633005
email enquiries@creative-plus.co.uk
website www.creative-plus.co.uk
Managing Director Beth Johnson

Provides all editorial and design from concept to final files for books, partworks and magazines. Specialises in female interest, children's, gardening, illustrated non-fiction. Opportunities for freelancers. Founded 1989.

Design Eye Ltd

226 City Road, London EC1V 2TT
tel 020-7812 8601
website www.quarto.com/co_ed_designeye_uk.htm
Publisher Sue Grabham

Co-edition publisher of innovative Books-Plus for children. Highly illustrated, paper-engineered, novelty and component-based titles for all ages, but primarily children's preschool (3+), 5–8 and 8+ years. Mainly non-fiction, early concepts and curriculum-based topics for the trade in all international markets. Opportunities for freelance paper engineers, artists, authors, editors and designers. Unsolicited MSS not accepted. Founded 1988.

Diagram Visual Information Ltd

34 Elaine Grove, London NW5 4QH
tel 020-7485 5941
email info@diagramgroup.com
website www.diagramgroup.com
Directors Bruce Robertson, Patricia Robertson

Research, writing, design and illustration of reference books, supplied as disks. Founded 1967.

Eddison Sadd Editions Ltd

St Chad's House, 148 King's Cross Road, London WC1X 9DH
tel 020-7837 1968
email info@eddisonsadd.com
website www.eddisonsadd.com
Directors Nick Eddison, Ian Jackson, David Owen, Sarah Rooney

Illustrated non-fiction books, kits and gift titles for the international co-edition market. Broad, popular list includingMind, Body & Spirit, health, self-help and relationships. Incorporates BOOKINABOX Ltd. Founded 1982.

Edition

PO Box 1, Moffat, Dumfriesshire DG10 9SU
tel (01683) 220808
email jh@cameronbooks.co.uk
Director Jill Hollis

Illustrated non-fiction. Design, editing, typesetting and production from concept to finished book for galleries, museums, institutions and other publishers. Founded 1976.

Elwin Street Ltd

3 Percy Street, London W1T 1DE
tel 020-7700 6785
email silvia@elwinstreet.com
email sorrel@elwinstreet.com
website www.elwinstreet.com
Director Silvia Langford, *Editorial Director* Sorrel Wood, *Rights Manager* Elena Battista

Illustrated adult non-fiction: reference, popular sciences, lifestyle, gastronomy, health and fitness, parenting, gift and humour. UK trade imprint: Modern Books.

Graham-Cameron Publishing & Illustration

59 Hertford Road, Brighton BN1 7GG
tel (01273) 385890
email enquiry@gciforillustration.com
and Helen Graham-Cameron, Graham-Cameron Illustration, The Art House, Uplands Park, Sheringham, Norfolk NR26 8NE

tel (01263) 821333
website www.gciforillustration.com
Partners Helen Graham-Cameron, Duncan Graham-Cameron

Educational and children's books; information publications; sponsored publications. Illustration agency with 37 artists. Do not send unsolicited MSS. Founded 1985.

Hart McLeod Ltd

14a Greenside, Waterbeach, Cambridge CB25 9HP
tel (01223) 861495
email jo@hartmcleod.co.uk
website www.hartmcleod.co.uk
Director Joanne Barker

Primarily educational and general non-fiction with particular expertise in illustrated books, school texts, English Language Teaching and electronic and audio content. Opportunities for freelancers and work experience. Founded 1985.

Heart of Albion

113 High Street, Avebury, Marlborough, Wilts. SN8 1RF
tel (01672) 539077
email albion@indigogroup.co.uk
website www.hoap.co.uk
Director Bob Trubshaw

Specialises in Wiltshire and Leicestershire local interest titles; also folklore, mythology and social history. Publishes up to 10 titles a year. See website for submission details. Founded 1989.

HL Studios Ltd

Riverside House, Two Rivers, Station Lane, Witney, Oxon OX28 4BH
tel (01993) 706273
email info@hlstudios.eu.com
website www.hlstudios.eu.com

Primary, secondary academic education (geography, science, modern languages) and co-editions (travel guides, gardening, cookery). Multimedia (CD-Rom programming and animations). Opportunities for freelancers. Founded 1985.

The Ivy Press Ltd

210 High Street, Lewes, East Sussex BN7 2NS
tel (01273) 487440
email applications@ivy-group.co.uk
website www.ivy-group.co.uk
Creative Director Michael Whitehead, *Managing Director* Stephen Paul, *Publisher* Susan Kelly

Packagers and publishers of illustrated trade books on art, lifestyle, popular culture, design, health and Mind, Body & Spirit. Opportunities for authors and freelancers. Founded 1996.

Lexus Ltd

60 Brook Street, Glasgow G40 2AB
tel 0141 556 0440
email peterterrell@lexusforlanguages.co.uk
website www.lexusforlanguages.co.uk
Director P.M. Terrell

Publisher of language books, especially language learning material and phrasebooks. Lexus Travelmate and Chinese Classroom series. Insider China. UK4U (written in Chinese). Dual language books: Cross Over into Gaelic series (Maggie Midge, Scottish Folk Tales). ScotlandSpeak. Dual language books for young children, Mess on the Floor, with audio app (French, German, Spanish and Scottish Gaelic). Founded 1980.

Little People Books

The Home of BookBod, Knighton, Radnorshire LD7 1UP
tel (01547) 520925
email littlepeoplebooks@thehobb.tv
website www.littlepeoplebooks.co.uk
Directors Grant Jessé (production & managing), Helen Wallis (rights & finance)

Packager of audio, children's educational and textbooks, digital publications. Parent company: Grant Jessé UK.

Market House Books Ltd

Suite B, Elsinore House, 43 Buckingham Street, Aylesbury, Bucks. HP20 2NQ
tel (01296) 484911
email books@mhbref.com
website www.markethousebooks.com
Directors Jonathan Law (editorial), Anne Kerr (production)

Book packagers with experience in producing reference books from small pocket dictionaries to large multi-volume colour encyclopedias and from specialist academic reference books to popular books for crossword enthusiasts. Deals with publishers worldwide. Services offered include: start-to-finish project management; commissioning of writers and editors; writing and rewriting; editing and copy-editing; proof-reading; checking of final pages; keyboarding; typesetting; page design and make-up; text conversion; data manipulation; database management. Founded 1970.

Orpheus Books Ltd

6 Church Green, Witney, Oxon OX28 4AW
tel (01993) 774949
email info@orpheusbooks.com
website www.orpheusbooks.com
website www.Q-files.com
Executive Directors Nicholas Harris, Sarah Hartley

Children's illustrated non-fiction/reference books and ebooks. Orpheus Books are the creators of Q-files.com, the free online children's encyclopedia. Founded 1993.

Paragon Publishing

4 North Street, Rothersthorpe, Northants NN7 3JB
tel (01604) 832149

email mark.webb@tesco.net
website www.intoprint.net
Proprietor Mark Webb

Packagers of non-fiction books: architecture, design, educational, textbooks, electronic (academic & professional), languages, linguistics, sports and games. All editorial and design services to complete pdf files, kindle, epub, website and print on demand: b&w and colour. Founded 1992.

Quantum Publishing

6 Blundell Street, London N7 8BH
tel 020-7700 6700
email kerry.enzor@quarto.com
website www.quarto.com
Publisher Kerry Enzor

Co-edition publisher and packager of a wide range of non-fiction titles; including healthy eating, fitness, history, Mind, Body & Spirit and craft Part of the Quarto Group. Founded 1995.

The Quarto Group, Inc.

The Old Brewery, 6 Blundell Street, London N7 9BH
tel 020-7700 9000
email info@quarto.com
website www.quarto.com
Chairman Timothy Chadwick, *Ceo* Marcus Leaver, *Chief Financial Officer* Mick Mousley, *Director, Quarto International Co editions Group* David Breuer, *President & Ceo, Quarto Publishing Group USA* Ken Fund, *Managing Director, Quarto Publishing Group UK* David Inman

The Quarto Group is a leading global illustrated book publisher and distribution group. It is composed of 3 publishing divisions: Quarto International Co-editions Group; Quarto Publishing Group USA; and Quarto Publishing Group UK; plus Books & Gifts Direct (a direct seller of books and gifts in Australia and New Zealand) and Regent Publishing Services, a specialist print services company based in Hong Kong. Quarto International Co-editions Group creates illustrated books that are licensed and printed for third party publishers for publication under their own imprints in over 30 languages around the world. The division includes: Quarto Publishing, Quarto Children's Books, words & pictures, Qu:id, Quintessence, Quintet Publishing, QED, RotoVision, Marshall Editions, Marshall Editions Children's Books, Small World Creations, Fine Wine Editions, Apple Press, Global Book Publishing, Iqon Editions Ltd., Ivy Press and Quantum Publishing. Book categories: practical art and crafts, graphic arts, lifestyle, reference, food and drink, gardening, popular culture.

Tangerine Designs Ltd*

5th Floor, The Old Malthouse, Clarence Street, Bath BA1 5NS
website www.tangerinedesigns.co.uk

Packagers and international co-edition publishers of children's books. Brands include: *The Little Dreamers, Jolly Maties, Baby Eco, Little Eco*. Specialising in novelty books, book-plus and innovations. Submissions accepted from UK only; must enclose sae if return required. See website for submissions procedure. Founded 2000.

The Templar Company Ltd

The Granary, North Street, Dorking, Surrey RH4 1DN
tel (01306) 876361
email info@templarco.co.uk
email submissions@templarco.co.uk (submissions)
website www.templarco.co.uk
Directors Mike McGrath (managing), Amanda Wood (creative), Helen Bowe (sales & marketing)

Publisher and packager of high-quality illustrated children's books, including novelty books, picture books, pop-up books, board books, fiction, non-fiction and gift titles. Send submissions via email.

Toucan Books Ltd

The Old Fire Station, 140 Tabernacle St, London EC2A 4SD
tel 020-7250 3388
website www.toucanbooks.co.uk
Directors Robert Sackville West, Ellen Dupont

International co-editions; editorial, design and production services. Founded 1985.

Windmill Books Ltd

1st Floor, 9–17 St Albans Place, London N1 0NX
tel 020-7424 5640
Children's Publisher Anne O'Daly

Book, partwork and continuity set packaging services for trade, promotional and international publishers. Opportunities for freelancers.

Working Partners Ltd

9 Kingsway, London WC2B 6XF
tel 020-7841 3939
email enquiries@workingpartnersltd.co.uk
website www.workingpartnersltd.co.uk
Managing Director Chris Snowdon, *Operations Director* Charles Nettleton

Children's and young adult fiction series. Genres include: animal fiction, fantasy, horror, historical, detective, magical, adventure. No unsolicited MSS or illustrations. Pays advance and royalty; retains copyright on all workd. Selects writers from unpaid writing samples based on specific brief. Looking to add writers to database: to register: www.workingpartnersltd.co.uk/apply/ Founded 1995.

Working Partners Two (division)
Managing Director Charles Nettleton
Adult fiction. Aims to create novels across most adult genres for UK, USA and international houses. See above for submission guidelines. Founded 2006.

Book clubs

Baker Books

Manfield Park, Cranleigh, Surrey GU6 8NU
tel (01483) 267888
email enquiries@bakerbooks.co.uk
website www.bakerbooks.co.uk

International school book club for children aged 3–16. Operates in international and English-medium schools.

Bibliophile

5 Datapoint, South Crescent, London E16 4TL
tel 020-7474 2474
email orders@bibliophilebooks.com
website www.bibliophilebooks.com
Secretary Annie Quigley

Promotes value-for-money reading. Upmarket literature and classical music on CD available from mail order catalogue (10 p.a.). Over 3,000 titles covering art and fiction as well as travel, history and children's books. Founded 1978.

The Book People Ltd

Park Menai, Bangor LL57 4FB
tel 0845 602 4040
email sales@thebookpeople.co.uk
website www.thebookpeople.co.uk

Popular general fiction and non-fiction, including children's and travel. Monthly.

The Folio Society

44 Eagle Street, London WC1R 4FS
tel 020-7400 4222
website www.foliosociety.com

Publishers of beautiful illustrated books.

Letterbox Library

Unit 151 Stratford Workshops, Burford Road, London E15 2SP
tel 020-8534 7502
email info@letterboxlibrary.com
website www.letterboxlibrary.com

Specialises in children's books that celebrate inclusion, equality and diversity.

The Poetry Book Society

The Dutch House, 307–308 High Holborn, London WC1V 7LL
tel 020-7831 7468
email info@poetrybooks.co.uk
website www.poetrybooks.co.uk
website www.poetrybookshoponline.com
website www.childrenspoetrybookshelf.co.uk

Runs a quarterly poetry book club, with poet selectors choosing the best new collection of the quarter. Also runs online poetry bookshop and distributes and sells CDs for the Poetry Archive. Awards the TS Eliot Prize for Poetry. See also page 331.

Red House

PO Box 142, Bangor LL57 4FBZ
tel 0845 606 4280
email enquiries@redhouse.co.uk
website www.redhouse.co.uk

A member of The Book People family. Aims to help parents to select the right books for their children at affordable prices. Founded 1979.

Scholastic Book Fairs

Westfield Road, Southam, Warks. CV47 0RA
tel 0845 603 9091 (freephone)
website www.scholastic.co.uk/bookfairs
Managing Director Steven Thompson

Sells directly to children, parents and teachers through 25,000 week-long events held in schools throughout the UK.

Writing short stories

Tania Hershman shares her passion for short stories. She introduces the multitude of different forms a short story can take and how to go about writing your own. She also outlines the possibilities for seeing your own short stories published.

The first short stories I read, as a child, were Roald Dahl's *Tales of the Unexpected*, which are horrifyingly wonderful. I couldn't believe so much could happen in only a few pages. Thus my interest in the short story was piqued. Later on, in my late twenties, I read Ali Smith's *Other Stories and Other Stories*, and was similarly astonished. This is *also* a short story? A short story can *also* be so quiet, intimate and just as powerful? And with that, my love for the form was sealed. Having wanted to be a writer from a very early age, I decided to set out to learn how to write short stories.

Short story writers

Some of my favourite short story writers are: Donald Barthelme, Richard Brautigan, Roald Dahl, Anthony Doerr, Janice Galloway, A.L. Kennedy, Ian McEwan, Lorrie Moore, Flannery O'Connor, Grace Paley, George Saunders, Ali Smith, Jeanette Turner Hospital and Tobias Woolf.

What is a short story?

In one respect there is a simple answer: a short story is short, and it's a story. What is short? As short as you like, down to five or six words even, some would say. And at the other end of the scale, the short story butts up against the novella at around 20,000 words, or roughly 100 pages. So, there's a lot of space inside the word 'short'. The question of what constitutes a story is more difficult. Beginning, middle and end? The more we try to define, the less clear it becomes, so let's say we know a complete story when we read one, as opposed to an excerpt from something else.

It's easier to say what a short story is not: it's not a mini-novel; it's not a poem without line breaks. However, it can sometimes seem like either of these. What it comes down to is that the short story is its own thing, a unique creature. Great short stories are great not *despite* their length but because of it. Great short story writers understand the rhythms of brevity, and that what is left out of a short story is just as important as the words it contains. Readers of short stories are required to fill in the gaps themselves, to do a little work, and

Tips for writing short stories

1. There is no one way to write, there are no rules, everyone does it differently. Pick and choose from other people's writing tips or make up your own rules, and find the way that works best for you.
2. Pin a note above your writing desk that says, 'No-one is ever going to read this' so that you can write freely without any inhibitions!
3. When you write, don't forget that everything is in the service of the story: characters, setting, plot, structure, voice, style, beginning, middle, end. Nothing is sacred.
4. Don't try and write for a particular market or competition; write the kinds of things you love to read. Surprise yourself, delight yourself, tell yourself stories.
5. Don't be afraid to take risks, to stray away from the known into chaos, to get away from labels and boxes. Feel free to make your writing messy, raw and original rather than neat, safe and familiar.

being involved in the story rather than just watching it unfold makes reading them very rewarding.

There are as many types of short story as there are great short stories. They can be any genre at all – science fiction, historical fiction, mystery, crime, paranormal romance, humour, lit fic, chick lit, magical realism, surrealism – or any combination of these. There are no restrictions on content, style or voice. They can be told in the first person, third person, or even the second person ('You wake up in the morning…') or the first person

Literary magazines

Some of my favourite literary magazines are listed here; they all accept short stories.

Bare Fiction
website www.barefiction.co.uk
Flash fiction, short stories, poetry, plays and more in a large print mag, plus annual contests.
website www.ceasecows.com

Cease, Cows
website www.ceasecows.com
Exploring the contemporary and the strange, flash fiction and prose poetry, online.

Conjunctions
website www.conjunctions.com
Innovative writing across fiction, non-fiction and poetry, in print and online.

Contrary Magazine
website http://contrarymagazine.com
A quarterly of poetry, short stories and reviews that highlight exceptional writing.

Frogmore Papers
website www.frogmorepress.co.uk
A quarterly journal of new writing.

Gutter
See page 60.

Interzone
See page 63.

LabLit
website www.lablit.com
'The culture of science in fiction and fact.'

The Letters Page
website www.theletterspage.ac.uk
A fabulous, correspondence-themed literary journal.

Litro
See page 67.

Memorious
website www.memorious.org
A journal of new verse and fiction.

PANK Magazine
website www.pankmagazine.com
Emerging and experimental poetry and prose.

Riptide
website www.riptidejournal.co.uk
Short stories with an undercurrent.

SHORT Fiction
website www.short-fiction.co.uk
Beautifully illustrated annual journal focusing on short stories.

Southword
website www.munsterlit.ie/Southword/issues_index.html
New writing from Ireland.

Stinging Fly
website www.stingingfly.org
A beautifully printed magazine showcasing new Irish and international writing with a particular interest in short stories.

Subtropics
website www.english.ufl.edu/subtropics/index.html
The literary magazine from the University of Florida.

Synaethesia Magazine
website www.synaesthesiamagazine.com
Themed online magazine of art, fiction, poetry and non-fiction articles and interviews. Showcasing weird, unusual, thought-provoking and occasionally bizarre fiction and poetry.

Visual Verse
website http://visualverse.org
An online anthology of art and poetry, short fiction and non-fiction, between 50 and 500 words.

Wigleaf
website http://wigleaf.com
Features stories under 1,000 words.

plural ('When we wake up it is still dark…'). Short stories can be 'experimental' – for example, they might take the form of a list or a recipe, or even a PowerPoint presentation (see also *Flash fiction* page 248). It is often easier to ask a reader to suspend disbelief and enter into an entirely bizarre world for only a few pages rather than something much longer.

There is a plethora of writing workshops and courses (see page 655) on offer face to face and online, and undergraduate and postgraduate courses in creative writing (see page 660). The short story world is buzzing with activity.

How to write a short story

There is no right or wrong way to write a short story. Some writers 'splurge' a first draft onto the page and then spend time revising the story. Others write the first paragraph and can't move on until they know what happens next, and generally this is how I write, revising as I go. The American writer Lorrie Moore says she writes the beginning of a short story, then the end, then the middle. A new story comes to me as a first line which demands to be written down. Other writers see an image or hear a voice. Something which took me a long time to internalise is that nothing is sacred in your first draft – not the characters, the plot, the location, the tense (past, present, future), or who is telling the story (main character, narrator…). Anything can be changed, cut entirely or moved around. Where you start writing may not be – and is often not – where the story should actually start. You don't have to start with a blank page: you could grab the nearest book, open it at random, pick a sentence and use that as your first line. Or go to YouTube, pick a video and use it as inspiration. A method that works for me is to compile a set of six prompt phrases taken from six different poems by various authors and write for a fixed amount of time, incorporating these phrases in my story.

Where you finish writing is often not where the story should end. Most of us have a tendency to overwrite endings, trying to tie up all the loose ends, but a good ending is vital. It's not possible to have a fantastic short story with a weak ending, one that stops abruptly so you turn the page and are surprised to find it has finished, or one that peters out, or an ending that goes on and on and doesn't know when to stop. I was told early on that the ending of a short story should be surprising yet inevitable. This is easier said than done. Ending a short story well comes with practice; it's an instinct you develop from reading many short stories as well as writing.

Publishing short stories

It is an excellent time to be a short story writer as the short story is getting a lot of attention. Canadian short story writer Alice Munro won the 2013 Nobel Prize for Literature; Lydia Davis, American writer of short and very short stories, won the 2013 Man Booker International Prize; and American short story writer George Saunders won the inaugural 2014 Folio Prize for Literature, which is open to all works of fiction.

There are many places where you can submit your work. When you have a short story ready to send out, a good place to start is with a literary magazine. There are now thousands of literary magazines being published worldwide, both online and in print – and sometimes as audio magazines. The literary magazine is not – as its name might imply – just for 'literary fiction' (another term that is easier to define by what it's *not*) but covers all genres. A literary journal may ask for stories that are only in a particular genre or on a particular theme, or under a certain length, or it may be open to all. Online databases of writers' markets such as Duotrope.com (a small annual fee is charged) allow you to search according to various parameters.

Always read a magazine before submitting anything. Each literary magazine has submission guidelines that should be followed to the letter. One way editors cut down on reading the hundreds of submissions they receive is to discard those that fail to stick to their guidelines – for example, if a story is double the permitted length, or if a science fiction story is sent to a magazine that only wants realist fiction. The majority of literary magazines and competitions stipulate that short stories must not have been previously published, and putting them online where anyone can read them – for example on your blog – counts as 'previously published'. The majority of literary magazines don't charge a fee to submit work but neither do they pay contributors, other than with a copy of the issue in which they are published (if it is a print journal). Although you won't make a living from publishing in literary magazines, it's wonderful to see your name in print (or pixels) and to have your story where it will find readers. It also helps to build your reputation as a writer.

Anthologies are another place where short stories are published. A publisher (mostly small independent presses) will issue a 'Call for Submissions', which is sometimes on a theme or it may be an open call. These can be found on publishers' websites, or via resources such as Duotrope.com and Places for Writers (www.placesforwriters.com). Authors with stories accepted usually receive one or two copies of the anthology and there is sometimes a small payment to the contributors.

BBC Radio 4 has two short story slots, the 15-minute *Afternoon Reading* on Fridays and the Short Reading on Sunday evenings (see *Stories on radio* on page 355), and the BBC pays well for short stories. Look out for the Opening Lines competition, which is for writers new to radio (see box), and for published writers there's also the annual BBC National Short Story Award (see page 536).

There are an increasing number of competitions for short stories. Usually an entry fee is payable, but always check into a competition's reputation before sending off your money and story. Look for competition listings in reputable magazines such as *Mslexia*, *The New*

Small presses that publish short story collections

Black Inc Books
website www.blackincbooks.com

Black Lawrence Press
website www.blacklawrence.com

Cinnamon Press
website www.cinnamonpress.com

Comma Press
website www.commapress.co.uk

Dzanc Books
website http://dzancbooks.org

FC2
website http://fc2.org

Mud Luscious Press
website http://mudlusciouspress.com

Rose Metal Press
website http://rosemetalpress.com

Route
website http://route-online.com

Salt Publishing
website http://saltpublishing.com

Small Beer Press
website http://smallbeerpress.com

Stinging Fly Press
website www.stingingfly.org/stinging-press

Writer and other sources (see box). If something sounds too good to be true, it may well be! While prizes can be up to £1,000 for the winning story – occasionally more – there can, of course, only be one winner. But competitions sometimes offer cash prizes – and publication – to finalists as well, and to be included in a competition anthology such as those published by the Bristol Short Story Prize (www.bristolprize.co.uk), the Asham Award (for women only, www.ashamaward.com), or the Bridport Prize (see page 538) is a very prestigious accomplishment. (See also *Prizes and awards* on page 534 for other short story competitions.) Competitions often make public not just the winners but also the longlisted and shortlisted stories, and to see your story on one of these lists is a great confidence boost – no, you didn't win, but your story rose close to the top out of hundreds, perhaps thousands of entries.

Another place where you can submit your stories is one of the growing number of 'live lit' events, where, if your story is accepted, you will either be invited to the venue to read it or it will be read by an actor (see box on page 246).

Be ready for rejection

It isn't wise to begin submitting anything until you are ready to receive a rejection. There is never a time in the life of a writer when rejection doesn't feature. It just gets easier to deal with as you understand that it is not a rejection of *you* personally and that there are many reasons why an editor may not pick your story. For example, perhaps it doesn't fit with his vision for that particular issue of the magazine; or maybe it was a topic that she personally doesn't like to read about; or it could be that you haven't got the ending right yet (sometimes editors can give marvellous feedback in rejection letters and I have found this very useful). Similarly, not getting anywhere in a competition doesn't necessarily mean the story isn't good. Competitions, too, are judged by human beings, with their own likes and dislikes.

I didn't submit anything for publication during my first seven years of writing short stories. Instead, I went to workshops (the Arvon Foundation, now Arvon, see page 655; and the Iowa Summer Writing Festival in the USA, www.iowasummerwritingfestival.org) and was learning how to write and how to read as a writer. There is no rush: don't risk being put off entirely by receiving a rejection too soon.

Short story competitions and contests

COMPETITION LISTINGS

Mslexia
See page 70.

The New Writer
website www.newwriteronline.com

Opening Lines
website www.bbc.co.uk/programmes/b007tmq5

Poets and Writers' Magazine Tools for Writers
website www.pw.org/toolsforwriters

Places for Writers
website www.placesforwriters.com

CRWROPPS list on Yahoo
website http://groups.yahoo.com/group/crwropps-b

CHAPBOOK CONTESTS

Black River Chapbook Contest
website http://blacklawrence.homestead.com/BRCCContestPage.html

The Diagram Chapbook Contest
website http://thediagram.com/contest.html

Doire Press Chapbook Competition
website http://doirepress.com/HOME.html

Gertrude Press Chapbook Competition
website www.gertrudepress.org/index.php/chapbook-contest/guidelines

Publishing a short story collection

A short story collection may be planned, perhaps with a theme linking the stories (although this is not necessary), or just something that happens when you realise you have enough stories for a book (roughly 30,000 words). If you decide you have a collection, there are several ways to look for a book deal. The traditional route is through a literary agent, although they commonly respond that it is very hard to sell a short story collection without the promise of a novel. Sending your manuscript straight to one of the large publishing houses will probably elicit a similar response. The main publishers of short story collections today are the small, independent presses, often operating on a not-for-profit basis. You

Short story festivals and live events

SHORT STORY FESTIVALS

See also *Festivals for writers, artists and readers* on page 563.

Cork International Short Story Festival (Ireland, September)

See page 565.

Kikinda Short Story Festival (Serbia, July)
website http://kikindashort.org.rs

National Short Story Day
website www.nationalshortstoryday.co.uk

National Short Story Week

See page 569.

Small Wonder: The Short Story Festival

See page 571.

LIVE SHORT STORY EVENTS

Are You Sitting Comfortably?
website www.thewhiterabbit.org.uk/projects/are-you-sitting-comfortably

London. 'A cosy evening of cracking stories, cute cakes and comfortable chairs.'

Bad Language
website http://badlanguagemcr.wordpress.com

Manchester. Promoting new writing in Manchester: a night of spoken word, prose and poetry.

Berko Speakeasy
website www.berkospeakeasy.co.uk

Berkhamsted. 'A cabaret of short stories.'

'Don't Eat The Mic(rophone)'
website www.scottishpoetrylibrary.org.uk/learn/poets/regular-open-mic-performance-poetry

Glasgow. Showcasing live poetry and short story recital, as well as drama and music.

Fictions of Every Kind
website http://sjbradleybooks.blogspot.co.uk

Leeds. DIY writers' social night organised by writer S.J. Bradley.

Grit Lit
website www.facebook.com/GritLit

Brighton. Exists to promote writing with an edge. Each writer gets a slot of approx. 15 minutes.

Inky Fingers
website http://inkyfingersedinburgh.wordpress.com

Edinburgh. A series of events for people who love words.

Liars League
website http://liarsleague.typepad.com

London. A monthly live fiction night, where professional actors read new short stories by writers from around the world.

Short Stories Aloud
website www.facebook.com/groups/151381574984462
email sarahefranklin@gmail.com
Contact Sarah Franklin

Oxford. Short stories read aloud by actors.

Story Fridays
website www.awordinyourear.org.uk/story-fridays

Bath. Writer-performers read stories inspired by a theme.

The Word Factory
website www.thewordfactory.tv

London. 'A series of intimate short story salons bringing brilliant writers and readers together.'

Rattle Tales
website http://rattletales.org

Brighton. A night of interactive storytelling run by local writers.

can submit to them directly, without an agent. They usually ask for three stories, and then the full manuscript if they are interested in your writing. You don't need to submit only to UK-based independent publishers – try further afield too.

Alternatively, you could enter your collection into a contest which has publication as the first prize. A number of American university presses run such contests, and the concept is spreading. There are also 'chapbook' contests (see box on page 245): a chapbook used to refer to slim, often hand-bound, poetry collections, but the term is also now applied to short story collections. The small presses that publish short story chapbooks often invest a great deal in presentation, hand-stitching the covers and experimenting with different formats.

Both my collections are published by very dynamic small presses, which invest a great deal of love and care into each book they produce. Being published by a small press may not carry the prestige of a 'big name' publishing house, and authors will often have to do a great deal of the book promotion themselves and are unlikely to receive an advance on sales. However, these presses pride themselves on their investment and individual attention to every book and author they publish, and small press published books do win major literary prizes. For example, *Grace, Tamar and Laszlo the Great* by Deborah Kay Davies (Parthian Books 2009) won the Wales Book of the Year.

Self-publishing, both in print and as an ebook is becoming increasingly popular, especially with short story writers as their chances of being published by a large publishing house are slim. However, this costs money and the writer is responsible for every element of the publishing process, including marketing and promotion. If you decide to head down this path, hire an editor to edit your stories first. For further information on self-publishing see *Self-publishing for beginners* on page 582 and other articles in the *Digital and self-publishing* section starting on page 573.

A passionate affair

I love short stories. This is a passionate affair that I hope will never end. I read upwards of 1,000 short stories a year – some because I am paid to (as a judge of short story contests, as a mentor, and as an editor) but mostly for pleasure – and I frequently find new favourite authors. I am continuously astonished at what writers can do with the short story form, reinventing it time and time again, making it their own. My greatest advice? Read. Read as many short stories as you can to inspire your own writing, to show you possibilities of what a short story can be – and then you can reinvent it for yourself. Good luck!

Tania Hershman is the author of two story collections: *My Mother Was An Upright Piano: Fictions* (Tangent Books 2012) and *The White Road and Other Stories* (Salt 2008; commended for the 2009 Orange Award for New Writers), and co-author of *Writing Short Stories: A Writers' & Artists' Companion* (Bloomsbury 2014). Tania's award-winning short stories and poetry have been widely published in print and online and broadcast on BBC Radio. She is founder and curator of ShortStops (www.shortstops.info), celebrating short story activity across the UK and Ireland. She is currently a Royal Literary Fund Fellow at Bristol University and studying for a PhD in Creative Writing at Bath Spa University. Her website is www.taniahershman.com.

See also...

• Details of the *Writers' & Artists' Yearbook* Short Story Competition, page vii

Flash fiction

Peter Blair introduces the short short story, most commonly known as flash fiction.

Flash fiction, or the short short story, is more popular now than ever. Its brevity makes it particularly suited to writing workshops, public performance and onscreen reading. A proliferation of websites, apps, e-zines and print journals are devoted to the form, conventional literary magazines increasingly publish flashes alongside poetry and longer prose, and high-profile commercial magazines have run flash features. Numerous anthologies and single-author collections have appeared, some of them bestsellers.

Flash fiction has its antecedents in such ancient forms as parables, fables and folk tales. It has a long history in China, where it is known as the palm-size or smoke-long story: a story that can be read in the time it takes to finish a cigarette. In Japan, Nobel Laureate Yasunari Kawabata wrote 'palm-of-the-hand' stories. In Latin America, there is a dazzling tradition influenced by Jorge Luis Borges. Israeli flash specialist Etgar Keret is internationally renowned, and short-shorts are popular in many European countries. In the USA, the 'short short story' label was first used in 1926 to describe fiction then appearing in newspapers and magazines, typically a column or page in length. Influences included Ernest Hemingway, whose 'A Very Short Story' is little over 600 words and whose shortest 'story' is just six: 'For sale. Baby shoes. Never worn.' The short-short flourished but its popularity waned in the 1950s and the form became more or less dormant until it re-emerged in 1986 with the first of the high-selling 'sudden fiction' anthologies edited by Robert Shapard and James Thomas. The term 'flash fiction' was subsequently coined by Thomas, and popularised by his co-edited 1992 anthology *Flash Fiction*. Jerome Stern's influential *Micro Fiction* followed in 1996. In 2013, Lydia Davis won the Man Booker International Prize.

While writers in the UK had dabbled in very short forms, flash leapt the Atlantic in 2004 when the *Guardian* ran a series of luminous 'short short stories' by US writer Dave Eggers, collected the next year as a Pocket Penguin. Accomplished collections by British authors followed, *Flash: The International Short-Short Story Magazine* was founded in 2008, and the first annual National Flash-Fiction Day was held in 2012.

The long and the short of it

Edgar Allan Poe's definition of the short story as fiction brief enough to be read in a 'single sitting' has inevitably led to flash being labelled 'flush fiction'. More common terms alluding to the time taken to read (or even write) a short-short are fast fiction, furious fiction, instant fiction, minute-long story, four-minute fiction and the evocative smoke-long. Other names refer to the diminutive size of the stories (micro fiction, microscript, nano fiction, mini fiction, skinny fiction, bite-size story, ficlet), often by describing the small space they take up (pocket-size story, postcard fiction, napkin fiction). 'Minute fiction' neatly invokes both time and space. 'Quick fiction' suggests not just speed, but stories that are intelligent, alive and incisive, that cut to the quick of things. 'Mobile phone fiction' dates back to the early days of text messaging, while the spread of hand-held electronic devices gives new meaning to 'palm-size' and 'palm-of-the-hand'. 'Byte' (punning on 'bite') is used by some tech-savvy flashers. Twitter Fiction or Twiction (stories of up to 140 characters), broadly Twitter Lit, Twit Lit or Twitterature, can be found via the hashtag #vss (very short story), but has also appeared in print publications.

The usual yardstick, however, is number of words. The path-breaking anthologies defined 'sudden fiction' as 1,500 or 2,000 words maximum, 'flash fiction' as up to 750 words, and 'micro fiction' as up to 250 words. But the foremost flash journals set different limits: *SmokeLong Quarterly's* maximum is 1,000 words; *Vestal Review's* is 500; *Flash* magazine's is 360, alluding to the number of degrees in a circle and reflecting its aim of including stories told from all angles and by writers from all points of the compass. Many consider micro fiction to be 100 words or fewer; 'hint fiction' designates stories of up to 25 words. Fixed-length forms are also popular. The stories in Pulitzer-winner Robert Olen Butler's *Severance* are each exactly 240 words, for example, but more common are the drabble

Flash fiction reading

Anthologies

Mark Budman and Tom Hazuka (eds), *You Have Time for This* (2007)
Calum Kerr and Valerie O'Riordan (eds), *Jawbreakers* (2012)
Christopher Merrill *et al* (eds), *Flash Fiction International* (2015)
Robert Shapard and James Thomas (eds), *Sudden Fiction* (1986)
Jerome Stern (ed.), *Micro Fiction* (1996)
James Thomas *et al.* (eds), *Flash Fiction* (1992)
Peter Wild (ed.), *The Flash* (2007)
Alan Ziegler (ed.), *Short* (2014)

Translations

Yasunari Kawabata, *Palm-of-the-Hand Stories* (2006) (Japan)
Etgar Keret, *Suddenly, A Knock at the Door* (2012) (Israel)
Shouhua Qi (ed.), *The Pearl Jacket* (2008) (China)
Ana María Shua, *Microfictions* (2009) (Argentina)
Robert Walser, *Microscripts* (2010) (Switzerland)

Fixed-length flashes [words per story]

Robert Olen Butler, *Severance* (2008) [240]
Rachel Fershleiser and Larry Smith (eds), *Not Quite What I was Planning* (2008) [6]
Steve Moss (ed.), *The World's Shortest Stories* (1999) [55]
Dan Rhodes, *Anthropology* (2005) [100]

Themed flashes

Mark Budman *et al.* (eds), *Sudden Flash Youth* (2011)
Robert Olen Butler, *Intercourse* (2008)
David Eagleman, *Sum: Forty Tales from the Afterlives* (2009)
Vanessa Gebbie, *Storm Warning: Echoes of Conflict* (2010)
Tom Hazuka (ed.), *Flash Fiction Funny* (2013)
Dan Rhodes, *Marry Me* (2013)

Genre flash fiction

Michael A. Arnzen, *100 Jolts* (2004) (horror)
Isaac Asimov *et al.* (eds), *100 Great Fantasy Short Stories* (1984)
Isaac Asimov *et al.* (eds), *Microcosmic Tales* (1980) (science fiction)
Isaac Asimov *et al.* (eds), *Miniature Mysteries* (1983)
Kevin Crossley-Holland, *Short Too!* (2011) (for children)

Social media

Alexander Aciman and Emmett Rensin, *Twitterature* (2009)
Lou Beach, *420 Characters* (2011) (Facebook fiction)
Sean Hill, *Very Short Stories* (2012) (tweets)
Gemma Seltzer, *Speak to Strangers* (2011) (blook)

Other recommended collections

Margaret Atwood, *Murder in the Dark* (1994)
Lydia Davis, *Can't and Won't* (2014)
Dave Eggers, *Short Short Stories* (2005)
David Gaffney, *Sawn-Off Tales* (2006)
Tania Hershman, *My Mother Was an Upright Piano: Fictions* (2012)
Liesl Jobson, *100 Papers* (2008)
J. Robert Lennon, *Pieces for the Left Hand* (2005)
David Swann, *Stronger Faster Shorter* (2015)
Tony Williams, *All the Bananas I've Never Eaten* (2012)
Barry Yourgrau, *Wearing Dad's Head* (1999)

Flash non-fiction

Judith Kitchen (ed.), *Short Takes* (2005)
Judith Kitchen and Mary Paumier Jones (eds), *In Short* (1996) and *In Brief* (1999)
Jan Morris, *Contact!* (2009)
Craig Taylor, *Londoners* (2011)

(100 words), dribble (50 words), 69er, 55 fiction and the Hemingway-inspired six-worder. Some suggest that stories can be shorter still, citing Julius Caesar's '*veni, vidi, vici*' and even single-word nicknames.

Such short forms are ideal for writers wanting to try out different settings, characters and scenarios, though they quickly use up inspiration. For readers, flashes offer novelty and variety, but make intense cognitive and emotional demands. 'Flash' refers not just to length but also effect and depth: the reader experiences a moment of insight, a 'sudden' apprehension, 'in a flash'. Engaging with story after story, when the after-image of the previous flash has barely begun to fade, produces flash fatigue. If a short story is one brief enough to read in a single sitting, flashes might be distinguished by *how many* can be read in a sitting. They cannot easily be blinked, or flushed, away. They are not flash-in-the-pan.

Writing flash fiction

The flash can be thought of as a slimmed-down short story ('skinny fiction'), and the short story as a fleshed-out flash. Flashes are feats of compression, condensation or concentration. Some argue that, to qualify as a story, this compressed form must retain such key elements as setting, character (desiring and developing) and plot (entailing conflict and resolution). Others suggest that, to compensate for compression, the flash should be even richer than the short story in implication, inference or suggestion. A flash may nevertheless be successful if one or more of these elements is slight or even absent. Flashes tend to be limited in scope: most have few characters (frequently unnamed), and many concentrate on a single scene, often beginning in the middle of an action. Others are even narrower in focus; a wafer-thin 'slice of life' can be nourishing, if served with skill.

An example of flash fiction

'Clean-up in Foxhole 12' by Steve Kissing

At the checkout, the clerk picked up my jar of black olives, scanned it, and said, 'I know why you got these.' He then winked, and said, 'It's good to know there are others out there, right here in this crappy little town of ours.' I wasn't sure what he meant. Nor did I bother to ask. I just wanted to get out of there. Fast.

On the drive home, I kept thinking about what the clerk could possibly have meant. And why he thought I fit his profile, whatever that may be. I envisioned his living room, stacked high with jars of black olives, him at the computer, instant-messaging with other black-olive aficionados from around the world. The thought depressed me.

Once home, I put on my comfy clothes and did what I always do with my black olives: cut them in half and used them as helmets on my handmade WWI figurines. It was the night I had promised to treat them – and myself – to a re-enactment of the Battle of Tanga.

The small frame of the flash can carry no flab; and the shorter the story, the leaner it must be. Frisk your flash for superfluous words, phrases, characters and subplots. Excise and revise. Every word must count, and contribute to a single effect. The title should lure, the first line hook, subsequent lines reel the reader in. It is often felt that flashes should end with an epiphany, or revelation. A common formula stipulates a trick ending, an ironic twist in the tale; a less sophisticated version is the punchline ending, which can make what comes before seem a contrived set-up for a smart-alecky pay-off, reducing the flash to a gag. (Worse still is ending with an explicit statement – a moral or message, at worst – that spells out what should already be implicit.) There's certainly life in the squibby, whizz-bang micro, provided the final reveal is subtly prepared for and deftly done. But the trick ending is becoming less common in flashes, particularly longer ones, as the form matures. Good flashes have small surprises (interesting details, striking descriptions, quiet realisations) throughout, rather than a big surprise at the end. They bear re-reading. The final sentence should resonate, but it needn't be flashy.

Steve Kissing's 'Clean-up in Foxhole 12' (see box) creates character economically through first-person narration (common in flash), concisely evokes small-town America and a pretentious counter-culture, and presents the protagonist-narrator's hobby as quirkily subversive, perhaps even sinister. It will change the way you look at olives.

Getting published

While many generalist literary magazines accept flash fiction, a number of e-zines and print journals are dedicated to the form. These include *Flash*, which also carries reviews, *SmokeLong Quarterly*, *Vestal Review*, *NANO Fiction*, *Sleeping Fish* and *Wigleaf*. Some periodicals welcome genres that overlap with flash fiction: the prose poem (in which the emphasis is on language and imagery, rather than character or narrative); and very short 'creative non-fiction' (such as the flash memoir and lyric essay), to which *Brevity* is devoted. *The Southeast Review*'s 'World's Best Short-Short Story Contest' and the Bridport, Fish and Lightship Prizes are amongst the biggest for a single flash. Some contests (a good one is run by Rose Metal Press, http://rosemetalpress.com) offer publication of a chapbook.

The flash is much-anthologised, but there is also an increasing market for single-author collections. While many of these have come from major houses, independent publishers and small presses include Canongate (page 156), Granta (page 168) and Salt (page 198) in the UK, and McSweeney's (www.mcsweeneys.net), PANK (www.pankmagazine.com) and Rose Metal Press in the USA. Oxford University Press (page 186) publishes a 'Short' series for children. When approaching a publisher, high-quality flashes or a distinctive voice might be enough. But a record of periodical publication, competition success and public reading can help, as can a strong online presence and following on social media; some books first appeared on blogs, Facebook or Twitter. Think of an anthology or collection not as a series of stand-alone flashes but as an organised whole that is more than the sum of its parts. Careful juxtapositions can be suggestive; some single-author collections are sequences, and a sequence can constitute a novel-in-flashes. A marketable concept, theme, genre, fixed length or word limit can be decisive, particularly when encapsulated in a striking title. See box on page 249 for reading suggestions and an indication of ways in which flash fiction is packaged for book publication.

Peter Blair is Senior Lecturer at the University of Chester, where he teaches English and Creative Writing, is Programme Leader of the MA in Modern and Contemporary Fiction, and researches South African literature. He is on the Editorial Board of University of Chester Press. He has published essays, articles, reviews, stories and poems, and has judged literary competitions. He has edited anthologies of short fiction and poetry, and is founding editor (with Ashley Chantler) of *Flash: The International Short-Short Story Press* and *Flash: The International Short-Short Story Magazine* (www.chester.ac.uk/flash.magazine).

Further reading

Allen, Roberta, *Fast Fiction: Creating Fiction in Five Minutes*, Story Press, 1997

Masih, Tara L. (ed.), *The Rose Metal Press Field Guide to Writing Flash Fiction*, Rose Metal Press, 2009

Mills, Mark (ed.), *Crafting the Very Short Story: An Anthology of 100 Masterpieces*, Prentice Hall, 2003

Wilson, Michael, *Flash Writing: How to Write, Revise and Publish Stories Less Than 1,000 Words Long*, Virtualbookworm.com, 2004

Graphic novels: how to get published

With more graphic novels and comic books being made into films and shortlisted for book prizes, publisher Emma Hayley suggests that there has never been a more exciting time for writers and artists to get their 'GN' published.

When Mary and Bryan Talbot's graphic novel *Dotter of Her Father's Eyes* (Jonathan Cape 2012) was named winner of the biography section in the 2012 Costa Book Awards, it was the first time a graphic novel had won this prestigious literary prize. While others have won major literary awards in the past – Chris Ware won the Guardian First Book Award in 2001 for *Jimmy Corrigan: The Smartest Kid on Earth* (Jonathan Cape 2000), and Art Spiegelman won the Pulitzer in 1992 for *Maus* (Penguin 1986/91) – the Costa jury's award marked a renewed enthusiasm for the medium, as well as its acceptance by the broader literary establishment.

Essential books about graphic novels

- Scott McCloud, *Understanding Comics: The Invisible Art* (William Morrow Paperbacks 1994)
- Scott McCloud, *Reinventing Comics* (William Morrow Paperbacks 2000)
- Scott McCloud, *Making Comics* (William Morrow Paperbacks 2006)
- Will Eisner, *Comics and Sequential Art* (WW Norton 2008)
- Will Eisner, *Graphic Storytelling* (David & Charles 2001)
- Michael Dooley and Stephen Heller, *Education of a Comics Artist* (Allworth Press 2005)
- Alan Moore, *Writing for Comics* (Avatar Press 2003)
- Paul Gravett, *1001 Comics You Must Read Before you Die* (Cassell 2011)
- Paul Gravett, *Graphic Novels: Stories to Change Your Life* (Collins Design 2005)

Journalists are dedicating more space to graphic novel reviews, and high-street retailers are devoting more space on their bookshelves to a wider range of graphic novels than ever before. The growth of the graphic novel and comic book market is clear: in the UK it grew from £2m in 2002 to £16m in 2012. That's a staggering *700% increase* over 10 years. This isn't the first time that the market has enjoyed a growth, but it is the first time that such a consistent period of growth has been seen since its peak in the mid-80s with the birth of such classics as *Watchmen*, *Maus* and *The Dark Knight Returns*.

What is a graphic novel?

The term 'graphic novel' was coined in 1964 by American comics reviewer and publisher Richard Kyle, but comics in book form have been around at least since the early 19th century. Not everyone agrees on the definition of a graphic novel: it is generally agreed, however, that it must contain sequential artwork, the narrative of which need not necessarily include words.

The word 'novel' is potentially misleading, since it elsewhere exclusively suggests a work of fiction. It is important to remember, however, that the medium of the *graphic* novel contains many different genres – including reportage, biography and history, as well as the more traditional forms of sci-fi, horror and romance. Essentially, the difference between a graphic novel and a comic is its length: while a comic may contain 24 or 32 pages, a graphic novel will be long enough to warrant a spine. But while a six-issue comic series might be collected into a graphic novel, there are many graphic novels that were only ever conceived as integral, 'long-form' works.

Despite some creators still disliking it (preferring to call their work a 'comic book', plain and simple), the term 'graphic novel' has gone a long way to overcoming preconceptions and prejudice. The usual stereotypical associations of 'comics' with children, geeks, male teenagers or middle-aged nerds (think 'Comic Book Guy' in *The Simpsons*) have to a large degree been replaced by the notion that this unique medium can be a sophisticated form of literature appealing to a broad range of readers.

Getting noticed

The best way to start getting your work noticed is to self-publish short comics. There is no stigma associated with self-publishing in the graphic novel world; in fact there is a long tradition of self-publishing which is actively encouraged. Write or draw your comic, print off some copies, hire yourself a table at a comic 'con' (convention) (see box) and sell it. If you've had an idea, executed it well and sold it, not only will you feel an enormous sense of accomplishment, but you will also have demonstrated your commitment – and this will not go unnoticed by a potential future publisher.

Taking part in a comic con is in any case a great way of meeting people in the industry, from fellow creators and enthusiasts to editors and publishers. Some publishers who exhibit at comic cons will be willing to do 'portfolio reviews', reading and appraising your work – it's a great chance to get your face, name and work in front of a publisher. If you catch them on their stand at a busy time, then at least drop off your pitch (see **Your pitch** overleaf) and give them your card.

Festivals and comic conventions

UK

There are numerous comic cons in the UK. Here are some of the bigger ones:

LICAF: The Lakes International Comic Art Festival
(Kendal, The Lake District)
website www.comicartfestival.com

Thought Bubble
(Leeds)
website http://thoughtbubblefestival.com

MCM Expo
(London, Birmingham, Ireland, Manchester, Belfast, Midlands)

Check this website for a complete list: http://www.comicconventions.co.uk

EUROPE

You'll find comic cons happening throughout Europe including in Copenhagen, Helsinki, Barcelona, Erlanger, Lucca and Holland. Be sure not to miss:

Angoulẹme International Comics Festival
website www.bdangouleme.com.

Book accommodation early to avoid disappointment.

NORTH AMERICA

North America boasts a huge number of comic cons of differing sizes. The big ones include:

Comic-Con International
(San Diego)
website www.comic-con.org

New York Comic Con
website www.newyorkcomiccon.com

Smaller cons include:

APE: Alternative Press Expo
(San Francisco)
website www.comic-con.org/ape

SPX: Small Press Expo
(Bethesda)
website www.spxpo.com

MoCCA festival: Museum of Comic and Cartoon Art
(New York)
website www.societyillustrators.org/Events-and-Programs/Special-Events/2015/MoCCA-Fest-2015/MoCCA-Fest.aspx

TCAF: Toronto Comic Arts Festival
website http://torontocomics.com

Social media A good presence on social media can be a prerequisite for some publishers. Make sure you are on the latest social media networks, whether that's Twitter, Facebook or Instagram, etc, and be prepared to build your fan base. One way would be to ask fellow creators to start following you and getting them to endorse or 'like' your work and ideas. Word of mouth is a powerful way to get attention.

Prizes and awards Another way of enhancing your profile (and broadening your experience of working to a brief) is to enter as many competitions as you can, of which there are an increasing number. The two main awards are the *Observer*/Cape/Comica graphic short story prize and Myriad's First Graphic Novel competition. If your artistic style is more manga-oriented, the Japanese Embassy's annual 'Manga Jiman' contest may be for you. This is a great way of getting your work seen by a wider public, and even if you don't win, your ambition will be noticed by industry professionals.

Know your publisher

Before pitching to a publisher, make sure you've studied their catalogue or website thoroughly. If they don't publish superhero books, don't send them a superhero pitch. Look at the different series they publish, look at the page count ('extent') and size of their books, and try to conform as much as possible with their formats. Check to see if they have any submission guidelines on their website (they usually will) and supply your pitch in accordance with these.

Covering letter Make sure that you spell the name of your publisher correctly. This may seem basic advice, but you'd be surprised at the number of people who send their covering letters in a rush and make rudimentary errors. Don't let that be you: you may fall at the first hurdle. Spend time on composing your covering letter – it doesn't need to be very long (publishers are busy people), but it does need to introduce you and your work as concisely and effectively as possible. Also ensure that you are addressing your letter to the right person, by finding out the name of the commissioning editor or publishing director.

Your pitch

Getting your pitch to stand out from the rest is one of the most important things you can do. Plan your approach well. One excellent way is to get endorsements for your pitch from those already in the industry, such as other well-known creators. A sentence or two is all that's needed. This shows good marketing skills and gives your project weight. Bribes such as chocolate coins or cookies have been known to send waves of excitement and appreciation through a publisher's office – this may not guarantee your work gets published, but it does get it noticed! The most important way to stand out from the crowd, however, is to make sure that the presentation of your submission is of the highest possible quality.

Usually a publisher will want to see a number of pages of sequential art (I would recommend at least eight pages), together with a 'synopsis' (brief summary of the whole book). A whole script isn't necessary at pitch stage. In fact, to begin with, less is definitely more. Make sure that those pages are of the highest standard possible. If you are a novice letterer, it's worth persuading a more experienced letterer to do it for you; if you're not brilliant at creating speech bubbles, ask someone else to help. Make sure that you don't let your good idea slip under the radar because of a sub-standard presentation.

Agents

Unlike most authors of prose fiction, creators of graphic novels don't need an agent. The graphic novel world is still small enough for you personally to get to know the editors and

Sequential art courses

Swindon College of Art
website http://micros.swindon-college.ac.uk/sofart_course/national-diploma-graphic-design

Royal Drawing School
website http://royaldrawingschool.org/courses/public-courses/drawing-comics-and-graphic-novels
website http://royaldrawingschool.org/courses/public-courses/drawing-the-graphic-novel-1

Staffordshire University
website http://staffs.ac.uk/course/08W91000.jsp

University of the Arts London
website www.arts.ac.uk/chelsea/courses/short-courses/browse-short-courses/illustration/comic-book-art
website www.arts.ac.uk/csm/courses/short-courses/graphic-design/illustration/cartooning-fundamentals

Raindance London
website www.raindance.org/london/course/introduction-to-comic-book-graphic-novel-scriptwriting

Glyndwr University
website www.glyndwr.ac.uk/en/Undergraduatecourses/DesignIllustrationGraphicNovelsandChildrensPublishing

University of Exeter
website https://humanities.exeter.ac.uk/english/modules/eas3166/description

Emerson College
(online course)
website www.emerson.edu/academics/professional-studies/certificate-programs/graphic-novel-writing-illustration

University of Cambridge Institute of Education
website www.ice.cam.ac.uk/component/courses/?view=course&cid=16446
('From Watchmen to Maus and beyond: the modern graphic novel')
The *Guardian* also runs masterclasses in graphic novel creation curated by SelfMadeHero.

Books

Building your library

- Art Spiegelman, *The Complete MAUS* (Penguin 2003)
- Alan Moore and Dave Gibbons, *Watchmen*, International Edition (DC Comics 2014)
- Marjane Satrapi, *The Complete Persepolis* (Random House 2007)
- Frank Miller, *Batman Dark Knight Returns* (DC Comics 2006)
- Frank Miller, *Sin City* series (DC Comics, 2010 onwards)
- Neil Gaiman, *Sandman* series (DC Comics, 2010 onwards)
- Chris Ware, *Jimmy Corrigan: The Smartest Kid on Earth* (Jonathan Cape 2001)
- Chris Ware, *Building Stories* (Jonathan Cape 2012)
- Craig Thompson, *Blankets* (Top Shelf 2003)
- Charles Burns, *Black Hole* (Jonathan Cape 2005)
- David B., *Epileptic* (Jonathan Cape 2006)
- Bryan Lee O'Malley, *Seconds* (SelfMadeHero 2014)
- Glyn Dillon, *The Nao of Brown* (SelfMadeHero 2012)
- Scott McCloud, *The Sculptor* (SelfMadeHero 2015)
- Posy Simmonds, *Tamara Drewe* (Jonathan Cape 2009)
- Daniel Clowes, *Ghost World* (Jonathan Cape 2000)
- Will Eisner, *A Contract with God* (WW Norton 2007)
- Joe Sacco, *Palestine* (Jonathan Cape 2003)
- Adrian Tomine, *Shortcomings* (Faber & Faber 2012)
- Alison Bechdel, *Fun Home: A Family Tragicomic* (Jonathan Cape 2006)

publishers who make the decisions. However, if you're trying to get your work published in the US, and you don't have the necessary contacts, then an agent could be a useful way in. Many creators are very good at creating, but not so good at selling themselves. If that's you, then perhaps finding an agent is a good option – though of course they don't work for free.

Collaborations

Some publishers will still accept pitches from a writer without an artist already attached, and vice versa. Increasingly, though, publishers prefer the pitch to be submitted by an established artist-and-writer team, while others prefer to work with a single creator who does both the writing and the artwork. If you're a writer or an artist looking for a collaborator, then there are a number of 'meet-ups' where you can find fellow creators.

Creator meet-ups

WIP Comics
website www.meetup.com/WipComics

Laydeez do Comics
website https://laydeezdocomics.wordpress.com

Process at Gosh
website https://twitter.com/processcomics

Get qualified

A huge number of creators with a background in filmscript or play writing imagine they can easily turn their hand to writing a graphic novel, but it's a different medium and it has different rules. True, if you are used to thinking in visual terms you'll have a head start, but there are unique storytelling techniques you should learn and absorb before taking the plunge. Below is a list of practical books that might be of help to you. On the other hand, if you've never written any kind of script in any medium before, then you should look at the various courses on offer.

Go for it!

If you're passionate about your project, the best thing you can do is believe in yourself and go for it. If it doesn't work out at first, don't be hard on yourself. One of my heroes is the filmmaker and comic book writer Alejandro Jodorowsky, whose recent documentary about his doomed attempt to film the sci-fi film *Dune* in the 1970s stands as a triumphant testament to the fact that something that might be deemed a failure can, in so many other ways, prove to be a success. Good luck!

Emma Hayley founded London-based publishing house SelfMadeHero in 2007 after spotting a gap in the UK market for high quality graphic novels for adults. Before launching her own company, she worked as a journalist, a film PR and as an editorial director for several small publishers. She was named UK Young Publishing Entrepreneur of the Year, as part of the British Book Industry Awards 2008. See http://www.selfmadehero.com/about.php.

Successful co-authoring

Louise Voss and Mark Edwards wrote their first thriller while living 6,000 miles apart, which they say helped prevent arguments. They pride themselves on writing lightning-fast page-turners and have their motto, 'All Thriller, No Filler', pinned above their desks. Here they jointly describe their experience of writing as co-authors.

When we make public appearances, or talk to anyone about our writing, the first question we get asked, without fail, is *How does co-writing work?* There are a fair number of writing teams out there, but most of them use one name: Nicci French, Tania Carver, Scott Mariani, Lars Kepler, P.J. Tracy. We can't answer for those duos, many of whom are husband and wife teams whereas we are just friends, but here is a glimpse into what it's like writing with a partner, loosely using our fourth novel, *Forward Slash*, as a case study.

It's a process we've unconsciously honed over the duration of our writing partnership – over 15 years now. When we first 'met', our friendship was conducted solely via email. Louise had seen Mark on a BBC documentary about aspiring writers, and was moved to send him a brief 'good luck' email via his then agent. We didn't meet in person until we'd been corresponding for about 18 months after that, and we always just talked about writing. This led very naturally into a process of editing each other's works-in-progress, and from there it wasn't too much of a stretch to start co-writing something new together.

Our first book, *Killing Cupid*, was easy to create because of the structure: 'he said, she said' alternating chapters. We took it in turns to write a chapter, edited the other's chapter, sent it back, and carried on – it was immediately stimulating and fun as, although we had a rough idea of what might happen in the other's next chapter, there was always an element of surprise to the results. We used to say it was as though the writing elves came along in the night and did half the work for us. The whole thing was done by email, as we lived on opposite sides of the world, and we had no plan or outline. We literally made it up as we went along.

Oh, how we miss those simple days! Now, our novels involve a lot of hair-tearing, wailing and gnashing of teeth – endless texts, emails, Skype chats, meetings, Post-it notes and index cards. This is partly to do with our ageing brains, but mostly down to the increased complexity of our books.

From idea to outline

We start by firing ideas at each other. Ideas, as most writers know, are cheap. Sometimes it's hard to know which ideas are worth developing, but having a partner helps enormously. It's not unusual for us to have a list of 20 'great' ideas that we argue about until we've decided which one is most likely to (a) excite us and be enjoyable to write, and (b) be a world-conquering bestseller (ever the optimists).

Once we have the germ of an idea we usually meet up and have a very long, rambling discussion that we somehow turn into an outline. From that, we work out a chapter plan that develops and shifts as we go along.

When you start a novel, it's a little like having a blank map that you need to fill in. We tend to plot out about the first quarter of the book. In *Forward Slash* we knew that a young woman, Becky, had disappeared after using online dating sites and that her sister, Amy, was going to try to find her. But we needed to know what had happened to Becky and what first steps Amy would take. Once we'd worked that out, we started writing, knowing that our first drafts of the early chapters would probably end up being thrown away.

Working with a master

In recent years we have been using Dropbox, an online file-sharing service, to save our work. We create a master document – leading to lots of text messages telling the other person we're 'in the master', which we find endlessly amusing because it sounds a bit rude. Each chapter is written in a separate document. So, 15 years later, we still use the same basic method as we did at the start: Mark will write a chapter, then send it to Louise for editing. She will edit straight away and send back. Rather than rewrite each other's work, we tend to write comments such as 'Do you really think she would wear black leather?'; 'I think you're giving this away too early.' It's vital to be completely honest and not worry about hurting the other person's feelings. That's why we are able to work together so well. We don't take offence. In fact, that is possibly the most important reason why we have a successful partnership: we respect each other's abilities and aren't afraid to say 'You could do much better'.

Who writes what

Apart from *Killing Cupid*, we always write from multiple points of view, which might be as a result of being a partnership. In *Forward Slash*, a novel in which the main characters are Amy, Becky, a cop and a serial killer, Mark wrote all of the cop and the serial killer and some of Amy's scenes, while Louise wrote most of Amy and all of Becky.

This is because we have preferences for the kind of scenes we gravitate towards. As gender-stereotypical as it sounds, Mark writes most of the action/violent sequences and Louise writes the emotional scenes. We take it in turns to write the sex scenes, and like to keep people guessing as to which of us writes which particular one! (An additional perk of a writing partnership is that Mark can tell his mum that Louise writes ALL the sex scenes, and vice versa.) Mark also got the job of writing the science scenes in *All Fall Down* and *Catch Your Death*, because he was slightly less rubbish than Louise at science at school. Louise writes most of the descriptions of people and places, partly because Mark is the kind of person who can't even remember the colour of the carpet in his living room.

Sometimes we will edit the prose directly, removing semi-colons and pointing out if the other person has made 15 references to eyes in one chapter (as Mark did, shortly after having an eye operation). Louise tends to edit out a lot of Mark's swearing. He will suggest she cuts some of the descriptions of countryside and wellies. Mark's instinct is to write lean, stripped-down prose and Louise is more lyrical. But we have learned to write as a third person, Voss Edwards – or Vedwards – and these days we often find it hard to tell who has written which part. We write in a unified voice, though Louise will still often embellish Mark's prose and he will trim her more flowery passages.

We meet up every month or so, get our laptops out and discuss where the story is going and brainstorm the difficult bits – the tricky parts of the plot, the motivations of the characters, how are we going to get from A to C via B? If anyone listened in to our conversations they would wonder how we ever get anything done as we switch from topic to topic at a ridiculous rate and both have terrible memories. We have to write everything down in our plan.

After about six months, we have a first draft – *Forward Slash* came in at almost 100,000 words. The next step was to do our own edit, which we do quickly, both reading through and making comments in the margins of the master document, discussing any issues that come up and making changes. When we write, we often get stuck over a particular detail – for example, how is X going to escape from Y? – and we will leave a big note in the manuscript saying 'Fix this later'. At the end, we have to go back and fix it. There is no point in sitting inactive for days – it's better to press on, knowing you can always change something later on.

Self-publishing and traditional publishing

Our first two novels were initially self-published, and were later 'traditionally' published after they were successful, and the latest two were written under contract. It's a very different experience writing a book for a publisher, mostly because of the involvement of your editor. For us, the editorial input is the best thing about having a publisher. They help with ideas, give guidance and, at the end send you a very long email with full details of everything you need to change. Undoubtedly having an editor results in a better book (although the HarperCollins version of *Killing Cupid* is identical to the self-published one, which we were pleased about) but at the time it makes you feel like hiding under a duvet and thinking that you might be happier driving a bus for a living.

Publishers also provide copy-editors, who point out all the inconsistencies and overuse of words like 'just', and proofreaders. Even though we read and check each other's work endlessly, a lot of mistakes sneak through. This is why it's so important for anyone who self-publishes to hire a professional proofreader, otherwise a lot of one-star reviews will await you.

Writing the second draft, following the editor's comments, is where co-writing really pays off. Most of it involves making decisions and finding creative solutions to problems – much easier with two people. So we meet regularly, spending many evenings at Louise's kitchen table thrashing out the details, often wanting to drink wine and forget about this bloody book, but making each other keep working until we figure out exactly what to change. We then divide up the work and set to work on the manuscript. With *Forward Slash* we used a Google spreadsheet which we could edit simultaneously to help us keep track of the many changes – although Louise forgot to use it so we were working off two different lists, which caused some of the wailing mentioned above.

The pros and cons of co-writing

This is one of the disadvantages of co-writing – keeping track of everything. When you write a book solo, you might have a notebook, a load of Post-its stuck to your wall, or perhaps you keep everything in your head. This isn't possible when there are two of you. We have to keep track of everything that is going on, and it's much harder to keep a firm grasp of the finer details of the plot and the characters when somebody else wrote half of the work in progress.

We also find that sometimes we have completely different ideas about what is going on, why something has happened and what will happen next, which leads to all sorts of bewilderment. This gets even worse when one of us accidentally saves the master document without the other person's latest changes, which has happened a few times, and which would probably be grounds for divorce were we married. We always blame Dropbox rather than the other person, though.

However, the advantages are many. As well as all the pros mentioned already – such as idea generation and only having to do half the work – it also helps a lot when it comes to that vital part of being a writer that nobody tells you about: promotion. This is hugely time-consuming, but we are able to share all the tweeting, blog post writing, personal appearances and so on.

Finally, the biggest advantage of all: having a co-writer means you have somebody to share everything with – the pain and the triumphs – and somebody who shares your obsession. Most writers are preoccupied by their work and their writing careers to say the least. There are only so many times your spouse can listen to you bang on about your latest idea or your current Amazon ranking. But we both find all of this endlessly fascinating. We could talk about our books 24 hours a day and never get bored, long after the eyes of everyone we know have glazed over.

Louise Voss and **Mark Edwards** are the co-authors of six novels including the bestselling *From the Cradle*, the first in the DI Lennon series, with Book 2, *The Blissfully Dead* following in September 2015. Mark and Louise can be found on Facebook.com/vossandedwards and on Twitter, @mredwards and @LouiseVoss1, and they blog regularly on www.vossandedwards.com. Mark and Louise are additionally publishing solo novels whilst they continue to co-write.

How to write an award-winning first novel

Following the award of 2013 Costa Book of the Year for his debut novel, *The Shock of the Fall*, Nathan Filer shares his thoughts on how focusing on achievable goals can ease the experience of writing your first novel.

On a rainy spring day in 2009, I shuffled into a lecture theatre at the University of Bristol to watch a presentation entitled 'Evidence-based Approaches to Positive Psychology'. I was deeply, deeply miserable.

Depression – somewhat ironically – was my bread and butter. I'd spent the last two years of my working life surrounded by filing cabinets in a cramped office, a short walk up the road from the lecture theatre. Here I helped to administer large trials – comparing side-effects of antidepressants, the effectiveness of talking therapies, that sort of thing. It was good work, important work. The problem: I wasn't any good at it. My aptitude for statistics is woeful. I'm slow with databases and spreadsheets. My heart was elsewhere.

At home, hidden away in a cardboard box, were the first 20 pages of a novel that I'd been planning to write for years, only where was the time?

Then on that rainy spring day, slumped at my desk, composing a newsletter, I noticed an email arrive: it was a reminder that all were welcome to the lunchtime lecture, starting in 15 minutes. I reread the title. Evidence-based Approaches to Positive Psychology. These things tend to suffer from lofty verbosity. Translate: How To Be Happy.

I grabbed my coat.

The notes I made during the lecture remain pinned to the wall above my writing desk, six years and one novel later. They don't contain any insights on shaping a compelling plot. Nothing on characterisation or how to write convincing dialogue. There are no well-worn wisdoms on the importance of cutting adverbs. Writing a first novel demands far more than the words we place on the page. Here are my thoughts on how to do it and, moreover, for making the experience a happier one.

Have specific goals

The operative word here is 'specific'. My stack of pages hidden away, my hope to be a writer one day – were a start, but it was too vague.

It didn't bother me that I would often put aside my manuscript for a month, three months, six months at a time. Why should it? I'd write it eventually. The problem, the lecturer explained, is that when our goals aren't specific, it's too easy to convince ourselves that we're getting there when we're not. Then at the other end of the journey, we tend not to properly savour the attainment of ill-defined goals, because it is less certain that we've reached them.

Here's what I did. I replaced 'I want to be a writer' (something I'm still not convinced I've achieved) with 'I'll write something today'.

That's pretty specific.

The first evening, in a frenzy of positivity, I wrote a page. The next day I deleted it. But I also wrote a new paragraph. That went too. By the end of the week I'd written 2,000 words that would never make it into *The Shock of the Fall*, and I had also written a sentence that would become the opening line. It was there, waiting.

Make sure your goals are achievable

As my novel grew, as I found the voice of my central character and knew with greater certainty how his story would unfold – I set myself tougher goals.

Today I will fix that irksome issue with the chronology. This week I will complete chapter four. Next week I shall write to an agent, etc.

My vague desire to write a novel had now been replaced with the clear intent to write *this* novel, to tell this specific story. That felt great, because now it felt achievable.

All too often we set ourselves unachievable goals. Then we feel bad for failing (more on failure in a bit). Many writers set themselves word count targets, and for some this is helpful. I tried it a few times – setting out to write 1,000 words a day. That isn't so much, but I still struggled. I'm precise. I edit as I go along. My style isn't suited to generating work quickly. So I set myself an achievable goal instead. I told myself that it didn't matter if I only wrote ten words, or if I deleted 50. All I had to do was spend the time at my desk. A lot of time.

I couldn't quit my job, but I could write in the evenings. Two hours every evening, without fail. Five hours on a weekend. That was achievable. It worked for a while too, but writing can be hard and lonely and disheartening. I'd written to an agent, sent off 30 pages. Then the rejection letter arrived. I took that day off, took the week off. Stopped.

Be prepared to fail along the way

I'm glad my lecture notes are pinned to my wall. It's obvious, I know, but we can all do with a reminder sometimes. 'The important thing,' the lecturer had explained, scanning the room before fixing her gaze on me. 'The important thing, is to see failures along the way for what they are. Set-backs in a longer journey. Not the end of the road.'

I wonder if there is a novelist alive who hasn't run into some kind of failure in their career. A rejection letter is a hiccup. Three rejection letters – that's three hiccups. What about 30?

I'd say if you get 30 rejection letters there's a chance that your novel isn't any good. That's not the same as you not being any good. However much of ourselves we pour into our writing, it's never the whole of us.

Besides, you're not trying to be a writer, remember? You're trying to write *this specific novel*. If it doesn't work out, consider writing another one. My debut – a book that won me a big prize and garnered much praise and attention – wasn't the first novel I had written. It's just the first one that got published.

Years before, I completed a children's book. It had a talking worm in it. That manuscript got a whole heap of rejections. But they weren't automated rejections. Not all of them, anyway. There was encouragement amongst them, kind words about the style. I was being told that it wasn't bad. The rejection letter for my 'second debut' went a step further: It's good. It's not for us. But it's good.

Base your affirmations on fact

Good isn't great. But good is good. Good might be good enough.

I think it's important to give ourselves a pep talk from time to time, a word of congratulations, a pat on the back. Writing is, on the whole, a solitary experience. We could be waiting a long time to hear praise from anyone else.

The key is to base our affirmations on fact. If you tell yourself you are the world's most remarkable storyteller, you've a long way to fall. But you can be good. That description you wrote earlier, capturing the precise moment when your character realises the truth – that was bloody good. It would stand up in any novel.

Savour these moments. It might be your private burden to suffer the anxieties of writing, but it's also your unique privilege to be first in line to enjoy what you create.

Be flexible in how you get there

Nearly 100 pages in, I hit a wall.

A first novel is a huge undertaking; we learn about ourselves as writers along the way. Sitting alone at my computer – even with the pep talks – was no longer working out. So I changed my approach and enrolled on an MA in creative writing. I didn't plan this at the outset, but that doesn't matter. The specific, achievable goal is what matters. I had committed to writing my novel; not to doing so without help.

For me, to be in a place with other writers sharing feedback and encouragement was very useful. Also useful was to be reminded that my novel wasn't the only one being written. I could contribute positively to other people's work. I could help other writers enjoy their successes. That felt good.

But writing courses bring their own challenges. When sharing early drafts with people, there's a danger of being buffeted around by conflicting advice.

Take responsibility

So remember, above all else, this is *your* novel. If it is published then it will be your name on the cover. You can't write a book by committee.

That doesn't mean we should close our ears to all suggestions. If we share an early draft of a chapter with ten friends, and all ten come back saying that the scene with the meringue doesn't work, then probably it's worth reworking the scene with the meringue. But if only one person says it doesn't work – well, your opinion counts too. I saw people who forgot this, who afforded other people's ideas a greater weight than their own.

I was fortunate. By the time I enrolled on the course I had a clear sense of the story I wanted to tell, and this made it easier to be selective about the advice I took. If your reader fully understands what a scene is intended to achieve, and can explain why it's not achieving this – that's valuable advice. If they just don't have a taste for meringue, but you do – that's not so useful. Take responsibility. Keep the (delicious) meringue.

Focus on the stuff you can control

If we're seeking representation from an agency, we can buy the *Writers' & Artists' Yearbook*; we can be sure to select agents who are accepting work in our genre; we can carefully read submission guidelines and fastidiously adhere to them. These are the things we can control. What we can't control, is whether or not the agent chooses to represent us, and if our writing gets published.

If our novel does get published, we can't control how it's received or how well it sells. Heck – we new authors rarely even get a say on what the book cover looks like. There is so much in the world of publishing that is beyond our influence.

Put it all aside.

Don't give another thought to writing a prize-winning first novel. Think instead about your next sentence, and you might just be on the way.

Six years on from that rainy spring day, my debut novel is on the shelves and has been well received (better than the talking worm, anyway).

But that doesn't mean it's all a breeze. I keep the notes from that lecture pinned to my wall and still use them.

Writing is hard and I falter often.

As for being a writer – I think that's always a work in progress.

When I received the request to write for this *Yearbook* I wasn't at all sure how to go about it or what I wanted to share. So I set myself a goal: 'Spend an hour at the keyboard'. This article is the result. Here's wishing you every success with your novel, and more importantly, every happiness.

Nathan Filer won the Costa First Novel Award and then the 2013 Costa Book of the Year for *The Shock of the Fall.* His debut novel was subject to an 11-way auction and bought by HarperCollins, and the paperback is published by the Borough Press (2014) and was the recipient of the Writers' Guild Award for Best First Novel in January 2015. Nathan now lectures on creative writing for Bath Spa University.

See also...

- *Prizes and awards*, page 534
- *Prize winners*, page 562
- *Open evening*, page 638

On writing: essential advice for writers

Author Ben Schott provides some clear-cut advice for the budding writer (including 'Never give writing advice').

A writer giving writing advice to other writers: it's almost the definition of hubris. I don't always follow George Orwell's 'six rules' for writing … and he was George Orwell. Moreover, as a writer of non-fiction books and journalism, I have no idea whether any of my experience applies to novelists, playwrights, poets or librettists. Or even to fellow sappers in the trenches of fact. But since I was asked, and *Geschäft ist Geschäft*, here goes:

1 Write. I am amazed by the number of would-be writers who aren't always writing. Writing is in no small part a *craft* – and every craftsman improves through industrious iteration. Imagine an aspiring pianist who didn't practice every day. Absurd.
2 Don't be imprisoned by routine. The Web is awash with banal infographics that detail the working hours of famous authors. What does it matter if Kafka wrote at midnight, or Austen napped after tea? Carve out time whenever you can and, more importantly, whenever it works for you.
3 It's *never* about the equipment. In his day Tiger Woods could have trounced nearly all of the world's golfers with only a rusty seven-iron. Who cares if you write shorthand with a quill, or hammer away on an Underwood? Get the right words in the right order, and don't trip over the furniture.
4 Find and cherish a good editor. The best editor is someone you write to impress, and the person who spots the flaws you've diligently camouflaged. Remember, as publishing becomes more about profit and loss, the best editor may not be your *actual* editor.
5 People say, 'Write about what you know.' I don't know. I say, 'Write about what enthuses you.' More often than not, the things that enthuse me are those I must leave the house to research.
6 Leave the house.
7 Don't bury the lede. Throat-clearing paragraphs are sometimes the only way to approach a project, but that doesn't mean they should remain up top, or at all. And, as the great Michael Kinsley said, 'Once you have the lede, the rest is just typing.'
8 Read. Everything and anything. From great literature to laundry instructions. A writer is always writing, just as a photographer is always 'seeing'.
9 Read your work out loud. Seriously. I can't stress this enough. You don't have to declaim it from a balcony, but even muttering the words *sotto voce* will identify the weak spots in your logic and prose.
10 Be leery of 'writers block'. Is there any other job where people get 'blocked'? Coalminers don't. Nor do midwives, bricklayers, coders or health-and-safety executives. Most professions demand writing – just look at the profusion of technical journals. Yet doctors, lawyers, academics and scientists rarely complain about being blocked like (aspiring) writers often do.
11 If you are stuck, constrict your options. George Perec wrote an entire novel without

using the letter E. Then Gilbert Adair translated it from French into English, again with no Es. Think *inside* the box and, if all else fails, channel the Oulipians.

12 Love language in all its forms. There is a time for sesquipedalian orotundity and a time for disarming brevity. Shakespeare deployed both 'honorificabilitudinitatibus' and 'cruel to be kind'.

13 I genuinely don't care about splitting infinitives, starting sentences with 'and' or 'but', or using 'iconic' to mean 'famous'. All of these 'sins' have been committed by writers far better than me. Pedantry is rarely the mother of creativity.

14 Rewrite. I can't tell you how often I rewrite my work. My best sentences – admittedly a low bar – might have been re-worked a dozen times. Every word should count. Every phrase should balance.

15 Don't number lists until you've finished. I've had to renumber this piece at least five times.

16 Back up your files regularly. I keep important files in more than one location and, as a project gets close to completion, carry a copy of the latest version with me on a thumb drive.

17 In journalism, the editor is your first audience. If you don't have good relationships with editors, you're going to have a hard time getting published. Be accurate, prompt, available, honest and polite. Don't pitch the same idea to more than one editor at a time; don't send attachments unless asked; keep everything a fact-checker might need; put your phone number on every email; be open to feedback; and be prepared to swallow your pride.

18 Editors usually work only on deadline. If your piece is not on deadline, your editor will get around to it later. Or not.

19 Don't be afraid to nudge an editor for a reply … gently.

20 Read your contracts. Even if you have an agent, be interested and get involved in the detail. Don't sign anything until you have read and understood it.

21 Read your royalty statements, no matter how unconscionably impenetrable: it's your money.

22 When faced with a choice between protecting your intellectual property or getting more money, err on the side of IP.

23 Aim to sell everything at least twice. Turn a speech into an article, a short story into a radio play, and a novel into a Hollywood epic. (*This* is why IP is important.)

24 Accept rejection with grace. Perhaps the editor is a blockhead; perhaps your idea was junk. Either way, the stars were out of alignment: move on.

25 No writer is a hero to his proofreader or fact-checker. These pros have saved my life more often than I care to admit, and I try always to express my gratitude.

26 Don't read online comments.

27 Don't read reviews – not even the good ones.

28 Never Google yourself.

29 If Twitter or Facebook is the answer, it's probably the wrong question.

30 Envying other writers is simply insane.

31 Book publicity is an incredibly tough job. With a few (immediately obvious) exceptions, publicists try their very best and work damn hard. Do everything you can to help, and be easy and fun to work with.

32 The amount of additional writing you have to do *after* publication is just absurd. But such is the brave new world of book promotion, so buckle down.

33 The line between self-promotion and self-respect is gossamer thin; on book tour, it's non-existent.

34 Give up. Everyone has bad days (and fallow months) when compiling even the simplest sentence feels like wading through treacle. But if the process is really *that* tough, *that* soul-destroying, *that* unbearably horrific, then perhaps (whisper it softly) writing is not for you.

35 Never give writing advice – it's a hostage to fortune. As Orwell wrote: 'Look back through this essay, and for certain you will find that I have again and again committed the very faults I am protesting against.' (I think 'against which I am protesting' reads better, George.)

Ben Schott is a writer, journalist and photographer, author of *Schott's Original Miscellany* (Bloomsbury Publishing 2002), four subsequent *Miscellanies* and the *Schott's Almanac* series. He writes for *The Times* and is a Contributing Columnist to the *New York Times*. See more at www.benschott.com.

The only book you will ever need

Susan Hill, writer and publisher, extols the virtues of the *Writers' & Artists' Yearbook* and describes how it helped her become a published author.

When I was studying for my A levels, and then working my way through the reading list sent in advance of going to university, I spent a lot of time in the Literature stacks of our public library which provided me with everything I wanted – those were the days. I became quite good friends with the librarian who looked after that section. One day, I summoned up the courage to tell him I was writing a novel and asked how I could find out about publishers. 'The only book you will ever need,' he said, leading me downstairs to the reference section, 'is this.' And he pulled out the latest *Writers' & Artists' Yearbook*.

I have never looked back, as a writer or, much later, when I became a small publisher. It is still extremely useful to me, but then it was the door to a new life, with key attached.

This, the Writers' Bible, will not actually teach you how to write your book, but it will do everything else for you. I get emails almost weekly, asking for advice about how to find an agent, how to submit a book to a publisher and which publisher, how to prepare a manuscript and, more recently, whether or not to self-publish. Every reply contains the best bit of help I can give, which is to buy a copy of the latest edition of the *Writers' & Artists' Yearbook*.

There are two sides to the writing life, and if one – the actual writing – is the most rewarding, the other is the most fun. My mother ran a small clothing factory, at a time when it was unheard heard of for a woman to do such a thing, and from her I inherited my fascination with business and how it works. I love the mechanics of the book trade, the way everything fits together – book manufacturing, publishing, distribution, marketing. I always wanted to learn about how a bookshop or a book chain, a publishing house or an agency, actually works – the logistics, the challenges, the risks and pitfalls. I absorbed so much information from the *Writers' & Artists' Yearbook* over many years, and when I came to start my own small publishing company, Long Barn Books, the latest edition never left my side.

I do not recommend that everyone go as far as I did and actually start a publishing house, but if you are a published author, or about to be one, I certainly think you should find out as much as you can about how it all works. Gaining an insight into what other people do to your book will help you to see things from other points of view. If you know how hard it is to make a profit from publishing and why, if you understand what a literary agent does for the money they take from you, if you discover how difficult life is for small bookshops now, you will have acquired valuable knowledge and some ammunition if you need it.

Agents frequently complain that they receive far too many manuscripts which are unsuitable for them. Why? Because people have not troubled to study exactly which agent represents their sort of book – information they can find readily in this *Yearbook*. The same goes for publishers. If they state clearly 'no unsolicited manuscripts' or 'submissions only through an established agent', then that is what they mean, so why waste your time and irritate them by submitting your book independently?

The majority of published writers do not earn a large amount. I certainly didn't for many years. I couldn't afford accountants and legal advisers, but from this *Yearbook*

I learned about tax, allowable expenses, and also copyright and libel. When you have a small income you need to manage it carefully and the cost of an annual copy of this *Yearbook* (an allowable expense) is money well spent.

Money, money, money. Grants. Prizes. Sitting on your own with just the words for company is the writer's way of life. You have to love it. I love it. But can we please get away from the airy-fairy notion of the writer being above the business side? There is less of it about, but it still exists, and that attitude won't help you stick to a budget or deal with HMRC or ask your agent why your latest statement seems to be alarmingly incorrect. (They never are – it is probably your own optimistic calculations that are wrong.)

Writing has not changed for me. I still love what I do; I still feel the butterflies of excitement when I start a new book. Writing the first line and being happy with it and able to go on from there, is the best feeling in the world – only rivalled by the very first time you see your work in a printed volume, bound and jacketed and in a bookshop. That thrill lessens a bit after some years and a few dozen books, but the excitement of writing 'Chapter One. Page One', never ever does. Writing is my thing. People ask me how they should learn to write and I have only one answer: 'Read, read, read – read those writers who are better than you or I will ever be,' and read attentively. Watch what they do. Every book will teach you something new and different. It will also enrich you, divert, entertain and delight you. Be careful not to copy other writers, even by accident – just read and learn. Your raw material will be uniquely yours, but the greatest writers of every genre and time will teach you what to do with it.

For everything else, as my librarian showed me over 50 years ago, you just need the *Yearbook* you have in your hand.

Susan Hill is the author of more than 56 books, which include literary and detective novels, collections of short stories and ghost stories, non-fiction and children's fiction. She has won the Whitbread (now Costa), Somerset Maugham and John Llewelyn Rhys awards, amongst others, and has been shortlisted for the Man Booker Prize. Her ghost story, *The Woman in Black*, published in 1983, is in its twenty-sixth year as an adaptation in London's West End and now is also a film. She is a respected reviewer, critic, broadcaster and editor, and in 1997 she set up her own publishing company, Long Barn Books. Her website is www.susanhill.org.uk.

See also

- *How to get published*, page 101
- *The publishing process*, page 109

Notes on becoming a novelist

William Boyd reveals how his first novel came to be published.

In the early 1970s when I was at university I started to fantasise about becoming a novelist. The trouble was that I literally hadn't a clue about how to set about realising my vague but heartfelt dream. It's hard to imagine today – in this internet age, with hundreds of creative writing courses on offer, writers' blogs and literary festivals and all the rest – how arcane and remote the business of becoming a novelist appeared to be at that time. It seemed like trying to join some incredibly exclusive club. I didn't know anyone who was a writer or who was connected in any way to the publishing industry; I had no idea how to submit a book to a publishing company or even what job a 'literary agent' did.

However, I bought myself a typewriter and started to write. I wrote a novel and then another; I wrote student journalism, prose sketches and bad poems and even entered a play for a one-act play competition at my local theatre. In my random way I was actually doing the right thing, I now realise. I was writing as hard as I could, fulfilling my apprenticeship, making mistakes and learning from them.

Then in 1976 I moved to Oxford to do a PhD and for the first time met 'real' writers. Talking to them made the road to publication seem a little less obscure, a little less hit or miss. It struck me, then – and this also shows how times have changed – that my best chance of being published was through writing short stories and so I duly started to write short stories and send them off. I submitted stories to any magazine that published them – and there were quite a few in those days – literary magazines, women's magazines, the BBC's 'Morning Story' slot. I had my share of rejections but slowly but surely, over the next couple of years, I began to have stories published and broadcast. My stories appeared in *London Magazine*, *Company*, *Punch*, *Good Housekeeping*, *Mayfair* and the *Literary Review* amongst others. When I had had about nine stories published I thought – hang on, there's almost a short story collection here, and I decided to submit my stories to a publisher. In fact I sent my collected stories off to two publishers, simultaneously. I recommend this ploy – it saves a lot of time – and in the unlikely event they both reply positively it becomes what's known in Hollywood as a 'high-class problem' – the kind of problem no one complains about.

The publishers I chose were Jonathan Cape and Hamish Hamilton. Both of them were highly regarded and were also regular publishers of short story collections (again, how times have changed). As a last-minute afterthought I added a PS to my letters of submission relating the fact that I had written a novel featuring a character – an overweight, drunken, young diplomat called Morgan Leafy – that appeared in two of the short stories.

A few weeks later the magic letter arrived from Hamish Hamilton, from the managing director himself, Christopher Sinclair-Stevenson. He said he would like to publish my story collection. Even better, he said he'd also like to publish the novel I had written – but, crucially, he wanted to publish the novel first. Slight problem – slight high-class problem – I hadn't written the novel… So I told a white lie – I had to retype the manuscript in its entirety, I said – and in a torrid heat of creative dynamism wrote my novel *A Good Man in Africa* in about ten weeks and sent it off. And the rest, so to speak, is history. In 1981 my novel was published and, six months later, so was my short story collection. I didn't have an agent, I didn't know anyone influential, I had no introduction to an editor or publisher – I did it entirely on my own. And I'm still waiting for a reply from Jonathan Cape.

William Boyd CBE is the author of novels including *A Good Man in Africa* (1981), winner of the Whitbread Literary Award and the Somerset Maugham Award; *An Ice Cream War* (1982), winner of the John Llewellyn Rhys Prize and shortlisted for the Booker Prize; *Any Human Heart* (2002); *Restless* (2006), winner of the Costa Novel Award, the Yorkshire Post Novel of the Year and a Richard & Judy selection; *Ordinary Thunderstorms* (2009); and *Waiting for Sunrise* (Bloomsbury 2012). His James Bond novel, *Solo*, was published in 2013 by Jonathan Cape. He is also the author of several collections of short stories, screenplays and non-fiction writing.

Finding my agent

Martina Cole describes how her writing career started.

The *Writers' & Artists' Yearbook* holds a very dear place in my heart. Without it, I would never have been published as quickly, or as well, of that much I am sure.

I had written my first novel, *Dangerous Lady*, when I was 21 and it had been a dream of mine to become an author. I wasn't expecting fortune, or fame; all I had ever wanted was to see my name on the cover of a book. Books are probably the most important things in my life, apart from the family of course! I have loved books since I was a small child, when my father, a merchant seaman, brought home from his travels a cardboard theatre. When I opened the crimson faux velvet curtains, hidden behind them were the smallest books I had ever seen. The stories they contained were all old Aesop fables, and fairy tales, and I was absolutely entranced.

After that, a book was second nature to me. I even played truant from school so I could lie all day long in the park reading books from the local library – books I had taken out in my parents' names as well as my own. Books I would never otherwise have been allowed to read at such a young age. My parents died never knowing they had library memberships!

So, when I wrote *Dangerous Lady* all those years ago, it was the start of my writing career, though I didn't know it at the time.

Over the next nine years I wrote three more novels, film scripts, television scripts, and even a play for the theatre. But I had no confidence in myself as a writer, and I wrote for the sheer pleasure of it. I'm sure many of the people reading this are doing exactly the same thing!

Coming up to 30 was my personal watershed. I was running a nursing agency and had been offered a partnership. I was also moving house, so there were big upheavals all round. I was going to throw out all my writing efforts, and put away the dream of being an author. Then I glanced through *Dangerous Lady* – and I knew instinctively that it was much better than I had ever realised and that I had to at least try and fulfil my ambition, whatever the outcome might be.

I purchased then read the *Writers' & Artists' Yearbook* from cover to cover, and was fascinated by this world I craved but knew absolutely nothing about. It told me the correct way to set out a manuscript, both for a novel and for television, who published what, and more importantly, where I could find them! It was a mine of information, and it gave me the push I needed to pursue my dream.

I found my agent, Darley Anderson, tucked away among the pages, and taking a deep breath I rang him up – I nearly passed out when he answered the phone himself. I explained that I had written a book, what it was about, and he said, 'Send it to me, I'm intrigued'.

I posted it to him on the Thursday night, and he phoned me on the Monday at teatime: Darley's first words were, 'You are going to be a star!' It was the start of a long and happy friendship. It was also the beginning of my career in publishing.

When I am at a writers' conference, or a library event, I always tell the audience they must purchase the *Writers' & Artists' Yearbook*. On signings, if I am approached by someone who is writing a novel and I think they are serious about it, I purchase the book for them, and tell them that if they get published I want the first signed copy!

When I was asked to write this article, I was thrilled because all those years ago when I bought my first copy of the *Yearbook* I never dreamt that one day I would be lucky enough to actually be a small part of it. It's a truly wonderful introduction to the world of literature, and it also contains everything you need to know about writing for television, film *et al.* If it's relevant to what you are writing about, be it a novel or a newspaper article, you can find it in this *Yearbook*.

There's so much of interest, and so much that the budding writer needs explained. By the time I finally had a meeting with Darley in person, the *Writers' & Artists' Yearbook* had helped me understand exactly what I needed to ask about, and more importantly, what to expect from the meeting itself.

I wish you all the very best of luck. Publishing is a great business to be a part of.

I wrote for years in my spare time, for free – I loved it. It was a part of me and who I was. I still love writing, every second of it. I was asked once by a journalist if I ever got lonely – writing is such a solitary occupation, as we all know. But I said no. I spend all day with people that I've created. I put the wallpaper on the walls, and I give them families, lives to live, cars to drive, and in some cases I have even killed them! Not many people can that say about their jobs.

The *Writers' & Artists' Yearbook* is a wonderful tool for any budding writer, so use it and enjoy it. Good luck.

Martina Cole is the bestselling author of 21 highly successful novels. When *The Good Life* went straight to No 1 on the *Sunday Times* hardback fiction bestseller list in 2014, it was Martina's thirteenth original fiction No 1 in a row. *The Take*, which won the British Book Award for Crime Thriller of the Year in 2006, was adapted for Sky One, as was *The Runaway*. Three of her novels have been adapted for the stage: *Two Women*, *The Graft* and *Dangerous Lady* were all highly acclaimed when performed at the Theatre Royal Stratford East. Her books have now sold over 13 million copies. Her new novel *Get Even* was published by Headline in 2015.

See also...

- *How to get an agent*, page 392
- *Getting hooked out of the slush pile*, page 394
- *Letter to an unsolicited author*, page 404
- *How to attract the attention of a literary agent*, page 407

Becoming a comic writer

Marina Lewycka describes how she became a comic writer and makes suggestions on looking at life from a comic writer's point of view. She also offers insights on why the same piece of comic writing can make some people laugh aloud but leave others totally baffled.

When I wrote *A Short History of Tractors in Ukrainian*, I certainly did not think I was embarking on a book in the comic genre; my intention was to write something deep and meaningful about the human condition. My two previous unpublished novels had been rather serious and angst-ridden works. I had wanted to write Literature with a capital L, but alas no one, it seemed, wanted to read my efforts. By the time I was in my late fifties I had more or less given up on the possibility of getting published, but some strange compulsion kept me writing, and I found myself chuckling quite a bit as I wrote. Freed from the obligation to write Literature, my style had lightened up, and so had my view of the human condition.

Getting published was a pleasant surprise, but I was a bit bemused to find myself in 2006 winning the Bollinger Everyman Wodehouse Prize (the UK's only literary award for comic fiction; see page 537). So that's where I've been going wrong, I thought. I must be a comic writer, not a writer of Literature. It was lovely to receive letters from readers who said they had laughed out loud while reading my book. But other readers wrote to me saying they did not know why the book had been described as comic, because they found it profoundly sad. And they had a point. The comic and the tragic are closer than we think. It's the human condition.

With that prize, the die was cast, and keen to experiment with my new craft, I set about writing another comic novel, *Two Caravans*. I was even more bemused to find myself being shortlisted for a prize for political writing.

I soon found that when it comes to comic writing, you can't please everyone. Not long after my third novel *We Are All Made of Glue* was published, I received a letter from a reader in Australia.

'Dear Ms Lewycka, I very much enjoy reading your books, but I am shocked that your spelling is so bad. Don't your publishers employ an editor? In *We Are All Made of Glue* there were two big spelling mistakes on page 14. Because of this, I do not feel able to recommend your books to my friends.'

Needless to say, I immediately turned to page 14 and read:

'My mother had always been a great advocate of past-sell-by-date shopping… She didn't think much of Listernia and Saminella…'

The offending words, for my correspondent, were Listernia and Saminella, which were the character's mangled pronunciation of Listeria and Salmonella. But the reader just didn't get it. In the novel, the narrator's mother uses long words she can't pronounce because she has pretensions to education and culture, and so does my snooty Australian correspondent. How could she be so stupid, I exclaimed under my breath? I wanted to pen a reply pointing out the brilliance of my joke, but alas there was no return address.

That's one of the dangers with comedy – it doesn't travel well. This joke had obviously not made it to this reader in Australia, despite the fact that English and Australian are almost the same language.

Comedy also travels badly in time. The scenes in Shakespeare that had the 16th-century groundlings rolling with laughter, mostly leave modern audiences cold. A good director can still get across the meaning, but the essential quality of comedy is lost when you have to explain it. We may just raise a faint smile, as if to say, 'Oh, I see what you mean.'

And humour even travels badly between generations. The things my parents thought were hilarious seem to me just faintly silly. The jokes that have me and my friends laughing out loud make my daughter and her friends snigger with embarrassment. The things they laugh at, I don't even understand, because they usually refer to music or films or people that I have no knowledge of.

When *Various Pets Alive and Dead* was published, the very same jokes which delighted some reviewers made others groan. For every reviewer who admired a burlesque scene, there was one who derided it as slapstick.

English language and culture are rich in humour: irony, satire, farce, wordplay, wit, silliness, absurdity, teasing. It comes in many forms, and the first rule is that there is no rule to judge whether something is intrinsically funny or not; it all rests on the judgement of the individual. What we find funny is essentially subjective. A good rule of thumb is that if you're chuckling to yourself as you write, the chances are that at least some other people will laugh when they read what you've written. But you can be certain that for every person laughing there will be someone else rolling their eyes and tutting.

Getting the most from rules

Comedy depends on recognition that certain rules commonly accepted by a social group are being broken. Its audience knows those rules, and the humour draws a warm circle of shared understanding around the insiders, 'people like us' who 'get' the joke, and excludes those who are baffled by it. What and who we laugh at defines us just as surely as the clothes we wear or the music we listen to or the books on our shelves.

Language is of course a set of rules, and breaking the rules of language is a rich source of humour. But you have to know the accepted expression to be amused by the mistakes people make. My books, like my life, are peopled by characters of many nationalities. When I was as a child, I learnt 'correct' English at school, while my home was always full of people who got along perfectly well with their own version of it. Later, a spell as a teacher of English to speakers of other languages left me with a lifelong fascination with the way that foreign people talk.

There are as many varieties of 'bad English' as there are languages, and the mistakes a non-native speaker makes often mirror the grammar of their own language. A Slavic native speaker leaves out definite and indefinite articles, whereas a German inserts them even where they don't belong in English, for example in front of abstract nouns. Speakers of Arabic often don't distinguish between 'p' and 'b'. People who speak gendered languages tend to ascribe gender to everything. When I gave Dog a voice in *Two Caravans*, I had to create a new language for him. I studied dogs and I talked to their owners. I learnt that their sense of smell is predominant. They keep tracking and back-tracking over the same ground, in a purposeful, not a random way. But they have no nose at all for punctuation. Even bad English must have its own internal logic. That poses a particular challenge for translators.

In Ukraine my humorous descriptions of Ukrainians have caused controversy because soon after the book was first published it was translated into Russian, not into Ukrainian, and the Russian translators translated all the 'bad English' as Ukrainian. Nor were my Ukrainian characters popular, for despite the great tradition of Ukrainian humour, including Gogol and Bulgakov, modern Ukrainians have only recently achieved independent nationhood, and they want to be taken seriously on the world stage.

Comic writers inevitably offend somebody; it's a risk you have to take, and most writers set their own limits. Just because you can upset someone doesn't mean you have to go out of your way to do so. I draw the line at humour that targets the vulnerable and weak, or diminishes someone's self-esteem. But I prefer humour that also expresses affection, and, like teasing, can offer us the gift of self-knowledge. We can transcend our foibles when we learn to laugh at them. This is one thing I particularly admire and love about the English sense of humour; the English do make fun of others, but they are supremely good at laughing at themselves.

Thinking about writing comedy

Although there is no formula to writing comedy, there has been an enormous amount of academic theory on the subject. From Aristotle through to Lacan and Umberto Eco, thinkers have provided many fascinating insights, but believe me, it's not a bundle of laughs. Umberto Eco is among the most accessible, as witty and stylish in his academic writing as he is in fiction. However, the more one tries to analyse or explain comedy, the more elusive it becomes. In fact when a joke or a comic scene has to be explained, it loses its power to make us laugh. Comedy has to grab you by surprise. It's one of those quirks of the human condition, like the fact that you can't tickle yourself.

If you want to write comedy, the most useful approach is probably to expose yourself to the comic side of life:

- Cultivate eccentric friends and relatives – seek them out, observe their ways, treat them nicely, and let them inhabit your books.
- Be curious – some might say nosy. Ask the slightly impertinent question, peep through the open door, read over the passenger's shoulder, listen in on the hushed conversation. Comedy is often found hidden away among secrets.
- Break rules – talk to strangers, shamelessly explore your host's house, get into arguments. A comic situation often starts out seeming perfectly normal, then incrementally becomes more and more absurd as boundaries are transgressed.
- Keep a notebook – however memorable a joke or an anecdote seems at the time, you will not be able to recall it in an hour's time.
- When things are getting hectic, imagine pushing them one stage further. Ask yourself – what if…?
- Or you can short-cut all these by immersing yourself in the zany world of wonderful comic writers, from Chaucer to Dickens to P.G. Wodehouse to Howard Jacobson. It's hard to imagine a more enjoyable 'homework'.

Comedy, like all drama, originates from a combination of people and circumstances. The same sorts of people often seem to find themselves drawn to tragic or comic situations. You probably have plenty among your acquaintances, and whether their story is comic or tragic depends on how it ends. I am particularly fond of:

- People in the grip of an obsession, like Mrs Bennet in *Pride and Prejudice*
- People who take themselves too seriously, like Adrian Mole or the characters created by Ricky Gervais

• People who are perpetual victims or losers, like Eeyore
• People who live in a world of their own imagining like Don Quixote
• People driven beyond the bounds of reasonable behaviour by an overriding need or desire, like Valentina in *A Short History of Tractors in Ukrainian.*

Now try placing one of these types of characters in a volatile situation, where some social norms are in danger of being transgressed. Maybe they misunderstand who someone is, or what someone has said, or they have misread the situation. Maybe there are too many people, or a dangerous combination of people together at the same time. Maybe money, honour or love are at stake. You can be sure that something will go terribly wrong. But instead of crying, we will laugh. It's the human condition.

Marina Lewycka was born in a refugee camp in Germany in 1946 and moved to England with her family when she was about a year old. She has been writing for most of her life, and in 2005 published *A Short History of Tractors in Ukrainian* which has sold more than a million copies in the UK alone. This was followed by *Two Caravans* in 2007, *We Are All Made of Glue* in 2009 and *Various Pets Alive and Dead* in 2012 – all published by Penguin.

Notes from a successful crime author

Mark Billingham shares his experiences of writing success.

I am a writer because I'm a reader. That I'm a *crime* writer, however, is probably down to a desire to get free books. I'd always written stuff of one sort or another: silly stories at school, terrible poetry at university, so-so plays for community theatre companies. I'd drifted into a career in stand-up and writing comedy for television but my passion as a reader was for crime fiction, primarily of the darker and more disturbing kind.

Devouring the work of my favourite writers from both sides of the Atlantic fired my imagination and fed my head and heart, but as I had also developed an obsession for collecting the first editions of these authors, it was doing very little for my bank balance. My wife made the choice quite a simple one: get the books for free or get a divorce.

I'm still amazed at how easy it was – how little time and effort was involved. A couple of phone calls to the publicity departments of several big publishers, a bit of blather about how I was reviewing for my local paper, and suddenly the books came tumbling through the letterbox: package after package carried manfully to the door by my less-than-delighted postman. I did indeed start to review for my local paper and soon I was writing longer pieces, then articles for national magazines, and it wasn't very long before I was asked if I'd like to interview a couple of crime writers – this was major!

I can vividly remember the enormous and terrifying thrill of interviewing such crime-writing giants as Michael Connelly and Ian Rankin, and I still get a secret buzz from the fact that I can now count them among my friends. (This, for me, remains one of the greatest pleasures in becoming a published writer; that if you're lucky, those whose work you've admired for many years can end up propping up bars with you in exotic countries at ungodly hours.) So, I was a reader who adored crime fiction, who was lucky enough to be writing *about* it and who, occasionally, talked to those who actually *wrote* it.

Writing it myself, however, at the time seemed completely out of the question. Talking now to unpublished writers, I discover that such terror at the thought of sitting down and writing a novel is hugely common. Some of them are like housebricks for heaven's sake! Now, I tell those as daunted as I was then, that if you write 1,000 words a day for a month, you're more or less a third of the way through a novel. It all sounds terribly straightforward of course, but it certainly didn't feel like that as I began trying to write my own crime novel.

One of the most common pieces of advice given to aspiring writers is to read, and it was at the point of starting what would become my first book, that I saw just how important this was. I was writing in an already overcrowded genre, and having read a great deal within it (or should that be *around* it?) I had a pretty good idea what not to write – that is, I knew those areas to which claims had already been successfully staked by others. Having decided therefore that my detective would not be a deerstalker-wearing cocaine fiend, or an Edinburgh-based Rolling Stones fan, I tried quite simply to write the sort of crime novel I enjoyed reading. I always imagine that such a stunningly basic notion would be obvious to all those who want to write. However, I'm constantly amazed to meet those claiming to have studied the industry carefully and to have spotted a sizeable gap on the bookshelves. Those who announce confidently that the world is finally ready for the crime-fighting antique-dealer/amateur veterinarian who, while not cooking and listening to opera, cracks tough cases with the help of a cat, in the mid-18th century Somerset countryside. If this is really what you're driven to write, then all power to you, but if you simply try and fill what you perceive to be a gap in the market, you're on a hiding to nothing.

I fully believed myself to be on a hiding to somewhat less than this, when I picked half a dozen agents from the *Writers' & Artists' Yearbook* and sent off the first 30,000 words of my novel. From this point on in the career path of almost any published writer, luck will play a part, and I must confess that I had more than my fair share of the very good sort.

Being taken on by an agent is wonderful, and if you're very fortunate, you will be taken on by a good one. Getting published is one thing but it helps if that publisher has enough faith in the book to spend a decent amount on marketing it – an amount so much more important than your advance. My still incomplete manuscript landed on all the right desks, and it was while in the incredible position of having to choose between agents, that I received the single best piece of advice I was given, or am able to pass on. Don't imagine that things are going well. Imagine that they are going badly. Imagine that *nobody* wants to publish your book, that the rejection letters come back in such numbers that the Royal Mail lays on special deliveries. When that happens, who will be the agent who will give you up as a bad lot, and who will be the one willing to fight? Which one will say 'well, if *they* don't want it I'm going to try X'? This is the agent to choose. In the course of any writer's life, a good agent, not to mention a good editor, will probably need to show more than once that they aren't afraid of a good scrap.

As far as further advice goes – beyond the encouragement to read and to write something every day – it is important to remember that lies (white or whoppers) and luck (of both kinds) may play a disproportionately large part in the way things turn out. Oh, and if you could avoid writing crime novels about a north London copper with a weakness for Tottenham Hotspur and Hank Williams, I'd be very grateful.

However, one small drawback to getting published and finding yourself trying to produce a book a year, is that you suddenly have far less time to read. This is hugely upsetting, and in my case doubly ironic considering that, with requests for reviews and endorsements, I now get more free books than ever. In fact, the only person unhappy about the way things turned out is my postman.

Mark Billingham is the author of an award-winning series of novels featuring London-based Detective Inspector Tom Thorne, the latest of which is *The Bones Beneath* (Little, Brown 2014). He has also worked for many years as a stand-up comedian but now prefers to concentrate on crime writing, as those who read the books are not usually drunk and can't throw things at him.

Writing bestselling women's fiction

Penny Vincenzi offers some insight on how she writes her bestselling novels. She highlights the value of writers really knowing the characters they create.

Well, that's a tough one! How to write bestselling women's fiction… Writing: yes, I can tell you about that. Writing women's fiction: yes, I can do that too. But bestselling women's fiction – that's a tough one. You need a bit of magic, a lot of luck, and an ability to believe in yourself – and a refusal to give up. I'll do my best to tell you what I know. Let's start with the writing.

First of all, you know if you're a writer because you'll be doing it already. I believe writers are born not made. You won't suddenly think, 'I don't like nursing, I wonder if I might be a writer instead.' (Although you can certainly do both, and lots of very successful writers have started out as nurses, doctors or vets; the medical profession is rich in plots…) You don't have to think about whether you want to write; you just know.

I started writing stories when I was eight, in the form of fake Enid Blytons, usually about a page long. My stories were hardly works of literature, but they were what I did when other children were sticking stamps in albums or building Meccano models, or playing with dolls. And I really couldn't stop: I was enthralled, happy, utterly satisfied. Two years later I typed my stories on my mother's typewriter with lots of carbon copies, stapled them into a magazine called *Stories* and handed them out in the school playground. (There were few takers.)

Later on, I wrote for the parish magazine and the school magazine (I was the editor), and then moved on to getting paid for writing captions to photographs in *Tatler* magazine where I worked as secretary to the editor. It was humble stuff: 'Lord and Lady Smith enjoying a joke on the stairs' sort of thing. But I knew that when I was writing, I was happy; I felt I was in the right place at the right time. Look out for that feeling; it's all-important.

Writing and inspiration

The next thing you should know is that writing is hard work. A lot of it is sheer hard grind. There is a tendency to romanticise it, but it is not romantic at all. I don't believe in inspiration – unless inspiration is what you call one of those bolt from the blue ideas that gets your spine tingling as it hits you and you recognise it as something that could form a rattling good plot, or really great chapter, or even one wonderful scene. But you are just as likely to get one of those ideas when you're stuck in a traffic jam or leafing through a magazine at the dentist's, or listening to someone chatting on the number 22 bus, as when (as many people seem assume) gazing misty eyed at some beautiful scenery or listening to a glorious piece of music (although don't knock it if it does come then).

You should write because you want to, and more than that even, because you have to. Having got the idea, you then have to start working on it; your book won't get written without you; the words won't drift into your head, page after wonderful page, without effort.

But I'm running away with myself; and also making out writing to be rather joyless when actually it's one of the most joyful, rewarding, exciting things you can possibly do. When I've had a good day at the plot-face, as I call it, I could fly; I feel literally and perfectly happy.

You need to practise writing; it's a bit like playing the piano, and writing a little every day is better than producing a chunk once a month. Reading is essential too; the more you read, carefully and attentively, paying proper attention to how the author tells the story, weaves the plot, creates the characters, the more you will learn. Read as much and as widely as you can – biographies, thrillers, memoirs and classics, as well as modern fiction.

Squeeze out the time somehow so you can write, however busy you are; getting up an hour earlier never hurt anyone. And don't think you need to have some complex program for your computer – or indeed a computer at all, although it helps. An exercise book and a ballpoint pen will suffice. 'Just do it…' as the song says.

Writing women's fiction

Because I write women's fiction, I feel qualified to tell you about it. I could never write a detective story because I'd be rubbish at the plotting side of it, or a learned literary work because I'm neither learned nor literary; and I couldn't write a self-help book because that sort of thing just doesn't interest me (although I do know they have huge value).

My fiction career began because I wanted to tell stories and I had a cracking idea. I suddenly felt there might be more to life than writing articles about beauty, or even doing interviews with celebrities and then writing about them, which at the time I loved. That writing experience taught me a lot about things like construction and creating a mood and a sense of place, all vital ingredients to successful fiction writing.

So, having cracking ideas is essential. All my books are what one of my editors called 'what-ifs' – each has a strong idea that grabs the reader when she first picks up the book and makes her want to explore it. For instance, a book about a village and the people who live in it sounds charming. But if the village in that book was threatened by a developer moving in and potentially wrecking its most precious beauty spot, describing who opposes him and how, and the relationships formed and/or threatened by him, plus the secrets that get unearthed in the process of the opposition – then you have a plot.

Thus, in *Dilemma* the 'what-if' is: 'What if your husband asked you to perjure yourself to keep him out of jail?', and in *Windfall*, 'what if you inherited an enormous sum of money, how would it affect you, your marriage and your relationships?', and in *The Decision*, 'what if you and your husband were battling over custody of your only child?' People can put themselves into these situations, and wonder: what would I do, how would I behave? And so on.

The greatest and most important rule about writing is an old one: write what you know. If you don't know about something – say, banking or the art world – but feel the subject suits your story, do a lot of research on it. Ignorance of a subject shows horribly in half a page. On the other hand, just because you've done the research it doesn't mean you have to use every syllable of it – that would be boring. Readers get very involved in the world you create; they like to find themselves in a new place – whether it's the world of modelling, law or journalism, they like to be told about something new. A sense of place is important too, from windswept beaches to plush restaurants and from Paris to Peru. If you bring those places alive, your readers will follow you to and through them. It all helps to bring everything in the book to life.

Know your characters

The most important thing about writing fiction for women is the characters you create. They need to leap off the page. For male fiction, in my view, it's less vital as the plot will do a lot more. I think that women need to bond, to become totally involved with their heroines, and to feel she is, for the duration of the book, part of their own lives. Again and again, when I give talks about writing, that's what people say: 'I loved Lady Celia' (in the *Lytton* trilogy), 'I can't get over what happened to Barty' (also in the *Lytton* trilogy and a great favourite of readers), and 'I got so worried about Jocasta [in *Sheer Abandon*] I couldn't sleep'.

And indeed if you start discussing women's favourite fiction, it's the characters people talk about – Jane (in *Jane Eyre*), Cathy (in *Wuthering Heights*), Scarlett (in *Gone with the Wind*) and Lizzie (in *Pride and Prejudice*) as much, if not more, than the book as a whole. A great heroine will, as you write, take over the book and the plot.

I never know what is going to happen in my books. Many writers work in this way, being taken by surprise at what their characters do and actually refusing to do what the writer tells them. The only book I ever planned carefully was my first, *Old Sins*, where I had wanted my heroine to marry her stepson. It was a nice neat plot: her first husband, who was about 25 years older than she was, had died, and I thought and indeed wrote in the synopsis that she would fall in love with his son. But she didn't and moreover, as I continued writing she just wouldn't. Every time I wrote the scene that brings them together, it was awkward and embarrassing. I panicked; what was I going to do with her? Why wasn't my neat plot working out? And then it hit me: she liked older men; of course she did, there was no way she would fall in love with a beautiful boy. So I listened to her for a bit and then abandoned the enforced marriage and allowed to her to choose someone else much more suitable.

It was a huge and truly valuable lesson. I've followed and listened to my characters ever since and I'd advise you to do the same. You need to know them really well – not just what they look like, but their likes and dislikes, what they are afraid of, what makes them happy, what makes them miserable, what they're afraid of. It doesn't all need to be spelt out though. Knowing your characters well makes them leap off the page, and makes your fiction sing and speak to people. It's a wonderful feeling when you create interesting, strong characters and just let them go and you follow them.

Becoming a bestseller

I was lucky; my first book was indeed successful. And I know I had a lot of luck to make it so. I also had some hard-headed practical advice given to me. I knew I needed to have an agent – don't even think about trying to sell your book to a publisher direct. It's difficult to find a good agent who is willing take you on. Agents won't take on an author unless they think they can sell their work. They know all the editors, and which of them will suit your work. Look in this *Yearbook* to find out which agents specialise in what areas. If you're lucky enough to find an agent, listen very attentively to what he or she advises. If they say your typescript is too long, or the language is too flowery, or your grammar isn't too great, or the plot is too convoluted, do what you're told and remember that you're lucky to have an expert working on your book with you.

I was truly lucky to have had a wonderful agent and an amazing editor first off and I never cease to be thankful for both of them. My story would have been very different, and less happy without them.

A good, memorable title is crucial, as is a striking cover. Publishers know a great deal about both and how to make a book stand out from the enormous number of books published every year. So if – and that's a big 'if' – your book is sold to a publisher, you still need a lot of what I call magic.

You need an idea that will catch people's fancy and ensnare their imaginations, a cover that catches the eye on the bookstalls, and a title that promises a heady dash of intrigue in the relationships you've created. It's almost impossible to define but if you can also deliver a considerable element of charm in your characters, that will make people talk about them. If your book provides a positive experience, your readers will want more of it and will also enjoy your other books.

I hope you enjoy your writing and I wish you good luck with it. I think writing is the best fun and if you can promise people fun too, then you could, very possibly, hit the jackpot. Be brave and go for it: believe in yourself and don't be talked out of writing the book you want to write!

Penny Vincenzi published her first novel, *Old Sins*, in 1989 and has since written 15 bestselling novels, including *The Decision* and the number one bestsellers *The Best of Times* and *An Absolute Scandal*. Her most recent book is *Love in the Afternoon and Other Delights* (Headline 2013).

Notes from a successful romantic novelist

Katie Fforde describes how she became published and why she likes writing romantic fiction.

If you want to get a group of writers into a panic, put them on a panel and then ask them, one at a time, what their working practice is. The first one answers confidently enough – after all they probably have several books on the shelves by this time. But the others listen in consternation, convinced that what they do is wrong and they are not proper writers even though the world is reading their books.

This is because there are as many writing methods as there are writers, and it's important to work out what kind of writer you are.

If you are reading this there is a chance that you are a writer; but in case you're not sure, do check. It's hard enough to write if you like doing it, but if you think you might prefer painting water colours or needlepoint, please try those first. At least you might get an acceptable still life or cushion relatively quickly. It takes a long time to write a novel.

I discovered I wanted to write – almost more than anything else in the world – as soon as I started. My mother had given me a writing kit for Christmas. This consisted of paper, pens, a dictionary, a thesaurus and yes, a copy of the *Writers' & Artists' Yearbook*, as well as Tipp-Ex and a nice box to keep it all in.

Having made a New Year's Resolution that I would start writing that year, I started in January. I cleaned the house, made sure my children were out of the way and put the first sheet of paper into my typewriter. When I'd got over my nerves – which I dealt with by starting to rewrite someone else's book – and began a story I'd had in my head for years, I realised what had been missing in my life for so long. I had a lovely family, a lovely house and a lovely dog, and yet I wasn't content. What had been missing was a creative outlet.

One of the joys of starting to write is that no one needs to know you are doing it until you choose to tell them. Most other things people do require a bit of going out in public. While it would be a bit difficult to hide it from the people you live with, the rest of the world doesn't need to know. In fact, I suggest you don't tell anyone unless you're sure they will understand. There is nothing more irritating than being asked 'how the book is going' by people who assume you just need to write one to become a millionaire.

There are annoying examples of people who got their first novel published and became an instant bestseller – some of those authors are even my friends – but I prefer to think it's better to be a tortoise than a hare. If you get there the long slow way at least you know what you've done and can do it again. That said, I have a Pollyanna side to my nature and will always see the advantages to any of life's setbacks if I possibly can. It took me eight years before I found a publisher and ten years – from starting – before I had a book on the shelves.

Now that you're feeling a bit more positive about it, knowing how long it took me to achieve publication, I'll go on with my tips.

My top tip, which I'm assuming you do already, is to read a lot. I believe if you never ever went to any sort of writing course or never read a 'how to' book on writing, you would still be able to write to a publishable standard just by reading enough novels. It would take you longer, probably, because you could set yourself an impossibly high standard and consequently never become Henry James. But once you've decided what sort of book you want to write, which I hope would be the sort of book you want to read, read as many of the genre as you can fit into your busy life.

My second tip – which I sometimes describe as the gift I'd give to baby writers if I was a fairy godmother – is perseverance. This pig-headedness (a less polite but more accurate word) got me through receiving all those rejections. Every time I was rejected I became more determined that one day I would have a book published. But you do have to be very determined. I'd quite like to be a size ten, too, but I'm never going to be one because I don't want it quite enough.

My third tip, which I'll say more about later, is to emulate Nelson's favourite captains and be lucky.

So why did it take me so long? I think it does take quite a long time to learn to write – for most of us anyway – but also I was aiming at a market that wasn't quite suitable for me. I was trying to write for Mills & Boon. Like many people, I read these by the shelf-load and assumed, in my complete ignorance, that because they were easy to read they were easy to write. Not so! But I am eternally grateful to the literary agents that sent me some very encouraging rejection letters, and trying to fit my story into 50,000 words forced me to keep to the point. There is no room in those books for characters who have no function, for any little scene that doesn't further the plot or for a hero who isn't extremely attractive.

How did I finally get a book deal? This is where the luck comes in. I had been a member of the Romantic Novelists' Association for some years (I am now its President) and through its New Writers' scheme (which alas is now hugely oversubscribed) my writing came to the attention of an agent, who was new to the business and so had time to look for new writers and to work with them. This agent told me she couldn't do anything with the books I had been writing but that she liked my style and together we discussed what my next novel should be like. She asked for 100 pages before the end of the year. I felt I couldn't write what amounted to half a Mills & Boon novel and not check I was on the right track so I sent her the first chapter. She liked it and I got into the habit of sending her chunks which she would read and comment on, sometimes asking for changes, at other times saying, crack on with it. This wonderful woman had sold the novel before I'd finished it.

But then came the hard work. There is no tougher writing course than your first professional edit, and although it was hard – no actual blood but certainly sweat and tears – I pity writers who don't have this experience. My lovely story had too little plot and putting one in after it had been written was akin to putting in the foundations to a house after it is built. It is possible with the help of Acrow props and rigid steel joists, but it is not the way round to do it. Books need plots in the same way that bodies need skeletons and it's better to work out what yours is before starting.

My second huge stroke of luck after finding a wonderful agent was to be picked for the WHSmith Fresh Talent promotion. This meant cardboard cutouts of me and the other authors were in the window of every WHSmith shop in the country and our books were reviewed by almost every newspaper. This massive exposure was a terrific start to any writing career.

So what keeps me going nowadays, 20 or so books on? One thing is that I keep having ideas which I want to write and I think this is something that develops along with other neural pathways that you forge. My antennae are constantly twitching when I watch television, go to a party or sit on a train. I am fascinated by relationships and want to explore new ones, and I also like falling in love. If you write romantic fiction you have to fall in love with your hero or you can't expect your readers to. Falling in love with your hero is the affair you're allowed to have and it is a lot less complicated to arrange.

Why do people buy my books? It's hard to say but I'm very glad that they do. I think it's because readers can recognise themselves in my characters and this is the same whatever age you are – I have readers of all ages, from school age girls to elderly women. I and three other authors were asked this question at a literature festival recently and we none of us really knew. The general consensus was, life is tough for a lot of people and everyone needs a bit of escape. Some people like a nice gritty crime novel or an edge-of-the-seat thriller, but some like a story where you know the baby – and probably even the dog – is not going to die. You know you're guaranteed a few hours off from your own life in a safe place.

This is why I like writing romantic fiction. I enjoy spending time with people I like, to whom nice things happen. I like being able to choose the wallpaper and have the garden I could never have. I also like deciding it's time we had a good summer, and write about one.

And the very best thing about being a writer is meeting people who have enjoyed your books, read them to cheer themselves up when they were ill (although I do take it amiss when it's implied that you have to be ill to read my books) or going through some sort of hard time. That is the very best reward.

So, if you feel fit for the fight (as Bonnie Tyler might have said) gather your tools and do your research. First of all, decide what you like to read. Don't try and write anything just because it's the current favourite unless you love it. You probably won't succeed if your heart isn't in it; if you do you'll be stuck writing chaste romance novels when you yearn to write raunchy thrillers, and the market will have changed by the time it hits the shelves anyway.

And please do your research before you even think of submitting anything. It may seem blindingly obvious, but the number of people who send their work to any agent in this *Yearbook* without checking that they even handle fiction is enormous.

Be brave and get someone else to read at least part of your book before you submit it. It does have to be someone you can trust to be brutally frank, who will tell you if they don't know who any of the characters are, and if they couldn't care less. It's better to find out things like this before you let the professionals near it.

Make sure you present your script exactly as it's requested. Don't email books to agents who only want hard copy. Make sure the copy is clean and easy to read. Write a covering letter that will encourage the agent to look at the book and if a synopsis is asked for, write one. (Some people find it easier to write after the book is finished.)

If you are lucky enough to receive comments from an agent, take them to heart unless you know them to be wrong. If they say your characters come across as older than they are supposed to be, watch a bit of 'yoof' television and learn some modern slang. If they say no one wants to read about undertakers, consider carefully if this is true. It's possible you've written the one that people would enjoy.

If you're brave enough to join a writers' group, make sure it's not a mutual appreciation society. It's more productive to be told your dialogue is poor than for people to wonder why on earth no one has yet snapped up your masterpiece.

Be in it for the long haul. If (or when) you're rejected, allow yourself a certain amount of time to gnash your teeth and eat chocolate and then get back to it. If you want it enough you will get there and there's no time to waste feeling sorry for yourself. Writing mustn't seem like a hobby, it must be your passion. Eventually it might also become your profession.

Katie Fforde is a *Sunday Times* No 1 bestselling author. Her first book was *Living Dangerously* (1995) and she has written 20 more novels since. Her most recent books are *A French Affair* (2013), *The Perfect Match* (2014) and *A Vintage Wedding* (2015), all published by Century. She has published three short story collections, *From Scotland with Love*, *Staying Away at Christmas* and *A Christmas Feast*. Her hobbies, when she has time for them, are singing in a choir and flamenco dancing. Her website is www.katiefforde.com.

Notes from a successful writer of erotic fiction

As writers, our desire is always to touch our readers, but as erotica writers, our aim is to go further than most and bring actual, physical pleasure. This is a challenge and also a privilege, but it's also a lot of fun, says the anonymous writer of this article.

Why erotica and why now?

Erotic fiction can be defined as sexually arousing stories that still aspire to be beautiful or literary in some fashion, exalting the carnal act beyond the merely physical. In many ways, it also honours the erotic, empowering the sexual as opposed to degrading it as much of pornography is considered to – although of course, the edges between the two are blurred.

Erotica isn't a new genre, and many of us include Anaïs Nin's *Delta of Venus* or Nancy Friday's *My Secret Garden* as formative works. But in recent years, women's sexuality has been increasingly expressed in a more open manner, and the growth of ebooks has enabled this previously hidden genre to flourish. What was on the fringes has now become mainstream. When 60 million people read *Fifty Shades of Grey*, and many of them read it openly in public, then you know things have changed, and that's fantastic.

As a feminist, I am cheering on this new development because women deserve the chance to experiment and express their sexuality, and words are one of the ways we become aroused. Of course, there is plenty of erotica written for and by men, but it is the feminine expression that has changed substantially with the digital market. I have always read erotica as part of a healthy and varied sex life, both for pleasure alone and with partners. I have written some over the years but never considered submitting it to a publisher because of concerns about privacy, and the fact that this is only one part of my writing career. But last year, seeing the possibilities with self-publishing and ebooks, I took the plunge under an assumed name and now love the freedom to write and help others explore their sexuality.

On pseudonyms

But, let's face it, writing erotic fiction is not something that will make your Mum happy, or your friends proud. It's likely to get you blackballed at the school gates and talked about behind your back. For, however much people like to read it and enjoy private pleasure, society is still judgmental enough to punish the writer, however good the story is. So privacy is often important and why many in the genre write under pseudonyms.

That doesn't mean we're ashamed of our sexuality. Definitely not. It just means we don't want the hassle of dealing with any backlash, especially if we also write children's fiction, or academic papers, or anything else really.

It's easy enough to write under a pseudonym. Choose a name that resonates but isn't obvious. Set up a Gmail account under that name and use it for all correspondence. Use that name on your Amazon page (if you already have one, you can set up a different account). Set up a separate website if you want to market the brand. Use a PO Box for your mailing address and don't mention the pseudonym to anyone – simple, yet effective, and you're free to write whatever you choose.

Of course, E.L. James (a pseudonym) was 'outed' once she sold gazillions of books, but that's only likely to happen if you hit the heights of success. And if that happens, you probably won't care anymore.

Top tips for writing erotic fiction

• **Know and love the genre.** There are many writers jumping into erotica because of the big money that a few authors are making, but like any style of writing, you need to know the genre. You also need to enjoy reading it in order to write it well. Authenticity and respect for the reader are important and you can only deliver on expectations if you understand them. For erotica, I would go even further – if it's not exciting you, it's unlikely to excite the reader, but if you're enjoying it, that makes for a really fun writing day!

• **Understand that not everyone likes the same thing.** During the peak of the *Fifty Shades* discussion, it became evident that the books were way too hardcore for vanilla lovers, but also offended some in the BDSM community who thought it too mainstream for their more refined tastes. Sex is certainly one area where we all have our preferences. Not everyone likes to admit to fantasies that don't fit their external persona, and sometimes people are ashamed of what turns them on but they still want to read about it. So write whatever you want, as there will be a niche for it, but understand that not everyone will like the same things you do.

• **Deliver on your brand.** Like any writer, you will start to set your reader's expectations through your work. If you're writing with a certain tone and setting with specific character types, it will upset your readers if you change to something completely different. A good example here is the use of certain words for sexual organs that can either be more romantic and erotic, or be harder and likely to offend some people. There are also sub-genres within erotica, for example people who like lesbian romantic erotica might be completely turned off by erotic horror. Those who love furry erotica may not enjoy alien abduction stories. Make it clear through your branding, cover design and sales description what people are going to get and satisfy that reader every time.

• **Learn the vocabulary and consult a sexy thesaurus.** You would be surprised how fast you run out of words for specific physical motions, body parts and noises that are crucial to the graphic nature of erotica. Luckily there are sites online where other erotica writers have compiled specific thesaurus entries to help you out in that second draft, as well as lots of other resources.

• **It's fiction, so make it a story.** You still need characters and setting, scenes and tension, dialogue and a story arc. You also need graphic sex that people can engage with, otherwise the book is more 'romance' than erotica, but make sure you also include the thoughts of your characters, their motivations and feelings. You want your reader to be inside the head of the character who is experiencing the fantasy and as turned on as they are. Use all of the senses in your descriptions and indulge in the details of the erotic experience. Try starting the story with erotic tension between characters, then building up the relationship through conflict before getting into the foreplay and sex. Ending the story with a resolution is just as important. You want the reader to be satisfied in every way, but also wanting to read more of your work.

• **It's a fantasy.** The success of *Fifty Shades* was as much to do with the characters of Ana and Christian and the fantasy of wealth and power as it was to do with sex. People read erotica to escape their lives for a time, so indulge the fantasy world in whatever you're writing, and don't make the reader feel guilty or ashamed for what they might enjoy.

• **Have fun!** My other books are dark thrillers and serious non-fiction – not a laugh a minute, I'll admit. But when I write erotica, I am actually giggling out loud as it is so much fun. Try letting yourself go and really indulging your imagination, especially under the freedom of a pseudonym.

Can you make lots of money as an erotica writer?

Most authors will never reach the dizzy heights of E.L. James' income but in this new world of digital publishing, plenty of authors are making extremely good monthly incomes from their writing, especially in the romance/erotica niche.

However, they all adhere to a few principles. They write good books that satisfy their readers, and they write a lot of them. You won't make a living wage from just one book in any genre, so consider how erotic writing fits into your wider career as an author and how much time you can put aside to create a body of work.

How to sell your erotic fiction

There are traditional markets for erotica but also a growing number of authors who choose to self-publish, especially because of the popularity of reading ebooks for this genre, the creative freedom, the speed to market and the higher royalties.

• **Publish on Amazon KDP and Kobo Writing Life**, as both sites are popular with 'active romance' readers. You can also use Smashwords.com as a distributor for the other ebook sites and sell directly there in another popular erotica market.

• **Experiment with short stories, novellas and full-length works.** Readers of erotica consume ebooks like candy, so you want to have more of them available as fast as possible. Most erotica books are short anyway, but you can also experiment with short stories, anthologies or novellas. This will also give you more digital shelf space and more chance of being discovered, and will help you write faster. Try writing a series character to save having to invent new people every time.

• **Experiment with pricing.** Giving away books for free is a good way to get your work noticed at the beginning when you don't have an existing audience. You can use KDP Select for a 90-day period with exclusivity or you can use Smashwords.com or Kobobooks.com with free pricing. Try to promote your free period or your sale on sites that have established email lists.

• **Start your own email list of readers.** Include a link at the back of your books to a page on your website where readers can sign up to be notified about the next book. This will grow over time and enable you to control sales spikes when you release a new book which is the best way to impact the bestseller charts.

• **Get book reviews on erotica blogs.** Find other erotica writers who write similar types of scenes and then search for bloggers who enjoyed those books. Google 'erotica book reviews' to find plenty of sites to start your research. This is the best way to get in front of a reader audience who enjoy your type of fiction.

• **Network with readers and other erotica writers.** As with writers in any genre, you should be an avid reader in the erotica genre, so you can naturally hang out with other readers on forums, review blogs, Goodreads.com and other places where readers talk about books. As with any networking, it's not about you; it's about connection over things you love to talk about and share anyway. Your profile will contain details of your books. You should also be connecting with other writers as this is a great way to join a community and learn what is working for others.

The author of this article, who prefers to remain anonymous, writes in the thriller and erotica genres.

Notes from a successful crossover author

Neil Gaiman explains how he 'learned to stop worrying and became a crossover author'.

I didn't set out to be a crossover author, it just never occurred to me not to be. To put it another way, what I wanted to be was the kind of writer who told whatever stories he wanted in whatever medium he wanted, and I seem, more or less, to have got to that place. So, I can tell you how I did it. I'm just not sure I could tell you how you could do it too.

My first book was a children's book. I was about 22 when I wrote it, and I sent it to one publisher, and it came back with a nice note from the editor saying that it wasn't quite right for them, and I put it away for ever. I was a journalist for a while (it would be accurate to say that all I knew of being a journalist when I began was what I had gleaned from the 1983 edition of the *Writers' & Artists' Yearbook*). Then I wrote comics – mostly for grown-ups – and once I'd learned to write comics to my own satisfaction and thought it might be good fun to go and explore prose fiction, I was spoiled. The joy of writing comics is that it's a medium that people mistake for a genre: nobody seemed to mind whether I lurched from historical to fantasy to spy stories to autobiography to children's fiction, because it was all comics – a freedom that I treasured.

I started writing my first real children's book in 1991, a scary story for my daughter, Holly, called *Coraline*. I showed the first few chapters to my editor at Gollancz, Richard Evans. Now, Richard was a good editor and a smart man, and had just midwifed a book by Terry Pratchett and me, *Good Omens*, into existence. The next time I was in the Gollancz offices he took me to one side and said, 'Neil. I read the *Coraline* chapters, and I loved it. I think it's the best thing you've ever written. But I have to warn you, it's unpublishable'. I was puzzled: 'Why?' 'Well, it's a horror novel aimed at children and adults,' he told me, 'and I don't think we could publish a horror novel for children, and I really don't know how anyone could publish anything for adults and children at the same time.'

So I put the book away. I planned to keep writing it, in my own time, but there wasn't a lot of my own time about, and I managed about a thousand words on it during the next few years. I knew that unless someone was waiting for it, unless it had a chance of being read, I wasn't going to write it.

By now I had published a couple of books with Avon, and I sent it to my editor, Jennifer Hershey. 'It's great,' she said. 'What happens next?' I told her I wasn't really sure, but if she sent me a contract we would both find out! She did. The contract was for about 5% of what I'd got as an advance for my last novel, but it was a contract, and Jennifer said she would worry about how the book was published when I handed it in.

Two years passed. I didn't have any more time, so I kept a notebook beside my bed and finished the book and handed it in. But I still had an adult novel, *American Gods*, to finish before *Coraline* would be published. Avon was taken over by HarperCollins, a publisher with a healthy children's publishing division, and somewhere in there it was decided that *Coraline* would be published by HarperCollins Children's. In the UK, the book was sold to Bloomsbury.

It was still a horror novel, still aimed at both adults and children, but the publishing landscape had changed in the previous handful of years. The success of the few books that had crossed over from children's fiction to the adult world – the Harry Potter books, Philip Pullman's *His Dark Materials*, the Lemony Snicket books – made it at least a feasible goal.

Coraline was published in the summer of 2002, which was, coincidentally, the first summer without a new Harry Potter book. Journalists had column inches to fill, and they wrote about *Coraline*, imagining a movement of adult novelists now writing children's books. In both the USA and the UK, it's fair to say, adults bought the book at first, not children. That came later, as teachers enjoyed reading it and began introducing it in schools, and news of it spread by word of mouth.

The Wolves in the Walls followed, written by me and illustrated by artist Dave McKean. A children's picture book, again, it was initially bought by adults who liked what I wrote and what Dave painted – essentially the graphic novel audience who had come with us from comics. But it was read to children, and became popular with them, and now most of the copies I sign at signings are for younger readers.

I don't think you can plan for something to be a crossover book. But you can do things to make it easier. In my case, it was useful that I already had a large readership, one that had followed me from comics into prose, and who didn't seem to mind that none of my prose books resembled each other very much, except in having been written by me. It was also wonderful that I had supportive publishers in the USA and the UK, who were willing to take different approaches to the material.

When I wrote *The Graveyard Book*, a book that began with me wondering what would happen if you took Kipling's *The Jungle Book* and relocated it to a graveyard, I wasn't really sure who I was writing it for. I just wanted it to be good. Dave McKean did a book cover for the US edition while I was still writing it, but once the book was done it was obvious that the cover was wrong. It looked like a book for ten year-olds, and only for ten-year-olds. While the book I'd written would work for children, it worked just as well for adults, and we didn't want to exclude them. With tremendous good humour, Dave went back to the drawing board and produced a dozen new sketches. One of them seemed perfect – it showed a gravestone, which became the outline of a boy's face in profile. It could as easily have been a children's book cover or the cover of a Stephen King book; no one picking it up would feel excluded. (Another of Dave's sketches, of a baby walking on a bloody knife-edge in which a graveyard could be seen, would have been perfect for a book aimed at adults, but was thought a bit too edgy for children.)

In the UK, Bloomsbury had come up with their own strategy: two editions of *The Graveyard Book*, one aimed at children, one at adults. The children's edition would be illustrated by Chris Riddell, the adult edition by Dave McKean – and Dave's baby-on-a-knife-edge cover was ideal for what they wanted, something that was unashamedly aimed at adults.

You can do your best to write a book for children that adults will like (or the other way around – in the USA the Young Adult Library Services awards celebrate the books for adults that young readers latch on to); you can try not to mess up the publishing end of things (that first cover for the US version of *The Graveyard Book*, which looked like a book that only 'middle grade readers' might have enjoyed would have been a mis-step); you can try to bring an existing audience with you, if you have one, and a way of letting them know what you've done. But I'm not sure that any of this will guarantee anything. Publishers are less intimidated by crossover books now that there have been many successes, but the mechanics of bookselling, the fact that books have to go somewhere in a bookshop, and that somewhere may be in a place that adults or children don't go, that the adult and children's divisions of publishers are staffed by different people in different groups who don't always talk to each other or have the same objectives (or even the same catalogues) – all of these things serve to make it harder to be a crossover author and encourage you to stay put, to write something people will know where to shelve, to write the same sort of thing you wrote before.

I suppose you become a crossover author by taking risks, but they had better be the kind of risks that you enjoy taking. Don't set out to be a crossover author. Write the books you have to write, and if you write one that crosses boundaries, that finds readers in a variety of ages and types, then do your best to get it published in a way that lets all of them know it's out there. Good luck.

Neil Gaiman is the *New York Times* bestselling author of the novels *The Ocean at the End of the Lane, Neverwhere, Stardust, American Gods, Anansi Boys* and *Good Omens* (with Terry Pratchett); the *Sandman* series of graphic novels; and the short story collections *Smoke and Mirrors* and *Fragile Things*. He is also the author of books for readers of all ages including the novels *The Graveyard Book, Coraline* and *Odd and the Frost Giants*; the short story collection *M is for Magic* and the picture books *Fortunately, the Milk, The Wolves in the Walls, The Day I Swapped My Dad for Two Goldfish, Crazy Hair, The Dangerous Alphabet* and *Blueberry Girl*. Neil's most recent children's book is *Chu's Day* (Bloomsbury 2014). He is the winner of numerous literary honours. Originally from England, he now lives in the USA. He is listed in the *Dictionary of Literary Biography* as one of the top ten living post-modern writers and he says he owes it all to reading the *Writers' & Artists' Yearbook* as a young man. Visit him at www.neilgaiman.com.

Notes from a successful children's author

J.K. Rowling shares her experiences of writing success.

I can remember writing *Harry Potter and the Philosopher's Stone* in a cafe in Oporto. I was employed as a teacher at the language institute three doors along the road at the time, and this café was a kind of unofficial staffroom. My friend and colleague joined me at my table. When I realised I was no longer alone I hastily shuffled worksheets over my notebook, but not before Paul had seen exactly what I was doing. 'Writing a novel, eh?' he asked wearily, as though he had seen this sort of behaviour in foolish young teachers only too often before. '*Writers' & Artists' Yearbook*, that's what you need,' he said. 'Lists all the publishers and … stuff,' he advised, before ordering a lager and starting to talk about the previous night's episode of *The Simpsons*.

I had almost no knowledge of the practical aspects of getting published; I knew nobody in the publishing world, I didn't even know anybody who knew anybody. It had never occurred to me that assistance might be available in book form.

Nearly three years later and a long way from Oporto, I had almost finished *Harry Potter and the Philosopher's Stone*. I felt oddly as though I was setting out on a blind date as I took a copy of the *Writers' & Artists' Yearbook* from the shelf in Edinburgh's Central Library. Paul had been right and the *Yearbook* answered my every question, and after I had read and reread the invaluable advice on preparing a manuscript, and noted the time-lapse between sending said manuscript and trying to get information back from the publisher, I made two lists: one of publishers, the other of agents.

The first agent on my list sent my sample three chapters and synopsis back by return of post. The first two publishers took slightly longer to return them, but the 'no' was just as firm. Oddly, these rejections didn't upset me much. I was braced to be turned down by the entire list, and in any case, these were real rejection letters – even real writers had got them. And then the second agent, who was high on the list purely because I like his name, wrote back with the most magical words I have ever read: 'We would be pleased to read the balance of your manuscript on an exclusive basis…'.

J.K. Rowling is the bestselling author of the *Harry Potter* series (Bloomsbury), published between 1997 and 2007, which have sold over 450 million copies worldwide, are distributed in more than 200 territories, translated into 78 languages and have been turned into eight blockbuster films. The first in the series, *Harry Potter and the Philosopher's Stone*, was the winner of the 1997 Nestlé Smarties Gold Prize and *Harry Potter and the Goblet of Fire* (2000) broke all records for the number of books sold on the first day of publication. She has also written two small volumes that appear as the titles of Harry's schoolbooks within the novels: *Fantastic Beasts and Where to Find Them* and *Quidditch Through the Ages* (Bloomsbury 2011) which were published in aid of Comic Relief. *The Tales of Beedle the Bard* was published in 2008 in aid of J.K. Rowling's children's charity Lumos and in 2015 her Harvard Commencement Speech was published as a book, *Very Good Lives*, also in aid of Lumos. In 2012 J.K. Rowling's digital company Pottermore was launched, where fans can enjoy her new writing and immerse themselves deeper in the wizarding world, and purchase the ebooks of the Harry Potter series. J.K. Rowling has written a novel for adults: *The Casual Vacancy* (Little Brown 2012) and crime novels under the pseudonym Robert Galbraith: *The Cuckoo's Calling* (Little Brown 2013) and *The Silkworm* (Little Brown 2014).

Writing historical fiction

Historical fiction gives writers the freedom to use 'informed imagination', rich in authentic detail, to breathe life into history, explains historian and novelist Alison Weir. She explores important aspects of the genre and describes the bridge between biography and fiction in her work, seeing encouraging trends in the market.

Filling in the gaps: enhancing history?

Writing a biography of Eleanor of Aquitaine was my first attempt at recreating the life of a medieval woman, piecing together myriad fragments of evidence in an attempt to construct a cohesive narrative – such is the challenge of medieval biography. It was, to some extent, a frustrating exercise, because there will always be gaps that we cannot hope to fill: no one thought to record what the beautiful Eleanor actually looked like, for example, how much political influence she actually exerted, or why she separated from her husband, Henry II. I found myself itching to fill those gaps, knowing that a historian oversteps the bounds of legitimate speculation at his or her peril, for we can only infer so much from historical sources.

It was while I was researching this biography, it occurred to me that I wanted to write a novel about Eleanor, one in which I could develop ideas and themes that had no place in a history book, but which – based on sound research and educated guesses – could help to illuminate her life and explain her motives and actions. A historian uses such inventiveness at their peril – but a novelist has the power to get inside their subject's head, and that can afford insights that would not be permissible to a historian, and yet can have a legitimate value of their own.

Having decided to have a go at writing a novel, I had to choose a subject. Eleanor of Aquitaine was off limits at the time, because my contract precluded a competing book. A reader had suggested that I write a biography of Lady Jane Grey, and it occurred to me that Jane's tragic tale would be an ideal subject for a novel: it was short, it was dramatic and unbearably poignant, and I knew it well, having researched it for an earlier book. Three months later the novel was finished.

My agent thought it a riveting story, but said I should come down off the fence and forget I was a historian, as the book read like 'faction'. But I had no more time to work on it, so I put it away and forgot about it until 2003, when I rewrote it using the first person and the present tense, a format in which no history book would ever be written. It was this novel that was commissioned by Hutchinson and was published in 2006 as *Innocent Traitor*. Since then I have published four more historical novels, including one on Eleanor of Aquitaine.

From historical fact to fiction: providing authentic detail

Writing historical fiction affords me a sense of freedom: it is liberating not to have to keep within the strict confines of contemporary sources. I can use my imagination to fill those frustrating gaps, although I strongly feel that what a historical novelist writes must be credible within the context of what is known about the subject. You cannot simply indulge in flights of fancy. That sells short both those who know nothing about the subject, and those who know a great deal. I know – because my readers regularly, and forcefully, tell me so – that people care that what they are reading in a historical novel is close to the truth, if allowing for a little dramatic licence and the novelist's informed imagination.

Consequently I feel that I have a great responsibility towards my readers – and also my subjects, who were, after all, real people. In my novels, I adhere to the facts where they exist, using my informed imagination where they do not. History does not always record people's motives, emotions and reactions, or the intimate details of their relationships or their love lives, so there is plenty of scope for invention there – and I have to confess to having been quite inventive in that respect!

The setting must be authentic. Too many historical novels fall down because the author has not done enough background research. They know the story superficially, but they don't know the period or the social and cultural context. It's an advantage to have studied the history in depth. I find that I am constantly looking up minor details in the interests of authenticity, such as the kind of books that were printed by the Caxton press in Lady Jane Grey's time, the kind of food that Eleanor of Aquitaine would have eaten, or even the Welsh folk song sung by Elizabeth I's nursery maid. One can't afford to be sloppy because this is 'just' fiction.

Readers of history books love such details – I've heard that time and again – and I've found that it's often in the details that we gain a broader picture. For example, Peter Englund's book on the Great War, *The Beauty and the Sorrow* (Knopf Publishing 2011), briefly mentions a soldier watching the body of a fallen comrade decompose over days; he has come to see it as just chemicals and rags. But that speaks volumes about how men coped with the unimaginable carnage of that war. And maybe historians can learn something from historical novelists about bringing history vividly to life.

Finding an authentic voice

A major challenge to any author embarking on a historical novel is the use of language. There are tough choices, and you will never please everyone. You could, if you were stupid enough, adopt pseudo-Tudor speak and alienate your readers with words and phrases such as 'prithee' or 'hey nonny nonny'; or you could go to the other extreme, as Suzannah Dunn does in *The Queen of Subtleties* (Doubleday 2005), where she has Anne Boleyn calling her father 'Dad'. Although I flinched at that, her novel worked well, thanks to the excellent characterisations.

Having spent many years studying Tudor sources, I have become familiar with the idioms of language in use then – although we can never fully know how people actually spoke, only how their words were written down, which may not be the same thing. Wherever possible, I use my characters' own historical quotes, or the quotes of others, lifting them from historical sources but modernising them slightly so that they do not stand out awkwardly in a 21st-century text. In order to appeal to as wide – and as young – an audience as possible, I confess to deliberately using a few modern idioms where I think they sound better than their Tudor equivalent, even if they are anachronistic. But it's impossible to please everyone with the language in a historical novel: while one reviewer of *Innocent Traitor* deplored what he saw as anachronisms, another said I had got the language just right. In my subsequent novels I have used the past tense and the third person, which allows for greater versatility in telling the story.

Inventive freedom: from historical evidence to 'what if ... ?'

How far dare a novelist make things up or manipulate the facts in a novel about a real historical figure who may also be famous? My feeling is that you should have some historical evidence, however flimsy, on which to base your storyline. For a historian, such evidence may not be convincing, but it might be a gift to a novelist. For example, in *The Other Boleyn Girl* (Harper 2007), Philippa Gregory has Anne Boleyn, desperate to have a son, contemplating committing incest with her brother because he is the only man who can safely be relied upon not to betray their intimacy to others. The historical Anne was charged with incest in the indictment drawn up against her, and while other evidence strongly suggests that these were trumped-up charges, a novelist can use them as the basis of a good plot. I have no argument with that.

The issue of Elizabeth I's much-vaunted virginity has been endlessly debated by scholars, so in my view it is quite legitimate for novelists such as Susan Kay in *Legacy* (Bodley Head 1985) and Robin Maxwell in *The Queen's Bastard* (Review 1999) to depict the Queen having a full physical relationship with the Earl of Leicester.

I myself took a similar liberty, going against what I believe as a historian, in my second novel, *The Lady Elizabeth* (Hutchinson 2008). That storyline was based purely on unreliable gossip and a coincidence over dates, but had this contemporary evidence not existed, I would not have ventured so far. Given that it does exist, and even though, as a historian, I would discount it, as a novelist I have the freedom to ask: what if?

My fourth novel, *A Dangerous Inheritance* (Hutchinson 2012), was the sequel to *Innocent Traitor*, with a dramatic sub-plot involving the bastard daughter of Richard III and a few hints of the supernatural, which I have woven into all my novels. But in this one the theme is more prominent – and you might say that Josephine Tey's *The Daughter of Time* (Macmillan 1951) was an inspiration. Yet this book is very different from that much-outdated classic, and it is the first of my novels in which I wrote a fictional tale that had no historical foundation. Even so, it is based on extensive research and set within the context of two documented lives – and an enduring mystery. You could say that I have learned to relax into fiction writing – but my quest for authenticity remains as enthusiastic as ever.

I feel strongly that, where a novelist invents material in a historical novel about real persons or events, they should always include an author's note explaining what is fact and what is fiction. If the book is largely fictional, that should be made clear. Does it matter? Of course it matters, when we are dealing with real history. It is a matter of concern to historians that fiction – in well-publicised novels and films – is often taken as fact.

Publishers, trends and sales

Where do publishers come into this? I want to say from the start that my own publishers have always been supportive of my pursuit of authenticity. But publishers do not have the autonomy they once had, and they need to survive in a difficult world. Supermarket giants, for example, have enormous power: they squeeze publishers' profits (see a 'buy one, get one free' offer and you might depend on it that one has been printed free); they reject jackets and titles as not being commercial enough for their customers, which can result in the dumbing down of a book, making both the publishers and the author very unhappy. I fought for my novel on Eleanor of Aquitaine to be titled *A Marriage of Lions*, which reflects the parallels between evolving heraldry and Eleanor's turbulent marriage to Henry II. But that was rejected out of hand, and I ended up submitting no fewer than 90 titles until a compromise was reached and we went for *The Captive Queen*. It's a title I still hate – it's inane, and echoes so many others on the market. And it has since become clear that many readers preferred *A Marriage of Lions*.

Having made my case somewhat passionately for authenticity in historical novels, which ones would I recommend? Apart from those already mentioned, I must mention C. J. Sansom's compelling Shardlake series; Edward Rutherfurd's epics *Sarum* (Arrow 1991), *London* (Century 1997) and *The Forest* (Century 2000); Sarah Gristwood's *The Girl in the Mirror* (Harper Press 2012); Derek K. Wilson's *The First Horseman* (Sphere 2013); and, of course, Hilary Mantel's *Wolf Hall* (Fourth Estate 2009) and *Bring Up The Bodies* (Fourth Estate 2012), in which she wonderfully evokes a world, even though as a historian I find her portrayal of Thomas Cromwell over-sympathetic. Historical novels have become a respected genre because of novels such as these.

The tide is turning, I think. Having seen the BBC's well-paced and fairly authentic adaptation of *Wolf Hall* (2015), and the huge interest in it, I am more optimistic than I was. Maybe we don't always have to knuckle under to the powerful factors that come into play in the publishing and interpretation of history: market forces; the need to drive sales; the impact of films and blockbuster novels. It seems that people are again seeking – and enjoying – excellence in historical fiction. But historians might not win all the battles. As one lady remarked when she heard me pointing out some inaccuracies to a friend as we toured a well-known castle – 'Please stop spoiling it for me!'

Alison Weir is the top-selling female historian (and the fifth bestselling historian overall) in the UK, and has sold over 2.7 million books worldwide. She has published 16 history books, including *The Six Wives of Henry VIII* (Bodley Head 1991), *The Princes in the Tower* (Bodley Head 1992), *Elizabeth the Queen* (Jonathan Cape 1998), *Eleanor of Aquitaine* (Jonathan Cape 1999), *Henry VIII: King and Court* (Jonathan Cape 2001), *Katherine Swynford* (Jonathan Cape 2007) and *The Lady in the Tower* (Jonathan Cape 2009). Alison has also published four historical novels, including *Innocent Traitor, The Lady Elizabeth* (Hutchinson 2008) and *The Marriage Game* (Hutchinson 2014). Her latest biography is *Elizabeth of York* (Jonathan Cape 2013). She is soon to publish a biography of Margaret Douglas, Countess of Lennox.

See also...

- *Notes from a successful biographer*, page 307

Changing voices

Alexander McCall Smith suggests that within each writer there is probably more than one author wishing to be expressed and that writers should be ready to push themselves and explore the unfamiliar, to try a new voice. In this article he examines the options and points out when it would be prudent to not write in a different voice.

Every author is used to being asked for a tip for those starting off in the profession. The one that I have tended to give is this: never get stuck on your first novel – move on to the next. That advice comes from meeting so many people who have spent years – sometimes decades – rewriting their first novel. That, in my view, is a bad mistake, particularly if that first novel is unsuitable for publication, as so many first novels are. So why not make one's second novel one's first?

But then comes the question: what other tips? That needs a bit more thought, but my second tip is probably this: be versatile. Being prepared to write more than one sort of thing is, I think, one of the most important abilities that any aspiring writer should seek to develop. Of course there are plenty of writers who find their exact niche and stick to it very successfully: I find it hard to think, for example, of any romantic novels written by John le Carré, or spy thrillers by Barbara Cartland, for that matter. Writers who have the good fortune to master a genre and make it very much their own can indeed get away with doing the same sort of book for their entire careers, but for most people the ability to write on different subjects or in different voices is a very useful weapon in the professional armoury.

Of course there are all sorts of pressures going the other way, not least being those that come from publishers. One of the things that the first-time author may not realise is that publishers prefer to take a long view. When they agree to publish your first book, they are probably already thinking of the second. The commercial reason for this is obvious: a publisher is going to invest time and money in a book that will probably have a reasonably short shelf-life. It is not surprising, then, that they are thinking of your future career and about how your second book can do better than your first. All that is reasonable enough: it takes time to build up a following.

With this long-term strategy in mind, publishers will be keen to pigeon-hole you and present you as a writer of a certain sort of book. If, for example, you write a steamy novel about 50 shades of something or other, your publisher is not going to be pleased if your next book is on moral philosophy or even – and this would cause even greater problems for your publisher – theology. If you write a thriller, then that is how you are going to be marketed – as a writer of thrillers.

This process of categorisation, of course, can be to your advantage. Crime novels, for instance, sell better than many other categories, and to be labelled as a crime writer may help an author get started on a lucrative career. And crime fiction can be extremely well written and psychologically profound; there is no shame in being considered a genre writer, as long as one does not allow the demands of genre to be too constraining. There is a world of difference, though, between the narrow, formulaic romantic novel and the novel about love. The former will be of little literary merit; the latter may be quite the opposite.

Some will be wary of identification with a genre, as being placed in a particular one may be considered limiting. Yet the boundaries of genre may be vague. Think of Patricia

Highsmith with her Ripley novels and her other titles too: those are every bit as good – if not better – than many so-called literary novels, and of course will be read, and enjoyed, by a much wider audience. Ian McEwan is another interesting example: his compelling novel, *Enduring Love*, could be considered crime fiction, or even a thriller, as could his exquisitely frightening novel, *Saturday*. And yet McEwan crosses literary boundaries with ease because he writes so well.

Writing for children brings particular dangers. Children's books are obviously a very distinct genre, marketed and perceived by the public in a very distinctive way. If your first book is a children's book, beware: you will be labelled by publishers – and possibly by everybody else – as a writer of books for children and you may never be able to present yourself as anything but that. I have personal experience of this: at an earlier stage of my writing career I wrote about 30 books for children and remember feeling very frustrated that I could not persuade the people who published those books to consider the manuscripts I wrote for adults. I felt trapped, and I know a number of writers who had a similar experience. It takes a real effort and not infrequently a stroke of luck to venture out from the world of children's books.

Of course there is no real reason why an author should not write for children as well as adults and go backwards and forwards between the genres. Roald Dahl is an example of somebody who did that: his short stories for adults are exceptionally well crafted, but are definitely not children's fare. His children's classics, though, can be read with enjoyment by adults, whether or not one is reading them aloud to one's children or for private pleasure. That is the mark, I think, of the great storyteller: he or she is of universal appeal.

But let us imagine that you are now launched, whether or not with a first book that fits into any narrow genre. What should you do about your second book? Should you try to do much the same thing as you did in the first? An initial question is whether you are interested in writing a sequel. That will depend on the nature of the first book: some books lend themselves to sequels more naturally than others. If you have created strong characters, you may wish to continue those characters and expose them to new challenges. That, of course, is how most real lives are lived: they go on for years – each of us, in a way, finds ourself in a family saga of one sort or another.

A series can be attractive to both author and publisher. From the author's point of view there is a particular pleasure in returning to characters and places with which you are already familiar. Creating a new chapter in a life that you have already got to know in an earlier novel can be rather like sitting down for a chat with an old friend, and may present chances to say much more about character and background than you were able to say in the first encounter. From the publisher's point of view, half the battle of marketing a book is over if there is a readership that already recognises – and likes – the principal character. That is why it is relatively easy for publishers of crime fiction to sell the latest exploits of well-known detectives: everybody knows those detectives and is eager to hear from them. But the same can be said too of other series: readers of Patrick O'Brian were lining up to read about Jack Aubrey and Stephen Maturin as soon as the next instalment was due, just as they did for Harry Potter and his friends.

Again, though, a warning note needs to be sounded. A successful series can become a treadmill for an author and may also frustrate the author's desire to do something different. So it is a good idea to make it clear to publishers that one wants to be able to write something different from time to time. A good publisher will be perfectly happy to allow this if the author has been reasonably successful with an existing series; indeed the publisher should see this as a way of expanding the author's readership as well as allowing existing readers to sample something different from a writer they have come to know.

My own experience of this has involved writing a number of standalone novels as well as a number of existing, regular series. I have found these standalones to be a valuable way of saying things that I might not have been able to say in any of my series, as well as giving me an opportunity to spread my wings stylistically. There is also the sheer stimulation involved in being able to do something new – to accept new challenges.

Recently I had one such challenge presented to me by a publisher with whom I had worked in the past. Roger Cazalet, one of the most highly regarded of British publishers, came to me with the suggestion that I should write a new version of Jane Austen's *Emma*. It took me, I think, not much longer than 30 seconds to say yes to this proposal. Not only would this enable me to work again with Roger – and the relationship with your publisher is a very important matter – but it would also allow me to step into the world of Jane Austen, a writer whom I, like virtually everybody else, admire so greatly. I was aware, though, that this was yet another genre of fiction that I was straying into: that of the use of fictional characters developed by another author altogether.

Using another author's characters seems to have become a rather popular pursuit. Not only are people doing it with Jane Austen – there are innumerable versions now of *Pride and Prejudice* – but they are doing it for a whole list of well-known fictional characters. There were the Flashman novels, for instance, that involved the reappearance of the bully in *Tom Brown's Schooldays*. There are also the now fairly numerous reappearances of James Bond, from the pen of various distinguished modern novelists such as William Boyd and Sebastian Faulks. This is itself now a whole new literary genre.

I found writing a new *Emma* one of the most enjoyable literary experiences of my life. Part of that, of course, was the sheer pleasure of Austen's story, but much of the attraction lay in the fact that it was a new thing for me to do. I had not done this sort of thing before, and there was the exciting challenge of an entirely fresh project. And that, I think, is the important thing for any author to remember: you must be ready to push yourself, to explore the unfamiliar, to try a new voice. I am not suggesting that one picks up and then abandons literary styles and genres with careless abandon: what I am suggesting is that within each one of us there is probably more than one author waiting for a chance of self-expression. Let those voices out. Cultivate them. And even if one ends up writing widely differing types of books, there is likely to be the same vision behind each of them that will make them authentically you. And that, of course, is the bit that you must always listen to and never silence – for any reason at all.

Alexander McCall Smith CBE, a former professor of Medical Law, is one of the world's most prolific and most popular authors. His *No 1 Ladies' Detective Agency* series has sold over 20 million copies, and his various series of books have been translated into over 40 languages. These include the 44 *Scotland Street* novels, the *Isabel Dalhousie Novels* series, the *von Igelfeld* series, and the *Corduroy Mansions* novels. Alexander is also the author of collections of short stories, academic works, and over 30 books for children. He has received numerous awards for his writing, including the British Book Awards Author of the Year Award in 2004 and holds honorary doctorates from nine universities in Europe and North America. His most recent novel is *The Novel Habits of Happiness* (Little, Brown 2015). *Emma: A Modern Retelling*, part of the Austen Project, in which six contemporary authors were invited to re-imagine the six complete novels of Jane Austen, was published by the Borough Press in 2014.

Literary translation

There is more to literary translation than merely translating, as Danny Hahn explains. A self-confessed lobbyist, advocate and proselytiser for the profession, he describes the increasing breadth and diversity of 'being a translator'. He gives advice on how to get started, practical information on the work, and reveals a highly supportive and dynamic working community.

The easy bit

What does a literary translator do? A literary translator takes a literary text in one language, and writes it again in another. It's not particularly difficult, so long as you don't care whether your translation is any good. But … what about not merely translating, but translating *well*? That's another matter entirely.

We all strive towards an ideal, a perfect translation, even while knowing that such a thing is impossible. Because rewriting a text in a new language doesn't just mean carrying over the sense, it means carrying over everything: the rhythm, the register, the associations, the resonances, the voice. All these things are deeply embedded in the original language, one might say they are inextricable from it – so how could it be possible to keep all of them when you're changing every single word? No, it's *impossible* – simple as that. And yet we translators do it anyway.

Being a literary translator demands all manner of unusual, overlapping skills, but there are just two that are absolutely essential. You need to be: 1) an uncommonly close, sensitive and wise reader; 2) a fantastically accomplished and versatile writer. And in two different languages, of course, because that's what translation is, after all – a process of reading, in language A, followed by a process of writing in which you deploy language B with such spectacular skill that everything you've read is somehow recreated, even if every single word is different. You read a line like 'The cat sat on the mat' and write a line in another language that keeps all of it: the meaning (feline, seated, carpet); the simple, almost childish register; the six absolutely consistent monosyllables; and the fact that the verb and both nouns all rhyme. Want to try it? Like I say – impossible!

How, practically, do translators work?

Literary translators in the UK are freelancers, hired usually by a publisher to do a single job (translate a novel, say). There are a number of publishing houses or imprints that have a particular focus on international literature in translation – Harvill Secker, Pushkin Press, And Other Stories, Peirene Press and others – but as it becomes more mainstream, translations are nowadays to be found (albeit in small numbers) on all kinds of literary and commercial publishing lists.

Translators do pitch ideas to publishers, but in the overwhelming majority of cases it's the publisher who initiates a project. The publisher finds a book they'd like to publish in English (at one of the big trade fairs, perhaps, such as the Frankfurt or London Book Fair), then they recruit a translator to do the job. (Sometimes they run a kind of beauty contest, with maybe three translators each doing a sample, for the publisher to choose the best match for the voice they're after.)

There will be a contract between publisher and translator, specifying the terms of the agreement, which will include a delivery deadline, a rate of payment and a royalty. Payment is calculated on the basis of the word count of the job (I currently charge £90 per 1,000 words of my translation, which is pretty typical, though rates can be negotiated up or down) and this is usually considered an 'advance' on future royalties. That is to say, it's like a royalty payment on credit, which has to be earned back before any more royalties start being paid out. The payment is usually made half on signature of the contract and half on delivery of the translation.

The translator will deliver the new text, which will go through a number of editorial stages; it won't usually get a major structural edit as an Anglophone work might, but there will be some editing, copy-editing and proofreading – with the translator involved at every stage. (The translator should have the right to veto unwelcome editorial changes, though most translators – like most writers – are happy to be well edited.)

Eventually the translation will be published, perhaps both in print and ebook form; the translator's name should be clearly credited (ideally on the jacket, but otherwise on the title page), and the translator's copyright in the work asserted. In very rare cases a publisher will ask a translator to agree to a contract in which he or she signs over their copyright, but this should be forcefully resisted! Once the book is out in the world, the translator may well be invited to be a part of promoting it – alongside, or instead of, the original author.

Getting started

Literary translation, like any writing, doesn't have anything as sensible as a career path one might tidily follow. It's not a job that requires a certain series of qualifications, or clear stages of apprenticeship to be served before attaining the hallowed status of Literary Translator (from which time great work just sort of appears magically whenever you need it...).What it does have, however, is an incredible collegial community, a network, which it's really easy to get into; and more support for starting-out literary translators than there has ever been.

Organisations like BCLT (see box) run residential summer schools and all kinds of other workshops; there's a mentoring scheme which pairs new translators with experienced translators in the same language for six months; and there are also now dozens of postgraduate programmes for studying literary translation, some more practice-based, others with a stronger focus on theory. There's a new Emerging Translators Network, too, which is mostly an online community but also hosts occasional events.

And there are plenty of opportunities to meet other translators in the community, whether it's at the Literary Translation Centre at the London Book Fair every April, which hosts its own programme of events at the Fair every year; or at the International Translation Day event in London, which gathers the whole tribe – translators but also interested publishers, students, writers, funders – for a day of discussions. International Translation Day itself is 30 September, St Jerome's Day (he's the patron saint of translators), so the London event is always around that time.

However much you might hate the idea of 'networking', getting yourself known to publishers is an important part of finding your way into this industry, and the existing events, programmes and networks certainly make this easier. You might also want to write to publishers direct and pitch ideas for books you think they should publish (and commission you to translate for them, naturally). Send a cover letter, some information about the book and its author, and an excellent short sample translation. It's very unusual that these cold pitches come to fruition but, if they (and your sample work in particular) are

Organisational support

The UK is blessed with a number of extremely effective and collaborative organisations working in the literary translation world. These are just a few of them. Sign up to their newsletters (and/or like on Facebook, follow on Twitter, etc) and you'll quickly get a sense of who else is out there.

The British Centre for Literary Translation (BCLT)

See page 499

Based at the University of East Anglia, the BCLT has recently changed its focus from public, professional and industry work to concentrate on its academic side. It hosts an annual summer school (in partnership with Writers' Centre Norwich, see below), and the annual Sebald Lecture. Speakers have included Seamus Heaney, Susan Sontag and Margaret Atwood.
website www.bclt.org.uk

English PEN

The founding centre of the PEN International network, English PEN works at the overlap between literature and free speech. Best known perhaps for its work with imprisoned authors around the world, its activities range much wider. Its strapline is 'Freedom to write, freedom to read', and it helps to make as wide a range of books as possible available to English-speaking readers, specifically by supporting literary translation. PEN offers grants to publishers to help cover the translation costs of publishing and promoting foreign books. It is a main player in the consortium of organisations that oversee the Literary Translation Centre at London Book Fair and International Translation Day.
website www.englishpen.org (See also PEN International in *Societies, associations and clubs* page 492.)

The Emerging Translators Network (ETN)

Just as it sounds, the ETN is a network for emerging translators. It operates mostly as an online forum, offering a welcoming and supportive environment for early-career literary translators and would-be literary translators to exchange information and advice.
website https://emergingtranslatorsnetwork.wordpress.com

Free Word

See page 508

The Free Word Centre in London is home to a number of organisations – both residents (such as English PEN, above) and associates (such as BCLT) – that work in the areas of literature, literacy and free expression.

Free Word has chosen translation as one of the focuses of its work, which has included three pairs of translators in residence who use their time at the Centre to collaborate with resident organisations, work with local schools, programme public events on a translation theme, and so on. Free Word is now the organisation responsible for International Translation Day.
website https://freewordcentre.com

Literature Across Frontiers (LAF)

Founded in 2001, this 'European Platform for Literary Exchange, Translation and Policy Debate' is based in Wales but works right across Europe (and beyond). With a wide network of partners, the organisation uses literature and translation to encourage intercultural dialogue, through workshops and publications, etc, focusing particularly on less-translated languages. It also carries out research into aspects of the translation market.
website www.lit-across-frontiers.org

The Translators Association (TA)

See page 529

Part of the Society of Authors, membership is limited to those who have published a book-length work or equivalent (though there is also associate membership for those who have been offered a first contract, even if it hasn't yet been completed). Among the many benefits is legal advice including clause-by-clause vetting of your contracts.
website http://societyofauthors.org/translators-association

Writers' Centre Norwich

This literature development agency is moving to new premises in 2015–16 and evolving into the National Centre for Writing. The transition will involve taking on much of the professional and public work that used to be done by BCLT, including the running of translation mentorships, programming public events that look at literary translation and translated literature, and publishing the journal for literary translators, *In Other Words*.
website www.writerscentrenorwich.org.uk

good enough, they are at least a useful calling card; even if they don't buy this book, publishers may remember you and later invite you to audition for something else they acquire. Offer to do reader's reports, too – these are a good way of honing your own critical skills, as well as allowing publishers to get to know you. And don't be shy about pitching short-form translations to magazines; publishing the odd short story or poem is a good way to get in the door. There are plenty of good places to start that are particularly receptive to international writing: *Words without Borders*, *Granta*, *Modern Poetry in Translation*, *The White Review*, *Asymptote*, and many others.

I've mentioned the translation 'community' quite a lot, but it's also worth thinking of smaller, more focused communities within it, which may exist for particular languages or regions. Find other translators who work in your language and look for other possible language-specific allies. For example most European countries, and some outside Europe, have organisations that exist to promote their literatures. Drop the appropriate ones a note and introduce yourself; they're usually grateful to meet translators who want to help them get their writers into the wider world, and they'll be useful to you.

'Being a translator'

The world of the professional literary translator in the UK has transformed in the last five or six years, and in almost every respect for the better. So much of this has come about thanks to the dynamism of translators themselves and the way the profession has come to think about itself, and in particular what it means to be a translator. I draw that distinction a lot these days, between 'translating' and 'being a translator', which seem to me entirely different things.

Translating is the core of the work, of course – taking an old text and writing a new one. That strange alchemical process (as one of my colleagues beautifully put it) of turning gold into gold. But that's not how I spend most of my time.

I talk to publishers about books – things that interest me, things that interest them; I read foreign-language submissions on their behalf and write reports. I talk to foreign agents and publishers and writers, too, to get a sense of what's going on in the publishing world out of which I'd translate. I am, in short, part of a big, transnational, translingual, literary conversation. I review translations for newspapers, and write about translation as I'm doing now. I do public events about literary translation and translated literature. I run workshops for newer translators than me (including in universities and schools, primary as well as secondary) and assorted programmes to make translation better, better paid, and more appreciated. In other words, I'm a lobbyist, an advocate, a proselytiser – as most translators are, I think. There's a sense in the profession of a kind of common mission (it seems rather zealous when I say that); we all feel there should be more translation, and more diverse translation, and that translations and translators should be profoundly cherished by the reading public.

That's what 'being a translator' means to me. Yes, doing the translating, but also being part of a community, a conversation – you might almost say a movement; it means seeing one's role as broad and flexible, seeing oneself as a significant and active player in the publishing world, not just an occasional, grateful hired hand. The community itself is an extraordinarily warm and welcoming one, and it's never been easier to join. Our profession and the market for our work are both growing – it's a good time for translating, and for being a translator, too.

Danny Hahn is a writer, editor and translator. He has translated about 20 novels from Portuguese, Spanish and French, including translations of fiction by José Eduardo Agualusa and José Luís Peixoto, and non-fiction by writers ranging from Portuguese Nobel Literature Laureate José Saramago to Brazilian footballer Pelé. He has also written several works of non-fiction and one children's picture book, as well as editing reference books for adults and reading guides for children and teenagers. Formerly National Programme Director of the British Centre for Literary Translation, he is the current chair of the Society of Authors and a former chair of the UK Translators Association (2012–15). His most recent publication is the new edition of the *Oxford Companion to Children's Literature* (Oxford University Press 2015).

Notes from a successful biographer

Claire Tomalin shares her thoughts about what writing a successful biography entails.

A good biography is driven by the curiosity of the writer, a passion to get as close as possible to understanding what is going on in another life. Anyone can write a biography, provided they are prepared to put in a lot of work: research, reading, travel and, more than anything else, thought. As much as I dare to, I write for my own pleasure. I am fired by curiosity, by following a thread here, a filament there. I want to explore the past as one might explore a foreign country. In the process, I want to educate myself, and there is no better way to do this than to research, and then attempt to write a book.

Researching a biography can be even more fascinating than reading a story someone else has imagined, because of the detective element. You follow a trail that may lead to a series of closed doors or dead ends or, if you are lucky, to discoveries that change a part or the whole of the perspective on a person or a period. The central figure of a biography may become a prism through which you view a whole society, a whole period.

I am not sure about rules for biography, but I believe you must like your subject. Better still if you fall in love with her, or him, because there has to be an element of obsession. Devoting several years or decades of your own life to thinking and writing about someone else's life is like being married. There are ups and downs, days when you are irritated or disappointed, others when you are delighted and surprised. And you have to keep at it. This is alongside your real life, which tends to get sidelined while the notional, biographical marriage takes up increasing energy and space. Biographers do occasionally choose to write about someone they loathe and produce a hymn of hate, and that must be obsessive too. It is not something I would attempt. Serious dispassionate studies of monsters such as Stalin and Hitler are something different again, and make up a special category, requiring particular historical skills and iron nerves.

In both historical and literary biography it is important to create the world around your subject, both the physical and the intellectual. Context matters as much as character, and a biography that skimps on it is thin and unsatisfying. You need to let your reader see the houses, landscapes and cities, hear the noises in the streets, know what was being joked and argued about, how children were reared at the time, how people took their pleasures, how they wore their clothes and hair, what they disapproved of, what excited them, what they were ready to fight for, how the social classes interacted – and so on.

So you need a jackdaw mind, ready to search and pick about in many subjects – politics, painting and sculpture, topography, psychology, sociology, the theatre, fashion, military and naval history, medicine. For most of my books I have found myself in the Wellcome Library of Medical History, finding out about the illnesses of my subjects – from Katherine Mansfield's gonorrhoea to Pepys's kidney and bladder stones – and I have corresponded with physicians and surgeons, all wonderfully instructive and entertaining. You have to be a bit cautious too, because retired doctors enjoy making posthumous diagnoses and may get carried away (like the one who became convinced that Thomas Hardy and his wife had syphilis).

You must master the handwriting of your subject and other members of her/his circle. Carry a magnifying glass with you to help you with the tricky bits, and I find copying it helps me to learn a hand. It gets easier as you go on. You must also find your way about archives, county records, libraries and museums, parish records and the public record office – plus websites and Google. Sadly, many archives are now on microfiche, fiddly to use and cruelly hard on the eyes. When I was working on Pepys [*Samuel Pepys: The Unequalled Self*] I thought I was going blind myself – luckily I was wrong.

Do your own picture research. You should also suggest the order of the illustrations and caption them yourself, so interestingly that they will turn a hesitant browser in a bookshop into a buyer. The advice came to me from my first editor, the late Tony Godwin, and I have followed it strictly. This is the journalistic side of your work, not to be despised.

You need academic skills too. You must write down all your sources carefully and legibly – book, volume, page, manuscript reference number, etc – as you go along, and keep them in a safe place. When I wrote my first book I was innocent of this, and it took me a long time to check my sources after I thought I had finished, returning to the British Library and other archives to do the work again. There was one reference I could not find, and naturally this was the one readers kept asking me about. Now I always put sources on my computer next to the quotation or fact as soon as I get back from a research trip – if you use a laptop you can do it at once. And never fail to back up your files! Another piece of advice from a scholarly friend: always read through and check quotations in your text at proof stage, to make sure you have copied them exactly, and indicated cuts. Sometimes there is no correct answer to a question. Hardy called his novel *Tess of the D'Urbervilles* in some editions and *Tess of the d'Urbervilles* in others, and reference books continue to give both: whichever you use, somebody will write pointing out your mistake.

If possible, visit the places where your subject lived, and walk where he or she walked. The historian Richard Cobb advised me to go on horseback, or at least on a bicycle, when researching subjects who lived before modern transport arrived, so as to see the landscape as they experienced it. He also told me I should make sure to search archives where there might just possibly be something of interest, however unlikely it seemed. Following his advice, I wrote to the town archives in Le Havre, which had been bombed flat in the Second World War, to ask if they had a record of the birth of Mary Wollstonecraft's daughter, Fanny, in 1794. Two weeks later an official envelope from the archivist arrived with a photocopy of Fanny's birth certificate (for '*le vingt cinquième jour Floréal l'an second de la république française*') which no one, it seemed, had looked at for nearly 200 years. It also certified that her parents were married, which they were not. I nearly cried with joy and tenderness for that little *Françoise*, who certainly never saw her own birth certificate.

Researching Mrs Jordan, I searched for material by writing to as many of her descendants as I could track down – she had 13 children – and found letters written by her sons in the first decade of the 19th century. The first batch were in a fairly remote country house, and their owner kindly brought them out in a dusty box in which they were crumbling away – I had arrived just in time. In a still more distant location there were other letters, and superb portraits of her I had never seen or heard of. More material surfaced after the hardback was published, with letters and portraits appearing as I went round giving talks about it, and successive editions of the paperback crammed in these extra discoveries. Biographies don't die, they become your life companions.

They also bring you friends. While researching Katherine Mansfield I was able to visit her friend Ida Baker, then in her nineties, living alone in a cottage in the New Forest, almost blind and very deaf, for a precious conversation about her memories. The discovery of an unknown short story by Mary Shelley in Italy took me to a 100-room house in San Marcello Pistoiese in the Apennines, still lived in by the great-granddaughter of the little girl for whom Mary Shelley had written her story. They were an enchanting family and greatly generous to me.

Not all research is so adventurous or such fun as this of course. There are long hours of tedious work, disappointments and moments of horror when you find that someone else is working on the same subject and is due to publish their book six months before yours. Since there is nothing you can do about this, you have to take it as calmly as you can. But do everything possible to avoid the double review, a dreadful thing which compares and contrasts your two efforts and is usually dull and likely to kill both books stone dead.

You will never write a definitive biography, because such a thing does not exist. New material appears, attitudes change. The best you can hope to do is approach your subject in good faith. There will always be things you don't know and can't find out. For me, the constraints of biography are part of the attraction, the tug between the known and the unknown, the fact that you have to accept that there are multitudinous gaps in what you know and which your narrative must deal with. One absolute rule must be that, when you speculate, declare that you are doing so, and give the grounds for your speculation – otherwise you are writing romantic fiction, not biography.

You may make money from a biography if you are lucky, but I doubt if that is the usual first reason for writing one. It occurs to me that we embark on the study of other people's lives for the same reason we read fiction, go to plays or watch films: to get the feeling of being inside another skin. As Katherine Mansfield wrote, 'one life is not enough'. And there is much more to it than that. It is a journey on which you explore another century, enlarge your understanding, perhaps do justice to a forgotten figure, and with any luck cast light on the variety of human activity and achievement. One Oxford academic complained that a biography was 'nosy', but I would say it is a condition of intelligent human beings to be curious about other lives – to be just that, nosy.

Claire Tomalin worked in publishing and then journalism for many years, becoming literary editor first of the *New Statesman* and then of the *Sunday Times*, which she left in 1986 in order to write full time. She is the author of *The Life and Death of Mary Wollstonecraft*, which won the Whitbread First Book Prize 1974; *Shelley and His World* (1992); *Katherine Mansfield: A Secret Life* (1988), *The Invisible Woman: The Story of Nelly Ternan and Charles Dickens* (1991), which won the NCR Book Award 1991, the Hawthornden Prize and the James Tait Black Memorial Prize for Biography 1990, and was also released as a feature film in 2014 ; *Mrs Jordan's Profession* (1995); *Jane Austen: A Life* (1997); *Several Strangers* (1999), a collection of reviews and personal memoirs; *Samuel Pepys: The Unequalled Self* (2002), which won the Samuel Pepys Award and the Whitbread Book of the Year 2002; and *Thomas Hardy: The Time-Torn Man* (2006). She has edited selected *Poems of Thomas Hardy* (2006), *Poems of John Milton* (2008) and *Poems of John Keats* (2009) for Penguin Classics. Her most recent book is *Charles Dickens: A Life* (Viking 2011). She was Chair of judges for the Samuel Johnson Prize for Non-Fiction in 2014.

Notes from a successful MBS author

William Bloom reveals the trials of writing for the mind, body & spirit market.

What's it all about? What's the meaning of life? What's my purpose? How am I meant to live? These Big Questions are at the heart of the Mind, Body & Spirit (MBS) movement and its books. Not surprisingly, the quality of answers ranges across a wide spectrum, from self-centred truisms to wisdom. It was ever so with philosophy and religion.

Free of the pulpit and the university chair, yet attempting to wrestle with these core issues, the MBS movement – also known as New Age, personal development and holistic – is an easy target. As a popular movement it does not appear to have gravitas or roots or a secure intellectual method. It is also a recent phenomenon. Just as each generation tends to decry the next generation's music, so philosophers and religionists do not like the look of this new creature in their territory. The glitterati, the media intellectuals, are also suspicious.

So, first things first: in general, as an MBS author in the UK, expect no respect! Almost without exception, the book pages of the national media will not give you any space except perhaps to make some snobbish wisecracks. The media likes to make fun of New Age ideas. But far from being a small niche fashion, MBS is now a nationwide lifestyle approach, which the glitterati themselves may adopt when its design elements (e.g. feng shui) are attractive or its healthcare strategies (e.g. stress control using visualisation) are pragmatically useful. There are also books and authors who cross over between MBS and more mainstream niches, such as Elizabeth Gilbert's *Eat, Pray, Love*, the Dalai Lama's *The Art of Happiness* and Alain de Botton's *Religion for Atheists*.

The general cynicism of Grub Street is not helped by the number of authors in the MBS field whose work is indeed flaky, but, if you are a would-be MBS author or publisher, you cannot help but notice that books on angels, spooks and manifesting prosperity are nevertheless perennial sellers.

On the more positive side, however, MBS material often initiates and supports the very best in holistic and integrative healthcare. For example, the increasing awareness of the relationship between emotions, diet, social tensions and health has been pioneered by MBS bestsellers such as Deepak Chopra, Daniel Goleman and Louise Hay. The notion of self-managed healthcare is deeply embedded in the holistic approach. The philosophical connection between the concepts of sub-atomic physics and mysticism, the alliance of feminism and eco-spirituality, the inclusive recognition that all religious traditions share important core features – these valuable elements in today's culture have all been initiated and nurtured by MBS authors.

As a body of knowledge and cultural movement, MBS presents a general worldview that opposes, to one degree or another, mainstream traditional culture. From an MBS perspective, mainstream culture might be provocatively caricatured as status-driven, emotionally crass and devoted to a crude materialistic billiard ball model of the universe in which only the solid is real and which rejects any concepts to do with altered states of consciousness, metaphysics or the notion of energy/vitality as an important force in human affairs. MBS asserts a more fluid model of an interconnected, interdependent universe in which matter, energy and consciousness are aspects of the same spectrum and interchangeable.

To better understand the MBS field it is perhaps useful to place it in its historical and cultural context and see it as part of the democratisation of information. It is a cliché now to notice that a few hundred years ago enquirers into the meaning of life would have been severely restricted in their research. Predominantly illiterate and with travel so difficult, their enquiry would have been limited to local authorities. Priests and 'wise women' would have been sources of information and we can only guess at the quality of their answers. We can surmise that their responses would have been clothed mainly in their particular culture. There was no interfaith movement, nor much multiculturalism. To enquire fully into the big questions would have required literacy and travel, both scarce resources. Even if you possessed both, there was no centre of education that housed information on *all* the world's religious traditions and their techniques; nor for example was there a body of study which we call psychology.

The mushrooming of literacy and communications since the 19th century has transformed all of that. Answers to the great questions can be found today in thousands of different sources. Over the last decades, for the first time in human history, the spiritualities, beliefs and philosophies of *all* cultures are now accessible. The sacred books of all traditions are available and there is at least one website that claims to provide the texts of all of them.

Teachings that were previously passed on one to one, teacher to student – such as tai chi or yoga – are also now part of the public domain. The esoteric strategies of traditional faiths – for example meditation, visualisation, body posture and prayer – historically restricted to the mystics of those traditions, are also completely publicly accessible and integrated into a modern life style.

This is no shallow revolution. Freedom of information has dismantled the dominating hierarchies of restricted information – in religion more than in any other domain of knowledge. Historically the power of religious organisations, of all faiths, was maintained by the claim that only an ordained few had access to the truth. At one level, in terms of literacy, this was indeed a horribly accurate statement. In terms of social status it was also violent and repressive.

MBS can, in my opinion, be seen as the cultural movement that is exploring and expressing this new-found freedom. All the old secrets are now on display. The dominance based on a monopoly of claimed truth or a monopoly of information is dismantled. This new culture is young and in its developmental stages. It is so young that it hardly even recognises itself, let alone takes itself seriously, which would be a good first step for a movement that wants others to take it seriously. But it is also sizeable and growing. Research and polls on religious belief demonstrate that at least 20% of the UK population now identifies itself as 'spiritual but not religious'. This is the core MBS market.

In this historical context of cultural upheaval, it is no wonder that traditional religionists survey this scene and decry the smorgasbord, the spiritual supermarket. It seems to offer no grounding in a rooted community, a trustworthy tradition or a set of ethics.

To a degree these protests are justified. The inevitable forces of commercialisation

Domains of MBS

- New Science
- Psychology
- Gaia – The Living Earth
- Health and Healing
- Feminism and the Goddess
- Shamanic and Magical Traditions
- Mystic and Esoteric Religion
- Modern Prophesy

and popularisation have indeed appropriated some precious spiritual jewels and dumbed them down, sometimes beyond recognition. (Yoga for perfect skin.) But that vulgarisation has always existed in the field of religious belief, from saints' bones and lascivious monks through to shrouds and cure-all snake oil.

The impression of being a spiritual supermarket is, however, a strength. One of the most positive features of MBS is its openness to the many domains that help us enquire into the meaning of life. When I first edited *The Penguin Book of New Age and Holistic Writing* in 2000, I organised these domains in a way that is still relevant (see box). In one form or another you will find similar sections, located close to each other, in most bookshops. What these books have in common is that they are all accessible to a popular audience and are not academic. Within each of the categories there are substantial bestsellers. Publishers, of course, are looking to repeat them. At the time of writing this article, authors such as Deepak Chopra, Neil Donald Walsh, Caroline Myss and Eckhart Tolle are performing strongly. In fact, one set of statistics suggests that Tolle has now sold more books than the Dalai Lama or the Pope. In the past, writers such as John Grey, M. Scott Peck and Louise Hay have topped the bestseller lists. As I mentioned above, there is currently a fashion for books on angels, spiritualist mediums, positive psychology, happiness and how to use the energy of thought for personal success. Previous flavours of the month have included subjects such as relationships, creativity, quantum physics, detoxing, past lives and energy medicine.

Is there a secret to success in this field? I once heard a cynical commissioning editor saying that the recipe for an MBS bestseller is to: (a) Tell people what they already know; (b) Wrap it up so that they think they are reading it for the first time; (c) Write it so that the reader feels intelligent for understanding the material and is therefore part of a cutting edge or spiritual elite. This means that pioneering authors, the originators of concepts, may be overshadowed by the more populist authors who transform original and unique material into a more accessible form. So another piece of advice for MBS authors seeking success is to not be original, but to develop the original material of others. (I am of course waiting philosophically for other authors to make a mint out of my work.) This, of course, is not always the case. Fritjof Capra's *Tao of Physics* and Daniel Goleman's *Emotional Intelligence* are good examples of bestselling and pioneering books.

So – as an MBS author, as in most literary fields, you have a wide range of options. You can offer your work as a flaky mishmash of half-baked truisms laid out in the supermarket smorgasbord of commercialised religion, psychology and philosophy. Or you can be part of an important cultural liberation movement in which adults, free of traditional prejudices and with an open heart and mind, are supported in exploring the most profound questions about life and its meaning.

William Bloom is one of the UK's most experienced teachers, healers and authors in the field of holistic development. His books include *The Endorphin Effect* (2001), *Feeling Safe* (2002) and *Psychic Protection* (1996), all published by Piatkus Little, Brown, and *Soulution: The Holistic Manifesto* (Hay House 2004). His most recent book is *The Power of Modern Spirituality* (Piatkus 2011). See more at www.williambloom.com.

Writing about food

Food writer and journalist Rose Prince is often told she has a fabulous job – and she has to agree. Here she explains how she came into this line of work, and describes its different aspects and challenges in a changing publishing world.

'So how did you become a food writer?', people ask. That is an extremely good question. As with so many aspects of journalism there is no fixed course or apprenticeship. It has in fact always been better to come to a career in food writing knowing a lot more about food than you do about the media. Why? Because food, while obviously being our daily fuel, is also the product of an industry and while a margin of that industry is something we can celebrate, a greater part is shrouded in dishonesty and technology designed less to nourish consumers than the wallets of multinational food producers.

'Food writing' is multi-limbed: cookery writing in magazines, newspapers, cookbooks and now, of course, on the web forms the greater part. Its visual side – the accompanying photography – makes it the most commercial. Food travelogue is a beautiful aspect of the job, bringing stories from far-flung places, but one that is becoming trickier to achieve since expense budgets have been cut. Feature writing and investigative reporting have become important and might cover stories about food producers, animal welfare, environment or the gruesome agendas of factories and supermarket chains. Nutrition has seeped into food editorial with its spurious claims and wacky diets and of course there are restaurant reviews, though this arm of food writing is somehow set apart from the others.

I do not have a degree. After a somewhat scanty education in a girls' boarding school – more an academy for brides than an education establishment – I drifted through the 1980s without much enjoyment (or husband). I cooked a lot for myself and my friends; it was the leisure I loved. I had been lucky to have both a grandmother who lived in France since before my birth and a mother who was not just a good cook but a great stylist who always found the new interesting ingredient, book or recipe before anyone else. She and Mary, my grandmother, were a great influence. I joke that in primary school in the 1960s I was the only one in class to smell of garlic, but it was true. So I had a food education from people who really cared and took an interest.

During my unhappy '80s 'drift' it was food that comforted me and in which I took a growing interest. And here is a theory, though one not proven: food writers need to experience that comfort, that consolation; it is necessary to ignite something that is more than appetite for their subject, to be able to project its sensory side to their readers. It is simply not good enough to say something is delicious – it is how food makes you feel.

Food writers like Elizabeth David, Nigel Slater, Nigella Lawson or the great American M.F.K. Fisher are sensitive people whose lives with good food have also been punctuated with a degree of personal pain. Elizabeth David was once described to me by a person who had known her well as someone who 'seemed to be without a skin, sort of raw'. That is not to say that you cannot write about food unless you had a miserable childhood, but understanding the joy that great food can bring to anyone, from any background, makes for a great communicator. Empathy meets salivation, you could say.

For a time, I thought I would be a food broadcaster. I met the producer of BBC Radio 4's *Food Programme* and was asked to make a package about a Hampshire butcher. It was themed on butchers' shops becoming a dying breed in the early 1990s, something close to my heart. I wondered why the producer wanted me to do it when I could barely operate the record button on my stereo. 'Because it takes a lot longer to teach a radio reporter your knowledge of food than it does to show you how to use a DAT machine', she said.

As it happened, I was not a great broadcaster. My voice was watery and I shook with nerves. Anyway, I wanted to write. I had begun to read about food while working in a cookbook shop three years before. Every morsel of information seemed fascinating and all I wanted was more. I became critical, deciding between the good and bad. I advise anyone who wants to write about food to read up, but also to be discriminating. For my part, it was the recognition of interesting food writing and appealing, original, tempting recipes that helped me to write closer to the level expected by editors.

Food and cookery writing – newspapers and magazines

Two decades ago, food editorial was largely devoted to cookery articles. Problems in the food industry were tackled by environmental correspondents, by the health writers or consumer affairs journalists. The coverage of agriculture issues tended to veer on the side of a post-war, 'more-(food)-is-more' philosophy dictated by agribusiness and barely concerned with the problems looming in the sector. When the scandals of salmonella and BSE hit the news in the 1990s, however, editorial opened up for food writers passionately campaigning for a revolution in the industry that favoured artisan producers of sustainable produce. It was at this time that I began to look up the appropriate editors and send in proposals.

When I finally submitted an idea that resulted in a commission to write a long food feature for a Sunday supplement, I thought, 'Oh, s***'. Writing the piece ultimately became a matter of not being found out – I would write it to the standard of the writers I loved, or get as close as possible. I waited for the editor's response but heard only from a sub-editor (a good sign that the story had made sense and was at least readable). The following week there was another commission, and so it began. . . . That was nearly 20 years ago.

I am aware that this is what most people would define as a 'break'; jumping from nobody to a writer because an idea landed in the right place. Yet it is the idea, the original thought, that gets you there. Every time you submit an idea, aim for it to have the 'I did not know that' factor, the element of surprise that every editor respects. Again, read a lot about food and you will know if the subject had a recent airing. It annoys the overburdened editor to receive a suggestion that appeared in a rival publication six months ago. Always run a search and never agree to do a piece unless your publication can run with it first. This is what is exciting about the job.

Of course, a journalist employed by a publication can become a specialist writer and many do. There is an advantage to working as a freelancer or a contracted writer working from home, however, because you arc unchained, able to do fieldwork, whether literally tramping round Welsh hill-farms or indulging in the food writer's greatest perk – having a long lunch with plenty of wine.

Food writing and PR

Not long after your first article has been published, the bombardment begins – from the food reps (or 'PRs'). The food industry spends a fortune on PR and the responsible food writer's job is to see through the rose-tinted haze of euphemism and cover-up, weigh up the promise that a new trend has begun against the likelihood that the notion was dreamt up in a conference room, and be careful not to be bribed. If you want to write about an idea put forward by a PR (and PRs who know what type of stories you look for and target you intelligently should be respected), it must always be your choice and not because you feel obliged having been love-bombed with free samples. I work upon one rule of thumb when it comes to PR-led stories: if they help shoppers make better choices, fine, but if shoppers are having the jumper pulled over their eyes, avoid.

Should the PR story involve a time-consuming assignment, or travelling abroad, do your homework and ask a lot of questions before proposing the story. I remember setting out to write about a mustard producer in France, believing it to be very artisan, pure and unadulterated. I took a wrong turning while touring the plant in Dijon, only to find a room filled with sacks of unpleasant chemical preservatives. Another time, in South Africa, I took a £200 taxi at the newspaper's expense to see a sun-dried fruit producer.

'What's that?', I asked the farmer, pointing to a tank on the production line.

'Caustic soda – we dip the peaches in it to remove the skins', he said.

That one hit the dust and I had a lot of explaining to do when retrieving my expenses.

Online

As a writer who has enjoyed the great years of print, I look at the online revolution and hope that it is a development for the good. Digital has brought the bloggers – a vast number of unedited critics and creative cooks who must earn the trust of readers *without* the supporting foundations of national newspapers and magazine publishers. When bloggers gain great numbers of followers on social media the publishers get interested, so this has become a way 'in' for aspirational writers. There is one fly in the ointment so far: if a blogger's following is online and read for free, why – except for the purposes of adorning a coffee table – would the same readers buy a book by the same author?

I guess that while digital and online is establishing itself in these early years, a balance will be found. So far, the texture of printed books and larger-format magazines with complementary cut-out-and-keep values make the print sector relevant. TV chefs' books (a zone apart from the food writing I am discussing) continue to do well in the digital age. Food sections in digital newspapers are expanding and in some cases are classy too. New food writers will find much to occupy them in the future, but for the sake of the readers we hope realistic writing fees will deter PR-led material taking over the content.

Cookery books

Earlier I mentioned how, when working in a bookshop dedicated to food in the early 1990s, I fell in love with food writing. The books I began to collect then, from all over the world and varying eras, formed the foundation of everything I have done since. The esoteric, way-out, provincial cookbooks, beautifully written by scholarly cooks, inspire me the most. Such books once achieved relatively large sales.

Could similarly influential books be published now? Not in the same volume. The process towards authoring a book is much altered by TV cookery. Let's say the independent cookery author struggles when retailers are drunk on sales of ghostwritten TV link-ups that reach half a million or more. The more room taken up on the tables of bookshops by the publications of TV cooks, the less room there is for a pretty book about the vegetable cuisine of Eastern Crete by a hitherto unknown author. Amazon, however, is good for the small book, should it get the right publicity, and all authors should tour independent bookshops and book festivals for face-to-face contact with readers.

Where, you have to ask yourself before approaching an agent or publisher, is your shop window? A columnist on a national publication, a successful chef with a trending, award-winning restaurant – and obviously a TV chef – will likely be published because they are visible and can promote their books naturally. Those running well-liked pop-ups, farm shops and some food producers can do very well too, but the author who writes about food in their own right has to work the hardest to get sales going.

But remember – there is always the fresh idea, beautifully realised in a gorgeous-looking book that hits the mood of the moment and becomes the year's big independent success story. I believe there are many more of these to be written and printed, ebooks notwithstanding, so go for it and write those proposals. Waking at 4 a.m. so you can write to fit around family and other work commitments, going through several gruelling edits and enduring sleepless nights while the book is finally on the presses – all this is worth the moment when your book arrives, your hands are on the cover and you can smell its newly bound pages. Now you are an author, and yes, it is a wonderful job.

Rose Prince is the author of *The New English Kitchen: Changing the Way You Shop, Cook and Eat* (Fourth Estate 2005), *The Savvy Shopper* (Fourth Estate 2006), *The New English Table: Over 200 Recipes That Will Not Cost The Earth* (Fourth Estate 2008), *Kitchenella* (Fourth Estate 2010), and *The Pocket Bakery* (W&N 2013). She has published three editions of *The Good Produce Guide* (Hardie Grant 2009–12). *How to Make Good Food Go Further: Recipes and Tips from The New English Kitchen* was published on Kindle in 2014. She writes monthly columns for the *Daily Telegraph* and the *Tablet* and contributes regularly to the *Daily Mail*, the *Spectator* and other publications. See more at http://www.roseprince.co.uk.

See also...

- *Writing features for newspapers and magazines*, page 13
- *Writing for magazines*, page 8

Being a travel writer

Sara Wheeler paints a vivid picture of life and work as a travel writer, through her own experiences and those of inspirational writers of the past. She reflects on the freedom and flexibility of travel writing as a genre, the personal qualities it demands, and how a sense of place is best captured through the details of daily life.

The happiest moment of my life presented itself one cool February afternoon in the Transantarctic mountains, many years ago. I was hiking up a valley. Fearful of losing my bearings, I stopped to fish an American Geological Survey map out of my pack and spread it on the ice. Tracing my route by topographical landmarks (including an especially pointy mountain glaciologists had baptised 'The Doesn'tmatterhorn'), my finger came to a straight line drawn with a ruler and marked 'Limit of Compilation'. Beyond that, the sheet was blank. I had reached the end of the map…

Getting off the map

Travel writing aims to take the reader off the map, literally and metaphorically. Throughout my own professional life, travel has loaned a vehicle in which to explore the inner terrain of fears and desires we stumble through every day. Writing about travel allows flexibility and freedom within the rigid framework of train journeys, weather and knackered tent. The creative process is an 'escape from personality' (T.S. Eliot said that), and so is the open road. And a journey goes in fits and starts, like life. Not history, not memoir, but a hybrid blend of the two with a generous dose of topographical description, travel writing is *sui generis* – either that, or anything you want it to be, provided the narrative conjures a sense of place. It is a baggy genre. Why not be playful?

In the 5th century BC, Herodotus sniffed around Egypt. Coming upon a handsome obelisk, he asked a gang of workers nearby the meaning of the hieroglyphics carved on the base. 'That', the labourers solemnly announced, 'records the number of onions eaten by the men who constructed the obelisk.' Travel writing can break ground too. In the 14th century, Ibn Battuta set out from the land now known as Morocco and deployed his pen (or was it a quill?) to unveil points east hitherto undreamt of by his contemporaries.

I got started some decades ago with a book on Evia, the second largest Greek island (known to classicists as Euboia). I had studied both ancient and modern Greek at university, had lived in the country for more than a year, and was incubating plenty of ideas about all things Greek. I got a commission, but the resulting book was a labour of love: too much labour, too much love and not enough art (though it's still in print … yeah!). My agent said, 'Next time, go somewhere you don't know anything about.' So I went to Chile, because I had always been fascinated by its shape.

Inspirational writers

Many of the writers who inspired me were on the road and at their desks in the early decades of the 20th century – a kind of golden age for travel writing in Britain. I'm thinking of Evelyn Waugh's *Labels: A Mediterranean Journal* (Duckworth 1930), Norman Douglas' *Old Calabria* (Secker & Warburg 1915), Arthur Grimble's *A Pattern of Islands* (John Murray 1952) and of course Robert Byron, the travel writer's travel writer, whose *Road to Oxiana* (Macmillan 1937) perfectly embraces the frivolous and the deeply serious – a killer combo.

In the '70s, the genre enjoyed a renaissance inspired by Paul Theroux, who set off by train to India, and then to Patagonia. In the aftermath, as the craze worked itself out, a superfluity of travelogues took a bogus motif as their central theme – you know the kind of thing: *Up Everest with One Hand Tied Behind My Back.* The trope reached its logical conclusion with Tony Hawks' bestselling *Round Ireland with a Fridge* (Ebury Press 1998) (he hitchhiked the length of the country with a small item of white goods). This idea has had its day, I feel, and prospective writers would do better to find a more authentic theme.

The 'pattern in the carpet'

The most important thing, in a book or a short piece, is the pattern in the carpet. Travel literature must be *about* something, and not just an account of a great trip. During the glorious six months I spent travelling down Chile, I assumed that journey's end would be Cape Horn. But I learned that the country claimed a slice of Antarctica, which appeared on all the maps – even those on badges on Boy Scouts' arms – like a slice of cake suspended in the Southern Ocean. Damn! So I hitched a lift on a Chilean air-force plane to a snowy base and, as I climbed a hill with a volcanologist and heard him tap-tapping ice into a specimen jar, I looked out at an ice desert bigger than the United States and saw my next book: a travel journey across the Antarctic. I subsequently spent seven months in 'the Big White' and the experience gave me a taste for extreme environments. Some years later I followed up with a book on the Arctic. For both, I had to get people to cooperate, as many of my destinations were not on commercial routes; indeed some, like the far eastern Russian region of Chukotka, were closed to foreigners. Dogged persistence required. Never Give Up!

Books and other ventures...

My chief endeavour, in my working life, has been books: travel books and biographies of travellers, of Captain Scott's man Apsley Cherry-Garrard, for example, author of the polar classic *The Worst Journey in the World* (Constable & Co. 1922). But, as for most of my peers, there have been many short pieces along the way. I write essays, reviews and squibs for love – and for money. The freelance travel writer has many avenues to explore. Some of these pieces really are essays – new introductions to classic works of travel literature, for example; some you could call incidental journalism. This latter might be an enemy of promise, but it gets me out of the house, often to places I would not otherwise go. Dropping in to a village in Kerala for six days might not yield any profound experience, but it offers suggestions and opens up possibilities.

There is a difference between the magazine assignment, for which the writer must travel fast and purposefully, and the book, for which the journey evolves its own inner logic. When I turned 50 my publisher suggested I collect some of my incidental articles in a volume which we called *Access All Areas: Selected Writings 1990–2011* (Jonathan Cape 2011). Editing that book revived pleasures of crossing unimportant African borders using a kidney donor card as ID; of sharing a bathroom with a harp seal; of mixing a cocktail of six parts vodka and one part something else (they didn't revive much of that, because I can't remember what happened next...).

The power of detail

I often hear it said that tourism has murdered travel writing. I don't think so. Mass travel has liberated the form. No amount of package tours will stop the ordinary quietly going on everywhere on earth. When I lived in Chile in the early '90s I found my weekly trawl round the supermarket gripping beyond belief: watching women decide between this jar of *dulce de leche* or that one, weighing out their cherimoyas, loading up with boxes of washing powder. In Greece a decade earlier I often joined girlfriends at their weekly weigh-in at the local pharmacy (domestic scales had to wait for more prosperous times). So you don't *actually* have to be off the map. Don't you sometimes find daily life almost unbearably poetic?

Minute curiosity is a requirement of the travel writer – and of the biographer, novelist and poet. The significance of the trivial is what makes a book human. Out there on the road, I have often found that the most aimless and boring interludes yielded, in the long run, the most fertile material. Every journey created energy, joy and, above all, hope. There was always a dash of human dignity to lift a story out of absurdity and farce, however ugly the background. The world everywhere and simultaneously is a beautiful and horrible place.

In short, the notion that all the journeys have been made is just another variation of the theme that the past exists in technicolour while the present has faded to grey – that everything then was good, and everything now is bad. A theme, in other words, as old as literature. I add the point that there are no package tours to the Democratic Republic of Congo, still the heart of darkness, or to the parts of Saudi Arabia where women live in a perpetual ethical midnight.

Tools of the trade

Having established her pattern in the carpet, the writer must work hard to conjure a sense of place: she has to make the reader see, hear, taste, feel and smell (though not all at the same time). Specificity is the key, as it is to all writing. Don't tell the reader so-and-so was eating, or reading – tell them *what* he was eating or reading. Themes and characters can function as scaffolding. Other trusty tools include the use of dialogue, which works on prose like yeast. Quotations from your diary or letters or emails can vary the texture of your narrative. And history is your friend – use judiciously selected quotations from those who have gone before you. I often cruise the topography shelves in the stacks of the London Library, on the lookout.

And do I need to add that to be any kind of writer you have to read all the time? If you are aiming to pursue a career in the field I describe, you can start by devouring one volume by each of the writers I cite here – preferably within a month. Get the habit. Make notes about what you like and don't like. I still keep a log of that kind, and I refer to it all the time.

Travelling heroines

Let me end with a few words from and about the travel writer who inspired me above all others: Mary Kingsley. She belonged to that tribe of tweed-skirted Victorians who battled through malarial swamps, parasols aloft, or scaled the unnamed Pamirs trailed by a retinue of exhausted factotums. History has tended to write them off as benignly mad eccentrics, but the best among their volumes have stood the test of time: Isabella Bird's *A Lady's Life in the Rocky Mountains* (1874), Harriet Tytler's *An Englishwoman in India* (1903–06), Kate Marsden's *On Sledge and Horseback to Outcast Siberian Lepers* (1893) (candidate for title of the millennium?). It is Kingsley, however, who carries the prize with her masterpiece

Travels in West Africa (1897), a book enjoyed by millions since it first appeared more than a century ago. The author's influence on those following in her tracks can scarcely be overestimated. After all, not only did she do what countless men told her could not be done, but she also turned the experience into literature – and had the time of her life to boot.

She was born in London in 1862, high noon of imperial splendour. Amazingly, given the sophistication of her publications, she never went to school. Blue-eyed and slender, with a long face and hair the colour of wet sand, she was 31 when she set off on her first proper trip to Africa in August 1893. *Travels in West Africa* tells the story of Kingsley's second, 11-month voyage. Her ship reached Freetown, Sierra Leone, on 7 January 1895, and she headed southwards through those countries now known as Ghana, Nigeria, Cameroon, Equatorial Guinea and Gabon. The trip involved almost unimaginable hardship. Approaching the Gabonese river Remboué, our heroine wades through swamps for two hours at a stretch, up to her neck in fetid water with leeches round her neck like a frill. She marches 25 miles through forest so dense that the sky is never once visible, and falls 15 feet into a game pit laid with 12-inch ebony spikes ('It is at these times,' she writes, 'you realise the blessing of a good thick skirt.'). Kingsley responds profoundly to the African landscape. 'I believe the great swamp region of the Bight of Biafra is the greatest in the world,' she writes, 'and that in its immensity and gloom it has a grandeur equal to that of the Himalayas.' Like all the very best travel scribes – one thinks of Sybille Bedford, Norman Lewis, Jonathan Raban, and, on form, Freya Stark – Kingsley brilliantly paints a landscape onto the page. The reader can see the silver bubbles of Lake Ncovi as the canoe carves a frosted trail, the rich golden sunlight of late afternoon, or the wreaths of indigo and purple over the forest as day sinks into night. 'To my taste', she writes, 'there is nothing so fascinating as spending a night out in an African forest, or plantation… And if you do fall under its spell, it takes all the colour out of other kinds of living.' Indeed.

Sara Wheeler, FRSL is a travel writer, biographer and journalist. Her books include *Travels in a Thin Country: A Journey Through Chile* (Little, Brown 1994), *Terra Incognita: Travels in Antarctica* (Jonathan Cape 1996), *Cherry: A Biography of Apsley Cherry-Garrard* (Jonathan Cape 2001) and *Too Close to the Sun: A Biography of Denys Finch Hatton* (Jonathan Cape 2006). Her most recent book is *O My America!* (Jonathan Cape 2013).

See also...

- *Notes from a successful biographer*, page 307
- *Writing for magazines*, page 8
- *Writing for newspapers and magazines*, page 13

Books

The world of the literary editor

Claire Armitstead gives an insight into the role of a literary editor.

When I started out as literary editor in 1999, reviews were commissioned by phone, written in wonky typewriter script, delivered by fax – and 50% of them never made it into the paper. Newspaper space was tight and publishing had entered the bloat years: it was no longer possible for even the best-managed set of literary pages to accommodate more than a fraction of the hundreds of books that poured into the office every week, and we were struggling to come to terms with this new reality.

Today, the books still pour in, but the internet has transformed the way we deal with them and confronted us with a whole new tidal wave of titles. We are no longer simply national newspapers, but international media operations with readers in every continent. Our space is limitless but our resources are shrinking – and we are once again struggling to come to terms with tough new realities.

All this coincides with a publishing revolution that is changing not only the volume of books produced each year but their very nature. If someone had told me five years ago that we would soon be reviewing a self-published novel about sado-masochism, I would have redirected them to *Playboy* magazine. But we did review *Fifty Shades of Grey*, albeit after a traditional publisher had picked it up. Whatever the arguments about its artistic validity, it was the biggest book of the year, and arguably of the decade so far – as significant in its way as the first in the *Harry Potter* series. To review one *Fifty Shades* was a no-brainer, but what about the thousands of pale shadows that have leapt out behind it?

Some things, though, haven't changed. The big grey mail bags still pile into the office twice a day, bulging with traditionally published books. Of the 400 or so books that are delivered every week, no more than 30 will make it into the review pages. While the internet has given us all manner of new ways to draw attention to books – from blogging to audio slideshows and video – reviews still belong to the old print culture.

Why should this be? One reason is economic: reviews take time to write and cost money to commission, and these resources are as yet mostly locked up in print. Another is cultural: people still want to write and read reviews on paper, just as they still want to read physical books. Though this might look quixotic in the era of online booksellers hosting online reader reviews, there is a strength in it. I oversee two weekly literary sections – the *Guardian Review* and the books pages of the *Observer News Review*. They are separately edited and have distinct personalities and policies, though both feed into the *Guardian* books website.

Review is a high-end section, which is currently strong on social history and literary fiction, and has a unique commitment to weekly reviews of poetry and children's books. The *Observer* section is smaller, and tends to review more populist writing, with a particular strength in graphic fiction. These two sections create a reviewing 'space' wider than could be filled by any single outlet. To the outsider, though, the similarities undoubtedly look more obvious than the differences. Both are unashamedly biased towards UK publishing; neither review many celebrity biographies. Nor do we do self-help books or the misery memoirs that top the library charts year after year. Though we all have our quirks, this crossover exists for all newspaper review sections, which means that the vast majority of books published each year will never be reviewed by any of us.

Perhaps surprisingly, since the newspaper books sections are part of news operations, none of us tend to review the top-selling books – teen vampire fiction, for instance, or commercial chick lit, or cookery books. Reviews have long been irrelevant anyway to the mass-market end of the business, which has other ways of selling itself. But to regard reviews in terms of impact on sales is to miss the whole point of book reviewing, which is a complicated negotiation between the culture of writing and reading.

The role of the newspaper books pages is not to sell books: it is to entertain, inform and stimulate readers, many of whom have little time in their lives to actually read books at all. The most obvious function of the review is to tell people whether a book is good or bad. But there is a whole spectrum between those two extremes, and this is often where the character and colour of the books sections lie. A book may be well written but essentially dull or badly written but packed with fascinating facts. Reviewers can offer a digest of the stuff people want to know about. They can mediate and simplify, bringing an academic thesis into the language of journalism and placing it within the available reading time of an ordinary person's working day. This is particularly true of non-fiction reviews – after all, a reader can be very interested in advances in quantum physics and very unlikely to get through Stephen Hawking's *A Brief History of Time.*

Commissioning the reviews

The job of deciding what to send out for review ranges from the diligent (the twice-yearly hack through all the publishing catalogues to compile a list for potential review of every upcoming book in the next season) to what might pass as mere partying. Yes, publishers do still hold book launches, but no, they are not all about getting drunk and behaving badly: it is often through meeting people that you pick up the 'buzz' about an exciting new writer, or an old one who has just been rediscovered. The best commissioning is often the result of lateral thinking inspired by a chance conversation: the former Archbishop of Canterbury, Rowan Williams, on the poet R.S. Thomas, for instance, or Jonathan Coe on Alexei Sayle.

Then comes the physical business of handling the books, which all have to be unpacked, stacked and tracked. Once the obvious no-hopers have been discarded, the dozens of more or less worthy contenders have to be whittled down to fit the available space. Books are separated into original fiction and non-fiction, with a separate bookcase for paperback re-issues. There are three editors on the *Guardian Review* desk who are each responsible for commissioning reviews in a particular area, in collaboration with the section editor. These are the gatekeepers, who convert the fantasy commissions of our brainstorming sessions into a realistic number of reviews. It does not mean that we are huddled away in our own little corners – on the contrary, the indefinable spark of a books desk depends on the hours that every editor is prepared to spend reading that marginal proof by an unknown writer on the bus home and enthusing about it in the office the next day. The commissions I am proudest of are reviews of those completely unexpected gems that only emerge from the most conscientious scouting.

But there are logistical limits to this sort of eureka commission. We have space for eleven 200-word paperback reviews a week, more than half of which will be cut-down versions of the original hardback reviews. Big reviews of first editions are more tricky: we may know that we will carry an average of six fiction and six non-fiction reviews a week, but until the review has arrived, we can never be absolutely sure what it will be like – ecstatic, condemning, indifferent; even long or short. This is where the literary editor's job is closer to news than to features. A features editor can set the agenda, by choosing a subject, deciding how many words to commission on it and instructing a writer how to write them. A literary commissioner can choose a book for a critic to review, but can never tell that critic what to think.

Choosing the reviewer

For a variety of social, historical and economic reasons, literary critics are regarded as more compromised than those in any other art form. There is some truth in this, if only because writers are always reviewed by other writers. There is none of the separation of crafts and industries that exists between reviewers and actors, ballet dancers or concert pianists.

In addition, there is no tradition in the UK of giving jobs to literary critics, as there is for other art forms, so most reviewers have 'day jobs' – usually their own writing, or some sort of teaching, both of which bring dependencies and compromises. It's the literary editor's job to steer a path between these conflicts of interest to that ideal reviewer, who will be knowledgeable but not compromised, wise, reasonable and witty. People often ask if critics actually read the books they are reviewing, which touches on another important part of the editor's role: to ensure that reviewers are properly attentive and to challenge them if they are not.

Placing the reviews

Once we have decided which books to send out, chosen a reviewer and taken delivery of their review, the next step is deciding where to place it and, just as importantly, what to place it with. Nobody would want to read page after page of bad-tempered reviews, yet equally, no one would trust pages in which every review was a rave. The challenge is to respect the opinion of the critic, while creating pages that have life and variety and which – in journalistic terms – 'talk to' each other. Serious reviews need to be leavened with playful ones, which explains the occasional inclusion of a blistering review of a predictably bad book.

One new aspect of this balancing act is that, though they are commissioning for print, good editors increasingly have an eye on how their reviews will play on the website, where the reader numbers (and opinions) are brutally clear. Our online readers are very different to the traditional newspaper readership: they are younger, more international and often gleefully pedantic. They love books about spelling and grammar, hate anyone they see as over-hyped, and are quick to ridicule anything they think is wrong or sub-standard.

New opportunities and challenges

This negotiation with print and online readerships is posing the greatest new challenge of all to the role of the literary editor. The *Guardian* is now a 'digital first' operation, which means we often run reviews on the website before they appear in the paper. A review on a website is fundamentally different to that same review in a newspaper: it is no longer a mandarin utterance, but an opinion-piece that is open for discussion by people who do not have to put their real names to their own, sometimes vicious, opinions. The old joke that today's newspaper is tomorrow's fish and chip wrapping is no longer true. Online books sections live in the 'long tail' – in hardback reviews which resurface as soon as the paperback appears, or pieces about unknowns who suddenly become prize-winners. So publication of a review online is only the start of its life, and part of the editor's job is to monitor the conversation, encourage critics to join in and defend them from unwarranted attacks.

The wonderful side of this new engagement with readers is the expansion of our intelligence-gathering networks. The *Guardian* has a devoted community of readers who congregate around our weekly 'Tips, links and suggestions' blog to exchange enthusiasms, as well as responding directly to reviews. They were the first to alert us to performance poet Kate Tempest, who won the 2012 Ted Hughes Award for New Work in Poetry (see page 545), and it was through them that we discovered *Down the Rabbit Hole*, a Mexican novella published in 2011 by the new publisher And Other Stories, which went on to become the first book in translation to be shortlisted for the *Guardian* First Book Award.

These online readers also, increasingly, write their own reviews – not least on our children's website, which for the last three years has been carrying up to three reviews a day by site members aged 17 or under, as well as family reviews of picture books. One teen review of *The Hunger Games* has been read more than 6,000 times and is still being picked up two years after it was published. Consider the impact of this new reviewing culture on children's publishing – a literary sector that has traditionally struggled to get any space at all in newspapers. The shift towards reader-reviewing is also happening on our adult website. It means that for the first time in newspaper history, books are being reviewed by the people who buy and read them, rather than by hired hands.

However, authority still matters. One of our regular correspondents, AggieH, explained it eloquently: 'Random reader reviews don't interest me. I don't browse for them, here or elsewhere. But if I am aware of their existence, I do read reviews by posters whose judgement I have learned to trust. Much in the same way that I read reviews by a few selected serious book bloggers.'

Back in 1999, we were limited to reviews on paper; today we have a weekly books podcast, video interviews, and a Twitter following of some 500,000 people all over the world. Each medium has its own personality and potential, but in the end what readers are looking for is informed choices and authoritative opinion within a known context. Which brings us full circle back to the critic and the book, and to the difficult negotiations between inside knowledge and independence, expertise and humility, seriousness and the willingness to entertain. Technologies may change, but as long as there are writers and readers in the world, reviewers will remain in hot pursuit.

Claire Armitstead is head of books for the *Guardian*, the *Observer* and guardian.co.uk.

Poetry

Becoming a published poet

Julia Copus shares insights and advice on getting your poetry published and tells her own personal story from first poem in print to published collections and beyond.

Poetic beginnings

Strictly speaking, I had my first poem published when I was seven. I'd sent it to a girls' comic called *Tammy*, and because I'd forgotten to add my name, the acceptance letter was addressed to 'Tammy Reader' and very nearly got thrown away. Luckily, rather than putting the letter straight back in the post unopened and marked 'return to sender', my mother thought to ask me if I knew anyone of that name. With the £2 postal order they'd enclosed by way of payment, I bought a miniature Pippa doll in a sparkling green evening dress. I say it was lucky because I think encouragements of this kind are tremendously important and though I'd have to wait a long time to see my next poem in print, that early success planted in me the notion that such things were possible.

Throughout school, I loved writing, and filled my exercise books with stories of Alice-like adventures where no one was quite as they seemed and holes in tree roots provided portals into other worlds. I continued writing poems too, and reading a few – mainly classics – but it wasn't until after university that poetry really clicked into place, like the bolt of a great door sliding open. My boyfriend had given me a copy of Sylvia Plath's novel *The Bell Jar* (Heinemann 1963) to read. It was one of those books that left me wanting to know more about the author, so I got hold of a biography and read that too. Finally, I came to the poems. Here was much of the same material (*The Bell Jar* is largely autobiographical) but framed in such a way that the words – visceral and super-charged – left me changed; after looking up from Plath's *Collected Poems* (Harper & Row 1981), the world seemed like a very different place. Mixed with inevitable admiration were feelings of envy and, beyond that, excitement. How had the poet pulled off this conjuring act? I wasn't sure, but somewhere inside me I felt it was something I might be able to emulate.

I spent the next few months trying; you might even say I am trying still, though the traces of Plath – very evident in those early poems – are, I hope, no longer visible. Influences are a good thing and poets, like painters, sculptors and musicians, can learn a great deal from copying the old masters but, for readers, the appeal of poems written 'in the style of...' is limited.

Competitions and other submissions

When I had five or six poems to my name, I entered a local poetry competition, judged by the poet Michael Baldwin who had been friends with Ted Hughes, and Iwon third prize; I entered another and won first. These were small contests but the affirmation they provided for a novice was vital. I sent off to the Poetry Library in London for a list of magazines and started submitting poems to *Envoi* because it said it welcomed new, as well as established, poets. (The Library still publishes the most comprehensive list, now available online at www.poetrylibrary.org.uk/magazines).

I was careful from the start to follow the standard advice: never send more than six poems; always type the poems; include the briefest of covering letters plus return postage. Though my very first submission was rejected, the editor enclosed an enthusiastic note saying which poems he liked best, where he thought they might be improved, and asking me to send again. Soon, he was accepting my poems and I began sending elsewhere too.

Poetry magazines play a crucial role in the life of any poet, and in the early stages they can act as a barometer of our progress in general, and of the success of individual poems. Until we feel secure enough to allow a second reader into our confidence, we must act as our own readers, editors and critics. For the uncertain, fledgling poet, the impersonal process of submitting to magazines is a godsend: sending a poem out to an unknown editor often feels less daunting than sharing it with someone we know. Editors aren't always right, but the chances are that if a poem is repeatedly rejected you need to work on it, or even start again from scratch. And if you can see beyond the disappointment, a rejection slip can be a useful ally, allowing you to gauge what does and does not work. It's also true that not all rejection slips are the same: if yours is accompanied by an encouraging note – still better a request to 'send more poems' – don't dismiss it. The editor in question has to like your poems a lot to make that kind of effort.

A year or so after I started sending work out to magazines, I read about an award exclusively for poets under 30, run by the Society of Authors. This was the Eric Gregory Award, which you can read about elsewhere in this book. By now I had amassed 19 poems that I felt could stand on their own feet. I filled in the form and off they went in their manila envelope to London. Winning one of the five Eric Gregory Awards for that year was a real turning point for me, as it has been for so many poets – Seamus Heaney, Andrew Motion and Carol Ann Duffy among them, but many less well-known names too. I'd go as far as to say that some poetry publishers are on the lookout for the latest 'Gregory winners'; there's no question that the prize opens doors.

Do you need an agent?

People sometimes want to know if an agent will help them in their work as a poet. My answer is no – at least not until you are well established. Even then, while some renowned poets have agents, at least as many of them don't. Remember that an agent will take a commission (generally 15% of everything you earn through your writing). I secured an agent about a year ago, but not for my poetry. I was embarking on two new projects – a children's book and a biography. In the case of the children's book, I wanted someone to help me make sense of the contract I'd been offered and to make sure I was getting a fair deal; in the case of the biography – another field that was new to me – I felt an agent would have a better chance of placing the book in the first place, and would probably be able to secure me a better deal than I could get by myself. Though I'm very glad I found the agent I now have, she has little to do with securing me poetry readings and commissions; to be honest, I had managed perfectly well for 15 years as a published poet without any outside help.

One thing is certain: an agent is not needed to help you place a poetry book with a publisher.

Publishing your first book of poetry

So *how* do you go about publishing a book of poetry? When is the right time? And how big a body of work should you present?

It would certainly be unwise to submit a manuscript to a publisher without first having placed at least a handful of poems (and preferably more) in reputable literary magazines. If you're able to tell a busy publisher that you have a good track record of magazine publication behind you, they are far more likely to take your manuscript seriously. Given that the average poetry collection contains around 56 pages of poetry, once you have, say, 40 poems together, *and you are convinced of their quality*, you might consider submitting your manuscript. Many publishers provide submission guidelines on their websites; in the first instance, they usually want to see a maximum of 15 poems (Faber asks for six; Bloodaxe 'up to a dozen'). If they like those, they will soon ask to see more.

My own route to publication

What of my own story? When the time came, I (along with every poet I know of) went not through an agent but direct to a publisher – and in my case I took a less than conventional route. It is not a route I'd advise others to take, incidentally, but here's how it happened...

After my early reading of Plath, I wanted to find out what poets had been up to in more recent years. The first contemporary poetry collection I read was *Electroplating the Baby* by Jo Shapcott (Bloodaxe Books 1988), which I'd found by chance in Maidstone Reference Library. I was very struck by the poems – surreal, engaging and disarmingly direct in tone. I was also quite taken by the eye-catching cover and started to look out for (and, crucially, *read*) other Bloodaxe titles in bookshops and libraries, as well as books by other publishers.

Soon afterwards I saw an advert in one of the poetry magazines for a competition that was being run by the Kitley Trust. I made up my mind to enter it – not for the prize money, which was £10 for each of the ten winning entries, but because it was being judged by Neil Astley, editor of Bloodaxe Books. I was lucky enough to win one of those prizes, and in due course I travelled up to the prize-giving in Sheffield. At the end of the afternoon, I did something I now shudder to remember: I took a sheaf of 15 poems from my bag and asked Neil if he would read them on the train home. In my defence I can say that, as a shy 24 year-old, I was certainly acting more out of naivety than bravado.

Fortunately for me, the gamble paid off. I remember the moment when Neil Astley's response arrived in the post. It came in a fat Jiffy® bag, postmarked 'Hexham'. I knew by the thickness of the envelope that it wasn't a rejection slip, and ripped it open so fast I cut my thumb on one of the staples. I still have the original letter, complete with its smeared insignia of blood. It says, 'Thank you for leaving me with a sample selection. I was very impressed. Can you send more?' The letter goes on to stress that it would be in my best interests not to publish a book prematurely but to wait until I had 'a consistently strong volume of work'. Sound advice – and over the following year or so I continued publishing in magazines and occasionally sending bundles of poems off to the Bloodaxe offices. The book began to take shape and before I knew it I was at the stage of choosing an image for the cover.

What comes next? Opportunities and possibilities

Perhaps it sounds strange but, for me, holding a book with my name on the cover was not the thrill you might expect. I think that is as it should be. If your overriding ambition is 'to be a published poet', it's unlikely you will ever write really good poems. For one thing, having a book published means that you are no longer anonymous, and for a writer there is great power and freedom in anonymity. Still, I am enormously grateful.

Rather like one of those magical portals I wrote about at primary school, my first book opened up for me a world of new experiences and also professional possibilities: residencies, fellowships, commissions, teaching. In addition, it led to my writing in more forms than I might otherwise have tried. I have gone on to write essays, reviews, radio programmes, children's books – even a pocket writing guide. This is not unusual. Once you have a book published, it is far easier to publish another; it is up to you, then, which direction you want to go in. Poets are, I think, at an advantage here. I know of several who have gone on to be first-class prose writers – novelists, short story writers, essayists – and for a few, they find that the new genre suits them better. It is certainly likely to be more lucrative: most poetry books do not sell in vast quantities. Partly for economic reasons, my own writing has followed several tributaries; even so, the source has always been poetry.

Julia Copus is a poet and children's author. She has published three collections of poetry, *The Shuttered Eye* (Bloodaxe 1995), *In Defence of Adultery* (Bloodaxe 2003) and *The World's Two Smallest Humans* (Faber & Faber 2012); all three are Poetry Book Society Recommendations. Her awards include First Prize in the National Poetry Competition and the Forward Prize for Best Single Poem (2010). She has recently published her second picture book for children, *The Hog, the Shrew and the Hullabaloo* (Faber & Faber 2015).

See also...

- *Poetry organisations*, page 331
- *Notes from a passionate poet*, page 329

Notes from a passionate poet

Benjamin Zephaniah describes his route to being published.

'How did you first get published?' and 'Can you give me any advice on getting published?' must be the two questions I am most regularly asked as I go poeting around this planet. And what really gets me is that for most of my poetic life I have found them so hard to answer without doing a long talk on race and culture, and giving a lesson on the oral traditions of the Caribbean and Africa. I'm trying hard not to do that now but I have to acknowledge that I do come out of the oral tradition and to some extent I am still very much part of the Jamaican branch of that tradition, which has now established itself in Britain. In reality, getting published wasn't that hard for me: I came to the page from the stage. I didn't wake up one day and decide to join the oral tradition, I simply started performing in churches and community centres, on street corners and at political rallies, and I really didn't care about being published in books – I used to say I just want to be published in people's hearts. Now I don't want to sound like a royal seeking sympathy or a surgeon evaluating her or his work, I just feel there's something very special about hearing people recite a poem of yours back to you when you know that it has never been written down: it means that they must have heard me recite the poem and it had such an impact on them that it left an impression on their minds – but I say hearts because it sounds more sensitive.

Someone with a PhD once told me that the most important thing I could do was to get published, so for what seemed like an eternity (in fact it was just a couple of months) I became the most depressed kid on the block as the rejections flooded in, and I took each rejection very personally. I soon stopped punishing myself and went back to performing. Within the black and Asian communities there was a large network of venues to perform in and I was happy there, performing for 'my people'. But it wasn't long before I started to make a bit of a name for myself in what we now call the mainstream, and then the publishers came running back to me, many of them apologising and saying that the person who sent the rejection letter to me had now moved on and they weren't very good anyway. I didn't blame the publishers; I wasn't angry with them. It was a time when the British publishing industry simply didn't understand Reggae and Dub poetry, and the performance scene as we know it today had hardly taken root. It's not practical to advise all budding poets to go down the route that I chose. Some poets simply don't want to perform whilst others want something published before they take to the stage – they literally want something to cling to as they recite – but I have to say there is nothing like looking your audience in the face and delivering your work to them in person.

I used to be able to give a run down of the poetry publishing and performance scene in Britain in about 30 minutes, but not any longer, with the internet and all that, the universe has changed. Not only are there hundreds of ways to get your poetry published, you can now publish your performance and have a worldwide hit without ever actually having a book or leaving your bedroom. You don't even have to tread the boards to become a performance poet. The choice is now yours: you can be a Dub poet, a pub poet, a cyber poet, a graffiti poet, a rap poet, a naked poet, a space poet, a Myspace poet, or a street poet. You can be a geek poet, a YouTube poet, an underground poet, a Facebook poet, a sound poet, and if you like to keep it short you can be a Twitter poet. You can go any way you want, but you must never forget to be a poet. You must never forget why you started writing (or performing) and you must love your art. The love I had for words as a baby has never left me, and when I was getting all those rejection letters and feeling so unwanted, my love for poetry never waned.

And another thing: read poetry. Many people tell me that they love poetry but after a minute or so of investigation I find that they only love their own poetry, and in many cases they only understand their own poetry. You can get a lot of help from teachers or in workshops, but reading other people's poetry is the best way of understanding poetry, it is the best way of getting into the minds of other poets. This great book that you now have in your hands and learned people who understand the industry are able to give you much better advice on getting published than I can, and if you do get published your publisher or agent should be offering you all the practical help you need. But you have to have the passion, you have to have the inspiration, you have to be a poet. Stay true.

Benjamin Zephaniah has been performing poetry since he was 11 years old. He has also written 13 books of poetry, four novels, and recorded five music CD albums. He spends much of his time encouraging young people to write and perform poetry and has received 16 honorary doctorates in recognition of his work. His latest releases are a martial arts travelogue called *Kung Fu Trip* (Bloomsbury 2011), *To Do Wid Me*, a book and DVD of live performances (Bloodaxe Books 2013) and *Terror Kid* (Hot Key Books 2014). He is currently Professor of Poetry and Creative Writing at Brunel University. His website is www.benjaminzephaniah.com.

Poetry organisations

Poetry is one of the easiest writing art forms to begin with, though the hardest to excel at or earn any money from. Below are some organisations which can help poets take their poetry further.

WHERE TO GET INVOLVED

The British Haiku Society

Flat 4, 2 Clifton Lawn, Ramsgate, Kent, CT11 9PB
email membership@britishhaikusociety.org.uk
website www.britishhaikusociety.org.uk

The Society runs the prestigious annual James W. Hackett International Haiku Award and the annual British Haiku awards in two categories – haiku and haibun. It is active in promoting the teaching of haiku in schools and colleges, and is able to provide readers, course/workshop leaders and speakers for poetry groups, etc. Founded 1990.

Literature Wales

(formerly Academi)
Cambrian Buildings, Mount Stuart Square, Cardiff Bay, Cardiff CF10 5FL
tel 029-2047 2266
email post@literaturewales.org
website www.literaturewales.org

The Welsh National Literature Promotion Agency, which has a huge resource available for poets and poetry. It organises events and tours, promotes poets and poetry, offers poetry advice, locates poetry publishers, offers financial help to poets and to organisers wishing to book poets, and much more. To take advantage of its services you have to live or be in Wales, which has the largest number of poets per 1,000 population anywhere in the Western World.

The Poetry Book Society

The Dutch House, 307–308 High Holborn, London WC1V 7LL
tel 020-7831 7468
email info@poetrybooks.co.uk
website www.poetrybooks.co.uk
website www.poetrybookshoponline.com
website www.childrenspoetrybookshelf.co.uk

This unique book club for readers of poetry was founded in 1953 by T.S. Eliot, and is funded by Arts Council England. Every quarter, selectors choose one outstanding publication (the PBS Choice), and recommend four other titles; these are sent to members, who are also offered substantial discounts on other poetry books. The PBS also administers the T.S. Eliot Prize (see page 541), produces the quarterly membership magazine, the *Bulletin*, and provides teaching materials for primary and secondary schools.

The Poetry Business

Bank Street Arts, 32–40 Bank Street, Sheffield S1 2DS
tel 0114 346 3037
email office@poetrybusiness.co.uk
website www.poetrybusiness.co.uk

Dedicated to helping writers reach their full potential by running supportive workshops.

Poetry Can

12 Great George Street, Bristol BS1 5RH
tel 0117 933 0900
email admin@poetrycan.co.uk
website www.poetrycan.co.uk

Poetry Can is one of the few literature organisations in the UK specialising in poetry. It organises events such as the Bristol Poetry Festival, runs a lifelong learning programme and offers information and advice in all aspects of poetry.

Poetry Ireland

32 Kildare Street, Dublin 2, Republic of Ireland
tel +353 (0)1 6789815
email info@poetryireland.ie
website www.poetryireland.ie

Poetry Ireland is the national organisation dedicated to developing, supporting and promoting poetry throughout Ireland. It is the only professional and dedicated national organisation for literature in Ireland. For over 35 years the organisation has supported poets and writers at all stages of their careers through both performance and publication opportunities, creating meaningful encounters between writers and the public. The organisation delivers through four core strands: Publication, Readings, the provision of an Information & Resource Service, and Education & Outreach. Through its Education & Outreach remit, Poetry Ireland offers a broad spectrum of services within the literary arts – from poetry to children's fiction, storytelling and drama.

The Poetry Society

22 Betterton Street, London WC2H 9BX
tel 020-7420 9880
email info@poetrysociety.org.uk
website www.poetrysociety.org.uk

The Poetry Society is Britain's leading voice for poets and poetry. Founded in 1909 to promote a more general recognition and appreciation of poetry, the Society has nearly 4,000 members. With innovative education, commissioning and publishing programmes, and a packed calendar of performances, readings and competitions, the Society champions poetry in its many forms.

The Society offers advice and information to all, with exclusive offers and discounts available to members. Every quarter, members receive copies of *Poetry Review* and the Society's newsletter, *Poetry News*. The Society also publishes education resources; organises high-profile events including an Annual Lecture and National Poetry Day celebrations; runs Poetry Prescription, a critical appraisal service available to members; and provides an education advisory and training service, school membership, youth membership and a website.

A diverse range of events and readings take place at the Poetry Café beneath the Society's headquarters in London's Covent Garden. The Society also programmes events and readings throughout the UK.

Competitions run by the Society include the annual National Poetry Competition, with a first prize of £5,000; the biennial Corneliu M. Popescu Prize for Poetry Translated from a European Language into English; the Ted Hughes Award for New Work in Poetry; SLAMbassadors UK; and the Foyle Young Poets of the Year Award.

The Seamus Heaney Centre for Poetry

c/o School of English, Queen's University Belfast, Belfast BT7 1NN
tel 028-9097 1070
email g.hellawell@qub.ac.uk
website www.qub.ac.uk/schools/SeamusHeaneyCentreforPoetry

The Seamus Heaney Centre for Poetry (SHC) was established in 2003 and is designed to promote both the writing and criticism of poetry, fiction and script-writing. The Centre houses an extensive library of contemporary poetry volumes. It hosts regular creative writing workshops, a poetry reading group, and an ongoing series of readings and lectures by visiting poets and critics from all over the world. The current director of the SHC is Professor Fran Brearton. Its founding director, the eminent poet Ciaran Carson, runs its writing group. Other staff include award-winning poets Sinead Morrissey, Leontia Flynn and Medbh McGuckian, novelists Glenn Patterson, Garrett Carr and Darran McCann and script-writers Tim Loane and Jimmy McAleavey, all of whom teach on undergraduate and postgraduate courses in creative writing.

Survivors' Poetry

NHS Support and Recovery Unit,
1 St Mary's Terrace, London W2 1SU
tel 01273 202876
email info@survivorspoetry.org.uk
website www.survivorspoetry.org
Director Simon Jenner

A national charity which promotes the writing of survivors of mental distress. A Survivor may be a person with a current or past experience of psychiatric hospitals, ECT, tranquillisers or other medication, or a user of counselling services, a survivor of sexual abuse and any other person who has empathy with the experiences of survivors.

Tower Poetry

Christ Church, Oxford OX1 1DP
tel (01865) 286591
email info@towerpoetry.org.uk
website www.towerpoetry.org.uk

Tower Poetry exists to encourage and challenge everyone who reads or writes poetry. Funded by a generous bequest to Christ Church, Oxford, by the late Christopher Tower, the aims of Tower Poetry are to stimulate an enjoyment and critical appreciation of poetry, particularly among young people in education, and to challenge people to write their own poetry.

WHERE TO GET INFORMATION

Your local library is a good first port of call, and should have information about the poetry scene in the area. Many libraries are actively involved in speading the word about poetry as well as having modern poetry available for loan. Local librarians promote writing activities with, for example, projects like Poetry on Loan and Poetry Places information points in West Midlands Libraries.

Alliance of Literary Societies (ALS)

email ljc1049@gmail.com
website www.allianceofliterarysocieties.org.uk
President Jenny Uglow

The ALS is the umbrella organisation for literary societies and groups in the UK. Formed in 1973, it provides support and advice on a variety of literary subjects, as well as promoting cooperation between member societies. Its journal, *ALSo…*, appears annually. Founded 1973.

Arts Council England

Head Office 21 Bloomsbury Street, London WC1B 3HF
tel 0845 300 6200
email enquiries@artscouncil.org.uk
website www.artscouncil.org.uk

Arts Council England has five regional offices (in addition to the national head office) and local literature officers can provide information on local poetry groups, workshops and societies (see page 492). Some give grant aid to local publishers and magazines and help fund festivals, literature projects and readings, and some run critical services.

Arts Council of Wales

Bute Place, Cardiff CF10 5AL
tel 0845 8734 900
email info@artswales.org.uk
website www.artswales.org.uk

The Arts Council of Wales is an independent charity, established by Royal Charter in 1994. It has three regional offices and its principal sponsor is the Welsh

Government. It is the country's funding and development agency for the arts, supporting and developing high-quality arts activities. Its funding schemes offer opportunities for arts organisations and individuals in Wales to apply, through a competitive process, for funding towards a clearly defined arts-related project.

National Association of Writers' Groups (NAWG)

65 Riverside Mead, Peterborough PE2 8JN
email chris.huck@ymail.com
website www.nawg.co.uk

NAWG aims to bring cohesion and fellowship to isolated writers' groups and individuals, promoting the study and art of writing in all its aspects. There are many affiliated groups and associate (individual) members across the UK.

The Northern Poetry Library

Morpeth Library, Gas House Lane, Morpeth, Northumberland NE61 1TA
tel (01670) 620390
email morpethlibrary@northumberland.gov.uk
website www.northumberland.gov.uk

The Northern Poetry Library is the largest collection of contemporary poetry outside London and has over 15,000 titles and magazines covering poetry published since 1945. Founded 1968.

The Poetry Trust

9 New Cut, Halesworth, Suffolk IP19 8BY
tel (01986) 835950
email info@thepoetrytrust.org
www.thepoetrytrust.org

The Poetry Trust is one of the UK's flagship poetry organisations, delivering a year-round live and digital programme, creative education opportunities, courses, prizes and publications. Over the last decade the Poetry Trust has been running creative workshops for teachers, and this extensive experience has been condensed into a free user-friendly handbook (pdf download), *The Poetry Toolkit*. The Trust also produces *The Poetry Paper*, featuring exclusive interviews and poems.

The Saison Poetry Library

Level 5, Royal Festival Hall, London SE1 8XX
tel 020-7921 0943/0664 WAYB
email info@poetrylibrary.org.uk
website www.poetrylibrary.org.uk
website www.poetrymagazines.org.uk
Membership Free with proof of identity and current address

The UK's largest collection of modern and contemporary poetry from 1912 onwards. It is open to everyone and free to join (see above stipulations). Members can borrow from the extensive loan collections, including audio items and take advantage of the library's eloan service through which ebooks can be loaned at distance. The extensive collection of current poetry magazines gives a window in to the breadth of poetry in the UK and beyond. The library runs a monthly event series called Special Edition, a programme of exhibitions which run throughout the year, a book club and an occasional tutored workshop for budding poets called The Poetry Butcher. The library's website features publishers' information, poetry news and a list of UK-wide events; the digital archive at www.poetrymagazines.org.uk is a free database of contemporary poems from UK magazines.

The Scottish Poetry Library

5 Crichton's Close, Canongate, Edinburgh EH8 8DT
tel 0131 557 2876
email reception@spl.org.uk
website www.scottishpoetrylibrary.org.uk

The Scottish Poetry Library is the place for poetry in Scotland for the regular reader, the serious student or the casual browser. It houses over 40,000 items: books, magazines, pamphlets, recordings and the Edwin Morgan Archive of his published works. The core of the collection is contemporary poetry written in Scotland, in Scots, Gaelic and English, but historic Scottish poetry as well as contemporary works from almost every part of the world are also available. All resources, advice and information are readily accessible, free of charge. The SPL holds regular poetry events, including reading and writing groups, details of which are available on the library website. Closed Saturday, Sunday and Monday. Founded 1984.

ONLINE RESOURCES

There is a wealth of information available for poets at the click of a mouse: the suggestions below are a good starting point.

British-Irish Poets

website www.jiscmail.ac.uk/cgi-bin/webadmin?A0=BRITISH-IRISH-POETS

Email discussion list (innovative poetry).

The Poetry Archive

website www.poetryarchive.org

World's premier online collection of recordings of poets reading their work. Free of charge. Features the voices of contemporary English-language poets as well as poets from the past, including C. Day Lewis, Paul Farley and Dorothea Smartt. The Archive is added to regularly.

The Poetry Free-for-All

website www.everypoet.org./pffa

Online community where visitors can post their own poems and comment on others'.

The Poetry Kit

website www.poetrykit.org

Collates a wide variety of poetry-related information, including events, competitions, courses and more, for an international readership.

Poetry Space

website www.poetryspace.co.uk

Specialist publisher of poetry and short stories, as well as news and features, edited by Susan Jane Sims. Operates as a social enterprise with all profits being used to publish online and in print, and to hold events to widen participation in poetry. Poetry submissions accepted all year round for *Poetry Space Showcase Quarterly*, an online and print publication aimed at over 16s. Poems are selected each quarter by a guest editor and if not chosen have another chance with the next guest editor. Poetry submissions also accepted for consideration for pamphlet and full collection publication. Poets are requested to send in a sample of six poems before a full manuscript will be considered; unsolicited manuscripts will not be read. Occasional submission calls for themed anthologies. Periodic calls for short story submissions for pamphlet series (*Poetry Space Shorts*) and for photographs to use on the website. Subscribers to the Friends of Poetry Space membership scheme receive *Showcase Quarterly* and a surprise pamphlet from the catalogue. Submissions for all of the above should be sent to susan@poetryspace.co.uk. Founded 2010.

The Poetry Toolkit

website www.thepoetrytrust.org

The Poetry Trust has been running creative workshops for teachers for over a decade, and this extensive experience has been condensed into a free user-friendly handbook (pdf download), *The Poetry Toolkit.*

Poets and Writers

website www.pw.org

US-based online magazine and e-newsletter on the craft and business of writing, including writing prompts.

Prac Crit

website www.praccrit.com

Online journal of poetry and criticism, published three times a year. Features interviews, essays and the reflections of poets themselves; close analysis of poems a hallmark.

Sabotage Reviews

website www.sabotagereviews.com

Poetry review site. Welcomes reviews of 1,500 words or fewer on poetry, fiction and the spoken word but check website guidelines carefully prior to submitting (http://sabotagereviews.com/about/guidelines) – full poetry collections or novels are rarely covered on the site.

Write Out Loud

website www.writeoutloud.net/directory

Directory listing publications, festivals, competitions and other poetry resources.

WHERE TO CELEBRATE POETRY

Festival information should be available from Arts Council England offices (see page 492). See also *Festivals for writers, artists and readers* on page 563. As well as the list below, major poetry festivals each year include Ledbury, Bridlington, Aldeburgh and Cheltenham. Poetry also features prominently at the Glastonbury and Latitude Festivals.

The British Council

10 Spring Gardens, London SW1A 2BN
tel 020-7389 3194
email general.enquiries@britishcouncil.org
website http://literature.britishcouncil.org

Visit the website for a list of forthcoming festivals.

Poems in the Waiting Room (PitWR)

12 Abingdon Court Lane, Cricklade, Wilts. SN6 6BL
email helenium@care4free.net
website www.poemsinthewaitingroom.org

PitWR is a registered arts in health charity which supplies short collections of poems for patients to read while waiting to see their doctor. First established in 1995, the poems cover both the cannon of English verse and contemporary works – poetry from Quill to Qwerty.

StAnza: Scotland's International Poetry Festival

email info@stanzapoetry.org
website www.stanzapoetry.org

StAnza is international in outlook. Founded in 1988, it is held each March in St Andrews, Scotland's oldest university town. The festival is an opportunity to engage with a wide variety of poetry, to hear world class poets reading in exciting and atmospheric venues, to experience a range of performances where music, film, dance and poetry work in harmony, to view exhibitions linking poetry with visual art and to discover the part poetry has played in the lives of a diverse range of writers, musicians and media personalities. The simple intention of StAnza is to celebrate poetry in all its forms.

WHERE TO PERFORM

Poetry evenings are held all over the UK and the suggestions listed below are worth checking out. Others can be found by visiting your local library or your Arts Council office, or by visiting the What's on section of the Poetry Society website (www.poetrysociety.org.uk/events). The Poetry Library (www.poetrylibrary.org.uk/events) is also an excellent source for upcoming poetry events. The list below also features a number of poetry groups at which members can share their work.

Allographic

tel 07904 488009
email info@allographic.co.uk
website www.allographic.co.uk
Contact Fay Roberts

Cambridge-based live events with new and upcoming names from the spoken word scene and a set of workshops for aspirant poets, storytellers and other writers and performers.

Apples and Snakes

The Albany, Douglas Way, London SE8 4AG
tel 0845 521 3460
email info@applesandsnakes.org
website www.applesandsnakes.org

Performance poetry and spoken word in London and throughout England: see website for full details and contact names.

Bad Language

The Castle Hotel, 66 Oldham Street, Manchester M4 1LE
email badlanguagemcr@gmail.com
website http://badlanguagemcr.com
Contact Joe Daly

Literature organisation and spoken word night dedicated to the promotion and development of new writing. See website for up-to-date listing of forthcoming events.

Bang Said the Gun

The Roebuck, 50 Great Dover Street, London SE1 4YG
email info@bangsaidthegun.com
website www.bangsaidthegun.com
Contact Daniel Cockrill

High-energy weekly spoken word night with a limited open-mic section.

Blind Poetics

32 West Nicolson Street, Edinburgh EH8 9DD
tel 07930 134910
email blindpoetics@gmail.com
website www.blindpoetics.wordpress.com

Free monthly spoken word (poetry, short stories, flash fiction etc) event with a feature performer and an open mic.

BookSlam

The Clapham Grand, 21–25 St John's Hill, London SW11 1TT
email info@bookslam.com
website www.bookslam.com
Contact Elliott Jack

Describes itself as 'London's best literary club night', featuring top writers and live music. A mix of new and established acts.

Burn After Reading

Seven Dials Club, 42 Earlham Street, London WC2H 9LA
email barpo@jsamlarose.com
website http://barpoetry.tumblr.com
Contacts Jacob Sam-La Rose and Jasmine Cooray

Community of young and emerging poets, and writers of both spoken word and 'page' poetry.

CB1 Poetry

The Gonville Hotel, Gonville Place, Cambridge CB1 1LY
tel (01223) 366611
email cb1poetry@fastmail.fm
website www.cb1poetry.org.uk

Regular readings featuring new and well-known artists. Previous participants include Owen Sheers, George Szirtes, Don Paterson and Emily Berry. Check website for dates and times of meetings.

Chill Pill

The Albany, Douglas Way, London SE8 4AG
website http://chill-pill.co.uk
Contact Deanna Rodger

Laid-back London-based club night where up-and-coming poets share the stage with established spoken word acts.

Coffee House Poetry

PO Box 16210, London W4 1ZP
tel 020-7370 1434
email coffpoetry@aol.com
website www.coffeehousepoetry.org

Meetings take place at The Troubador, 263–267 Old Brompton Road, London SW5 9JA.

Forked

Barbican Theatre, Plymouth PL1 2NJ
email gina@applesandsnakes.org
website www.applesandsnakes.org/page/141/South+West
Editor Gina Sherman

Plymouth-based poetry night in association with Apples and Snakes.

451

Nuffield Theatre, University Road, Southampton SO17 1TR
email pete@applesandsnakes.org
website www.applesandsnakes.org/page/142/South+East

Contact Pete Hunter

Southampton-based bi-monthly celebration of the spoken word.

Hammer and Tongue

170 Campbell Road, Oxford, OX4 3NR
tel 07906 885069
email steve@hammerandtongue.com
website www.hammerandtongue.com
President Steve Larkin

Poetry slam events in London (Camden and Hackney), Bristol, Brighton, Cambridge and Oxford. See website for timings and contact details.

Hit the Ode

website www.applesandsnakes.org/page/108/Events?region=4
Programme Co-ordinator Bohdan Piasecki

Spoken word poetry in Birmingham. Each Hit the Ode features an act from the West Midlands, one from elsewhere in the UK and one international guest.

Inky Fingers

email hello@inkyfingers.org.uk
website www.inkyfingers.org.uk

Grassroots spoken word organisation running a series of wordy events in Edinburgh, from open mic nights to reading and performance workshops.

Jawdance

Rich Mix, 35–47 Bethnal Green Road, London E1 6LA
email russell@applesandsnakes.org
website www.applesandsnakes.org
Contact Russell Thompson

Poetry, film, music and multimedia night, currently every fourth Wednesday of the month. Check website for details.

JibbaJabba

The Cumberland Arms, James Place Street, Newcastle-upon-Tyne NE6 1LD
email kirsten@applesandsnakes.org
website http://applesandsnakes.org/page/148/North+East
Contact Kirsten Luckins

Monthly spoken word night in partnership with Apples and Snakes.

Poetry Swindon Open Mic

email poetryswindon@yahoo.co.uk
website www.poetryswindon.org

Poets wishing to read or perform are invited to do so for up to five minutes. Takes place on the second Tuesday of each month at The Victoria. 88 Victoria Road, Swindon SN1 3BD.

Poetry Unplugged at the Poetry Café

22 Betterton Street, London WC2 9BX
tel 020-7420 9888
email poetrycafe@poetrysociety.org.uk
website www.poetrysociety.org.uk/content/cafe/
Host Niall O'Sullivan

Open mic session, welcoming to new poets. Every Tuesday, sign-up between 6pm and 7pm; note that spaces are limited.

Poets' Café

21 South Street, Reading RG1 4GU
website www.readingarts.com/southstreet
Host A.F. Harrold

Poetry reading events with guest readers, and an open mic. Usually third Friday of each month but check website for details.

Polari

Royal Festival Hall, South Bank Centre, Belvedere Road, London SE1 8XX
email paulburston@btinternet.com
website www.polariliterarysalon.co.uk
Contact Paul Burston

Multi-award-winning LGBT literary salon, held once a month at the South Bank Centre (see website for details). Focuses on established authors but has some pre-arranged spots per event for up-and-coming LGBT writers.

Rainbow Poetry Recitals

2 Old Farm Court, Shoreham BN43 5FE
tel (01273) 465423
email rainbow.poetry@hotmail.co.uk
Administrator Hugh Hellicar

Poetry meetings and recitals at two branches in London and four in Sussex. Membership £7 p.a. Poetry appreciation and members' poems. Founded 1994.

Rally & Broad

email rallyandbroad@gmail.com
website www.rallyandbroad.com
Contacts Jenny Lindsay and Rachel McCrum

Spoken word and music night based around Edinburgh and Glasgow.

SoapBox

email amy@getonthesoapbox.co.uk
website www.getonthesoapbox.co.uk
Contact Amy Wragg

Based in Norfolk and Suffolk, SoapBox promotes and organises live music, poetry and comedy events in a variety of settings, from pubs to arts centres, festivals and street performances.

That's What She Said

The Peckham Pelican, 92 Peckham Road, London SE15 5PY
website http://forbookssake.net/events
Contact Paul Forster

Feminist spoken word and poetry night curated by For Books' Sake. Currently bi-monthly at The Peckham Pelican.

The Bus Driver's Prayer

93 Feet East, The Old Truman Brewery,
150 Brick Lane, London E1 6QL
email richardpurnell1@gmail.com
website http://busdriversprayerevents.wordpress.com
Editor Richard Purnell

Offbeat poetry, comedy and music.

Tongue Fu

Rich Mix, 35–47 Bethnal Green Road,
London E1 6LA
email tonguefupoetry@gmail.com
website www.tonguefu.co.uk
Founders Chris Redmond and Riaan Vosloo

Lively spoken word night; describes itself as 'a riotous experiment in live literature, music, film and improvisation'. See website for information on forthcoming events.

Tongues&Grooves

tel 07775 244573
email enquiries@tongues-and-grooves.org.uk
website www.tongues-and-grooves.org.uk
Co-founder Maggie Sawkins

Hosts poetry performance events and creative writing workshops in the Portsmouth area. Founded 2003.

WORD!

The Y Theatre, East Street, Leicester LE1 6EY
email secretagentartist@hotmail.com
website http://wordpoetryleic.blogspot.co.uk
Comperes Lydia Towsey, Tim Sayers and Pam Thompson

Longest-running poetry and spoken word night in the Midlands. First Tuesday of the month, sign-up at 7pm, events typically run 8–10.30pm.

COMPETITIONS

There are now hundreds of competitions to enter and as the prizes increase, so does the prestige associated with winning such competitions as the National Poetry Competition.

To decide which competitions are worth entering, make sure you know who the judges are and think twice before paying large sums for an anthology of 'winning' poems which will be read only by entrants wanting to see their own work in print. The Poetry Library publishes a list of competitions each month (available free on receipt of a large sae). See also *Becoming a published poet* on page 325 and *Prizes and awards* on page 534.

Literary prizes are given annually to published poets and as such are non-competitive. An A–Z guide to literary prizes can be found on the Booktrust website (www.booktrust.org.uk/prizes).

WHERE TO WRITE POETRY

Apples and Snakes

The Albany, Douglas Way, London SE8 4AG
tel 0845 521 3460
email info@applesandsnakes.org
website www.applesandsnakes.org

Organisation for performance poetry in England, with a reputation for producing innovative work that raises the profile of spoken word and pushes the boundaries of the artform for artists, audiences and participants. Runs a variety of programmes for poets, including participatory workshops. Founded 1982.

Arvon

Lumb Bank – The Ted Hughes Arvon Centre,
Heptonstall, Hebden Bridge,
West Yorkshire HX7 6DF
tel (01422) 843714
email lumbbank@arvon.org
Totleigh Barton, Sheepwash, Beaworthy, Devon EX21 5NS
tel (01409) 231338
email totleighbarton@arvon.org
The Hurst – The John Osborne Arvon Centre,
Clunton, Craven Arms, Shrops. SY7 0JA
tel (01588) 640658
email thehurst@arvon.org
website www.arvon.org

Arvon's three centres run five-day residential courses throughout the year for anyone over the age of 16, providing the opportunity to live and work with professional writers. Writing genres explored include poetry, narrative, drama, writing for children, songwriting and the performing arts. Bursaries are available to those receiving benefits. Founded 1968.

Cannon Poets

22 Margaret Grove, Harborne, Birmingham B17 9JH
Meets at The Moseley Exchange, The Post Office Building, 149–153 Alcester Road, Moseley, Birmingham B13 8JP usually on the first Sunday of each month (except August) at 2pm
website www.cannonpoets.org.uk

Cannon Poets have met monthly since 1983. The group encourages poetry writing through:

- workshops run by members or visitors
- break-out groups where poems are subjected to scrutiny by supportive peer groups
- 10-minute slots where members read a selection of their poems to the whole group
- publication of its journal, *The Cannon's Mouth* (quarterly).

Members are encouraged to participate in poetry events and competitions.

City Lit

Keeley Street, London WC2B 4BA
tel 020-7492 2600

email infoline@citylit.ac.uk
website www.citylit.ac.uk

Offers classes on poetry appreciation as well as practical workshops.

Kent & Sussex Poetry Society

Camden Centre, Market Square, Tunbridge Wells, Kent TN1 2SW
email info@kentandsussexpoetrysociety.org
website www.kentandsussexpoetry.com
Secretary Mary Gurr

A local group with a national reputation. Organises monthly poetry readings (third Tuesday of each month), workshops and an annual poetry competition.

The Poetry School

81 Lambeth Walk, London SE11 6DX
tel 020-7582 1679
website www.poetryschool.com

Teaches the art and craft of writing poetry (to adults, with very occasional focus on children's poetry). Offers courses, small groups and one-to-one tutorials, from one-day workshops to year-long courses, in London and in other city locations across England. Activities for beginners to advanced writers, both unpublished and published. Face-to-face, downloadable and online activities. Three new programmes a year plus social network for poets at www.campus.poetryschool.com.

Shortlands Poetry Circle

Ripley Arts Centre, 24 Sundridge Avenue, Bromley
tel (01689) 811394
email shortlands@poetrypf.co.uk
website www.poetrypf.co.uk/shortlands.html, https://shortlandspoetrycircle.wordpress.com (blog)

Tŷ Newydd

Llanystumdwy, Cricieth, Gwynedd LL52 0LW
tel (01766) 522811
email tynewydd@literaturewales.org
website www.tynewydd.org

Tŷ Newydd runs residential writing courses encompassing a wide variety of genres, including poetry, and caters for all levels, from beginners to published poets. All the courses are tutored by published writers. Writing retreats are also available.

Wey Poets (Surrey Poetry Centre)

Friends Meeting House, 3 Ward Street, Guildford GU1 4LH
tel (01483) 562206
email weyfarers@yahoo.co.uk
email bb_singleton@hotmail.com
website www.weyfarers.com
Contact Belinda Singleton

Group meets third Wednesday of the month, 7–9.30 for workshop, September to June (except first Wednesday in December). Additional speaker events on first Wednesday in November, March, April and May. (Please see website for any changes.) Supportive workshops for original poetry. Small, long-standing group with quality input. New members/visitors and enquiries very welcome.

HELP FOR YOUNG POETS AND TEACHERS

National Association of Writers in Education (NAWE)

PO Box 1, Sheriff Hutton, York YO60 7YU
tel/fax (01653) 618429
email pjohnston@nawe.co.uk
website www.nawe.co.uk
Deputy Director Anne Caldwell

National organisation which aims to widen the scope of writing in education, and coordinate activities between writers, teachers and funding bodies. It publishes the magazine *Writing in Education* and has created a writers' database that can identify writers who fit the given criteria (e.g. speaks several languages, works well with special needs, etc.) for schools, colleges and the community. Publishes *Reading the Applause: Reflections on Performance Poetry by Various Artists.* Write for membership details. NAWE's mission is to further knowledge, understanding and enjoyment of creative writing and to support good practice in its teaching and learning at all levels. NAWE promotes creative writing as both a distinct discipline and an essential element in education generally. Its membership includes those working in Higher Education, the many freelance writers working in schools and community contexts, and the teachers and other professionals who work with them. NAWE incorporates The Writer's Compass (formerly literaturetraining), providing information and advice on professional development for writers and other literature professionals. It runs a national database of writers, publishes two journals – *Writing in Education* and *Writing in Practice* – and a national conference.

Poetry Society Education

The Poetry Society, 22 Betterton Street, London WC2H 9BX
tel 020-7420 9880
email education@poetrysociety.org.uk
website www.poetrysociety.org.uk/education

The Poetry Society has an outstanding reputation for its exciting and innovative education work. For over 30 years it has been introducing poets into classrooms, providing comprehensive teachers' resources and producing lively, accessible publications for pupils. It develops projects and schemes to keep poetry flourishing in schools, libraries and workplaces, giving work to hundreds of poets and allowing thousands of children and adults to experience poetry for themselves.

Through projects such as the SLAMbassadors UK, the Foyle Young Poets of the Year Award and Young Poets Network, the Poetry Society gives valuable encouragement and exposure to young writers and performers.

Schools membership offers Poetry Society publications, books and posters, a subscription to *Poems on the Underground* and free access to a consultancy service giving advice on working with poets in the classroom. Youth membership is available (for age 11–18; £15 p.a.) and offers discounts, publications, poetry books and posters.

The Poetry Trust – see The Poetry Trust on page 333

The Saison Poetry Library (Children's Collection)

Level 5, Royal Festival Hall, London SE1 8XX
tel 020-7921 0664
email info@poetrylibrary.org.uk
website www.poetrylibrary.org.uk

The Children's Collection comprises c. 20,000 items for young poets of all ages, including poetry on CD and DVD. The library has an education service for teachers and writing groups, with a separate collection of books and materials for teachers and poets who work with children in schools. Group visits can be organised inviting children to interact with the collection in various exciting ways from taking a Poetry Word Trail across Southbank Centre, to exploring how the worlds of science and poetry interact, and from engaging with war poetry via the Letters Home booklet to becoming a Poetry Library Poetry Explorer. Nursery schools can also book a Rug Rhymes session for under-5s. Children of all ages can join for free and borrow books and other materials. A special membership scheme is available for teachers to borrow books for the classroom. Contact the library for membership details and opening hours.

Young Poets Network

website www.youngpoetsnetwork.org.uk

Online resource from The Poetry Society of features about reading, writing and performing poetry, plus new work by young poets and regular writing challenges. Aimed at young people up to 25.

YOUNG POETRY COMPETITIONS

Children's competitions are included in the competition list provided by the Poetry Library (free on receipt of a large sae).

Foyle Young Poets of the Year Award

The Poetry Society, 22 Betterton Street, London WC2H 9BX
tel 020-7420 9880
email education@poetrysociety.org.uk
website www.poetrysociety.org.uk/content/competitions/fyp

Free entry for children aged 11–17 years with unique prizes. Annual competition. Poems must be written in English. Opens March and closes for entries on the 31st July each year. Founded 2001.

SLAMbassadors

The Poetry Society, 22 Betterton Street, London WC2H 9BX
tel 020-7429 9894, 020-7420 4818, 07847 378892, 07847 372 892
email jtaylor@poetrysociety.org.uk
website http://slam.poetrysociety.org.uk
Contact Joelle Taylor

An annual poetry slam championship for 12–18 year-olds. Young people across the UK are invited to enter by filming themselves performing a spoken word piece or rap and submitting it online for consideration by judges. Prizes include the opportunity to perfom at a showcase event, workshops with respected spoken word artists and further professional development opportunities. Established 2002.

Christopher Tower Poetry Prize

Christ Church, Oxford OX1 1DP
tel (01865) 286591
email info@towerpoetry.org.uk
website www.towerpoetry.org.uk/prize/

An annual poetry competition (open from November to March) from Christ Church, Oxford, open to 16–18 year-olds in UK schools and colleges. The poems should be no longer than 48 lines, on a different chosen theme each year. Prizes: £3,000 (1st), £1,000 (2nd), £500 (3rd). Every winner also receives a prize for their school.

FURTHER READING

Baldwin, Michael, *The Way to Write Poetry*, Hamish Hamilton, 1982, o.p.
Chisholm, Alison, *The Craft of Writing Poetry*, Allison & Busby, 1997, repr. 2001
Chisholm, Alison, *A Practical Poetry Course*, Allison & Busby, 1994, o.p.
Corti, Doris, *Writing Poetry*, Writers News Library of Writing/Thomas & Lochar, 1994
Fairfax, John, and John Moat, *The Way to Write*, Penguin Books, 2nd edn revised, 1998

Finch, Peter, *How to Publish Your Poetry*, Allison & Busby, 4th edn, 1998, o.p.
Forbes, Peter, *Scanning the Century: The Penguin Book of the Twentieth Century in Poetry*, Viking, 1999, o.p.
Greene, Roland, *et al.*, *Princeton Encyclopedia of Poetry and Poetics*, Princeton University Press, 4th edn, 2012
Hamilton, Ian, *The Oxford Companion to Twentieth-century Poetry*, Clarendon Press, 1994
Hyland, Paul, *Getting into Poetry: A Readers' & Writers' Guide to the Poetry Scene*, Bloodaxe, 2nd edn, 1992, o.p.
Livingstone, Dinah, *Poetry Handbook for Readers and Writers*, Macmillan, 1993, o.p.
Maxwell, Glyn, *On Poetry*, Oberon Books, 2012
O'Brien, Sean (ed), *The Firebox: Poetry from Britain and Ireland after 1945*, Picador, 1998, o.p.
Padel, Ruth, *52 Ways of Looking at a Poem: A Poem for Every Week of the Year*, Vintage, 2004
Padel, Ruth, *The Poem and the Journey: 60 Poems for the Journey of Life*, Vintage, 2008
Reading the Applause: Reflections on Performance Poetry by Various Artists, Talking Shop, 1999
Riggs, Thomas (ed.), *Contemporary Poets*, St James Press, 7th edn, 2003
Roberts, Philip Davies, *How Poetry Works*, Penguin Books, 2nd edn, 2000
Sampson, Fiona, *Writing Poetry: The Expert Guide*, Robert Hale, 2009
Sansom, Peter, *Writing Poems*, Bloodaxe, 1993, reprinted 1997
Sweeney, Matthew and John Hartley Williams, *Write Poetry and Get It Published*, Hodder and Stoughton, 2010
Whitworth, John, *Writing Poetry*, A&C Black, 2nd edn, 2006

See also...

- *Publishers of poetry*, page 759
- *Becoming a published poet*, page 325
- *Notes from a passionate poet*, page 329

Television, film and radio
Adaptations from books

Kate Sinclair describes how books are selected and adapted for other media.

Although every writer wants to create their own work and find their own voice, adaptation is a good way both to generate income and to learn about the disciplines of different media: how to write for other formats.

Writers may be approached to adapt their own work from one medium to another during their career. For example, John Mortimer originally wrote *A Voyage Round My Father* for the radio and later adapted it for stage, film and finally, for television. There are also opportunities for both writers and directors to adapt someone else's work from one performance medium to another or from a novel to any of the above.

Every year classic novels are made into adaptations for all media and it is a growing trend. These may be for the theatre, such as *The Curious Incident of the Dog in the Night-time* based on Mark Haddon's award-winning book adapted by Simon Stephens or for radio such as *Life and Fate*, Vasily Grossman's novel adapted by Mike Walker and Jonathan Myerson (the Classic Serial, Radio 4). Television carries dramatisations like *Wolf Hall*, based on a book by Hilary Mantel and adapted superbly by Peter Straughan (BBC), and feature film screenplays such as *The Wolf of Wall Street*, adapted by Terence Winter based on a non-fiction book by Jordan Belfont and directed by Martin Scorsese, or the award-winning *Argo* adapted by Chris Terrio, based on a book by Tony Mendez. Although these are usually costly to produce, involving large casts and – particularly in the visual media – the considerable expense of recreating the period in which they were written, they command loyal audiences and seem to be in steady demand. These classic projects also generate significant income both from DVD/video sales and from sales to overseas companies and networks. Some adapters are as well known as writers who concentrate on their own work. For example, Andrew Davies has become almost a household name for his television dramatisations of *Middlemarch*, *Bleak House* and, more recently, *Northanger Abbey* and *Little Dorritt*.

Producers in radio, television and film are also in regular contact with publishers and literary agents to keep abreast of contemporary novels that may work well in another format. I work as an Executive Producer finding books, both fiction and non-fiction, for screenwriters, directors or producers for feature films. Both television producers and film companies are also sent books with potential by the publicity departments of publishing houses and writers may also make direct approaches to producers and commissioners with material that they feel they can successfully transcribe for that particular medium. There is clearly a market for adaptations of all types. For example, I found *Slumdog Millionaire* for Film4 on reading 50 pages of an unpublished book, *Q&A* by Vikas Swamp, and also *Salmon Fishing in the Yemen* by Paul Torday as an unpublished manuscript. Both of these books were brilliantly adapted by Simon Beaufoy. The added stimulus for the adapter is, as well as having a ready-made story, exploring technically how another writer writes – their use of language, the way they structure a narrative, their characterisation. It presents the opportunity to learn from the skill and subtlety of great writers together with the challenge of finding ways to transport a story from one form to another, with a multitude of creative possibilities to explore.

What to adapt, and why?

Just because a narrative works in one format doesn't guarantee that it will in another. Form and story are often inextricably bound together. Something works as a radio play precisely because it appeals to a listening audience and is able to exploit the possibilities of sound. A novel may be very literary and concentrate on a character's inner thoughts, and not on external action. While this may be fine for reading quietly alone, it could leave a theatre, television or film audience bored and longing for something to happen.

That said, the key ingredient is story and there are some stories which seem to work in almost any media and which have almost become universal (though different treatments bring out different aspects of the original). For example, Henry James's *The Turn of the Screw* was written as a novella. It subsequently became a much-performed opera, with a libretto by Myfanwy Piper and music by Benjamin Britten; an acclaimed film, retitled *The Innocents* with the screenplay by John Mortimer; and a television adaptation for ITV by Nick Dear. What makes a narrative like this transmute so successfully?

At the most basic level it must be dramatic. Radio, television and film, like the theatre, need drama to hold their audiences. Aristotle's premise that 'all drama is action', and should have protagonists whom we identify with, antagonists who oppose them, and the reversals, climaxes and resolutions which typify a dramatic structure. This is not necessarily the case for a novel; it is easy to be seduced by a tale that has personal resonance or beautiful language and forget the basic template which has, after all, worked for thousands of years. It may seem obvious, but reminding yourself of this when considering the suitability of any material for adaptation could spare you a rejection or a great deal of later reworking.

Knowing the media

The other important consideration is a detailed knowledge of the final medium. The adapter needs to understand why that particular story is specifically suited to it. Ideally they will have experience of writing for that form, as well as an awareness of the current market for the project. It is vital to know precisely what is currently being produced and by whom. Staff and policies change very quickly, so the more up-to-date your research is, the better your chance of creating a successful adaptation and being able to get it accepted.

If you are adapting for the theatre, how often do you go and when was the last time you saw a production that wasn't originally written for the stage? As well as observing how successful it was, both artistically and in box office terms, would you know whether that company or theatre regularly programmes adaptations, and if so, what sort? Do they, like Shared Experience, have a reputation primarily for classics, or do they, like the National Theatre, produce versions of contemporary novels? Are you sufficiently aware of the tastes of the current artistic director and the identity of the theatre to know whether to send your project to the West Yorkshire Playhouse or the Arcola Theatre? This is not necessarily just a question of scale or level, but more a reflection of contemporary trends and the specific policy of each of these buildings. Whilst the overall remit of a theatre or company may remain the same – if they are funded to produce only new plays, it is unlikely that this will alter – individual personnel and fashions will change regularly and it is important to keep in touch.

Television and radio

The same holds true for all the other media and, if anything, is even more important in radio and television. All of the broadcast media are now subject to the rigorous demands of ratings, which in turn make for extremely precise scheduling. Channels have strong identities, and conversations with producers and commissioners will inevitably involve a discussion of which slot a project is suited to and what has recently been shown or broadcast. Up-to-the-minute knowledge of the work being produced by a company or broadcaster is therefore essential, and regularly seeing that work and being able to talk about it, even more so. For example, BBC Radio 3's *Wire* is specifically for new work by contemporary writers and therefore isn't suitable for a classic adaptation of a novel. Radio 4 produces the Classic Serial on Sunday afternoons and *Women's Hour* has a regular serialisation slot that can be contemporary or classic and is often an adapted novel. Biographies, autobiographies and non-fiction works are also frequently abridged and read on Radio 4 at 9.45am on weekdays. For a detailed knowledge of this output there can be no substitute for studying the *Radio Times*, seeing what is programmed, and listening to what gets produced in which slots. Being able to envisage the eventual destination for a chosen adaptation helps you to choose the right project and place it successfully.

In television this process of research is more complex. As well as strong competition between the BBC and the larger independent broadcasters (ITV, Channel 4, Sky, etc) to secure an audience, there is also considerable rivalry between the hundreds of independent production companies to receive commissions. The ratings war means that scheduling is paramount and big dramatic adaptations are often programmed at exactly the same time by the BBC and ITV. Familiarity with the output of each channel is crucial when suggesting projects for adaptation, either to a commissioner or a production company. Again, watching dramatisations and noting what format they are in, who is producing them, and when they are being broadcast, is all part of the job.

It is helpful to know that, as a general rule, both adaptations and writing commissioned directly for television tend to be divided into several basic categories (not including soaps). Single dramas are usually high-profile though few and far between, event pieces broadcast at prime times such as Bank Holidays and are usually 90 minutes long. Series consist of a number of weekly parts shown over several weeks (3, 4, 6 and 8 are all common), each part lasting 30–60 minutes. Finally, there are two-part dramas – serials – or high-profile pieces which take place on consecutive nights, somctimes five in a row, with each part between one and two hours long. The percentage of adaptations will generally be lower than newly commissioned drama, although this is entirely dependent upon the type of slot and the broadcaster. For example, the BBC has considerably more per hour for drama than Channel 4 has, and produces many more dramatisations of classic novels, particularly recently. Likewise, ITV has currently been producing more contemporary drama in terms of adaptations with an emphasis on crime. Its period serials such as *Downton Abbey* or *Mr Selfridge* have most recently been original drama rather than being book based. Channel 4, when it commissions adaptations, tends to focus on cutting-edge contemporary novels, such as *Any Human Heart* by William Boyd. And there are of course always exceptions to all these trends, which is why it is necessary to be an aware and regular viewer.

If you want to adapt for film, the nature of what will work and when seems to be more open-ended, though it is of course important to go regularly to the cinema and know what

Successful collaborations

Film

The Imitation Game (Andrew Hodges, screenplay Graham Moore)
The Wolf on Wall Street (Jordan Belfort, screenplay Terence Winter)
Lincoln (Doris Kearns Goodwin, screenplay Tony Kushner)
Argo (Tony Mendez, screenplay Chris Terrio)
Salmon Fishing in the Yemen (Paul Torday, screenplay Simon Beaufoy)
Jane Eyre (Charlotte Bronte, screenplay Moira Buffini)
Tinker, Tailor, Soldier, Spy (John Le Carré, adaptation Bridget O'Connor and Peter Straughan)
The Best Exotic Marigold Hotel (Deborah Moggach, screenplay Ol Parker)
The Social Network (Ben Mezrich, screenplay Aaron Sorkin)
127 Hours (Aron Ralston, screenplay Danny Boyle and Simon Beaufoy)
Up in the Air (Walter Kim, screenplay Jason Reitman and Sheldon Turner)
Slumdog Millionaire (Vikas Swamp, screenplay Simon Beaufoy)
The Diving Bell and the Butterfly (Jean-Dominique Bauby,screenplay Ronald Harwood)
The Motorcycle Diaries (Ché Guevara, screenplay Joe Rivera)
Enduring Love (Ian McEwan, screenplay Joe Penhall)
Trainspotting (Irvine Welsh, screenplay John Hodges)
Lord of the Rings (J.R.R. Tolkien, screenplay Fran Walsh)
The House of Mirth (Edith Wharton, screenplay Terence Davies)
Jude (George Eliot, screenplay Hossein Amini)
Persuasion (Jane Austen, screenplay Nick Dear)

Television

Wolf Hall (Hilary Mantel, adaptation Peter Straughan)
Death Comes to Pemberley (P.D. James, adaptation Juliette Towhidi)
The Girl (Donald Spoto, adaptation Gwyneth Hughes)
Great Expectations (Charles Dickens, adaptation Sarah Phelps)
Any Human Heart (William Boyd, adaptation William Boyd)
Lark Rise to Candleford (Flora Thompson, adaptation Bill Gallagher)
Bleak House (Charles Dickens, adaptation Andrew Davies)
Middlemarch (George Elliott, adaptation Andrew Davies)
The Forsyte Saga (John Galsworthy, adaptation Stephen Mallatratt)
Brideshead Revisited (Evelyn Waugh, adaptation John Mortimer)
The Buddha of Suburbia (Hanif Kureshi, adaptation Roger Michell and Hanif Kureshi)
Longitude (Dava Sobel, adaptation Charles Sturridge)

Theatre

The Curious Incident of the Dog in the Night-time (Mark Haddon, adaptation Simon Stephens)
War Horse (Michael Morpurgo, adaptation Nick Stafford)
Coram Boy (Jamilla Gavin, adaptation Helen Edmundson)
Nana (Emile Zola, adaptation Pam Gems)
The Magic Toyshop (Angela Carter, adaptation Bryony Lavery)

Radio

Life and Fate (Vasily Grossman, adaptation Mike Walker and Jonathan Myerson)
The Worst Journey in the World (Apsley Cherry-Garrard, adaptation by Stef Penny)
The Old Curiosity Shop (Charles Dickens, adaptation Mike Walker)

has been produced recently. This may be to do with the nature of distribution – the fact that most films are on in a number of cinemas for several weeks – and the time it takes to make a film – often years between the initial idea and eventual screening. However, you still need to keep up to date with who is producing what and when. It is worth noting, though, that there is a very strong relationship between books and film, and that around 50% of all Oscar-winning films are based on books.

The rights

Once you have selected your material and medium, it is vital to establish who has the rights to the original and whether these are available for negotiation. Sometimes this involves a bit of detective work. If the writer is dead, it is necessary to find out whether there is an estate and if the work is still subject to copyright. Copyright law is extremely complex and varies around the world so it is essential to seek expert advice concerning the current rules for any potential project, depending on the country of origin (page 672). It is usually possible to begin the search for the copyright holder and source of rights from the imprint page of the novel, play, film script, etc. If this information is not given, try the publisher, the Society of Authors (see page 485) or the Authors' Licensing and Collecting Society (ALCS, page 687).

In the case of a living writer, you will need to establish who their literary agent is – if they have one – and contact them to see if adaptation is possible and how much it will cost. The scale of costs will depend upon the medium. Rights for a stage adaptation are often separate from film or television options. If a book or play has already been optioned, this means that it is probably not available for a period of at least 12–18 months. Should the purchaser of the option choose not to renew, or fail to produce the adaptation within the required timescale, rights may become available again. Many agreements include an extension clause for a further fixed time period, however, and this is particularly common in film as the end-product is rarely produced within 18 months.

Large film companies, particularly in Hollywood, will often buy the rights to a book or script outright, sometimes for a substantial sum. The proposed version may never get made but legally the original will not be available for adaptation by anyone else. If the writer or material is famous enough, or if they have a good agent, a time limit will be part of the original agreement. Complete buy-outs are less common in the UK.

The cost of acquiring rights varies significantly with the scale of the project, the profile of the writer and the intended medium. Usually an initial payment will be needed to secure the rights for a fixed period, followed by the same amount again, should an extension be necessary. In addition, there is nearly always some form of royalty for the original writer or estate in the form of a percentage of the overall profits of the final production, film, or broadcast. This will normally have a 'floor' (minimum amount or reserve) which must be paid whether or not the final work is financially successful and a 'ceiling' (purchase price). There may also be additional clauses for consultancy. With television, film or radio, there may be a further payment for repeat formats, and in the theatre the rate may well alter if the production transfers. Sometimes, with a low-budget production such as a fringe show or short film, a writer or estate will waive any initial rights fee and only expect a royalty. Whether you use a 'deal memo' to formalise your agreement or a more comprehensive 'long form agreement', it is always worth seeking expert help to make sure you have covered everything you need to.

Legalities aside, time spent forming a relationship with the writer of the original, or whoever manages their estate, has another much more important creative function, that of getting closer to the source material.

How to adapt

I don't believe it is possible to lay down a set of rules for adapting, any more than one could invent a meaningful template for creative writing. The only observation I can offer, therefore, is personal and a reflection of my own taste. When I recommend or commission an adaptation, either for film, television or in the theatre, my first requirement is that something in the original story has hooked me and I want to see the original given another life and another audience. I have to be able to imagine that it has the potential to work dramatically in a different format and can often already see or hear fragments of it.

At this stage I ask myself a lot of questions about the material. How strong is the story and how engaging are the characters? Why should it be done in another medium? How is it possible to achieve the narrative, the characters, the tone, the sequences of action, in a way that is different but still truthful, a sort of creative equivalent, like a metaphor? For me, it is all about thinking laterally and being enthused about the new possibilities another form will generate from the original, or vice versa.

This process generally leads me back to the source, be it book, film or play, in order to dig over everything about it and its writer. As well as looking at other adaptations to see what parts of the original have been enhanced or cut, I like to meet and talk to the writer. If they are no longer alive I try to find out about them from books and/or people who knew them. I want to know what interested them; what were they thinking when they were writing; even what they looked at every day. If possible, I like to go and visit the places they have written about or the place in which they wrote. This process of total immersion helps me to get under the skin of the original.

While this is entirely personal, it raises an interesting question which I believe any adapter needs to answer for themselves. How closely do you wish to be faithful to the original material and how much do you intend to depart from it? Choosing not to stick closely to the source may be the most creative decision you make but you must understand why you are doing it and what the effect will be. After all, two different trains of thought, styles and imaginations need to be fused together for this transformation to be complete and it is important that the balance between them works. I once spoke to a writer who was commissioned to adapt a well-known myth for Hollywood. Several drafts later, when he had been asked to alter all the key elements of the story to the point where it was unrecognisable, he decided to quit. It was the right decision and the film was a flop.

While respect for the writer and the source material is fundamental, there are of course lots of examples where enormous lateral and creative changes have been made to make a story work to optimum effect in its new medium. What matters ultimately is the integrity of the final product. At its best, it is like a marriage of two minds, celebrating the talents of both writer and adapter in an equally creative partnership.

Kate Sinclair is an Executive Producer for The Forge finding and developing projects from books for television adaptation. Previously she worked for Film4, where she found in manuscript *Slumdog Millionaire* and *Brick Lane* for them. She was also Executive Producer for Company Pictures and the Literary Consultant for the UK Film Council, a consultant for Aardman Animations, Free Range and See Saw Films and a Development Producer for Kudos Films, for whom she found *Salmon Fishing in the Yemen*. She has also worked as a theatre director and is currently producing, writing and directing her own feature film projects with Feet Films Ltd.

See also...

- *The calling card script for screen, radio and stage*, page 347
- *Stories on radio*, page 355

The calling card script for screen, radio and stage

Breaking in to the competitive world of scriptwriting can be achieved by submitting an impressive calling card script. Paul Ashton explains the considerations to take into account so that your script is as good as it possibly can be before you send it off to be read.

Many, perhaps most, contemporary professional scriptwriters turn chameleon at some point in their career to work across different mediums, formats and genres – not just to survive, but to thrive. As time marches on, the possibilities open up and some of the seemingly traditional boundaries between different kinds of scriptwriting break down. It has never been more pertinent for scriptwriters to be flexible, and stay flexible. And the ever-intensifying competition from other aspiring scriptwriters means it is equally important to be armed with a great calling card script.

Where did I go wrong?

The 'how to' of writing scripts will always divide opinion, but the reasons why so many scripts and writers fall short in the eyes of the industry seem to soldier on perennially. From my experience as an industry 'gatekeeper' who has ultimately said 'no' to many thousands of scripts and writers, the common, recurring problems with the majority include all the usual fundamental mistakes, inconsistencies, lack of thought and care or plain old cliché surrounding:

- Medium and form (what IS it?)
- Genre and tone (what KIND of thing is it?)
- Idea and premise (what is it trying to explore and SAY?)
- Story (what is engaging the reader's ATTENTION from the start through to the finish?)
- Structure (where is it GOING and does it get there in SURPRISING ways?)
- Characters (are they distinct? do I CONNECT with them emotionally?)
- Scenes (do they come to dramatic LIFE in the moment?)
- Dialogue (are the characters VOICED convincingly, authentically and expressively?)
- Ending (is the conclusion coherent and SATISFYING?)

The honest truth is that these are the difficulties faced every day, by every story and every writer. Never send out a script if you have not gone back, looked again, rewritten, and given yourself the space to get as many of these things as right as you can. It is certainly possible to over-develop a script by forever tinkering and rewriting all the personality out of it. Your script doesn't need to be perfect or utterly slick. But most scripts from aspiring writers do feel under-developed. And your script does need to be ready to be read, because once it has been rejected by someone they will not want to see it again, no matter how much more you develop it. Each script only really has one shot with any given commissioner, producer, director, development executive or literary manager.

Two things (or rather one, stated two different ways) that you should always remember and you ignore at your peril:

- Writing anything really well is *always* really difficult
- There are no simple short cuts to writing well – it is *always* really difficult.

Who am I writing for?

Awareness of market and audience is another perennial problem with aspiring writers. Often the writer isn't thinking enough about who might produce their work and who the audience might be. (Or at the other end of the spectrum, they are worrying far too hard about getting a commission and trying/failing desperately to second guess what producers want.) Then there are those who write to satisfy their own creative urge, who write only for themselves. Drama and comedy are audience-driven forms; without an audience, your work means nothing. But there is some hope for the egotist – because one thing you really must never forget is your own voice, your unique, original perspective on the world of your story. This is the thing the gatekeepers are really looking for, possibly more than anything else.

So to answer the question: you must always be writing for an audience, but you should always be writing to express yourself.

What is a calling card script?

Written well, it is a script that simply speaks your voice. It is interesting, engaging, intriguing, and in some way unusual. It shows what you can do. It is an opportunity to be truly original. It shows the choices you make when you are not writing to a strict brief or commission. It demonstrates your skill and hints at your potential. It opens doors and starts a dialogue. It is the start of a writer's journey, not the final goal or end point of it. It is a means to any number of ends – yet must not feel like it's been written solely to be expedient, solely to impress, solely to second-guess.

A calling card script is not necessarily the first script you write. You must apply the same rigour to every script until you complete one that you feel speaks your voice. And if you really want to write professionally, then the calling card must not be the only script you ever write. You must *always* be writing anew – again, and again, and again. No matter how successful you ultimately might be, each new original script you write is a kind of calling card of who you are as a writer at any given point in your career. A statement of your intent. An expression of your voice.

What should my script look like?

Film

- Make it no less than 80 and no more than 120 pages long.
- It must be original and a complete, single, self-contained story.
- Think about genre; think about the *big* screen.

Television

- The 60-page pilot episode is ideal – whether for a returning series or a finite serial.
- Do not create your own soap opera and never send out a spec episode of an existing programme in the UK.
- Think about where in the small screen schedule it would sit.

Radio

- Aim for the 45-minute single drama.
- The Radio 4 Afternoon Drama is the main window of opportunity, for which you can write all kinds of stories.
- Think about sound and acoustic setting; don't overwrite the dialogue.

Theatre

- You can write with fewer formal restrictions for theatre.
- Make it nothing less than one hour, or much more than two, in length.
- Think hard about the kind of space/place where you imagine it being staged.

What are you looking for at the moment?

This is the single most repeated question from aspiring (and/or desperate) writers. And it is impossible to answer simply. Commissioners, producers, development executives and literary managers across the new writing industries all like to be surprised. They like to be seen to take risks. They like to be responsible for breaking new talent as well as getting the very best out of established talent. They like being able to identify a new idea as worthy of a commission, development and production investment. They like stamping their personality over their 'slate'. They are looking not only for ideas they have never seen before, but also ideas with which as large an audience as possible can fall in love. This is not crude populism or 'commercialism', by the way. It is the meaning of storytelling: to reach, touch, move, entertain, enthuse, inspire, anger, haunt and surprise as many people as possible. From tiny studio theatre through to prime-time television and movie blockbusters – everyone wants their particular house to be a *full* house.

Audiences are more discerning, intelligent, hungry, critical, demanding and knowing than you suspect they are, or than we ever give them credit for. You need to know what has and hasn't worked for audiences – and why – in order to know what has already been done and shouldn't be done again in quite the same way. Don't just repeat. Learn from what you see and hear. Dissect it. Analyse it. Criticise it. Digest it. Accept it. Even if you don't like it. And move on to what's distinct about your idea. If you want to write a Radio 4 Afternoon Drama, you need to know what that slot in the schedule is and does. It's always best if you already love a slot/form. It's good if you can learn to love the potential in it. But if you feel nothing for it whatsoever then you are simply being strategic, and this will be seen for what it is very quickly. Write something you care about. Write about what matters to you.

Further information for writers and film-makers

SUPPORT IN THE UK FILM INDUSTRY

British Film Institute
website www.bfi.org.uk

The lead organisation for film in the UK, investing National Lottery funds in British film-making activity. The BFI Film Fund coordinates the NET.WORK, which is comprised of the following UK-wide support:

Creative England
website www.creativeengland.co.uk

Regional Talent Centres were created to support new and emerging film-makers achieve their first feature film through short film production, feature film development and skills training.

Northern Ireland Screen
website www.northernirelandscreen.co.uk

Film Agency for Wales
website www.filmagencywales.com

Creative Scotland
website www.creativescotland.com

Film London
website www.filmlondon.org.uk

BRITISH BROADCASTERS SUPPORTING FILM

BBC Films
website www.bbc.co.uk/bbcfilms

Film4
website www.film4.com/film4-productions

It is important not to write simply for the sake of expediency – because you think it's the kind of thing you ought to write, or everyone else seems to be writing, or, worst of all, because you reckon it will be 'easier'. These scripts are spotted a mile off, and weeded out quickly. What producers are really looking for is a writer with a distinct voice who can deliver an original story that an audience will love. Your calling card script will probably never be made – but if it's good, then it will get you noticed. And that notice is the thing that will get you closer to becoming a real scriptwriter.

So you think your script is ready to be noticed?

If you do think your script is indeed ready to be read, then here's a checklist of key things to do first – and then do next:

- **Don't send it straight out**. Put it in a drawer for a couple of weeks. Give yourself one last chance to spot any problems/errors.
- **Do your research**. Know your market, know your audience. Put in the legwork on where to send it, what opportunities exist, who is and is not accepting scripts, whose taste you might chime with. (If you have a commercially minded romantic comedy, then is the producer of edgy low-budget social realist films really the best place to send your film script?)
- **Follow their guidelines**. Read what they say carefully. If you directly ignore or contradict their guidelines then don't be surprised if and when they reject your script, unread. You may not like their requirements and remits if they don't suit what you want, but they are always there for a reason so ignore them at your peril.
- **Write a simple cover letter/email**. Don't synopsise your script or go into laborious detail. If your writing is strong, then let your script do the talking; if the writing isn't strong enough, then no amount of prefacing or explaining will change that. Long missives immediately put people off reading and enjoying a script.
- **Don't make irrelevant claims, outrageous promises or damaging admissions**. The person reading doesn't need to know if you think it happens to be better than so-and-so other produced script was (and if you're unlucky they may have been involved with said script, and then you've made an irredeemable *faux pas*). Nor does it really matter if it got a distinction on your MA. Or the script reading service you used told you it ought to get made. Or that your friends loved it. Or that 'it's never been done before' (unless you've seen everything ever made – which nobody has – then this is an impossible assertion). Never tell them it's 'meant to be ambiguous' or 'it gets better later on' or you 'know there are areas you could improve it', when what you are really admitting is that you don't know the ending, it isn't very good at the beginning, and it isn't ready to be read. Never claim 'it's the best script you will read all year' as you have no idea what else they will read that year (nor which high-profile award-winning writer they happen to be working with right now).
- **Don't lie about your experience or be economical with the truth**. Really, don't. The creative industries are ultimately quite small, a lot of people know one another, and truth outs pretty easily and quickly. Whatever experience you do have, you should talk it up; but you should never make it up. Be honest.
- **Be confident in what you think you've achieved**. But don't be arrogant – and do prepare for the worst. For the people looking at your script, it will be just one amongst hundreds or even thousands that year, and you always face stiff competition from other writers.

- **Start your next script**. Don't sit waiting anxiously for a response. Real writers write, all the time, obsessively. Keep writing. And try new things. Never written a radio play? Try it. Want to master final draft screenplay format? Try it.
- **Show initiative**. Don't sit around waiting for floods of interest and commissions to jam up your letterbox/inbox. Find out what useful industry events and networking opportunities of any kind exist within reachable distance to you, and go to them, meet people, network. Use whatever contacts you might have, however tenuous they might seem.
- **Be resilient**. Don't be offended by silence; the volume of spec emails has made life harder for most in the industry. And everyone is rejected at some point. *Everyone.* Learn to deal with rejection, roll with the punches, don't simmer with resentment, argue with someone's decision, or lash out in rejected anger. If someone simply doesn't connect with your work then no amount of telling them that they should will change that. Move on and try to find the person that does connect with it. Learn to bounce back better, stronger – happier.

Coda

Embrace the necessary difficulty of writing well. Invest in your own voice. Never be satisfied. Be honest. Be prepared. Be realistic. Be idealistic. Be brave. Be obsessive. Stay sane.

And be lucky.

Paul Ashton is a Senior Film Executive at Creative England, where he leads the Sheffield Talent Centre as part of the BFI NET.WORK to support new and emerging film-makers towards getting their first feature films made. Paul was previously Development Producer at BBC writersroom (www.bbc.co.uk/writersroom), and before that freelanced across film, television, radio and theatre. He has been involved in finding, developing and producing Academy- and BAFTA-nominated films, and BAFTA, RTS, Sony and Prix Italia award-winning drama and comedy for television and radio. Paul is the author of *The Calling Card Script: A Writer's Toolbox for Stage, Screen and Radio* (Methuen Drama 2011).

See also...

- *Adaptations from books*, page 341
- *Notes from a successful soap scriptwriter*, page 352
- *Stories on radio*, page 355
- *Writing for the theatre*, page 371
- *Bringing new life to classic plays*, page 367

Notes from a successful soap scriptwriter

As the longest serving member of the *Archers'* scriptwriting team, Mary Cutler shares her thoughts about writing for soaps.

A few years ago I was introduced by a friend to someone struggling to establish herself as a playwright. 'I so envy you,' she said, 'writing for the *Archers*. I love soaps.' 'If you love soaps, maybe you should be writing them,' I suggested. I met her again some time later and she said, 'I want to thank you: I took your advice. I gave it a try, and now I'm writing for Emmerdale.' So there you are, dear readers. Ten magic words from me might transform your life. I will try to explore why you might love writing for soaps, or equally helpfully, I hope, why you might not.

I have been writing for the *Archers* for 36 years (the programme was first broadcast on Radio 4 in 1951) and such a long career is by no means unique in soaps. During these years I have had a guaranteed audience for my work, and what's more, an affectionate and engaged audience. I've worked collaboratively with some extremely talented people, while retaining control of my own words. I have had the opportunity to cover almost every dramatic situation – tragic, comic, social, political – I could ever have wanted to, in every possible dramatic form. Yes, you may ask – though I hope not as the question fills me with fury – but what about your own work? This is my own work. Who else wrote all those scripts?

The production process

The process of getting a script ready to be recorded starts with the monthly Wednesday script conference. This is attended by all the writers (there are eight of us in the team at the moment) and the production team. We each have in front of us the large script pack which would have been emailed to us on the previous Friday. We meet to decide on the storyline for the next writing month, for which four of the writers present will each be writing a week's worth of episodes. Those four writers then pitch their week based on the ideas in the pack. But we all work on the storyline together – the writers, whether writing or not – and all the production team, at all levels. That is one of the things I like most. I have never felt plotting was a particular strength of mine, but if someone will give me a starting line I can run from it. The delight of a good script conference is when we start with a strong idea which everyone expands and improves on until it's a thing of beauty, and no one can remember whose idea it was first, and it doesn't matter.

To be part of this engrossing process you have to speak. Most soaps have a script conference element where you will be expected to voice, and if necessary, defend your ideas. That doesn't mean you have to shout, or talk all the time – indeed, these would be positive disadvantages. But you need to stand your ground, especially about what a character might or might not do, and also be ready to yield gracefully if you lose the argument. One of our characters was once torn between two lovers, and the team were, too. On the day of the final decision there was a bad hold-up on the motorway, and three writers rooting for one lover didn't arrive until midday, by which time the other had carried the day. Those writers each had to find their own way to make that decision work for them when they wrote their scripts.

After the script conference, the storyline is emailed two days later to all the writers and members of the production team to arrive on Friday evening. The writers for that month have until Monday morning to each write their synopsis, which is a scene-by-scene break down of what they intend to write in their six episodes. If it is a well-structured and imaginative synopsis, all that now needs to be written is the dialogue. A script editor speaks with each of the writers for that month the next day, and they then have 12 days to write six scripts – an hour and a quarter of radio. Not everyone can work that fast. One of the best weeks of the *Archers* I ever heard was also that writer's last: he said he could never do it again in the time. It's not a case of locking yourself in your garret and seeing where the muse takes you. The storyline must be covered: while the writer for one week is working on their scripts, the writer for the following week's episodes is writing theirs starting from the point where the storyline is left on the previous week. As all the scripts are written simultaneously each writer needs to let the others know what they're doing. How each writer chooses to dramatise the story is entirely up to them, so there's a lot of scope for individual creative work. There are constraints on the structure of the programme, such as the financial restriction on the number of actors which can be used. Writers may need to tell a story without a character being present because the actor is working elsewhere. Alternatively a writer may swap episodes within their week, or with other writers, to get the actors they need, though we try not to do that.

Until the script editor sees the writing for all four weeks, she can't tell if stories are going too fast or too slow, have become repetitive, or picked up the wrong tone. There may well be changes to be made following the synopsis discussion. It is only after the synopsis is agreed that the office starts ringing the actors to see if they are still available. Some of them may not be, in which case a writer may have to rethink their beautiful structure and clever stories. But those are just normal run-of-the-mill changes. When we lost the delightful and distinguished actress who played Julia Pargeter (who died suddenly and unexpectedly after a happy day in the recording studio) the team had to deal with not only their individual sorrow and distress, but the fact that this meant rewriting and re-recording scripts that had been completed in the studio, and rewriting those that were about to be recorded, as well as rethinking those that were about to be written. I had two days to turn round my part of this massive undertaking. When the foot-and-mouth crisis hit British farming in 2001 our fictional world was being rewritten practically day by day, so a good soap scriptwriter needs to be fast and flexible. When the Princess of Wales died our redoubtable editor had one day to get something appropriate on air.

My scriptwriting break

So how did scriptwriting for soaps become the job for me? I had always wanted to write, and had been writing since I was quite small. I thought I was going to be a novelist, and wrote several highly autobiographical, very literary quasi novels while at school and university. I should have noticed that the only person prepared to pay me was the editor of *Jackie* magazine to whom I sold three highly autobiographical, although not quite so literary, stories. Then at university I stopped having saleable teenage fantasies, and started having unsaleable literary ones. Real life took over – I decided my ambition to be a writer was a fantasy – I would concentrate on my burgeoning career as a teacher, and stop writing.

But I found I couldn't stop. When I realised how I think – rather than seeing images or words, I hear voices (a perpetual radio broadcast!) – I started to write radio plays. To my delight, I found that I could write dialogue till the cows came home(!) though whether it was about anything that would interest even the cows was another matter. I sent my radio plays to the BBC, and sometimes they came back with kind comments (once I was even invited to meet a producer) – and sometimes they just came back. But I persisted.

I am a life-long fan of the *Archers* (I remember Grace Archer dying when I was six and I used to play Phil Archer and his pigs with my little brothers – naturally I was Phil). When an old school friend started writing for the *Archers* I was fascinated to hear her first week on air: it simultaneously sounded like the *Archers* I had known and loved but also very like my friend – her sense of humour, her preoccupations. I idly wondered what I might find out about my own writing if I tried using these well-loved characters to express myself. So after I heard her Friday episode, I sat down to write the following Monday's, purely as a writing exercise and just for fun, and sent it off.

Some time later I received a letter from the recently appointed editor of the *Archers* saying that although he wasn't looking for new writers my script interested him. He also invited me to meet him. When I went to Pebble Mill the editor offered me a trial week, which I did in the Easter holidays. Following that, he offered me a six-month contract. So my big break was a combination of persistence (I had been sending radio plays to the BBC for at least three years, and writing stories since I could hold a pencil) and sheer luck – the new editor *was* looking for new writers, despite what he'd said in his letter. My script also had the necessary ingredients of craft and, dare I say it, talent. I had, without knowing it, written a script of the right length, with the right number of scenes and the right number of characters – all those years of listening had given me a subliminal feel for the form. According to the editor, my first good line was two-thirds of the way down the first page. I can still remember it: 'She can get up a fair lick of speed when she's pushed'. (Maybe you had to be there but I still think it has a certain ring to it!) But it was also a script I wrote for fun for a programme I loved and admired.

Mary Cutler has been a scriptwriter for the *Archers* since 1979. She has dramatised five of Lindsey Davis's *Falco* novels for Radio 4, the last one being *Poseidon's Gold*, and three dramatic series – *Live Alone and Like It, Three Women and a Boat* and *Three Women and a Baby* for *Women's Hour*. She has also written for the stage and television, including some scripts for *Crossroads* before she was told that her particular talents did not quite fit its special demands. She'd still like to write a novel.

Stories on radio

Getting a story read on BBC Radio 4 is very competitive. Di Speirs outlines how work is selected.

Before they were ever written down, we told stories to each other. And there remains a natural empathy between the written tale and the spoken word. The two make perfect partners in a medium where the imagination has free rein – in other words – radio. And that partnership is particularly effective on the BBC's speech networks, BBC Radio 4 and 4Extra, which play host to more stories than any other UK stations. Stories, of course, can and do appear in many guises there, from original plays to dramatised adaptations, but above all they work on air as themselves, read by some of the finest actors of our day and listened to by upwards of one million listeners on most slots.

There are two main reading slots for books on Radio 4: the morning non-fiction reading at 9.45am, which is repeated in the late evening and has an audience of around 3.5 million weekly, and every weekday evening a *Book at Bedtime* episode can lull you towards (although hopefully not to) sleep, just after *The World Tonight* at 10.45pm. There are also two slots a week, on Friday at 3.30pm and at 7.45pm on a Sunday where both commissioned and extant short stories are broadcast, and on Radio 4 Extra you can find occasional outings in the *Short Story Zone* for five pieces from short story collections.

A number of different producers, both in-house and independent, produce readings for these slots – finding the books and stories, getting them commissioned by Radio 4 and then producing the final programmes. The process of successfully translating the written work to the airwaves is as intimate as that of any editor within a publishing house. There is nothing like structuring the abridgement of a novel or a short story – which reduces an author's meticulously crafted work down to 2,000 words an episode – to focus the mind on the essential threads and hidden subtleties of a work, be it originally 3,500 perfectly chosen words or an intricately plotted 300-page novel. The author Derek Longman once described the abridging of his *Diana's Story* (one of the most popular readings ever on *Woman's Hour*) as akin to the book 'having gone on a diet'. You aim to retain the essence, but in a trimmer, slimmer version.

Once cut to the bone, finding the right voice to convey and enhance the story is crucial, as performance, in part, compensates for what has been lost. Casting is vital; so is direction in the studio where different stories demand very different approaches: listen to the output and you'll hear everything from a highly characterised monologue to a narrator-driven piece which demands that the actor also creates a cast of dozens of distinct voices. From the cues that introduce a story, to the music that sets the right mood, a producer works to move a story from the author's original vision into a different but sympathetic medium. As authors mourn what is discarded, it is important to remember what is added by good quality production and top class performance. And of course to remember how effective readings are at taking a book to a whole new audience.

So how do you get your story on air and to all those eager listeners? What is Radio 4 looking for and what works best?

It would be disingenuous to say that it is any easier to get your work read on radio than to get it published. In truth, given the finite number of slots and the volume of submissions it's a tough call. But here are a few hints and guidelines that may help.

Book of the Week

The *Book of the Week* slot is the one that reflects current publishing more than any other. With 52 books a year broadcast on or very close to their original publication date, in five 13-minute episodes, the non-fiction remit is broad and the slot covers everything from biography to humour, politics to travel. Memoir is always an important part of the mix, but so too are good, accessible science books with a narrative thread that can engage the listener, and few subjects are out of bounds if the prose lifts off the page and can catch the attention of what is, by necessity, a largely active and busy audience at that time in the morning.

Submissions come through publishers and agents and in reality are always of published material. (The only exceptions are the occasional fast turnaround commissioned 'letters' in response to events.) The books need to sustain their story over five episodes but also to work as individual episodes, for this is an audience that won't necessarily hear all of the book (though the BBC's 'Listen Again' facility on iPlayer is increasingly changing this pattern). Overly academic prose doesn't work, nor do too many names and facts. The key is a story and, as below, a voice.

Book at Bedtime

Book at Bedtime is a mix of classic and new fiction. The slot is mostly serialised fiction although occasional harder hitting short story collections – for instance by writers like Julie Orringer and Anne Enright – do find their way in, as do the odd weeks of poetry (*Paradise Lost* and *The Prelude* have been read in the past). The novels divide into, roughly, a quarter classic fiction, a quarter more recent popular fiction, a quarter established names on publication (e.g. new novels, usually transmitted on publication by popular writers, from Donna Tartt to John le Carré, Colm Toibin to Kazuo Ishiguro); and a quarter newer voices, including a high proportion of debut novels (Ross Raisin's *Waterline*, Kyung-sook Shin's *Please Look After My Mother*, Anna Funder's *All that I Am*, Amy Sackville's *The Still Point*) and some short stories (e.g. Polly Samson, Clare Keegan). What they all share is a quality of writing that works when you pare it to the core. Abridging a work will show up its literary qualities and its flaws – and there is nowhere to hide. Listen to the slot and you will be aware of both the variety (from classics to crime, domestic dramas to lyrical translations) and the quality of the writing.

There are few other hard-and-fast rules – a linear plot, with sub-plots that can be reduced or lost, is preferable – *The Vanishing Act of Esme Lennox* by Maggie O'Farrell was a demanding listen in terms of jumps in time and place but the characters were so vivid and the story so powerful it worked; myriad characters are best avoided, but are manageable with a classic (where familiarity helps). Length is also an important issue. The usual run for a book is 10 episodes over 2 weeks; for almost any novel over 350 pages this becomes a cut too far. Exceptions can be made but they are exceptions; *Atonement* by Ian McEwan, *Merivel, A Man of His Time* by Rose Tremain and *The Interpretation of Murder* by Jed Rubenfeld all ran at 15 episodes, but for new work this is a rarity. (Short novels can run over five episodes.)

New book submissions

New novels are found almost entirely through submissions from agents and publishers to individual producers – the best ones both understand Radio 4 and know the predilections of the main players and play to their tastes. It is extremely rare that an author submits directly; even rarer for them to be successful in what is the most competitive readings slot of all. However, the passion of an individual agent or editor can make a real difference in getting a book read by the producer, which is the first step in the process. Bear in mind that in my office alone we receive upwards of 50 manuscripts and proof sets a week – a lot of work for a team of four producers. Having a reputable champion who can expand on why your novel really is potentially right for the slot is a genuine plus in getting to the top of the scripts pile.

We usually see work at the manuscript or proof stage; this is increasingly submitted online though this is not essential, or even always desirable, as many producers still prefer to read from paper. New titles are ideally broadcast at or near to the hardback publication date, and so producers need to see them in time to get them commissioned and made – ideally six to nine months in advance. And however passionate a producer is about an individual title, the choice is finally in the hands of the commissioning team at Radio 4 who know what else lies in the complex schedule across the network, and must always weigh individual merits against the broader picture.

What makes a good book to read on Radio 4?

Radio 4 is looking for the quality of the writing, coherence of plot (bear in mind though that complex sub-plots can sometimes be stripped out by skilful abridgers), a comprehensible, identifiable and preferably fairly small cast and perhaps above all, a sense of engagement with the listener. Although crime is always popular, broadcasting copious amounts of blood and gore at bedtime is unlikely to endear the BBC to the public. Psychological work – like *Engleby* by Sebastian Faulks – works better. Think too, when descriptions are cut, do the clues in the plot stand out like a sore thumb? Consider whether the subject matter is likely to fit with the Radio 4 audience – who are almost certainly much broader-minded and certainly more eclectic than you might imagine – and also highly literate. There is a very real desire to reflect as wide a range of fiction as possible – from a bestseller by Sadie Jones to a Bangladeshi debut from Tahmima Anan, from a suddenly discovered classic from Irene Nemirovsky to the cutting edge of David Mitchell. It's a broad spectrum but there are of course some issues surrounding language, violence and sexual content; these can be surmountable in many cases – judicious pauses are effective and radio is, after all, a medium that allows the imagination to fill in the blanks as far as you may want to. However, there is no point in submitting a novel filled with expletives or subject matter that will simply shock for the sake of it.

Think too about the voice of a novel – this applies, as much does here, to the short story too. It's an aural medium. Does your book have a 'voice' – can you hear it leaping off the page? Would you want to hear it read to you? And will that be easy to do? There are problems with any story or novel that veers from the third to the first person continually. It can be done – Anna Funder's *All That I Am* was a gift for three narrators, but remember that although every year Radio 4 runs several novels with multiple narrators, they are more expensive to produce and as budgets get ever leaner, slots are even more limited. Be realistic. The competition for this slot is the fiercest of all – and with approximately 26 titles a year, a good number of which are from the ever-popular classic canon, there are really only around a dozen opportunities for the year's new titles.

Short Readings

Fifty-two weeks of the year, twice a week, Radio 4 broadcasts a short story or occasionally short non-fiction – approximately 100 stories annually are commissioned by producers around the country. The rest comprise of the re-reading of old masters and selections from newly published collections, by writers such as Alice Munro, Jennifer Egan, Helen Simpson, Edith Pearlman, Sana Kraskiov and Mary Costello. Like novels, these collections are submitted by publishers and agents.

The BBC is arguably the largest single commissioner of short stories in the UK, possibly even the world. It is hugely committed to the short story, that most difficult and often underrated of literary forms, and does provide an unparalleled opportunity for writers who want to explore the genre. However, as with *Book at Bedtime*, the competition here is severe.

Stories are usually grouped around a theme and often in runs of threes. Sometimes stories broadcast from literary festivals, such as Edinburgh, Latitude and Hay-on-Wye. Writers for these are often selected from the festival's own programme, either to write original material or to perform something they are already reading.

The majority of other weeks are commissioned by producers around a theme that they've discussed with the commissioning editor. The scope is very wide. There have been stories drawn from the three Benelux countries and others inspired by Tom Waits under the umbrella title 'The Heart of a Saturday Night'. A series of 'Heartbreak' was followed by a series of 'Passion' and later by 'Wedding Feasts', while thornier subjects such as 'Addiction' have allowed writers to explore a surprising variety of subjects from caffeine to love. 'Madame Bovary Speaks' allowed writers to play with various angles from Flaubert's novel while a returning series like 'Curly Tales' plays with the storytelling form and enjoys turning it upside down. These themed runs offer producers a wonderful opportunity to approach both well-known writers (who usually have a record in short story writing) and to give new writers – perhaps spotted in an anthology or a magazine, or because of a strong debut novel, or through the advocacy of an agent – a chance to get their work on air. Many acclaimed short story writers, like Jackie Kay, Helen Dunmore and Peter Ho Davies, have a long history with Radio 4, and are commissioned regularly because they understand the demands and the possibilities of the slot.

Unsolicited stories

There are some opportunities for writers to submit work for consideration: for instance once a year the London Readings Unit runs a returning series called *Opening Lines* for writers specifically 'New to Radio' and accepts submissions in a creative window for a specific and limited period, and BBC Scotland produces a series of unsolicited *Scottish Shorts*. A number of the independent suppliers are also committed to finding new talent. Very occasionally a story is commissioned on a theme, following on from an unsolicited submission, but this is rare. The short story is a demanding form, and skill and practise is perhaps more vital here than anywhere else. Producers have a certain but sadly limited amount of time to work with an author in an editorial capacity. With only 2,000 words there's no room for waste and yet you must, as Alice Munro (the Canadian doyenne of the short story) says, 'create a world in a glance'. The subjects may be wide but the bar is high – the best writers in the country and beyond are writing for this slot and you have to match that standard. You may have a better chance of being considered by aiming your story locally (some local BBC radio stations run short fiction from time to time). Be aware of which independent and regional teams work in your geographic area, as the Radio 4 slots reflect the regions and nations of the UK.

But above all, as with *Book at Bedtime*, listen to the slot to hear both the range and also what works well. Listen to how writers use the unique qualities of radio – the chance to write a powerful monologue or to use sound or location within a tale – to enhance their story, create a sense of place or person, to flesh out what is in reality a brief moment in time. There are real ways to be experimental in both storytelling and production, and producers are always on the lookout for those alongside perfectly pitched and flawless prose.

Finally, for the past 10 years the BBC has been a partner with Booktrust, in the BBC National Short Story Award (see page 536), which was established to celebrate and foster the art of the short story. With an award of £15,000 to the winner, it is one of the largest in the world for a single story. We have received over 7,500 entries from published writers either from, or resident in, the UK since the award began. It is certainly clear that the short story is alive and well across the UK and choosing the winners has been a tremendously hard task each time. If you are a published writer, do consider entering next time around. The BBC NSSA is part of the wider 'Story' campaign, run by Booktrust, which exists to support all short story writers (www.theshortstory.org.uk). In 2015, to celebrate the 10th anniversary of this Grand-Daddy of short story prizes, and to encourage teenage would-be authors, we have launched the BBC Young Writers Award to run alongside the main one.

In all the readings slots, Radio 4 is looking for terrific writing, a good story and an ear-catching 'voice'. Despite the fierce competition, producers love to 'discover' new writers for the network and every year sees new talent getting their work on air. Keep listening, get to know the slots, and if you have a story – long or short – that demands to be read aloud, try to find a champion for it. Good luck.

Di Speirs worked in theatre and for the Australian Broadcasting Corporation before joining the BBC as a producer for *Woman's Hour*. She edited the *Woman's Hour* serial for three years and produced the first ever *Book of the Week*. She is now Editor, Books for BBC Radio and Music – responsible for the output of the BBC London Readings Unit (about a third of *Book of the Week*, a quarter of *Book at Bedtime*, short stories on Radio 4, Radio 3 essays and occasional adaptations), as well as Radio 4's Book Club and Open Book, and World Book Club and works closely with the BBC Arts Online team producing Books at the BBC. She has been instrumental in the BBC National Short Story Award since its inception in 2005 and is a regular judge on the panel. She judged the 2008 Asham Award, Chaired the Orange Award for New Writers in 2010 and was a nominator for Rolex Mentor and Protégé Arts Initiative 2012.

See also...

- *Writing short stories*, page 241
- *Adaptations from books*, page 341
- *The calling card script for screen, radio and stage*, page 347

Television and radio

The information in this section has been compiled as a general guide for writers, artists, agents and publishers to the major companies and key contacts within the broadcasting industry. As personnel, corporate structures and commissioning guidelines can change frequently, readers are encouraged to check the websites of companies for the most up to date situation.

REGULATION

Ofcom is the regulator for the communications industries in the UK and has responsibility for TV and radio, as well as telecommunications and wireless services. Advertising is regulated by the Advertising Standards Authority and on-demand TV services are regulated by the Authority for Television On Demand.

Ofcom

Riverside House, 2A Southwark Bridge Road, London SE1 9HA
tel 020-7981 3000, 0300 123 3000
website www.ofcom.org.uk
Chief Executive Sharon White

Ofcom is accountable to parliament and exists to: further the interests of consumers by balancing choice and competition with the duty to encourage plurality, protect viewers and listeners, promote diversity in the media and ensure full and fair competition between communications providers.

Advertising Standards Authority

Mid City Place, 71 High Holborn, London WC1V 6QT
tel 020-7492 2222
website www.asa.org.uk
Chief Executive Guy Parker

The Advertising Standards Authority is the UK's independent regulator of advertising across all media. Its work includes acting on complaints and taking action against misleading, harmful or offensive advertisements.

Authority for Television On Demand (ATVOD)

27 Sheet Street, Windsor, Berks. SL4 1BN
tel (01753) 860498
email atvod@atvod.co.uk
website www.atvod.co.uk
Chief Executive Pete Johnson

ATVOD is the independent co-regulator for the editorial content of UK video-on-demand services that fall within the statutory definition of on-demand programme services.

TELEVISION

There are five major TV broadcasters operating in the UK: the BBC, ITV, Channel 4 (S4/C in Wales), Channel 5 and Sky. In Ireland, RTÉ is the country's public service broadcaster.

The BBC

website www.bbc.co.uk

The BBC is the world's largest broadcasting organisation, with a remit to provide programmes that inform, educate and entertain. Established by a Royal Charter, the BBC is a public service broadcaster funded by a licence fee. Income from the licence fee is used to provide services including:

- 10 national TV channels plus regional programming
- 10 national radio stations
- 40 local radio stations
- BBC Online
- BBC World Service

Anyone in the UK who watches or records TV programmes (whether via TV, online, mobile phone, games console, digital box, etc) at the time they are broadcast needs a TV licence. The Government sets the level of the licence fee – in 2010 it was frozen at £145.50 per annum until the end of the current BBC Charter period in 2016.

In addition, the BBC operates separate commercial ventures whose profits help to fund public services.

Governance

BBC Trust

The BBC Trust is the governing body of the BBC. It is made up of 12 trustees, led by Rona Fairhead. It is the guardian of both licence fee revenue and the public interest in the BBC. More specifically, it sets the BBC's strategy, approves licence fee expenditure, establishes objectives for the BBC, ensures that services meet audiences' expectations and provide good value for money, and it serves as the final point of appeal for complaints.

The Trust is separate from the BBC's Executive Board, which is led by the Director-General.

Executive Board

The Executive Board is responsible for the operational delivery of services, as well as ensuring that editorial and creative output adheres to the guidelines set by the Trust.

The Executive Board is lead by Director-General Tony Hall and is supported by six non-executive directors.

Structure

A number of separate operational areas manage the day-to-day working of the BBC. These include:

- Executive Board
- Management Board
- TV
- Radio
- News Group
- Strategy & Digital
- BBC North
- Finance & Business

In addition there are three commercial subsidiaries:

- BBC Worldwide
- BBC Global News
- BBC Studios and Post Production

What does the BBC do?

It is not possible to list here information about all BBC activities, functions and personnel. The following provides a selective overview of the BBC's main services and key contact information we consider most relevant to our readership.

Television

The BBC operates 10 regional national TV channels, providing entertainment, news, current affairs and arts programming for the whole of the UK: BBC One, BBC Two, BBC Three, BBC Four, CBBC, CBeebies, BBC News, BBC Parliament, BBC HD and BBC Alba.

BBC Three is set to cease operations as a TV channel but will remain as an online service.

Director, TV Danny Cohen

Service controllers

Controller BBC One Charlotte Moore
Controller BBC Two and BBC Four Kim Shillinglaw
Controller BBC Three Damian Kavanagh
Acting Controller BBC Daytime Jo Street
Controller Children's Alice Webb
Director of Sport Barbara Slater

BBC Strategy & Digital

BBC Online's services include news, sport, weather, CBBC and BBC iPlayer. BBC Online sites are developed to provide audiences with access to content on a variety of devices including tablets, smartphones, computers and internet-connected TVs. BBC Online also provides access to the BBC's radio and TV programme archives, through BBC iPlayer. Another interactive service, BBC Red Button, provides audiences with access to content that is directly related to what is being broadcast.

Director, Strategy & Digital James Purnell
Director, BBC Digital Ralph Rivera

News Group

The largest of the BBC's departments in terms of staff, with over 8,000 employed around the UK and throughout the rest of the world. BBC News incorporates network news (the newsroom, news programmes such as Newsnight, political programmes such as Daily Politics, and the weather team), English Regions and Global News.

Director, News & Current Affairs James Harding
Director, World Service Group Fran Unsworth

BBC North

BBC North covers Sport, Children's 5 Live, some parts of Learning and Future Media.

Director, BBC England Peter Salmon

Finance & Business

This operational area manages all aspects of the BBC's finance and operations.

Managing Director, Finance & Operations Anne Bulford

BBC Worldwide

BBC Worldwide Ltd is the primary commercial arm and a wholly owned subsidiary of the BBC. Its aim is to support the BBC's public service remit and maximise profits on its behalf by commercialising content from the BBC around the world. BBC Worldwide helps to keep the licence fee as low as possible. Geographic markets are grouped into three regions: North America; UK, Australia and New Zealand; and Global Markets. The three global business areas are Content, Digital and Brands.

Ceo Tim Davie

BBC Studios & Post Production

Works with media companies to create and manage content across all genres for a diverse range of broadcasters and platforms, including ITV, Channel 4 and Sky, as well as the BBC. A wholly owned subsidiary of the BBC.

Managing Director David Conway

BBC World Service Group

This division incorporates BBC World Service and BBC Global News.

Director, World Service Group Fran Unsworth

Commissioning

For full details of editorial guidelines, commissioning, production and delivery guidelines, and how to submit a proposal, see www.bbc.co.uk/commissioning.

Developing and producing programmes is complex and requires substantial knowledge of production and broadcasting. BBC Pitch is the BBC's commissioning tool designed for UK-based production companies and BBC in-house production teams to submit content proposals for BBC Network Television. See www.bbc.co.uk/commissioning/tv/articles/pitch. Individuals and members of the public cannot use BBC Pitch. If you are a member of the public with an idea, see www.bbc.co.uk/commissioning/tv/ideas-from-the-public.

Who's who in commissioning?

Television (genre commissioning)
CBBC *Controller & Portfolio Head* Cheryl Taylor
CBeebies *Controller & Portfolio Head* Kay Benbow
Comedy *Controller* Shane Allen, *Commissioning Editors* Gregor Sharp, Kristian Smith, Chris Sussman
Daytime & Early Peak *Acting Controller* Jo Street, *Commissioning Editors* Aisling O'Connor, Carla-Maria Lawson, Alex McLeod, Gerard Melling
Drama *Controller* Ben Stephenson, *Commissioning Editors* Lucy Richer, Matthew Read, Joe Oppenheimer (films), *Head of Independent Drama* Polly Hill
Entertainment *Controller* Mark Linsey, *Commissioning Editors* Jo Wallace, Rachel Ashdown, Ed Sleeman, Ruby Kuraishe, Pinki Chambers, Alan Tyler
Factual (covers arts, current affairs, documentaries, features & formats, history & business, learning, music, religion & ethics, science & natural history, Open University, acquisitions, BBC iPlayer): *Commissioning Heads* Mark Bell (arts), Clive Edwards (current affairs), Maxine Watson (documentaries), Alison Kirkham (features & formats), Sam Bickley (documentaries on BBC Three), Martin Davidson (history & business), Abigail Appleton (BBC Learning), Jan Younghusband (music), Aaqil Ahmed (religion & ethics), Tom McDonald (science & natural history), Sue Deeks (acquisitions, films & series), Caroline Ogilvie (Open University)
Sport *Director* Barbara Slater

BBC Regions
England *Director* Peter Salmon
Northern Ireland *Director* Peter Johnston
Scotland *Director* Ken MacQuarrie
Cymru Wales *Director* Rhodri Talfan Davies

BBC writersroom

website www.bbc.co.uk/writersroom

BBC writersroom is the first port of call at the BBC for unsolicited scripts and new writers. It champions writing talent across a range of genres and is always on the lookout for writers of any age and experience who can show real potential for the BBC. Visit the website to discover:

- how and when to submit a script;
- new opportunities for writers;
- writing tips and success stories;
- interviews and top tips from writers.

The BBC writersroom blog provides a wealth of behind-the-scenes commentary from writers and producers who have worked on BBC TV and radio programmes: www.bbc.co.uk/blogs/writersroom.

Education and training

The BBC has adopted a recruitment system called the BBC Careers Hub. It allows candidates to apply for jobs, source interview tips, learn about the BBC's recruitment processes and get advice about CVs, applications and assessments: www.bbc.co.uk/careers/home.

Trainee Schemes

website www.bbc.co.uk/careers/trainee-schemes

For full details of the BBC's trainee schemes see website.

Work Experience

website www.bbc.co.uk/careers/work-experience

For full details of the BBC's work experience placements see website.

BBC College of Production

website www.bbc.co.uk/academy/production

A free, online learning resource providing practical advice and information on all aspects of working in TV, radio and online.

BBC College of Technology

website www.bbc.co.uk/academy/technology

A free, online learning environment which focuses on providing resources connected with broadcast engineering, software technology and business systems.

BBC College of Journalism

website www.bbc.co.uk/academy/journalism

The College is responsible for the training of BBC news staff and provides in-depth information about core skills, legal and ethical matters and writing techniques. Features a wide range of hints, tips and style guides for writers.

Work in Broadcast

website www.bbc.co.uk/academy/work-in-broadcast

This site provides a wealth of information for anyone wanting to work for the BBC, whether as an employee or freelance.

Writer's Lab

website www.bbc.co.uk/writersroom/writers-lab

The Writer's Lab provides interviews, advice, toolkits, guidelines and other resources to help and support your writing.

ITV plc

The London Television Centre, Upper Ground, London SE1 9LT

tel 020-7157 3000
website www.itv.com, www.itvplc.com

The ITV network is responsible for the commissioning, scheduling and marketing of network programmes on ITV1 and its digital channel portfolio including ITV2, ITV3, ITV4 and CiTV. It is the UK's largest commercial TV network. In addition to TV broadcasting services, ITV also delivers programming via a number of platforms, including ITV Player.

ITV Studios is the UK's largest production company and produces over 3,500 hours of original content annually. ITV Studios (UK) produces programming for the ITV network's own channels as well as other UK broadcasters including the BBC, Channel 4, Channel 5 and Sky. ITV also has an international production business which produces for local broadcasters in the USA, Australia, France, Germany and Scandinavia.

Management team
Ceo Adam Crozier
Group Communications and Corporate Affairs Director Mary Fagan
Director of Television Peter Fincham
Managing Director, Commercial Kelly Williams
Managing Director Kevin Lygo
Managing Director, Online, Pay TV, Interactive and Technology Simon Pitts
Group Legal Director Andrew Garard
Group Finance Director Ian Griffiths
Human Resources Director David Osborn

Commissioning

ITV's commissioning areas include entertainment and comedy, factual, daytime, drama, sport, current affairs, digital and online. Information, FAQs and guidelines for commissioning can be found at www.itv.com/commissioning.

Entertainment & Comedy

email comedy.commissioning@itv.com
Director of Entertainment Elaine Bedell, *Commissioning* Claire Zolkwer, Asif Zubairy, Kate Maddigan, Peter Davey, Amanda Stavri

Factual

email factual.commissioning@itv.com
Director of Factual Richard Klein, *Controller* Jo Clinton-Davis, *Commissioning* Katy Thorogood, Priya Singh

Daytime

email daytime.commissioning@itv.com
Director of Daytime Helen Warner, *Commissioning* Clare Ely, Jane Beacon

Drama

email drama.commissioning@itv.com
Director of Drama Steve November, *Controller* Victoria Fea, *Commissioning* Charlie Hampton, *Head of Drama Series* Jane Hudson

Sport

Director of Sport Niall Sloane

Current Affairs

email currentaffairs.commissioning@itv.com
Controller of Current Affairs and News Operations Ian Squires

Digital

Director of Digital Channels and Acquisitions Angela Jain, *Controller* Paul Mortimer

Recruitment, training and work experience

Information about training schemes, work experience and recruitment at ITV can be found at www.itvjobs.com, including details of ITV Insight, a volunteering scheme which enables people seeking experience in the TV industry to gain hands-on experience.

ITV network regions

The ITV Network is made up of the following regions:
ITV Anglia www.itv.com/news/anglia
ITV Border www.itv.com/news/border
ITV Central www.itv.com/news/central
ITV Granada www.itv.com/news/granada
ITV London www.itv.com/news/london
ITV Meridian www.itv.com/news/meridian
ITV TyneTees www.itv.com/news/tyne-tees
ITV Wales www.itv.com/news/wales
ITV West Country (East) www.itv.com/news/west
ITV West Country (West) www.itv.com/news/westcountry
STV Group www.stv.tv (Scotland)
UTV www.u.tv (Northern Ireland)
Channel Television (Wales) www.channelonline.tv/channelonline (Channel Islands)

Channel 4

124 Horseferry Road, London SW1P 2TX
tel 020-7396 4444
website www.channel4.com

Channel 4 is a publicly-owned, commercially-funded, not-for-profit public service broadcaster and has a remit to be innovative, experimental and distinctive. Its public ownership and not-for-profit status ensure all profit generated by its commercial activity is directly reinvested back into the delivery of its public service remit. As a publisher-broadcaster, Channel 4 is also required to commission UK content from the independent production sector and currently works with over 400 creative companies across the UK every year. In addition to the main Channel 4 service, its portfolio includes: E4, More4, Film4, 4Music, 4seven, channel4.com and brand new digital service, All 4, which presents all of C4's on-demand content, digital innovations and live linear channel streams in one place online for the first time.

Management team

Chief Executive David Abraham
Chief Creative Officer Jay Hunt
Chief Marketing & Communications Officer Dan Brooke
HR Director Diane Herbert

Commissioning

Information about commissioning and related processes and guidelines can be found at www.channel4.com/info/commissioning.

Arts

Commissioning John Hay

Comedy

Head of Comedy Phil Clarke, *Commissioning* Nerys Evans, Fiona McDermott, Rachel Springett, Laura Riseam

Daytime

Head of Daytime David Sayer, *Commissioning* Sagina Shabaya

Documentaries

Head of Documentaries Nick Mirsky, *Commissioning* Emma Cooper, David Brindley, Anna Miralis, Amy Flanagan, Madonna Benjamin

Drama

Head of Drama Piers Wenger, *Deputy Head of Drama* Beth Willis, *Head of Development* Surian Fletcher-Jones, *Commissioning* Roberto Troni, *Head of International Drama* Simon Maxwell

Entertainment

Head of Entertainment Justin Gorman, *Commissioning* Tom Beck, Syeda Irtizaali, Madeleine Knight

Factual Entertainment

Head of Factual Entertainment Liam Humphreys, *Commissioning* Rich Evans, Lucy Leveugle, Tina Flintoff (on maternity leave), Ian Dunkley, Tom Beck

Features

Head of Features Gill Wilson, *Commissioning* Alex Menzies, Kate Teckman, Stef Wagstaffe, Lizi Wootton, Helen Cooke

Formats & Music

Head of Formats Dominic Bird, *Commissioning* Jilly Pearce (on maternity leave), Simone Haywood, Danny Carvalho, *Commissioning – Music* Jonny Rothery, *Commissioning – Education* Bec Milligan (on maternity leave), Emily Jones

Nations and Regions

Nations and Regions Manager Ian MacKenzie, *Nations and Regions Executive* Susie Wright, *Disability Executive* Alison Walsh, *Project Lead Paralympics and TV Events* Lara Akeju

News & Current Affairs

Head of News & Current Affairs Dorothy Byrne, *Commissioning* Siobhan Sinnerton, Daniel Pearl, Tom Porter

Online

Head of Online Richard Davidson-Houston, *Commissioning* Jody Smith, Adam Gee, Colin Macdonald, Isaac Densu, James Rutherford

Specialist Factual

Head of Specialist Factual David Glover, *Commissioning* Sara Ramsden, John Hay, Rob Coldstream

4Talent

website http://4talent.channel4.com
Industry Talent Specialist Priscilla Baffour

Through 4Talent, Channel 4 aims to help people wanting to work in the broadcasting industry gain experience, qualifications and career development.

There are a range of options including apprenticeship, graduate and scholarship programmes, work experience, training, events and workshops. For full details see website.

Channel 5

10 Lower Thames Street, London EC3R 6EN
tel 020-8612 7000
website www.channel5.com
Director of Programmes Ben Frow

Brands include Channel 5, 5* and 5USA, and an on-demand service, Demand 5. Channel 5 works with independent production companies to provide its programmes.

Commissioning

Information about commissioning and related processes and guidelines can be found at: http://about.channel5.com/programme-production/commissioning

Factual, News and Current Affairs

Commissioning Emma Westcott, Simon Raikes, Jason Wells

Factual Entertainment, Features and Entertainment

Commissioning Greg Barnett, Chloe Skinner

Acquisitions

Head of Acquisitions Katie Keenan, *Programme Acquisition Executive – Series* Marie-Claire Dunlop, *Programme Acquisition Executive – Film* Sebastian Cardwell

Children's Programming

Head of Children's Jessica Symons, *Children's Programmes Coordinator* Josie Grierson

RTÉ

Donnybrook, Dublin 4, Republic of Ireland
email info@rte.ie
website www.rte.ie
Director General Noel Curran

RTÉ (Raidio Teilifis Éireann) is Ireland's national public service broadcaster. A leader in Irish media, RTÉ provides comprehensive, free-to-air multimedia services.

Commissioning

RTÉ works in partnership with independent producers to create many of Ireland's favourite TV programmes. RTÉ commissions content in the following areas: lifestyle and formats, entertainment, young people, regional, diversity, wildlife and education, factual, drama, sport, religion, comedy, talent development and music. Full details of RTÉ's commissioning guidelines, specifications and submissions can be found at www.rte.ie/commissioning.

S4C

Parc Ty Glas, Llanishen, Cardiff CF14 5DU
tel 0870 600 4141
website www.s4c.co.uk

S4C is the only Welsh language TV channel in the world, broadcasting over 115 hours of programming weekly on sport, drama, music, factual, entertainment and events. See website for full details of commissioning and production guidelines and personnel.

Management team
Ceo Ian Jones
Director of Content and Broadcast Daffydd Rhys
Director of Communications and Information Steve Thomas
Director of Partnerships Catrin Hughes Roberts
Director of Corporate and Commercial Elin Morris

DIGITAL TV PROVIDERS

Sky

Grant Way, Isleworth TW7 5QD
tel 0333 100 0333
website http://corporate.sky.com
Chief Executive Jeremy Darroch

BT

81 Newgate Street, London EC1A 7AJ
Customer postal address BT Correspondence Centre, Providence Row, Durham DH98 1BT
tel 020-7356 5000 (switchboard) or 0800 800 150 (customers)
website http://home.bt.com
Ceo Gavin Patterson

Virgin Media

Media House, Bartley Wood Business Park, Hook, Hants RG27 9UP
website www.virginmedia.com
Ceo Tom Mockridge

Freesat

23–24 Newman Street, London W1T 1PJ
tel 0345 313 0051
website www.freesat.co.uk
Managing Director Emma Scott

YouView

3rd Floor, 10 Lower Thames Street, London EC3R 6YT
email info@youview.com
website www.youview.com
Ceo Richard Halton

Organisations connected to television broadcasting

BARB

20 Orange Street, London WC2H 7EF
tel 020-7024 8100
email enquiries@barb.co.uk
website www.barb.co.uk
Chief Executive Justin Sampson

The Broadcasters Audience Research Board is the official source of viewing figures in the UK.

Public Media Alliance

University of East Anglia, Norwich NR4 7TJ
tel (01603) 592335
email info@publicmediaalliance.org
website www.publicmediaalliance.org
Contact Sally-Ann Wilson

World's largest association of public broadcasters. Previously known as the Commonwealth Broadcasting Association

Ipsos MediaCT

(specialist division of Ipsos MORI)
79–81 Borough Road, London SE1 1FY
tel 020-7347 3000
website www.ipsos-mori.com
Managing Director Ipsos MediaCT Liz Landy, *Ceo Ipsos MORI* Ben Page

Involved in the running of BARB and RAJAR.

RADIO

UK domestic radio services are broadcast across three wavebands: FM, medium wave and long wave. A number of radio stations are broadcast in both analogue and digital and there are growing numbers of stations broadcasting in digital alone. Digital radio (DAB – digital audio broadcasting) is available through digital radio sets, car radios, online, and on games consoles and mobile devices such as smartphones and tablets. Radio provision in the UK comprises of public service radio programming provided by the BBC and programming provided by independent, commercial stations.

BBC Radio

The BBC operates 10 national radio stations offering music and speech programming for the whole of the UK: Radio 1, Radio 1 Xtra, Radio 2, Radio 3, Radio 4, Radio 4 Extra, Radio Five Live, Radio Five Live Sports Extra, Radio 6 Music and Asian Network. In addition, there are over 40 regional/local radio stations.
Director, Radio Helen Boaden
Service controllers
Controller Radio 1/1Xtra Ben Cooper
Controller Radio 2, 6 Music and Asian Network Bob Shennan
Controller Radio 3 & BBC Proms Alan Davey
Controller Radio 4/Radio 4 Extra Gwyneth Williams
Controller Radio 5 Live/Radio 5 Live Sports Extra Jonathan Wall
Controller Radio & Music Multiplatform Mark Friend

Commissioning

For full details of commissioning and delivery guidelines, see www.bbc.co.uk/commissioning/radio/. For details of how to pitch programme ideas to BBC Radio, see www.bbc.co.uk/commissioning/radio/articles/pitching-to-radio.
Radio 1/1Xtra *Controller* Ben Cooper, *Commissioning Editor* Robert Gallacher
Radio 2 *Controller* Bob Shennan, *Commissioning Editor* Robert Gallacher
Radio 3 *Controller* Alan Davey, *Commissioning* David Ireland
Radio 4/4 Extra *Controller* Gwyneth Williams, *Commissioning Editors* Jeremy Howe, Tony Phillips, Mohit Bakaya, Sioned Wiliam
Radio 5 Live/5 Live Sports Extra *Controller* Jonathan Wall, *Commissioning Editor* Richard Maddock
Radio 6 Music *Controller* Bob Shennan, *Commissioning Editor* Robert Gallacher
World Service *Controller (English)* Mary Hockaday, *Commissioning Editors* Steve Titherington (senior), Tony Phillips
Asian Network *Controller* Bob Shennan, *Head of Programmes* Mark Strippel
Radio & Music Multiplatform *Controller* Mark Friend, *Programme Manager* Helen Cox

Commercial radio

There are around 300 commercial radio stations operating in the UK, most of which serve a local or regional area. A small number of commercial radio stations operate nationally, including Classic FM, Absolute Radio, talkSport and LBC. The majority of commercial radio stations are owned by one of three groups:

Global Radio
website www.thisisglobal.com

Bauer Media
website www.bauermedia.co.uk

UTV Media
website www.utvmedia.com

Organisations connected to radio broadcasting

Media UK
website www.mediauk.com

This website provides detailed listings of UK radio stations plus information about TV, newspapers, magazines and media ownership in the UK.

RAJAR
6th Floor, 55 New Oxford Street, London WC1A 1BS
tel 020-7395 0630
website www.rajar.co.uk
Chief Executive Jerry Hill

RAJAR – Radio Joint Audience Research – is the official body in charge of measuring radio audiences in the UK. It is jointly owned by the BBC and the RadioCentre on behalf of the commercial sector.

The Radio Academy
3rd Floor, 55 New Oxford Street, London WC1A 1BS
tel 020-3174 1180
website www.radioacademy.org
Ceo Paul Robinson

The Radio Academy is a registered charity dedicated to the promotion of excellence in UK radio broadcasting and production. For over 30 years the Radio Academy has run the annual Radio Academy Awards, which celebrate content and creativity in the industry.

RadioCentre
6th Floor, 55 New Oxford Street, London WC1A 1BS
tel 020-7010 0600
email info@radiocentre.org
website www.radiocentre.org
Chief Executive Siobhan Kenny

RadioCentre is the voice of UK commercial radio and works with government, policy makers and regulators, and provides a forum for industry-wide debate and discussion.

Theatre

Bringing new life to classic plays

What makes a successful, comfortably off, academic publisher chuck in a safe career and try his hand in the slippery and financially unrewarding world of theatre? Mike Poulton describes how frustration with the style and tone of English productions of classic masterpieces in the past, and persistent neglect of such fine works, drove him to make his successful move into translation and adaptation. He shares his personal golden rules, practical advice and insights.

Becoming an adaptor of classic plays – the motivation

I suppose I became an adaptor of classic plays because, as an avid theatregoer since late childhood, I became increasingly unhappy with what I was seeing and hearing. I had read a lot of Schiller at university and become gripped by it. Why did these powerful epic dramas never, or very rarely, seem to make it into our theatres? Theatre back then was still a going concern, comparatively speaking, and every proud provincial capital supported its producing house. I had also read a lot of Chekhov. On the rare occasions I did see English productions of these Russian masterpieces, they seemed slow, unfunny – sometimes even turgid. Yet in the audiences for them there was an apparent reverence, which seemed unrelated to all the very English over-emoting that was projected woodenly from the acres of silver birch forest on the stage. It was sometimes possible to believe you had wandered out of a *Cherry Orchard* and ended up in *Brief Encounter*. My discontent grew and grew. The material was so much livelier – so much more thrilling in the imagination. I felt cheated. And later, with the arrogance of youth, I deluded myself into a belief that I could do better.

At a rare performance of a Chekhov or an Ibsen play it would seem clear to me that what the actors on the stage were saying, and how they said it, bore very little relationship to how people spoke in *real life* – either now or at the time the plays were written. It was as if the theatre had a style of delivery it reserved unto itself – as did, say, the Church and the BBC. What's more, in a cast of 20 characters, each of them, whatever their status, spoke in the same way. Generals, postmasters and small children all used the same speech patterns and vocabulary – unless they were clowns (who always spoke Mummerset). But for the most part the cast delivered lines with a single voice, and it wasn't difficult to work out that that voice must be the *translator's* voice. I didn't have the same problem with English writers; Shakespeare, though of a different age, seemed real and immediate. It was just that, with the Greeks, the Russians and the European greats performed in translation, there was a middleman, an often dry and academic voice, getting in the way. The immediacy and drive of the original was lost – buried under the literalness of the English text.

An example: in Schiller's great play *Don Carlos* there's a scene where Carlos, the Crown Prince, pleads with his father for a military command and is refused. One very old translation says: 'In this, your refusal, by continually denying my requests you humiliate your son.' Another even older version says: 'Whatever I ask, and I ask for only a very little, is met with your repeated refusals.' It would be difficult for even the most accomplished actor to breathe life into either of those utterances, or even get his tongue round them. So

I went back to the original German. What Schiller makes Carlos say ends in the line: 'Mir alles, alles, alles so verweigern.' This repetition is a gift to an actor when translated as: 'Think how you'll dishonour me, if you refuse me everything – everything – everything! What will the world say of me?' Schiller knew his trade – he knew what an actor needed. The old translations ignored the needs of the actor, and ignored the spirit and passion of the original, in favour of a pedantic slavery to the literal meaning of words. I also began to notice, particularly in performances of Chekhov, that the old translators imposed a tone on their literal translations – refusing to let the characters speak for themselves – and geared their versions towards the tragic, if not the downright dull. I knew, from reading him, that Chekhov had a wonderfully subversive sense of humour. If you watch a Chekhov play in the original with an audience of Russians, they spend half the evening in tears and the other half doubled up with laughter. In English performances that laughter was absent. I realised that the translator was ignoring, once again, the spirit of the original and imposing his or her own opinions and voice on the play. And it was a solemn voice.

But perhaps my strongest motive for wanting to bring great plays to life was a sense of neglect. European theatre eagerly embraces English drama. In any major town in France, Germany or Italy chances are that there will be a Shakespeare and other English (or Irish) work in the theatre programme during the season. (Last year, Montaubon even had posters for *L'eventail de Lady Windermere*.) But in the past it was not a two-way street. English-speaking audiences tended to stick to what they knew. They were not very adventurous. Today though, prompted by some adventurous directors and producing houses, things are improving. There is a vast treasure house of forgotten classics waiting to be brought back to life.

Neglect is still rife. We hardly know how to value our own great works, let alone the masterpieces of the rest of the world. We are unlikely to see a production of *The Great Duke of Florence*, or *The Maid of Honour*, or *The Lie of the Day*, *The World in a Village*, or *Tony Lumpkin in Town*, or even to remember who wrote them. So what chance do Turgenev's *The Old Bachelor*, Goldoni's *The New House*, or Schiller's *Maid of Orleans* stand of a production? Happily, more of a chance today than 20 years ago, but these neglected works still need a producer and a translator to champion them.

Translating classic plays – some practical advice

My rule when starting out was … never accept a commission. I preferred to get a version the way I wanted it and only then to start approaching theatres and artistic directors. I only worked with authors I knew and loved, and had befriended. It's not easy to make a friend of Schiller, say, because he's been dead for such a long time. But I felt I had to get to know him so well I could reach a point where I could confidently answer on his behalf. I did this by reading and re-reading everything he ever wrote. If you want to know how Chekhov thinks, for example, read all his short stories and his letters.

At all costs … avoid living authors. The dead ones are a lot less trouble and won't take 50% of your royalties – should there be any. You must believe in the greatness of your author, otherwise why would championing his or her works be a worthwhile expenditure of your time? And, on the question of time, the rule is to work out how long you think you need and double it. When working at full stretch, Ibsen could write a play in a month. To translate that play can't be done successfully, I believe, in under seven.

Another rule of mine was … never translate and adapt a play with the object of making money. I could never have begun a career as a translator/adaptor had I not previously had a successful career as an academic publisher. If you're passionate about the play you want to put before an audience, then some slight financial reward may follow. On occasion you might find you have a smash hit on your hands – but such occasions are, in financial terms, rare. I honestly don't know how playwrights new to the business support themselves. In my first year – almost 20 years ago – I had two plays at Chichester. One went into the West End and both went to Broadway. But that was only after working more than a year for nothing, endless readings and workshops, and more good luck and support from the Chichester theatre than I had the right to expect.

Starting out

Every new translator needs to start somewhere. My starting point was a play by Turgenev called *Alien Bread*. I read it in a very old and unplayable translation but I had a strong sense that underneath its lines lay a very powerful play – and great roles for two leading actors. With a lot of help from Russian friends I wrote a version of it I called *Fortune's Fool* and it won a lot of prizes on Broadway. It was a lucky break – and we all need lucky breaks.

So the first thing an adaptor has to do is to look for and find an extraordinary play by an extraordinary but neglected author. Ignore the ones that are out there already, Chekhov, Ibsen, Schiller even. There are plenty of other great works mouldering unregarded on dusty shelves. A fundamental Christian belief is in the communion of saints and the company of angels. The souls of the righteous, saints and martyrs exist in heaven, conversing with the various orders of angels, and with all those down here on Earth waiting to be redeemed and marked out for higher things. I like to imagine that similar communion exists among the great writers of the past. They no longer move on earth but their voices remain – waiting to be translated into English.

Collaboration

Surprisingly, it would be a mistake to think that adapting a play is a solitary business. It's not something you ought to try on your own. If, say, you're working on a Russian play, you have to surround yourself with Russians who will explain to you every layer of meaning in every line. If you are not fluent in the language of the original you have to commission a literal translation – an expensive business – but a good translator is invaluable. I tend to go through the literal translation with the translator in great detail, and then go back to the original and read the two versions together line by line. Only when you are confident that you've absorbed every shade of meaning in the original, and understand it in the context of its time, do you begin your own work – which is to translate the 'spirit' of the original play. This process has very little to do with the words or the order in which they're set down on the page.

I work in drafts. When I have the first rough draft in a speakable form I get a group of actors together and hear it read aloud. However much time you spend pacing up and down and reading your own lines, you'll never accomplish much. You have to sit and listen, notebook in hand, to others reading your work. Then you can begin the serious work of adaptation. For the second draft you'll probably need the cooperation of a theatre. You might need between 10 and 20 actors to spend a week trying out your material. Most actors are very willing to help, but they need feeding! Unless you have a large private income, you're going to need a sponsor, or the involvement of a theatre. And you're only going to get that once you're past Draft One. You might then need another 'workshop' or even two more before you feel you have a script you can confidently take into rehearsal.

I recently adapted *Wolf Hall* and *Bring Up The Bodies* from Hilary Mantel's novels. I could not have done this without the commitment and faith of the Royal Shakespeare Company. And this came because I'd previously worked on six other productions there and the new Artistic Director must have thought I was a good risk. The first draft of *Wolf Hall* was about two-thirds longer than the draft we took into rehearsal a year later. But without the input of 20 RSC actors we'd have never have got the project off the ground, into The Swan, into the West End and onto Broadway. Nobody said it would be easy. I certainly couldn't have called on such resources earlier in my career. Patience is everything.

Maintaining the backlist

Once you have a backlist, a great deal of time is spent in maintenance. I would argue that a 'version' – as we call a play translated and adapted from a classical original these days – has a life in the theatre of five or six years at most. William Archer, the first great translator of Ibsen, now seems florid and unspeakable. Some time ago Michael Mayer breathed new life into Ibsen and became the translator everybody turned to. Now others have overtaken him. A new translation, after a year or so, needs fine-tuning, an overhaul, or in some cases a complete rebuild. For example, my version of Ibsen's *Ghosts* has had six productions in the last 15 years, and for each I have given it a major rethink and a substantial rewrite. Language, we know, is fluid but I wonder if we're aware of how rapidly it dates. I look at my published versions of Schiller, Chekhov, Euripides and Ibsen on my shelves and I think of them in a very different way from the originals standing next to them. The originals are like fine wine maturing and improving. My translations – all translations – are like bottles of milk, open, and rapidly going sour.

The audience

Finally, the most important consideration of all in any adaptation or translation is the audience. If you want to produce a really successful adaptation of any play, go obsessively to the theatre for 20 or 30 years and study your audience. (What makes them laugh? What makes them freeze? What bores them? What gets them on the edge of their seats?) After that you're ready to start.

Mike Poulton is a translator and adaptor of classic plays and novels who began writing for the theatre in 1995 after an earlier successful career as an academic publisher. His first two productions, Chekhov's *Uncle Vanya* and Turgenev's *Fortune's Fool,* were staged the following year at the Chichester Festival Theatre and later went to Broadway. His adaptation of Schiller's *Don Carlos* won an Olivier Award in 2005. Other productions have included Euripides' *Ion*, Schiller's *Wallenstein*, Malory's *Morte d'Arthur* and Dickens' *A Tale of Two Cities*. His Olivier-nominated stage adaptations of Hilary Mantel's *Wolf Hall* and *Bring Up the Bodies* played in Stratford, the West End and on Broadway in 2014/15.

See also...

- *Adaptations from books*, page 341
- *Literary translation*, page 302
- *Writing for the theatre*, page 371

Writing for the theatre

From the perspective of a playwright, David Eldridge describes the process of writing a play, its production, through to a run at a theatre.

Writing the play

Ideas for plays can come from anywhere. Political anger, a riff of dialogue, an image, some experience in your life, a newspaper article, a dream or fantasy, or from a particular actor you admire. As Caryl Churchill says, 'What's the difference between an idea for a play [*sic*]? I think the only difference is that you want to make [it] into a play, the point at which [it] become[s] an idea for a play is when you get some sort of technical or physical way of turning it into a play'. Wherever your ideas for plays come from, the key thing is that you are fired up by your idea.

So you have your idea – a biting political satire or a fantastical farce fuelled by a lost dog – and you've decided whether it's going to be a stichomythic two-hander or a surreally big cast piece. It could be that your story will be told in a form with which an audience is familiar and that inspires you – Chekhovian four-act movement or a fragmented narrative inspired by the plays of Martin Crimp. But what next? Some writers are planners by nature and have everything mapped out on A4 or in notebooks, and spend weeks structuring the drama before any physical action or dialogue is written. Stephen Jeffreys and Simon Stephens are good examples of playwrights who work in this way. But for others, like Robert Holman or David Storey, often even thinking of the possible shape of a play is an anathema, and structuring is a block to them. They like to start with an image or a line, or even a blank page, and find out what 'it' is as they go along. I'm somewhere in the middle; I need to do a little bit of planning to get me going and to avoid false starts, but if there's too much plotting in advance it becomes drained of life. It's true, too, that each play I've written has been made in a different way. So it seems there's not only as many ways to write a play as there are playwrights, but each playwright may write differently from one play to the next.

In the absence of a right way to do it, the best thing is just to get on and do your own thing, what feels right for you – anything really, as long as you write. 'Don't get it right, get it written', is how it goes. I always remind myself that I'm under no obligation to show anyone what I've written, so I try not to fear anything. If what I write is rubbish, I can just chuck it away. If what I write is promising but not perfect, I can come back to it later and improve it. The main thing is to write and get to the end. And when you've got to the end, you go back to the beginning again and work on it until you can do no more.

Final draft to producer

When you feel your play is complete and that you've done all you can on it for now, what next? Resist reaching for the stamps or hitting the 'Send' button on your email, and have some time away from it – at least a week or two. Often after the intensive work on a first draft, one comes back to it feeling refreshed both in perspective and in terms of renewed energy. And when you can do no more to improve your script, get one or two (certainly no more than three) people to read it. You need people who will read the script properly and give an honest and generous opinion. They may be a partner, a friend, a colleague or, if you are lucky enough to have such a connection, someone who works in the theatre. Choose your readers carefully because you don't want anyone who will focus solely on criticising your script and consequently demoralise you at this stage, and neither do you want unqualified praise as they think this is what you want to hear.

I tend to send out what is in reality a third draft. I usually do a second draft after leaving it for between two and four weeks and then a third draft, which is provoked a bit by the responses or questions of one or two trusted readers. That's my practice now as an established writer, just as it was when I started writing. Today, almost all my work is commissioned but when I first began writing and would send out a play unsolicited, I had some wise advice from playwright Mark Ravenhill. He said I should concentrate on submitting my play to two or three theatres where I believed the play might be of interest and welcome, and where I would like to work. I still think that's good advice. One must be realistic about how few plays that are sent unsolicited actually attract the attention of producing theatres. And plays that are sent unsolicited to too many theatres can often have a feeling of being dog-eared and rejected by everyone, making it harder for those plays to get on anywhere.

Since the mid-1990s, many theatres have grown substantive play development programmes and it is a normal requirement now for new plays to undergo substantial rewrites with the producer's notes in mind. Readings and workshops often take place to see how the scripts work with actors. There's a wide-ranging philosophical debate within the theatre about how much theatres ought to be actively involved in the rewriting of plays and what good it does. My feeling is that writers ought to take on the ideas of theatre professionals when they are good, to be unafraid of saying when you are unsure, and to say 'no' when you don't like the proposed changes to your script. While a network of collaboration brings a play to life, writers must take responsibility for their authorship. Active collaboration is good; passive concession is bad.

Around this time, it may be appropriate to get an agent. Most theatres will recommend agents and help you meet those who might be sympathetic to your work.

Rehearsals, production and previews

The play is going ahead. Often the first person you hear from is the theatre's director of marketing as they need to prepare the copy and images for your play for the season's brochure and other publicity. In new writing theatres it is normal for most elements of the pre-production and production of a play to involve the writer. This includes input on the choice of director and creative team, casting the actors, progress of the set design, the development of a marketing and sales strategy, press and media interviews, and even invitations to attend fundraising events for the theatre.

But of course the most significant contribution that the writer makes is to the rehearsal process, particularly in the first week of rehearsal. The acting company and creative team are hungry to mine the writer for every scrap of useful information which may help the play's production. The writer is very much at the centre of the process and what he or she says about their play or how it may be acted and staged has great power. I know from experience how invaluable a playwright's contribution can be to the production of his or her play, both from discussion of the text in rehearsals and from informal discussions during tea breaks, at lunch, or in the pub after rehearsals. Generally, most of what a writer says is useful but care needs to be taken not to squeeze the air out of the contributions of others.

Sometimes rewrites in rehearsals can be challenging. Changing the odd word or line isn't often contentious but when whole scenes are being cut or rewritten, the excitement of making the play better on the rehearsal room floor should be approached with caution. Actors tend to think of the script from their character's perspective rather than seeing the writer's whole vision. And, as the point of rehearsal is to practise something until it is right, I'd be wary of actors or directors who want to make changes too quickly.

After the first week or so it is usual and advisable for the writer to not attend rehearsals. The middle part of rehearsals become sticky and the actors may grapple with learning their lines. When the writer makes a return towards the end of rehearsals to see bits of the play worked without scripts or a run through, the writer's fresh perspective is very useful to the director.

As public performances approach, the playwright can make everyone feel good about the work by encouraging the company after rehearsals, buying the first drink in the pub, and making the tea during breaks. However, sometimes the writer has to be brave if things aren't right and late changes need to be made to adjust a performance or the staging, etc.

Some writers don't attend all the previews but I do, as most directors continue working and rehearsing the play right up until opening night. You can learn a huge amount by watching the play with an audience, but I have two points of caution. Firstly, you have to be realistic about what is achievable before the opening night. Secondly, while it is important to learn from audience responses, particularly if the storytelling isn't clear or a joke doesn't work properly, I'd stay away from the discussion forums of theatre websites which are routinely populated by strange people who get off on abusing early performances of plays.

Opening nights are nerve-racking evenings for the writer and seeing the critics and guests forming a crush at the theatre bar can prompt the urge to run away, and for this reason some directors and playwrights don't watch their press night performances. I couldn't be absent as I feel I have to be there for my actors, but it is gruelling and all you can do is will the actors and stage crew on and keep your nerve.

The working writer

Hopefully, the play is a hit and it's a great experience. I tend to see the play once a week because you can learn so much from seeing it again and again and experiencing how it changes and grows over its run.

Often, however successful (or not) a first play is, just the fact that it has been produced will attract the interest of other theatre producers, often radio interviews and sometimes television. If your agent is doing their job, he or she will have brought some of these people to see your play with the hope of opening up future opportunities for you. Offers of commissions for rival theatres, finding yourself pitching radio, television and film ideas, and sometimes being approached to adapt an old play, book or film are all commonplace, particularly if your play is a success.

But the most important thing for the working playwright is to focus on the next play. The longer you leave it after your first play closes the harder it gets to begin something new, and the bigger deal it will seem. So my advice is just to start where you began all those months and years ago and think about something which in some way intrigues you. And off you go.

David Eldridge is the author of *Under the Blue Sky*, *The Knot of the Heart*, *In Basildon* and many other plays and adaptations, such as his new version of *Miss Julie* by August Strindberg, which ran to critical acclaim at the Royal Exchange Theatre in 2012. His new play *Holy Warriors* was premiered at Shakespeare's Globe in 2014 and his screenplay of Hallie Rubenhold's *The Woman in Red* was broadcast on BBC2 in 2015. David teaches Creative Writing at Birkbeck, University of London. You can find him on Twitter @deldridgewriter.

See also...

- *The calling card script for screen, radio and stage*, page 347

Writing about theatre: reviews, interviews and more

Mark Fisher compares popular perceptions of the theatre critic with the realities, and outlines what it takes to succeed in the business.

The critic

In the award-winning movie *Birdman*, Michael Keaton plays Riggan Thomson, a mainstream Hollywood actor trying to earn some late-career credibility. He's banking on people seeing him in a different light if he has a Broadway hit with his adaptation of a Raymond Carver story. As opening night approaches, the stakes are high. He loses his lead actor, his last-minute replacement is an unpredictable maverick and his budget is at breaking point.

As the tensions mount, he comes across Tabitha Dickinson in a bar. Played by Lindsay Duncan, she is the lead theatre critic of the *New York Times* and seems to exist less as a character in her own right than as a projection of his actorly neuroses.

In the short time she is in the film, this is what we learn about her:

(1) She is always alone. We first see her perched at the end of a counter having a drink and writing longhand in a notepad. In the theatre, she sits at the end of a row and leaves before the rest of the audience.

(2) She is prepared to wield the power of the *New York Times* to shut down a show that she hasn't even seen – at least, she says she is. Having decided Thomson is indulging in a vanity project, she regards him as a threat to Broadway's artistic standards. She tells him she will give him a bad review on principle.

(3) She gets it all wrong. When, finally, she does file a rave review, she appears not to have realised that the onstage violence was a genuine suicide attempt.

Watching the movie as a theatre critic, I naturally tried to weigh this portrayal against my own experience. If I were the sensitive type, I'd be worried. This is especially the case because the majority of fictional critics share the same characteristics. In films, novels and television programmes, my profession is dominated by misanthropic loners, arrogant opinion-mongers, writers who love the sound of their own voice and destructive zealots who detest the theatre – unless, of course, they happen to be having an affair with someone on stage. Variations on this theme include Addison DeWitt in *All About Eve*, Sheridan Whiteside in *The Man Who Came to Dinner* and Moon and Birdboot in Tom Stoppard's *The Real Inspector Hound*.

Critical characteristics

For anyone considering a career as a theatre critic, it's reasonable to wonder not so much whether the characteristics described above pertain to you, but whether you're prepared for other people to see you in this light. To the theatre profession, you can seem like the only sober guest at the party, the spoilsport who is all head and no heart, the one who's prepared to break the magic spell that keeps the whole enterprise alive. They may not want to be your friend any more.

In reality, the quality common to nearly all the critics I have known is their love of theatre. The job involves long journeys to out-of-the-way venues, spending evenings at

Theatre

work when you could be with friends and family, and sitting through mediocre shows that were not made for someone like you in the first place. Only someone with blind optimism and a passionate belief in the artform would sign up to such working conditions. I've seen cynical critics write entertainingly, but they invariably burn out in a matter of months. In real life, the negativity of a fictional critic is not sustainable.

There is a kind of truth, though, in the solitariness of *Birdman*'s Tabitha. Theatre criticism suits lone wolves. You may be friendly and sociable in the right circumstances, but when it comes to the job, it's just you, your opinion and a blank computer screen. It's not something you can do collectively. You can't get a friend to help. Everything is down to you. This takes a certain resourcefulness. You need to be self-motivated or, at least, motivated by the pressure of a deadline (and not freaked by it) and happy in your own company. You have to be content to work antisocial hours in sociable circumstances. When those around you are on their feet applauding or wiping the tears from their eyes, you have to be thinking of a catchy first sentence.

Becoming a critic

When I told people I was writing a book called *How to Write About Theatre* (Methuen Drama 2015), some questioned my timing. After all, if you read anything about criticism these days, it tends to be about newspapers cutting back on their arts coverage and laying critics off. Shouldn't I have called it *How Not to Write About Theatre*? Certainly, it seems unlikely that a journalist starting today would have quite the career trajectory I have enjoyed. I was employed in the late 1980s by the *List* magazine, then a fortnightly arts and entertainment guide, and now, since 2015, a predominantly online publication. My first job there was as a production assistant, but with my drama degree and previous interest in writing, it was perhaps inevitable that I would start contributing to the theatre section. Eventually I became the theatre editor and then took up a freelance career in which I founded and edited a quarterly theatre magazine, became theatre critic for the *Herald* in Glasgow and, latterly, Scottish theatre critic for the *Guardian*.

Even if I add that most of the money I have earned has come from feature writing rather than reviewing, there's no question that today's critics have fewer paid opportunities open to them. There are, however, more opportunities than ever for unpaid criticism – and more people than ever writing about theatre. No need for contacts or job interviews, you can just set up a blog right now and start writing. This is having two beneficial effects. One is that a wider range of voices are being heard and the old cultural hegemony – what Nicholas Hytner called the 'dead white men' of the critical establishment – is breaking down. The other is that the idea of what constitutes a 'proper' review is being upturned: the interactive and responsive nature of the internet is well suited to a discursive form of criticism, one that needn't be the final word, just an addition to the debate.

The good news for writers is that it's now possible to make an impression from a standing start. If you have something to say and an arresting way of saying it, you can build up a reputation on the internet without the endorsement of a traditional media publication. The bad news – until somebody comes up with a better idea – is that you're likely to have to treat your writing as a kind of loss leader, an investment in your future career that may (or may not) pay dividends at some later date. The industrious Matt Trueman (http://matttrueman.co.uk) is a case in point. From being a predominantly online critic, he has gone on to pick up paid work from publications including the *Guardian*, the *Stage*, *What's On Stage* and *Variety*.

How typical this route will be in the future remains to be seen, although, as a former editor, I would expect anyone with a serious interest in becoming a professional theatre critic to be doing the job without waiting to be asked. Whether you get published in a student newspaper, a zine, your own website or someone else's, you'll never get a foothold on the critical ladder unless you first do it of your own volition. Without that, you will have no opportunity to develop your writing skills, learn how to translate a live experience into words and extend your knowledge of contemporary theatre. It's also a way to advertise yourself. If you can't show an editor examples of your work, he or she will have nothing to go on and no reason to employ you.

For the first-time critic, the question of authority comes into play. 'Who do you think you are, passing comment on other people's work – what makes you so special?' Your self-confidence is the only adequate answer to this question, especially as there is no expected qualification for the job. Yes, you can study drama, yes, you can take a course in journalism – and there's a strong case to say you should – but nobody will ask to see your certificates. Criticism is a practical occupation and the evidence of whether you can do it or not is in your writing. Taking a course will widen your knowledge, develop your skills and give you confidence, but it will be your passion for communication and passion for theatre, as well as an insatiable desire to get better at both, that will make you a good critic.

Features, interviews and other writing

If you have such a passion, there's no reason you should confine your writing to criticism. On the contrary, there are many more opportunities for writing about theatre – and at greater length – than in reviewing it. For the keen-eyed journalist, the theatre is a rich source of material. The people who work in it, the relationship it has with the wider community, the ideas it deals with and the pragmatics of putting it on all offer potential stories.

Feature writing can range from interviews with the theatremakers to research-based pieces inspired by the themes of a production. If one of the creative team has a fascinating story to tell, you may be able to write a human-interest piece that is only tangentially connected to the show. You may find outlets for think-pieces and blogs about theatrical issues or news stories about artistic fall-outs and funding problems. Think too about publications aimed at special-interest groups such as lighting designers, educationalists and marketing managers. You may also find other ways to exploit your specialist knowledge – I have given seminars to theatre students and led cultural tours for foreign visitors, for example.

Staff or freelance?

My assumption underlying all this is that you will be working freelance. That's not entirely fair because, of course, there are many full-time staff with some responsibility for theatre, whether it be a BBC arts reporter, a theatre editor on a national newspaper or an in-house critic. I worked as an editor back at the *List* magazine from 2000 to 2003, but have been freelance for the majority of my career. Staff jobs have the advantage of relative security, a team of colleagues, pension schemes, wage rises and some kind of career structure. Unsurprisingly, there is tough competition to get one.

It takes a particular temperament to cope with the freelance life. You have to be resilient, thick-skinned and comfortable with unpredictability. If you can't stomach the thought of not knowing where next week's money is going to come from, it probably isn't for you. But in uncertain economic times, when increasing numbers are shifting into portfolio careers, your adaptability can be an asset. It's also a little more likely that you'll be able to spread your knowledge of theatre around a number of publications than to find one publication that can sustain a single theatre-related job.

If that's a life you're happy to lead, then be prepared for a few knocks, keep on generating the ideas and say yes to anything that comes your way (worry about practicalities later). As with any journalistic writing, you need to be accurate, reliable and punctual. If you have a dazzling turn of phrase, your editors will like you even more, but most important is being easy to work with. And as far as the theatre community is concerned, the more you can let your passion and erudition show through, the better they will appreciate you and the more you will enjoy yourself.

Mark Fisher is one of Scotland's foremost commentators on the arts. With over 25 years' experience, he is the Scottish theatre critic for the *Guardian*, a former editor of the *List* and a freelance contributor to *Variety*, the *Scotsman* and *Scotland on Sunday*. He is the author of *The Edinburgh Fringe Survival Guide* (Methuen Drama 2012) and *How to Write About Theatre* (Methuen Drama 2015).

See also...

- *FAQs for writers*, page 707
- *Income tax*, page 709
- *National Insurance contributions and social security benefits*, page 719
- *The writer's ultimate workspace*, page 621

Theatre producers

This list is divided into metropolitan theatres (below), regional theatres (page 381) and touring companies (page 386). See also the articles in this section, which start on page 371 and *Literary agents for television, film, radio and theatre* on page 761.

There are various types of theatre companies and it is helpful to know what they include. Metropolitan new writing theatre companies which specialise in new writing; these are largely London-based theatres (Hampstead Theatre, Royal Court, Bush Theatre, Soho Theatre) but also include Royal Exchange Manchester, Everyman Theatre Liverpool, West Yorkshire Playhouse etc. Regional repertory theatre companies are theatres based in towns and cities across the country which may produce new plays as part of their repertoire. Commercial producing managements are unsubsidised profit-making theatre producers who may occasionally be interested in new plays to take on tour or to present in the West End. Small and/or middle-scale touring companies are companies (mostly touring) which may exist to explore or promote specific themes or are geared towards specific kinds of audiences.

Individuals also have a role. Independent theatre practitioners include, for example, actors who may be looking for interesting plays in which to appear, and independent theatre producers such as young directors or producers who are looking for plays to produce at the onset of their career. There are also drama schools and amateur dramatics companies. See the *Actors and Performers Yearbook 2016* (Bloomsbury Methuen Drama 2015) for further information.

Theatre

LONDON

Bush Theatre

7 Uxbridge Road, London W12 8LJ
tel (admin) 020-8743 3584
email info@bushtheatre.co.uk
website www.bushtheatre.co.uk
Artistic Director Madani Younis

The Bush has produced hundreds of groundbreaking premieres since its inception in 1972 – many of them Bush commissions – and hosted guest productions by leading companies and artists from around the world. Check the website for the unsolicited commissions policy and guidelines on when and how to submit.

Michael Codron Plays Ltd

Aldwych Theatre Offices, Aldwych, London WC2B 4DF
tel 020-7240 8291

Finborough Theatre

118 Finborough Road, London SW10 9ED
tel 020-7244 7439
email admin@finboroughtheatre.co.uk
website www.finboroughtheatre.co.uk
Artistic Director Neil McPherson

Presents new writing, revivals of neglected plays from 1800 onwards, music theatre and UK premieres of foreign work, particularly from Ireland, Scotland, the USA and Canada. Unsolicited scripts are accepted, but see literary policy on website before sending. Founded 1980.

Robert Fox Ltd

6 Beauchamp Place, London SW3 1NG
tel 020-7584 6855
email info@robertfoxltd.com
website www.robertfoxlimited.com

Independent theatre and film production company. Stages productions mainly in the West End and on Broadway. Not currently accepting submissions. Founded 1980.

Hampstead Theatre

Eton Avenue, London NW3 3EU
tel 020-7449 4200
email literary@hampsteadtheatre.com
website www.hampsteadtheatre.com
Literary Manager Will Mortimer

The company's theatre, built in 2003, was designed with writers in mind, allowing for flexible staging within an intimate main house auditorium and a second studio space. The theatre accepts unsolicited plays from UK-based writers only. All plays are read but feedback is given only on plays that the theatre is interested in pursuing; responses are usually given within four months. Plays can be accepted only by email (scripts@hampsteadtheatre.com) during the submission window (1 July to 31 December). See website for full details of the submission process and new writing initiatives.

Bill Kenwright Ltd

BKL House, 1 Venice Walk, London W2 1RR
tel 020-7446 6200
email info@kenwright.com
website www.kenwright.com
Managing Director Bill Kenwright

Commercial producing management presenting revivals and new works for the West End and for touring theatres. Recent productions include: *Blood Brothers, Dreamboats and Miniskirts, Joseph and the Amazing Technicolor Dreamcoat* and *The Sound of Music.* Currently not receiving or responding to unsolicited scripts.

King's Head Theatre

115 Upper Street, London N1 1QN
tel 020-7226 8561
website www.kingsheadtheatre.com
Contact Adam Spreadbury-Maher, Artistic Director

Off-West End theatre producing premieres of plays and musicals.

Lyric Hammersmith

Lyric Square, King Street, London W6 0QL
tel 020-8741 6850
email enquiries@lyric.co.uk
website www.lyric.co.uk
Artistic Director Sean Holmes, *Executive Director* Jessica Hepburn

West London's largest producing and receiving theatre. Unsolicited scripts for in-house productions not accepted.

Neal Street Productions Ltd

1st Floor, 26–28 Neal Street, London WC2H 9QQ
tel 020-7240 8890
email post@nealstreetproductions.com
website www.nealstreetproductions.com
Founders Sam Mendes, Pippa Harris, Carol Newling

Independent theatre and film producer of new work and revivals. No unsolicited scripts. Founded 2003.

The Old Red Lion Theatre

418 St John Street, London EC1V 4NJ
tel 020-7837 7816
email info@oldredliontheatre.co.uk
website www.oldredliontheatre.co.uk
Artistic Director Stewart Pringle

Interested in contemporary pieces, especially from unproduced writers. No funding: incoming production company pays to rent the theatre. All submissions via email. Founded 1977.

Orange Tree Theatre

1 Clarence Street, Richmond, Surrey TW9 2SA
tel 020-8940 0141
website www.orangetreetheatre.co.uk
Artistic Director Paul Miller

Producing venue. New works presented generally come from agents or through writers' groups. The theatre asks that writers contact the theatre first by email (literary@orangetreetheatre.co.uk) with a synopsis of their proposed project rather than send unsolicited scripts.

Polka Theatre

240 The Broadway, London SW19 1SB
tel 020-8543 8320
email stephen@polkatheatre.com
website www.polkatheatre.com
Artistic Director Peter Glanville

Theatre of new work, with targeted commissions. Exclusively for children aged 0–14, the Main Theatre seats 300 and the Adventure Theatre seats 70. It is programmed 18 months–2 years in advance. Founded 1967.

The Questors Theatre

12 Mattock Lane, London W5 5BQ
tel 020-8567 0011
email enquiries@questors.org.uk
website www.questors.org
Executive Director Andrea Bath

Largest independent community theatre in Europe. Produces around 20 shows a year, specialising in modern and classical world drama. No unsolicited scripts.

Royal Court Theatre

(English Stage Company Ltd)
Sloane Square, London SW1W 8AS
tel 020-7565 5050
email info@royalcourttheatre.com
website www.royalcourttheatre.com
Literary Manager Chris Campbell

Programmes original plays that investigate the problems and possibilities of our time. Looks for outstanding plays which are formally or thematically original and are unlikely to be produced elsewhere.

Royal National Theatre

South Bank, London SE1 9PX
tel 020-7452 3333
website www.nationaltheatre.org.uk
Literary Administrator Sarah Clarke

Limited opportunity for the production of unsolicited material, but submissions considered from the UK and Ireland. No synopses, treatments or email submissions. Send to Literary Department, together with an sae for return of the script if required.

Soho Theatre

21 Dean Street, London W1D 3NE
tel 020-7478 0117

email judiellard@sohotheatre.com
website www.sohotheatre.com
Artistic Director Steve Marmion

Aims to discover and develop new playwrights, produce a year-round programme of new plays and attract new audiences. Producing venue of new plays, cabaret and comedy. The Writers' Centre offers an extensive unsolicited script-reading service and provides a range of development schemes such as writers' attachment programmes, commissions, seed bursaries and more. Three venues: the main Soho Theatre has 150 seats; Soho Upstairs is self-contained and seats 90; and Soho Downstairs is a 150-seat capacity cabaret space. Also theatre bar, restaurant, offices, rehearsal, writing and meeting rooms. Founded 1972.

Tabard Theatre

2 Bath Road, London W4 1LW
tel 020-8995 6035
email info@tabardtheatre.co.uk
website www.tabardtheatre.co.uk

Hosts a variety of live entertainment, from classical adaptations to revivals and new musical works. Also produces in-house shows.

Theatre Royal, Stratford East

Gerry Raffles Square, London E15 1BN
tel 020-8534 7374
website www.stratfordeast.com
Artistic Director Kerry Michael, *Executive Director* Mary Caws

Middle-scale producing theatre. Specialises in new writing, including developing contemporary British musicals. Welcomes new plays that are unproduced, full in length, and which relate to its diverse multicultural, Black and Asian audience.

The Tricycle Theatre Company

Tricycle Theatre, 269 Kilburn High Road, London NW6 7JR
tel 020-7372 6611
email info@tricycle.co.uk
website www.tricycle.co.uk
Artistic Director Indhu Rubasingham

Presents at least six productions per year, aiming to provoke debate and engage. Many of these are commissioned and written specifically for the theatre, or are programmed in collaboration with national or international companies. Unable to accept unsolicited submissions.

Unicorn Theatre

147 Tooley Street, London SE1 2HZ
tel 020-7645 0560
email hello@unicorntheatre.com
website www.unicorntheatre.com
Artistic Director Purni Morell, *Executive Director* Anneliese Davidsen

Produces a year-round programme of theatre for children and young people under 21. In-house productions of full-length plays with professional casts are staged across two auditoria, alongside visiting companies and education work. Unicorn rarely commissions plays from writers who are new to it, but it is keen to hear from writers who are interested in working with the theatre in the future. Do not send unsolicited MSS, but rather a short statement describing why you would like to write for the Unicorn and a CV or a summary of your relevant experience.

White Bear Theatre Club

138 Kennington Park Road, London SE11 4DJ
tel 020-7793 9193
email info@whitebeartheatre.co.uk
website www.whitebeartheatre.co.uk
Artistic Director Michael Kingsbury

Metropolitan new writing theatre company. Welcomes scripts from new writers. Founded 1988.

Young Vic Theatre Company

66 The Cut, London SE1 8LZ
tel 020-7922 2922
email info@youngvic.org
website www.youngvic.org
Artistic Director David Lan

Leading London producing theatre. Founded 1969.

REGIONAL

Abbey Theatre Amharclann na Mainistreach

26 Lower Abbey Street, Dublin 1, Republic of Ireland
tel +353 (0)1 8872200
email info@abbeytheatre.ie
website www.abbeytheatre.ie
Director Fiach Mac Conghail

Ireland's national theatre. Produces new Irish writing and contemporary productions of classic plays.

Yvonne Arnaud Theatre Management Ltd

Millbrook, Guildford, Surrey GU1 3UX
tel (01483) 440077
email yat@yvonne-arnaud.co.uk
website www.yvonne-arnaud.co.uk
Contact James Barber

Producing theatre which also receives productions.

The Belgrade Theatre

Belgrade Square, Coventry CV1 1GS
tel 024-7625 6431
email admin@belgrade.co.uk
website www.belgrade.co.uk
Artistic Director Hamish Glen

Repertory theatre producing drama, comedy and musicals. Does not accept unsolicited scripts; email short synopses first to admin@belgrade.co.uk.

Birmingham Repertory Theatre Ltd

Broad Street, Birmingham B1 2EP
tel 0121 245 2000
email stage.door@birmingham-rep.co.uk
website www.birmingham-rep.co.uk
Artistic Director Roxana Silbert

Producing theatre company and pioneer of new plays whose programme includes new versions of the classics as well as contemporary writing. Recently refurbished alongside the Library of Birmingham, the theatre now includes a new 300-seat studio theatre. Founded 1913.

The Bootleg Theatre Company

23 Burgess Green, Bishopdown, Salisbury, Wilts. SP1 3EL
tel (01722) 421476
website www.bootlegtheatre.co.uk
Contact Colin Burden

New writing theatre company whose recent productions include *Girls Allowed* by Trevor Suthers and *The Squeaky Clean* by Roger Goldsmith. Also produces compilation productions of monologues/duologues: these have included *People Skills* and *Tales from the Street* with contributions from Alison Clink, Rosie Finnegan, Gwynne Power, Karen Bartholomew and Annie L Cooper. Forthcoming productions include *Deal With It* as well as further compilations of new work. Founded 1985.

Bristol Old Vic

King Street, Bristol BS1 4ED
tel 0117 949 3993
email admin@bristololdvic.org.uk
website www.bristololdvic.org.uk

Oldest theatre auditorium in UK (opened in 1766). See website for more details. Founded 1946.

Chichester Festival Theatre

Oaklands Park, Chichester, West Sussex PO19 6AP
tel (01243) 784437
website www.cft.org.uk
Artistic Director Jonathan Church

Stages annual Summer Festival Season April–Oct in Festival and Minerva Theatres together with a year-round education programme, autumn touring programme and youth theatre Christmas show. Unsolicited scripts are not accepted.

Clwyd Theatr Cymru

Mold, Flintshire CH7 1YA
tel (01352) 756331
email william.james@clwyd-theatr-cymru.co.uk
website www.clwyd-theatr-cymru.co.uk
Literary Manager William James

Produces a season of plays each year performed by a core ensemble, along with tours throughout Wales (in English and Welsh). Plays are a mix of classics, revivals, contemporary drama and new writing. Considers plays by Welsh writers or with Welsh themes. Also the home of Clwyd Theatr Cymru Theatre for Young People (www.clwyd-theatr-cymru.co.uk/en/young_clwyd).

Colchester Mercury Theatre Ltd

Balkerne Gate, Colchester, Essex CO1 1PT
tel (01206) 577006
email info@mercurytheatre.co.uk
website www.mercurytheatre.co.uk
Artistic Director Daniel Buckroyd

Regional repertory theatre presenting works to a wide audience. Produces some new work, mainly commissioned. Runs local Playwrights' Group for adults with a serious commitment to writing plays.

Contact Theatre Company

Oxford Road, Manchester M15 6JA
tel 0161 274 0600
website www.contactmcr.com
Artistic Director Matt Fenton, *Head of Creative Development* Suzie Henderson

Multidisciplinary arts organisation focused on working with and for young people aged 13–35.

Curve

Rutland Street, Leicester LE1 1SB
tel 0116 242 3560
email contactus@curvetheatre.co.uk
website www.curveonline.co.uk
Chief Executive Fiona Allan, *Artistic Director* Nicolai Foster

Regional producing theatre company.

Derby Theatre

Theatre Walk, Westfield, St Peter's Quarter, Derby DE1 2NF
tel (01332) 255800
email tickets@derbyplayhouse.co.uk
website www.derbytheatre.co.uk
General Manager Gary Johnson, *Artistic Director* Sarah Brigham

Regional producing and receiving theatre.

Druid Theatre Company

Druid Theatre, Flood Street, Galway, Republic of Ireland
tel +353 (0)91 568660
email info@druid.ie
website www.druid.ie
Artistic Director Garry Hynes

Producing company presenting a wide range of national and international plays. Emphasis on new Irish writing.

The Dukes

Moor Lane, Lancaster LA1 1QE
tel (01524) 598505

email info@dukes-lancaster.org
website www.dukes-lancaster.org
Artistic Director Joe Sumsion

See website (given above) for information about the theatre's productions and programming approach.

Dundee Repertory Theatre

Tay Square, Dundee DD1 1PB
tel (01382) 227684
email info@dundeereptheatre.co.uk
website www.dundeereptheatre.co.uk
Artistic Directors Philip Howard, Jemima Levick

Regional repertory theatre company with resident ensemble. Mix of classics, musicals and new commissions.

Everyman Theatre

7 Regent Street, Cheltenham, Glos. GL50 1HQ
tel (01242) 512515
email admin@everymantheatre.org.uk
website www.everymantheatre.org.uk
Creative Director Paul Milton

Regional presenting and producing theatre promoting a wide range of plays. Small-scale experimental, youth and educational work encouraged in The Studio Theatre. Contact the Creative Director before submitting material.

Exeter Northcott Theatre

Stocker Road, Exeter, Devon EX4 4QB
tel (01392) 223999
email info@exeternorthcott.co.uk
website www.exeternorthcott.co.uk
Artistic and Executive Director Paul Jepson, *Associate Director (ENGAGE)* Polly Agg-Manning

460-seat venue offering a varied programme of shows and touring productions.

The 42nd Theatre Company

17c Durham Avenue, Bromley, Kent BR2 0QE
tel 020-3525 0591
email literary@the42ndtheatrecompany.com
website www.the42ndtheatrecompany.com
Artistic Director Adam Bambrough, *Head of Literary Development* Sophia Danes-Gharboui

Small theatre company specialising in new writing. Submissions welcome: see website for guidelines. All work commissioned will be compensated. Founded 2013.

Harrogate Theatre

Oxford Street, Harrogate, North Yorkshire HG1 1QF
tel (01423) 502710
email info@harrogatetheatre.co.uk
website www.harrogatetheatre.co.uk
Artistic Director Phil Lowe

Predominately a receiving house, Harrogate Theatre rarely produces productions in-house. Unsolicited scripts not accepted.

HOME: Theatre

2 Tony Wilson Place, First Street, Manchester M15 4FN
tel 0161 228 7621
email info@homemcr.org
website www.homemcr.org
Artistic Director Walter Meierjohann

World classic drama, international and new writing, adaptations and cross-art projects. Produces one family show a year. Formed following the merger of Cornerhouse and Library Theatre Company. HOME's brand-new purpose-built centre for international contemporary art, theatre and film is due to open during 2015.

Live Theatre

Broad Chare, Quayside, Newcastle upon Tyne NE1 3DQ
tel 0191 232 1232
email info@live.org.uk
website www.live.org.uk
Enquiries Wendy Barnfather, *Script Submissions* Degna Stone

New writing theatre company and venue. Stages three to four productions per year of new writing, comedy, musical comedy, etc.

Liverpool Everyman and Playhouse

Liverpool and Merseyside Theatres Trust Ltd, 5–11 Hope Street, Liverpool, L1 9BH
tel 0151 708 3700
email info@everymanplayhouse.com
website www.everymanplayhouse.com
Executive Director Deborah Aydon, *Artistic Director* Gemma Bodinetz, *Literary Associate* Lindsay Rodden, *Literary Assistant* Hayley Greggs

Produces and presents theatre.

The New Theatre: Dublin

The New Theatre, Temple Bar, 43 East Essex Street, Dublin 2, Republic of Ireland
tel +353 (0)1 6703361
email info@thenewtheatre.com
website www.thenewtheatre.com
Artistic Director Anthony Fox

Innovative theatre producing plays by classic as well as Irish writers whose work deals with issues pertaining to contemporary Irish society. Welcomes scripts from new writers. Seats 66 people. Founded 1997.

New Vic Theatre

Etruria Road, Newcastle under Lyme ST5 0JG
tel (01782) 717954
email admin@newvictheatre.org.uk
website www.newvictheatre.org.uk
Artistic Director Theresa Heskins, *Executive Director* Fiona Wallace

Europe's first purpose-built theatre-in-the-round, presenting classics, musical theatre, contemporary plays and new plays.

The New Wolsey Theatre

Civic Drive, Ipswich, Suffolk IP1 2AS
tel (01473) 295900
website www.wolseytheatre.co.uk
Chief Executive Sarah Holmes, *Artistic Director* Peter Rowe

Mix of producing and presenting in main house and studio. Hosts annual Pulse Fringe Festival. Founded 2000.

Northern Stage (Theatrical Productions) Ltd

Barras Bridge, Newcastle upon Tyne NE1 7RH
tel 0191 242 7210
email info@northernstage.co.uk
website www.northernstage.co.uk
Executive Director Susan Coffer

The largest producing theatre company in the north east of England. Presents local, national and international theatre across three stages and runs an extensive participation programme.

Nottingham Playhouse

Nottingham Playhouse Trust Ltd, Wellington Circus, Nottingham NG1 5AF
tel 0115 947 4361
website www.nottinghamplayhouse.co.uk
Artistic Director Giles Croft

Works closely with communities of Nottingham and Nottinghamshire. Takes six months to read unsolicited MSS.

Nuffield Theatre

University Road, Southampton SO17 1TR
tel 023-8031 5500
email info@nuffieldtheatre.co.uk
website www.nuffieldtheatre.co.uk

Repertory theatre producing straight plays and occasional musicals, on a range of scales. A mix of re-imagined classics and new plays.

Octagon Theatre

Howell Croft South, Bolton BL1 1SB
tel (01204) 529407
email info@octagonbolton.co.uk
website www.octagonbolton.co.uk
Chief Executive Roddy Gauld, *Artistic Director* Elizabeth Newman

Fully flexible professional theatre. Year-round programme of own productions and visiting companies. Capacity: 320–90 depending on configuration. Also houses Bill Naughton Studio Theatre for outreach, children's theatre, new work and emerging artists. Capacity: 100.

The Oldham Coliseum Theatre

Fairbottom Street, Oldham OL1 3SW
tel 0161 624 1731
email mail@coliseum.org.uk
website www.coliseum.org.uk
Chief Executive and Artistic Director Kevin Shaw

Interested in new work, particularly plays set in the North. Its annual First Break writing festival aims to showcase the best in new writing and emerging talent. The theatre's learning and engagement department runs a variety of outreach programmes and courses for young people, adults and schools.

Perth Theatre

185 High Street, Perth PH1 5UW
tel (01738) 472700
email info@horsecross.co.uk
website www.horsecross.co.uk
Associate Director (Theatre) Kenny Miller

Combination of three- and four-weekly repertoire of plays and musicals, incoming tours, one-night variety events and studio productions.

Queen's Theatre, Hornchurch

(Havering Theatre Trust Ltd)
Billet Lane, Hornchurch, Essex RM11 1QT
tel (01708) 462362
email info@queens-theatre.co.uk
website www.queens-theatre.co.uk
Chair, Havering Theatre Trust Dennis Roycroft

500-seat producing theatre serving outer East London with a permanent company of actors/musicians presenting eight main house and two TIE productions each year. Unsolicited scripts may be returned unread. Also offers writers' groups at various levels.

Royal Exchange Theatre Company Ltd

St Ann's Square, Manchester M2 7DH
tel 0161 833 9333
email suzanne.bell@royalexchange.co.uk
website www.royalexchange.co.uk
Executive Director Fiona Gasper, *Literary Associate* Suzanne Bell

Varied programme of major classics, new plays, musicals, contemporary British and European drama. Focus on new writing, writer development, creative collaborations and community participation.

Royal Lyceum Theatre Company

Royal Lyceum Theatre, 30b Grindlay Street, Edinburgh EH3 9AX
tel 0131 248 4800
email info@lyceum.org.uk
website www.lyceum.org.uk
Artistic Director Mark Thomson

Edinburgh's busiest repertory company, producing a diverse year-round programme of classic, contemporary and new drama. Interested in work of Scottish writers.

Royal Shakespeare Company

The Royal Shakespeare Theatre, Waterside, Stratford-upon-Avon, Warks. CV37 6BB

tel (01789) 296655
email literary@rsc.org.uk
website www.rsc.org.uk
Artistic Director Gregory Doran, *Deputy Artistic Director* Erica Whyman, *Literary Manager* Pippa Hill

Based in Stratford-upon-Avon, the Company produces a core repertoire of Shakespeare alongside modern classics, new plays and the work of Shakespeare's contemporaries. The Company commissions new plays, new translations and new adaptations that illuminate the themes and concerns of Shakespeare and his contemporaries for a modern audience. The Literary department does not accept unsolicited work but rather seeks out writers it wishes to work with or commission, and monitors the work of emerging writers in production in the UK and internationally. Writers are welcome to invite the Literary department to readings, showcases or productions by emailing the address above. The RSC intends to re-open its studio theatre, The Other Place, in 2016 with a programme of cutting-edge new work.

Salisbury Playhouse

Malthouse Lane, Salisbury, Wilts. SP2 7RA
tel (01722) 320117; box office (01722) 320333
email info@salisburyplayhouse.com
website www.salisburyplayhouse.com
Artistic Director Gareth Machin, *Executive Director* Sebastian Warrack

Regional producing and presenting theatre with a broad programme of classical and contemporary plays in two auditoria. Does not accept unsolicited scripts. The Playhouse is committed to a programme of original drama with a particular focus on South West writers. Please check website for current information on script submission.

Stephen Joseph Theatre

Stephen Joseph Theatre, Westborough, Scarborough, North Yorkshire YO11 1JW
tel (01723) 370540
email enquiries@sjt.uk.com
website www.sjt.uk.com
Artistic Director Chris Monks

Regional repertory theatre company presenting approx. eight productions a year, many of which are premieres. Contact Henry Bell, Associate Director for script submissions. Visit website for further details. Enclose a sae with all submissions. Send treatments rather than MSS in first instance.

Sheffield Theatres

(Crucible, Crucible Studio & Lyceum)
55 Norfolk Street, Sheffield S1 1DA
tel 0114 249 5999
website www.sheffieldtheatres.co.uk
Chief Executive Dan Bates, *Artistic Director* Daniel Evans

Large-scale producing house with distinctive thrust stage; studio; Victorian proscenium arch theatre used mainly for touring productions.

Sherman Cymru

Senghennydd Road, Cardiff CF24 4YE
tel 029-2064 6900
email margaret.jones@shermancymru.co.uk
website www.shermancymru.co.uk
Artistic Director Rachel O'Riordan, *Executive Director* Margaret Jones

Produces new work and revivals when possible/appropriate. Seeks to stage high-quality and innovative drama and dance with a local, national or international perspective. Develops writers by Welsh and Welsh-based writers, both in English and Welsh, and dance, with a local, national and international perspective. Supports writers through a writer in residence and in association with other Wales-based writers' initiatives/groups. Participatory work with youth theatres (age 5 to 25), community engagement, and mentorship of new artists. Currently unable to read and respond to unsolicited scripts. Founded 2007.

Show of Strength Theatre Company Ltd

74 Chessel Street, Bedminster, Bristol BS3 3DN
tel 0117 902 0235
email info@showofstrength.org.uk
website www.showofstrength.org.uk
Creative Producer Sheila Hannon

Small-scale company committed to producing new and unperformed work. Founded 1986.

Swansea Grand Theatre

Singleton Street, Swansea SA1 3QJ
tel (01792) 475715
email gerald.morris@swansea.gov.uk
website www.swanseagrand.co.uk
Strategic Finance Operations Manager Gerald Morris, *Programme, Marketing and Development Manager* Paul Hopkins, *Marketing Manager* Helen Dalling

Regional receiving theatre.

Theatre Royal & Drum Theatre Plymouth

Royal Parade, Plymouth PL1 2TR
tel (01752) 668282
website www.theatreroyal.com
Artistic Director Simon Stokes

Stages small, middle and large-scale drama and music theatre. Commissions and produces new plays in the award-winning Drum Theatre. The theatre no longer accepts unsolicited playscripts but will consider plays that come through known channels – theatre practitioners, regional and national scriptwriters groups, and agents. Predominantly a receiving house, the Theatre Royal produces some shows (especially musicals) which transfer to the West End.

Theatre Royal, Bath

Sawclose, Bath BA1 1ET
tel (01225) 448815
website www.theatreroyal.org.uk
Director Danny Moar

One of the oldest theatres in Britain. Comprising three auditoria – the Main House, the Ustinov Theatre and the Egg theatre for children and young people – the Theatre Royal offers a varied programme of entertainment all year round.

Theatre Royal Windsor

32 Thames Street, Windsor, Berks. SL4 1PS
tel (01753) 863444
email info@theatreroyalwindsor.co.uk
website www.theatreroyalwindsor.co.uk
Executive Producer Bill Kenwright

Regional producing theatre presenting a wide range of productions, from classics to new plays.

Traverse Theatre

10 Cambridge Street, Edinburgh EH1 2ED
tel 0131 228 3223
website www.traverse.co.uk
Artistic Director Orla O'Loughlin

Produces and presents new theatre work from Scotland and internationally. Scripts submissions are accepted at certain points throughout the year; please see the website for submission guidelines and further information.

Watford Palace Theatre

20 Clarendon Road, Watford, Herts. WD17 1JZ
tel (01923) 235455
website www.watfordpalacetheatre.co.uk
Contact Artistic Director, Brigid Larmour

Regional theatre. Produces and co-produces seasonally, both classic and contemporary drama and new writing. Accepts unsolicited scripts from writers in Hertfordshire.

The West Yorkshire Playhouse

Playhouse Square, Quarry Hill, Leeds LS2 7UP
tel 0113 213 7800
website www.wyp.org.uk
Artistic Director James Brining

Twin auditoria complex; community theatre. Has a policy of encouraging new writing from Yorkshire and Humberside region. Send script with a sae for its return to the Associate Director (Literary).

York Citizens' Theatre Trust Ltd

Theatre Royal, St Leonard's Place, York YO1 7HD
tel (01904) 658162
website www.yorktheatreroyal.co.uk
Chief Executive Liz Wilson, *Artistic Director* Damian Cruden

Repertory productions, tours.

TOURING COMPANIES

Actors Touring Company

ICA, 12 Carlton Terrace, London SW1Y 5AH
tel 020-7930 6014
email atc@atctheatre.com
website www.atctheatre.com
Artistic Director Ramin Gray

Small to medium-scale company producing international new writing.

Eastern Angles

Sir John Mills Theatre, Gatacre Road, Ipswich IP1 2LQ
tel (01473) 218202
email admin@easternangles.co.uk
website www.easternangles.co.uk
Contact Ivan Cutting

Touring company producing new work with a regional theme. Stages three to four productions per year. Welcomes scripts from new writers in the East of England region. Founded 1982.

Graeae Theatre Company

Bradbury Studios,
138 Kingsland Road London E2 8DY
tel 020-7613 6900
email info@graeae.org
website www.graeae.org
Artistic Director Jenny Sealey MBE, *Operations Director* Kevin Walsh, *Finance Director* Charles Mills, *Access and Production Co-ordinator* Helen Jackson-Lyall

Small to mid-scale touring company. Welcomes scripts from disabled writers. Founded 1980.

Headlong Theatre

17 Risborough Street, London SE1 0HG
tel 020-7620 4440
email info@headlongtheatre.co.uk
website http://headlong.co.uk
Artistic Director Jeremy Herrin

A mid/large-scale touring company presenting three–four productions per year: revivals and adaptations of established masterpieces, modern classics and new work.

The Hiss & Boo Company Ltd

1 Nyes Hill, Wineham Lane, Bolney, West Sussex RH17 5SD
tel (01444) 881707
email email@hissboo.co.uk
website www.hissboo.co.uk
Managing Director Ian Liston

Little scope for new plays, but will consider comedy thrillers/chillers and plays/musicals for children. Produces pantomimes. No unsolicited scripts – email first. Plays/synopses will be returned only if accompanied by a sae.

Hull Truck Theatre Co. Ltd

50 Ferensway, Hull HU2 8LB
tel (01482) 224800
email admin@hulltruck.co.uk
website www.hulltruck.co.uk
Artistic Director Mark Babych

Producing and receiving theatre with a national reputation for new writing. Premieres of new plays, including own commissions, have included works by John Godber, Alan Plater, Richard Bean, Amanda Whittington, Nick Lane and David Windass; new commissions include Tom Wells and Morgan Sproxton.

The London Bubble

(Bubble Theatre Company)
5 Elephant Lane, London SE16 4JD
tel 020-7237 4434
email admin@londonbubble.org.uk
website www.londonbubble.org.uk
Creative Director Jonathan Petherbridge

M6 Theatre Company

Studio Theatre, Hamer C.P. School,
Albert Royds Street, Rochdale, Lancs. OL16 2SU
tel (01706) 355898
email admin@m6theatre.co.uk
website www.m6theatre.co.uk
Contact Gilly Baskeyfield

Touring theatre company specialising in creating and delivering high-quality, innovative theatre for young audiences.

New Perspectives Theatre Company

Park Lane Business Centre, Park Lane, Basford, Nottingham NG6 0DW
tel 0115 927 2334
email info@newperspectives.co.uk
website www.newperspectives.co.uk
Artistic Director Jack McNamara

Touring theatre company, staging approximately four to six new productions a year, many of which are new commissions. The company tours new writing and adaptations of existing works to theatres, arts centres, festivals and rural village halls around the country. Founded 1973.

NITRO

(formerly Black Theatre Co-operative Ltd)
Unit 36, 88–90 Hatton Gardens, London EC1N 8PG
tel 020-77609 1331
email info@nitro.co.uk
website www.nitro.co.uk
Artistic Director Felix Cross, *Executive Producer* Diane Morgan

Commissions and produces new and innovative musical theatre writing by black writers, that expresses the contemporary aspirations, cultures and issues that concern black people.

Northumberland Theatre Company (NTC)

The Playhouse, Bondgate Without, Alnwick, Northumberland NE66 1PQ
tel (01665) 602586
email admin@northumberlandtheatre.co.uk
website www.northumberlandtheatre.co.uk
Artistic Director Gillian Hambleton

Performs a wide cross-section of work: new plays, extant scripts, classic and modern. Particularly interested in non-naturalism, physical theatre and plays with direct relevance to rural audiences.

Out of Joint

7 Thane Works, Thane Villas, London N7 7NU
tel 020-7609 0207
email ojo@outofjoint.co.uk
website www.outofjoint.co.uk
Contact Max Stafford-Clark

Touring company producing new plays and occasional revivals. Welcomes scripts. Founded 1993.

Paines Plough

4th Floor, 43 Aldwych, London WC2B 4DN
tel 020-7240 4533
email office@painesplough.com
website www.painesplough.com
Artistic Directors George Perrin, James Grieve

Commissions and produces new plays by British and Irish playwrights. Tours at least six plays per year nationally for small and midscale theatres. Also runs The Big Room, a concierge-style development strand for professional playwrights – see website for further details. Welcomes unsolicited scripts and responds to all submissions. Seeks original plays that engage with the contemporary world and are written in a distinctive voice.

Proteus Theatre Company

Proteus Creation Space, Council Road, Basingstoke, Hants RG21 3DH
tel (01256) 354541
email info@proteustheatre.com
website www.proteustheatre.com
Artistic Director and Chief Executive Mary Swan

Small-scale touring company particularly committed to new writing and new work, education and community collaborations. Produces three touring shows per year plus several community projects. Founded 1979.

Real People Theatre Company

37 Curlew Glebe, Dunnington, York YO19 5PQ
tel/fax (01904) 488870
email sueann@curlew.totalserve.co.uk
website www.realpeopletheatre.co.uk
Artistic Director Sue Lister

Women's theatre company. Welcomes scripts from women writers. Founded 1999.

Red Ladder Theatre Company

3 St Peter's Buildings, York Street, Leeds LS9 8AJ
tel 0113 245 5311
email rod@redladder.co.uk
website www.redladder.co.uk
Artistic Director Rod Dixon

Theatre performances with a radical and dissenting voice. National touring of theatre venues and community spaces. Commissions one or two new plays each year. Runs the Red Grit Project, a free theatre training programme for over 18s.

Shared Experience Theatre

Oxford Playhouse, 11–12 Beaumont Street, Oxford OX1 2LW
tel (01865) 305305
email admin@sharedexperience.org.uk
website www.sharedexperience.org.uk
Artistic Director Polly Teale

Middle-scale touring company presenting two productions per year: innovative adaptations or translations of classic texts, and some new writing. Tours nationally and internationally. Founded 1975.

Sphinx Theatre Company

Ovalhouse Theatre, 52–54 Kennington Oval, London SE11 5SW
email info@sphinxtheatre.co.uk
website www.sphinxtheatre.co.uk
Artistic Director Sue Parrish

Specialises in writing, directing and developing roles for women.

Talawa Theatre Company

Ground Floor, 53–55 East Road, London N1 6AH
tel 020-7251 6644
email hq@talawa.com
website www.talawa.com
Artistic Director Michael Buffong

Script-reading service available three times a year. Visit the website for further details of submission windows.

Theatre Absolute

Shop Front Theatre, 38 City Arcade, Coventry CV1 3HW
tel (02476) 158340
email info@theatreabsolute.co.uk
website www.theatreabsolute.co.uk
Contact Julia Negus

Independent theatre producer of contemporary work. In 2009, Theatre Absolute opened the Shop Front Theatre in Coventry, a 50-seat flexible professional theatre space for new writing. performances, script development, theatre lab, and other live art events. The company is funded project to project and unfortunately not able to receive unsolicited scripts. Founded 1992 by Chris O'Connell and Julia Negus.

Theatre Centre

Shoreditch Town Hall, 380 Old Street, London EC1V 9LT
tel 020-7729 3066
email admin@theatre-centre.co.uk
website www.theatre-centre.co.uk
Artistic Director Natalie Wilson

Young people's theatre company producing plays and workshops which tour nationally and internationally. Productions are staged in schools, arts centres and other venues. Founded 1953.

Literary agents

How literary agencies work

Catherine Clarke gives an insight into literary agents, both large and small.

When I joined Felicity Bryan as a literary agent in June 2001, I knew I would be making one or two adjustments to my professional mindset. But I didn't fully appreciate how different working for a small agency would be from the publishing job I had left behind – several years as a publishing director for trade books at Oxford University Press, having come up through the editorial route. OUP is a large organisation with a corporate structure and hierarchy, and several divisions which operate effectively as separate companies, not only in the UK but in offices all over the world. I was now joining an agent who had previously been a director at Curtis Brown in London, and had successfully set up her own business in 1988, and who up until this point had operated on her own, with an assistant and a bookkeeper, from a small, pretty office in north Oxford. It was with something of a sigh of relief that I left behind the regular weekly and monthly meetings with colleagues from various publishing departments, which even when they were fun and useful seemed to take up such an inordinate amount of time, and set about learning what the differences were between representing authors and publishing them.

The first eye-opening lesson was that even though the agency itself consisted of just two agents and two staff, it functioned as the hub of a vast, informal network of relationships, not only within the UK but right across the globe. On the day that I started work, an auction was in progress for a new book proposal, a memoir co-written with a ghostwriter. The authors were based in London, but the publishers bidding for it (by phone and email on this occasion) were in Germany. The bids were relayed to Felicity Bryan by our German translation sub-agent at Andrew Nurnberg Associates in London, specialists in translation rights. Felicity called the authors to keep them up to speed with what was happening, and eventually made a recommendation to them for which offer to accept. The deal, once it was done and announced in the trade press, kick-started auctions for the book in many other territories, including the UK and the USA. While all this was happening, Felicity picked up the phone and talked to a London-based agent who deals with film and television rights and agreed that, given the intense interest in the book, it would be a good time to submit it to production companies in London and Los Angeles and get the proposal on track for a film option or sale. The authors were, naturally, over the moon.

Meanwhile I, the novice agent, was learning fast from this on-the-job induction, and was also busy setting up meetings with editors and publishing directors in all the London publishing houses, particularly those who specialised in serious non-fiction – books by historians, literary biographers, and philosophers mostly, as that was my own background as a publisher, and the areas where my earliest clients would be coming from. I wanted to find out what books were selling well for each editor, and what they were looking for. In several cases they were looking for books on particular subjects, and asked if I could help find authors for them.

By the time I attended my first Frankfurt Book Fair in October 2001, I had a small list of my own clients and a few deals already done with UK publishers. In my Filofax (now we all carry Moleskine® notebooks) I had a miniaturised schedule of 50 or so half-hour meetings with European and US publishers in the International Rights Centre, and several invitations to evening parties. I had already had a number of conversations about 'hot' books and who was buying what with publishers at the check-in at Heathrow airport and again waiting at the baggage claim at Frankfurt. Over the mindbogglingly expensive white wine at the Frankfurterhof bar late at night, thronging with publishers from all over the world, I handed over proposals for books that resulted in deals (which took place later, after the adrenalin rush of the Fair was over and everyone could make a sober decision on what they wanted to buy). During the evening I met the New York-based agent who was to become my first port of call for selling my clients' books on my behalf in the US market (later I added two other US agents who had different tastes and close publishing relationships so I could match each project to a really enthusiastic co-agent). I felt well and truly launched by the time I flew back home. The following spring the London Book Fair was to prove just as intense and influential, and when I went on to develop a list of children's writers, the Bologna Children's Book Fair became another annual springtime fixture in my diary for selling rights, meeting new publishers, checking up on how existing deals were progressing, and for trailing exciting new projects that were still in the offing. Very soon I was factoring in a regular trip to New York to see publishers and co-agents, so I could get a sense of the rather different market patterns and pressures in the USA, and also talk up my clients' books.

That experience is probably not very different for any agent, whatever the size of their business, though some will have less emphasis on the international markets. It undoubtedly helps as an agent starting out to have colleagues or contacts already in the business who can effect introductions and help build the necessary networks.

So what might a prospective writer take into account when looking for an agent to represent them?

There are many literary agencies in the UK – the membership of the Association of Authors' Agents is around 90 – and they vary in size from one person working entirely on their own to very large organisations with many agents and support staff. Most agencies are somewhere in between, with several book agents specialising in fiction or non-fiction, children's and adult, or more usually a mixture, and with support staff or freelance services such as royalty management and accounts. The very large agencies, such as Curtis Brown or United Agents also have agents who specialise in film and television rights, scriptwriters, directors, presenters and actors; in other words, they manage a wide range of creative talent. Jonathan Lloyd, Chairman of Curtis Brown, says, 'Compared to almost all publishers, agencies, even the bigger ones, are tiny, but an impressive client list helps us to protect our clients and the "one-stop-shop" ability allows us to exploit clients in the fullest and most effective way.'

At the other end of the spectrum, Rachel Calder at the Sayle Literary Agency, in Cambridge, feels that small is definitely beautiful: 'A small agency can afford to work in the medium- and long-term interest of their writers, not just the short term, because they are under less pressure from having to contribute to large overheads... they can be more flexible in reacting to changing industry circumstances, and still be acting in the writers' best interests.' As Sally Holloway, former publisher and an associate agent with the Felicity Bryan Agency, says, 'Smaller agents, like smaller publishers, are much more aware of their own bottom line, and therefore will pursue that last little foreign rights deal.'

For the writer, several factors might come into the reckoning if they are thinking about who should represent them. The first is that a relationship with an agent is, ideally, for life, or at least for the longer-term career, and should not be entered into lightly on either part. Whether the agent is part of a small or larger agency is not so great a consideration as whether the writer and agent trust one another's judgement and ability to deliver: whether they can both foresee a happy and fruitful collaboration. For some writers, being part of a list of high-profile writers – or more generally of famous 'talent' – may be the highest comfort factor; they might be less concerned about having the full attention of an agent with a very big list of clients than being part of a particular 'brand' created by that list. For others, that is less of a factor than having a hands-on agent who will work hard with the writer to get a proposal or novel into the best possible shape and then doggedly pursue the best deals in all potential markets – and that would not necessarily mean the highest advances. Of course, most agents can happily combine these qualities.

Because literary agenting is a business based not only on contacts and relationships but also personal tastes, every agency will have a slightly different ethos or feel. As Rachel Calder says, 'A good agent is committed to their author's work and career, has excellent industry contacts at home and abroad, wide publishing experience, confidence about their abilities and good literary judgement… what matters is how good the deals are that the agent does for those writers.'

Catherine Clarke is Managing Director at Felicity Bryan Associates.

See also...

- *How to get an agent*, page 392
- *Getting hooked out of the slush pile*, page 394
- *Being an agent in the digital age*, page 398
- *Letter to an unsolicited author*, page 404
- *How to attract the attention of a literary agent*, page 407

How to get an agent

Philippa Milnes-Smith demystifies the role of the literary agent.

This article is for all those who are prepared to dedicate themselves to the pursuit of publication. If you are currently experiencing just a vague interest in being a writer or illustrator, stop reading now. You are unlikely to survive the rigorous commercial assessment to which your work will be subjected. If you are a children's writer or illustrator do not think that the process will be any easier. It's just as tough, if not tougher.

So, what is a literary agent and why would I want one?

If you can answer a confident 'yes' to all the questions below, and have the time and resources to devote to the business of being an author, you might not need an agent:

• Do you have a thorough understanding of the publishing market and its dynamics?
• Do you know who are the best publishers for your book and why? Can you evaluate the pros and cons of each? Do you know the best editors within these publishers?
• Are you up to navigating the fast-changing world of digital publishing?
• Are you financially numerate and confident of being able to negotiate the best commercial deal available in current market conditions?
• Are you confident of being able to understand fully and negotiate a publishing or other media contract?
• Do you know the other opportunities for your work beyond publishing and how these might be exploited? Could you deal with the complexities of a franchise?
• Do you enjoy the process of selling yourself and your work?

An agent's job is to deal with all of the above on your behalf. A good agent will do all of these well – and let you get on with the important creative work of being an author. And they should be able to see the long-term strategy and opportunities.

So, is that all an agent does?

Some agents will provide more editorial and creative support; some will be subject specialists; some will involve themselves more in marketing and promotion; all should work in their clients' best interests.

I definitely do want an agent. Where do I begin?

Firstly, using this *Yearbook* and the internet, identify the agents to whom your book will appeal. Then really think about who will buy your book and why. An agent will only take someone on if they can see how and why they are going to make money for the client and themselves. An agent also knows that if he/she does not sell a client's work, the relationship isn't going to last long. Then do some further research online about both the agent and agency.

So the agent just thinks about money?

Good agents also care about the quality of work and the clients they represent. And they commit themselves to doing the best job they can. They also know that good personal relationships count. This means that, if and when you get as far as talking to a prospective agent, you should ask yourself the questions: 'Do I have a good rapport with this person? Do I understand and trust what they are saying?' Follow your instinct – more often than not it will be right.

So how do I convince an agent that I'm worth taking on?

Start with the basics. Make your approach professional and only approach an appropriate agent who deals with the category of book you are writing/illustrating. Check to whom you should send your work and whether there are any specific ways your submission should be made, and only make an electronic submission if the agency in question states that it is acceptable. For hard copy submissions, only submit neat, typed work on single-sided A4 paper. Send a short covering letter with your manuscript explaining what it is, why you wrote it, what the intended audience is and providing any other *relevant* context. Always say if and why you are uniquely placed and qualified to write a particular book. Provide your professional credentials, if any. If you are writing an autobiography, justify why it is of public interest and why your experiences set you apart. Supply a relevant CV or short autobiographical piece. Send a stamped addressed envelope for the return of your manuscript if you wish to have it returned. But in addition make your approach personal and interesting. You want to make the agent *want* to read your work. And you might only get one go at making your big sales pitch to an agent.

And if I get to meet an agent?

Treat it like a job interview (although hopefully it will be more relaxed than this). Be prepared to talk about your work and yourself. An agent knows that a prepossessing personality in an author is a great asset for a publisher in terms of publicity and marketing – they will be looking to see how good your interpersonal and presentation skills are. Authors are often required to do publicity interviews and events as well as use social networking to promote their work.

And if an agent turns my work down? Should I ask them to look again? People say you should not accept rejection.

No means no. Don't pester. It won't make an agent change his/her mind. Instead, move on to the next agency – the agent there might feel more positive. The agents who reject you may be wrong. But the loss is theirs.

Even if an agent turns my work down, isn't it worth asking for help with my creative direction?

No. Agents will often provide editorial advice for clients (some go as far as running their own creative groups) but are under no obligation to do so for non-clients. Submissions are usually sorted into two piles of 'yes, worth seeing more' and 'rejections'. Creative courses and writers' and artists' groups are better options to pursue for teaching and advice (see *Creative writing courses* on page 655). It is, however, vital to practise and develop your creative skills. If you want to get your work published, you will be competing with professional writers and artists – and those who have spent years working daily at their craft. The time you spend on your writing is still the most important you can spend.

Philippa Milnes-Smith is a literary agent and children's and YA specialist at the agency LAW (Lucas Alexander Whitley). She was previously Managing Director of of Puffin Books and is a past president of the Association of Authors' Agents.

See also...

• *Getting hooked out of the slush pile*, page 394
• *Letter to an unsolicited author*, page 404
• *How to attract the attention of a literary agent*, page 407

Getting hooked out of the slush pile

Literary agents wade through slush piles to find a manuscript that shines out and entices them to read more. Madeleine Milburn offers some helpful tips on how to get your submission noticed, read and hooked by an agent.

I started the Madeleine Milburn Literary, TV & Film Agency at the beginning 2012, after ten years of experience at two major UK literary agencies. I've always had a really positive attitude towards my 'slush pile' as it's where I've found 99% of my authors. 'Slush' can conjure some unfairly pejorative images, but it also offers agents the opportunity to wade through these shadowy waters of talent to find that one treasure: a book that melts the icy heart of the literary agent into a slushy pulp. I receive up to 50 submissions a day and read them all – but it takes something very special to make me want to read more.

Don't look for an agent too soon

The first, and most important, question when you are thinking of submitting your work to an agent is: am I ready? This might seem like a strange question but it is worth asking. Your book is finished, you've written a smashing covering letter, managed to condense the plot into a one-page synopsis – you've even written the dedication. But you would be surprised how many people submit before they are quite 'there'.

Slush pile

slush pile noun *informal* A stack of unsolicited manuscripts that have been sent to a publishing company for consideration.

slush noun [mass noun] **1** Partially melted snow or ice. **1.1** Watery mud. **2** *informal* Excessive sentiment.

Asking some pertinent questions will help you to see where you stand. How long ago did you finish the book? Have you come back to it with fresh eyes and read and reread it? Have you asked anyone for a second opinion? Have you self-edited your manuscript – gone through it critically to make sure the pace is right and the characters are authentic? Have you made sure that it captivates the reader from start to finish?

Read your work aloud, and go through it with a fine toothcomb to weed out any repetition or aspects that don't move the plot along at lightning pace. Once you get past the massive hurdle of getting your full manuscript requested, you'll need to make the agent fall in love with the *entire* book. Unfortunately, so many times, I've loved the opening chapters of a novel only to be sorely let down by a rushed and unsuccessful outcome. This is your big chance – don't fudge it!

Find an appropriate agent

Having read, reread and polished your manuscript until it's positively shining, you need to find an appropriate agent to submit it to. Start by looking at some agency websites to see what kind of books they represent, or what they are looking to represent. Look out for authors whose work is similar to your own. Has the agent specified that they would welcome a book in the genre you're writing in? Is the agency actively seeking new talent? Are they launching debut authors as well as securing new deals for their existing authors? Do they actively help with their authors' publicity efforts? Do they appear to be aware of all the digital options? This is so important in our digital age.

Explore alternative ways of getting to know about agents, such as joining a writing group, reading book trade news, following agents on Twitter and going to literary events.

It's often been said that your agent will become your business partner and, whilst I agree with this, I also see the relationship as a close working-friendship. Your agent should be someone who you feel comfortable talking with. The very best agents are those who care deeply about their authors and their work, and who will fight for them at every stage of their writing career. If you are fortunate enough to have more than one agent offering you representation, choose the agent who is most passionate about your work, and who is ambitious for you.

Unless you wish to be represented by a particular agent, there is no need to submit to agents on an exclusive basis. You don't want to be waiting for months for a response. A strong voice will always stand out no matter whether you have submitted exclusively or not.

Sell your book compellingly

Submission packages for agencies are usually of a similar format. Most require you to send a covering letter, synopsis and the all-important first three chapters. When you feel that your manuscript is as good as it can be and you are ready to submit to an agent, here are some key tips to consider.

The title

Use a strong and compelling title that grabs an agent's attention. Bestselling titles resonate with a reader before they open a book, for instance *Gone Girl*, *Room*, *Before I Go to Sleep*, *The Husband's Secret* and *The Boy in the Striped Pyjamas*. Don't use a title that only makes sense to a reader once they have read the story. Think of how you, as a reader, approach books in bookshops. What grabs your attention?

The covering letter

A covering letter should include a brief introduction, for example, 'I am currently seeking representation for my debut novel…', followed by an intriguing sentence that will draw the reader into your story; a slightly longer, enticing blurb; a reason why you have chosen the agent you are submitting to; a short profile; and a brief sentence or two about what you are/will be working on next.

Pitch your book in your letter, *not* in your synopsis. The letter is the place to get an agent excited about your opening chapters and where you need to 'sell' your book. Read the back cover blurb of books in the genre you are writing in, and study why they rouse your attention and interest. Practice pitching your book in a single sentence to get to the core of your story. You need to position your book straight away and make it evident to the agent what genre you are writing in.

Imagine your book on the shelves of a bookshop. Where would it sit? Next to Lee Child or Helen Fielding? I want to see that a writer has researched the market and knows that there is a readership for their work. An editor who loves your book will need to persuade the rest of the publishing team that there is a market for it. But when comparing yourself to another author, please don't say you are 'the next' Dan Brown; instead express the hope that your work will appeal to 'readers of' Dan Brown.

Only mention your achievements that are relevant to the book you are submitting. I applaud Duke of Edinburgh adventurers, dirt road bikers, members of Save the Whale foundations and other wonderfully colourful hobbyists, but unless the activity is specifically relevant to your book, for now, please keep the information short and sweet. Use the covering letter to sell the story, not yourself. I'd love to hear everything about you later, over a coffee, if I ask you to meet up.

Pitch just one book in your letter. If you have written more than one book, choose the one you'd like to launch your writing career with. If an agent loves the book you are submitting, he or she will be interested in all of your work. If you write both adult and children's stories, pick one (for now). A prospective editor will want your next book to appeal to the same readers as your first book – and I like to do two- or even three-book deals with publishers to ensure that they are committed to developing an author's career.

The synopsis

A synopsis is a straightforward chronological account of the *most important* things that happen in a story. A lot of agents read this last, or only read it if they want to see more chapters. Don't include every single detail; try to stick to one A4 page. Also, if there are any twists or plot revelations, don't keep them hidden. The agent needs to see how original your plotting is compared to what is currently on the market, so this aspect can be crucial to deciding whether your manuscript is requested.

The opening chapters

Your first three chapters are extremely important as, together with your covering letter, they are what an agent judges your work by. They need to be strong, enticing and compelling. There must be a strong sense of atmosphere, empathy or intrigue. Be wary of including irrelevant background information or context at this stage: it never grips readers' attention when they are not yet familiar with the characters. At worst, it can also slow the pace and be boring.

Strong characters are so important. Everyone remembers characters rather than the intricate details of a plot – just think James Bond, Jack Reacher, Sherlock Holmes and Harry Potter. Let your readers do the work. Create suspense and hook us in with a central character so that we are desperate to know more about them and read on.

Don't make your chapters too long to get around the three-chapter limit. I sometimes get asked whether I'd like to see more than three chapters because theirs are relatively short and, to be similarly brief, the answer is 'no thank you'. I don't count a Prologue as a chapter though.

Checklist for submitting to an agent

- Make sure your book has a strong title.
- Research the market and check that the length of your novel is appropriate for the genre you are writing in.
- Print out the manuscript and check that all spelling is correct. You will be surprised at how many errors you find.
- Take care to follow the instructions that are specific to each agency. For instance, I like to see 1.5 line spacing for the opening chapters and a one-page synopsis.
- Create a strong and attention-grabbing one-line hook that captures the heart of your story and will entice people to buy and read your book.
- Write a compelling back cover blurb.
- Consider all the selling points for your book. Write a summary of the book's appeal: be clear who the audience is and confident that they will identify with the book. Know the strengths of your manuscript and why it is unique. Think about what previous experience you have that could help promote your book.
- Tailor your profile to be relevant to your writing career. State if you are on a creative writing course, are a member of any writing clubs or societies and if you have won any writing competitions.
- If you have been published before, it is important to be upfront about it. Provide any writing history and say whether you have had an agent in the past.
- Write a synopsis that summarises your book's plot in chronological order with the ending included.

I personally read everything that comes into my 'slush pile'. I represent a wide range of adult, young adult and children's fiction, and would be delighted to look at your work.

Madeleine Milburn is a literary agent (see page 429) and in 2011 was chosen as one of the book trade's Rising Stars in the *Bookseller*. Madeleine Milburn's agency blog provides an insight into her literary agency and the book trade as a whole (www.mmla.co.uk). She is always on the lookout for new writers, self-published authors, or authors who are mid-career. Her Twitter handle is @agentmilburn.

Being an agent in the digital age

Even when liaising with traditional publishers for printed books, a strong digital thread is embedded in the work of literary agent Gordon Wise as he pursues possible commercial opportunities for his clients' work.

There's a question on a lot of writers' lips right now, devil's advocate or otherwise. What, when there are many routes to getting published via digital platforms – and seemingly numerous stories of writers finding untold riches through following them – is the role of the agent or publisher in a digital environment? Well, here's my take on why the agent's role should be more relevant than ever. (I hope the publishers will speak up for themselves...)

The perfect match

When I left my last in-house publishing job I knew I wanted to work in an environment where it was possible to adapt quickly to change, and where I could consider a range of projects that had strong prospects, rather than only what my company 'did'. That's exactly what an agent is able to do.

As an agent, I often say to prospective clients that I will take them on when I feel they have shown me work that I could, in theory, sell the next day. Immediacy excites an agent; something being fresh and new spurs you on to call perhaps a dozen influential editors to share your enthusiasm and get the project not only into their inbox but opened up on their desktop or downloaded to their e-reader in the hope that they will make a swift offer. Of course, in reality many projects take weeks or months of development to get them to that stage, but the principle remains: there has to be a sense of fresh promise for every book you are trying to sell.

And this is the link to digital. For the digital world is all about immediacy, instant sharing, a constant flow of information, multiple choices, fresh discovery. If something is wrong or isn't working, you can take it down or change tack straight away. If something's not for you, seek and you shall find an alternative that is. Philosophically, agenting and the digital environment couldn't be more compatible.

Many people claim it is hard to make money in the digital realm, even though any list of the rich will highlight a pantheon of online millionaires. Agenting sits at the point where creativity and commerce meet.

The digital thread

Not long after I became an agent in 2005, Penguin hosted its first presentation to agents about the work it was doing in the digital realm. What impressed me most was how a consideration of digital means of communication and ways of working had been adopted as a thread that ran through every area of the company's activities. The technical advantages were obvious, in terms of production or operations, as ebooks were just starting to come on stream in a serious way. But it was also exciting to see, for example, how the Penguin website had been marshalled to provide a colony of microsites around book and author brands – from household name thriller writers to its top children's characters – providing competitions and exclusive material and forums and space for reader engagement; and to hear that the junior publicists being recruited had an aptitude and familiarity with then-nascent social media. Digital wasn't something that Penguin was opting into; it was something it couldn't possibly not embrace. A book is digital from the writer's very first computer keystroke, and every stage from that point on needs to maximise the opportunities available to it in the digital sphere.

When a new agency launched, I remember the partners telling me that their goal was to mirror the range of a publisher's list within their own, so they would have something for any editor with whom they engaged. For an agent, competence in the digital space must similarly apply: an agent, author and publisher are all partners in their commercial endeavour, and need to be speaking the same language and operating in the same space. In a world where self-publishing can be achieved in the space of perhaps half an hour on a user-friendly platform or website, what use is the agent or publisher unless they have mastery of at least the basic publishing tools that are available to anyone using Google, and can indeed add considerably more to that?

The challenge of choice

But coming back to Penguin and its presentation: the appeal of what they were doing was to harness opportunities to book projects, to manage the digital offering, and to package it for readers. The internet is a vast and constantly rolling space; opportunities and ideas need focus and presentation in order for mere mortals to get their heads around them. And this is what agents do. They were doing it before the advent of digital. In contrast, publishers are mostly reactive, and rely on projects washing up on their literary shores or being introduced for their consideration. They rarely have an effective process for successfully managing unsolicited submissions; even more rare is the idea of devoting resources to speculative development. They make acquisitions following consensus from a team of perhaps 15, which leaves little room for spontaneity or backing a hunch. But the everyday world of the agent is one of constant surprise and discovery. When I go to work each morning, I never know quite what's going to cross my desk, and the challenge is to identify what is going to benefit from development and yield a commercial result for all three parties – author, agent and publisher – and a satisfying and stimulating experience for the reader.

It's about more than just books

When I became an agent, I also wanted to make sure that I wasn't in an environment that was 'only' about books. My first job in publishing was as a bookseller, and even in a space that was first and foremost about books, you learned from the nature of customers' enquiries that books are not the only thing on people's minds. They're also thinking, for example, about what's on television that night (or wondering what their digibox viewing service has selected for them), or their boxed set of DVDs that they are only halfway through, or about the live music or film experience they're planning for that weekend. Books are possibly one of the most richly rewarding forms of entertainment, but they're not alone in the marketplace in terms of things clamouring to have time devoted to them. I wanted to work in an environment where there was a continuum of entertainment ideas in the air. I liked the concept of books sharing continuity with the ideas from the stage or screen (large or small) that people were responding well to. In physical form, for me, that meant Curtis Brown, Europe's largest and longest-established broad-range talent agency. And that range is exactly what the digital spectrum also offers.

An agent who is on top of their game in the digital age will not only be looking for sales in the digital space. While the balance is shifting – and one of the exciting things is that we don't yet know where it will settle – the current core of the publishing business model is still the traditional physical realm. But to every aspect of this there is now a digital implication, and that consideration of the digital thread has to be embedded in the agent's work when pursuing all possible opportunities for maximising their clients' work. This not only includes selling their novel in print and/or ebook in the home market, but also introducing it to transatlantic and translation publishers and getting the best terms for those sales that also factor in the benefits that a publishing house can bring in terms of distribution, marketing and publicity. It means carefully considering the value of audio rights in physical and download, and even 'subsidiary' rights such as serialisation online and/or as a physical product. It involves considering what connections can be made with broadcast, traditional print and online media to boost an author's profile and awareness of their work; it may involve sponsored podcast work to complement their work as a public speaker at literary festivals or on the corporate or after-dinner circuit. Agents need to have a strategy for the proper management of film, television and performance rights, and know the contractual implications of granting certain digital rights to a publisher in the light of this. A strategy is also required for managing digital piracy, the flipside to digital opportunity (although some see this as a digital marketing strategy in itself). It may even extend to things that can't be done online, such as merchandising – lunchboxes and t-shirts and mugs – as in the case of my cartoonist client Andy Riley.

Encompassing the digital realm

Few authors would be able to manage such a large portfolio of activities independently; inherently, publishers are not in a position to do this to the author's maximum advantage. A good agent will have the resources for the 360-degree agenting that the digital world demands. Here are some examples of this from my own list.

For the publication of John Yorke's *Into the Woods: A Five Act Journey Into Story*, his publicist at Particular Books and I negotiated a feature article in the *Guardian Review* which highlighted key 'takeaway' tips from the book, to run shortly in advance of publication. He and I had also been working with the Professional Writing Academy (PWA) to create an online course using the book's tenets, and PWA's landing page was set to go live in time for publication. When the *Guardian* piece ran, PWA and I were able to tweet links to Amazon, the course site and the Curtis Brown web page for the book, engaging in what's known as a 'virtuous circle'. The book entered the Amazon top 100, and as a result of the *Guardian's* outreach we had an approach from a proactive US publisher with whom I was able to close a deal at the London Book Fair three weeks later.

Although the same set of connections or possibilities for multi-platform adaptations don't apply to every project, the willingness and ability to connect must be there. I cannot claim that my efforts at social media were the driver for the book. But my role was (a) to be a link in the chain, (b) to instigate elements of the project, (c) to develop the means of communication about it, and (d) to close deals on what could be commercialised out of the process.

Where an author has a body of work, the digital environment provides enormously exciting prospects for multi-platform and multi-format exposure, which would be impossible to achieve without professional literary management. I represent the works of

Winston Churchill, and we're in the process of concluding a decade's work in transferring all his papers from microfilm to a dynamic interactive scholarly product from Bloomsbury Academic, coordinating global publication of his published works in ebook with digital pioneers Rosetta, the reissue of the landmark multi-volume official biography, and building a public-facing online hub to promote education and leadership in 2015, the year that marks the 50th year of his passing and the 70th anniversary of the end of the Second World War. All this on top of managing traditional publishing relationships which range from licences to Penguin Classics to a special edition of his essay 'Painting as a Pastime' with specialist publisher Unicorn Press.

I'm also actively engaged with Virago in the UK and Open Road (a US digital publisher and multimedia content company) to launch digital editions of the works of the great mid-20th century writer Mary Renault, whose books about Ancient Greece were beloved by earlier generations and which are ripe for rediscovery by readers of Madeline Miller and George R.R. Martin. Virago will produce handsome new print editions with forewords by contemporary authors, while digital formats will enable us to introduce readers to her 'lost' early works – the books that launched her career, but which have not been available for decades.

Some digital nuts and bolts for *your* publishing strategy

Manuscript length

In all of the above, perhaps I am putting the cart before the horse. Without attempting to cover the whole topic of how to be successful with your creative writing, let's consider a couple of digital resource basics. Firstly, your work must be a manageable length. Successful novels tend to be 70,000–100,000 words long; there are of course many exceptions to this and a number of classics and bestsellers fall either side of this rule but they only work for particular reasons. To get a more objective view on the length and readability of your work, I recommend doing two things – one very physical, one very digital:

1. Print out the whole manuscript on single sides of A4 paper with the type set at 12 point, double-spaced, with generous margins. You will see just how much of a doorstop you will be foisting on the unsuspecting reader. The expense, in terms of toner and paper, of doing this more than a couple of times should deter you from over-writing unless you have very good reason to expect a similar investment in time and consumables from your readers.
2. Transfer your file on to an e-reading device to display its standardised font and format. This will enable you to have a much closer experience of reading your book as though you were a third party, allowing you to see more objectively its strengths and weaknesses, and dissuading you from blipping over passages that have ceased to catch your over-trained eye.

Submitting your manuscript

In this *Yearbook*, listings for each agency (see page 411) and publisher (see page 148) provide submission guidelines, including whether they consider unsolicited submissions, and if they accept them electronically. Also consult the websites of the publishers and agents you're thinking of approaching. If the company doesn't have a website or it isn't very good, this will give you a pretty good indicator of how it approaches digital matters. Today, for an industry which has digital at its very core and endless ways of gaining from the development of the digital sphere, not to be digitally well-engaged with even your online shop front is inexcusable.

From looking at its website, the submission policy of the publisher or agency should be evident. If it doesn't encourage submissions online, and you don't have a personal introduction to a particular agent, respect this. Agents have far too many emails coming in already, juggling as they are the needs and projects of their existing clients, and you'll only come across badly if you get in the way of that. And hassling by Twitter is not the way to win friends. Present yourself in the way that you yourself would want someone introduced to you: not as spam, but as a properly curated experience. Do what they ask – and take into account the advice that many others offer elsewhere in this *Yearbook* – and you'll be taken much more seriously.

A publisher's focus is more on promoting the actual books it has under licence than the long-term career interests of their author. Curtis Brown has spent a number of years developing a highly sophisticated website to promote its clients and their work. While I, together with the other agents in the company, would expect an author to have his or own digital presence in some form, we know that every author will have different strengths and resources available to them in this respect. As part of our role, we would reinforce and bring some focus in the digital realm to the work of the authors we represent. We create news stories about clients and their work on a rolling basis; we provide links to their own websites; we even stream in their Twitter feeds.

Curtisbrowncreative.co.uk was one of the first agency submission portals and it is linked to the work of our in-house creative writing school. Its interactive submission form prompts writers to supply all the information we're looking for about them and their work in order to be able to consider it properly, as well as a dynamic way of feeding back and responding. The agency can't promise representation for everyone who submits work to us, but we can promise the best possible consideration based on how you present yourself and your work and our experienced view of the market prospects for it.

Getting your message across

When it comes to submissions, keep it simple. The stories of gimmicks that are meant to induce an agent to take notice of a writer's work or take a client on are legion, and I doubt there is any evidence that this made their approaches more successful. Basically, the idea and its execution has to be good and original, and hold the reader's attention in a world where – not least because of digital opportunities – attention spans are not long and the competition for a reader's attention is stiff.

What to download from all this

Here are three lots of under-140 characters' worth of things to keep in mind as you head towards publication:

- Think about the digital implications of your every writing activity. Digital's not going away so make it work for you.
- Audition agents and publishers in the light of this, but also listen to why they do and don't do what they do.
- Turn the question around: look at the whole package publishers and agents provide, not just what you could have done yourself anyway.

Just because something has a beginning, middle and an end and is properly spelled won't make it exceptional. Agents want to work with writers within whom, if you were to snap them in half like a stick of rock, you find the qualities of their work running right through them. Agents want to work with writers who have done their research and can identify from the profile of their client list that they are the right match for them. And while all work submitted should be (a) complete, and (b) already as good as it possibly can be, good agents will also be prepared to work with writers whose work in their view isn't quite 'there' on first reading of the manuscript. Besides making introductions and handling the business transactions, this is a fundamental 'added value' offered by an agent: if they judge it to be worth both sides' time, based on their experience and knowledge of readers' and editors' tastes an agent will inspire the confidence that with the right developmental encouragement the author can take their writing to the next level.

Show evidence of what you have done to get your work read by others. Most literary festivals have creative writing events built into them (see page 563), there are many excellent creative writing courses (see page 655), and some reading groups have a new writing element to them. And this is even before you consider the online possibilities afforded by sites like Wattpad.com, or indeed confident and well-informed self-publishing that shows you know how to reach your readership. An agent who takes you on will show a piece of your work to a number of publishers around the world; those publishers in turn want it to appeal to thousands and thousands of people. If the agent is the first person to read your work other than you, the stakes are very high if it falls short for want of work on aspects that could have been identified through some simple roadtesting.

Fancy presentation and social media

Fancy presentation is something you would consider in conjunction with your agent. For instance, for one client we put a short film on YouTube featuring her talking about her work, as her personality was intrinsic to the success of the idea. For another, we were able to direct publishers to a popular Tumblr site he had created. But these were mechanisms to reinforce what was already at root a good idea; they were vehicles, not the ideas themselves. Good agents in the digital age will be looking for clients who have command of and familiarity with digital assets such as these, or show an aptitude for them. And explore social media as a writing resource: follow your favourite authors to see what they are saying about the writing life, and look at the profiles of agents and publishers you think might be right for your work as well as discussion threads like #writingtip.

Everyone has a different level of engagement with social media. I personally don't use Facebook; it's never clicked with the way I like to present myself. I tweet sporadically – not as much as the gurus recommend, but to the level that works for me; it also gives me a toehold in the social media space and a way of interacting with others for whom it is their forte. As an unpublished writer, an agent or publisher can't reasonably expect you to have social media followings that run to the tens of thousands – although you will be an extremely attractive prospect if you do – but they will like to see that you have been experimenting in that space, to have considered how best to show yourself off there, to be saying interesting things and making connections about your work. One day, they will be expecting you to speak at literary festivals, do feature pieces about yourself and your work, and be engaging on broadcast media. Social media is part of the training ground for that, and the more development work you can do on that front yourself, the more interesting you will look as a publishing business proposition.

Gordon Wise has worked in publishing for over 20 years, first as a bookseller and then as an editor and publisher. He is a senior agent at Curtis Brown (www.curtisbrown.co.uk) and Vice President of the Association of Authors' Agents (www.agentsassoc.co.uk).

Letter to an unsolicited author

With the benefit of 20 years of experience as a literary agent, Simon Trewin gives valuable advice to unpublished authors on how and when to approach a literary agent with their manuscript.

Dear Author,

Being an agent is not rocket science. There is no agent training school and there is no course that I know of that exclusively trains people to do what I do. All I do, quite simply, is read work, decide if it ticks a number of boxes and then try to seek a publishing home for it. It is as clear and as simple as that – I am not a literary critic, I don't run a creative writing school and I'm not a publisher but I *am* entrepreneurial, I am clear in my mind as to my particular strengths and weaknesses and I am also a nurturer of talent. On top of all of that I continually love the fact that there are thousands and thousands of writers out there looking for book deals. So far so good.

There is an illustrated edition of *Jack and the Beanstalk* that I used to read to my son Jack when he was little and we both loved one particular page – it showed a tiny Jack knocking on the huge wooden door of the giant's castle. The door was reinforced with rivets and there was an intimidating sense of austere formality about it. Jack knocked and knocked on that door but no one came and it felt poignant and it felt uneven. I am absolutely aware that this is how unsolicited and unrepresented authors feel when they are in search of an agent – that they are knocking on a massive door which never seems to open. The reality of course is that on the other side of the publishing door there isn't an ogre or a huge author-eating giant but there are in fact hundreds of busy agents running around doing great work and all faced with a common quest – to find exciting new authors to add to their growing lists. We all want to find the Next Big Thing and any agent who says otherwise is telling porky pies. It is good to remind myself as an agent, and to remind all authors out there at the beginning of their journeys that when I started out as an agent an author called Joanne Rowling was still sitting in a café somewhere scribbling the adventures of a young wizard boy at a school called Hogwarts. She wrote to the agent Christopher Little and the rest is history. As the advert for the lottery once said, 'It could be you…'.

We are all looking for our own J.K. Rowling but, unfortunately, many writers put unnecessary barriers in between their work and the potential of an agent picking it up. There is no exact science to breaking into publishing but there are many things you should avoid like the plague.

Agents are a curious bunch (I'm not sure what the collective noun for agents should be – maybe a 'clause of agents'?) and the community I inhabit is made up of not only the mad, the bad and the dangerous to know (as in any profession) but on the whole by a huge number of truly inspiring entrepeneurial people who spend every waking hour as passionate advocates of the powers of prose. If you take a look at various agent websites (and you really should) you will see a diverse list of clients who reflect their agent's idiosyncrasies, their passion and their interests and this should be encouraging to any author in search of representation.

We agents need you – without authors we would be sitting at our desks sucking our pens and looking at empty bookshelves – but we also need you to help us make efficient use of our time and our skills. With 20 years' experience as an agent I can tell you that many prospective authors don't do themselves any favours when they approach the door. The 'nos' fall into many categories:

(a) **The Arrogant.** I once received a submission which said, and I quote, 'Dear Mr Terwin (*sic*) I am probably one of the best writers currently working in the English language and, frankly, you are lucky to be seeing this picaresque novel which my tutor at Oxford has already described as "heart-stoppingly wonderful". Personally I don't think I need an agent but someone mentioned your name as being one of the less bad ones so I am giving you an opportunity to persuade me otherwise. If you would like to visit me in Oxford next Wednesday lunchtime that would be convenient.' Sincerely, etc. Frankly I didn't bother reading any more – I knew that we weren't going to get on. I have nothing against writers being confident and passionate and displaying their work to the best of its potential but this crossed the line!

(b) **The Impersonator.** I received a mediocre thriller one day and read about 50 pages and sent it back with a note saying I didn't feel it was going to be a good fit for my list. The next morning a very indignant man called me and told me in no uncertain terms that I was mistaken. 'Oh yes,' said I, 'why is that?' He then proceeded to tell me that he had read the top ten thrillers of the previous year and had decoded each of them onto a graph. When there was a cliffhanger he coloured in the appropriate square on his chart with green crayon, when there was an explosion he whipped out the red crayon, and when there was a sex scene he used blue and so on. He then wrote his own novel based on this equation of what constituted the statistically average 'bestselling novel' and was amazed that I didn't immediately snap it up. What he had done of course was create an impersonation of a thriller rather than a thriller itself, and the book he sent me was very hollow indeed. He hadn't invested anything of himself in it and it really showed. My feeling is that you should write from the inside out and take that storytelling fire in your belly and get it down on paper. Don't analyse the market or the genre – just write.

(c) **The Misguided.** I sing in the bath. I enjoy it and I can just about carry a tune but I don't believe that I am entitled to a record deal and a seven-night residency at the O2. That doesn't bother me because, as I said, I enjoy it. Some of the manuscripts I receive are just not very good but still they come with covering letters reeking of entitlements and that say, 'My friends and family think this is better than most books being published right now'. I would be very apprehensive about suggesting to any author that they use their friends and family's reaction to their work as a selling point. Have you ever told a friend that their ugly baby was anything other than 'beautiful'? Of course not. Go figure! Don't trust anyone's judgement who you share Christmas dinner with.

(d) **The Scattergun.** I am all for authors who have a multiplicity of talents and who write prose, poetry, genre fiction, verse drama and children's books but I would advise them against sending examples of ALL OF THEM AT ONCE to an agent with a note saying, 'I love all this stuff – you decide what I should write next'. I want to hear your undivided passion for one area of your writing because if I become your agent I will need to sell you in a very focused way to a publisher. Variety may be the spice of life but I would suggest you write to an agent about one major project at a time – your publisher will want to launch you as a mini-brand and will want to package you and continue to publish you in a coherent manner that creates a sense of expectation from your growing readership.

(e) **The Misdirected.** Even though I am very open on my website as to what my likes and dislikes are, I still receive material that is in direct opposition to those stated preferences. I don't understand or represent science fiction or fantasy; I don't have an interest in sagas; I don't represent young children's books; I don't represent academic books; I don't represent illustrated books. I'm very clear about this but still, on a daily basis, letters arrive that say things like, 'Dear Simon, I know you say that you don't represent x, y or z, but I hope that once you've read my material you'll make an exception'. The short answer to that is *no* – I know it sounds harsh but it is there to save you time and to make sure that you send your precious work to someone who is actively wanting to read it.

(f) **The Underdeveloped.** It is virtually impossible to secure a book deal for fiction in the current climate on anything less than the full manuscript, so you shouldn't approach an agent without having completed several drafts of your masterwork. Ideally you will also have put it to one side for a couple of months so you can achieve that all-important 'distance' from your work. This is crucial but it is amazing how many people approach me saying something like, 'I know the second half doesn't work at all and I will probably change the main character entirely but I would love your thoughts now'. My thoughts on this are clear – do not submit your work until you are happy to be judged by it. Again I know this sounds harsh but you wouldn't go into a job interview and say, 'I'm probably completely wrong for this job and sorry I am still wearing my pyjamas and I am half an hour late but let's have a chat… if that's all right with you'. Take the process really seriously and present yourself in a professional way to a professional agent and you will achieve so much more.

Your one aim is to put no barriers between you, your prose and my assessment of it and it really isn't that difficult. The important thing to remember throughout this entire process is that I am sitting at my desk waiting for something wonderful to come into my life. I am looking to find storytellers – non-fiction and fiction – who can make me, for a brief moment or two, forget that I am reading a book. Authors who have a distinctive voice that carries me with it to strange lands of the imagination or simply to a place where I am viewing the mundane from an off-kilter perspective. I am looking, simply, for books that I will feel proud to share with my peers in the publishing world and who will feel the same passion for them that I do.

If you can avoid transgressing any of the great sins of approaching an agent that I have outlined then you will raise the odds of securing an agent and publication by a factor of at least ten. And if you can avoid doing as one author did when he wrote to me and said, 'I have tried 14 publishers and nine agents and they have all said "no" so I am now approaching you', then even better!

This year I am particularly looking for interesting, original debuts in fiction and non-fiction which helps us to decode the world today.

Simon Trewin is a partner at William Morris Endeavor Entertainment and runs the literary department in their London office. He can be reached at sct@wmeentertainment.com and WME's submission policy can be seen at www.wmeauthors.co.uk.

See also...

- *How to get an agent*, page 392
- *Getting hooked out of the slush pile*, page 394
- *How to attract the attention of a literary agent*, page 407

How to attract the attention of a literary agent

Having a literary agent can help you to get published. When an agent takes on a writer publishers are far more likely to take notice of that writer's work. Alison Baverstock gives advice on how to attract the attention of a literary agent.

With certain genres, literary agents perform a valuable sifting function for publishing houses. They are people with lots of publishing experience, who are offered a wide variety of work, in various stages of development. The agents bring the material they favour to the attention of the publishers they think will like it too. There is also the affirmation that comes from having an agent; the comfort of knowing someone who understands the business as a whole, has plenty of choice, and yet has chosen to back you. Of course that's not to say that all great potential writers have agents, or that all new authors taken on by publishing houses have agents, just that amongst the newly published, there will probably be more authors with agents than authors without. Stories of titles that are self-published, are then spotted by publishers and their creators offered advances for future books are more and more common, but the process is still often agented – those who self-publish having found out in the process that effective publishing is much harder than it looks and they would prefer to concentrate on writing.

The nature of literary agents

Many agents have been publishers themselves. It follows that they like to specialise (usually in the kind of titles they used to publish, or in which they have a strong personal interest) and that they have an encyclopedic view of the industry.

Agents tend to work a bit like advertising agencies, in that they often have just one major client in each field. So just as an advertising agency would not represent two directly competing accounts, it would be unlikely that a literary agent would take on two authors whose books were very similar.

Generalising further, literary agents are gregarious, fond of being noticed (they tend to dress quite strikingly), are good talkers (they certainly seem to know everyone), dramatic travellers (fond of hopping on and off planes in a blaze of self-generated publicity), are good negotiators (their livelihood depends on it as well as that of the authors they represent) and are not immune to vanity – so mentioning that you heard them speak, or making it clear you know who they are and particularly want to be represented by *them*, tends to go down well.

What's in it for the agent?

I always think the secret of a good business proposal is to look at it from your would-be collaborator's viewpoint rather than your own. Thus when seeking sponsorship, you get a far better response if you explain what the potential sponsor will get out of a relationship with you than if you tell them how much you need the money. To paraphrase J.F. Kennedy, 'Think not what an agent can do for you, but what you can do for an agent.' Taking the same approach, agents are looking for writers (a) with talent (and can you prove it by providing quotes from satisfied readers/reviewers?); (b) who can sustain their writing beyond one book (and thus will be ongoing earners and repay the initial investment of time they make in you); (c) who are topical (all agents and publishers claim to be looking for the 'next big thing'); (d) who are different, or have a new slant to bring to an existing strand of publishing; and (e) who are *promotable* (a key publishing term meaning interesting or memorable to the media). How you come over (or are likely to come over) in the press/on the air will be a key factor in deciding whether or not to take you on.

The money side of things needs a little more consideration. Whilst literary agents are book lovers and enjoy what they do, if their service fails to make a profit it is unlikely to be there in future, so as well as a talent for writing they are looking for financial remuneration. An agent may be willing to help you shape your novel, provide advice on your style, advise you on how to prepare for an interview, but they will be doing these things in the hope that you will reward them with material that sells rather than out of pure altruism.

Whatever advance the author gets, their agent usually gets 15%-plus of it, so it is in the agent's interest to sell the material for the highest amount of money, or to the publishing house that is most likely to make a long-term success of the writer's career. This may lead the cynical to conclude that agents are more likely to be interested in media-friendly (or just media-based) authors than pure literary genius, but it is through success of key names that they are able to take a punt on new writers. An agency that confined itself to literary fiction alone, and ignored the popular market completely, would probably not last long.

Top tips for securing the attention of an agent

1. Do your research. Consult *Literary agents UK and Ireland* starting on page 411 of this *Yearbook*, look at what kind of writers each agent represents and note their specialities. If they say they do not take science fiction, do not assume you are helpfully extending their range by offering it. Send an email outlining what you have in mind and ask who is the right person within their firm to send it to. Don't assume that if the agency is called 'Snodgrass and Wilkins' you must talk only to one of the two key names. The chances are their books will be full already – or they may be long deceased (and so if you write to them by name your lack of research will be immediately obvious). A more junior member of staff may be hungrier for new authors, and don't forget that their judgement will be backed – because they are a staff member and presumably have been taken on by the partners to search for new talent. And one day they too may be on the letterhead.

2. Don't necessarily be put off by the request for 'no unsolicited submissions'. You might decide to interpret this as 'No ill-considered submissions' – which means you have done your research and think what you are sending them will appeal to them personally and be a good fit for their wider list of clients. All agents need some new writers; you have to make the case for their next choice being you.

3. Send in what they ask for, not more or less. Note whether they request print or email submissions and send your material in exactly the format they ask for. Three chapters and a synopsis means just that, it is not code for 'anything over three chapters' or 'as near as you can get to three chapters'. Send the first three chapters, not three chosen at random. If the first three are not also the best, think carefully before sending anything.

4. Ensure the book has a really good title. It's tempting to think that writing the book is the really important thing and that the title can grow out of the writing later. Wrong. The title is extremely important. It should catch the agent's attention and stick in the memory. Think how the same thing works for you in bookshops. I recently bought a copy of *Fifty* *is Not a Four-letter Word* by Linda Kelsey simply because I liked the title. I was looking for a present for a friend and I thought her fancy would be tickled by it too.

Heather Holden-Brown of the hhb agency says: 'The title matters hugely. I want something that excites me, and that will draw a similarly instant reaction from any publisher I mention it to. So go for something that is topical, intriguing or witty and to the point.'

5. Write a synopsis. This should be an outline of what kind of book you are writing, it is not your chance to give a detailed listing of what is in each chapter. It should start by ensuring the agent can grasp in their mind very precisely what kind of writer is on offer – this is important because it may enable them to think what kind of publisher it would appeal to.

If you can, say which section of the bookshop your title would be stocked in (don't just say the table at the front!) and list writers whose books are already in this category. Booksellers are very loathed to stock titles they don't know where to put, and agents may be unwilling to back a title that has no natural home. A friend of a friend wanted to write a book on the menopause and to call it *How Long Before I Can Hang-glide?*. A bookseller persuaded her that whilst this would make a very good subtitle, people looking for books on the subject would be in danger of not finding it – unless they were by chance looking in the sports section.

6. Write a book blurb for your work. Think what goes on the back of most books and how important it is in attracting attention to the title inside. A book blurb should be a fair representation of the style of the book, should tempt the reader to want to know more *now*, and should not give away the ending. Writing a book blurb is harder than you think, and is an excellent way of getting yourself noticed by an agent.

7. Send an interesting CV on yourself. This is not the time to rehash your formal one; a literary agent is not interested in how you did at 'O'/GCSE or 'A' level. Rather, what they do need to know is what you have done that makes you an interesting proposition to a publishing house. Remember agents are interested in how 'promotable' any potential new author is. This could be your job, your family commitments or your past experience. Don't assume that what you consider boring or mundane will be viewed in the same light by those you are approaching. A background working in the City is not the normal path to becoming a novelist and so may be well received by an agent. Similarly your domestic arrangements may be equally ordinary to you but interesting when combined with the fact that you have written a book.

Take an imaginative approach to your past and think creatively. A friend of mine once used a revolving door in an American hotel at the same time as a well-known actor and would proudly boast that she had 'been around in New York with Cary Grant.' I have four children and have always moved house mid-pregnancy, hence the scan and the birth never took place in the same hospital. Whereas this is entirely a function of my husband's peripatetic job, my publishers got quite excited when I told them. What have you done that can be made to sound interesting?

8. Do you have anyone else who can say what you write is good? This does not have to be a celebrity (although they are always useful) but what about other readers, writers and friends with relevant job titles? It's not hard to get testimonials for your work – many people like to be asked; some will oblige out of pure friendship, others for the publicity it may bring them.

9. Can you prove that there is a market for what you write? When an agent approaches a publisher to enthuse about a new author they will have to justify the claims they make on your behalf, and the newer the feel of what you want to write, the harder they will have to work. It's not good enough to say 'everyone will want to read' this new title. So, find out the viewing figures for programmes that relate to the book you want to write, or the sales of magazines that have a strong overlap with your material. Think laterally. For example, I co-wrote a book on raising teenagers (*Whatever!*, Piatkus 2005) and found that there were lots of books on parenting babies, but relatively little on parenting older children. It seemed to me that our subject was really modern morality; how to provide guidance in a fast-changing world. To prove there is a market I took as examples the healthy book sales of popular philosophy titles by A.C. Grayling and the number of people who have taken an Alpha course (over 3 million in the UK and 18 million worldwide so far). The agent I approached told me this widening of the issue really made a difference to how he viewed my proposal.

If you have already self-published material say how many sales/downloads have been achieved so far. The old stigma about agents being reluctant to consider those who have self-published has gone; today it is a good route to demonstrating demand for your writing.

10. Write a really good letter (or email for online submissions) to accompany the package you send to an agent. This may take you a long time but a good letter of introduction is well worth the trouble. It should outline all of the above: what kind of book you want to publish, how far down the road you have got, what is noteworthy about you as a person, who else thinks so.

Some agents acknowledge what they receive, others do not. You could ask them to email receipt, or enclose a stamped addressed postcard with a reminder to let you know they have received it. This is a further opportunity to remind them you are a human being, so try a witty postcard or add a caption to an image to make the point that you are dying to hear from them! For inspiration, look at the card selection in a local art gallery and think which picture sums up your mood as you wait for them to respond.

Finally, do remember that agents are individuals, and perhaps more individualistic than the key protagonists in many other professions. Just as many are instantly recognisable, they also have very individual taste. It follows that what does not appeal to one may well appeal to another. So if your first choice does not immediately sign you up, there may be others who will think differently. But they will only find out about you if you have the gumption to keep going. In the long run, getting an agent on your side is invariably worth the effort.

Carole Blake of Blake Friedmann says: 'We receive at least 20 unsolicited manuscripts a day, our books are full and to be honest we are looking for reasons to say no – but I still get such excitement from a really new voice writing something that grabs my attention. I have known the world stand still as I ignore the rest of the post and just read on until I have finished. When that happens it's really special – and I will fight to get that author published. Sometimes it takes years, but if I believe in an author I will keep going.'

Dr Alison Baverstock is Associate Professor of Publishing at Kingston University, where she co-founded MA Publishing. A former publisher, and winner of the Pandora Prize for Services to Publishing, she has written widely about publishing and writing. Her books include *Marketing Your Book: An Author's Guide* (Bloomsbury 2007, 2nd edn), *Is There a Book in You?* (Bloomsbury 2006), *The Naked Author: A Guide to Self-publishing* (Bloomsbury 2011) and, most recently, the fifth edition of *How to Market Books* (Routledge 2015). Her website is www.alisonbaverstock.com and you can follow her on Twitter @alisonbav.

Literary agents UK and Ireland

The *Writers' & Artists' Yearbook*, along with the Association of Authors' Agents and the Society of Authors, takes a dim view of any literary agent who asks potential clients for a fee prior to a manuscript being placed with a publisher. We advise you to treat any such request with caution and to let us know if that agent appears in the listings below. However, agents may charge additional costs later in the process but these should only arise once a book has been accepted by a publisher and the author is earning an income. We urge authors to make the distinction between upfront and additional charges. Authors should also check agents' websites before making an enquiry and should familiarise themselves with submission guidelines.

*Member of the Association of Authors' Agents

A & B Personal Management Ltd

PO Box 64671, London NW3 9LH
tel 020-7794 3255
email b.ellmain@aandb.co.uk
Directors R.W. Ellis, R. Ellis

Full-length MSS, scripts for TV, theatre, cinema; also novels, fiction and non-fiction. No unsolicited material. Email or telephone before submitting anything. Founded 1982.

A for Authors Ltd

73 Hurlingham Road, Bexleyheath, Kent DA7 5PE
tel (01322) 463479
email enquiries@aforauthors.co.uk
website www.aforauthors.co.uk
Directors Annette Crossland, Bill Goodall

Fiction, literary and commercial/mass market, including (but not exclusively) crime, thriller, women's, historical and also YA. Home 15%, overseas/translation 20%, film/TV 15% (home)/20% (overseas). No sci-fi/horror, short stories or poetry. Send synopsis plus first three chapters or 50pp, whichever is shorter, preferably by email as Word attachments. No reading fee.

Sheila Ableman Literary Agency*

36 Duncan House, 7–9 Fellows Road, London NW3 3LZ
tel 020-7586 2339
email sheila@sheilaableman.co.uk
website www.sheilaableman.com
Contact Sheila Ableman

Non-fiction including history, science, biography, autobiography (home 15%, USA/translation 20%). Not taking any new clients at present. No reading fee. Founded 1999.

The Agency (London) Ltd*

24 Pottery Lane, London W11 4LZ
tel 020-7727 1346
email info@theagency.co.uk
website www.theagency.co.uk
Children's Book Agent Hilary Delamere

Represents authors and illustrators of children's books for all ages, preschool to teen fiction (home 15%, overseas 20%); works in conjunction with overseas subagents. The Agency also represents screenwriters, directors, playwrights and composers (10%). Adult novels represented only for existing clients. For film/TV/theatre executives, please email. No unsolicited material. Founded 1995.

Aitken Alexander Associates Ltd*

18–21 Cavaye Place, London SW10 9PT
tel 020-7373 8672
email reception@aitkenalexander.co.uk
website www.aitkenalexander.co.uk
Contacts Gillon Aitken, Clare Alexander, Sally Riley, Lesley Thorne, and in the US office Anna Stein (Directors), Matthew Hamilton, Lucy Luck, Imogen Pelham; children's & YA fiction: Gillie Russell; film/TV/stage rights: Lesley Thorne, Leah Middleton.
Associated Agents Mary Pachnos, Anthony Sheil

Fiction and non-fiction (home 15%, USA 20%, translation 20%, film/TV 15%). No plays or scripts. Email preliminary letter with half-page synopsis and first 30pp of sample material to submissions@aitkenalexander.co.uk. No reading fee.

Clients include Lisa Appignanesi, Jo Baker, Pat Barker, Colin Barrett, Kevin Barry, Lloyd Bradley, Paul Brannigan, Mike Brearley, Jung Chang, Clare Clark, John Cornwell, John Crace, Sarah Dunant, Diana Evans, Roopa Farooki, Sebastian Faulks, Helen Fielding, Germaine Greer, Julia Gregson, Mark Haddon, Mohammed Hanif, Philip Hoare, Peter Hook, Laird Hunt, Virginia Ironside, Oliver James, Liz Jensen, Alan Johnson, Dom Joly, J.M. Ledgard, Ben Lerner, Mark Lowery, Paul Mason, Charles Moore, Lucy Moore, Caroline Moorehead, William Nicholson, Catherine O'Flynn, Jonathan Raban, Piers Paul Reid, Paul Rees, Louise Rennison, Michèle Roberts, Jennie Rooney, Gabriel Roth, Edward St Aubyn, James Scudamore, Maria Semple, Nicholas Shakespeare, Gillian Slovo, Brix Smith, Francis Spufford, Rory Stewart, Bilal Tanweer, Colin Thubron, Robert Twigger, Amanda Vickery, Penny Vincenzi, Willy Vlautin, Daisy Waugh, Paul Willetts,

A.N. Wilson, Andrew Wilson, Robert Wilson, Hanya Yanagihara, Adam Zamoyski. UK only – Harper Lee, J.D. Salinger.

Estates – John Betjeman, Gordon Burn, Bruce Chatwin, Paul Gallico, Ian Hamilton, Ngaio Marsh, Mary Norton.

Translation and film/TV only for associated agents – James Bowen, Estate of John Fowles, Garry Jenkins. Founded 1977.

The Ampersand Agency Ltd*

Ryman's Cottages, Little Tew, Oxon OX7 4JJ
tel (01608) 683677/683898
email info@theampersandagency.co.uk
website www.theampersandagency.co.uk
Contacts Peter Buckman, Anne-Marie Doulton, Jamie Cowen

Literary and commercial fiction and non-fiction (home 15%, USA 15–20%, translation 20%). No reading fee. Writers should consult the website for more information and submission guidelines.

Clients include Quentin Bates, Helen Black, Sharon Bolton, Druin Burch, J.D. Davies, Will Davis, Catherine Deveney, Jamie Doward, Cora Harrison, Phillip Hunter, Jin Yong, Mark Latham, Leo Murray, Tim O'Rourke, Matthew Pritchard, Mark Roberts, Adrian Selby, Ivo Stourton, Vikas Swarup, Henry Venmore-Rowland, Michael Walters and the estates of Georgette Heyer, Angela Thirkell, Winifred Foley and John James. Founded 2003.

Darley Anderson Literary, TV and Film Agency*

Estelle House, 11 Eustace Road, London SW6 1JB
tel 020-7386 2674
email enquiries@darleyanderson.com
website www.darleyanderson.com
website www.darleyandersonchildrens.com
Contacts Darley Anderson (international thrillers, women's fiction, love stories and cat books), Camilla Wray (crime, thrillers, suspense, general fiction, women's fiction, YA books), Clare Wallace (children's fiction, women's fiction, accessible literary), Mary Darby (Head of Rights), Rosanna Bellingham (Financial Controller), Sheila David (TV and Film), Sophie Mcleman (PA to Darley Anderson), Emma Winter (Rights Executive)

All commercial fiction and non-fiction; children's fiction (for all ages including young adult and crossover), non-fiction, picture books and illustration (home 15%, USA/translation 20%, film/TV/radio/illustrators 20%). No poetry, academic books, scripts or screenplays. Send covering letter, short synopsis and first three chapters. Return postage/sae essential for reply. Overseas associates APA Talent & Literary Agency (LA/Hollywood) and leading foreign agents worldwide.

Special interests (fiction): all types of thrillers, crime and mystery. All types of American and Irish novels. All types of popular women's fiction and accessible literary/Richard and Judy Book Club-type fiction. Also comic fiction. Children's fiction for all ages (including young adult and crossover), picture books and illustration.

Special interests (non-fiction): autobiographies, biographies, sports books, 'true-life' women in jeopardy, revelatory history and science, popular psychology, self improvement, diet, beauty, health, fashion, animals, humour/cartoon, cookery, gardening, inspirational, religious.

Clients include Rosie Blake, Constance Briscoe, James Carol, Chris Carter, Cathy Cassidy, Lee Child, Martina Cole, John Connolly, Jane Costello, A.J. Cross, Caroline Crowe, Jason Dean, Margaret Dickinson, Clare Dowling, Kerry Fisher, Martyn Ford, Tana French, Helen Grant, David Hewson, Polly Ho Yen, Tara Hyland, Emma Kavanagh, Annie Murray, Phaedra Patrick, Lesley Pearse, Adam Perrott, Adrian Plass, Jo Platt, Dave Rudden, Rebecca Shaw, Kim Slater, Sean Slater, Erik Storey, Tim Weaver, Lee Weeks, Kimberley Willis, David Wishart.

ANDLYN

tel 020-3290 5638
email submissions@andlyn.co.uk
website www.andlyn.co.uk
Founder and Agent Davinia Andrew-Lynch

Specialises in children's fiction and content. Represents authors of picture books, middle grade and YA fiction. This also includes graphic novels for these age groups. Particularly looking for storytellers whose material has cross-media/platform potential. Commission: 15% home and audio, 20% US, foreign/translation, film/TV, multiplatform and online media rights. No reading fee. See website for submission guidelines. Established 2015.

Anubis Literary Agency

7 Birdhaven Close, Lighthorne, Warwick CV35 0BE
tel (01926) 642588
Contact Steve Calcutt

Genre fiction: science fiction, fantasy and horror (home 15%, USA/translation 20%). No other material considered. Send 50pp with a one-page synopsis (sae essential). No reading fee. No telephone calls. Works with The Marsh Agency Ltd on translation rights. Founded 1994.

Diane Banks Associates Ltd*

email submissions@dianebanks.co.uk
website www.dianebanks.co.uk
Contact Diane Banks

Commercial fiction and non-fiction (home 15%, overseas and rights in other media 20%). Fiction: women's, crime, thrillers, literary fiction with a strong storyline, young adult. Non-fiction: memoir, real-life stories, celebrity, autobiography, biography, business, popular history, popular science, self-help, popular psychology, fashion, health & beauty. No poetry, children's, academic books, plays, scripts or short stories. Send brief cv, synopsis and first three chapters as Word or Open Document attachments. Aims to give initial response within two weeks. No reading fee.

Authors include Prof. Brian Cox, Prof. Jon Butterworth, Dani Atkins, Kate Riordan, Adam Palmer, Alex Higgins, Andy Taylor (Duran Duran), Miss S, Shelina Janmohamed, Marisa Merico, Sophie Hayes. Founded 2006.

Tassy Barham Associates

231 Westbourne Park Road, London W11 1EB
tel 020-7792 5899
email tassy@tassybarham.com
Proprietor Tassy Barham

Specialises in representing European and American authors, agents and publishers in Brazil and Portugal, as well as the worldwide representation of Brazilian authors. Founded 1999.

Bath Literary Agency

5 Gloucester Road, Bath BA1 7BH
tel (01225) 314676
email gill.mclay@bathliteraryagency.com
website www.bathliteraryagency.com
Contact Gill McLay

Specialist in fiction for children and young adults. Also accepts submissions in non-fiction and picture books. For full submission details, refer to the website. No reading fee. Founded 2011.

The Bell Lomax Moreton Agency*

Suite C, 131 Queensway, Petts Wood, Kent BR5 1DG
tel 020-7930 4447
email info@bell-lomax.co.uk
website www.bell-lomax.co.uk
Executives Eddie Bell, Pat Lomax, Paul Moreton, June Bell, Josephine Hayes, Helen Mackenzie-Smith, Lauren Clarke, Sarah McDonnell

Quality fiction and non-fiction, biography, children's, business and sport. No unsolicited MSS without preliminary letter. No poetry, screenplays or scripts. No reading fee. Founded 2000.

Lorella Belli Literary Agency (LBLA)*

54 Hartford House, 35 Tavistock Crescent, London W11 1AY
tel 020-7727 8547
email info@lorellabelliagency.com
website www.lorellabelliagency.com
Proprietor Lorella Belli

Fiction and general non-fiction (home 15%, overseas/dramatic 20%). Particularly interested in first-time writers, journalists, international and multicultural writing, books on Italy and successful self-published authors. No children's, science fiction, fantasy, academic, poetry, original scripts. No reading fee. May suggest revision. Send an enquiry letter or email before submitting work. Does not return materials unless the correct sae postage is provided. Enclose a stamped acknowledgement card with submission if receipt acknowledgment is required. Works with dramatic and overseas associates; represents American, Canadian and Australian agencies in the UK. Sells translation rights on behalf of British publishers, literary agents and independent authors.

Clients include Shahena Ali, Jennifer Armentrout/J. Lynn, Bookouture, Susan Brackney, Zoë Brân, Gesine Bullock-Prado, Scott Carney, Sally Corner, Crux Publishing, D.B. Nielsen, Renita D'Silva, Kasey Edwards, Carrie Elks, Marcus Ferrar, Emily Giffin, 'Girl on the Net', Kent Greenfield, Jenny Han/Siobhan Vivian, Helena Hunting, Sophie Jackson, Linda Kavanagh, Ed Kritzler, Dinah Lee Kung, Christopher Lascelles, Diane and Bernie Lierow, William Little, Sharon Maas, Elisabetta Minervini, Nisha Minhas, Alanna Mitchell, Rick Mofina, Sandro Monetti, Farnoosh Moshiri, Kirsty Moseley, Angela Murrills, Annalisa Coppolaro-Nowell, Judy Nunn, Jennifer Ouellette, Panoma Press, Robert J. Ray, Burt Reynolds, Sheila Roberts, Anneli Rufus, Dave Singleton, Sole Books, Rupert Steiner, Katie Stephens, Justine Trueman, Victoria Van Tiem, Diana Winston, P.P. Wong, Carol Wright. Founded 2002.

The Bent Agency*

21 Melliss Avenue, Richmond TW9 4BQ
email info@thebentagency.com
website www.thebentagency.com
Agents Gemma Cooper, Molly Ker Hawn (UK); Jenny Bent, Heather Flaherty, Louise Fury, Susan Hawk, Victoria Lowes, Beth Phelan, Brooks Sherman (US)

Represents authors of fiction for adults, children and teenagers, and selected non-fiction with commercial appeal. Offices in the UK and US. Unsolicited submissions welcome by email only: query and first ten pages pasted into body of email. See complete guidelines at www.thebentagency.com/submission.php. Founded 2009.

Berlin Associates Ltd

7 Tyers Gate, London SE1 3HX
tel 020-7836 1112
email submissions@berlinassociates.com
website www.berlinassociates.com
Agents Marc Berlin, Stacy Browne, Matt Connell, Alexandra Cory, Rachel Daniels, Julia Mills, Laura Reeve, Fiona Williams, Emily Wraith, Julia Wyatt

A boutique agency representing writers, directors, producers, designers, composers and below-the-line talent across theatre, film, TV, radio and new media. No prose/fiction. The majority of new clients are taken on through recommendation or invitation, however, if you would like your work to be considered for representation, email a cv along with a brief outline of your experience and the work you would like to submit for consideration.

The Blair Partnership*

Middlesex House, Fourth Floor,
34–42 Cleveland Street, London W1T 4JE
tel 020-7504 2520
email info@theblairpartnership.com
email submissions@theblairpartnership.com
website www.theblairpartnership.com
Founding Partner Neil Blair, *Managing Partner* Dan Marks, *Agents* Zoe King, Liz Bonsor

Considers all genres of fiction and non-fiction for adults, young readers and children. Will consider unsolicited MSS. Email a covering letter, a one-page synopsis and the first ten pages to: submissions@theblairpartnership.com.

A multi-platform rights management agency, works in partnership with some of the best creative talent in the world to build their brands by effective management of their IP throughout the world and across books, film, TV, digital and all other media and platforms.

Clients include the Class of 92/Salford FC, the Alexander Wilson estate, Frank Lampard, Maajid Nawaz, J.K. Rowling, Pete Townshend and a select number of talented debut writers including Claire Barker, Michael Byrne, Simon David Eden, Tatum Flynn, Dan Freedman, the Freeman Brothers, Keaton Henson, Inbali Iserles, Karl James, Jennifer Kincheloe, Kieran Larwood, Sophie Nicholls, Justine Pattison and Zoom Rockman.

Blake Friedmann Literary, TV & Film Agency Ltd*

First Floor, Selous House, 5–12 Mandela Street, London NW1 0DU
tel 020-7387 0842
email info@blakefriedmann.co.uk
website www.blakefriedmann.co.uk
Agents Books: Carole Blake, Isobel Dixon, Juliet Pickering, Tom Witcomb; Film/TV: Julian Friedmann, Christine Glover, Conrad Williams, Daniel Nixon, Ellen Gallagher

Full-length MSS. Fiction: crime, thrillers, women's fiction, literary fiction and YA; a broad range of non-fiction (home 15%, overseas 20%). Media Department handles film and TV rights, and represents scriptwriters, playwrights and directors. Represented worldwide in 26 markets. Preliminary letter, synopsis and first three chapters preferred via email. No reading fee. See website for full submission guidelines.

Authors include Tim Baker, Edward Carey, Elizabeth Chadwick, Barbara Erskine, Liz Fenwick, Paul Finch, Janice Galloway, David Gilman, Ann Granger, Ken Hom, Kerry Hudson, Peter James, Deon Meyer, Lawrence Norfolk, Joseph O'Connor, Sheila O'Flanagan, Laurie Penny, Monique Roffey, Tess Stimson, Julian Stockwin, Ivan Vladislavić.

Scriptwriters, playwrights and directors include Gaby Chiappe, Roger Spottiswoode, Andy Briggs, Marteinn Thorisson, Debbie O'Malley and Greg Latter. Founded 1977.

The Book Bureau Literary Agency

7 Duncairn Avenue, Bray, Co. Wicklow, Republic of Ireland
tel +353 (0)12 764996
email thebookbureau@oceanfree.net
email thebookbureau123@gmail.com
Managing Director Geraldine Nichol

Full-length MSS (home 15%, USA/translation 20%). Fiction preferred – thrillers, crime, Irish novels, literary fiction, women's commercial novels and general fiction. No horror, science fiction, children's or poetry. Strong editorial support. No reading fee. Preliminary letter, synopsis and three sample chapters (single line spacing); return postage required. Works with agents overseas.

BookBlast Ltd

PO Box 20184, London W10 5AU
tel 020-8968 3089
email gen@bookblast.com
website www.bookblast.com

Full-length MSS (home 12%, overseas 20%), TV and radio (15%), film (20%). Fiction and non-fiction. Literary and general adult fiction and non-fiction (memoir, travel, popular culture, multicultural writing only). No reading fee. Editorial advice given to own authors. Initiates in-house projects. Also offers translation consultancy and literary PR services. Film, TV and radio rights mainly sold in works by existing clients. Founded 1997.

Bright Literary Agency

Studio 102, 250 York Road, London SW11 3SJ
email mail@thebrightgroupinternational.com
website www.brightgroupinternational.com
Contact Vicki Willden-Lebrecht

A boutique children's literary agency born out of the success of The Bright Agency, a leading children's illustration agency with a global client list. Works across all genres of children's publishing including novelty, picture books and fiction. Email submissions in pdf or Word format only to literarysubmissions@brightgroupinternational.com. See website for full submission guidelines. Founded 2009.

Alan Brodie Representation

Paddock Suite, The Courtyard,
55 Charterhouse Street, London EC1M 6HA
tel 020-7253 6226
email abr@alanbrodie.com
website www.alanbrodie.com
Managing Director Alan Brodie, *Agents* Sarah McNair, Lisa Foster, Caroline Underwood, Victoria Williams, *Musical Theatre Consultant* Caroline Underwood

Specialises in stage plays, literary estates, radio, TV and film (home 10%, overseas 15%). No prose, fiction or general MSS. Represented in all major countries. No unsolicited scripts; recommendation from known professional required. Founded 1996.

Jenny Brown Associates*

33 Argyle Place, Edinburgh EH9 1JT
tel 0131 229 5334
email info@jennybrownassociates.com
website www.jennybrownassociates.com
Contact Jenny Brown, Mark Stanton, Lucy Juckes, Allan Guthrie, Kevin Pocklington, Francesca Dymond

Literary fiction, crime writing and writing for children; non-fiction: biography, history, nature, sport, music, popular culture; play and screen scripts (home 12.5%, overseas/translation 20%). No poetry, science fiction, fantasy or academic. No reading fee. Check website for submission guidelines.

Clients include Lin Anderson, Jennie Erdal, Gavin Extence, Gavin Francis, Alex Gray, Doug Jackson, Kathleen Jamie, Doug Johnstone, William McIlvanney, Sara Maitland, Jonathan Meres, Sara Sheridan, Natasha Solomons. Founded 2002.

Felicity Bryan Associates*

2A North Parade, Banbury Road, Oxford OX2 6LX
tel (01865) 513816
email agency@felicitybryan.com
website www.felicitybryan.com

Fiction and general non-fiction with emphasis on history, biography, science and current affairs (home 15%, overseas 20%). No scripts for TV, radio or theatre, no crafts, how-to, science fiction, light romance or poetry. No email submissions.

Clients include Carlos Acosta, David Almond, Karen Armstrong, Mary Berry, Simon Blackburn, Archie Brown, Marcus Chown, Artemis Cooper, Edmund de Waal, John Dickie, Sally Gardner, A.C. Grayling, Tim Harford, Gill Hornby, Sadie Jones, Liza Klaussmann, Simon Lelic, Diarmaid MacCulloch, Martin Meredith, James Naughtie, John Julius Norwich, Iain Pears, Rosamunde Pilcher, Matt Ridley, Eugene Rogan, Meg Rosoff, Miriam Stoppard, Roy Strong, Adrian Tinniswood, Anna Whitelock, Lucy Worsley and the estate of Humphrey Carpenter.

Juliet Burton Literary Agency*

2 Clifton Avenue, London W12 9DR
tel 020-8762 0148
email juliet.burton@btinternet.com
Contact Juliet Burton

Handles fiction and some non-fiction. Special interests include crime and women's fiction. No science fiction/fantasy, children's, short stories, plays, film scripts, articles, poetry or academic material. Commission: home 15%, US & translation 20%. Approach in writing in the first instance with synopsis and two sample chapters and sae. No reading fee.

Clients include Kay Brellend, Barbara Cleverly, Marjorie Eccles, Edward Enfield, Anthea Fraser, June Hampson, Veronica Heley, Peter Helton, Mick Herron, Avril Joy, Maureen Lee, Priscilla Masters, Gwen Moffat, Barbara Nadel and Pam Weaver. Founded 1999.

Capel & Land Ltd*

29 Wardour Street, London W1D 6PS
tel 020-7734 2414
email firstname@capelland.co.uk
website www.capelland.com
Agents Georgina Capel, Philippa Brewster, Romily Withington, Rachel Conway

Literary and commercial fiction, history, biography; film and TV (home/overseas 15%). No reading fee; see website for submission guidelines.

Clients include Simon Barnes, Julia Copus, Flora Fraser, John Gimlette, Adrian Goldsworthy, Katharine Grant, Andrew Greig, Tristram Hunt, Tobias Jones, Leanda de Lisle, Colleen McCullough, Adam Nicolson, Louise O'Neill, Stella Rimington, Andrew Roberts, Ian Sansom, Simon Sebag Montefiore, Diana Souhami, Elizabeth Speller, Louis Theroux, Lesley Thomson, Fay Weldon. Founded 1999.

Casarotto Ramsay & Associates Ltd

Waverley House, 7–12 Noel Street, London W1F 8GQ
tel 020-7287 4450
email info@casarotto.co.uk
website www.casarotto.co.uk
Directors Jenne Casarotto, Giorgio Casarotto, Mel Kenyon, Jodi Shields, Rachel Holroyd

MSS – theatre, films, TV, sound broadcasting only (10%). Works in conjunction with agents in USA and other foreign countries. Preliminary letter essential.

The Catchpole Agency

53 Cranham Street, Oxford OX2 6DD
tel 07789 588070
email james@thecatchpoleagency.co.uk
email celia@thecatchpoleagency.co.uk
website www.thecatchpoleagency.co.uk
Proprietors James and Celia Catchpole

Agents for authors and illustrators of children's books from picture books through to young adult novels. Commission from 10% to 15%. See website for contact and submissions details. Founded 1996.

Chapman & Vincent*

7 Dilke Street, London SW3 4JE
email chapmanvincent@hotmail.co.uk
Directors Jennifer Chapman, Gilly Vincent

Handles illustrated non-fiction work only, often acting as a packager. Not actively seeking new clients but will consider email enquiries without attachments. No reading fee. Works with The Elaine

Markson Agency. Commission: home 15%; US and Europe 20%.

Clients include George Carter, Leslie Geddes-Brown, Lucinda Lambton and Eve Pollard. Founded 1992.

Teresa Chris Literary Agency Ltd*

43 Musard Road, London W6 8NR
tel 020-7386 0633
email teresachris@litagency.co.uk
website www.teresachrisliteraryagency.co.uk
Director Teresa Chris

All fiction, especially crime, women's commercial, general and literary fiction. No science fiction, horror, fantasy, short stories, poetry, academic books (home 10%, overseas 20%). No reading fee. Send introductory letter describing work, first three chapters and sae. Representation in all overseas territories. Founded 1988.

Anne Clark Literary Agency

PO Box 1221, Harlton, Cambridge CB23 1WW
tel (01223) 262160
email submissions@anneclarkliteraryagency.co.uk
website www.anneclarkliteraryagency.co.uk
Contact Anne Clark

Specialist in fiction for children and young adults, also picture book texts (home 15%, overseas 20%). Submissions by email only. See website for submission guidelines. No reading fee. Founded 2012.

Mary Clemmey Literary Agency*

6 Dunollie Road, London NW5 2XP
tel 020-7267 1290
email mcwords@googlemail.com

High-quality fiction and non-fiction with an international market (home 15%, overseas 20%, performance rights 15%). No children's books or science fiction. TV, film, radio and theatre scripts from existing clients only. Works in conjunction with US agent. No reading fee. No unsolicited MSS and no email submissions. Approach first by letter (including sae).

US clients include Lynn C. Franklin Associates Ltd, The Miller Agency, Roslyn Targ, Weingel-Fidel Agency Inc. Founded 1992.

Jonathan Clowes Ltd*

10 Iron Bridge House, Bridge Approach, London NW1 8BD
tel 020-7722 7674
email admin@jonathanclowes.co.uk
website www.jonathanclowes.co.uk
Directors Jonathan Clowes, Ann Evans, Nemonie Craven, Olivia Guest

Literary and commercial fiction and non-fiction, film, TV, theatre (for existing clients) and radio (home 15%, overseas 20%). See website for submission guidelines. No reading fee. Email for general enquiries. Works in association with agents overseas. Founded 1960.

Clients include Dr David Bellamy, Arthur Conan Doyle Characters Ltd, Simon Critchley, Len Deighton, Brian Freemantle, Victoria Glass, Francesca Hornak, Carla Lane, David Nobbs, Gruff Rhys and the literary estates of Doris Lessing, Elizabeth Jane Howard, Michael Baigent and Richard Leigh.

Rosica Colin Ltd

1 Clareville Grove Mews, London SW7 5AH
tel 020-7370 1080
Directors Sylvie Marston, Joanna Marston

All full-length MSS (excluding science fiction and poetry); also theatre, film and sound broadcasting (home 10%, overseas 10–20%). No reading fee, but may take 3–4 months to consider full MSS. Send synopsis only in first instance, with letter outlining writing credits and whether MS has been previously submitted, plus return postage.

Authors include Richard Aldington, Simone de Beauvoir (in UK), Samuel Beckett (publication rights), Steven Berkoff, Alan Brownjohn, Sandy Brownjohn, Donald Campbell, Nick Dear, Neil Donnelly, J.T. Edson, Bernard Farrell, Rainer Werner Fassbinder (in UK), Jean Genet, Franz Xaver Kroetz, Don McCamphill, Heiner Müller (in UK), Graham Reid, Alan Sillitoe, Botho Strauss (in UK), Rina Vergano, Anthony Vivis, Wim Wenders (in UK). Founded 1949.

Conville & Walsh Ltd*

Haymarket House, 28–29 Haymarket, London SW1Y 4SP
tel 020-7393 4200
email firstname@convilleandwalsh.com
website www.convilleandwalsh.com
Directors Clare Conville, Patrick Walsh, Jake Smith-Bosanquet

Handles all genres of fiction, non-fiction and children's worldwide (home 15%, US and translation 20%). Submissions welcome: first three chapters, cover letter, synopsis by email or post with sae. No reading fee. Part of the Curtis Brown Group of Companies; simultaneous submission accepted.

Fiction clients include notable prize winners such as D.B.C. Pierre, Sarah Hall, Nathan Filer, Lisa O'Donnell, Ali Shaw, M.L. Stedman and Simon Wroe. Other novelists include Tim Clare, Esther Freud, Kirsty Gunn, Matt Haig, Nick Harkaway, Rachel Joyce, Stephen Kelman, Howard Marks, John Niven, Favel Parrett, S.J. Watson, Isabel Wolff.

Non-fiction clients include Jim al-Khalili, Belle de Jour, Marcus Berkmann, Helen Castor, Misha Glenny, Thomas Harding, Natalie Haynes, Tom Holland, Gavin Pretor-Pinney, Tali Sharot, Simon Singh, Tim Spector, Clive Stafford-Smith, Zoe Williams, Ben Wilson and Richard Wiseman. Artists represented for books include Steven Appleby, David

Shrigley and the estate of Francis Bacon. Children's and young adult list includes John Burningham, Damian Dibben, Steve Voake, Paula Rawsthorne, Katie Davies, Rebecca James, P.J. Lynch, Piers Torday and the estate of Astrid Lindgren. Founded 2000.

Jane Conway-Gordon Ltd*

38 Cromwell Grove, London W6 7RG
tel 020-7371 6939
email jane@conway-gordon.co.uk
website www.janeconwaygordon.com

Full length MSS (home 15%, overseas 20%). No poetry, science fiction or children's. Represented in all foreign countries. No reading fee but preliminary letter and return postage essential. Founded 1982.

Coombs Moylett Maclean Literary Agency

120 New Kings Road, London SW6 4LZ
tel 020-8740 0454
email lisa@cmm.agency
website www.cmm.agency
Contacts Lisa Moylett, Jamie Maclean

Specialises in well-written commercial fiction, particularly in the genres of historical fiction, crime/mystery/suspense and thrillers, women's fiction across a spectrum ranging from chick-lit sagas to contemporary and literary fiction. Also looking to build a children's list concentrating on YA fiction. Considers most non-fiction particularly history, biography, current affairs and cookery. Works with foreign agents. Commission: home 15%, overseas 20%, film/TV 20%. No reading fee. Does not handle poetry, plays or scripts for film and TV.

Creative Authors Ltd

11a Woodlawn Street, Whitstable, Kent CT5 1HQ
email write@creativeauthors.co.uk
website www.creativeauthors.co.uk
Director Isabel Atherton

Fiction, women's fiction, literary fiction, non-fiction, humour, history, science, autobiography, biography, business, memoir, mind, body & spirit, health, cookery, arts and crafts, crime, children's fiction, picture books, young adult, graphic novels and illustrators (home 15%, overseas 20%). Only accepts email submissions.

Authors and illustrators include Mark Beaumont, Bompas & Parr, Robert Kelsey, Fiona McDonald, Cassie Liversidge, Anthony Galvin, Sarah Herman, Tristan Donovan, Kelly Lawrence, Lucy Scott, John Robb, Bethany Straker, Nick Soulsby, Dr Keith Souter. Founded 2008.

The Creative Rights Agency

17 Prior Street, London SE10 8SF
tel 020-8149 3955
email info@creativerightsagency.co.uk
website www.creativerightsagency.co.uk
Contact Richard Scrivener

Specialises in male interest fiction, 'lager sagas', thrillers, memoirs, contemporary culture and sports. Submit via email: sample chapters, synopsis and author biog. Also handles film/tv and licensing rights. Founded 2009.

Rupert Crew Ltd*

6 Windsor Road, London N3 3SS
tel 020-8346 3000
email info@rupertcrew.co.uk
website www.rupertcrew.co.uk
Directors Doreen Montgomery, Caroline Montgomery

International representation, handling accessible literary and commercial fiction and non-fiction for the adult and children's (8+) markets. Home 15%; overseas, TV/film and radio 20%. No picture books, plays, screenplays, poetry, journalism, science fiction, fantasy or short stories. No reading fee. No unsolicited MSS: see website for current submission guidelines. Founded 1927 by F. Rupert Crew.

Curtis Brown Group Ltd*

Haymarket House, 28–29 Haymarket, London SW1Y 4SP
tel 020-7393 4400
email cb@curtisbrown.co.uk
website www.curtisbrown.co.uk
website www.curtisbrowncreative.co.uk
website www.curtisbrownbookgroup.wordpress.com
Chairman Jonathan Lloyd, *Joint Ceos* Ben Hall and Jonny Geller, *Directors* Jacquie Drewe, Nick Marston, Sarah Spear
Books Jonny Geller (Managing Director), Felicity Blunt, Sheila Crowley, Anna Davis, Jonathan Lloyd, Lauren Pearson (Children's & Young Adult), Norah Perkins (Estates), Vivienne Schuster, Karolina Sutton, Stephanie Thwaites (Children's & Young Adult), Gordon Wise
Film/TV/Theatre Nick Marston (Chairman), Ben Hall (Managing Director), Jessica Cooper, Amanda Davis, Sam Greenwood, Nish Panchal, Cynthia Okoye, Joe Phillips, Lily Williams, Camilla Young
Actors Sarah Spear (Managing Director), Lara Beach, Grace Clissold, Oriana Elia, Mary FitzGerald, Maxine Hoffman, Jessica Jackson, Lucy Johnson, Alexander Lindsey-Renton, Sarah MacCormick, Grant Parsons, Edward Smith, Kate Staddon, Frances Stevenson, Sam Turnbull, Olivia Woodward
Presenters Jacquie Drewe (Chair)
CUBA Pictures Nick Marston (Ceo), Dixie Linder

Represents prominent writers of fiction and non-fiction, from winners of all major awards to international bestsellers, and formats ranging from print and audio to digital and merchandise. In fiction, works across many genres, both literary and those aimed at a popular audience, and looks for strong voices and outstanding storytellers in general fiction, crime, thrillers, psychological suspense, mainstream fantasy, historical fiction, young adult and children's books. Non-fiction list includes leading commentators and thinkers, historians, biographers, scientists and writers of quality narrative non-fiction. Represents a number of well-known personalities, from world-renowned politicians to business leaders and comedians. Curtis Brown also manages the international careers of authors, with strong relationships in translation and US markets. The Book Department works closely with a team of media agents, offering full-service representation in film, TV and theatre. New initiatives include a creative writing school, Curtis Brown Creative, established with the aim of finding and fostering new talent; Studio 28, an in-house digital publishing venture; and the Curtis Brown Books Group, to build an online reading community.

No longer accepts submissions by post. For more information on submissions and individual agents, please consult www.curtisbrowncreative.co.uk. Simultaneous submissions with Conville and Walsh (see separate entry), also a member of the Curtis Brown Group of Companies. Founded 1899.

Judy Daish Associates Ltd

2 St Charles Place, London W10 6EG
tel 020-8964 8811
email judy@judydaish.com
website www.judydaish.com
Agents Judy Daish, Howard Gooding, Tracey Elliston

Theatre, film, TV, radio (rates by negotiation). No unsolicited MSS. No reading fee. Founded 1978.

Caroline Davidson Literary Agency*

5 Queen Anne's Gardens, London W4 1TU
tel 020-8995 5768
email enquiries@cdla.co.uk
website www.cdla.co.uk

Handles exceptional novels and non-fiction of originality and high quality (12.5%). Visit website for further information. All submissions must be in hard copy. Email submissions are not considered. For non-fiction send letter with cv and detailed, well thought-out book proposal, including chapter synopsis. With fiction, send letter, cv, summary and the first 50pp of your work. CDLA does not handle plays, film scripts, poetry, children's/YA, fantasy, horror, crime or sci-fi. No reply without large sae with correct return postage/IRC. No reading fee.

Authors include Simon Akam, Peter Barham, Andrew Beatty, the estate of Maggie Black, Andrew Dalby, Jan Davison, Emma Donoghue, Chris Greenhalgh, Richard Hobday, Andrew Russell, Helena Whitbread. Founded 1988.

Felix de Wolfe

20 Old Compton Street, London W1D 4TW
tel 020-7242 5066
email info@felixdewolfe.com
website www.felixdewolfe.com
Agents Caroline de Wolfe, Wendy Scozzaro

Theatre, films, TV, sound broadcasting, fiction (home 10–15%, overseas 20%). No reading fee. Works in conjunction with many foreign agencies. No unsolicited submissions.

DGA Ltd

55 Monmouth Street, London WC2H 9DG
tel 020-7240 9992
email assistant@davidgodwinassociates.co.uk
website www.davidgodwinassociates.com
Directors David Godwin, Heather Godwin

Literary fiction and general non-fiction. No reading fee; send MS with synopsis and cover letter to sebastiangodwin@davidgodwinassociates.co.uk. Founded 1995.

DHH Literary Agency

23–25 Cecil Court, London WC2N 4EZ
tel 0207-836 7376
email submission@dhhliteraryagency.com
website www.dhhliteraryagency.com

Fiction, women's commercial fiction, crime and literary fiction. Non-fiction special interests include history, science, cookery and humour. Also children's fiction and non-fiction. No plays or scripts, poetry or short stories. Send informative preliminary email with first three chapters and synopsis. No reading fee. Will suggest editorial revisions where appropriate. New authors welcome. Founded 2008.

Diamond Kahn & Woods Literary Agency

Top Floor, 66 Onslow Gardens, London N10 3JX
tel 020-3514 6544
email info@dkwlitagency.co.uk
email submissions.ella@dkwlitagency.co.uk
email submissions.bryony@dkwlitagency.co.uk
website www.dkwlitagency.co.uk
Directors Ella Diamond Kahn, Bryony Woods

Accessible literary and commercial fiction (including all major genres) and non-fiction for adults; and children's, young adult and crossover fiction (home 15%, US/translation 20%). Interested in new writers. No reading fee, email submissions only. Send three chapters and synopsis to one agent only. See website for further details on agents, their areas of interest and submission guidelines.

Clients include Vanessa Curtis, Virginia Macgregor, S.E. Lister, Chris Lloyd, Nicole Burstein, David Owen, Ishbelle Bee, L.H. Johnson, Samantha Collett, Sharon Gosling, Sylvia Bishop.

Elise Dillsworth Agency

9 Grosvenor Road, Muswell Hill, London N10 2DR
email submissions@elisedillsworthagency.com
website www.elisedillsworthagency.com
Owner/Literary Agent Elise Dillsworth

Represents literary and commercial fiction and non-fiction in the area of memoir, biography, travel and cookery, with a keen aim to reflect writing that is international (home 15%, overseas 20%). Does not represent science fiction, fantasy or children's books. Send preliminary letter, synopsis and first three chapters (or approximately 50 pages). Postal and email submissions accepted. See website for full submission guidelines.

Authors include Zoe Adjonyoh, Robert Antoni, Vanessa Bolosier, Anthony Joseph, Oonya Kempadoo, Irenosen Okojie, Yewande Omotoso, Saima Mir and Minoli Salgado. Founded 2012.

Robert Dudley Agency

135A Bridge Street, Ashford, Kent TN25 5DP
tel 07879 426574
email info@robertdudleyagency.co.uk
website www.robertdudleyagency.co.uk
Proprietor Robert Dudley

Non-fiction only. Specialises in history, biography, sport, management, politics, military history, current affairs (home 15%, overseas 20%; film/TV/radio 20%). No reading fee. Will suggest revision. Email submissions preferred. All material sent at owner's risk. No MSS returned without sae.

Authors include Nigel Barlow, Steve Biko, Michael Broers, Prit Buttar, Ian Gardner, David Hanrahan, Halik Kochanski, Mungo Melvin, Richard Ogorkiewicz, Chris Parry, Tim Phillips, Brian Holden Reid, Chris Sidwells, Martyn Whittock, Dan Wilson. Founded 2000.

Toby Eady Associates Ltd

3rd Floor, 9 Orme Court, London W2 4RL
tel 020-7792 0092
website www.tobyeadyassociates.co.uk
Contact Toby Eady

Fiction and non-fiction (home 15%, overseas/film/TV 20%). Special interests: China, Middle East, Africa, India. No film/TV scripts or poetry. Approach by personal recommendation. Send submissions to submissions@tobyeadyassociates.co.uk.

Clients include Nada Awar Jarrar, Sister Wendy Beckett, Jason Burke, Mark Burnell, John Carey, Tim Clissold, Bernard Cornwell, Yasmin Crowther, Yu Dan, Janet Davey, Shereen El Feki, Gavin Esler, Fadia Faqir, Ching-He Huang, Susan Lewis, Diane Wei Liang, Julia Lovell, Francesca Marciano, Patrick Marnham, Richard Lloyd Parry, Deborah Scroggins, Samia Serageldin, Rachel Seiffert, John Stubbs, Zhu Wen, Alison Wong, Fan Wu, Xinran Xue. Estates of Peter Cheyney, Ted Lewis, Margaret Powell, Mary Wesley. Founded 1968.

Eddison Pearson Ltd*

West Hill House, 6 Swains Lane, London N6 6QS
tel 020-7700 7763
email info@eddisonpearson.com
website www.eddisonpearson.com
Contact Clare Pearson

Children's and young adult books, fiction and non-fiction, poetry (home 10%, overseas 15–20%). Small, personally run agency. Enquiries and submissions by email only; email for up-to-date submission guidelines by return. No reading fee. May suggest revision where appropriate.

Authors include Valerie Bloom, Sue Heap, Caroline Lawrence, Robert Muchamore.

Edwards Fuglewicz*

49 Great Ormond Street, London WC1N 3HZ
tel 020-7405 6725
Partners Ros Edwards, Helenka Fuglewicz

Literary and commercial fiction (but no children's fiction, science fiction or horror); non-fiction: biography, history and narrative non-fiction (including animal stories), (home 15%, USA/translation 20%). No email submissions. Founded 1996.

Faith Evans Associates*

27 Park Avenue North, London N8 7RU
tel 020-8340 9920
email faith@faith-evans.co.uk

Small agency (home 15%, overseas 20%). Co-agents in most countries. List full. No phone calls or submissions.

Authors include Melissa Benn, Eleanor Bron, Midge Gillies, Ed Glinert, Vesna Goldsworthy, Jim Kelly, Helena Kennedy, Tom Paulin, Sheila Rowbotham, Harriet Walter, Elizabeth Wilson, and the estates of Madeleine Bourdouxhe and Lorna Sage. Founded 1987.

Frank Fahy

129 Delwood Close, Castleknock, Dublin 15, Republic of Ireland
tel +353 (0)86 2269330
email frank.fahy0@gmail.com
website www.frank-fahy.com
Agent Frank Fahy

Adult and children's fiction and non-fiction (home 15%, overseas 20%). *Authors* include Sheila Agnew, Dr Frances Fahy, Amy Lynch, Barnaby Newbolt, Dr Henrike Rau, Susan Weir.

Janet Fillingham Associates

52 Lowther Road, London SW13 9NU
tel 020-8748 5594
website www.janetfillingham.com
Agents Janet Fillingham, Kate Weston

Film, TV and theatre only (home 15%, overseas 15–20%). No books. Strictly no unsolicited MSS; professional recommendation required. Founded 1992.

Film Rights Ltd

11 Pandora Road, London NW6 1TS
tel 020-8001 3040
email information@filmrights.ltd.uk
website www.filmrights.ltd.uk
Directors Brendan Davis, Joan Potts

Theatre, films, TV and sound broadcasting (home 10%, overseas 15%). No reading fee. Represented in USA and abroad. Founded 1932.

Laurence Fitch Ltd

(incorporating The London Play Company 1922)
11 Pandora Road, London NW6 1TS
tel 020-8001 3040
email information@laurencefitch.com
website www.laurencefitch.com
Directors F.H.L. Fitch, Joan Potts, Brendan Davis

Film and TV (home 10%, overseas 15%).

Authors include Carlo Ardito, John Chapman, Peter Coke, Ray Cooney OBE, Dave Freeman, John Graham, Robin Hawdon, Jeremy Lloyd (plays), Dawn Lowe-Watson, Glyn Robbins, Edward Taylor and the estate of Dodie Smith.

Fox & Howard Literary Agency*

39 Eland Road, London SW11 5JX
tel 020-7223 9452
email fandhagency@googlemail.com
website www.foxandhoward.co.uk
Partners Chelsey Fox, Charlotte Howard

General non-fiction: biography, history and popular culture, reference, business, mind, body & spirit, health and personal development, popular psychology (home 15%, overseas 20%). Check website for submission details. Founded 1992.

Fox Mason Ltd*

36–38 Glasshouse Street, London W1B 5DL
tel 020-7287 0972
email info@foxmason.com
website www.foxmason.com
Director Ben Mason

Literary and commercial fiction and narrative non-fiction (home 15%, overseas 20%) for worldwide exploitation. Submissions via website only. Clients include Sinclair Mckay, Nadifa Mohamed, Lynn Shepherd, Jacques Strauss, Kate Tempest, Robert Thorogood, Levison Wood. Established 2010.

FRA*

(formerly Futerman, Rose & Associates)
91 St Leonards Road, London SW14 7BL
tel 020-8255 7755
email enquiries@futermanrose.co.uk
website www.futermanrose.co.uk
Contacts Guy Rose, Alexandra Groom

Fiction, biography, show business, current affairs, teen fiction and scripts for TV and film. No children's, science fiction or fantasy. No unsolicited MSS. Send brief résumé, synopsis, first 20pp and sae.

Clients include Lolicia Aitken, Jill Anderson, Larry Barker, Nick Battle, Christian Piers Betley, Kevin Clarke, Richard Digance, Iain Duncan Smith, Sir Martin Ewans, John French, Susan George, Paul Hendy, Michael Kelly, Sara Khan, Keith R. Lindsay, Eric MacInnes, Paul Marx, Tony McMahon, Vartan Melkonian, Joseph Miller, Max Morgan-Witts, Judge Chris Nicholson, Mary O'Hara, Ciaran O'Keeffe, Antonia Owen, Tom Owen, Zoe Paphitis, Liz Rettig, Kenneth G. Ross, Peter Sallis, Paul Stinchcombe QC, Gordon Thomas, Bill Tidy, Toyah Willcox, Simon Woodham, Allen Zeleski. Founded 1984.

Fraser Ross Associates

6 Wellington Place, Edinburgh EH6 7EQ
tel 0131 553 2759, 0131 657 4412
email lindsey.fraser@tiscali.co.uk
email kjross@tiscali.co.uk
website www.fraserross.co.uk
Partners Lindsey Fraser, Kathryn Ross

Writing and illustration for children's books, fiction and non-fiction for adults. See website for client list and submission guidelines. Submissions can be emailed to fraserrossassociates@gmail.com. Founded 2002.

Furniss Lawton*

94 Strand on the Green, London W4 3NN
tel 020-8987 6804
email info@furnisslawton.co.uk
website furnisslawton.co.uk
Agents Eugenie Furniss, Rowan Lawton, Rory Scarfe

Fiction: general commercial, thrillers, historical, crime, suspense, women's fiction, literary and young adult. Non-fiction: biography, memoir, cookery, business, history, popular science psychology. Submissions by email only to info@furnisslawton.co.uk. Home 15%, overseas 20%.

Authors include Kevin Brooks, Julian Clary, Lindsey Kelk, Raymond Khoury, Tom Knox, Piers Morgan, Tasmina Perry, Matthew Reilly, Alexandra Shulman.

Jüri Gabriel

35 Camberwell Grove, London SE5 8JA
tel 020-7703 6186
email juri@jurigabriel.com

Quality fiction and non-fiction (i.e. anything that shows wit and intelligence); radio, TV and film, but selling these rights only in existing works by existing clients (home 10%, overseas 20%, performance rights 10%). Submit three sample chapters plus a 1–2 page synopsis and sae in the first instance. Will suggest revision where appropriate. No short stories, articles, verse or books for children. No reading fee. Jüri Gabriel was the chairman of Dedalus (publishers) for nearly 30 years.

Authors include Jack Allen, Nick Bradbury, Tom Clempson, Miriam Dunne, Paul Genney, Pat Gray, Mikka Haugaard, Robert Irwin, Andrew Killeen, 'David Madsen', Richard Mankiewicz, David Miller, John Outram, Philip Roberts, Julian Sayarer, Roger Storey, Jeremy Weingard.

Eric Glass Ltd

25 Ladbroke Crescent, London W11 1PS
tel 020-7229 9500

email eglassltd@aol.com
Director Janet Glass

Full-length MSS only; also theatre, films, and TV. No unsolicited MSS. Founded 1932.

Graham Maw Christie*

37 Highbury Place, London N5 1QP
email enquiries@grahammawchristie.com
website www.grahammawchristie.com
Contacts Jane Graham Maw, Jennifer Christie

General non-fiction: autobiography/memoir, business, web-to-book, humour and gift, food and drink, craft, health, lifestyle, parenting, self-help/how to, popular science/history/culture/reference, TV tie-in. No fiction, children's or poetry. No reading fee. Email submissions only. Will suggest revisions. Also represents ghostwriters. See website for submission guidelines.

Authors include Jane Brocket, Simon Dawson, Julia Deering, Oli Doyle, Cassandra Ellis, Michael Foley, Louise Glazebrook, Leah Hardy, Dr Jessamy Hibberd, Dr Philippa Kaye, Cathryn Kemp, Dannii Martin, Rosie Millard, Lisa Lam, Alex Monroe, James Ramsden, Amanda Riley, Juliet Sear, Jo Usmar, Richard Wilson, Suzi Witt. Founded 2005.

Annette Green Authors' Agency

5 Henwoods Mount, Pembury,
Tunbridge Wells TN2 4BH
tel (01892) 263252
website www.annettegreenagency.co.uk
Partners Annette Green, David Smith

Full-length MSS (home 15%, overseas 20%). Literary and general fiction and non-fiction, popular culture, history, science, teenage fiction. No dramatic scripts, poetry, science fiction or fantasy. No reading fee. Preliminary letter, synopsis, sample chapter and sae essential.

Authors include Andrew Baker, Tim Bradford, Bill Broady, Natasha Carthew, Katherine Clements, Terry Darlington, Elizabeth Haynes, Frances Kay, Claire King, Maria McCann, Adam Macqueen, Ian Marchant, Stephen May, Imogen Robertson, Kirsty Scott, Deborah Swift.

Christine Green Authors' Agent*

2D02, Southbank Technopark, 90 London Road, London SE1 6LN
tel 020-7401 8844
email info@christinegreen.co.uk
website www.christinegreen.co.uk
Contact Christine Green

Literary and commercial fiction, narrative (novelistic) non-fiction. General, young adult, women's, crime and historical fiction welcome, but note no genre sci-fi or fantasy, travelogues, self-help, picture books, scripts or poetry. Commission: home 15%, overseas 20%. Works in conjunction with agencies in Asia, Europe and Scandinavia. No reading fee. Preliminary queries by email welcome. Email submissions only. Founded 1984.

Louise Greenberg Books Ltd*

The End House, Church Crescent, London N3 1BG
tel 020-8349 1179
email louisegreenberg@msn.com

Full-length MSS (home 15%, overseas 20%). Literary fiction and non-fiction. No reading fee. Return postage and sae essential. No telephone enquiries. Founded 1997.

Greene & Heaton Ltd*

37 Goldhawk Road, London W12 8QQ
tel 020-8749 0315
email submissions@greeneheaton.co.uk
email info@greeneheaton.co.uk
website www.greeneheaton.co.uk
Contacts Carol Heaton, Judith Murray, Antony Topping, Nicola Barr, Jamie Coleman, Chris Wellbelove, Claudia Young

Fiction and non-fiction (home 15%, USA/translation 20%). No poetry or original scripts for theatre, film or TV. Email submissions accepted, but no reply guaranteed, or send a covering letter, synopsis and first three chapters with sae and return postage. Handles translation rights directly in all major territories.

Clients include Hugh Aldersey-Williams, Steven Amsterdam, Lisa Ballantyne, Lucy Atkins, Laura Barnett, Elizabeth Buchan, Emma Chapman, Lucy Clarke, Suzannah Dunn, Catherine Dunne, Sabine Durrant, Marcus du Sautoy, Travis Elborough, Hugh Fearnley-Whittingstall, Michael Frayn, Andrea Gillies, Helen Giltrow, Bill Granger, Maeve Haran, Oliver Harris, P.D. James, Anna Krien, M.D. Lachlan, William Leith, Dan Lepard, Ian Leslie, Colette McBeth, James McGee, S.G. MacLean, Thomasina Miers, Lottie Moggach, Carmen Reid, C.J. Sansom, Sarah Waters, Katherine Webb, Kerry Wilkinson, Benjamin Wood, Jackie Wullschlager. *Children's authors* include Helen Craig, Josh Lacey, Lucy Christopher, Viviane Schwarz. Founded 1963.

The Greenhouse Literary Agency

4th Floor, 9 Kingsway, London WC2B 6XF
tel 020-7841 3959
email submissions@greenhouseliterary.com
website www.greenhouseliterary.com
Director Sarah Davies, *UK Agent* Polly Nolan, *US Agent* John Cusick

Specialist children's book agency with a reputation for impressive transatlantic deals. Represents fiction from picture books through to teen/young adult (USA/UK 15%, elsewhere 25%). Represents both UK and Commonwealth (Polly Nolan) and North American (Sarah Davies and John Cusick) authors. No non-fiction. No reading fee. Queries by email only, see website for details.

Authors include Jennifer Bell, Julie Bertagna, Romily Bernard, Caroline Carlson, Sarwat Chadda, Donna Cooner, Harriet Goodwin, Swapna Haddow, Jill Hathaway, Dawn Kurtagich, Lindsey Leavitt, Jon Mayhew, Wendy Mills, Megan Miranda, Sinéad O'Hart, C.J. Omololu, Gavin Puckett, Jeyn Roberts, Erica L. Scheidt, Tess Sharpe, Tricia Springstubb, Julie Sykes, Blythe Woolston, Brenna Yovanoff. Founded 2008.

Gregory & Company Authors' Agents*

3 Barb Mews, London W6 7PA
tel 020-7610 4676
email info@gregoryandcompany.co.uk (general enquiries)
email maryjones@gregoryandcompany.co.uk (submissions)
website www.gregoryandcompany.co.uk
Contacts Jane Gregory (UK, US, film rights), Claire Morris (translation rights), Stephanie Glencross and Mary Jones (editorial), Irene Baldoni (rights assistant), Ruth Murray (assistant)

Fiction (home 15%, USA/translation/radio/film/TV 20%). Special interests (fiction): literary, commercial, women's fiction, crime, suspense and thrillers. Particularly interested in books which will also sell to publishers abroad. No science fiction, fantasy, poetry, academic or children's books, original plays, film or TV scripts (only published books are sold to film and TV). No reading fee. Editorial advice given to own authors. No unsolicited MSS: send preliminary letter with cv, synopsis (3pp maximum), first 10pp of typescript and future writing plans plus return postage. Submissions can also be sent by email but due to volume will only respond if interested in reading more. Represented throughout Europe, Asia and USA. Founded 1987.

David Grossman Literary Agency Ltd

118B Holland Park Avenue, London W11 4UA
tel 020-7221 2770

Full-length MSS (home 10–15%, overseas 20% including foreign agent's commission, performance rights 15%). Works in conjunction with agents in New York, Los Angeles, Europe, Japan. No reading fee but preliminary letter required. No submissions by fax or email. Founded 1976.

Gunn Media

50 Albemarle Street, London W1S 4BD
tel 020-7529 3745
email douglas@gunnmedia.co.uk
Directors Doug Kean, Sarah McFadden

Commercial fiction and non-fiction including literary, thrillers and celebrity autobiographies (home 15%, overseas 20%).

Authors include Mhairi McFarlane, Dr Liam Fox, Paul Burrell, Mill Millington.

Marianne Gunn O'Connor Literary Agency

Morrison Chambers, Suite 17, 32 Nassau Street, Dublin 2, Republic of Ireland
email mgoclitagency@eircom.net
Contact Marianne Gunn O'Connor

Commercial and literary fiction, non-fiction, biography, children's fiction (home 15%, overseas 20%, film/TV 20%). Email enquiry with a half-page outline. Translation rights handled by Vicki Satlow Literary Agency, Milan.

Clients include Patrick McCabe, Cecelia Ahern, Susie Lau aka Stylebubble, Shane Hegarty, Terry Edwards and George Craig, Kathleen McMahon, Kate Kerrigan, Claudia Carroll, Sinead Moriarty, Louise Douglas, Liz Nugent, Emily Gillmor Murphy, Helen Falconer, Kieran Crowley, Noelle Harrison, Christy Lefteri, Julia Kelly, Alison Walsh, Maureen Gaffney, Alan Gilsenan, Chris Binchy, John Lynch, Mike McCormack, Paddy McMahon, David McWilliams.

The Hanbury Agency Ltd, Literary Agents*

28 Moreton Street, London SW1V 2PE
tel 020-7630 6768
email enquiries@hanburyagency.com
website www.hanburyagency.com

Represents general fiction and non-fiction. See website for submission guidelines. Also offers media/PR service to authors.

Authors include George Alagiah, Tom Bergin, Simon Callow, Jimmy Connors, Luke Dormehl, Tim Jarvis, Imran Khan, Roman Krznaric, Judith Lennox, Katie Price, Kate Raworth, Jerry White. The agency has a strong stable of ghostwriters. Founded 1983.

Hardman & Swainson

4 Kelmscott Road, London SW11 6QY
tel 020-7223 5176
email caroline@hardmanswainson.com
email joanna@hardmanswainson.com
email hannah@hardmanswainson.com
website www.hardmanswainson.com
Directors Caroline Hardman, Joanna Swainson

Literary and commercial fiction, crime and thiller, women's, accessible literary, YA and older children's fiction. Non-fiction, including memoir, biography, popular science, history, philosophy. No poetry or screenplays (home 15%, US/translation/film/TV 20%). No reading fee. Will work editorially with the author where appropriate. Submissions by email only to submissions@hardmanswainson.com.

Clients include Rebecca Wait, Dinah Jefferies, Abby Clements, Liz Trenow, Vanessa Greene, Michele Gorman, Alastair Gunn, Cathy Bramley, Ali McNamara, Giovanna Fletcher, Liz Trenow, Sara Crowe, Eleanor Wood, Stuart David, Nick Russell-Pavier, Ann Morgan and Prof. Daniel M. Davis. Founded 2012.

Antony Harwood Ltd

103 Walton Street, Oxford OX2 6EB
tel (01865) 559615

email mail@antonyharwood.com
website www.antonyharwood.com
Contacts Antony Harwood, James Macdonald Lockhart, Jo Williamson (children's)

General and genre fiction; general non-fiction (home 15%, overseas 20%). Will suggest revision. No reading fee.

Clients include Amanda Craig, Louise Doughty, Alan Glynn, Peter F. Hamilton, Alan Hollinghurst, A.L. Kennedy, Douglas Kennedy, Dorothy Koomson, Chris Manby, George Monbiot, Garth Nix. Founded 2000.

A.M. Heath & Co. Ltd*

6 Warwick Court, London WC1R 5DJ
tel 020-7242 2811
website www.amheath.com
Contacts Bill Hamilton, Victoria Hobbs, Euan Thorneycroft, Jennifer Custer (foreign rights), Oliver Munson, Julia Churchill (children's)

Full-length MSS. Literary and commercial fiction and non-fiction, children's (home 15%, USA/translation 20%), film/TV (15–20% by agreement). No screenplays, poetry or short stories except for established clients. No reading fee. Digital submission via website.

Clients include David Abulafia, Christopher Andrew, Anita Brookner, Lauren Beukes, Lindsey Davis, Katie Fforde, Conn Iggulden, Cynan Jones, Claire Kendal, Deborah Levy, Marina Lewycka, Sarah Lotz, Hilary Mantel, David Mark, Maggie O'Farrell, Mario Reading, Matt Rudd, Kamila Shamsie, Robert Tombs, Holly Webb, Tim Willocks. Founded 1919.

Rupert Heath Literary Agency*

50 Albemarle Street, London W1S 4BD
tel 020-7060 3395
email emailagency@rupertheath.com
website www.rupertheath.com
Agents Rupert Heath

Fiction: literary, thrillers, crime, historical, general; non-fiction: history, biography and autobiography, science, nature, politics and current affairs, popular culture and the arts (15% UK, 20% overseas, 20% film/TV/dramatic). Visit website before submitting material. Email submissions preferred. International associates worldwide.

Authors include Michael Arnold, Ros Barber, A.K. Benedict, Mark Blake, Andy Bull, Stephen Collishaw, Paddy Docherty, Reni Eddo-Lodge, Dayo Forster, Sarah Govett, Claire Harcup, Martin Lampen, Jo Litchfield, Nina Lyon, Scott Mariani, Lorna Martin, Russell Senior, Merryn Somerset Webb, Robyn Young. Founded 2001.

hhb agency ltd*

6 Warwick Court, London WC1R 5DJ
tel 020-7405 5525
email heather@hhbagency.com
email elly@hhbagency.com
email jack@hhbagency.com
website www.hhbagency.com
Contacts Heather Holden-Brown, Elly James, Jack Munnelly

Non-fiction: journalism, history and politics, contemporary autobiography and biography, books about words, popular culture, entertainment and TV, business, family memoir, food and cookery a speciality. Fiction: commercial and literary, women's, historical and crime. 15%. No reading fee. Founded 2005.

Sophie Hicks Agency

email info@sophiehicksagency.com
website www.sophiehicksagency.com
Agents Sophie Hicks, Sarah Williams

Fiction, non-fiction and children's books (UK/US 15%, translation 20%). No poetry or scripts. Email submissions only, see website for guidelines. No reading fee. Represented in all foreign markets.

Authors include: Sarah Bannan, Herbie Brennan, Paul Burston, Eoin Colfer, DJ Connell, Emerald Fennell, Tristan Gooley, Maunika Gowardhan, Benedict Jacka, James Macmanus, Paddy O'Reilly, @Queen_UK, Danny Scheinmann, Kit Whitfield and Tom Whipple. Founded 2014.

David Higham Associates Ltd*

7th Floor, Waverley House, 7–12 Noel Street, London W1F 8GQ
tel 020-7434 5900
email dha@davidhigham.co.uk
website www.davidhigham.co.uk
Managing Director Anthony Goff, *Books* Veronique Baxter, Georgia Glover, Anthony Goff, Andrew Gordon, Lizzy Kremer, Caroline Walsh, *Foreign Rights* Alice Howe, *Film/TV/Theatre* Nicky Lund, Georgina Ruffhead

Agents for the negotiation of all rights in literary and commercial fiction, general non-fiction in all genres, children's fiction and picture books, plays, film and TV scripts (home 15%, USA/translation 20%, scripts 10%), offering a full service across all media. Represented in all foreign markets either directly or through sub-agents. See website for submissions policy. No reading fee.

Clients include literary prize winners: J.M. Coetzee, Tim Winton, Penelope Lively, Alice Sebold, Naomi Alderman; best-selling authors: Jane Green, Alexander McCall Smith, Carole Matthews; eminent estates: Graham Greene, Dylan Thomas, John Wyndham; historians: Paul Kennedy, Felipe Fernandez-Armesto; food writers: Claudia Roden, Simon Hopkinson, Rachel Khoo; popular science: John Gribbin; current affairs: John Pilger, Owen Jones, Peter Oborne; biographers: Hilary Spurling, Victoria Glendinning; popular narrative: Lynne Truss; and performers: Stephen Fry, Joanna Lumley, Hugh Laurie. The children's list features Roald Dahl,

Jacqueline Wilson, Lauren Child and Michael Morpurgo. Founded 1935.

Vanessa Holt Ltd*

59 Crescent Road, Leigh-on-Sea, Essex SS9 2PF
tel (01702) 473787
email v.holt791@btinternet.com

General fiction and non-fiction (home 15%, overseas 20%, TV/film/radio 15%). Works in conjunction with foreign agencies in all markets. No reading fee. No unsolicited MSS and submissions preferred by arrangement. No overseas submissions. Founded 1989.

Valerie Hoskins Associates Ltd

20 Charlotte Street, London W1T 2NA
tel 020-7637 4490
email vha@vhassociates.co.uk
website www.vhassociates.co.uk
Proprietor Valerie Hoskins, *Agent* Rebecca Watson

Film, TV and radio; specialises in animation (home 12.5%, overseas max. 20%). No unsolicited MSS; preliminary letter essential. No reading fee, but sae essential. Works in conjunction with US agents.

Tanja Howarth Literary Agency

19 New Row, London WC2N 4LA
tel 020-7240 5553
email tanja.howarth@btinternet.com

General fiction and non-fiction, thrillers, contemporary and historical novels (home 15%, USA/translation 20%). No unsolicited MSS, no submissions by email. No reading fee. Specialists in handling German translation rights for Verlag Kiepenheuer & Witsch, Hoffmann & Campe Verlag, AVA-international and others.

Clients include Sebastian Fitzek, Markus Heitz, Frank Schaetzing, Patrick Sueskind, Ferdinand von Schirach, and the estate of Heinrich Boell. English authors represented are Trevor Hoyle, Tom Callaghan and the estate of Zoe Barnes. Founded 1970.

Clare Hulton Literary Agency*

email info@clarehulton.co.uk
website www.clarehulton.com
Director Clare Hulton

Specialises in non-fiction especially cookery and lifestyle, pop culture, music, humour, television tie-ins, popular philosophy, self-help, commercial non-fiction, history and memoir. Non-fiction submissions consisting of a synopsis and sample chapter should be sent by email. Does not accept unsolicited fiction, YA or children's proposals. Founded 2012.

IMG UK Ltd

OBL, One Burlington Lane, London W4 2TH
tel 020-8233 5000
email sarah.wooldridge@img.com
Literary Director Sarah Wooldridge

Celebrity books, sports-related books, non-fiction and how-to business books (home 15%, USA 20%, elsewhere 25%). No theatre, fiction, children's, academic or poetry. No emails. No reading fee.

Authors include Sir Steve Redgrave, Michael Johnson, Colin Montgomerie, John McEnroe, Katherine Grainger, Ken Brown, Nicole Cooke, Dave Aldred. Founded 1960.

Independent Talent Group Ltd

Oxford House, 76 Oxford Street, London W1D 1BS
tel 020-7636 6565
website www.independenttalent.com
Directors Duncan Heath, Susan Rodgers, Lyndsey Posner, Sally Long-Innes, Paul Lyon-Maris *Literary Agents* Susan Rodgers, Jessica Sykes, Catherine King, Greg Hunt, Hugo Young, Michael McCoy, Duncan Heath, Paul Lyon-Maris, Laura Rourke

Specialises in scripts for film, theatre, TV, radio (home 10%, overseas 10%).

Shelley Instone Literary Agency

56 Queens Road, London SW14 8PJ
tel 020-8876 8209
email info@shelleyinstoneliteraryagency.co.uk
website www.shelleyinstoneliteraryagency.co.uk
Director Shelley Instone

Represents the voices of established and debut authors in adult fiction, children's fiction and non-fiction. Works in conjunction with rights specialist Louisa Pritchard and the Knight Hall Agency for TV and film. Specialist area is in children's from junior fiction (5–9) to middle grade (9–12). Also YA and NA (13+). Commission: home 15%, overseas 20%. See website for submission guidelines.

Authors include Ciara Hegarty and Sally Poyton.

Intercontinental Literary Agency Ltd*

Centric House, 390–391 Strand, London WC2R 0LT
tel 020-7379 6611
email ila@ila-agency.co.uk
website www.ila-agency.co.uk
Contacts Nicki Kennedy, Sam Edenborough, Mary Esdaile, Clementine Gaisman, Katherine West, Jenny Robson

Represents translation rights only. Founded 1965.

Janklow & Nesbit (UK) Ltd*

13a Hillgate Street, London W8 7SP
tel 020-7243 2975
email submissions@janklow.co.uk
website www.janklowandnesbit.co.uk
Agents Will Francis, Rebecca Carter, Claire Conrad, Hellie Ogden, Jessie Botterill, *Translation rights:* Rebecca Folland

Commercial and literary fiction and non-fiction. No poetry, plays, film/TV scripts. No reading fee. Send informative covering letter with full outline (non-fiction), synopsis and first three sample chapters (fiction) by email to submissions@janklow.co.uk. US rights handled by Janklow & Nesbit Associates in New York. Founded 2000.

JFL Agency Ltd

48 Charlotte Street, London W1T 2NS
tel 020-3137 8182
email agents@jflagency.com
website www.jflagency.com
Agents Alison Finch, Dominic Lord, Gary Wild

TV, radio, film, theatre (10%). No novels, short stories or poetry. Initial contact by preliminary email; do not send scripts in the first instance. See website for further information.

Clients include Humphrey Barclay, Claire Bennett, Tim Brooke-Taylor, Ian Brown, Grant Cathro, Bill Dare, Ed Dyson, Phil Ford, Rob Gittins, Wayne Jackman, Jane Marlow, Caimh McDonnell, Giles New and Keiron Self, Jim Pullin, David Semple, James Serafinowicz, Pete Sinclair, Paul Smith, Fraser Steele.

Johnson & Alcock Ltd*

Clerkenwell House, 45–47 Clerkenwell Green, London EC1R 0HT
tel 020-7251 0125
website www.johnsonandalcock.co.uk
Contacts Michael Alcock, Andrew Hewson, Anna Power, Ed Wilson

All types of commercial and literary fiction, and general non-fiction (home 15%, USA/translation/film 20%). Young adult and children's fiction (ages 9+). No poetry, screenplays or board/picture books.

For fiction and non-fiction, send first three chapters, full synopsis and brief covering letter with details of writing experience. For email submission guidelines see website. No reading fee but return postage essential. Founded 1956.

Robin Jones Literary Agency

6B Marmora Road, London SE22 0RX
tel 020-8693 6062
email robijones@gmail.com
Director Robin Jones

Adult fiction and non-fiction: literary and commercial. Russian language, and themed fiction and non-fiction especially welcomed. Full MSS required though 50pp sample, synopsis and cover letter detailing writing experience sufficient in first instance. Works with co-agents in some territories and for some dramatic, film and TV rights.

Clients include Philip Lymbery, Waqas Ahmed, D.C. Pae, Sir David Madden, Michael Madden, Ashley Stokes, Nasrin Alavi, Paul Jackson. (Home 15%, overseas 20%). No reading fee. Co-founder of literary publisher Unthank Books (www.unthankbooks.com), Unthank School of Writing (www.unthankschool.com) and Unthank Literary Festival (www.unlitfestival.com). Founded 2007.

Tibor Jones & Associates

Unit 12B, Piano House, 9 Brighton Terrace, London SW9 8DJ
tel 020-7733 0555
email enquiries@tiborjones.com
website www.tiborjones.com
Director Kevin Conroy Scott

Literary fiction and non-fiction, category fiction, music autobiographies and biographies. Send first 5pp, synopsis and covering letter via email.

Authors include V.W. Adams, Sulaiman Smy Addonia, Sophia Al-Maria, Sarah Bilston, Brian Chikwava, Jason Cowley, Lewis Crofts, Peter Culshaw, Kevin Cummins, Alice de Smith, Colin Grant, Matthew Green, Oscar Guardiola-Rivera, Hala Jaber, Rem Koolhaas, Denise Meredith, Hans Ulrich Obrist, Tali Sharot, Brian Schofield, Christopher Winn, Tod Wodicka. Founded 2007.

Jane Judd Literary Agency*

18 Belitha Villas, London N1 1PD
tel 020-7607 0273
website www.janejudd.com

General non-fiction and fiction (home 10%, overseas 20%). Special interests: women's fiction, historical fiction, narrative non-fiction and biography. No short stories, film/TV scripts, poetry or plays. No reading fee, but preliminary letter with synopsis, first chapter and sae essential. Works with agents in the US and most foreign countries. Founded 1986.

Michelle Kass Associates Ltd*

85 Charing Cross Road, London WC2H 0AA
tel 020-7439 1624
Proprietor Michelle Kass

Full-length MSS. Literary fiction (home 10%, overseas 15–20%) and scripts for film and TV. Works with agents around the world. No reading fee. No email submissions. No unsolicited material, phone in first instance. Founded 1991.

Keane Kataria Literary Agency

1 Queen Square, Bath BA1 2HA
email info@keanekataria.co.uk
website www.keanekataria.co.uk
Partners Sara Keane, Kiran Kataria

Boutique agency welcoming quality commercial fiction, accessible literary fiction, non-fiction, short stories (home 15%, USA/translation 20%). No children's, science fiction/fantasy, academic, poetry, plays, film or TV scripts. Submissions via email only: covering email, synopsis and first three chapters. See website for further submission guidelines. No reading fee. Founded 2014.

Frances Kelly Agency*

111 Clifton Road, Kingston-upon-Thames, Surrey KT2 6PL
tel 020-8549 7830

Full-length MSS. Non-fiction: general and academic, reference and professional books, all subjects (home 10%, overseas 20%, TV/radio 10%). No reading fee, but no unsolicited MSS; preliminary letter with synopsis, cv and return postage essential. Founded 1978.

Knight Features Ltd

20 Crescent Grove, London SW4 7AH
tel 020-7622 1467
email info@knightfeatures.co.uk
website www.knightfeatures.com
Contacts Gaby Martin, Sam Ferris

Biography, history, humour and puzzles. No poetry, cookery or travel. No fiction. No unsolicited MSS. Send letter accompanied by synopsis, samples and sae.

Clients include David J. Bodycombe, Frank Dickens, Gray Jolliffe, Mike Shackleton, Barbara Minto. Founded 1985.

Knight Hall Agency Ltd

Lower Ground Floor, 7 Mallow Street, London EC1Y 8RQ
tel 020-3397 2901
email office@knighthallagency.com
website www.knighthallagency.com
Contacts Charlotte Knight, Martin Knight, Emily Hayward-Whitlock, Tanya Tillett, Katie Langridge

Specialises in writers for stage, screen and radio but also deals in TV and film rights in novels and non-fiction (home 10%, overseas 15%). No reading fee.

Clients include Simon Beaufoy, Jeremy Brock, Liz Lochhead, Tim Lott, Martin McDonagh, Simon Nye, Ol Parker, Lucy Prebble, Philip Ridley, Laura Wade. Founded 1997.

LAW (Lucas Alexander Whitley Ltd)*

14 Vernon Street, London W14 0RJ
tel 020-7471 7900
website www.lawagency.co.uk
Contacts Adult: Mark Lucas, Julian Alexander, Araminta Whitley, Alice Saunders, Peta Nightingale, Ben Clark, Jennifer Hunt; Children's: Philippa Milnes-Smith, Elizabeth Briggs

Full-length commercial and literary fiction, non-fiction, fantasy, young adult and children's books (home 15%, USA/ translation 20%). No plays, poetry or textbooks. Film, TV and stage handled for established clients only. Represented in all markets. Unsolicited MSS considered. See website for further information about the clients and genres represented and essential information on submissions. No reading fee. Founded 1996.

LBA Books*

91 Great Russell Street, London WC1B 3PS
tel 020-7637 1234
email info@lbabooks.com
website www.lbabooks.com
Directors Luigi Bonomi, Amanda Preston

Fiction and non-fiction (home 15%, overseas 20%). Keen to find new authors and help them develop their careers. Fiction: commercial and literary fiction, thrillers, crime, psychological suspense, young adult, children's, women's fiction, fantasy. Non-fiction: history, science, parenting, lifestyle, cookery, memoir, TV tie-in. No poetry, short stories or screenplays. Send preliminary letter, synopsis and first three chapters. No reading fee. Works with foreign agencies and has links with film and TV production companies including Endemol, Tiger Aspect, BBC Worldwide, HatTrick, Plum Pictures, Zodiak and Sega.

Authors include Will Adams, Sarah Alderson, Kirstie Allsopp, Professors Anthony Barnosky & Liz Hadley, Virginia Bergin, J.T. Brannan, Diana Bretherick, Amanda Brooke, Fern Britton, Jo Carnegie, Rebecca Cobb, Gennaro Contaldo, Ping Coombes, Josephine Cox, Dean Crawford, Mason Cross, Matthew Dunn, Judy Finnigan, Nick Foulkes, Tom Fox, David Gibbins, Rachel Hamilton, Richard Hammond, Helen Hancocks, Matt Hilton, Eva Holland, Honey & Co., John Humphrys, Annabel Kantaria, Simon Kernick, Victoria Lamb, John Lucas, Rachael Lucas, Colin McDowell, Richard Madeley, Lucy Mangan, Lucinda Martin, James May, Julie Mayhew, Gavin Menzies, Dreda Say Mitchell, Seth Patrick, Ivor Peters, Gervase Phinn, Louisa Reid, Alice Roberts, Mike Rossiter, Cate Sampson, Karen Swan, Prof. Bryan Sykes, Alan Titchmarsh, Phil Vickery, Sir Terry Wogan, Laura Wood, Emma Yarlett. Founded 2005.

Susanna Lea Associates Ltd*

34 Lexington Street, London W1F 0LH
tel 020-7287 7757
email uk-submission@susannalea.com
website www.susannaleaassociates.com
Directors Susanna Lea, Kerry Glencorse

General fiction and non-fiction. No plays, screenplays or poetry. Send query letter, brief synopsis, the first three chapters and/or proposal via the website. Established in Paris 2000; New York 2004; London 2008.

Barbara Levy Literary Agency*

64 Greenhill, Hampstead High Street, London NW3 5TZ
tel 020-7435 9046
email blevysubmissions@gmail.com
Director Barbara Levy, *Associate* John Selby (solicitor)

Full-length MSS. Fiction and general non-fiction (home 15%, overseas by arrangement). Film and TV rights for existing clients only. No reading fee, but preliminary letter with synopsis and sae essential, or by email. Translation rights handled by the Buckman Agency; works in conjunction with US agents. Founded 1986.

Limelight Celebrity Management Ltd*

10 Filmer Mews, 75 Filmer Road, London SW6 7JF
tel 020-7384 9950

email mail@limelightmanagement.com
website www.limelightmanagement.com
Contacts Fiona Lindsay, Roz Ellman

Full-length and short MSS. Food, wine, health, crafts, gardening, interior design, literary fiction, biography, travel, history, women's fiction, crime, fashion, business, politics (home 15%, overseas 20%), TV and radio rights (10–20%); will suggest revision where appropriate. No reading fee. Founded 1991.

Lindsay Literary Agency

East Worldham House, Alton, Hants GU34 3AT
tel (01420) 83143
email info@lindsayliteraryagency.co.uk
website www.lindsayliteraryagency.co.uk
Directors Becky Bagnell, Kate Holroyd Smith

Children's books, middle grade, teen/YA, picture books. No reading fee. Will suggest revision.

Authors include Pamela Butchart, Sam Gayton, Ruth Hatfield, Peter Jones, Mike Lancaster, Rachel Valentine. Founded 2008.

Christopher Little Literary Agency LLP*

(in association with Curtis Brown Group Ltd))
48 Walham Grove, London SW6 1QR
tel 020-7736 4455
email info@christopherlittle.net
website www.christopherlittle.net
Contact Christopher Little

Commercial and literary full-length fiction and non-fiction (home 15%; USA, Canada, translation, audio, motion picture 20%). No poetry, plays, science fiction, fantasy, textbooks, illustrated children's or short stories. Film scripts for established clients only. No unsolicited submissions.

Authors include Paul Bajoria, Ginny Elliot MBE, Janet Gleeson, Cathy Hopkins, Carol Hughes, General Mike Jackson (Sir), Oskar Cox Jensen, Philip Kazan, Lise Kristensen, Alastair MacNeill, Pippa Mattinson, Robert Mawson, Bruce McCabe, Kate McCann, Haydn Middleton, Shiromi Pinto, A.J. Quinnell, Robert Radcliffe, Darren Shan, Wladyslaw Szpilman, Pip Vaughan-Hughes, John Watson, Anne Zouroudi. Founded 1979.

London Independent Books

26 Chalcot Crescent, London NW1 8YD
tel 020-7722 7160
Proprietor Carolyn Whitaker

Specialises in commercial, fantasy and teenage fiction. Full-length MSS (home 15%, overseas 20%). Will suggest revision of promising MSS. No reading fee.

Authors include Alex Bell, John Donaghue, Tim Mackintosh-Smith, Glenn Mitchell, Connie Monk, Richard Morgan, Steve Mosby, Dan Smith, Chris Wooding. Founded 1971.

Andrew Lownie Literary Agency*

36 Great Smith Street, London SW1P 3BU
tel 020-7222 7574
email lownie@globalnet.co.uk
email david.haviland@andrewlownie.co.uk
website www.andrewlownie.co.uk
Director Andrew Lownie, *Fiction agent* David Haviland

Handles fiction and non-fiction, working in association with a range of sub-agents around the world. Non-fiction submissions should include synopsis, author profile, chapter summaries and sample material. Fiction submissions should comprise synopsis and three chapters. The non-fiction list includes biography, history, reference, current affairs and packaging journalists and celebrities for the book market (home and US 15%, translation and film 20%). Recent sales include the memoirs of Kerry Katona, *Made in Chelsea*'s Spencer Matthews and *The Only Way is Essex*'s Sam Faiers and Kirk Norcross, and Marina Chapman's *The Girl With No Name.* Represents inspirational memoirs (Cathy Glass, Casey Watson) and ghostwriters. Also handles commercial fiction in all genres, particularly crime, thrillers and historical. No reading fee. Will suggest revision.

Authors include Richard Aldrich, Juliet Barker, the Joyce Cary estate, Roger Crowley, Tom Devine, Duncan Falconer, Timothy Good, David Hasselhoff, John Hatcher, Kris Hollington, Robert Hutchinson, Lawrence James, Ian Knight, Frank Ledwidge, Christopher Lloyd, Sean Longden, the Julian Maclaren-Ross estate, Norma Major, Neil McKenna, Sean McMeekin, Tim Newark, Linda Porter, Martin Pugh, Sian Rees, David Roberts, Desmond Seward, David Stafford, Daniel Tammet, Peter Thompson, Mei Trow, Christian Wolmar; *The Oxford Classical Dictionary*, *The Cambridge Guide to Literature in English*. Founded 1988.

Lucas Alexander Whitley – see LAW (Lucas Alexander Whitley Ltd)

Luithlen Agency

88 Holmfield Road, Leicester LE2 1SB
tel 0116 273 8863
website www.luithlenagency.com
Agents Jennifer Luithlen, Penny Luithlen

Children's fiction, all ages to YA (home 15%, overseas 20%), performance rights (15%). See website for submission information. Founded 1986.

Lutyens & Rubinstein*

21 Kensington Park Road, London W11 2EU
tel 020-7792 4855
email submissions@lutyensrubinstein.co.uk
website www.lutyensrubinstein.co.uk
Contacts Sarah Lutyens, Felicity Rubinstein, Jane Finigan

Fiction and non-fiction, commercial and literary (home 15%, overseas 20%). Send material by email with a covering letter and short synopsis.

Submissions not accepted by hand or by post. Founded 1993.

David Luxton Associates Ltd

23 Hillcourt Avenue, London N12 8EY
website www.davidluxtonassociates.co.uk

Agency specialising in non-fiction especially sport, memoir, politics and history. Also handles rights for Judith Murdoch Literary Agency, Eve White Literary Agency and Graham Maw Christie. Unable to accept unsolicited submissions. Please consult website for submission guidelines.

Duncan McAra

28 Beresford Gardens, Edinburgh EH5 3ES
tel 0131 552 1558
email duncanmcara@mac.com

Literary fiction; non-fiction: art, architecture, archaeology, biography, military, Scottish, travel (home 15%, USA/translation 20%). Preliminary letter with sae essential. No reading fee. Member of the Association of Scottish Literary Agents. Founded 1988.

Eunice McMullen Ltd

Low Ibbotsholme Cottage, Off Bridge Lane, Troutbeck Bridge, Windermere, Cumbria LA23 1HU
tel (01539) 448551
email eunicemcmullen@totalise.co.uk
website www.eunicemcmullen.co.uk
Director Eunice McMullen

All types of children's fiction, particularly picture books and older fiction (home 15%, overseas 15%). No unsolicited scripts. Telephone or email enquiries only. Founded 1992.

Authors include Margaret Chamberlain, Sam Childs, Caroline Jayne Church, Ross Collins, Emma Dodd, Charles Fuge, Cally Johnson Isaacs, Sarah Massini, David Melling, Angela McAllister, Angie Sage, Gillian Shields. Founded 1992.

Andrew Mann Ltd*

United House, North Road, London N7 9DP
email info@andrewmann.co.uk
website www.andrewmann.co.uk
Contacts Tina Betts, Louise Burns

MSS for fiction/non-fiction. Preferences are for upmarket commercial and literary fiction, women's commercial fiction, crime and thrillers, particularly psychological thrillers, historical fiction and narrative non-fiction. Also handles children's fiction (home 15%, USA/Europe 20%). Email submissions only, first three chapters. Associated with agents worldwide. No reading fee. See submission guidelines on website before submitting work. Founded 1968.

Marjacq Scripts*

Box 412, 19–21 Crawford Street, London W1H 1PJ
tel 020-7935 9499
email enquiries@marjacq.com
website www.marjacq.com
Contact Philip Patterson (books), Sandra Sawicka (foreign rights), Luke Speed (film/TV)

All full-length MSS (direct 15%, sub-agented 20%), including commercial and literary fiction and non-fiction, crime, thrillers, commercial, women's fiction, graphic novels, children's, science fiction, history, biography, sport, travel, health. No poetry. No musicals. Send first three chapters with synopsis, preferably by email. May suggest revision. Film and TV rights, screenplays, documentaries: send full script with 1–2pp synopsis/outline. Interested in documentary concepts and will accept proposals from writer/directors: send show reel with script. Sae essential for return of submissions.

Clients include: Richard Asplin, Charles Barker, Sean Bates, Sean Black, C.M. Change, J.J. Connolly, John Connor, Gaelle Denis, Stephen Duggan, Katie Ellwood, Fern Elsdon-Baker, Campbell X, Helen FitzGerald, James Follett, Christopher Goffard, Jasper Graham, Stephen Graham, Jonny Grant, Ben Hatch, Rebecca Hobbs, Will Hodgkinson, SJI Holliday, Jenefer Hughes, Ros Jay, Greg Jonkatys, Anthony Lappe, E.A. Larkin, Damien Lewis, Ed Lilly, Howard Linskey, Stuart MacBride, George Markstein (estate), Ben Marlow, Graham Oakley, Greg Read, Jack Sheffield, Brian Sibley, Will Simpson, William Sutton, Michael Taylor, Jaz Towner, Toby Wagstaff, Andy Walker, R.D. Wingfield (estate), Tom Vater, Luca Veste, Matt Winn, Tom Winship, Tom Wood, M.P. Wright. Founded 1974.

The Marsh Agency Ltd*

50 Albemarle Street, London W1S 4BD
tel 020-7493 4361
website www.marsh-agency.co.uk

Founded as international rights specialists for British, American and Canadian agencies. Expanded to act as agents to handle fiction and non-fiction, specialising in authors with international potential (home 15%, overseas/TV/film 20%). See website for agent details and submission guidelines. No reading fee. Unsolicited submissions considered. No poetry, plays, scripts, children's or picture books. Founded 1994, incorporating Paterson Marsh Ltd and Campbell, Thomson and McLaughlin Ltd as of April 2011.

Blanche Marvin Agency

21A St John's Wood High Street, Flat 4, London NW8 7NG
tel 020-7722 2313
Directors Blanche Marvin, Niki Marvin

Books, plays, performance rights. Authors include Christopher Bond, Mike Dorrell. Does not accept any unsolicited material.

MBA Literary and Script Agents Ltd*

62 Grafton Way, London W1T 5DW
tel 020-7387 2076

website www.mbalit.co.uk
Book agents Diana Tyler, Laura Longrigg, David Riding, Susan Smith, Sophie Gorell Barnes, *Film/TV/Radio/Theatre agent* Diana Tyler

Fiction and non-fiction, children's books (home 15%, overseas 20%) and TV, film, radio and theatre scripts (TV/theatre/radio 10%, films 15%). See website for submission guidelines. Works in conjunction with agents in most countries. UK representative for Harlequin.

Clients include Sita Brahmachari, Jeffrey Caine, Neil Forsyth, Michele Hanson, estate of B.S. Johnson, Julian Jones, Robert Jones, estate of Anne McCaffrey, Clare Morrall, Stef Penney, estate of Peter Tinniswood, Cathy Woodman. Founded 1971.

Madeleine Milburn Ltd Literary, TV & Film Agency*

10 Shepherd Market, Mayfair, London W1J 7QF
tel 020-7499 7550
email submissions@madeleinemilburn.com
website www.mmla.co.uk
Director Madeleine Milburn, *Assistant* Cara Lee Simpson, *Rights Executive* Rachael Sharples

Represents a dynamic and prize-winning range of adult, young adult and children's fiction. Richard and Judy choices, crime, thrillers, suspense, mystery, horror, psychological suspense, women's fiction, love stories, tear-jerkers, romantic comedy, chick lit, romance, women in jeopardy, war, narrative memoir, historical, family drama, saga, relationships, comedy, mainstream fantasy, science fiction, genre-bending and general fiction, American, Irish, Australian and translated fiction. Children's fiction for all ages including 6–8 years, 9–12 years, teen, YA, new adult and books that are read by both children and adults. Also considers narrative non-fiction, history, memoirs, science books, popular psychology, self-help, film/TV tie-ins and picture books.

Represents British, American and international authors. Manages the international careers of writers. Handles all rights in the UK, US and foreign markets including film/TV/radio and digital (home 15%, USA/translation/film 20%). International associates worldwide including Creative Artists Agency (CAA) in LA for film. Enhances author careers in print and digital format. Also manages successful self-published authors.

No longer accepts submissions by post. See submission guidelines and agency news on website. No reading fee. Works editorially with all clients.

Authors include Holly Bourne, Nuala Casey, Simon Cherry, C.J. Daugherty, Jemma Forte, Victoria Fox, Emma Garcia, S.B. Hayes, Sophie Hart, Carolyn Jess-Cooke, Belinda Jones, Fionnuala Kearney, Anouska Knight, Caleb Krisp, Luana Lewis, Dave Lowe, Janet MacLeod Trotter, Geoffrey Malone, Holly Martin, Lynda Page, Talli Roland, Karen Ross, Matt Ralphs, J.J. Salem, Radhika Sanghani, Mel Sherratt, C.L. Taylor, Rupert Wallis, Anna Lou Weatherley, Eliza West, Lara Williamson. Founded 2012.

Mulcahy Associates*

First Floor, 7 Meard Street, London W1F 0EW
email enquiries@ma-agency.com
website www.ma-agency.com
Contacts Ivan Mulcahy, Sallyanne Sweeney

Fiction: commercial and literary fiction, crime/thrillers, women's fiction, young adult, children's and picture books; non-fiction: memoir, inspirational stories, economics, biography, history, sport, lifestyle (home 15%, overseas/ translation 20%). Send a covering letter, synopsis and first three chapters/50pp. See website for full submission guidelines.

Clients include Ha-Joon Chang, David Mitchell, Martin Pistorius, Wendy Wallace, Lisa McInerney, Steven Lenton, Jon Walter.

Toby Mundy Associates Ltd

6 Bayley Street, Bedford Square, London WC1B 3HE
tel 020-3713 0067
email enquiries@tma-agency.com
website www.tma-agency.com
Contact Toby Mundy

A management company that represents writers, speakers and brands. Also creates bespoke content for organisations. Works in association with Ed Victor. Fiction and non-fiction (home 15%, USA/translation 20%). Wide range of genres including history, science, biography, autobiography, politics and current affairs, literary fiction, crime, thrillers. No plays, poetry, sci-fi/horror or short stories. Email preliminary letter, brief cv and first 30pp of sample material to submissions@tma-agency.com. No reading fee. Founded 2014.

Judith Murdoch Literary Agency*

19 Chalcot Square, London NW1 8YA
tel 020-7722 4197
website www.judithmurdoch.co.uk
Contact Judith Murdoch

Full-length fiction only, especially accessible literary, crime and commercial women's fiction (home 15%, overseas 20%). No science fiction/fantasy, poetry, short stories or children's. Approach by post, sending the first two chapters and synopsis. Send email address or return postage; no email submissions. Editorial advice given; no reading fee. Translation rights handled by Rebecca Winfield (email: rebecca@rebeccawinfield.com).

Clients include Diane Allen, Trisha Ashley, Anne Bennett, Anne Berry, Frances Brody, Anne Doughty, Leah Fleming, Caro Fraser, Elizabeth Gill, Maggie Hope, Alex Howard, Lola Jaye, Sheila Jeffries, Pamela Jooste, Catherine King, Jill McGivering, Alison Mercer, Barbara Mutch, Kitty Neale, Carol Rivers, Jacqui Rose, Mary Wood. Founded 1993.

Andrew Nurnberg Associates International Ltd*

20–23 Greville Street, London EC1N 8SS
tel 020-3327 0400

email contact@andrewnurnberg.com
website www.andrewnurnberg.com

Represents adult and children's international authors, agent and publisher clients in the fields of literary/commercial fiction and general non-fiction for the sale of rights throughout the world via our offices in the UK and overseas.

Deborah Owen Ltd

78 Narrow Street, Limehouse, London E14 8BP
tel 020-7987 5119/5441
Contact Deborah Owen

Small agency specialising in only two authors: Delia Smith and David Owen. No new authors. Founded 1971.

PBJ & JBJ Management

22 Rathbone Street, London W1T 1LA
tel 020-7287 1112
email suzanne@pbjmgt.co.uk
website www.pbjmgt.co.uk
Chairman Peter Bennett-Jones, *Managing Director* Caroline Chignell, *Agents* Janette Linden, Suzanne Milligan, Kate Haldane

Represents writers, performers, presenters, composers, directors, producers and DJs (theatre 15%, film/TV/radio 12.5%). Specialises in comedy. No reading fee. Founded 1987.

Maggie Pearlstine Associates*

31 Ashley Gardens, Ambrosden Avenue, London SW1P 1QE
tel 020-7828 4212
email maggie@pearlstine.co.uk
Contact Maggie Hattersley

Small agency representing a select few authors. No new authors. Translation rights handled by Aitken Alexander Associates Ltd.

Authors include Matthew Baylis, Sir Menzies Campbell, Jamie Crawford, Mark Douglas-Home, Toby Green, Roy Hattersley, Dr Paul Keedwell, Charles Kennedy, Quentin Letts, Mark Leonard, Gary Mulgrew, Prof. Lesley Regan, Sir Malcolm Rifkind, Winifred Robinson, Lucy Saxon, Christopher Ward. Founded 1989.

Jonathan Pegg Literary Agency*

32 Batoum Gardens, London W6 7QD
tel 020-7603 6830
email info@jonathanpegg.com
email submissions@jonathanpegg.com
website www.jonathanpegg.com
Founder & Agent Jonathan Pegg

Specialises in full-length quality fiction and non-fiction. No reading fee. Email submissions accepted; see website for submission guidelines. Founded 2008.

Catherine Pellegrino & Associates

148 Russell Court, Woburn Place, London WC1H 0LR
email catherine@catherinepellegrino.co.uk
website www.catherinepellegrino.com
Director Catherine Pellegrino

Provides a full agenting service for children's writers, from picture books through to new adult. Founded 2011.

PFD (Peters Fraser & Dunlop Ltd)*

Drury House, 34–43 Russell Street, London WC2B 5HA
tel 020-7344 1000
email info@pfd.co.uk
website www.petersfraserdunlop.com
Ceo Caroline Michel, *Coo* Robert Caskie, *Books* Caroline Michel, Michael Sissons, Fiona Petheram, Annabel Merullo, Nelle Andrew, Laura Williams, *Books & Journalism* Robert Caskie, *Books & Theatrical Rights* Adam Gauntlett, *Children's & Audio Rights* Silvia Molteni, *Books & Foreign Rights* Rachel Mills, Alexandra Cliff, Marilia Savvides, *Estates* Camilla Shestopal, *Broadcast & Presenters* Naomi Joseph, *TV & Film Rights* Jonathan Sissons, *Public Speaking* James Caroll

Represents authors of fiction and non-fiction, presenters and public speakers throughout the world. Covering letter, synopsis or outline and first three chapters as well as author biographies should be addressed to the books department or individual agents. Return postage necessary. No reading fee. See website for submission guidelines. Does not represent scriptwriters. Founded 1924.

Pollinger Limited*

(formerly Laurence Pollinger Ltd, successor of Pearn, Pollinger and Higham)
Drury House, 34–43 Russell Street, London WC2B 5HA
tel 020-7404 0342
email info@pollingerltd.com
website www.pollingerltd.com
Managing Director Lesley Pollinger, *Agents* Tim Bates, Katy Loffman

All types of general trade adult and children's fiction and non-fiction books. For submission guidelines see website.

Clients include Kimberley Chambers, Michael Coleman, Catherine Fisher, Philip Gross, Tim Hayward, Hayley Long, Kelly McKain, Robert M. Pirsig, Nicholas Rhea, Robert Sellers and Jaqueline Yallop. Also the estates of H.E. Bates, Rachel Carson, D.H. Lawrence, Carson McCullers, John Masters, Alan Moorehead, Eric Frank Russell, Clifford D. Simak and other notables. Founded 1935.

Shelley Power Literary Agency Ltd*

20 Powell Gardens, South Heighton, Newhaven BN9 0PS
tel (01273) 512347
email sp@shelleypower.co.uk
Contact Shelley Power

General fiction and non fiction. Full length MSS (home 12.5%, USA/translation 20%). No children's books, YA, sci-fi, fantasy, poetry, screenplays or plays. Works in conjunction with agents abroad. No reading fee, but preliminary letter essential – may be sent by email. Founded 1976.

Redhammer Management Ltd

186 Bickenhall Mansions, Bickenhall Street, London W1U 6BX
tel 020-7486 3465
email admin@redhammer.info
website www.redhammer.info
Vice President Peter Cox

Specialises in works with international potential (home 17.5%, overseas 20%). Unpublished authors must have major international potential, ideally book, film and/or TV. Submissions must follow the guidelines given on the website. Do not send unsolicited MSS by post. No radio or theatre scripts. No reading fee.

Clients include Martin Bell, Mark Borkowski, Peggy Brusseau, Michelle Paver, Mal Peet, David Yelland. Founded 1993.

The Lisa Richards Agency

108 Upper Leeson Street, Dublin 4, Republic of Ireland
tel +353 (0)1 6375000
email faith@lisarichards.ie
email info@lisarichards.ie
website www.lisarichards.ie
Contact Faith O'Grady

Handles fiction and general non-fiction (Ireland 10%, UK 15%, USA/translation 20%, film/TV 15%). Approach with proposal and sample chapter for non-fiction and 3–4 chapters and synopsis for fiction (sae essential). No reading fee. *Overseas associate* The Marsh Agency for translation rights.

Clients include Des Bishop, Niall Breslin (Bressie), Helena Close, June Considine (aka Laura Elliot), Matt Cooper, Damian Corless, Chris Dooley, Austin Duffy, Christine Dwyer Hickey, Simon Fitzmaurice, John Giles, Antonia Hart, Tara Heavey, Maeve Higgins, Kitty Holland, Paul Howard (aka Ross O'Carroll-Kelly), Amy Huberman, Arlene Hunt, Roisin Ingle, Alison Jameson, Declan Lynch, Darragh Martin, Aisling McDermott, Ronan McGreevy, Rory O'Neill/Panti, Colm O'Regan (Irish Mammies), Pauline McLynn, David O'Doherty, Mary O'Donoghue, Mark O'Sullivan, Damien Owens, Roz Purcell, Nicolas Roche, Daniel Seery, The Happy Pear Cookbook, Sheena Wilkinson. Founded 1998.

Richford Becklow Agency

85 Ashburnham Road, London NW10 5SA
tel 020-3737 1068
email enquiries@richfordbecklow.co.uk
website www.richfordbecklow.com
Contact Lisa Eveleigh

Literary and commercial fiction and non-fiction: first novels, history, biography, young adult and popular culture particularly welcome (home 15%, overseas 20%). No fiction for middle grade and younger readers accepted. No reading fee. No postal submissions; will only respond to email submissions (enquiries@richfordbecklow.co.uk) as outlined on the website and will not return postal submissions.

Authors include Hugo Barnacle, Carol Clewlow, Natalie Klein, R.P. Marshall, Grace Wynne-Jones, Mary Alexander, Karen Clarke, Caroline Ashton, K.E. Coles, Sophie Parkin, Katherine Price, Anne Corlett, Lakshmi Raj Sharma, Stephen Buck. Founded 2011.

Rocking Chair Books Ltd

2 Rudgwick Terrace, St Stephens Close, London NW8 6BR
email representme@rockingchairbooks.com
website www.rockingchairbooks.com
Contact Samar Hammam

Focuses on adult commercial fiction, literary fiction, graphic novels and non-fiction for publication around the world (home 15%, translation/adaptation rights 20%). No children's, YA or science fiction (unless they are crossover). Also works with other agencies to represent their translation or English language rights, including Mulcahy Associates and the Raya Agency. Submission by email only.

Rogers, Coleridge & White Ltd*

20 Powis Mews, London W11 1JN
tel 020-7221 3717
email info@rcwlitagency.com
website www.rcwlitagency.com
Chairman Gill Coleridge, *Managing Director* Peter Straus, *Finance Director* Nelka Bell, *Directors* Stephen Edwards, Georgia Garrett, Laurence Laluyaux, David Miller, Peter Robinson, Zoe Waldie, Claire Wilson, *Agents* Sam Copeland, Jennifer Hewson, Cara Jones, Rebecca Jones (foreign).

Full-length book MSS, including children's books (home 15%, USA 20%, translation 20%). See website for submissions information. No reading fee. Note that due to the volume of unsolicited queries, it is policy to respond (usually within six weeks) only if interested in the material. Founded in 1967 by Deborah Rogers (1938–2014), who received the highest honour in the trade, the London Book Fair Lifetime Achievement Award, in 2014.

Elizabeth Roy Literary Agency

White Cottage, Greatford, Nr Stamford, Lincs. PE9 4PR
tel (01778) 560672
website www.elizabethroy.co.uk

Children's fiction and non-fiction – writers and illustrators (home 15%, overseas 20%). Send preliminary letter, synopsis and sample chapters with names of publishers and agents previously contacted.

Return postage essential. No reading fee. Founded 1990.

Uli Rushby-Smith Literary Agency

72 Plimsoll Road, London N4 2EE
tel 020-7354 2718
email uli.rushby-smith@btconnect.com
Director Uli Rushby-Smith

Fiction and non-fiction, literary and commercial (home 15%, USA/foreign 20%). No poetry, picture books, plays or film scripts. Send outline, sample chapters (no disks) and return postage. No reading fee. Founded 1993.

The Sayle Literary Agency*

1 Petersfield, Cambridge CB1 1BB
tel (01223) 303035
email info@sayleliteraryagency.com
website www.sayleliteraryagency.com
Proprietor & Agent Rachel Calder

Fiction: general, literary and crime. Non-fiction: current affairs, social issues, travel, biographies, history (home 15%, USA/translation 20%). No plays, poetry, textbooks, children's, technical, legal or medical books. No reading fee. See website for submission guidelines. Translation rights handled by The Marsh Agency Ltd. Film and TV rights handled by Sayle Screen Ltd. US rights handled by Dunow, Carlson and Lerner. Represents UK rights for Darhansoff and Verill (USA) and The Naher Agency (Australia). Founded 1896.

Sayle Screen Ltd

11 Jubilee Place, London SW3 3TD
tel 020-7823 3883
email info@saylescreen.com
website www.saylescreen.com
Agents Jane Villiers, Matthew Bates, Tania Hurst-Brown

Specialises in scripts for film, TV, theatre and radio. No reading fee. Unable to consider unsolicited material unless recommended by producer, development executive or course tutor. If this is the case, email a cv, covering letter and details of your referee or course tutor to the relevant agent. Please do not email more than one agent at a time. Every submission carefully considered, but responds only to submissions it wishes to take further; not able to return material sent in. Represents film and TV rights in fiction and non-fiction for The Sayle Literary Agency, Greene & Heaton Ltd and Peter Robinson Ltd. Works in conjunction with agents in New York and Los Angeles.

The Science Factory Ltd*

Scheideweg 34c, 20253 Hamburg, Germany
tel +49 (0)40 4327 2959 (Germany), 020-7193 7296 (Skype)
email info@sciencefactory.co.uk
website www.sciencefactory.co.uk
Director/Agent Peter Tallack (Germany), *Agent* Tisse Takagi (New York)

Serious popular non-fiction, particularly science, history and current affairs, by academics and journalists (home 15%, overseas 20%). No fiction. In first instance send proposal with chapter summaries and sample chapter (not the first). Email submissions only (material sent by post not returned). No reading fee. May suggest revision.

Authors include Anjana Ahuja, Anil Ananthaswamy, Jim Baggott, David Bainbridge, Jesse Bering, Lee Billings, Piers Bizony, Daniel Bor, Dennis Bray, Daniel Clery, Matthew Cobb, Enrico Coen, Michael Corballis, Trevor Cox, Seth Darling, Nicholas Dunbar, John Duncan, Graham Easton, Richard Elwes, Georgina Ferry, Lone Frank, Marianne Freiberger, David Hand, Bob Holmes, Simon Ings, Harris Irfan, Stephen Joseph, James Kingsland, Adam Kucharski, Ehsan Masood, Arthur I. Miller, Mark Miondownick, Samer Nashef, Ted Nield, Michael Nielsen, Paul Parsons, Aarathi Prasad, John Rhodes, Angela Saini, Ian Sample, Nicholas J. Saunders, Menno Schilthuizen, Doug Sisterson, P.D. Smith, Ian Stewart, Thomas Suddendorf, Frank Swain, Jeremy Taylor, Rachel Thomas, Roberto Trotta, Mark Van Vugt, Geerat J. Vermeij, Matt Wilkinson, Adam Zeman. UK-registered limited company established 2008.

Scott Ferris Associates

22 Dunns Lane, Mumbles, Swansea SA3 4AA
tel (01792) 360453
email riversscott@btinternet.com
Partners Gloria Ferris and Rivers Scott

General fiction and non-fiction (home 15%, overseas/TV/radio 20%). No unsolicited MSS or submissions by email. Preliminary letter and postage essential. Reading fee by arrangement. Founded 1981.

Linda Seifert Management Ltd

Screenworks Room 315, 22 Highbury Grove, London N5 2ER
tel 020-3214 8293
email contact@lindaseifert.com
website www.lindaseifert.com
Agents Edward Hughes, Nick Turner

Represents writers, directors and producers for film, TV and radio only – no book authors (home 10%, overseas 20%). Client list ranges from the highly established to the emerging talent of tomorrow – see website for details. Established 2002.

The Sharland Organisation Ltd

The Manor House, Manor Street, Raunds, Northants NN9 6JW
tel (01933) 626600
email tso@btconnect.com
website www.sharlandorganisation.co.uk
Directors Mike Sharland, Alice Sharland

Specialises in film, TV, stage and radio rights throughout the world (home 15%, overseas 20%). Preliminary letter and return postage is essential. No reading fee. Works in conjunction with overseas agents. Founded 1988.

Anthony Sheil in association with Aitken Alexander Associates

18–21 Cavaye Place, London SW10 9PT
tel 020-7373 8672
website www.aitkenalexander.co.uk
Proprietor Anthony Sheil

Quality fiction and non-fiction (home 15%, overseas 20%). No plays, film/TV scripts, poetry, short stories or children's fiction. Send preliminary letter with half-page synopsis and first consecutive 30pp of sample material. Include return postage. No reading fee.

Authors include Caroline Alexander, Catrine Clay, Mick Conefrey, the estate of Patrick Leigh Fermor, the estate of John Fowles, the estate of John Keegan, Harriet Tuckey, Robert Wilson.

Sheil Land Associates Ltd

(incorporating Richard Scott Simon Ltd 1971 and Christy & Moore Ltd 1912)
52 Doughty Street, London WC1N 2LS
tel 020-7405 9351
email info@sheilland.co.uk
Agents UK & US Sonia Land, Vivien Green, Piers Blofeld, Ian Drury, Gaia Banks *Film/theatre/TV* Lucy Fawcett, Ella Tayler Baron *Foreign Rights* Gaia Banks, Melissa Mahi

Quality literary and commercial fiction and non-fiction, including: politics, history, military history, gardening, thrillers, crime, romance, drama, science fiction, fantasy, young adult, biography, travel, cookery, humour, UK and foreign estates (home 15%, USA/translation 20%). Also film, TV, radio and theatre scripts. Welcomes approaches from new clients to start or to develop their careers. Please see website for submission instructions. No reading fee. Overseas associates Georges Borchardt, Inc. (Richard Scott Simon). *US film and TV representation* CAA, APA and others.

Clients include Sally Abbott, Peter Ackroyd, Max Adams, Charles Allen, Pam Ayres, Christopher Bartley, Hugh Bicheno, Melvyn Bragg, Steven Carroll, Lana Citron, David Cohen, Alexandra Connor, Anna del Conte, Elspeth Cooper, Elizabeth Corley, Seamus Deane, Angus Donald, Nadine Dorries, Joe Dunlop, Janet Edwards, Chris Ewan, Robert Fabbri, Ann Featherstone, N.S. Fountain, Alan Gilbey, Robert Green, Dr Claire Guest, Graham Hancock, Felicity Hayes-McCoy, Peter Higgins, Susan Hill, Aby King, Mark Lawrence, Richard Mabey, Magnus MacFarlane-Barrow, The Brothers McLeod, Gareth Patterson, Roger Pearce, Cath Quinn, David Robinson, Graham Rice, Doug Richard, Leo Ruikbie, Stephanie Saulter, Anthony Seldon, Diane Setterfield, Laura Summers, Martin Stephen, Jeffrey Tayler, Rose Tremain, Boris Volodarsky, Prof. Stanley Wells, Neil White, Julia Widdows, J.C. Wilsher, Martin Windrow, and the estates of Catherine Cookson, Helen Forrester, Richard Holmes, Patrick O'Brian, Penelope Mortimer, Jean Rhys, Tom Sharpe, Barry Unsworth, F.A. Worsley and Stephen Gately. Founded 1962.

Caroline Sheldon Literary Agency Ltd*

71 Hillgate Place, London W8 7SS
tel 020-7727 9102
email carolinesheldon@carolinesheldon.co.uk
email felicitytrew@carolinesheldon.co.uk
website www.carolinesheldon.co.uk
website www.carolinesheldonillustrators.co.uk
Contacts Caroline Sheldon, Felicity Trew

Fiction and non-fiction and children's books (home 15%, USA/translation 20%, film/TV 15%). Special interests: fiction – all fiction for women, sagas, suspense, contemporary, chick lit, historical fiction, fantasy and humour; non-fiction – true life stories, animal stories, memoirs and humour; children's – fiction for all age groups, contemporary, comic, fantasy and illustration for children's books.

Send submissions by email only with Submissions/ Title of work/Name of author in subject line. Include full introductory information about yourself and your writing and the first three chapters only or equivalent length of work.

Does not represent TV or film scripts except for existing book writing clients. No reading fee. Gives editorial advice on work of exceptional promise. Founded 1985.

Jeffrey Simmons

15 Penn House, Mallory Street, London NW8 8SX
tel 020-7224 8917
email jasimmons@unicombox.co.uk

Specialises in fiction (no science fiction, horror or fantasy), biography, autobiography, show business, personality books, law, crime, politics, world affairs. Full-length MSS (home from 10%, overseas from 15%). Will suggest revision. No reading fee, but preliminary letter essential.

Sinclair-Stevenson

3 South Terrace, London SW7 2TB
tel 020-7581 2550
Directors Christopher Sinclair-Stevenson, Deborah Sinclair-Stevenson

Full-length MSS (home 15%, USA/translation 20%). General – no children's books. No reading fee; will suggest revision. Founded 1995.

Robert Smith Literary Agency Ltd*

12 Bridge Wharf, 156 Caledonian Road, London N1 9UU

tel 020-7278 2444
email robertsmith.literaryagency@virgin.net
website www.robertsmithliteraryagency.com
Directors Robert Smith, Anne Smith

Non-fiction only: autobiography and biography, topical subjects, history, lifestyle, popular culture, entertainment, sport, true crime, health and nutrition, illustrated books (home 15%, overseas 20%). No unsolicited MSS. No reading fee. Will suggest revision.

Authors include Sarbjit Athwal, Richard Baker, Peta Bee, Paul Begg, Ralph Bulger, Gary Chapman, Judy Cook, Rick Cressman, Clive Driscoll, Rosie Dunn, Russell Edwards, Stewart Evans, Sarah Flower, Helen Foster, Becci Fox, Astrid Franse, Stephen Fulcher, Charlotte Green, Neil and Christine Hamilton, Alan Hicken, Naomi Jacobs, Albert Jack, Heidi Kingstone, Roberta Kray, Carol Ann Lee, Angela Levin, Ann Ming, James Moore, Michelle Morgan, Zana Morris, Alan Moss, Kim Noble, Theo Paphitis, Howard Raymond, Lyn Rigby, Keith Skinner, Monica Weller, Wynne Weston-Davies. Founded 1997.

The Standen Literary Agency

4 Winton Avenue, London N11 2AT
tel 020-8245 2606
website www.standenliteraryagency.com
Director Yasmin Standen

Interested in discovering new writers and launching the careers of first-time writers. Literary and commercial fiction, YA and children's fiction – middle grade upwards (home 15%, overseas 20%). Non-fiction: get in touch to see if genre is represented. Send submissions by email only; no submissions by post. Send first three chapters, a synopsis (one side of A4) and a covering letter, all double-line spaced. Submissions may be made via the website. No reading fee. See website for further information.

Authors include: Zara Kane, Fran Smith, Christina Banach, Anwesha Arya, Andrew Murray. Founded 2004.

Elaine Steel Writers' Agent*

49 Greek Street, London W1D 4EG
tel (01273) 739022
email info@elainesteel.com
website www.elainesteel.com
Contact Elaine Steel

Represents screen, radio, theatre and book writers. Does not read unsolicited material. Any consideration for representation must be by email and accompanied by a cv together with a short outline of the work to be submitted. Founded 1986.

Abner Stein*

10 Roland Gardens, London SW7 3PH
tel 020-7373 0456
website www.abnerstein.co.uk
Contacts Caspian Dennis, Sandy Violette

Fiction, general non-fiction and children's (home 15%, overseas 20%). Not taking on any new clients at present.

Micheline Steinberg Associates

Studio 315, ScreenWorks, 22 Highbury Grove, London N5 2ER
tel 020-3214 8292
email info@steinplays.com
website www.steinplays.com
Agents Micheline Steinberg, Jack Buckley

Represents writers/directors for theatre, opera, television, film, radio and animation. Film and TV rights in fiction and non-fiction on behalf of book agents (home 10%, overseas 10–20%). Works in association with agents overseas. No unsolicited submissions. Industry recommendation preferred. Founded 1987.

Rochelle Stevens & Co

2 Terretts Place, Upper Street, London N1 1QZ
tel 020-7359 3900
email info@rochellestevens.com
website www.rochellestevens.com
Directors Rochelle Stevens, Frances Arnold

Drama scripts for films, TV, theatre and radio (10%). Send preliminary letter, cv, short synopsis and opening 10pp of a drama script by post (sae essential for return of material). See website for full submission guidelines. No reading fee. Founded 1984.

Shirley Stewart Literary Agency*

3rd Floor, 4A Nelson Road, London SE10 9JB
tel 020-8293 3000
Director Shirley Stewart

Specialises in literary fiction and general non-fiction (home 10–15%, overseas 20%). No poetry, plays, film scripts, science fiction, fantasy or children's books. No reading fee. Send preliminary letter, synopsis and first three chapters plus return postage. Founded 1993.

Sarah Such Literary Agency

81 Arabella Drive, London SW15 5LL
tel 020-8876 4228
email info@sarahsuch.com
website sarahsuchliteraryagency.tumblr.com
Director Sarah Such

High-quality literary and commercial non-fiction and fiction for adults, young adults and children with a particular focus on literary and commercial debut novels, biography, memoir, history, popular culture and humour (home 15%, TV/film 20%, overseas 20%). Always looking for exciting new writers with originality and verve. No reading fee. Will suggest revision. Submit synopsis and a sample chapter (as a

Word attachment by email) plus author biography. No postal submissions unless requested. No unsolicited MSS or telephone enquiries. TV/film scripts for established clients only. No radio or theatre scripts, poetry, fantasy, self-help or short stories. Translation representation: The Buckman Agency, The English Agency (Japan) Ltd. Film/TV representation: Lesley Thorne, Aitken Alexander Associates Ltd.

Authors include Matthew De Abaitua, Nick Barlay, Salem Brownstone, Ali Catterall, Rob Chapman, Ian Critchley, John Harris Dunning, Rob Harris, John Hartley, Marisa Heath, Wayne Holloway-Smith, Vina Jackson, Maxim Jakubowski, Antony Johnston, Louisa Leaman, Mathew Lyons, Sam Manning, Vesna Maric, David May, Kit McCall, Benjamin Myers QC, Ben Osborne, Marian Pashley, Greg Rowland, John Rowley, Caroline Sanderson, Tony De Saulles, Nikhil Singh, Sara Starbuck, Michael Wendling. Founded 2006.

The Susijn Agency Ltd

820 Harrow Road, London NW10 5JU
tel 020-8968 7435
email info@thesusijnagency.com
website www.thesusijnagency.com
Agents Laura Susijn, Priya Bora

Specialises in world rights in English- and non-English-language literature: literary fiction and general non-fiction (home 15%, overseas 20%, theatre/film/TV/radio 15%). Send synopsis and three sample chapters. No reading fee.

Authors include Peter Ackroyd, Uzma Aslam Khan, Robin Baker, Tessa De Loo, Gwynne Dyer, Olivia Fane, Radhika Jha, Yan Lianke, Jeffrey Moore, Mark Mulholland, Parinoush Sainee, Karl Shaw, Sunny Singh, Hwang Sok-yong, Paul Sussman, Alex Wheatle, Adam Zameenzad. Founded 1998.

Emily Sweet Associates

35 Barnfield Road, London W5 1QU
tel 07980 026298
website www.emilysweetassociates.com
Director Emily Sweet

Represents quality fiction and general non-fiction including history, biography, current affairs, topical non-fiction and cookery. No children's or YA. Founded 2014.

The Tennyson Agency

10 Cleveland Avenue, London SW20 9EW
tel 020-8543 5939
email submissions@tenagy.co.uk
website www.tenagy.co.uk
Theatre, Radio, Television & Film Scripts Christopher Oxford, Adam Sheldon

Scripts and related material for theatre, film and TV only (home 15%, overseas 20%). No reading fee.

Clients include Tony Bagley, Kristina Bedford, Alastair Cording, Caroline Coxon, Iain Grant, Jonathan Holloway, Philip Hurd-Wood, Steve Macgregor, Antony Mann, Elizabeth Moynihan, Ken Ross, Karl Sabbagh, Matthew Salkeld, Graeme Scarfe, Diane Speakman, Diana Ward and the estate of Julian Howell. Founded 2002.

Jane Turnbull*

Mailing address Barn Cottage, Veryan Churchtown, Truro TR2 5QA
tel (01872) 501317
email jane@janeturnbull.co.uk
London Office 58 Elgin Crescent, London W11 2JJ
tel 020-7727 9409
website www.janeturnbull.co.uk

High quality non-fiction; biography, history, natural history, lifestyle, humour; TV tie-ins, some literary fiction (home 15%, USA/translation 20%), performance rights (15%). Works in conjunction with Aitken Alexander Associates Ltd for sale of translation rights. No reading fee. Preliminary letter (NOT email) essential; no unsolicited MSS. Founded 1986.

United Agents LLP*

(incorporating AP Watt)
12–26 Lexington Street, London W1F 0LE
tel 020-3214 0800
email info@unitedagents.co.uk
website www.unitedagents.co.uk
Agents Sarah Ballard, Caroline Dawnay, Jon Elek, Natasha Fairweather, Ariella Feiner, James Gill, Margaret Halton, Jodie Hodges (children's/young adult writers and illustrators), Caradoc King, Robert Kirby, Amy Mitchell, Zoe Ross, Rosemary Scoular, Linda Shaughnessy, Charles Walker, Anna Webber, Jane Willis, Mildred Yuan.

Fiction and non-fiction (home 15%, USA/translation 20%). No reading fee. See website for submission details. Founded 2008 and 1875.

Jo Unwin Literary Agency

c/o Rogers, Coleridge and White, 20 Powis Mews, London W11 1JN
email jo@rcwlitagency.com
website www.jounwin.co.uk
Contact Jo Unwin

Represents authors of literary fiction, commercial women's fiction, YA fiction and fiction for children aged 9+ (picture books only accepted if written by established clients). Also represents comic writing and narrative non-fiction.

Authors include Richard Ayoade, Charlie Brooker, Karen Campbell, Jenny Colgan, Nina Stibbe.

Ed Victor Ltd*

6 Bayley Street, Bedford Square, London WC1B 3HE
tel 020-7304 4100
website www.edvictor.com

Fiction, non-fiction, children's and film/TV (home 15%, USA 15%, film/TV 15%, translation 20%).

Authors include John Banville, Candice Bergen, Edna O'Brien, Tina Brown, Max Brooks, Alastair Campbell, Eric Clapton, Sir Ranulph Fiennes, Frederick Forsyth, James Fox, Mark Frost, A.A. Gill, Jack Higgins, Nigella Lawson, Kathy Lette, Ben Macintyre, Andrew Marr, Keith Richards, Andrew Lloyd Webber, U2, and the estates of Douglas Adams, Raymond Chandler, Dame Iris Murdoch, Sir Stephen Spender, Josephine Hart. Founded 1976.

Wade and Co. Literary Agency Ltd

33 Cormorant Lodge, Thomas More Street, London E1W 1AU
tel 020-7488 4171
email rw@rwla.com
website www.rwla.com
Directors Robin Wade

General fiction and non-fiction, excluding children's books (home 15%, overseas 20%). No poetry, plays, picture books or short stories. See website for submission guidelines. Email submissions preferred. New authors welcome. No reading fee. Founded 2001.

Watson, Little Ltd*

Suite 315, ScreenWorks, Highbury Grove, London N5 2ER
tel 020-7388 7529
email office@watsonlittle.com
website www.watsonlittle.com
Contact James Wills (Managing Director), Donald Winchester (Agent), Laetitia Rutherford (Agent)

Fiction: literary, commercial women's, crime and thriller. Non-fiction: history, science, popular psychology, memoir, humour, cookery, self-help. Children's fiction and non-fiction. No poetry, TV, play or film scripts. (Commission: home 15%, USA/ Translation 20%.) Send informative preliminary letter, synopsis and sample chapters. *Overseas associates* The Marsh Agency Ltd; *Film and TV associates* Ki Agency and The Sharland Agency; *US associates* Howard Morhaim Literary Agency and The Gersh Agency.

Authors include Susan Blackmore, Martin Edwards, Christopher Fowler, Tim Hall, Greg Jenner, Alex Marwood, Margaret Mahy, Colin Wilson, James Wong, Evie Wyld.

Josef Weinberger Plays Ltd

(formerly Warner/Chappell Plays Ltd)
12–14 Mortimer Street, London W1T 3JJ
tel 020-7580 2827

Specialises in stage plays. Works in conjunction with overseas agents. No unsolicited MSS; preliminary letter essential. Founded 1938.

Whispering Buffalo Literary Agency Ltd

97 Chesson Road, London W14 9QS
tel 020-7565 4737
email info@whisperingbuffalo.com
website www.whisperingbuffalo.com
Director Mariam Keen

Commercial/literary fiction and non-fiction, children's and young adult fiction (home 15%, overseas 20%). Special interest in book-to-screen adaptations; TV and film rights in novels and non-fiction handled in-house. No reading fee. Will suggest revision. Founded 2008.

Eve White*

54 Gloucester Street, London SW1V 4EG
tel 020-7630 1155
email eve@evewhite.co.uk
website www.evewhite.co.uk
Contact Eve White, Jack Ramm

Commercial and literary fiction and non-fiction, children's fiction and film/TV tie-ins (home 15%, overseas 20%). No reading fee. Will suggest revision where appropriate. See website for up-to-date submission requirements. No submissions by post.

Authors include Andy Stanton, Rae Earl, Saskia Sarginson, Mark Haysom, Jane Shemilt, Fergus McNeill, Yvvette Edwards, Tracey Corderoy, Ruth Warburton, Ruth Ware, Kate Maryon, Elli Woollard, Sarah Naughton, Michaela Morgan, Simon Nicholson, Ivan Brett, Susanna Corbett, Abie Longstaff, Rachael Mortimer, Ciaran Murtagh, Kate Scott, Sarah Ockwell-Smith, Adam Britten. Founded 2003.

Isabel White Literary Agent

email isabel@isabelwhite.co.uk (trade)
email query.isabelwhite@googlemail.com (submissions)
website www.isabelwhite.co.uk
Proprietor Isabel White

Fiction and non-fiction (home 15%, overseas 20%). Books only – no film, TV or stage plays, poetry, short stories or academic monographs. Not currently accepting submissions. No reading fee.

Authors include Suzi Brent, Iain Clark, Graeme Kent. Founded 2008.

Dinah Wiener Ltd*

12 Cornwall Grove, London W4 2LB
tel 020-8994 6011 *mobile*
email dinah@dwla.co.uk
Director Dinah Wiener

Fiction and general non-fiction (home 15%, overseas 20%), film and TV in association (15%). No plays, scripts, poetry, short stories or children's books. No reading fee, but preliminary letter and return postage essential. Founded 1985.

WME*

(William Morris Endeavour, UK)
Centre Point, 100 New Oxford Street, London WC1A 1DD

tel 020-7534 6800
website www.wmeauthors.co.uk
Books Simon Trewin, Elizabeth Sheinkman, Cathryn Summerhayes, Jo Rodgers, *TV* Isabella Zoltowski, Coz Jackson

Literary and commercial fiction, crime, thrillers, young adult fiction, memoir, self-help, history, popular culture (film/TV 10%, UK books 15%, USA books/translation 20%). No children's picture books. For submission guidelines see website. Worldwide talent and literary agency with offices in New York, Beverly Hills, Nashville and Miami.

The Writers' Practice

28 Denmark Street, London WC2H 8NJ
tel 0845 680 6578 *mobile* 07940 533243
email jemima@thewriterspractice.com
website www.thewriterspractice.com
Literary Agent & Editorial Consultant Jemima Hunt, *Editorial Consultant, manuscripts and scripts* Jeremy Page, *Editorial Consultant, YA* Hannah Sheppard

The Writers' Practice is a boutique literary agency and editorial consultancy comprising a small team of published authors and scriptwriters, editors and creative writing teachers. Jemima Hunt is interested in commercial and literary fiction and specialises in memoir and narrative non-fiction. She works closely with writers on all aspects of book development. Founded 2011.

The Wylie Agency (UK) Ltd

17 Bedford Square, London WC1B 3JA
tel 020-7908 5900
email mail@wylieagency.co.uk
website www.wylieagency.co.uk
President Andrew Wylie

Literary fiction and non-fiction (home 10%, overseas 20%, USA 15%). No unsolicited MSS; send preliminary letter with two sample chapters and sae in first instance. Founded 1996.

Susan Yearwood Literary Agency

2 Knebworth House, Londesborough Road, London N16 8RL
tel 020-7503 0954
email fiction@susanyearwood.com
email non-fiction@susanyearwood.com
email childrens@susanyearwood.com
website www.susanyearwood.com
Contact Susan Yearwood

Literary and commercial fiction (home 15%, overseas 20%), including crime/thriller, women's and general. Non-fiction. Send first 30pp and a synopsis via email. No reading fee. Founded 2007.

Clients include Prajwal Parajuly and Piers Buckman.

Zeno Agency Ltd*

Primrose Hill Business Centre, 110 Gloucester Avenue, London NW1 8HX
tel 020-7096 0927
website www.zenoagency.com
Director John Berlyne

Specialises in science fiction, fantasy and horror in publishing and related fields. Also selected other fiction genres (crime, thrillers, YA, historical, etc) and occasional appropriate non-fiction (home and direct overseas 15%, overseas via sub-agents 20%). See website for client list and submission guidelines. No reading fee. Founded 2008.

Literary agents overseas

This list includes only a selection of agents across the English-speaking world. Selected lists of agents in non-English speaking territories can be found at www.writersandartists.co.uk/listings. Before submitting material, writers are advised to visit agents' websites for detailed submission guidelines and to ascertain terms.

AUSTRALIA

Australian Literary Management

2–A Booth Street, Balmain, NSW 2041
tel +61 (0)9 818 8557
email alpha@austlit.com
website www.austlit.com

For full details of genres represented and submission guidelines, see website. Does not consider scripts of any kind or books for children by unpublished authors. Does not accept self-published work or writing by non-Australian authors.

The Author's Agent

PO Box 577 Terrigal, NSW 2260
email brian.cook@theauthorsagent.com.au
website www.theauthorsagent.com.au

Specialises in adult fiction, narrative non-fiction and children's books. Does not accept submissions by email. For detailed guidelines, see website.

Cameron Creswell Agency

Suite 75, 61 Marlborough Street, Surry Hills, NSW 2010
+61 (0)2 9319 7199
email literary@cameronsmanagement.com.au
website www.cameronsmanagement.com.au
Literary Agent Jo Butler

Genres represented vary. See website for current details. Only accepts submissions in accordance with guidelines on website. No reading fee. Founded 1978.

Curtis Brown (Australia) Pty Ltd

PO Box 19, Paddington, NSW 2021
tel +61 (0)2 9361 6161
email reception@curtisbrown.com.au
website www.curtisbrown.com.au

No reading fee.

Jenny Darling & Associates

email office@jennydarling.com.au
website www.jennydarling.com.au
Contact Jenny Darling

Adult fiction and non-fiction, some YA (home 15%, international/translation 20%, film/TV 20%). Send up to 5,000 words or the first three chapters by email with short synopsis. Does not accept material by post. No reading fee. Founded 1998.

Drummond Agency

PO Box 572, Woodend, VIC 3442
tel +61 (0)3 5427 3644
email info@drummondagency.com.au
website www.drummondagency.com.au

Considers both fiction and non-fiction for adults and YA fiction but no fantasy or sci-fi. Query by telephone, email or letter. Do not send attachments unless requested. See website for full submission guidelines and author listing.

Authors include Randa Abdel-Fattah, Vikki Wakefield, Claire Zorn, Deborah Burrows, Margareta Osborn, Yvette Walker. Founded 1999.

Golvan Arts Management

PO Box 766, Kew, Victoria 3101, Australia
email golvan@ozemail.com.au
website www.golvanarts.com.au

Represents a wide range of writers including writers of both adult and children's fiction and non-fiction, poetry, screenwriters and writers of plays. Also represents visual artists and composers. See the General Information section on the website before making contact.

HLA Management

Postal address: PO Box 1536 Strawberry Hills, Sydney, NSW 2012
email hla@hlamgt.com.au
website www.hlamgt.com.au

Represents directors, writers, designers, directors of photography, film editors, choreographers, composers, comedians and presenters. Does not represent actors. No unsolicited material. Requests for representation by referral.

HMMG Pty Ltd

Fox Studios Australia, FSA 38, 38 Driver Avenue, Moore Park, NSW 2021
email hmm@harrymmiller.com
website www.harrymmiller.com.au

Accepts submissions for the following genres: non-fiction (strong female, animals, biography, memoir) and reality-based fiction. Does not accept submissions for poetry, short stories, sci-fi, fantasy, screenplays or academic textbooks. For detailed submission guidelines, see website.

Margaret Kennedy Agency

PO Box 1433, Toowong 4066, Brisbane
email info@margaretkennedy.com
website www.margaretkennedy.com

See website for detailed submission guidelines. Query via email, no attachments.

The Naher Agency

PO Box 249, Paddington, NSW 2021
website www.naher.com.au

Specialises in quality fiction and non-fiction for adults. Does not represent fantasy, sci-fi, YA, children's or self-help. Make initial query via form on website.

CANADA

Acacia House Publishing Services Ltd

51 Chestnut Avenue, Brantford, Ontario N3T 4C3
tel +1 519-752-0978
email bhanna.acacia@rogers.com
Managing Director Bill Hanna

Literary fiction/non-fiction, quality commercial fiction, most non-fiction (15% English worldwide, 25% translation, performance 20%). No horror or occult. Works with overseas agents. Query first with sample of 50pp max. Include return postage. No reading fee. Founded 1985.

Authors' Marketing Services Ltd

PO Box 84668, 2336 Bloor Street West, Toronto M6S 4Z7
tel +1 416-763-8797
email authors_lhoffman@compuserve.com
website www.hoffmanagency.ca
Principal Agent Larry Hoffman

Adult fiction, biography and autobiography (home 15%, overseas 20%). Reading fee charged for unpublished writers; will suggest revision. Founded 1978.

Rick Broadhead & Associates

47 St. Clair Avenue West, Suite 501, Toronto M4V 3A5
email info@rbaliterary.com
website www.rbaliterary.com

See website for submission guidelines and genres represented. Email queries preferred.

The Bukowski Agency Ltd

14 Prince Arthur Avenue, Suite 202, Toronto M5R 1A9
email info@bukowskiagency.com
website www.bukowskiagency.com
Agent Denise Bukowski

Specialises in international literary fiction and up-market non-fiction for adults. Does not represent genre fiction, children's literature, plays, poetry or screenplays. See website for submission guidelines. Founded 1986.

The Cooke Agency

email agents@cookeagency.ca
website www.cookeagency.ca
Agents Dean Cooke, Sally Harding, Suzanne Brandreth, Ron Eckel, Rachel Letofsky

Literary fiction, commercial fiction (including science fiction, fantasy, crime and horror), women's commercial fiction, non-fiction (specifically narrative-driven works in the areas of popular culture, practical non-fiction in the areas of health and wellness, science, history, politics and natural history), and middle-grade and young adult books. No children's picture books, poetry or screenplays. Accepts only electronic queries, no attachments. See website for submission guidelines. Founded 1992.

Helen Heller Agency

4–21 Heath Street West, Toronto M5P 1N7
email info@helenhelleragency.com
website www.helenhelleragency.com

Specialises in adult and young adult fiction and non-fiction. Does not open attachments sent with emails. Query letters and any writing samples should be contained within the body of an email. No phone enquiries. See website for full list of genres represented and submission guidelines.

Robert Lecker Agency

4055 Melrose Avenue, Montreal H4A 2S5
email robert.lecker@gmail.com
website www.leckeragency.com

Specialises in books on entertainment, music, popular culture, popular science, intellectual and cultural history, food and travel. Does not represent children's, screenplays, poetry, self-help or spiritual. See website for submission guidelines. Do not send MSS or any other material without first querying by email.

Anne McDermid & Associates Ltd

64 Bloem Avenue, Toronto M6E 1S1
email info@mcdermidagency.com
website www.mcdermidagency.com

Represents literary and commercial novelists of high quality as well as writers of non-fiction in the areas of memoir, biography, history, literary travel, narrative science, investigative journalism, popular culture and lifestyle. Represents a small number of children's and YA writers in the fields of sci-fi and fantasy. Query by email. No unsolicited submissions or telephone queries. See website for full submission guidelines.

P.S. Literary Agency

20033-520 Kerr Street, Oakville, Ontario L6K 3C7
email info@psliterary.com
website www.psliterary.com
President & Principal Curtis Russell, *Vice President & Senior Literary Agent* Carly Watters, *Associate Literary Agent* Maria Vicente

Represents both fiction and non-fiction works to publishers in North America, Europe and throughout the world. Categories include commercial, literary, women's fiction, mystery, thriller, romance, LGBTQ, young adult, middle grade, picture books, memoir, history, politics, current affairs, business, wellness, cookbooks, sports, humour, pop science, pop psychology, pop culture, design and lifestyle. Does not accept submissions via mail or telephone. Send queries to query@psliterary.com. Do not send email attachments unless specifically requested.

Beverley Slopen

131 Bloor Street West, Suite 711, Toronto M5S 1S3
email beverley@slopenagency.ca
website www.slopenagency.com
Agent Beverley Slopen

Represents a diverse list of authors in fields ranging from literary and commercial fiction to history, non-fiction, anthropology, biography and selected true crime and self-help. See website for full submission guidelines.

Carolyn Swayze Literary Agency Ltd

7360-137th Street, Suite 319, Surrey, BC V3W 1A3
email reception@swayzeagency.com
website www.swayzeagency.com
Proprietor Carolyn Swayze

Literary fiction, a limited list of commercial fiction and non-fiction. No science fiction, poetry, screenplays or children's picture books. Eager to discover lively, thought-provoking narrative non-fiction, especially in the fields of science, history, travel, politics and memoir. No telephone calls: make contact by email or post. Send query including synopsis and short sample. Provide resume, publication credits, writing awards, education and experience relevant to the book project. If querying by post include email or sase for return of materials. No original artwork or photographs. Allow six weeks for a reply.

Westwood Creative Artists

94 Harbord Street, Toronto M5S 1G6
email wca_office@wcaltd.com
website www.wcaltd.com

Represents literary fiction, quality commercial fiction including mysteries and thrillers and non-fiction in the areas of memoir, history, biography, science, journalism and current affairs. See website for submission guidelines.

NEW ZEALAND

Glenys Bean Writer's Agent

PO Box 639, Warkworth 0941, New Zealand
email info@glenysbean.com
Directors Fay Weldon, Glenys Bean

Adult and children's fiction, educational, non-fiction, film, TV, radio (10–20%). Send preliminary letter, synopsis and sae. No reading fee. Founded 1989.

Playmarket

Suite 4, 35–38 Cambridge Terrace, Te Aro, Wellington
PO Box 9767, Marion Square, Wellington 6141
tel +64 (0)4 382 8462
email info@playmarket.org.nz
website www.playmarket.org.nz
Director Murray Lynch

Playwrights' agent, advisor and bookshop. Representation, licensing and script development of New Zealand plays and playwrights. Currently licences over 400 productions of New Zealand plays each year, in New Zealand and around the world. Founded 1973.

Total Fiction Services

PO Box 46–031, Park Avenue, Lower Hutt 5044
tel +64 (0)4 565 4429
email tfs@elseware.co.nz
website www.elseware.co.nz

General fiction, non-fiction, children's books. No poetry, or individual short stories or articles. Enquiries from New Zealand authors only. Email queries but no attachments. Hard copy preferred. No reading fee. Also offers assessment reports, mentoring and courses.

USA

**Member of the Association of Authors' Representatives*

The Axelrod Agency*

55 Main Street, PO Box 357, Chatham, NY 12037
tel +1 518-392-2100
email steve@axelrodagency.com
President Steven Axelrod

Full-length MSS. Fiction (home 15%, overseas 20%), film and TV rights (15%); will suggest revision where appropriate. Works with overseas agents. No reading fee. Founded 1983.

The Bent Agency*

159 20th Street, 1B, Brooklyn, NY 11232, USA
email info@thebentagency.com
website www.thebentagency.com
Agents Jenny Bent, Gemma Cooper, Louise Fury, Molly Ker Hawn, Susan Hawk, Victoria Lowes, Beth Phelan, Brooks Sherman, Heather Flaherty

Represents a diverse range of genres including history, humour, lifestyle, inspiration, memoir, literary fiction, children's and commercial fiction. Only accepts email queries. See website for detailed query and submission guidelines.

Georges Borchardt Inc.*

136 East 57th Street, New York, NY 10022
tel +1 212-753-5785
website www.gbagency.com
Directors Georges Borchardt, Anne Borchardt, Valerie Borchardt

Full-length and short MSS (home/British/ performance 15%, translations 20%). Agents in most foreign countries. No unsolicited MSS. No reading fee. Founded 1967.

Bradford Literary Agency

5694 Mission Center Road, Suite 347, San Diego, CA 92108
email queries@bradfordlit.com
website www.bradfordlit.com

Currently looking for fiction (romance, urban fantasy, women's, mystery, thrillers, children's and YA) and non-fiction (business, relationships, biography, memoir, self-help, parenting, narrative humour). Not currently looking for poetry, screenplays, short stories, westerns, horror, new age, religion, crafts, cookbooks or gift books. Query by email only. For detailed submission guidelines, see website. No reading fee.

Brandt & Hochman Literary Agents Inc.*

1501 Broadway, Suite 2310, New York, NY 10036
tel +1 212-840-5760
website www.brandthochman.com
Contact Gail Hochman

Full-length and short MSS (home 15%, overseas 20%), performance rights (15%). No reading fee.

The Helen Brann Agency Inc.*

94 Curtis Road, Bridgewater, CT 06752
tel +1 860-354-9580
email hbrann@helenbrannagency.com
President Helen Brann

Barbara Braun Associates Inc.*

7 East 14th Street. 19F, New York, NY 10003, USA
email bbasubmissions@gmail.com
website www.barbarabraunagency.com
President Barbara Braun

Represents literary and commercial fiction and serious non-fiction (home 15%, overseas 20%). Does not represent poetry, sci-fi, fantasy, horror or screenplays. Send queries by email. See website for full submission guidelines.

Browne & Miller Literary Associates*

410 South Michigan Avenue, Suite 460, Chicago, IL 60605
tel +1 312-922-3063
email mail@browneandmiller.com
website www.browneandmiller.com
Contact Danielle Egan-Miller

General fiction and non-fiction (home 15%, overseas 20%). Select young adult projects. Works in conjunction with foreign agents. Will suggest revision; no reading fee. Founded 1971.

Maria Carvainis Agency Inc.*

1270 Avenue of the Americas, Suite 2320, New York, NY 10020
tel +1 212-245-6365
email mca@mariacarvainis.com
President & Literary Agent Maria Carvainis

Adult fiction and non-fiction (home 15%, overseas 20%). All categories of fiction (except science fiction and fantasy), especially literary and mainstream; mystery, thrillers and suspense; historical, Regency; young adult. Non-fiction: biography and memoir, health and women's issues, business, finance, psychology, popular science, popular culture. No reading fee. Query first; no unsolicited MSS. No queries by fax or email. Works in conjunction with foreign, TV and movie agents.

Frances Collin Literary Agent*

PO Box 33, Wayne, PA 19087-0033
tel +1 610-254-0555
email queries@francescollin.com
Owner Frances Collin, *Agent* Sarah Yake

Home 15%, overseas 20%, performance rights 20%. Specialisations of interest to UK writers: literary fiction, mysteries, women's fiction, history, biography, science fiction, fantasy. No screenplays. No reading fee. No unsolicited MSS. Query via email only. Query letter in the body of the email, no attachments. Works in conjunction with agents worldwide. Founded 1948; successor to Marie Rodell-Frances Collin Literary Agency.

Don Congdon Associates Inc.*

110 William Street, Suite 2202, New York, NY 10038
tel +1 212-645-1229
email dca@doncongdon.com
website www.doncongdon.com
Agents Michael Congdon, Susan Ramer, Cristina Concepcion, Maura Kye-Casella, Katie Grimm, Katie Kotchman

Full-length and short MSS. General fiction and non-fiction (home 15%, overseas 20%, performance rights 15%). Works with co-agents overseas. No reading fee but no unsolicited MSS – query first with sase (no IRCs) or email for reply. Does not accept phone calls from querying authors. Founded 1983.

The Doe Coover Agency*

PO Box 668, Winchester, MA 01890
tel +1 781-721-6000
email info@doecooveragency.com
website www.doecooveragency.com
Contact Doe Coover (non-fiction), Colleen Mohyde (fiction), Frances Kennedy

Specialises in non-fiction: business, history, popular science, biography, social issues, cooking, food writing, gardening; also literary and commercial fiction (home 15%, overseas 10%). No poetry or screenplays. Email queries only; see website for submission guidelines. Founded 1985.

Richard Curtis Associates Inc.

171 East 74th Street, Floor 2, New York, NY 10021
tel +1 212-772-7363

website www.curtisagency.com
President Richard Curtis

All types of commercial non-fiction (home 15%, overseas 25%, film/TV 15%). Foreign rights handled by Baror International. Founded 1970.

Curtis Brown Ltd*

10 Astor Place, New York, NY 10003
tel +1 212-473-5400
Branch office 1750 Montgomery Street, San Francisco, CA 94111
tel +1-415-954 8566
website www.curtisbrown.com
Ceo Timothy Knowlton, *President* Peter Ginsberg (at CA branch office); Contact agents directly (see Agent page of website for details) Noah Ballard, Ginger Clark, Katherine Fausset, Jonathan Lyons, Laura Blake Peterson (*Vice President*), Mitchell Waters, *Film & TV rights* Holly Frederick, *Translation rights* Jonathan Lyons

Fiction and non-fiction, juvenile, film and TV rights. No unsolicited MSS. See individual agent's entry on the Agents page of the website for specific query and submission information. No reading fee; no handling fees. Founded 1914.

Liza Dawson Associates

350 Seventh Avenue, Suite 2003, New York, NY 10001
website www.lizadawsonassociates.com
Ceo Liza Dawson, *Cfo, Foreign Rights Manager* Havis Dawson; Caitlin Blasdell, Hannah Bowman, Monica Odom, Caitie Flum. (To query agents by email, the address style is queryfirstname, e.g. queryliza@lizadawsonassociates.com)

A full-service agency which draws on expertise as former publishers. Fiction: thrillers, mysteries, women's fiction, romance, historical fiction, sci-fi, fantasy, literary, magical realism. Non-fiction: women's issues, cross-cultural, narrative history, memoir, humour, mathematics, science, religion, theatre, pop culture, current events. See website for submission guidelines and email contacts.

Authors include: Annie Barrows, Marie Bostwick, Bob Brier, Pierce Brown, Stella Cameron, Robyn Carr, Kameron Hurley, Michael Losier, Brian McClellan, Victoria Christopher Murray, Carla Norton, Tawni O'Dell, Jean Sasson, Brian Stavely, Charles Stross, Rebecca Zanetti.

DeFiore and Company*

47 East 19th Street, 3rd Floor, New York, NY 10003
email info@defioreandco.com
email submissions@defioreandco.com
website www.defioreandco.com
Contacts Brian DeFiore, Laurie Abkemeier, Matthew Elblonk, Kate Garrick, Debra Goldstein, Meredith Kaffel, Caryn Karmatz Rudy, Adam Schear, Rebecca Strauss

Fiction and non-fiction (home 15%, overseas 20%). No poetry, science fiction, fantasy or romance. Query by email but if you must send by post, include sase to ensure a response. Founded 1999.

Sandra Dijkstra & Associates*

PMB 515, 1155 Camino Del Mar, Del Mar, CA 92014
tel +1 858-755-3115
website www.dijkstraagency.com
Contacts Sandra Dijkstra, Elise Capron, Jill Marr, Roz Foster, Thao Le, Andrea Cavallaro, Jessica Watterson

Fiction: contemporary, women's, literary, suspense and thrillers. Non-fiction: narrative, history, business, psychology, self-help, science and memoir/biography (home 15%, overseas 20%). Works in conjunction with foreign and film agents. Email submissions only. Please see website for the most up-to-date guidelines. No reading fee. Founded 1981.

Donadio & Olson Inc.*

121 West 27th Street, Suite 704, New York, NY 10001
tel +1 212-691-8077
email mail@donadio.com
website www.donadio.com
Associates Edward Hibbert, Neil Olson, Carrie Howland

Literary fiction and non-fiction.

Dunham Literary, Inc.*

110 William Street, Suite 2202, New York, NY 10038–3901
email dunhamlit@gmail.com
website www.dunhamlit.com
Contact Jennie Dunham, Bridget Smith

Literary fiction and non-fiction, children's books (home 15%, overseas 20%). Send query by post or to query@dunhamlit.com. No reading fee. Founded 2000.

Dunow, Carlson & Lerner*

27 West 20th Street, Suite 1107, New York, NY 10011
email mail@dclagency.com
website www.dclagency.com

Represents literary and commercial fiction, narrative non-fiction, memoir, popular culture and YA fiction. Queries should be made by post (include sase) or email (no attachments).

Dystel & Goderich Literary Management*

1 Union Square West, New York, NY 10003
tel +1 212-627-9100
website www.dystel.com
Contacts Jane D. Dystel, Miriam Goderich, Michael Bourret, Jim McCarthy, Lauren Abramo, Stacey Glick, Jessica Papin, John Rudolph, Rachel Stout

General fiction and non-fiction (home 15%, overseas 19%, film/TV/radio 15%): literary and commercial fiction, narrative non-fiction, self-help, cookbooks, parenting, science fiction/fantasy, children's and young adults. Send a query letter with a synopsis and up to 50pp of sample MS. Will accept email queries. No reading fee. Will suggest revision. Founded 1994.

The Ethan Ellenberg Literary Agency*

548 Broadway, Suite 5E, New York, NY 10012
tel +1 212-431-4554
email agent@ethanellenberg.com
website www.ethanellenberg.com
President & Agent Ethan Ellenberg

Fiction and non-fiction (home 15%, overseas 20%). Commercial fiction: sci-fi, fantasy, romance, thrillers, suspense, mysteries, children's and general fiction; also literary fiction with a strong narrative. Non-fiction: history, adventure, true crime, science, biography. Children's fiction: interested in young adult, middle grade and younger, of all types. Will consider picture books and other illustrated works. No scholarly works, poetry, short stories or screenplays.

Will accept unsolicited MSS and seriously consider all submissions, including first-time writers. For fiction submit synopsis and first three chapters. For non-fiction send a proposal (outline, sample material, author cv, etc). For children's works send complete MS. Illustrators should send a representative selection of colour copies (no orginal artwork). Unable to return any material from overseas. See website for full submission guidelines. Founded 1983.

Diana Finch Literary Agency*

116 West 23rd Street, Suite 500, New York, NY 10011
tel +1 917-544-4470
email diana.finch@verizon.net
website www.dianafinchliterary.blogspot.com
Owner and Agent Diana Finch

Memoirs, narrative non-fiction, science, history, environment, business, literary fiction, YA fiction (domestic 15%, foreign 20%). No reading fee. Queries by email or via website preferred, no attachments. No queries by telephone.

Clients include Azadeh Moaveni, Antonia Juhasz, Loretta Napoleoni, Owen Matthews, Greg Palast, Thaisa Frank, Eric Simons, Thomas Goltz, Mark Schapiro, Joanna Russ (estate). Founded 2003. Previously agent with Ellen Levine Literary Agency.

FinePrint Literary Management*

115 West 29th Street, 3rd Floor, New York, NY 10001
website www.fineprintlit.com
Ceo Peter Rubie, *President* Stephany Evans, three other agents

Represents fiction and non-fiction. Each agent has specific genre interests; these are detailed on the website. Query by email to the appropriate agent, including a query letter, synopsis and first two chapters but do not send any attachments without an invitation to do so.

Folio Literary Management*

The Film Center Building, 630 9th Avenue, Suite 1101, New York, NY 10036
website www.foliolit.com

Represents both first-time and established authors. Seeks upmarket adult fiction, literary fiction, commercial fiction that features fresh voices and/or memorable characters, narrative non-fiction. Folio Jr is devoted exclusively to representing children's book authors and artists. Consult agents' submission guidelines on the website before making contact.

Jeanne Fredericks Literary Agency Inc.*

221 Benedict Hill Road, New Canaan, CT 06840
tel +1 203-972-3011
email jeanne.fredericks@gmail.com
website www.jeannefredericks.com

Quality non-fiction, especially health, science, women's issues, gardening, antiques and decorative arts, biography, cookbooks, popular reference, business, natural history (home 15%, overseas 20%). No reading fee. Query first by email or mail, enclosing sase. Member of Authors Guild and AAR. Founded 1997.

Samuel French Inc.

235 Park Avenue South, 5th Floor, New York, NY 10003
tel +1 866-598-8449
email info@samuelfrench.com
President & Ceo Nate Collins

Play publishers; authors' representatives. No reading fee.

Sarah Jane Freymann Literary Agency

tel +1 212-362-9277
email submissions@sarahjanefreymann.com
website www.sarahjanefreymann.com
Contacts Sarah Jane Freymann, Steven Schwartz, Katherine Sands, Jessica Sinsheimer

Book-length fiction and general non-fiction. Special interest in serious non-fiction, mainstream commercial fiction, contemporary women's fiction, Latino American, Asian American, African American fiction and non-fiction, all children's books. Non-fiction: women's issues, biography, health/fitness, psychology, self-help, spiritual, natural science, cookbooks, pop culture. Works in conjunction with Abner Stein in London. No reading fee. Query with sase. Founded 1974.

The Friedrich Agency*

19 West 21st Street, Suite 201, New York, NY 10010
email mfriedrich@friedrichagency.com
email lcarson@friedrichagency.com
website www.friedrichagency.com
Agents Molly Friedrich, Lucy Carson

Represents literary and commercial fiction for adults and YA, plus narrative non-fiction and memoir. Accepts queries by email and post. Query only one agent. No unsolicited MSS. No attachments to query emails unless invited. See website for detailed submission guidelines.

Gelfman Schneider ICM Partners*

850 Seventh Avenue, Suite 903, New York, NY 10019
tel +1 212-245-1993
email mail@gelfmanschneider.com
Directors Jane Gelfman, Deborah Schneider

General adult fiction and non-fiction (home 15%, overseas 20%). No reading fee. Send sase for return of material. Query by post only. Works in conjunction with ICM Partners and Curtis Brown, London.

Global Lion Intellectual Property Management, Inc.

PO Box 669238, Pompano Beach, FL 33066
tel +1 754-222-6948
email peter@globallionmgt.com
website www.globallionmanagement.com
President/Ceo Peter Miller, *Associates* Hugh Walter, Zachary Yerian

Specialises in commercial fiction (especially thrillers), true crime, all types of non-fiction, all books with global publishing and film/TV potential (15% US/ Canada, 25% overseas), and films and television programmes (10–20%). Works in conjunction with agents worldwide. Initial submissions should include a synopsis, author biography, manuscript sample and details of personal social media and self-promotion.

Authors and *clients* include Sir Ken Robinson, Jean Pierre Isbouts, Raymond Benson, Rhodi Hawk, Bob Deutch, Anthony DeStefano. Founded 1976.

Barry Goldblatt Literary LLC*

320 Seventh Avenue, #266, Brooklyn, New York, NY 11215
tel +1 718-832-8787
email query@bgliterary.com
website www.bgliterary.com
Contact Barry Goldblatt

Represents young adult and middle grade fiction, as well as adult science fiction and fantasy. No non-fiction. Has a preference for quirky, offbeat work. Query only.

Frances Goldin Literary Agency*

57 East 11th Street, Suite 5B, New York, NY 10003
tel +1 212-777-0047
email agency@goldinlit.com
website www.goldinlit.com
Agents Frances Goldin, Ellen Geiger, Matt McGowan, Sam Stoloff, Sarah Bridgins

Fiction (literary and high-quality commercial) and non-fiction, particularly books with a progressive political orientation. Send query with sase. No unsolicited MSS. Founded 1977.

Goodman Associates, Literary Agents*

500 West End Avenue, New York, NY 10024
tel +1 212-873-4806
Partners Arnold P. Goodman, Elise Simon Goodman

Adult book length fiction and non-fiction (home 15%, overseas 20%). No reading fee. Accepts new clients by referral only. Founded 1976.

Sanford J. Greenburger Associates Inc.*

55 Fifth Avenue, New York, NY 10003
tel +1 212-206-5600
website www.greenburger.com
Contacts Heide Lange, Faith Hamlin, Daniel Mandel, Matt Bialer, Brenda Bowen, Lisa Gallagher, Courtney Miller-Callihan, Nicholas Ellison, Chelsea Lindman, Lindsay Ribar, Rachel Dillon Fried

Fiction and non-fiction, film and TV rights. See website for submission guidelines. No reading fee.

The Joy Harris Literary Agency Inc.*

381 Park Avenue South, Suite 428, New York 10016
tel +1 212-924-6269
email joyharris@jhlitagent.com
email adamreed@jhlitagent.com
website www.joyharrisliterary.com
President Joy Harris

John Hawkins & Associates Inc.*

80 Maiden Lane, Suite 1503, New York, NY10038
tel +1 212-807-7040
email jha@jhalit.com
website www.jhalit.com
Agents Moses Cardona (President), Warren Frazier, Anne Hawkins

Fiction, non-fiction, young adult. No reading fee. Founded 1893.

The Jeff Herman Agency LLC

PO Box 1522, Stockblidge, MA 01262
tel +1 413-298-0077
email jeff@jeffherman.com
website www.jeffherman.com

Business, reference, popular psychology, technology, health, spirituality, general non-fiction (home/ overseas 15%); will suggest revision where appropriate. Works with overseas agents. No reading fee. Founded 1986.

Hill Nadell Literary Agency

6442 Santa Monica Blvd., Suite 201, Los Angeles, CA 90038
tel +1 310-860-9605
email queries@hillnadell.com
website www.hillnadell.com
Agents Bonnie Nadell, Dara Hyde

Full-length fiction and non-fiction (home 15%, overseas 20%). Send query letter initially with first chapter. If you would like your materials returned, include adequate postage. Due to the high volume of submissions the agency receives, a response to all emailed queries cannot be guaranteed. Works in conjunction with agents in Scandinavia, France,

Germany, Holland, Japan, Spain and more. No reading fee. Founded 1979. Founded 1979.

ICM Partners*

730 Fifth Avenue, 3rd Floor, New York, NY 10019
tel +1 212-556-5600
London office 5th Floor, 28–29 Haymarket, London SW1Y 4SP
tel 020-7393 4400
website www.icmpartners.com

No unsolicited MSS.

InkWell Management

521 Fifth Avenue, 26th Floor, New York, NY 10175
tel +1 212-922-3500
email info@inkwellmanagement.com
email submissions@inkwellmanagement.com
website www.inkwellmanagement.com
Contacts Kimberly Witherspoon, Michael V. Carlisle, Richard Pine, Lizz Blaise, Lyndsey Blessing, William Callahan, Catherine Drayton, David Forrer, Jolie Hale, David Hale Smith, Allison Hunter, Alexis Hurley, Nathaniel Jacks, George Lucas, Alyssa Mozdzen, Jacqueline Murphy, Charlie Olsen, Eliza Rothstein, Hannah Schwartz, Lauren Smythe, Lisa Vanterpool, Jenny Witherell, Monika Woods

Fiction and non-fiction (home/overseas 15%). See website for submission guidelines. Founded 2004.

Janklow & Nesbit Associates

445 Park Avenue, New York, NY 10022
tel +1 212-421-1700
email info@janklow.com
website www.janklowandnesbit.com
Chairmen Morton L. Janklow, Lynn Nesbit

Commercial and literary fiction and non-fiction. No unsolicited MSS. Works in conjunction with Janklow & Nesbit (UK) Ltd. Founded 1989.

Keller Media Inc.

578 Washington Boulevard, No. 745, Marina Del Rey, CA 90292
website www.kellermedia.com
Ceo/Senior Agent Wendy Keller

Non-fiction for adults: business (all types), self-improvement, parenting, relationships, wellness, health and non-traditional health, science, nature, history, politics, psychology, personal finance and ecology/green movement. Autobiographies considered only by well-known people. No children's books, poetry, memoirs, screenplays or illustrated books. To submit a query, see www.kellermedia.com/query/. Founded 1989.

Virginia Kidd Agency Inc.

538 East Hartford Street, PO Box 278, Milford, PA 18337
tel +1 570-296-6205
website www.vk-agency.com

Fiction, specialising in science fiction and fantasy (home 15%, overseas 20–25%). Send synopsis (1–3pp), cover letter and sase. Founded 1965.

Harvey Klinger Inc.*

300 West 55th Street, Suite 11V, New York, NY 10019
website www.harveyklinger.com
Agents Harvey Klinger, David Dunton, Sara Crowe, Andrea Somberg

Commercial and literary adult and children's fiction and non-fiction – serious narrative through to self-help psychology books by authors who have already established strong credentials in their respective field. (Home 15%, overseas 25%). See website for submission guidelines and submission form. Founded 1977.

The Knight Agency*

email submissions@knightagency.net
website www.knightagency.net

Represents both first-time and established authors across a wide range of genres. For the genre interests of individual agents and detailed submission guidelines, see website. All queries should be made by email. Queries must be addressed to a specific agent, with no attachments.

kt literary*

9249 S. Broadway 200–543, Highlands Ranch, CO 80129
tel +1 720-344-4728
email contact@ktliterary.com
website www.ktliterary.com
Contact Kate Schafer Testerman, Sara Megibow, Renee Nyen

Primarily middle-grade and young adult fiction. No picture books. In adult, also seeking romance, science fiction, fantasy, and erotica (Sara Megibow only). Email a query letter and the first 3pp of manuscript in the body of the email (no attachments) as per website instructions. No snail mail.

Clients include Maureen Johnson, Stephanie Perkins, Matthew Cody, Ellen Booraem, Trish Doller, Amy Spalding, Roni Loren, Tiffany Reisz, Stefan Bachmann, Jason Hough. Founded 2008.

Susanna Lea Associates

331 West 20th Street, New York, NY 10011
tel +1 646-638-1435
email us-submission@susannalea.com
website www.susannalea.com

General fiction and non-fiction with international appeal. No plays, screenplays or poetry. Send query letter, brief synopsis, the first three chapters and/or proposal via website. Established in Paris 2000, New York 2004, London 2008.

Levine Greenberg Literary Agency Inc*

307 Seventh Avenue, Suite 2407, New York, NY 10001
email query@levinegreenberg.com
website www.levinegreenberg.com
Principal Jim Levine

Represents literary and commercial fiction (mystery and suspense, women's, romance, YA and middle grade) and non-fiction across a diverse range of genres. Unable to accept submissions sent by mail. Prefers electronic submissions via the form on the website or by email. Refer to the How to Submit section of the website before querying or submitting work.

Julia Lord Literary Management*

38 West Ninth Street, New York, NY 10011
email query@julialordliterary.com
website www.julialordliterary.com

Currently looking for submissions in the following genres: narrative non-fiction, reference, biography, history, lifestyle, sports, humour, science, adventure, general fiction, historical fiction, YA fiction, thrillers, mysteries. Email and postal queries accepted. See website for detailed query and submission guidelines.

Donald Maass Literary Agency*

Suite 801, 121 West 27th Street, New York, NY 10001
tel +1 212-727-8383
email info@maassagency.com
website www.maassagency.com
Agents Donald Maass, Jennifer Jackson, Cameron McClure, Stacia Decker, Amy Boggs, Katie Shea Boutillier, Jennifer Udden

Specialises in fiction, all genres (home 15%, overseas 20%). See website for submission guidelines. Founded 1980.

Margret McBride Literary Agency*

PO Box 9128, La Jolla, CA 92038
tel +1 858-454-1550
email staff@mcbridelit.com
website www.mcbrideliterary.com
President Margret McBride

Business, mainstream fiction and non-fiction (home 15%, overseas 25%). No poetry or children's books. No reading fee. See website for submission guidelines. Founded 1981.

McIntosh & Otis Inc.*

353 Lexington Avenue, New York, NY 10016
tel +1 212-687-7400
email info@mcintoshandotis.com
website www.mcintoshandotis.com
Agents Eugene H. Winick, Elizabeth Winick Rubinstein, Shira Hoffman, Christa Heschke

Adult and juvenile literary fiction and non-fiction. No unsolicited MSS; query first via email, see website for instructions. No reading fee. Founded 1928.

Carol Mann Agency*

55 Fifth Avenue, New York, NY 10003
tel +1 212-206-5635
email submissions@carolmannagency.com
website www.carolmannagency.com
Associates Carol Mann, Laura Yorke, Gareth Esersky, Myrsini Stephanides, Joanne Wyckoff, Lydia Blyfield

Psychology, popular history, biography, pop culture, health, advice/relationships, current affairs/politics, parenting, business, memoir, humour, science, general non-fiction, fiction (home 15%, overseas 20%). Works in conjunction with foreign and film agents. Submission guidelines: fiction, send a query and the first 25 pages; non-fiction, send a query, synopsis/proposal and the first 25 pages. Founded 1977.

The Evan Marshall Agency*

1 Pacio Court, Roseland, NJ 07068-1121
tel +1 973-287-6216
email evan@evanmarshallagency.com
President Evan Marshall

General fiction (home 15%, overseas 20%). Works in conjunction with overseas agents. Will suggest revision; no reading fee. Do not query. Accepting new clients by professional referral only. Founded 1987.

William Morris Agency Inc.

1325 Avenue of the Americas, New York, NY 10019
tel +1 212-586-5100
website www.wma.com

Jean V. Naggar Literary Agency Inc.*

216 East 75th Street, Suite 1E, New York, NY 10021
tel +1 212-794-1082
email jvnla@jvnla.com
website www.jvnla.com
President Jennifer Weltz, *Agents* Alice Tasman, Elizabeth Evans, Laura Biagi

Mainstream commercial and literary fiction, non-fiction (psychology, science biography, history), young readers (picture, middle grade, young adult). Home 15%, overseas 20%. Works in conjunction with foreign agents. Submit queries via form on website. No reading fee. Founded 1978.

Harold Ober Associates Inc.*

425 Madison Avenue, New York, NY 10017
tel +1 212-759-8600
website www.haroldober.com
Directors Phyllis Westberg, Pamela Malpas, Jake Elwell, Craig Tenney

Full-length MSS (home 15%, UK/overseas 20%), performance rights (15%). No screenplays or playscripts. No email or fax queries; see website for submission instructions. No reading fee. Founded 1929.

Fifi Oscard Agency Inc.

110 West 40th Street, New York, NY 10018
tel +1 212-764-1100
email agency@fifioscard.com
website www.fifioscard.com
Agents Peter Sawyer, Carolyn French, Carmen La Via, Kevin McShane, Ivy Fischer Stone, Jerome Rudes, Laura R. Paperny

Full-length MSS (home 15%, overseas 20%), theatrical performance rights (10%). See website for genres represented and submission guidelines.

The Richard Parks Agency*

PO Box 693, Salem, NY 12865
email rp@richardparksagency.com
website www.richardparksagency.com

Represents literary and commercial fiction and trade non-fiction in a wide range of subject areas (home 15%, overseas 20%). Does not handle children's books, poetry, plays or screenplays. Query by mail only with sase. No unsolicited MSS or email queries.

James Peter Associates Inc.

PO Box 358, New Canaan, CT 06840
tel +1 203-972-1070
email gene_brissie@msn.com
website www.jamespeterassociates.com
Contact Gene Brissie

Non-fiction, especially history, politics, popular culture, health, psychology, reference, biography (home 15%, overseas 20%). Will suggest revision. No reading fee. Foreign rights handled by JPA. Founded 1971.

Alison Picard, Literary Agent

PO Box 2000, Cotuit, MA 02635
tel +1 508-477-7192
email ajpicard@aol.com

Adult fiction and non-fiction, children's and young adult (15%). No short stories, poetry, plays, screenplays or sci-fi/fantasy. Please send query via email (no attachments). No reading fee. Founded 1985.

Rees Literary Agency*

14 Beacon Street, Suite 710, Boston, MA 02108
email reesagency@reesagency.com
website www.reesagency.com
Contact Helen Rees, *Agents* Ann Collette, Lorin Rees, Nicole LaBombard, Rebecca Podos

Business books, self-help, biography, autobiography, political, literary fiction, memoirs, history, current affairs (home 15%). No reading fee. Submit query letter with sase. Founded 1982.

Renaissance Management

PO Box 17379 Beverly Hills, CA 90209
tel +1 323-848-8305
Contact Alan Nevins

Full-length MSS. Fiction and non-fiction, plays, film and TV rights, performance rights. No unsolicited MSS; query first, submit outline. No reading fee.

The Angela Rinaldi Literary Agency*

PO Box 7875, Beverly Hills, CA 90212–7875
tel +1 310-842-7665
email amr@rinaldiliterary.com
website www.rinaldiliterary.com
President Angela Rinaldi

Mainstream and literary adult fiction; non-fiction (home 15%, overseas 25%). No reading fee. Founded 1994.

Russell & Volkening Inc.*

c/o Lippincott, Massie, McQuilkin,
27 West 20th Street, Suite 305, New York, NY 10011
tel +1 212-352 2055 +1 212-352-2059
email randv@lmqlit.com
website www.lmqlit.com
Contacts Derek Parsons, Amanda Panitch

Schiavone Literary Agency, Inc.

Corporate offices 236 Trails End, West Palm Beach, FL 33413–2135
tel 516-966-9294
email profschia@aol.com
3671 Hudson Manor Terrace No 11H, Bronx, NY 10463–1139
tel +1 718-548-5332
email jendu77@aol.com
400 East 11th Street, Suite 7, New York, NY 10009
email kvn.mcadams@yahoo.com
website www.publishersmarketplace.com/members/profschia
Ceo James Schiavone, *President* Jennifer DuVall, *Executive vice president* Kevin McAdams

Fiction and non-fiction, specialising in celebrity biography and memoirs (home 15%, overseas 20%). No reading fee. Accepts only one-page email queries (no attachments). No longer accepts queries by post. Founded 1996.

Susan Schulman, A Literary Agency LLC*

454 West 44th Street, New York, NY 10036
tel +1 212-713-1633
email susan@schulmanagency.com
website www.schulmanagency.com

Agents for negotiation in all markets (with co-agents) of fiction and general non-fiction, children's books, academic and professional works, and associated subsidiary rights including plays and film (home 15%, UK 7.5%, overseas 20%). No reading fee. Return postage required.

Scott Meredith Literary Agency LP

55 Broadway, Suite 2002, New York, NY 10006-3008
tel +1 646-274-1970

website www.scottmeredith.com
President Arthur Klebanoff

General fiction and non-fiction. Founded 1946.

The Spieler Agency

27 West 20th Street, Room 305, New York, NY 10011
tel +1 212-757-4439
website www.thespieleragency.com
Agents Joe Spieler, Eric Myers, John Thornton, Victoria Shoemaker

History, politics, ecology, business, consumer reference, biography, spirituality, serious non-fiction; some fiction (home 15%, overseas 20%). See website for submission guidelines. Founded 1982.

Philip G. Spitzer Literary Agency, Inc.*

50 Talmage Farm Lane, East Hampton, NY 11937
tel +1 631-329-3650
email lukas.ortiz@spitzeragency.com
website www.spitzeragency.com
Agents Philip Spitzer, Lukas Ortiz, Lucas Hunt

General fiction and non-fiction; specialises in mystery/suspense, sports, politics, biography, social issues.

The Strothman Agency*

PO Box 231132, Boston, MA 02123
email info@strothmanagency.com
website www.strothmanagency.com

Specialises in history, science, narrative journalism, nature and the environment, current affairs, narrative non-fiction, business and economics, YA fiction and non-fiction, middle grade fiction and non-fiction. Only accepts electronic submissions. Query by email to strothmanagency@gmail.com but first see website for detailed submission guidelines.

Emma Sweeney Agency*

245 East 80th Street, Suite 7E, New York, NY 10075-0506
email query@emmasweeneyagency.com
website www.emmasweeneyagency.com

Specialises in general fiction, historical fiction and narrative non-fiction including memoir, history, science and religion. Only accepts electronic queries. Query by email with a description of plot/proposal and a brief cover letter containing how you heard about the agency, previous writing credits and a few details about yourself. Do not send attachments unless requested; instead, paste the first ten pages of your novel/proposal into the text of your query email.

Trident Media Group

41 Madison Avenue, New York, NY 10010
tel +1 212-333-1511
email info@tridentmediagroup.com
website www.tridentmediagroup.com

Full-length MSS: see website for genres represented (home 15%, overseas 20%); in conjunction with co-agents, theatre, films, TV (15%). Will suggest revision. See website for submission guidelines.

Austin Wahl Agency Inc.

1820 North 76th Court, Elmwood Park, IL 60707–3631
tel +1 708-456-4780
President Thomas Wahl

Full-length and short MSS (home 15%, overseas 20%), theatre, films, TV (10%). No reading fee; professional writers only. Founded 1935.

Watkins/Loomis Agency Inc.

PO Box 20925, Park West Finance Station, New York, NY 10025
tel +1 212-532-0080
email assistant@watkinsloomis.com
website www.watkinsloomis.com
President Gloria Loomis

Fiction and non-fiction. No unsolicited MSS. *Representatives* Abner Stein (UK), the Marsh Agency Ltd (foreign).

Waverly Place Literary Agency

189 Waverly Place, Suite 4, New York, NY 10014–3135, USA
email waverlyplaceliterary@aol.com
website www.waverlyplaceliterary.com
Agent Deborah Carter

Fiction and non-fiction (home 15%, overseas 20%). Special interests: literary novels and short story collections with popular appeal, mysteries/thrillers, espionage fiction/non-fiction, historical fiction, literary narrative non-fiction, memoirs and biography about extraordinary people and experiences, travel, history, pop culture, music, the arts, fashion, nostalgia, antiques and anything not mentioned here that authors feel would be of interest to the agent; and children's fiction/non-fiction. Particularly interested in multicultural fiction for adults and children. Special call for first novels with characters in their 20s and 30s. No category romance, chick lit, science fiction, fantasy, horror, religion, spirituality, gratuitous violence, a sentimental outlook, stories of victimhood or illness. Prefers queries by email with no attachments. If no response within two weeks, query again.

Wolf Literary Services*

email queries@wolflit.com
website www.wolflit.com
President Kirsten Wolf, *VP/Senior Agent* Adriann Ranta, *Agent* Kate Johnson, *Junior Agent/Subsidiary Rights Manager* Allison Devereux

Specialises in dynamic, quirky books written for all ages. The fact that a book is surprising, weird, fresh, dark, heartbreaking, tear-jerking or side-splitting is more important than genre. Send a query letter along with a 50-page writing sample (fiction) or a detailed proposal (non-fiction) by email. Samples may be submitted as an attachment or in the body of the email. See website for detailed guidelines.

Authors include Sarah Gerard, Kendare Blake, Ian Doescher. Founded 2008.

Writers House LLC*

21 West 26th Street, New York, NY 10010
tel +1 212-685-2400
website www.writershouse.com

Fiction and non-fiction, including all rights; film and TV rights. See website for submission guidelines and contact details for agents. Founded 1974.

The Wylie Agency Inc.

250 West 57th Street, Suite 2114, New York, NY 10107
tel +1 212-246-0069
email mail@wylieagency.com
website www.wylieagency.com

Literary fiction/non-fiction. No unsolicited MSS accepted. London office: the Wylie Agency UK Ltd.

Art and illustration

Freelancing for beginners

Fig Taylor describes the opportunities open to freelance illustrators and discusses types of fee and how to negotiate one to your best advantage.

Full-time posts for illustrators are extremely rare. Because commissioners' needs tend to change on a regular basis, most artists have little choice but to freelance – offering their skills to a variety of clients in order to make a living.

Illustration is highly competitive and a professional attitude towards unearthing and targeting potential commissioners, presenting, promoting and delivering your work will be vital to your success. Likewise, a realistic understanding of how the industry works and of your place within it will be key. Without adequate research into your chosen field(s) of interest, you may find yourself approaching inappropriate clients – a frustrating and disheartening experience for both parties and a waste of your time and money.

Who commissions illustration?

Magazines and newspapers

Whatever your illustrative ambitions, you are most likely to receive your first commissions from editorial clients. The comparatively modest fees involved allow art editors the freedom to take risks, so many are keen to commission newcomers. Briefs are generally fairly loose though deadlines can be short, particularly where daily and weekly publications are concerned. However, fast turnover also ensures a swift appearance in print, thus reassuring clients in other, more lucrative, spheres of your professional status. Given then that it is possible to use magazines as a springboard, it is essential to research them thoroughly when seeking to identify your own individual market. Collectively, editorial clients accommodate an infinite variety of illustrative styles and techniques. Don't limit your horizons by approaching only the most obvious titles and/or those you would read yourself. Consider also trade and professional journals, customer magazines (such as inflight magazines and those produced for supermarkets) and those available on subscription from membership organisations or charities. You will often find obscure titles in the reference section of public or university libraries, where the periodicals they subscribe to will reflect the subjects taught. Seeking out as many potential clients as possible will benefit you in the long term. In addition to the titles listed in this *Yearbook*, the Association of Illustrators (AOI) publishes an *Editorial Directory* which gives specific client contact details, and is updated annually. Don't just confine yourself to the world of print either; online publications commission illustration – and gifs – too. There are also a number of useful online resources to further aid your research such as www.magforum.com, www.magpile.com and www.issuu.com.

Book publishing

With the exception of children's picture books, where illustration is unlikely to fall out of fashion, some publishers are using significantly less illustration than they once did. However, those invested in digital publishing are constantly exploring new formats and platforms enabling books to be experienced in new ways and this could open up fresh avenues for illustrators in time. While publishers of traditional mass market fiction genres, such as science fiction and fantasy, still favour strong, representational, full-colour work on their covers, photography has begun to predominate in others, such as the family saga and historical romance. However, the prevailing trend for using fashion illustration in lifestyle-related advertising has strongly influenced the packaging of contemporary women's fiction, where quirky, humorous and graphic styles have become synonymous with the genre. A broader range of styles can be accommodated by those smaller publishers specialising in literary, upmarket fiction, though many opt to use stock imagery in order to operate within a limited budget. While specialist and technical illustrators still have a vital part to play in non-fiction publishing, there is some decorative work being commissioned for lifestyle-related subjects, particularly those considered to appeal to women (such as mind, body & spirit titles). Overall, however, photography currently predominates.

Children's publishers use a wide variety of styles, covering the gamut from baby books, activity and early learning, through to full-colour picture books, covers for young adults and black-and-white line illustrations for the 8–11-year-old age group (particularly for boys, who tend to be more reluctant readers than girls). Author/illustrators are particularly welcomed by picture book publishers – though some have a policy of working only with those represented by a literary agent. Whatever your style, being able to develop believable characters and sustain them throughout a narrative is paramount. Some children's book illustrators initially find their feet in educational publishing. However, all ages are catered for within this area, including adults with learning difficulties, those learning languages for business purposes and teachers working right across the educational spectrum. Consequently, a wide variety of illustrators can be accommodated, even those working in comic book or manga styles. With the exception of educational publishing, which tends to have a faster turnover, most publishing deadlines are civilised and mass market covers particularly well paid. There are numerous publishing clients listed elsewhere in this *Yearbook* and visiting individual websites is a good way to get a flavour of the kind of illustration they may favour. In addition, the AOI publishes a *Publishing Directory*, which is updated yearly and gives specific client contact details.

Greeting cards

Many illustrators are interested in providing designs for cards and giftwrap. Illustrative styles favoured include decorative, graphic, humorous, fine art, children's and cute. For specific information on the gift industry which, unlike the areas covered here, works on a speculative basis, see *Card and stationery publishers that accept illustrations and photographs* on page 476.

Design companies

Both designers and their clients (who are largely uncreative and will, ultimately, be footing the bill) will be impressed and reassured by relevant, published work so wait until you're in print before approaching them. Although fees are significantly higher than those in newspapers, magazines and book publishing, this third-party involvement generally results in a more restrictive brief. Deadlines may vary and styles favoured range from conceptual through to realistic, decorative, humorous and informational – with those involved in multimedia and web design favouring illustrators with character development and flash animation skills.

Magazines such as *Creative Review* and the online-based *Design Week* (both published by Centaur Media Plc) will keep you abreast of developments in the design world and help you identify clients' individual areas of expertise. Meanwhile, online directories such as www.designdirectory.com and www.creativematch.com carry listings, though there are any amount of well-curated blogs produced by and dedicated to the work of graphic designers you could scour for leads. Individual contact names are also available at a price from database specialists File FX, who can provide creative suppliers with up-to-date information on commissioners in all spheres. A similar service is provided by Bikinilists, an online annual subscription-based resource that specialises in providing categorised contact data. The AOI's annually updated *Advertising Directory* also incorporates a number of design consultancies.

Advertising agencies

As with design, you should ideally be in print before seeking advertising commissions. Fees can be high, deadlines short and clients extremely demanding. A wide range of styles are used and commissions might be incorporated into direct mail or press advertising, featured on websites, billboards, hoardings or animated for television. Fees will vary, depending on whether a campaign is local, national or even global and how many forms of media are used to attract the target demographic's attention.

Most agencies employ at least one art buyer to look at portfolios, both in person and online. A good one will know what campaigns each creative team is currently working on

Useful addresses

Association of Illustrators (AOI)
Somerset House, Strand, London WC2R 1LA
tel tel 020-7759 1010
email info@theaoi.com
website www.theaoi.com, www.aoiportfolios.com

The UK's professional trade organisation. organisers of the World Illustration Awards and the London Transport Museum Prize for Illustration, and publishers of *Varoom* magazine, *The Illustrator's Guide to Law and Business Practice* and various client directories. See also page 495.

Bikinilists
Unit 18, Govanhill Workspace, 69 Dixon Road, Glasgow G42 8AT
tel 0141 636 3901
website www.bikinilists.com

Maintains an up-to-date database of creative commissioners to creative practitioners. Provides a boutique platform and support to those wishing to create and send promotional email marketing campaigns.

Centaur Media Plc
79 Wells Street, London W1T 3QN
website www.creativereview.co.uk, www.designweek.co.uk

Publishes *Creative Review* magazine and free online resource, *Design Week*.

Contact Creative UK LLP
Old Main Block, Redhill Aerodrome, Kingsmill Lane, Surrey RH1 5YP
tel (01737) 241399
email info@contact-creative.com
website www.contact-creative.com

Publishes *Contact Creative Illustration and Design* and offers a variety of services for practitioners to promote their work in print, by email and online.

File FX
7 Shepperton House, 83–93 Shepperton Road, London N1 3DF
tel 020-7226 6646
email info@filefx.co.uk
website www.filefx.co.uk

Specialises in providing creative suppliers with up-to-date information on commissioning clients in all spheres.

and may refer you to specific art directors or vice versa. These days many art buyers are open to being approached by freelance illustrators, providing the illustrator has some published work. *Creative Review* and the weekly *Campaign* (see page 43) carry agency news, while the AOI also publishes an *Advertising Directory*, updated annually.

Portfolio presentation

In general, UK commissioners prefer to see someone with a strong, consistent, recognisable style rather than an unfocused jack-of-all-trades type and, in time, the internet will probably make this requirement universal, as the world shrinks and the talent pool widens. Thus, when assembling your professional portfolio – whether print or digital (and most illustrators have both) – try to exclude samples which are, in your own eyes, weak, irrelevant, uncharacteristic or simply unenjoyable to do and focus on your strengths instead. Should you be one of those rare, multi-talented individuals who finds it hard to limit themselves stylistically, try splitting conflicting work into separate portfolios/sections (or even websites) geared towards different kinds of clients to avoid confusion.

A lack of formal training need not be a handicap providing your portfolio accurately reflects the needs of the clients you target. Some illustrators find it useful to assemble 'mock-ups' using existing magazine layouts. By responding to the copy and replacing original images with your own illustrations, it is easier to see how your work will look in context. This is particularly relevant to conceptual illustrators, as commissioners are paying for the way you think in addition to your style/technique. Eventually, as you become established you'll be able to augment these with published pieces.

If you are presenting a print portfolio, ideally it should be of the hard or soft, bound, zip-up, ring-bound variety and never exceed A2 in size. A3 or A4 is industry standard these days as clients usually have little desk space; portfolio boxes are also acceptable, though you could run the risk of samples going astray. Alternatively, you may choose to give a laptop or tablet presentation, in which case strive to keep it simple and well organised as if it were a print one. In other words, have a finite number of images and a set running order. If clients wish to see further samples, you have the option of showing some afterwards. Either bring your own device or borrow one with which you are familiar. (Make sure it is fully charged and that you have emergency laptop back-up such as a power brick, USB sticks, CDs, etc. If your presentation involves talking a client through your website or blog rather than files or slideshows, check you will have wireless internet access and, if not, take screen captures.) Complexity of style and diversity of subject matter will dictate how many samples to include but if you are opting for a print portfolio presentation, all should be neatly mounted on lightweight paper or card, or printed out filling the page and placed inside protective plastic sleeves. Originals, high-quality photographs, computer printouts and laser copies are acceptable to clients but tacky out-of-focus snapshots are not. Also avoid including multiple sketchbooks and life drawings, which are anathema to clients. It will be taken for granted that you know how to draw from observation.

Interviews and beyond

Making appointments can be hard work but clients take a dim view of spontaneous visits from passing illustrators. However, face-to-face meetings where geographically practicable can be vital to launching an illustrator's career. Having established the contact name (either from a written source or by asking the company directly), and making sure your work is suitable to the needs of your target, clients are still best initially approached by letter or telephone call. Emails can be overlooked, ignored or simply end up in the company spam filter. Some publishing houses are happy to see freelances, though others prefer a pdf or web link or even an old fashioned print portfolio 'drop-off'. Most commissioners will automatically take photocopies of your work for reference. However, it's advisable to have some kind of promotional material to leave behind such as a CD, postcard, broadsheet or advertising tearsheet. Always ask an enthusiastic client if they know of others who might be interested in your work. Personal recommendation almost always guarantees an interview.

Cleanliness, punctuality and enthusiasm are more important to clients than how you dress – as is a professional attitude to taking and fulfilling a brief. A thorough understanding of each commission is paramount from the outset. You will need to know your client's requirements regarding roughs; format and – if relevant – size and flexibility of artwork; preferred medium if you work in more than one; and whether the artwork is needed in colour or black and white. You will also need to know when the deadline is. Never, under any circumstances agree to undertake a commission unless you are certain you can deliver on time and always work within your limitations. Talent is nothing without reliability.

Self-promotion

There are many ways an illustrator can ensure their work stays uppermost in the industry's consciousness, some more expensive than others. On the affordable front, images can be emailed in a variety of formats, put onto CD or DVD, posted in a blog, or showcased on a website/online portfolio. Social networking platforms, such as Twitter, Pinterest, Tumblr, Facebook and Instagram, can also be invaluable when raising your professional profile. Advertising in source books such as Contact Creative UK's *Contact Creative Illustration and Design*, while available free to commissioners in two formats, doesn't come cheap to advertisers. However, such publications have a long shelf life and are well respected by industry professionals. Competitions are another effective means of self promotion. The annual World Illustration Awards and the London Transport Museum Prize for Illustration, both run by the Association of Illustrators, are open to students and new graduates as well as professional illustrators. There are eight categories in the former and all shortlisted work is published online by the AOI. Category winning work and other shortlisted work is profiled in an annual exhibition and awards catalogue. Keep your eyes open for other competitions too. Even comparatively low-key online challenges such as *Illustration Friday* have resulted in illustrators getting commissions.

As commissioners routinely use internet resources, websites have become an essential method of self-promotion. Make sure yours loads quickly, is simple and straightforward to negotiate and displays decent-sized images. Use your 'About Me' section to discuss the way you work and the type of commissions you've had or hope to work on. Likewise incorporate links to where else your work can be found on the internet. Advertisers in *Contact Creative Illustration and Design* automatically qualify for a web portfolio of 20 images with links back to individual websites. Since *Contact Creative* offers a variety of web-based marketing tools, it is also possible for illustrators to promote their work on the website without appearing in the annual. Currently, both AOI members and non-members can promote their work online at www.aoiportfolios.com, though members can do so at a reduced rate.

Be organised

Once you are up and running, it is imperative to keep organised records of all your commissions. Contracts can be verbal as well as written, though details – both financial and otherwise – should always be confirmed in writing (an email fulfils this purpose) and duplicated for your files. Likewise, keep corresponding client faxes, letters, emails and order forms. The AOI publication *The Illustrator's Guide to Law and Business Practice* offers a wealth of practical, legal and ethical information. Subjects covered include contracts, fee negotiation, agents, licences, royalties and copyright issues.

Money matters

The type of client, the purpose for which you are being commissioned and the usage of your work can all affect the fee you can expect to receive, as can your own professional attitude. Given that it is *extremely* inadvisable to undertake a commission without first agreeing on a fee, you will have to learn to be upfront about funds.

Licence *v.* copyright

Put simply, according to current EU legislation, copyright is the right to reproduce a piece of work anywhere, *ad infinitum*, for any purpose, for a period ending 70 years after the death of the person who created it. This makes it an extremely valuable commodity.

By law, copyright automatically belongs to you, the creator of your artwork, unless you agree to sell it to another party. In most cases, clients have no need to purchase it, and the recommended alternative is for you to grant them a licence instead, governing the precise usage of the artwork. This is far cheaper from the client's perspective and, should they subsequently decide to use your work for some purpose other than those outlined in your initial agreement, will benefit you too as a separate fee will have to be negotiated. It's also worth noting that even if you were ill-advised enough to sell the copyright, the artwork would still belong to you unless you had also agreed to sell it.

Rejection and cancellation fees

Most commissioners will not expect you to work for nothing unless you are involved in a speculative pitch, in which case it will be up to you to weigh up the pros and cons of your possible involvement. Assuming you have given a job your best shot, i.e. carried out the client's instructions to the letter, it's customary to receive a rejection fee even if the client doesn't care for the outcome: 25% is customary at developmental/rough stage and 50% at finished artwork stage. (Clear this with the client before you start, as there are exceptions to the rule.) Cancellation fees are paid when a job is terminated through no fault of the artist or, on occasion, even the client. Customary rates in this instance are 25% before rough stage, 33% on delivery of roughs and 100% on delivery of artwork.

Fixed *v.* negotiable fees

Editorial and publishing fees are almost always fixed with little, if any, room for haggling and are generally considerably lower than advertising and design fees, which tend to be negotiable. A national full-colour 48-sheet poster advertising Marks & Spencer is likely to pay more than a local black-and-white press ad plugging a poodle parlour. If, having paid your editorial dues, you find yourself hankering after commissions from the big boys, fee negotiation – confusing and complicated as it can sometimes be – will become a fact of life. However you choose to go about the business of cutting a deal, it will help if you disabuse yourself of the notion that the client is doing you a whopping favour by considering you for the job. Believe it or not, the client *needs* your skills to bring his/her ideas to life. In short, you are worth the money and the client knows it.

Pricing a commission

Before you can quote on a job, you'll need to know exactly what it entails. For what purpose is the work to be used? Will it be used several times and/or for more than one purpose? Will its use be local or national? For how long is the client intending to use it? Who is the client and how soon do they want the work? Are you up against anyone else (who could possibly undercut you)?

Next, ask the client what the budget is. Believe it or not there's a fair chance they might tell you. Whether they are forthcoming or not, don't feel you have to pluck a figure out of thin air or agree to their offer immediately. Play for time. Tell them you need to review your current workload and that you'll get back to them within a brief, specified period of time. If nothing else, haggling over the phone is less daunting than doing it face to face. If you've had no comparable commissions to date and are an AOI member, check out the going rate by contacting them online for pricing advice (or check out their survey on illustration fees and standards of pricing in the members-only section of the AOI website). Failing that, try speaking to a friendly client or a fellow illustrator who's worked on similar jobs.

When you begin negotiating, have in mind a bottom-line price you're prepared to do the job for and always ask for slightly more than your ideal fee as the client will invariably try to beat you down. You may find it useful to break down your asking price in order to explain exactly what it is the client is paying for. How you do this is up to you. Some people find it helpful to work out a daily rate incorporating overheads such as rent, heating, materials, travel and telephone charges, while others prefer to negotiate on a flat fee basis. There are also illustrators who charge extra for something needed yesterday, time spent researching, model hire if applicable and so on. It pays to be flexible, so if your initial quote exceeds the client's budget and you really want the job, tell them you are open to negotiation. If, on the other hand, the job looks suspiciously thankless, stick to your guns. If the client agrees to your exorbitant demands, the job might start to look more appetising.

Getting paid

Once you've traded terms and conditions, done the job and invoiced the client, you'll then have the unenviable task of getting your hands on your fee. It is customary to send your invoice to the accounts department stating payment within 30 days. It is also customary for them to ignore this entreaty, regardless of the wolf at your door, and pay you when it suits them. Magazines pay promptly, usually within 4–6 weeks; everyone else takes 60–90 days – no matter what.

Be methodical when chasing up your invoice. Send out a statement the moment your 30 days has elapsed and call the accounts department as soon as you like. Take names, note dates and the gist of their feeble excuses, and keep on chasing. Don't worry about your incessant nagging scuppering your plans of further commissions as these decisions are solely down to the art department, and they think you're a gem. Should payment still not be forthcoming three months down the line, it might be advisable to ask your commissioner to follow things up on your behalf. Chances are they'll be horrified you haven't been paid yet and things will be speedily resolved. In the meantime, you'll have had a good deal of practice talking money, which can only make things easier next time around.

And finally...

Basic book-keeping – making a simple, legible record of all your financial transactions, both incoming and outgoing – will be crucial to your sanity once the tax inspector starts to loom. It will also make your accountant's job easier, thereby saving you money. If your annual turnover is less than £81,000, it is unnecessary to provide HM Revenue & Customs with detailed accounts of your earnings. Information regarding your turnover, allowable expenses and net profit may simply be entered on your tax return. Although an accountant is not necessary to this process, many find it advantageous to employ one. The tax system is complicated and dealing with HM Revenue & Customs can be stressful, intimidating and time consuming. Accountants offer invaluable advice on tax allowances, National Insurance and tax assessments, as well as dealing expertly with HM Revenue & Customs on your behalf – thereby enabling you to attend to the business of illustrating.

Further reading

- Fig Taylor, *How To Create A Portfolio and Get Hired* (Laurence King Publishing 2010, 2nd edn 2013)
- Derke Brazell and Jo Davies, *Becoming a Successful Illustrator* (Fairchild Books, *Creative Careers* series, 2013)
- Darrel Rees, *How To Be An Illustrator* (Laurence King Publishing 2008, 2nd edn 2014)

Fig Taylor initially began her career as an illustrators' agent in 1983. She has been the resident 'portfolio surgeon' at the Association of Illustrators since 1986 and also operates as a private consultant to non-AOI member artists. She lectures extensively in Professional Practice to illustration students throughout the UK and is the author of *How to Create a Portfolio and Get Hired* (Laurence King Publishing 2010, 2nd edn 2013).

See also...

- *Art agents and commercial studios*, page 472
- *Getting your greeting cards published*, page 463
- *Copyright questions*, page 667
- *Income tax*, page 709
- *National Insurance contributions and social security benefits*, page 719

How to get ahead in cartooning

Earning a living from creating cartoons is highly competitive. But if you feel that you were born to be a cartoonist, Martin Rowson offers some advice on how to get your work published.

I can't say precisely when I first realised I wanted to be a cartoonist. I personally believe that cartoonists are born and not made so perhaps I should be talking about when I realised I *was* a cartoonist. I do know that, aged ten, I nicked my sister's 1950s British history textbook, which was illustrated throughout by cartoons (from Gillray via Tenniel to Low) and somewhere inside me stirred an unquantifiable yearning to draw – to express myself in the unique style that is the equally unique talent of the 'cartoonist'. So, shortly afterwards I started copying the way Wally Fawkes (better known by his *nom de plume* 'Trog') drew the then Prime Minister Edward Heath.

I've spent most of my life drawing. I drew cartoons for school magazines, designed posters for school societies which invariably turned into political cartoons displayed, in the good old-fashioned way, on walls. I also developed a useful party trick of caricaturing teachers on blackboards. I did Art 'O' and 'A' levels (only a grade B in the latter) but that didn't have much to do with cartoons, and I certainly never contemplated for a moment going to art school. Instead I went to Pembroke College, Cambridge, to read English Literature, and as things turned out I hated it and I spent most of my time doing cartoons for two-bit student magazines, which partly explains how I ended up with a truly terrible degree. More on this later.

At the same time I was half-heartedly putting together a portfolio of work, in the hope that what I'd always done for fun (despite the fact that it was also a compulsion) might just end up being what I did for a living. I'd occasionally send off the portfolio to magazines, never to hear anything back. Then, shortly after graduating I had an idea for a series which I hoped would appeal to a particular demographic at the time (1982). It was called 'Scenes from the Lives of the Great Socialists' and consisted of a number of stylised depictions of leading socialist thinkers and politicians from history, with the added value of an appallingly bad pun thrown into the mixture. One example is 'Proudhon and Bakunin have tea in Tunbridge Wells', which showed the 19th century French and Russian anarchists sitting round a tea table, with Bakunin spitting out his cup of tea and exclaiming 'Proudhon! This tea is disgusting! This isn't proper tea at all!', to which Proudhon replied 'Ah, my dear Bakunin, but Property is Theft!'

I sent about half a dozen of these drawings to the *New Statesman* (then going through one of its periodic lefty phases) and, as usual, heard nothing for months. Then, just before Christmas 1982, in bed suffering from chickenpox, I received a phone call from the art director who said they were going to publish four of the cartoons in their Christmas issue, and would like me to do a series. (I was paid £40 a cartoon, which throughout 1983 meant I was earning £40 a month, which also meant I still had to sign on in order to stay alive.) Thus began my career as a cartoonist.

My three-year deadline

Now living in London, I found myself an agent and *She* magazine was the first offer to come in. They proposed to pay their standard fee of £6 for anything they published. I instructed my agent to inform them that this barely covered my expenses for materials and postage and they could forget it (although I used two other words, one of them also beginning with 'f') – I don't know if he passed on the message. Then someone wanted to do a book of the *New Statesman* cartoons, with the offer of an advance of £750. This took my earned income for that year to somewhere perilously close to a thousand pounds.

At around this time I went to a College reunion and remember skulking around in my Oxfam suit listening with growing irritation to my contemporaries outlining how they'd got into computing/merchant banking/systems analysis or whatever at just the right time, and were earning 50 times more than I was. But I knew I was in for the long haul. As a slight nod to my father's ceaseless injunctions that it was time I got a proper job, I'd set myself a limit of three years, sort of promising that, if I wasn't making a fist of it by then I'd give up (although I doubt I actually meant it).

Luckily, a year into my putative career other contemporaries from university were starting out in journalism, and found they could earn important brownie points from their editors by bringing in a cartoonist to liven up the dull magazines they worked for. That's how I found myself working for *Satellite and Cable TV News* and *One Two Testing....* The fact that I neither knew nor cared about what I was illustrating and lampooning didn't matter. It was work, and also an essential lesson in how to master a brief, however obscure.

However, the true catalyst for my career came when another university acquaintance started working on *Financial Weekly* and, for the usual self-aggrandising reasons, suggested to the editor that they might use me. Again, this was something I knew and cared nothing about but it offered plenty of scope to lampoon truly awful people and of course frequently crossed over into political satire, where my real interest lay. More significantly, the editor himself was so nice, kind and amenable that he consequently drove his staff mad with frustration to the point that they would leave for better things. And when they went, they often took me with them.

Part of the *Financial Weekly* diaspora fled to Eddie Shah's infant *Today* newspaper, and so, just inside my self-imposed three-year time limit, I was producing a daily pocket cartoon for the business pages as well as drawing editorial cartoons for both *Today* and its short-lived sister paper *Sunday Today*. From there, another university friend brought me onto the books pages of the *Sunday Correspondent* and, in doing so, to broadsheet respectability. After that I never really had to solicit for work again. I'd reached cartooning critical mass; the people commissioning knew who I was and, more importantly, knew my work so the hard part was over. And, rather nicely, when I went to another College reunion, I discovered that all the smart boys in computing and banking had been sacked in the recession of the early 1990s.

How can other people get ahead in cartooning?

At one level you could say, between gritted teeth, that all that I've written above proves is that it's just about the old boy network – not what you know but who you know. To an extent that's true, but I'd like to think that none of the publications I'd worked for would have given me a second glance if I couldn't cut the mustard and deliver the goods. So, what do you need to get ahead in cartooning?

First of all, and most importantly, you need to recognise whether or not you truly are a cartoonist, and to do that you need to know what cartoons are. It won't do just to be able to draw; nor is it enough to have a sense of humour. You need to combine the two, and understand that in so doing you are creating something that can't be expressed in any other way. This requires a mindset which, I believe, is innate. Moreover, I don't believe you can teach people how to be cartoonists – they have to teach themselves, and from an early age at that. If you copy other cartoonists to find out how it's done, then slowly but surely you'll develop a style of your own which you feel comfortable with.

Once you recognise what you are, and that you're determined to embark on a career that, like poetry or acting, offers a dream of glamour out of all proportion to its guaranteed financial reward, you then need to create a frame of mind which combines, in equal measure, arrogance and sloth. In other words, you *know* that you're good, and actually better than anyone else who's ever lived, but you're also, crucially, too lazy to do anything else, like accountancy.

Then comes the hard part, which is not for the faint-hearted. You have to work very hard, to make sure what you're producing is really good, and is the best you can do (of which you will always, ultimately, be the best judge). If you're a caricaturist, practice your caricature (and by all means steal other, more established cartoonists' tricks in order to develop your own; after all, they do). If you're a gag cartoonist, hone the gag and work on the drawing so it's clear what's going on (cartooning is the last bastion of realism in the visual arts – abstract cartoons don't work). If you're a political cartoonist, immerse yourself in current affairs and, most importantly, either develop or clearly express your point of view, which can be either right or left wing (a fair, unopinionated cartoonist is as useless and boring as a newspaper columnist with no opinions and nothing to say). A good editorial cartoon is a newspaper column by other means, and is best described as visual journalism, using tricks – like irony, humour, violence and vile imagery – that the big boys in newspaper punditry are too dumb to understand. But remember – while you go through this stage you'll be papering your bedroom wall with rejection slips.

Practical advice

Always try to make your artwork look professional. This means using good paper drawn on in indelible ink, centrally placed. This might sound obvious, but I've seen many cartoons by aspiring cartoonists drawn in crayon on lined file paper going right up to the edge of the sheet. This won't even get halfway out of the envelope before any editor bins it.

Second, always remember that, although you are a genius you have to start somewhere, and some work is always better than no work. If you want to get into newspapers or magazines (which is all there really is if you want to earn some money and not just feel complacent about your beautiful website), identify parts of the press that would benefit from your input.

Journalists producing gardening or travel or, most of all, personal finance sections are crying out for something to liven their pages, something other than a photo which will mark them out as different. In other words, be arrogant enough to be sufficiently humble to illustrate copy you'd never in a million years personally read. Many famous and established cartoonists still knock out stuff for trade papers of crashing obscurity and dullness, this being as good a way as any other of paying the mortgage.

Once you've identified a potential gap in the market, *always* submit your idea or portfolio to the editor of that section, and *never* send it to the art director (despite my experience with the *New Statesman*). There are several reasons for this. First, art directors are inundated with unsolicited work, and so the odds are immediately pitched against you. Second, there's the danger that, in the endless little territorial feuds that pertain in journalism, you will become the exclusive property of the art director who, because he or she hates the gardening editor, will never pass your work on. Third, the section editor will be flattered and delighted to receive something different from the usual dross of press releases and letters of pedantic complaint. If your work tickles their fancy, then you're in, and a section editor always pulls rank over an art director, whatever anyone may imagine.

From these first steps, you will have the beginnings of a portfolio of published work which will stand you in excellent stead on your way to reaching that critical mass of recognition I mentioned earlier.

Finally, never forget that cartoons are something different from anything else. While they combine text journalism and illustration, they end up as something greater than their component parts. In a way, a cartoon is a kind of voodoo, doing harm to someone (whether a politician or a castaway on a desert island) at a distance with a sharp object, which in this case is a pen. It's hard to get established, the number of successful cartoonists earning a decent wedge is tiny and there will always be a generational logjam as the clapped-out old has-beens whose work enrages and disgusts you cling tenaciously to the precious few slots. But if you're determined and tough enough, stick with it and you, too, could become one of those clapped-out has-beens. Until then, just bear in mind that it's a small and crowded profession, and despite everything I've said, the last thing I need is anyone good coming along and muscling in on my territory. In my heart of hearts, I should really advise all aspiring young cartoonists to give up now. Such churlishness apart, however, I'll stick with wishing you good luck.

Martin Rowson is a cartoonist and writer whose work appears regularly in the *Guardian*, the *Daily Mirror*, the *Independent on Sunday* and many other publications. His awards include Political Cartoonist of the Year in 2001, 2003 and 2010, Caricaturist of the Year in 2011, and he produced the Political Cartoon of the Year in 2002 and 2007. His books include comic book versions of *The Waste Land*, *Tristram Shandy* and *Gulliver's Travels*, and *Stuff*, a memoir of clearing out his late parents' house which was longlisted for the Samuel Johnson Prize for Non-fiction. He is Chairman of the British Cartoonists' Association, a trustee of the British Humanists Association and a former vice-president of the Zoological Society of London.

See also...

- *Freelancing for beginners*, page 451
- *Design and Artists Copyright Society*, page 689
- *Marketing yourself online*, page 602
- *Managing your online reputation*, page 607

Getting your greeting cards published

The UK population spends £1.6 billion a year on greeting cards - more than it spends on tea and coffee. Sharon Little of the Greeting Card Association suggests how to find a route into this fiercely competitive business.

There are estimated to be around 800 greeting card publishers in the UK, ranging in size from 'one man bands' to multinational corporations. Not all publishers accept freelance artwork, but a great many do. Remember, whatever the size of the company, all publishers rely on good designs.

The Greeting Card Association

The GCA is the trade association for the greeting card industry.

The GCA website

www.greetingcardassociation.org.uk is the hub for information and contacts for the greeting card industry in the UK.

Its free resources section provides comprehensive information for new publishers, artists, writers and anyone interested in the greeting card industry. They are also on Facebook (www.facebook.com/GreetingCard Association) and Twitter (http://twitter.com/GCAUK).

The GCA Members' Directory

The GCA has over 400 publisher members. You can search its online Members' Directory for publishers looking for artists (www.greetingcardassociation.org.uk/members-directory).

Finding the right publishers

While some publishers concentrate on producing a certain type of greeting card (e.g. humorous, fine art or juvenile) the majority have diversified and publish a variety of greeting card ranges. This of course makes it more difficult for you as an artist to target the most appropriate potential publishers for your work. There are various ways in which you can research the market, quickly improve your publisher knowledge and therefore reduce the amount of wasted correspondence.

Go shopping

Browse the greeting card displays in card shops, varietal stores (WH Smith, Boots), department stores and gift shops. This will give you an insight not only as to what is already out in the market but also which publishers may be interested in your work. Most publishers include their contact details on the back of their cards.

Trade fairs

There are a number of trade exhibitions held during the year at which publishers exhibit their greeting card ranges to retailers and overseas distributors. By visiting these exhibitions, artists will be able to gain both a broad overview of the design trends in the industry and also the current ranges of individual publishers.

Some publishers are willing to meet artists and look through artists' portfolios on the stand; others are not. Be careful not to get in the way of the publisher selling their cards to the buyers – they have spent a lot of time and money on exhibiting in order to attract buyers. If you believe your work could be relevant for them, ask for a contact name and follow it up afterwards. Some larger companies may suggest you contact their art director or design manager, while for smaller businesses it may be the managing director of the company who deals with the design aspect. It is a good idea to have a supply of business cards handy, perhaps illustrated with some of your work, to leave with the publisher.

Sending samples of your work

The first step is to establish whether the publisher accepts work from freelance artists and ascertain their requirements for an artist's submission.

Before you send publishers examples of work, do your research and make sure that the artwork you send is suitable and applicable. It is best to send several examples of your work to show the breadth of your artistic skills; up to 10 or 15 designs is a good amount, preferably as jpgs or pdfs at a decent resolution. You should also provide links to your website and blog. Be sensible when sending work; don't send lots of very large files all in one go as email attachments.

Remember that publishers work a long way in advance. Christmas ranges, for example, are launched to the retailers in January; Spring season ranges (Valentine's Day, Mother's Day, Easter and Father's Day) are generally launched in June/July. Development of a range may take up to six months prior to launching.

When interest is shown

Some publishers respond to artists straightaway, while others prefer to deal with a pile of artists' submissions once a month. Following up your submission with a phone call is natural; however do avoid badgering immediately after you have submitted work – remember that publishers receive numerous submissions and that this can be a long process. Do not be disheartened if you hear nothing for a few weeks.

Caution!

When contacting card publishers, **don't:**

- Send original hard copies.
- Waste your time sending a long letter of introduction. It is unlikely to be read.
- Send very large files as email attachments.
- Sell similar designs to more than one publisher; it may tarnish your reputation.
- Chase the publisher for a response immediately after submitting work.
- Take rejection personally.

When a publisher does contact you, it may be to request more submissions on a specific design style or of a specific character. This speculative development work is usually carried out free of charge. A publisher interested in buying your artwork will then issue you with

Best practice

Follow this valuable advice if you want to get your work published.

Do:

- Your homework. A little time spent researching the market will save you a lot of time, money and frustration in the long run.
- Ring the company before sending copies of your designs to check who to send them to and if they accept freelance work.
- Remember that few greeting card display racks show each card in its entirety, so ensure that some of the design 'action' appears in the top half.
- Remember that most wholesale designs will need to include a caption, or space for one.
- Present your work well.
- Send 10 to 15 examples of your work, preferably as jpg or pdf files at a decent resolution.
- Provide links to your website and blog.
- Put your name and address on the back of every hard copy design.
- Enclose a sae (correct size and postage) if you wish your work to be returned.
- Agree how you will be paid.

a contract. This may cover aspects such as: the terms of payment; rights of usage of the design (e.g. is it just for greeting cards or will it include gift wrap, stationery and so on?); territory of usage (most publishers these days will want worldwide rights), ownership of copyright or license period.

Rates of pay

There is no set industry standard rate of pay for greeting card artists; rough guidelines are given here. Publishers will pay for an individual design or a range of designs. Rates include:

- *Flat fee* – the publisher makes a one-off payment to the artist for ownership of a design for an unlimited period. The fee can be anything from £150–£250 for one design, with a sliding scale coming into play for more than one design.
- *Licensing fee* – this grants the publisher the right to use artwork for specified types of products and for a specified number of years, after which the full rights revert to the artist. Artists are paid in the region of £150+ per design for this.
- *Licensing fee + royalty* – similar to above, but also with a royalty payment on each card sold. Artists would generally receive £100+ licensing fee plus 3% of trade price for each card sold.
- *Advance royalty deal* – the artist is paid a goodwill advance on royalties. In the case of a range, the artist would receive a goodwill advance of say £500–£1,000 and 5% additional royalty payment once the threshold is reached.
- *Royalty only* – the artist will receive regular royalty payments based on the number of cards sold. Royalties are generally paid quarterly. Artists should expect a sales report and royalty statement.

Fees and advances are generally paid on completion of artwork. Most publishers will expect to be granted worldwide rights. This means that any artist being paid royalties will also receive royalty payments for sales overseas, although these will be on a pro rata basis linked to the export trade price.

Sharon Little is Chief Executive Officer of the Greeting Card Association. Article text adapted from guidance at www.greetingcardassociation.org.uk, where additional information is also available. See also http://www.facebook.com/GreetingCardAssociation; http://twitter.com/GCAUK; http://www.youtube.com/GCAClips.

See also...

- *Card and stationery publishers that accept illustrations and photographs,*page 476
- *Freelancing for beginners,* page 451

The freelance photographer

Becoming a successful freelance photographer is as much about marketing as photographic talent. Professional photographer Ian Thraves highlights possibilities for freelancers.

Having an outstanding portfolio is one thing, but to receive regular commissions takes a good business head and sound market knowledge. Although working as a professional photographer can be tough, it is undoubtedly one of the most interesting and rewarding ways of earning a living.

Entering professional photography

A good starting point is to embark on one of the many college courses available, which range from GCSE to degree level, and higher. These form a good foundation, though most teach only the technical and artistic aspects of photography and very few cover the basics of running a business. But a good college course will provide students with the opportunity to become familiar with photographic equipment and develop skills without the restrictions and pressures found in the workplace.

In certain fields, such as commercial photography, it is possible to learn the trade as an assistant to an established photographer. A photographer's assistant will undertake many varied tasks, including preparing camera equipment and lighting, building sets, obtaining props and organising locations, as well as general mundane chores. It usually takes only a year or two for an assistant to become a fully competent photographer, having during that time learnt many technical aspects of a particular field of photography and the fundamentals of running a successful business. There is, however, the danger of a long-standing assistant becoming a clone of the photographer worked for, and it is for this reason that some assistants prefer to gain experience with various photographers rather than working for just one for a long period of time. The Association of Photographers (AOP) can help place an assistant.

However, in other fields of photography, such as photojournalism or wildlife photography, an assistant is not generally required, and photographers in these fields are usually self-taught.

Identifying your market

From the outset, identify which markets are most suitable for the kind of subjects you photograph. Study each market carefully and only offer images which suit the client's requirements.

Usually photographers who specialise in a particular field do better than those who generalise. By concentrating on one or two subject areas they become expert at what they do. Those who make a name for themselves are invariably specialists, and it is far easier for the images of, for example, an exceptional fashion photographer or an award-winning wildlife photographer to be remembered than the work of someone who covers a broad range of subjects.

In addition, photographers who produce work with individual style (e.g. by experimenting with camera angles or manipulating images to create unusual and distinctive effects) are far more likely to make an impact. Alternative images that attract attention and can help sell a product or service are always sought after. This is especially true of advertising photography, but applies also to other markets such as book and magazine publishers, who are continually seeking eye-catching images, especially for front cover use.

Promoting yourself

Effective self-promotion tells the market who you are and what service you offer. A first step should be to create an outstanding portfolio of images, tailored to appeal to the targeted market. Photographers targeting a few different markets should create an individual portfolio for each rather than presenting a single general one, including only a few relevant images. A portfolio should only contain a photographer's most outstanding work. Including substandard images will show inconsistent quality, leaving a potential client in doubt about the photographer's ability.

Images should be presented in a format that the client is used to handling. Usually, a high-quality printed portfolio, backed up by a well-designed website is adequate. Many photographers also produce an additional portfolio in the form of a DVD slideshow or movie. These can be very cheap to create and duplicate and can be handed or posted out to potential and existing clients. Any published material (often referred to as 'tearsheets') should also be added to a portfolio. Tearsheets are often presented mounted and laminated in plastic.

Business cards and letterheads should be designed to reflect style and professionalism. Consider using a good graphic designer to create a logo for use on cards, letterheads and any other promotional literature. Many photographers produce postcard-size business cards and include an image as well as their name and logo.

Other than word of mouth, advertising is probably the best way of making your services known to potential clients. Whether targeting local or global markets, web-based advertising has become the photographer's preferred method of gaining business. Compared to print advertising media, web-based marketing is generally much cheaper and more

Professional organisations

The Association of Photographers (AOP)
Studio 9, Holborn Studios,
49/50 Eagle Wharf Road, London N1 7ED
tel 020-7739 6669
email info@aophoto.co.uk
website www.the-aop.org
See page 495.

BAPLA (British Association of Picture Libraries and Agencies)
59 Tranquil Vale, Blackheath, London SE3 0BS
tel 020-8297 1198
email enquiries@bapla.org.uk
website www.bapla.org.uk
See page 497.

British Institute of Professional Photography (BIPP)
The Coach House, The Firs, High Street,
Whitchurch, Aylesbury, Bucks. HP22 4SJ
tel (01296) 642020
email info@bipp.com
website www.bipp.com
See page 500.

Master Photographers Association
Jubilee House, 1 Chancery Lane, Darlington,
Co. Durham DL1 5QP
tel (01325) 356555
email membership@thempa.com
website www.masterphotographersassociation.co.uk
See page 515.

The Royal Photographic Society
Fenton House, 122 Wells Road, Bath BA2 3AH
tel (01225) 325733
email reception@rps.org
website www.rps.org
See page 522.

accessible to potential markets, plus it allows the photographer more opportunity to showcase a greater number of portfolio images, supported by an unlimited amount of text/copy. However, for more specific commercial markets (such as advertising and design), high-quality printed directories are still popular. These include titles like *The Creative Handbook* and *Contact Photography* (see page 469), which both still take pride-of-place on the bookshelves of many who work in the creative marketplace.

Cold calling by telephone is probably the most cost-effective and productive way of making contacts, and these should be followed up by an appointment to meet potential clients in person, if possible.

Photographers should regard the internet as a primary promotion medium. A cleverly designed website is essential and is a stylish and cost-effective way to expose a photographer's portfolio to a global market, as well as being a convenient way for a potential client to view a photographer's work. Your website address should be included in all business stationery and other forms of advertising.

Creating a website can be much cheaper than advertising using conventional published print media. However, its design should be carefully composed and is probably best left to a professional website designer. Although many images and details about your business can be placed on a website, one limiting factor is the time it can take to navigate an over-complicated site. Unless this is a relatively quick process the viewer may lose patience.

In addition to a traditional website, many photographers have taken to 'blogging' as another form of web-based marketing. The beauty of a blog is the ease at which the owner can update the content. Updatable items may include your latest images, news articles and equipment reviews, plus any other interesting posts that relate to the industry. Blogs and other types of social media, such as Twitter, Facebook and LinkedIn, can all work hand-in-hand to increase a photographer's 'fan-base' or 'following', all serving to strengthen a photographer's market presence on a global basis.

A well-organised exhibition of images is a very effective way of bringing a body of work to the attention of current and potential new clients. Some photographers promote themselves by throwing a preview party with refreshments for friends, colleagues and specially invited guests from the industry. A show that is well reviewed by respected newspaper and magazine journalists can generate additional interest.

As a photographer's career develops, the budget for self-promotion should increase. Many established photographers will go as far as producing full-colour mailers, posters, and even calendars, which all contain examples of their work.

Digital photography

Most photographers now use digital cameras, and image-enhancement and manipulation using computer technology are widely used in the photographic industry. There are various levels of quality produced by digital cameras and photographers should consider the requirements of their market prior to investing in expensive hardware which is prone to rapid change and improvement. At the cheaper level, digital SLR cameras (DSLRs) manufactured by companies such as Nikon and Canon can produce outstanding quality images suitable for many end uses. Cameras like these are used predominantly for press, PR and general commercial work.

At a higher level, many commercial studio photographers have invested in a medium or large format 'digital capture back', which is a high-quality chip that can be adapted to fit many of the conventional studio cameras. This system is far more expensive, but is capable of producing file sizes which closely compare, if not exceed, the quality of a high-resolution scan from large format film. Thus the images are suitable for any end use, such as top-quality advertisements. Photographers thinking of supplying stock libraries with digital images should consider the quality of the camera they use. Stock libraries often supply a diverse range of clients, including advertising, and will therefore only accept the highest standard in order to meet the demands of the market.

Image-enhancement and manipulation using a computer program such as Adobe Photoshop provides photographers with an onscreen darkroom where the possibilities for creating imaginative images are endless. As well as being useful for retouching purposes and creating photo compositions, it provides the photographer with an opportunity to create images that are more distinctive.

Using a stock library

As well as undertaking commissions, photographers have the option of selling their images through a photographic stock library or agency. There are many stock libraries in the UK, some specialising in specific subject areas, such as wildlife photography, and others covering general subjects.

Stock libraries are fiercely competitive, all fighting for a share of the market, and it is therefore best to aim to place images with an established name, although competition amongst photographers will be strong. Each stock library has different specific requirements and established markets, so contact them first before making a submission. Some agencies will ask to see a large number of images from a photographer in order to judge for consistency of quality and saleability, while others will consider an initial submission of just a few images.

Useful information

Bureau of Freelance Photographers
Vision House, PO Box 474, Hatfield AL10 1FY
tel (01707) 651450
email info@thebfp.com
website www.thebfp.com
Membership £54 p.a.
Helps the freelance photographer by providing information on markets and a free advisory service. Publishes *Market Newsletter* (monthly).

DIRECTORIES

Centaur Communications
Centaur Media PLC, Wells Point, 79 Wells Street, London W1T 3QN
tel 020-7269 1450
website www.creativereview.co.uk
Publishes *The Creative Handbook.*

Contact Creative UK LLP
PO Box 397, Reigate, Surrey RH2 2ES
tel (01737) 241399
website www.contact-creative.com
Publishes *Contact Photography.*

Images placed with a library usually remain the property of the photographer and libraries do not normally sell images outright to clients, but lease them for a specific use for a fee, from which commission is deducted. This means that a single image can accumulate many sales over a period of time. The commission rate is usually around 50% of every sale generated by the library. This may sound high, but it should be borne in mind that the library takes on all overheads, marketing costs and other responsibilities involved in the smooth running of a business, allowing the photographer the freedom to spend more time taking pictures.

As a result of the current boom in online advertising, many libraries now offer video clips, in addition to still photographs. The majority of professional DSLR cameras are now capable of capturing 1080p high-definition video footage and this has opened new doors to photographers willing to diversify and exploit the new demand for high-quality video.

Photographers should realise, however, that stock photography is a long-term investment and it can take some time for sales to build up to a significant income. Clearly, photographers who supply the right images for the market, and are prolific, are those who do well, and there are a good number of photographers who make their entire living as full-time stock photographers, never having to undertake commissioned work.

Royalty-free CD companies

Many stock photography agencies now market royalty-free images on CD or as 'virtual CD' downloads. This method of purchasing images as sets is popular with graphic designers since it is possible to create their own in-house image library of popular subjects. Once the CD has been purchased, the images can be used commercially as often as required without paying any further fees. Images are usually purchased as themes, such as health and beauty, sports and fitness, business and industry, etc. Typically, a stock agency will obtain images from photographers by either purchasing them outright, or by paying royalties based on CD sales.

Although photographers may be tempted to sell images in this way in order to gain an instant fee, they should be aware that placing images with a traditional stock library can be far more fruitful financially in the long term, since a good image can accumulate very high fees over a period of time and go on selling for many years to come. Furthermore, the photographer always retains the rights to his or her own images.

Running your own library

Photographers choosing to market their own images or start up their own library have the advantage of retaining a full fee for every picture sale they make. But it is unlikely that an individual photographer could ever match the rates of an established library, or make the same volume of sales per image. However, the internet continually progresses, offering new marketing avenues for photographers and providing many opportunities to sell images worldwide. Previously, only an established stock library would have been able to do this. Before embarking on establishing a 'home' library, photographers should be aware that the business of marketing images is essentially a desk job which involves a considerable amount of admin work and time, which could be spent taking pictures.

When setting up a picture library, your first consideration should be whether to build up a library of your own images, or to take on other contributing photographers. Many photographers running their own libraries submit additional images to bigger libraries to increase the odds of making a good income. Often, a photographer's personal library is made up of work rejected by the larger libraries, which are usually only interested in images that will regularly sell and generate a high turnover. However, occasional sales can generate a significant amount of income for the individual. Furthermore, a photographer with a library of specialised subjects stands a good chance of gaining recognition with niche markets, which can be very lucrative if the competition for those particular subjects is low.

If you take on contributing photographers, the responsibility for another's work becomes yours, so it is important to draw up a contract with terms of business for both your contributing photographers and your clients. Since images are now predominantly distributed as digital files, via CD/DVD or broadband, there is no real problem with loss or damage, which used to be a big problem in the days of film-based originals. However, another issue has emerged since the advent of digital technology in the form of copyright abuse, which is now rife in the industry. Therefore, if representing another's work, it will be the library or agent's responsibility to protect image copyright on behalf of the photographer and also take any necessary legal steps in cases where copyright has been abused.

Reproduction fees should also be established on a strict basis, bearing in mind that you owe it to your contributing photographers to command fees that are as high as possible when selling the rights to their images. It is also essential that you control how pictures will be used and the amount of exposure they will receive. The fees should be established according to the type of client using the image and how the image itself will be reproduced. Important factors to consider are where the image will appear, to what size it will be reproduced, the size of the print run, and the territorial rights required by the client. However, many online agencies have now simplified their pricing structure and base fees on the specific image file size that's required by the client. A smaller file size (or lower resolution) limits the extent to which an image can be reproduced and therefore dictates final reproduction quality.

Working in any field of professional photography is fiercely competitive and successful practitioners commonly spend a great deal of time researching their client's needs and then marketing accordingly – the ultimate goal to ensure their name is always ahead of the ever-increasing competition.

Ian Thraves is a self-employed photographer and former picture editor at Bruce Coleman The Natural World Photo Agency (www.thravesphoto.co.uk).

See also...

- *Freelancing for beginners*, page 451
- *Marketing yourself online*, page page 602
- *Managing your online reputation*, page page 607
- *Design and Artists Copyright Society*, page 689
- *Copyright questions*, page 667

Art agents and commercial art studios

Before submitting work, artists are advised to make preliminary enquiries and to ascertain terms of work. Commission varies but averages 25–30%. The Association of Illustrators (see page 495) provides a valuable service for illustrators, agents and clients.

*Member of the Society of Artists Agents
†Member of the Association of Illustrators

Advocate Art

56 The Street, Ashtead, Surrey KT21 1AZ
tel 020-8879 1166
email mail@advocate-art.com
website www.advocate-art.com
Director Edward Burns

Has 7 agents representing 300 artists and illustrators. Bespoke Illustration for children's books, greeting card and fine art publishers, gift and ceramic manufacturers. For illustrators' submission guidelines see website. New: animation, design and original content represented through LaB; Writers and Artists colLaBorate. Also original art gallery, stock library and website in German, Spanish and French. Founded as a co-operative in 1996.

Allied Artists/Artistic License

tel 07971 111256
email info@allied-artists.net
website www.alliedartists-illustration.com
Contact Gary Mills

Represents over 40 artists specialising in realistic figure, cute and stylised illustrations for children's books, magazines, adult books, plates, prints, cards editorial and advertising. Extensive library of stock illustrations. Commission: 33%. Founded 1983.

Arena*†

Arena Illustration Ltd, 31 Eleanor Road, London E15 4AB
tel 020-8555 9827
website www.arenaillustration.com
Contact Tamlyn Francis

Represents 26 artists illustrating mostly for book covers, children's books and design groups. Average commission 25%. Founded 1970.

The Art Agency

The Lodge, Cargate Lane, Saxlingham Thorpe, Norwich NR15 1TU
tel (01508) 471500
email artagency@me.com
website www.the-art-agency.co.uk

Represents more than 40 artists producing top-quality, highly accurate and imaginative illustrations across a wide variety of subjects and for all age groups, both digitally and traditionally. Clients are children's fiction and non-fiction publishers. Include sae with submissions. Do not email portfolios. Commission: 30%. Founded 1992.

The Art Market*

51 Oxford Drive, London SE1 2FB
tel 020-7407 8111
email info@artmarketillustration.com
website www.artmarketillustration.com
Director Philip Reed

Represents 40 artists creating illustrations for publishing, design and advertising. Founded 1989.

Artist Partners Ltd*

2E The Chandlery, 50 Westminster Bridge Road, London SE1 7QY
tel 020-7401 7904
email chris@artistpartners.demon.co.uk
website www.artistpartners.com
Managing Director Christine Isteed

Represents artists, including specialists in their field, producing artwork in every genre for advertising campaigns, storyboards, children's and adult book covers, newspaper and magazine features and album covers. New artists are only considered if their work is of an exceptionally high standard, in which case submission should be by post only and include a sae. Commission: 30%. Founded 1951.

The Artworks*†

12–18 Hoxton Street, London N1 6NG
tel 020-7729 1973
email mail@theartworksinc.com
website www.theartworksinc.com
Contact Lucy Scherer, Stephanie Alexander-Jinks, Alex Gardner

Represents 22 illustrators for design and advertising work as well as for book jackets, illustrated gift books and children's books. Commission: 25% advances, 15% royalties.

Beehive Illustration

42A Cricklade Street, Cirencester, Glos. GL7 1JH
tel (01285) 885149

email contact@beehiveillustration.co.uk
website www.beehiveillustration.co.uk
Contact Paul Beebee

Represents 200 artists specialising in ELT, education and general children's publishing illustration. Commission: 25%. Founded 1989.

Central Illustration Agency

17b Perseverance Works, 38 Kingsland Road, London E2 8DD
tel 020-3222 0007
email info@centralillustration.com
website www.centralillustration.com
Contact Benjamin Cox

Represents 70 artists producing illustrations for design, publishing, animation and advertising. Commission: 30%. Founded 1983.

Column Arts Agency

104–108 Floodgate Street, Digbeth, Birmingham B5 5SR
tel 07803 244202
email hi@columnartsagency.co.uk
website www.columnartsagency.co.uk
Artists' Agent & Project Manager William Ashbury

Column Arts Agency are an illustration, design and animation agency that represents a range of author-cum-illustrators, artists and commercial creatives. Represents the talented portfolios of individuals in both the UK and US. Founded 2012.

Creative Coverage

Nightingale Terrace, 53 Botley Road, Park Gate, Southampton, Hants SO31 1AZ
tel (01489) 564536
email info@creativecoverage.co.uk
website www.creativecoverage.co.uk
Co-founders Tim Saunders & Caroline Saunders

Fine art book publisher and artists agent. All aspects of marketing for professional artists. Founded January 2013.

David Lewis Agency

3 Somali Road, London NW2 3RN
tel 020-7435 7762 *mobile* (07931) 824674
email davidlewis34@hotmail.com
website www.davidlewisillustration.com
Director David Lewis

Considers all types of illustration for a variety of applications but mostly suitable for book and magazine publishers, design groups, recording companies and corporate institutions. Also offers a comprehensive selection of images suitable for subsidiary rights purposes. Send return postage with samples. Commission: 30%. Founded 1974.

Début Art & The Coningsby Gallery†*

30 Tottenham Street, London W1T 4RJ
tel 020-7636 1064
email info@debutart.com
website www.debutart.com
website www.coningsbygallery.com
Directors Andrew Coningsby, Jonathan Hedley

Representing 140+ of the world's leading illustrators, motion artists and illustrative designers. Commission: 30%/25%. Worldwide commissioning client and artist base. Submissions from new illustrators always welcome via email. Founded 1985.

Eastwing†*

99 Chase Side, Enfield EN2 6NL
tel 020-8367 6760
email representation@eastwing.co.uk
website www.eastwing.co.uk
Partners Andrea Plummer, Gordon Allen *Contact* Abby Glassfield

Represents 31 artists who work across advertising, design, publishing, editorial. Commission: 25–30%. Founded 1985.

Eye Candy Illustration

Field Cottage, Saintbury WR12 7PX
tel 020-8291 0729
email info@eyecandyillustration.com
website www.eyecandyillustration.com
Managing Director Mark Wilson

Represents more than 50 artists producing work for advertising campaigns, packaging, publishing, editorials, greeting cards, merchandising and a huge variety of design projects. Submit printed samples with sae or email low-res jpg files via website. Founded 2002.

Ian Fleming Associates – see Phosphor Art Ltd

Folio Illustrators' & Designers' Agents

10 Gate Street, Lincoln's Inn Fields, London WC2A 3HP
tel 020-7242 9562
email info@folioart.co.uk
website www.folioart.co.uk
website www.folioboutique.com

All areas of illustration. Founded 1976.

Good Illustration Ltd

11–15 Betterton Street, London WC2H 9BP
tel 020-8123 0243, (US) +1 347-627-0243
email draw@goodillustration.com
website www.goodillustration.com
Directors Doreen Thorogood, Kate Webber, Tom Thorogood

Represents over 50 artists for advertising, design, publishing and animation work. Send return postage with samples. Commission: 25% publishing, 30% advertising. Founded 1977.

Graham-Cameron Illustration

59 Hertford Road, Brighton BN1 7GG
tel (01273) 385890

email enquiry@gciforillustration.com
and Helen Graham-Cameron, Graham-Cameron Illustration, The Art House, Uplands Park, Sheringham, Norfolk NR26 8NE
tel (01263) 821333
website www.gciforillustration.com
Partners Helen Graham-Cameron, Duncan Graham-Cameron

Represents 37+ artists and undertakes all forms of illustration for publishing and communications. Specialises in educational, children's and information books. Telephone before sending A4 sample illustrations with sae or email samples or a link to a website. Do not send MSS. Founded 1985.

The Guild of Aviation Artists

Trenchard House, 85 Farnborough Road, Farnborough, Hants GU14 6TF
tel (01252) 513123
email admin@gava.org.uk
website www.gava.org.uk
President Michael Turner FGAvA, *Secretary/ Administrator* Susan Gardner

Specialising in aviation art in all hand-applied mediums and comprising approx. 450 members, the Guild sells, commissions and exhibits members' work. Founded 1971.

Illustration Ltd*†

2 Salamanca Place, Albert Embankment, London SE1 7HB
tel 020-7720 5202
email hello@illustrationweb.com
website www.illustrationweb.com
Contact Juliette Lott, Victoria Pearce, Alice Ball, Mike Cowley, Harry Lyon-Smith

Represents 150 artists producing illustrations and animation for international advertisers, designers, publishers and editorial clients. Artists should send submissions via the website. Founded 1929.

Image by Design Licensing

Suite 3, 107 Bancroft, Hitchin, Herts. SG5 1NB
tel (01462) 422244
email lucy@ibd-licensing.co.uk
website www.ibd-licensing.co.uk
Contact Lucy Brenham

Quality artwork, design and photography for a wide range of products including greeting cards, wall art, stationery, calendars, ceramics, table top, jigsaws, giftware and needlecraft. New artists always considered. Founded 1987.

B.L. Kearley Ltd

16 Chiltern Street, London W1U 7PZ
tel 020-7935 9550
email christine.kearley@kearley.co.uk
website www.kearley.co.uk
Agent C.R. Kearley

Represents over 30 artists and has been supplying top-quality illustrations for over 60 years. Mainly specialises in children's book and educational illustration for the domestic market and overseas. The company is known for realistic figurative work. Also specialises in the sale of original book illustration artwork from own artists dating back to the founding of the company. Commission 25%. Founded 1948.

Kids Corner

The Old Candlemakers, West Street, Lewes BN7 2NZ
tel 020-7593 0500
email info@meiklejohn.com
website www.kidscornerillustration.co.uk
Managing Director Claire Meiklejohn

Illustration Agency, representing a collection of highly talented illustrators, from award-winning to emerging artists for children's publishing. Styles include fun, cute, stylised, picture book, young fiction, reference, graphic, traditional, painterly and digital. Established 2015.

Lemonade Illustration Agency

Hill House, Suite 231, 210 Upper Richmond Road, London SW15 6NP
tel (07891) 390750
email lucy@lemonadeillustration.com
and 347 Fifth Ave, New York, NY 10016, USA
website www.lemonadeillustration.com
Contact Lucy Quinn

Represents over 100 illustrators, storyboard artists and animators who create illustrations for all kinds of media from TV to children's books. Also has a specialist division, Fizzy, which represents 50 artists who provide styles suited for the children's picture book and educational market. Any submissions from illustrators by email must contain a website link (no attachments) or hard copies of samples can be sent by post with a sae. Lemonade serves clients worldwide through offices in London, New York and Taipei.

Frances McKay Illustration

17 Church Road, West Mersea, Essex CO5 8QH
tel (01206) 383286
email frances@francesmckay.com
website www.francesmckay.com
Proprietor Frances McKay

Represents Represents 20+ artists for illustration mainly for children's books. For information on submissions please look at the website. Submit email low-res scans or colour copies of recent work; sae essential for return of all unsolicited samples. Commission: 25%. Founded 1999.

Meiklejohn Illustration*

The Old Candlemakers, West Street, Lewes BN7 2NZ
tel 020-7593 0500
email info@meiklejohn.co.uk
website www.meiklejohn.co.uk
Managing Director Claire Meiklejohn

Illustration Agency, representing a collection of highly talented illustrators, covering a wide range of style, from traditional, children's publishing, photorealistic, cartoon to contemporary.

N.E. Middleton Artists' Agency

email kathy.bishop@btinternet.com
website www.nemiddleton.co.uk

Designs for greeting cards, stationery, prints, calendars, china and jigsaws. Submissions by email only, following link from website.

Monkey Feet Illustration

tel 07760 162374
email enquiries@monkeyfeetillustration.co.uk
website www.monkeyfeetillustration.co.uk
Director Adam Rushton

Presenting portfolios of over 50 artists creating work for children's book publishers, design agencies, greeting cards companies and toy manufacturers. Founded 2002.

NB Illustration

40 Bowling Green Lane, London EC1R 0NE
tel 020-7278 9131
email info@nbillustration.co.uk
website www.nbillustration.co.uk
Directors Joe Najman, Charlotte Dowson, Paul Najman

Represents 50+ artists and will consider all material for the commercial illustration market. Sae essential. Commission: 30%. Founded 2000.

New Division*

The Old Candlemakers, West Street, Lewes BN7 2NZ
tel 020-7593 0505
email info@newdivision.com
website www.newdivision.co.uk
Managing Director Claire Meiklejohn

Illustration Agency, representing a collection of highly talented illustrators, from award-winning artists to talented new graduates. Boutique agency represents a select group of lifestyle, fashion and stylised artists. Founded 1983.

The Organisation*

The Basement, 69 Caledonian Road, London N1 9BT
tel 0845 054 8033
email lorraine@organisart.co.uk
website www.organisart.co.uk
Contact Lorraine Owen

Represents over 60 international illustrators. Contemporary and traditional styles for all areas of publishing. Stock illustration also available. See website for submission guidelines. Founded 1987.

Oxford Designers & Illustrators Ltd

Suite M, Kidlington Centre, High Street, Kidlington, Oxford OX5 2DL
tel (01865) 512331
email roger@odi-design.co.uk
website www.o-d-i.com
Directors Roger Noel (general managing), Andrew King (managing)

Studio of 15 staff working for educational publishers and businesses. Design for print and the web. All types of artwork including scientific, technical, medical, natural history, figures, 3D, cartoons, animation, maps and diagrams – computer generated and hand drawn. Not an agency. Founded 1968.

Phosphor Art Ltd*

tel 020-7064 4666
email info@phosphorart.com
website www.phosphorart.com
Directors Jon Rogers, Catriona Wydmanski

Represents 46 artists and specialises in innovative graphic digital illustration with artists working in watercolour, oil and gouche methods as well as pen and ink, scraper, charcoal and engraving styles. Also animation. Incorporates Ian Fleming Associates and The Black and White Line. Commission: 33.3%.

Plum Pudding Illustration

Park House, 77–81 Bell Street, Reigate, Surrey RH2 7AN
tel (01737) 244095
email letterbox@plumpuddingillustration.com
website www.plumpuddingillustration.com
Director Mark Mills *Associate Director* Hannah Whitty

Represents 80+ artists, producing illustrations for children's publishing, advertising, editorial, greeting cards and packaging. See website for submission procedure. Commission: 30%. Founded 2006.

Sylvie Poggio Artists Agency

36 Haslemere Road, London N8 9RB
tel 020-8341 2722
email sylviepoggio@blueyonder.co.uk
website www.sylviepoggio.com
Directors Sylvie Poggio, Bruno Caurat

Represents 40 artists producing illustrations for publishing and advertising.

Vicki Thomas Associates

195 Tollgate Road, London E6 5JY
tel 020-7511 5767
email vickithomasassociates@yahoo.co.uk
website www.vickithomasassociates.com
Consultant Vicki Thomas

Considers the work of illustrators and designers working in greetings/gift industries, and promotes work to gift, toy, publishing and related industries. Email sample images, covering letter and CV. Commission: 30%. Founded 1985.

Card and stationery publishers that accept illustrations and photographs

Before submitting work, artists and photographers are advised to ascertain requirements of the company they are approaching, including terms and conditions. Only top quality material should be submitted; inferior work is never accepted.

*Member of the Greeting Card Association

The Almanac Gallery*

Waterwells Drive, Gloucester, Glos. GL2 2PH
tel (01452) 888999
email submissions@greatbritishcards.co.uk
website www.greatbritishcards.co.uk

Specialises in contemporary art cards. Brands include Animal Magic; Ailsa Black; Copper Tree; Almanac Wildlife Colour Foil; Over The Rainbow; Almanac Art; MODA; Gaia: Barry Goodman; Shawn St Peter; Ken Eardley; Indian Summer; and Natural History Museum Wildlife Photographer of The Year – **see The Great British Card Company**.

Card Connection Ltd*

Park House, South Street, Farnham, Surrey GU9 7QQ
tel (01252) 892300
email enquiries@cardconnection.co.uk
website www.card-connection.co.uk
Managing Director Michael Johnson

Everyday and seasonal designs. Styles include cute, fun, traditional, contemporary, humour and photographic. Humorous copy and jokes plus sentimental verse. Founded 1992.

CardsWorld Ltd t/a 4C For Charity

114 High Street, Stevenage, Herts. SG1 3DW
tel 0845 230 0046
email design@charitycards.org
website www.charitycards.org

Contemporary and traditional Christmas cards for the corporate and charity market (London, international and festive themes). Submit low-res artwork by email no larger than 5MB. No verses or cute styles. Works with 70+ charities. Founded 1966.

Caspari Ltd*

Linden House, John Dane Player Court, East Street, Saffron Walden, Essex CB10 1LR
tel (01799) 513010
email info@caspari.co.uk
website www.casparionline.com

Traditional fine art/classic images; 5 x 4in transparencies. No verses. Founded 1990.

Colneis Marketing Ltd*

York House, 2–4 York Road, Felixstowe IP11 7QQ
tel (01394) 271668
email colneiscards@btconnect.com
website www.colneisgreetingcards.com
Proprietor John Botting

Photographs (preferably medium format) and colour artwork of nature and cute images. Founded 1994.

Colour House Graphics Ltd*

York House, 2–4 York Road, Felixstowe IP11 7QQ
tel (01394) 271668
email colourhousegraphics@hotmail.com
website www.colourhousegraphics.co.uk
Contact John Batting

Contemporary styles of painting of subjects relating to people's everyday lives. Particularly interested in sophisticated, loose, graphic styles. No verses. Founded 1990.

Simon Elvin Ltd*

Wooburn Industrial Park, Wooburn Green, Bucks. HP10 0PE
tel (01628) 526711
email studioadmin@simonelvin.com
website www.simonelvin.com
Art Director Fiona Buszard *Studio Manager* Rachel Green

Female/male traditional and contemporary designs, female/male cute, wedding/anniversary, birth congratulations, fine art, photographic animals, flowers and male imagery, traditional sympathy, juvenile ages, special occasions and giftwrap.

Looking for submissions that show flair, imagination and an understanding of greeting card design. Artists should familiarise themselves with the ranges, style and content. Submit a small collection of either colour copies or prints (no original artwork) and include a sae for return of work. Alternatively email jpg files.

Gallery Five Ltd*

The Old Bakery, 1 Bellingham Road, London SE6 2PN
tel 020-8697 1629
website www.galleryfive.co.uk

Send samples of work FAO 'Gallery Five Art Studio'. Colour photocopies, Mac-formatted zip/CD acceptable, plus sae. No verses.

Gemma International Ltd*

Linmar House, 6 East Portway, Andover, Hants SP10 3LU
tel (01264) 388400
email esales@gemma-international.co.uk
website www.gemma-international.co.uk
Directors William Harris, A. Parkin, T. Rudd-Clarke, David Wesson

Cute, contemporary, leading-edge designs for children, teens and young adults. Founded 1984.

Graphic Humour Ltd

PO Box 717, North Shields, Tyne & Wear NE30 4WR
tel 0191-280 5019
email enquiries@graphichumour.com
website www.graphichumour.com

Risqué and everyday artwork ideas for greeting cards; short, humorous copy. Founded 1984.

The Great British Card Company

(incorporating Paper House, Medici Cards and The Almanac Gallery)
Waterwells Drive, Gloucester, Glos. GL2 2PH
tel (01452) 888999
email art@paperhouse.co.uk
website www.greatbritishcards.co.uk

Publishers of everyday, Christmas and spring greeting cards, notecards, gift wrap and gift bags. Particularly welcomes new humorous submissions. For a full listing of brands published please visit website.

Green Pebble

Roos Hall Studio, Bungay Road, Beccles, Suffolk NR34 8HE
tel (01502) 710427
email ruby@greenpebble.co.uk
website www.greenpebble.co.uk
Publisher Michael Charles

Publisher of fine art greeting cards and associated products by artists. See website for style before submitting. Send a minimum of 6 design thumbnails via email. Founded 2010.

Hallmark Cards Plc*

Hallmark House, Bingley Road, Heaton, Bradford BD9 6SD
tel (01274) 252523
email creativesubmissions@hallmark-uk.com
website www.hallmark.co.uk

See website for freelance opportunities and submission details.

Hotchpotch Publishing Ltd

PO Box 264, Hampton, Middlesex TW12 2ZT
tel 020-8941 0126
email art@hotchpotchpublishing.com
website www.hotchpotchpublishing.com
Senior Designer/Studio Co-ordinator Helen Wallace

Colour artwork for greeting cards, giftwrap and social stationery. Founded 1997.

Leeds Postcards

4 Granby Road, Leeds LS6 3AS
email xtine@leedspostcards.com
website www.leedspostcards.com
website shop online at www.leedspostcards.co.uk
Contact Christine Hankinson

Publisher and distributor of postcards; feminism, animal rights and socialism shows the drift. Send only suitable and relevant jpg files to email above. If published, paid by advance royalty on print run.

Lima Design

1 Lordship Lane, London SE22 8EW
tel 020-8693 4257
email lara@lima-designlimited.co.uk
website www.limadesign.co.uk
Proprietor Lisa Breakwell

Produces contemporary, design-conscious cards which are all hand applied using resisters and capacitors, ribbon, indoor sparklers, animal-shaped rubber bands, metallic thread and beads. Founded 2002.

Ling Design Ltd*

Westmoreland House, Westmoreland Street, Bath BA2 3HE
tel (01225) 489760
email info@lingdesign.co.uk
website www.lingdesign.co.uk
Creative Director Isabel Scott Evans

Artwork for greeting cards, stationery and giftwrap.

Medici Cards

Waterwells Drive, Gloucester, Glos. GL2 2PH
tel (01452) 888999
email submissions@greatbritishcards.co.uk
website www.greatbritishcards.co.uk

Specialises in market leading art and photographic cards. Brands include National Geographic; English Heritage; Royal Horticultural Society; and Medici Cards Blue Label – **see The Great British Card Company**.

Miko Greetings*

85 Landcroft Road, East Dulwich, London SE22 9JS
tel 020-8693-1011
email info@miko-greetings.com
website www.miko-greetings.com
Head Creative, Illustrator, Managing Director, Mik Brown/Miko, *Creative Photographer* Toby Brown, *Proof Checker* Annie Horwood

High-end, quality, sophisticated, creative, humorous illustrated cards. Visually stunning photographic cards. Inside mostly blank for any occasion. A small company with a big ambition. Founded 2014.

Paper House

Waterwells Drive, Gloucester, Glos. GL2 2PH
tel (01452) 888999

email art@paperhouse.co.uk
website www.greatbritishcards.co.uk

Producers of everyday and seasonal greeting cards. Brands: Humour Factory; Birdwit; Two Fat Gherkins; Eric The Penguin; Look At It This Way; Fred & Ginger; Darkroom; Elgin Court; Young At Heart; Just My Type; Retrotopia; Histericals; Dollop Of Sauce; Off The Bone; Peter Cross; LaffSmacked; Wildlife; Villager Jim; Peony Rose; The Great Outdoors; The Country Diary Of An Edwardian Lady; Bee Brown; Special Days; Bebunni; Hi There; Word For Word – **see The Great British Card Company**.

Paperlink Ltd*

356 Kennington Road, London SE11 4LD
tel 020-7582 8244
email info@paperlink.co.uk
website www.paperlink.co.uk
Directors Louise Tighe, Tim Porte, Tim Purcell

Publishers of ranges of humorous and contemporary art greeting cards. Produce products under licence for charities. Founded 1986.

Pineapple Park*

Unit 9, Henlow Trading Estate, Henlow Camp, Beds. SG16 6DS
tel (01462) 814817
email sally@pineapplepark.co.uk
website www.pineapplepark.co.uk
Main contact Sally Kelly *Directors* Peter M. Cockerline, Sarah M. Parker

Illustrations and photographs for publication as greeting cards. Contemporary, cute, humour: submit artwork or laser copies with sae. Photographic florals always needed. Humour copy/jokes accepted without artwork. Founded 1993.

Powell Publishing

Millyard House, Millyard Way, Eythorne, Dover, Kent CT17 4NL
tel (01304) 833550
email richard@powellpublishing.co.uk
website www.powellpublishing.co.uk
Directors D.J. Powell *Art & Design Manager* Richard Oram

Greeting cards publishers. Interested in Christmas designs for the charity card market. Division of Powell Print Ltd.

Nigel Quiney Publications Ltd*

Cloudesley House, Shire Hill, Saffron Walden, Essex CB11 3FB
tel 01799 520200
email carl.pledger@nigelquiney.com
website www.nigelquiney.com
Contact Carl Pledger (Head of Product)

Everyday and seasonal greeting cards including fine art, photographic, humour, contemporary and cute. Submit by email or colour copies, photographs, transparencies or disk by post: no original artwork.

Really Good*

The Old Mast House, The Square, Abingdon, Oxon OX14 5AR
tel (01235) 537888
email ello@reallygood.uk.com
website www.reallygood.uk.com
Director David Hicks

Always looking for fun, trendy and quirky artwork to publish on cards, stationery or gifts. Check the website first, and if there is a fit, email website/blog link or small jpg or pdf files to view. Please do not post submissions. Really Good is the sister company of Soul. Founded 1987.

Felix Rosenstiel's Widow & Son Ltd

Fine Art Publishers, 33–35 Markham Street, London SW3 3NR
tel 020-7352 3551
email artists@felixr.com
website www.felixr.com

Invites offers of artwork of a professional standard for reproduction as picture prints for the picture framing trade. Any type of subject considered. See website for submission details.

Royle Publications Ltd – see Medici Cards

J. Salmon Ltd

100 London Road, Sevenoaks, Kent TN13 1BB
tel (01732) 452381
email enquiries@jsalmon.co.uk
website www.jsalmon.co.uk

Picture postcards, calendars, greeting cards and local view booklets.

Santoro London

Rotunda Point, 11 Hartfield Crescent, London SW19 3RL
tel 020-8781 1100
email submissions@santorographics.com
website www.santoro-london.com
Directors Jason Freeman

Publishers of innovative and award-winning designs for greeting cards, giftwrap and gift stationery. Bold, contemporary images with an international appeal. Subjects covered: contemporary, pop-up, cute, quirky, fashion, retro. Submit samples as colour copies or digital files (jpg or pdf files). Founded 1985.

Second Nature Ltd*

10 Malton Road, London W10 5UP
tel 020-8960 0212
email rods@secondnature.co.uk
website www.secondnature.co.uk
Publishing Director Rod Schragger

Contemporary artwork for greeting cards and handmade cards; jokes for humorous range; short modern sentiment; verses. Founded 1981.

Solomon & Whitehead Ltd

Lynn Lane, Shenstone, Staffs. WS14 0DX
tel (01543) 483000

Fine art prints, limited editions and originals, framed and unframed.

Soul*

Old Mast House, The Square, Abingdon, Oxon OX14 5AR
tel (01235) 537816
email smile@souluk.com
website www.souluk.com
Director David Hicks

Publishers of contemporary trend gifts, cards and stationery. Also wrapping paper and notebooks. Look at the website, and if there is a fit please email website/blog link, or small jpg or pdf files to view. Please do not post artwork. Soul is the sister company of Really Good.

Noel Tatt Group/Impress Publishing*

Appledown House, Barton Business Park, Appledown Way, New Dover Road, Canterbury, Kent CT1 3TE
tel (01227) 811600
email mail@noeltatt.co.uk
website www.noeltatt.co.uk
Directors Jarle Tatt, Diane Tatt, Richard Parsons, Ian Hylands

General everyday cards – broad mix; Christmas. Will consider verses. Founded 1964.

UK Greetings Ltd

Mill Street East, Dewsbury, West Yorkshire WF12 9AW
tel (01924) 465200
website www.ukgreetings.co.uk
Sales and Marketing Director James Conn *Director of Marketing* Ceri Stirland

All types of artwork, any size; submit as colour roughs, colour copies or transparencies. Especially interested in humorous artwork and ideas.

Wishing Well Studios (cbg)*

The Granary, Wallgate, Wigan WN1 1BA
tel (01243) 792642
email nicky.harrison@cbg.co.uk
website www.wishingwell.co.uk
Contact Nicky Harrison

Part of Carte Blanche Group. Rhyming and prose verse 4–24 lines long; also jokes. All artwork styles considered but do not send originals (enclose a sae for return of work). Email attachements no larger than 3MB.

Woodmansterne Publications Ltd*

1 The Boulevard, Blackmoor Lane, Watford, Herts. WD18 8UW
tel (01923) 200600
website www.woodmansterne.co.uk

Publisher of greeting cards and social stationery featuring fine and contemporary art and photography (colour and b&w). Submit colour copies, photographs or jpg files by email.

Societies, prizes and festivals

Festivals for writers

Experienced festival director Judith Heneghan gives advice on what to expect from literary and writers' festivals, and how to prepare for and take full advantage of the opportunities they have to offer.

Festivals for writers are proliferating at an astonishing rate. Every summer, new events are launched, some in village halls or community centres, others in libraries or universities or stately homes – or maybe even in a yurt in a field. Yet, at first glance, 'festival' is a curious word to apply to writerly activity. It conjures up a party: celebratory, loud, full of people wearing colourful clothes and, quite possibly, wellies. Will there be music, stand-up comedy, food stalls selling over-priced burgers and dodgy toilet facilities? Where does the writing come in?

Well, in my view, the best 'festivals of words' have a clear sense of purpose, place or community. They may have international reach or remain small and local with individually ticketed events or week-long packages, but they understand their audiences and are committed to their goals. Such festivals offer all kinds of opportunities for writers.

The literary festival

Literary festivals, or book festivals, are primarily festivals for readers. Typically they offer readings, book signings, storytelling, author interviews, Q&A, panel discussions and debates, generally on a 'per event' basis. Their audiences expect to be stimulated and entertained and they are a wonderful way for writers to reach new readers, sell copies of their books, boost fragile egos, leave the shed behind for a weekend and – let's be honest – *socialise.*

How do you get a gig?

If you have a publicist, let them know you're interested and they'll probably do the work for you. However, many writers need to do the leg-work themselves.

First, *research* the kinds of events put on by a particular festival. Is there a theme? Do they have a track-record of inviting emerging writers as well as 'big names'?

Then *get in touch with the festival director* several months before they launch their programme with a brief message of introduction. Mention your book, provide snippets of any reviews and details of any prizes, suggest an engaging title for an event and let them know if you've made other public appearances. Are there any video clips of you talking about your book?

If you are new to the circuit, consider whether you might be more comfortable with a joint appearance or an interview-style presentation. Debut novelist Claire Fuller says she prefers this 'in conversation with…' format as it reduces the pressure and is, she believes, more interesting for the audience.

Check the details – assume nothing!

If you are booked to do an event, great. But the research doesn't stop there – find out about:

• *Marketing*. How will the event be marketed? Will your event be publicised individually or merely in the general programme?
• *Expenses*. Be sure to ask questions about rates and expenses, as some festivals pay a modest fee or cover travel and accommodation only, but many expect authors or their publishers to foot the bill. And writers need to eat.
• *Technical matters*. Issues with microphones and screens, or lack of them, can take writers by surprise. Find out if you can stand or walk around at your event and let them know if you need to sit down.
• *Sales*. Ask whether the festival arranges for books to be on sale and, if not, liaise with your publisher or the festival bookseller.

This type of detail can significantly affect your festival experience. However, you too have a responsibility to your audience who have paid good money to come and listen to you. Are you confident in front of a crowd? Do you enjoy taking questions from the floor? Have you a clear reading voice and interesting anecdotes to relate and will you be comfortable with an audience of 300, or 30, or possibly just three people?

The book festival circuit can form a significant and rewarding aspect of a writer's life, but don't do it unless you enjoy it.

The writers' festival

The writers' festival, in contrast, is a festival for writers. Attendees typically consist of new, unpublished or emerging writers who are seeking fresh inspiration or who wish to hone their craft, receive constructive critical feedback, meet like-minded creative types in a supportive environment and network with industry insiders. Smaller festivals may focus on a particular genre or theme while the larger ones usually cater for all forms of writing with a broad range of workshops, panels, writing competitions, networking receptions, talks and full-day courses. Increasingly, literary and book festivals offer some of these services too, but the writers' festival still tends to provide a more immersive experience, typically over one, two or three days.

The one-to-one appointment

As publishers close their doors to unsolicited submissions and the unappealingly named 'slush piles' grow ever more precipitous, writers seek new ways to circumvent such difficulties. One of the biggest festival attractions for any writer seeking publication is the opportunity to have a one-to-one meeting with a literary agent or commissioning editor. The format is usually quite simple. Your work is read beforehand by an industry professional. You get critical feedback, a commercial appraisal and the chance to establish a personal contact. Agents and editors too seem to welcome the opportunity to scout for new talent and meet potential authors face to face. Time-slots are managed by the festival team. What's not to like?

Your one-to-one appointment: some dos and don'ts

• Do your research to find out what each editor, agent or book doctor is looking for and how they want it presented.
• Write down any questions you have about your work.
• Arrive on time – a typical appointment lasts 10-15 minutes and you'll want to make the most of it.
• Listen carefully and make notes so that you can remember the details later.
• Don't take criticism personally – view it as an opportunity to reflect on and improve your work.

However, writers are wise to do their homework first. If it's publication you seek, make an appointment with someone who is looking for the kind of work you produce. Visit their website, check their entry in the *Writers' & Artists' Yearbook*, follow them on Twitter, research the kinds of writers they represent. Usually the festival organisers will ask for a writing sample and cover letter in advance which they forward to the agent or editor or 'book doctor' who may be an experienced author or writing tutor. Treat this as you would any formal submission: be courteous and concise. Get their name right! Then, when the time comes for your meeting, use it as a learning experience. Listen carefully to any feedback and remember that the professional you are talking to is a human being too; their opinion is subjective and personal but you have asked them to consider your submission using their specialist knowledge and experience. If you are told that the work 'isn't ready' or 'it's not for me', then be sure to ask why. If they ask to see more, be sure to deliver!

The festival at Winchester

The University of Winchester Writers' Festival is now in its 35th year and as such was one of the first of its kind to nurture emerging writers. I was appointed Director in 2013 so there's a lot of history behind me and I'm still learning, though the purpose of the festival is as clear now as it has always been: writers need supporting in a creative and critically engaged environment.

The festival takes place over three days towards the end of June within the pleasant campus at the University of Winchester. Many attendees say it is an intense experience, with a choice of ten all-day masters' courses for more experienced writers, 32 Saturday talks and nine Sunday workshops for those at an earlier stage in their writing or embarking on a new project. These talks and workshops are delivered by literary agents and commissioning editors, experienced authors, poets and industry specialists who also participate in hundreds of 15-minute one-to-one appointments.

New last year was our Writers' Room – a quiet space for thinking, day-dreaming or undertaking one of the guided writing exercises. However, the festival weekend is also a celebration, so we run an open mic, incorporate 'fringe' events such as book launches, signings and impromptu readings, and invite a world-renowned author such as Sebastian Faulks to give the keynote address.

Then of course there are the writing competitions run by most writers' festivals. This year we ran ten competitions at Winchester, ranging from 'Poetry' and 'First Three Pages of a Novel' to 'Writing Funny Fiction for Children', 'Flash Fiction' and 'Pitch a TV Drama'. You don't have to attend the festival to enter and, in keeping with our ethos, entrants can, for a small additional fee, receive a written adjudication. Prizes, similarly, include consultations with agents, scriptwriting software, writing courses and, naturally, copies of the Writers' & Artists' Yearbook. A win boosts a writer's confidence and often helps attract publishing interest.

So, my job is principally that of juggler. I devise the programme and book the speakers while seeking a balance of genre, form, events for beginners and experienced writers, and an appropriate mix of traditional craft concerns and industry innovations and developments. Along with the Events Manager, I deal with advertising, design, campus facilities and our website, as well as speaking to writers' groups and students. During the festival itself, my role is that of facilitator and introducer; thankfully we are most ably supported by a fantastic team of volunteers and campus staff. Naturally I want the speakers to have a positive and productive experience, but most of all I want the festival attendees – writers all – to feel welcomed, supported and inspired.

And the downside?

There are potential pitfalls. One is mild exhaustion. An immersive writers' festival can feel intensive, challenging and revealing. My advice would be to take a bit of time to reflect on and digest the experience. If it has been worthwhile you probably *should* feel tired, so give yourself the day off afterwards if you can!

The second issue is one of cost. Festivals can be expensive. At Winchester we pay all our speakers and we pay their expenses; we pay for conference services, for rooms, for catering and bar staff. Advertising isn't cheap and we don't make a profit, but neither do we want to limit the opportunities we offer to the well-off or the already established. For this reason we have recently instituted a Festival Scholarship Scheme for young writers aged 18-25 who may apply to attend for free. If you want to attend a writers' festival but are prevented by the cost, find out if the festival offers any bursaries as we do at Winchester. Sometimes attendees apply successfully for grants in their local area. It is getting harder and harder to find alternative sources of funding, but do ask the question; it would be a great shame to miss out.

Take the plunge

Whether you are a published writer looking to promote your book by appearing at a literary festival, or an emerging writer seeking support, inspiration and networking opportunities at a writers' festival, these gatherings can help you to feel part of a creative and dynamic writing community. Attend with an open mind, ready to learn.

And a final word on the subject of those one-to-one appointments and more informal networking opportunities. Good things do happen. Each year at Winchester, writers meet the agents and editors who will help their debuts take flight.

Worth celebrating, I think.

Judith Heneghan is the Director of the Winchester Writers' Festival. She began her career as a commissioning editor for Teach Yourself at Hodder but now lectures in Creative Writing at the University of Winchester where she runs the MA Writing for Children. Her fiction includes *Stonecipher* (Andersen Press 2005) and *The King of Kites* (Evans 2009) and she has written over 50 non-fiction books for children, including the recent *Plant Life* series for Wayland. She was a Trustee of the inaugural Winchester Poetry Festival held in September 2014.

See also...

• *Festivals for writers, artists and readers*, page 563

The Society of Authors

The Society of Authors is an independent trade union, representing writers' interests in all aspects of the writing profession.

Founded over 100 years ago, the Society now has more than 9,000 members. It has a professional staff, responsible to a Management Committee of 12 authors, and a Council (an advisory body meeting twice a year) consisting of 60 eminent writers. Specialist groups within the Society serve particular needs: the Broadcasting Group, the Children's Writers and Illustrators Group, the Educational Writers Group and the Translators Association (see page 529). There are also groups representing Scotland and the North of England.

Membership

The Society of Authors
84 Drayton Gardens, London SW10 9SB
tel 020-7373 6642
email info@societyofauthors.org, membership@societyofauthors.org
website www.societyofauthors.org
Chief Executive Nicola Solomon

Membership entitles authors to advice on all aspects of the writing profession and confidential clause-by-clause vetting of any contract offered. Members also receive a quarterly journal, free ALCS membership and a wide range of benefits, including offers on books and professional insurance.

Membership is available to authors who have had a full-length work published, broadcast or performed commercially. Membership is also open to those who have had published or commercially performed an equivalent body of literary work; owners or administrators of a deceased author's estate; those who have been published on a non-traditional basis (e.g. self published or on a print-on-demand/ebook-only basis) and who meet sales criteria to indicate profit. Those who do not meet the criteria for Membership may apply to become an Associate, for instance if they have been offered a contract for publication or agent's representation.

Both Members and Associates are subject to election, and to the payment of subscription fees. The annual subscription fee (tax deductible) is £95, or £68 for those who are 35 and under and not yet earning a significant income from writing. From the second year of subscription, discounted and quarterly Direct Debit options are available and there are concessionary rates for over 65s who are no longer earning a significant amount of income from writing. See website for full details.

The Society and members

Through its permanent staff (including a solicitor), the Society is able to give its members a comprehensive personal and professional service covering the business aspects of authorship, including:

- advising on negotiations, including the individual vetting of contracts, clause by clause, and assessing their terms both financial and otherwise;
- helping with members' queries, major or minor, over any aspect of the business of writing;
- taking up complaints on behalf of members on any issue concerned with the business of authorship;
- pursuing legal actions for breach of contract, copyright infringement, and the non-payment of royalties and fees, when the risk and cost preclude individual action by a member and issues of general concern to the profession are at stake;
- holding conferences, seminars, meetings and social occasions;
- producing a comprehensive range of publications, free of charge to members, including the Society's quarterly journal, the *Author*.

The Society frequently secures improved conditions and better returns for members. It is common for members to report that, through the help and facilities offered, they have saved more, and sometimes substantially more, than their annual subscription.

Further membership benefits include special offers and discounts on books, places to stay, insurance and other products and services, and free membership of the Authors' Licensing and Collecting Society (ALCS; see page 687).

The Society and authors

The Society lobbies Members of Parliament, ministers and government departments on all issues of concern to writers, litigates in matters of importance to authors and campaigns for better terms for writers. It is recognised by the BBC for the purpose of negotiating rates for writers' contributions to radio drama, as well as for the broadcasting of published material. It was instrumental in setting up the ALCS, which collects and distributes fees from reprography and other methods whereby copyright material is exploited without direct payment to the originators.

> 'It does no harm to repeat, as often as you can, "Without me the literary industry would not exist: the publishers, the agents, the sub-agents, the accountants, the libel lawyers, the departments of literature, the professors, the theses, the books of criticism, the reviewers, the book pages – all this vast and proliferating edifice is because of this small, patronised, put-down and underpaid person."' – *Doris Lessing*

The Society keeps in close touch with the Association of Authors' Agents, the Booksellers Association and Publishers Association, the British Council, the Department for Culture, Media and Sport, the National Union of Journalists and the Writers' Guild of Great Britain. It is a member of the European Writers Council and the British Copyright Council.

Awards

The following awards are administered:

• the Authors' Foundation and Kathleen Blundell Trust, which give grants to assist authors working on their next book;

• the Francis Head Bequest and the Authors' Contingency Fund, which assist authors who, through physical mishap, are temporarily unable to maintain themselves or their families;

• Travelling Scholarships, which give honorary awards;

• two prizes for first novels: the Betty Trask Awards and the McKitterick Prize;

• the Somerset Maugham Awards for a full-length published work;

• two poetry awards: the Eric Gregory Awards and the Cholmondeley Awards;

• the Tom-Gallon Award for short story writers;

• two radio drama prizes: the Imison Award for a writer new to radio drama and the Tinniswood Award;

• awards for translations from Arabic, Dutch/Flemish, French, German, Greek, Italian, Portuguese, Spanish and Swedish into English;

• educational and medical book awards.

The Writers' Guild of Great Britain

The Writers' Guild of Great Britain (WGGB) is the TUC-affiliated trade union for writers.

WGGB is a trade union affiliated to the TUC and represents writers working in film, television, radio, theatre, books, poetry, animation and videogames. Formed in 1959 as the Screenwriters' Guild, the union gradually extended into all areas of freelance writing activity and copyright protection. In 1974, when book authors and stage dramatists became eligible for membership, substantial numbers joined. In June 1997 the Theatre Writers' Union membership unified with that of the WGGB to create a larger, more powerful writers' union.

Apart from necessary dealings with Government and policies on legislative matters affecting writers, the WGGB is, by constitution, non-political, has no involvement with any political party, and members pay no political levy.

WGGB employs a permanent general secretary and other permanent staff and is administered by an Executive Council of 20 members. WGGB comprises professional writers in all media, united in common concern for one another and regulating the conditions under which they work.

Membership

The Writers' Guild of Great Britain (WGGB)
First Floor, 134 Tooley Street, London SE1 2TU
tel 020-7833 0777
email admin@writersguild.org.uk
website www.writersguild.org.uk
General Secretary Bernie Corbett
Full Membership: Members pay approximately 1.2% of earnings from professional writing using a banding system (min. £180, max. £1,800 p.a.)
Candidate Membership: £100 p.a. (restricted to writers who have not had work published or produced at WGGB-approved rates)
Affiliate Membership: £275 p.a. (for people who work professionally with writers, e.g. agents, technical advisers)

Members receive a weekly email newsletter every Friday afternoon. The WGGB website contains full details of collective agreements and WGGB activities, plus a 'Find a Writer' service and a dedicated Members' area; information is also made available on Twitter and Facebook. Other benefits include: legal advice and contract vetting; free training; member events, discounts and special offers, including free entry to the British Library reading rooms.

WGGB agreements

WGGB's core function is to negotiate minimum terms in those areas in which its members work. Those agreements form the basis of the individual contracts signed by members. Further details are given below. WGGB also gives individual advice to its members on contracts and other matters which the writer encounters in his or her professional life. It also organises informative and social events for members, and maintains a benevolent fund to help writers in financial trouble.

Television

WGGB negotiates minimum terms agreements with the BBC, ITV, Pact (Producers' Alliance for Cinema and Television, see page 518) and has also talked to Channel 4 about internet services. There is also a minimum terms agreement in place with TAC (representing Welsh-language television producers).

WGGB TV agreements regulate minimum fees, residuals and royalties, copyright, credits, and general conditions for television plays, series and serials, dramatisations and adaptations, soaps, sitcoms and sketch shows. One of the WGGB's most important achievements has been the establishment of pension rights for members. The BBC, ITV and independent producers pay a pension contribution on top of the standard writer's fee on the understanding that the WGGB member also pays a contribution.

The swtich to digital television, video-on-demand and download-to-own services, mobile phone technology and the expansion of the BBC's commercial arm have seen WGGB in constant negotiation over the past decade. WGGB now has agreements for all of the BBC's digital channels and for its joint venture channels. In May 2012 WGGB signed ground-breaking new agreements with the BBC extending minimum terms over online services such as iPlayer. From April 2015 the first payments under the Writers Digital Payments scheme were paid out to writers whose work had been broadcast on BBC iPlayer and ITV Player (Writers Digital Payments is a not-for-profit company set up by WGGB and the Personal Managers' Association).

WGGB is now in negotiations with Pact to agree new minimum terms for writers commissioned by independent television producers for all digital television channels and online services.

Film

In 1985 an important agreement was signed with the two producer organisations: the British Film and Television Producers' Association and the Independent Programme Producers' Association (now known as Pact). Since then there has been an industrial agreement covering UK film productions. Pension fund contributions have been negotiated for WGGB members in the same way as for the BBC and ITV. The Agreement was renegotiated in February 1992 and consultations on an updated arrangement, led by the WGGB Film Committee, are in progress. WGGB has recently published updated guidelines for film writers.

Radio

WGGB has a standard agreement for Radio Drama with the BBC, establishing a fee structure that is reviewed annually. This agreement was comprehensively renegotiated in 2005, with input from the WGGB Radio Committee, resulting in an agreement covering various new developments such as digital radio. In 1985 the BBC agreed to extend the pension scheme already established for television writers to include radio writers. WGGB has special agreements for Radio 4's *The Archers* and for the online streaming of BBC Radio services (iPlayer). A separate agreement covers the reuse of old comedy and drama material on digital BBC Radio 4 Extra.

Books

WGGB fought long, hard and successfully for the loans-based Public Lending Right (see page 140) to reimburse authors for books lent in libraries. The scheme is now administered by the British Library and WGGB is represented on its advisory committee.

WGGB has an active Books Committee, which works on behalf of book writers and poets. Recently, the committee has been discussing and advising members about new trends in self-publishing, print-on-demand services and ebooks.

Theatre

In 1979 WGGB, together with the Theatre Writers' Union, negotiated the first industrial agreement for theatre writers. The Theatres National Committee Agreement (TNC) covers the Royal Shakespeare Company, the Royal National Theatre Company and the English Stage Company at the Royal Court. When their agreement was renegotiated in 2007, WGGB achieved a long-standing ambition of a minimum fee of £10,000 for a new play; this has since risen to £12,126.

In June 1986, a new agreement was signed with the Theatrical Management Association (now UK Theatre), which covers 95 provincial theatres. In 1993, this agreement was comprehensively revised and included a provision for a year-on-year increase in fees in line with the Retail Price Index. The agreement is now being renegotiated.

After many years of negotiation, an agreement was concluded in 1991 between WGGB and the Independent Theatre Council (ITC), which represents 200 of the smaller and fringe theatres as well as educational and touring companies. This agreement was revised in 2002 and the minimum fees are reviewed annually. WGGB is currently talking to the ITC about updating the agreement again and making it more user-friendly.

The WGGB Theatre Committee holds an annual forum for Literary Managers, runs a Theatre Encouragement Award scheme and has regular meetings with Arts Council England to inform its theatre policy.

Other activities

WGGB is in touch with Government and national institutions wherever and whenever the interests of writers are in question or are being discussed. It holds cross-party Parliamentary lobbies with Equity and the Musicians' Union to ensure that the various artforms they represent are properly cared for.

Working with the Federation of Entertainment Unions, WGGB makes its views known to Government bodies on a broader basis. It keeps in touch with Arts Council England, the BBC Trust, Ofcom and other national bodies.

WGGB is an active affiliate of the British Copyright Council, Creators' Rights Alliance and other organisations whose activities are relevant to professional writers. It has an Anti-Censorship Committee, which has intervened strongly to protect freedom of speech.

Internationally, WGGB plays a leading role in the International Affiliation of Writers Guilds, which includes the American Guilds East and West, the Canadian Guilds (French and English), and the Irish, Mexican, French, Israeli, South African and New Zealand Guilds. When it is possible to make common cause, the Guilds act accordingly. WGGB takes a leading role in the European Writers' Council and the Fédération des Scénaristes d'Europe. WGGB is becoming more involved with matters at the European level where the harmonisation of copyright law, the regulation of a converged audiovisual/telecommunications industry and the regulation of collecting societies are of immediate interest.

On a day-to-day basis, WGGB helps with problems on behalf of individual members, gives advice on contracts, and takes up issues that affect the lives of its members as professional writers. Members have access to free legal advice and professional contract vetting. Other member benefits include access to free and discounted training, a weekly e-bulletin, exclusive events and discounts, and a dedicated online members' area. In addition, full members are entitled to submit a profile for inclusion in the WGGB online *Find A Writer* directory; pay no joining fee for membership to Writers Guild of America East or West; and are eligible for Cannes accreditation. Regular committee meetings are held by various specialist WGGB Craft Committees.

WGGB has active branches in most parts of the UK. They organise a range of events such as panel discussions, talks and social occasions.

Each year WGGB presents the much-prized Writers' Guild Awards, covering all the areas in which its members work. These are the only cross-media awards in which writers are honoured by their peers, and as such are highly valued by the recipients.

WGGB has sponsored the creation of the Writers' Foundation (UK), a registered charity that funds cultural and educational activities of benefit to the entire writing community. The Foundation can be contacted via the WGGB office.

The writer is an isolated creator in a world in which individual voices are not always heard. WGGB brings writers together to make common cause on many important matters, making full use of its collective strength.

The Alliance of Independent Authors

The ALLi is a professional association of self-publishing writers and advisors.

The Alliance of Independent Authors (ALLi) is a global collaborative collective of self-publishing writers. It was founded in 2012 at the London Book Fair by former trade published author and literary agent, Orna Ross, in response to her personal experience of self-publishing and she has been named 'One of the 100 most influential people in publishing' for this work.

ALLi has an Advisory Board of world-class authors and educators, bloggers and service providers, all of whom hold the self-publishing choice in high esteem and all with exceptional knowledge and skills. Their contribution is supplemented by ALLi's global ambassadors, who aid writers to create vibrant self-publishing literary communities in their local areas or online.

A rapidly growing organisation, with members all over the world, ALLi invites 'indie' authors to come together in a spirit of mutual cooperation, empowerment and service to the reading and writing community. As well as encouraging ethics and excellence in the writing, printing, formatting and promotion of self-published books, ALLi advances, supports and advocates for the interests of independent, self-publishing authors everywhere. Its Open Up To Indie Authors Campaign promotes the interests of indie authors within the literary and publishing industries – engaging with booksellers, festivals, prize-giving committees, libraries, book clubs and the media.

ALLi's core mission is the democratisation of writing and publishing.

Membership

The Alliance of Independent Authors
Free Word Centre, 60 Farringdon Road,
London EC1R 3GA
email press@allianceindependentauthors.org
website http://allianceindependentauthors.org, www.SelfPublishingAdvice.org

At ALLi, 'independent' is an inclusive description, including trade-published, self-published and hybrid authors. There are 4 grades of membership:

Author Membership is open to writers or translators of books for adults who have self-published a full-length title (55,000+ words); writers of children's/young adult books who have self-published; and previously trade-published writers or translators who are now preparing to self-publish.

Partner Membership is open to organisations or sole traders offering necessary services to self-publishing authors and bloggers (e.g. editing, design, publicity, printing, distribution, etc) or an individual who works within an organisation that offers such services. All partner members are vetted by the ALLi watchdog desk.

Professional Membership is open to full-time self-publishing authors who earn their living through book sales, though this may be in some cases combined with service to the writing and reading community. All applications for professional membership are carefully assessed on a case-by-case basis.

Associate Membership is open to writing/publishing students with an interest in self-publishing and non-published writers (or translators) preparing a book for self-publication.

Benefits include self-publishing advice and guidance; collaboration and contacts; discounts and deals, author promotion and advancement, and campaigns on behalf of indie authors. See website for full information.

Societies, associations and clubs

The societies, associations and clubs listed here will be of interest to both writers and artists. They include appreciation societies devoted to specific authors, professional bodies and national institutions. Some also offer prizes and awards (see page 534).

AITA/IATA International Amateur Theatre Association

Secretariat, 19 Dorset Avenue, London UB2 4HF
email secretariat@aitaiata.org
website www.aitaiata.org
President Rob Van Genechten (from July 2015), *Vice-President* Roger Ellis, *English Speaking Secretary* Aled Rhys-Jones, *French Speaking Secretary* Beatrice Cellario, *Spanish Speaking Secretary* Jorge Crespi, *Treasurer* Villy Dall, *Children & Youth* Josef Hollos

Aims to encourage, foster and promote exchanges of community and non-professional theatre and of student, educational and adult theatre activities at international level. To organise international seminars, workshops, courses and conferences, and to collect and collate information of all types for national and international dissemination.

All Party Parliamentary Writers Group

tel 020-7264 5700
email barbara.hayes@alcs.co.uk
website www.allpartywritersgroup.co.uk
Chair John Whittingdale MP, *Administrator* Barbara Hayes

The Group has some 60 Members from both Houses and seeks to represent the interests of all writers; to safeguard their intellectual property rights and ensure they receive a fair level of recognition and reward for their contribution to the economy and society as a whole. Founded 2007.

Alliance of Independent Authors – see page 491

Alliance of Literary Societies

email ljc1049@gmail.com
website www.allianceofliterarysocieties.org.uk
Chair Linda J. Curry, *Hon. Treasurer and Membership Secretary* Julie Shorland
Membership Charge depends on size of society

Membership comprises 120+ affiliated literary societies. Aims to act as a valuable liaison body between member societies as a means of sharing knowledge, skills and expertise, and may also act as a pressure group when necessary. The Alliance can assist in the preservation of buildings, places and objects which have literary associations. Produces two newsletters a year, plus a literary magazine. Holds an annual literary weekend, hosted by a different member society each year.

American Literary Translators Association (ALTA)

900 East 7th Street, PMB 266 Bloomington, IN 47405-3201
email erica@literarytranslators.org
website www.literarytranslators.org
Managing Director Erica Mena

A broad-based professional association dedicated to the promotion of literary translation through services to literary translators, forums on the theory and practice of translation, collaboration with the international literary community, and advocacy on behalf of literary translators. Founded 1978.

American Society for Indexing (ASI)

1628 E. Southern Ave. 9-223, Tempe, AZ 85282, USA
tel +1 480-245-6750
email info@asindexing.org
website www.asindexing.org
Executive Director Gwen Henson

Increases awareness of the value of high-quality indexes and indexing; offers members access to educational resources that enable them to strengthen their indexing performance; keeps members up to date on indexing technology; advocates for the professional interests of indexers.

American Society of Composers, Authors and Publishers

website www.ascap.com

An organisation owned and run by its members, it is the leading performance rights organisation representing over 450,000 songwriters, composers and music publishers.

Arts Club

40 Dover Street, London W1S 4NP
tel 020-7499 8581
email membership@theartsclub.co.uk
website www.theartsclub.co.uk

A private members' club founded in 1863 for all those connected with or interested in the arts, literature and science.

Arts Council England

tel 0845 300 6200
email enquiries@artscouncil.org.uk
website www.artscouncil.org.uk

The national development agency for the arts in England, distributing public money from Government and the National Lottery. Arts Council England's main funding programme is Grants for the Arts, which is open to individuals, arts organisations, national touring companies and other people who use the arts in their work. Founded 1946.

East
Eastbrook, Shaftesbury Road, Cambridge CB2 8BF
tel 0845 300 6200

East Midlands
Room 005-005A, Arkwright Building, Nottingham Trent University, Burton Street, Nottingham NG1 4BU
tel 0845 300 6200

London
21 Bloomsbury Street, London WC1B 3HF
tel 0845 300 6200

North East
Central Square, Forth Street, Newcastle upon Tyne NE1 3PJ
tel 0845 300 6200

North West
The Hive, 49 Lever Street, Manchester M1 1FN
tel 0845 300 6200

South East
Sovereign House, Church Street, Brighton BN1 1RA
tel 0845 300 6200

South West
Third Floor, St Thomas Court, Thomas Lane, Bristol BS1 6JG
tel 0845 300 6200

West Midlands
82 Granville Street, Birmingham B1 2LH
tel 0845 300 6200

Yorkshire
21 Bond Street, Dewsbury, West Yorkshire WF13 1AX
tel 0845 300 6200

Arts Council/An Chomhairle Ealaíon

70 Merrion Square, Dublin 2, Republic of Ireland
tel +353 (0)1 6180200
website www.artscouncil.ie
Arts Directors Liz Meaney, Stephanie O'Callaghan, *Acting Head of Literature* Liz Powell, *Head of Visual Arts* Claire Doyle

The national development agency for the arts in Ireland. Founded 1951.

Arts Council of Northern Ireland

77 Malone Road, Belfast BT9 6AQ
tel 028-9038 5200
email info@artscouncil-ni.org
website www.artscouncil-ni.org
Chief Executive Roisín McDonough, *Head of Drama & Literature* Damian Smyth, *Head of Visual Arts* Suzanne Lyle

Promotes and encourages the arts throughout Northern Ireland. Artists in drama, dance, music and jazz, literature, the visual arts, traditional arts and community arts can apply for support for specific schemes and projects. The value of the grant will be set according to the aims of the application. Artists of all disciplines and in all types of working practice, who have made a contribution to artistic activities in Northern Ireland for a minimum period of one year within the last five years, are eligible.

Arts Council of Wales

Bute Place, Cardiff CF10 5AL
tel 0845 873 4900
email info@artscouncilofwales.org.uk
website www.artswales.org.uk

National organisation with specific responsibility for the funding and development of the arts in Wales. Arts Council of Wales receives funding from the Welsh Government and also distributes National Lottery funds for the arts in Wales. From these resources, Arts Council of Wales makes grants to support arts activities and facilities. Some of the funds are allocated in the form of annual revenue grants to full-time arts organisations such as Literature Wales. It also operates schemes which provide financial and other forms of support for individual artists or projects. Arts Council of Wales undertakes this work in both the English and Welsh languages. Wales Arts International is the unique partnership between the Arts Council of Wales and British Council Wales, which works to promote knowledge about contemporary arts and culture from Wales and encourages international exchange and collaboration.

North Wales Regional Office
Princes Park II, Princes Drive, Colwyn Bay LL29 8PL
tel (01492) 533440

Mid and West Wales Regional Office
4–6 Gardd Llydaw, Jackson Lane, Carmarthen SA31 1QD
tel 0845 873 4900

South Wales Office
Bute Place, Cardiff CF10 5AL
tel 0845 873 4900

Aslib (The Association for Information Management)

Howard House, Wagon Lane, Bingley BD16 1WA
tel (01274) 777700
website www.aslib.co.uk
Director Rebecca Marsh, *Editor-in-Chief* Graham Coult

Actively promotes best practice in the management of information resources. It represents its members and lobbies on all aspects of the management of and legislation concerning information at local, national and international levels. Aslib provides consultancy and information services, professional development training, conferences, specialist recruitment, internet products, and publishes primary and secondary journals, conference proceedings, directories and monographs. Founded 1924.

Association for Scottish Literary Studies (ASLS)

c/o Dept of Scottish Literature, 7 University Gardens, University of Glasgow G12 8QH
tel 0141 330 5309
email office@asls.org.uk
website www.asls.org.uk
President Ian Brown, *Secretary* Ronnie Young, *Director* Duncan Jones
Membership £47 p.a. individuals; £12 UK students; £75 corporate

Promotes the study, teaching and writing of Scottish literature and furthers the study of the languages of Scotland. Publishes annually *New Writing Scotland*, an anthology of new Scottish writing; an edited text of Scottish literature; a series of academic journals; and a newsletter (two p.a.) Also publishes *Scotnotes* (comprehensive study guides to major Scottish writers), literary texts and commentary CDs designed to assist the classroom teacher, and a series of occasional papers. Organises three conferences a year. Founded 1970.

Association of American Correspondents in London (AACL)

AACL, PO Box 645, Pinner HA5 9JJ
email secretary@theaacl.co.uk
website www.theaacl.co.uk
Contact Monique Jessen

An independent, not-for-profit organisation whose members represent North American media organisations with staff based in London.

Association of American Publishers

71 Fifth Avenue, 2nd Floor, New York, NY 10003-3004,
USA and 455 Massachusetts Avenue NW, Suite 700, Washington, DC 20001, USA
tel +1 212-255-0200 (NY); +1 202-347-3375 (DC)
email info@publishers.org
website www.publishers.org
President & Ceo Tom Allen

AAP is the largest trade association for US books and journal publishers, providing advocacy and communications on behalf of the industry and its priorities nationally and worldwide. Founded 1970.

Association of Art Historians (AAH)

70 Cowcross Street, London EC1M 6EJ
tel 020-7490 3211
email admin@aah.org.uk
website www.aah.org.uk
Ceo Pontus Rosen, *Deputy Chief Executive and Communications Officer* Claire Davies, *Membership and Admin Officer* Carina Persson
Membership Options for individual and institutional membership

Formed to promote the professional practice and public understanding of art history and visual culture. Publishes *Art History* journal, *Careers in Art History* booklet and Artists' Papers Register (APR) online listings. Organises events, funding, resources and an annual conference. Founded 1974.

The Association of Authors' Agents

c/o Greene & Heaton, 37 Goldhawk Road, London W12 8QQ
tel 020-8749 0315
website www.agentsassoc.co.uk
President Sam Edenborough, *Secretary* Claudia Young

The AAA exists to provide a forum which allows member agencies to discuss issues arising in the profession; a collective voice for UK literary agencies in public affairs and the media; and a code of conduct to which all members commit themselves. Founded 1974.

Association of Authors' Representatives Inc.

676A, Suite 312 9th Avenue, New York, NY 10036, USA
tel +1 212-840-5770
email administrator@aaronline.org
website www.aaronline.org
Administrator Jody Klein

A professional organisation of over 400 agents who work with book authors and playwrights.

Founded 1991.

Association of British Science Writers (ABSW)

email info@absw.org.uk
website www.absw.org.uk
President Martin Ince

Association of science writers, editors, and radio, film and TV producers concerned with the presentation and communication of science, technology and medicine. Aims to improve the standard of science writing and to assist its members in their work. Runs the annual ABSW Science Writers' Awards and the Biennial UK Conference of Science Journalists. Membership details/application through website only.

Association of Canadian Publishers

174 Spadina Avenue, Suite 306, Toronto, Ontario M5T 2C2, Canada
tel +1 416-487-6116
email admin@canbook.org
website www.publishers.ca
Executive Director Carolyn Wood

Represents approximately 135 Canadian-owned and controlled book publishers from across the country. Founded 1976.

Association of Christian Writers

Administrator Mrs Mandy Johnson, Bethany, 7 Eversley Walk, Nottingham NG5 5NL
tel 07979 198556
email admin@christianwriters.org.uk
website www.christianwriters.org.uk
Membership £28 p.a. (£25 DD), £33 (overseas)

Registered charity that aims to see excellence in writing, either overtly Christian or shaped by a Christian perspective, in every area of the media, reaching the widest range of people across the UK and beyond; and to inspire and equip people to use their talents and skills with integrity to compose, write and market quality material which comes from a Christian world view. Founded 1971.

Association of Freelance Editors, Proofreaders and Indexers

Contact 1 Brenda O'Hanlon (Co-chair)
tel +353 (0)1 2952194
email brenda@ohanlonmedia.com
Contact 2 Averill Buchanan (Co-chair)
tel 07875 857278
email averill@averillbuchanan.com
Contact 3 Kate Murphy (Treasurer/Secretary)
tel +353 (0)1 8135898
email kemurphy@online.ie
website www.afepi.ie

Based in Dublin. Protects the interests of members and serves as a point of contact between publishers and members. Membership is available to experienced professional editors, proofreaders and indexers.

The Association of Illustrators

Somerset House, Strand, London WC2R 1LA
tel 020-7759 1010
email info@theaoi.com
website www.theaoi.com
Contact Membership Coordinator

Trade association which supports illustrators, promotes illustration and encourages professional standards in the industry. Publishes *Varoom* magazine (four p.a.); presents an annual programme of events; annual competition, exhibition and tour of the World Illustration Awards in partnership with the Directory of Illustration (www.theaoi.com/awards). Founded 1973.

The Association of Learned and Professional Society Publishers

Chief Executive Audrey McCulloch, 1–3 Ship Street, Shoreham-by-Sea, West Sussex BN43 5DH
tel (01442) 828928
email audrey.mcculloch@alpsp.org
website www.alpsp.org

The Association of Learned and Professional Society Publishers (ALPSP) is the international membership trade body which works to support and represent not-for-profit organisations and institutions that publish scholarly and professional content around the world. Its membership also encompasses those that partner with and provide services to not-for-profit publishers. ALPSP has over 320 members in 40 countries, who collectively publish over half the world's total active journals, as well as books, databases and other products.

The Association of Photographers (AOP)

Studio 9, Holborn Studios, 49/50 Eagle Wharf Road, London N1 7ED
tel 020-3327 7203
email info@aophoto.co.uk
website www.the-aop.org
Membership £280 p.a.

Contact Gwen Thomas, Director of Business & Legal Services

Exists to protect and promote the interests of fashion advertising and editorial photographers. Founded 1968.

The Jane Austen Society

Membership Secretary Sharron Bassett, Sospiri, 9 George Street, Dunfermline, Fife KY11 4TQ
email memsec@jasoc.org.uk
website www.janeaustensoci.freeuk.com
Membership £28 from 1 January to 31 December each year; £33 joint membership for 2 people living at the same address; £10 student membership (UK), on production of tutor reference or ID; £38 overseas.

Aims to promote interest in, and enjoyment of, the life and works of Jane Austen (1775–1817). Regular publications, meetings and conferences. Eleven branches in UK. Founded 1940.

Australia Council

PO Box 788, Strawberry Hills, NSW 2012, Australia
located at 372 Elizabeth Street, Surry Hills, NSW 2010, Australia
tel +61 (0)2 9215 9000
email mail@australiacouncil.gov.au
website www.australiacouncil.gov.au
Ceo Tony Grybowski

Provides a broad range of support for the arts in Australia, embracing music, theatre, literature, visual arts, crafts, Aboriginal arts, community and new media arts. It has an office of the Chief Executive and five divisions.

Australian Copyright Council

PO Box 1986, Strawberry Hills, NSW 2012, Australia
tel +61 (0)2 8815 9777
email info@copyright.org.au
website www.copyright.org.au
Executive Director Fiona Phillips

The Australian Copyright Council is an independent, non-profit organisation. It represents the peak bodies for professional artists and content creators working in Australia's creative industries and Australia's major copyright collecting societies. The Council comprises 24 organisations or associations of owners and creators of copyright material, including the Australian Society of Authors, the Australian Writers' Guild and the Australian Publishers Association.

Acts as an advocate for the contribution of creators to Australia's culture and economy; the importance of copyright for the common good. Works to promote the understanding of copyright law and its application, lobbies for appropriate law reform and fosters collaboration between content creators and consumers. Provides easily accessible and affordable practical, user-friendly information, legal advice, education and forums on Australian copyright law for content creators and consumers. Founded 1968.

Australian Publishers Association (APA)

60–89 Jones Street, Ultimo, NSW 2007, Australia
email office@publishers.asn.au
website www.publishers.asn.au
Ceo Maree McCaskill

The Australian Publishers Association is the peak industry body for Australian book, journal and electronic publishers. Founded 1948.

The Australian Society of Authors

Suite C1.06, 22–36 Mountain Street, Ultimo, NSW 2007, Australia
tel +61 (0)2 9211 1004
email asa@asauthors.org
website www.asauthors.org
Executive Director Angelo Loukakis

Aims to be the principal advocate for the professional and artistic interests of Australian authors by: protecting basic rights to freedom of expression; working to improve income and conditions; and promoting Australian writing and literary culture.

Australian Writers' Guild (AWG)

5 Blackfriars Street, Chippendale, NSW 2008
tel +61 (0)2 9319 0339
email admin@awg.com.au
website www.awg.com.au
Executive Director Jacqueline Elaine

The professional association for all performance writers, i.e. writers for film, TV, radio, theatre, video and new media. The AWG is recognised throughout the industry in Australia as being the voice of performance writers. Founded 1962.

Authors Aloud UK

72 Castle Road, St Albans, Herts AL1 5DG
tel (01727) 893992
email info@authorsalouduk.co.uk
website www.authorsalouduk.co.uk
Partners Anne Marley, Naomi Cooper, Annie Everall

Authors Aloud UK is an author booking agency which brings together authors, illustrators, poets, storytellers and trainers with schools, libraries and festivals to promote enthusiasm for reading, both for enjoyment and information. Authors Aloud UK is happy to take on new speakers, published by mainstream children's publishers, who meet the relevant criteria and guidelines. Keen to work with new and debut authors who wish to visit schools and libraries.

Authors' Club

c/o National Liberal Club, Whitehall Place, London SW1A 2HE
tel 020-7733 8594
email info@authorsclub.co.uk
website www.authorsclub.co.uk
President John Walsh, *Chairman* Chris Schuler, *Deputy Chairperson* Sunny Singh
Membership Apply to Deputy Chairperson

Founded by Sir Walter Besant to provide a social club for all those professionally engaged with literature, the Authors' Club welcomes as members writers, publishers, critics, journalists, and academics. Holds monthly lunches addressed by guest authors, evening discussions, and administers the Authors' Club Best First Novel Award, the Art Book Prize and the Stanford Dolman Travel Book of the Year Award. Founded 1891.

Authors' Licensing and Collecting Society Ltd – see page 687

Axisweb

Studio 17/18, 46 The Calls, Leeds LS2 7EY
tel 0113 242 9830
email info@axisweb.org
website www.axisweb.org
Director Sheila McGregor
Membership Artist/art professional membership from £15 p.a. (early career) and £28.50 (full membership)

Axisweb gives artists and art professionals a platform to showcase their work, find work opportunities, stay informed and make useful connections. The online directory of selected artists and art professionals is an essential research tool for anyone interested in keeping in touch with UK contemporary art. Axisweb also commissions features from a wide network of specialist contributors across the UK, who highlight artists, ideas and new developments.

How you can get involved: apply to have a profile on the site and access the members-only work opportunities, sign up for e-bulletins, engage with members or pitch to write a feature. Axisweb was established as a charity in 1991 and is funded by Arts Council England.

BAFTA (British Academy of Film and Television Arts)

195 Piccadilly, London W1J 9LN
tel 020-7734 0022

email info@bafta.org
website www.bafta.org
Chief Executive Amanda Berry OBE

The UK's pre-eminent, independent charity supporting, developing and promoting the art forms of the moving image (film, TV and games) by identifying and rewarding excellence, inspiring practitioners and benefiting the public. BAFTA's awards are awarded annually by its members to their peers in recognition of their skills and expertise. In addition, BAFTA's year-round learning programme offers unique access to some of the world's most inspiring talent through workshops, masterclasses, lectures and mentoring schemes, connecting with audiences of all ages and backgrounds across the UK, Los Angeles and New York. Founded 1947.

BANA (Bath Area Network for Artists)

The Old Malthouse, Comfortable Place,
Upper Bristol Road, Bath BA1 3AJ
tel 07526 428280
email enquiries@banaarts.co.uk
website www.banaarts.co.uk
Membership From £20 p.a.

An artist-led network that is committed to developing members' professional practice through connecting their creativity. BANA aims to raise the profile of arts activity in and around the Bath area, to establish and strengthen links between artists, artists' groups and art promoters, and advocate for increased investment in local arts activities. Founded 1998 and a company limited by guarantee since 2003.

BAPLA (British Association of Picture Libraries and Agencies)

59 Tranquil Vale, Blackheath, London SE3 0BS
tel 020-8297 1198
email enquiries@bapla.org.uk
website www.bapla.org.uk
Membership & Communications Manager Susanne Kittlinger

The British Association of Picture Libraries and Agencies (BAPLA) is the trade association for picture libraries in the UK, and has been a trade body since 1975. Members include the major news, stock and production agencies as well as sole traders and cultural heritage institutions.

The Beckford Society

The Timber Cottage, Crockerton,
Warminster BA12 8AX
tel (01985) 213195
email sidney.blackmore@btinternet.com
website www.beckfordsociety.org
Membership £20 p.a. minimum

Aims to promote an interest in the life and works of William Beckford of Fonthill (1760–1844) and his circle. Encourages Beckford studies and scholarship through exhibitions, lectures and publications, including *The Beckford Journal* (annual) and occasional newsletters. Founded 1995.

The Arnold Bennett Society

Secretary Carol Gorton, 4 Field End Close,
Trentham, Stoke-on-Trent ST4 8DA
email arnoldbennettscty@btinternet.com
website www.arnoldbennettsociety.org.uk
Membership £15 p.a. individuals; £17.50 p.a. family. Add £2 if living outside Europe

Aims to promote the study and appreciation of the life, works and times not only of Arnold Bennett (1867–1931), but also of other provincial writers with particular relationship to north Staffordshire.

The E.F. Benson Society

The Old Coach House, High Street, Rye,
East Sussex TN31 7JF
tel (01797) 223114
website www.efbensonsociety.org
Secretary Allan Downend
Membership £12 p.a. single; £15 p.a. for two people at same address; £20 overseas

Aims to promote interest in the author E.F. Benson (1867–1940) and the Benson family. Arranges annual literary evening, annual outing to Rye (July) and other places of Benson interest, talks on the Bensons and exhibitions. Archive includes the Austin Seckersen Collection, transcriptions of the Benson diaries and letters. Publishes postcards, anthologies of Benson's works, a Mary Benson biography, books on Benson and an annual journal, *The Dodo*. Also sells out-of-print Bensons to members. Founded 1984.

Bibliographical Society

c/o Institute of English Studies,
University of London, Senate House, Malet Street,
London WC1E 7HU
tel 020-7782 3279
email admin@bibsoc.org.uk
website www.bibsoc.org.uk

Acquisition and dissemination of information on subjects connected with historical bibliography. Publishes the journal *The Library*. Founded 1892.

The Blackpool Art Society

The Studio, Wilkinson Avenue,
Off Woodland Grove, Blackpool FY3 9HB
tel (01253) 768297
email sec@blackpoolartsociety.co.uk
website www.blackpoolartsociety.co.uk
Hon. Secretary Carol Sanderson

Various exhibitions (members' work only). Studio meetings, demonstrations, workshops, lectures, out-of-door sketching. New members always welcome. See website for more details. Founded 1884.

Book Aid International

39–41 Coldharbour Lane, London SE5 9NR
tel 020-7733 3577

email info@bookaid.org
website www.bookaid.org
Director Alison Hubert

Works in partnership with libraries in Africa providing books, resources and training to support an environment in which reading for pleasure, study and lifelong learning can flourish.

Book Marketing Society

5th Floor, Endeavour House,
189 Shaftesbury Avenue, London WC2H 8JR
email jo@bookmarketingsociety.co.uk
website www.bookmarketingsociety.co.uk
Executive Jo Henry

The Book Marketing Society was launched with the objective of becoming the representative body of marketing within the book industry. As such, it champions marketing professionalism with the ultimate goal of expanding the UK book market. Anyone who works for a book publisher, book retailer or book wholesaler is eligible for membership, including those working in associated areas of the publishing and book retailing industry. Founded 2004.

The Booksellers Association of the United Kingdom & Ireland Ltd

6 Bell Yard, London WC2A 2JR
tel 020-7421 4640
email mail@booksellers.org.uk
website www.booksellers.org.uk
Chief Executive T.E. Godfray

A membership organisation for all booksellers in the UK and Ireland, representing over 95% of bookshops. Key services include National Book Tokens and World Book Day. Founded 1895.

Book Trust

(formerly the National Book League, founded 1925)
G8 Battersea Studios, 80 Silverthorne Road, London SW8 3HE
tel 020-7801 8800
email query@booktrust.org.uk
website www.booktrust.org.uk
Director Diana Gerald, *Chair of Board* Karen Brown

Book Trust is a charity that works to transform lives through inspiring a love of reading. Reading for pleasure has a dramatic impact on social mobility, attainment and mental health, and Book Trust works to ensure that all children and families in the UK have access to books and are supported in developing a love of reading.

Book Trust is responsible for a number of successful national reading promotions, sponsored book prizes and creative reading projects aimed at encouraging readers to discover and enjoy books.

The George Borrow Society

Membership Secretary Michael Skillman,
60 Upper Marsh Road, Warminster, Wilts. BA12 9PN
email mkskillman@blueyonder.co.uk
website http://georgeborrow.org
Membership £25 p.a.; £37.50 joint members at same address; £10 students

Promotes knowledge of the life and works of George Borrow (1803–81), traveller and author. Publishes *Bulletin* (bi-annual). Founded 1991.

British Academy

10 Carlton House Terrace, London SW1Y 5AH
tel 020-7969 5200
email pubs@britac.ac.uk
website www.britishacademy.ac.uk
President Prof. Lord Stern of Brentford, *Publications Secretary* Prof. Mary Morgan, *Chief Executive & Secretary* Dr Robin Jackson

The national academy for the humanities and social sciences: an independent and self-governing fellowship of scholars, elected for distinction and achievement in one or more branches of the academic disciplines that make up the humanities and social sciences. Its primary purpose is to promote research and scholarship in those areas: through research grants and other awards, the sponsorship of a number of research projects and of research institutes overseas; the award of prizes and medals (including the Crawshay prizes for critical literary studies by a female scholar); and the publication both of sponsored lectures and seminar papers and of fundamental texts and research aids prepared under the direction of Academy committees. It also acts as a forum for the discussion of issues of interest and concern to scholars in the humanities and the social sciences, and it provides advice to the Government and other public bodies. Founded 1901.

British Academy of Songwriters, Composers and Authors

British Music House, 26 Berners Street,
London W1T 3LR
tel 020-7636 2929
email info@basca.org.uk
website www.basca.org.uk
Contact Graham Jackson, Head of Membership

The Academy represents the interests of composers and songwriters across all genres, providing advice on professional and artistic matters. It administers a number of major events, including the annual Ivor Novello Awards and British Composer Awards.

British Association of Journalists

General Secretary Nick Townsend, 89 Fleet Street,
London EC4Y 1DH
tel 020-7353 3003
email office@bajunion.org.uk
website www.bajunion.org.uk
Membership £18.25 per month for national newspaper staff, national broadcasting staff and national news agency staff; £10.50 p.m. for other

seniors including magazine journalists, photographers, PRs, freelancers; £7.50 p.m. under age 24

Non-political trade union for professional journalists. Aims to protect and promote the industrial and professional interests of journalists. Founded 1992.

British Association of Picture Libraries and Agencies – see BAPLA (British Association of Picture Libraries and Agencies)

British Centre for Literary Translation (BCLT)

School of Literature, Drama & Creative Writing, University of East Anglia, Norwich Research Park, Norwich NR4 7TJ
tel (01603) 592785
email bclt@uea.ac.uk
website www.bclt.org.uk

BCLT raises the profile of literary translation in the UK through events, publications, activities and research aimed at professional translators, the publishing industry, students and the general reader.

Activities include the annual Sebald Lecture in London, Summer School and public talks and events. It is joint sponsor of the John Dryden Translation Prize. Member of the international RECIT literary translation network. Founded 1989 by the author and UEA Professor W.G. Sebald.

British Copyright Council

2 Pancras Square, London N1C 4AG
tel (01986) 788122
email info@britishcopyright.org
website www.britishcopyright.org
Vice-President Geoffrey Adams, *President of Honour* Maureen Duffy, *Chairman* Trevor Cook, *Directors* John Smith, Andrew Yeates, Peter Leatham, Richard Combes, Frances Lowe, Nicola Soloman, Gwen Thomas, *Ceo and Company Secretary* Janet Ibbotson, *Treasurer* Hugh Jones

Aims to defend and foster the true principles of copyright and its acceptance throughout the world, to bring together bodies representing all who are interested in the protection of such copyright, and to keep watch on any legal or other changes which may require an amendment of the law.

The British Council

10 Spring Gardens, London SW1A 2BN
email general.enquiries@britishcouncil.org
website www.britishcouncil.org
Chair Sir Vernon Ellis, *Chief Executive* Ciarán Devane, *Director of Arts* Graham Sheffield

The British Council connects people worldwide with learning opportunities and creative ideas from the UK, and builds lasting relationships between the UK and other countries. It has 6,000 staff in offices, teaching centres, libraries, and information and resource centres in the UK and 110 countries and territories worldwide.

Working in close collaboration with book trade associations, British Council offices participate in major international book fairs.

The British Council is an authority on teaching English as a second or foreign language. It also gives advice and information on curriculum, methodology, materials and testing.

The British Council Literature Department works with hundreds of writers and literature partners in the UK and collaborates with offices overseas to broker relationships and create activities which link thousands of artists and cultural institutions around the world, drawing them into a closer relationship with the UK. The Department works with writers, publishers, producers, translators and other sector professionals across literature, publishing and education. With them they develop innovative, high-quality programmes and collaborations that provide opportunities for cultural exchange with the UK.

The Visual Arts Department promotes the UK's visual arts sector internationally. It stages and supports contemporary art projects in areas of the developing world via exhibitions, training and development, professional study visits and the management of the British Pavilion at the Venice Biennale and an expansive collection of 20th- and 21st-century British art.

The British Fantasy Society

email secretary@britishfantasysociety.org
website www.britishfantasysociety.org
Membership £35 p.a. single; £40 joint; £45 Europe; £60 rest of world

For devotees of fantasy, horror and related fields, in literature, art and the cinema. There is a small-press library and an annual convention, FantasyCon, and fantasy awards sponsored by the Society. Founded 1971.

BFI (British Film Institute)

21 Stephen Street, London W1T 1LN
tel 020-7255 1444
website www.bfi.org.uk
Chair Greg Dyke, *Chief Executive* Amanda Nevill

The BFI is the lead organisation for film in the UK with the ambition to create a flourishing film environment in which innovation, opportunity and creativity can thrive by:

• connecting audiences to the widest choice of British and World cinema;
• preserving and restoring the most significant film collection in the world for today and future generations;
• championing emerging and world class film makers in the UK, investing in creative, distinctive and entertaining work;

• promoting British film talent to the world; and
• growing the next generation of film makers and audiences.

The BFI is a Government arm's-length body and distributor of Lottery funds for film. The BFI serves a public role which covers the cultural, creative and economic aspects of film in the UK. It delivers this role:
• as the UK-wide organisation for film, a charity core funded by Government;
• by providing Lottery and Government funds for film across the UK; and
• by working with partners to advance the position of film across the UK.

The BFI is a registered charity governed by Royal Charter. Founded 1933.

British Guild of Agricultural Journalists

General Secretary Nikki Robertson, 444 Westwood Heath Road, Coventry CV4 8AA
tel 024-7642 1491
email gajsec@gmail.com
website www.gaj.org.uk
President Lord Curry of Kirkharle, *Chairman* Ben Briggs
Membership £68 p.a.

Established in 1944, the Guild promotes high standards among journalists, photographers and communicators who specialise in agriculture, horticulture, food production and other rural affairs, and contributes towards a better understanding of agriculture.

British Guild of Beer Writers

Secretary Adrian Tierney-Jones, Woodcote, 2 Jury Road, Dulverton, Somerset TA22 9DU
tel (01398) 324314
email atierneyjones@gmail.com
website www.beerwriters.co.uk
Membership £40 p.a

Aims to improve standards in beer writing and at the same time extend public knowledge of beers and brewing. Awards are given annually to writers and broadcasters judged to have made the most valuable contribution to this end. Publishes a directory of members with details of their publications and their particular areas of interest, which is circulated to the media. Founded 1988.

The British Guild of Travel Writers

335 Lordship Road, London N16 5HG
tel 020-8144 8713
email secretariat@bgtw.org
website www.bgtw.org

Arranges meetings, discussions and visits for its 260+ members (who are all professional travel journalists) to promote and encourage the public's interest in travel. Publishes a monthly newsletter (for members only), website and annual Yearbook, which contains details of members and lists travel industry PRs and contacts. Annual awards for journalism (members only) and the travel trade. Founded 1960.

The British Haiku Society

Flat 4, 2 Clifton Lawn, Ramsgate, Kent, CT11 9PB
email bhsenquiries2@virginmedia.com
website www.britishhaikusociety.org

The society runs the prestigious annual British Haiku Awards, in three categories: haiku, tanka and haibun. It is active in promoting the teaching of haiku in schools and colleges and is able to provide readers, course/workshop leaders and speakers for poetry groups etc. Founded 1990.

British Institute of Professional Photography

The Coach House, The Firs, High Street, Whitchurch, Aylesbury, Bucks. HP22 4SJ
tel (01296) 642020
email info@bipp.com
website www.bipp.com
Chief Executive Chris Harper

Represents all who practise photography as a profession in any field; to improve the quality of photography; establish recognised qualifications and a high standard of conduct; to safeguard the interests of the public and the profession. Admission can be obtained by submission of work and other information to the appropriate examining board. Fellows, Associates and Licentiates are entitled to the designation FBIPP, ABIPP or LBIPP in accordance with the qualification awarded. Organises numerous meetings and conferences in various parts of the country throughout the year; publishes *The Photographer* magazine (bi-monthly), plus various pamphlets and leaflets on professional photography. Founded 1901; incorporated 1921.

British Interactive Media Association (BIMA)

4th Floor, 77 Kingsway, London WC2B 6SR
tel 020-3538 6607
email info@bima.co.uk
website www.bima.co.uk
Membership Open to any organisation or individual with an interest in multimedia

Established to promote a wider understanding of the benefits of interactive multimedia to industry, government and education and to provide a regular forum for the exchange of views amongst members. Founded 1984.

The British Science Fiction Association Ltd

email info@bsfa.co.uk
website www.bsfa.co.uk
Chair Donna Bond

For authors, publishers, booksellers and readers of science fiction, fantasy and allied genres. Publishes *Focus*, an amateur writers' magazine; *Vector*, a critical magazine and the Orbiter Service, a network of email/postal writers' workshops. Trophies are awarded annually to the winner in each category of the BSFA Awards: best UK-published novel (previous winners include Christopher Priest, Adam Roberts, China Mieville), best short story, best artwork, best non-fiction. Founded 1958.

British Society of Comedy Writers

President Kenneth Rock, 61 Parry Road, Ashmore Park, Wolverhampton, West Midlands WV11 2PS
tel (01902) 722729
email info@bscw.co.uk
website www.bscw.co.uk
Membership £75 p.a. full, £40 p.a. subscriber

Aims to bring together writers and industry representatives in order to develop new projects and ideas. Holds an annual international comedy conference, networking days and workshops to train new writers to professional standards. Founded 1999.

British Society of Magazine Editors

137 Hale Lane, Edgware, Middlesex HA8 9QP
tel 020-8906 4664
email admin@bsme.com
website www.bsme.com

The only society in the UK exclusively for magazine and website editors. Represents the needs and views of all magazine editors and acts as a voice for the industry.

Broadcasting Entertainment Cinematograph and Theatre Union (BECTU)

373–377 Clapham Road, London SW9 9BT
tel 020-7346 0900
email info@bectu.org.uk
website www.bectu.org.uk
General Secretary G. Morrissey

Aims to defend the interests of writers in film, TV and radio. By virtue of its industrial strength, the Union is able to help its writer members to secure favourable terms and conditions. In cases of disputes with employers, the Union can intervene in order to ensure an equitable settlement. Its production agreement with PACT lays down minimum terms for writers working in the documentary area. Founded 1991.

The Brontë Society

Brontë Parsonage Museum, Haworth, Keighley, West Yorkshire BD22 8DR
tel (01535) 642323
email bronte@bronte.org.uk
website www.bronte.org.uk

Caring for and promoting the collections and literary legacy of the Brontë family; exhibitions and events; contemporary art projects; learning and engagement programmes. Publishes *Brontë Studies* and the *Brontë Gazette* three times a year. The museum is open all year round, except in January.

The Browning Society

Hon. Secretary Jim Smith, 64 Blyth Vale, London SE6 4NW
email browningsociety@hotmail.co.uk
website www.browningsociety.org
Contact Jim Smith, Hon. Secretary
Membership £15 p.a.

Aims to widen the appreciation and understanding of the lives and poetry of Robert Browning (1812–89) and Elizabeth Barrett Browning (1806–61), as well as other Victorian writers and poets. Founded 1881; refounded 1969.

The John Buchan Society

Membership Secretary Dr Dee Dunne-Thomas, 31 Walmley Ash Road, Walmley, Sutton Coldfield B76 1JA
tel 0121 351 3121
email thomasmdrb@btinternet.com
website www.johnbuchansociety.co.uk
Membership £20 p.a. – full; overseas and other rates on application

Promotes a wider understanding of the life and works of John Buchan (1875–1940). Encourages publication of Buchan's works, and supports the John Buchan Story Museum in Peebles. Holds regular meetings and social gatherings; produces a newsletter and a journal. Founded 1979.

Bureau of Freelance Photographers

Vision House, PO Box 474, Hatfield AL10 1FY
tel (01707) 651450
email mail@thebfp.com
website www.thebfp.com
Chief Executive John Tracy
Membership £54 p.a. UK; £70 p.a. overseas

Exists to help the freelance photographer by providing information on markets, and free advisory service. Publishes *Market Newsletter* (monthly). Founded 1965.

Byron Society (Newstead Abbey)

Acushla, Halam Road, Southwell, Notts. NG25 0AD
website www.newsteadabbeybyronsociety.org
Chairman P.K. Purslow
Membership £22 p.a.

Aims to promote research into the life and works of Lord Byron (1788–1824) through seminars, discussions, lectures and readings. Publishes *The Newstead Review* (annual, £12.50 plus postage). Founded 1988.

Randolph Caldecott Society

Secretary Kenn Oultram, Blue Grass Cottage, Clatterwick Lane, Little Leigh, Northwich, Cheshire CW8 4RJ

tel (01606) 891303 (office), (01606) 781731 (evening)
website www.randolphcaldecott.org.uk
Membership £12.50 p.a. individual; £17.50 p.a. families/corporate

Aims to encourage an interest in the life and works of Randolph Caldecott (1846–86), the Victorian artist, illustrator and sculptor. Meetings held in Chester. Liaises with the American Caldecott Society. Founded 1983.

Cambridge Bibliographical Society

University Library, West Road, Cambridge CB3 9DR
email cbs@lib.cam.ac.uk
website www.lib.cam.ac.uk/cambibsoc

Aims to encourage the study of bibliography, including book and MS production, book collecting and the history of libraries. It publishes *Transactions* (annual) and a series of monographs, and arranges a programme of lectures and visits. Founded 1949.

Campaign for Freedom of Information

Unit 109 Davina House, 137–149 Goswell Road, London EC1V 7ET
tel 020-7490 3958
email admin@cfoi.demon.co.uk
website www.cfoi.org.uk

A non-profit organisation working to improve public access to official information and to ensure that the Freedom of Information Act is implemented effectively.

Campaign for Press and Broadcasting Freedom

2nd Floor, Vi & Garner Smith House, 23 Orford Road, London E17 9NL
tel 07729 846146
email freepress@cpbf.org.uk
website www.cpbf.org.uk

Organisation dedicated to the promotion of diverse, democratic and accountable media. Founded 1979.

Canadian Authors Association

6 West Street North, Suite 203, Orillia, Ontario L3V 5B8
tel +1 705-325-3926
email admin@canadianauthors.org
website www.canadianauthors.org
President Matthew Bin, *Executive Director* Anita Purcell

Provides writers with a wide variety of programmes, services and resources to help them develop their skills in both the craft and the business of writing. A membership-based organisation for writers in all areas of the profession. Branches across Canada. Founded 1921.

Canadian Publishers' Council

250 Merton Street, Suite 203, Toronto, Ontario M4S 1B1, Canada
tel +1 416-322-7011
website www.pubcouncil.ca
Executive Director Jacqueline Hushion

Represents the interests of Canadian publishing companies that publish books and other media for schools, colleges and universities, professional and reference markets, the retail and library sectors. Founded 1910.

CANSCAIP (Canadian Society of Children's Authors, Illustrators & Performers)

720 Bathurst Street, Suite 501, Toronto, Ontario M5S 2R4, Canada
tel +1 416-515-1559
email office@canscaip.org
website www.canscaip.org
Administrative Director Helena Aalto
Membership $85 p.a.

A non-profit support network for children's artists. Promotes children's literature and performances throughout Canada and internationally. Founded 1977.

Careers Writers' Association

email reedwendy@btinternet.com
website www.parentalguidance.org.uk
Membership £40 p.a.

Society for established writers and editors of print and web-based materials on all careers-related issues, including study options, career choice and change, labour market information and specific vocational areas. Runs a careers website for parents to help them advise young people in their care. Details of members' publications and specific expertise are available on the website. Holds twice-yearly meetings. Founded 1979.

The Lewis Carroll Society

6 Chilton Street, London E2 6DZ
email membership@lewiscarrollsociety.org.uk
website www.lewiscarrollsociety.org.uk
Membership £20 p.a. UK; £23 Europe; £26 elsewhere. Special rates for institutions

Aims to promote interest in the life and works of Lewis Carroll (Revd Charles Lutwidge Dodgson) (1832–98) and to encourage research. Activities include regular meetings, exhibitions, and a publishing programme that includes the first annotated, unexpurgated edition of his diaries in nine volumes, the Society's journal *The Carrollian* (two p.a.), a newsletter, *Bandersnatch* (quarterly) and the *Lewis Carroll Review* (occasional). Founded 1969.

Lewis Carroll Society (Daresbury)

Secretary Kenn Oultram, Blue Grass Cottage, Clatterwick Lane, Little Leigh, Northwich, Cheshire CW8 4RJ

tel (01606) 891303 (office), (01606) 781731 (evening)
Membership £7 p.a.; £10 families/corporate

Aims to encourage an interest in the life and works of Lewis Carroll (1832–98), author of *Alice's Adventures*. Meetings take place at Carroll's birth village (Daresbury, Cheshire). Founded 1970.

Cartoonists Club of Great Britain

Secretary John Stilgoe, 160 Ashby Road, Hinckley, Leics. LE10 1SW
email secretary@thecartoonistsclub.com
email membership@thecartoonistsclub.com
website www.ccgb.org.uk
Membership £44 p.a. or £11 per quarter

Aims to encourage social contact between members and endeavours to promote the professional standing and prestige of cartoonists.

The Chartered Institute of Journalists

General Secretary Dominic Cooper, 2 Dock Offices, Surrey Quays Road, London SE16 2XU
tel 020-7252 1187
email memberservices@cioj.co.uk
website www.cioj.co.uk
Membership £195 p.a. maximum

The senior organisation of the profession, the Chartered Institute has accumulated funds for the assistance of members. A Freelance Division links editors and publishers with freelancers and a Directory is published of freelance writers, with their specialisations. There are special sections for broadcasters, motoring correspondents, public relations practitioners and overseas members. Occasional contributors to the media may qualify for election as Affiliates. Founded in 1884; incorporated by Royal Charter in 1890.

Chartered Institute of Linguists (CIOL)

Dunstan House, 14a St Cross Street, London EC1N 8XA
tel 020-7940 3100
email info@ciol.org.uk
website www.ciol.org.uk

An international professional membership organisation. It promotes proficiency in modern languages worldwide amongst professional linguists, including translators, interpreters and educationalists, as well as those in the public and private sectors for whom languages are an important skill. The IoL Educational Trust, an associated charity, is an accredited awarding body offering high-level exams.

The Institute helps to ensure equal access for all to the public services (law, health, local government) by providing interpreting qualifications in most of the languages spoken in the UK. Founded 1910.

The Chartered Society of Designers

1 Cedar Court, Royal Oak Yard, Bermondsey Street, London SE1 3GA
tel 020-7357 8088
email info@csd.org.uk
website www.csd.org.uk
President Jake Leith

Works to promote and regulate standards of competence, professional conduct and integrity, including representation on government and official bodies, design education and awards. The services to members include general information, publications, guidance on copyright and other professional issues, access to professional indemnity insurance, as well as the membership magazine *The Designer*. Activities in the regions are included in an extensive annual programme of events and training courses.

The Children's Book Circle

website www.childrensbookcircle.org.uk
Membership £25 p.a.

Provides a discussion forum for anybody involved with children's books. Monthly meetings are addressed by a panel of invited speakers and topics focus on current and controversial issues. Holds the annual Patrick Hardy lecture and administers the Eleanor Farjeon Award. Founded 1962.

Children's Books Ireland

17 North Great George's Street, Dublin 1, Republic of Ireland
tel +353 (0)1 8727475
email info@childrensbooksireland.com
website www.childrensbooksireland.ie
Director Elaina Ryan, *Publications and Communications Manager* Jenny Murray, *Programme Manager* Aoife Murray

Children's Books Ireland (CBI) is the national children's books resource organisation of Ireland. Its mission is to make books part of every child's life. Champions and celebrates the importance of authors and illustrators and works in partnership with the people and organisations who enhance children's lives through books. Core projects include: the CBI Annual Conference; the CBI Book of the Year Awards and its shadowing scheme for school groups and book clubs; the annual nationwide reading campaign which promotes books and reading and which coincides with the publication of Recommended Reads, a guide to the best books of the year; nationwide Book Clinics and *Inis* magazine in print and online, a forum for discussion, debate and critique of Irish and international books. CBI administers the Laureate na nÓg project on behalf of the Arts Council and runs live literature events throughout the year. Founded 1996.

CILIP (Chartered Institute of Library and Information Professionals)

7 Ridgmount Street, London WC1E 7AE
tel 020-7255 0500
email info@cilip.org.uk
website www.cilip.org.uk
Membership Varies according to income

The leading professional body for librarians, information specialists and knowledge managers. CILIP's vision is a fair and economically prosperous society underpinned by literacy, access to information and the transfer of knowledge. CILIP is a registered charity, no. 313014. Offices in London, Wales, Scotland and Northern Ireland.

Circle of Wine Writers

Administrator Andrea Warren, Scots Firs, 70 Joiners Lane, Chalfont St Peter, Bucks. SL9 0AU
tel (01753) 882320
email administrator@circleofwinewriters.org
website www.circleofwinewriters.org
Membership By election, £75 p.a.

An association for those engaged in communicating about wines and spirits. Produces *Circle Update* electronic newsletter (five p.a.), organises tasting sessions as well as a programme of meetings and talks. Founded 1960.

The John Clare Society

tel (01353) 668438
email l.j.curry@bham.ac.uk
email sueholgate@hotmail.co.uk
website http://johnclaresociety.blogspot.com/
Membership £15 p.a. UK individual; other rates on application

Promotes a wider appreciation of the life and works of the poet John Clare (1793–1864). Founded 1981.

Classical Association

email office@classicalassociation.org
website www.classicalassociation.org
Hon. Secretary Dr E.J. Stafford

Exists to promote and sustain interest in classical studies, to maintain their rightful position in universities and schools, and to give scholars and teachers opportunities for meeting and discussing their problems.

The William Cobbett Society

1 Meadow View Cottages, Spring Grove, Burlesdon SO31 8BB
email information@williamcobbett.org.uk
website www.williamcobbett.org.uk

Aims to make the life and work of William Cobbett (1763–1835) better known. Founded 1976.

The Wilkie Collins Society

Membership Secretary Paul Lewis, 4 Ernest Gardens, London W4 3QU
email paul@paullewis.co.uk
website www.wilkiecollins.org
Membership £12 p.a. EU; £18 international

Aims to promote interest in the life and works of Wilkie Collins (1824–89). Publishes a newsletter, an annual scholarly journal and reprints of Collins's lesser known works. Founded 1981.

Comhairle nan Leabhraichean/The Gaelic Books Council

32 Mansfield Street, Glasgow G11 5QP
tel 0141 337 6211
email rosemary@gaelicbooks.org
website www.gaelicbooks.org
Director Rosemary Ward

Stimulates Scottish Gaelic publishing by awarding publication grants for new books, commissions new works from established and emerging authors and provides editorial advice and guidance to Gaelic writers and publishers. Has a bookshop in Glasgow that stocks all Gaelic and Gaelic-related books in print. All stock is listed on the website and a paper catalogue is also available. Founded 1968.

The Joseph Conrad Society (UK)

The Honorary Secretary c/o The Polish Social and Cultural Association, 238–246 King Street, London W6 0RF
email theconradian@gmail.com
website www.josephconradsociety.org
Chairman Robert Hampson, *Honorary Secretary* Hugh Epstein, *Editor* Allan Simmons

Activities include an annual international conference; publication of *The Conradian* and a series of pamphlets; and maintenance of a substantial reference library as part of the Polish Library at the Polish Social and Cultural Association. Administers the Juliet McLauchlan Prize, a £200 annual award for the winner of an essay competition, and travel grants for scholars wishing to attend Conrad conferences. Founded 1973.

Copyright Clearance Center Inc.

222 Rosewood Drive, Danvers, MA 01923, USA
tel +1 978-750-8400
website www.copyright.com

Aims to remove the complexity from copyright issues and make it easy for businesses and academic institutions to use copyright-protected materials while compensating publishers and content creators for their work.

Copyright Council of New Zealand Inc.

PO Box 331488, Takapuna 0740, North Shore City, New Zealand
tel +64 (0)9 486 6250
email info@copyright.org.nz
website www.copyright.org.nz

The aim of the Copyright Council is to protect, preserve, develop and promote the rights of copyright creators and owners to New Zealand's best, long-term advantage. It currently has 22 members representing a wide spectrum of organisations.

The Copyright Licensing Agency Ltd – see page 685

Creative Scotland

Waverley Gate, 2–4 Waterloo Place,
Edinburgh EH1 3EG
tel 0330 333 2000
email enquiries@creativescotland.com
website www.creativescotland.com

Creative Scotland is the public body that supports the arts, screen and creative industries across all parts of Scotland on behalf of everyone who lives, works or visits there. Through distributing funding from the Scottish Government and the National Lottery, Creative Scotland enables people and organisations to work in and experience the arts, screen and creative industries in Scotland by helping others to develop great ideas and bring them to life.

Crime Writers' Association

email info@thecwa.co.uk
email director@thecwa.co.uk
website www.thecwa.co.uk
Director Lucy Santos
Membership Associate membership open to publishers, journalists, booksellers specialising in crime literature and literary agents

Membership is open to crime writers, reviewers, editors or agents, plus anyone whose business is concerned with publishing, bookselling or representing crime writers. Provisional membership is available for writers with a valid contract whose first book will be published within the next two years. The CWA was founded in 1953. Membership benefits include a monthly full colour magazine *Red Herrings*. CWA members can promote their work through the Crime Readers' Association.

The Critics' Circle

Contact Rick Jones, c/o 17 Rosenthal Road, Catford, London SE6 2BX
tel 020-8698 2460
email criticscircleallsections@gmail.com
website www.criticscircle.org.uk
President Jeffery Taylor, *Hon. General Secretary* Rick Jones, *Hon. Treasurer* Peter Cargin
Membership By invitation of the Council

Aims to promote the art of criticism, to uphold its integrity in practice, to foster and safeguard the professional interests of its members, to provide opportunities for social intercourse among them, and to support the advancement of the arts. Such invitations are issued only to persons engaged professionally, regularly and substantially in the writing or broadcasting of criticism of dance, drama, film, literaure, music and the visual arts. Founded 1913.

Cwlwm Cyhoeddwyr Cymru

Bethan Mair, Y Berth, 29 Coed Bach, Portarddulais, Abertawe, Swansea SA4 8RB
tel 07779 102224
email geiriau@gmail.com
website www.bedwen.com

Represents and promotes Welsh-language publishers and organises Bedwen Lyfrau, the only national Welsh-language book festival, held annually in May. Founded 2002.

Walter de la Mare Society

3 Hazelwood Close, New River Crescent, Palmers Green, London N13 5RE
website www.walterdelamare.co.uk
Hon. Secretary and Treasurer Frances Guthrie
Membership £15 p.a.

To promote the study and deepen the appreciation of the works of Walter de la Mare (1873–1956) through a magazine, talks, discussions and other activities. Founded 1997.

Design and Artists Copyright Society – see page 689

Dickens Fellowship

The Charles Dickens Museum, 48 Doughty Street, London WC1N 2LX
tel 020-7405 2127
email postbox@dickensfellowship.org
website www.dickensfellowship.org
Joint Hon. Secretaries Mrs Lee Ault, Paul Graham
Membership £17 p.a.

Based in the house occupied by Charles Dickens (1812–70) during the period 1837–9. Publishes *The Dickensian* (3 p.a.). Founded 1902.

Directory of Writers' Groups

39 Lincoln Way, Harlington, Beds. LU5 6NG
tel (01525) 873197
email writerscircles@yahoo.co.uk
website www.writers-circles.com
Editor Diana Hayden

Directory of writers' groups and courses published annually since 1999; print and ebook.

The Arthur Conan Doyle Society

PO Box 1360, Ashcroft, BC V0K 1A0, Canada
tel +1 250-453-2045
email sirhenry@telus.net
website www.ash-tree.bc.ca/acdsocy.html

Promotes the study of the life and works of Sir Arthur Conan Doyle (1859–1930). Publishes *ACD* journal (bi-annual) and occasional reprints of Conan Doyle material. Occasional conventions. Founded 1989.

Early English Text Society

Faculty of English, St Cross Building, Manor Road, Oxford OX16 0TR
website www.eets.org.uk
Hon. Director Prof. V. Gillespie, *Executive Secretary* Prof. D. Wakelin

Membership £30 p.a.

Aims to bring unprinted early English literature within the reach of students in sound texts. Founded 1864.

Edinburgh Bibliographical Society

Rare Book Collections, National Library of Scotland, George IV Bridge, Edinburgh EH1 1EW
email h.vincent@nls.uk
website www.edinburghbibliographicalsociety.org.uk
Secretary H. Vincent, *Treasurer* R. Betteridge
Membership £15 p.a.; £20 corporate; £10 full-time students

Encourages bibliographical activity through organising talks for members, particularly on bibliographical topics relating to Scotland, and visits to libraries. See website for submission guidelines and prizes. Publishes *Journal* (annual, free to members) and other occasional publications. Founded 1890.

Editors' and Proofreaders' Alliance of Northern Ireland (EPANI)

tel 07875 857278
email info@epani.org.uk
website www.epani.org.uk
Manager Averill Buchanan

Aims to establish and maintain high professional standards in editorial skills in Northern Ireland. Membership is free, but a small fee is charged for inclusion in EPANI's online directory. Full details can be found on the website. Founded 2011.

The George Eliot Fellowship

Chairman John Burton, 39 Lower Road, Barnacle, Coventry CV7 9LD
tel 024-7661 9126
email jkburton@tiscali.co.uk
website www.georgeeliot.org
President Jonathan G. Ouvry
Membership £18 p.a. (£15 concessions) individuals; £23 p.a. (£20 concessions) for couples; £15 p.a. students (under 25)

Promotes an interest in the life and work of George Eliot (1819–80) and helps to extend her influence; arranges meetings, study days and conferences; produces an annual journal (*The George Eliot Review*), newsletters and other publications. Works closely with educational establishments in the Nuneaton area. Awards the annual George Eliot Fellowship Prize (£500) for an essay on Eliot's life or work, which must be previously unpublished and not exceed 4,000 words. Hopes to open a George Eliot Visitor Centre at Griff, Nuneaton, before 2016. Founded 1930.

English Association

University of Leicester, University Road, Leicester LE1 7RH
tel 0116 229 7622
email engassoc@leicester.ac.uk
website www.le.ac.uk/engassoc
Chair Martin Halliwell, *Chief Executive* Helen Lucas

Aims to further knowledge, understanding and enjoyment of English literature and the English language, by working towards a fuller recognition of English as an essential element in education and in the community at large; by encouraging the study of English literature and language by means of conferences, lectures and publications; and by fostering the discussion of methods of teaching English of all kinds.

English Speaking Board (International) Ltd

9 Hattersley Court, Burscough Road, Ormskirk L39 2AY
tel (01695) 573439
email admin@esbuk.org
website www.esbuk.org
Ceo Peter Wren
Membership £39.50 p.a. individuals; £75 p.a. corporate; £20 for new individual members joining after 1 July

Aims to foster all activities concerned with oral communication. Offers assessment qualifications in practical speaking and listening skills for candidates at all levels in schools, vocational and business contexts; also for those with learning difficulties and those for whom English is an acquired language. Also provides training courses in teaching and delivery of oral communication. Offers membership to all those concerned with the development and expression of the English language. Members receive *Speaking English* (two p.a.); articles are invited on any special aspect of spoken English.

The English-Speaking Union

Dartmouth House, 37 Charles Street, London W1J 5ED
tel 020-7529 1550
email esu@esu.org
website www.esu.org
Membership Various categories

Aims to promote international understanding and human achievement through the widening use of the English language throughout the world. The ESU is an educational charity which sponsors scholarships and exchanges, educational programmes promoting the effective use of English, and a wide range of international and cultural events. Members contribute to its work across the world. Founded 1918.

Equality in Publishing

The Publishers Association, 29b Montague Street, London WC1B 5BW
tel 020-7691 9191
website www.equalityinpublishing.org.uk

Established to promote equality across publishing, bookselling and agenting by driving forward change and increasing access to opportunities within the industry.

European Broadcasting Union

Geneva Headquarters, L'Ancienne Route 17A, CH–1218 Grand-Saconnex (Geneva), Switzerland
tel +41 (0)22-717 2111
email ebu@ebu.ch
website www.ebu.ch
Director General Ingrid Deltenre

The European Broadcasting Union (EBU) is the world's foremost alliance of public service media (PSM) organisations with 73 Members in 56 countries in Europe and beyond. Its mission is to defend the interests of PSM and to promote its indispensable contribution to modern society and sustaining democracy. The EBU is a centre of media industry knowledge and expertise, particularly in the areas of broadcast technology and innovation, training research and European media law. The EBU operates the EUROVISION and EURORADIO networks to produce and deliver top quality live sport and news as well as entertainment, culture and music content.

Fabian Society

61 Petty France, London SW1H 9EU
tel 020 7227 4900
email info@fabians.org.uk
website www.fabians.org.uk
General Secretary Andrew Harrop, *Head of Editorial* Ed Wallis

Publishes a quarterly magazine, books, pamphlets, policy reports and blog. Current affairs, political thought, economics, education, environment, foreign affairs, social policy. Also controls NCLC Publishing Society Ltd. Founded 1884.

TheFED – A Network of Writing and Community Publishers

Flat 2 Clydesdale, 5 College Road, Buxton, Derbyshire SK17 9DZ
tel 07549 862495
email fedonline1@gmail.com
website www.thefed.btck.co.uk
Membership Secretary/Treasurer Louise Glasscoe
Membership £25 p.a. funded groups; £15 unfunded; £10 waged individuals; £5 unwaged/low income

TheFED continues the work started by the Federation of Worker Writers and Community Publishers. Details of the 2016 annual festival of writing and AGM at Syracuse University's London campus at Faraday House, 48–51 Old Gloucester Street, London WC1N 3AE will be advertised on the website. Admission: members £10 (in advance) or £12 (on the door); non-members £15 (in advance) or £17 (on the door) – includes information packs, lunch, refreshments and workshops.

Federation Against Copyright Theft Ltd (FACT)

Europa House, Church Street, Old Isleworth, Middlesex TW7 6DA
tel 020-8568 6646
email contact@fact-uk.org.uk
website www.fact-uk.org.uk
Director General Kieron Sharp

Aims to protect the interests of its members and others against infringement in the UK of copyright in cinematograph films, TV programmes and all forms of audiovisual recording. Founded 1982.

Federation of British Artists

17 Carlton House Terrace, London SW1Y 5BD
tel 020-7930 6844
email info@mallgalleries.com
website www.mallgalleries.org.uk

Administers nine major National Art Societies as well as the Threadneedle Prize at the Mall Galleries, The Mall, London SW1.

Federation of European Publishers

Rue Montoyer 31 Bte 8, B–1000 Brussels, Belgium
tel +32 2-7701110
email info@fep-fee.eu
website www.fep-fee.eu
President Pierre Dutilleul, *Director General* Anne Bergman-Tahon

Represents the interests of European publishers on EU affairs; informs members on the development of EU policies which could affect the publishing industry. Founded 1967.

Federation of Spanish Publishers' Association

(Federación de Gremios de Editores de España)
email fgee@fge.es
website www.federacioneditores.org
President Daniel Fernández

A non-profit, private professional association created to represent, manage, enhance and defend the general common interests of Spanish publishers on a national, European and international level. Founded 1978.

Federation of Writers (Scotland)

email ettadunn@hotmail.com
website www.writersfederation.org.uk
Executive Convener Etta Dunn, *Ambassador and Events Convener* Marc R. Sherland

The Federation aims to support writers of all abilities across Scotland from the inception of the idea through to publication. Maintains a directory of writing groups, making it easier for writers to establish contacts in their area. Also organises performances of work in progress and completed pieces. In addition to these services, the Federation holds regular meetings, seminars and workshops and helps with the process of getting published. Has its own imprint, New Voices Press, which publishes an annual anthology of members' work in addition to regular chapbooks of collections from selected members. Membership of the Federation is free; donations gratefully received.

The Fine Art Trade Guild

Unit 2, Wye House, 6 Enterprise Way,
London SW18 1FZ
tel 020-7381 6616
email info@fineart.co.uk
website www.fineart.co.uk
Ceo Louise Hay

Promotes the sale of fine art prints and picture framing in the UK and overseas markets; establishes and raises standards amongst members and communicates these to the buying public. The Guild publishes *Art Business Today*, the trade's longest established magazine, and various specialist books. Founded 1910.

FOCAL International Ltd (Federation of Commercial AudioVisual Libraries International Ltd)

79 College Road, Harrow, Middlesex HA1 1BD
tel 020-3178 3535
email info@focalint.org
website www.focalint.org
Commerical Manager Anne Johnson, *General Manager* Julie Lewis

A not-for-profit trade association for the commercial audio visual library industry, with over 300 members. Founded 1985.

The Folklore Society

c/o The Warburg Institute, Woburn Square,
London WC1H 0AB
tel 020-7862 8564
email enquiries@folklore-society.com
website www.folklore-society.com
President Prof. James H. Grayson, *Hon. Secretary* W.J. Roberts
Membership £45 p.a.

Collection, recording and study of folklore. Founded 1878.

Foreign Press Association in London

Award House, 7–11 St Matthew Street,
London SW1P 2JT
tel 020-3727 4319
email christopherwyld@fpalondon.org
email terrypage@fpalondon.org
website www.fpalondon.org
Director Christopher Wyld
Membership Full membership open to those working for news media organisations with headquarters overseas. Associate membership also available.

Aims to promote access for journalists from overseas. Founded 1888.

Free Painters & Sculptors

Registered office 14 John Street, London WC1N 2EB
email info@freepaintersandsculptors.co.uk
website www.freepaintersandsculptors.co.uk

Promotes group shows twice a year in prestigious galleries in London. Sponsors all that is exciting in contemporary art.

Free Word

Free Word Centre, 60 Farringdon Road,
London EC1R 3GA
tel 020-7324 2570
email info@freewordonline.com
website www.freewordonline.com
Fees for associates International Associates £100 p.a., Associates range from £150 to £450 p.a. All prices exclude VAT.

Free Word is an international centre for literacy, literature and free expression. Develops local, national and international collaborations that explore the transformative power of words. Manages a building which hosts organisations working across literature, literacy and free expression. Current residents are: Apples & Snakes, ARTICLE 19, Arvon, English PEN, The Literary Consultancy and The Reading Agency. Hosts a year-round programme of events inspired by literature, literacy and free expression: through conferences, debates and exhibitions, book launches, films and school programmes, Free Word promotes, protects and democratises the power of words. With residents, associates and other partners, Free Word develops a programme of cultural projects to explore important contemporary issues. Works worldwide with writers and thinkers.

Free Word Centre is a hub for work, study and discussion. The centre provides flexible meeting rooms, exhibition/event spaces, a lecture theatre, and a lively public cafe.

French Publishers' Association

(Syndicat National de l'Edition)
115 Blvd St Germain, 75006 Paris, France
tel +33 (0)1 4441 4050
website www.sne.fr

The Gaelic Books Council – see Comhairle nan Leabhraichean/The Gaelic Books Council

The Garden Media Guild

Katepwa House, Ashfield Park Avenue,
Ross-on-Wye, Herefordshire HR9 5AX
tel (01989) 567393
email admin@gardenmediaguild.co.uk
website www.gardenmediaguild.co.uk
Chairman Deborah Stone
Membership £65 p.a.

Aims to raise the quality of garden writing, photography and broadcasting, to help members operate efficiently and profitably, to improve communication between members and to promote liaison between members and the broader horticultural industry. The Guild administers annual awards to encourage excellence in garden writing, photography, trade and consumer press journalism, TV and radio broadcasting. Founded 1991.

The Gaskell Society

37 Buckingham Drive, Knutsford,
Cheshire WA16 8LH
tel (01565) 651761
email pam.griffiths@talktalk.net
website www.gaskellsociety.co.uk
Secretary Mrs Pam Griffiths
Membership £23 p.a.; £28 joint annual member/ European member/institutions; £15 student in full time education; £30 non-European member

Promotes and encourages the study and appreciation of the work and life of Elizabeth Cleghorn Gaskell (1810–65). Holds regular meetings in Knutsford, London, Manchester and Bath, visits and residential conferences; produces an annual journal and bi-annual newsletters. Founded 1985.

Gay Authors Workshop

Kathryn Byrd, BM Box 5700, London WC1N 3XX
email eandk2@btinternet.com
Membership £8 p.a.; £4 unwaged

Exists to encourage writers who are lesbian, gay or bisexual. Quarterly newsletter, bi-annual magazine and monthly meetings. Founded 1978.

German Publishers' and Booksellers' Association

(Börsenverein des Deutschen Buchhandels e.V.)
Braubachstraße 16, 60311 Frankfurt am Main, Germany/ Postfach 10 04 42,
60001 Frankfurt am Main
tel +49 (0)69 13060
email info@boev.de
website www.boersenverein.de
General Manager Alexander Skipis, *President* Heinrich Riethmuller

The leading organisation for publishing companies, booksellers and the intermediate book trade in Germany. Founded 1825.

Graham Greene Birthplace Trust

Yan Christensen, 9 Briar Way, Berkhamsted HP4 2JJ
tel (01442) 873604
email secretary@grahamgreenebt.org
website www.grahamgreenebt.org
Membership £12 p.a.; £32 for 3 years

Exists to study the works of Graham Greene (1904–91). The Trust promotes the Annual Graham Greene Festival and Graham Greene trails. It publishes a quarterly newsletter, occasional papers, videos and CDs, and maintains a small library. It administers the Graham Greene Memorial Awards. Founded 1997.

The Greeting Card Association

United House, North Road, London N7 9DP
tel 020-7619 0396
website www.greetingcardassociation.org.uk
Chief Executive Sharon Little

The trade association for greeting card publishers. See website for information and contacts for freelance designing and writing for greeting cards. Official magazine: *Progressive Greetings Worldwide* (see page 0). Founded 1919.

Guernsey Arts Commission

North Esplanade, St Peter Port Guernsey GY1 2LQ
tel (01481) 709747
email info@arts.gg

The Commission's aim is to help promote, develop and support the arts in Guernsey through exhibitions, a community arts programme and public events.

The Guild of Aviation Artists

(incorporating the Society of Aviation Artists)
Trenchard House, 85 Farnborough Road, Farnborough, Hants GU14 6TF
tel (01252) 513123
email admin@gava.org.uk
website www.gava.org.uk
President Michael Turner, *Secretary/Administrator* Susan Gardner
Membership £65 p.a. Full (by invitation); £50 Associates (by selection); £30 Friends

Formed to promote aviation art through the organisation of exhibitions and meetings. Holds annual open exhibition in July in London; £1,000 prize for 'Aviation Painting of the Year'. Quarterly members' newsletter. Founded 1971.

Guild of Food Writers

Administrator Jonathan Woods,
255 Kent House Road, Beckenham, Kent BR3 1JQ
tel 020-8659 0422
email guild@gfw.co.uk
website www.gfw.co.uk
Membership £85 p.a.

Aims to bring together professional food writers including journalists, broadcasters and authors, to print and issue an annual list of members, to extend the range of members' knowledge and experience by arranging discussions, tastings and visits, and to encourage the development of new writers by every means, including competitions and awards. There are 14 awards and entry is not restricted to members of the Guild. Founded 1984.

Guild of Health Writers

Dale Lodge, 88 Wensleydale Road, Hampton, Middlesex TW12 2LX

tel 020-8941 2977
email admin@healthwriters.com
website www.healthwriters.com
Membership £50 p.a.; Student £12 p.a.

The Guild of Health Writers is a national, independent membership organisation representing Britain's leading health journalists and writers. It was founded to encourage the provision of readable and accurate health information to the public. Members write on every aspect of health and wellbeing, from innovative medical science to complementary therapies and lifestyle issues. They value the training and networking opportunities that the Guild provides. Founded 1994.

The Guild of International Songwriters & Composers

Ebrel House, 2a Penlee Close, Praa Sands, Penzance, Cornwall TR20 9SR
tel (01736) 762826
email songmag@aol.com
website www.songwriters-guild.co.uk
Secretary Carole Jones
Membership £60

Gives advice to members on contractual and copyright matters; assists with protection of members rights; assists with analysis of members' works; international collaboration register free to members; outlines requirements to record companies, publishers, artists. Publishes *Songwriting & Composing* (quarterly).

The Guild of Motoring Writers

The Guild of Motoring Writers' Secretariat, 40 Baring Road, Bournemouth BH6 4DT
tel (01202) 422424
email generalsec@gomw.co.uk
website www.gomw.co.uk.co.uk

The Guild of Motoring Writers is the largest organisation of its kind in the world representing automotive journalists, photographers, broadcasters and artists. Based in the UK, it represents more than 450 working members in 25 countries. It aims to raise the standard of motoring journalism, to encourage motoring, motorsport and road safety, promote professional training of journalists, works closely with the motor industry and provides a link between fellow members around the world and to safeguard the interests of members in relation to the aims of the Guild. Founded 1944.

Guild of Railway Artists

Chief Executive Officer F.P. Hodges, 45 Dickins Road, Warwick CV34 5NS
tel (01926) 499246
email frank.hodges@virgin.net
website www.railart.co.uk

Aims to forge a link between artists depicting railway subjects and to give members a corporate identity; also stages railway art exhibitions and members' meetings and produces books of members' works. Founded 1979.

Hakluyt Society

c/o The Map Library, The British Library, 96 Euston Road, London NW1 2DB
tel (01428) 64185
email office@hakluyt.com
website www.hakluyt.com
President Michael Barritt

Publication of original narratives of voyages, travels, naval expeditions, and other geographical records. Founded 1846.

Hampshire Writers' Society

University of Winchester, Winchester, Hants SO22 4NR
tel (01962) 712307
email hampshirewriters@gmail.com
website www.hampshirewriterssociety.co.uk

Welcomes all aspiring and published writers to enjoy a broad range of talks, readings, panels and performances by renowned authors, poets, playwrights, producers, children's authors, literary agents, commissioning editors and industry specialists. Meetings are held on the second Tuesday of each month (except July and August) 7 pm for 7.30 pm in The Stripe Theatre, University of Winchester. Annual membership £30, visitors £5, students free. Enter the monthly writing competition which is adjudicated and prizes awarded at the meeting. Phone or email for the programme of events.

The Thomas Hardy Society

c/o Dorset County Museum, High West Street, Dorchester, Dorset DT1 1XA
tel (01305) 251501
email info@hardysociety.org
website www.hardysociety.org
Membership £24 p.a.; £35 overseas

Aims to promote and celebrate the work of Thomas Hardy (1840–1928). Publishes *The Thomas Hardy Journal* (annual) and *The Hardy Society Journal* (2 p.a.). Biennial conference held in Dorchester. Founded 1967.

Harleian Society

College of Arms, Queen Victoria Street, London EC4V 4BT
tel 020-7236 7728
email norroy&ulster@college-of-arms.gov.uk
website http://harleian.org.uk
Chairman T. Woodcock CVO, DL, FSA, Garter King of Arms, *Hon. Secretary* T.H.S. Duke, Norroy and Ulster of Arms

Instituted for transcribing, printing and publishing the heraldic visitations of Counties, Parish Registers and any manuscripts relating to genealogy, family history and heraldry. Founded 1869.

Hesketh Hubbard Art Society

17 Carlton House Terrace, London SW1Y 5BD
tel 020-7930 6844
email info@mallgalleries.com
website www.mallgalleries.org.uk
President Simon Whittle
Membership £215 p.a.

Weekly life drawing classes.

The Hilliard Society of Miniaturists

c/o 26 St Cuthbert Avenue, Wells, BA5 2JW
email hilliardsociety@aol.com
website www.hilliardsociety.org
President Sarah Whitehouse, *Executive Secretary* Heather Webb
Membership From £60 p.a.

Aims to increase knowledge and promote the art of miniature painting. Annual exhibition held in June at Wells; produces a newsletter. Member of the World Federation of Miniaturists. Founded 1982.

The James Hilton Society

Hon. Secretary Dr J.R. Hammond,
49 Beckingthorpe Drive, Bottesford,
Nottingham NG13 0DN
website www.jameshiltonsociety.co.uk
Membership £13 p.a. (£10 concessions)

Aims to promote interest in the life and work of novelist and scriptwriter James Hilton (1900–54). Publishes quarterly newsletter and an annual scholarly journal, and organises conferences. Founded 2000.

Historical Novel Society

Contact Richard Lee, Marine Cottage, The Strand, Starcross, Devon EX6 8NY
tel (01626) 891962
email richard@historicalnovelsociety.org
website http://historicalnovelsociety.org/
Membership £30 p.a.

Promotes the enjoyment of historical fiction. Based in the US and UK but welcomes members (who can be readers or writers) from all over the world. Publishes print magazines, organises conferences and has an active website. Founded 1997.

The Sherlock Holmes Society of London

General enquiries Roger Johnson,
Press & Publicity Officer (shjournal@btinternet.com)
Membership Secretary David Jones
(audav@hotmail.co.uk)
website www.sherlock-holmes.org.uk
Chairman Elaine Hamill
(appledore.towers@btinternet.com)

The Society is open to anyone with an interest in Sherlock Holmes, Dr John H. Watson and their world. A literary and social society, publishing a bi-annual scholarly journal and occasional papers, and holding meetings, dinners and excursions. Founded 1951.

Horror Writers Association (HWA)

244 5th Avenue, Suite 2767, New York, NY 10001
email hwa@horror.org
website www.horror.org
President Lisa Morton
Membership $69 p.a. (individual); $48 (supporting); $115 (corporate); $89 (family)

A worldwide organisation of 1,300 writers and publishing professionals dedicated to promoting the interests of writers of horror and dark fantasy. There are five levels of membership: for new writers, established writers, professionals, academics and non-writing horror professionals. The HWA gives the iconic Bram Stoker Awards® on an annual basis, as well as hosting horror conventions, and provides a range of services to its horror writer, editor and publisher membership base. Founded 1987.

Housman Society

80 New Road, Bromsgrove, Worcs. B60 2LA
tel (01527) 874136
email info@housman-society.co.uk
website www.housman-society.co.uk
Chairman Jim Page
Membership £15 p.a. (UK), £20 p.a. (overseas)

Aims to foster interest in and promote knowledge of A.E. Housman (1859–1936) and his family. Sponsors a lecture at the Hay Festival. Publishes an annual journal and bi-annual newsletter. Founded 1973.

Incorporated Society of Musicians

4–5 Inverness Mews, London W2 3JQ
tel 020-7629 4413
email membership@ism.org
website www.ism.org
President Prof. Barry Ife CBE, *Chief Executive* Deborah Annetts
Membership £164 p.a.

Professional body for musicians. Aims to promote the art of music; protect the interests and raise the standards of the musical profession; provide services, support and advice for its members. Publishes *Music Journal* (six p.a.) and a yearbook annually. Founded 1882.

Independent Press Standards Organisation (IPSO)

Gate House, 1 Farringdon Street, London EC4M 7LG
email inquiries@ipso.co.uk
website www.ipso.co.uk

IPSO is the independent regulator of the newspaper and magazine industry. It exists to promote and uphold the highest professional standards of journalism in the UK and to support members of the public in seeking redress where they believe that the Editors' Code of Practice has been breached.

Independent Publishers Guild

PO Box 12, Llain, Login SA34 0WU
tel (01437) 563335
email info@ipg.uk.com
website www.ipg.uk.com
Chair Oliver Gadsby
Membership Open to new and established publishers and book packagers

Provides an information and contact network for independent publishers. Also voices concerns of member companies within the book trade. Founded 1962.

Independent Theatre Council (ITC)

The Albany, Douglas Way, London SE8 4AG
tel 020-7403 1727
email admin@itc-arts.org
website www.itc-arts.org
Chief Executive Charlotte Jones
Membership Rates start at £175 + vat

The Independent Theatre Council exists to enable the creation of high quality professional performing arts by supporting, representing and developing the people who manage and produce it. It has around 500 members from a wide range of companies, venues and individuals in the fields of drama, dance, opera, musical theatre, puppetry, mixed media, mime, physical theatre and circus. Founded 1974.

Institute of Designers in Ireland

The Fumbally Exchange, 5 Dame Lane, Dublin 2, Republic of Ireland
email info@idi-design.ie
website www.idi-design.ie

Irish design profession's representative body, covering every field of design. Founded 1972.

Institute of Internal Communication

Suite G10, Gemini House, Sunrise Parkway, Linford Wood, Milton Keynes MK14 6PW
tel (01908) 232168
email enquiries@ioic.org.uk
website www.ioic.org.uk

The market leader in internal communications for those involved in corporate media management and practice by providing professional, authoritative, dynamic, supportive and innovative services. Founded 1949.

The Institute of Translation & Interpreting (ITI)

Suite 165, Milton Keynes Business Centre, Linford Wood, Milton Keynes MK14 6GD
tel (01908) 325250
email info@iti.org.uk
website www.iti.org.uk

The Institute of Translating & Interpreting was founded in 1986 as the only independent professional association of practising translators and interpreters in the UK. It is now one of the primary sources of information on these services to government, industry, the media and the general public. With the aim of promoting the highest standards in the profession, ITI serves as a focal point for all those who understand the importance of translation and interpreting to the economy and community. This is important in light of the growth in global communications and changes in UK and EU legislation requiring that foreign nationals have access to help through an interpreter or translator. ITI offers guidance to those entering the profession and advice to both people offering their language services and their potential customers.

International Association of Conscious & Creative Writers (IACCW)

PO Box 3703, Trowbridge BA14 6ZW
tel (01380) 871331
email info@iaccw.com
website www.iaccw.com
Founder/Creative Director Julia McCutchen
Membership Free, or full at £97 p.a.

Membership-based organisation for writers offering monthly teleseminar training and interviews with best-selling authors and experts from around the world. Topics include all aspects of creativity, writing and contemporary publishing options, plus marketing and building an author platform. The range of member benefits includes a complimentary audio CD set presenting the current year's best interviews collection, a welcome pack and opportunities to share information and resources. Highlights the importance of discovering an authentic voice both on the page and in the world. Established 2010.

International Publishers Association

23 avenue de France, 1202 Geneva, Switzerland
tel +41 22-704 1820
email secretariat@internationalpublishers.org
website www.internationalpublishers.org
President Richard Charkin, *Secretary-General* Jens Bammel

A federation of national, regional and specialist publishers' associations. Its membership comprises more than 60 organisations from more than 50 countries in Africa, Asia, Australia, Europe and the Americas. Founded 1896.

International Society of Typographic Designers

ISTD Ltd, PO Box 7002, London W1A 2TY
email mail@istd.org.uk
Co-chairs Andy Uren, Becky Chilcott, *Past President* Freda Sack

Working closely with graphic design educationalists and the professional community, the International Society of Typographic Designers establishes, maintains and promotes typographic standards through the forum of debate and design practice. Membership is awarded to practising designers, educators and students who demonstrate, through the quality of their work, their commitment to achieving the highest possible quality of visual communication. It publishes a journal, *Typographic*. Students of typography and graphic design are encouraged to gain membership of the Society by entering the annual student assessment scheme. Founded 1928.

International Visual Communication Association (IVCA)

1st Floor, 23 Golden Square, London W1F 9JP
tel 020-7287 1002
email info@ivca.org
website www.ivca.org
Chief Executive Officer Marco Forgione
Membership membership@ivca.org

For those who work in business communication. Aims to promote the industry and provide a collective voice; provides a range of services, publications and events to help existing and potential users to make the most of what video, film, multimedia and live events can offer their business. Founded 1987.

The Irish Copyright Licensing Agency

25 Denzille Lane, Dublin 2, Republic of Ireland
tel +353 (0)1 6624211
email info@icla.ie
website www.icla.ie
Executive Director Samantha Holman

Licences schools and other users of copyright material to photocopy extracts of such material, and distributes the monies collected to the authors and publishers whose works have been copied. Founded 1992.

Irish Translators' and Interpreters' Association

Irish Writers' Centre, 19 Parnell Square, Dublin 1, Republic of Ireland
tel +353 (0)87 673 8386
email secretary@translatorsassocation.ie
website www.translatorsassociation.ie
Hon. Secretary Mary Phelan
Membership professional, associate, affiliate, institutional and student

Promotes translation in Ireland, the translation of Irish authors abroad and the practical training of translators, and promotes the interests of translators and interpreters. Maintains a detailed register of translators and interpreters. Founded 1986.

Irish Writers' Centre

19 Parnell Square, Dublin 1, Republic of Ireland
tel +353 (0)1 872 1302
email info@writerscentre.ie
website www.writerscentre.ie
Director Valerie Bistany

The national resource centre for Irish writers. It runs workshops, seminars and events related to the art of writing, hosts professional developments seminars for writers, provides space for writers, writing groups and other literary organisations. It also provides information to writers and the general public.

Irish Writers' Union/Comhar na Scríbhneoirí

Irish Writers' Centre, 19 Parnell Square, Dublin 1, Republic of Ireland
tel +353 (0)86 233 0084
email iwu@ireland-writers.com
website www.ireland-writers.com
Chairperson Sean Carabini, *Secretary* Kate Walsh

The Union aims to advance the cause of writing as a profession, to achieve better remuneration and more favourable conditions for writers and to provide a means for the expression of the collective opinion of writers on matters affecting their profession. Founded 1986.

The Johnson Society

Johnson Birthplace Museum, Breadmarket Street, Lichfield, Staffs. WS13 6LG
tel (01543) 264972
email info@thejohnsonsociety.org.uk
website www.johnsonnew.wordpress.com
General Secretary Ann Lakin

Aims to encourage the study of the life and works of Dr Samuel Johnson (1709–84); to preserve the memorials, associations, books, manuscripts and letters of Dr Johnson and his contemporaries; and to work with the local council in the preservation of his birthplace.

Johnson Society of London

Membership Secretary Christopher T.W. Ogden, 16 Laurier Road, London NW5 1SG
email memsec@johnsonsocietyoflondon.org
website www.johnsonsocietyoflondon.org
President Lord Harmsworth
Membership Single £25 p.a.; joint £30 p.a., student £20 p.a.

Aims to study the life and works of Dr Johnson (1709–84), and to perpetuate his memory in the city of his adoption. Founded 1928.

Journalists' Charity

Dickens House, 35 Wathen Road, Dorking, Surrey RH4 1JY
tel (01306) 887511
email enquiries@journalistscharity.org.uk
website www.journalistscharity.org.uk
Director David Ilott

For the relief of hardship amongst journalists, their widows and dependants. Financial assistance and retirement housing are provided.

The Sheila Kaye-Smith Society

Secretary Christine Hayward, 22 The Cloisters, St John's Road, St Leonards-on-Sea, East Sussex TN37 6JT
tel (01424) 422139
Membership £8 p.a. single; £12 joint

Aims to stimulate and widen interest in the work of the Sussex writer and novelist, Sheila Kaye-Smith (1887–1956). Produces a newsletter (three p.a.) now incorporating *The Gleam* and occasional papers; also organises talks and an annual walk. Founded 1987.

Keats-Shelley Memorial Association

Bedford House, 76A Bedford Street, Leamington Spa CV32 5DT
tel (01926) 427400
Chairman Hon. Mrs H. Cullen, *Hon. Secretary* David Leigh-Hunt
Membership £15 p.a. minimum

Owns and supports house in Rome where John Keats died, as a museum open to the public; celebrates the poets Keats (1795–1821), Shelley (1792–1822) and Leigh Hunt (1784–1859). Regular meetings; poetry competitions; annual *Review;* two literary awards; and progress reports. Founded 1903.

Kent and Sussex Poetry Society

Contact John Arnold, 39 Rockington Way, Crowborough, East Sussex TN6 2NJ
tel (01892) 662781
email kentandsussexpoetry@gmail.com
website www.kentandsussexpoetry.com
Secretary Mary Gurr, *President* Laurence Lerner, *Chairman* Clive Eastwood
Membership £15 p.a. full; £10 country members/concessions

Based in Tunbridge Wells, the Society was formed to create a greater interest in poetry. Well-known poets address the Society, a Folio of members' work is produced and a full programme of recitals, discussions, competitions (see page 547) and readings is provided. Founded 1946.

The Kipling Society

Hon. Secretary John Lambert, 31 Brookside, Billericay, Essex CM11 1DT
email john.lambert1@btinternet.com
website www.kipling.org.uk
Membership £24 p.a.; £12 under age 23

Aims to encourage discussion and study of the work and life of Rudyard Kipling (1865–1936), to assist in the study of his writings, to hold discussion meetings, to publish a quarterly journal and website, with a Readers' Guide to Kipling's work, and to maintain a Kipling Library in London.

The Charles Lamb Society

BM Elia, London WC1N 3XX
website www.charleslambsociety.com
Chairman Nicholas Powell, *Membership Secretary* Cecilia Powell
Membership Personal: £18/$35 p.a. (single), £24 (double); Corporate: £24/$48 p.a.

Publishes the academic journal *The Charles Lamb Bulletin* (twice a year). The Society's extensive library of books and MSS by and about Charles Lamb (1775–1834) is housed at the Guildhall Library, Aldermanbury, London EC2P 2EJ. Founded 1935.

The Lancashire Authors' Association

website www.lancashireauthorsassociation.co.uk
Membership Secretary Heather Thomas

For writers and lovers of Lancashire literature and history. Founded 1909.

The D.H. Lawrence Society

D.H. Lawrence Birthplace Museum, 8a Victoria Street, Eastwood, Nottingham NG16 3AW
tel (01773) 717353
email dhlawrencesociety@gmail.com
Membership £18 p.a. UK; £20 rest of world; £16 UK retired persons and students

Aims to bring together people interested in D.H. Lawrence (1885–1930), to encourage study of his work, and to provide information and guides for people visiting Eastwood. Founded 1974.

The T.E. Lawrence Society

PO Box 728, Oxford OX2 9ZJ
email telsocchair@gmail.com
website www.telsociety.org.uk
Membership £21 p.a. UK; £26 overseas (discounts available for membership benefits received via email)

Promotes the memory of T.E. Lawrence (1888–1935) and furthers education and knowledge by research into his life; publishes *Journal* (bi-annual) and *Newsletter* (quarterly). Founded 1985.

League of Canadian Poets

312–192 Spadina Avenue, Toronto, Ontario M5T 2C2, Canada
tel +1 416-504-1657
email joanna@poets.ca
website www.poets.ca
Executive Director Joanna Poblocka
Membership $185 p.a.

Aims to promote the interests of poets and to advance Canadian poetry in Canada and abroad. Administers three annual awards; runs National Poetry Month; publishes a newsletter and *Poetry Markets for Canadians, Who's Who in The League of Canadian Poets*, and *Poets in the Classroom* (teaching guide). Founded 1966.

Literature Wales

Literature Wales, 4th Floor, Cambrian Buildings, Mount Stuart Square, Cardiff CF10 5FL
tel 029-2047 2266
email post@literaturewales.org
North West Wales Office: Tŷ Newydd, Llanystumdwy, Cricieth, Gwynedd LL52 0LW

tel (01766) 522811
email tynewydd@literaturewales.org
website www.literaturewales.org
Chief Executive Lleucu Siencyn

The national company responsible for developing and promoting literature in Wales. Its activities include Wales Book of the Year, the National Poet of Wales, Writers on Tour funding scheme, Young People's Laureate for Wales, Bardd Plant Cymru, residential writing courses at Tŷ Newydd, funding and advice for writers, the Dinefwr Literature Festival, Young People's Writing Squads and an annual Literary Tourism events programme.

Literature Wales represents the interests of Welsh writers in all genres and languages, both inside Wales and internationally. It offers advice, support, bursaries, mentoring and opportunities to meet other writers. It works with the support of the Arts Council of Wales and the Welsh Government. It is one of the resident organisations of the Wales Millennium Centre, where it runs the Glyn Jones Centre.

Little Theatre Guild of Great Britain

Guild Secretary Caroline Chapman, Satley House, Satley, near Bishop Auckland, Co. Durham DL13 4HU
tel (01388) 730042
website www.littletheatreguild.org

Aims to promote closer cooperation amongst the little theatres constituting its membership; to act as a coordinating and representative body on behalf of the little theatres; to maintain and advance the highest standards in the art of theatre; and to assist in encouraging the establishment of other little theatres.

LLL Productions (Lewes Live Literature)

c/o Lewes Town Hall, High Street, Lewes, East Sussex BN7 2QS
tel (07972) 037612
email info@leweslivelit.co.uk
website www.leweslivelit.co.uk
Artistic Director Mark Hewitt
Takes place At any time – see website for dates

A live literature production company developing multimedia touring productions with writers. Occasional one-off events or festivals and an ongoing programme of workshops for writers.

Magazines Canada (Canadian Magazine Publishers Association)

425 Adelaide Street West, Suite 700, Toronto, Ontario M5V 3C1, Canada
tel +1 416-504-0274
email info@magazinescanada.ca
website www.magazinescanada.ca
Chief Executive Officer Mark Jamison

The national trade association representing Canadian-owned, Canadian-content consumer, cultural, speciality, professional and business media magazines.

The Marlowe Society

email frieda.barker@marlowe-society.org
website www.marlowe-society.org
Chairman George Metcalfe, *Membership Secretary* Frieda Barker
Membership £18 p.a.; £15 concessions; £30 joint (couple); £500 life.

Registered charity that aims to extend appreciation and widen recognition of Christopher Marlowe (1564–93) as the foremost poet and dramatist preceding Shakespeare, whose development he influenced. Holds meetings and cultural visits, and issues a bi-annual magazine and an occasional research journal. Founded 1955.

The John Masefield Society

Chairman Bob Vaughan, 40 Mill Way, Bushey, Herts WD23 2AG
tel (01923) 246047
email robert.vaughan110@gmail.com
website www.ies.ac.uk/cmps/projects/masefield/society/jmsws.htm
Membership £5 p.a.; £10 overseas; £8 family/institution

Aims to stimulate interest in, and public awareness and enjoyment of, the life and works of the poet John Masefield (1878–1967). Holds an annual lecture and other, less formal, readings and gatherings; publishes an annual journal and frequent newsletters. Founded 1992.

Master Photographers Association

Jubilee House, 1 Chancery Lane, Darlington, Co. Durham DL1 5QP
tel (01325) 356555
email membership@thempa.com
website www.masterphotographersassociation.co.uk
Ceo Colin Buck
Membership £165 p.a.

Exists to promote and protect professional photographers. Members qualify for awards of Licentiate, Associate and Fellowship.

The Media Society

website www.themediasociety.com
President Geraldine Sharpe-Newton
Membership £35 p.a.

Exists to promote and encourage collective and independent research into the standards, performance, organisation and economics of the media and hold regular discussions, debates, etc on subjects of topical or special interest and concern to print and broadcast journalists and others working in or with the media. Founded 1973.

Mediawatch-UK

(formerly National Viewers' and Listeners' Association)
Director Vivienne Pattison, 3 Willow House, Kennington Road, Ashford, Kent TN24 0NR

tel (01233) 633936
email info@mediawatchuk.org
website www.mediawatchuk.org
website mediawatch-UK.blogspot.com
Membership £15 p.a.

Aims to encourage viewers and listeners to react effectively to programme content; to initiate and stimulate public discussion and parliamentary debate concerning the effects of broadcasting, and other mass media, on the individual, the family and society; to secure effective legislation to control obscenity and pornography in the media. Founded 1965.

William Morris Society

Kelmscott House, 26 Upper Mall, London W6 9TA
tel 020-8741 3735
email info@williammorrissociety.org.uk
website www.williammorrissociety.org.uk
Secretary Penny Lyndon

Aims to spread knowledge of the life, work and ideas of William Morris (1834–96); publishes newsletter (quarterly) and journal (two p.a.). Library and collections open to the public Thurs and Sat, 2–5pm. Founded 1955.

Music Publishers Association Ltd

6th Floor, 2 Pancras Square, London N1C 4AG
tel 020-3741 3800
email info@mpaonline.org.uk
website www.mpaonline.org.uk
Membership Details available on request

Trade organisation representing over 270 UK music publisher members: promotes and safeguards its members' interests in copyright, trade and related matters. Sub-committees and groups deal with particular interests. Founded 1881.

The Mythopoeic Society

Corresponding Secretary Edith Crowe,
The Mythopoeic Society, PO Box 6707, Altadena, CA 91003-6707, USA
email correspondence@mythsoc.org
website www.mythsoc.org
Membership with electronic *Mythprint* $12 p.a. (USA)

A non-profit international literary and educational organisation for the study, discussion and enjoyment of fantastic and mythic literature, especially the works of Tolkien, C.S. Lewis and Charles Williams. The word 'mythopoeic' (myth-oh-PAY-ik or myth-oh-PEE-ic), meaning 'mythmaking' or 'productive of myth', aptly describes much of the fictional work of the 3 authors who were also prominent members of an informal Oxford literary circle (1930s–1950s) known as the Inklings. Membership is open to all scholars, writers and readers of these literatures. The Society sponsors 3 periodicals: *Mythprint* (a bulletin of book reviews, articles and events), *Mythlore* (scholarly articles on mythic and fantastic literature), and *Mythic Circle* (a literary annual of original poetry and short stories). Each summer the Society holds an annual conference. Founded 1967.

National Acrylic Painters' Association (NAPA)

website www.napauk.org

Promotes interest in, and encourages excellence and innovation in, the work of painters in acrylic. Holds an annual exhibition and regional shows: awards are made. Worldwide membership. Publishes a newsletter known as the *International NAPA Newspages*. Founded 1985; American Division established 1995, now known as International Society of Acrylic Painters (ISAP).

National Association of Press Agencies (NAPA)

Suite 308, Queens Dock Business Centre, 67–83 Norfolk Street, Liverpool L1 0BG
tel 0870 240 0311
email enquiries@napa.org.uk
website www.napa.org.uk
Chairman Jon Harris
Membership £250 p.a.

A network of independent, established and experienced press agencies serving newspapers, magazines, TV and radio networks. Founded 1983.

National Association of Writers' Groups (NAWG)

email chris.huck@ymail.com
website www.nawg.co.uk
Secretary Chris Huck
Membership £40 p.a. per group; £20 Associates (individuals)

Aims 'to advance the education of the general public throughout the UK, including the Channel Islands, by promoting the study and art of writing in all its aspects'. Publishes *LNK*, a bi-monthly magazine. Festival of Writing held annually in August/September. New members always welcome. Founded 1995.

National Campaign for the Arts (NCA)

17 Tavistock Street, London WC2E 7PA
tel 020-7240 4698
email nca@artscampaign.org.uk
website www.artscampaign.org.uk
NCA Team Simon Trevithick, Maddy Radcliff

The UK's only independent lobbying organisation representing all the arts. It provides a voice for the arts world in all its diversity and seeks to safeguard, promote and develop the arts and win public and political recognition for their importance as a key element in our national culture. The NCA is a membership organisation.

National Council for the Training of Journalists (NCTJ)

The New Granary, Station Road, Newport, Essex CB11 3PL

tel (01799) 544014
email info@nctj.com
website www.nctj.com

A registered charity which aims to advance the education and training of trainee journalists, including press photographers. Full-time courses run at 40 colleges/universities in the UK. Distance learning programmes and short courses are also available.

National Literacy Trust

68 South Lambeth Road, London SW8 1RL
tel 020-7587 1842
email contact@literacytrust.org.uk
website www.literacytrust.org.uk

An independent charity that aims to help change lives through literacy. It campaigns to improve public understanding of the importance of literacy, as well as delivering projects and working in partnership to reach those most in need of support.

National Society for Education in Art and Design

3 Mason's Wharf, Potley Lane, Corsham, Wilts. SN13 9FY
tel (01225) 810134
email info@nsead.org
website www.nsead.org
General Secretary Lesley Butterworth, *Assistant General Secretary* Sophie Leach

The leading national authority concerned with art, craft and design across all phases of education in the UK. Offers the benefits of membership of a professional association, a learned society and a trade union. Has representatives on national and regional committees concerned with art and design education. Publishes *International Journal of Art and Design Education* online (three p.a.; Wiley Blackwell) and *AD* magazine for teachers. Founded 1888.

National Society of Painters, Sculptors and Printmakers

Hon. Treasurer Colin Michael, 161 Village Way, Beckenham, Kent BR3 3NL
tel 020-8663 3392
email colinmichael@btconnect.com
email sophiefuller@btconnect.com
website www.nationalsociety.org/
Membership Associate £60; full £120

Formed to communicate innovative painting, sculpture and printmaking with a wide audience. Newsletter (four p.a.) for members. An annual exhibition at the Menier Gallery, Southwark Street, London SE1. Founded 1931.

National Union of Journalists

Headland House, 308–312 Gray's Inn Road, London WC1X 8DP
tel 020-7278 7916
email info@nuj.org.uk
website www.nuj.org.uk

Trade union for journalists and photographers, including freelancers, with 38,000 members and 136 branches in the UK, Republic of Ireland, Paris, Brussels and the Netherlands. It covers the newspaper press, news agencies, magazines, broadcasting, periodical and book publishing, public relations departments and consultancies, information services and new media. The NUJ mediates disputes, provides training and general and legal advice. Official publications: *The Journalist* (bi-monthly), the online *Freelance Directory* and *Freelance Fees Guide*, *The NUJ Code of Conduct* and policy pamphlets.

NCTJ – see National Council for the Training of Journalists (NCTJ)

The Edith Nesbit Society

21 Churchfields, West Malling, Kent ME19 6RJ
email edithnesbit@googlemail.com
website www.edithnesbit.co.uk
Membership £8 p.a. (single); £10 p.a. (joint); £15 (organisations/overseas)

Aims to promote an interest in the life and works of Edith Nesbit (1858–1924) by means of talks, a regular newsletter and other publications, and visits to relevant places. Founded 1996.

New English Art Club

website www.newenglishartclub.co.uk
President Richard Pikesley, *Membership Secretary* Louise Balaam

The New English represents the very best of contemporary British figurative painting. Members of the public can send in work to the Annual Open Exhibition at The Mall Galleries, The Mall, London SW1, open to all working in painting, drawing, pastels and prints.

New Writers UK

PO Box 9310, Nottingham NG5 0DZ
tel 07969 516158
email julie@newwritersuk.co.uk
website www.newwritersuk.co.uk
Founder & President Julie Malone, *Membership Secretary* Rachel Littlewood
Membership £30 p.a. (includes group PLI of up to £5m)

New Writers UK supports and advises independently published authors and those who do not have financial backing or marketing to promote their books. This is an organisation of authors working on a voluntary basis to assist other authors and encourage imaginative literacy in young people and adults. New members welcome. NWUK holds a number of events throughout the year, produces an online quarterly newsletter and has links with

Facebook, Twitter and LinkedIn. NWUK has an associate membership of copy editors, proofreaders, graphic designers, reviewers and illustrators. Established 2006.

New Writing North

PO Box 1277, Newcastle upon Tyne NE99 5BP
email office@newwritingnorth.com
website www.newwritingnorth.com

The literature development agency for the North of England. Specialises in developing writers and acts as a broker between writers, producers, publishers and broadcasters. Flagship projects include Northern Writers' Awards, Gordon Burn Prize and Durham Book Festival.

New Writing South

9 Jew Street, Brighton, East Sussex BN1 1UT
tel (01273) 735353
email admin@newwritingsouth.com
website www.newwritingsouth.com
Director Chris Taylor
Membership £45 p.a. (concessions available from £20 p.a.)

New Writing South supports and encourages writers at all stages of their careers and new writing in all its forms. Activities include script-reading service, workshops, mentoring, masterclasses and events. Membership benefits comprise booking discounts, fortnightly e-news and networking opportunities.

The Creative Learning Team works in schools, places of work and throughout the community to inspire imagination, encourage creative thinking and get young people and adults writing. New Writing South is open to all creative writers in south east England.

New Zealand Association of Literary Agents

PO Box 46-031, Park Avenue, Lower Hutt 5044, New Zealand
email tfs@elseware.co.nz
website www.elseware.co.nz

Set up to establish standards and guidelines for literary agents operating in New Zealand. All members subscribe to a code of ethics which includes working on commission and not charging upfront fees for promotion or manuscript reading.

New Zealand Writers Guild

PO Box 47 886, Ponsonby, Auckland 1144, New Zealand
tel +64 (0)9 360 1408
email info@nzwg.org.nz
website www.nzwritersguild.org.nz

Aims to represent the interests of New Zealand writers (TV, film, radio and theatre); to establish and improve minimum conditions of work and rates of compensation for writers; to provide professional services for members. Founded 1975.

News Media Association

292 Vauxhall Bridge Road, London SW1V 1AE
tel 020-7963 7480
email nma@newsmediauk.org
website www.newsmediauk.org

Serves and promotes the shared interests of national, regional and local news media publishers in the UK by working across a broad range of issues which affect the industry.

Outdoor Writers and Photographers Guild

1 Consul Street, Manchester M22 4WN
tel 0161-270 3126
email secretary@owpg.org.uk
website www.owpg.org.uk
Membership £80 p.a.

Association of the leading practitioners in outdoor media; represents members' interests to representative bodies in the outdoor industry; circulates members with news of media opportunities; provides a forum for members to meet colleagues and others in the outdoor industry.

Presents annual literary and photographic awards. Members include writers, journalists, broadcasters, illustrators, photographers, editors and publishers. Founded 1980.

Wilfred Owen Association

29 Arthur Road, London SW19 7DN
website www.wilfredowen.org.uk
Membership £10 p.a. individual; £15 p.a. couple; £8 concessions; £13 couple concession; £15 overseas; £20 overseas couple. Special rates for joint membership of The Wilfred Owen Association and the Siegfried Sassoon Fellowship

Aims to commemorate the life and work of Wilfred Owen (1893–1918), and to encourage and enhance appreciation of his work through visits, public events and a bi-annual journal. Founded 1989.

Oxford Bibliographical Society

Bodleian Library, Broad Street, Oxford OX1 3BG
email membership@oxbibsoc.org.uk
website www.oxbibsoc.org.uk
Membership £20 p.a.

Exists to encourage bibliographical research. Founded 1922.

Pact (Producers' Alliance for Cinema and Television)

3rd Floor, Fitzrovia House,
153–157 Cleveland Street, London W1T 6QW
tel 020-7380 8230
email info@pact.co.uk
website www.pact.co.uk
Chief Executive John McVay

The UK trade association that represents and promotes the commercial interests of independent feature film, television, animation and interactive media companies. Headquartered in London, it has regional representation throughout the UK, in order to support its members. An effective lobbying organisation, it has regular and constructive dialogues with government, regulators, public agencies and opinion formers on all issues affecting its members, and contributes to key public policy debates on the media industry, both in the UK and in Europe. It negotiates terms of trade with all public service broadcasters in the UK and supports members in their business dealings with cable and satellite channels. It also lobbies for a properly structured and funded UK film industry and maintains close contact with other relevant film organisations and government departments.

The Pastel Society

tel (01304) 619921
email cherylculver@btinternet.com
email info@mallgalleries.com
website www.thepastelsociety.org.uk
President Cheryl Culver, *Membership Secretary* Brian Plummer

Pastel and drawings in all dry media. Annual Exhibition open to all artists working in dry media held at the Mall Galleries, The Mall, London SW1. Members elected from approved candidates' list. Founded 1898.

PEN International

Brownlow House, 50–51 High Holborn, London WC1V 6ER
tel 020-7405 0338
email info@pen-international.org.uk
website www.pen-international.org.uk
International President John Ralston Saul, *International Secretary* Hori Takeaki
Membership Apply to Centres

A world association of writers. PEN was founded by C.A. Dawson Scott under the presidency of John Galsworthy, to promote friendship and understanding between writers and to defend freedom of expression within and between all nations. The initials PEN stand for Poets, Playwrights, Editors, Essayists, Novelists – but membership is open to all writers of standing (including translators), whether men or women, without distinction of creed or race, who subscribe to these fundamental principles. PEN takes no part in state or party politics.

Membership of any one Centre implies membership of all Centres; at present 145 autonomous Centres exist throughout the world. Associate membership is available for writers not yet eligible for full membership and for persons connected with literature. Founded 1921.

English PEN Centre

email enquiries@englishpen.org
website www.englishpen.org

Scottish PEN Centre

email info@scottishpen.org
website www.scottishpen.org

Irish PEN Centre

email info@irishpen.com.com
website www.irishpen.com

The Personal Managers' Association Ltd

30 Bristol Gardens, Brighton, BN2 5JR
tel 0845 602 7191
email info@thepma.com
website www.thepma.com

Membership organisation for agents representing talent in film, television and theatre.

The Picture Research Association

tel 07825 788343
email chair@picture-research.org.uk
website www.picture-research.org.uk

Founded in 1977, the PRA is a professional organisation of picture researchers and picture editors specifically involved in the research, management and supply of visual material to the media industry. Its aims are:

• To promote the recognition of picture research, management, editing, picture buying and supplying as a profession requiring particular skills and knowledge.
• To bring together all those involved in the picture profession and provide a forum for information exchange and interaction.
• To encourage publishers, TV and video production organisations, internet companies, and any other users of images to use the PRA freelance register and engage a member of PRA to obtain them, thus ensuring that professional standards and copyright clearances are adhered to and maintained.
• To advise those specifically wishing to embark on a profession in the research and supply of pictures for all types of visual media information, providing guidelines and standards in so doing.

Registered members are listed on the website and can be located through the Find Researchers page, along with lots of useful information about the picture industry.

Player–Playwrights

Secretary Peter Thompson, 9 Hillfield Park, Muswell Hill, London N10 3QT
email publicity@playerplaywrights.co.uk
website www.playerplaywrights.co.uk
Membership £12 in first year and £8 thereafter (plus £2.50 per attendance)

Meets on Monday evenings upstairs in the North London Tavern, 375 Kilburn High Road, London NW6 7QB. The society reads, performs and discusses plays and scripts submitted by members, with a view to assisting the writers in improving and marketing their work. Newcomers and new acting members are always welcome. Founded 1948.

The Poetry Book Society – see page 331

The Poetry Society – see page 331

The Beatrix Potter Society

c/o The Lodge, Salisbury Avenue, Harpenden, Herts. AL5 2PS
tel (01582) 769755
email beatrixpottersociety@tiscali.co.uk
website www.beatrixpottersociety.org.uk
Membership £25 p.a. UK (£31 overseas); £30/£36 commercial/institutional

Promotes the study and appreciation of the life and works of Beatrix Potter (1866–1943) as author, artist, diarist, farmer and conservationist. Regular lecture meetings, conferences and events in the UK and USA. Quarterly newsletter. Small publishing programme. Founded 1980.

The Powys Society

Hon. Secretary Chris Thomas, Flat D, 87 Ledbury Road, London W11 2AG
tel 020-7243 0168
email chris.d.thomas@hotmail.co.uk
website www.powys-society.org
Membership £22 p.a. UK (£26 overseas)

Aims to promote the greater public recognition and enjoyment of the writings, thought and contribution to the arts of the Powys family, particularly John Cowper (1872–1963), Theodore (1875–1953) and Llewelyn (1884–1939) Powys, and the many other family members and their close friends. Publishes an annual scholarly journal (*The Powys Journal*) and three newsletters per year as well as books by and about the Powys family, and holds an annual weekend conference in August, as well as organising other activities throughout the year. Founded 1967.

The J.B. Priestley Society

Membership Secretary Tony Reavill, Eldwick Crag Farm, High Eldwick, Bingley, W. Yorkshire BD16 3BB
email reavill@globalnet.co.uk
website www.jbpriestleysociety.com
General Secretary Rod Slater, *Information Officer* Michael Nelson (m.nelson928@btinternet.com)
Membership £15 p.a. single, £20 family, £10 concessions

Aims to widen the knowledge, understanding and appreciation of the published works of J.B. Priestley (1894–1984) and to promote the study of his life and career. Holds lectures and discussions and shows films. Publishes a newsletter and journal. Organises walks to areas with Priestley connections, Annual Priestley Night and other social events. Founded 1997.

Printmakers Council

Ground Floor Unit, 23 Blue Anchor Lane, London SE16 3UL
tel 07531 883250
email printpmc@googlemail.com
website www.printmakerscouncil.com
Chairman Margaret Ashman
Membership £70 p.a.; £30 students

Artist-led group which aims to promote the use of both traditional and innovative printmaking techniques by:

- holding exhibitions of prints;
- providing information on prints and printmaking to both its membership and the public;
- encouraging cooperation and exchanges between members, other associations and interested individuals. Founded 1965.

Private Libraries Association

Hon. Secretary Jim Maslen, 29 Eden Drive, Hull HU8 8JQ
email maslen@maslen.karoo.co.uk
website www.plabooks.org
President Giles Mandelbrote, *Hon. Journal Editors* David Chambers, David Butcher, James Freemantle
Membership £30 p.a.

International society of book collectors and lovers of books. Publications include *The Private Library* (quarterly), annual *Private Press Books*, and other books on book collecting. Founded 1956.

Professional Cartoonists' Organisation

Secretary Huw Aaron, 57 Bishops Road, Whitchurch, Cardiff CF14 1LW
email info@procartoonists.org
website www.procartoonists.org
Membership £80 p.a.

An organisation dedicated to the promotion of UK cartoon art in new media and old. Cartoons provide much-needed humour and satire to society and are a universally appreciated, effective method of communication for business. The organisation showcases UK cartoonists via its magazine, *Foghorn*, cartoon news blog (*Bloghorn*), and public events such as the annual Big Draw and cartoon festivals. Established 2006.

Professional Publishers Association

35–38 New Bridge Street, London EC4V 6BW
tel 020-7404 4166
email info1@ppa.co.uk
website www.ppa.co.uk
Chief Executive Barry McIlheney

Represents around 220 companies, ranging from consumer magazine publishers to business-to-business data and information providers, customer magazine publishers and smaller independent companies.

PRS for Music

Copyright House, 29–33 Berners Street,
London W1T 3AB
tel 020-7580 5544
website www.prsformusic.co.uk

PRS for music represents the rights of over 100,000 members in the UK. It licenses organisations to play, perform or make available copyright music on behalf of members and those of overseas societies, distributing royalties fairly and efficiently. Promotes and protects the value of copyright.

The Publishers Association

29B Montague Street, London WC1B 5BW
tel 020-7691 9191
email mail@publishers.org.uk
website www.publishers.org.uk
Ceo Richard Mollet, *President* Dominic Knight, *Director of Publisher Relations* Emma House, *Operations Director* Mark Wharton, *Director of Policy and Communications* Susie Winter

The leading representative voice for books, journal, audio and electronic publishers in the UK. The Association has over 100 members and its role is to support publishers in their political, media and industry stakeholder communications. Founded 1896.

Publishers Association of New Zealand (PANZ)

B3, 72 Apollo Drive, Rosedale, Auckland 0632, New Zealand
tel +64 (0)9 280 3212
email anne@publishers.org.nz
website www.publishers.org.nz
Association Director Anne de Lautour

PANZ represents book, educational and digital publishers in New Zealand. Members include both the largest international publishers and companies in the independent publishing community.

Publishers' Association of South Africa (PASA)

House Vincent, Wynberg Mews, 1st Floor, Unit 104, Brodie Road, Wynberg, South Africa
tel +27 (0)21 762 9083
email pasa@publishsa.co.za
website www.publishsa.co.za

PASA is the largest publishing industry body in South Africa and is committed to creativity, literacy, the free flow of ideas and encouraging a culture of reading. It aims to promote and protect the rights and responsibilities of the publishing sector in South Africa.

Publishers Licensing Society Ltd (PLS)

55–56 Russell Square, London WC1B 4HP
tel 020-7079 5930
email pls@pls.org.uk
website www.pls.org.uk
Chairman Mark Bide, *Chief Executive* Sarah Faulder

PLS serves the UK publishing industry by working to protect publishers' rights, and leads on industry-wide initiatives involving rights management and collective licensing. It is a not-for-profit organisation and has mandates from over 2,700 publishers. PLS is dedicated to protecting and strengthening the copyright framework by motivating good practice in rights management. One of the most important ways it does this is by facilitating licence solutions that protect rights and provide revenue for publishers through collective licensing. PLS strives to ensure a high level of service that works on behalf of publishers and readers to uphold copyright legislation. Founded 1981.

Publishers Publicity Circle

email publisherspublicitycircle@gmail.com
Secretary/Treasurer Ruth Warburton

Enables all book publicists to meet and share information regularly. Monthly meetings provide a forum for press journalists, TV and radio researchers and producers to meet publicists collectively. Awards are presented for the best PR campaigns. Monthly newsletter includes recruitment advertising. Founded 1955.

Publishing Ireland – Foilsiú Éireann

25 Denzille Lane Dublin 2, Republic of Ireland
tel +353 (0)1 6394868
email info@publishingireland.com
website www.publishingireland.com
President Michael McLoughlin

Publishing Scotland

(formerly Scottish Publishers Association)
Scott House, 10 South St Andrew Street,
Edinburgh EH2 2AZ
tel 0131 228 6866
email enquiries@publishingscotland.org
website www.publishingscotland.org
Chief Executive Marion Sinclair

A network for trade, training and development in the Scottish publishing industry.

Founded 1973.

ReadWell

26 Nailsworth Mills, Avening Road, Nailsworth, Glos. GL6 0BS
tel 0870 240 1124
email reading@readathon.org
website www.readwell.org.uk

In consultation with hospital and education staff in several children's hospitals, ReadWell was established in 2010 to help children in hospital through the therapeutic powers of reading. ReadWell brings books and storytellers to hospitalised children to help take their minds off their situation, ease their worries and entertain them. Carefully-chosen books are also available to help ensure that children don't suffer educationally by falling behind at school. ReadWell currently provides services to children's hospitals in Bristol, Birmingham and Oxford, with ambitions to expand the service across all UK children's hospitals and children's wards over the coming months and years.

The Romantic Novelists' Association

Chairman Eileen Ramsay, *Hon. Secretary* Julie Vince
email rnahonsec@romanticnovelistsassociation.org
website www.romanticnovelistsassociation.org

Aims to promote romantic fiction and encourage good writing within the genre. Represents more than 700 writers, agents, editors and other publishing professionals. See also page 555.

Royal Academy of Arts

Burlington House, Piccadilly, London W1J 0BD
tel 020-7300 8000
website www.royalacademy.org.uk
President Christopher Le Brun, *Keeper* Eileen Cooper

Royal Academicians are elected from the most distinguished artists in the UK. Holds major loan exhibitions throughout the year including the Annual Summer Exhibition (June–Aug). Also runs Royal Academy Schools for 60 postgraduate students in painting and sculpture.

Royal Birmingham Society of Artists

RBSA Gallery, 4 Brook Street, St Paul's, Birmingham B3 1SA
tel 0121 236 4353
email rbsagallery@rbsa.org.uk
website www.rbsa.org.uk
Membership Friends £34 p.a.

The Royal Birmingham Society of Artists (RBSA) is an artist-led charity, which supports artists and promotes engagement with the visual arts through a range of exhibitions, workshops and events. The Society is one of the oldest in the UK. It owns and runs its own exhibition venue, the RBSA Gallery, which is located near Birmingham's historic Jewellery Quarter and the city centre. The RBSA Gallery has a changing programme of exhibitions across its two upper floors, ground floor solo show spaces, and ground floor Craft Gallery. The programme includes various yearly, two-yearly and three-yearly open exhibitions, providing opportunities for all artists working in all media. The Gallery is open seven days a week and admission is free. See website for opening times.

Royal Institute of Oil Painters

17 Carlton House Terrace, London SW1Y 5BD
tel 020-7930 6844
email enquiries@theroi.org.uk
website www.theroi.org.uk
President Ian Cryer

Promotes and encourages the art of painting in oils. Open Annual Exhibition at the Mall Galleries, The Mall, London SW1.

Royal Institute of Painters in Water Colours

17 Carlton House Terrace, London SW1Y 5BD
tel 020-7930 6844
email info@riwatercolours.org
website www.riwatercolours.org
President Ronald Maddox
Membership Elected from approved candidates' list

Promotes the appreciation of watercolour painting in its traditional and contemporary forms, primarily by means of an annual exhibition at the Mall Galleries, The Mall, London SW1 of members' and non-members' work and also by members' exhibitions at selected venues in Britain and abroad. Founded 1831.

The Royal Literary Fund

3 Johnson's Court, off Fleet Street, London EC4A 3EA
tel 020-7353 7159
email eileen.gunn@rlf.org.uk
website www.rlf.org.uk
President Sir Ronald Harwood CBE, *Chief Executive* Eileen Gunn

The RLF is a benevolent fund for writers in financial difficulties. It does not offer grants to writers who can earn their living in other ways, nor does it provide financial support for writing projects, but it helps authors who have fallen on hard times due to personal or professional setbacks. Applicants must have published several works of approved literary merit. Applicants are requested to send copies of their books with their completed application forms. Founded 1790.

The Royal Musical Association

Executive Officer Dr Jeffrey Dean, 4 Chandos Road, Chorlton-cum-Hardy, Manchester M21 0ST
tel 0161 861 7542
email exec@rma.ac.uk
website www.rma.ac.uk
President Prof. Mark Everist, *Treasurer* Valerie James
Membership See website for details

Promotes the investigation and discussion of subjects connected with the art and science of music. Founded 1874.

The Royal Photographic Society

Fenton House, 122 Wells Road, Bath BA2 3AH
tel (01225) 325733
email reception@rps.org
website www.rps.org
Membership UK £111; overseas £99; discounts for over 65s, under 25s, students, the disabled

The Society aims to promote photography in all its forms and to support and encourage individuals to develop their skills, which it does through exhibitions, workshops and a distinctions and qualifications programme. The Society has 14 specialist interest groups. It also acts as an advocate for photography and photographers. Membership is open to anyone with an interest in photography. Founded 1853.

The Royal Scottish Academy of Art and Architecture

The Mound, Edinburgh EH2 2EL
tel 0131 225 6671
email info@royalscottishacademy.org
website www.royalscottishacademy.org
Director Colin R. Greenslade

Led by eminent artists and architects, the Royal Scottish Academy (RSA) is an independent voice for cultural advocacy and one of the largest supporters of artists in Scotland. The Academy administers a number of scholarships, awards and residencies and has an historic collection of Scottish artworks and an archive, recognised by the Scottish Government as being of national significance. The Academy cherishes its independence from local or national government funding, relying instead on bequests, legacies, sponsorship and earned income. This allows the RSA the autonomy to develop and present a wide range of initiatives without restriction. For information on open submission exhibitions, artist scholarships and residencies, or to discuss making a bequest to the Academy, contact the RSA office or visit the website. Founded 1826.

The Royal Society

6–9 Carlton House Terrace, London SW1Y 5AG
tel 020-7451 2500
email library@royalsociety.org
website royalsociety.org
President Sir Paul Nurse KT, PRS, *Treasurer* Prof. Anthony Cheetham FRS, *Biological Secretary* Sir John Skehel FRS, *Physical Secretary* Prof. Alex Halliday FRS, *Foreign Secretary* Sir Martyn Poliakoff FRS, *Executive Director* Dr Julie Maxton

The Royal Society for Asian Affairs

25 Eccleston Place, London SW1W 9NF
tel 020-7235 5122
email info@rsaa.org.uk
website www.rsaa.org.uk
President Lord Davies of Abersoch CBE, *Chairman of Council* Sir David John KCMG, *Secretary* Alan R.J. Attryde
Membership £75 single; £100 joint (UK and Overseas); younger members 18–30 £20; benefactor life members £1,500; corporate members £500

For the study of all Asia present and recent past; fortnightly lectures, etc; library. Publishes *Asian Affairs* (three p.a.), free to members. Founded 1901.

Royal Society for the Encouragement of Arts, Manufactures and Commerce (RSA)

8 John Adam Street, London WC2N 6EZ
tel 020-7930 5115
email general@rsa.org.uk
website www.thersa.org

Works to remove the barriers to social progress, driving ideas, innovation and social change through an ambitious programme of projects, events and lectures. Supported by over 27,000 Fellows, an international network of influencers and innovators from every field and background across the UK and overseas. Welcomes women and men of any nationality and background who will support the organisation's aims. Its activities are detailed in the *RSA Journal*. Founded 1754.

Royal Society of British Artists

17 Carlton House Terrace, London SW1Y 5BD
tel 020-7930 6844
email info@mallgalleries.com
website www.mallgalleries.org.uk
President James Horton

Incorporated by Royal Charter for the purpose of encouraging the study and practice of the arts of painting, sculpture and architectural design. Annual Open Exhibition at the Mall Galleries, The Mall, London SW1, open to artists working in any two- or three-dimensional medium.

Royal Society of Literature

Somerset House, Strand, London WC2R 1LA
tel 020-7845 4678
email info@rsliterature.org
website www.rsliterature.org
Membership £50 p.a.

For the promotion of literature and encouragement of writers by way of lectures, discussions, readings, and by publications. Administers the V.S. Pritchett Memorial Prize, the Royal Society of Literature Ondaatje Prize, and the Royal Society of Literature/ Jerwood Awards. Founded 1820.

Royal Society of Marine Artists

17 Carlton House Terrace, London SW1Y 5BD
tel 020-7930 6844
email info@rsma-web.co.uk
website www.rsma-web.co.uk
President Elizabeth Smith

The aim of the society is to promote and encourage the highest standards of marine art and welcomes submissions for their Annual Open Exhibition at The Mall Galleries in London, which is usually held in October (more information at www.mallgalleries.org.uk). Membership is achieved by a consistent record of success in having work selected and hung at this event and ultimately by election by the membership.

The Royal Society of Miniature Painters, Sculptors and Gravers

email info@royal-miniature-society.org.uk
website www.royal-miniature-society.org.uk

President Rosalind Peirson PRMS, CFA (OXON), PPHS, MAA, MSAF, *Executive Secretary* Claire Hucker
Membership By selection and standard of work over a period of years (ARMS associate, RMS full member)

Annual Open Exhibition in October at the Mall Galleries, The Mall, London SW1. Hand in October; schedules available from the website. Applications and enquiries to the Executive Secretary. Founded 1895.

Royal Society of Painter-Printmakers

Bankside Gallery, 48 Hopton Street, London SE1 9JH
tel 020-7928 7521
email info@banksidegallery.com
website www.banksidegallery.com
website www.re-printmakers.com
President Mychael Barratt PRE HON RWS
Membership Open to British and overseas artists. An election of Associates is held annually; for details check the website. New members are elected by the Council of the Society based on the quality of their work alone, in a tradition reaching back over one hundred years. Friends membership is open to all those interested in artists' original printmaking

Holds three members' exhibitions per year. Founded 1880.

Royal Society of Portrait Painters

17 Carlton House Terrace, London SW1Y 5BD
tel 020-7930 6844
email enquiries@therp.co.uk
website www.therp.co.uk
website www.mallgalleries.org.uk
President Robin Lee Hall

Annual Exhibition at the Mall Galleries, The Mall, London SW1, of members' work and that of selected non-members. Five high-profile artists' awards are made: the Seven Investment Conversations Prize (£15,000), the Ondaatje Prize for Portraiture (£10,000), the De Laszlo Prize (£3,000), the Prince of Wales's Award for Portrait Drawing (£2,000), the Changing Faces Prize (£2,000). Also commissions consultancy service throughout the year. Founded 1891.

Royal Television Society

7th Floor, 3 Dorset Rise, London EC4Y 8EN
tel 020-7822-2810
email info@rts.org.uk
website www.rts.org.uk

The leading forum for discussion and debate on all aspects of the TV community. In a fast-changing sector, it reflects the full range of perspectives and views. Holds awards, conferences, seminars, lectures and workshops. Founded 1927.

Royal Watercolour Society

Bankside Gallery, 48 Hopton Street, London SE1 9JH
tel 020-7928 7521
email info@banksidegallery.com
website www.royalwatercoloursociety.co.uk
President Thomas Plunkett PRWS, Hon RE
Membership Open to British and overseas artists; election of Associates held annually. Friends membership is open to all those interested in watercolour painting

Arranges lectures and courses on watercolour paintings; holds an annual open exhibition in February. Exhibitions in the spring and autumn. Founded 1804.

Royal West of England Academy

Queens Road, Clifton, Bristol BS8 1PX
tel 0117 973 5129
email info@rwa.org.uk
website www.rwa.org.uk
Director Alison Bevan, *President* Janette Kerr

An art academy/gallery/museum and drawing school whose objectives are to advance the education of the public in the fine arts and in particular to promote the appreciation and practice of the fine arts and to encourage and develop talent in the fine arts. Founded 1844.

The Ruskin Society

email secretary@theruskinsociety.com
website www.theruskinsociety.com
Membership £10 p.a.

Aims to encourage a wider understanding of John Ruskin (1819–1900) and his contemporaries. Organises lectures and events which seek to explain to the public the nature of Ruskin's theories and to place these in a modern context. Affiliated to the Ruskin Foundation. Founded 1997.

SAA (Society for All Artists)

PO Box 50, Newark, Notts. NG23 5GY
tel 0800 980 1123
email info@saa.co.uk
website www.saa.co.uk
Membership from £29.50 p.a.

Aims to encourage and inspire all artists. Members range from complete beginners to professionals. SAA is the largest art society with over 46,000 members, and welcomes new members. Membership includes paintings insurance for exhibitions and third party public liability, exclusive discounts and offers on art materials from the society's *Home Shop* catalogue and the inspirational *Paint* magazine (bi-monthly). Founded 1992.

The Malcolm Saville Society

5 Churchfield, Harpenden, Herts. AL5 1LJ
email mystery@witchend.com
website www.witchend.com
Membership £15 p.a. (£17.50 Europe; £21 elsewhere)

Aims to remember and promote interest in the work of Malcolm Saville (1901–82), children's author.

Regular social activities, library, contact directory and magazine (four p.a.). Founded 1994.

The Dorothy L. Sayers Society

Gimsons, Kings Chase, Witham, Essex CM8 1AX
tel (01376) 515626
email info@sayers.org.uk
website www.sayers.org.uk
Chair Seona Ford, *Secretaries* Lenelle Davis, Jasmine Simeone
Membership £18 p.a. UK and worldwide for electronic version of Bulletin. Paper version (mailed): £20 UK, £23 Europe, £26 rest of world; under 25 rates available

Aims to promote and encourage the study of the works of Dorothy L. Sayers (1893–1957); to collect archive materials and reminiscences about her and make them available to students and biographers; to hold an annual conference and other meetings; to publish *Proceedings*, pamphlets and a bi-monthly Bulletin; to make grants and awards. Founded 1976.

Scattered Authors' Society

email membership@scatteredauthors.org
website www.scatteredauthors.org

Aims to provide a forum for informal discussion, contact and support for professional writers in children's fiction. Founded 1998.

Scottish Arts Club

24 Rutland Square, Edinburgh EH1 2BW
tel 0131 229 8157
email scottishartsclub@btconnect.com
website www.scottishartsclub.co.uk

Art, literature, music.

Scottish Association of Writers

3 The Loan, Bo'ness, EH51 0HN
email secretary@sawriters.org.uk
website www.sawriters.org.uk
President Marc Sherland, *Secretary* Jen Butler, *Treasurer* Jacklin Murray

An organisation promoting writing in Scotland. Annual conference attended by writers who are members of affiliated clubs and alternating annual satellite events; Write Up North and Write Down South. Competitions organised throughout the year in a range of categories (Contact the Competition Secretary: competition@sawriters.org.uk). Website features group and writer resources. For further information about joining the Association, contact the Affiliation Secretary: affiliation@sawriters.org.uk Founded 1969.

Scottish Book Trust (SBT)

Sandeman House, Trunk's Close, 55 High Street, Edinburgh EH1 1SR
tel 0131 524 0160
email info@scottishbooktrust.com
website www.scottishbooktrust.com

Scottish Book Trust (SBT) is Scotland's national agency for the promotion of reading, writing and literature. Programmes include: Bookbug, a free universal book-gifting programme which encourages families to read with their children from birth; an ambitious school's programme including national tours, the virtual events programme Authors Live and the Scottish Children's Book Awards; the Live Literature funding programme, a national initiative enabling Scottish citizens to engage with authors, playwrights, poets, storytellers and illustrators; a writer development programme, offering mentoring and professional development for emerging and established writers; and a readership development programme featuring a national writing campaign as well as Book Week Scotland during last week in November. SBT also has a website full of information for readers and writers, including writing tips, booklists, podcasts, competitions and blogs for all ages.

Scottish Fellowship of Christian Writers

c/o Ian McGregor, Flat 1/1, 3 Grantley Street, Glasgow G41 3PT
email info@sfcw.info
website www.sfcw.info
Membership Secretary Ian McGregor
£10 p.a.

To encourage Christians living in Scotland to make use of their creative writing talents. Over 100 members. Founded 1980.

Scottish Newspaper Society

17 Polwarth Grove, Edinburgh EH11 1LY
email info@scotns.org.uk
website www.scotsns.org.uk
Represents the interests of the Scottish newspaper industry.

Seven Stories – National Centre for Children's Books

30 Lime Street, Ouseburn Valley, Newcastle upon Tyne NE1 2PQ
tel 0845 271 0777
email info@sevenstories.org.uk
website www.sevenstories.org.uk

Seven Stories champions the art of children's books to ensure its place as an integral part of childhood and national cultural life. The world of children's books is celebrated through exhibitions, events and an archive. Seven Stories celebrates books, where books are made, where they come from and how we can enjoy and share them. It is housed in a specially converted warehouse. Arts Council England and Newcastle City Council regularly fund Seven Stories' work, giving children's literature status and establishing new ways of engaging young audiences.

The Shaw Society

c/o 1 Buckland Court, 37 Belsize Park, London NW3 4EB

tel 020-7435 6497
email contact@shawsociety.org.uk
website www.shawsociety.org.uk
Chairman Phillip Riley
Membership £20/$40 p.a.

Works towards the improvement and diffusion of knowledge of the life and works of Bernard Shaw (1856–1950) and his circle. Publishes *The Shavian*.

Society for Editors and Proofreaders (SfEP)

Apsley House, 176 Upper Richmond Road, London SW15 2SH
tel 020-8785 6155
email administrator@sfep.org.uk
website www.sfep.org.uk

Works to promote high editorial standards and achieve recognition of its members' professional status, through local and national meetings, an annual conference, discussion forums and a regular e-magazine. The Society publishes an online directory of ordinary and advanced members. It also runs a programme of reasonably priced open and in-house workshops/training days, which help newcomers to acquire basic editorial skills, and enable experienced editors and proofreaders to update their skills or broaden their competence. Training also covers aspects of professional practice or business for the self-employed. The Society supports moves towards recognised standards of training and accreditation for editors and proofreaders and has developed its own Accreditation in Proofreading qualification. It has close links with the Publishing Training Centre and the Society of Indexers, is represented on the BSI Technical Committee dealing with copy preparation and proof correction (BS 5261), and works to foster good relations with all relevant bodies and organisations in the UK and worldwide. Founded 1988.

The Society for Theatre Research

c/o The National Theatre Archive, 83–191 The Cut, London SE1 8LL
email contact@str.org.uk
website www.str.org.uk
Hon. Secretary Jenny Bloodworth

Publishes journal *Theatre Notebook* (three p.a.) and at least one major book per annum, holds lectures and makes annual research grants (current annual total sum approx. £5,000). Also awards an annual prize of up to £500 for best book published in English on the historical or current practice of the British Theatre.

Society of Artists Agents

website www.saahub.com

Formed to promote professionalism in the illustration industry and to forge closer links between clients and artists through an agreed set of guidelines. The Society believes in an ethical approach through proper terms and conditions, thereby protecting the interests of the artists and clients. Founded 1992.

The Society of Authors – see page 485

The Society of Botanical Artists

Executive Secretary Mrs Pam Henderson, 1 Knapp Cottages, Wyke, Gillingham, Dorset SP8 4NQ
tel (01747) 825718
email pam@soc-botanical-artists.org
website www.soc-botanical-artists.org
President Sandra Wall Armitage
Membership Through selection. £150 p.a.; £20 friend members

Aims to encourage the art of botanical painting. Annual Open Exhibition held in April/May at Westminster Central Hall, London SW1. Submit work in February/March. Entry schedules available from the Executive Secretary from January on receipt of sae. Founded 1985.

Society of Children's Book Writers and Illustrators (SCBWI)

email ra@britishscbwi.org
website www.britishislesscbwi.org
Regional Adviser, SCBWI–British Isles Natascha Biebow
Membership approx. £50 p.a.

An international network for the exchange of knowledge between professional writers, illustrators, editors, publishers, agents, librarians, educators, booksellers and others involved with literature for young people. Sponsors conferences on writing and illustrating children's books and multimedia – in New York (February, annual), Los Angeles (August, annual) and Bologna (spring, bi-annual) – as well as dozens of regional conferences and events throughout the world. Publishes a quarterly newsletter, *The Bulletin*, and information publications. Awards grants for: works in progress, portfolios, humour, marketing your book, excellence in non-traditional publishing and diversity in books. The SCBWI also presents the annual Golden Kite and Crystal Awards for the best fiction and non-fiction books.

The SCBWI British Isles region meets regularly for speaker, networking or professional development events, including the professional series PULSE events for published members, agents' party, masterclasses for writers and illustrators and a fiction and picture book retreat. Also sponsors local and online critique groups and publishes Words and Pictures blog magazine (www.wordsandpics.org), which includes up-to-date events and marketing information, interviews and articles on the craft of children's writing and illustrating. The biennial Undiscovered Voices competition offers new talent an opportunity to be discovered by publishers (www.undiscoveredvoices.com). The yearly 2-day Writers' and Illustrators' Conference includes workshops, one-to-one manuscript and portfolio reviews, a mass book launch and the opportunity to meet publishing professionals. Founded 1971.

The Society of Civil and Public Service Writers

email membership@scpsw.co.uk
website www.scpsw.co.uk
Membership £15 p.a.; Poetry Workshop add £7

Welcomes serving and retired members of the Civil Service, Armed Forces, Post Office and BT, the nursing profession, and other public servants. Members can be aspiring or published writers. Holds annual competitions for short stories, articles and poetry, plus occasional competitions for longer works. Offers postal folios for short stories and articles; holds an AGM and occasional meetings; publishes *The Civil Service Author* (quarterly) magazine. Poetry Workshop offers magazine, postal folio, anthology and weekend. Send sae for details. Founded 1935.

Society of Editors

Director Bob Satchwell, University Centre, Granta Place, Mill Lane, Cambridge CB2 1RU
tel (01223) 304080
email office@societyofeditors.org
website www.societyofeditors.org
Membership £230 p.a. depending on category

Formed from the merger of the Guild of Editors and the Association of British Editors, the Society has more than 400 members in national, regional and local newspapers, magazines, broadcasting and digital media, journalism education and media law. It campaigns for media freedom, self regulation, the public's right to know and the maintenance of standards in journalism. Founded 1999.

Society of Graphic Fine Art

email enquiries@sgfa.org.uk
website www.sgfa.org.uk
President Jackie Devereux PSGFA, *Hon. Secretary* Dr Susan E. Poole SGFA
Membership by annual election. Dates of elections and membership fees may be obtained from the website.

The Society of Graphic Fine Art (The Drawing Society) exists to promote and exhibit works of high quality in colour or black and white, with the emphasis on good drawing and draughtsmanship, in pencil, pen, brush, charcoal or any of the forms of original printmaking. The Society holds an annual Open Exhibition with prizes and awards in many categories. The Society's journal can be found at http://sgfajournal.wordpress.com. Founded 1919.

Society of Heraldic Arts

53 Hitchen Street, Baldock, Hertfordshire, SG7 6AQ
email sha.honsec@gmail.com
website www.heraldic-arts.com
Secretary John J. Tunesi of Liongam, *Membership Secretary* Gwynn Ellis-Hughes
Membership Craft £35 p.a.; Associate £17.50

Aims to serve the interests of heraldic artists, craftsmen, designers and writers, to provide a 'shop window' for their work, to obtain commissions on their behalf and to act as a forum for the exchange of information and ideas. Also offers an information service to the public. Candidates for admission as craft members should be artists or craftsmen whose work comprises a substantial element of heraldry and is of a sufficiently high standard to satisfy the requirements of the Society's advisory council. Founded 1987.

Society of Indexers – see page 636

The Society of Limners

Contact Richard East, 16 Tudor Close, Hove, East Sussex BN3 7NR
tel (01273) 770628
email info@societyoflimners.co.uk
website www.societyoflimners.co.uk
Membership £45 p.a., £25 Friends (open to non-exhibitors); £50/£30 overseas

The Society's aims are to promote an interest in miniature painting (in any medium), calligraphy and heraldry and encourage their development to a high standard. New members are elected after the submission of four works of acceptable standard and guidelines are provided for new artists. Members receive up to three newsletters a year and an annual exhibition is arranged. At least one painting weekend is held each year and a seminar every two years. Founded 1986.

The Society of Medical Writers

Dr R. Cutler, 30 Dollis Hill Lane, London NW2 6JE
website www.somw.org.uk

Aims to recruit members from all branches of the medical profession, together with all professions allied to medicine, to foster interest in literature and in writing – not solely about medicine but also about art, history, music, theatre, etc. Members are encouraged to write fiction, poetry, plays, book reviews, non-fiction articles. Poetry, short story and biography (Roger Bacon Award) prizes, for best non-fiction and best written clinical paper. Publishes *The Writer* (two p.a.) and a register of members and their writing interests. Holds a bi-annual conference in which various aspects of literature and writing are explored in a relaxed and informal atmosphere. Founded 1989.

Society of Scribes and Illuminators (SSI)

Hon. Secretary 6 Queen Square, London WC1N 3AT
email honsec@calligraphyonline.org
website www.calligraphyonline.org

Membership £40 Fellows; £32 Lay members; £26 Friends

Aims to promote and preserve the art of calligraphy, bringing the beauty of handwritten letters to the modern world, moving with the times to embrace contemporary lettering whilst upholding the traditions of the craft. Founded 1921.

The Society of Sussex Authors

Secretary Jane Bwye, 44c Wannock Lane, Lower Willingdon, Eastbourne BN20 9SD
tel (01323) 482025
email jbwye@yahoo.co.uk
Membership £12 p.a.

Aims to encourage social contact between members, and to promote interest in literature and authors. Membership is open to writers living in Sussex who have had at least one book commercially published or who have worked extensively in journalism, radio, TV or the theatre. Founded 1969.

Society of Wildlife Artists

17 Carlton House Terrace, London SW1Y 5BD
tel 020-7930 6844
website www.swla.co.uk
President Harriet Mead

Aims to promote and encourage the art of wildlife painting and sculpture. Open Annual Exhibition at Mall Galleries, The Mall, London SW1, for any artist whose work depicts wildlife subjects (botanical and domestic animals are not admissable).

The Society of Women Artists

Executive Secretary Rebecca Cotton, Foxcote Cottage, Foxcote, Andoversford, Cheltenham, Glos. GL54 4LP
tel 07528 477002
email rebeccacottonswa@gmail.com
website www.society-women-artists.org.uk
President Sue Jelley SPF
Membership Election by invitation, based on work submitted to the exhibition

Receiving day in April for annual open exhibition held in June/July at Mall Galleries, The Mall, London SW1. Founded in 1855, the Society continues to promote art by women.

Society of Women Writers & Journalists (SWWJ)

email enquiries@swwj.co.uk
website www.swwj.co.uk
Contact Barbara Field-Holmes

The Society of Women Writers & Journalists was formed to support professional women writers 120 years ago and that support is still as strong as ever.

This forward-looking Society offers a number of benefits to fully paid up members who write in many differing genres. Founded 1894.

Society of Young Publishers

The Secretary, c/o The Publishers Association, 29B Montague Street, London WC1B 5BW
email sypchair@thesyp.org.uk
website www.thesyp.org.uk
Membership Open to anyone employed in publishing or hoping to be soon; £30 p.a. standard; £24 student/unwaged

Organises monthly events which offer the chance to network and hear senior figures talk on topics of key importance to the publishing industry. Runs a job database advertising the latest vacancies and internships as well as a blog, PressForward, and a print magazine, *InPrint*. Also has branches in Oxford, Scotland and the North. Founded 1949.

South African Writers' Circle

email southafricanwriterscircle@gmail.com
website www.sawriters.org.za
Membership R190 p.a. (single), R255 (couple); R145 (pensioners); concessions available

Aims to help and encourage all writers, new and experienced, in the art of writing. Publishes a monthly newsletter, and runs competitions with prizes for the winners. Founded 1960.

Southwest Scriptwriters

email info@southwestscriptwriters.co.uk
website www.southwestscriptwriters.co.uk
Artistic Director Tim Massey
Membership £6 p.a.

Workshops members' drama scripts for stage, screen, radio and TV with the aim of improving their chances of professional production, meeting at Watershed in Bristol. Also hosts talks by professional dramatists. Projects to present members' work to a wider audience have included theatre and short film productions, as well as public rehearsed readings. Bi-monthly e-newsletter. Founded 1994.

Sports Journalists' Association of Great Britain (SJA)

c/o Start2Finish Event Management, Unit 92, Capital Business Centre, 22 Carlton Road, Surrey CR2 0BS
tel 020-8916 2234
website www.sportsjournalists.co.uk
President Sir Michael Parkinson
Membership £30 p.a. (full); £20 (associate)

Represents sports journalists across the country and is Britain's voice in international sporting affairs. Offers advice to members covering major events, acts as a consultant to organisers of major sporting events on media requirements. Member of the BOA Press Advisory Committee. Founded 1948.

Spread the Word

The Albany, Douglas Way, London SE8 4AG
tel 020-8692 0231 extension 249
email info@spreadtheword.org.uk
website www.spreadtheword.org.uk

Spread the Word is London's writer development agency. Provides advice, information, craft and career support for the writers of London. Works with writers at all stages of development from those beginning to engage with writing to those who are professional career writers, across all forms and genres. Spread the Word is a national portfolio organisation of Arts Council England. Founded 1995.

The Robert Louis Stevenson Club

Secretary John W.S. Macfie, 17 Heriot Row, Edinburgh EH3 6HP
tel 0131 556 1896
email mail@stevenson-house.co.uk
Membership £25 p.a.; £180 for 10 years

Aims to foster interest in Robert Louis Stevenson's life (1850–94) and works through various events and its newsletter. Founded 1920.

Sussex Playwrights' Club

Hon. Secretary, 24 Highcroft Villas, Brighton BN1 5PS
email mail@sussexplaywrights.com
website www.sussexplaywrights.com

Founded 1935.

Swedish Publishers' Association

(Svenska Förläggareföreningen)
Drottninggaten 97, 113 60 Stockholm, Sweden
tel +468-7 361940
email info@forlaggare.se
website www.forlaggare.se
Director Kristina Ahlinder

Works to promote an open and free book market with space for new publishers to establish themselves and to grow. Members are professional publishers working across all genres and formats and account for around 70% of sales in the industry.

Founded 1843.

The Tennyson Society

Central Library, Free School lane, Lincoln LN2 1EZ
tel (01522) 687837
email kathleen.jefferson@lincolnshire.gov.uk
website www.tennysonsociety.org.uk
Membership £14 p.a.; £16 family; £25 institutions

Promotes the study and understanding of the life and work of the poet Alfred, Lord Tennyson (1809–92) and supports the Tennyson Research Centre in Lincoln. Holds lectures, visits and seminars; publishes the *Tennyson Research Bulletin* (annual), Monographs and Occasional Papers; tapes/recordings available. Founded 1960.

Theatre Writers' Union – see page 487

Angela Thirkell Society

Chairman Mrs P. Aldred, 54 Belmont Park, London SE13 5BN
tel 020-8244 9339
email penny.aldred@ntlworld.com
website www.angelathirkellsociety.co.uk
Membership £10 p.a.

Aims 'to honour the memory of Angela Thirkell (1890–1960) as a writer, and to make her works available to new generations'. Publishes an annual journal, and encourages Thirkell studies. Founded 1980.

The Edward Thomas Fellowship

21 Verlands, Congresbury, Bristol BS49 5BL
tel (01934) 825357
email ianandbreeda@btinternet.com
website www.edward-thomas-fellowship.org.uk
Secretary Ian Morton
Membership single £10 p.a.; joint £15 p.a.

Aims to perpetuate the memory of Edward Thomas (1878–1917), poet and writer, foster an interest in his life and work, to assist in the preservation of places associated with him and to arrange events which extend fellowship amongst his admirers. Founded 1980.

Dylan Thomas Society of Great Britain

email geoff@dylanthomasbirthplace.com
website thedylanthomassocietyofgb.co.uk
Chairman Geoff Haden
Membership £10 p.a. single; £15 p.a. double; Patrons £25

Aims to promote an interest in the works of Dylan Thomas (1914–53) and other writers. Founded 1977.

The Tolkien Society

email membership@tolkiensociety.org
website www.tolkiensociety.org
Membership £30 p.a.; £2 p.a. (Entings (under 16s))

The Translators Association

84 Drayton Gardens, London SW10 9SB
tel 020-7373 6642
email info@societyofauthors.org
website www.societyofauthors.org/translators-association

Specialist unit within the membership of the Society of Authors (see page 485), exclusively concerned with the interests and special problems of translators into English whose work is published or performed commercially in Great Britain. Members are entitled to advice on all aspects of their work, including remuneration and contractual arrangements with publishers, editors and broadcasting organisations. Founded 1958.

The Trollope Society

PO Box 505, Tunbridge Wells, TN2 9RW
tel (01747) 839799
email info@trollopesociety.org
website www.trollopesociety.org
Chairman Michael Williamson JP DL
Membership UK: £26 p.a.; international: £36

Has produced the first ever complete edition of the novels of Anthony Trollope (1815–82). Founded 1987.

The Turner Society

BCM Box Turner, London WC1N 3XX
website www.turnersociety.org.uk
Chairman Andrew Wilton
Membership £25 p.a. individuals; £25 p.a. overseas surface mail; £37.50 p.a. overseas airmail, Life Member £500

Aims to foster a wider appreciation of all facets of the work of J.M.W. Turner RA (1775–1851); to encourage exhibitions of his paintings, drawings and engravings. Publishes *Turner Society News* (two p.a.). Founded 1975.

V&A Publishing

Victoria and Albert Museum, South Kensington, London SW7 2RL
tel 020-7942 2966
email vapubs@vam.ac.uk
website www.vandapublishing.com
Publisher Mark Eastment, *PR and Marketing* Julie Chan, *Sales* Susannah Priede, *Rights* Nina Jacobson

Popular and scholarly books on fine and decorative arts, architecture, contemporary design, fashion and photography. Founded 1980.

Ver Poets

tel (01582) 715817
email gregsmith480@gmail.com
website www.verpoets.org.uk
Secretary Gregory Smith
Membership £18 p.a. UK; £24 overseas; £12 students

Encourages the writing and study of poetry. Holds evening meetings and daytime workshops in the St Albans area. Holds members' competitions and the annual Open Competition. Founded 1966.

Visiting Arts

c/o ICA, The Mall, London SW1Y 5AH
tel 020-3463 4560
email information@visitingarts.org.uk
website www.visitingarts.org.uk
Director Yvette Vaughan Jones

Aims to strengthen intercultural understanding through the arts. It provides information and intelligence in order to strengthen intercultural dialogue, and creates opportunities to experience intercultural exploration. This is done through mediated performances, exhibitions, and by initiating and promoting collaborations. Visiting Arts seeks to expand the skills and knowledge of existing cultural players and develop new talent to ensure a wide, diverse and sustainable group of players.

Visiting Arts creates, produces and distributes authoritative directories and help-sheets, targeted briefings and the latest advice through print, web and word of mouth. It organises seminars, conferences and networking events to deepen intercultural understanding; establishes and fosters opportunities for ground-breaking artist exchanges; promotes cutting edge exhibitions; and contributes to some of the world's biggest and most innovative festivals. It works with the most exciting next generation of artists and cultural players, inviting them to the UK, expanding knowledge and horizons and championing intercultural working.

Visiting Arts is an independent registered charity. It is funded by the British Council, Arts Council England, Creative Scotland, the Arts Council of Wales, the Arts Council of Northern Ireland and the Department of Culture, Media and Sport. Founded 1977.

Voice of the Listener & Viewer Ltd (VLV)

The Old Rectory Business Centre, Springhead Road, Northfleet DA11 8HN
tel (01474) 338716
email info@vlv.org.uk
website www.vlv.org.uk
Administrator Sue Washbrook

An independent, non-profit-making membership association, free from political, commercial and sectarian affiliations, working for quality and diversity in British broadcasting. VLV represents the interests of listeners and viewers as citizens and consumers across the full range of broadcasting issues. VLV is concerned with the structures, regulation, funding and institutions that underpin the British broadcasting system but also takes note of developments in Europe and the wider world. It holds regular conferences and seminars and publishes The Bulletin and an e-newsletter. VLV is a charitable company limited by guarantee. Founded 1983.

The Walmsley Society

Secretary Fred Lane, April Cottage, 1 Brand Road, Hampden Park, Eastbourne, East Sussex BN22 9PX
website www.walmsleysoc.org
Membership Secretary George Featherston, 3 Dobson Terrace, Redcar TS10 3LG

Aims to promote and encourage an appreciation of the literary and artistic heritage left to us by Leo Walmsley (1892–1966) and J. Ulric Walmsley (1860–1954). Founded 1985.

Mary Webb Society

Secretary Sue Higginbotham, Old Barn Cottage, 10 Barrow Hall Farm, Village Road, Great Barrow, Chester, Cheshire CH3 7JH
tel (01829) 740592
email suehigginbotham@yahoo.co.uk
website www.marywebbsociety.co.uk

For devotees of the literature and works of Mary Webb (1881–1927) and of the beautiful Shropshire countryside of her novels. Publishes a bi-annual journal, organises summer schools and other events in various locations related to Webb's life and works. Archives, lectures; tours arranged for individuals and groups. Founded 1972.

The H.G. Wells Society

Eric Fitch, 20 Upper Field Close, Hereford HR2 7SW
email secretaryhgwellssociety@hotmail.com
website www.hgwellsusa.50megs.com
Publicity Officer Dr Emelyne Godfrey (juststruckone@hotmail.com), *Secretary* Eric Fitch
Membership £20 p.a. UK, £24 EU, £27 p.a. rest of world; retired/student/unwaged: £13 p.a. UK, £17 EU, £20 rest of world; Institutions: £25 p.a. UK, £30 EU, £35 rest of world.

Promotes an active interest in and an appreciation of the life, work and thought of H.G. Wells (1866–1946). Publishes *The Wellsian* (annual) and *The Newsletter* (bi-annual). Founded 1960.

Welsh Academy – see Literature Wales

Welsh Books Council/Cyngor Llyfrau Cymru

Castell Brychan, Aberystwyth, Ceredigion SY23 2JB
tel (01970) 624151
email castellbrychan@cllc.org.uk
website www.cllc.org.uk
website www.gwales.com
Ceo Elwyn Jones

A national body funded directly by the Welsh Government which provides a focus for the publishing industry in Wales. Awards grants for publishing in Welsh and English. Provides services to the trade in the fields of editing, design, marketing and distribution. The Council is a key enabling institution in the world of books and provides services and information in this field to all who are associated with it. Founded 1961.

The Oscar Wilde Society

22 Edric Road, London SE14 5EL
email michael.seeney@btinternet.com
website www.oscarwildesociety.co.uk
Membership Secretary Cressida Battersby, *Hon. Secretary* Michael Seeney

Aims to promote knowledge, appreciation and study of the life, personality and works of the writer and wit Oscar Wilde (1854–1900). Activities include meetings, lectures, readings and exhibitions, and visits to associated locations. Members receive a journal, *The Wildean* (two p.a.), and a newsletter, *Intentions* (five p.a.). Founded 1990.

Charles Williams Society

Secretary Richard Sturch, 35 Broomfield, Stacey Bushes, Milton Keynes MK12 6HA
email charles_wms_soc@yahoo.co.uk
website www.charleswilliamssociety.org.uk

Aims to promote interest in the life and work of Charles Walter Stansby Williams (1886–1945) and to make his writings more easily available. Founded 1975.

The Henry Williamson Society

General Secretary Sue Cumming, 7 Monmouth Road, Dorchester, Dorset DT1 2DE
tel (01305) 264092
email zseagull@aol.com
Membership Secretary Margaret Murphy, 16 Doran Drive, Redhill, Surrey RH1 6AX
tel (01737) 763228
email mm@misterman.freeserve.co.uk
website www.henrywilliamson.co.uk
Chairman Will Harris
Membership £15 p.a.

Aims to encourage a wider readership and greater understanding of the literary heritage left by Henry Williamson (1895–1977). Two meetings annually; also weekend activities. Publishes an annual journal. Founded 1980.

The P.G. Wodehouse Society (UK)

Tony Ring, 34 Longfield, Great Missenden, Bucks. HP16 0EG
tel (01494) 864848
website www.pgwodehousesociety.org.uk
Membership £22 p.a.

Aims to promote enjoyment of P.G. Wodehouse (1881–1975). Publishes *Wooster Sauce* (quarterly) and *By The Way* papers (four p.a.) which cover diverse subjects of Wodehousean interest. Holds events, entertainments and meetings throughout Britain. Founded 1997.

Women in Publishing (WiP)

email info@wipub.org.uk
website www.wipub.org.uk
Membership £27.50 p.a.

Promotes the status of women within publishing; encourages networking and mutual support among women; provides a forum for the discussion of ideas, trends and subjects to women in the trade; offers advice on publishing careers; supports and publicises women's achievements and successes. Each year WiP presents two awards: the Pandora Award is given in recognition of significant personal contributions by women to publishing, and the New Venture Award is presented to a recent venture which reflects the interests and concerns of women or minority groups in the 21st century. Founded 1979.

Virginia Woolf Society of Great Britain

Stuart N. Clarke, Membership Secretary, Fairhaven, Charnleys Lane, Banks, Southport PR9 8HJ
tel (01704) 225232
email stuart.n.clarke@btinternet.com
website www.virginiawoolfsociety.co.uk
Membership £18 p.a.; £23 Europe; £26 outside Europe

Acts as a forum for British admirers of Virginia Woolf (1882–1941) to meet, correspond and share their enjoyment of her work. Publishes the *Virginia Woolf Bulletin*. Founded 1998.

The Wordsworth Trust

Dove Cottage, Grasmere, Cumbria LA22 9SH
tel (01539) 435544
email enquiries@wordsworth.org.uk
website www.wordsworth.org.uk
Membership Officer Hannah Stratton
Membership £25 p.a. (individual)

To preserve and enhance Dove Cottage, the Collection and the historic environment of Town End for future generations; to give people of all ages the chance to fulfil their creative potential; to develop the education and lifelong learning programmes for the benefit of the widest possible audience. Founded 1891.

Worshipful Company of Stationers and Newspaper Makers

Stationers' Hall, London EC4M 7DD
tel 020-7248 2934
email admin@stationers.org
website www.stationers.org
Master Helen Esmonde, *Clerk* William Alden MBE DL

One of the Livery Companies of the City of London. Connected with the printing, publishing, bookselling, newspaper and allied trades. Founded 1403.

Writers Advice Centre for Children's Books

Shakespeare House, 168 Lavender Hill, London SW11 5TG
tel 020-7801 6300
email info@writersadvice.co.uk
website www.writersadvice.co.uk
Managing Editor Louise Jordan

Dedicated to helping new and published children's writers by offering both editorial advice and tips on how to get published. The Centre also runs an online children's writing correspondence course and publishes a small list of its own under the name of Wacky Bee Books (www.wackybeebooks.com). Founded 1994.

Writers Guild of America, East Inc. (WGAE)

250 Hudson Street, 7th Floor, New York, NY 10013, USA
tel +1 212-767-7800
website www.wgaeast.org

Represents writers in screen, TV and new media for collective bargaining. It provides member services including pension and health, as well as educational and professional activities. Founded 1954.

Writers Guild of America, West Inc. (WGAW)

7000 West 3rd Street, Los Angeles, CA 90048, USA
tel +1 323-951-4000
website www.wga.org

Union representing and servicing 12,000 writers in film, broadcast, cable and multimedia industries for purposes of collective bargaining, contract administration and other services, and functions to protect and advance the economic, professional and creative interests of writers. Monthly publication, *Written By*, available by subscription. Founded 1933.

Writers Guild of Canada

366 Adelaide Street West, Suite 401, Toronto, Ontario M5V 1R9, Canada
tel +1 416-979-7907; toll free +1-800-567-9974
email info@wgc.ca
website www.wgc.ca
Executive Director Maureen Parker

Represents over 2,000 professional writers of film, TV, animation, radio, documentary and digital media. Negotiates and administers collective agreements with independent producers and broadcasters. The Guild also publishes *Canadian Screenwriter* magazine.

The Writers' Guild of Great Britain – see page 487

Writers Guild of Ireland

(formerly the Irish Playwrights and Screenwriters Guild)
Art House, Curved Street, Temple Bar, Dublin 2, Republic of Ireland
tel +353 (0)1 6709970
email info@script.ie
website www.script.ie
Chairperson Thomas McLaughlin

Represents writers' interests in theatre, radio and screen. Founded 1969.

Writers in Oxford

email wio_membership@yahoo.co.uk
website www.writersinoxford.org
Chair Denise Cullington
Membership £25 p.a.

Promotes social mixing, networking and professional discussion among published writers in and around Oxfordshire. Activities include: suppers, literary talks, parties and outings. Publishes a regular newsletter, *The Oxford Writer*. Founded 1992.

The Writers' Union of Canada

460 Richmond Street West, Suite 600, Toronto, Ontario M5V 1Y1
tel +1 416-703-8982
email info@writersunion.ca
website www.writersunion.ca

National arts service organisation for professionally published book authors. Founded 1973.

Yachting Journalists' Association

June-Marie Hamilton, Crimsham Manor, Lagness, Chichester PO20 1LN

tel (01243) 264173
email secretary@yja.co.uk
website www.yja.co.uk
Membership £40 p.a.

President Lord Ambrose Greenway, *Honorary Secretary* June-Marie Hamilton

Aims to further the interests of yachting, sail and power, and yachting journalism. Members vote annually for the Yachtsman of the Year and the Young Sailor of the Year Award and host several important functions annually on both the British and international maritime calendar. Founded 1969.

The Yorkshire Dialect Society

Publicity Officer Eric Scaife, 298 Selby Road, Leeds LS15 0PS
email enquiries@yorkshiredialectsociety.org.uk
website www.yorkshiredialectsociety.org.uk
Membership £12 p.a.

Aims to encourage interest in: dialect speech, the writing of dialect verse, prose and drama; the publication and circulation of dialect literature; the study of the origins and the history of dialect and kindred subjects. Organises meetings; publishes *Transactions* (annual) and *The Summer Bulletin* free to members; list of other publications on request. Founded 1897.

Francis Brett Young Society

Secretary Mrs J. Hadley, 92 Gower Road, Halesowen, West Midlands B62 9BT
tel 0121 422 8969
email michael.hall10@gmail.com
website www.fbysociety.co.uk
Chairman Dr Michael Hall
Membership Individuals: £7 p.a., £70 life; Joint: £10 p.a., £100 life; Full-time students: £5 p.a.; Societies and institutions £7 p.a.

Aims to provide opportunities for members to meet, correspond, and to share the enjoyment of the works of Francis Brett Young (1884–1954). Publishes a journal (two p.a.). Founded 1979.

Prizes and awards

This list provides details of many British prizes, competitions and awards for writers and artists, including grants, bursaries and fellowships, as well as details of major international prizes. See page 763 for a quick reference to its contents.

The Aeon Award

Albedo One, 8 Bachelor's Walk, Dublin 1, Republic of Ireland
email fraslaw@yahoo.co.uk
website www.albedo1.com

An annual contest for short fiction (up to 10,000 words) in genres of fantasy, science fiction, horror or anything in between. A grand prize of €1,000 will be awarded to the winner (2nd prize €200, 3rd €100) plus publication in Albedo One. The contest runs for four rounds throughout the year; deadlines are 31 March (1st round), 30 June (2nd round), 30 September (3rd round) and 30 November (final round). At the end of each round the best story submissions will be shortlisted for the award. Email submissions only to fraslaw@yahoo.co.uk. Entry fee: €7.50.

ALCS Educational Writers' Award

The Society of Authors, 84 Drayton Gardens, London SW10 9SB
tel 020-7373 6642
email info@societyofauthors.org
website www.societyofauthors.org/education-book-prize

This is an annual award alternating each year between books in the 5–11 and 11–18 year age groups. It is given to an outstanding example of traditionally published non-fiction (with or without illustrations) that stimulates and enhances learning. The work must have been first published in the UK, in the English language, within the previous two calendar years. Deadline 30 June.

The Hans Christian Andersen Awards

International Board on Books for Young People, Nonnenweg 12, Postfach CH–4009 Basel, Switzerland
tel +41 61-272 2917
email ibby@ibby.org
website www.ibby.org

The Medals are awarded every two years to a living author and an illustrator who by the outstanding value of their work are judged to have made a lasting contribution to literature for children and young people. *2014 winners*: Nahoko Uehashi (author), Roger Mello (illustrator).

Arts Council England

Arts Council England, 21 Bloomsbury Street, London WC1B 3HF
tel 0845 300 6200
email enquiries@artscouncil.org.uk
website www.artscouncil.org.uk

Arts Council England presents national prizes rewarding creative talent in literature. These are awarded through the Council's flexible funds and are not necessarily open to application: the David Cohen Prize for Literature, and the Independent Foreign Fiction Prize.

Arts Council England, London

Arts Council England, 21 Bloomsbury Street, London WC1B 3HF
tel 0845 300 6200
email enquiries@artscouncil.org.uk
website www.artscouncil.org.uk

Arts Council England, London is the regional office for the capital, covering 33 boroughs and the City of London. Grants are available through the 'Grants for the Arts' scheme throughout the year to support a variety of projects.

Contact the Literature Unit for more information, or see website for an application form.

The Arts Council/An Chomhairle Ealaíon

70 Merrion Square, Dublin 2, Republic of Ireland
tel +353 (0)1 6180200
email info@artscouncil.ie
website www.artscouncil.ie

Outlines all of its funding opportunities for individuals, groups and organisations on website. Also publishes an email newsletter that provides monthly updates on grants and awards, news and events, and arts policy. Register to receive the newsletter by visiting www.artscouncil.ie/en/newsletter.aspx.

Arts Council site YouWriteOn.com Book Awards

tel 07948 392634
email edward@youwriteon.com
website www.youwriteon.com

Arts Council-funded site publishing awards for new fiction writers. Random House and Orion, the publishers of authors such as Dan Brown and Terry Pratchett, provide free professional critiques for the highest rated new writers' opening chapters and short stories on YouWriteOn.com each month. The highest rated writers of the year are then published, three in each of the adult and children's categories, through

YouWriteOn's free paperback publishing service for writers. The novel publishing awards total £1,000. Writers can enter at any time throughout the year: closing date is 31 December each year. Join YouWriteOn.com to participate. Previous YouWriteOn.com winners have been published by mainstream publishers such as Random House, Orion, Penguin and Hodder including Channel 4 TV Book Club winner and bestseller *The Legacy* by Katherine Webb. Founded 2005.

The Australian/Vogel's Literary Award

email vogel@allenandunwin.com
website www.allenandunwin.com

An annual award of $20,000 for a chosen unpublished work of fiction, Australian history or biography. Entrants must be under 35 years of age on the closing date and must normally be residents of Australia. The MS must be between 30,000 and 100,000 words and must be an original work entirely by the entrant written in English. It cannot be under consideration by any publisher or award. See website for details. Closing date: 31 May. Founded 1980.

Authors' Club Awards

website www.authorsclub.co.uk

Best First Novel Award

The Authors' Club Best First Novel Award was inaugurated in 1954 and past winners have included Brian Moore, Alan Sillitoe, Paul Bailey, Diran Adebayo, Jackie Kay, Susan Fletcher, Nicola Monaghan, Anthony Quinn, Jonathan Kemp and, most recently, Jack Wolf. The £2,500 prize is open to any debut novel written in English and published in the UK during the previous calendar year: novels first published in another country will not be considered. All imprints may submit two titles. Please send two copies of each title to Suzi Feay, The Authors' Club, c/o The National Liberal Club, 1 Whitehall Place, SW1A 3HE. Please mark packages 'BFNA' and send a confirmation email to suzifeay@aol.com with details of the titles submitted.

The Art Book Prize

The Art Book Prize (formerly the Banister Fletcher Prize) is presented each year for the best book on architecture or the arts (architecture, fine art, painting, sculpture, photography, graphic art, design etc). The book needs to be published in the previous calendar year, with a preferred emphasis on works illuminating art for the intelligent lay reader. It must be in English, but may be published anywhere in the world. Please send two copies of each title to Sunny Singh, The Authors' Club, c/o The National Liberal Club, 1 Whitehall Place, SW1A 3HE. Please mark packages 'Art Book Prize' and send a confirmation email to ssingh@authorsclub.co.uk with details of the titles submitted.

The Stanford-Dolman Best Travel Book Award

The award is presented annually for the best literary travel book (no guidebooks accepted) published in the previous calendar year. It is open to writers from across the globe, although submissions must be available in English. Instituted by the Reverend Dr William Dolman in 2005, the £5,000 prize is now jointly sponsored by Stanfords, the world's largest travel bookshop. Please send two copies of each title to John Walsh, The Authors' Club, c/o The National Liberal Club, 1 Whitehall Place, SW1A 3HE. Please mark packages 'Stanford-Dolman Award' and send a confirmation email to j.walshindependent@gmail.com with details of the titles submitted.

The Authors' Contingency Fund

Sarah Baxter, The Society of Authors,
84 Drayton Gardens, London SW10 9SB
tel 020-7373 6642
email sbaxter@societyofauthors.org
website www.societyofauthors.org

This fund makes modest grants to established, published authors who find themselves in sudden financial difficulty. Apply for guidelines and application form.

The Authors' Foundation

The Society of Authors, 84 Drayton Gardens, London SW10 9SB
tel 020-7373 6642
email info@societyofauthors.org
website www.societyofauthors.org/grants-works/progress

Founded in 1984 to mark the centenary of the Society of Authors, the Authors' Foundation provides grants to writers to assist them while writing books. There are two rounds of grants each year, awarded in the summer and in the winter. The aim is to provide funding (in addition to a proper advance) for research, travel or other necessary expenditure. Grants are available to novelists, poets and writers of non-fiction.

Applicants are welcome who have been commissioned by a commercial British publisher to write a full-length work of fiction, poetry or non-fiction and need funding (in addition to the publisher's advance) for important research, travel, or other more general expenditure; or those without a contractual commitment by a publisher but who have had at least one book published commercially by a British publisher, and there is a strong likelihood that a further book will be published in Britain. Closing dates: 30 April and 30 September.

BAFTA (British Academy of Film and Television Arts)

195 Piccadilly, London W1J 9LN
tel 020-7734 0022
email info@bafta.org
website www.bafta.org
Chief Executive Amanda Berry OBE

The UK's pre-eminent independent charity supporting, developing and promoting the art forms of the moving image (film, TV and games) by identifying and rewarding excellence, inspiring practitioners and benefiting the public. BAFTA's awards are awarded annually by its members to their peers in recognition of their skills and expertise. In addition, BAFTA's year-round learning programme offers unique access to some of the world's most inspiring talent through workshops, masterclasses, lectures and mentoring schemes, connecting with audiences of all ages and backgrounds across the UK, Los Angeles and New York. Founded 1947.

Baileys Women's Prize for Fiction

Book Trust, G8 Battersea Studios,
80 Silverthorne Road, London SW8 3HE
tel 020-7801 8800
email query@booktrust.org.uk
website www.booktrust.org.uk
Contact Laura Mell

The Baileys Prize for Fiction, part managed by Book Trust, features five debut novels and celebrates excellence, originality and accessibility in writing by women in English from throughout the world. Known from 1996 to 2012 as the Orange Prize for Fiction and in 2013 as the Women's Prize for Fiction, it is the UK's most prestigious annual book award for fiction written by a woman and also provides a range of educational, literacy or research initiatives to support reading and writing.

The Baileys Women's Prize for Fiction is awarded annually for the best full novel of the year written by a woman and published in the UK. Any womanwriting in English – whatever her nationality, country of residence, age or subject matter – is eligible. The winner receives a cheque for £30,000 and a limited edition bronze figurine known as a 'Bessie', created and donated by the artist Grizel Niven. The 2014 winner was Eimear McBride for her novel *A Girl is a Half-Formed Thing* (Galley Beggar Press/ Faber).

Bardd Plant Cymru (Welsh-Language Children's Poet Laureate)

Welsh Books Council, Castell Brychan, Aberystwyth, Ceredigion SY23 2JB
tel (01970) 624151
email castellbrychan@wbc.org.uk
website www.cllc.org.uk

The main aim is to raise the profile of poetry amongst children and to encourage them to compose and enjoy poetry. During his/her term of office the bard will visit schools as well as helping children to create poetry through electronic workshops.

The scheme's partner organisations are: S4C, the Welsh Books Council, Urdd Gobaith Cymru and Literature Wales.

Verity Bargate Award

Soho Theatre, 21 Dean Street, London W1D 3NE
email writers@sohotheatre.com
website www.sohotheatre.com

This biennial award is made to the writer of a new and previously unperformed full-length play. It is the only award in the UK designed specifically for emerging writers and is only eligible to playwrights with less than three professional credits. The winner receives: a prize of £5,000 in respect of an exclusive option to produce the play and a residency at the Soho Theatre. Closing date for submissions: to be announced. See website for information on workshops and events associated with the award. Established 1982.

BBC National Short Story Award

Book Trust, G8 Battersea Studios,
80 Silverthorne Road, London SW8 3HE
tel 020-7801 8800
email bbcnssa@booktrust.org.uk
website www.booktrust.org.uk
Contact Jenny Holder

Part of the Book Trust campaign to celebrate short stories, a prize of £15,000 is awarded for the winning story, plus £3,000 for the runner-up and £500 for the three other shortlisted writers. One of the most prestigious prizes for a single short story, the BBC NSSA is run in partnership with Book Trust. Closing date: February.

The David Berry Prize

Administrative Secretary of the Royal Historical Society, University College London, Gower Street, London WC1E 6BT
tel 020-7387 7532
email m.ransom@royalhistsoc.org
website http://royalhistsoc.org/prizes/

Candidates may submit an essay/article of between 6,000 and 10,000 words in length on any subject dealing with Scottish history. Essays/articles already published or selected for future publication are eligible. Value of prize: £250. Closing date: 31 December each year.

Besterman/McColvin Medals – see The ISG Reference Awards

The Biographers' Club Slightly Foxed Best First Biography Prize

Prize Administrator, 79 Arlington Avenue, London N1 7BA
tel 020-7359 7769
email ariane.bankes@googlemail.com
website www.biographersclub.co.uk
Contact Ariane Bankes

The Prize is awarded to the best book written by a first-time biographer as chosen by a panel of judges which, in 2015, includes writer, columnist and playwright Damian Barr, biographer Fiona MacCarthy and Radio 4 *Today* presenter, James Naughtie. The Prize, worth £3,500, is sponsored by *Slightly Foxed, The Real Reader's Quarterly*. Only entries submitted by publishers will be accepted for consideration. Literary memoirs are also eligible but celebrity autobiographies and ghostwritten books are not eligible.

To qualify, books must have a publication date between 1 September and 31 August (proofs are acceptable). Four copies of each book should be submitted no later than 1 July (enclose a press release to confirm publication date) along with an entry form (downloadable from the website) and entry fee of £20 per title. Delivery address: The Slightly Foxed Best First Biography Prize, c/o David Roberts, 133 Albert Street, London NW1 7NB

The Biographers' Club Tony Lothian Prize

Prize Administrator, 79 Arlington Avenue,
London N1 7BA
tel 020-7359 7769
email ariane.bankes@googlemail.com
website www.biographersclub.co.uk
Contact Ariane Bankes

The £2,000 Tony Lothian Prize (sponsored by her daughter, Elizabeth, Duchess of Buccleuch) supports uncommissioned first-time writers working on a biography. Applicants should submit a proposal of no more than 20 pages including a synopsis and ten-page sample chapter (double-spaced, numbered pages), cv and a note on the market for the book and competing literature (all unbound), to the prize administrator. Entry fee: £15. For further details and mandatory entry form, see website.

Luke Bitmead Bursary

The Luke Bitmead Bursary, Legend Press,
The Old Fire Station, 140 Tabernacle Street,
London EC2A 4SD
tel 020-7300 7370
email bitmeadbursary@legendpress.co.uk
website www.legendtimesgroup.com
Judging Coordinators Lucy Chamberlain & Lauren Parsons

The Luke Bitmead Bursary is now one of the UK's biggest prizes for unpublished authors. The award is free to enter, with the winner receiving a publishing contract and £2,500. Submissions can be sent from May to August to bitmeadbursary@legendpress.co.uk (Please check the website for entry details and deadlines). Founded 2006.

Blue Peter Book Awards

Book Trust, G8 Battersea Studios,
80 Silverthorne Road, London SW8 3HE
tel 020-7801 8800
email bluepeter@booktrust.org.uk
website www.booktrust.org.uk
Contact Katherine Woodfine

Awarded annually, winners are shortlisted by a panel of expert adult judges, then a group of young *Blue Peter* viewers judge the two categories, which are: the Best Story and the Best Book with Facts. Winning books are announced on *Blue Peter* in March. Established 2000. *2015 winners*: Pamela Butchart (illustrated by Thomas Flintham) for *The Spy Who Loved School Dinners* and Andy Seed (illustrated by Scott Garrett) for *The Silly Book of Side-Splitting Stuff*.

The K Blundell Trust

The Society of Authors, 84 Drayton Gardens,
London SW10 9SB
tel 020-7373 6642
email info@societyofauthors.org
website www.societyofauthors.org/grants-works-progress

Grants are given to published writers under the age of 40 to assist them with their next book. This work must 'contribute to the greater understanding of existing social and economic organisation' and can be fiction or non-fiction. Closing dates: 30 April and 30 September. Download from the website or send sae for an information sheet.

The Boardman Tasker Prize

Steve Dean, 8 Bank View Road, Darley Abbey,
Derby DE22 1EJ
email steve@people-matter.co.uk
website www.boardmantasker.co.uk

This annual prize of £3,000 is given for a work of fiction, non-fiction or poetry, the central theme of which is concerned with the mountain environment. Authors of any nationality are eligible but the work must be published or distributed in the UK. Entries from publishers only. Founded 1983.

The Bollinger Everyman Wodehouse Prize for Comic Fiction

Four Colman Getty, 20 St Thomas Street,
London SE1 9BF
tel 020-3697 4243
email lucy.hinton@fourcolmangetty.com

UK's only prize for comic fiction. Awarded to the most original comic novel of the previous 12 months. The winner receives a case of Bollinger Special Cuvée, a jeroboam of Bollinger, a complete set of the Everyman Wodehouse collection and a rare breed pig named after the winning novel. Eligible novels are published in the UK between 1 May and 30 April. The winner is announced at the Hay Festival in late May/early June. Closing date: February; shortlist announced in mid-April. Launched in 2000 on the 25th anniversary of the death of P.G. Wodehouse.

The *Bookseller* Industry Awards

Crowne House, 56–68 Southwark Street,
London SE1 1UN
tel 020-3358 0387
email blake.brooks@bookseller.co.uk
website www.thebookseller.com/bookseller-industry-awards/2015

Marketing and Events Coordinator Blake Brooks

Awards to celebrate the best in bookselling, publishing, and other aspects of the UK book industry. Closing date: February.

Alfred Bradley Bursary Award

website www.bbc.co.uk/writersroom

This biennial development opportunity is awarded to a writer or writers resident in the North of England. This scheme allows the winning writer to devote a period of time to writing and to develop an idea for a radio drama commission. Founded 1992.

The Branford Boase Award

8 Bolderwood Close, Bishopstoke, Eastleigh, Hants SO50 8PG
tel 023-8060 0439
email anne.marley@tiscali.co.uk
website www.branfordboaseaward.org.uk

An annual award of £1,000 is made to a first-time writer of a full-length children's novel (age 7+) published in the preceding year; the editor is also recognised. Its aim is to encourage new writers for children and to recognise the role of perceptive editors in developing new talent. The Award was set up in memory of the outstanding children's writer Henrietta Branford and the gifted editor and publisher Wendy Boase who both died in 1999. Closing date for nominations: end of December. Founded 2000.

The Bridport Prize

The Bridport Prize, PO Box 6910, Dorset DT6 9BQ
email info@bridportprize.org.uk
website www.bridportprize.org.uk

Annual prizes are awarded for poetry and short stories (1st £5,000, 2nd £1,000, 3rd £500) in both categories, and £1,000 for short short stories (under 250 words). Entries should be in English, original work, typed or clearly written, and never published, read on radio/TV/stage. Winning stories are read by a leading London literary agent, without obligation, and an anthology of winning entries is published each autumn. Top four poems are submitted to the Forward Poetry Prizes and top 13 eligible stories are submitted to the National Short Story Award and *The Sunday Times* Short Story Prize. Send sae for entry form or enter online. Closing date: 31 May each year.

A new award, the Peggy-Chapman Andrews First Novel Award, was launched in 2014. Enter first chapter(s) of novel, up to 8,000 words plus 300-word synopsis. 1st prize £1,000 plus mentoring and possible publication. Closing date 31 May each year. Send sae for entry form or enter online.

British Academy Medals and Prizes

The British Academy, 10 Carlton House Terrace, London SW1Y 5AH
tel 020-7969 5200
email secretary@britac.ac.uk
website www.britishacademy.ac.uk

A number of prizes and medals are awarded for outstanding work in various fields of the humanities and social sciences on the recommendation of specialist committees: Burkitt Medal (Biblical Studies); Derek Allen Prize (made annually in turn for Musicology, Numismatics and Celtic studies); Brian Barry Prize in Political Science; Edward Ullendorff Medal (Semitic languages and Ethiopian studies); Sir Israel Gollancz Prize (English studies); Grahame Clark Medal (Prehistoric Archaeology); Kenyon Medal (Classical Studies and Archaeology); Rose Mary Crawshay Prize (English Literature); Serena Medal (Italian studies); Leverhulme Medal and Prize (Humanities and Social Sciences); John Coles Medal for Landscape Archaeology; Wiley Prize in Psychology; Wiley Prize in Economics.

British Council Award for ELT Writing

The Society of Authors, 84 Drayton Gardens, London SW10 9SB
tel 020-7373 6642
email info@societyofauthors.org
website www.societyofauthors.org/british-council-elt-award

This is an annual award of £2,000 that recognises an outstanding contribution by an English Language Teaching author or authors. The work must have been first published in English in the UK within the previous calendar year. Deadline 28 February.

British Czech & Slovak Association Writing Competition

24 Ferndale, Tunbridge Wells, Kent TN2 3NS
tel (01892) 543206
email prize@bcsa.co.uk
website www.bcsa.co.uk
Contact BCSA Prize Administrator

Annual competition (1st prize: £300; 2nd prize: £100) for fiction or non-fiction on the theme of the links between Britain and the Czech and Slovak Republics, at any time in their history, or society in transition in those republics since the Velvet Revolution in 1989. Winning entries published in *British Czech & Slovak Review*. Length: 2,000 words max. Entry is free. Closing date: 30 June each year. Established 2002.

British Fantasy Awards

56 Leyton Road, Birmingham B21 9EE
tel 0121-241 5580
email bfsawards@britishfantasysociety.org
website www.britishfantasysociety.org
Awards Administrator Stephen Theaker

The British Fantasy Awards have been awarded since 1972 in up to 14 categories including best novel, novella, short story and collection, and are presented each autumn at FantasyCon to works published the previous year. Past winners include Neil Gaiman,

Angela Slatter, Lavie Tidhar and Tanith Lee. Publishers, writers, editors and readers are able to contribute to a list of eligible works. The shortlist is currently decided by a vote of British Fantasy Society members and FantasyCon attendees, and the winners decided by a jury.

British Sports Book Awards

c/o Agile Marketing, Magnolia House,
172 Winsley Road, Bradford-on-Avon,
Wiltshire BA15 1NY
tel (01225) 865776
email danielle@agile-ideas.com
website www.britishsportsbookawards.co.uk
Contact Danielle Bowers

Sports books published in the UK in hardback or paperback in the calendar year are eligible. Categories include biography, cricket, football, golf, illustrated, motorsports and rugby. Nominations are called in December/January over a four-week period. Winners are announced at an annual awards ceremony in early June. See website for full details.

The Caine Prize for African Writing

Lizzy Attree, Director, The Menier Gallery,
Menier Chocolate Factory, 51 Southwark Street,
London SE5 1RU
tel 020-7378 6234
email info@caineprize.com
website www.caineprize.com

An annual award of £10,000 for a short story published in English (may be a published translation into English) by an African writer in the five years before the closing date, and not previously submitted. Indicative length 3,000–10,000 words. Shortlisted writers will each be awarded £500. Submissions only by publishers. Closing date: 31 January each year. Founded 1999.

Carnegie Medal – see The CILIP Carnegie and Kate Greenaway Awards

The CBI Book of the Year Awards

Children's Books Ireland,
17 North Great George's Street, Dublin 1,
Republic of Ireland
tel +353 (0)1 8727475
email info@childrensbooksireland.ie
website www.childrensbooksireland.ie

These awards are made annually to authors and illustrators born or resident in Ireland and are open to books written in Irish or English. The awards are: CBI Book of the Year, the Eilis Dillon Award (for a first children's book), the Honour Award for Fiction, the Honour Award for Illustration, the Special Judges' Award and the Children's Choice Award. Schools and reading groups nationwide take part in a shadowing scheme: each group reads the shortlisted books and engages with them using the suggested questions and activities in the CBI shadowing packs. Each group then votes for their favourite book, the results of which form the basis for the Children's Choice Award. Closing date: December for work published between 1 January and 31 December of an awards year. Winners announced in May. Founded 1990.

Cheltenham Illustration Awards

email cheltillustrationawards@glos.ac.uk
website www.cheltenham-illustration-awards.com

Exhibition and Annual submissions are invited and can be freely interpreted in a narrative context. Submissions of work are free and open to all students, emerging and established illustrators and graphic novelists. A selection panel will assess entries. The selected work will be showcased in an exhibition and published in the Cheltenham Illustration Awards Annual, which will be distributed to education institutions and publishers. Deadline for submissions. June. See website for further information.

The Children's Laureate

Book Trust, Studio G8, Battersea Studios,
80 Silverthorne Road, London SW8 3HE
tel 020-7801 8800
email childrenslaureate@booktrust.org.uk
website www.childrenslaureate.org.uk
Contact Katherine Woodfine

The idea for the Children's Laureate originated from a conversation between (the then) Poet Laureate Ted Hughes and children's writer Michael Morpurgo. The post was established in 1999 to celebrate exceptional children's authors and illustrators and to acknowledge their importance in creating the readers of tomorrow. Quentin Blake was the first Children's Laureate (1999–2001), followed by Anne Fine (2001–2003), Michael Morpurgo (2003–2005), Jacqueline Wilson (2005–2007), Michael Rosen (2007–2009), Anthony Browne (2009–2011), Julia Donaldson (2011–2013) and Malorie Blackman (2013–2015).

Cholmondeley Awards

The Society of Authors, 84 Drayton Gardens,
London SW10 9SB
tel 020-7373 6642
email info@societyofauthors.org
website www.societyofauthors.org

These honorary awards are to recognise the achievement and distinction of individual poets. Submissions are not accepted. Total value of awards about £8,000. Established by the then Dowager Marchioness of Cholmondeley in 1965.

The CILIP Carnegie and Kate Greenaway Awards

CILIP, 7 Ridgmount Street, London WC1E 7AE
tel 020-7255 0650

email ckg@cilip.org.uk
website www.carnegiegreenaway.org.uk

Recommendations for the following two awards are invited from members of CILIP (the Chartered Institute of Library and Information Professionals), who are asked to submit a preliminary list of not more than two titles for each award, accompanied by a 50-word appraisal justifying the recommendation of each book. The awards are selected by the Youth Libraries Group of CILIP.

Carnegie Medal

Awarded annually for an outstanding book for children (fiction or non-fiction) written in English and first published in the UK during the preceding year or co-published elsewhere within a three-month time lapse.

Kate Greenaway Medal

Awarded annually for an outstanding illustrated book for children first published in the UK during the preceding year or co-published elsewhere within a three-month time lapse. Books intended for older as well as younger children are included, and reproduction will be taken into account. The Colin Mears Award (£5,000) is awarded annually to the winner of the Kate Greenaway Medal.

Arthur C. Clarke Award

website www.clarkeaward.com

An annual award of £2,015 plus engraved bookend is given for the best science fiction novel with first UK publication during the previous calendar year. Titles are submitted by publishers. Founded 1985.

The David Cohen Prize for Literature

Book Trust, G8 Battersea Studios,
80 Silverthorne Road, London SW8 3HE
tel 020-7801 8800
email prizes@booktrust.org.uk
website www.booktrust.org.uk
Contact Laura Mell

Established in 1993, the David Cohen Prize for Literature is one of the UK's most distinguished literary prizes. It recognises writers who use the English language and are citizens of the United Kingdom or the Republic of Ireland, encompassing dramatists as well as novelists, poets and essayists. Former winners include Harold Pinter, William Trevor, Doris Lessing, Seamus Heaney, Hilary Mantel and, most recently in 2015, Tony Harrison.

The biennial prize, of £40,000, is for a lifetime's achievement and is donated by the John S. Cohen Foundation. Established in 1965 by David Cohen and his family, the trust supports education, the arts, conservation and the environment. Arts Council England provides a further £12,500 (The Clarissa Luard Award), which the winner of the David Cohen Prize awards to a literature organisation that supports young writers or an individual writer under the age of 35.

Commonwealth Short Story Prize

Commonwealth Foundation, Marlborough House, Pall Mall, London SW1Y 5HY
email writers@commonwealth.int
website www.commonwealthwriters.org

The Short Story Prize is part of Commonwealth Writers, the cultural initiative from the Commonwealth Foundation, which inspires, develops and connects writers and storytellers in a range of disciplines. It then links them to groups which seek to bring about social change. The Commonwealth Short Story Prize is awarded for the best piece of unpublished short fiction (2,000–5,000 words) in English. The overall winner receives £5,000. Regional winners receive £2,500. Short stories translated into English from other languages are also eligible.

The Pol Roger Duff Cooper Prize

Artemis Cooper, 54 St Maur Road, London SW6 4DP
tel 020-7736 3729
website www.theduffcooperprize.org

An annual prize for a literary work in the field of biography, history, politics or poetry published in English and submitted by a recognised publisher during the previous 12 months. The prize of £5,000 comes from a Trust Fund established by the friends and admirers of Duff Cooper, 1st Viscount Norwich (1890–1954) after his death.

Cordon d'Or – Gold Ribbon Culinary Academy Awards

7312 6th Avenue North, St Petersburg, FL 33710, USA
email cordondor@aol.com
website www.cordondorcuisine.com
website www.culinaryambassadorofireland.com
Contact Noreen Kinney, President

Awards for authors, writers, journalists, photographers, newsletters, websites, cookbooks and culinary literature. Overall winner receives $1,000. See website for details. Founded 2003.

Costa Book Awards

(formerly the Whitbread Book Awards)
The Booksellers Association, 6 Bell Yard, London WC2A 2JR
tel 020-7421 4640
email naomi.gane@booksellers.org.uk
website www.costabookawards.com
Contact Naomi Gane

The awards celebrate and promote the most enjoyable contemporary British writing. There are five categories: Novel, First Novel, Biography, Poetry and Children's. Each category is judged by a panel of three judges and the winner in each category receives £5,000. Nine final judges then choose the Costa Book of the Year from the five category winners. The overall winner receives £30,000. Authors of submitted books must have been resident in the UK or Ireland for over six months of each of the previous three years (although UK or Irish nationality is not essential). Books must have been first published in the UK or Ireland between 1 November of the previous year and 31 October of the current year. Books previously published elsewhere are not eligible. Submissions must be received from publishers. Closing date: end of June.

The Rose Mary Crawshay Prize

The British Academy, 10–11 Carlton House Terrace, London SW1Y 5AH
tel 020-7969 5200
website www.britishacademy.ac.uk

The Rose Mary Crawshay Prize, worth £500, is awarded each year to a woman of any nationality for a historical or critical work on any subject connected with English literature which has been published in the three years preceding the award. Nominations are invited from Fellows of the British Academy and, under the original terms of the prize, preference is given to a work regarding Byron, Shelley or Keats. Founded 1888.

Creative Scotland

tel 0330 333 2000
email enquiries@creativescotland.com
website www.creativescotland.com

Support is offered to writers, playwrights and publishers through Open Project Funding. See www.creativescotland.com for details. See also Scottish Children's Book Awards (page 557).

CWA Dagger Awards

Crime Writers' Association, PO Box 3408, Norwich, NR3 3WE
email director@thecwa.co.uk
website www.thecwa.co.uk

CWA Awards for crime writing: the Diamond Dagger, the Goldsboro Gold Dagger, the Ian Fleming Steel Dagger, the John Creasey Dagger, the International Dagger, the Non-fiction Dagger, the Dagger in the Library, the Short Story Dagger, the Debut Dagger, the Endeavour Historical Dagger. See website for details. The CWA Margery Allingham Short Story Competition is open to unpublished stories of up to 3,000 words. The competition is open to both published and unpublished authors. See website for details.

The Roald Dahl Funny Prize

Book Trust, G8 Battersea Studios,
80 Silverthorne Road, London SW8 3HE
tel 020-7801 8800
email prizes@booktrust.org.uk
website www.booktrust.org.uk
Contact Claire Shanahan

Founded by Michael Rosen, Children's Laureate (2007–9), this prize is unique in its aim to honour the funniest children's books of the year. This is part of the wider objective of promoting and drawing attention to humour in children's literature. The winners of the two categories, the Funniest Book for Children Aged 6 and Under and the Funniest Book for Children Aged 7–14, are awarded £2,500 each, as well as both receiving a bottle of wine from the Dahl family's wine cellar. Fiction, non-fiction and poetry are welcomed in each category. The Prize is currently on hold.

The Rhys Davies Trust

Prof. Meic Stephens, The Secretary,
The Rhys Davies Trust, 10 Heol Don, Whitchurch, Cardiff CF14 2AU

The Trust aims to foster Welsh writing in English and offers financial assistance to English-language literary projects in Wales, directly or in association with other bodies.

Deutsche Börse Photography Prize

The Photographers' Gallery, 16–18 Ramillies Street, London W1F 7LW
tel 020-7087 9300
email info@tpg.org.uk
website www.thephotographersgallery.org.uk

Aims to reward a living photographer, of any nationality, who has made the most significant contribution to the medium of photography during the past year (1st prize £30,000). Founded in 1996 by the Photographers' Gallery.

Dundee International Book Prize

email bookprize@dundee.ac.uk
website www.dundeebookprize.com

A prize (£10,000 and the chance of publication by Cargo) awarded for an unpublished novel by a debut author. Founded 1996.

Edge Hill Short Story Prize

Edge Hill University, St Helens Road, Ormskirk, Lancs. L39 4QP
tel (01695) 584121
email ailsa.cox@edgehill.ac.uk
website www.edgehill.ac.uk/shortstory
Contact Ailsa Cox

This prize is awarded annually by Edge Hill University for excellence in a published single author short story collection. The winner will receive £5,000 and a Readers' Choice prize of £1,000 is awarded to a writer from the shortlist. Publishers are entitled to submit collections published during the preceding year. Authors must be born or normally resident in the British Isles (including Ireland). Deadline: 1 March.

The T.S. Eliot Prize

Poetry Book Society, The Dutch House,
307–308 High Holborn, London WC1V 7LL

tel 020-7831 7468
email info@poetrybooks.co.uk
website www.poetrybooks.co.uk

An annual prize of £20,000, with £1,500 for each of the ten shortlisted poets, is awarded by the Poetry Book Society to the best collection of new poetry published in the UK or the Republic of Ireland during the year. Submissions are invited from publishers in the summer. The prize money is provided by Valerie Eliot. The prize is accompanied by a shadowing scheme for schools, which enables students to read the best new poetry and shadow the judges. Founded 1993.

The Desmond Elliott Prize

Emma Manderson, Administrator,
The Desmond Elliott Charitable Trust,
84 Godolphin Road, London W12 8JW
tel 020-8222 6580
email ema.manderson@googlemail.com
website www.desmondelliottprize.org

An annual prize for a first novel written in English by an author resident in the UK or Ireland and published in the UK. Worth £10,000 to the winner, the prize is named after the literary agent and publisher, Desmond Elliott, who died in 2003. Qualities the judges will be looking for are: a debut novel of depth and breadth with a compelling narrative, original and arresting characters, vividly written and confidently realised. Founded 2007.

Encore Award 2015

email encoreprize@hotmail.co.uk
website www.encoreaward.com

The prize of £10,000 is awarded annually to a UK or Commonwealth writer whose second novel is first published in the UK between 1 January and 31 December 2015. All books must be submitted via the publisher; direct submissions from authors cannot be accepted. Self-published books or those published by vanity publishers cannot be accepted. The closing date for submissions is 1 November. Submission suggestions should be sent by email. Founded 1990.

The European Poetry Translation Prize

Competition Organiser, The Poetry Society,
22 Betterton Street, London WC2H 9BX
tel 020-7420 9880
email info@poetrysociety.org.uk
website www.poetrysociety.org.uk

Awarded biennially by the Poetry Society, the European Poetry Translation Prize (formerly the Popescu Prize) rewards a published collection of poetry translated from a European language into English. Previous winners include Alice Oswald, Judith Wilkinson and David Constantine. Founded 2003.

The European Publishers Award

website www.europhotobookaward.eu

Annual competition for the best set of photographs suitable for publication as a book. All photographic material must be completed and unpublished in book form and be original. Projects conceived as anthologies are not acceptable. Copyright must belong to the photographer. See website for details. Founded 1994.

The Geoffrey Faber Memorial Prize

An annual prize of £1,000 is awarded in alternate years for a volume of verse and for a volume of prose fiction, first published originally in the UK during the two years preceding the year in which the award is given which is, in the opinion of the judges, of the greatest literary merit. Eligible writers must be not more than 40 years old at the date of publication of the book and a citizen of the UK and Colonies, of any other Commonwealth state or of the Republic of Ireland. The three judges are reviewers of poetry or fiction who are nominated each year by the literary editors of newspapers and magazines which regularly publish such reviews. Faber and Faber invite nominations from reviewers and literary editors. No submissions for the prize are to be made. Established in 1963 by Faber and Faber Ltd, as a memorial to the founder and first Chairman of the firm.

The Alfred Fagon Award

email info@alfredfagonaward.co.uk
website www.alfredfagonaward.co.uk

An annual award of £6,000 for the Best New Play of the Year (which need not have been produced) for the theatre in English. TV and radio plays and film scripts will not be considered. Only writers of Caribbean and African descent resident in the UK are eligible. Applicants should submit two copies of their play plus sae for return of their script and a CV which includes details of the writer's Caribbean and African connection. Closing date: end August. Founded 1997.

The Eleanor Farjeon Award

website www.childrensbookcircle.org.uk

An annual award which may be given to an individual or an organisation. Librarians, authors, publishers, teachers, reviewers and others who have given exceptional service to the children's book industry are eligible for nomination. It was instituted in 1965 by the Children's Book Circle (page 503) for distinguished services to children's books and named after the much-loved children's writer Eleanor Farjeon.

Financial Times and McKinsey Business Book of the Year Award

email bookaward@ft.com
website www.ft.com/bookaward

This award aims to identify the book that provides the most compelling and enjoyable insight into modern business issues including management, finance and economics. Submissions should be made via the publisher. The winner will receive £30,000 and each runner up £10,000. Closing date: end June.

Fish Publishing Prizes

Fish Publishing, Durrus, Bantry, Co. Cork, Republic of Ireland
email info@fishpublishing.com
website www.fishpublishing.com

International writing prizes set up to publish and encourage new writers. There are a number of prizes available including the Fish Short Story Prize, the Fish Short Memoir Prize, the Fish Flash Fiction Prize and the Fish Poetry Prize. For full details see website. Established 1994.

The Folio Prize

email suzy@thefolioprize.com
email fionam@fmcm.co.uk
website www.folioprize.com
Executive Director Suzy Lucas, *Strategic Director & PR* Fiona McMorrough

The Folio Prize is the first major English language book prize open to writers from around the world. Its aim is simple: to celebrate the best fiction of our time, regardless of form or genre, and to bring it to the attention of as many readers as possible. Through The Folio Prize Academy, an international group of people who write, review and delight in books, it will discover and promote excellence in writing, encouraging people to put great literature at the centre of their lives. The prize is worth £40,000.

The Folio Prize is open to all works of fiction written in English and published in the UK. All genres and forms of fiction are eligible. The format of first publication may be print or digital. See the website for dates and submission guidelines.

The Paul Foot Award

c/o Private Eye, 6 Carlisle Street, London W1D 3BN
tel 020-7437 4017
email maisie.glazebrook@private-eye.co.uk
website www.private-eye.co.uk
Contact Maisie Glazebrook

Private Eye magazine and *The Guardian* newspaper set up the award for investigative and campaigning journalism in memory of revered investigative journalist Paul Foot. See the website for details.

E.M. Forster Award

American Academy of Arts and Letters, 633 West 155th Street, New York, NY 10032, USA
tel +1 212-368-5900
email academy@artsandletters.org
website www.artsandletters.org

The distinguished English author, E.M. Forster, bequeathed the American publication rights and royalties of his posthumous novel *Maurice* to Christopher Isherwood, who transferred them to the American Academy of Arts and Letters, for the establishment of an E.M. Forster Award, currently $20,000, to be given annually to a British or Irish writer for a stay in the USA. Applications for this award are not accepted.

Forward Prizes for Poetry

Forward Prizes for Poetry, c/o The Royal Society for Literature, Somerset House, Strand, London WC2R 1LA
tel 020-7845 4655
email info@forwardartsfoundation.org
website www.forwardartsfoundation.org

Three prizes are awarded annually:

• The Forward Prize for Best Collection published in the UK and Republic of Ireland between 1 October and 30 September (£10,000);
• The Felix Dennis Prize for Best First Collection published between 1 October and 30 September (£5,000); and
• The Forward Prize for Best Single Poem in memory of Michael Donaghy, published but not as part of a collection between 29 March and 27 March (£1,000).

All poems entered are also considered for inclusion in the *Forward Book of Poetry*, an annual anthology. Entries for the Best Collection and Best First Collection must be submitted by book publishers and, for Best Single Poem, by editors of newspapers, periodicals and magazines in the UK and Ireland. Entries accepted online or via postal form. See website for details. Entries from individual poets of their unpublished or self-published work will not be accepted. Established 1992.

Miles Franklin Literary Award

tel +61 (0)2 8295 8100
email milesfranklin@thetrustcompany.com.au
website www.milesfranklin.com.au

This annual award is for a novel or play first published in the preceding year, which presents Australian life in any of its phases. More than one entry may be submitted by each author. Biographies, collections of short stories or children's books are not eligible. See website for details. Founded 1954.

The Lionel Gelber Prize

Prize Manager, The Lionel Gelber Prize, c/o Munk School of Global Affairs, University of Toronto, 1 Devonshire Place, Toronto, Ontario M5S 3K7, Canada
tel +1 416-946 8901
email gelberprize.munk@utoronto.ca
website www.utoronto.ca/munk/gelber

This international prize is awarded annually in Canada to the author of the year's most outstanding work of non-fiction in the field of international relations. Submissions must be published in English or in English translation. Books must be submitted by the publisher. Full eligibility details are on website. Established 1989.

Gladstone History Book Prize

Administrative Secretary, Royal Historical Society, University College London, Gower Street, London WC1E 6BT
tel 020-7387 7532
email m.ransom@royalhistsoc.org
website http://royalhistsoc.org/prizes/

An annual award (value £1,000) for a history book. The book must:

• be on any historical subject which is not primarily related to British history;
• be its author's first solely written history book;
• have been published in English during the previous calendar year;
• be an original and scholarly work of historical research.

One non-returnable copy of an eligible book should be submitted by the publisher before 31 December. Should the book be shortlisted, two further copies will be required.

The Goethe-Institut Award for New Translation

The Society of Authors, 84 Drayton Gardens, London SW10 9SB
tel 020-7373 6642
email info@societyofauthors.org
website www.societyofauthors.org/german-embassy-award-translators

This award is open to British translators of literature who translate from German into the English language. The winner will be awarded prize money of €1,000, a place at the International Translator's seminar including a visit to the Leipzig Book Fair and a four-week working stay at the Literarisches Colloquium Berlin following the Leipzig Bookfair. The next award will be in 2016.

The Gourmand World Cookbook Awards

Pintor Rosales 50, 28008, Madrid, Spain
tel +34-91-541-67-68
email pilar@gourmandbooks.com
email edouard@gourmandbooks.com
website www.cookbookfair.com
President Edouard Cointreau

The annual Gourmand World Cookbook Awards were created by Edouard Cointreau in 1995. Entries are free and any book published within the year can be entered by anyone sending three copies of the book to the Gourmand Library at: Luis Velez de Guevara, 8, bajo A, 28012, Madrid, Spain. The Gourmand Library was created in 2013 to house the reference collection of cookbook and wine book titles of the awards. For futher details about past winners, see the website.

Kate Greenaway Medal – see The CILIP Carnegie and Kate Greenaway Awards

The Eric Gregory Trust Fund

The Society of Authors, 84 Drayton Gardens, London SW10 9SB
tel 020-7373 6642
email info@societyofauthors.org
website www.societyofauthors.org/eric-gregory

These awards are for poets under the age of 30, made annually for the encouragement of young poets who can show that they are likely to benefit from an opportunity to give more time to writing. Candidates must be British subjects by birth, but not a national of Eire or any of the British dominions or colonies, and be ordinarily resident in the UK or Northern Ireland. Candidates must be under the age of 30 on 31 March in the year of the Award (i.e. the year following submission). The work submitted may be a published or unpublished volume of poetry, drama-poems or belles-lettres, and no more than 30 poems should be submitted. Closing date: 31 October.

Griffin Poetry Prize

The Griffin Trust for Excellence in Poetry, 363 Parkridge Crescent, Oakville, Ontario L6M 1A8
tel +1 905-618 0420
email info@griffinpoetryprize.com
website www.griffinpoetryprize.com

Two annual prizes of Can$65,000 will be awarded for collections of poetry published in English during the preceding year. One prize will go to a living Canadian poet, the other to a living poet from any country. Collections of poetry translated into English from other languages are also eligible and will be assessed for their literary quality in English. Submissions only from publishers. Closing date: 31 December. Founded 2000.

The Guardian Children's Fiction Prize

email childrensprize@guardian.co.uk
website www.guardian.co.uk/books/guardianchildrensfictionprize

The *Guardian's* annual prize is for a work of fiction for children published by a British or Commonwealth writer. See website for eligibility, submission guidelines and closing dates.

The Guardian First Book Award

email firstbook@guardian.co.uk
website www.theguardian.com/books/guardianfirstbookaward

The award recognises and rewards new writing by honouring an author's first book. For full details, see website.

The Guardian Research Fellowship

Academic Administrator, The Guardian Research Fellowship, Nuffield College, Oxford OX1 1NF
tel (01865) 278542

A biennial Fellowship to be held for one year at Nuffield College, Oxford, to research or study any project related to the experience of working in the media. It is hoped that the Fellow will produce a book or substantial piece of written work. The Fellow will be asked to give the *Guardian* lecture following the end of their Fellowship. The Fellowship is open to people working in newspapers, TV, the internet or other media. Founded 1987.

Hawthornden Fellowships

The Administrator, International Retreat for Writers, Hawthornden Castle, Lasswade, Midlothian EH18 1EG
tel 0131 440 2180
email office@hawthornden.org

Applications are invited from novelists, poets, dramatists and other creative writers whose work has already been published. The Retreat provides four-week fellowships in a peaceful setting. Application forms are available from January for Fellowships awarded in the following year. Deadline for applications 30 June.

The Hawthornden Prize

The Administrator, International Retreat for Writers, Hawthornden Castle, Lasswade, Midlothian EH18 1EG
email office@hawthornden.org

This prize of £10,000 is awarded annually to the author of what, in the opinion of the judges, is the best work of imaginative literature published during the preceding calendar year by a British author. Books are chosen rather than received by submission.

Francis Head Bequest

Sarah Baxter, The Society of Authors, 84 Drayton Gardens, London SW10 9SB
tel 020-7373 6642
email sbaxter@societyofauthors.org
website www.societyofauthors.org

This fund provides grants to published British authors over the age of 35 who need financial help during a period of illness, disablement or temporary financial crisis. Apply for guidelines and application form.

The Hessell-Tiltman History Prize

English PEN, 60 Farringdon Road, London EC1R 3GA
tel 020-7324 2535
email enquiries@englishpen.org
website www.englishpen.org/events/prizes/hessell-tiltman-prize

An annual prize of £2,000 awarded to a non-fiction work of high literary merit covering any historical period until the end of the 1960s. Biography and autobiography are excluded. Submissions must come through publishers. Full details can be found on the English PEN website. Founded 2002.

William Hill Sports Book of the Year Award

Graham Sharpe/Romaine Snijder, William Hill Organisation, Greenside House, 50 Station Road, London N22 4TP
tel 020-8918 3731
website www.williamhillmedia.com

This award is given annually in November for a book with a sporting theme. The title must be in the English language, and published for the first time in the UK during the relevant calendar year. Total value of prize is £30,000, including £27,000 in cash. 2015 winner: *Night Games* by Anna Krien (Yellow Jersey Press). Founded 1989.

The Calvin and Rose G. Hoffman Memorial Prize for Distinguished Publication on Christopher Marlowe

The Hoffman Administrator, The King's School, 25 The Precincts, Canterbury, Kent CT1 2ES
tel (01227) 595544
email bursar@kings-bursary.co.uk

This annual prize is awarded to the writer of the best distinguished scholarly essay on Christopher Marlowe. Closing date: 1 September.

L. Ron Hubbard's Writers and Illustrators of the Future Contests

email writersofthefutureuk@gmail.com
website www.writersofthefuture.com
Administrator Andrea Grant-Webb

Aims to encourage new and aspiring writers and illustrators of science fiction and fantasy. In addition to the quarterly prizes there is an annual prize of £2,500 for each contest. All 24 winners are invited to the annual L. Ron Hubbard Achievement Awards, which include a series of writers' and illustrators' workshops, and their work is published in an anthology.

Writers of the Future Contest

Entrants should submit a short story of up to 10,000 words or a novelette of less than 17,000 words. Prizes of £600 (1st), £450 (2nd) and £300 (3rd) are awarded each quarter. Founded 1984.

Illustrators of the Future Contest

Entrants should submit three b&w illustrations on different themes. Three prizes of £300 are awarded each quarter. Founded 1988.

The Ted Hughes Award for New Work in Poetry

Competition Organiser, The Poetry Society, 22 Betterton Street, London WC2H 9BX
tel 020-7420 9880
email tedhughesaward@poetrysociety.org.uk
website www.poetrysociety.org.uk

An annual award of £5,000 for a living UK poet, working in any form, who has made the most exciting contribution to poetry over the year. Organised by the Poetry Society and funded by Carol Ann Duffy with the honorarium which the Poet Laureate traditionally receives from H.M. the Queen.

The Imison Award

Jo McCrum, The Broadcasting Committee,
The Society of Authors, 84 Drayton Gardens,
London SW10 9SB
tel 020-7373 6642
email info@societyofauthors.org
website www.societyofauthors.org/imisonaward

This annual prize of £1,500 (sponsored by the Peggy Ramsay Foundation) is awarded to any new writer of original audio drama first produced and broadcast (nationally or online) in the UK between 1 October 2015 and 31 October 2016. Founded 1994.

The Impress Prize for New Writers

Innovation Centre, Rennes Drive,
University of Exeter, Devon EX4 4RN
tel (01392) 950910
email enquiries@impress-books.co.uk
website www.impress-books.co.uk
Contacts Richard Willis, Colin Morgan

This prize aims to find exciting new, unpublished writing talent. The winner will receive a publishing contract from Impress Books and will be chosen from a shortlist by a panel of judges working in the book industry. Entry fee: £15. Established 2006.

Independent Foreign Fiction Prize

Book Trust, G8 Battersea Studios,
80 Silverthorne Road, London SW8 3HE
tel 020-7801 8800
email iffp@booktrust.org.uk
website www.booktrust.org.uk
Contact Jenny Holder

This prize honours the best work of fiction by a living author which has been translated into English and published in the UK during the prize year. Uniquely, this prize gives the winning author and translator equal status: they each receive £5,000. The prize ran until 1995 and was then revived in 2000 with the support of Arts Council England, which continues to fund the award in association with Champagne Tattinger and the *Independent*. This prize also forms part of the Book Trust campaign to celebrate translated fiction. The Independent Foreign Fiction Prize 2016 will invite publishers to submit entries from 8 August to 16 September 2015.

2014 winners: *The Iraqi Christ* written by Hassan Blasim, translated from Arabic by Jonathan Wright (Comma Press). Established 1990.

International IMPAC Dublin Literary Award

The International IMPAC Dublin Literary Award,
Dublin City Library & Archive,
138–144 Pearse Street, Dublin 2, Republic of Ireland
tel +353 (0)1 6744802
email literaryaward@dublincity.ie
website www.impacdublinaward.ie
website www.impacdublinaward.com
Contact Award Administrator

This award is the largest and most international prize of its kind. Administered by Dublin City Public Libraries, nominations are made by libraries in capital and major cities throughout the world. Novels are nominated solely on the basis of 'high literary merit'. Books may be written in any language, but must be translated into English.

The prize is €100,000 which is awarded to the author if the book is written in English. If the winning book is in English translation, the author receives €75,000 and the translator €25,000. The Award, an initiative of Dublin City Council. Established 1996.

International Playwriting Festival

87 Great Titchfield Street, London W1W 6RL
website www.internationalplaywritingfestival.com
Festival Patron Thelma Holt CBE

The International Playwriting Festival has been discovering and promoting the work of new playwrights since 1986. Over the years it consolidated the role of the Warehouse Theatre Company as a powerhouse of new writing. Warehouse Phoenix has now taken over this role which it will continue to enhance. The IPF is held in two parts: the first is a competition with entries from all over the world accepted between April–November which is judged by a panel of distinguished theatre practitioners; the second is a showcase of the selected plays (with a view to a later full scale production) which is held the following May. The IPF's international partners, *Premio Candoni* in Italy and *Theatro Ena* in Cyprus enable the work of selected writers to be presented across Europe. See rules and entry details on the website.

The Bord Gáis Energy Irish Book Awards

137 Hillside, Dalkley, County Dublin,
Republic of Ireland
+353 (0)85 1449574
email bert@agile-ideas.com
website www.irishbookawards.ie
IBA Executive Director Alastair Giles, *IBA Project Administrator* Bert Wright

The Irish Book Awards began life as The Hughes & Hughes Irish Novel of the Year and slowly developed into a multi-category awards project for Irish publishing as a whole. Each year 400 books are submitted for consideration in ten categories, each separately sponsored. Over 40,000 readers vote to select the winners in each category. Libraries and bookshops showcase the best books of the year in the critical sales period of the fourth quarter. Bord Gáis Energy is the headline sponsor.

The Lifetime Achievement Award has been awarded to literary greats such as John McGahern, William Trevor, Edna O'Brien, Maeve Binchy and Seamus Heaney. Exclusively Irish, inclusive in every other sense, the Bord Gáis Energy Irish Book Awards brings together the entire literary community, including readers, authors, booksellers, publishers and librarians, like no other awards.

Books must have been published within the current awards year, i.e. between 1 November and 31 October the following year. Authors must be Irish by birth, citizenship or long-term residence. Books must be original and not reprints or translations/ adaptations of previously-published books. Submissions open: 31 March; shortlist announced: late October; Awards ceremony: late November.

The ISG Reference Awards

CILIP, 7 Ridgemount Street, London WC1E 7AE
tel 020-7255 0500
email isgrefawards@cilip.org.uk
website www.cilip.org.uk/isg

The Besterman/McColvin Medals

Awarded annually for outstanding works of reference that have become available and relevant to the library and information sector in the UK within the preceding year. There are two categories, one for electronic formats and one for printed works. Recommendations are invited from Members of CILIP (the Chartered Institute of Library and Information Professionals), publishers and others, who are asked to submit a preliminary list of not more than three titles via email. Winners receive a certificate.

The Walford Award

Awarded annually to an individual for outstanding contribution to the world of reference and information services. Recommendations may be made for the work of a living person or persons, or for an organisation. The winner receives a certificate and a cheque for £50.

Jewish Quarterly – Wingate Literary Prizes

website www.jewishquarterly.org

Annual prize of £4,000 awarded for a work of fiction or non-fiction which best stimulates an interest in and awareness of themes of Jewish concern among a wider reading public. Founded 1977.

Samuel Johnson Prize for Non-Fiction

Four Colman Getty, 20 St Thomas Street, London SE1 9BF
tel 020-3697 4200
email info@samueljohnsonprize.com
website www.thesamueljohnsonprize.co.uk
Contact Sarah Watson

This annual prize is the biggest non-fiction prize in the UK and is worth £20,000. Closing date: June/July. Founded 1999.

Kent and Sussex Poetry Society Open Poetry Competition

The Competition Organiser, 26 Courtlands, Teston, Maidstone, Kent ME18 5AS
email kentandsussexpoetry@gmail.com
website www.kentandsussexpoetry.com

This competition is open to all unpublished poems, no longer than 40 lines. Prizes: 1st £1,000, 2nd £300, 3rd £100, 4th, four at £50. Closing date: 31 January. Entry fee £5 per poem (£4 per poem if submitting 3+ poems). Founded 1985.

Kerry Group Irish Novel of the Year Award

Listowel Writers' Week, 24 The Square, Listowel, Co. Kerry, Republic of Ireland
tel +353 (0)68 21074
email info@writersweek.ie
website www.writersweek.ie
Contacts Maire Logue, Eilish Wren

An annual award of €15,000 for a published novel by an Irish author; must be published between 1 February 2015 and 1 February 2016. No entry fee. Submit six copies. Closing date 1 February 2016. Listowel Writers' Week is an acclaimed literary festival devoted to bringing together writers and audiences at unique and innovative events in the historic and intimate surroundings of Listowel, County Kerry. Events include workshops, readings, seminars, lectures, book launches, art exhibitions and a comprehensive children's and teenagers' programme. Founded 1971.

The Kitschies

c/o BGV/Makerversity, Somerset House, London WC2R 1LA
email submissions@thekitschies.com
website www.thekitschies.com
Director Glen Mehn

The Kitschies reward the year's most progressive, intelligent and entertaining works that contain elements of the speculative or fantastic. Open for submissions in late spring/early summer and closed in late autumn/early winter, with awards presented in late winter each year. Prizes total £2,500 thanks to sponsor Fallen London, and there is no fee to enter. Founded 2009.

Kraszna-Krausz Awards

email info@kraszna-krausz.org.uk
website www.kraszna-krausz.org.uk

Awards totalling over £10,000 are made each year for the best photography book and best moving image book published in English. Entries to be submitted by publishers only. The Foundation also presents the Outstanding Contribution to Publishing Award and supports the National Media Museum First Book Award. Instituted in 1985.

Leverhulme Research Fellowships

The Leverhulme Trust, 1 Pemberton Row, London EC4A 3BG
tel 020-7042 9861

email agrundy@leverhulme.ac.uk
website www.leverhulme.ac.uk

The Leverhulme Trust Board offer annually approximately 90 fellowships to experienced researchers in aid of original research. These awards are not available as replacement for past support from other sources. Applications in all subject areas are considered, with the exception of clinical medical or pharmaceutical research. Applications must be completed online by early November 2015 for 2016 awards. Refer to the website for further details. Founded 1933.

Listowel Writers' Week Poetry Competitions

Listowel Writers' Week, 24 The Square, Listowel, Co. Kerry, Republic of Ireland
tel +353 (0)68 21074
email info@writersweek.ie
website www.writersweek.ie
Contacts Maire Logue, Eilish Wren

Holds four poetry competitions (poetry single, poetry collection, poetry book, short poem), with various prizes. Contact as above for full details and submission guidelines. No entry form required. Closing date for poetry book 29 January 2016. Closing date for other poetry competitions, 29 February 2016. Founded 1971.

The London Hellenic Prize

The Hellenic Centre, 16–18 Paddington Street, London W1U 5AS
email enquiries@londonhellenicprize.org
website www.londonhellenicprize.org
Prize Coordinator Michael Moschos, *Assistant* Jason Leech

Established in 1996 by the London Hellenic Society, the Prize (formerly the Criticos Prize) is worth £10,000 and runs annually with a submission deadline of 31 January for books published in the preceding calendar year. It is awarded to authors of original works written in (or translated into) English and inspired by Greece or Greek exploits, culture or history at any time from the ancient past to the present day. Although the Prize will always strive to recognise works of excellence, any winner must be accessible to a broad readership. Individual applicants or their publishers may submit any number of titles (two copies of each). Further details are available on the website or by contacting the email address above.

London Press Club Awards

c/o London & Partners, 6th Floor, 2 More Riverside, London SE1 2RR
tel 020-7520 9082
email info@londonpressclub.co.uk
website www.londonpressclub.co.uk

The London Press Club is a membership organisation for journalists and other media professionals. It organises debates, Q&As and social events at exclusive venues across the capital, as well as the annual Press Ball. The London Press Club Awards take place each spring, honouring the following categories: Daily Newspaper of the Year, Sunday Newspaper of the Year, Business Journalist of the Year, Scoop of the Year, Blog of the Year, Reviewer of the Year, Broadcast Journalist of the Year, the Edgar Wallace Award and Londoner of the Year.

The Elizabeth Longford Grants

The Society of Authors, 84 Drayton Gardens, London SW10 9SB
tel 020-7373 6642
email info@societyofauthors.org
website www.societyofauthors.org/grants-works-progress

One grant of £2,500 is available each half year to a historical biographer working on a commissioned book. Sponsored by Flora Fraser and Peter Soros. Entry dates: 30 April and 30 September. See website or send sae for information.

The Elizabeth Longford Prize for Historical Biography

The Society of Authors, 84 Drayton Gardens, London SW10 9SB
tel 020-7373 6642
email info@societyofauthors.org
website www.societyofauthors.org

A prize of £5,000 is awarded annually for a historical biography published in the year preceding the prize. Established in 2003 in affectionate memory of Elizabeth Longford, the acclaimed biographer, and sponsored by Flora Fraser and Peter Soros. See website or send sae for information. Submissions are not accepted.

The Sir William Lyons Award

The Guild of Motoring Writers' Secretariat, 40 Baring Road, Bournemouth BH6 4DT
tel (01202) 422424
email generalsec@gomw.co.uk
website www.gomw.co.uk

Sponsored by Jaguar Cars in memory of Sir William Lyons, founder and president of Jaguar Cars, this annual award – trophy, £2,000 and two years' provisional membership of The Guild of Motoring Writers – was set up to encourage young people to foster interest in motoring and the motor industry through automotive journalism. Open to any person of British nationality resident in the UK aged 17–23 years at the closing date of 1 October. Full details are available on the website.

The McKitterick Prize

The Society of Authors, 84 Drayton Gardens, London SW10 9SB
tel 020-7373 6642

email info@societyofauthors.org
website www.societyofauthors.org/mckitterick

This annual award of £4,000 is open to first published novels (excluding works for children) and unpublished typescripts by authors over the age of 40. Closing date: 31 October. Endowed by the late Tom McKitterick. Download or send sae for entry form.

The Franco-British Society's Enid McLeod Literary Prize

Isabelle Gault, Executive Secretary,
Franco–British Society, 3 Dovedale Studios,
465 Battersea Park Road, London SW11 4LR
email francobritsoc@gmail.com
website www.francobritishsociety.org.uk

This annual prize is given for a full-length work of literature which contributes most to Franco–British understanding. It must be first published in the UK between 1 January and 31 December, and written in English by a citizen of the UK, British Commonwealth or the Republic of Ireland. Closing date: 31 December.

Bryan MacMahon Short Story Award

Listowel Writers' Week, 24 The Square, Listowel,
Co. Kerry, Republic of Ireland
tel +353 (0)68 21074
email info@writersweek.ie
website www.writersweek.ie
Contacts Maire Logue, Eilish Wren

An annual award for the best short story (up to 3,000 words) on any subject. Prize: €2,000. Entry fee: €10. No entry form required, enter online. Closing date: 29 February 2016. There is a subsidiary award, Writers' Week Originals Short Story, for stories of up to 1,500 words. Listowel Writers' Week is an acclaimed literary festival devoted to bringing together writers and audiences at unique and innovative events in the intimate and historic surroundings of Listowel, County Kerry. Events include workshops, readings, seminars, lectures, book launches, art exhibitions and a comprehensive children's and teenagers' programme. Founded 1971.

The Macmillan Prize for Children's Picture Book Illustration

Macmillan Children's Books, 20 New Wharf Road,
London N1 9RR
email macmillanprize@macmillan.co.uk

Four prizes are awarded annually for unpublished children's book illustrations by art students in higher education establishments in the UK. Prizes: £1,000 (1st), £500 (2nd), £250 (3rd) and the Lara Jones award for the entrant that shows most promise as an illustrator of books for babies and very young children (£500).

Man Asian Literary Prize

email info@manasianliteraryprize.org
website www.manasianliteraryprize.org
Contact Prize Manager, Marina Ma

An annual award (US$10,000) for an unpublished Asian novel in English. Submissions accepted from May. See website for details. Supported financially by the Man Group plc. Founded 2007.

The Man Booker International Prize

Four Colman Getty, 20 St Thomas Street,
London SE1 9BF
tel 020-3697 4243
email info@fourcolmangetty.com
website www.themanbookerprize.com

A prize of £60,000 to complement the annual Man Booker Prize by recognising one writer's achievement in continued creativity, development and overall contribution to world fiction. The prize does not invite submissions; a list is drawn up by the judges. It is awarded once every two years to a living author who has published fiction either originally in English, or generally available in translation in the English language.

The Man Booker International Prize echoes and reinforces the annual Man Booker Prize for Fiction in that literary excellence is its sole focus. The winner is announced in May. Sponsored by Man Group plc.

The Man Booker Prize

Four Colman Getty, 20 St Thomas Street,
London SE1 9BF
tel 020-3697 4243
email info@fourcolmangetty.com
website www.themanbookerprize.com

This annual prize for fiction of £50,000, including £2,500 to each of six shortlisted authors, is awarded to the best novel published each year. It is open to novels written in English by citizens of the British Commonwealth and Republic of Ireland and published for the first time in the UK by a British publisher, although previous publication of a book outside the UK does not disqualify it. Entries only from UK publishers who may each submit novels based on their previous longlisting with scheduled publication dates between 1 October of the previous year and 30 September of the current year, but the judges may also ask for other eligible novels to be submitted to them. In addition, publishers may submit eligible titles by authors who have either won or been shortlisted in the past. Sponsored by Man Group plc.

The Manchester Fiction Prize

Contact James Draper, Manager,
The Manchester Writing School at MMU,
Dept of English,
Manchester Metropolitan University,
Rosamund Street West, Off Oxford Road,
Manchester M15 6LL
tel 0161 247 1787
email writingschool@mmu.ac.uk
website www.manchesterwritingcompetition.co.uk

The Manchester Writing School, the home of creative writing within the Department of English at

Manchester Metropolitan University (MMU), hosts this competition which is designed to attract and celebrate the best new writing from around the world. Entrants are asked to submit a short story of up to 2,500 words in length. An award of £10,000 will be made each year to the overall winner, or winners. The deadline for entries for the 2016 competition is 30 September and the award ceremony will be held in November. See website for further information.

The Manchester Poetry Prize

Contact James Draper, Manager,
The Manchester Writing School at MMU,
Dept of English,
Manchester Metropolitan University,
Rosamond Street West, Off Oxford Road,
Manchester M15 6LL
tel 0161 247 1787
email writingschool@mmu.ac.uk
website www.manchesterwritingcompetition.co.uk

The Manchester Writing School, the home of creative writing within the Department of English at Manchester Metropolitan University (MMU), hosts this competition which is designed to attract and celebrate the best new writing from around the world. Entrants are asked to submit a portfolio of three to five poems totalling up to 120 lines. An award of £10,000 will be made to the overall winner, or winners. The deadline for entries for the 2016 competition is 30 September and the award ceremony will be held in November. See website for further information.

The Michael Marks Awards for Poetry Pamphlets

Wordsworth Trust, Dove Cottage, Grasmere,
Cumbria LA22 9SH
tel (01539) 435544
website www.wordsworth.org.uk

Inaugurated by the British Library in 2009 to raise the profile of poetry pamphlets and also recognise and reward the enormous contribution that poets and their pamphlet publishers make to the poetry world in the UK. There are two awards worth £5,000 each:

- The Michael Marks Poetry Award to recognise a single outstanding work of poetry published in pamphlet form in the UK during the eligible period. This award is open to self-published work.
- The Michael Marks Publishers' Award to recognise an outstanding UK publisher of poetry in pamphlet form, based on their publishing programme during the eligible period.

See website for full details and submission guidelines. Supported by the Michael Marks Charitable Trust. Deadline: August.

Marsh Award for Children's Literature in Translation

Administered by The English-Speaking Union (on behalf of the Marsh Christian Trust),
Dartmouth House, 37 Charles Street,
London W1J 5ED
tel 020-7529 1590
email education@esu.org
website www.esu.org/marsh

This biennial award of £3,000 is given to the translator of a book for children (aged 4–16) from a foreign language into English and published in the UK by a British publisher. The award celebrates the high quality and diversity of translated literature for young readers. Ebooks, encyclopedias and other reference books are not eligible. Next award: January 2017 (entries accepted from Spring 2016).

The John Masefield Memorial Trust

Sarah Baxter, The Society of Authors,
84 Drayton Gardens, London SW10 9SB
tel 020-7373 6642
email sbaxter@societyofauthors.org
website www.societyofauthors.org

This trust makes occasional grants to professional poets who find themselves with sudden financial problems. Apply for guidelines and application form.

The Somerset Maugham Awards

The Society of Authors, 84 Drayton Gardens,
London SW10 9SB
tel 020-7373 6642
email info@societyofauthors.org
website www.societyofauthors.org/somerset-maugham

These annual awards are for writers under the age of 35. Candidates must be British subjects by birth, and ordinarily resident in the UK or Northern Ireland. Poetry, fiction, non-fiction, belles-lettres or philosophy, but not dramatic works, are eligible. Entries should be submitted by the publisher. Closing date: 30 November.

Sheridan Morley Prize for the Best Theatre Biography

Administered by Anne Bond, 33 Rodney Court,
Maida Vale, London W9 1TH
email anne@ruthleon.com
website www.thesheridanmorleyprize.org
Contact The Administrator

In memory of the late critic and biographer Sheridan Morley, a cash prize of £2,000 is awarded to the winner chosen by the panel of judges chaired by critic, broadcaster and biographer Ruth Leon. Awarded in the spring of each year for theatrical biographies published in English in the preceding calendar year. Launched 2008.

The Mythopoeic Fantasy Award for Adult Literature

email correspondence@mythsoc.org
website www.mythsoc.org

Given to the fantasy novel, multi-volume novel or single-author story collection for adults published during the previous year that best exemplifies the spirit of the Inklings.

The Mythopoeic Scholarship Award in Myth and Fantasy Studies

email correspondence@mythsoc.org
website www.mythsoc.org

Given to scholarly books on specific authors in the Inklings tradition, or to more general works on the genres of myth and fantasy.

The Mythopoeic Scholarship Award in Inklings Studies

email correspondence@mythsoc.org
website www.mythsoc.org

Given to books on J.R.R. Tolkien, C.S.Lewis and/or Charles Williams that make significant contributions to Inklings scholarship.

Specsavers National Book Awards

c/o Agile Marketing, Magnolia House,
172 Winsley Road, Bradford-on-Avon,
Wilts. BA15 1NY
tel (01225) 865776
email cath@agileuklimited.com
website www.nationalbookawards.co.uk

The National Book Awards showcases the best of British writing and publishing whilst celebrating books with wide popular appeal, critical acclaim and commercial success. *Award categories* include: popular fiction, non-fiction, food and drink, new writer, children's book, biography, author, international author, audiobook and outstanding achievement.

National Poetry Competition

Competition Organiser, The Poetry Society,
22 Betterton Street, London WC2H 9BX
tel 020-7420 9880
email info@poetrysociety.org.uk
website www.poetrysociety.org.uk

One of the UK's major annual open poetry competitions. Accepts poems up to 40 lines long on any theme (previously unpublished and written in English). Prizes: 1st £5,000, 2nd £2,000, 3rd £1,000, plus seven commendations of £100. Judged by a panel of three leading poets. For rules and an entry form send a sae or visit the website. Closing date: 31 October each year. Founded 1978.

New Angle Prize for East Anglian Literature

Ipswich Institute, Reading Room & Library,
15 Tavern Street, Ipswich IP1 3AA
tel (01473) 253992
email library@ipswichinstitute.org.uk
website www.ipswichinstitute.org.uk/NAP.html
Prize Coordinator Hugh Pierce

The New Angle Prize is a biennial award (inaugurated in 2009) for a recently published book of literary merit, associated with or influenced by the UK region of East Anglia (defined here as Norfolk, Suffolk, north Essex, Cambridgeshire and the Fens).

The 2017 award will be open to works of fiction or poetry, first published between 1 January 2015 and 31 December 2016. Previous winners have been Mark Cocker (*Crow Country*, Jonathan Cape, 2007) and Jim Kelly (*Death Watch*, Penguin, 2010) and Jules Pretty (*This Luminous Coast*, Full Circle Editions, 2011). Previous judges have included Ronald Blythe, D.J. Taylor, Nicci Gerrard and Esther Freud. Current sponsors of the £2,000 single category first prize (£500 for runner-up) are Suffolk-based Goetlee Solicitors.

New Zealand Post Book Awards

c/o Booksellers New Zealand, 16–20 Willis Street,
Wellington 6011, New Zealand
tel +64 (0)4 472 1908
email awards@booksellers.co.nz
website www.nzpostbookawards.co.nz

Annual awards to celebrate excellence in, and provide recognition for, the best books published annually in New Zealand. Awards are presented in four categories: fiction, poetry, illustrated non-fiction and general non-fiction. The winner of each category wins $10,000. One category winner is chosen as the *New Zealand Post* Book of the Year and receives an additional $15,000. Special awards include the Maori Language Award, the People's Choice Award, the Booksellers' Choice Award and the three Best First Book Awards for poetry, fiction and non-fiction. Eligible authors' and illustrators' books must have been published in New Zealand in the year preceding the submissions closing date. Closing date: May. Founded 1996.

New Zealand Post Book Awards for Children and Young Adults

c/o Booksellers New Zealand, 16–20 Willis Street,
Wellington 6011, New Zealand
tel +64 (0)4 472 1908
email awards@bookawardstrust.org.nz
website www.bookawardstrust.org.nz

Annual awards to celebrate excellence in, and provide recognition for, the best books for children and young adults published annually in New Zealand. Awards are presented in four categories: non-fiction, picture book, junior fiction and young adult fiction. The winner of each category wins $7,000. One category winner is chosen as the *New Zealand Post* Margaret Mahy Book of the Year and receives an additional $7,500. Check the website for full eligibility criteria, as submissions dates occasionally change. Founded 1990. Subsidiary Awards: Maori Language Award, for books wholly in te reo Maori. The winner receives $1,000. First books are eligible for the Best First Book Award, the winner receives $2,000.

Nielsen Gold and Platinum Book Awards

tel (01483) 712300
email mo.siewcharran@nielsen.com
Head of Marketing Mo Siewcharran

The Nielsen Book Gold and Platinum Awards were established in 2000 and are presented to authors and publishers that have achieved exceptional sales. To qualify for a Gold Award sales of 500,000 copies must be achieved, and 1m copies must be achieved for a Platinum Award. Publishers have to claim the awards and can either order awards for presentation to their authors or for themselves.

The Nobel Prize in Literature

email comments@nobelprize.org
website www.nobelprize.org

This is one of the awards stipulated in the will of the late Alfred Nobel, the Swedish scientist who invented dynamite. No direct application for a prize will be taken into consideration. From 1901 to 2014, 27 of the 111 Nobel Laureates in Literature wrote/write in English. Rabindranath Tagore (1913) wrote in Bengali and English, Samuel Beckett (1969) wrote in French and English and Joseph Brodsky (1987) wrote in Russian and English. For a full list of literature Laureates, visit www.nobelprize.org/nobel_prizes/literature/laureates/index.html.

Northern Writers' Awards

New Writing North, PO Box 1277,
Newcastle upon Tyne NE99 5BP
email office@newwritingnorth.com
website www.northernwritersawards.com

Awards (£1,000–£5,000) are aimed at developing writers at different stages in their careers. A panel of professional writers shortlists and makes awards once a year. Awards are open to residents of the greater North: North East, North West, Yorkshire and Humberside. See website for details. Deadline for applications: end January/early February.

The Observer/Jonathan Cape/Comica Graphic Short Story Prize

website www.comicafestival.com

An annual graphic short story competition offering a £1,000 cash prize and the chance to see your story printed in the Observer. Founded 2007.

OCM Bocas Prize for Caribbean Literature

email info@bocaslitfest.com
website www.bocaslitfest.com

An annual prize for literary books by Caribbean writers (writers must have been born in the Caribbean or hold Caribbean citizenship). Books published in the calendar year 2015 will be eligible for the 2016 prize. There are two deadline dates for entries: books published before November 2015 (which should be received by the prize administrators by mid-November) and books published between 1 November and 31 December 2015 (which should be received by the prize administrators by the first week of January 2016). Books are judged in three categories: poetry; fiction (including novels and short stories); and literary non-fiction (including books of essays, biography, autobiography, history, current affairs, travel and other genres which demonstrate literary qualities and use literary techniques, regardless of subject matter. Textbooks, technical books, coffee-table books, specialist publications and reference works are not eligible. There is an entry fee of US$25.00. The overall winner will receive an award of US$10,000.

The inaugural OCM Bocas Prize for Caribbean Literature, presented in April 2011, was won by Derek Walcott's collection of poems *White Egrets*. The 2012 prize was won by Earl Lovelace's novel *Is Just a Movie*, the 2013 prize was won by Monique Roffey's novel *Archipelago*, and the 2014 prize was won by Robert Antoni's novel *As Flies to Whatless Boys*.

Frank O'Connor International Story Award

Frank O' Connor House, 84 Douglas Street, Cork, Ireland
tel +353 (0)21 431 2955
email munsterlit@eircom.net
website www.munsterlit.ie
website www.frankoconnor-shortstory-award.net

This prestigious international short story award in the memory of Frank O'Connor is the single biggest prize in the world for a collection of short stories. The Frank O'Connor International Short Story prize is worth €25,000 to the winning author of a collection of short stories published for the first time, in English, anywhere in the world between 1 July and 30 June. Deadline for entries: March. See website for submission guidelines.

The Orwell Prize

King's College London, Virginia Woolf Building,
22 Kingsway, London WC2B 6NR
tel 020-7848 7930
email alex.bartram@theorwellprize.co.uk
website www.theorwellprize.co.uk
Contact Alex Bartram

The Orwell Prize is awarded annually for books and journalism that come closest to George Orwell's ambition to make political writing into art. Deadline for entry is mid-January. All work with a British or Irish connection first published in the calendar year before the date of the prize is eligible. Please see website for further details. Founded 1994.

PEN Ackerley Prize for Autobiography and Memoir

English PEN, 60 Farringdon Road,
London EC1R 3GA

tel 020 7324 2535
email enquiries@englishpen.org
website www.englishpen.org

An annual prize of £2,000 is given for an outstanding work of literary autobiography/memoir written in English and published during the previous year by an author of British nationality. No submissions: books are nominated by the judges only. Founded 1982.

The People's Book Prize

23 Berkeley Square, London W1J 6HE
tel 020-7665 6605
email thepeoplesbkpr@aol.com
website www.peoplesbookprize.com
Founder and Prize Administrator Tatiana Wilson, *Patron* Frederick Forsyth OBE, *Founding Patron* Dame Beryl Bainbridge DBE

The People's Book Prize awards prizes in five categories: fiction, non-fiction, children's, first time author (the Beryl Bainbridge First Time Author Award), and best achievement. Titles must be submitted by publishers, with a limit of one title per category. For entry rules and submission guidelines, see the website.

The Samuel Pepys Award

Paul Gray, Haremoor House, Faringdon, Oxon SN7 8PN
tel 07802 301297
email plgray@btinternet.com
website www.pepys-club.org.uk

A biennial prize is given to a book published in English making the greatest contribution to the understanding of Samuel Pepys, his times, or his contemporaries. The winner receives £2,000 and the Robert Latham Medal. Founded by the Samuel Pepys Award Trust in 2003 on the tercentenary of the death of Pepys. Closing date: 30 June 2017 (for books published between 1 July 2015 and 30 June 2017).

Charles Pick Fellowship South Asia

School of Literature, Drama and Creative Writing, University of East Anglia, Norwich NR4 7TJ
tel (01603) 593564
email charlespickfellowship@uea.ac.uk
website www.uea.ac.uk/literature/fellowships

The Charles Pick Fellowship is dedicated to the memory of the distinguished publisher and literary agent, Charles Pick, whose career began in 1933 and continued until shortly before his death in January 2000. He encouraged young writers at the start of their careers with introductions to other writers and offered practical and financial help. The Charles Pick South Asian Fellowship seeks to continue this spirit of encouragement by giving support to the work of a new and, as yet, unpublished writer of fictional or non-fictional prose based in South Asia. The writer should be from South Asia (Afghanistan, Bangladesh, Bhutan, India, Kazakhstan, Kyrgyzstan, Maldives, Burma/Myanmar, Nepal, Pakistan, Sri Lanka, Turkmenistan, Tajikistan, Uzbekistan), but does not need to be domiciled there. The 2014/15 Charles Pick South Asia Fellows: Mahreen Sohail and Avinab Datta.

The Plough Prize

The Plough Arts Centre, 9–11 Fore Street, Great Torrington, Devon EX38 8HQ
tel (01805) 624624
website www.theploughprize.co.uk

Poetry competition; poems should contain no more than 40 lines. Visit website for full entry criteria and submission guidelines. Entry fee £5 per poem.

The Poetry Business Book & Pamphlet Competition

Competition Administrator The Poetry Business, Bank Street Arts, 32–40 Bank Street, Sheffield S1 2DS
tel 0114 346 3037
email office@poetrybusiness.co.uk
website www.poetrybusiness.co.uk
Directors Peter Sansom, Ann Sansom

An annual award is made for a poetry collection. The judges select up to five short collections for publication as pamphlets; on further submission of more poems, one of these will be selected for a full-length collection. To be published under the Poetry Business's Smith/Doorstop imprint. All winners share a cash prize of £2,000. Poets over the age of 18 writing in English from anywhere in the world are eligible. Founded 1986.

The Portico Prize

Miss Emma Marigliano, Librarian, Portico Library, 57 Mosley Street, Manchester M2 3HY
tel 0161 236 6785
email librarian@theportico.org.uk
website www.theportico.org.uk

This biennial prize is awarded for a published work of fiction or non-fiction, of general interest and literary merit set wholly or mainly in the North of England with prizes for fiction and non-fiction totalling up to £20,000. Founded 1985.

Prequel to Cannes Feature Film Script Competition

Creative Thoughts Productions Ltd
tel (01202) 691994, 07763 988662
email rosiecreativethoughts@btinternet.com
website www.creativethoughtsproductions.co.uk
website www.prequeltocannes.biz
Contact Rosie Jones

This prize gives writers the opportunity to receive industry feedback on their script. All entries which meet the terms and conditions of entry will have the chance to win one of the two cash prizes; have their script (max. 90 pages) read by a film production company; receive a three-page feedback document on the merits and opportunities of their script from a professional film industry script reader. Full submission details are available on the website. Entry fee. Previous winners include Dom Carver, *Faith* (now optioned for a feature film) and Lisa Barass (Dyer), *Since you've been gone* (published as a novel by Crooked Cat Publishers in 2013).

Prequel to Cannes Short Film Script Competition

Creative Thoughts Productions Ltd
tel (01202) 691994, 07763 988662
email rosiecreativethoughts@btinternet.com
website www.creativethoughtsproductions.co.uk
website www.prequeltocannes.biz
Contact Rosie Jones

Competition for film scripts. Cash prizes will be awarded to writers of the top three scripts by a prestigious film industry judging panel. Scripts will be read by a professional script reader and selected production companies, and a one-page script summary on the strengths and opportunities of the script will be supplied. Entry fee. *Previous winners*: Alice D. Cooper, Rob Greens, Tracy Jane Murrey, James Dwyer, Barry Staff, Martin Adams. In 2013 Rosie Jones was appointed by the National Trust as their first Writer in Residence, see http://rosiejones.weebly.com. Founded 2009.

The Press Awards

Society of Editors, University Centre, Granta Place, Cambridge CB2 1RU
tel (01223) 304080
email office@societyofeditors.org
website www.pressawards.org.uk

Annual awards for British journalism judged by a number of influential judges as well as representatives from all the national newspaper groups.

The V.S. Pritchett Memorial Prize

The Royal Society of Literature, Somerset House, Strand, London WC2R 1LA
tel 020-7845 4678
email info@rsliterature.org
website www.rsliterature.org

An annual prize of £1,000 is awarded for a previously unpublished short story of up to 5,000 words. Entry fee: £5 per story. Closing date for entries: June. See website for full details and submission guidelines. Entrants must be citizens of the UK, the Republic of Ireland or Commonwealth countries or have been resident in one the aforementioned countries for the past three years. Founded 1999.

The Radio Academy Awards

The Radio Academy Awards, The Radio Academy, 3rd Floor 55 New Oxford Street, London WC1A 1BS
tel 020-3174 1180
email info@radioacademyawards.org
website www.radioacademyawards.org

The Radio Academy Awards recognise the best in the UK radio industry and celebrate outstanding achievement. The Awards offer stations, presenters and production companies an annual opportunity to enter work in a range of categories reflecting today's UK radio landscape. Entries close in February with nominations announced in April and the winners revealed at a ceremony in May. See website for further information. Founded 1982.

The Peggy Ramsay Foundation

G. Laurence Harbottle, Hanover House, 14 Hanover Square, London W1S 1HP
tel 020-7667 5000
email laurence.harbottle@harbottle.com
website www.peggyramsayfoundation.org

Grants are made to writers of stage plays who have had at least one professional production and occasionally to theatrical organisations to facilitate new writing for the stage. Awards are made at intervals during each year. A total of approx. £200,000 is expended annually. Founded 1992.

The Red House Children's Book Award

123 Frederick Road, Cheam, Sutton, Surrey SM1 2HT
website www.redhousechildrensbookaward.co.uk

This award is given annually to authors of fiction for children published in the UK. Children participate in the judging of the award. Awards are made in the following categories: Books for Younger Children, Books for Young Readers and Books for Older Readers. Founded in 1980 by the Federation of Children's Book Groups.

Trevor Reese Memorial Prize

Institute of Commonwealth Studies, School of Advanced Study, University of London, Senate House, Malet Street, London WC1E 7HU
tel 020-7862 8853
email ics@sas.ac.uk
website www.commonwealth.sas.ac.uk/reese.htm

The Trevor Reese Memorial Prize was established by the Institute of Commonwealth Studies in 1979. It is in the name of Dr Trevor Reese, a distinguished scholar of Australian and Commonwealth history, who was Reader in Imperial Studies at the Institute until his death in 1976. He was the author of several leading works in his field, and was both founder and first editor of the *Journal of Imperial and Commonwealth History*. The prize was established with the proceeds of contributions to a memorial fund by friends and colleagues of Trevor Reese throughout the Commonwealth and United States. The prize of £1,000 is awarded every three years to the author of a work which has made a wide-ranging, innovative and scholarly contribution in the broadly-defined field of Imperial and Commonwealth History. The next award of the prize will be in 2016, for books in the relevant field published in 2013, 2014 or 2015. Queries regarding this prize should be sent by email.

The Romantic Novel of the Year Awards

email RONAawards@romanticnovelistsassociation.org
website www.romanticnovelistsassociation.org
RoNA Awards Organiser Nicola Cornick

The Romantic Novelists' Association gives annual awards for the very best romantic fiction. These awards, presented in early March, consist of six categories: Contemporary, Epic, Historical, Romantic Comedy, Young Adult, and the RoNA Rose (for shorter/category) romantic novels. The winners go forward to a panel of judges that selects an overall winner for the Romantic Novel of the Year Award, presented at the same event. The awards are open to both members and non-members of the RNA. Novels must be first published between 1 January and 31 December of the year of entry. Four copies of each novel are required and there is a small entry fee. The entry form can be found on the website or obtained from the organiser. For further information, go to the RNA website.

The Joan Hessayon Award is only open to members of the Romantic Novelists' Association's New Writers' Scheme who submit a MS from January until the end of August. All will receive a critique. Any MSS subsequently accepted for publication become eligible for the Award.

The Royal Society of Literature Jerwood Awards for Non-Fiction

The Royal Society of Literature, Somerset House, Strand, London WC2R 1LA
tel 020-7845 4678
email paulaj@rslit.org
website www.rslit.org

Awards offering financial assistance to authors engaged in writing their first major commissioned works of non-fiction. Three awards – one of £10,000 and two of £5,000 – will be offered annually to writers working on substantial non-fiction projects. The awards are open to UK and Irish writers and writers who have been resident in the UK for at least three years. See website for further details.

The Royal Society of Literature Ondaatje Prize

The Royal Society of Literature, Somerset House, Strand, London WC2R 1LA
tel 020-7845 4679
email paulaj@rslit.org
website www.rslit.org/rsl-ondaatje-prize

This annual £10,000 award, administered by the Royal Society of Literature and endowed by Sir Christopher Ondaatje, is awarded to a book of literary merit, fiction, poetry or non-fiction, best evoking the spirit of a place. See website for full details and submission guidelines. The writer must be a citizen of the UK, Commonwealth, Republic of Ireland or have been a resident of the UK for three years. See website for further details.

The Royal Society Winton Prize for Science Books

The Royal Society, 6–9 Carlton House Terrace, London SW1Y 5AG
tel 020-7451 2513
email sciencebooks@royalsociety.org
website https://royalsociety.org/awards/science-books
Events Officer, Public Engagement Rebecca Jones

This prestigious prize is open to authors of science books written for a non-specialist audience. The winner will receive £25,000 and each shortlisted author will receive £2,500. Eligible books should be written in English and, from late 2015 onwards, their first publication in the UK must have been between 1 October and 30 September the following year.

Publishers may submit any number of books for the Prize. Entries may cover any aspect of science and technology but educational textbooks published for professional or specialist audiences are not eligible. The Prize is sponsored by Winton Capital Management. Founded 1988.

The Royal Society Young People's Book Prize

The Royal Society, 6–9 Carlton House Terrace, London SW1Y 5AG
tel 020-7451 2254
email sciencebooks@royalsociety.org
website https://royalsociety.org/awards/young-people
Events Officer, Public Engagement David Chapman

This prize is open to books for under-14s that have science as a substantial part of their content, narrative or theme. An expert adult panel choose the shortlist, but the winner is chosen by groups of young people in judging panels across the UK. The winning entry receives £10,000 and shortlisted entries receive £1,000.

Entries open in November each year. Pure reference works including encyclopedias, educational textbooks, and descriptive books are not eligible. The Prize is offered thanks to the generosity of an anonymous donor. Founded 1988.

RSPCA Young Photographer Awards (YPA)

Brand Marketing and Content Department Department, RSPCA, Wilberforce Way, Southwater, Horsham, West Sussex RH13 9RS
email ypa@rspca.org.uk
website www.rspca.org.uk/ypa

Annual awards are open to anyone aged 18 or under. The aim of the competition is to encourage young people's interest in photography and to show their appreciation and understanding of the animals around them. See website for a full list of categories and submission guidelines. Founded 1990.

RTÉ Radio 1 Francis MacManus Awards

RTÉ Radio Centre, Donnybrook, Dublin 4, Republic of Ireland
website www.rte.ie/radio1/francis-macmanus-short-story

An annual competition for short stories of 1,800–2,000 words, open to writers born or living in Ireland. First prize €3,000. Entries, in Irish or English, should not have been previously published or broadcast. See website for details. Winning entries are broadcast on RTÉ Radio 1.

RTÉ Radio Drama P.J. O'Connor Drama Awards

RTÉ Radio Drama, Radio Centre, Donnybrook, Dublin 4, Republic of Ireland
email radiodrama@rte.ie
website www.rte.ie/dramaonone

Rubery Book Award

PO Box 15821, Birmingham, B31 9EA
email enquiries@ruberybookaward.com
website www.ruberybookaward.com

An annual award for published books on any subject, with prizes totalling £1,300. Books published by independent presses and self-published books are eligible. Short story competition for unpublished short stories on any subject, prizes totalling £700; the best stories will be published in an anthology. See website for entry fees and submission guidelines. Deadline (book award) end April; (short story competition) end October.

Runciman Award

The Administrator, The Anglo-Hellenic League, 16–18 Paddington Street, London W1U 5AS
tel 020-7486 9410
email info@anglohellenicleague.org
website www.anglohellenicleague.org

An annual award of £9,000 to promote Anglo–Greek understanding and friendship. Works must be wholly or mainly about some aspect of Greece or the world of Hellenism, which has been published in English in any country in its first edition during the previous year. Shortlisted books must be available for purchase to readers in the UK at the time of the award ceremony. No category of writing will be excluded from consideration, e.g. history, literary studies, biography, travel and topography, the arts, architecture, archaeology, the environment, social and political sciences or current affairs; fiction, poetry or drama. Works in translation, with the exception of translations from Greek literature, will not be considered. Sponsored by the National Bank of Greece and named after Sir Steven Runciman, former Chairman of the Anglo-Hellenic League. Established 1985.

The Saltire Society Awards

The Saltire Society, 9 Fountain Close, 22 High Street, Edinburgh EH1 1TF
tel 0131 556 1836
email saltire@saltiresociety.org.uk
website www.saltiresociety.org.uk
Contacts Jim Tough, Executive Director; Sarah Mason, Programme Manager

Books published between 1 September and 31 August are eligible for awards. **The Scottish Book of the Year** is an annual award selected from the Saltire Society Book Award categories. The categories are as follows:

Scottish First Book of the Year

Annual award open to any author who has not previously published a book. Authors of Scottish descent or living in Scotland, or any book which deals with the work or life of a Scot or with a Scottish problem, event or situation are eligible.

Scottish Fiction Book of the Year

Annual award for all fiction by an author of Scottish descent or living in Scotland, or for any book which deals with the work or life of a Scot or with a Scottish problem, event or situation.

Scottish Non-Fiction Book of the Year

Annual award for non-fiction books such as biography, travel and political writing. Authors of Scottish descent or living in Scotland, or any book which deals with the work or life of a Scot or with a Scottish problem, event or situation are eligible.

Scottish History Book of the Year

Annual award for a work of Scottish historical research from authors of Scottish descent or living in Scotland, or for any book which deals with the work or life of a Scot or with a Scottish problem, event or situation. Editions of texts are not eligible. Nominations are invited from professors of Scottish history and editors of historical reviews.

Scottish Poetry Book of the Year

Annual award for a collection of new poetry from authors of Scottish descent or living in Scotland, or for any book which deals with the work or life of a Scot or with a Scottish problem, event or situation. Collections which include previously published are not eligible (excludes magazine/pamphlet publication).

Scottish Research Book of the Year

Annual award for a books representing a significant body of research by authors of Scottish descent or living in Scotland, or for any book which deals with the work or life of a Scot or with a Scottish problem, event or situation. Research books must offer insight or dimension to the subject and add to the knowledge and understanding of Scotland and the Scots.

Walter Scott Prize for Historical Fiction

c/o StonehillSalt PR, Haddington House,
28 Sidegate, Haddington, East Lothian EH41 4BU
tel (01620) 829800
email rebecca@stonehillsalt.co.uk
email amanda@bordersbookfestival.org
website www.walterscottprize.co.uk
Administration, Publicity & Marketing Rebecca Salt, *Administration & Entries* Amanda Graham

The Walter Scott Prize for Historical Fiction was founded in 2010 by the Duke and Duchess of Buccleuch and Alistair Moffat, the Chair of Judges. Awarded annually, it rewards fiction of exceptional quality which is set in the past (according to Walter Scott's subtitle for Waverley, at least 'sixty years since'). The Prize is among the richest UK book prizes, with a total value of £30,000. The winner receives £25,000, and shortlisted authors receive £1,000 each. The Prize is awarded at the Borders Book Festival in Melrose each June, with a shortlist announced in March or April. Previous winners of the Walter Scott Prize for Historical Fiction include Hilary Mantel, Andrea Levy, Sebastian Barry, Tan Twan Eng and Robert Harris.

Books must be written in English and have had their principal and first publication in the UK, Eire or the Commonwealth during the calendar year. Books written in English by authors of British nationality first published outside the UK, Eire or the Commonwealth are also eligible provided they are also published in the UK in that calendar year. Books must be submitted by publishers, and self-published authors are not eligible.

The Kim Scott Walwyn Prize

Book Trust, G8 Battersea Studios,
80 Silverthorne Road, London SW8 3HE
tel 020-7801 8800
email ksw@booktrust.org.uk
website www.booktrust.org.uk
Contact Katherine Woodfine

Founded in 2003, the Kim Scott Walwyn Prize honours the life and career of Kim Scott Walwyn (who was Publishing Director at Oxford University Press and who died in 2002) and celebrates exceptional women in publishing. It has now been awarded nine times, with the 2014 Prize going to Anne Perry, Editor at Hodder & Stoughton and founder of The Kitschies. The Prize is managed by the Prize Committee and Book Trust and is run in partnership with the Society of Young Publishers and the Publishing Training Centre (PTC). It is open to any woman who has worked in publishing in the UK for up to seven years and recognises the professional achievements and promise of women in the industry.

For the first time in 2013 nominations were invited, as well as applicants being able to nominate themselves. Applications must be supported by two referee statements. The winner of the Prize receives £1,000, sponsored by the SYP, and a two-day training course of their choice at the PTC. Shortlisted candidates will also receive a one-day training course courtesy of the PTC.

Scottish Book of the Year – see The Saltire Society Awards

Scottish Children's Book Awards

Scottish Book Trust, Sandeman House,
Trunk's Close, 55 High Street, Edinburgh EH1 1SR
tel 0131 524 0160
website www.scottishbooktrust.com/scba

Scotland's largest book awards for children and young people. Awards totalling £12,000 are given to new and established authors of published books in recognition of high standards of writing for children in three age group categories: Bookbug Readers (3–7 years), Younger Readers (8–11 years) and Older Readers (12–16 years). A shortlist is drawn up by a panel of children's book experts and then a winner in each category is decided by children and young people by voting for their favourites in schools and libraries across Scotland. An award of £3,000 is made for the winner in each category and £500 for runners-up. Books published in the preceding calendar year are eligible. Authors must be resident in Scotland. Guidelines available on request. Closing date: 31 March. Award presented: February. Administered by Scottish Book Trust, in partnership with Creative Scotland.

Scottish First Book of the Year – see The Saltire Society Awards

Scottish Research Book Award – see The Saltire Society Awards

The André Simon Memorial Fund Book Awards

1 Westbourne Gardens, Glasgow G12 9XE
tel 07801 310973
email katie@andresimon.co.uk
website www.andresimon.co.uk
Secretary Kate Lander

Celebrating excellent new writing in the fields of food and drink. Two awards of £2,000 are given annually, one each for the best new books on food and on drink. There is also a Special Commendation of £1,000 in either category. All works first published in the calendar year of the award are eligible (publisher entry only). Closing date: November each year. Awards are given in the spring of the following year. Founded 1978.

The Jill Smythies Award

The Linnean Society of London, Burlington House, Piccadilly, London W1J 0BF

tel 020-7434 4479
email info@linnean.org
website www.linnean.org

Established in honour of Jill Smythies whose career as a botanical artist was cut short by an accident to her right hand. The rubric states that 'the Award, to be made by Council usually annually consisting of a silver medal and a purse ... is for published illustrations, such as drawings and paintings, in aid of plant identification, with the emphasis on botanical accuracy and the accurate portrayal of diagnostic characteristics. Illustrations of cultivars of garden origin are not eligible.' Closing date for nominations: 30 November. Founded 1988.

Spear's Book Awards

John Carpenter House, John Carpenter Street, London EC4Y 0AN
tel 020-7936 6445
email josh.spero@spearswms.com
website www.spearswms.com

These annual awards celebrate the best writing talent and British books of the year – from finance to fiction. The awards – Novel of the Year, Biography of the Year, Financial History of the Year, Business Book of the Year, Family History of the Year, Memoir of the Year, Large Format Illustrated Book of the Year, Outstandingly Produced Book, Best First Book and Lifetime Achievement – are presented at a glamorous sit-down lunch for 100 guests. All books must have been first published or made available in English (electronic versions excluded) between 1 May and 30 April of the following year. Established 2009.

The Sunday Times EFG Private Bank Short Story Award

Book Trust, G8 Battersea Studios, 80 Silverthorne Road, Battersea, London SW8 3HE
tel 020-7801 8800
email sundaytimesEFG@booktrust.org.uk
website www.booktrust.org.uk
Contact Claire Shanahan

Launched in 2009 by Lord Matthew Evans, former chairman of EFG Private Bank and Cathy Galvin from *The Sunday Times*, The Sunday Times EFG Short Story Award is the richest prize for a single short story in the English language open to any novelist or short story writer from around the world who is published in the UK. Worth £30,000 to the winner, and £1,000 to each of the shortlisted authors, the annual award aims to promote and celebrate the excellence of the modern short story, and has attracted entries from some of the world's finest writers. Winners of the competition, which is open to stories of up to 6,000 words written in English, have come from all over the world, and have included the Pulitzer prize-winning American writer Junot Diaz, C.K. Stead from New Zealand and Kevin Barry from Ireland. Last year's recipient of the award was the Pulitzer winner Adam Johnson for his haunting story *Nirvana*.

The James Tait Black Memorial Prizes

English Literature, School of Literatures, Languages and Cultures, The University of Edinburgh, 50 George Square, Edinburgh EH8 9LH
tel 0131 650 3619
website www.ed.ac.uk/about/people/tait-black

The James Tait Black Fiction and Biography Prizes

Two prizes of £10,000 are awarded annually: one for the best biography or work of that nature, the other for the best work of fiction, published during the calendar year 1 January to 31 December. The adjudicators are Professors of English Literature at the University of Edinburgh, with the assistance of teams of postgraduate readers. Eligible novels and biographies are those written in English and first published or co-published in Britain in the year of the award. Both prizes may go to the same author, but neither to the same author a second time.

Publishers should submit a copy of any appropriate biography, or work of fiction, as early as possible with a note of the date of publication, marked 'James Tait Black Prize'. Closing date for submissions: 1 December. Founded in memory of a partner in the publishing house of A&C Black, these prizes were instituted in 1918.

The James Tait Black Prize for Drama: University of Edinburgh in association with Playwrights Studio Scotland

A prize of £10,000 for the best original new play written in English, Scots or Gaelic. Judges will award the accolade to a professionally produced play which displays an original voice in theatre and one that they feel has made a significant and unique contribution to the art form. The prize is open to any new work by playwrights from any country and at any stage in their career. The judges will be students and staff of the University's School of Literatures, Languages and Cultures and representatives from the Playwrights Studio Scotland.

Plays must be formally commissioned and have had a full professional production. Eligible plays will have been produced between 1 January and 31 December in the year preceding the year of the award. A typed copy of the script and a digital copy must be sent with details of the first production, which should include venue, company and date, and proof of production if possible. The submissions must come from the producing company or the agent of the playwright, and should be submitted to the Department of English Literature by the date specified on the website. Please complete the submission form which can be downloaded from the website and enclose it with your hard copy.

Applications which do not have the submission form complete will be considered ineligible. For full criteria visit: www.ed.ac.uk/news/events/tait-black/drama or contact nicola.mccartney@ed.ac.uk.

Reginald Taylor and Lord Fletcher Essay Competition

John McNeill, Hon. Secretary,
British Archaeological Association, 18 Stanley Road, Oxford OX4 1QZ
email jsmcneill@btinternet.com

A prize of a medal and £500 is awarded biennially for the best unpublished essay of high scholarly standard, which shows original research on a subject of archaeological, art-historical or antiquarian interest within the period from the Roman era to AD1830. The successful competitor will be invited to read the essay before the Association and the essay may be published in the Association's *Journal*. Competitors should notify the Hon. Editor in advance of the intended subject of their work. Next award: Spring 2016. The essay should be submitted not later than 1 November 2015 to the Honorary Editor, Dr Zoe Opacic, Department of History of Art, Birkbeck College, 43–46 Gordon Square, London WC1H 0PD. Founded in memory of E. Reginald Taylor FSA and Lord Fletcher FSA.

International Dylan Thomas Prize

tel (01792) 606245
website www.swansea.ac.uk/dylan-thomas-prize

The £30,000 University of Wales Dylan Thomas Prize is awarded to the best eligible published or produced work in the English language, written by an author under 39. See website for full details. Founded 2005.

The Times/Chicken House Children's Fiction Competition

Chicken House, 2 Palmer Street, Frome, Somerset BA11 IDS
tel (01373) 454488
email chickenhouse@doublecluck.com
website www.doublecluck.com
Contact Kesia Lupo

This annual competition is open to unpublished writers of a full-length children's novel (age 7–18). Entrants must be over 18 and novels must not exceed 80,000 words in length. The winner will be announced in *The Times* and will receive a worldwide publishing contract with Chicken House with a royalty advance of £10,000. The winner is selected by a panel of judges which includes children's authors, journalists, publishers, librarians and other key figures from the world of children's literature. Submissions are invited between April and October, with a shortlist announced the following February and the winner chosen at Easter. See website for further details.

Tir na n-Og Awards

Welsh Books Council, Castell Brychan, Aberystwyth, Ceredigion SY23 2JB
tel (01970) 624151
email wbc.children@wbc.org.uk
website www.wbc.org.uk

The Tir na n-Og Awards were established with the intention of raising the standard of children's and young people's books in Wales. Three awards are presented annually by the Welsh Books Council and are sponsored by the Chartered Institute of Library and Information Professionals Cymru/Wales and Cymdeithas Lyfrau Ceredigion:

• The best English-language book of the year with an authentic Welsh background. Fiction and factual books originally in English are eligible; translations from Welsh or any other language are not eligible. Prize: £1,000.
• The best original Welsh-language book aimed at the primary school sector. Prize: £1,000.
• The best original Welsh-language book aimed at the secondary school sector. Prize: £1,000.

Founded 1976.

The Tom-Gallon Trust Award

The Society of Authors, 84 Drayton Gardens, London SW10 9SB
tel 020-7373 6642
email info@societyofauthors.org
website www.societyofauthors.org/tom-gallon-trust-and-olive-cook-award

An annual award of £1,000 is made on the basis of a submitted short story to fiction writers of limited means who have had at least one short story accepted for publication. Send a sae or download entry forms from the website. Closing date: 31 October.

The Translation Prizes

The Society of Authors, 84 Drayton Gardens, London SW10 9SB
tel 020-7373 6642
email info@societyofauthors.org
website www.societyofauthors.org/grants-and-prizes

The Society of Authors administers a number of prizes for published translations into English. There are prizes for translations of Arabic, Dutch, French, German, Italian, Spanish and Swedish works. Closing date 28 February and 31 March for Saif Ghobash Banipal Prize. Entries should be submitted by the publisher.

The Betty Trask Awards

The Society of Authors, 84 Drayton Gardens, London SW10 9SB
tel 020-7373 6642
email info@societyofauthors.org
website www.societyofauthors.org/betty-trask

These awards are for the benefit of authors under the age of 35 and are given on the strength of a first novel (published or unpublished) of a traditional or romantic nature. It is expected that prizes totalling approximately £20,000 will be presented each year.

The winners are required to use the money for a period or periods of foreign travel. Send a sae or download an entry form from the website. Closing date: 30 November. Made possible through a generous bequest from the novelist Betty Trask.

The Travelling Scholarships

The Society of Authors, 84 Drayton Gardens, London SW10 9SB
tel 020-7373 6642
email info@societyofauthors.org
website www.societyofauthors.org/travelling-scholarships

These are honorary awards established in 1944 by an anonymous benefactor. Submissions are not accepted.

The V&A Illustration Awards

Victoria & Albert Museum, London SW7 2RL
email villa@vam.ac.uk
website www.vam.ac.uk/illustrationawards

These annual awards are given to practising book and magazine illustrators living or publishing in the UK for work first published during the 12 months preceding the closing date of the awards. Awards are made in the following categories: book cover, book illustration and editorial illustration.

Venture Award

website www.flippedeye.net/venture

Annual poetry pamphlet award worth £1,750 named after Wilfred Albert Venture. Open to anyone over the age of 16. Enter up to 15 A4 pages of poetry of any length. Entries by email only to venture@flippedeye.net. See website for full details and submission guidelines.

Ver Poets Open Competition

Competition Secretary Gill Knibbs, 181 Sandridge Road, St Albans, Herts. AL1 4AH
tel (01727) 762601
email gillknibbs@yahoo.co.uk
website www.verpoets.org.uk

A competition open to all for poems of up to 30 lines of any genre or subject matter, which must be unpublished work in English. Prizes: £600 (1st), £300 (2nd), £100 (3rd). Send two copies of each poem with no name or address; either put address on separate sheet or send sae or email for entry form. Closing date: 30 April. Anthology of winning and selected poems with Adjudicator's Report usually available from mid-June, free to those included. See website for details.

Wales Book of the Year Award

Literature Wales, 4th Floor, Cambrian Buildings, Mount Stuart Square, Cardiff CF10 5FL
tel 029-2047 2266
email post@literaturewales.org
website www.walesbookoftheyear.co.uk
website www.literaturewales.org
Literature Wales Chief Executive Lleucu Siencyn

The Wales Book of the Year Award is presented to the best Welsh and English-language works first published in the year preceding the ceremony in the fields of creative writing and literary criticism in three categories: Poetry, Fiction and Creative non-fiction. The English-language poetry award is titled the Roland Mathias Poetry Award. A panel of three English-language and three Welsh-language judges decide on three titles in each category to compile the Short List which is announced in spring. The winners of each category will then be announced at the Award Ceremony in the summertime, where one overall winner in each language will also be chosen from the three category winners. Wales Book of the Year is organised by Literature Wales, the national company for the development of literature.

The Walford Award – see The ISG Reference Awards

Warwick Prize for Writing

Warwick Prize for Writing, Communications Office, University House, University of Warwick CV4 8UW
tel 024-7615 0708
email prizeforwriting@warwick.ac.uk
website www.warwick.ac.uk/go/prizeforwriting/

An international cross-disciplinary biennial prize, founded in 2009, awarded for an excellent and substantial piece of writing in the English language, in any genre or form. Nominations are invited from University of Warwick and Monash University staff, students, honorary and emeritus professors, and honorary graduates. See website for full details.

Wasafiri New Writing Prize

The Open University in London, 1–11 Hawley Crescent, London NW1 8NP
email wasafiriprize@open.ac.uk
website www.wasafiriprize.org/wasafiri-new-writing-prize.asp
Assistant Editor Nisha Obano

The Wasafiri New Writing Prize is awarded in three categories (Poetry, Fiction and Life Writing) and is open to anyone worldwide who has not published a complete book in the category they wish to enter. Entries should be no longer than 3,000 words or five poems max., and should be submitted with an entry form and payment. See website for submission guidelines and entry fees. Judges in 2015 include Yasmin Alibhai-Brown, Toby Litt, Roger Robinson and Susheila Nasta. Founded 2009.

The Wellcome Trust Book Prize

tel 020-7611 8612
email bookprize@wellcome.ac.uk
website www.wellcomebookprize.org
Contact Tim Morley

Celebrates the best of medicine in literature by awarding £30,000 each year for the finest fiction or non-fiction book centred around medicine. This prize aims to stimulate interest, excitement and debate about medicine and literature, reaching audiences not normally engaged with medical science. See www.wellcomebookprize.org for further details. Founded 2009.

The Whitfield Prize

Administrative Secretary, Royal Historical Society, University College London, Gower Street, London WC1E 6BT
tel 020-7387 7532
email m.ransom@royalhistsoc.org
website http://royalhistsoc.org/prizes/

The Prize (value £1,000) is announced in July each year for the best work on a subject within a field of British or Irish history. It must be its author's first solely written history book, an original and scholarly work of historical research and have been published in the UK or Republic of Ireland in the preceding calendar year. One non-returnable copy of an eligible book should be submitted by the publisher before 31 December to the Administrative Secretary. Should the book be shortlisted, two further copies will be required.

Wildlife Photographer of the Year

The Natural History Museum, Cromwell Road, London SW7 5BD
tel 020-7942 5015
website www.nhm.ac.uk/wpy

This annual award is given to the photographer whose individual image is judged to be the most striking and memorable. Open to all ages. Entry fee £30; free for under 17s.

Winchester Writers' Festival Competitions and Scholarships

University of Winchester, Winchester, Hants SO22 4NR
tel (01962) 827238
email judith.heneghan@winchester.ac.uk
website www.writersfestival.co.uk
Festival Director Judith Heneghan

Ten writing competitions are attached to this major international festival of writing, which takes place in June. Entrants do not have to attend the Festival and can opt to receive a written adjudication. Categories are First Three Pages of a Novel, Poetry, Short Stories, Flash Fiction, Children's Picture Book, Children's Funny Fiction, Memoir, Writing Can Be Murder, Young Writers' Poetry Competition and Pitch a TV Drama. Deadline for entries: mid May. Fee £7 without written adjudication; £12 with written adjudication. Prizes include editorial consultations, writing software, writing courses and books. First place winning entries and their adjudications will be published in the Festival anthology. The Festival also offers ten scholarships for young writers aged 18–25 to attend the Festival for free.

The Wolfson Foundation

The Prize Administrator, The Wolfson Foundation, 8 Queen Anne Street, London W1G 9LD
tel 020-7323 5730 ext. 216
website www.wolfson.org.uk

Annual awards are made to encourage and recognise books by British historians that can be enjoyed by a general readership and will stimulate public interest in history. The awards total up to £50,000. Authors must be British citizens and normally resident in the UK. Books must be published in the calendar year preceding the year of the award. Details on the submission process are available online. Founded 1972.

David T.K. Wong Fellowship

School of Literature, Drama and Creative Writing, University of East Anglia, Norwich NR4 7TJ
tel (01603) 592713
email davidtkwongfellowship@uea.ac.uk
website www.uea.ac.uk/literature/fellowships

The David T.K. Wong Fellowship is a unique and generous annual award of £26,000 to enable a fiction writer who wants to write in English about the Far East to spend a year in the UK, at the University of East Anglia in Norwich. The Fellowship is named for its sponsor Mr David T.K. Wong, a retired Hong Kong businessman, who has also been a teacher, journalist and senior civil servant, and is a writer of short stories himself. The Fellowship will be awarded to a writer planning to produce a work of prose fiction in English which deals seriously with some aspect of life in the Far East (Brunei, Cambodia, Hong Kong, Indonesia, Japan, Korea, Laos, Macau, Malaysia, Mongolia, Myanmar, Peoples' Republic of China, Philippines, Singapore, Taiwan, Thailand and Vietnam). The 2014/15 David T. K.Wong Fellow: Jack Wang.

World Illustration Awards

Association of Illustrators, Somerset House, Strand, London WC2R 1LA
tel 020-7759 1012
email awards@theaoi.com
website www.theaoi.com/awards/
Awards Manager Sabine Reimer

The World Illustration Awards, in partnership with the Directory of Illustration, is an awards programme that sets out to celebrate contemporary illustration across the globe. A panel of international judges create a shortlist, which is displayed at an exhibition in Somerset House and subsequently tours the UK.

An accompanying publication of a selection of shortlisted work is distributed to commissioners worldwide. Entries can be submitted by practising illustrators or students from around the world, created in any medium into one of eight categories. Two awards are given for Best in each category and to one overall winner of Professional and New Talent respectively. Call for entries: November 2015 to February 2016; shortlist announced late April 2016; exhibition and publication October 2016; UK tour for one year thereafter.

Writers' & Artists' Yearbook 2016 Short Story Competition

website www.writersandartists.co.uk

See information panel on page vii of this edition or visit our website for details.

YouWriteOn.com – see Arts Council site YouWriteOn.com Book Awards

PRIZE WINNERS

This is a selection of high-profile literary prize winners from 2014–15 presented chronologically. Entries for many of the these prizes are included in the *Yearbook*, starting on page 534.

May 2014

Independent Foreign Fiction Prize
The Iraqi Christ by Hassan Blasim (translated from Arabic by Jonathan Wright)
Commonwealth Short Story Prize
Let's Tell This Story Properly by Jennifer Nansubuga Makumbi

June

Baileys Women's Prize for Fiction
A Girl is a Half-Formed Thing by Eimear McBride
The CILIP Carnegie Medal
The Bunker Diary by Kevin Brooks
The CILIP Kate Greenaway Medal
This Is Not My Hat by John Klassen

September

BBC National Short Story Award
Kilifi Creek by Lionel Shriver

October

The Nobel Prize in Literature
Patrick Modiano
The Man Booker Prize
The Narrow Road to the Deep North by Richard Flanagan
The Bridport Prize
Clear Recent History by Natalya Anderson (Poetry); *Scenes of a Long Term Nature* by Tracy Slaughter (Short Story); *Romans Chapter 1 Verse 29* by Kit de Waal (Flash Fiction)

November

National Book Awards (USA)
Redeployment by Phil Klay (Fiction); *Age of Ambition: Chasing Fortune, Truth, and Faith in the New China* by Evan Osnos (Non-fiction); *Brown Girl Dreaming* by Jacqueline Woodson (Young People's Literature); *Faithful and Virtuous Night* by Louise Glück (Poetry)

December

Specsavers National Book Awards
The Miniaturist by Jessie Burton (Book of the Year)

January 2015

T.S. Eliot Prize for Poetry
Fire Songs by David Harsent
Costa Book of the Year
H is for Hawk by Helen Macdonald

February

David Cohen Prize for Literature
Tony Harrison
Red House Children's Book Award
The Day the Crayons Quit by Drew Daywalt and Oliver Jeffers

March

Blue Peter Book Awards
The Spy Who Loved School Dinners by Pamela Butchart (Best Story); *The Silly Book of Side-Splitting Stuff* by Andy Seed (Best Book with Facts)
The Folio Prize
Family Life by Akhil Sharma

April

Waterstones Children's Book Prize
Blown Away by Rob Biddulph (Best Illustrated Book and Overall Winner); *Half Bad* by Sally Green (Best Fiction for Teenagers); *Murder Most Unladylike* by Robin Stevens (Best Younger Fiction)
The Sunday Times EFG Private Bank Short Story Award
A Sheltered Woman by Yiyun Li
The Pulitzer Prize (USA)
All the Light We Cannot See by Anthony Doerr (Fiction); *Digest* by Gregory Pardlo (Poetry); *Encounters at the Heart of the World: A History of the Mandan People* by Elizabeth A. Fenn (History); *The Sixth Extinction: An Unnatural History* by Elizabeth Kolbert (General Non-fiction); *The Pope and Mussolini: The Secret History of Pius XI and the Rise of Fascism in Europe* by David I. Kertzer (Biography or Autobiography); *Between Riverside and Crazy* by Stephen Adly Guirgis (Drama); *Anthracite Fields* by Julia Wolfe (Music)

Festivals for writers, artists and readers

There are hundreds of arts festivals held in the UK each year – too many to mention in this *Yearbook*. We give here a selection of literature, writing and general arts festivals which include literature events. Space constraints and the nature of an annual publication together determine that only brief details are given; contact festival organisers for a full programme of events. A directory of literature-related festivals is maintained by the British Council. Visit http://literature.britishcouncil.org/festivals.

Ageas Salisbury International Arts Festival

87 Crane Street, Salisbury, Wilts. SP1 2PU
tel (01722) 332241
email info@salisburyfestival.co.uk
website www.salisburyfestival.co.uk
Takes place May–June

A thriving, annual multi-arts festival that includes strong music and literature programmes.

Aldeburgh Poetry Festival

The Poetry Trust, 9 New Cut, Halesworth, Suffolk IP19 8BY
tel (01986) 835950
email info@thepoetrytrust.org
website www.thepoetrytrust.org
Director Ellen McAteer
Takes place annually on the first weekend in November

Takes place on 6–8 November 2015 across venues in Aldeburgh and at Snape Maltings. Annual festival of contemporary poetry with readings, workshops, talks, discussions, public masterclass and children's event. Founded 1989.

Appledore Book Festival

Brenda Daly, Festival Office, Docton Court Gallery, 2 Myrtle Street, Appledore, Bideford, Devon EX39 1PH
email info@appledorebookfestival.co.uk
website www.appledorebookfestival.co.uk
Takes place 26 September–4 October 2015

Founded by children's author Nick Arnold this annual festival includes a schools programme covering north Devon and public events for all ages; also book fairs and a bookshop. Founded 2007.

Asia House Festival of Asian Literature

Asia House, 63 New Cavendish Street, London W1G 7LP
tel 020-7307 5454
email enquiries@asiahouse.co.uk
website www.asiahouse.co.uk
Takes place May

The only festival in the UK dedicated to writing about Asia and Asians. It covers Asia in the broadest context, from the Persian Gulf in the west to Indonesia in the east.

Aspects Irish Literature Festival

email info@aspectsfestival.com
website www.apectsfestival.com

An annual celebration of contemporary Irish writing with novelists, poets and playwrights. Includes readings, discussion, workshops, comedy, music and an Aspects showcase day for young writers.

Autumn International Literary Festival

University of East Anglia, Norwich NR4 7TJ
tel (01603) 456161
email literaryevents@uea.ac.uk
website www.uea.ac.uk/litfest
Contact Festival Administrator
Takes place Late September–early December

An annual festival of events bringing established writers of fiction, biography and poetry to a public audience in the Eastern region.

Ballymena Creative Citizen Programme

The Braid Ballymena Town Hall, Museum & Arts Centre, 1–29 Bridge Street, Ballymena, Co. Antrim BT43 5EJ
tel 028-2563-5900
email braid.enquiries@ballymena.gov.uk
website www.thebraid.com
Contact Hannah Gibson
Takes place March–May

Bath Literature Festival

Bath Festivals, Abbey Chambers, Kingston Buildings, Bath BA1 1NT
tel (01225) 462231 Box Office (01225) 463362
email info@bathfestivals.org.uk
website www.bathfestivals.org.uk/literature
Takes place February/March

An annual festival with leading guest writers. Includes readings, debates, discussions and workshops, and events for children and young people.

Ulster Bank Belfast Festival at Queen's

Queen's University, Lanyon North, University Road, Belfast BT7 1NN
tel 028-9097 1034
email belfastfestival@qub.ac.uk
website www.belfastfestival.com
Festival Director Richard Wakely
Takes place October/November

Ireland's leading contemporary international arts festival. Includes literature events.

Beverley Literature Festival

Wordquake, Council Offices, Skirlaugh, East Riding of Yorkshire HU11 5HN
tel (01482) 392745
email bevlitfestival@eastriding.gov.uk
website www.bevlit.org
Festival Director Dorcas Taylor
Takes place 1–10 October 2015

Beverley Literature Festival is one of the UK's leading literature festivals. The festival includes authors' events, readings, panel events, workshops, children's activities, performances and readings.

Birmingham Literature Festival

Unit 204, Custard Factory, Gibb Street, Birmingham B9 4AA
tel 0121 246 2770
email sara@writingwestmidlands.org
website www.birminghamliteraturefestival.org
Programmes Director Sara Beadle
Takes place 8–17 October 2015

Promoting excellent writing, with events ranging from the local to the international, the Festival reflects the diversity of the city, a place made beautiful by its patchwork of industry, culture, art, history and commerce. Events include in conversations, book readings, book launches, performances, poetry slams, quizzes, writing workshops, reading days/afternoons and much more. A project of Writing West Midlands.

Bread and Roses

c/o Five Leaves Bookshop, 14a Long Row, Nottingham NG1 2DH
email bookshop@fiveleaves.co.uk
website www.fiveleavesbookshop.co.uk
Contact Ross Bradshaw
Takes place November

An annual weekend of radical politics, music and literature held at various venues in Nottingham. The initial weekend in 2014 featured Owen Jones, Iain Sinclair and Natalie Bennett, leader of the Green Party. The only book festival supported by trade unions.

Bridlington Poetry Festival

Wordquake, Council Offices, Skirlaugh, East Riding of Yorkshire HU11 5HN
tel (01482) 392745
email brid.poetryfest@eastriding.gov.uk
website www.bridlington-poetry-festival.com
Festival Directors Dorcas Taylor, Antony Dunn
Takes place June

One of the UK's leading poetry festivals held in the beautiful coastal surroundings of Sewerby Hall and Gardens. A residential poetry school runs alongside the festival. Founded 2010.

Brighton Festival

29 New Road, Brighton BN1 1UG
tel (01273) 700747
email info@brightonfestival.org
website www.brightonfestival.org
Takes place May

An annual arts festival with an extensive national and international programme featuring theatre, dance, music, opera, literature, outdoor and family events.

Bristol Poetry Festival and Bristol Spring Poetry Festival

Poetry Can, 12 Great George Street, Bristol BS1 5RH
tel 0117 933 0900
email admin@poetrycan.co.uk
website www.poetrycan.co.uk
Festival Director Colin Brown
Takes place April–May and September

A celebration of language, imagination and life. Features award-winning poets and performers from all over the UK and abroad. Venues include Arnolfini and various Bristol locations.

Buxton Festival

3 The Square, Buxton, Derbyshire SK17 6AZ
tel (01298) 70395
email info@buxtonfestival.co.uk
website www.buxtonfestival.co.uk
Artistic Director Stephen Barlow, *Chief Executive* Randall Shannon
Takes place July

The incredible opera and music programme is complemented by a much envied Literary Series, featuring distinguished authors, which takes place every morning and afternoon.

Canterbury Festival

8 Orange Street, Canterbury, Kent CT1 2JA
tel (01227) 452853
email info@canterburyfestival.co.uk
website www.canterburyfestival.co.uk
Takes place 17–31 October 2015

An annual international arts festival with 200 events in two weeks.

Charleston Festival

The Charleston Trust, Charleston, Firle, Lewes, East Sussex BN8 6LL

email info@charleston.org.uk
website www.charleston.org.uk
Takes place 10 days at end of May

Charleston, country home of Bloomsbury artists Duncan Grant and Vanessa Bell, hosts an annual literary festival involving writers, performers, politicians and thinkers – both high profile and up and coming, national and international.

The Times and The Sunday Times Cheltenham Literature Festival

109–111 Bath Road, Cheltenham, Glos. GL53 7LS
tel (01242) 511211
website www.cheltenhamfestivals.com
Takes place 2–11 October 2015

This annual festival is the largest of its kind in Europe. Events include talks and lectures, poetry readings, novelists in conversation, exhibitions, discussions, workshops and two large bookshops. *Book It!* is a festival for children within the main festival with an extensive programme of events. Brochures are available in August. Founded 1949.

Chester Literature Festival

website www.chesterliteraturefestival.co.uk
Takes place October

A leading literature festival, grown in stature and scale in recent years, with scores of events spread over a fortnight featuring writers from the internationally acclaimed to emerging local talent. The festival incorporates GobbleDeeBook, an annual week-long children's literature festival with workshops, plays and parties as well as events featuring dozens of children's authors.

City of London Festival

Fitz Eylwin House, 25 Holborn Viaduct, London EC1A 2BP
email info@colf.org
website www.colf.org
Director Paul Gudgin

Every summer the Festival takes over the City's most beautiful venues with hundreds of ticketed and free arts events for everyone.

Cork International Short Story Festival

Frank O'Connor House, 84 Douglas Street, Cork, Republic of Ireland
tel +353 (0)21 4312955
email info@munsterlit.ie
website www.munsterlit.ie
website www.corkshortstory.net
Takes place September

Run by the Munster Literature Centre, this festival includes readings, seminars and public interviews, and is host to several short story awards, including the Frank O'Connor Short Story Award. The Centre also hosts the annual Cork Spring Poetry Festival.

Cúirt International Festival of Literature

Galway Arts Centre, 47 Dominick Street, Galway, Republic of Ireland
tel +353 (0)91 565886
email info@galwayartscentre.ie
website www.cuirt.ie
Progamme Director Dani Gill
Takes place 19–24 April 2016

An annual week-long festival to celebrate writing, bringing together national and international writers to promote literary discussion. Events include readings, performances, workshops, seminars, lectures, poetry slams and talks. The festival is renowned for its convivial atmosphere ('cúirt' means a 'bardic court or gathering'). Founded 1985.

The Daunt Books Festival

83 Marylebone High Street, London W1U 4QW
tel 020-7224 2295
email marylebone@dauntbooks.co.uk
website www.dauntbooks.co.uk
Festival Organiser Emily Rhodes

The Daunt Books Festival takes place in a beautiful Edwardian premises in Marylebone. This annual celebration of literature goes to show that a bookshop is not just a place to buy books but a space to bring readers together, to foster a literary community and to have a great deal of fun in the process. Key speakers have included Michael Palin, Antonia Fraser, Colin Thubron, Owen Jones, Tracy Chevalier, Sebastian Barry, William Fiennes, Robert Muchamore and Michael Morpurgo.

Dinefwr Literature Festival

Literature Wales, 4th Floor, Cambrian Buildings, Mount Stuart Square, Cardiff CF10 5FL
tel 029-2047 2266
email post@literaturewales.org
website www.dinefwrliteraturefestival.co.uk
Takes place June

Dinefwr Literature Festival takes place at the beautiful Dinefwr Park and Castle in Carmarthenshire. The bilingual (Welsh/English) festival features an eclectic mix of literature, music, comedy, children's activities and nature walks. The line-up includes award-winning novelists, performance poets, children's authors, singer-songwriters and scriptwriters, plus fringe acts appealing to children and adults alike. The festival is organised by Literature Wales in partnership with National Trust, Cadw and University of Wales Trinity Saint David, and is supported by Arts Council of Wales.

Dublin Book Festival

c/o Dublin UNESCO City of Literature, 138–144 Pearse Street, Dublin 2, Republic of Ireland
tel +353 (0)1 4425713
email info@dublinbookfestival.com
website www.dublinbookfestival.com

Dublin Book Festival brings together the best of Irish publishing, offering a chance for the voices of both established and up and coming authors to be heard. Held in Smock Alley Theatre, the festival's events include book launches, interviews, workshops, a children's and schools programme and lots more.

Durham Book Festival

New Writing North, PO Box 1277,
Newcastle upon Tyne NE99 5PB
email office@newwritingnorth.com
website www.durhambookfestival.com
Takes place October

A book festival for new and established writers, taking place in the historic city of Durham.

Edinburgh International Book Festival

5A Charlotte Square, Edinburgh EH2 4DR
tel 0131 718 5666
email admin@edbookfest.co.uk
website www.edbookfest.co.uk
Director Nick Barley
Takes place August

Europe's largest public celebration of books and reading. In addition to a unique independent bookselling operation, more than 800 UK and international writers appear in over 750 events for adults and children. Programme details available in June.

Ennis Book Club Festival

Clare County Library, Mill Road, Ennis, Co. Clare, Republic of Ireland
tel +353 (0)87 9723642
email info@ennisbookclubfestival.com
website www.ennisbookclubfestival.com
Takes place First weekend in March

An annual literary weekend which brings together book club members, book lovers and writers. Includes lectures, readings, discussions, workshops and exhibitions.

Essex Poetry Festival

Flat 3, 1 Clifton Terrace, Southend-on-Sea,
Essex SS1 1DT
email adrian@essex-poetry-festival.co.uk
website www.essex-poetry-festival.co.uk
Contact Adrian Green
Takes place October

A poetry festival across Essex. Also includes the Young Essex Poet of the Year Competition.

Festival at the Edge

39 Fawdry Street, Whitmore Reans,
Wolverhampton WV1 4PA
tel 07544 044126
email info@festivalattheedge.org
website www.festivalattheedge.org
Takes place July

A storytelling festival with a mix of stories, music and performance, held in Much Wenlock, Shropshire.

The Festival of Writing

The Writers' Workshop, The Studio, Sheep Street,
Charlbury OX7 3RR
tel 0345 459 9560
email info@writersworkshop.co.uk
website www.writersworkshop.co.uk
Events Director Laura Wilkins
Takes place in York 4–6 September 2015

A festival for aspiring writers providing the opportunity to meet literary agents, publishers, professional authors and book doctors. Keynote speakers from across the industry. Also workshops, competitions, networking events, Q&A panels and the chance to pitch work directly to literary agents.

Folkestone Book Festival

tel (01303) 760740
email info@folkestonebookfest.com
website www.folkestonebookfest.com
Takes place 20–29 November 2015

An annual festival with over 40 events, including a Children's Day.

Free the Word!

PEN International, Brownlow House,
50–51 High Holborn, London WC1V 6ER
tel 020-7405 0338
email info@internationalpen.org.uk
website www.internationalpen.org.uk/events-festivals/free-the-word
Takes place April

Free the Word! is a festival for authors and readers which bridges the divide between national literatures. Presents writers from countries worldwide at events in London.

Guildford Book Festival

c/o Tourist Information Office, 155 High Street,
Guildford GU1 3AJ
tel (01483) 444334
email director@guildfordbookfestival.co.uk
website www.guildfordbookfestival.co.uk
Takes place 11–18 October 2015

An annual festival. Diverse, provocative and entertaining, held throughout the historic town and drawing audiences from throughout London and the south-east. Author events, workshops and schools programme. Its aim is to further an interest and love of literature by involvement and entertainment. Founded 1989.

Harrogate History Festival

32 Cheltenham Parade, Harrogate,
North Yorkshire HG1 1DB
tel (01423) 562303
email info@harrogate-festival.org.uk
website www.harrogateinternationalfestivals.com/history/

Takes place 22–25 October 2015

Four days of events celebrating the best of historical writing, as well as inspiring talks and discussions on historical topics.

The Hay Festival

Festival Office, The Drill Hall, 25 Lion Street, Hay-on-Wye HR3 5AD
tel (01497) 822620 (admin)
email admin@hayfestival.org
website www.hayfestival.org
Takes place May/June

This annual festival of literature and the arts in Hay-on-Wye, Wales, brings together writers, musicians, film-makers, historians, politicians, environmentalists and scientists from around the world to communicate challenging ideas. More than 700 events over ten days. Within the annual festival is a festival for families and children, Hay Fever, which introduces children, from toddlers to teenagers, to their favourite authors and holds workshops to entertain and educate. Programme published April.

Huddersfield Literature Festival

School of Humanities, Music and Media, University of Huddersfield HD1 3DH
tel (01484) 430228
email huddlitfest@gmail.com
website www.litfest.org.uk
Festival Director Michelle Hodgson

The festival programmes events to support and showcase new, emerging and established writers/ artists, including author talks, writing and performance workshops, multi-arts performances, innovative spoken word events and the Huddersfield Manga Con, Majikkon. Founded 2006.

Ilkley Literature Festival

9 The Grove, Ilkley LS29 9LW
tel (01943) 601210
email admin@ilkleyliteraturefestival.org.uk
website www.ilkleyliteraturefestival.org.uk
Festival Director Rachel Feldberg, *Festival Manager* Gail Price, *Administrator* Laura Beddows
Takes place 2–18 October 2015

The north of England's oldest, largest and most prestigious literature festival with over 250 events, from author discussions to workshops, readings, literary walks, children's events and a festival fringe. Founded 1973.

Independent Bookshop Week

website www.independentbooksellersweek.org.uk
Takes place June

Independent Bookshop Week is an annual celebration of independent bookshops and is part of the IndieBound campaign (www.indiebound.org.uk) to promote independent bookshops, strong reading communities and the idea of shopping locally and sustainably. Independent Bookshop Week brings together bookshops, publishers and consumers through events such as National Reading Group Day, author visits and storytime sessions, and offers from publishers.

International Literature Festival Dublin

c/o Dublin City Council, Arts Office, The Lab, Foley Street, Dublin 1, Republic of Ireland
tel +353 (0)1 2225455
email info@ilfdublin.com
website www.ilfdublin.com
Takes place May

The International Literature Festival Dublin (formerly the Dublin Writers Festival) is Ireland's premier literary event and gathers the finest writers in the world to debate, provoke, delight and enthral. The Festival continues to champion Dublin's position as a UNESCO City of Literature, celebrating the local alongside the global and the power of words to change the world. With readings, discussions, debates, workshops, performances and screenings, the Festival creates a hotbed of ideas for all ages to enjoy. Founded 1998.

Jewish Book Week

Jewish Book Council, ORT House, 126 Albert Street, London NW1 7NE
tel 020-7446 8771
email info@jewishbookweek.com
website www.jewishbookweek.com
Festival Coordinator Sarah Fairbairn
Takes place Feb/March

A festival of Jewish writing, with contributors from around the world and sessions in London and nationwide. Includes events for children and teenagers.

King's Lynn Festival

Bishops Lynn House, 18 Tuesday Market Place, King's Lynn, Norfolk PE30 1JW
tel (01553) 767557
email info@kingslynnfestival.org.uk
website www.kingslynnfestival.org.uk
Administrator Ema Holman
Takes place 17–30 July 2016

An annual arts festival with a music focus, including literature events featuring leading guest writers. Founded 1951.

King's Lynn Literature Festivals

email enquiries@lynnlitfests.com
website www.lynnlitfests.com
Chairman Tony Ellis
Takes place Sept/March

Poetry Festival (25–27 Sept 2015): An annual festival which brings 12 published poets to King's Lynn for the weekend for readings and discussions.

Fiction Festival (March 2016): An annual festival which brings ten published novelists to King's Lynn for the weekend for readings and discussions.

Kingston Readers' Festival

Kingston University, River House,
53–57 High Street, Kingston upon Thames KT1 1LQ
tel 020-8417 9000
email events@kingston.ac.uk
website www.kingston.ac.uk/krf
Festival Director Sandy Williams
Takes place April/May

A small non-profit-making limited company with charitable and educational aims to:

- Foster and celebrate a love of reading.
- Promote a broad range of events for all ages, including short story, poetry and writing for performance competitions.
- Develop an outreach programme comprising workshops and authors' talks.
- Promote the work of Kingston University and the Rose Theatre, Kingston.
- Raise money for local good causes and other reading-related charities. Established 2002.

Knutsford Literature Festival

website www.knutsfordlitfest.org
Takes place October

An annual festival to celebrate writing and performance, with distinguished national, international and local authors. Events include readings and discussions, a literary lunch and theatrical performances.

Laureate na nÓg

Children's Books Ireland,
17 North Great George's Street, Dublin 1, Ireland
tel +353 (0)18 727475
email info@childrenslaureate.ie
email info@childrensbooksireland.ie
website www.childrenslaureate.ie

This is a project recognising the role and importance of literature for children in Ireland. This unique honour was awarded for the first time in 2010. The position is held for a period of two years. The laureate participates in selected events and activities around Ireland and internationally during their term.

The laureate is chosen in recognition of their widely recognised high-quality children's writing or illustration and the considerably positive impact they have had on readers as well as other writers and illustrators. Laureate na nÓg 2014–2016: Eoin Colfer. The 2016–2018 Laureate na nÓg will be announced in May 2016.

Ledbury Poetry Festival

Master's House, St Katherines, Bye Street,
Ledbury HR8 1EA
tel (01531) 6341563
email manager@poetry-festival.co.uk
website www.poetry-festival.co.uk
Festival Manager Phillippa Slinger
Takes place July

An annual festival featuring top poets from around the world, together with a poet-in-residence programme, competitions (see rules and download form from website), workshops, community events and exhibitions.

Listowel Writers' Week

24 The Square, Listowel, Co. Kerry,
Republic of Ireland
tel +353 (0)68 21074
email info@writersweek.ie
website www.writersweek.ie
Festival Managers Eilish Wren, Maire Logue
Takes place 1–5 June 2016

Listowel Writers' Week is an acclaimed literary festival devoted to bringing together writers and audiences at unique and innovative events in the historic and intimate surroundings of Listowel, County Kerry. At the heart of the annual celebration is a commitment to developing and promoting writing talent, underpinned by an organisation that works to the values of partnership, inclusivity and civic responsibility. Events include workshops, readings, seminars, lectures, book launches, art exhibitions and a comprehensive children's and teenagers' programme. Founded 1971.

Litfest

The Storey, Meeting House Lane, Lancaster LA1 1TH
tel (01524) 62166
email marketing@litfest.org
website www.litfest.org
Takes place 15–19 October 2015

Annual literature festival featuring prose and poetry from local, national and international writers. Litfest is the literature development agency for Lancashire with a year round programme of reading and occasional workshops.

London Literature Festival

Southbank Centre, Belvedere Road, London SE1 8XX
tel 020-7960 4200
email customer@southbankcentre.co.uk
website www.southbankcentre.co.uk/whatson/festivals-series/london-literature-festival
Takes place October

A two-week festival featuring international and prize-winning authors, historians, poets, performers and artists, children's events, specially commissioned work, debate and discussion, interactive and improvised writing and performance. Founded 2007.

Lowdham Book Festival

c/o The Bookcase, 50 Main Street,
Lowdham NG14 7BE
tel 0115-966 4143
email info@fiveleaves.co.uk
website www.lowdhambookfestival.co.uk
Contact Jane Streeter

Takes place June

An annual ten-day festival of literature events for adults and children, with a daily programme of high-profile national and local writers. The last day always features dozens of free events and a large book fair.

Manchester Children's Book Festival

The Manchester Writing School at MMU,
Dept of English,
Manchester Metropolitan University,
Rosamond Street West, Off Oxford Road,
Manchester M15 6LL
tel 0161 247 2424
email mcbf@mmu.ac.uk
website www.mcbf.org.uk
Festival Directors Carol Ann Duffy (Creative Director), James Draper (Director: Marketing & Development), Kaye Tew (Director: Education & Partnerships)
Takes place 24 June–3 July 2016

An annual festival celebrating the very best writing for children, inspiring young people to engage with literature and creativity across the curriculum, and offering extended projects and training to ensure the event has an impact and legacy in classrooms.

Manchester Literature Festival

The Department Store, 5 Oak Street,
Manchester M4 5JD
tel 0161 832 5502
email office@manchesterliteraturefestival.co.uk
website www.manchesterliteraturefestival.co.uk
Directors Cathy Bolton and Sarah-Jane Roberts

An annual two-week festival in October celebrating the best new literature from around the world.

May Festival

Events Team, University of Aberdeen,
King's College, Aberdeen AB24 3FX
tel (01224) 273874
email festival@abdn.ac.uk
website www.abdn.ac.uk/mayfestival
Takes place May

The May Festival programme aims to engage people of all ages and backgrounds, providing a culturally-enriching experience of the North East, Scotland and beyond. It aims to build on the success of research projects and past and present activities such as Word, Director's Cut, the British Science Festival and the music concert series. Events include debates, lectures, readings, workshops and concerts spanning areas such as literature, science, music, film, Gaelic, food and nutrition.

National Eisteddfod of Wales

40 Parc Ty Glas, Llanisien, Cardiff CF14 5DU
tel 0845 409 0300
email gwyb@eisteddfod.org.uk
website www.eisteddfod.org.uk
Chief Executive Elfed Roberts
Takes place August

Wales's largest cultural festival. Activities include competitions in all aspects of the arts, fringe performances and majestic ceremonies. In addition to activities held in the main pavilion, it houses over 300 trade stands along with a literary pavilion, a music studio, a movement and dance theatre, an outdoor performance stage and a purpose-built theatre. The event is set in a different location each year; Montgomeryshire in 2015 and Monmouthshire in 2016.

National Short Story Week

email admin@shortstoryweek.org.uk
website www.nationalshortstoryweek.org.uk
Director Ian Skillicorn
Takes place 16–22 November 2015

An annual awareness week aimed at encouraging more people to write, read and listen to short stories. Events held around the UK with involvement from publishers, writers, libraries, universities, writing organisations and readers. See website for details of the Annual Young Writers' competition. Founded 2010.

Noirwich Crime Writing Literary Festival

School of Literature, Drama and Creative Writing,
University of East Anglia, Norwich NR4 7TJ
tel (01603) 592738
email henry.sutton@uea.ac.uk
website www.writerscentrenorwich.org.uk/noirwich.aspx
Takes place September

Noirwich Crime Writing Festival celebrates the sharpest noir and crime writing over four days of author and academic events, film screenings and writing masterclasses in Norwich, UNESCO City of Literature. A collaboration between the Crime Writers' Association, the University of East Anglia, Waterstones and Writers' Centre Norwich.

Norfolk & Norwich Festival

Augustine Steward House, 14 Tombland,
Norwich NR3 1HF
tel (01603) 877750
email info@nnfestival.org.uk
website www.nnfestival.org.uk
Takes place annually in May

Off the Shelf Festival of Words Sheffield

Room 311, Town Hall, Pinstone Street,
Sheffield S1 2HH
tel 0114 273 4716
email offtheshelf@sheffield.gov.uk
website www.offtheshelf.org.uk
Takes place 10–31 October 2015

A diverse and exciting and exciting literature festival with more than 150 events including well-known author talks, writing workshops, poetry, family activities, debates, competitions and exhibitions.

Oundle Festival of Literature

email oundlelitfest@hotmail.co.uk
website www.oundlelitfest.org.uk
Festival Manager Helen Shair
Takes place March and throughout the year

Featuring a full programme of author events, poetry, philosophy, politics, storytelling, biography, illustrators and novelists for young and old. Includes events for children.

FT Weekend Oxford Literary Festival

Registered Office, Greyfriars Court, Paradise Square, Oxford OX1 1BE
tel (01865) 286074
email info@oxfordliteraryfestival.org
website www.oxfordliteraryfestival.org
Festival Chief Executive Sally Dunsmore
Takes place March/April

An annual festival for both adults and children. Presents topical debates, fiction and non-fiction discussion panels, and adult and children's authors who have recently published books. Topics range from contemporary fiction to discussions on politics, history, science, gardening, food, poetry, philosophy, art and crime fiction.

Poetry International

Literature Department, Southbank Centre, Belvedere Road, London SE1 8XX
website www.southbankcentre.co.uk
Contact Anna Selby
Takes place July

The biggest poetry festival in the British Isles, bringing together a wide range of poets from around the world. Includes readings, workshops and discussions. The Literature + Spoken Word department also runs a year-round programme of readings, talks and debates.

Port Eliot Festival

Port Eliot Estate Office, St Germans, Saltash, Cornwall PL12 5ND
tel (01503) 232783
email info@porteliotfestival.com
website www.porteliotfestival.com

The idyllic Port Eliot estate in Cornwall plays host to the UK's most imaginative arts festival; over 100 performances on ten different stages, presenting a wealth of creative talent from the worlds of books, music, fashion, food and film. Port Eliot aims to raise the spirits of and inspire its audience, and the festival prides itself on offering something a little bit different.

Quite Literary

The Plough Arts Centre, 9–11 Fore Street, Torrington, Devon EX38 8HQ
tel (01805) 622552
email richard@theploughartscentre.org.uk
website www.theploughartscentre.co.uk
Contact Richard Wolfenden-Brown
Takes place Throughout the year

An occasional literature programme including workshops, readings, performances and exhibitions, as part of a larger programme of arts work, including community and educational workshops, projects, residencies and performances. For info on The Plough Prize international poetry competition, visit www.theploughprize.co.uk.

Raworths Literature Series

32 Cheltenham Parade, Harrogate, North Yorkshire HG1 1DB
tel (01423) 562303
email info@harrogate-festival.org.uk
website www.harrogateinternationalfestivals.com/raworths-literature-series/
Takes place July

Four days of literary events designed to inspire and stimulate.

Readathon

Read for Good, 26 Nailsworth Mills, Avening Road, Nailsworth, Glos. GL6 0BS
tel 0845 606 1151
email reading@readathon.org
website www.readathon.org

Readathon is the UK-wide sponsored reading event for schools, encouraging children of all ages to read for pleasure, motivated by the knowledge that the money they raise will help seriously ill children via Readathon's partner charities. Readathon may be run at any time of year to suit each school's preference. Pupils choose their own reading material, which needn't just be books. Pre-readers may listen to stories or share picture books. Each school receives book vouchers worth 20% of its sponsorship total. Founded 1984.

Richmond upon Thames Literature Festival, Arts Service

Orleans House Gallery, Riverside, Twickenham TW1 3DJ
tel 020-8831 6000
email artsinfo@richmond.gov.uk
website www.richmondliterature.com
Takes place Throughout November

An annual literature festival featuring a diverse programme of authors, commentators and leading figures from sport, television, politics and journalism in a range of interesting and unique venues across the borough. The festival includes something for everyone, with an exciting programme for all ages and interests.

Rye Arts Festival

Literary Events Director, Little Maxfield, Fourteen Acre Lane, Three Oaks, Hastings, East Sussex TN35 4NB

tel (01797) 224442
website www.ryeartsfestival.co.uk
Literary Events Director Catherine Bingham
Takes place Last 2 weeks of September (15 days)

Annual festival of literary events featuring biographers, novelists, political and environmental writers with book signings and discussions. Runs concurrently with festival of music and visual arts.

Small Wonder: The Short Story Festival

The Charleston Trust, Charleston, Firle, Lewes, East Sussex BN8 6LL
tel (01323) 811626
email festivals@charleston.org.uk
website www.charleston.org.uk
Takes place 23–27 September 2015

Charleston, country home of the Bloomsbury set, hosts this respected annual short story jamboree. Small Wonder celebrates the most innovative short fiction in a variety of forms from top practitioners of the art, and also incorporates a fringe programme of participatory events for all ages.

Spring Literary Festival

University of East Anglia, Norwich NR4 7TJ
tel (01603) 592286
email literaryevents@uea.ac.uk
website www.uea.ac.uk/litfest
Contact Festival Administrator
Takes place February to April

An annual festival of events bringing established writers of fiction, biography and poetry to a public audience in the Eastern region.

St Ives Literature Festival

tel (01736) 753899
email info@stiveslitfest.co.uk
website www.facebook.com/StIvesLiteratureFestival
Contact Bob Devereux
Takes place Second week in May

Organised in association with a number of Cornwall and West Country publishers, the festival consists of readings, talks, workshops and performance events.

StAnza: Scotland's International Poetry Festival

tel (01334) 475000 (box office), (01334) 474610 (programmes)
email info@stanzapoetry.org
website www.stanzapoetry.org
Festival Director Eleanor Livingstone
Takes place March

The festival engages with all forms of poetry: read and spoken verse, poetry in exhibition, performance poetry, cross-media collaboration, schools work, book launches and poetry workshops, with numerous UK and international guests and weekend children's events. Founded 1997.

States of Independence

c/o Five Leaves Publications, PO Box 8786, Nottingham NG1 9AW
email info@fiveleaves.co.uk
website www.statesofindependence.co.uk
Contact Ross Bradshaw
Takes place March

An annual one-day festival celebrating independent publishing. Held in mid-March at De Montfort University in Leicester. Involves independent publishers from the region and elsewhere in the country. A free event with 30 sessions and a book fair.

Stratford-upon-Avon Poetry Festival

Shakespeare Centre, Henley Street, Stratford-upon-Avon CV37 6QW
tel (01789) 204016
email info@shakespeare.org.uk
website www.shakespeare.org.uk
Takes place June/July

An annual festival to celebrate poetry past and present with special reference to the works of Shakespeare. Events include: evenings of children's verse, a Poetry Mass and a local poets' evening. Sponsored by The Shakespeare Birthplace Trust.

Swindon Festival of Literature

Lower Shaw Farm, Shaw, Swindon, Wilts. SN5 5PJ
tel (01793) 771080
email swindonlitfest@lowershawfarm.co.uk
website www.swindonfestivalofliterature.co.uk
Festival Director Matt Holland
Takes place May

An annual celebration of live literature through prose, poetry, drama and storytelling, with readings, discussions, performances and talks in theatres, arts centres, parks and pubs. A festival of ideas with leading authors, speakers and performers.

Theakstons Old Peculier Crime Writing Festival

32 Cheltenham Parade, Harrogate, North Yorkshire HG1 1DB
tel (01423) 562303
email crime@harrogate-festival.org.uk
website www.harrogateinternationalfestivals.com/crime/
Takes place July

Four days of events featuring the best of UK and international crime writers.

The Dylan Thomas Festival

The Dylan Thomas Centre, Somerset Place, Swansea SA1 1RR
tel (01792) 463980
email dylanthomas.lit@swansea.gov.uk
website www.dylanthomas.com

Events Manager Jo Furber
Takes place 27 October–9 November each year

An annual festival celebrating the life and work of Swansea's most famous son: performances, lectures, debates, poetry, music and film. Also, regular events throughout the year and talks and tours by arrangement.

Warwick Words – Festival of Literature and Spoken Word

The Court House, Jury Street, Warwick CV34 4EW
tel (07944) 768607
email info@warwickwords.co.uk
website www.warwickwords.co.uk
Takes place beginning of June and October

Founded 1999.

Ways With Words Festivals of Words and Ideas

Droridge Farm, Dartington, Totnes, Devon TQ9 6JG
tel (01803) 867373
email admin@wayswithwords.co.uk
website www.wayswithwords.co.uk
Contact Kay Dunbar

Leading writers give talks, interviews and discussions. Events: Words by the Water Festival of Words and Ideas (Cumbria, March), The Telegraph Ways With Words Festival of Words and Ideas (Devon, July), the Southwold Literature Festival (Suffolk, November) and writing and art holidays in Italy and Devon.

Wells Festival of Literature

Old Ditch Farm, Lynch Lane,
Westbury Sub Mendip BA5 1HW
tel (07885) 225991
email speakers@wellsfestivalofliterature.org.uk
website www.wellsfestivalofliterature.org.uk
Takes place 9–17 October 2015

An 8-day festival, featuring leading writers of fiction and non-fiction, poets and performers. Programme includes talks, discussions, workshops, bookclub and competitions. Events in local schools and the community throughout the year. Takes place in the historic Wells Bishop's Palace. Founded 1992.

Wigtown Book Festival

Wigtown Festival Company, County Buildings, Wigtown, Dumfries & Galloway DG8 9JH
tel (01988) 402036
email mail@wigtownbookfestival.com
website www.wigtownbookfestival.com
Festival Manager Anne Barclay
Takes place 25 September–4 October 2015

An annual celebration of literature and the arts in Scotland's National Book Town. Over 180 events including author events, theatre, music, film and children's and young people's programmes.

The Winchester Writers' Festival

University of Winchester, Winchester,
Hants SO22 4NR
tel (01962) 827238
email judith.heneghan@winchester.ac.uk
email sara.gangai@winchester.ac.uk
website www.writersfestival.co.uk
Festival Director Judith Heneghan, *Events Manager* Sara Gangai
Takes place University of Winchester, third weekend in June

This festival of writing, celebrating its 35th year in 2015, attracts emerging writers from the UK and around the world who come for one-day masters' courses, talks, workshops and over 750 one-to-one appointments with 60 internationally renowned authors, poets, playwrights, literary agents and commissioning editors to help them harness their creativity and develop their writing, editing and marketing skills. Ten writing competitions, including Poetry, Short Stories, First Three Pages of the Novel, Flash Fiction, Children's Picture Books, Children's Funny Fiction, Memoir, Young Writers' Poetry Competition, Writing Can Be Murder and Pitch a TV Drama are open to all with prizes including editorial consultations. All first place winners are published in the annual Festival anthology. For information and registration, visit the website.

World Book Day

6 Bell Yard, London WC2A 2JR
tel 0906 265 0004 (helpline)
email wbd@education.co.uk
website www.worldbookday.com
Takes place first Thursday in March

An annual celebration of books and reading aimed at promoting their value and creating the readers of the future. Every schoolchild in full-time education receives a £1 (€1.50) book token and events take place all over the UK and Ireland in schools, bookshops and libraries. World Book Day was designated by UNESCO as a worldwide celebration of books and reading and is marked in over 30 countries. It is a partnership of publishers, National Book Tokens, booksellers and interested parties who work together to promote books and reading for the personal enrichment and enjoyment of all.

Digital and self-publishing
Electronic publishing

Ebooks continue to change the face of the publishing industry and possibilities for e-publishing are rapidly developing all the time. With new author-to-reader routes opening up, Philip Jones sets the scene and explains the implications for authors.

Markets, growth and sales

In the UK, the ebook market is now a fixed entity, with digital sales for most trade publishers now making up about 30% of their total books revenue. The market growth that was extreme between 2010 and 2013 has plateaued, with most publishers having recorded ebook sales growth in the teens over the past 12 to 18 months, a sharp deceleration from the growth seen in prior years. One might think from this that the rate of change has also lessened. However, the truth about digital publishing is that its significance is, if anything, even more fundamental than first imagined. Even if the pace of ebook growth continues to slow and stabilise – as many predict it will – the wider impact of digital on the book business runs deep and by no means in one direction.

At the beginning of 2014 the ebook market was dominated – as it has been throughout its creation and growth – by Amazon and its Kindle device, and by the end of 2014 little had changed in this regard. Challengers came – Apple, Google, Nook, Kobo, Blinkbox-books – but did not make a dent. In the case of Blinkbox the effort was too much, with Tesco closing its ebook retailer at the beginning of 2015.

For authors and publishers, the ebook market may have become a large and healthy part of their overall business; for retailers not called Amazon it remains a desert. But there was some innovation seen in 2014, with the launch of subscription services Oyster, Scribd and Mofibo (among others) who have inked deals with many major publishers in an attempt to expand the market beyond those readers already locked into Amazon. Subscription ebook vending is said to be perfect for tablets (devices on which many users already pay for subscription content) and this will become a major new front in digital reading in the years to come.

However, for now, it seems the market in 2014 was not much different from the previous year. We are, as before, stymied by the lack of verifiable data from this new marketplace; Amazon is the main player but does not share its numbers either with its investors, the news media, or third-party data companies such as Nielsen BookScan, which tracks physical book sales. Nevertheless, as in previous years, the *Bookseller* has collated the digital sales numbers from all the major trade publishers, providing a good view of most of the digital market. Domestic ebook sales for the five groups – Penguin Random House, Hachette, HarperCollins, Pan Macmillan – totalled 49m units in 2014, a 15.3% rise on 2013. Three of the five publishers recorded double-digit growth, with only Simon & Schuster down – albeit marginally – on 2013. By contrast, the top five publishers recorded an 18% rise in digital volume in 2013 over 2012, which followed that huge 105% gain in 2012 (on 2011).

For the past few years, the *Bookseller* has used the numbers provided by the big groups to make some assumptions about the overall digital market. The top five publishers represent 56% of BookScan's print volume in 2014; if we assume their digital market share is broadly in line with this, we can argue that the overall ebook market in 2014 amounted to 87.8m units, representing a year-on-year rise of 18.5% (compared with 20% in 2013). From this we extrapolate an overall market value of £370m, which is obtained by using the average selling price for digital content up to October as recorded by Nielsen consumer research.

How do these numbers chime with those reported elsewhere? The best source for publisher data is the *Publishers Association Statistics Yearbook*, which takes sales from across its membership, but reports the invoiced value (not the price paid at tills). Its figure for consumer ebook sales in 2013 was £263m, compared with £222m in 2012, representing growth of 18%. It had yet to release 2014 numbers when this edition went to press, but in July 2014 it had reported that publishers' digital sales grew 10% in the first quarter.

This context is important to understand when trying to figure out the growth rates of a market that is still in its infancy, and prone to tantrums. Last year in the *Yearbook* I wrote that – in the UK at least – the rate of growth in the ebook market was exaggerated in 2012 because of the *Fifty Shades* trilogy, which also then further skewed the perceived slowdown in sales growth in 2013; for example in 2012 the companies that would become Penguin Random House reported ebook sales volume growth of 169%, but one year later their ebook sales business fell by 20%. By contrast, Hachette followed a more understandable pattern, recording growth of 82% in 2012, 58% in 2013 and 7% in 2014. If we remove the Penguin Random House numbers from the calculations altogether, the market growth over the past three years has been as follows: 95% in 2012, 40% in 2013, and 13% in 2014.

If that looks familiar, it should; in the US, ebook sales registered treble-digit growth rates until 2012 when that market came off the boil and (in volume terms) recorded growth of around 50%, which then relented further in 2013, when the rate dropped to 10%. By this calculation, we are still about a year behind the Americans, meaning that all eyes should be turned to the States when it releases its 2014 full-year numbers to see what the ebook market has in store for us in 2015. So far, growth has been flat.

There are one or two conclusions worth reflecting on. The first follows the view put forward by HarperCollins UK chief executive Charlie Redmayne that the traditional Christmas sales spike has 'all but' disappeared, confirming what Waterstones MD James Daunt said in early 2015 that e-readers are no longer a Christmas gift item. Also, the shift to tablet reading, alongside the rise of subscription services, are likely to change the narrative again. As Kindle's Russ Grandinetti suggested in January 2015, stability is not on the menu. The good news seems to be that the book business is better at absorbing the shocks than we once thought.

The biggest question mark, however, remains over how big the market is that we do *not* see, as represented by authors who choose to self-publish, whether that is via Amazon's Kindle Direct Publishing platform, or those rivals offered by Nook and Kobo, or by using one of the print-on-demand players such as Blurb or Ingram. No sales made via these routes are being tracked (or indeed are trackable without the intervention of a third party such as Amazon). Estimates from Nielsen BookScan suggest that self-published ebooks account for as much as 20% of the market by volume, and perhaps 15% by value (self-publishers tend to sell their ebooks at prices well below the average), meaning that a reasonable estimate for the ebook market in the UK is that it is now about £400m, and growing – with self-publishers a not-insubstantial part of that overall digital market.

E-publishing highlights

Not everything is digitally equal, however. Even within trade publishing there are variances: commercial genre fiction far outsells literary fiction digitally. One of the biggest books of 2015 so far has been Paula Hawkins' *The Girl on the Train* (Transworld Digital 2015), that hit the top spot in January, and in the first quarter of 2015 was the sixth bestselling title in the physical book charts. However, sales of its digital edition have outpaced even those for its print book. In January and February it sold more than 111,000 ebooks, 60% of its overall digital and print book sales.

Emma Healey's *Elizabeth is Missing* (Penguin Books 2015), by contrast, has seen digital sales maxing-out at about 40% of its overall sales. The difference? *The Girl on the Train* is only out in hardback and therefore is more expensive as a print book than its digital equivalent, but also *Elizabeth is Missing* is more literary than Hawkins' thriller. We see similar patterns across the *Bookseller*'s monthly ebook rankings: commercial fiction transfers well across to the newer format, while non-fiction titles and children's books continue to do better in print. And, price matters. The remark, made by many, that throwaway books do well digitally and 'books for keeps' do less well, still holds true.

With regard to the overall book market, we do know that the number of print books sold has fallen consistently since its high point in 2008, thanks first to the recession, then a minor collapse in celebrity titles, and now the transfer to digital reading. This downturn has been in the range of 3%–5% annually, but since the beginning of 2000 the rate of decline has accelerated with paperback fiction sales consistently down as digital has risen.

Having said that, 2014 was not a bad year for print. Just as digital growth has slowed, so has the downturn in print. Nielsen BookScan's measure of the print market showed total consumer sales of £1.4 billion in 2014, down 1.3%. This is the lowest total since 2002, but also the lowest drop for three years. Fiction sales fell 5.3%, non-fiction was down 4%. But there was remarkable growth in one sector, children's books, which saw sales grow 9%, meaning that the children's book business is now bigger than adult fiction.The irony is that the big trend in 2014 was a digital one, albeit one that resulted in print book sales. Children's publisher Egmont created four of the biggest books of 2014 by turning the online game Minecraft into a book franchise; new publisher Blink Publishing turned prominent YouTube star (vlogger) Alfie Deyes into an author with the arrival of *The Pointless Book*; while Penguin Random House made fellow vlogger Zoe Sugg (aka Zoella) into a publishing phenomenon – her *Girl Online* became the fastest-selling debut since records began. There may be a generation that spends much of its time online playing, watching, engaging, but it also appears to be one that wants to own physical books.

Publishers' horizons

For publishers, a stable market is a good one, and we should begin to see a trickle-down effect in terms of better publishing and great investment in authors. Pan Macmillan MD Anthony Forbes Watson said that in 2014 the book trade 'rekindled its love affair with the physical book'. The big worry, from the perspective of digital, is that this does not also lead to the spurning of the ebook, a market within which there remains great potential.

Last year, I noted that some publishers got burnt betting the bank on continued strong ebook growth. In 2015 they may get caught out simply by looking the other way. All the big publishers in the UK are somehow on the move: Penguin Random House has announced 2015 as its year of implementation, after 2014 proved to be another year of planning following their mega-merger in 2013. Hachette UK – the second biggest trade publisher in the UK – has just begun the process of housing all of their businesses under one roof for the first time, in a move that its chief executive Tim Hely Hutchinson said would lead to a redefinition of federalism. In the meantime, HarperCollins has moved from West London to East London, and now shares a building with its sister company News International – including in that stable *The Times*, the *Sun*, and the *Wall Street Journal*.

All of this contributed to the wider market. Adding in the *Bookseller*'s estimates for the digital market, the overall books market grew by 4% in 2014, the first year of growth since the *Fifty Shades*-dominated year of 2012. Digital and print (in lots of different ways) combined to grow the overall books business in 2014. It may be too soon to call this market (there is still too much changing for certainty) but there are suggestions that the market may now – with the wider economic recession lifting – have turned a corner. In early 2015, the *Bookseller*'s tracker for the market over the past 12 months (compared with the previous 12 months) moved into positive territory for the first time in half a decade.

As far as digital is concerned, the word on the street is complacency. How publishers ready themselves for what happens now that the first wave of digital has come to an end will be key. At Penguin Random House its main focus appears to be on discoverability and marketing to the consumer, not on selling direct. 'We want to connect. We don't need to make the transaction,' said its chief executive Markus Dohle last year.

Publishers are thinking hard about three things: how they reach readers; how they go about reaching readers; and what they should do once they've reached those readers. In 2015, Penguin Random House will launch a consumer website around the 'Penguin' brand; HarperCollins will continue to experiment with different models (subscription) and by selling direct to the consumer; Pan Macmillan will continue to grow its broadcasting arm, with books shows produced for YouTube. All publishers will continue to look for talent that already has an audience.

Publishers may be tempted to bank the ebook cash that came from strong digital growth, but that looks unwise. Publishers need to supercharge their push into an expanding digital environment that is hungry for content, and different in ways they are only beginning to understand.

What's in it for writers?

How does this changing market affect writers? When we talk about the fundamental impact digital is having on the book business, nowhere is this more apparent than in the traditional publishing world's relationship with authors.

Authors now have more ways to find readers than ever before, and often without the intervention of an intermediary. Successful self-publishing is now no longer the exception that proves the rule, it is becoming the exception that threatens the rule. Writers such as Hugh Howey, whose fiction title *Wool* was 2012's stand-out self-published hit, are showing not only that they publish successfully, but that they can bring publishers to heel. Simon & Schuster in the USA bought print rights to *Wool*, but the author refused the company digital rights.

Howey's way is not for every writer but what it shows is that publishers now have to market themselves to each and every writer, not just in competition against other publishers, but in competition to not having a publisher at all. And most publishers have a strong message. The biggest-selling book of many years, *Fifty Shades of Grey*, sold far more copies after it was traditionally published by Random House than it did before this, and ever could have done. The first title in the trilogy sold 1.6 million copies as an ebook in 2012, but it sold 4.5 million copies as a print book. Not all publishing stories will be so stark, but publishing still works. It doesn't stop working because self-publishing also works and, in sheer numbers, traditional publishing still sells far more books across a far wider range of titles and authors. Furthermore, if you are writing a book that is not commercial fiction or a genre title, traditional publishing remains the only viable route to market.

Nevertheless, as you write your book, or begin to think about sending it out for submission, there are new questions to ask yourself. Do you wait for a publisher to discover you? Or do you publish direct to a retailer's website? Do you use a third-party aggregator? Or pay for professional help?

In 2014, Howey launched AuthorEarnings.com, a website that claimed to have analysed charts data from a range of ebook retailers (most notably Amazon). His conclusion was that indie writers took a quarter of all ebook sales (on any given day), but independent writers were earning 47% of the total author revenue from genre fiction sales because they received more compensation from each sale than traditionally published writers did from their publisher. Many commentators took issue with the findings, the logic, and even the reliability of the data. But Howey raised an important issue for publishers. In a world with so many new options open to writers, is big publishing's 'value-add' still significant enough to prevent authors taking what promises to be a more lucrative route sideways? Probably. But it is a question that is not going away.

A report commissioned by the Authors' Licensing and Collecting Society (ALCS; see page 687) in 2014 noted that the most successful self-publishing ventures had an average rate of return of 154% (and a typical 'median' rate of return of 40%). But it remained a risky option, partly because of the costs associated with self-publishing. The report found that the bottom 20% of self-publishers made losses of £400 or more. Nevertheless, in 2014 there appeared to be fewer headliners along the lines of Howey or James. Indie writers make a huge noise about their success, but even self-publishing companies such as Smashwords noted a slowdown in sales growth for this sector. In part, this was because publishers have simply got better about their business. In 2014, the headlines were about which books sold and where they'd come from (Alfie Deyes, Zoella, Minecraft, David Walliams), and in the main it was publishers making this happen.

All that glisters

Furthermore, Amazon's success in digital and its dominance within the self-publishing market has also becomes its biggest problem. The lack of genuine competition, beyond that provided by Nook Press and Kobo Writing Life, is also limiting the noise. Sites such as WattPad, where writers promote and improve their work, are increasingly being used by both self-publishers and publishers as ways of meeting and interacting with readers in a more neutral territory.

That said, should you choose to self-publish, then Amazon's Kindle Direct Publishing platform remains the compelling option. It offers clarity, high rewards, and a route to the largest audience of ebook readers. For a writer, Amazon offers a short-term solution to the reader, but it is not a risk-free decision. During 2014 it launched Kindle Unlimited, a subscription offer seemingly hurried out in order to compete with the perceived threat of newer ebook vendors Oyster and Scribd, whose business model was the near mythical 'Spotify for ebooks'. Amazon placed many independently published titles into the service without asking authors to opt-in, and set up a pool of money that they would share based on the number of reads. Many authors quickly opted out as they feared (like traditional publishers) that their sales would be cannibalised. Though the jury is out on this, there was a sense of a bond of trust between platform and author having been stretched – though not quite to breaking point.

Despite this, the range of services marketing to authors has grown exponentially, with the arrival and growth in importance of the Alliance of Independent Authors helping to add an informed voice within the community. Because – and this is important – as an author you will at some point need to engage an expert. Even successful self-published writers will engage an editor, a cover designer, and perhaps even a 'social media guru'. This market is now well served, and certainly more honourable than it was even a few years ago. But, as ever, be careful what you pay for up-front, and make sure you understand what you are getting in return for your money. The rebranding of the self-published into 'indie' writers has not meant an end to the traditional vanity operations (see page 145); many have simply transformed into online author platforms offering to publish a book and make it available worldwide for a fee. Just as there is much more to publishing than simply printing a book, there is also much more to digital publishing that merely acquiring an ISBN.

Consult the giant ebook aggregators, such as Ingram (www.ingrambook.com), Lulu (www.lulu.com) and Smashwords (www.smashwords.com); these companies will ensure the ebook basics are covered and that the ebooks are featured on third-party websites at a fraction of the cost of a typical vanity publisher. And if you get this far, it's only just the beginning – the digital route to consumers is proving to be no less complicated than the print circuit, as both ebooksellers and e-reading devices proliferate.

Publishers are even waking up to the noise that authors might actually be prepared to pay them: Penguin bought the huge self-publishing services company Author Solutions in 2012, while a number of others, including Simon & Schuster, offered self-publishing options as part of their panoply of offerings. It's a shift that should work for both sides; publishers are experts and, if they choose not to invest in a title, why shouldn't the author choose to buy those services instead? But in truth, this is still a young and developing model and one that authors should be careful about choosing. Publishers are still at their best when they are backing a book at their own risk. The author has already made their investment in writing the book; a good publisher will want to match that with an investment of their own.

An agent should still be your first call, of course, but don't expect the agent of the future to be the only, or even the best, conduit to a publisher. Some agents may actually be just too busy publishing themselves (or at least trying it out); some may be concentrating on fewer and bigger brands, while others may be looking at how the books fare on the digital slush pile before making a commitment. Having too many options can be as tough as having too few.

New wine

Even if you do find an agent, and they in turn find a publisher, don't expect an advance – at least not a big one. However, you should expect (and push for) a bigger digital royalty (you may not think that spending 90% of your negotiating time on 30% of the market is a wise idea, but watch that market grow and think again). Publishers *are* making more money from digital – so should you. Ask for a strategic plan for both print and digital (and occasionally app) versions of your writing. Interrogate them about the marketing plan; publishers may want to offer less up-front, but they need to deliver more on publication than ever before if they are going to remain competitive.

Sadly, none of this is going to make it easier to make that first deal. However, look at new publishers, or old publishers publishing in new bottles; the rise of digital-only lists will be a growing phenomenon, with the launch of many digital-only or digital-first lists, such as Little, Brown's Blackfriars, HarperCollins' Impulse, Canelo, Bonnier's twenty7, or even Amazon Publishing's growing suite of imprints. Just make sure that publishers treat these digital-only lists as they would their other lists – digital is no longer a second-class ride. As Bonnier Publishing Fiction's Mark Smith said recently, digital can be used to create a story around a book or author that can then lead to a different type of publishing – usually print publication. At the moment, even the more successful self-published writers are struggling to get their books into bookshops, a route the traditional publishers still mine most effectively.

Talent does out, however. Publishers are beginning to look for new talent more aggressively; they'll be jumping earlier to get at that talent and, in the case of HarperCollins' Authonomy platform or Penguin's Bookcountry, they will be looking to incubate that talent in their own walled gardens.

Publishers such as HarperCollins' Borough Press and even Random House's Jonathan Cape have been experimenting with a period for 'open submissions', suggesting that even as more gets published, and the routes to readers clear, publishers remain desperate to root out the talent. Perhaps the biggest burden to getting published these days is not that a gatekeeper won't entertain you, but that they are so busy dealing with the rush through the gates!

Major players

In the UK (as in the USA) Amazon still dominates digital sales, with a market share of perhaps 80% of consumer ebook sales. It also dominates device sales. The Kindle is by far the most popular device for pure digital reading, with Nook, Apple and Kobo coming up falteringly from the rear. In the UK, with Waterstones stocking the Kindle, there is little serious competition to Amazon. Kobo, Apple and Nook are said to be growing but are yet to make a dent. Ebooks by Sainsbury's is slowly emerging as a contender, but remains hobbled by a lack of device. In a sense, all of these players are competing on the content side for that small bit of ebook business that is not locked in to the Kindle.

And then there are the tablets. These devices are for interacting with multimedia content, including enhanced ebooks and book apps. Here Apple remains the major player, with its iPad and iPhone devices the runaway leaders. Kobo (Kobo Arc), Amazon (Kindle Fire), Nook (NookTablet), Google (Nexus) are also making ground, while cheaper smaller devices have also come onto the market.

We do not yet know how much e-reading goes on using tablets, or whether heavily illustrated books (such as children's picture books) will migrate, but we do know that Apple has yet to pull off this trick, and that is worrying. In fact, though products (good ones too) continue to be developed across the range of multimedia tablets, we are still no closer to answering the fundamental question: is this what consumers want?

Apple's share of the ebooks market via the iBookstore has disappointed (its market share in the USA is about 20% and decreasing, and in the UK perhaps half that). This is not due to the lack of devices in people's hands (hundreds of millions, in fact) or because those users are not engaging with book content on them (people read ebooks via their Kindle apps, and download separate books apps). The reason is simply that Apple has not yet come up with a compelling retail platform on which to sell enhanced digital content. Its iBooks Authors, and iBooks2 platforms are both creditable entities, but they are not yet delivering on the numbers. Nothing has changed in the past year to shift this view, though Apple continues to push at it, putting iBooks in 2014 among those apps preloaded onto its devices.

We may yet see creative authors or publishers build a new kind of storybook or non-fiction title – one with music, images, animation and voice-over – that engages the reader and sells at a reasonable price. Certainly publishers are continuing to show a willingness to try and reinvent the product. Some argue that they simply haven't got it right yet, others that the market does not exist. Now the publishers feel more settled, we may yet see them have another go.

The much neglected audiobook market offers hope. It has been revitalised by digital downloads and stores that stock a wide range of audio titles, a far cry from the dusty tucked-away shelf often spotted in high street bookshops. Inevitably Amazon, through its subsidiary Audible, is dominant here now, and has even put the tools into the hands of authors via its ACX platform (recently launched in the UK), meaning that authors can now create their own audiobook versions.

Multimedia developers would be wise to figure out what consumers want first, before simply 'building it'. The reader has so far proved more interested in reading than interacting.

Reading rules

So, having lived through this first wave of digital, what can we say with any kind of certainty about the future? Actually, very little. Readers like reading, and many of them like writing too. Despite the great disruptions we've seen, the bits in between the reader and writer remain largely stable and stabilising. The shift in 2014 was, again, not at either pole but in this middle ground; publishers simply got better at getting books from authors to readers – both digitally and in print.

In a previous edition of this *Yearbook* I said that print would survive, but in truth this might have best been expressed through gritted teeth. Last year, I said that print will survive and that it might even find a better, firmer, less threatened space in which to thrive. That still holds, and in 2014 we saw a sense of how that might play out, with those print books not selling digitally finding more room to breathe in bookstores, as digital continues to expand in those narrow areas where it has already made a dent; an accommodation between the formats serving different reading needs. The ebook did not kill off the printed book; the printed book will not now kill off the ebook.

But this only works if the delicate balance we see now is maintained. And there is much that could change that: pricing, discoverability, self-publishing, a declining high street, and the tablet, are all part of a future still waiting to be written.

Philip Jones is editor of the *Bookseller*, and co-founder of the digital blog FutureBook.net.

See also...

- *News, views and trends in book publishing*, page 128
- *Self-publishing for beginners*, page 582
- *What do self-publishing providers offer?*, page 586
- *Marketing, publicising and selling self-published books*, page 597

Self-publishing for beginners

Reasons for self-publishing are varied. Many highly respected contemporary and past authors have published their own works. Peter Finch outlines the implications of such an undertaking.

Everyone's doing it.

Despite the economic downturn, or maybe because of it, there's a boom going on. After a decade or so of change, technology has finally delivered. Never has it been so easy to get published. So long, of course, that you are willing to do the work and take the risks yourself.

Why bother?

You've tried all the usual channels and been turned down; your work is uncommercial, specialised, technical, out of fashion; you are concerned with art while everyone else is obsessed with cash; you need a book out quickly; you want to take up small publishing as a hobby; you've heard that publishers make a lot of money out of their authors and you'd like a slice – all reason enough. But be sure you understand what you are doing before you begin.

But isn't this cheating?

It can't be real publishing – where is the critical judgement? Publishing is a respectable activity carried out by firms of specialists. Writers of any ability never get involved. But they do.

Start self-publishing and you'll be in good historical company: Horace Walpole, Balzac, Walt Whitman, Virginia Woolf, Gertrude Stein, John Galsworthy, Rudyard Kipling, Beatrix Potter, Lord Byron, Thomas Paine, Mark Twain, Upton Sinclair, W.H. Davies, Zane Grey, Ezra Pound, D.H. Lawrence, William Carlos Williams, Alexander Pope, Robert Burns, James Joyce, Anaïs Nin and Lawrence Stern. All these writers at some time in their careers dabbled in doing it themselves. William Blake did nothing else. He even made his own ink, handprinted his pages and got Mrs Blake to sew on the covers.

But today it's different?

Not necessarily. This is not vanity publishing we're talking about although if all you want to do is produce a pamphlet of poems to give away to friends then self-publishing will be the cheapest way. Self-publishing today can be a valid form of business enterprise. Being twice shortlisted for major literary prizes sharpened Timothy Mo's acumen. Turning his back on mass-market paperbacks, he published *Brownout on Breadfruit Boulevard* on his own. Canadian author W.P. Young got onto the *USA Today* bestseller list with his Christian fiction *The Shack*. G.P. Taylor's *Shadowmancer*, which topped the UK bestsellers for 15 weeks, began as a self-published title. So, too, did the infamous *Fifty Shades of Grey*, which began life as *Twilight* fan fiction on the internet.

Can anyone do it?

Certainly. If you are a writer then a fair number of the required qualities will already be in hand. The more able and practical you are then the cheaper the process will be. The utterly inept will need to pay others to help them, but it will still be self-publishing.

Where do I start?

With research. Read up on the subject. Make sure you know what the parts of a book are. You will not need to become an expert but you will need a certain familiarity. Don't rush. Learn. See *Glossary of publishing terms* on page 625.

What about ISBNs?

International Standard Book Numbers – a standard bibliographic code, individual to each book published – are used by booksellers and librarians alike. They are issued by the Nielsen ISBN Agency at a cost for newly registering publishers of £144 including VAT for 10. Prices are subject to change. Self-publishers may balk at this apparently inordinate expense but the ISBN is the device used by the trade to track titles and, if you are serious about your book, including one should be regarded as essential. There are full details of the Agency's services on its website (www.isbn.nielsenbook.co.uk); see also *FAQs about ISBNs* on page 133.

Next?

Put your book together – be it the printed-out pages of your novel, your selected poems or your story of how it was sailing round the world – and see how large a volume it will make. If you have no real idea of what your book should look like, go to your local bookshop and hunt out a few contemporary examples of volumes produced in a style you would like to emulate. Take your printout and your examples round to a number of local printers and ask for a quote.

How much?

It depends. How long is a piece of string? Unit cost is important: the larger the number of copies you have printed the less each will cost. Print too many and the total bill will be enormous. Printing has gone through a revolution in the past decade. The arrival of POD (print on demand; see page 135) and other digital technologies have reduced costs and made short runs much more economic. But books are still not cheap.

Can I make it cost less?

Yes. Do some of the work yourself. If you want to publish poems and you are prepared to use a text set on your computer, you will make a considerable saving. Most word processing programs have publishing facilities which will enhance the look of your text. Could you accept home production, run the pages off on a decent printer, then staple the sheets? Editions made this way can be very presentable.

For longer texts, savings can be made by supplying the work as a digital file directly to a printer. But be prepared to shop around.

Who decides how it looks?

You do. No one should ever ask a printer simply to produce a book. You should plan the design of your publication with as much care as you would a house extension. Spend as much time and money as you can on the cover. It is the part of the book your buyer will see first. If you're stuck, employ a book designer.

How many copies should I produce?

Poetry books can sell about 200 copies, new novels sometimes manage 1,000, literary paperbacks 10,000, mass-market blockbusters half a million. But that is generally where there is a sales team and whole distribution organisation behind the book. When using traditional methods of production do not, on the one hand, end up with a prohibitively high unit cost by ordering too few copies. Fifty of anything is usually a waste of time. On the other hand, can you really sell 3,000? Will shops buy in dozens? They will probably only want twos and threes. Take care. Research your market first. If you worry then use

POD as it allows for tiny print runs and avoids the risk of having to hold stock. The downside is that POD can significantly increase the unit cost.

How do I sell it?

With all your might. This is perhaps the hardest part of publishing. It is certainly as time consuming as both the writing of the work and the printing of it put together. To succeed here you need a certain flair and you should definitely not be of a retiring nature. If you intend selling through the trade your costing must be correct and worked out in advance. Independent shops – those that remain – will want at least 35% of the selling price as discount. National chains will demand more. You'll need about the same again to cover your distribution, promotion and other overheads, leaving the final third to cover production costs and any profit you may wish to make. Multiply your unit production cost by at least four. Commercial publishers often multiply by as much as nine.

Do not expect the trade to pay your carriage costs. Your terms should be at least 35% post free on everything bar single copy orders. Penalise these by reducing your discount to 25%. Some shops will suggest that you sell copies to them on a sale or return basis. This means that they only pay you for what they sell and then only after they've sold it. This is a common practice with certain categories of publications and often the only way to get independent books into certain shops; but from the self-publisher's point of view it should be avoided if at all possible. Cash in hand is best but expect to have your invoices paid by cheque or bank transfer at a later date. Phone the shops you have decided should take your book or turn up in person and ask to see the buyer. Letters and sample copies sent by post will get ignored. Get a freelance distributor to handle all of this for you if you can. But expect to be disappointed. Independent book representatives willing to take on a one-off title are as rare as hen's teeth. Expect to have to go it alone.

Successful selling through Amazon, the holy grail for many publishers, is easier than you might think. The company encourages individuals to include their titles on their website. Fulfilment of orders can be done either directly by the self-publisher or, where there is sufficient demand, through Amazon's own warehouses. There is no financial risk but you will have to give Amazon a commission. Check their website for details. Worth doing? You'd be a fool not to.

What about promotion?

A vital aspect often overlooked by beginners. Send out as many review copies as you can, all accompanied by slips quoting selling price and name and address of the publisher. Never admit to being that person yourself. Invent a name: it will give your operation a professional feel. Ring up newspapers and local radio stations ostensibly to check that your copy has arrived but really to see if they are prepared to give your book space. Buying advertising space rarely pays for itself but good local promotion with 100% effort will generate dividends.

What about depositing copies at the British Library?

Under the Copyright Acts the British Library, the Bodleian Library, Oxford, the University Library, Cambridge, the National Library of Scotland, the Library of Trinity College Dublin and the National Library of Wales are all entitled to a free copy of your book which must be sent to them within one month of publication. One copy should go direct to the Legal Deposit Office at the British Library, Boston Spa, Wetherby, West Yorkshire LS23 7BY.

The other libraries use the Agency for the Legal Deposit Libraries, 161 Causewayside, Edinburgh EH9 1PH (www.legaldeposit.org.uk). Contact them directly to find out how many copies they require.

And what if it goes wrong?

Put all the unsolds under the bed or give them away. It has happened to lots of us. Even the big companies who are experienced at these things have flops. It was an adventure and you did get your book published. On the other hand you may be so successful that you'll be at the London Book Fair selling the film rights and wondering if you've reprinted enough.

What about working online?

No self-respecting author should be without their own personal website. From here you can advertise yourself and your works, and offer downloadable samples or complete books. This method of self-promotion is highly recommended.

The power of blogging and social networking should also not be ignored. Self-publishers will benefit enormously from setting up a Facebook page devoted to their titles, from sending out tweets pushing the works and from writing a blog about the whole process. None of this will cost anything more than time. Do it now.

The internet is also thick with operators offering to promote or publish work electronically. These range from companies which post sample chapters and then charge readers a fee for the complete work to professional ebook developers who offer books fully formatted for use on hand-held and other devices.

Peter Finch is a poet, author and psychogeographer. Until recently, he was Chief Executive of Literature Wales, the Literature Development Agency. He is a former bookseller and small publisher and author of *How to Publish Yourself*. His website is www.peterfinch.co.uk.

Further reading

Baverstock, Alison, *The Naked Author – The Complete Guide to Self-publishing*, Bloomsbury, 2011

Buchanan, Mike, *The Joy of Self-publishing: Self-publishing and Publishing with the Print-on-Demand and Digital Print Models of Lightning Source*, LPS Publishing, 2010

Hamilton, April, *The Indie Author: Self-publishing Strategies Anyone Can Use*, Writers Digest Books, 2010

Holley, Michael J., *The Beginners Guide To Self-Publishing A Book: A Step by Step Manual*, Beach Hut Publishing, 2014

McCann, Kevin and Green, Tom, *Get Started in Self-Publishing*, Teach Yourself, 2013

Peppitt, Ed, *How to Self-publish: A Guardian Masterclass*, Kindle edn 2012

Ross, Marilyn and Collier, Sue, *The Complete Guide to Self-Publishing*, Writer's Digest Books, 5th edn 2010

Ryan Howard, Catherine, *Self-printed: The Sane Person's Guide to Self-Publishing*, CreateSpace Independent Publishing Platform, 3rd edn 2014

The Self-publishing Magazine, www.selfpublishingmagazine.co.uk

See also...

- *Promoting and selling your book*, page 119
- *What do self-publishing providers offer?*, page 586
- *Marketing, publicising and selling self-published books*, page 597

What do self-publishing providers offer?

Jeremy Thompson presents the options for engaging an author services company.

Now that self-publishing is widely accepted and it is easier to do it than ever before, authors are presented with a broader range of opportunities to deliver their book or ebook to readers. This brings with it a greater responsibility to you, the author and publisher, to make the right choices for your publishing project. The various options for self-publishing may seem bewildering at first, and each has their pros and cons. But some relatively simple research will prove invaluable in ensuring you make the right choices for your book.

Motivation influences method

There are many reasons why authors choose to self-publish, and contrary to popular belief, the decision to do so is not usually motivated by the aspiration to be a bestselling novelist! That is only one reason; others include the wish to impart knowledge to a wider audience; the desire to publish a specialist book with a relatively small target audience; the fulfilment of a hobby; publishing as part of a business or charity; and yes, vanity (a wish to see one's name on a book cover is fine, as long as you have realistic expectations of your work).

Understanding why you are self-publishing is important, as the reasons for doing so can help point to the best way in which to go about it. For example, if you are publishing simply for pleasure, and have few expectations that your book will 'set the world alight', then you'd be wise not to invest in a large number of copies; using 'print on demand' (POD) or producing an ebook could be the way forward. If you have a book that you're publishing to give away or sell as part of your business to a relatively captive audience, then a short print run of, say, 300 copies might be wise, as the more copies you print, the greater the economies of scale. If you want your novel to reach as many readers as possible and to sell it widely, you'll need to have physical copies to get into the supply chain and in front of potential readers, so opt for a longer print run of perhaps 500 or more copies.

Decisions on how to self-publish are often influenced by the money you are prepared to invest in (and risk on) your project. Making a decision on what self-pubishing route to take based on financial grounds alone is fine, as long as you understand the implications of that decision. For example, as the name implies, print-on-demand (POD) books are only printed when someone actually places an order for a copy; there are no physical copies available to sell. As POD books are largely sold on a 'firm sale' basis, bookshops will rarely stock them, so most POD sales will be made through online retailers. In addition, as the POD unit cost is higher than if a quantity of books are printed in one go, the retail price of a book is likely to be fairly high in order to cover the print cost and retailer's discount, and make you, the publisher, some profit. Authors often assume that POD is some miracle form of low-cost book publishing, but if that were so, why aren't all the major commercial publishers distributing all of their books in this way? The disadvantages of POD include limited distribution and high print cost; these can work for many types of book, like specialist non-fiction titles or academic books that command high cover prices, but it can be difficult to make it cost-effective for mass market books. (For further information, see *Print on demand* on page 135.)

At the other end of the scale, printing 3,000 copies of a novel will only pay off if you can get that book onto the retailers' shelves and in front of potential readers, or if you have some other form of 'captive' readership that you can reach with your marketing. Distribution to retailers works largely on the 'sale or return' model, using distribution companies and sales teams to sell new books to bookshops (and whatever you may have heard to the contrary, bookshops are still the largest sellers of books in the UK). If you can't get your book into that distribution chain, you are limiting the prospect of selling your 3,000 copies, and money tied up in unsaleable stock is wasted.

Publishing an ebook is also an increasingly popular method of self-publishing, but it too has its pros and cons. On the up side, it can be done very cheaply and quickly; the flip side is that, as hundreds of new ebooks are published each day, how do you get yours noticed? Making your ebook available through one retailer (e.g. Kobo) effectively limits your potential readership... what about readers with a Kindle, a Sony Reader or a Nook? How and where should you market your ebook?

As a self-publisher, you need to make sure you understand the limitations of each form of publishing method before you decide on the best route for your book(s). It can make the difference between success or failure for your book.

Choosing an author services company

In its truest sense, self-publishing means that you as author undertake all the processes undertaken by a commercial publisher to bring a book to market: editing, design, production, marketing, promotion and distribution. If you're multi-talented and have a lot of spare time, then you may want to do all of these things yourself, but for most authors it's a question of contracting an author services company to carry out some or all of the tasks required. It should be noted that most author services companies make their money by selling their services to you as the author; very few have a lot of market knowledge and even fewer offer any real form of active marketing or have a retail distribution set-up. Choosing the right company to work with is crucial in ensuring that your self-publishing expectations stand a chance of being met. Author services companies come in various guises, but they can broadly be broken into three categories:

- **DIY POD services.** You upload your manuscript and cover design, and your book (or ebook) is simply published 'as is'. It's relatively cheap, and great if you are not too concerned about the design quality of your book and POD or electronic distribution is what you want.
- **Assisted services companies.** These companies offer typesetting and cover design, and perhaps some limited distribution and marketing options. If you're looking for a better product and some basic help in selling your book then this could be right for you.
- **Full service companies.** These suppliers tend to work at the higher quality end of the self-publishing market, offering authoritative advice, bespoke design, active trade and media marketing and, in a couple of cases, real bookshop distribution options.

In addition, there is a plethora of companies and individuals offering component parts of the book production and marketing process, such as copy-editing, proofreading, cover design, public relations, etc.

The key for any self-publisher in choosing a company to work with is research. Having decided why you are self-publishing and set your expectations from doing so, the next step is to see who offers what, and at what cost, and to match the right company with what you are seeking. A search on the internet for 'self-publishing' will present you with many choices, so explore the company websites, compare what is being offered, and generally get a feel for what each says they do. Are they just selling services to authors, or are they selling their authors' books? Do they offer active marketing or just 'marketing advice'? Don't take their word for it, though: seek independent advice from other authors or independent industry commentators – there are plenty out there. Which companies are widely recommended by authors and experts alike, and which are not?

Having identified some services that look as if they will help you meet your publishing expectations, you need to establish how much it will cost. Get detailed quotations from companies and compare like-for-like. Ask questions of those companies if anything is in doubt: ask to see a contract; ask for a sample of their product (many companies still produce appalling quality books!). Talk to someone at each of the companies you are considering, and ask to speak to one of their current authors. Time spent at this stage will ensure that you get a good feel for the company you're considering working with, and that can be the difference between a happy self-publishing experience and a disastrous one.

Marketing and distribution

Authors often concentrate on producing a book or ebook and ignore the part of the equation that actually sells the book. Examine carefully what author services companies offer in this respect. Distribution includes all the processes involved in getting a book or ebook in front of potential readers, but many companies offer only a limited, online-only service. Marketing is the process of alerting both the media (whether in print, on air or online) and potential readers that a book is available. Similarly, very few companies spend much effort to actively market their authors' work. The right choice of marketing and distribution service can make or break a book even before production has started.

As the author and self-publisher, you must decide how the world will find out about your book, and how to get it into the hands of readers. You will need to make decisions on whether POD distribution or wider retail distribution is required; whether the marketing services offered by an author services company are enough for your book; or if a public relations company might be the way forward. And, of course, all of this has a cost implication. (See *Marketing, publicising and selling self-published books* on page 597.)

A brave new world

Self-publishing offers authors a host of opportunities to get their projects published and available to readers. Making the right decisions to meet your expectations for your book or ebook in the early stages of the publishing process will pay dividends in ensuring both an enjoyable self-publishing experience, and one that successfully meets your goals.

Understand your motivations for self-publishing; set realistic expectations for your book or ebook; research the production options well; understand distribution choices; give marketing the importance it requires; and above all, enjoy your self-publishing experience!

Jeremy Thompson founded Troubador Publishing (www.troubador.co.uk) in 1996 and started the Matador (www.troubador.co.uk/matador) self-publishing imprint in 1999, which has since helped over 5,000 authors to self-publish. Troubador also publishes the *Self-Publishing Magazine* (quarterly, print and online), runs the annual Self-Publishing Conference and holds a 'Self-Publishing Experience' (in its third year in 2015). Troubador also runs Indie-Go (www.indie-go.co.uk), offering component author services, and Matador Distribution & Marketing, offering distribution and marketing to books published independently or using another self-publishing company.

Being a self-published author

Mel Sherratt describes her route from aspiring writer to successful self-published author, and offers advice on how to stay ahead in a challenging business.

I've wanted to write for as long as I can remember. My first ever short story was about a gobstopper called Gerry who was kidnapped by the Black Jacks and Fruit Salads in a sweet shop.

When I was in my teens, I used to go to the library every week to see which 'how-to-write' books on writing were new or available. I borrowed books about writing children's novels, crime, romance, horror, screenplays, short stories, magazine articles – you name it, I wanted to try it. It was most disappointing when there were no new books to read, and equally exciting when a new one popped up on the shelves. I just wanted to write.

My route to success

I tried for 12 years to get a traditional deal before self-publishing my debut novel, *Taunting the Dead* (2011). In the early 2000s, I would religiously wait for the new edition of the *Writers' & Artists' Yearbook* to come out. I'd sit down with a notepad and write a list of agents I could approach, what genres they represented and their submission details. Any new agents that hadn't been included the year before were a bonus! Back then, most submissions – the first three chapters, a synopsis and covering letter, had to be sent by snail mail. Then came the wait. Most of the rejections slips would be delivered on a Saturday – so that would be another weekend ruined.

I found my first agent in 2004, when I was writing contemporary women's fiction (which I have since self-published on Kindle Direct Publishing Services under a pen name). By that time, I had written the first of the three novels in my first series, *The Estate Series*, which are about fear and emotion, friendships and gritty lifestyles. As well as enjoying books by Martina Cole and Lynda la Plante, I began to read more authors I admired in the crime genre, such as Peter James, Ian Rankin and Mark Billingham. From all of them I learned about hooks, scene-setting, character-building, cliffhangers, how to show not tell, how less is often more, and evoking a sense of place. As I began to find my love for crime, I wanted to portray much more than fear and emotion in my own books. I wanted to delve deeper into darker storylines, often with a crime that was solved by the police. So my writing went from shopping and gossip, to gossip and emotion, to emotion and fear, to justice and murder.

When *Taunting The Dead* was originally rejected by several publishers, I was devastated. It was the fifth book I had written, and it wasn't the first of my books to be turned down. *Somewhere to Hide* and *Behind a Closed Door*, the first two books in *The Estate Series*, had been rejected because they were too much of a mixture between women's fiction and crime. So when I wrote something more 'to type', it then became too similar to Martina Cole or Lynda la Plante. Was I still trying to find my own voice? *Taunting the Dead* did go to acquisition meetings, but in the end it wasn't accepted – again because it didn't fit into an established niche.

So I changed tack. I decided to self-publish *Taunting the Dead* to see if a traditional publisher might then take an interest. But getting the book noticed wasn't easy. You can't just put a book online and expect it to sell. It needs to be marketed – discoverability being the main objective. I had been a blogger for several years prior to publication and had built up a lot of support online which helped to spread the word about my self-published novel. I discovered that through my blog and Twitter I was able to create a 'network' of contacts who would recommend my books of their own accord.

I studied what was popular in the Kindle charts: the bestsellers and series that were selling well, books by unknown authors as well as books by bestselling writers, debut novelists and established ones too. I checked out covers and blurbs, and which genres were selling consistently.

Why self-publishing worked for me

When I first self-published in 2011–12, I was worried that if I couldn't get a publisher to sign up my gritty novel, making it available direct to the public might scupper my writing 'career' before it had really started. But in fact, using the strategy I had adopted for *Taunting the Dead*, over the space of six months I self-published three more books in a series.

I write under a number of different genres – police procedurals, psychological thrillers, women's fiction with a punch, and contemporary women's fiction novels under a pen name. But the main thing I like to write about is emotion, whether that is fear and emotion or love and emotion. These subjects cover a vast area of the commercial fiction market. Readers who enjoy digital copies devour books so quickly that they always want more. I very often find that if a reader likes one of my books, they tend to seek out the others.

For novels that I publish with traditional publishers, I work well in advance of publication date; it is months after the manuscript is finished that the book is scheduled for release. I have a fantastic editing and cover design team, promotion, and the backing of a great editor who schedules everything in for me. Until a writer has had a structural edit of a book, they are unlikely to know how valuable such interventions are. Only now do I realise the huge difference between development editing and copy edits. My editor has added the glitter to my words.

In between the times I have work to do for my publisher, I concentrate on my other books. With the self-published novels, I can try new things all the time. I can try out free promotions, lower prices for a limited period or change prices on a regular basis to tempt new and existing readers. Last year, I changed the covers on *The Estate Series* to give it a boost. I'm constantly refreshing things, such as tweaking the product description (or blurb). You have to be organised – a good project manager; most of the time I am, but it often means working evenings and weekends to fit everything in.

What have I learned along the way?

Just like any fledgling business, I learned as I went along and I strive to keep learning a little more every day. Having lots of books to market is a challenge. I am writing number 11 now – imagine trying to keep tabs on all those! There are many people who help keep my business afloat. I have a bookkeeper who looks after all my accounts for me (I'm terrible with figures) and I have an accountant who deals with the more complicated side of things. I have a cover designer, who also does all my banners and advertising images. I hire a structural editor and a copy-editor. I'm in the process of finding a PR aide. And my husband is a great sounding board for plots and twists. He helps keep my ideas realistic: 'That's a bit *Die Hard 7*, Mel,' he'll say. 'You need to bring it back to *Die Hard 4*.'

Why I chose to work with an agent

After I parted company with my second agent early in 2012, due to my success with self-publishing, I was approached by seven agents in a matter of weeks. I'm now able to work with a fantastic lady, Madeleine Milburn, who really understands my work. Through her, I've been offered two 2-book deals and I feel my writing is going from strength to strength. My agent encourages me to be who I am – a gritty, raw writer, producing work steeped in emotion.

Madeleine came looking for me. I still remember the Saturday afternoon I received an email from her. She had been reading my books, checking out my website and my online presence, and asked if we could meet. We had learned a lot about each other over a stream of emails and when we met in person, we clicked. Madeleine told me what she could do for me and has since put her plans into action. For example, I'm finally getting foreign rights deals. There's a lot of self in self-publishing and sometimes I just want to sit down and write. Madeleine takes some of the burden from me, leaving me with more time to do what I love. She even tells me to stop worrying, to get a grip if I'm panicking, and gives me a stern telling-off when the self-doubt eats at me too much.

I've been represented by Madeleine for nearly three years and, not only has she become a great friend, she is also my business partner. She treats me as an equal. We can chat about strategies and sales and long-term plans, and we bounce ideas off one another too. I have knowledge of self-publishing and try to keep up to date with what is going on in the digital world and she in turn keeps me up to date with the publishing world she inhabits.

Prizes and other successes

In 2014, I was one of the first four authors to appear on a panel for 'indies' at Crimefest. From there, I was delighted to take part in a panel at Theakston Old Peculiar Crime Writing Festival, called 'The Good Old Days', tracking several writers' stories to success. I've been going to Harrogate for this festival for the past five years, and it was at the top of my writer's bucket list to get up on that stage. This was topped when I found out that I was longlisted, and then shortlisted, for the Crime Writer's Association Dagger in the Library Award 2014, which was voted for by readers. That was a fantastic feeling and, as it was in December last year, it ended an incredible year.

What next?

Having decided to make *Taunting the Dead* the first in a series, in 2015 I released two further books with my publisher, *Follow the Leader* and *Only the Brave*, and now I'm working on a fourth book. I'm still self-publishing books and am planning what to do in

Some advice

These are my top pieces of advice for any writer:

- Write, write, write.
- Read, read, read in the genre you want to conquer.
- Edit until you are sick of the work.
- Hire an editor to work with you.
- Get the best cover you can if you're going to publish it yourself.
- Stay positive on social media – it leads to so many opportunities and great friendships.
- Read about marketing yourself.
- Experiment and have fun.

2016–17. For me, writing has turned into a business. It's very exciting. It's very scary too. But that's what keeps me on my toes. So, for now, I'm going to do what I do best – and that is to keep learning and keep writing. I have a saying – 'Keep on keeping on.' I feel very lucky to do what I do, but there were numerous times over those 12 years of rejection that I would convince myself that I couldn't do it, that I didn't have what it takes ...

If there is a writer inside you, you'll do it because you have to. It compels you, even if you're getting nowhere to start with. Words have always been a huge part of my life. I love making things up! By writing more, your skills will improve, your words will get better and others will take notice. I still can't quite believe it when I get reviews and emails from readers saying how much they have enjoyed my books. Self-publishing *Taunting the Dead* helped me to start my career as well as my own business. Now I see writers not only taking the self-publishing path but choosing to pursue that route rather than a traditional publishing deal. Either way is fine – and doing both is good too. Writers have more choices now; that's real progress.

Mel Sherratt is a writer of psychological thrillers, suspense, police procedurals and women's fiction 'with a punch'. She self-published *Taunting the Dead* in 2011 and a further two books in the series, *Follow the Leader* and *Only the Brave* in 2015. She has also published *Watching Over You* (2014) and four titles in her psychological suspense *The Estate Series*. See more at http://melsherratt.co.uk/ or on Twitter @writermels.

See also...

- *Finding my agent*, page 272
- *Getting hooked out of the slush pile*, page 394
- *Notes from a successful crime author*, page 278
- *On writing: essential advice for writers*, page 265
- *Notes from a hybrid author*, page 593

Notes from a hybrid author

Nick Spalding's success with writing comedy fiction and self-publishing ebooks led him to be noticed by publishers and literary agents. Deals followed that have seen him published in print both in the UK and abroad. Epitomising a new breed of 'hybrid author', he describes his publishing choices so far and stresses the value of always keeping your options open.

I'm not sure if the term 'hybrid author' is one that sits all that well with me, to be honest. It makes me sound like some kind of hideous experiment, conducted in one of those sterile laboratories you see in badly made sci-fi horror movies. In my mind's eye, I can see myself stumbling out of a glass pod, surrounded by cold gas, covered in green goo and moaning loudly about royalty payments. There's probably a Kobo grafted onto one hand, an iPad grafted onto the other, and a Kindle shoved up my arse. Not a pretty sight.

Nevertheless, hybrid author is the accepted term for what I am, so I'm just going to have to lump it. What authors don't have to lump these days is a single path to publication. You now have more options than ever when it comes to getting your book into the grubby hands of readers all over the world.

You can submit the book to agents and publishers in order to get your book into print 'the old-fashioned way', with one of the large publishing companies that have dominated the industry for decades, or you can go smaller scale and try to get your work published via one of the new digital-only publishers that have sprung up in recent years. Lastly, you can choose to self-publish both ebook and paperback versions of your book via the various companies available online that provide such a service – the most powerful and successful of which, of course, is Amazon. The most important word here is *choice*. Writers have a clear choice these days – and consequently far greater control over their careers.

It was Amazon's KDP (Kindle Direct Publishing) platform that gave me my springboard to a career as a writer. Without it, I wouldn't be covered in all that green goo and walking round with a Kindle up my backside – metaphorically speaking.

So what exactly is a hybrid author then? I would describe a hybrid author as one who uses as many different paths to publication as possible. A hybrid author is a writer who likes to keep his or her options open. Someone who keeps a foot in as many camps as they possibly can – without rupturing something important.

The publishing industry is about as predictable as an episode of *Game Of Thrones*, so I think it's vitally important to avoid putting all your eggs in one basket – if you are lucky enough to have more than one basket available to you. I do, so that's why I continue to self-publish books, alongside securing traditional publishing contracts when appropriate (and I always find it *very* appropriate when people offer me a lot of cash, funnily enough).

My road to being a successful hybrid author was largely through trial and error, with a fair bit of luck thrown in for good measure. Five years ago, I wrote a semi-fictional memoir, *Life...With No Breaks*, in a 30-hour period as an experiment, and had no idea what to do with it. So when the Amazon KDP service came to my attention it seemed like the perfect place for it to find a home.

I then wrote a second memoir called *Life... On A High* and a fantasy adventure called *The Cornerstone*, and released both in the summer of 2011. My sales then started to pick up – proving that the more books you have out, the more books you sell, as your platform grows and people start to recognise your brand name.

Then one evening I was discussing with my girlfriend what to do next. I wanted to write a book that would appeal to as many ebook readers as possible, and from the year or so I'd spent self-publishing it had become very apparent that a majority were female. A popular genre for female readers is romance, so I decided to combine Spalding-style humour with a romantic storyline. *Love. . . From Both Sides* was born – and the rest (as people who like to indulge in obvious cliché would say) is history.

Love. . . From Both Sides was released in September 2011. In the first six months of its life, it shifted 1,500 copies. Not a bad haul if you're just starting out – but I'd been around a while, had built a pretty good reputation, and all of my other books were selling far better. I was quite the disappointed lad, I can tell you.

It took a cover change and a price drop for *Love. . . From Both Sides* to take off. I cut the price from £1.49 to 99p, and added two cartoon images of Jamie and Laura to the cover. That was at the start of March 2012. By the end of April I'd sold over 36,000 copies, and developed a nosebleed.

Given the rampant sales, I figured I'd better write a sequel, so in the middle of May I released *Love. . . And Sleepless Nights* and sat back to await developments. And developments turned out to be combined sales of 300,000 for the two books by the end of October, along with another 100,000 sales of my other three titles.

You don't sell that many books without somebody sitting up and paying attention. I started to get emails from both agents and publishers during the summer, and by the autumn I'd sewn up a deal with Hodder & Stoughton to republish *Love. . . From Both Sides* and *Love. . . And Sleepless Nights*, along with a third title, which ended up being *Love. . . Under Different Skies.*

So why change from a purely self-published author, to one also published by a traditional publishing company? My decision was due to a combination of things. The first – and I'm not going to lie to you here – was the rather large advance Hodder offered. The second was the fact they could get me into the paperback market – something which I was unable to do as a self-publisher. Thirdly – and separate to the Hodder deal – having an agent enabled me to secure several foreign rights deals, which I would not have been able to negotiate on my own.

I believed (and still do) that forming a relationship with an agent and a publisher is still ultimately the best way to secure a long-term livelihood as a writer. Self-publishing is a brilliant way to establish a career, but for longevity you need help.

That help doesn't just have to come from agents or publishers though. Your fellow authors can be incredibly helpful too. Around the time I was writing *Love. . . Under Different Skies*, I was fortunate enough to be asked to join a collective of successful authors, working together under the banner of Notting Hill Press. Made up of several of the UK's best romance and humour writers, Notting Hill Press is an absolutely fantastic thing to be a part of, and I was more than happy to place *Life. . . With No Breaks* and its sequel with them. I'm still fairly new to this industry, so having a group of experienced and talent authors to turn to for advice has been a godsend. I now have five titles published with NHP (and still I retain control over all of my rights) and plan on publishing even more with them over the coming years.

After all that excitement, the next step in my career was to write and sell a new book called *Fat Chance* (Lake Union Publishing 2014). This was an entirely new project, so I was bloody nervous about getting a deal for it. It's one thing to write sequels to a story that you know is already popular; it's quite another to write about an entirely new set of characters in a brand new setting. Luckily, my agent stepped up to the plate again magnificently, and scored me a contract with the newly created publishing arm over at Amazon.

This was an absolutely brilliant deal for me, as Amazon are the industry leaders right now when it comes to selling books, so who better to be published by? I'm sure that *Fat Chance* has done better with their Lake Union imprint than it would have with any other publisher, given the clout that Amazon can exert when it comes to promotion and publicity. Proof? At the time of writing this article, *Fat Chance* is in the Amazon UK Kindle Top Ten. Needless to say, I hope to have further titles with Amazon Publishing over the next few years.

So right now I find myself in the position of being published by Hodder & Stoughton with the *Love. . .* series, published by Amazon with *Fat Chance*, a member of Notting Hill Press with five other titles, and still self-published under my own steam with a further three. You don't get much more hybrid than that! Unless I buy my own printing press and start churning books out to throw at passers by in the street, I think I've covered as many bases as I possibly can for the moment.

None of this means I am guaranteed any kind of success in the future of course, but by diversifying as much as possible, I feel that I've given myself the best chance of having some longevity in this business.

So what does all this tell you – other than the fact I am a jammy bastard, obviously? Probably that the way an author goes about his or her work in the 21st century is vastly different from the way things were 15 years ago. The march of technological progress has multiplied the avenues through which a writer can sell a book to the reading public, and changed his or her relationship with publishers and agents.

Making sure you investigate each and every avenue open to you is a must. Even if you choose not to walk down them (and I'm fully aware of how laboured this metaphor is becoming – don't worry, I won't mention it again after this sentence) you should at least consider each one thoroughly, because not doing so may cut off a potential revenue stream for your work. And if there's one thing no writer should ever do, it's miss out on an opportunity to make money!

Are there downsides to being a hybrid author? Yes, absolutely. Juggling all these different ways of working can be extremely stressful. I am not only a writer, I am also a marketer, a publicist, an editor, a proofreader, a webmaster, an admin secretary, an amateur accountant and an online researcher. I would stick a broom up my backside and sweep the floor at the same time, but the Kindle keeps getting in the way.

It's not a career choice for everyone, certainly. But it's the only way to be a writer that I've ever known, so I don't know any better! Being a hybrid has worked for me in the past, and I very much hope it will continue to do so in the future. While it is a lot of hard work, it is also a lot of fun, and I wouldn't change it for the world.

What I would change is the first paragraph of this feature, because I am painfully aware that while I've tried my best to give you an idea of what it's like to be a hybrid author, there's every chance that the only thing you're actually going to take away from this article is the image of a snot-covered Nick Spalding with a Kindle stuck up his arse.

Nick Spalding previously worked in the communications industry, mainly in media and marketing. Because Nick concluded that talking rubbish for a living can get tiresome (for anyone other than a politician), he thought he'd have a crack at writing comedy fiction – and has sold over half a million books to date. His books include six novels and two memoirs; the fourth book in his *Love. . .* series, *Love. . . Among the Stars* (Notting Hill Press), was released on Kindle in 2015. You can contact him via Twitter: @spalding_author and Facebook: www.facebook.com/spaldingauthor. See also his website and blog: spaldings-racket.blogspot.co.uk.

See also...

- *Being a self-published author*, page 589
- *Electronic publishing*, page 573
- *Marketing yourself online*, page 602
- *Self-publishing for beginners*, page 582

Marketing, publicising and selling self-published books

Self-published authors need to accomplish what an in-house marketing and publicity department of a traditional publisher would do for their authors. But they have the advantage of deciding for themselves how best to target the media. Ben Cameron, publicist, explains how to do it.

The publishing world has undergone two revolutions almost simultaneously over the last couple of years – the ebook revolution and the self-publishing revolution. Publishers are no longer the gatekeepers that they once were and the playing field has been nearly levelled.

If we compare self-publishing to travelling, travel agents used to book everything for us – flights, excursions, hotels, transfers, etc. Now we are more than likely to do it all ourselves, saving money and giving us more control. Self-publishing is similar and without a publisher to do it for you, you need to consider printing, editing, cover design, layout, distribution, website and, the last link in the chain, publicity and marketing.

Anyone can self-publish and consequently there are a lot of people in competition for readers. To be picked out of the crowd the most important thing is to make your book as good as it can be. That means having the editing, formatting and cover design done by experienced professionals. You will never sell a significant number of books, no matter what your marketing strategy is, without your book being (and looking) right for your audience.

When preparing the text to go on the back cover, don't be tempted to throw something together with little thought. If you do, you may just doom your 75,000-word masterpiece in a mere 200 words. The importance of a good book description, whether for the back cover or a website listing, is extremely underrated; it must be written carefully, with your readers in mind. Take a step back and consider your book as if you are a reader seeing it for the first time. Why should I buy it? Why is this particular book better than the others? What will it do for me? A good back cover blurb will answer those questions in 200 words or less, with every word precisely chosen.

Press releases

Book press releases should generally be contained within a single page, include an image of the book's front cover, a succinct description of the book and author, the publication date and other publishing details, and contact information. You can also create other kinds of releases, such as an author release (focusing on what the author can talk about in interviews, rather than what the book is about) or a news release (connecting the author or book to some event that is currently in the news). These should contain quotes from the author and can be a longer, although they still need to be concise.

Keep a single master book press release but feel free to adapt it for different media and purposes. For example, a release about a book on the great wines of the world could emphasise the taste of the wine for food magazines, and focus more on the vineyards and regions for travel magazines. Identify all the different subject areas in relation to your book and cater to each of them. Think like a journalist: what sort of stories would you be looking for? Hone all your press releases to perfection.

Use your biography

Remember that your publicity campaign isn't only about your book. In fact, when it comes to interviews, the media's interest needs to be in you and what you have to say.

Unless your book is an autobiography it will not encapsulate the entire 'you' as a person. Make the most of your interests, experience and knowledge outside of the subject of your book. I once publicised a fiction thriller by an author who was formerly a cameraman and worked on well-known films. I attracted a huge amount of media attention for his stories about working in Hollywood, all of which mentioned his (unrelated) book and drove sales! Whatever your experience and interests, there are magazines and websites that may want to know what *you* have to say.

Be sure to include a biography on your website, as it is often the first place that journalists go to when researching author details. Writing a blog is another way to maximise your background and interests.

Media lists

Identify your key audiences – both mainstream and niche – and make a list of media outlets that reach them. List relevant media in all the various types, including magazines, newspapers, online publications, television, radio and blogs. You can conduct much of this research online, but it doesn't hurt to browse in your local newsagent and note the publications that seem a good fit for your book.

While you can research the media yourself, compiling media lists and tracking down names and addresses is extremely time-consuming. You can cut corners by buying a list from a publicity company like Smith Publicity (www.smithpublicity.com) or Handle Your Own PR UK (www.handleyourownpr.co.uk), or by sending your press release through a mailing service such as PRWeb (www.prweb.com) or PR Newswire (www.prnewswire.co.uk). There are also very sophisticated media databases such as Cision (www.cision.com), Gorkana (www.gorkana.com) and Vocus (www.vocus.com), but these are typically for publishers and publicity agencies only because subscriptions to them cost thousands of pounds. Keep in mind that the quality of the contacts on your list is more important than the quantity.

Pitching

Remember that you are pitching 'stories' to the media, not your book(s). Think like a journalist when you tell people why they should be interested and, more importantly, why their audience should be interested. You can pitch by post, email or phone (or any combination, such as mailing review copies and following up with a phone call), but keep in mind that emails are easily ignored. If you phone, remember that journalists are extremely busy. Get straight to the point and be polite, even if they are not interested.

Different media have different 'lead times', i.e. how far in advance they work. A local radio station could have you on air in a couple of days, while a monthly magazine may be working on their Christmas issue in July. So as much as you can, try to approach your contacts at the appropriate time.

Print media

There are generally two types of articles about books in a newspaper or magazine – reviews and features. There is no area of book publicity that has changed more over the last few years than the 'book review'. Traditional reviews – the kind that you read in your newspaper

– used to dominate the publishing industry (see *The world of the literary editor* on page 321). But now these reviews are dying off as circulations decrease, culture sections get smaller and staff writers dwindle. And at the same time, the number of books being published is growing exponentially. The result is that traditional newspaper reviews tend to be dominated by big name authors whose books are going to sell a lot anyway. These reviews are certainly prestigious, but probably don't add to sales.

However, online reviews are flourishing. Technology has opened up publishing to almost anyone, and not just for books. If you go to a restaurant, you might review your experience of it online when you get home; if you get a tooth capped you might critique the dentist; and if you read a book you let everyone know what you thought about it. Reviewing is now part of people's everyday experience, and while our opinions may not be held in the same esteem as those of the literary editors, there are rather more of us doing it. Star ratings on Amazon, Goodreads and other websites are an average of many reviews – they are not just one person's opinion. Online reviews reach consumers directly and it only takes a tap of a mouse to turn that review into a sale.

Feature articles are stories and interviews about authors and topics related to a book but not specifically about the book, and they are a valuable way of getting traditional print media coverage (and sales). Features tend to be widely read and are usually intended for a more general audience, not just those interested in books. For example, while publicising a novel set in a business school, the author (who was also a banker in the City) mentioned his interest in a fairly obscure sub-genre of rock music. I talked to a music journalist who

Ten top publicity tips for the self-published author

1. Make your book as good and as inviting as it can possibly be. Pay attention to editing, cover design, layout, description blurb, etc. Do everything you can to make it stand out from the competition.

2. Be realistic about what you can do – and get help with what you can't. If you are not an outgoing personality, hate talking about yourself or are just time-poor, you may not be able to do everything that needs to be done. Call in the experts!

3. Have a media pack ready. Be prepared with compatible files of your front cover, press release, a biography, a professional 300 dpi photo of yourself and anything else that you think might help publicise your book.

4. Maximise your listings on websites (Amazon, Goodreads, etc). Make sure that everything is included, the information is correct and that it is well written.

5. Write articles for websites and blogs. Short articles (700–1,000 words) about the subject of your book, or anything else that matters to you, can be pitched to online news and information sources and can have your name and book title in the by-line.

6. Be truly social in your social marketing. Be personal, interactive and not too 'salesy' – show that you are a real person! Authenticity goes far in the social media realm.

7. Pay attention to bloggers. They can be far more influential than you might think. Treat them with respect and be personal in your interactions with them.

8. Practice for interviews. Be able to describe your book in 10–15 seconds in a way that anyone can understand. But don't be too scripted; be chatty and personable to ensure the interview appears natural.

9. Get out and about. Don't hide away in your writing shed! Signings at your local bookshop and other outlets are the perfect place to start.

10. No medium is too small. Don't discount smaller media and local papers; they can lead to bigger things – and often do!

was writing about the music for a national newspaper and she loved that a banker was improbably very knowledgeable about the music. Her article included quotes from the author and a mention of the book.

Chances are, you are an expert in something. You may not see it that way and it may not be related to your book, but if you think about it there is bound to be something that you know a lot about. By-line articles are written by you about something that you have special knowledge of or experience with, and can be pitched to online or print media. Op-eds are similar but, instead of being factual, they encapsulate your opinion about something in the news. Both article styles are usually 700–1,200 words long and can be a great way to spread the word and establish yourself as a writer, and your book title and website would normally be included in the credit line at the end.

Broadcast media

If you manage to get booked onto a radio or television show, you may well feel nervous about it. Replace your panic with preparation: practise talking about your book and your subject matter with others and in front of a mirror, be able to describe your book in 10–15 seconds, and remind yourself that you know what you are talking about. When you are actually 'on-air' be chatty, personable and talk about your book without trying to 'sell' it. And if the host fails to do so, be sure to plug your website address before the interview wraps so the audience can find out more about you and your book.

Local publicity

One thing that I have disagreements with clients about more than any other is local media. Ambitious authors often cannot be bothered with their local free paper – they only want massive readerships! However, local stories do have a way of finding their way to the national media outlets. It's not unusual for a national journalist to notice a news item in a local paper or hear something on a local radio station that they feel has a wider interest – and then for the story to be taken to a larger audience. Every author should think of media placements as building a resume for their book; each review, article, interview, etc will help solidify your author platform and pave the way for bigger opportunities.

Blogs

Most people consider media contacts in order of 'importance', with television being the golden ticket and blogs being something that you try once all other possibilities have been exhausted. However, for many books blogs can be a more efficient, achievable and targeted form of publicity than any other. The trick to getting great blog coverage is in your research and approach. Like other media, blogs do not exist to reprint every press release that is sent to them and bloggers can get annoyed when someone sends them a communication that shows no knowledge of or concern for what they write about. It can be seen as rude, and a blogger, like an angry person with a megaphone, has the power to shout back at you very loudly indeed. They can write a bad review or pick apart your carefully constructed press release, or worse.

So read the blogs you intend to target, and be positive and personal in your approach to the bloggers. Tell them that you love them. Tell them that you care about what they care about – and mean it! Enough blogs exist for you to find plenty that will be interested in your book, whatever it is about.

Social media

Social media is counter-intuitive: Those who do it well can sell a huge number of books almost effortlessly and those who do it poorly can waste a lot of time getting nowhere. The key is to really enjoy the interaction and get to know people – it's called social for a reason! Understand which platforms would be good for your book and make the most of them. Facebook is great for showcasing your book and letting people know how it can help them. Twitter is the best way of getting to know others in the book business – writers, publishers, agents, bloggers, and even reviewers. Pinterest is a visual medium and is great for photography, travel, cooking, and art and crafts. LinkedIn is about business networking and has some interesting publishing forums you can explore.

Social media is not a replacement for publicity through 'traditional' media. It works best as a way of amplifying the results that you achieve with newspapers, magazines, etc. For example, if you have a glowing review in *The Times* or an interview on *Woman's Hour*, tweeting about it is an efficient way to spread the word to an even larger audience. Few people, however, can sell a significant number of books through social media alone.

Ebooks

Publicising books that are only available as ebooks can be tricky in the UK as many media outlets won't consider them. The other difficulty is actually getting your ebook to reviewers and journalists in a format that they can read. NetGalley (www.netgalley.com) is a subscription-based website that is used by publishers and publicists to enable reviewers to read ebooks securely on any device. If your publicist or self-publishing company can upload your book to NetGalley it is a real advantage. It can also be worthwhile to set up your book on a print-on-demand platform simply to have something physical to send out to the media (see *Print on demand* on page 135).

For many UK authors, one fantastic consequence of publishing in ebook is that their book is available in the USA when it wouldn't have been otherwise. Even if you did not intend this to happen, you will want to encourage people there to read it. But for most people it is simply unworkable to do their own book promotion in the USA, especially if the media or the customs (it is done differently) are unfamiliar. It is also expensive to post books and phone the media.

If you do decide to try to take America by storm, it certainly helps to have someone on your side who knows the media, has the personal contacts and is physically there in the right time zone. If you are hiring a publicity company to promote your book in the USA, be certain that the person running your campaign is actually based there. In order for them to give you value for your investment they need to know the US media market intimately and have the contacts to make things happen.

A final note on sales

And finally, remember that publicity is only a part of the process of selling a book. Publicity is pointless if people are unable to find your book, or the cover or description are uninviting, or if it is too expensive. Sales rarely happen quickly for self-published books; as the author, you need to build an audience, and if you take a long-term view of sales you will be less frustrated in the short run and do much better over time.

Ben Cameron is the founder and Managing Director of Cameron Publicity and Marketing Ltd (www.cameronpm.co.uk), a full-service publicity and marketing source for independent authors and publishers. Ben has over 20 years of experience in publicity, publishing and bookselling in the UK.

Marketing yourself online

Simon Appleby and Mathew F. Riley outline how writers can use the internet to get noticed.

Make some noise!

Some basic things have not changed since the last edition of this *Yearbook* was published. Writers are writing. Readers are reading. This is good, but whether you're a published writer with an ongoing deal, or an aspiring writer with a whole load of ideas, or even a finished manuscript, the challenge will always be the same: how do you get your name known, your words read, your manuscripts taken on, your book bought, and then sell *more* books to justify a second book? Whether you're looking for a traditional publishing deal, considering self-publishing, or have some other approach in mind, this article is intended to help you promote your work online.

Important aspects of the literary environment are unquestionably changing: more people are reading and writing online; and readers have *become* writers. The ceaseless development of the internet enables anyone to say anything at any time to anyone who's reading (some types of e-reader even allow you to share your thoughts with other people reading the same book at the same time). Whether fiction, news, opinion or reviews, everybody's having their say, shouting the loudest to lure readers to their writing; readers and critics wanting to attract writers and publishers to their reviews. One more change: risk-averse publishers (and agents) look to the internet for inspiration and increasingly do so to gauge marketability. Much of your activity should be geared towards demonstrating to a publisher that people like your work and would pay to read more of it. Hence an author who is entrepreneurial, has developed a loyal fan-base, and a positive vibe about their work, has a chance of standing out from the crowd, with more to put on their CV and evidence that they really have put in the effort to get people reading their work. You probably won't need reminding that the global phenomenon *Fifty Shades of Grey* started life on an internet fan fiction forum, the ultimate reminder that there are many ways to be discovered as a writer.

The technologies, platforms and communities involved in online promotion are constantly evolving, but the concepts behind developing a manageable approach to promoting your writing on the internet, *to get you closer to your readers and them closer to you*, will absolutely hold true. This article won't give you detailed DIY instructions, but it will hopefully provide you with a focus with which to develop your presence on the internet in a structured and achievable fashion.

There's a lot of noise out there, and to be heard you will have to make some of your own. So, how do you do it? The technical side of things is not rocket science – the numerous (and free) solutions available out there do most of it for you, but it does take persistence and require an idea of where you want to be, and who you want to talk to. At the risk of teaching an old dog new tricks this means setting aside an amount of time to plan your approach. Just like writing. Once you've put the building blocks in place, it *is* writing. And (you already know this) when you start writing, you won't be able to stop!

Set up your own blog

Chances are you're already doing this, but if not you probably should. To get started, check out authors who are selling themselves well (and badly). Look at professional authors with well-designed websites, as well as lesser-known authors who are simply utilising the blogging platforms available to all of us. Note which blogging platforms these authors are using and investigate them for yourself. You don't need to have an all-singing, all-dancing, beautifully designed website and blog from day one – we have seen household names using basic, off-the-shelf blog themes, which is fine because what they are writing is interesting and entertaining.

A blog is *your* website. It can be whatever you want it to be. Publish some or all of your work to find out what people think about it, discuss other authors' work, the writing market, the process you go through in your writing. Give readers extra content they cannot get anywhere else. Study the statistics (try to avoid becoming addicted!) that your blog automatically provides and look at any sites that link to yours. Make yourself accessible. When someone sends you a message or leaves you a comment it's an opportunity to enter into a discussion about your writing. Get back to them while they're still interested. Make your blog the centre of your online universe, and explore the threads that will grow from this centre – but remember, what you write will be available on the internet for a long time, so be sure to think about how you talk about yourself, your life and about other writers, and don't put anything in writing that you wouldn't want a potential reader or publisher of your work to see.

Social networking and communities

To help people find your blog, and want to read it, you must exploit and be a willing participant of the social internet.

There are innumerable communities on the internet – each one an island floating on an ocean of 'noise'. Navigating your way to these oases of context is vital and you'll find them just as you find a good book – by searching according to your tastes, and listening to the recommendations of your friends. It won't happen overnight, but keep at it and slowly but surely it will work: your friends and visitors increase, your words are read and your name and reputation spreads. Here are the main categories to think about:

- **Writing communities** – where you can get your work evaluated and rate the work of others. These are both a source of useful feedback and encouragement, and a place to get noticed by publishers (even leading to book deals for the best).
- **General book communities** – where book owners, librarians, collectors and authors come together, an instant source of like-minded people.

Ten good author websites

Joe Abercombie
website www.joeabercrombie.com

Antony Beevor
website www.antonybeevor.com

John le Carré
website www.johnlecarre.com

Bernard Cornwell
website www.bernardcornwell.net

Gillian Flynn
website www.gillian-flynn.com

Anthony Horowitz
website www.anthonyhorowitz.com

E.L. James
website www.eljamesauthor.com

J.K. Rowling
website www.jkrowling.co.uk

Will Self
website www.will-self.com

Marcel Theroux
website www.thisworldofdew.com

• **Forums** – these can be wide ranging or frighteningly focused on one subject, but if you find one you like, hang around and join in. But remember, you should not expect to drop in, plug your work and have other users be grateful for your contribution if you don't stick around.
• **Social networking** – this is the broadest category, encompassing thousands of sites large and small. Find the one that's right for you.

'Friends'

Set up a Facebook page and a Twitter profile. Thousands of writers have already done so, and they're talking to each other and their fans right now. Facebook and Twitter are *all* about talking. Use these platforms to promote your work – friendships may even develop too. It's an excuse to talk to complete strangers and you'll soon find things in common. Search for the topics that interest you, the areas you write about and the markets you work in. It's no exaggeration to say that you'll be sure to find people and groups who like what you do. As well as your profile you can set up pages for your books and invite people to be fans. You can import the content from your blog and send people updates as your content changes. All this can be done automatically. You may get the impression that some users spend their entire lives on Twitter (and perhaps they do), but ten minutes a couple of times a day is all you'll need after the initial set-up.

Increasingly worthy of mention too is LinkedIn – while in the past this was the province of traditional professionals, you will find many authors, agents and publishing people on there, and there are numerous groups where topics of interest to authors are discussed. You may be able to use it to find collaborators (perhaps an illustrator or photographer), and a smartly completed LinkedIn profile is the equivalent of an online CV – essential if you want to be taken seriously.

A tool for every job

As in life, so online, there is a tool for every possible situation. We can't tell you everything a good toolkit should contain, but we can suggest some general principles and a few key tools, all of which are free and easy to use.
• **Stay on 'brand'** – keep handy a standard biography and a decent photo of yourself when setting up user profiles. It helps to represent yourself consistently wherever people encounter you. Try always to use the same username as well. Keep a note of the profiles you set up and periodically update them.
• **Social conversation** – use social networking sites, micro-blogging services (i.e. Twitter) and your own site to get engaged with your current and potential readers and your fellow authors.
• **Share and enjoy** – for any type of content you create, there's a platform to share it on, whether it's video (YouTube, Vimeo), photos (Flickr, Photobucket), audio/podcasts (Soundcloud) and, of course, writing of all kinds. When you share content, consider whether it needs to be under copyright or whether Creative Commons licensing (http://creativecommons.org) might help it be more widely seen.
• **Listening tools** – when you know people are talking about you and your work, or linking to your website, you can drop in and make a contribution, or link to the content in question. For this, Google Alerts is your friend. More broadly, use Really Simple Syndication (RSS) to follow the blogs that interest you and keep track of new writers, industry trends and

more, as this may also provide you with topics to blog about. We suggest NewsBlur or Feedly, but there are numerous feed readers available.

• **Keep current** – wherever there is information about you, make sure it's current and as detailed as possible. If you have one, keep your Wikipedia entry up to date (taking care to stay factual); update information about yourself on sites such as LibraryThing (www.librarything.com); and if you have one, make sure your publisher knows about your online activities so they can promote them.

Engagement

As a writer spending time online, you are inevitably going to come in contact with criticism of your work at some point, perhaps even abuse. Keep your cool and remember, when deciding how to react to something, one of these four responses will usually be appropriate:

• **Endorse** – if something's really positive (a good review, or creativity inspired by your work) link to it, shout about it, tell your publisher, encourage the creator.

• **Engage** – enter into discussion with fans and critics alike on their forum of choice; respond to constructive criticism professionally and never take it personally.

• **Ignore** – if you can't say anything nice....

• **Enforce** – if anyone is getting abusive, infringing your rights or just going too far, take measured steps to do something about it (like contacting their forum moderator or ISP), but never descend to their level. Anything you say in anger may come back to haunt you later.

One other thing – *never* pretend to be someone you're not, anywhere, for any reason. Always represent yourself honestly as 'the author in question'. Successful authors, who shall remain nameless here, have seriously damaged their credibility and careers through the practice of 'sockpuppetry', leaving glowing reviews of their own work under false names and trashing their rivals' books.

Online PR

This is a glorified way of saying 'Talk to people about your work in order to get them to write about it'. If you are willing to put in the time to contact bloggers and offer review copies, interviews, competition prizes or other content they can use, some of them are likely to respond positively. Understand their pressures – they want to find things to write about, and that's where you come in, but they may get many offers every single day.

Use some of the same organisational skills that you use researching and talking to agents and publishers – much as you do when you look through the *Writers' & Artists' Yearbook* for suitable publishers and agents, do your homework on blogs too. Read a blog thoroughly before you approach the blogger to make sure your work is right for that blog, and read any submission guidelines the site may have. Keep a record of who you contact and when, to make sure you don't repeat yourself. Follow up after a suitable time any sites that offer to look at your work. Present yourself professionally: it's all good common sense, but in our experience that doesn't mean everyone does it properly.

> *I went down the independent publishing route and got my book out in the USA and UK with BookSurge, a branch of Amazon. The pivotal moment for me was reading an article in the* Guardian, *'Is it curtains for critics?', describing the eclipse of professional critics by bloggers, and mentioning an influential book blogger, dovegreyreader. I emailed her and*

most of the other bloggers listed on her page, asking if they would review an independently published book. Most said they would, and most of those read and reviewed my book. This led to enquiries by publishers. The result: War on the Margins: A Novel *was released by Duckworth Publishers in the UK in July 2009. – Libby Cone*

Getting creative on a budget

You can get creative and get noticed even if you have little or no money to spend: write a blog or an article 'in character'. Set up a Twitter feed in your character's name, or write micro-fiction. Enlist the services of friends and family, and their cameras, video cameras, computers and, most importantly, skills to create images or videos that you can promote yourself with. We know you're creative, or you wouldn't be reading this, so we bet you can think of something imaginative (and don't get hung up on being wholly original, or you might never get started).

What does the future look like?

You don't need us to tell you this is a hard question to answer – especially for anything relating to the online world. What we do know is that the internet is rapidly eroding the barriers between writers, readers and publishers, posing new challenges for all three groups, and that's without mentioning the changes being wrought by the growth of the ebook market. This is an opportunity for you as a writer: it's a chance to get feedback earlier, from more people than ever before; a chance to hone your own marketing and presentational skills not just to literary agents, but to a much broader base of enthusiastic bloggers and fans; and most importantly, a chance to take your destiny into your own hands in a way that writers would not have imagined possible only a few years ago.

So let us hear you make some noise!

Simon Appleby and **Mathew F. Riley** have a combined total of 30 years' experience working with digital media, including setting up many publisher and author websites. They own and run Bookswarm (www.bookswarm.co.uk), an agency dedicated to providing digital marketing services to publishers and authors.

See also...

- *Managing your online reputation*, page 607
- *Book blogs*, page 610

Managing your online reputation

These days, most people who want to find out about someone they haven't met instinctively reach for their phone, laptop or other device and key the name into Google. Antony Mayfield offers guidelines to help determine what is found as a result.

Managing your reputation has become part of every professional's career these days, and for aspiring and published authors alike it is especially important to understand what the web says about you and why that matters. Rather than think of this as another onerous responsibility in the ever-expanding job description of the professional writer, however, it may be better to view managing what the web says about you as both an opportunity and part of a powerful new way of working.

As the saying goes, reputation is what you do plus what others say about you. Translated for the web age, that means when someone puts your name into a search engine or social networking website, your reputation is what they find about you and your work.

Most importantly, for writers looking to get published, an established online reputation being part of a strong network or community of peers and fans adds to the chances that a book will be a success. This is not just about direct sales: an online community that values a writer's work will be likely to help spread the word, write reviews and generally support that writer's efforts.

In the best tradition of *Writers' & Artists' Yearbook*, the advice in this article comes from a personal perspective, and should be taken and made your own. One of the most important things to understand about the web is that it is a machine, a tool, and you should feel like it works for you rather than the other way around.

Understanding your online world

Just as being a good writer means being a good reader, it helps to get to know your online world and pay attention to what is going on there. Who are the people who are talking about subjects you are interested in and write about, or if you have a public profile already, where are they talking about your work?

It can even be helpful to sketch a map of what your online world looks like: over here are the people blogging about your subject matter, over there the specialist community site dedicated to it, over there the Twitter conversations.

Being found for yourself

The next job is to look at what people find when they look for you online. What happens when you key your name into Google, Facebook, or other websites? If you have a common name, what keywords would a stranger (a publisher or journalist wanting to know more about you, for instance) use to narrow their search? Would they add the name of your school or university, the town where you live, your employer or profession for instance?

One fairly useful measure of success for your efforts in managing your reputation is how much easier you can make it for others to find you online and how much useful stuff they find (on your sites and others). Ideally, you want the first page on Google – or any other search engine – that appears for your name to be yours. Not least, this means that whatever the rest of the world says about you, you get your say first.

A page you can call home

Developing your online presence these days can mean having profiles on several websites (for most authors at least a personal website or blog, Twitter and Facebook). Ensure that one is your hub, where you organise your online presence and connect to others. Also, if you are a non-fiction author or looking to attract offers of work as well as readers for your books, a complete LinkedIn profile is a must.

Some people find that a Facebook page (a fan page, not a personal profile) can serve this purpose. Bear in mind, though that not everyone has a Facebook account and a few even object to it – so making this your central online presence can have drawbacks.

For me, the most versatile and future-proof approach is to have a personal blog or website and to link writing and other content you put there to other sites and social networks.

Ideally, a hosted WordPress (www.wordpress.com) blog at a personal web address is the way to go (a little help from a moderately tech-savvy friend can get you up and running). Alternatives like SquareSpace (www.squarespace.com) charge a reasonable monthly fee and make it relatively simple to run a professional-looking blog or personal web page.

Another option is to use a personal homepage service like Flavors.me or About.me. These are attractive, simple web pages which are easy to set up, free or low-cost and can sit on your personal web address. Your homepage will link to and even show excerpts from your Twitter, Facebook and other social websites. This is a low maintenance approach, but will still stand a good chance of appearing high in the search engine listings for your name.

Public and private lives online

Early on in managing your online reputation, there is an important personal policy you need to draw up. How much of your life are you going to live in public? To put it another way, where are you going to draw the line between your personal life and your work as a writer?

For some people, living publicly is something they are very happy to do. For others, they want a complete division between their professional persona and their private self. Most people draw their personal division somewhere in between.

It is not just a case of protecting your personal privacy. The word 'over-share' crept into the dictionaries a few years ago, largely to describe people sharing too many personal details online. It is not just a privacy issue as you may annoy readers of your blog or Twitter by posting a stream of personal trivia.

Once you are clear on your approach to public and private, pay careful attention to what you are posting and where. If you use services like Facebook for personal and family communication, take some time to understand the privacy settings and how you can use them to make sure that you are, for instance, not sharing 200 photos of a birthday party with your professional Facebook page instead of just your family and friends.

Make it a way of working

You already have a job that takes up most of your time: writing. The danger of online reputation management is that it can either be too daunting a job to take on at all, or become an addictive distraction (I'll just check my Twitter feed, just look at the visitor statistics on my blog, etc).

The best way of adding to your online presence and growing your reputation is to be useful to the communities around you, your networks of contacts, connections and readers. As a writer this can be done by complementing your working routine (research, reading, thinking) with social media tools.

Thinking of your blog as a public notebook can be a liberating and useful experience. At a conference on storytelling, science fiction writer and blogger Cory Doctorow shared his approach to blogging as a way of collecting ideas and research. I noted his method (on my own blog) like this:

• Blog about why something is interesting in five sentences.
• By doing that you are creating a searchable database.
• If it is interesting, people will annotate it with comments.
• After a while, there are enough posts and emerging themes that the case for a long-form piece of writing becomes clear.

Dealing with the dark side of online reputation

Many people feel trepidation about writing on the web because of a fear of being attacked by unkind commentators and critics. This shouldn't be an issue for authors though, right? If it is, then consider the web an excellent opportunity to develop a thicker skin when it comes to criticism.

There is a useful maxim among community managers and web editors that is worth sharing: 'don't feed the trolls'. Trolls are people who – usually anonymously – like to bait others with deliberately provocative comments online. The simple advice therefore, is to ignore them and refuse to be drawn into arguments you are unlikely ever to win.

Lastly, remember that when it comes to any online space, even a seemingly intimate or private one, you are on the record when you post anything on the web, and a permanent record at that. Effectively, all electronic communication – emails, texts and instant messages included – should be thought of as semi-public.

Useful resources and links

Managing your online reputation then, is an art that authors should learn. It should not interfere with the day job much though; think of it as a way of making the most of what you already have in terms of thoughts, ideas, reputation and writing. If you want to find out more, see my blog (www.antonymayfield.com/writers) for a list of resources and links to the websites and services mentioned in this article, along with some others that would be useful for any author looking to manage their online reputation.

Antony Mayfield is a founding partner of Brilliant Noise, a digital strategy consultancy working with major brands, media and marketing agencies. He founded the content and social media teams at iCrossing, which became the largest independent digital marketing firm in the world, before being sold to Hearst Media in 2010. His book, *Me and My Web Shadow* (Bloomsbury 2010), is about how to manage your personal reputation online.

See also...

• *Marketing yourself online*, page 602
• *Book blogs*, page 610

Book blogs

This is a small selection of the best book blogs as compiled by the editors of the *Yearbook*.

The Artist's Road

website http://artistsroad.wordpress.com
Founder Patrick Ross

Blog created to record the cross-USA road trip that the author Patrick Ross took in the summer of 2010 while interviewing over 40 artists with the aim of discussing the motivations, challenges and rewards of their lifestyles, and passing on their creative wisdom. It now details his insights into living an 'art-committed life' through writing and creativity.

Books & Such

website www.booksandsuch.com/blog
Founder Janel Kobobel Grant

Blog from a literary agent's perspective, advising on writing query letters and improving MSS before submitting them to agents. Also addresses how to find an agent and get published. Highlights the importance of the editing process in adding to writing quality. Discusses the merits of both traditional publishing paths and how to decide which option is right for you.

Nathan Bransford

website http://blog.nathanbransford.com
Founder Nathan Bransford

From the perspective of an author and former literary agent advising about the writing, editing and publishing process, based on his own experience. Added tips on improving plots, dialogue and characters, writing a query letter and synopsis and finding a literary agent. Analyses and debates a range of topics including ebooks and their pricing, social media options, marketing, cover design and plot themes. Includes a publishing glossary and FAQs.

Cornflower Books

website www.cornflowerbooks.co.uk
Founder Karen Howlett

Reviews a wide range of books and has a monthly online book club, debates cover designs and includes a 'writing and publishing' section. Also includes interviews with well-known authors about their books, writing process and routine. Selects 'books of the year' in different genres, and discusses literary festivals and prizes.

Courage 2 Create

website http://thecourage2create.com
Founder Ollin Morales

Ollin Morales shares the experience of writing his first novel: pitfalls to avoid, dealing with stress, overcoming challenges, how his lifestyle benefits from writing, and inspirational quotes. Blog chapters describe his creative journey and what he has learned about life through the writing process.

The Creative Penn

website www.thecreativepenn.com
Founder Joanna Penn

Focuses on the writing process and how to market and sell your book. Advises writers on dealing with criticism, finding an agent and writing query letters. Debates traditional publishing, 'hybrid' and self-publishing options, and also advises on POD, ebook publishing as well as online and social media marketing. Includes audio/video interviews with mainly self-published authors.

Dear Author

website www.dearauthor.com
Founder Jane Litte

Focuses on romantic novels. All reviews are written in the form of a letter to the author. Includes interviews with authors about their books and writing style.

Fiction Notes

website www.darcypattison.com
Founder Darcy Pattison

Darcy Pattison is a published non-fiction writer and children's author, as well as an experienced speaker. Her blog collates her own articles and thoughts on children's writing, reviews of her work and information on her speaking engagements where she specialises in novel revision and metamorphosis.

Jane Friedman

website http://janefriedman.com
Founder Jane Friedman

Focuses on digital publishing and discusses the future of publishing. Provides tips for writers on how to beat writers' block, DIY ebook publishing, marketing your writing and publicising it online through blogs, social media and websites to create your 'author platform' and publish your book. Includes guidance on copyright and securing permissions.

Goins, Writer

website http://goinswriter.com
Founder Jeff Goins

Focuses on advising authors about their writing journey and how to enhance their writing style.

Highlights how authors can build a core fanbase 'tribe' through a focused approach and adding value to social media and blogs.

Helping Writers Become Authors

website www.helpingwritersbecomeauthors.com
Founder K.M. Weiland

Tips on story structure, creating memorable characters and plot development. Advice about finding writing inspiration and the writing process, as well as addressing the story revision and MS editing stages. Includes an extensive list of books for aspiring authors.

Live Write Thrive

website www.livewritethrive.com
Founder C. S. Lakin

Set up by a writer specialising in fiction, fantasy and YA, this blog focuses on helping writers discover what kind of copy-editing and critiquing services their work will need once it is finished. As a copy-editor and writing coach, Lakin offers her own editorial services and advice on how to choose the right editor. There are also articles by guest bloggers and a variety of useful posts, including tips on grammar.

A Newbie's Guide to Publishing

website http://jakonrath.blogspot.co.uk
Founder Joe Konrath

Blog by a self-published author which discusses the writing process and focuses on self-publishing, encourages writers to self-publish ebooks, and looks at developments and trends in this area. Includes interviews with self-published authors about their books, and guest posts.

Positive Writer

website www.positivewriter.com
Founder Bryan Hutchinson

A motivational and inspirational blog for creatives, particularly writers, focusing on how to overcome doubt and negativity and to unlock your inner creativity. It includes handy tips on marketing and interviews with other authors.

Ready Steady Book

website www.readysteadybook.com/Blog.aspx
Founder & Managing Editor Mark Thwaite

Includes reviews of books in the literary fiction, poetry, history and philosophy genres, with added links for purchase. Highlights up-coming book events and has an extensive selection of interviews with authors and publishers. A range of articles discuss authors' works and literary themes.

Romance University

website http://romanceuniversity.org
Co-founders Tracey Devlyn, Kelsey Browning, Adrienne Giordano

An online 'university' for all who are hoping to learn the craft of writing romance. Three new blog post lectures are added by contributors and industry professionals weekly. Each Monday, posts focus on the theme of 'crafting your career', which include the business of writing, agents, publishing and self-publishing options, and marketing your work on social media and blogs. Wednesdays focus on 'the anatomy of the mind' in relation to different facets of romance writing. Fridays focus on the elements of the manuscript writing process, e.g. creating characters and plot.

Terribleminds

website http://terribleminds.com/ramble/blog
Founder Chuck Wendig

Comical, easy-to-read blog about author Chuck Wendig's trials and tribulations whilst writing.

There Are No Rules

website www.writersdigest.com/editor-blogs/there-are-no-rules

Blog by the editors of Writer's Digest. Focuses on the writing process, plot and character development, writing query letters and creating your author platform through social media and public speaking. Tips on how to overcome writing challenges, improve your writing and revise your MS so that it is more likely to be accepted by an agent. Includes a range of regular webinars with industry professionals including agents offering advice. Also discusses and advises on the self-publishing process.

The Write Life

website www.thewritelife.com
Founder Alexis Grant

This blog, by writers for writers, is designed to encourage individuals to connect and share experiences. There is no single expert, but a running dialogue connecting fellow writers during the stages in their writing journey. Posts tend to focus on how to become a writer rather than the writing process itself, with advice on blogging, freelancing, finding an agent, promoting and self-publishing amongst other topics.

The Write Practice

website http://thewritepractice.com
Founder Joe Bunting

Focuses on how to get published; includes advice for writers on different stages of the writing process and submitting MSS to agents (e.g. '8 Tips for Naming Characters', 'Your Dream vs. Rejection' and 'Bring Your Setting to Life').

Writer Unboxed

website http://writerunboxed.com
Co founders Therese Walsh (Editor-in-Chief) and Kathleen Bolton

Comical tips on the art and craft of writing fiction, the writing process, and marketing your work. Includes interviews with established authors also offering advice.

Writers Helping Writers

website http://writershelpingwriters.net
Co-founders Angela Ackerman and Becca Puglisi

Writing tools for authors, to help them visualise and create dynamic characters and improve their plot and writing, including a 'Character Pyramid Tool', 'Character Profile Questionnaire' and 'Reverse Backstory Tool'. Also provides multiple thesauruses such as the 'Character Trait Thesaurus', 'Emotion Thesaurus' and 'Setting Thesaurus' to help authors improve their descriptive writing. Downloadable advice sheets on blogs and social media marketing for authors also available.

Self-publishing providers

This is a selection of the ever-expanding list of companies that offer editorial, production, marketing and distribution support for authors who want to self-publish. As with all the organisations mentioned in the *Yearbook*, we recommend that you check carefully what companies offer and what they charge.

Acorn Independent Press Ltd

82 Southwark Bridge Road, London SE1 0AS
tel 020-3488 0820
email info@acornselfpublishing.com
website www.acornselfpublishing.com
Editorial Director Leila Dewji, *Sales & Marketing Director* Ali Dewji

Self-publishing service provider for authors at all stages of their careers. Offers three main packages, ranging from £1,100–£3,900, all of which come with personal service and the option to meet face-to-face prior and throughout the process.

Albury Books

Albury Court, Albury, Thame, Oxon OX9 2LP
tel (01844) 337000
email hannah@alburybooks.com
website www.alburybooks.com

International publishing house that collaborates with writers and illustrators to self-publish and/or re-publish their work through the Albury Bookshelf platform. Offers services for each stage of the publishing process including editing, illustration, layout and art direction. Provides ISBNs and print-on-demand or short print runs and co-edition deals. Offers marketing campaigns and submissions for awards. Each book published is listed for sale in the Albury online store and made available to major booksellers. Founded 2013.

Amolibros

Loundshay Manor Cottage, Preston Bowyer, Milverton, Somerset TA4 1QF
tel (01823) 401527
email amolibros@aol.com
website www.amolibros.com
Director Jane Tatam

Offers print and ebook design, production, copy-editing, and distribution through online retailers. Sales and marketing services include design and production of adverts, leaflets, author websites, distribution of press releases, and direct mail campaigns.

Author House UK

1663 Liberty Drive, Bloomington, IN 47403, USA
tel 0800 197 4150
website www.authorhouse.co.uk

Offers editorial services, interior and cover design, illustration, marketing and publicity advice and distribution for hardcover and paperback print-on-demand books, as well as ebook conversion and distribution services. Colour and b&w publishing packages start at £499, speciality packages at £949, and ebook-only packages at £299.

Author Solutions

1663 Liberty Drive, Bloomington, IN 47403, USA
website www.authorsolutions.com

Owns several self-publishing imprints, including iUniverse, Author House, Author House UK, Palibrio, Xlibris, and Trafford Publishing. US-based. A Penguin Random House company.

Authoright

5th Floor, 22 Upper Ground, London SE1 9PD
tel 020-7993 8225
email info@authoright.com
website http://authoright.com
CEO & Co-founder Gareth Howard, *COO & Co-founder* Hayley Radford

Offers structural editing, copy-editing and proofreading, ebook creation and distribution, manuscript layout and cover design. Additional services include: composing and distributing press releases; designing author websites; creating book trailers and author interview videos; establishing and maintaining social media profiles.

Azimuth Print Ltd

Unit 1, Bowling Hill Business Park, Chipping Sodbury, Bristol BS37 6JL
tel (01454) 319676
email sales@azimuthprint.co.uk
website www.azimuthprint.co.uk
Contact Mike Edmonds

Produces wirebound, perfect-bound and hardback books in a variety of sizes, in colour or b&w. Authors can send own artwork, use the artwork templates supplied by Azimuth Print or commission their designers. Also prints promotional materials including leaflets and posters. Founded 1989.

Be-Published.com

website http://be-published.com

Provides b&w, colour and speciality self-publishing in genres including fiction, non-fiction, poetry and science fiction. Editorial services offered include copy-editing, formatting and interior and cover design. Marketing services include creating and distributing press releases and printed publicity materials.

Berforts Information Press

23–25 Gunnels Wood Park, Gunnels Wood Road, Stevenage, Hertfordshire SG1 2BH
tel (01438) 312777
website www.berforts.co.uk

Specialises in litho and short-run digital printing of hardback and paperback books in b&w and full colour in a variety of sizes and bindings, including case binding and perfect binding. Also offers self-publishing help and advice; contact for free guide to book printing and self-publishing.

The Better Book Company

5 Lime Close, Chichester, West Sussex PO19 6SW
tel 0800 907 0018
email betterbook@mac.com
website http://thebetterbookcompany.com

Offers interior and cover design, editing, proofreading and printing services. Two sets of proofs are sent to the author for approval before printing.

Blue Ocean Publishing

St John's Innovation Centre, Cowley Road, Cambridge CB4 0WS
tel (01763) 208887
email publishing@blueoceanpublishing.biz
website www.blueoceanpublishing.biz

Professional, personal self-publishing of books, ebooks, brochures, CDs, DVDs and games for individuals and organisations. Advice on MSS, as well as complete design and editorial services are available, as is assistance with marketing, writing and distribution. Established 2007.

Blurb

website www.blurb.co.uk
Founder, President & Ceo Eileen Gittins

Provides downloadable book-making software, templates and customisable layouts for creating print books or ebooks with audio and video for iPad. Publications can be sold online through the Blurb bookshop and the iBookstore. Photobooks and trade books, novels or poetry can be printed in hardcover or softcover and in a variety of sizes. Prices are based on extent. Authors may retain 100% of the mark-up for a print book, or 80% of the retail price they set for an ebook sold through the Blurb bookstore; monies received from other retailers may vary. Discounts are available for volume orders on print books. For pricing details, see www.blurb.co.uk/pricing-calculator.

BookBaby

tel +1 503-961-6878
email books@bookbaby.com
website www.bookbaby.com

US-based provider offering ebook creation and distribution services as well as cover design and customisable author websites. BookBaby partners with Firstediting.com to provide editiorial services. Its print operations offer printing services across a range of formats. A variety of products is available but pricing and commission levels vary; see website for full details.

BookCurve.com

Enterprise Centre, Denton Island, Newhaven, East Sussex BN9 9BA
tel 0845 123 2699
email helpdesk@bookcurve.com
website www.bookcurve.com

Ebook distribution service from eBook Partnership. Worldwide distribution and management of ebook files for authors, publishers, businesses and non-profit organisations. Standard and fixed layout ebook files. Extensive network of retailers, libraries and subscription services. Set-up fee, but clients retain 100% of royalties. Client admin system, no fees for changes to listings.

BookPrinting UK

Remus House, Coltsfoot Drive, Woodston, Peterborough PE2 9BF
tel (01733) 898102
email info@bookprintinguk.com
website www.bookprintinguk.com

Offers colour and b&w printing and print-on-demand books in a range of bindings. Can provide custom illustration and interior layout options, as well as typesetting. Provides templates for formatting manuscript files before sending. Can also distribute print books direct to customers. Prints bookmarks, posters and flyers.

Cameron Publicity and Marketing Ltd

180 Piccadilly, London W1J 9HF
tel 020-7917 9812
email info@cameronpm.co.uk
website www.cameronpm.co.uk

Publicity and marketing campaigns for publishers and independent authors including media awareness, websites and social media. Founded January 2006.

The Choir Press

132 Bristol Road, Gloucester GL1 5SR
tel (01452) 500016
email enquiries@thechoirpress.co.uk
website www.selfpublishingbooks.co.uk
Contact Miles Bailey

Offers short- and long-run printing and print-on-demand options in a variety of sizes and bindings, as well as ebook conversion and distribution. Preferred formats for printed editions are illustrated non-fiction. Offers custom cover design or can incorporate author-supplied images. Copy-editing, structural editing and proofreading services also available. Founded 1982.

CompletelyNovel

website http://completelynovel.com

Provides online publishing tools for authors to upload their manuscript to create and distribute print-on-demand books and ebooks, and an online cover creator tool. A number of sales and distribution options are available. Website also offers self-publishing advice on topics including editing, cover design and social media marketing.

CreateSpace

website www.createspace.com

Publishing engine of Amazon. Allows writers and users to self-publish and distribute books, DVDs, CDs and video downloads on demand.

Crux Publishing

39 Birdhurst Road, London, SW18 1AR
tel 020-8871 0594
email hello@cruxpublishing.co.uk
website www.cruxpublishing.co.uk
Publisher Christopher Lascelles

Boutique digital publisher offering to produce, distribute and market selected high-quality, non-fiction titles. Operates an open submissions policy for new authors and digitally republishes backlist titles for existing authors. Works with individual authors to create and execute a unique marketing plan that drives sales. Founded December 2011.

eBook Partnership

Enterprise Centre, Denton Island, Newhaven, East Sussex BN9 9BA
tel 0845 123 2699
email helpdesk@ebookpartnership.com
tel (US) +1 855 373 4770
website www.ebookpartnership.com

Ebook conversion specialists. Standard and fixed layout formats for authors, publishers, businesses, charities and non-profits. Worldwide ebook distribution to online retailers, libraries and subscription services. Set-up fee; no commission on royalties. Also offers cover-design service; ISBNs; and print-book scanning service. Client admin system available for sales and royalty information. Founded 2010.

eBook Versions

27 Old Gloucester Street, London WC1N 3AX
website www.ebookversions.com

Offers ebook self-publishing and distribution through online retailers including Kindle, Apple iBookstore, Kobo, Nook and WH Smith. Packages begin at £95 and are based on conversion of a manuscript of up to 100,000 words. Print-on-demand and distribution options are also available. Can convert different types of books including comics, scientific and technical to ebooks, and creates illustrated and reference ebooks for large screen tablets incorporating audio, video and interactivity.

The Electronic Book Company

tel (01974) 272539
email info@theelectronicbookcompany.com
website http://theelectronicbookcompany.com
Founder Colin Timms

Offers ebook conversion, formatting and distribution for £199 for texts up to 60,000 words, plus £15 per additional 10,000 words. £5 per image. Custom cover design for £85. Authors retain 100% of net royalties from ebook sales. Offers proofreading with three different levels of editing, from £1.75 per page. Publishes a range of fiction and non-fiction genres. May help to market selected titles to their mailing list, and can edit books to incorporate US and international English language use.

Fast Print Publishing

9 Culley Court, Bakewell Road, Orton Southgate, Peterborough PE2 6XD
tel (01733) 404828
email info@fast-print.net
website www.fast-print.net

Offers print-on-demand and ebook self-publishing and distribution packages. Also offers proofreading (£11 per 1,000 words), page layout (£1.50 per 100 words), cover design and marketing services. Retail and distribution packages are also available to retailers including Waterstones, Amazon and Foyles.

Firsty Group

4 The Courtyard, London Road, Newbury, Berkshire RG14 1AX
tel (01635) 581185
email info@firstygroup.com
website http://firstygroup.com

Provides ebook conversion and distribution. Converts files to a range of formats including .ePub, .mobi/.prc and KF8 for Kindle, and fixed format for Apple. In addition creates apps, particularly for children's picture books, revision guides and reference books, which include animation, audio-visual interactive features, and social media integration. Also designs websites with e-commerce functions.

Grosvenor House Publishing

Crossweys, 28–30 High Street, Guildford GU1 3EL
tel (01483) 243450
website www.grosvenorhousepublishing.co.uk
Co-founders Kim Cross, Jason Kosbab

Publishes for a range of genres including children's and non-fiction in colour, b&w, print-on-demand, paperback, hardback and ebook formats. Offers a £795 publishing package which includes typesetting, five free print copies, an ISBN and print and ebook distribution via online retailers. Authors can design covers online. Marketing services include producing posters and postcards, and website set-up from template with two years' hosting. Ebook publishing costs £195 if the print edition of the book has been produced by the company and £495 otherwise. Print costs and royalties depend on book specification. A proofreading service is offered at a rate of £5 per 1,000 words. See website for full list of costs.

The Hilary Johnson Authors' Advisory Service

3 Maple Drive, South Wootton, King's Lynn, Norfolk PE30 3JL
tel (01553) 676611
email enquiries@hilaryjohnson.com
email hilary@hilaryjohnson.demon.co.uk
website www.hilaryjohnson.demon.co.uk
Contact Hilary Johnson

Provides a manuscript reading and critique service for fiction, short-story, children's and non-fiction authors. Specialist advice for genres including science fiction, romance, crime, thrillers, film/TV/radio scripts and poetry. Also offers copy-editing and proofreading. Assessment of covering letter and synopsis before submitting to literary agents is also available. Advises on manuscript presentation.

I_AM Self-Publishing

82 Southwark Bridge Road, London SE1 0AS
tel 020-3488 0565
email hello@iamselfpublishing.com
website www.iamselfpublishing.com

Produces print books and ebooks for self-publishing authors. Services include: design, typesetting, editing, proofreading, print-on-demand and short-run printing in b&w and full colour, ebook conversion, author branding and backlist re-publication. Also offers an authors' marketing course. Authors can opt for either a global, managed distribution service to the major ebook retailers for an 80% royalty, or an Amazon-only option to keep 100% of royalties. Packages range from £400–£1,900. Works with large media organisations, literary agencies and individual authors alike.

iBooks Author

website www.apple.com/ibooks-author

App that allows authors to create interactive e-textbooks and other types of ebooks, for example photo books, travel, or craft/cookery books for iPad. Features include video and audio, interactive diagrams, photos and 3D images. They can then be sold through the iBookstore. Authors choose fonts and template page layouts or design their own. Charts, tables, text, images and interactive features can also be added.

iUniverse

1663 Liberty Drive, Bloomington, IN 47403, USA
tel +1 812-330-2909
website www.iuniverse.com

Offers editorial (proofreading/copy-editing), cover and interior design, production and marketing services. (Services are available on an individual basis.) Also offers assistance with publicity campaigns, including press release, video and social media, as well as print-on-demand and ebook self-publishing and distribution services through online retailers. Packages range from $899 ('Select') to $4,299 ('Book Launch').

Kindle Direct Publishing

website https://kdp.amazon.com

Ebook self-publishing and distribution platform for Kindle and Kindle Apps. Its business model offers up to a 70% royalty (on certain retail prices between $2.99–$9.99) in many countries and availability in Amazon stores worldwide. POD options are available through CreateSpace, an Amazon company (see www.createspace.com). Note that KDP Select makes books exclusive to Amazon (which means they cannot be sold through an author's personal website, for example), but authors can share in the Global Fund amount every time the book is borrowed from the Kindle Owners' Lending Library.

Kobo Writing Life

website www.kobo.com/writinglife

Ebook self-publishing platform where authors can upload manuscripts and cover images, and Kobo then coverts the files into ebooks before distributing them through the Kobo ebookstore. Authors are able to set pricing and DRM territories, as well as track sales. Royalty rates of either 70% or 45% are offered, depending on price or territory (see user guide for details). Free to join.

Lavender and White

Snipe Lodge, Moycullen, County Galway, Republic of Ireland
tel +353 87 6814267
email info@lavenderandwhite.co.uk
website www.lavenderandwhite.co.uk
Editorial Director Jacqueline Broderick, *Editor* Sarah Lewis

Complete publishing solution for self-publishing authors. Editing, proofreading, cover design, typesetting, ebook conversion, print-on-demand, marketing and sell-through services. Also offers mentoring and ghostwriting services.

Costs vary depending on services required; email for a quote. Easy payment options available.

Lightning Source UK

Chapter House, Pitfield, Kiln Farm,
Milton Keynes MK11 3LW
tel 0845 121 4567
email enquiries@lightningsource.co.uk
website www.lightningsource.com

Established supplier and distributor of print-on-demand books and ebooks. No prices given on the website, but an exhaustive list of FAQs is provided.

Lulu

website www.lulu.com/gb/en

Self-publishing platform and distributor for ebooks and print-on-demand books through online retailers including Amazon and iBooks. Authors can upload a file and design their own cover for free. Optional paid-for services include cover design, editorial, publicity services and materials. Packages available from \$999–\$3,199. An 80% royalty after unit costs is available for books sold via Lulu Marketplace.

Margie's Mark

email margie@margiesmark.com
website http://margiesmark.com
Contact Margie Markevicius

Supplies graphic design services including logo design and can apply designs to social media accounts. Also offers book cover design and formatting for print and print-on-demand, and designs ebook ePub files. Provides website design and can offer website maintenance and update content. Also designs business cards and stationery.

Matador

Troubador Publishing Ltd, 9 Priory Business Park,
Wistow Road, Kibworth Beauchamp,
Leicester LE8 0RX
tel 0116 279 2299
email enquiries@troubador.co.uk
website www.troubador.co.uk/matador
Managing Director Jeremy Thompson

Offers print-on-demand, short-run digital- and litho-printed books and ebook production, with distribution through high-street bookshops and online retailers, plus worldwide ebook distribution. Author services include all book and ebook production, trade and retail marketing, plus bookshop distribution via Orca Book Services. Founded 1999.

Mereo Books

1A The Woolmarket, Dyer Street, Cirencester,
Gloucestershire GL7 2PR
tel (01285) 640485
email info@mereobooks.co.uk
website www.mereobooks.com
Director Tony Tingle, *Editor-in-Chief* Chris Newton

Specialises in editing, typesetting, and cover design of both fiction and non-fiction. Publishes in hardback, paperback and ebook formats. Also offers ghostwriting. Allocates ISBNs and distributes to online retailers including Amazon and Barnes & Noble, as ebooks or print-on-demand and from stock through Orca Book Services trade distribution. Books sold through Mereo website plus through trade sales representation with Eames Publishing Services and trade distribution by Orca Book Services, and listed with wholesalers. Costs dependent on specification. Mereo is part of Memoirs Publishing.

New Generation Publishing

The Old Fire Station, 140 Tabernacle Street,
London EC2A 4SD
tel 020-7300 7370 *tel* (01234) 711956
email info@newgeneration-publishing.com
website www.newgeneration-publishing.com

Provides publication in paperback, hardback and ebook with global distribution. Publishing packages range from £299 to £2,999. Services include layout, cover design, ISBN allocation, editing, proofreading, bookselling, bookstore placement, website design and manuscript critique. Distribution provided via online retailers, high-street shops, libraries and wholesalers. Promotional materials available including distributed press releases. Free marketing and promotional support service also offered. Offices in London and Buckinghamshire; author visits welcome.

Nook Press

website www.nookpress.com

Provides ebook self-publishing and distribution through Nook, and Barnes & Noble online store. Offers free online manuscript upload, writing, editing and formatting tools. When an ebook is sold, Nook retains a percentage of the list price. Ebooks are made available for reading on the Nook e-reader or using the app for android devices, iPad, iPhone and web browser. Also offers an online royalty tracking service.

Peppermint Books

Unit 2b, Church View Business Park,
Coney Green Road, Clay Cross, Chesterfield S45 9HA
tel (01246) 866165
email sales@peppermintbooks.co.uk
website www.peppermintbooks.co.uk

Produces short-run digitally printed perfect-bound paperback and hardback books in a variety of sizes, with a choice of different types of paper. Images can be included and ISBNs provided. A final proof print copy is sent to the author before the complete order is printed. Cover design using stock or author-supplied images is also available for £225. See the website for a price calculator for paperback book production.

PublishNation

Suite 544, Kemp House, 152 City Road,
London EC1V 2NX

email david@publishnation.co.uk
website www.publishnation.co.uk
Publisher David Morrison

Offers print-on-demand paperback and Kindle format ebooks, available through Amazon. Publication in both print and digital formats costs £195 or £125 for Kindle format. Images may be included from £2.95 each. A range of book sizes is available, as are free template book covers. Enhanced cover design costs £40. Marketing services include creation of a press release, social media accounts and author website. Standard proofreading is £7 per thousand words, while an 'express' option from £125 focuses on the beginning of the manuscript. Editorial critique reports range in price from £99 for manuscripts of up to 15,000 words to £219 for manuscripts of up to 120,000 words.

Red Button Publishing

email redbuttonpublishing@gmail.com
website http://redbuttonpublishing.net
Directors Karen Ings, Caroline Goldsmith

Offers consultancy services to authors who wish to self-publish. Provides ebook conversion, formatting and custom cover design. Additional services for self-publishers include editorial feedback, structural and line editing, and proofreading. Can advise the author about online retailers and setting up social media or blogs. Designs marketing materials including posters or website banners. Founded 2012.

Reedsy

email service@reedsy.com
website https://reedsy.com

Online collaboration site on which authors are able to connect with publishing professionals. Also offers a set of project management tools. Forthcoming expansion plans include coverting authors' files to .ePub and .mobi formats and then distributing and marketing to ebookstores. Founded 2014.

Rowanvale Books Ltd

Indycube, Trade Street Lane, Cardiff CF10 5DR
email info@rowanvalebooks.com
website www.rowanvalebooks.com
Managing Directors Cat Charlton, Sarah Scotcher

Provider of publishing services such as editorial, design, e-conversion, print, marketing, distribution and aftercare, as well as advisory services for writing and marketing, author website creation, and literary agent submission. Royalty rate to authors of 65% for ebook and hard copy sales. Global distribution to over 1,000 e-retailers as well as all major print retailers, and books also sold via own bookstore. Founded 2012.

Scotforth Books

Carnegie House, Chatsworth Road,
Lancaster LA1 4SL
tel (01524) 840555
email anna@carnegiepublishing.com
website www.scotforthbooks.com
Contact Anna Goddard

Specialises in the complete design and production of books of all kinds, from manuscript to finished printed copies. This can include, as required, editing/proofreading, processing and placement of pictures, page layout, covers and jacket design, printing and binding of any number of copies, sales and marketing advice and leaflet/poster design etc. Estimates are free of charge and author visits to discuss requirements welcomed.

Selfpublishbooks.ie

Springhill House, Carrigtwohill, Co. Cork, Republic of Ireland
tel +353 (0)21 4883370
email info@selfpublishbooks.ie
website www.selfpublishbooks.ie

Services include digital printing and binding options, including perfect binding and saddle stitching. Offers custom cover design or can include author-supplied images and artwork. Also offers editing, proofreading and formatting services. Can design promotional materials including posters and bookmarks and allocate ISBNs. Printing prices start from 100 copies but fewer can be printed on request.

The Self-Publishing Partnership

7 Green Park Station, Green Park Road, Bath BA1 1JB
tel (01225) 478444
email enquiries@selfpublishingpartnership.co.uk
website www.selfpublishingpartnership.co.uk
Contacts Douglas Walker, Garry Manning

Offers full self-publishing services, with personal guidance. Services include proofreading/copy-editing; page design and typesetting; and cover design (bespoke or standard) utilising author images if required. Also ebooks; ISBNs & legal cataloguing; and trade-order fulfilment (invoicing & distribution).

SilverWood Books

14 Small Street, Bristol BS1 1DE
tel 0117 910 5829
email info@silverwoodbooks.co.uk
website www.silverwoodbooks.co.uk
Publishing Director Helen Hart

Offers bespoke author services tailored to an individual project, as well as three publishing packages, with prices dependent on specification. Services offered include cover and page design, typesetting, ebook hand-formatting and conversion, print-on-demand, short-run, and lithographic printing, one-to-one support and coaching. Distributes to bookshops via wholesalers and to online retailers including Amazon. Also provides the Amazon Look Inside feature, and lists books in its own SilverWood online bookstore. UK wholesale distribution via Central Books. Nielsen Enhanced Data Listing. Marketing services include creating a press release, media target list, social media set-up, online book trailer campaign and virtual blog tours. Editorial services include an initial assessment and manuscript appraisal. Copy-editing from £7.30 per 1,000 words; proofreading from £6.75 per 1,000 words.

Smart Quill Editorial

email info@smartquilleditorial.co.uk
website http://smartquilleditorial.co.uk
Editorial Consultant Philippa Donovan

Offers editorial reports with different levels of structural evaluation from £350 to £950. Offers an agent submission report for £200 which analyses the covering letter, synopsis and first three chapters. Agent recommendation service and industry advice also available. Fiction, narrative non-fiction and picture books.

Spiderwize

Remus House, Coltsfoot Drive, Woodston, Peterborough, PE2 9BF
tel (01733) 898103
email info@spiderwize.com
website www.spiderwize.com

Offers print-on-demand self-publishing packages for several genres including fiction, autobiography and poetry. See website for full information.

Stairwell Books

161 Lowther Street, York YO31 7LZ
tel 01904 733767
email rose@stairwellbooks.com
website www.stairwellbooks.co.uk
Owner and Operations Alan Gillott, *Owner and Marketing* Rose Drew

Publisher of novels, memoirs, anthologies and collections focussed mainly but not exclusively on York and Yorkshire writers. Publishers of *Dream Catcher* international literary journal. Services include preparation and design of books, managing new book launches, event management, proofreading, content advice, fact-checking with particular reference to physical anthropology, archaeology and history, as well as a range of author services and writing projects. Founded 2002.

Tantamount

Coventry University Technology Park, Puma Way, Coventry CV1 2TT
tel 024 7722 0299
email hello@tantamount.com
website tantamount.com, www.authorbranding.co.uk

Specialists in tablet-based digital publications and author branding. Offers a wide range of editorial, design and publishing services to individual authors and publishing houses. Integrated online presence and self-publishing service allows writers to deal with a single supplier for all digital, design and publishing requirements, and also achieve a unified and coherent personal brand image for their work. Founded 2002.

2QT Publishing

Unit 5, Commercial Courtyard, Duke Street, Settle, North Yorkshire BD24 9RH
tel (01729) 268010
website www.2qt.co.uk
Director Catherine Cousins

Offers flexible, tailored packages. Services offered include cover design, manuscript critique, editing and proofreading. Provides ebook conversion and distribution from £250, and audiobook production and distribution. Offers print-on-demand and printing options. Allocates ISBNs and barcodes. Books also sold through the 2QT website.

Vook

151 W. 25th Street, New York, NY 10001, USA
email weloveauthors@vook.com
website https://vook.com

Offers ebook creation and distribution to online retailers including Amazon, iBooks, Barnes & Noble and Kobo. Manuscript files converted to .ePub and .mobi formats for Kindle and other e-readers. Provides free online sales tracking system. Also offers data-enhanced marketing advice and author support.

Westbow Press

1663 Liberty Drive Bloomington, IN 47403, USA
tel 00 1 866-928-1240
email lworman@westbowpress.com
website www.westbowpress.com
Director of Publishing Services Pete Nikolai, *Sales Customer Service Manager* Lisa Worman

Specialises in self-publishing options for Christian books. Packages range from $999 to $6,499. Services include custom cover and interior design, and custom illustrations. Also provides softcover and hardcover format printing and distribution, and ebook conversion and distribution. Offers editorial analysis, line editing, content editing and developmental editing. Offers a DIY audiobook option. Marketing services include press release writing and distribution, and video book trailer creation.

Wise Words Editorial

email info@wisewordseditorial.com
website www.wisewordseditorial.com

Provides proofreading services for fiction and non-fiction manuscripts and ebooks. Rate is £5/$8.50 per 1,000 words for proofreading documents over 50,000 words. Authors are sent a file showing edits as well as the final proofread file.

WRITERSWORLD

2 Bear Close Flats, Bear Close, Woodstock,
Oxon OX20 1JX
tel (01993) 812500
email enquiries@writersworld.co.uk
website www.writersworld.co.uk
Founder & Owner Graham Cook

Leading book publisher in self-publishing, print-on-demand books and book reprints. Also issues the ISBN on behalf of authors, pays them 100% of the royalties and supplies them with copies of their books at print cost. Established 2000.

Xlibris

Victory Way, Admirals Park, Crossways, Dartford, Kent DA2 6QD
tel 0800 056 3182
email info@xlibrispublishing.co.uk
website www.xlibrispublishing.co.uk

Established POD publisher, offering b&w, colour and speciality publishing packages, with prices starting at £599 (Basic). Speciality packages include poetry and children's. Services include design, editorial, ebook creation and distribution with online booksellers, website creation and marketing materials including a press release and book video. Royalties: 10% to author if sold via retail partner, and 25% if sold via Xlibris directly.

Resources for writers

The writer's ultimate workspace

Arranging for a space to write in a domestic environment can be a huge challenge for some people. Rib Davis gives the benefit of his experience of writing from home.

This is a work of fiction. It is based on fact – as much of the best fiction is – but there is certainly more of the wish than the accomplishment in what follows. I have been asked to write an article giving advice to the prospective writer about some of the day-to-day material conditions and habits of mind that one should attempt to establish in order to be able to work happily and efficiently. I assume that I was chosen on the basis that I have, over 30 years, failed to do these so spectacularly that I am now considered an expert in the field. I may not have learned much from my mistakes but at least I can list some of them, and let the reader do the learning.

Finding the ideal workspace

Where should the workspace be located? When we have to, we can write anywhere. At my most desperate I have written parts of scripts on trains, in crowded offices, in pubs and even leaning on a car steering wheel while waiting for the AA to rescue me. Such is the power of the deadline. Sometimes, strangely, I have produced some rather good work while battling with the distractions and other limitations of the immediate environment; I would hesitate, however, to recommend the practice too highly.

So what would be the ideal workspace location? It seems to be generally agreed that a writer (or writers, if you are working collaboratively) should work in a place where distractions are minimal. Some highly successful writers have taken this to the extreme of working in a shed or a caravan at the bottom of the garden, with only elves for company. I have never owned a caravan, and unless I learn to write seated on a bicycle I will always have trouble squashing into our slowly rotting shed, so that has never been an option. But where possible a degree of isolation – and particularly isolation from family activities and domestic duties – does seem desirable. Sustained concentration is extremely important for any sort of creative work, and such a location helps to facilitate it. In my own case, when I am actually scripting (as opposed to researching or planning) I usually find that I have to read my notes and then the latest part of the script for about an hour before I can even begin to put new words onto the page, so anything that breaks the concentration is unwelcome.

At the same time, though, we are only as strong as our will-power. Many of us could stick ourselves in an arctic igloo to write and yet still manage to find distractions (examining snowflakes can be so fascinating). For about a year I did my writing in a room at the back of a bookshop in Milton Keynes, well away from my home. It seemed to offer the ideal combination of relative isolation along with a congenial, supportive and vaguely arty environment. But the lure of the books and the customers ultimately proved too much; I soon found myself helping out at the till rather than tapping away at my *magnum opus*.

Perhaps my need to write was not sufficiently urgent. Certainly it is true that in those days I was driven by blind hope rather than deadlines, but I don't think that was the problem. The problem was (and is) fear: fear of writing badly, of not living up to one's own – and others' – expectations. For me, at least, it is this fear above all that gets in the way of creativity. First I fear the blank page (of course), then the writing, and then the finishing. This is why those awful distractions can seem, in fact, very welcome indeed. And it is part of the reason why we should try to avoid them as far as possible.

For a few years, remarkably, I did work in a suitable location. Quite simply, this was a room in the house that I was able to turn into my study. It was not totally cut off from the rest of Life, but it was sufficiently separate to allow generally uninterrupted concentration. My small son had difficulty understanding why, if I was behind the door, I refused to open it, but apart from that it worked well. For many decades, though, I did my writing on the living room table. My laptop and notes were moved away at mealtimes; people traipsed through the living room to get to the kitchen (why hadn't we thought of this when we bought the house?); the television was in the same room. In short, my workplace has been set in the teeming hub of the house. Big mistake.

Cordial domestic relations

A word on educating one's family. A writer's partner and/or children will generally recognise and respect the writer's need to focus on the work in hand, but there is at least one point which needs clarifying. When I write, I take breaks. These breaks can occur for a variety of reasons. Perhaps I have reached an interim target, or I have become stuck, or I am thirsty, or just tired. So I might stop and play the piano, or make a cup of coffee, or – exceptionally – even do some washing up, and then return to the writing with a clearer head. No problem, except that this might be observed, and the observing partner/child may think, 'Ah, so he doesn't mind his concentration being broken after all'. This can be a problem. You have to be selfish. You have to make clear that you can break your own concentration as and when you feel the need – you can wrong-note your way through a whole Beethoven sonata if you feel like it – but that does not give others the green light to break your concentration as and when they feel the need. Be unreasonable.

So much for location. Now, what should the workspace look like? My answer would simply be: pleasant. It should be a welcoming place, where you will feel comfortable and not oppressed. For me, this means well decorated in soft colours, with the desk facing out to a window, preferably with a view, and a temperature that's warm but not sleep-inducing. For others, windows may present yet another distraction, colours should be severe, the radiator should be off and the whole place should be tatty. The point is that you feel comfortable there and it feels like *your* space.

Where I have been able to, I have turned my space into an almost self-sufficient world. This requires at the very least coffee (stimulation), Scotch (counter the extreme effects of coffee) and a variety of non-laxative snacks (counter the other effects of coffee). Ideally I suppose an en suite bathroom would be a good idea, but we should keep to the feasible. When I am really rich and famous I will also have an extra piano in my study, but for now I make do with a stereo. I find music (at least, some music) can create a less intense atmosphere when I am researching or planning, but when I am actually scripting I tend to turn it off, as otherwise I find the writing being influenced moment-to-moment by every passing mood of the music, which does not tend to improve the quality of my literary product at all.

Working efficiently

Writing is of course more than simply tapping words onto a page. It is also thinking, researching, planning and finally doing all the administrative work connected to the sale and then either publication or production of the work, whether through an agent or otherwise. So your workspace must be able to accommodate all this too. Give yourself as much work surface as possible, so that you can refer to as many materials as you need simultaneously, and you can even have materials left out for more than one project at a time. And set up an efficient filing system from the start. Or if, as in my case, this is certainly not the start, do it now anyway. Do not simply put every new publisher's letter, piece of research and pizza takeaway leaflet together in an in-tray. The in-tray eventually overflows; you get a second one; that overflows too. You will eventually be surrounded by in-trays. File everything as it comes along, and don't hesitate to open a new file for even the germ of a new project.

This filing particularly applies to emails. One can make the mistake of thinking that because something is there on the computer it has been filed. It hasn't. Electronic documents – and emails most of all – can be just as much of a mess as a physical desktop. Keep your emails in folders.

Mention of emails leads me on to phones. Both can take over your whole existence if you allow them to; they will certainly try. Deal with emails when you are at your least productive as a writer. If you think of yourself as a 'morning person' then that is when you should be writing; do the emails in the evening. Or if mornings tend to be barren periods of grogginess and haze, those are the times for doing emails. And try to deal with all the day's emails in one sitting; certainly don't let them interrupt you whenever they feel like it. Set up your computer in such a way that it does not let you know when emails have arrived; instead, just check them once or twice per day.

Similarly, don't simply answer the phone whenever it rings. The phone can of course be very useful for your writing, particularly for research, but in general – switch it to silent. If the caller doesn't leave a message, it can't be very important.

A great deal of research is now done on the web, but I still like having books around. In particular, despite the existence of online dictionaries I still believe a writer should have a really good book dictionary (some of the larger ones give a date for each word usage, which is particularly helpful for period writing), and I also find a large thesaurus very useful (the original format, not the alphabetical kind; the latter is simpler to use but as it is necessarily so repetitive it contains far fewer options). Then, of course, there are always the books needed for the particular project in hand.

Most writers fit their research and other writing activities in with other work, whether writing-related or not. This means that time becomes a very precious commodity. I have always worked best when I have been able to arrange my writing time in large chunks, preferably whole days. An hour here or there really is hardly any use. And whenever possible I have tried to establish routines. The truth is that I have been particularly bad at this, perhaps because I have often had too many projects at different stages simultaneously, but I would still recommend adopting a daily routine as far as possible. It means there is just one less decision to have to make: your writing times have been decided and that's it.

Writer's block

So now you are all set. You have bought yourself Final Draft software (or something similar) and you have the workspace, the materials, the books, the filing – the lot. You write and write. You pin the best rejection slips onto the wall (we've all had them). You write and write. And then you don't. You get writer's block. I have had this. It is a particularly nasty affliction as in almost everyone else's eyes 'writer's block' translates as 'laziness'. This is not the place for a full discussion, but I can pass on a couple of pieces of advice I received, which worked for me. Firstly, don't always try to see the whole piece of work, as that may be overwhelming to you. Instead, focus on a particular section of it and nothing more. Secondly, when you have writer's block a whole day of writing ahead of you looks interminable. So don't do it. Strictly limit yourself to writing for two hours and no more. You may well find yourself writing with real urgency, trying to cram all that you can into those two allotted hours. Only much later can you gradually increase the limit back to a normal day.

Well, it worked for me. But then there are all sorts of writers. My old friend Jack Trevor Story had a writer's solution for insomnia: he wrote right through the night. Every night. It worked for him.

Now, as usual, I am going to try to learn from what I've written.

Rib Davis has been writing professionally for over 30 years. He has over 60 credits, including scripts for radio, television and stage, as well as two books on the art of writing scripts. Having finally sorted out his domestic arrangements he has now moved house, so is starting all over again.

Glossary of publishing terms

The selected terms in this glossary relate to the content of this *Yearbook* and cross-references are provided to guide readers to the relevant pages for more detail.

advance

Money paid by a publisher to an author before a book is published which will be covered by future royalties. A publishing contract often allows an author an advance payment against future royalties; the author will not receive any further royalties until the amount paid in advance has been earned by sales of the book. See page 109; page 114.

AI (advance information sheet)

A document that is put together by a publishing company to provide sales and marketing information about a book before publication and can be sent several months before publication to sales representatives. It can incorporate details of the format and contents of the book, key selling points and information about intended readership, as well as information about promotions and reviews. See page 109; page 119; page 124.

backlist

The range of books already published by a publisher that are still in print. See page 109.

blad (book layout and design)

A pre-publication sales and marketing tool. It is often a printed booklet that contains sample pages, images and front and back covers which acts as a preview for promotional use or for sales teams to show to potential retailers, customers or reviewers. See page 109.

blurb

A short piece of writing or a paragraph that praises and promotes a book, which usually appears on the back or inside cover of the book and may be used in sales and marketing material. See page 109.

book club edition

An edition of a book specially printed and bound for a book club for sale to its members. See page 240.

book proof

A bound set of uncorrected reading proofs used by the sales team of a publishing house and as early review copies. See page 109; page 119.

C format

A term most often used to describe a paperback edition published simultaneously with, and in the same format as, the hardback original.

co-edition

The publication of a book by two publishing companies in different countries, where the first company has originated the work and then sells sheets to the second publisher (or licenses the second publisher to reprint the book locally). See page 236.

commissioning editor

A person who asks authors to write books for the part of the publisher's list for which he or she is responsible or who takes on an author who approaches them direct or via an agent with a proposal. Also called acquisitions editor or acquiring editor (more commonly in the USA). A person who signs-up writers (commissions them to write) an article for a magazine or newspaper. See page 109.

copy-editor

A person whose job is to check material ready for printing for accuracy, clarity of message and writing style and consistency of typeface, punctuation and layout. Sometimes called a desk editor. See page 109; page 629.

copyright

The legal right, which the creator of an original work has, to only allow copying of the work with permission and sometimes on payment of royalties or a copyright fee. An amendment to the Copyright, Designs and Patents Act (1988) states that in the UK most works are protected for 70 years from the creator's death. The 'copyright page' at the start of a book asserts copyright ownership and author identification. See page 667; page 672.

distributor

Acts as a link between the publisher and retailer. The distributor can receive orders from retailers, ship books, invoice, collect revenue and deal with returns. Distributors often handle books from several publishers. Digital distributors handle ebook distribution.

edition

A quantity of books printed without changes to the content. A 'new edition' is a reprint of an existing title that incorporates substantial textual alterations. Originally one edition meant a single print run, though today an edition may consist of several separate printings, or impressions.

editor

A person in charge of publishing a newspaper or magazine who makes the final decisions about the content and format. A person in book publishing who has responsibility for the content of a book and can be variously a senior person (editor-in-chief) or day-to-day contact for authors (copy-editor, development editor, commissioning editor, etc). See page 109; page 629.

endmatter

Material at the end of the main body of a book which may be useful to the reader, including references, appendices, indexes and bibliography. Also called back matter.

extent

The number of pages in a book.

first edition

The first print run of a book. It can occasionally gain secondhand value if either the book or its author become collectable.

folio

A large sheet of paper folded twice across the middle and trimmed to make 4 pages of a book. Also a page number.

frontlist

New books just published (generally in their first year of publication) or about to be published by a publisher. Promotion of the frontlist is heavy, and the frontlist carries most of a publisher's investment. On the other hand, a backlist which continues to sell is usually the most profitable part of a publisher's list. See page 109.

impression

A single print run of a book; all books in an impression are manufactured at the same time and are identical. A 'second impression' would be the second batch of copies to be printed and bound. The impression number is usually marked on the copyright/imprint page. There can be several impressions in an edition, all sharing the same ISBN.

imprint

The publisher's or printer's name which appears on the title page of a book or in the bibliographical details; a brand name under which a book is published within a larger publishing company, usually representing a specialised subject area.

inspection copy

A copy of a publication sent or given with time allowed for a decision to purchase or return it. In academic publishing, lecturers can request inspection copies to decide whether to make a book/textbook recommended reading or adopt it as a core textbook for their course.

ISBN

International Standard Book Number. See page 133.

ISSN

International Standard Serial Number. An international system used on periodicals, magazines, learned journals, etc. The ISSN is formed of eight digits, which refer to the country in which the magazine is published and the title of the publication. See page 133.

kill fee

A fee paid to a freelance writer for material written on assignment but not used, typically a percentage of the total payment.

literary agent

Somebody whose job is to negotiate publishing contracts, involving royalties, advances and and rights sales on behalf of an author and earns commission on the proceeds of the sales they negotiate. See page 389; page 392; page 398; page 404; page 407.

marketing department

The department that originates the sales material – catalogues, order forms, blads, samplers, posters, book proofs and advertisements – to promote titles published. See page 109; page 119; page 124.

moral right

The right of people such as editors or illustrators to have some say in the publication of a work to which they have contributed, even if they do not own the copyright. See page 667; page 672.

out of print or o.p.

Relating to a book of which the publisher has no copies left and which is not going to be reprinted. Print-on-demand technology, however, means that a book can be kept 'in print' indefinitely.

packager

A company that creates a finished book for a publisher. See page 236.

page proofs

A set of proofs of the pages in a book used to check the accuracy of typesetting and page layout, and also as an advance promotional tool. These are commonly provided in electronic form, rather than in physical form. See page 109; page 119; page 629.

paper engineering

The mechanics of creating novelty books and pop-ups.

PDF/pdf
Portable Document Format. A data file generated from PostScript that is platform-independent, application-independent and font-independent. Acrobat is Adobe's suite of software used to generate, edit and view pdf files.

picture researcher
A person who looks for pictures relevant to a particular topic, so that they can be used as illustrations in, for example, a book, newspaper or TV programme. See page 466.

point of sale
Merchandising display material provided by publishers to bookshops in order to promote particular titles. See page 109.

prelims
The initial pages of a book, including the title page and table of contents, which precede the main text. Also called front matter.

pre-press
Before going to press, to be printed.

print on demand or POD
The facility to print and bind a small number of books at short notice, without the need for a large print run, using digital technology. When an order comes through, a digital file of the book can be printed individually and automatically. See page 135.

print run
The quantity a book printed at one time in an impression.

production controller
A person in the production department of a publishing company who deals with printers and other suppliers. See page 109.

proofreader
A person whose job is to proofread texts to check typeset page presentation and text for errors and to mark up corrections. See page 109; page 629.

publicity department
This department works with the author and the media on 'free' publicity – e.g. reviews, features, author interviews, bookshop readings and signings, festival appearances, book tours and radio and TV interviews – when a book is published. See page 109.

publisher
A person or company that publishes books, magazines and/or newspapers. See page 109.

publisher's agreement
A contract between a publisher and the copyright holder, author, agent or another publisher, which lays down the terms under which the publisher will publish the book for the copyright holder. See page 114.

publishing contract
An agreement between a publisher and an author by which the author grants the publisher the right to publish the work against payment of a fee, usually in the form of a royalty. See page 485.

reading fee
Money paid to somebody for reading a manuscript and commenting on it.

recto
Relating to the right-hand page of a book, usually given an odd number.

reprint
Copies of a book made from the original, but with a note in the publication details of the date of reprinting and possibly a new title page and cover design.

review copy
An advance copy of a book sent to magazines, newspapers and/or other media for the purposes of review. A 'book proof' may be sent out before the book is printed. See page 109; page 119; page 124; page 321; page 597.

rights
The legal right to publish something such as a book, picture or extract from a text. See page 109; page 114.

rights manager
A person who negotiates and coordinates rights sales (e.g. for subsidiary, translation or foreign rights). Often travels to book fairs to negotiate rights sales.

royalty
Money paid to a writer for the right to use his or her property, usually a percentage of sales or an agreed amount per sale. See page 109; page 114.

royalty split
The way in which a royalty is divided between several authors or between author and illustrator.

royalty statement
A printed statement from a publisher showing how much royalty is due to an author. See page 114.

sans serif
A style of printing letters with all lines of equal thickness and no serifs. Sans faces are less easy to read

than seriffed faces and they are rarely used for continuous text, although some magazines use them for text matter.

serialisation

Publication of a book in parts in a magazine or newspaper. See page 114.

serif

A small decorative line added to letters in some fonts; a font that uses serifs, such as Times. The addition of serifs (1) keeps the letters apart while at the same time making it possible to link one letter to the next, and (2) makes the letters distinct, in particular the top parts which the reader recognises when reading.

slush pile

Unsolicited manuscripts which are sent to publishers or agents, and which may never be read. See page 407; page 394.

STM

The accepted abbreviation for the scientific, technical and medical publishing sectors.

style sheet

A guide listing all the rules of house style for a publishing company which has to be followed by authors and editors. See page 629.

sub-editor

A person who corrects and checks articles in a newspaper before they are printed. See page 3.

subscription sale or 'sub'

Sales of a title to booksellers in advance of publication, and orders taken from wholesalers and retailers to be supplied by the publisher shortly before the publication date. See page 109.

subsidiary rights

Rights other than the right to publish a book in its first form, e.g. paperback rights; rights to adapt the book; rights to serialise it in a magazine; film and TV rights; audio, ebook, foreign and translation rights. See page 114.

territory

Areas of the world where the publisher has the rights to publish or can make foreign rights deals. See page 114.

trade discount

A reduction in price given to a customer in the same trade, as by a publisher to another publisher or to a bookseller.

trade paperback (B format)

A paperback edition of a book that is superior in production quality to a mass-market paperback edition and is similar to a hardback in size 198 x 129mm.

trim size or trimmed size

The measurements of a page of a book after it has been cut, or of a sheet of paper after it has been cut to size.

type specification or 'spec'

A brief created by the design department of a publishing house for how a book should be typeset. See page 114.

typeface

A set of characters that share a distinctive and consistent design. Typefaces come in families of different weights, e.g. Helvetica Roman, Helvetica Italic, Bold, Bold Italic, etc. Hundreds of typefaces exist and new ones are still being designed. Today, 'font' is often used synonymously with 'typeface' though originally font meant the characters were all the same size, e.g. Helvetica italic 11 point.

typescript or manuscript

The final draft of a book delivered by an author to the publishing house. This unedited text is usually a Word file on disk but may be typewritten. The term 'typescript' (abbreviated TS or ts) is now used more commonly than 'manuscript' (abbreviated MS or ms; pl. MSS or mss), though they are synonymous. See page 109; page 629.

typesetter

A person or company that 'sets' text and prepares the final layout of the page for printing. It can also now involve XML tagging for ebook creation. See page 109; page 629.

typographic error or typo

A mistake made when keying text or typesetting. See page 629.

verso

The left-hand page of a book, usually given an even number.

volume rights

The right to publish the work in hardback or paperback (this can now sometimes include ebook). See page 114.

XML tagging

Inserting tags into the text that can allow it to be converted for ebooks or for use in electronic formats.

Editing your work

If you have been lucky enough to secure a publisher for your work, a vital component of the process is editing. In this article, Lauren Simpson answers some commonly-asked questions.

What is editing?

Broadly speaking, 'editing' involves the refinement of a piece of writing (manuscript) to make it as near perfect as possible and thus ready to be published. Editing covers a whole range of interventions to a manuscript at different stages in its life, including restructuring, factual checking, copy-editing and proofreading.

Typically, when a manuscript is copy-edited, the editor will pay close attention to every word, reviewing and refining:

- spelling and grammar;
- syntax (the arrangement of words and phrases), structure and layout;
- factual and/or technical accuracy;
- whether the writing has the appropriate tone and content for the intended readership.

Some manuscripts need very little editing, while others need to be heavily edited or, in some cases, almost completely rewritten. It is essential that a manuscript is edited as comprehensively as time and budget allows – the aim being to ensure optimum sense and clarity for the reader. How much editing a particular manuscript will require depends on a number of factors, including:

- the complexity of the subject matter;
- whether or not a publisher's house style has to be imposed upon it;
- the quality of the writing;
- the expertise of the writer.

Should I edit my work before submitting the completed manuscript?

On completion of a manuscript, a diligent author should always go back over their work in order to eliminate spelling and grammatical mistakes ('typos') and to ensure that there are no inconsistencies (for example, in plot, dialogue, characterisation, physical descriptions, dates or sequences of events) or factual inaccuracies.

Before delivering your completed manuscript, you might also want to:

- read through your manuscript as an 'outsider' to identify errors that you may have overlooked while you were writing;
- consider how a reader might think/feel when reading your work, and revise anything they might not like or understand. This is not an easy task, so you might want to ask a trusted friend or colleague to read it through for you and suggest improvements.

Exercising 'good housekeeping' along these lines demonstrates that you are serious about your craft and can help save time and money down the editorial track. However, it is worth pointing out that any editing you undertake won't replace the editing that your publisher will carry out once your manuscript has been delivered, so there is no need to pay for your work to be edited in advance. For a cautionary note on editing your own work, see *Do self-published authors need to pay for an editor?* below.

What happens to my manuscript once it has been submitted?

While processes differ from publisher to publisher, the sequence of events from manuscript to printed copy can be broadly summarised as follows:

- The author (or their agent) delivers the completed manuscript to the publisher. The author should make every effort to submit the manuscript in accordance with the publisher's style guide and format requirements, to avoid the time and expense of revising the material at a later stage.
- The publisher arranges for the manuscript to be copy-edited and any queries arising from this process are passed to the author to be resolved in advance of typesetting/design.
- Copy-edited material is typeset or put through an electronic page layout or design process.
- Page proofs are produced and: (1) first page proofs are proofread by the publisher and the author; (2) corrections are incorporated and revised page proofs are produced; (3) revised page proofs are checked, corrected and signed off.
- The final, edited text is ready to be printed.

What do different types of editor do?

It is important to remember that no two publishing companies are the same and there are many different monikers applied to the editing professionals that you may come across: commissioning editor, copy-editor, managing editor, project editor, desk editor, sub-editor, assistant editor, chief editor… In addition, your work will almost certainly be pored over by one of the most important cogs in the editorial wheel – the proofreader.

Space constraints prevent a description of every editor listed above but an overview of the key editorial staff that you are likely to encounter will give you a good idea of the work they do.

Commissioning (or acquiring) editors identify books to publish in order to build up a publisher's list in a particular area or genre. They commission work by finding authors or responding to book proposals and, for fiction work, acquire most of their books through a literary agent. They are responsible for ensuring that authors deliver manuscripts to specification and on time.

Copy-editors check that content is accurate, clearly and logically expressed, conveys the desired message or tone, and comes together to form a coherent and cohesive whole. Copy-editors must be analytical in their approach and able to weed out factual errors as well as annotate diagrams, cross-check references and apply a publisher's house style to a text. They may also be required to have specialist knowledge of the subject matter, particularly in the case of science, maths and law.

Proofreaders scrutinise content in very fine detail to ensure that errors relating to syntax, spelling, grammar, punctuation, design and format are eliminated. Proofreaders have good technical language skills and an excellent eye for detail. The latter is especially important in order to deal effectively with errors in technical or complex text, or when checking that the copy-editor has applied a style guide correctly.

What are the differences between copy-editing and proofreading?

Copy-editing and proofreading are crucial stages of the publishing process and, while the two can often be confused or referred to interchangeably, there are important differences. The copy-editing function normally takes place when a manuscript is complete but before typesetting or design, allowing substantial revisions to be made at minimal cost.

Proofreading, on the other hand, typically takes place after a manuscript has been copy-edited and typeset/designed and serves to 'fine-polish' the text to ensure that it is free from editorial and layout inaccuracies.

Is all editing done electronically?

Traditionally, manuscripts were copy-edited on paper, which was labour-intensive and time-consuming. These days, nearly all copy-editing is carried out electronically, usually using Microsoft Word or a bespoke publishing system. The 'track changes' function allows the copy-editor to make alterations to the manuscript: deletions/additions can be highlighted so that the copy-editor's work can be easily monitored; comments and queries for the author or publisher can be inserted into the margins of the document; and the 'find and replace' function enables inaccuracies and inconsistencies to be corrected globally. Furthermore, tracking changes electronically allows changes to a manuscript to be accepted or rejected on an individual basis, giving them great control over the final version. Another advantage of copy-editing electronically is that an edited manuscript can be emailed – saving time and money.

How is proofreading carried out?

If a manuscript is very 'clean' (i.e. it does not contain many errors), a publisher may insist that the proofreading is carried out electronically. In this case, the proofreader will be sent the manuscript by email, usually in pdf format, and will annotate changes to the document on screen. However, proofreaders will usually receive a manuscript in hard copy and then mark up corrections directly onto the printed page, often using the protocols set down by the British Standards Institution (www.bsigroup.co.uk).

Mistakes to look out for when editing and proofreading

- Similar words used incorrectly, e.g. effect/affect.
- Phrases used inappropriately, e.g. 'should of' instead of 'should have'.
- Apostrophe misuse, especially in respect of its/it's.
- Words with similar spelling or pronunciation but with different meanings used incorrectly, e.g. their/they're/there.
- References in the text that do not correspond to footnotes.
- Inaccurate or inadequate cross-referencing.
- Index listings which cannot be found on the page given in the index.
- Text inadvertently reordered or cut during the typesetting process.
- Headings formatted as ordinary text.
- Running heads that do not correspond to chapter headings.
- Fonts and font sizes used incorrectly.
- Inconsistent use of abbreviations and acronyms.
- Formatting inconsistencies such as poorly-aligned margins or uneven columns.
- Captions/headings omitted from illustrations, photographs or diagrams.
- Illustrations/photographs/diagrams without appropriate copyright references.
- Missing bullet points or numbers in a sequenced list.
- Word processing errors, e.g. '3' instead of '£'.
- Incorrect layout of names, addresses, telephone numbers and email/web addresses.
- Incorrect use of trademarks, e.g. 'blackberry' instead of 'BlackBerry™'.
- Abbreviations/acronyms that have not been defined in full.
- Widows and orphans, e.g. text which runs over page breaks and leaves a word or a line stranded.
- Past and present tenses mixed within a piece of text.
- Use of plural verb conjugations with single subjects, e.g. 'one in five children are...' instead of 'one in five children is...'.

What are proofreading symbols and why do I need to know them?

Proofreading symbols (or marks) are the 'shorthand' that copy-editors and proofreaders use for correcting written material. Typesetters, designers and printers also require this knowledge as part of correcting page layout, style and format.

Once a manuscript has been copy-edited and typeset, authors will be sent a set of page proofs to look at and so it is important that they, too, have at least a basic understanding of proofreading symbols so that they can correct their proofs quickly, uniformly and without any ambiguity.

Proofreading marks/symbols fall into separate categories:

- general instructions;
- inserting, deleting and changing text;
- grammar and punctuation;
- altering the look/style/layout of text.

Depending on the nature of the changes needed, proofreading marks are typically positioned in the margin of the document, with some changes requiring a mark within the text or some additional instructions.

The full set of proofreading marks is defined by the British Standards Institution (BS 5261), however, most authors will be able to mark up proofs using only the most common symbols. The most useful marks can be found on page 633 and 634.

Are there any handy proofreading tips?

Effective proofreading takes time and practice but by following these tips you'll be able to spot mistakes quickly and accurately in no time.

- Set aside adequate time for proofreading. It requires concentration and should not be rushed.
- Before starting on a proofreading task, make sure you have easy access to a dictionary and thesaurus, and ensure that you have any relevant style guides for language style and format/design.
- If possible, proofread a document several times and concentrate on different aspects each time, e.g. sense/tone, format, grammar/punctuation/use of language.
- Spot typos by reading the text backwards – that way you will not be distracted by the meaning of the text.
- Always double-check scientific, mathematical or medical symbols as they can often be corrupted during the typesetting process. Accented characters and currency symbols can also cause problems.
- If possible, have a version of the copy-edited text to refer to while you proofread – it might help solve minor inaccuracies or inconsistencies more quickly.

Do self-published authors need to pay for an editor?

Self-published authors do not have to obtain or pay for editorial advice, but remember that if you want to sell a book that looks as good and reads as well as a professionally produced one, you should consider how you are going to achieve this. There are a host of individuals and companies available to review or edit your work at all stages in the writing process, from concept to publication. We even offer such editorial services here at Writers & Artists.

Marks/symbols for general instructions

INSTRUCTIONS	MARGIN	TEXT
Leave the text in its original state and ignore any marks that have been made, commonly referred to as 'stet'	✓ (circled)	---- under the characters to be left as they were
Query for the author/typesetter/ printer/publisher.	? (circled)	A circle should be placed around text to be queried
Remove non-textual marks	×	A circle should be placed around marks to be removed
End of change	/	None

Marks/symbols for inserting, deleting and changing text

INSTRUCTIONS	MARGIN	TEXT
Text to be inserted	New text, followed by ⋏	⋏
Additional text supplied separately	⋏ followed by a letter in a diamond which identifies additional text ◇A	⋏
Delete a character	₰	/ through the character
Delete text	₰	⊢⊣ through text
Delete character and close space	₰ (with close-up marks)	I (with close-up marks) through the character
Delete text and close space	₰ (with close-up marks)	⊢⊣ (with close-up marks) through text
Character to replace marked character	New character, followed by /	/ through the character
Text to replace marked text	New text, followed by /	⊢⊣ through text

Marks/symbols for grammar and punctuation

INSTRUCTIONS	MARGIN	TEXT
Full stop	⊙	⋏ at insertion point or through character /
Comma	,	As above
Semi-colon	;	As above
Colon	: (circled)	As above
Hyphen	⊢–⊣	As above
Single quote marks	‘ or ’ (in Y)	As above
Double quote marks	“ or ” (in Y)	As above
Apostrophe	’ (in Y)	As above
Ellipses or leader dots	... (circled)	As above
Insert/replace dash	1en (⊢⊣) Size of dash to be stated between uprights	As above

Marks/symbols for altering the look/style/layout of text

INSTRUCTIONS	MARGIN	TEXT
Put text in italics		under text to be changed
Remove italics, replace with roman text		Circle text to be changed
Put text in bold		under text to be changed
Remove bold		Circle text to be changed
Put text in capitals		under text to be changed
Put text in small capitals		under text to be changed
Put text in lower case	or	Circle text to be changed
Change character to superscript	under character	through character to be changed
Insert a superscript character	under character	at point of insertion
Change character to subscript	above character	through character to be changed
Insert a subscript character	above character	at point of insertion
Remove bold and italics		Circle text to be changed
Paragraph break		
Remove paragraph break, run on text		
Indent text		
Remove indent		
Insert or replace space between characters or words		at relevant point of insertion or through character
Reduce space between characters or words		
Insert space between lines or paragraphs	Mark extends into margin	or
Reduce space between lines or paragraphs	Mark extends into margin	or
Transpose lines		
Transpose characters or words		
Close space between characters		character character
Underline words	underline	circle words
Take over character(s) or word(s) to next line/column/page	Mark extends into margin	
Take back character(s) or word(s) to previous line/column/page	Mark extends into margin	

If you think a professional eye would enhance your text, be cautious and read the small print. Decide what type of edit your text requires, agree a fair price for the edit and try to employ a professional with a track record and recommendations. Look at the advice, rates and contacts provided by the Society of Editors and Proofreaders (www.sfep.org.uk).

Lauren Simpson is a freelance editor, writer and proofreader with 20 years' experience. She has contributed to and developed a wide range of publications covering subjects as diverse as agriculture, local government, marketing, business, English language teaching, boating, law, HR, social work, human rights and counselling & psychotherapy. Lauren also has experience of editing biography and autobiography, as well as manuscripts for self-published authors. In addition, she has been editor of a number of prestigious reference works including *The Municipal Year Book* and *Whitaker's Almanack*.

Further resources

All writers and editors need a quality dictionary to hand, such as *The Shorter Oxford English Dictionary* (2 volumes, 6th edn, 2007) or the single-volume *Oxford Dictionary of English* (3rd edn, 2010). Other good dictionaries, available in print, ebook and online are published by Collins and Chambers. See also www.oxforddictionaries.com, www.dictionary.com and www.collinslanguage.com.

Burchfield, R.W., *Fowler's Modern English Usage*, Oxford University Press, re-revised 3rd edn, 2004

Butcher, Judith; Drake, Caroline and Leach, Maureen, *Butcher's Copy-editing: The Cambridge Handbook for Editors, Copy-editors and Proofreaders*, Cambridge University Press, 4th edn, 2006

The Chicago Manual of Style: The Essential Guide for Writers, Editors, and Publishers, University of Chicago Press, 16th edn, 2010

New Oxford Dictionary for Writers and Editors: The Essential A-Z Guide to the Written Word, Oxford University Press, revised edn, 2014

New Hart's Rules: The Oxford Style Guide, Oxford University Press, 2014

Society for Editors and Proofreaders (SfEP), www.sfep.org.uk (see page 526)

The Publishing Training Centre offers courses on editing, proofreading and all aspects of publishing, www.train4publishing.co.uk

Indexing

A good index is essential to the user of a non-fiction book; a bad index will downgrade an otherwise excellent book. The functions of indexes, and the skills needed to compile them, are explained here by the Society of Indexers.

An index is a detailed key to the contents of a document, unlike a contents list, which shows only the sections into which the document is divided (e.g. chapters). An index guides readers to information by providing a systematic arrangement of entries (single words, phrases, acronyms, names and so on) in a suitably organised list (usually alphabetical) that refers them to specific locations using page, column, section, frame, figure, table, paragraph, line or other appropriate numbers or hyperlinks.

Professional indexing

A well-crafted analytical index produced by a skilled professional with appropriate subject expertise is an essential feature of almost every non-fiction book. A professional indexer not only has subject knowledge, but also analyses the document from the readers' perspectives, anticipating how they will approach the subject and what language they will use. The indexer analyses the content of the text and provides a carefully structured index to guide readers efficiently into the main text of the book.

A detailed, comprehensive and regularly updated directory of freelance professional indexers, *Indexers Available*, is on the Society of Indexers' website (see box). Professional competence is recognised in three stages by the Society. Professional Members (MSocInd) have successfully completed initial training (see below) or have many years' continuous experience. Advanced Professional Members (MSocInd(Adv)) have demonstrated skills and experience gained since their initial training, while Fellows of the Society of Indexers (FSI) have been through a rigorous assessment procedure to demonstrate the quality of their work.

Indexing fees depend on many factors, particularly the complexity of the text, but for an index to a straightforward text the Society recommends £23.00 an hour, £2.55 a page or £6.95 1,000 words (in 2014).

Indexing should normally be organised by the publisher, but may be left to the author to do or to arrange. It is rarely a popular task with authors, and they are often not well suited to the task, which takes objectivity, perspective, speed, patience, attention to detail and, above all, training, experience and specialist software. Moreover, authors are generally too close to the text by this stage. Authors who do need to construct their own indexes for whatever reason should consult the further reading list at the end of this article.

Ebooks and other electronic material

An index is necessary for ebooks and other electronic material. It is a complete myth that users of ebooks can rely solely on keyword-based retrieval systems; these pick out far too much information to be usable and far too little to be reliable. Only careful analysis by the human brain creates suitable index terms for non-fiction ebooks. There are no shortcuts for judging relevance, for extracting meaning and significance from the text, for identifying complex concepts, or for recognising different ways of expressing similar ideas. Index entries must also be properly linked to the text when a printed book is converted into an ebook.

The Society of Indexers

The Society of Indexers was founded in 1957 and is the only autonomous professional body for indexers in the UK. The main objectives of the Society are to promote high standards in all types of indexing and highlight the role of indexers in the organisation of knowledge; to provide, promote and recognise facilities for both the initial and the further training of indexers; to establish criteria for assessing conformity to indexing standards; and to conduct research and publish guidance, ideas and information about indexing. It seeks to establish good relationships between indexers, librarians, publishers and authors, both to advance good indexing and to ensure that the contribution of indexers to the organisation and retrieval of knowledge is properly recognised.

The Society holds an annual conference and publishes a learned journal, the *Indexer* (quarterly), a newsletter and *Occasional Papers on Indexing*. Additional resources are published on its website.

Further information

Society of Indexers
Woodbourn Business Centre, 10 Jessell Street, Sheffield S9 3HY
tel 0114 244 9561
email admin@indexers.org.uk
website www.indexers.org.uk
Membership (2015) £126 p.a. UK/Europe, £157.50 overseas; for corporate rates see website

Publishers and authors seeking to commission an indexer should consult *Indexers Available* on the website.

Indexing as a career

Indexing is often taken up as a second career, frequently drawing on expertise developed in some other field. Both intellectually demanding and creative, it requires considerable and sustained mental effort. Indexers need to be well-organised, flexible, disciplined and self-motivated, and resilient enough to cope with the uncertainties of freelance work. The Society of Indexers long-established training course, which has received the CILIP Seal of Recognition, gives a thorough grounding in indexing principles and plenty of practice on real documents. Based on the principle of open learning, it enables students to learn in their own way and at their own pace. A web-based platform offers access to study materials, practice exercises and quizzes, and links to a wide range of useful resources. Online tutorials are undertaken at various stages during the course. After completing the four assessed modules, which cover the core indexing skills, students undertake a book-length practical indexing assignment to prepare them for work in the commercial world. Successful completion of the course leads to Accreditation, designation as a Professional Indexer (MSocInd), and entry in the Society's online directory, *Indexers Available*.

Further reading

Booth, P.F., *Indexing: The Manual of Good Practice*, K.G. Saur, 2001

British Standards Institution, *British Standard Recommendations for Examining Documents, Determining their Subjects and Selecting Indexing Terms* (BS6529:1984)

'Indexes' (chapter from *The Chicago Manual of Style*, 16th edn), University of Chicago Press, 2010

International Standards Organisation, *Information and Documentation – Guidelines for the Content, Organization and Presentation of Indexes* (ISO 999:1996)

Mulvany, N.C., *Indexing Books*, University of Chicago Press, 2nd edn 2005

Stauber, D.M., *Facing the Text: Content and Structure in Book Indexing*, Cedar Row Press, 2004

Open evening

Toby Litt sets the scene for what writers can expect from taking part in a creative writing course.

'Hello – how are you? – thank you for coming. Could I ask your name? And you're interested in Creative Writing, are you? Good. *Great*. Well, what would you like to know?'

This is me, being open. We are sitting across from one another in one of the – for me anyway – cosily Stalinist halls of the Royal National Hotel in Bloomsbury. Between us is a table covered with prospectuses and brochures. On the covers of the prospectuses and brochures are contented-looking students, asking questions, writing answers. Occasionally, an announcement comes over the crunchy tannoy, and we have to wait for it to finish blasting before we can hear one another. It's a Birkbeck Open Evening, getting towards the end, about a quarter past seven. But that's good, because you haven't had to wait in a queue to speak to me. (Quite a few people are interested in Creative Writing these days, even if they're not entirely sure what it is.) You've just walked in, straight up to the table, and sat down – slightly out of breath after rushing from wherever – and now I'm asking you a question. Of course you expected this, but you're not entirely settled, so you say, 'Well, yes, I'm interested – *very* interested,' remembering to sound enthusiastic, 'but I'm not sure it's right for me.'

This is just what I hoped to hear. So, I begin finding out about you by asking whether you have done anything like a creative writing course before.

You tell me about the group at your local library, or the Arvon course you attended (but you really can't remember either of the tutors' names), or the BA you've already completed. Or you say that you haven't really done anything – except write, that is. You're a little more relaxed now; I seem friendly enough – smiling and saying yes. A little tired, but then both of us are. So you ask, 'How would I know if the course would be right for me?'

You settle back. It seems like I'm going to talk for a little while now, and you're right. As there's no one waiting behind you, I decide to give you the full answer. The ideal, forget time, forget embarrassment, answer.

In a way, it's easier to say who Creative Writing courses are *wrong* for. For example, me. When I was 20 or 21, I thought that there wasn't anyone around good enough for me to learn from. I thought that writing was about genius and that the learning-your-craft part was for non-geniuses. (I was a genius, *obviously*.) I thought that letting anyone else in to my work, my ideas, my mind, would damage my originality. I thought that Creative Writing courses were, as I used to put it, 'a load of swine sitting around waiting for a pearl to be tossed by the master'.

That changed when I met a writer called Jacqui Lofthouse, at a party. By this point, I was a little older than 21 and had written four and a half unpublished novels. We sat on someone's carpet, drank wine, chatted, and Jacqui changed my life. I think I mentioned the swine, and she laughed and said, no, the course she was on – with Malcolm Bradbury at the University of East Anglia – wasn't like that *at all*. In fact, most of the time Malcolm – (it was exciting to hear her speak about a published writer by their first name, but I stayed cool) – Malcolm didn't speak much at all. Just a little, at the end, to sum up. It was a *workshop*, and that meant that Jacqui did most of her learning from the other writers in the group. They were the ones who spoke or significantly didn't speak, who passionately disagreed, who gave feedback she could either take or leave. This had worked for Jacqui. Her novel, *The Temple of Hymen*, was going to be published.

In the years since sitting on the carpet with Jacqui, I've realised that she said just the right thing. If you're thinking of any kind of writing class, you need to ask yourself a very simple question: 'Am I prepared to do *anything* – to learn from *anyone* – in order to become a better writer?' Creative writing courses are less like sitting at the feet of the pearly-teethed master and are far more like Alcoholics Anonymous. 'Hello, my name is X and I am trying to write a historical novel set in Y.' 'Thank you, X.' When I was lucky enough to get onto the UEA course and be in one of Malcolm Bradbury's workshops, I saw that the learning-from-anyone part was the foundation. Because I learned at least as much from other students' negative examples as from their occasional positive comments about my work. I learned that what usually makes a writer bad is clinging on to something about their writing, something they feel is essential, but which is causing it to collapse inwards in some way or other. Self-love, in other words. Conceit. Most people never get to read unpublished writing, or even first drafts by published writers, so they have no idea of the kind of swampy sinkhole-filled morass that's out there. They get used to strolling along the paths of the landscaped garden, after the completion of the massive drainage project, after the dumping of new imported soil, after the carefully planned planting that looks so wonderfully *natural*.

So, to answer your question more directly: Creative Writing is right for *you* if you come to it with a basic humility. 'Okay, something's not working in what I'm doing. Probably a lot of things. I know that. And I'm prepared to do anything – and learn from anyone – in order to get better. I'm prepared to give up my self-love, and my idea of myself as a self-sufficient genius. I'm prepared to listen.'

This answer, even on an open evening, is a little more open than you expected. In fact, it's verging on the confessional. You didn't need to hear about the wine and the carpet – although it made the whole thing quite vivid. But you think you've got the basic concept: Creative Writing courses are hard on the ego. You decide to reciprocate by making yourself a little vulnerable. You say, 'I have all these ideas, and I make lots of starts – I've got dozens of those – but I can't seem to get them finished. What I'm really looking for is some *discipline*.'

And I say, 'A lot of people thinking about doing a writing course say that.' And discipline – or, at least, *structure* – is one of the things a workshop can offer. You'll have to put in a piece of work three or four times a term. (They call them semesters, now.) So, you'll have deadlines that aren't artificial or self-imposed. One of the most important things a creative writing class provides is an audience. It's a peer group as well. But firstly it's a set of readers who don't have a personal investment in you or your ego. (Not to start with, anyway.)

If you give the first 20 pages of your novel to your partner, or your best friend, or even to that writer you know through a friend of a friend, they are socially and emotionally involved with you. They are aware that they'll have to deal with the social and emotional aftermath of telling you the truth. Most writers, myself included, just want to hear, 'This is the greatest thing ever written. I laughed. I wept. I even pondered. You are a sublime genius. Don't change a comma.' Most writers don't want to hear, 'The main character is the most self-important tosser I've ever come across and, if they opened their mouth and spoke like this, could clear the 8.14 from Basingstoke', or 'You write like you're some kind of demented cross between the Pope, the Queen and the *Oxford English Dictionary*', or 'I was so bored I ate my index finger'.

Now, this is not the sort of feedback you're going to get in a Creative Writing class – because your readers there will themselves be writers, they will know about dwelling in the swampy morass of the first draft, and they will be starting from the basis of thinking, 'Here's a story, what's happening in it? What's not happening? How can it be improved?' They quite possibly (as we do at Birkbeck) will talk about the story as if the person who wrote it wasn't in the room. That may feel odd but also oddly liberating. The writing is *from* you and *of* you but it isn't *you yourself personally for ever*. It can be changed, improved, transformed. The main character can become loveable, the prose style can become delightful, the story can become unputdownable. This may be because you find your own particular truth in the usual workshop advice of 'Write what you know', 'Keep it simple, stupid' or 'Show don't tell'. This may be because you learn some technical stuff to do with point of view, narrative tone, time-management, or because someone in the class, talking about something else entirely, not your work at all, said just the right thing. This will almost certainly be because you, in writing terms, *get over yourself*. All writers need constantly to get over themselves, but they also need selves to get over. That's the paradox you'll be dealing with for the rest of your writing life.

Even for an open evening, this was beyond open. It's all getting a bit self-helpy, the other side of the table. But you feel it's fairly close to answering your question. You said you needed discipline. I'm saying that discipline isn't just about putting in the hours and decades at the laptop, it's about self-discipline. And it seems, from what I'm saying, that you can learn a lot about self-discipline from other people – more particularly, from a group of 10 or 12 passionately attentive strangers, gently moderated by someone they all respect, collectively trying to improve as writers.

You're feeling good. You decide to commit fully and ask the big question. You say, 'Will going on the course help get me published?'

And it was all going so well! But now I can't keep the look of disappointment from my face. Publication? That's what they really want to know about, isn't it? Choosing covers and doing interviews and rave reviews and saying you're a writer rather than a whatever, and having people say, 'Oh, how interesting!' But it's Open Evening, so I have to be open.

I have to say, 'If you write just for publication, you're doing the wrong thing. Leave now and don't come back. Publication is a tiny part of a writer's life. Most of a writer's life is – and I know you're ahead of me here – writing. Which means, being alone with your failures. They may only be verbal failures, but they often don't feel like it. They feel like my-entire-life-failures. I know people who've become astonishingly successful at writing – you'll have heard of them – films have been made of their work – but they discover they hate their job as much as anyone can. So, they move away from the being-alone bit by becoming screenwriters or writing journalism or finding something that lets another person through the door, that gives another person responsibility.'

Oh dear. I've said too much. Been too open. But it's late. I'm tired. And now they've just announced, through the crunchy tannoy, that the Open Evening is finishing. You look crestfallen. You say, 'I only meant – ' I wait. 'I only meant would it *help*?'

'Yes,' I say, with a smile, 'I think it will. If you have the right approach, it will help you become a better writer faster than you could on your own. And it's the better writers who get published – the ones who have repeatedly transformed their swamps into gardens.'

And we shake hands, and you head off back to your swamp, and I head off back to mine.

Toby Litt is a short story writer and novelist. He has published 12 books, including *Adventures in Capitalism* (Secker and Warburg 1996), *Exhibitionism* (Hamish Hamilton 2002), *I play the drums in a band called okay* (Hamish Hamilton 2008) and, most recently, *Life-Like* (Seagull Books 2014). He is currently working on *Wrestliana*, a non-fiction book about his great-great-great grandfather, William Litt, who was a poet, novelist, smuggler and champion wrestler. Toby's blog is at www.tobylitt.com.

See also...

- *The calling card script for screen, radio and stage*, page 347
- *Creative writing courses*, page 655

Writers' retreats

Some writers find that spending time at a writers' retreat proves bountiful. One author who has benefited from this experience is Maggie Gee.

Writers' retreats are not for everyone. They aren't, for example, for the poet who once said to me, *apropos* of Hawthornden Castle International Writers' Retreat, 'But it's so quiet. And Edinburgh is *half an hour away* by bus.' For him, to be half an hour from the metropolis was a penance.

Before going into the desert, think long and hard. Are you quarrelsome, or oversensitive, or both? The other writers will, for the most part, be busy and quiet, but mealtimes are generally communal. People are more vulnerable when they are off their own territory and away from loved ones. Do not always eat the last piece of cake (food gains an emotional significance when other props are missing) or be competitive about how much you have written, or how much you get paid. Actual numbers of words and pounds should never be quoted. Do not give a reading from your new work unless asked.

Ask yourself hard questions before you go. Do you mind very much being away from your loved ones, your cat, your garden? Will you be wracked by guilt? Are you addicted to television to relax? Do you feel anxious if you can't pick up emails or vary the monotony of your work with half-hourly binges on Google, Facebook or Twitter? Most retreats have no televisions and many deliberately have no internet connection.

But if you are a writer who can never get enough time uninterrupted by phone calls, plumbers, pets, children and the washing-machine, writers' retreats are absolute heaven. For me personally, three widely spaced four-week stays at Hawthornden Castle produced the first drafts of two novels, *Where are the Snows* (1991) and *The Flood* (2004), and the second half of my memoir, *My Animal Life* (2011). When I am away from all the things I ought to do at home, I become tenfold more productive.

Prose writers have to come to terms with the leaden truth that you cannot write a book without hours of immobility. I personally prefer concentrating those hours into a smaller number of weeks and months. I speak as one whose eighth novel (*The White Family*), took seven years to write and rewrite (no retreats), whereas *The Flood*, after 18 months of mulling over, took just a month to dream up and write at a retreat, and six months to rewrite at home. Poets enjoy retreats too: the second time I was at Hawthornden I was with Jean Sprackland, and the collection she wrote, *Hard Water*, was later shortlisted for the T.S. Eliot Prize and the Whitbread Award for Poetry.

In the USA there is a wide choice of retreats open to writers from the UK and elsewhere. Google will present you with a bewildering variety of retreats there, many of them luxurious, long established and highly competitive. Most of them are free, but you have to find the airfare. In the UK there are fewer choices and just one retreat is free, Hawthornden Castle in Scotland. Writers can only go there once every five years. You must make a formal application and if you are accepted you can look forward to a stay in a beautiful castle in dramatic wooded grounds. The rooms are small but attractive, the food is good and the five or six writers who are in residence at any one time pay only for their pre-prandial sherry. Arvon, famous for tutored retreats, also sometimes offers one-week untutored retreats – check the website. Ireland has scenic Anam Cara, on the coast of Western Cork.

It is common for American writers to spend much of their life going from retreat to retreat, but British writers are less well served at home. I can recommend only three retreats from personal experience: Hawthornden, as above; the Chateau de Lavigny, a very beautiful and special European mansion on the hilly slopes of Lac Leman above Lausanne; and El Gouna, an amazing free retreat in a hotel in an 'eco-village' in Egypt, not far from Hurghada, which sadly has not survived changing economic conditions.

El Gouna was a modern four-star hotel set beside dry, sparkling vistas over blue canals to the sea. I was there in May 2011, not long after the Revolution, and I wrote half my new novel in my cool room, printing it off and correcting it in the open air in the hot square which was hazy with aromatic smoke from the hubble-bubble pipes. Unforgettable, but perhaps too good to last.

Lavigny – ah, the Chateau de Lavigny. This free retreat was founded by Jane Rowohlt in memory of her husband, famous German paperback publisher Heinrich Mari Ledig-Rowohlt, who lived there and sometimes entertained the writers he published, among them his friend Vladimir Nabokov – my room was only a wall away from the narrow bed where my Russian hero had slept. I was there in summer, watched the cornfields below turn golden for the harvest, and took long walks through rows of vines, coming back to write the end of my novel about Uganda as I looked towards the white tip of Mont Blanc. Lavigny is beautiful, un-institutional, and truly international – I was there with an Egyptian, a Pole, an American, a Frenchwoman and a Scotsman.

It seems like a miracle that in our harsh capitalistic era the generosity of patrons still supports literature, as it has since medieval times. Benefit if you can, and don't despair if you don't get in to your chosen retreat first time – that's normal. Be resourceful. There are always bargain deals at out-of-season seaside hotels, or if you once went to a college or university, you could find out if they let *alumni* stay there cheaply in empty rooms. Many do, and they should have decent desks and chairs. As a last resort, send yourself on 'day retreats' to the local library or park, and don't go home until the pages are done. I like to flee to the British Library or my local cafe. Once the washing-machine, the telephone and the pets have fallen silent, the dream of the book will begin.

Maggie Gee OBE's most recent novel, *Virginia Woolf in Manhattan* (Telegram 2014) is a comedy that brings Virginia Woolf back to life in the 21st century in New York and Istanbul. She has written a memoir, *My Animal Life*; a collection of short stories, *The Blue*; and 12 acclaimed novels, including *The White Family*, shortlisted for the Orange Prize, and two comedies about the UK and Uganda, *My Cleaner* and *My Driver* (Telegram 2009). She was the first female Chair of the Royal Society of Literature (2004–8) and is currently one of its vice-presidents. An international conference about her work was held at St Andrew's University, Scotland, in 2012. She is Professor of Creative Writing at Bath Spa University.

WRITERS' RETREATS

Anam Cara

website www.anamcararetreat.com

An all-inclusive residential retreat, Anam Cara offers private and common working rooms and five acres of walking paths, quiet nooks and crannies, a river island and a labyrinth meadow. Set on a hillside between Coulagh Bay and Mishkish mountain on the Kealincha River, Anam Cara is a tranquil spot to provide sanctuary for people who seriously want to enhance their craft. Whether writers want to work by themselves or as part of a workshop, or special interest group, Anam Cara provides support, creature comforts and peace to help everyone produce their best work.

Arty Breaks

tel (01323) 736884 *mobile* 07944 420214
email debra@artybreaks.co.uk
website www.artybreaks.co.uk
Contact Debra Sabri

Join fellow writers for a weekend of writing in Eastbourne. Arty Breaks writing retreats are for all writers and would-be writers and include peer and author-led workshops. Full board for two nights in a seafront hotel is included. Take advantage of the ever-changing scenery of the seashore or take a trip to the spectacular Beachy Head to find your muse.

Arvon

Free Word, 60 Farringdon Road, London EC1R 3GA
tel 020-7324 2554
email national@arvon.org
website www.arvon.org
Chief Executive Ruth Borthwick

See individual entries for Arvon's three centres: The Hurst – The John Osborne Arvon Centre, Lumb Bank – The Ted Hughes Arvon Centre and Totleigh Barton. Arvon hosts week-long residential creative writing courses and retreats in four beautiful writing houses, set in inspiring countryside. Weeks include morning workshops, one-to-one tutorials with leading authors and plenty of time and space to write. Courses cover a range of genres including fiction, poetry, theatre, creative non-fiction, writing for children and many more. Arvon runs a grants system for those who would not be able to afford the full course fee.

Château de Lavigny International Writers' Residence

Le Château, Route d'Etoy 10, 1175 Lavigny, Switzerland. The head office address is: Fondation Ledig-Rowohlt, Av. Montbenon 2, Case postale 5475, 1002 Lausanne, Switzerland
tel +41 21-321 4545
email chlavigny@hotmail.com
website www.chateaudelavigny.ch

An international residence for writers in the canton of Vaud in Switzerland. The residence was created in 1996 by the Ledig-Rowohlt Foundation and has since welcomed each summer 20 or more writers from around the world. Writers come for four weeks, in groups of five or six, from early June through to mid-September. They are housed in the former home of German publisher Heinrich Maria Ledig-Rowohlt and his wife Jane, an 18th-century manor house among vineyards and hills overlooking Lake Geneva. Sessions are in English or French and writers must be published.

The Grange

9 Eastcliff Road, Shanklin, Isle of Wight PO37 6AA
tel (01983) 867644
email info@thegrangebythesea.com
website www.thegrangebythesea.com
Contact Jenni Canakis

The Grange is an offshoot of Skyros with its renowned Writers' Lab that has attracted some very well-respected authors. The Grange hosts weekend residential creative writing workshops in a 4-star B&B, in the old village of Shanklin on the south coast of the Isle of Wight. Nestled in greenery, it is very secluded, yet only moments from thatched pubs, cosy tearooms, the local train station, shops, restaurants and the long sandy beach. A beautiful and peaceful place to write.

Hawthornden Castle

International Retreat for Writers, Lasswade, Midlothian EH18 1EG
tel 0131 440 2180
email office@hawthornden.org
Contact The Director

Exists to provide a peaceful setting where published writers can work without disturbance. The Retreat houses up to six writers at a time, who are known as Hawthornden Fellows. Writers from any part of the world may apply for the fellowships. No monetary assistance is given, nor any contribution to travelling expenses, but fellows board as guests of the Retreat. Application forms are available from January for the following calendar year. Deadline for applications 30 June.

The Hurst – The John Osborne Arvon Centre

Arvon, The Hurst, Clunton, Craven Arms, Shropshire SY7 0JA
tel (01588) 640658
email thehurst@arvon.org
website www.arvon.org
Centre Director Natasha Carlish, *Centre Administrator* Dan Pavitt

Offers residential writing courses April to December. Grants available. The Hurst is situated in the beautiful Clun Valley in Shropshire, 12 miles from Ludlow, and is set in 30 acres of woodland, with gardens and a lake.

Irish Writers Centre

19 Parnell Square, Dublin 1, Republic of Ireland
tel +353 (0)1 8721302
email info@writerscentre.ie
website www.writerscentre.ie
Director Valerie Bistany

The national resource centre for Irish writers. It runs workshops, seminars and events related to the art of writing, hosts professional developments seminars for writers, provides space for writers, writing groups and other literary organisations. It also provides information to writers and the general public.

Isle of Wight Writing Courses and Workshops

F&F Productions, 39 Ranelagh Road, Sandown, Isle of Wight PO36 8NT
tel (01983) 407772
email felicity@writeplot.co.uk
website www.learnwriting.co.uk
website www.wightdiamondpress.com
Contact Felicity Fair Thompson

Residential and non-residential occasional weekends through the year for beginners and experienced writers. Individual advice and workshops. Time to write and to enjoy the beautiful Isle of Wight in comfortable and roomy B&B accommodation, two minutes from beach path and coastal walks to Sandown and Shanklin. Also offers postal MS critiques and one-to-one advice on film scripts and fiction.

Le Verger

Le Verger, Savignac-Lédrier, Dordogne, 24270 France
tel (01223) 316539 (UK)
email djlambert4@gmail.com
website www.retreatfrance.co.uk
Contact David Lambert

Le Verger offers residential writers' retreats or tutored courses (poetry, drama, fiction and life writing) from May to September. Le Verger is a comfortable *maison de campagne* outside a picturesque village in the rolling Dordogne countryside of south-west France. Shared or individual accommodation in the main house, The Piggery and writer's cabins, full board (with wine) for up to ten writers. Transfers to/from Limoges.

Limnisa Centre for Writers

Agios Georgios, 18030, Methana, Greece
tel +44 (0)7937 352800
email mariel@limnisa.com
website www.limnisa.com

International retreats and workshops for writers. Two hours by ferry from Piraeus, Limnisa stands in its own shaded garden with access to a tranquil beach, in a stunning position on the Methana Peninsula with views to Epidavros and the island of Aegina. Offers single rooms, studios or tents and all vegetarian meals. Check website for details and dates.

Lumb Bank – The Ted Hughes Arvon Centre

Arvon, Lumb Bank, Heptonstall, Hebden Bridge, West Yorkshire HX7 6DF
tel (01422) 843714
email lumbbank@arvon.org
website www.arvon.org
Centre Director Lucy Burnett, *Assistant Centre Director* Jill Penny, *Administrator* Becky Liddell

Offers residential writing courses April to December. Grants available. Lumb Bank is an 18th-century former mill-owner's house set in 20 acres of steep pasture land.

Annie McKie

Writer's Retreat, Keystone, Blakeney Hill, Glos. GL15 4BT
email annie@anniemckie.co.uk
website www.anniemckie.co.uk
Contact Annie McKie

A peaceful retreat in the Forest of Dean, Gloucestershire. Beautiful room with private access and en suite bathroom. Balcony with wide reaching views across woodland and the Severn Valley. A few steps from the garden gate take you into the Forest with its mile upon mile of public footpaths. Retreats are a minimum of two nights. The price includes all homemade vegetarian meals and an hour of one-to-one tuition. Additional feedback is available at an extra cost. All retreats are geared to the individual. Accepts only one guest at a time.

Moniack Mhor

Moniack Mhor, Teavarran, Kiltarlity, Beauly, Inverness-shire IV4 7HT
tel (01463) 741675
email info@moniackmhor.org.uk
website www.moniackmhor.org.uk
Centre Directors Cynthia Rogerson, Rachel Humphries

Moniack Mhor is Scotland's Creative Writing Centre, running open residential creative writing courses and partnership courses throughout the year, for adults and young people at all stages of a writing career. Tuition is by established writers, and retreats and residencies are also offered. Moniack Mhor also runs one-off events. High on a hill close to Loch Ness, the centre is an inspirational, inclusive and nurturing setting for writers to spend an intensive period focusing on their work.

Monkton Wyld Court

Elsdon's Lane, Charmouth, Bridport, Dorset DT6 6DQ
tel (01297) 560342
email info@monktonwyld.org
website http://monktonwyldcourt.co.uk/writers-retreats/

A Victorian country house in a secluded valley on the Dorset/Devon border. Monkton Wyld Court is an educational charity offering affordable, full-board, short- and long-term accommodation to writers of all sorts. In-house professional copy-editing services also available. Email or call to discuss availability.

responsibletravel.com

First Floor, Edge House, 42 Bond Street, Brighton BN1 1RD
tel (01273) 823700
email rosy@responsibletravel.com
email sarah@responsibletravel.com
website www.responsibletravel.com
Contacts Rosy Everitt (Helpdesk Manager), Sarah Bareham (Marketing Executive)

Offers a range of holidays, secluded retreats and specialist writing, painting and photography holidays. For writers and artists with confirmed commissions, can also help source press trips, dependent on the type of commission and publication involved.

Retreats for You

The Court, The Square, Sheepwash, Beaworthy, Devon EX21 5NE
tel (01409) 231252
email retreatsforyou@gmail.com
website www.retreatsforyou.co.uk
Contact Deborah Dooley

Offers writers and artists peace and quiet as well as plenty of good food. Simple, comfortable rooms with desks and kettles, in a thatched house with a huge log fire, surrounded by beautiful Devon countryside. Full board is provided and guests may be as sociable or as solitary as they please.

SCBWI-BI Picture Book Retreat

email picbookretreat@britishscbwi.org
website www.britishisles.scbwi.org/events
Contact Anne-Marie Perks

A creative weekend for picture book writers and illustrators. Jump start your writing, explore new techniques and experiment with words and art materials. There will be an optional project set for both writers and illustrators, and ample time for work on this or on personal projects. Every attendee will be assigned a faculty mentor and will have the chance to book a slot with a commissioning editor. Evenings will be open for informal critique sessions and discussions on technique, craft and the children's publishing industry. In 2016 the retreat will take place from 8–11 July at Holland House in Pershore, Worcestershire.

SCBWI-BI Writer's Retreat

email retreat@britishscbwi.org
website www.britishisles.scbwi.org/events
Contact Retreat Coordinator

Providing an ideal opportunity for space to write, away from day-to-day demands, the programme is streamlined to allow maximum writing time. In 2016, the retreat takes place from 6–9 May at Dunford House Conference Centre in Midhurst, West Sussex. Faculty includes editors, agents and a keynote author; one-to-ones with speakers will also be available.

Skyros Writers' Lab

9 Eastcliff Road, Shanklin, Isle of Wight PO37 6AA
tel (01983) 865566
email office@skyros.com
website www.skyros.com
Co-founders Dr Yannis Andricopolous, Dr Dina Glouberman

The Skyros Writers' Lab, situated on the island of Skyros in Greece, offers writers of all levels the opportunity to learn from distinguished writers, share the joys and struggles of the creative process, discover their strengths and polish their skills. Courses are open to novices with a passion for writing as well as writers with a book under their belt. Arrive with work in progress or just an empty page; all are welcome.

The Skyros Writers' Lab has built up an excellent reputation over the years for its visiting authors who have included Steven Berkoff, Mez Packer, Leigh Russell, Sophie Hannah, Rachel Billington, Margaret Drabble, Hanif Kureishi, D.M. Thomas, Sue Townsend, Marina Warner, Hugo Williams, Hilary Mantel, James Kelman, Barry Unsworth, Bernice Rubens and Alison Lurie.

Stiwdio Maelor

Maelor, Corris, Machynlleth SY20 9SP
tel 07759 451785
email stiwdiomaelor@gmail.com
website www.stiwdiomaelor.wordpress.com
Contact Veronica Calarco

Provides short-term residencies with low-cost accommodation for visual artists and writers. Writers and artists are able to take time out of their busy lives, visit a stunning area in North Wales, refocus on their work and find new inspiration. Founded 2014.

TLC Literary Adventures

The Literary Consultancy, Free Word Centre, 60 Farringdon Road, London EC1R 3GA
tel 020-7324 2563
email info@literaryconsultancy.co.uk
website www.literaryconsultancy.co.uk
website http://literaryconsultancy.co.uk/literary-adventures
Director Rebecca Swift

TLC's annual writing retreat is held at the idyllic Casa Ana in Andalucia, Spain. Workshops are led by award-winning novelist and inspiring tutor Rebecca Abrams and TLC Director Rebecca Swift. TLC Literary Adventures offers an environment where inspiration and improvisation meet. Guests have access to world-class teaching and get a chance to work, read, listen and relax in a stunning setting which opens the mind and the senses. The retreat is open to writers of fiction, memoir and general non-fiction. Groups are limited to a maximum of 12.

Totleigh Barton

Arvon, Totleigh Barton, Sheepwash, Beaworthy, Devon EX21 5NS
tel (01409) 231338
email totleighbarton@arvon.org
website www.arvon.org
Centre Directors Mary Morris, *Assistant Centre Director* Eliza Squire, *Administrator* Sue Walker

Offers residential writing courses April to December. Grants available. Totleigh Barton is a thatched, 16th-century manor house, surrounded by farmland in Devon, two miles from the village of Sheepwash.

Tŷ Newydd Writers' Centre

Tŷ Newydd Writers' Centre, Llanystumdwy, Cricieth, Gwynedd LL52 0LW
tel (01766) 522811

email tynewydd@literaturewales.org
website www.literaturewales.org
website www.tynewydd.org

Tŷ Newydd, the former home of Prime Minister David Lloyd George, has hosted residential creative writing courses for writers of all abilities for over 25 years. Whether you're interested in a poetry masterclass, writing for the theatre, developing a novel for young adults or conquering the popular fiction market, there'll be a course in our programme suitable for you. Courses are open to everyone over the age of 16 and no qualifications are necessary. Literature Wales staff based at Tŷ Newydd can advise on the suitability of courses, and further details about each individual course can be obtained by visiting the website, or contacting the team by phone or email.

Upton Cressett Foundation

Upton Cressett Hall, Upton Cressett, Nr Bridgnorth, Shrops. WV16 6UH
tel (01746) 714616
email enquiries@uptoncressett.co.uk
website www.uptoncressetthall.co.uk
Contact William Cash

Guest fellows are invited to stay and write in the Foundation's historic Grade I Elizabethan gatehouse for up to four weeks (off season) to make progress with a literary project. The idea is to give established writers an opportunity to make headway with a work-in-progress in a remote and beautiful creative environment away from domestic or second career distractions. This could be 100 pages of a novel, a major rewrite after an editor's marks, a new play/screenplay or a monograph. Previous fellows include Dr Lara Feigel, the historian Juliet Gardiner and the playwright Ella Hickson.

Urban Writers' Retreat

email hello@urbanwritersretreat.co.uk
website www.urbanwritersretreat.co.uk
Contact Charlie Haynes

Urban Writers' Retreat creates time and space so you can focus and just write. Escape the real world and all its distractions at one-day retreats in London and blissful residential retreats in the countryside, or get online courses and support to help you kick procrastination into touch.

The Write Retreat

The Write Retreat Ltd, Kerivoa, 22390, Bourbriac, Cotes d'Armor, Brittany, France
tel +33 (0)2 9643 6361
mobile +33 (0)6 3594 5754 (France), 07834 954993 (UK)
email info@thewriteretreat.com
website www.thewriteretreat.com
Contact Katherine Bolton-Parris

Set in historic Kerivoa in Brittany, The Write Retreat offers residential creative writing holidays and writing retreats throughout the year. Accommodation is in a renovated farmhouse within a secluded spot offering tranquility and peacefulness. Inspiring accompanied walks from the farmhouse include a Dolmen, Menhir, ancient woodlands and local villages. Free wi-fi. The food is mostly home grown, reared or baked and special diets can be catered for. Non-writing partners are welcome and there is one dedicated pet-friendly room.

Courses are bespoke and run by experienced creative writing tutor Katherine Parris (member of SWWJ, NAWG, IBBY).

Libraries

Libraries are no longer just repositories for books and a source of reference. Today, they provide an increasing range of different services, using a multitude of media to reach a more diverse audience than ever before.

TYPES OF LIBRARIES

• **Public libraries** are accessible to the general population and are usually funded by a local or district council. They typically offer a mix of lending and reference facilities. Public libraries are distinct from research libraries, subscription libraries and other specialist libraries in terms of their funding and access, but may offer some of the same facilities to its readers. Public library services are facing financial challenges and cuts to funding so many library authorities are looking towards new approaches to working with communities in order to build sustainable library services for the future.
• A list of **community libraries** in the UK can be found at www.publiclibrariesnews.com.
• An **academic library** is usually affiliated to an educational institution and primarily serves the students and faculty of that institution. Some are accessible to the public.
• A **subscription library** is one that is funded via membership or endowments. Access is often restricted to members but membership is sometimes extended to groups who are non-members, such as students.
• Many libraries belong to the Association of Independent Libraries and a list of members can be found on its website (see below).

TEN OF THE BEST

Britain has such a wealth of comprehensive and historic libraries that a full list of them is not possible in this publication. Here are just 10 of the best.

Barbican Library

Barbican Centre, Silk Street, London EC2Y 8DS
tel 020-7638 0569
email barbicanlib@cityoflondon.gov.uk
website www.cityoflondon.gov.uk/barbicanlibrary

The largest of the City of London's lending libraries with a strong arts and music section, a London collection, literature events programme, and reading groups.

Belfast Central Library

Royal Avenue, Belfast BT1 1EA
tel 028-9050 9150
email belfast.central@librariesni.org.uk
website www.ni-libraries.net

The library's reference library is the largest in stock terms in Northern Ireland. The library houses a number of special collections including a digital film archive and the Northern Ireland Music Archive.

Library of Birmingham

Centenary Square, Broad Street,
Birmingham B1 2ND
email enquiries@libraryofbirmingham.com
website www.libraryofbirmingham.com

The Library of Birmingham replaced Birmingham Central Library in September 2013 and is the largest public library in the UK and the largest regional library in Europe. Check the website for the latest information and updates.

Cardiff Central Library

The Hayes, Cardiff CF10 1FL
tel 029-2038 2116
email centrallibrary@cardiff.gov.uk
website www.cardiff.gov.uk/ENG/resident/Libraries-and-archives/Find-a-library/Pages/Central-Library.aspx

The largest public library in Wales, opened in 2009, houses 90,000 books, 10,000 of which are in Welsh.

Liverpool Central Library

William Brown Street, Liverpool L3 8EW
tel 0151 233 3069
email refbt.central.library@liverpool.gov.uk
website https://liverpool.gov.uk/libraries/find-a-library/central-library/

Liverpool Central Library has undergone major refurbishment and reopened in May 2013. The collection includes 15,000 rare books.

London Library

14 St James's Square, London SW1Y 4LG
tel 020-7930 7705
email reception@londonlibrary.co.uk
website www.londonlibrary.co.uk

Subscription lending library. With more than one million books and periodicals in over 50 languages, the collection includes works from the 16th century to the latest publications in print and electronic form. Membership is open to all.

Manchester Central Library

St Peter's Square, Manchester M2 5PD
email libraries@manchester.gov.uk
website http://www.manchester.gov.uk/info/500138/central_library

Manchester's main library, the second biggest public lending library in the UK, reopened in March 2014 after major refurbishment.

Mitchell Library

North Street, Glasgow G3 7DN
tel 0141 287 2999
email libraries@glasgowlife.org.uk
website www.glasgowlife.org.uk/libraries/the-mitchell-library/pages/home.aspx

The largest public reference library in Europe housing almost 2 million volumes. Holds an unrivalled collection of material relating to the City of Glasgow.

Newcastle City Library

City Library, Charles Avison Building,
33 Newbridge Street West,
Newcastle upon Tyne NE1 8AX
tel 0191 277 4100
email information@newcastle.gov.uk
website www.newcastle.gov.uk/leisure-libraries-and-tourism/libraries/branch-libraries-and-opening-hours/city-library

The city's main public library includes a café, exhibition spaces, a rare books and watercolours collection, a viewing deck and 6 floors of books.

Westminster Reference Library

35 St Martin's Street, London WC2H 7HP
tel 020-7641 6200 (press 2)
email referencelibrarywc2@westminster.gov.uk
website www.westminster.gov.uk/westminster-reference-library

Specialist public reference library with collections in Performing Arts and Art & Design. Hosts regular and varied events, includes an exhibition space and a Business Information Point. Also has a range of business resources including market research, company and legal databases.

LIBRARIES OF LEGAL DEPOSIT IN THE UK AND IRELAND

A library of legal deposit is a library that has the power to request (at no charge) a copy of anything published in the UK. There are 6 legal deposit libraries in the UK and Ireland. To obtain a copy of a book, 5 out of the 6 legal deposit libraries must make a request in writing to a publisher within one year of publication of a book, newspaper or journal. Different rules apply to the British Library in that all UK libraries and Republic of Ireland publishers have a legal responsibility to send a copy of each of their publications to the library, without a written request being made. The British Library is the only legal deposit library with its own Legal Deposit Office. Since April 2013, legal deposit also covers material published digitally and online, so that the legal deposit libraries can provide a national archive of the UK's non-print published material, such as websites, blogs, e-journals and CD-ROMs.

Agency for the Legal Deposit Libraries

161 Causewayside, Edinburgh EH9 1PH
tel 0131 623 4680
email publisher.enquiries@legaldeposit.org.uk
website www.legaldeposit.org.uk

The Agency for the Legal Deposit Libraries requests and receives copies of publications for distribution to 5 major libraries (not the British Library). It is maintained by 5 legal deposit libraries and ensures that they receive legal deposit copies of British and Irish publications. The legal deposit libraries belong to the agency, which sends out written requests on behalf of member libraries and acts as a depot for books received. The agency must request copies on behalf of the libraries within 12 months of the date of publication. On receiving such a request from the agency, a publisher must supply a copy for each of the requesting libraries under the terms of the Legal Deposit Libraries Act 2003 (UK) and the Copyright and Related Rights Act 2000 (Ireland).

Bodleian Libraries of the University of Oxford

Broad Street, Oxford OX1 3BG
tel (01865) 277162
email reader.services@bodleian.ox.ac.uk
website www.bodleian.ox.ac.uk

With 11 million volumes and 80,000 e-journals and vast quantities of materials in many other formats, the Bodleian Libraries together forms the second-largest library in the UK after the British Library, and is the main reference library of Oxford University.

The British Library

St Pancras Building, 96 Euston Road,
London NW1 2DB
tel 0330 333 1144 (switchboard), 020-7412 7676 (reader information, St Pancras), (01937) 546070 (reader information, enquiries, Boston Spa), 020-7412 7831 (humanities & sound archive), 020-7412 7702 (maps), 020-7412 7513 (manuscripts)
Legal Deposit Office: The British Library, Boston Spa, Wetherby, West Yorkshire LS23 7BQ
tel (01937) 546268 (books), (01937) 546267 (serials)
email legal-deposit-books@bl.uk
website www.bl.uk

The British Library holds books, journals, newspapers, sound recordings, patents, original MSS, maps, online images and texts, plays, digital books, and poet and author recordings. With a holding of 14 million UK books, 150 million published items from around the globe, almost a million journals and newspapers, and 3 million sound recordings, it is the largest library in the world in terms of number of items held.

Cambridge University Library

West Road, Cambridge CB3 9DR
tel (01223) 333000
email library@lib.cam.ac.uk
website www.lib.cam.ac.uk

Cambridge University Library houses its own collection and also comprises 4 other libraries within the university. The library dates back to the 15th century and now has a collection of 8 million books. It is the only legal deposit library that keeps a large percentage of its books on open access.

National Library of Scotland

George IV Bridge, Edinburgh EH1 1EW
tel 0131 623 3700
email enquiries@nls.uk
website www.nls.uk

The National Library of Scotland holds over 15 million printed items including 7 million books and more than 2 million maps. It is the world's central source for research relating to Scotland and the Scots. The library also holds a copy of the Gutenberg Bible, a First Folio of Shakespeare, and the last letter written by Mary Queen of Scots. In 2005 the library bought the John Murray Archive for £31 million and it contains important items relating to Jane Austen, Lord Byron and Sir Arthur Conan Doyle.

National Library of Wales

Aberystwyth, Ceredigion SY23 3BU
tel (01970) 632800
email gofyn@llgc.org.uk
website www.llgc.org.uk

The National Library of Wales was established in 1907 and holds over 5 million books, including many important works such as the first book printed in Welsh and the first Welsh translation of the Bible.

Trinity College Library Dublin

College Green, Dublin 2, Republic of Ireland
tel +353 (0)1 896 1127
email dutylibrarian@tcd.ie
website www.tcd.ie/library

Trinity College Library is the largest library in Ireland and is home to the *Book of Kells* – 2 of the 4 volumes are on permanent public display. The library houses sound recordings, maps, databases, and a digital collection.

DESIGNATED OUTSTANDING COLLECTIONS

The Designated Outstanding Collections scheme was established in 1997 by the Museums and Galleries Commission to identify collections of national and international importance in non-national museums and galleries. In 2005 the scheme was extended to include libraries and archives. The scheme is now administered by Arts Council England and there are 140 Designated Outstanding Collections in England. To find out if there is a Designated Outstanding Collection library near you, visit the Designation section of the Arts Council website (www.artscouncil.org.uk).

SPECIALIST LIBRARIES IN THE UK

Writers often need access to specialised information sources in order to research their work. The following listing provides a sample of the kind of specialist libraries the UK has to offer.

BBC Written Archives Centre

Peppard Road, Caversham Park, Reading RG4 8TZ
tel 0118-948 6281
email heritage@bbc.co.uk
website www.bbc.co.uk/historyofthebbc/research/wac

Home of the BBC's written records. Holds thousands of files, scripts and working papers from the BBC's formation in 1922 to the 1980s together with information about past programmes and the history of broadcasting. Does not have recordings or information about current programmes.

BFI National Archive and Reuben Library

21 Stephen Street, London W1T 1LN
tel 020-7255 1444
website www.bfi.org.uk

Established in 1935, the BFI National Archive is one of the largest film and television collections anywhere. Dating from the earliest days of film to the 21st century, it contains nearly a million titles. The archive contains over 50,000 fiction films, over 100,000 non-fiction titles and approx. 625,000 television programmes. The majority of the collection is British material but it also features internationally significant holdings from around the world. The Archive also collects films which feature key British actors and the work of British directors. Using the latest preservation methods, the BFI cares for a variety of often obsolete formats so that future generations can enjoy their film heritage. The BFI Reuben Library at BFI Southbank is home to a huge collection of books, journals, documents and audio recordings about the world of film and television.

British Library for Development Studies (BLDS)

Institute of Development Studies at the University of Sussex, Brighton BN1 9RE
tel (01273) 915659
email blds@ids.ac.uk
website www.blds.ids.ac.uk

Europe's largest research collection on economic and social change in developing countries.

British Newspaper Archive

tel (01382) 210100
website www.britishnewspaperarchive.co.uk

The British Newspaper Archive gives access to over 10 million historical local, national and regional newspaper pages from across the UK and Ireland.

The archive is published and managed by Brightsolid in collaboration with the British Library.

Catholic National Library

St Michael's Abbey, Farnborough Road, Farnborough, Hants GU14 7NQ
tel (01252) 543818
email library@catholic-library.org.uk
website www.catholic-library.org.uk

Holds over 70,000 books, pamphlets and periodicals on theology, spirituality and related subjects, biography and history.

Chawton House Library

Chawton, Alton, Hants GU34 1SJ
tel (01420) 541010
email info@chawton.net
website www.chawtonhouse.org

A collection of over 8,000 volumes focusing on women's writing in English from 1600 to 1830 including some manuscripts. The library also houses the Knight Collection.

City Business Library

Aldermanbury, London EC2V 7HH
tel 020-7332 1812
email cbl@cityoflondon.gov.uk
website www.cityoflondon.gov.uk/citybusinesslibrary

One of the leading business information sources in the UK.

City of London Libraries

– see City Business Library, Guildhall Library and Barbican Library (under 'Ten of the Best')

Library of the Commonwealth Secretariat

Commonwealth Secretariat, Marlborough House, Pall Mall, London SW1Y 5HX
tel 020-7747 6164 (librarian), 020-7747 6167 (archivist)
email library@commonwealth.int
website http://thecommonwealth.org/library-and-archives

Collection covers politics and international relations, economics, education, health, gender, environment and management. Holds a comprehensive collection of Commonwealth Secretariat publications and its archives.

Crafts Council Research Library

Crafts Council, 44A Pentonville Road, London N1 9BY
tel 020-7806 2500
email reception@craftscouncil.org.uk
website www.craftscouncil.org.uk

A unique collection of materials mapping the development of contemporary craft since the mid-20th century. Holdings include over 7,000 books and catalogues, and 100 journals and magazines. Online access to Photostore, the national register of makers, and funding resources also provided. Open every Weds and Thurs 10am–5pm. by appointment.

Goethe-Institut London Library

50 Princes Gate, Exhibition Road, London SW7 2PH
tel 020-7596 4000
email library@london.goethe.org
email infoservice@london.goethe.org
website www.goethe.de/london

Specialises in German literature, especially contemporary fiction and drama, film DVDs, and books/audiovisual material on German culture and recent history. New e-library gives access to Goethe Institut libraries in the UK, Ireland and the Netherlands and allows electronic downloading of ebooks, e-audiobooks and electronic newspapers for a predetermined period of time.

Guildhall Library

Aldermanbury, London EC2V 7HH
tel 020-7332 1868/1870
email guildhall.library@cityoflondon.gov.uk
website www.cityoflondon.gov.uk/guildhalllibrary

Specialises in the history of London, especially the City, as well as holding other significant collections including business history, maritime history, clock and watchmaking, food and wine.

Lambeth Palace Library

15 Galleywall Road, London SE1 7JU
tel 020-7898 1400
email archives@churchofengland.org
website www.lambethpalacelibrary.org

The historic library of the Archbishops of Canterbury and the principal library and record office for the Church of England.

Library Services, The Open University

Open University, Walton Hall, Milton Keynes, MK7 6AA
tel (01908) 659001
email lib-help@open.ac.uk
website www.open.ac.uk/library

The Open University's electronic library service.

Linen Hall Library

17 Donegall Square North, Belfast BT1 5GB
tel 028-9032 1707
email info@linenhall.com
website www.linenhall.com

Renowned for its Irish and Local Studies Collection ranging from early Belfast and Ulster printed books to the 250,000 items in the internationally acclaimed Northern Ireland Political Collection (NIPC). Also expansive General Lending Collection.

National Art Library

Victoria & Albert Museum, Cromwell Road, South Kensington, London SW7 2RL
tel 020-7942 2400
email vanda@vam.ac.uk
website www.vam.ac.uk/page/n/national-art-library/

A major reference library and the Victoria & Albert Museum's curatorial department for the art, craft and design of the book.

National Maritime Museum

Greenwich, London SE10 9NF
tel 020-8858 4422
email library@rmg.co.uk
website www.rmg.co.uk/national-maritime-museum

Specialist maritime research library.

Natural History Museum Library and Information Services

Cromwell Road, London SW7 5BD
tel 020-7942 5011 (main information desk), 020-7942 5507/5873 (archives), 020-7942 5460 (general library), 020-7942 6156 (Ornithology Library, Tring)
website http://www.nhm.ac.uk/research-curation/science-facilities/library/

Online catalogue contains all library material acquired since 1989 and about 80% of earlier items. The collections are of international importance with extensive holdings of early works, periodicals and current literature, including over 800,000 books, 20,000 periodical titles (about half of them current) and original watercolour drawings, as well as maps, manuscripts and archives of the Museum. Contact via the website.

RNIB National Library Service

Far Cromwell Road, Bredbury, Stockport SK6 2SG
tel 0303 123 9999
email library@rnib.org.uk
website www.rnib.org.uk/library

The largest specialist library for readers with sight loss in the UK. Offers a comprehensive range of books and accessible information for children and adults in a range of formats including braille, large print and unabridged audio. Also provides free access to online reference material, braille sheet music, themed book lists and a quarterly reader magazine.

Science Museum Library

Library Office, The Science Museum's Dana Centre, 165 Queens's Gate, London SW7 5HD
tel 020-7942 4242
email SMLinfo@sciencemuseum.org.uk
website www.sciencemuseum.org.uk/about_us/collections/science_library.aspx

In recent years the Science Museum Library has specialised in the history of science and technology as its key role as part of the National Museum of Science & Industry. The library is no longer based at Imperial College Road. A new Research Centre with library facilities will open in late 2015.

Tate Library & Archive

Tate Library and Archives, Tate Britain, Millbank, London SW1P 4RG
tel 020-7887 8838
email reading.rooms@tate.org.uk
website www.tate.org.uk/research/library

Broadly covers those areas in which the Tate collects. The library collects British art from the Renaissance to the present day and international modern art from 1900. The archive covers British art from 1900 and contains a wealth of unpublished material on artists, art world figures and organisations.

Wellcome Library

183 Euston Road, London NW1 2BE
tel 020-7611 8722
email library@wellcome.ac.uk
website http://wellcomelibrary.org/

One of the world's major resources for the study of medical history. They also have an expanding collection of material relating to contemporary medicine and biomedical science in society.

Wellcome Images

tel 020-7611 8348
email images@wellcome.ac.uk
website http://wellcomeimages.org/

Moving Image and Sound Collections

tel 020-7611 8766
email misc@wellcome.ac.uk

Westminster Music Library

Victoria Library, 160 Buckingham Palace Road, London SW1W 9UD
tel 020-7641 6200
email musiclibrary@westminster.gov.uk
website www.westminster.gov.uk/library-opening-hours-and-contact-details#reference

Housed in Victoria Library, the Westminster Music Library holds a wide range of scores, orchestral sets, books on music, music journals and a collection of Mozart sound recordings, formerly the GLASS collection.

Women's Library @ LSE

Lionel Robbins Building,
The London School of Economics and Political Science, 10 Portugal Street, Westminster, London WC2A 2HD
tel 020-7955 7229
email library.enquiries@lse.ac.uk
website www.lse.ac.uk/library/collections/featuredCollections/womensLibraryLSE.aspx

Houses the most extensive collection of women's history in the UK. Part of the London School of Economics.

Working Class Movement Library

Jubilee House, 51 The Crescent, Salford M5 4WX
tel 0161 736 3601
email enquiries@wcml.org.uk
website www.wcml.org.uk

Records over 200 years of organising and campaigning by ordinary men and women. The collection provides an insight into working people's daily lives. Collection contains: books, pamphlets, archives, photographs, plays, poetry, songs, banners, posters, badges, cartoons, journals, biographies, reports.

Zoological Society of London Library

Outer Circle, Regent's Park, London NW1 4RY
tel 020-7449 6293
email library@zsl.org
website www.zsl.org/about-us/library

ORGANISATIONS AFFILIATED TO LIBRARIES

Association of Independent Libraries

website http://independentlibraries.co.uk

Founded in 1989 to develop the conservation, restoration and public awareness of independent libraries in the UK. Together, its members possess over 2 million books and have many listed buildings in their care.

Association of Senior and Children's Education Librarians (ASCEL)

website www.ascel.org.uk

A national membership network of Senior Children's and Education Librarians. It aims to stimulate developments and share initiatives relating to children and young people using public libraries and educational services.

CILIP (Chartered Institute of Library and Information Professionals)

website www.cilip.org.uk

The leading body representing the information professions in the UK. Its aim is to encourage a literate, knowledgeable and connected society. See also page 503.

School Library Association (SLA)

website www.sla.org.uk

The main goal of the SLA is to support people involved with school libraries, promoting high quality reading and learning opportunities for all.

Society of Chief Librarians (SCL)

website www.goscl.com

SCL leads and manages public libraries in England, Wales and Northern Ireland. It is made up of the head of service of every library authority, and advocates for continuous improvement of the public library service on behalf of local people.

ONLINE LIBRARY RESOURCES

An electronic or digital library is an online collection of resources including text, visual, video and audio material which is stored and viewed in electronic formats. Digital libraries can be affiliated to existing local or national public, specialist or academic libraries or they exist as an electronic-only repository. Some charge a subscription; others are free.

Internet Archive

website https://archive.org

A non-profit organisation that was founded to build an internet library. Its purposes include offering permanent access to historical collections that exist in digital format for researchers, historians, scholars, people with disabilities and the general public.

London Library eLibrary

website elibrary.londonlibrary.co.uk

The e-library of the London Library makes available to members a wide range of electronic publications, databases and journals.

Open Library

website https://openlibrary.org

Provides an open, editable library catalogue, working towards providing a web page for every book ever published.

Oxford Digital Library

website www.odl.ox.ac.uk

Offers central access to digital collections of the Oxford libraries.

Public Library Online

website http://uk.publiclibraryonline.com/

Provides access to a large range of fiction and non-fiction titles, from a range of renowned publishers.

Questia

website www.questia.com

Provides an online research and paper writing resource and aims to help people find and cite high-quality scholarly research.

Scribd

website www.scribd.com

A digital library subscription service offering access to a large collection of ebooks and written works.

Welsh Libraries E-library

website http://welshlibraries.org/e-resources/e-books

Provides information on libraries and books held by all the libraries in Wales.

World Digital Library

website www.wdl.org

Offers, free of charge and in multilingual format, significant primary materials from countries and cultures around the world.

ORGANISATIONS THAT SUPPORT AND ENCOURAGE LIBRARY USE

There are many non-profit organisations which champion the use of libraries in the UK. These include:

Book Trust

website www.booktrust.org.uk

Book Trust's main aim is to give everyone access to books and the chance to benefit from reading. See also page 498.

The Community Knowledge Hub for Libraries

website http://libraries.communityknowledgehub.org.uk/

Unites expert guidance and resources with an interactive community of organisations and local authorities involved with community-managed and supported libraries.

The Library Campaign

website www.librarycampaign.com

Aims to advance the lifelong education of the public by the promotion, support, assistance and improvement of libraries through the activities of friends and user groups.

National Libraries Day

website www.nationallibrariesday.org.uk

The first National Libraries Day took place in February 2012 and is now an annual event in the UK dedicated to the celebration of libraries and librarians. Author talks and competitions, etc are arranged by local authorities, universities, other providers of library services and local community groups.

National Literacy Trust

website www.literacytrust.org.uk

Aims to improve the reading, writing, speaking and listening skills in the UK's most disadvantaged communities, in part through access to libraries. See also page 517.

Public Libraries News

website www.publiclibrariesnews.com

Promotes knowledge about libraries in the UK.

The Reading Agency

website http://readingagency.org.uk

Aims to give everyone an equal chance in life by helping people become confident and enthusiastic readers, and that includes supporting library use.

Voices for the Library

website www.voicesforthelibrary.org.uk

Provides information about the public library service in the UK and the role of professional librarians. Library users can share their stories about the difference public libraries have made to their lives on the website.

Creative writing courses

Anyone wishing to participate in a writing course should first satisfy themselves as to its content and quality. For day and evening courses consult your local Adult Education Centre. Details of postgraduate writing courses follow on page 660.

The All New Writers' Holiday at Fishguard

School Bungalow, Church Road, Pontnewydd, Cwmbran, South Wales NP44 1AT
tel (01633) 489438
email gerry@writersholiday.net
website www.writersholiday.net
Contact Gerry Hobbs

A six-day annual conference for writers of all standards from absolute beginner to bestselling author. The event includes 14 courses. Also weekend workshops.

Alston Hall College

Alston Lane, Longridge, Preston PR3 3BP
tel (01772) 784661
email alstonhall@lancashire.gov.uk
website www.alstonhall.com

Provides high quality day and residential courses.

Arvon

Arvon, Free Word Centre, 60 Farringdon Road, London EC1R 3GA
tel 020-7324 2554
email national@arvon.org
website www.arvon.org
Contacts Suzie Jones, Joe Bibby
Centres:
Lumb Bank – The Ted Hughes Arvon Centre, Heptonstall, Hebden Bridge, West Yorkshire HX7 6DF
tel (01422) 843714
email lumbbank@arvon.org
Contact Becky Liddell
Totleigh Barton, Sheepwash, Beaworthy, Devon EX21 5NS
tel (01409) 231338
email totleighbarton@arvon.org
Contact Sue Walker
The Hurst – The John Osborne Arvon Centre Clunton, Craven Arms, Shrops. SY7 0JA
tel (01588) 640658
email thehurst@arvon.org
Contact Dan Pavitt

Residential creative writing courses and retreats in beautiful rural locations, led by highly respected authors. A powerful mix of workshops, individual tutorials and time and space to write. Grants are available to help with course fees. Founded 1968.

The Book Doctor and Creativity Coach

Canalot Studios, Kensal Road, London W10 5BN
tel 020-8964 1444
email philippa_pride@yahoo.co.uk
website www.thebookdoctor.co.uk
Contact Philippa Pride

How to Free Your Creativity, Write a Book and Get it Published writing courses in the UK and abroad as well as one-to-one coaching and consultancy.

University of Cambridge

Institute of Continuing Education, Madingley Hall, Madingley, Cambridge CB23 8AQ
tel (01223) 746262
email enquiries@ice.cam.ac.uk
website www.ice.cam.ac.uk
Contact Admissions Team

A wide range of short and part-time courses at introductory and advanced levels on literature, creative writing, art and art history. See website for details.

Central St Martins College of Arts & Design, Short Course Office

Granary Square, 1 Granary Building, King's Cross, London N1 4AA
tel 020-7514 7015
email shortcourse@csm.arts.ac.uk
website www.csm.arts.ac.uk/shortcourses
Contact The Short Course Office

Evening and day courses for beginners and intermediate levels.

Chalk the Sun Creative Writing

PO Box 67647, London SW19 4FA
tel 07852 483001
email creativewriting@chalkthesun.co.uk
website www.chalkthesun.co.uk
Programme Director Ardella Jones

Offers creative writing courses from beginners to specialist workshops for novelists, children's writers and scriptwriters with a team which includes CBBC producer Jonathan Wolfman, screenwriter Gillian Corderoy, playwright Danusia Iwaszko, academic Jo Hepplewhite and editor Simon Sideri. Also runs reading events, an Italian writing retreat, courses in Andalusia, one-to-one development tutorials, personalised distance learning and editing services. Classes are taught in small groups in the relaxed atmosphere of the Balham Bowls Bar and Bread and Roses.

City Lit

Keeley Street, London WC2B 4BA
tel 020-7492 2652

email writing@citylit.ac.uk
website www.citylit.ac.uk

The largest writing department in the country, which offers courses in a wide range of genres, both fiction and non-fiction. An outstanding-rated Ofsted institution, City Lit provides courses for both the curious and the committed at affordable prices, both in the centre of London and online. Founded 1919.

Community Creative Writing and Publishing

Sea Winds, 2 St Helens Terrace, Spittal, Berwick-upon-Tweed, Northumberland TD15 1RJ
tel (01289) 305213
email mavismaureen@btinternet.com
Author/Tutor Moderator Maureen Raper MBE, (member of the Society of Authors and the Royal Society of Literature)

Classes in creative writing for beginners and intermediates in Writing for Radio and Television, Writing for Children, Writing Romantic Fiction. Writing groups monthly; reading groups monthly at Berwick Library. Distance learning available for all.

The Complete Creative Writing Course

tel 020-7503 6285
email maggie@writingcourses.org.uk
website www.writingcourses.org.uk
Contact Maggie Hamand

Inspiring creative writing courses held at the Groucho Club in Soho and nearby locations, starting in January, April and September on Mondays and Saturdays, daytime and evenings. Offers beginner, intermediate and advanced courses, and runs weekend workshops and a summer school. Tutors are all published writers and experienced teachers. Courses of six to eight three-hour sessions include stimulating exercises, feedback, discussion and homework. Cost ranges from £295 to £425 inclusive of VAT.

Cove Park

Peaton Hill, Cove, Dunbartonshire, Scotland G84 0PE
tel (01436) 850123
email information@covepark.org
website www.covepark.org
Director Julian Forrester

Cove Park is Scotland's international artist residency centre and offers a year-round programme of residencies for writers and artists. For details of the funded residency programme, see the website.

Between September and May Cove Park offers the opportunity for self-funded residencies and retreats for writers and artists. Artists may stay for one week or more at any time during this period, subject to availability. Residents stay in Cove Park's spectacular self-catering accommodation overlooking Loch Long. Prices from £50 per night for a two-night stay, with discounts for longer stays. A studio can be hired for £20 per day. For more information and bookings visit the website. Established 2000.

The Creative Writer's Workshop

Kinvara, Co. Galway, Republic of Ireland
tel +353 (0)86 2523428
email office@thecreativewritersworkshop.com
website www.thecreativewritersworkshop.com
Founder Irene Graham

Writing retreats and workshops in Fiction, Memoir and Autobiographical Fiction at magnificent locations on the West Coast of Ireland, for new, emerging and advanced writers. Also provides private writing sessions with book writing coach Irene Graham. Established 1991.

CreativeWordsMatter

Chinook, Southdown Road, Shawford, Hants. SO21 2BY
tel (01962) 712307
email b.a.large@gmail.com
website www.creativewordsmatter.co.uk
Contact Barbara Large MBE, FRSA, HFUW

Offers individual and group editorial advice; nurturing, mentoring and line-editing of manuscripts for publication; and helps writers to build partnerships with literary agents and commissioning editors. In addition, a team of professional writers offers talks, workshops and one-to-one appointments on all genres of adult and children's fiction and non-fiction to art centres, festivals, universities, colleges, schools and businesses to stimulate new ideas and to develop writing projects for pleasure and publication.

Day courses on How To Successfully Self-Publish Your Book are offered in conjunction with CPI Group UK, part of Europe's largest printing group, to help writers plan a strategy that will produce the best product; well-written, with an attractive cover and a joy to read.

Emerson College

Emerson College, Forest Row, East Sussex RH18 5JX
tel (01342) 822238
email info@emerson.org.uk
website www.emerson.org.uk

A holistic centre for education based on the works of Rudolph Steiner. Emerson is a rich environment for personal, artistic and spiritual growth. Visual arts courses held September to June every year; one-term and shorter blocks available. Founded 1962.

The Faber Academy

Faber and Faber Ltd, Bloomsbury House, 74–77 Great Russell Street, London WC1B 3DA
tel 020-7927 3827
email academy@faber.co.uk
website www.faberacademy.co.uk
Contact Ian Ellard

Drawing on Faber's 80 years of publishing experience, Faber Academy offers high-quality creative writing courses, run by hand-picked authors, editors and agents. Provides the time, space and support needed to write and write well.

Fictionfire Literary Consultancy

110 Oxford Road, Old Marston, Oxford OX3 0RD
tel 07827 455723
email info@fictionfire.co.uk
website www.fictionfire.co.uk
Contact Lorna Fergusson

Fictionfire offers creative writing day courses and weekend workshops/retreats in Oxford and St Ives, plus shorter Focus Workshops on specific writing topics. Guest talks and workshops can be arranged for writers' groups, libraries, conferences and festivals. Manuscript appraisal, editing, mentoring and consultation also available. Founded 2009.

Fire in the Head

tel (01548) 821004
email roselle@fire-in-the-head.co.uk
website www.fire-in-the-head.co.uk
website www.thewildways.co.uk
Contact Roselle Angwin

Poetry, novel, life writing, therapeutic writing, eco-writing, journaling and personal development; retreats; short courses; online/distance learning courses; mentoring.

The French House Party, Carcasonne

The Jaylands, Abberley, Worcs. WR6 6BN
mobile 07900 322791
email enquiries@frenchhouseparty.co.uk
website www.frenchhouseparty.eu
Director Moira Martingale

Learning retreat in South of France which includes creative writing and songwriting courses.

GKBCInc Writer Academy

tel 0845 838 0936
email academy@gkbcinc.com
website http://gkbcinc.com/join-our-writer-academy
Academy Development Officer Susannah Plomer

A free online scheme that helps aspiring writers of any age to improve their skills and get their work published. Learn to write to a brief and then receive expert editorial feedback on your work. Users have access to exclusive training courses and every piece will be published on one of GKBCInc's partner websites.

Indian King Arts

Garmoe Cottage, 2 Trefrew Road, Camelford, Cornwall PL32 9TP
tel (01840) 212161
email indianking@btconnect.com

Weekly morning poetry group, facilitated by Helen Jagger; occasional all day poetry workshops and readings by guest poets; and bi-monthly novel workshop led by Karen Hayes. Also the home of the Poetry Society's North Cornwall Stanza.

The Inkwell Group

The Old Post Office, Kilmacanogue, Co. Wicklow, Republic of Ireland
tel +353 (0)1 2765921, +353 087 2835382
website www.inkwellwriters.ie
website www.writing.ie
Contact Vanessa Fox O'Loughlin

The Inkwell Group works with writers at all stages of their career to improve their work and to achieve their goals. Inkwell is a literary scout for some of Ireland and the UK's top agents and has assisted bestselling and award-winning authors to publication. Inkwell developed www.writing.ie, Ireland's national writing resources magazine and the National Emerging Writer Programme with Dublin UNESCO City of Literature (free writing advice from experts on DVD and online). Founded 2006.

Irish Writers Centre

19 Parnell Square, Dublin 1, Republic of Ireland
tel +353 (0)1 8721302
email info@writerscentre.ie
website www.writerscentre.ie
Director Valerie Bistany

The national resource centre for Irish writers. It runs workshops, seminars and events related to the art of writing, hosts professional developments seminars for writers, provides space for writers, writing groups and other literary organisations. It also provides information to writers and the general public.

Kilkenny Campus NUI Maynooth

St. Kieran's College, College Road, Kilkenny, Republic of Ireland
tel +353 (0)56 7775910
email kilkenny.campus@nuim.ie
website http://kilkenny.nuim.ie

NUI Certificate in Creative Writing for Publication held over ten weekends.

Knuston Hall

Irchester, Wellingborough, Northants NN29 7EU
tel (01933) 312104
email enquiries@knustonhall.org.uk
website www.knustonhall.org.uk

Knuston Hall offers an extensive programme of courses and events which can be attended on a residential or non residential basis.

London Writers' Workshop

5a Arundel Square, London N7 8AT
tel 020-7609 1839
email londonwritersworkshop@hotmail.co.uk
website www.londonwritersworkshop.co.uk
Contact Susan Oudot

Offers a range of one-day workshops and courses led by acclaimed novelist and scriptwriter Susan Oudot and best-selling author David Wingrove. Workshops range from Basics in Creative Writing through to Developing Your Skills, with specialist classes on How to Write and Pitch TV Drama and Writing Science Fiction. The tutors are able to draw on their wide-ranging experience to answer students' questions about the book and broadcasting industries.

Marlborough College Summer School

Marlborough, Wilts. SN8 1PA
tel (01672) 892388
email admin@mcsummerschool.org.uk
website www.summerschool.org.uk
Contact John Blake

Marlborough College Summer School is expanding from three to four weeks running from 12 July to 8 August with over 500 courses on offer.

The ever-changing course programme is refreshed and developed annually. Students can attend for one, two, three or four weeks. There are various courses, including nine creative writing courses, with each course being five half days or full days Monday-Friday. Accommodation available. Founded 1975.

The Memoir Writing Club

tel +353 (0)86 2523428
email office@thememoirwritingclub.com
website www.thememoirwritingclub.com
Founder Irene Graham

The Memoir Writing Club developed from Irene Graham's twenty years tutoring fiction and memoir writing workshops using right-brain/left-brain learning techniques. Provides a 12-week online memoir writing course and a six-month online memoir mentoring programme. Courses include the memoir writing workbook, audio tutorials, live writing discussions and submission of work for private feedback. Live discussions available in international time zones. Also provides ghostwriting, co-authoring services and private writing sessions with book writing coach Irene Graham.

Middlesex University Summer School

Summer School Office, Middlesex University, The Burroughs, London, NW4 4BT
tel 020-8411 5782
email sschool@mdx.ac.uk
website www.mdx.ac.uk/study/summer

Offers a number of creative writing courses.

Missenden Abbey Adult Learning

Great Missenden, Bucks. HP16 0BD
tel (01296) 383582
email adultlearningbucks@buckscc.gov.uk
website www.missendenabbey-al.co.uk

Weekend writing courses.

Morley College

61 Westminster Bridge Road, London SE1 7HT
tel 020-7450 1889
email enquiries@morleycollege.ac.uk
website www.morleycollege.ac.uk

Offers a number of creative writing courses – one day, one week and part-time day and evening throughout the year.

The National Academy of Writing

email rena@thenationalacademyofwriting.org.uk
website www.thenationalacademyofwriting.org.uk
Director Richard Beard, *Course Coordinator* Rena Brannan

The National Academy of Writing (NAW) organises one-off events and short courses based around the NAW Public Edit, a unique format for detailed textual feedback delivered by writer and Academy Director Richard Beard. NAW courses may also involve tuition, one-to-one mentoring and workshops, as well as the input of established writers and industry professionals. Writers who have spoken at NAW events include Kazuo Ishiguro, Jojo Moyes, Sir Michael Holroyd, Minette Walters, Evie Wyld and many others. Courses run at various points in the year, in London and Cambridge. Established 2000.

Newcastle University

School of English, Percy Building, Newcastle upon Tyne NE1 7RU
tel 0191 222 7619
email melanie.birch@ncl.ac.uk
website www.ncl.ac.uk/elll/creative
Contact Melanie Birch

Creative Writing short courses, one week intensive Spring School, a postgraduate certificate and degrees at MA and PhD level.

North West Kent College

Oakfield Lane, Dartford DA1 2JT
tel 0800 074 1447, (01322) 629400
email enquiries@nwkcollege.ac.uk
website www.nwkmedia.com
Contact Neil Nixon, Pathway Leader, Professional Writing

Open College of the Arts

The Michael Young Arts Centre, Redbrook Business Park, Wilthorpe Road, Barnsley S75 1JN
tel 0800 731 2116
email enquiries@oca-uk.com
website www.oca.ac.uk

Distance learning writing courses to develop skills or gain credits towards a degree.

Open Studies – Part-time Courses for Adults: Office of Lifelong Learning

Office of Lifelong Learning, University of Edinburgh, Paterson's Land, Holyrood Road, Edinburgh EH8 8AQ
tel 0131 650 4400

email openstudies@ed.ac.uk
website www.lifelong.ed.ac.uk

Offers a large number of creative writing courses.

Oxford University Summer School for Adults

Dept for Continuing Education, Rewley House, 1 Wellington Square, Oxford OX1 2JA
tel (01865) 270396
email oussa@conted.ox.ac.uk
website www.conted.ox.ac.uk/oussa
Contact Programme Administrator

A 4-week programme consisting of over 40 week-long courses, including creative writing and specialist literature courses.

Pitch to Publication

tel 07952 724299
email pitchtopublication@gmail.com
Contacts Glynis Kozma, Liat Hughes Joshi

Pitch to publication is an eight-week online course with telephone tuition and coaching. It is designed to take prospective non-fiction authors to the point where they are ready to submit a well-honed pitch to agents and publishers. Taught by two experienced, published non-fiction writers. Open to all. Courses run every 8-10 weeks.

Pitstop Refuelling Writers' Saturday and Weekend Workshops

Shawford Hall, Shawford, Winchester, Hants. SO21 2BY (and other venues)
tel (01962) 712307
email b.a.large@gmail.com
website www.creativewordsmatter.co.uk

For new and established writers. Offers the opportunity, throughout the year, for aspiring writers to work in small groups, under the guidance of professional writers, to improve their writing projects towards the goal of publication. At each workshop a literary agent or commisioning editor will offer one-to-one appointments. Phone or email for a free brochure.

Scottish Universities', International Summer School

21 Buccleuch Place, Edinburgh EH8 9LN
tel 0131 650 4369
email suiss@ed.ac.uk
website www.summer-school.hss.ed.ac.uk/suiss
Directors Dr Linden Bicket, Dr Tom Farrington

A four-week creative writing course for undergraduates, postgraduates and teachers, as well as published writers keen to widen their skills.

Swanwick, The Writers' Summer School

Hayes Conference Centre, Swanwick, Derbyshire DE55 1AU
tel 07765 890733
email secretary@swanwickwritersschool.org.uk
website www.swanwickwritersschool.org.uk
Takes place 8–14 August 2015 / 6–12 August 2016

A week-long programme for writers of all ages, abilities and genres featuring courses, talks, workshops, panels and one-to-one sessions, all run by expert tutors. Attracts top speakers such as Simon Brett, Alex Gray, Peter James, Helen Lederer, Deborah Moggach and other best-selling authors, playwrights, screenwriters and comedy writers plus the literary agents and publishers who represent them. Full-board accommodation available on site; day tickets also available. Founded 1949.

Travellers' Tales

92 Hillfield Road, London NW6 1QA
email info@travellerstales.org
website www.travellerstales.org
Director Jonathan Lorie, Contributing Editor of *Traveller* magazine

UK's leading training agency for travel writers and travel photographers. Offers vocational courses with the UK's top travel photographers and travel writers in London, Marrakech, Istanbul and Andalusia including beginners' weekends, masterclasses and creative retreats. Hosts the Travellers' Tales Festival of the world's leading travel writers and photographers. Online tuition also available. Founded 2004.

Tŷ Newydd Writers' Centre

Tŷ Newydd, Llanystumdwy, Cricieth, Gwynedd LL52 0LW
tel (01766) 522811
email tynewydd@literaturewales.org
website www.literaturewales.org

Tŷ Newydd, the former home of Prime Minister David Lloyd George, has hosted residential creative writing courses for writers of all abilities for over 25 years. Whether you're interested in a poetry masterclass, writing for the theatre, developing a novel for young adults or conquering the popular fiction market, there'll be a course in our programme suitable for you. Courses are open to everyone over the age of 16 and no qualifications are necessary. Literature Wales staff based at Tŷ Newydd can advise on the suitability of courses, and further details about each individual course can be obtained by visiting the website, or contacting the team by phone or email.

The Writers Bureau

The Writers Bureau, 8–10 Dutton Street, Manchester M3 1LE
tel 0161 819 9922
email studentservices@writersbureau.com
website www.writersbureau.com
Director of Studies Diana Nadin

The Writers Bureau offers a wide range of writing-related distance-learning courses including: Creative

Writing, Freelance Journalism, Proofreading and Copy-Editing, Writing for Children, Copywriting, Poetry, How to Market Your Book, Non-Fiction Writing, Article Writing, Fiction Writing, Novel and Short Story Writing, Biographies, Memoirs and Family Histories, How to Write for Competitions, Writing for the Internet, Report Writing, Business Writing and Effective Time Management.

The courses are suitable for both beginners and writers wanting to brush up on their skills. The only requirement for enrolment is a good command of English and plenty of enthusiasm! Also holds annual writing competitions with cash and free courses as prizes. See www.wbcompetition.com.

The Writers' Workshop

The Studio, Sheep Street, Charlbury, Oxon OX7 3RR
tel 0345 459 9560
email info@writersworkshop.co.uk
website www.writersworkshop.co.uk
Contacts Harry Bingham, Laura Wilkins, Nikki Holt

Runs courses for every range of experience, all tutored by professional authors, including: How to Write a Novel, Screenwriting, Writing for Children, Writing Picture Books, Writing from Life, Self-editing your Novel, Creative Writing Flying Start and the Complete Novel Writing Course. Plus events, editorial critiques, mentoring and the Festival of Writing. See website for full details.

The Writing College

16 Magdalen Road, Exeter EX2 4SY
tel (01392) 499488
email enquiries@writingcollege.com
website www.writingcollege.com
Director Richard Littler

'The Complete Writer' correspondence course: 28 modules divided into the practice and art of writing, writing genres and the business of writing. An MS appraisal service is also available. Founded 2000.

Writing Magazine Creative Writing Courses

Warners Group Publications, Fifth Floor, 31–32 Park Row, Leeds
tel 0113 200 2917
email writingcourses@warnersgroup.co.uk
website www.writers-online.co.uk/writing-courses/

Writing Magazine creative writing courses offer aspiring and published writers a selection of nine writing courses that can be studied from the comfort of your own home. Courses are offered in a wide range of genres: Fiction, Article and Freelance Journalism, Short Story, Scriptwriting, Writing for Children, Poetry, Polish Your Writing Style, Make the Most of Your Life Experiences and Becoming a Successful Writer.

Courses can be tailored to suit experience and ambitions. All tutors are successful published writers who will work to develop your writing through one-to-one feedback and constructive critiques. No previous writing experience necessary, just a good understanding of the English language. Courses are available by email and post.

Writingclasses.co.uk

tel 0131-554 1857
email marianne@writingclasses.co.uk
website www.writingclasses.co.uk
Director Marianne Wheelaghan

Established to help beginner and emerging writers hone their writing skills and develop story ideas in a nurturing online environment. The school offers a range of short online courses, which run in real time from four to ten weeks throughout the year. Experienced tutors, who are professional writers, give full feedback on all written work and are available 24/7 to support students with all aspects of the course. Students come from throughout the UK and around the world. As long as you have a passion for telling stories and a desire to improve your writing skills, you can sign up for a writingclasses.co.uk course. Founded 2002.

www.writing.ie

The Old Post Office, Kilmacanogue, Co. Wicklow, Republic of Ireland
tel +353 (0)1 2765921, +353 (0)87 2835382
email vanessa@writing.ie
Contact Vanessa Fox O'Loughlin

A national online writing resources magazine packed full of author tips and assistance for new, emerging and established writers. Features author interviews plus information on competitions, submission opportunities, festivals and events as well as writing courses and workshops. Contains agent and publisher listings, guest blogs, plus services for writers listings, book reviews, writers' groups, book club information and giveaways. View the National Emerging Writer Programme (video), a joint project with Dublin UNESCO City of Literature, free online at www.writing.ie; vital tips and advice from three of Ireland's top writers, Carlo Gebler, Sinead Moriarty and Declan Hughes.

POSTGRADUATE COURSES

Aberystwyth University

Department of English and Creative Writing, Hugh Owen Building, Penglais Campus, Aberystwyth, Ceredigion SY23 3DY
tel (01970) 622534
email jxr@aber.ac.uk
website www.aber.ac.uk/en/english
Contact Julie Roberts

MA in Creative Writing. PhD in Creative Writing.

Bath Spa University

Dept of Creative Writing and Publishing, School of Humanities and Cultural Industries,

Bath Spa University, Newton Park, Newton St Loe, Bath BA2 9BN
tel (01225) 875875
email b.soyinka@bathspa.ac.uk
website www.bathspa.ac.uk

MA in Creative Writing. MA in Writing for Young People. MA in Scriptwriting. MA in Travel and Nature Writing. PhD in Creative Writing.

Birkbeck College, University of London

Malet Street, London WC1E 7HX
tel 020-7631 6000
email a.taylor@bbk.ac.uk
website www.bbk.ac.uk
Contact Anne Marie Taylor

MA in Creative Writing: full- and part-time evening teaching. Applications from students writing fiction for young adults welcome. Tutors include: Julia Bell, Toby Litt and Russell Celyn Jones. PhD students also welcome but prospective students should consult with individual tutors before making an application. BA Creative Writing: four-years part-time, evening study. Course covers all genres from fiction to playwriting to poetry and practical courses on publishing and journalism. Screenwriting: MA/ postgraduate certificate.

University of Bolton

University of Bolton, Deane Road Campus, Bolton BL3 5AB
tel (01204) 903903
website www.bolton.ac.uk
Contact Programme Leader, Creative Writing

MA in Children's Literature & Culture, MPhil/PhD in Creative Writing Specialisms.

Brunel University

College of Business, Arts and Social Science, Brunel University, Uxbridge, Middlesex UB8 3PH
tel (01895) 265599
email course-enquiries@brunel.ac.uk
website www.brunel.ac.uk/cbass/arts-humanities

MA Creative Writing: The Novel and MA Creative Writing.

Cardiff University

Cardiff School of English and Philosophy, John Percival Building, Colum Drive, Cardiff CF10 3EU
tel 029-2087 4722
email encap-pg@cardiff.ac.uk
website www.cf.ac.uk/encap
Contact Rachel Thomas

MA in Creative Writing.

University of Chichester

Bishop Otter Campus, College Lane, Chichester, West Sussex PO19 6PE
tel (01243) 816000
email s.barker@chi.ac.uk
email s.norgate@chi.ac.uk
website www.chi.ac.uk
Contacts Prof. Simon Barker, Head of Department; Stephanie Norgate, MA in Creative Writing Programme Coordinator

MPhil/PhD in English, Literary Theory or Creative Writing. MA in Creative Writing.

City University

City University, Northampton Square, London EC1V 0HB
email enquiries@city.ac.uk
website www.city.ac.uk

MA Creative Writing (Non-Fiction), MA Creative Writing (Literary Novels, Crime/Thriller Novels), MA Creative Writing (Screenplay and Screenwriting), MA Creative Writing & Publishing.

University of Cumbria

Bowerham Road, Lancaster LA1 3JD
tel (01524) 384328
website www.cumbria.ac.uk

MA in Scriptwriting. MA in Creative Writing.

De Montfort University

Art, Design and Humanities Admissions Team, De Montfort University, The Gateway, Leicester LE1 9BH
tel 0116 257 7555
email adh@dmu.ac.uk
website www.dmu.ac.uk/tvscriptwriting
Contact Art, Design and Humanities Admissions Team

MA in Television Scriptwriting. This long-established course concentrates on the craft of television scriptwriting and prepares students for the competitive world of professional writing. It offers direct links and networking opportunities within the industry by introducing students to professional writers, script editors, agents and producers through a regular programme of guest lectures, workshops, location visits and one-to-one mentoring.

University of East Anglia

Admissions Office, School of Literature, Drama and Creative Writing, Faculty of Arts and Humanities, University of East Anglia, Norwich Research Park, Norwich NR4 7TJ
tel (01603) 591515
email admissions@uea.ac.uk
website www.uea.ac.uk/ldc
Contact Admissions Office

MA in Creative Writing: Prose. MA in Creative Writing: Poetry. MA in Creative Writing: Scriptwriting. MA in Biography and Creative Non-fiction. PhD in Creative and Critical Writing, MFA Creative Writing: Prose, MA Crime Fiction.

Edge Hill University

Department of English and History, St Helens Road, Ormskirk L39 4QP
tel (01695) 584274
website www.edgehill.ac.uk

For MA in Creative Writing (full- and part-time, established 1989) and PhD programmes in creative writing, contact Prof. Robert Sheppard (shepparr@edgehill.ac.uk). For BA in Creative Writing, contact Rodge Glass (rodge.glass@edgehill.ac.uk).

University of Edinburgh

Graduate School of Literatures, Languages & Cultures, David Hume Tower, Edinburgh EH8 9JX
tel 0131 650 8443
email rjamieso@staffmail.ed.ac.uk
website www.ed.ac.uk/englit/
Programme Director Dr Robert Alan Jamieson

MSc in Creative Writing.

University of Essex

Wivenhoe Park, Colchester CO4 3SQ
tel (01206) 872624
email thorj@essex.ac.uk
website www.essex.ac.uk
Contact Dept of Literature, Film, and Theatre Studies

MA in Creative Writing.

University of Exeter

College of Humanities, Department of Drama, Thornlea, New North Road, Exeter EX4 4LA
tel (01392) 722427
email drama@exeter.ac.uk
website www.exeter.ac.uk/drama

MA in Theatre Practice with specialist pathways.

Falmouth University

Falmouth Campus, Woodlane, Falmouth, Cornwall TR11 4RH
tel (01326) 213730
email admissions@falmouth.ac.uk
website www.falmouth.ac.uk
Contact Admissions Team

Writing at Falmouth has a reputation for excellence in teaching, renowned MAs and internationally recognised research. Blending a solid foundation in the study of English literature and a practical engagement with the craft and vocation of creative writing and opportunities in journalism, Falmouth focuses on the development of imaginative thinking and professional skills that are more important than ever to writers. Falmouth offers a wide range of postgraduate MA courses including International Journalism, Multimedia Broadcast Journalism and Professional Writing.

University of Glasgow

University of Glasgow, 4 University Gardens, Glasgow G12 8QQ
tel 0141 330 5850
website www.gla.ac.uk/schools/critical

MLitt, MFA and DFA in Creative Writing.

University of Hull

Dept of English, University of Hull, Cottingham Road, Hull HU6 7RX
tel (01482) 465315
email pgenglish@hull.ac.uk
website www.hull.ac.uk
Contact Prof. Martin Goodman

MA/PhD in Creative Writing.

Kingston University

River House, 53–57 High Street, Kingston upon Thames, Surrey KT1 1LQ
tel 020-8417 2361
website www.kingston.ac.uk
Contact Postgraduate Admissions Administrator

Courses in Creative Writing, Journalism, Playwriting, Publishing and Translation Studies.

Lancaster University

Dept of English & Creative Writing, County College, Lancaster University, Lancaster LA1 4YD
tel (01524) 594169
email l.kellett@lancaster.ac.uk
website www.lancs.ac.uk/fass/english
Contact The Secretary

MA in Creative Writing. MA in Creative Writing by Distance Learning.

University of Leeds

Faculty of Performance, Visual Arts & Communications, Woodhouse Lane, Leeds LS2 9JT
tel 0113 343 8710
email admissions-pci@leeds.ac.uk
website www.leeds.ac.uk
Admissions Secretary Jane Richardson

MA in Writing for Performance and Publication.

Leeds Metropolitan University

School of Film, Television and Performing Arts, Northern Film School, Electric Press, 1 Millennium Square, Leeds LS2 3AD
tel 0113 812 3330
email r.m.allen@leedsmet.ac.uk
website www.leedsmet.ac.uk
Contact Richard Allen, Course Administrator

MA in Film-making.

Liverpool John Moores University

Faculty of Arts, Professional & Social Studies, Redmonds Building, Brownlow Hill, Liverpool L3 5UG
tel 0151 231 5175
email APSadmissions@ljmu.ac.uk
website www.ljmu.ac.uk
Contact Programme Administrator

MA in Screenwriting and MA in Writing.

University of London, Goldsmiths

Dept of English and Comparative Literature,
Goldsmiths, University of London,
London SE14 6NW
tel 020-7919 7752
email r.bolley@gold.ac.uk
website www.gold.ac.uk
Contact Richard Bolley, Departmental Administrator

MPhil/PhD in Creative Writing, MA in Creative and Life Writing, BA in English with Creative Writing. The Department of English and Comparative Literature is also the home of the Goldsmiths Writers' Centre and the Goldsmiths Prize.

University of London, Goldsmiths College

Dept of Theatre and Performance,
Goldsmiths College, University of London,
London SE14 6NW
tel 020-7919 7171
email drama@gold.ac.uk
website www.gold.ac.uk
Contact Drama Secretary

MA in Writing for Performance.

University of London, King's College

School of Humanities, University of London,
King's College, Strand, London WC2R 2LS
tel 020-7848 1773
email kelina.gotman@kcl.ac.uk
website www.kcl.ac.uk
Contact Dr Kelina Gotman

MA in Theatre and Performance Studies.

University of London, Royal Holloway

Dept of English, Royal Holloway,
University of London, Egham, Surrey TW20 0EX
tel (01784) 434455/437520
website www.rhul.ac.uk/English

Contact Jo Shapcott

MA in Creative Writing, taught in central London.

London College of Communication

LCC School of Media, Elephant & Castle,
London SE1 6SB
tel 020-7514 6599
email info@lcc.arts.ac.uk
website www.lcc.arts.ac.uk
Contact Admissions Team

MA in Screenwriting (two-year part-time degree).

The London Film School

London Film School, 24 Shelton Street,
London WC2H 9UB
tel 020-7836 9642
email screenwriting@lfs.org.uk
website www.lfs.org.uk
Contact Brian Dunnigan

MA in Screenwriting.

University of Manchester

Centre for New Writing, Mansfield Cooper Building,
University of Manchester, Oxford Road,
Manchester M13 9PL
tel 0161 306 1259
email info-cnw@manchester.ac.uk
website www.manchester.ac.uk/centrefornewwriting

Whether you want to study creative writing at an undergraduate, MA or PhD level, Manchester has a programme in poetry, prose or literature to meet your needs. MA and PhD in Creative Writing MA and PhD in Contemporary Literature and Culture and the newly launched MA in Screenwriting.

The Manchester Writing School at Manchester Metropolitan University

Department of English, Rosamond Street West,
Off Oxford Road, Manchester M15 6LL
tel 0161 247 1787
email writingschool@mmu.ac.uk
website www.manchesterwritingschool.co.uk
Contact (admission and generic enquiries) James Draper, Manager: The Manchester Writing School at MMU

MA in Creative Writing: Writing for Children & Young Adults; campus-based and international online distance learning, available to study full time (two years) or part time (three years). September and January enrolment. Scholarships available. Evening taught, with strong industry links and all students completing a full-length book. Tutors include Sherry Ashworth, N.M. Browne, Carol Ann Duffy, Livi Michael. Optional units in Teaching Creative Writing, Crime Fiction, Journalism Skills, Poetry for Music, Historical Fiction and Place Writing; also available as short courses. Home of the Manchester Children's Book Festival, Manchester Poetry and Fiction Prizes and children's writing anthology projects.

Middlesex University

tel 020-8411 5555
email d.rain@mdx.ac.uk
website www.mdx.ac.uk

MA Writing, PhD Creative Writing.

National Film and Television School

National Film and Television School,
Beaconsfield Studios, Station Road, Beaconsfield,
Bucks. HP9 1LG
tel (01494) 671234
email info@nfts.co.uk
website www.nfts.co.uk

MA in Screenwriting and Diploma in Script Development. See website for application information.

Newcastle University

School of English Literature,
Language and Linguistics, Percy Building,
Newcastle upon Tyne NE1 7RU

tel 0191 222 7199
email pgadmissions@ncl.ac.uk
website www.ncl.ac.uk/elll
Contact Postgraduate Admission Secretary

MA in Creative Writing. Postgraduate Certificate in Creative Writing. PhD in Creative Writing.

Northumbria University

Faculty of Arts, Design and Social Sciences,
Lipman Building, Newcastle upon Tyne NE1 8ST
tel 0191 227 4444
email ar.admissions@northumbria.ac.uk
email steve.chambers@northumbria.ac.uk
email tony.williams@northumbria.ac.uk
website www.northumbria.ac.uk
Contacts Steve Chambers, Programme Leader (MA Creative Writing), Tony Williams, Course Leader (PG Cert.)

MA in Creative Writing, storytelling in prose and script. PG Cert. in Creative Writing in the Classroom; a postgraduate course for teachers wanting to teach creative writing.

Nottingham Trent University

School of Arts and Humanities,
Nottingham Trent University, Clifton Lane,
Nottingham NG11 8NS
tel 0115 848 4200
email rory.waterman@ntu.ac.uk
email hum.enquiries@ntu.ac.uk
website www.ntu.ac.uk/creativewriting
Contact Dr Rory Waterman, Programme Leader

MA in Creative Writing. One of the longest-established programmes of its kind in the UK, with many highly successful graduate writers. Diverse options include: Fiction; Poetry; Writing for Stage, Radio and Screen; Children's and Young Adult Fiction.

Oxford University

Dept for Continuing Education,
1 Wellington Square, Oxford OX1 2JA
tel (01865) 280145
website www.conted.ox.ac.uk/mstcw

Short online courses in creative writing: Getting Started in Creative Writing, Writing Drama, Writing Fiction, Writing Fiction for Young Adults, Writing Lives, Writing Poetry. Three intakes a year: October, January and April. *Email*: onlinecourses@conted.ox.ac.uk.

Creative Writing Summer School held at Exeter College: July/August. *Email*: ipwriters@conted.ox.ac.uk.

Master of Studies in Creative Writing (two years part-time): covering prose fiction, narrative non-fiction, radio and TV drama, poetry, stage drama and screenwriting. *Email*: mstcreativewriting@conted.ox.ac.uk.

Also offers an Undergraduate Diploma in Creative Writing with more than 200 contact hours. Students develop their skills in three major areas: poetry, prose and drama.

Plymouth University

Faculty of Arts, University of Plymouth,
Drake Circus, Plymouth PL4 8AA
tel (01752) 585100
email anthony.caleshu@plymouth.ac.uk
email admissions@plymouth.ac.uk
website www.plymouth.ac.uk
Contact Dr Anthony Caleshu, Senior Lecturer in English and Creative Writing

MA/Postgraduate Diploma in Creative Writing.

Queen's University, Belfast

School of English, Queen's University, Belfast,
Belfast BT7 1NN
tel 028-9097 3320
email l.drain@qub.ac.uk
website www.qub.ac.uk/schools/SchoolofEnglish/
Contact Linda Drain (Postgraduate Secretary)

MA/Postgraduate Diploma in Creative Writing. PhD in Creative Writing.

The Royal Central School of Speech and Drama

Embassy Theatre, Eton Avenue, London NW3 3HY
tel 020-7722 8183
website www.cssd.ac.uk

MA/postgraduate diploma in Advanced Theatre Practice. MA and MFA in Writing for Stage and Broadcast Media.

University of St Andrews

School of English, University of St Andrews,
St Andrews, Fife KY16 9AR
tel (01334) 462668
email pgeng@st-andrews.ac.uk
website www.st-andrews.ac.uk/english/postgraduate
Contact Alexandra Wallace, PG Administrator

PhD, MFA or MLitt in Creative Writing: Poetry, Prose and Writing for Performance options available.

University of Salford

MediaCity UK, Plot B4, Salford Quays,
Salford M50 2HE
tel 0161 295 4545
email enquiries@salford.ac.uk
website www.salford.ac.uk
Contact Admissions Tutor

MA/Postgraduate Diploma in Television and Radio Scriptwriting.

Sheffield Hallam University

Faculty of Development and Society,
Sheffield Hallam University, City Campus,
Sheffield S1 1WB
tel 0114 225 5555

email fdsenquiries@shu.ac.uk
website www.shu.ac.uk/prospectus/subject/english

MA/Postgraduate Diploma/Postgraduate Certificate in Writing. Recognised by Don Paterson (winner of the Whitbread Poetry Prize and two-time winner of the T.S. Eliot Prize) as one of the leading postgraduate courses in England. There are two intakes per year and applications should be received by the end of October for the January intake and by the end of March for the September intake.

University of South Wales

School of Humanities and Social Science, University of South Wales, Treforest, Pontypridd CF37 1DL
tel (01443) 654195
email philip.gross@southwales.ac.uk
website http://courses.southwales.ac.uk/courses/297-mphil-in-writing
Contact Prof. Philip Gross, Course Director

MPhil/PhD in Writing programme. One of the original creative writing master's programmes in the UK, this is a research degree with one-to-one supervision enhanced by three weekend workshopping residencies per year. Also an international students' version with a single five-day residency.

University of Wales Trinity Saint David

School of Cultural Studies, Lampeter Campus, Ceredigion SA48 7ED
tel (01570) 422351
email p.wright@trinitysaintdavid.ac.uk
email registrycc@tsd.ac.uk
website www.trinitysaintdavid.ac.uk/en/
Contact Dr Paul Wright

MA in Creative Writing, MA in Creative and Script Writing.

University of Warwick

Dept of English and Comparative Literary Studies, Humanities Building, University of Warwick, Coventry CV4 7AL
tel 024-7652 4928
email english@warwick.ac.uk
website www.warwick.ac.uk
Contact Tracie Williams, Warwick Writing Programme Secretary

MA in Writing.

University of Winchester

Winchester SO22 4NR
tel (01962) 827234
email course.enquiries@winchester.ac.uk
website www.winchester.ac.uk
Contact Course Enquiries & Applications

MA Writing for Children and MA Creative and Critical Writing.

Copyright and libel

Copyright questions

Gillian Haggart Davies answers questions to draw out some of the legal issues and explain the basics of how copyright works, or should work, for the benefit of the writer.

What is copyright?

Copyright is a negative right in the sense that it is not a right of possession but is a right of *exclusion*. However, if you know your rights it can be a strong legal tool because copyright law affords remedies in both the civil and criminal courts. Material will automatically be protected by copyright without registration (in the UK) if it is original, i.e. not copied. The onus is on you, the writer, and your publisher to do the work of protecting, policing and enforcing your valuable intellectual property. Copyright is different in every country – registration is not possible in the UK, Japan or the Netherlands; it is optional in the USA (for some works), China and India; and mandatory for some works in other jurisdictions (e.g. for some works in the Kyrgyz Republic, Mauritius and Nepal). Unfortunately, generally speaking, people do not respect copyright and there are ongoing issues to do with copyright, especially online, with large expanses of 'grey areas'.

I am a freelance writer and submitted an article to a magazine editor and heard nothing back. Six months later I read a feature in a Sunday newspaper which looks very similar. Can I sue someone?

Pitching ideas can be fraught with difficulty. In legal terms you do not have any protection under copyright law for 'ideas', but only for 'the expression of those ideas' – for the way in which the ideas have been 'clothed in words' to paraphrase a Learned Judge. It could be argued that in many ways this distinction between ideas and their expression does not work for writing and 'literary works'. But that won't help you in court or get you legal recompense if you are ripped off.

In the situation described, you would need to prove that your work came first in time; that your work was seen by the second writer or publisher; and that the second person copied unlawfully a 'substantial part' of your work (this is qualitative not quantitative), which these days involves a very woolly and subjective judicial comparison of one work weighed against the other. You would also need to be able to counter any claims that the subject matter is not capable of being monopolised by you and show that there is actual language copying. Further, you might then have to fend off counter-arguments from the other party that you did not have copyright in the first place. The other writer can rely on a 'defence' that she has 'incidentally included' the text; or that her use is 'fair dealing' (because she is using it for a permitted purpose, for example of reporting news or current affairs; or that it is for research for non-commercial purposes; or for private use; or for 'criticism or review'; or that it is parody, pastiche or satire. These defences are actually referred to in the legislation as 'exceptions' and are very strict, i.e. they have always been difficult to make out.

In addition, as if all that were not complicated enough, the person doing the 'copying' or publishing could say that she had an 'implied licence' from you to do so; or that she had a common law right under trusts law: this would arise, say, if she and you had been accustomed to dealing with each other in such a way that you commonly gave her original work and she used/copied it.

Avoid these difficulties by taking practical pre-emptive steps: mark your speculative pieces 'in confidence' and add '© Your Name 201X'. Using the © symbol puts people on notice that you are aware of your rights. It would also have an effect later on if it came to litigation evidentially, i.e. if a person sees the copyright sign but nevertheless goes ahead and uses work without permission, the defence of 'innocent dissemination' cannot be relied upon.

You did not have copyright in the first place: if the subject matter is 'out there', i.e. common knowledge, copyright law may not protect the first work. The law is very contradictory in this area, as can be seen in these three cases which went to court: the persistent lifting of facts from another newspaper, even with rewriting, was deemed a copyright infringement; but copyright did protect a detailed sequence of ideas where precise wording was not copied; the fact that an author went to primary sources did not necessarily ensure that he was not copyright-infringing. However, copyright law does weigh heavily in favour of protecting the originator.

If a newspaper pays for an article and I then want to sell the story to a magazine, am I free under the copyright law to do so?

Yes, provided that you have not assigned copyright or licensed exclusive use to the newspaper. When selling your work to newspapers or magazines, make it clear in writing, that you are selling only First or Second Serial Rights, not your copyright.

Does being paid a kill fee affect my copyright in a given piece?

No, provided that you have not assigned or licensed your copyright to the magazine or newspaper. Broadly, never agree to an assignation; it is irreversible. Always license, and those parts of copyright you want to license, for example print-only; UK only; not television rights, etc. Copyright rights are infinitely divisible and negotiable. If you have inadvertently or purposely granted copyright permission to the publisher and the publisher prints the piece, and you have taken a kill fee, don't forget that you can at least also claim 'secondary licence' income from the collective pool of monies collected on behalf of UK authors by both the ALCS (see page 687) and PLR (see page 140) if you are named on the piece. This may amount to only a tiny amount of money but it may take the sting out of the tail.

I am writing an (unauthorised) biography of a novelist. Can I quote her novels – since they are published and 'public domain'?

Using extracts and quotes is a very difficult area and there is no easy answer to this. If the author has definitely been deceased for 70 years or more, you may be fine; the work may have passed into the 'public domain'. However, unpublished works require caution. In general, unpublished works are protected by copyright as soon as they are 'expressed' and copyright belongs to the author until/unless published and rights are transferred to a publisher. Protection for unpublished works lasts for 50 years (usually); Crown copyright lasts for 125 years for unpublished works – it's a legal minefield!

Generally, copyright law requires you to ask permission and (usually) pay a fee for reuse. There is no exact recipe for the amount of money payable or the number of words you can 'take' before you need to pay. A new law passed on 1 October 2014 says, somewhat vaguely, that you can take 'no more than is required for the specific purpose for which it is needed'. To quote from the legislation: 'Copyright in a work is not infringed by the use of a quotation from the work (whether for criticism or review or otherwise) provided that (a) the work has been made available to the public, (b) the use of the quotation is fair dealing with the work, (c) *the extent of the quotation is no more than is required by the specific purpose for which it is used* [emphasis added], and (d) the quotation is accompanied by a sufficient acknowledgement (*unless this would be impossible for reasons of practicality or otherwise* [emphasis added])' [Copyright and Rights in Performances (Quotation and Parody) Regulations 2014, No. 2356 (in force since 1 June 2014)]. But does this help? Is it not a bit woolly? In the biography example here, how much would 'no more than is necessary' be? A line from every work? A paragraph from every work? A page? The entirety of one work but excerpts only of others … or none at all? What if the biography is authorised, not unauthorised? These are all unanswered questions and untried by case law.

I want to use a quote from another book but don't know who owns the copyright. Can I just put it in quotes and use it?

If you cannot identify the source of the quote, we enter the murky waters of 'orphan works'. A new scheme is now in place whereby you can buy a licence to use an 'orphan work' from the IPO (Intellectual Property Office), for an application fee of £20 (for a single 'work', e.g. book), up to £80 for 30 'works', plus a licence fee, which will depend on the work and what you say about its use on the application form. The licence will last for seven years, which is the window of time allowed for a copyright owner to 'claim' the work (which goes on the IPO orphan works register when it becomes a licensed subject under the scheme).

The IPO will not grant an orphan-use licence if it thinks your use will be 'derogatory' of the copyright work, or if you are unable to show that you have made diligent attempts to trace the copyright owner, so the old rules about making such efforts now apply in statutory form.'Diligent' efforts to trace the copyright owner could include contacting publishers, searching the WATCH (Writers Artists and their Copyright Holders) database (www.watch-file.com, http://norman.hrc.utexas.edu/watch), and placing an advertisement in the *TLS*, the *Bookseller*, etc). Keep a record of all your efforts in case the copyright question comes back to bite you later, and use a disclaimer on your material. In an ideal world, all content would be tagged with details of what is permissible and how to contact the owner. [See www.alcs.co.uk/wiseup; BPP Legal Advice Clinic www.whatcanIdowiththiscontent.com; IPO orphan works https://www.gov.uk/apply-for-a-licence-to-use-an-orphan-work; and the section above relating to quoting from a novel.]

My publisher has forgotten to assert my copyright on the imprint page. What does that mean for me?

Technically, what is usually asserted on the imprint page is the moral right to be identified as author of the work. This 'paternity right' is lost if it is not 'asserted', so if it is not on the imprint page or anywhere else you lose the right. Moral rights are copyrights, separate to and additional to what we normally refer to as '('economic') copyright': they protect the personal side of creation, in that they are about the integrity of the work and the person/reputation of the creator. Whereas the 'main'/economic copyright protection is there to ensure you get revenues from your work, for example licence fees and royalties. Both economic copyrights and moral rights were conferred by the 1988 UK statute and derive from the Berne Convention. They exist separately, so you can keep moral rights and 'licence away' copyright (economic copyrights). And so in reverse, even if your moral right to be identified as author is lost, your other rights – economic copyright and the moral right to not have your work subjected to 'derogatory treatment' – remain with you. Moral rights cannot be licensed or assigned because they are personal to the author, but they can be 'waived'; for example, a ghostwriter may well waive the right to be identified as author. Moral rights are very flexible and useful, but are not widely used.

I've found an illustration I want to use for the cover of a book that I'm self-publishing. I chose the picture (dated 1928) on purpose because the artist is out of copyright and the picture is in the 'public domain'. Why is the picture library, which holds the image, charging a reproduction fee?

You have to pay a reproduction fee under copyright law because of the separate copyright issue for photography. Because the original artwork was photographed, copyright vests separately in the photograph (of the artwork) as opposed to the artwork itself. It is a controversial area and one where the UK/US legal systems are split. Make sure that standing behind this is a contract with your publishing services provider identifying you as the copyright holder. Do not cede any rights. You should be granting the publisher a non-exclusive licence to publish your book only.

I included someone's work on my blog, but as I blog for free and it's not a money-making exercise, can I be sued for copyright infringement?

Yes you can. If the person alleging copyright infringement can show she has copyright in the work, that you had access to her work, can show you copied the whole of that work or a 'substantial part' of it, and that you did not have permission, you could well be infringing criminal and civil copyright laws. The point of copyright law – the economic as opposed to the moral rights aspect – is to protect the economic interests of the original copyright owner. If she can demonstrate that her position has been undermined by your blog in terms of her market share having diminished and/or that sales have been adversely affected, etc or if she can show that you have not paid her any reuse fee or asked permission or acknowledged her authorship, you are on very thin ice.

I retweeted, edited, two lines from Twitter. I tweet for free and it's not a money-making exercise, can I be sued for copyright infringement?

A similar answer to the above. 'Yes' or at least 'probably yes'. A ruling of the Court of Justice of the European Union (CJEU) interpreting EU copyright law strongly suggests copyright vests in anything that is the original author's creation, and in the EU case in point (*Infopaq*, 2009) that applied to an 11-word extract. This is in spite of the fact that there is a broader general principle in copyright that an 'insubstantial part' of a work does not enjoy copyright protection in the first place, and therefore there could be no breach. If you had a good lawyer she could argue either way as this is a grey area. The situation in the USA may be different but seems certainly arguable. An alternative way of viewing the situation is that this is a 'quote', and therefore 'exceptional', i.e. non-infringing under new legislation introduced in 2014 (see above). But the issues have not been tested in court and again, I would say, are wide open to argument.

My book has been made available by a free book download site but I never agreed to this. What can I do?

Contact your publisher or ask the site direct (if it's a self-published work) to remove it from their website. If they do not act or do not respond, get legal advice: a lawyer will be able to issue a warning followed by a 'take down notice', followed if necessary by a court injunction. However, this is very difficult for cases worth under £10,000. And it is no understatement to say that the present system of access to justice and costs of lawyers and litigation will prove to be a significant hurdle for most writers. Take practical steps to protect copyright in your own works yourself by setting up a Google Alert for every title you own.

First steps legal advice may be available from the Society of Authors (see page 485), the Writers' Guild of Great Britain (see page 487), the National Union of Journalists (NUJ), the Society for Editors and Proofreaders (SfEP, page 526) or your local BusinessLink or an intellectual property specialist adviser like Own-It or Artquest (which deals with the visual arts but carries advice applicable to writers too).

Gillian Haggart Davies MA (Hons), LLB is the author of *Copyright Law for Artists, Designers and Photographers* (A&C Black 2010) and *Copyright Law for Writers, Editors and Publishers* (A&C Black 2011).

See also...

- *Writing for newspapers*, page 3
- *Writing for magazines*, page 8
- *Writing features for newspapers and magazines*, page 13
- *The Copyright Licensing Agency Ltd*, page 685
- *Design and Artists Copyright Society*, page 689
- *UK copyright law*, page 672
- *The laws of Privacy, Confidentiality and Data Protection*, page 691
- *Defamation*, page 696

UK copyright law

Jonathan Moss describes the main types of work which may qualify for copyright protection, or related protection as a design, together with some of the problems which may be faced by readers of this *Yearbook* in terms of protecting their own works or avoiding infringement of existing works in the UK. This is a technical area of the law, and one which is constantly developing; in an article of this length, it is not possible to deal fully with all the complexities of the law. It must also be emphasised that copyright is national in scope, so whilst works of UK authors will be protected in many other countries of the world, and works of foreign authors will generally be protected in the UK, foreign laws may deal differently with questions of subsistence, ownership and infringement.

Copyright law creates and protects a property right in a number of different kinds of works. UK copyright arises immediately upon creation of a relevant work, and provides its owner with the right to take action to prevent others from doing a number of 'restricted acts' without the owner's consent.

The major UK statute is the Copyright, Designs & Patents Act 1988 ('the Act') which came into force on 1 August 1989. It replaced the Copyright Act 1956, which had replaced the first modern Act, the Copyright Act 1911. All three Acts remain relevant because a property right which may last for many years (see below) and questions of the subsistence, ownership and protection of works may be tested according to the law in force at the time a work was made or first published.

Useful websites

www.ipo.gov.uk/

Useful information, guidance notes and legislation are available on the website of the UK Intellectual Property Office (previously the Patent Office).

www.wipo.int/

Website of the World Intellectual Property Organisation.

www.bailii.org/

Provides free and broadly comprehensive access to UK case-law and legislation, with links to equivalent foreign websites. Legislation on the site may be in an unamended form.

Since the 1988 Act came into force it has been amended pretty much continuously, mainly in the light of various EU Directives. An important change occurred on 1 January 1996, when the duration of copyright protection in respect of most works (see below) was extended from 'life of the author' plus 50 years to life plus 70 years. New rights have been created, such as the database right which came into existence on 1 January 1998, and the important Community registered and unregistered design rights which came into effect in 2003. Numerous other changes have been made, some of the most significant arose out of the Information Society Directive (2001/29), implemented by the Copyright and Related Rights Regulations 2003, which sought in particular to meet the challenges posed by the Internet and electronic rights management, and changes to remedies required by the Enforcement Directive (2004/48) and by the Digital Economy Act 2010. Further important changes were made by the Broadcasting Acts of 1990 and 1996. These continuing changes do mean that it is important to check that you are using the current version of the Act. The website of the UK Intellectual Property Office (see box) is a useful resource.

Continuing relevance of old law

In this article, I discuss the law as it currently stands, but where a work was made before 1 August 1989 one needs to consider the law in force at the time of creation (or, possibly, first publication) in order to assess the existence or scope of any rights. Particular difficulties arise with foreign works, which may qualify for protection in the UK as a matter of international obligation. Each Act has contained transitional provisions and these, as well as the substantive provisions of any relevant earlier Act, need to be considered where, for instance, you wish to use an earlier work and need to decide whether permission is needed and, if so, who may grant it. In addition, publishing or licence agreements designed for use under older Acts and prior to the development of modern technologies may be unsuitable for current use.

Copyright protection of works

Copyright does not subsist in ideas – that is the province of patents and the law of confidence. Copyright protects the expression of ideas, the particular form of the subject matter in which the author's idea has been expressed, not the idea itself. This distinction was examined in *Baigent & Leigh* v. *The Random House Group* [2007] FSR 24: Dan Brown was alleged to have copied the 'Central Theme', consisting of a series of historical facts, conjectures or theories, from the Claimants' book, *The Holy Blood and the Holy Grail*, in writing his bestselling novel *The Da Vinci Code*. Whilst the judge found evidence of copying, the Court of Appeal held that what Dan Brown took from HBHG 'amounted to generalised propositions, at too high a level of abstraction to qualify for copyright protection, because it was not the product of the application of skill and labour by the authors of HBHG in the creation of their literary work. It lay on the wrong side of the line between ideas and their expression.' (Lloyd LJ at para. 99). Copyright does not 'extend to clothing information, facts, ideas, theories and themes with exclusive property rights, so as to enable the Claimants to monopolise historical research or knowledge and prevent the legitimate use of historical and biographical material, theories… arguments… general hypotheses… or general themes' (Mummery LJ at para. 156).

The difficulty in seeking to apply this guidance to other cases is that the Court of Appeal emphasised that case-law cannot lay down any clear principle from which one may tell whether what is sought to be protected in any particular case is on the 'ideas' side of the dividing line, or on the 'expression' side. What can be said is that in cases of artistic copyright at least, '…the more abstract and simple the copied idea, the less likely it is to constitute a substantial part. Originality, in the sense of the contribution of the author's skill and labour, tends to lie in the detail with which the basic idea is presented.' (Lord Hoffman in *Designers Guild* v. *Russell Williams (Textiles) Ltd* [2000] 1 WLR 2416). What is more, these pre-2009 UK decisions may need to be re-evaluated in the light of the breadth of the CJEU's decision in *Infopaq* (see below).

One area of particular difficulty for establishing a dividing line between ideas and expression is photography. This problem was an issue in the case of *Temple Island Collections* v. *New English Teas* [2012] FSR 9 where a photographer had taken a picture of a red London bus going over Westminster Bridge with the houses of Parliament in the background. The picture had then been manipulated to remove all colour except for that of the red London bus. A similar, but not identical photo was then created by the defendant. The judge held that the later photograph was an infringing copy. Whether this case of similar works infringing will be applied outside of manipulated photographs remains to be seen, but at the time of writing it has not yet been followed in another case.

Of course, if someone has written an outline, script or screenplay for a television show, film, etc and that idea is confidential, then dual protection may arise in the confidential idea embodied in the documents and in the literary (and sometimes artistic) works in which the idea is recorded. If the idea is used, but not the form, this might give rise to an action for breach of confidence, but not for infringement of copyright. Copyright prevents the copying of the *material form* in which the idea has been presented, or of a substantial part of it, measured in terms of quality, not quantity (see further below). One result is that so-called 'format right' cases rarely succeed.

Section 1 of the Act sets out a number of different categories of works which can be the subject of copyright protection. These are:

- original literary, dramatic, musical or artistic works,
- sound recordings, films or broadcasts, and
- typographical arrangements of published editions.

These works are further defined in ss.3–8 (see box for examples).

However, no work of any description enjoys copyright protection until it has been recorded in a tangible form, as s.3(2) provides that no copyright shall subsist in a literary, musical or artistic work until it has been recorded in writing or otherwise.

On the other hand, all that is required to achieve copyright protection is to record the original work in an appropriate medium. Once that has been done, copyright will subsist in the work in the UK (assuming that the qualifying features set out below are present) without any formality of registration or otherwise. There is, for instance, no need to publish a work to protect it. However, where a work is unpublished, it will be more difficult for a party to prove that another party copied that work.

Nonetheless, you can derive practical benefits from keeping a proper record of the development, design and creation of a work. Drafts or preliminary sketches should be kept and dated, as should source or research material, so as to be able to show the development of your work. It is also a wise precaution (especially where works are to be submitted to potential publishers or purchasers) to take a complete copy of the documents and send them to yourself or lodge them with a responsible third party, sealed and dated, so as to be able to provide cogent evidence of the form or content of the work at that date. Such evidence may help the author, whether as claimant or defendant, to prove the independence of the creation of his work and its originality in a copyright infringement or breach of confidence action. If, as is often the case, a work is being prepared on a computer, it is advisable to keep separate electronic copies for each stage at which the work is potentially revealed to third parties.

Originality

Under the 1988 Act, literary, dramatic, artistic and musical works must be 'original' to qualify for copyright protection. According to the CJEU in *Infopaq* (above), originality means that a work must be 'its author's own intellectual creation'. Subject to that point, UK law does not impose any concept of objective originality. Originality relates to the 'expression of the thought', rather than to the thought itself. The policy of copyright protection and its limited scope (set out above) explain why the threshold requirement of originality does not impose 'any objective standard of novelty, usefulness, inventiveness, aesthetic merit, quality or value'; so, a work may be 'complete rubbish', yet have copyright protection (see again Mummery LJ in *Sawkins*). A work need only be original in the sense of being the product of skill and labour on the part of the author.

There may be considerable difficulty, at times, in deciding whether a work is of sufficient originality, or has sufficient original features to attract copyright, particularly if there have been a series of similar designs, see e.g. *L.A. Gear Inc.* [1993] FSR 121, *Biotrading* [1998] FSR 109. There are similar difficulties where there has been amendment of an existing work. In *Sawkins* (above), the question was whether or not the editorial work done by Dr Sawkins on works by the baroque composer, Lalande, had created new musical works. The result turned partly on the definition of 'music', but the nature of Dr Sawkins' input was such that he was found to have created an original musical work with its own copyright. So an adaptation of an existing work may have its own copyright protection (see *Cala Homes* [1995] FSR 818) but making a '*slavish* copy' of a work will not create an original work: (*Interlego AG* [1989] AC 217). This is a matter of degree – some copying may take skill (Jacob LJ in *Sawkins*). If the work gives particular expression to a commonplace idea or an old tale, copyright may subsist in it, for example in *Christoffer* v. *Poseidon Film Distributors Limited* (6/10/99) a script for an animated film of a story from Homer's *Odyssey* was found to be an original literary work. But, as the *Da Vinci* case showed, whilst copyright may subsist in the work, the unlicensed use only of facts or ideas contained in it may not infringe that copyright. Copyright protection will be limited to the original features of the work, or those features created or chosen by the author's input of skill and labour.

Historically, the titles of books and periodicals, headlines, or phrases like advertising slogans, were not generally given copyright protection, however much original thought was involved in their creation, because they were too short to be deemed literary works. Following *Infopaq*, that may no longer be the case, because the CJEU said that even a short part of a longer work may be entitled to copyright protection if that part also amounts to its author's 'own intellectual creation'. In *Newspaper Licensing Agency Ltd* v. *Meltwater Holding BV* [2011] RPC 7, it was therefore held that headlines were capable of being literary works, whether independently or as part of the articles to which they related, depending upon the process of creation and the identification of the skill and labour that had gone into them. The *Meltwater* case was appealed up to the Supreme Court and part of the case has now been referred to the CJEU, however the question on the appeal is whether or not temporary copies of these headlines created by browsing fall within an exception that allows a defence of copyright infringement for temporary copies.

The CJEU has also held, in relation to portrait photographs, that the level of creativity required for a work to be original is minimal (*Painer* [2012] ECDR 6). Thus for

Definitions under the Act

Literary work is defined as: 'any work, other than a dramatic or musical work, which is written, spoken or sung, and accordingly includes: (a) a table or compilation other than a database, (b) a computer program, (c) preparatory design material for a computer program and (d) a database.'

A musical work means: 'a work consisting of music, exclusive of any words or action intended to be sung, spoken or performed with the music.'

An artistic work means: '(a) a graphic work, photograph, sculpture or collage, irrespective of artistic quality, (b) a work of architecture being a building or model for a building, or (c) a work of artistic craftsmanship.' What constitutes a sculpture or work of artistic craftsmanship was discussed in relation to *Star Wars* stormtrooper helmets in *Lucasfilm* v. *Ainsworth*. The Supreme Court held that the stormtrooper helmet (and the rest of the armour) was a work of neither sculpture nor artistic craftsmanship, instead it was properly protected by design law.

These categories of work are not mutually exclusive, e.g. a film may be protected both as a film and as a dramatic work. See *Norowzian* v. *Arks* [2000] FSR 363. However, the position as to databases is particularly complicated: rights may arise under the Act or under the Database Directive 96/9, the question of how this works has been referred to the CJEU: see *Football Dataco Ltd* v. *Yahoo! UK Ltd* [2010] EWCA Civ 1380, 9 Dec 2010.

photographs the angle, composition and special techniques used may be enough to give even the most basic photograph copyright protection. Therefore, even very short excerpts of text, from a headline or from a book, or very simple photographs, could theoretically infringe another person's copyright. However, it is very hard to determine where exactly this line will get drawn.

Sound recordings or films which are copies of pre-existing sound recordings or films, and broadcasts which infringe rights in another broadcast are not protected by copyright.

Computer 'languages', and the ideas or logic underlying them, are not protected as copyright works; such protection extends only to the computer programs: see *Navitaire* v. *Easyjet* [2004] EWHC 1725. So it is legitimate to emulate a program for a computer game and produce a game with similar characteristics, as long as the program code and the graphics are not copied (*Nova Productions Limited* v. *Mazooma Games Limited* [2007] RPC 25). In the case of *SAS Institute* (2013 EWHC 69) the court held, following a response from the CJEU, that copyright in a computer program does not protect either the programming language in which it is written or its interfaces (specifically, its data file formats) or its functionality from being copied. The SAS case is currently under appeal and the issue of what copyright in software actually protects will not be fully resolved for a number of years.

Qualification

The Act is limited in its effects to the UK (and for example to colonies to which it may be extended by Order). It is aimed primarily at protecting the works of British citizens, or works first published in the UK. However, in line with various international conventions, copyright protection in the UK is also accorded to the works of nationals of many foreign states, as well as to works first published in those states, on a reciprocal basis.

There is a principle of equal treatment for works of nationals of other member states of the European Union, so that protection must be offered to such works here: see *Phil Collins* [1993] 3 CMLR 773.

The importance of these rules mainly arises when one is trying to find out whether a foreign work is protected by copyright here, for instance, to make a film based upon a foreign novel.

Traditionally, if a work was not protected in the UK then it could be copied in the UK, even if it was in copyright elsewhere, i.e. copyright was a territorial right limited in its scope. This is still the case, but a corollary of this was that a defendant could only be sued in the country where the infringement occurred. However, the recent decision of the Supreme Court in *Lucasfilm* v. *Ainsworth* [2012] 1 AC 208 means that an action can now be brought in England for the infringement of US copyright in the USA (e.g. if a party sells into the USA through the internet). This still requires an infringement to occur *in the USA* but this is relatively easy due to the presence of the internet.

Ownership

The general rule is that the copyright in a work will first be owned by its author, the creator of the work. The definition of 'author' in relation to films and sound recordings has changed over the years; currently, the author of a sound recording is its producer, and the authors of a film are the producer and principal director.

One important exception to the general rule is that the copyright in a work made by an employee in the course of his or her employment will belong to their employer, subject to any agreement to the contrary. However, this rule does not apply to freelance designers, journalists, etc and not even to self-employed company directors. This obviously may lead to problems if the question of copyright ownership is not dealt with when an agreement is made to create, purchase or use a work. In the absence of an appropriate agreement, the legal title may simply not be owned by the apparent owner, who will generally need it if he wishes to sue for infringement, and it is often difficult to formalise the position long after creation of the work. More importantly, perhaps, there have been numerous cases in which the extent of the rights obtained in a 'commissioned' work has been disputed, simply because of the lack of any clear agreement at the outset between the author and the 'commissioner'. See for example *Griggs* v. *Evans* (below). It is very important for writers and artists of all kinds to agree about ownership/terms of use at the outset and record them in writing, particularly where you are being paid to create a work – any such arrangement may be a 'commission'. It is equally important to understand the difference between an assignment and a licence (again, see below).

Where a work is produced by several people who collaborate so that each one's contribution is not distinct from that of the other(s), then they will be joint authors of the work, for example where two people write a play, each rewriting what the other produces, there will be a joint work. But where two people collaborate to write a song, one producing the lyrics and the other the music, there will be two separate copyright works, the copyright of which will be owned by each of the authors separately. The importance of knowing whether the copyright is joint or not arises:

- in working out the duration of the copyright, and
- from the fact that joint works can only be exploited with the agreement of all the joint authors, so that all of them have to join in any licence, although each of them can sue for infringement without joining the other(s) as a claimant in the proceedings.

Duration of copyright

With effect from 1 January 1996, copyright in literary, dramatic, musical or artistic works expires at the end of the period of 70 years from the end of the calendar year in which the author dies (s.12(1)). Where there are joint authors, then the 70 years runs from the death of the last of them to die. If the author is unknown, there will be 70 years protection from the date the work was made or (where applicable) first made available to the public. Previously, the protection was for 'life plus 50'. (NB See 'Infringement' below for important limits on the copyright protection of artistic works.)

The extended 70-year term also applies to films, and runs from the end of the calendar year in which the death occurs of the last to die of the principal director, the author of the screenplay or the dialogue, or the composer of any music created for the film (s.13B). This obviously may be a nightmare to establish, and there are certain presumptions in s.66A which may help someone wishing to use material from an old film.

However, sound recordings are still protected by copyright only for 50 years from the year of making or release (s.13A). This affects many 'classic' recordings of pop music, and (after much international negotiation) it is possible, though not certain, that the term may be extended to 70 or even 95 years. Broadcasts and computer-generated works get only 50 years protection.

The new longer term applies without difficulty to works created after 1 January 1996 and to works in copyright on 31 December 1995. The owner of the extended copyright will be the person who owned it on 31 December 1995, unless he had only a limited term of ownership, in which case the extra 20 years will be added on to the reversionary term.

Where copyright had expired here, but the author died between 50 and 70 years ago, the position is more complicated. EC Directive 93/98 provided that if a work was protected by copyright anywhere in the EU on 1 July 1995, copyright would revive for it in the other EU states until the end of the same 70-year period. This may make it necessary to look at the position in the states offering a longer term of protection, namely Germany, France and Spain.

Ownership of the *revived* term of copyright will belong to the person who was the owner of the copyright when the initial term expired, though if that person died (or a company, etc ceased to exist) before 1 January 1996, then the revived term will vest in his personal representatives.

Any licence affecting a copyright work which was in force on 31 December 1995 and was for the full term of the copyright continues to have effect during any extended term of copyright, subject to any agreement to the contrary.

The increased term offered to works of other EU nationals as a result of the Term Directive is not offered automatically to the nationals of other states, but will only apply where an equally long term is offered in their state of origin.

Where acts are carried out in relation to such revived copyright works as a result of things done whilst they were in the public domain, protection from infringement is available. A licence as of right may also be available, on giving notice to the copyright owner and paying a royalty.

Dealing with copyright works

Ownership of the copyright in a work gives the exclusive right to deal with the work in a number of ways, and essentially stops all unauthorised exploitation of the work. Ownership of the copyright is capable of being separated from ownership of the material form in which the work is embodied, depending upon the terms of any agreement or the circumstances. So, buying an original piece of artwork will not in general carry with it the legal title to the copyright, as an effective assignment must be in writing signed by the assignor (although beneficial ownership might pass: see below).

Copyright works can be exploited by their owners in two ways:

• **Assignment**. In an assignment, rights in the work are sold, with the owner retaining no interest in it (except, possibly, for a claim to royalties). An assignment must be in writing, signed by or on behalf of the assignor, but no other formality is required. One can make an assignment of future copyright under s.91: Where the author of a work not yet made agrees in writing that he will assign the rights in the future work to another, copyright vests in the assignee immediately upon the creation of the work, without further formalities.

• **Licensing**. A licence arises where permission is granted to another to exploit the right whilst the licensor retains overall ownership. Licences do not need to take any particular form, and may be granted orally. However, an exclusive licence (i.e. one which excludes even the copyright owner himself from exploiting the work) must be in writing if the licensee is to enjoy rights in respect of infringements concurrent with those of the copyright owner. Non-exclusive licensees get more limited rights. See ss.101 and 101A of the Act.

Agreements dealing with copyright should make it clear whether an assignment or a licence is being granted. There may be significant advantages for an author in granting only a licence, for a third party who acquires the assignee's rights will not necessarily be subject to the assignee's obligations, for example to pay royalties (see *Barker* v. *Stickney* [1919] 1 KB 121). However, an assignment may expressly provide for the rights to revert to the author if the assignee breaches the agreement (see *Crosstown Music* v. *Rive Droite Music* [2011] FSR 5). If it is unclear whether a licence or an assignment was intended or agreed, the Court is likely to find that the grantee took the minimum rights necessary for his intended use of the work, quite probably an exclusive licence rather than an assignment (*Ray* v. *Classic FM plc* [1998] FSR 622), unless the work was 'commissioned' from the author. This case, *Griggs* (see above), and many other similar disputes, show how very important it is, if you make an agreement to create a work for someone else, or ask someone to make a work for you or your business, to discuss who is to own the copyright, or what is to be the extent of any licence, and to record the agreed position in writing. The question of moral rights (see below) should also be considered by the parties.

Assignments and licences often split up the various rights contained within the copyright. So, for instance, a licence might be granted to one person to publish a novel in book form, another person might be granted the film, television and video rights, and yet another the right to translate the novel into other languages. Obviously, the author should seek to grant the narrowest possible rights on each occasion and retain other rights for future exploitation. All such agreements must be drafted carefully; the author must negotiate as best he can. Failure to make clear what is covered by a licence can lead to problems. It is particularly important to make clear what forms of exploitation are licensed, and whether the licence will extend to new technologies. See for example *MGN Ltd* v. *Grisbrook* [2011] ECDR 4: photos held in a picture library were not licensed for use on a website.

Assignments and licences may also confer rights according to territory, dividing the USA from the EU or different EU countries one from the other. Any such agreement should take into account divergences between different national copyright laws. Furthermore, when seeking to divide rights between different territories of the EU there is a danger of infringing the competition rules of the EU. Professional advice should be taken, as breach of these rules may attract a fine and can render the agreement void in whole or in part.

Licences can, of course, be of varying lengths. There is no need for a licence to be granted for the whole term of copyright. Well-drafted licences will provide for termination on breach, including the failure of the licensee to exploit the work, and on the insolvency of the licensee and will specify whether the rights may be assigned or sub-licensed.

Copyright may be assigned by will. A bequest of an original document, etc embodying an unpublished copyright work will carry the copyright.

Infringement

The main type of infringement is what is commonly thought of as plagiarism, that is, copying the work. In fact, copyright confers on the owner the exclusive right to do a number of specified acts, so that anyone doing those acts without his permission will normally infringe. It is not necessary to copy a work exactly or use all of it; it is sufficient if a substantial part is used. That question is to be judged on a qualitative not a quantitative basis, bearing in mind that it is the skill and labour of the author which is to be protected (see *Ravenscroft* v. *Herbert* [1980] RPC 193 and *Designers Guild*). The ECJ has recently held that an extract just 11 words long might be protected, if it reproduced 'the expression of the intellectual creation of their author' – see *Infopaq* (above), as might a newspaper headline: see *Meltwater* (above). Primary infringement, such as copying, can be committed innocently of any intention to infringe.

The form of infringement common to all forms of copyright works is that of copying. This means reproducing the work in any material form. Infringement may occur from direct copying or where an existing work provides the inspiration for a later one, for example by including edited extracts from a history book in a novel (*Ravenscroft*), using a photograph as the inspiration for a painting (*Baumann* v. *Fussell* [1978] RPC 485), or words from a verse of one song in another (*Ludlow Music* v. *Williams* [2001] FSR 271). Infringement will not necessarily be prevented merely by the application of significant new skill and labour by the infringer, nor by a change of medium.

In the case of a two-dimensional artistic work, reproduction can mean making a copy in three dimensions, and vice versa. However, s.51 of the Act provides that in the case of a 'design document or model' (for definition, see 'Design right' below) for something which is not *itself* an artistic work, it is no infringement to make an article to that design. This means that whilst it would be an infringement of copyright to make an article from a design drawing for, say, a sculpture, it will not be an infringement of copyright to make a handbag from a copy of the design drawing for it, or from a handbag which one has purchased.

Copying a film, broadcast or cable programme can include making a copy of the whole or a substantial part of any image from it (see s.17(4)). This means that copying one frame of the film will be an infringement. It is not an infringement of copyright in a film to reshoot the film (*Norowzian*) (though there would doubtless be an infringement of the copyright in underlying works such as the literary copyright in the screenplay).

Copying is generally proved by showing substantial similarities between the original and the alleged copy, plus an opportunity to copy. Surprisingly often, minor errors in the original are reproduced by an infringer.

Copying need not be direct, so that, for instance, where the copyright is in a fabric design, copying the material without ever having seen the original drawing will still be an infringement, as will 'reverse engineering' of industrial designs, for example to make unlicensed spare parts (*British Leyland* [1986] AC 577; *Mars* v. *Teknowledge* [2000] FSR 138).

Issuing copies of a work to the public (e.g. by putting them on sale) when they have not previously been put into circulation in the UK is also a primary infringement of all types of work.

Other acts which may amount to an infringement depend upon the nature of the work. It will be an infringement of the copyright in a literary, dramatic or musical work to perform it in public, whether by live performance or by playing recordings. Similarly, it is an infringement of the copyright in a sound recording, film, broadcast or cable programme to play or show it in public. Many copyright works will also be infringed by the rental or lending of copies of the work.

It is also an infringement to 'communicate' a work to the public, especially by making it available electronically, such as on the internet (s.20). See, for example, *Twentieth Century Fox* v. *Newzbin* [2010] EWHC 608 (infringement by facilitating illegal downloading). The Digital Economy Act 2010 is designed to control online infringement of copyright (especially in music, films and games) by imposing duties on ISPs, with an industry code to be approved or made by Ofcom.

It is also possible to infringe by making an adaptation of a literary, dramatic or musical work. An adaptation includes, in the case of a literary work, a translation, in the case of a non-dramatic work, making a dramatic work of it, and vice versa. A transcription or arrangement of a musical work is an adaptation of it.

There are also a number of 'secondary' (but nonetheless very common and commercially important) infringements – see box.

It is also an infringement to authorise another person to commit any act of primary infringement.

As copyright law is territorial, it is only an infringement of UK copyright to carry out the prescribed acts in the UK, save that it is possible to infringe by authorising an infringement in the UK even where the act of authorisation takes place abroad.

Exceptions to infringement

The Act provides a large number of exceptions to the rules on infringement.

UK design right

Many designs are excluded from copyright protection by s.51 (see above). Section 52 of the Act used to limit the term of copyright protection given to certain types of artistic works, if they were applied industrially, to 25 years from first industrial application. However, at the time of writing s.52 is in the process of being repealed and therefore many newly created designs now will receive protection for the full term of copyright rather than being limited to 25 years. Such artistic works may instead be protected by the UK unregistered 'design right' created by ss.213–64 of the Act or by Community design right. Like copyright, design right depends upon the creation of a suitable design by a 'qualifying person'.

UK unregistered design right is granted to original designs consisting of the shape or configuration (internal or external) of the whole or part of an article, not being merely 'surface decoration'. Even very simple designs may be protected. However, a design is not original if it was commonplace in the design field in question at the time of its creation, meaning a design of a type which would excite no 'peculiar attention' amongst those in the trade, or one which amounts to a run-of-the-mill combination of well-known features (*Farmers Build* [1999] RPC 461). Designs are not protected if they consist of a method or

'Secondary' infringements

Secondary infringements consist not of making infringing copies, but of dealing with existing infringing copies in some way. It is an infringement to import an infringing copy into the UK, and to possess in the course of business, or to sell, hire, offer for sale or hire, or distribute in the course of trade an infringing copy. However, none of these acts will be an infringement unless the alleged infringer knew or had reason to believe that the articles were infringing copies. What is sufficient knowledge will depend upon the facts of each case (see *LA Gear Inc.* [1992] FSR 121, *ZYX Records* v. *King* [1997] 2 All ER 132 and *Pensher Security* [2000] RPC 249). Merely putting someone on notice of a dispute as to ownership of copyright may not suffice to give him or her reason to believe in infringement for this purpose. But someone who is informed that he is infringing 'yet carries out no sensible enquiries, and does nothing in the face of continued assertions of the copyright' may become someone with 'reason to believe' the claim: *Nouveau Fabrics* v. *Voyage Decoration* [2004] EWHC 895; *Hutchison* [1995] FSR 365.

Other secondary infringements consist of permitting a place to be used for a public performance in which copyright is infringed and supplying apparatus to be used for infringing public performance, again, in each case, with safeguards for innocent acts.

principle of construction, or are dictated by the shape, etc of an article to which the new article is to be connected or of which it is to form part, the so-called 'must-fit' and 'must-match' exclusions. In *Ocular Sciences* [1997] RPC 289, these exclusions had a devastating effect upon design rights claimed for contact lens designs. See also *Dyson* v. *Qualtex* [2006] RPC 31 in which these exclusions were applied to spare parts for Dyson vacuum cleaners.

UK design right subsists in designs made by or for qualifying persons (see, broadly, 'Qualification', above) or first marketed in the UK or EU or any other country to which the provision may be extended by Order.

UK design right lasts only 15 years from the end of the year in which it was first recorded or an article made to the design, or (if shorter) ten years from the end of the year in which articles made according to the design were first sold or hired out. During the last five years of the term of protection, a licence to use the design can be obtained 'as of right' on payment of a proper licence fee. Hence, design right may give only five years 'absolute' protection, as opposed to the 'life plus 70' of copyright.

The designer will be the owner of the right, unless it was commissioned, in which case the commissioner will be the first owner. An employee's designs made in the course of employment will belong to the employer. The right given to the owner of a design right is the exclusive right to reproduce the design for commercial purposes. The rules as to assignments, licensing and infringement, both primary and secondary, are substantially similar to those described above in relation to copyright, as are the remedies available.

The law on UK registered designs coexists with the right given by the unregistered UK design right discussed above. The Registered Design Act 1949 has been amended (and expanded) in line with EU legislation, and permits the registration of designs consisting of the appearance of the whole or any part of a product resulting from features of the product itself, such as shape, materials, etc or from the ornamentation of the product. It covers industrial or handicraft items, their packaging or get-up, etc. Designs must be novel and not solely dictated by function. The range of designs which may be registered is wider than under the old law, and designs need not necessarily have 'eye appeal'. Such designs provide a monopoly right renewable for up to 25 years. For further explanation see the guidance on the Patent Office website.

Community designs

In addition to UK design right and registered designs, EU Regulation 6/2002 created two Community design regimes, one for registered and one for unregistered designs. It is increasingly common for designers to rely on Community design right, especially where there are problems in relying on UK design right, for example where a surface decoration, pattern or colouring is central to the design. Artists and industrial designers may wish to consider registering their designs, whilst infringements should now generally be considered under both the UK and Community design right regimes.

It is not possible in the space available here to describe these new regimes in detail but the Regulation is available online (http://oami.europa.eu/en/design/pdf/reg2002_6.pdf).

Moral rights

The Act also provides for the protection of certain 'moral rights'.

The right of 'paternity' is for the author of a copyright literary, dramatic, musical or artistic work, or the director of a copyright film, to be identified as the author/director, largely whenever the work is commercially exploited (s.77). See *Sawkins*.

However, the right does not arise unless it has been 'asserted' by appropriate words in writing (see end), or in the case of an artistic work by ensuring that the artist's name appears on the frame, etc. There are exceptions to the right, in particular where first ownership of the copyright vested in the author's or director's employer.

The right of 'integrity' protects work from 'derogatory treatment', meaning an addition to, deletion from, alteration or adaptation of a work which amounts to distortion or mutilation of the work or is otherwise prejudicial to the honour or reputation of the author/director. Again, infringement of the right takes place when the maltreated work is published commercially or performed or exhibited in public. There are various exceptions set out in s.81 of the Act, in particular where the publication is in a newspaper, etc and the work was made for inclusion in it or made available with the author's consent.

Where the copyright in the work vested first in the author's or director's employer, he or she has no right to 'integrity' unless identified at the time of the relevant act or on published copies of the work.

These rights subsist for as long as the copyright in the work subsists.

A third moral right conferred by the Act is not to have a literary, dramatic, musical or artistic work falsely attributed to one as author, or to have a film falsely attributed to one as director, again where the work in question is published, etc. This right subsists until 20 years after a person's death.

None of these rights can be assigned during the person's lifetime, but all of them either pass on the person's death as directed by his or her will or fall into his residuary estate.

A fourth but rather different moral right is conferred by s.85. It gives a person who has commissioned the taking of photographs for private purposes a right to prevent copies of the work being issued to the public, etc.

The remedies for breach of these moral rights again include damages and an injunction, although s.103(2) specifically foresees the granting of an injunction qualified by a right to the defendant to do the acts complained of, if subject to a suitable disclaimer.

Moral rights are exercisable in relation to works in which the copyright has revived subject to any waiver or assertion of the right made before 1 January 1996 (see details as to who may exercise rights in paragraph 22 of the Regulations).

NOTICE
JONATHAN MOSS hereby asserts and gives notice of his right under s.77 of the Copyright, Designs & Patents Act 1988 to be identified as the author of the foregoing article.

Jonathan Moss is a barrister in private practice in London, and specialises in patents, copyright, designs, trade marks, and similar intellectual property and 'media' work. He is also a qualified US lawyer, being a member of the New York State Bar.

Further reading

Cornish, William, *Intellectual Property: Patents, Copyrights, Trademarks & Allied Rights* (Sweet & Maxwell, 2010)
Bently, Lionel and Sherman, Brad, *Intellectual Property Law*, OUP, 2008
Garnett, Rayner James and Davies, *Copinger and Skone James on Copyright*, Sweet & Maxwell, 16th edn, 2010

Copyright Acts

Copyright, Designs and Patents Act 1998 (but it is vital to use an up-to-date amended version). See www.ipo.gov.uk

The Duration of Copyright and Rights in Performances Regulations 1995 (SI 1995 No 3297)

The Copyright and Rights in Databases Regulations 1997 (SI 1997/3032) amended by the Copyright and Rights in Databases (Amendment) Regulations 2003 (SI 2003/2501)

The Copyright and Related Rights Regulations 2003 (SI 2003 No 2498)

The Intellectual Property (Enforcement, etc) Regulations 2006 (SI 2006 No 1028)

The Performances (Moral Rights, etc) Regulations 2006 (SI 2006 No 18)

see also Numerous Orders in Council

Council Regulation 6/2002

Directive 2006/116/EC (codifying provisions)

See also...

- *Copyright questions*, page 667

The Copyright Licensing Agency Ltd

The Copyright Licensing Agency (CLA) licenses organisations to copy extracts from copyright publications on behalf of the authors, publishers and visual creators it represents.

CLA's licences permit limited copying from print and digital publications. This copying includes photocopying, scanning and emailing of articles and extracts from books, journals and magazines, as well as digital copying from electronic publications, online titles and websites. CLA issues its licences to schools, further and higher education, businesses and government bodies. The money collected is distributed to the copyright owners to ensure that they are fairly rewarded for the use of their intellectual property.

Why was CLA established?

CLA was set up by its owners, the Authors' Licensing and Collecting Society (ALCS, see page 687) and the Publishers Licensing Society (PLS), and has an agency agreement with the Design and Artists Copyright Society (DACS, page 689), which represents visual artists, such as photographers, illustrators and painters. CLA represents creators and publishers by licensing the copying of their work and promoting the role and value of copyright generally. By championing copyright it is helping to sustain creativity and maintain the incentive to produce new work.

Further information

The Copyright Licensing Agency Ltd
Saffron House, 6–10 Kirby Street,
London EC1N 8TS
tel 020-7400 3100
email cla@cla.co.uk
website www.cla.co.uk

How CLA helps creators and users of copyright work

CLA allows licensed users access to millions of titles worldwide. In return, CLA ensures that creators, artists, photographers and writers, along with publishers, are fairly recompensed by the payment of royalties derived from the licence fees which CLA collects and distributes.

Through this collective licensing system CLA is able to provide users with the simplest and most cost-effective means of obtaining authorisation for the photocopying and scanning of published works, albeit under strict copy limits.

CLA has licences which enable digitisation of existing print material, enabling users to scan and electronically send extracts from print copyright works.

In addition, CLA has launched a series of licences for business and government which allow users to reuse and copy from digital electronic and online publications, including websites. Writers and publishers can benefit further from the increased income generated from these enhanced licences, which operate under the same copy limits as the established photocopying licences.

Who is licensed?

CLA's licences are available to three principal sectors:

- education (schools, further and higher education);
- government (central departments, local authorities, public bodies); and
- business (businesses, industry and the professions).

CLA offers licences to meet the specific needs of each sector and user groups within each sector. Depending on the requirement, there are both blanket and transactional li licences available. Every licence allows copying from most books, journals, magazines and periodicals published in the UK. Most licences include digital copying permissions granted by copyright owners on an opt-in basis.

International dimension

Many countries have established equivalents to CLA and the number of such agencies is set to grow. Nearly all these agencies, including CLA, are members of the International Federation of Reproduction Rights Organisations (IFRRO).

Through reciprocal arrangements covering 36 overseas territories, including the USA, Canada and most EU countries, CLA's licences allow copying from an expanding list of international publications. CLA receives monies from these territories for the copying of UK material abroad, passing it on to UK rights holders.

Distribution of licence fees

The fees collected from licensees are forwarded to PLS, ALCS and DACS for distribution to publishers, writers and visual artists respectively. The allocation of fees is based on subscriptions, library holdings and detailed surveys of copying activity. CLA has collected and distributed to rights holders over £814 million since 1983. For the year 2012/13, £66.8 million was paid to creators and publishers in the UK and abroad.

Enabling access, protecting creativity

CLA believes it is important to raise awareness of copyright and the need to protect the creativity of artists, authors and publishers. To this end, it organises a range of activities such as copyright workshops in schools, seminars for businesses and institutions and an extensive programme of exhibitions and other events.

CLA believes in working positively together with representative bodies in each sector, meaning legal action is rare. However, organisations – especially in the business sector – are made aware that copyright is a legally enforceable right and not a voluntary option. CLA's compliance arm, Copywatch (www.copywatch.org), is active in these sectors to educate users and seek out illegal copying.

By supporting rights holders in this way, CLA plays an important role in maintaining the value of their work, thereby sustaining creativity and its benefit to all. Through protection of this sort the creative industries in the UK have been able to grow to support millions of jobs and contribute to the economy.

See also...

- *Copyright questions*, page 667
- *Authors' Licensing and Collecting Society*, page 687
- *Design and Artists Copyright Society*, page 689

Authors' Licensing and Collecting Society

The Authors' Licensing and Collecting Society is the rights management society for UK writers.

The Authors' Licensing and Collecting Society (ALCS) is the UK collective rights management society for writers. Established in 1977, it represents the interests of all UK writers and aims to ensure that they are fairly compensated for any works that are copied, broadcast or recorded.

A non-profit company, ALCS was set up in the wake of the campaign to establish a Public Lending Right (see page 140) to help writers protect and exploit their collective rights. Today, it is the largest writers' organisation in the UK with a membership of approximately 87,000. In the financial year of 2013/14, over £32 million (gross) in royalties were paid out to writers.

ALCS is committed to ensuring that the rights of writers, both intellectual property and moral, are fully respected and fairly rewarded. It represents all types of writers and includes educational, research and academic authors drawn from the professions: scriptwriters, adaptors, playwrights, poets, editors and freelance journalists, across the print and broadcast media.

Internationally recognised as a leading authority on copyright matters and authors' interests, ALCS is committed to fostering an awareness of intellectual property issues among the writing community. It maintains a close watching brief on all matters affecting copyright, both in the UK and internationally, and makes regular representations to the UK government and the European Union.

ALCS collects fees that are difficult, time-consuming or legally impossible for writers and their representatives to claim on an individual basis, money that is nonetheless due to them. To date, it has distributed over £380 million in secondary royalties to writers. Over the years, ALCS has developed highly specialised knowledge and sophisticated systems that can track writers and their works against any secondary use for which they are due payment. A network of international contacts and reciprocal agreements with foreign collecting societies also ensures that UK writers are compensated for any similar use overseas.

The primary sources of fees due to writers are secondary royalties from the following.

Membership

Authors' Licensing and Collecting Society Ltd
The Writers' House, 13 Haydon Street,
London EC3N 1DB
tel 020-7264 5700
email alcs@alcs.co.uk
website www.alcs.co.uk
Chief Executive Owen Atkinson

Membership is open to all writers and successors to their estates at a one-off fee of £36 for Ordinary membership. Members of the Society of Authors, the Writers' Guild of Great Britain, National Union of Journalists, Chartered Institute of Journalists and British Association of Journalists have free Ordinary membership of ALCS. Operations are primarily funded through a commission levied on distributions and membership fees. The commission on funds generated for Ordinary members is currently 9.75%. Most writers will find that this, together with a number of other membership benefits, provides good value.

Photocopying

The single largest source of income, this is administered by the Copyright Licensing Agency (CLA, see page 685). Created in 1982 by ALCS and the Publishers Licensing Society (PLS),

CLA grants licences to users for copying books and serials. This includes schools, colleges, universities, central and local government departments, as well as the British Library, businesses and other institutions. Licence fees are based on the number of people who benefit and the number of copies made. The revenue from this is then split between the rights holders: authors, publishers and artists. Money due to authors is transferred to ALCS for distribution. ALCS also receives photocopying payments from foreign sources.

Digitisation

In 1999, CLA launched its licensing scheme for the digitisation of printed texts. It offers licences to organisations for storing and using digital versions of authors' printed works that have been scanned into a computer. Again, the fees are split between authors and publishers.

Foreign Public Lending Right

The Public Lending Right (PLR) system pays authors whose books are borrowed from public libraries. Through reciprocal agreements, ALCS members receive payment whenever their books are borrowed from German, Belgian, Dutch, French, Austrian, Spanish, Estonian and Irish libraries. Please note that ALCS does not administer the UK Public Lending Right; this is managed directly by the UK PLR Office (see page 140).

ALCS also receives other payments from Germany. These cover the loan of academic, scientific and technical titles from academic libraries; extracts of authors' works in textbooks and the press, together with other one-off fees.

Simultaneous cable retransmission

This involves the simultaneous showing of one country's television signals in another country, via a cable network. Cable companies pay a central collecting organisation a percentage of their subscription fees, which must be collectively administered. This sum is then divided by the rights holders. ALCS receives the writers' share for British programmes containing literary and dramatic material and distributes it to them.

Educational recording

ALCS, together with the main broadcasters and rights holders, set up the Educational Recording Agency (ERA) in 1989 to offer licences to educational establishments. ERA collects fees from the licensees and pays ALCS the amount due to writers for their literary works.

Other sources of income include a blank tape levy and small, miscellaneous literary rights.

Tracing authors

ALCS is dedicated to protecting and promoting authors' rights and enabling writers to maximise their income. It is committed to ensuring that royalties due to writers are efficiently collected and speedily distributed to them. One of its greatest challenges is finding some of the writers for whom it holds funds and ensuring that they claim their money.

Any published author or broadcast writer could have some funds held by ALCS for them. It may be a nominal sum or it could run into several thousand pounds. Either call or visit the ALCS website – see box for contact details.

Design and Artists Copyright Society

Established by artists for artists, the Design and Artists Copyright Society (DACS) is the UK's leading visual arts rights management organisation.

As a not-for-profit organisation, DACS translates rights into revenues and recognition for a wide spectrum of visual artists. It offers three rights management services – Payback, Artist's Resale Right and Copyright Licensing – in addition to lobbying, advocacy and legal advice for visual artists.

Contact details

Design and Artists Copyright Society (DACS)
33 Old Bethnal Green Road, London E2 6AA
tel 020-7336 8822
email info@dacs.org.uk
website www.dacs.org.uk

DACS is part of an international network of rights management organisations. Today DACS represents 80,000 artists and in 2013 it distributed over £14 million in royalties to artists and their beneficiaries. See website for more information about DACS and its services.

Payback

Each year DACS pays a share of royalties to visual artists whose work has been reproduced in UK magazines and books or broadcast on UK television channels. DACS operates this service for situations where it would be impractical or near impossible for an artist to license their rights on an individual basis, for example when a university student wants to photocopy pages from a book that features their work.

Artist's Resale Right

The Artist's Resale Right entitles artists to a royalty each time their work is resold for more than €1,000 by an auction house, gallery or dealer. See website for details of eligibility criteria. DACS ensures artists receive their royalties from qualifying sales not just in the UK but also from other countries in the European Economic Area (EEA). Since 1 January 2012 in the UK, artists' heirs and beneficiaries can now benefit from these royalties.

Copyright Licensing

This service benefits artists and their estates when their work is reproduced for commercial purposes, for example on t-shirts or greetings cards, in a book or on a website. DACS can take care of everything on behalf of the artist, ensuring terms, fees and contractual arrangements are all in order and in their best interests. Artists who use this service are also represented globally through the DACS international network of rights management organisations.

Copyright facts

- Copyright is a right granted to visual artists under law.
- Copyright in all artistic works is established from the moment of creation – the only qualification is that the work must be original.
- There is no registration system in the UK; copyright comes into operation automatically and lasts the lifetime of the visual artist plus a period of 70 years after their death.
- After death, copyright is usually transferred to the visual artist's heirs or beneficiaries. When the 70-year period has expired, the work then enters the public domain and no longer benefits from copyright protection.

• The copyright owner has the exclusive right to authorise the reproduction (or copy) of a work in any medium by any other party.
• Any reproduction can only take place with the copyright owner's consent.
• Permission is usually granted in return for a fee, which enables the visual artist to derive some income from other people using his or her work.
• If a visual artist is commissioned to produce a work, he or she will usually retain the copyright unless an agreement is signed which specifically assigns the copyright. When visual creators are employees and create work during the course of their employment, the employer retains the copyright in those works.

See also...

- *Freelancing for beginners*, page 451
- *How to get ahead in cartooning*, page 459
- *Copyright questions*, page 667
- *The Copyright Licensing Agency Ltd*, page 685

The laws of Privacy, Confidentiality and Data Protection

In this article Keith Schilling guides writers and artists through the main principles of English law to assist them in gauging when specialist legal advice may be required.

Privacy and confidentiality issues may affect writers and artists (hereinafter 'the Writer') in a number of different ways, namely:

- **The Writer as a publisher.** In law a writer is also regarded as a publisher because he causes his work to be published. When writing/publishing an article, a press release, a work of non-fiction (and even a work of fiction), or a blog, the Writer needs to take care to ensure that the privacy rights of others are not infringed. Generally, the privacy rights of others are *engaged* when they have *a reasonable expectation of privacy in respect of the information in question.* This could include information disclosed orally or overheard, or contained in correspondence, journals, telephone calls or emails, or posted on social networking sites, if it concerns medical and family details, financial issues, sexual preferences or orientation or other information of a private nature. This potential liability is of particular importance in the field of book publishing (and the making of television programmes and films) since the Writer will generally give a warranty to the book publisher (or producer of the television programme or film) that nothing contained in the work will infringe the privacy or confidentiality rights of any third person and, if it does, the Writer agrees to fully indemnify the publisher. Often a book publisher will take out insurance and may carry out pre-publication checks but the insurance will not usually benefit the Writer and, if the pre-publication checks are inadequate or fail to identify a particular risk, it may be the Writer who has to make full restitution for all claims. The extent of his liability may go far beyond any financial benefit he is due to receive from the publication of his work. Due to Privacy law being a relatively recent development in English law, its importance is not always appreciated, particularly in the pre-publication process.
- **The Writer as public figure or celebrity.** The private life of a successful Writer may be of great interest to the public. This may result in the unwanted publication of details of the Writer's private life, as well as of the private life of members of his or her family. This can occur when, for example, the Writer is photographed surreptitiously whilst engaged in private activities such as sunbathing on holiday, or when on a family outing. Phone messages can be illicitly intercepted (as occurred on an industrial scale by the now defunct *News of the World*), or their computers, social networking sites or email accounts can be unlawfully accessed. In serious cases, media interest and the behaviour of the press and photographers may amount to harassmentand an injunction or compensation may be awarded accordingly by the courts. However, there is a significant threshold of seriousness to be met before a harassment claim can succeed. The test is an objective one and cannot merely be met because one was offended or insulted by what was written about them. In any event, the Writer may wish to take pre-emptive steps to prevent the publication of private information about himself or his family in the first place. This could include checking cyber security levels in respect of computers and mobile devices, managing his or her digital (online) reputation by removing, where appropriate and practicable, private

information available on the internet, checking the privacy settings of social networking sites used by her and her family or, in a more extreme case, by taking legal action to have private information taken down from the internet, before it is widely published.

• **The Writer as the originator of confidential ideas (or, conversely the Writer as the recipient of such ideas from another writer).** The law of Confidentiality may be invoked by the Writer where he or she submits an original idea, in confidence, for the consideration of a third party (perhaps a potential partner or television production company) and that other person decides to use those ideas without the consent of the Writer. This is a form of plagiarism but it is not a copyright infringement since it is said 'there is no copyright in ideas'. However, there may be confidentiality in ideas provided that certain conditions are met. Where a protectable idea has been stolen, the Writer may have been deprived not only of the fee that he or she might have received for their work but any repeat fees, any buy-out fees and, importantly, the loss of opportunity to enhance their reputation through the commercial exploitation of their idea.

• **The Writer as a Data Controller.** Whenever a Writer 'processes' any information that could identify a living individual, they are deemed to be a 'data controller' which means that they are subject to the Data Protection Act 1998 ('DPA'). The DPA defines 'processing' broadly, and it covers the collection, storage and use of such information including the disclosure of it, for example, by publication. The obligations imposed on data controllers under the DPA are contained within eight data protection principles which govern how 'personal data' should be processed, and include requirements in relation to information that should be given to individuals whose information is processed, and also requirements in relation to the security measures that must be taken to protect the information. The first principle provides that 'personal data' must be processed fairly and lawfully: that means that if a Writer publishes material that would be a breach of confidence, or a violation of an individual's right to privacy then the Writer would also fall foul of the DPA and would be liable to an individual for unlawful processing as well.

An individual has the right to seek compensation from a data controller who causes them damage or distress as a result of the unlawful processing of personal data.

There are several exemptions under the DPA which may mean that the publication of certain material does not automatically become unlawful if the principles of the DPA are not adhered to in full. The most pertinent to a Writer in relation to material used for publication is likely to be found under Section 32 of the DPA which provides an exemption to all of the principles of the DPA (apart from the seventh principle which deals with the security of data) where the processing is for the 'special purposes' of journalism, literature or art. The exemption may apply where there is (1) a view to publication, (2) publication would be in the public interest, and (3) compliance with the DPA would be 'incompatible' with the special purposes, i.e. that compliance with a particular part of the DPA would essentially prevent the publication. It is important to note that this is not a blanket exemption, and each part of the DPA must be considered in turn. Where a particular provision may be complied with without frustrating the journalistic, literary or artistic purpose of the processing then it must be complied with.

In each of the above four instances there is a tension, or conflict, between freedom of speech and rights of privacy or confidentiality. This article therefore outlines some of the principles which are applied to resolving those conflicts.

The law of Privacy

Article 8 of the European Convention on Human Rights was incorporated into English law by the Human Rights Act 1998 and states: 'Everyone has the right to respect for his private and family life, his home, and his correspondence'.

The case of *Naomi Campbell* v. *The Mirror* in 2004 established our modern law of privacy. The *Mirror* had published a series of photographs and an accompanying article which revealed that Campbell was attending a drug addiction support group, a fact which she had publicly denied.

The newspaper unsuccessfully argued that (1) the publication was in the public interest to expose her (false) denials of drug use, and (2) the photographs had been taken on a public street and, therefore, were not private.

Campbell accepted that the newspaper was entitled to publish the fact that she was receiving treatment for her addiction. She argued that publishing *details* of the treatment she was receiving, including how often she attended meetings of the group, was unnecessary and went too far. Publication of photographs of her leaving the treatment centre were objectionable as they might inhibit her future attendance, and others as well, and it was in the public interest that people should be able to attend unhindered.

The Court held that on these facts the publication by the *Mirror* had been in breach of Naomi Campbell's rights of privacy and she was awarded damages and an injunction.

Photographs

As the *Campbell* case shows, the courts regard photographs, and long lens photography, as particularly intrusive. A picture 'tells a thousand words' and can provide a degree of intrusive detail which a mere description cannot.

As such, where photographs are concerned, the courts are generally willing to afford claimants a higher degree of protection in the information depicted. However, photographs can be a very powerful medium to impart information and present a story. Whilst photographs published pursuant to a genuine 'public interest' (which does not mean 'what is of interest to the public') will undoubtedly be hard to challenge, photographs depicting, say, sexual relationships or activity intended to titillate, or private family activities, will be harder to justify.

Children and privacy

Children have a right to privacy which is distinct from that of their parents, even where a parent is world-famous. In 2008, Harry Potter author J.K. Rowling and her husband brought proceedings on behalf of their 19-month-old son against a paparazzi agency which was responsible for the publication of a picture of their son in his pram which was taken as she was walking to a café near her home. The photographs had been taken by a long lens camera and were published in a national newspaper. The court held that the child had a reasonable expectation of privacy and the law should protect children from unwarranted and unjustifiable media intrusion.

Free speech

Where there is a strong public interest in publication, then the publisher's right to freedom of expression (protected by Article 10 of the European Convention on Human Rights) *may* outweigh rights to privacy. In such cases, where privacy and freedom of expression rights are in conflict, the court must carry out a careful balancing act to decide which right should prevail, on those particular facts. There is no exhaustive list of what is or is not 'in the public interest'. It is possible to conclude, however, that some things possess a higher level of public interest than others, for example the reporting of a crime, political conduct and integrity, matters of national health and security, and matters of general public concern. Those who feel that there is a public interest in knowing about medical procedures undergone by an actress or intimate details of the sex lives of celebrities may have an uphill task in persuading a court that publication of this information is in the public interest.

Damages and injunctions

If a claim in privacy is made out at trial a claimant may be entitled to damages and legal costs. In 2008, Max Mosley was awarded £60,000 damages for invasion of his privacy – the highest award made to date – against the *News of the World* for publishing details of his sexual preferences (including a video on their website which was accessed over one million times). Mr Mosley continues to take legal action to remove the videos from the internet, or remove access to the videos from search engines.

However, most claimants will want to prevent the publication of the information in the first place, rather than recover damages after the event, and may therefore apply for an interlocutory (i.e. interim) injunction restraining publication. Such an injunction may prevent an article being published or could prevent a book, television programme or film being published and distributed in that form.

Key points

The relevant questions to ask in such cases are usually the following (bearing in mind that in the event of a dispute it will be for the court to answer them definitively):
• Is there a reasonable expectation of privacy in the relevant information?
• Does the privacy right outweigh other countervailing rights – in particular the right of free speech?
Before publication the Writer may wish to ask himself the following questions:
• Has the information in question already been published and, if so, to what extent? If it has been widely published it may no longer be entitled to protection. However, this is a balancing act as the courts have held that information that is accessible through a social networking site is not necessarily considered to be in the public domain and may still be protected against publication in newspapers. Has the person spoken openly about the particular information or otherwise consented to its publication?
• Are sensitive photographs involved and/or were they taken in inappropriate circumstances?
• Are the privacy rights of children or other private family members engaged?
• Is there an overwhelming public interest in the publication of this particular material?

Of course, it is much more advantageous to set up preventative measures to ensure that breaches of the Writer's privacy are minimised, rather than to end up in a public court battle. These include simple steps such as applying the highest privacy settings on social networking websites to more complex steps such as engaging in digital forensics and privatising the Writer's online footprint. In cases where litigation cannot be avoided, the Writer should seek specialist legal advice as there are measures that can be taken to minimise any damaging impact that a public court battle may have on a Writer's reputation.

The law of Confidentiality

Whilst the law of Privacy is apposite to protect private information, the law of Confidentiality may protect confidential ideas. In (Donald) *Fraser and Others* v. *Thames Television* in 1983, the claimants devised an idea for a television series and conveyed this idea orally to producers at Thames. Thames subsequently broadcast an award-winning series, called *Rock Follies*, based upon that idea. The court found that to be protectable such an idea must be:

- *Clearly identifiable*, in other words not too vague
- *Original*, i.e. not in the public domain
- *Of potential commercial attractiveness*
- *Capable of being realised in actuality* (These last two conditions were established by Thames broadcasting a series based upon the idea.)
- *Communicated in confidence* to the defendant.

This law may also protect, in appropriate circumstances, unpublished television formats which are often not protectable in copyright.

Key points

If you are submitting an idea for a novel, a television programme or format or a film, or a business idea, it is recommended that you:

- Reduce it into writing, and keep a copy in a safe place, electronically and/or with a trusted third party to establish the date on which it was created;
- Do not overexpose the idea by sending it out too widely as it could then be said it is no longer confidential;
- Prominently mark the document and any covering letter with the word 'Confidential'.

If you have *received* an idea which may be confidential, consider carefully whether you are entitled to use it.

These are developing areas of law and in a short article it is not possible to do justice to its many complexities or to identify all the instances where it may apply. Specialist legal advice should always be sought.

Keith Schilling is Chairman and Senior Partner at Schillings, an international multidisciplinary law firm specialising in privacy and reputation. Regarded as pre-eminent in this field, Keith is often involved in providing advice on issues that emanate from both traditional and non-traditional media sources; using his expertise in media, cyber, copyright, data protection and commercial litigation. Keith successfully represented Naomi Campbell, J.K. Rowling and Donald Fraser in the cases cited in the text. See more at www.schillings.co.uk/our-people/keith-schilling

See also...

- *Copyright questions*, page 667
- *UK copyright law*, page 672
- *Defamation*, page 696

Defamation

The law of defamation affects writers in particular, but also artists and others involved in the creative industries. In this article, Alex de Jongh summarises its main principles. However, specific legal advice should be taken when practical problems arise – or better still, prior to publication, if problems are anticipated. The law discussed is that of England and Wales. Scottish law is similar, but there are a number of differences and these are briefly described.

1. Introduction

Defamation is a tort (a civil wrong). Its purpose is to vindicate an injured party's reputation. Where the claimant is an individual, his or her reputation may be part of their right (under Article 8 of the European Convention on Human Rights, ECHR) to respect for their private and family life. The law seeks to balance that right against the competing right to freedom of expression under Article 10 of the ECHR.

Publication of a defamatory allegation can result in a civil claim for damages and/or an injunction to prevent repetition. Libel is no longer actionable under the criminal law.

There are two categories of defamation: libel and slander. A defamatory statement in permanent form is *libel*; where the form is transient, it is *slander*. 'Permanent form' includes writing, printing, drawings and photographs, radio and television broadcasts, film and tape recordings, and theatrical performances. Publications on the internet or in other electronic form will generally fall into the category of libel. Slander tends to be spoken, and claims are comparatively rare. Thus libel is more likely than slander to concern writers and artists professionally, and the slightly differing rules applicable to slander are not covered here.

Claims for libel almost invariably relate to the published word, but can be brought in respect of any other matter which conveys meaning, such as paintings or photographs. A colourful and often cited example is an 1894 claim against Madame Tussaud's, arising out of the positioning of a waxwork of the claimant adjacent to the entrance of the Chamber of Horrors (the claimant successfully argued that this amounted, by innuendo, to an allegation that he was guilty of murder, but recovered damages of only one farthing).

Law reform

Following a long process of parliamentary gestation, the Defamation Act 2013 ('2013 Act') came into force on 1 January 2014. The new law applies to all claims brought in respect of material published since that date.

2. The ingredients of a claim: what does the Claimant need to prove?

The claimant must prove that the statement about which s/he complains:

- is defamatory;
- refers to him or her (or is capable of being understood as referring to him or her); and
- has been published by the defendant to a third party.

Each of these requirements is discussed in greater detail below. If the claimant can establish all three elements, s/he has a *prima facie* case, and the burden shifts to the defendant. The defendant will escape liability if s/he can show that s/he has a good defence.

2.1. What is defamatory?

Before it is possible to decide whether a statement is defamatory, it is necessary to determine what it means. The meaning decided by a court will not necessarily be the same as the meaning intended by the publisher: intention is irrelevant.

The law will treat a given statement as having only one 'natural and ordinary' meaning, i.e. the meaning that an ordinary reasonable person would understand from it. This 'single meaning rule' is not, of course, reflective of the reality that a statement may be open to more than one equally valid interpretation. The natural and ordinary meaning will not necessarily be the literal meaning: the law recognises that the ordinary reader is not naive and will be able to detect (for example) a degree of sarcasm, irony or insinuation.

A statement may also have an 'innuendo meaning' (which can coexist with the natural and ordinary meaning). In the legal sense, this is not a simple insinuation which could be understood by anyone reading between the lines based on matters of general knowledge, but a meaning which will only be apparent to individuals with particular knowledge. The words may appear quite innocent but acquire a defamatory meaning when read by a person in possession of this special knowledge. For example, to state that a person has been seen entering a particular house would be an innocuous statement to some readers, but not to those who knew the address to be a brothel or a crack house.

Meaning is derived from a reading of the publication as a whole, so if a damaging allegation is made in one part but corrected with sufficient prominence in another (so called 'bane and antidote') the overall meaning will not be defamatory.

Having established their meaning, the claimant must show that the words complained of are defamatory. Trivial or frivolous claims should fall at the first hurdle: under the 2013 Act, a statement is not defamatory unless its publication has caused or is likely to cause 'serious harm' to the reputation of the claimant. If the claimant is a company (or any other body which 'trades for profit') and the 2013 Act applies, it must in addition establish that the words have caused or are likely to cause it 'serious financial loss'. So far there has been only limited guidance from the courts as to when and how the courts will require such loss to be proved, and how they will measure 'seriousness'.

There is no single definition of 'defamatory', but various tests have been established and it is sufficient that any one of these is satisfied. A statement is defamatory if it would tend to:

- lower the subject in the estimation of reasonable or right-thinking members of society; or
- bring the subject into ridicule, hatred or contempt with society; or
- make the subject shunned, avoided or cut off from society.

The first of these definitions is most commonly encountered in practice, but the others cannot be ignored. For example, it may seem surprising that a statement that an individual was 'hideous-looking' could be held to be defamatory, but that was the outcome of a 1997 case, on the grounds that the statement exposed the claimant to ridicule (however, mere 'vulgar abuse' will not be regarded as defamatory; it can be a fine dividing line). Similarly, an allegation that an individual is seriously ill or mentally unstable may imply no fault on the part of the claimant, but would be likely to cause them to be shunned or avoided.

A statement may be inaccurate (and damaging) but if it does not impact adversely on the claimant's reputation, it is not defamatory. Such a statement may still give rise to regulatory sanction (e.g. if it breaches the Ofcom or IPSO codes of conduct) or to a claim for malicious falsehood (see below). For example, merely to overstate a person's income is not defamatory; but it will be if the context implies s/he has not fully declared it to the tax authorities.

'Society' means right-thinking members of society generally. It is by reference to such people that the above tests must be applied. A libel claim will fail if the statement would bring the claimant into disrepute with a section of society, but not 'right-thinking' society as a whole. So, an allegation that an individual was a police informer may have brought the claimant into grave disrepute with the underworld, but would not be defamatory.

2.2. Identification – and who can sue

A claimant will usually be named, but an unnamed claimant may still be able to bring a claim: s/he may be identifiable to readers from other published information or pointers, which may range from an address or job description to references to physical characteristics. The intention of the publisher is irrelevant, so a statement intended to refer to one person may give rise to a claim by another person of the same name, if the statement could be understood to refer to him (even if this is based on knowledge derived from other sources rather than the publication itself). For example, in a 1996 case a newspaper article accused an author of plagiarism. It was illustrated with a photograph of an artist of the same name. The artist claimed, successfully, that some readers would understand that he, not the author, was the plagiarist in question.

Generalised references to classes of individuals are, broadly speaking, not successfully actionable, because it is not possible to establish that any individual has been identified. To say that 'all lawyers are corrupt' does not give any single lawyer a cause of action, because the statement does not point a finger at any individual. The smaller the class, however, the more likely it becomes that an individual within it will be able to show that they are identified by the libel.

As well as individuals, a company (subject to the requirement that the allegation has caused or is likely to cause it 'serious financial loss'), officials of unincorporated association or trustees of a charity can all be defamed, and bring libel claims seeking vindication.

Defamation claims cannot be brought by political parties or departments of central or local government (although individuals within them may be able to sue in respect of similar allegations).

Civil claims for defamation cannot be brought on behalf of the dead. Any claim will be extinguished if the claimant dies before the judge or jury deliver their verdict. In those circumstances, the claim 'abates', and cannot be carried on by the deceased's estate.

2.3. Publication – and who can be sued

There will be no civil claim for defamation if the statement has been made to the claimant alone. In order for a cause of action to arise, it must be communicated to a third party.

'Publication' in the legal sense is therefore much wider than (but includes) the lay usage applied to books and newspapers: any communications to a person other than the claimant is sufficient. It follows that the content of a book is published in the legal sense when the manuscript is first submitted to the publishing firm just as it is when the book is later placed on sale to the public. The first publication, however, is obviously much narrower in scope, and the extent of the publication will affect the measure of any damages awarded.

All those responsible for a given publication, including the author (or artist or photographer), the editor and the publisher, can be sued. Where publication takes place online, website publishers, internet hosts and service providers will similarly be treated as publishers. However, those whose involvement in the publication is limited may have a defence of innocent dissemination (see below). Defamation claims can no longer be funded by legal aid unless the Legal Aid Agency considers a case incapable of being fairly tried without it. Such cases will be extremely rare.

3. Defences

If the claimant can show that s/he has a *prima facie* cause of action, the defendant must establish a defence. There are several, although by far the most common are truth, honest opinion and privilege.

3.1. Truth

The defendant will have a complete defence to a libel claim if s/he can show that the imputation conveyed by the statement is a true or substantially true statement of fact.

The defendant must show that on the balance of probability, i.e. a greater than 50% likelihood, that the statement is substantially true. In other words, the law presumes that a defamatory statement is false, and the burden is on the defendant to show otherwise. The defendant does not have to show that the statement is entirely accurate. Minor errors will be disregarded, but s/he must show that the statement is sufficiently true so as to substantiate the 'sting' of the libel.

Where a number of distinct charges are made against a claimant, some of which cannot be shown to be substantially true, the defence will not fail if, in the light of what is shown to be substantially true, the unproven allegations do not seriously harm the claimant's reputation.

One point requires particular attention. It is insufficient for the defendant to prove that s/he has accurately repeated what a third person has written or said or that such statements have gone uncontradicted when made on occasions in the past. If X writes 'Y told me that Z is a liar', it is no defence to an action against X merely to prove that Y did indeed say that. His only defence is to prove that Z is a liar by establishing a number of instances of Z's untruthfulness. Nor does it help a defence of Truth to prove that the defendant genuinely believed what s/he published to be true. This may, however, form part of a qualified privilege defence (see below). Bona fide belief may also be relevant to the assessment of damages. Special care should be taken in relation to references to a person's convictions, however accurately described. Under the Rehabilitation of Offenders Act 1974, a person's less serious convictions may become 'spent' and reference to them may in certain circumstances incur liability. Reference to the 1974 Act and its subordinate legislation must be made in order to determine the position in any particular case.

3.2. Honest opinion

The 2013 Act abolished the common law defence of honest comment (previously known as 'fair comment'), and replaced it with a new statutory defence of 'honest opinion'.

Honest opinion protects the expression of a writer's genuinely held opinion. It applies to statements of comment, opinion or value judgement, as opposed to statements of fact (although the distinction between comment and fact is not always easy to draw in practice).

In order to establish the defence, the defendant must show: (i) that the statement was a statement of opinion; (ii) that it indicated the basis on which it was made; and (iii) that an honest person could have held the opinion on the basis of any fact which existed when the statement was published, or anything asserted as fact in a privileged statement published before the statement of opinion was published.

The defence will remain available if, for example, only three out of five factual claims can be proved true (or privileged), provided that these three are by themselves sufficient to sustain, and are proportionate to, the fairness of the comment.

However, the defence will fail if the claimant can show that the defendant did not hold the opinion or, where the statement is made by one person but published by another, that the publisher knew or ought to have known that the original maker of the statement did not hold the opinion expressed.

Matters of which criticism has been expressly or impliedly invited, such as publicly performed plays and published books, are a legitimate subject of comment. Criticism need not be confined merely to their artistic merit but equally may deal with the attitudes and opinions they expressed.

3.3. Privilege

The law recognises situations in which it is in the public interest that freedom of expression should trump a claimant's right to protect their reputation. Statements made on such occasions will be privileged, i.e. the publisher will have a defence, regardless of the truth or accuracy of the statement, and the harm it may do to the claimant's reputation. There are two broad categories of privilege: *absolute privilege*, where there will be a complete defence regardless of the truth of the statement and the motivation of the publisher; and *qualified privilege*, where the publisher's motives may prevent the defence from succeeding. The 2013 Act has somewhat widened the circumstances in which absolute and qualified privilege may arise.

3.3.1. Absolute privilege

A person defamed by a statement made on an occasion of absolute privilege has no remedy whatsoever, even if the statement is demonstrably false or the maker of the statement has an improper motive (malice) for making it.

Absolute privilege applies to statements in parliamentary proceedings and papers, statements made in the course of proceedings in the courts and certain tribunals, and reports published by certain quasi-judicial bodies.

It also applies to fair, accurate and contemporaneous reports of public judicial proceedings in the UK and abroad, and any international court or tribunal established by the UN Security Council or by an international agreement.

3.3.2. Qualified privilege

Qualified privilege differs from absolute privilege in that the defence will fail if the claimant can prove malice, i.e. an improper motive or carelessness or recklessness as to the truth of the publication. There are three subcategories of qualified privilege.

First, there are various examples of *statutory qualified privilege*, established under section 15 of the Defamation Act 1996 and widened by the 2013 Act. These are set out in Schedule 1 to the 1996 Act (as amended by the 2013 Act), and include fair and accurate reports of public proceedings before a legislature, a court, a government inquiry and an international organisation or conference anywhere in the world, and of certain documents, or extracts from such documents, issued by those bodies. There is no requirement to correct or publish explanations concerning these reports. Such an obligation does arise in respect of a separate category of potentially privileged reports. These include fair and accurate reports of notices or other matter issued for the information of the public by or on behalf of a legislature or government anywhere in the world, authorities performing governmental functions, and international organisations and conferences.

Second, there are instances of *qualified privilege at common law*. Here, the law recognises a statement made by a person with a legal, social or moral duty to make it, to someone with a legal, social or moral duty or interest in receiving it. Examples include employment references, credit references and statements made to the police in response to enquiries or in relation to a crime. Normally the scope of publication must be no wider than necessary: if the material is published to those with no interest in receiving it, the defence of qualified privilege will be lost.

Third, a qualified privilege will be available under section 4 of the 2013 Act where the statement was, or formed part of, a statement on a matter of public interest and the defendant reasonably believed (allowing for an appropriate degree of editorial judgement) that publishing it was in the public interest. This abolishes the similar common law defence (under which qualified privilege was extended to publications by the media to the public at large following the 1999 case of *Reynolds* v. *Times Newspapers*) and changes the emphasis from 'responsible journalism' to 'reasonable belief'. However, the factors which would be considered in determining whether a *Reynolds* defence would be available are likely to remain the relevant considerations when applying the new section 4 defence. These include the seriousness of the allegation, the nature of its source, the steps taken to verify it, the urgency of the publication, whether the claimant's side of the story has been obtained and reported, and the tone of the publication. Like *Reynolds*, the new defence protects a publisher who cannot show that what it published was true (or honest opinion) but can show that (a) the offending statement was, or formed part of, a statement on a matter of public interest; and (b) it reasonably believed that publishing the statement complained of was in the public interest. It can extend to 'neutral reportage' – accurate and impartial coverage of a dispute to which the claimant was a party – under section 4(3) of the 2013 Act.

3.4. Secondary responsibility

This defence may be available where the publisher publishes a defamatory statement inadvertently. 'Innocent disseminators', such as printers, distributors, broadcasters, internet service providers (ISPs) and retailers, who can show they took reasonable care and had no reason to believe what they were handling contained a libel, have a defence under section 1 of the Defamation Act 1996 or the Electronic Commerce Regulations 2002.

The defence will only be available if the broadcaster, ISP or other publisher is not the 'author, editor or publisher' of the offending words. Typically, this might occur where the offending statement is made by an interviewee in a live broadcast, or where user-generated content is published automatically on a website without prior moderation.

The 2013 Act (and the Defamation (Operators of Websites) Regulations 2013 – the 'Regulations') provide further protection for the operators of websites. Where defamatory statements are posted on a website by a third party (such as reader comments on a blog), the operator of the website will have a defence (even if content is moderated by the operator before being posted). If the claimant is capable of identifying the third party (so that s/he can sue him or her directly) the website operator has an absolute defence unless s/he has acted with malice (knowledge that the statement is untrue or recklessness as to its truth). If the claimant cannot identify the defendant, he must serve a notice on the website operator in the form prescribed in the Regulations. The defence will then be defeated if the website operator fails to respond in the manner required under the Regulations. Those steps are complicated and specific advice should be sought if you receive a notice under section 5 of the 2013 Act and the Regulations.

3.5. Offer of amends

Section 2 of the Defamation Act 1996 creates a procedure which aims to nip in the bud disputes in which the claimant has been defamed unintentionally. Under this procedure, the defendant must offer to publish a suitable correction and sufficient apology, and pay damages (if any) and the claimant's costs, to be assessed by a judge if not agreed. If an offer of amends is not accepted by the claimant, the defendant can rely on it as a defence, unless the claimant can prove malice. While reliance on an offer of amends prevents the defendant from relying on any other defences, it offers a considerable incentive to settle complaints and will save substantially on costs.

3.6. Other defences and restrictions

Peer-reviewed statements in scientific or academic journals. In response to concerns that libel law was having a 'chilling effect' on the freedom of speech of writers on academic (particularly medical and scientific matters), the 2013 Act creates a new defence for publishers of statements in scientific or academic journals. Statements in such journals will be privileged if (i) they relate to a scientific or academic matter; and (ii) prior to publication, their merit was reviewed independently by the journal's editor and one or more other people with appropriate expertise in the relevant field. This is a qualified rather than absolute privilege, so it is lost if the claimant can establish malice on the part of the defendant.

Limitation. A claim for libel can be defeated on the grounds that it has been issued too late: section 4 of the Limitation Act 1990 provides that (with very limited exceptions) any claim for libel must be issued within one year from date of publication. Before the 2013 Act, each new publication (e.g. every hit on a website) was regarded as a separate tort, giving rise to a fresh one-year limitation period. This put online publishers at a disadvantage. The 2013 Act introduces a 'single publication' rule, preventing claimants from suing more than a year after the date of the original publication, even if the material remains online. So, for example, an article published (and remaining available) online since 17 October 2013 would be treated as having been republished with every page view until the 2013 Act came into force on 1 January 2014, so the limitation period would expire on 31 December 2014. An article published online since 17 October 2014 would become immune from a libel claim after 16 October 2015. Note that this will not protect republication in a materially different manner, or by other publishers.

Strike out. A claim may be *struck out* on the grounds that it is an abuse of the process of the courts. For example, if the scope of the publication is so small as to be insignificant, the court may prevent the claim from continuing. The Court of Appeal did so in a case involving the *Wall Street Journal* in 2005, where there was evidence that the article in question had been viewed only five times in this jurisdiction, and that three of those viewings were by individuals closely connected to the claimants or their lawyers.

There are a number of other, rarely used, defences:

- *Consent:* there will be a defence where the claimant has given their consent to the publication in question. Consent may be express or implied.

• *Release* (aka accord and satisfaction): where the claimant has agreed that s/he will not sue (or continue to sue) the defendant in respect of a given publication, the terms of settlement have contractual force and may be relied on as a defence.

4. Remedies

A successful claimant will be compensated for the damage done to his or her reputation by an award of damages. He will usually also be awarded an injunction to prevent further publication of the offending words. The losing party will usually be ordered to pay the winner's costs. However, the costs claimed by the winning party will be assessed by the court, and it is unusual for the winner to recover 100% of his costs.

4.1. Damages

It is not necessary for the claimant to prove that s/he has actually suffered any loss: some damage is presumed. It is generally very difficult to forecast the amounts juries are likely to award; the Court of Appeal has power to reduce excessive awards of damages.

There are 4 categories of damages:

• *'Ordinary' or 'general' damages:* the law presumes that a successful claimant will suffer some damage to their reputation. This is compensated by an award of general damages. At the top end, these may be in the region of £270,000 for the most serious libels. At the bottom end, the court may award nominal damages of as little as £1 where the libel is trivial (and in such cases the claimant would be unlikely to recover his costs). Awards of general damages are considerably lower now than they have been in the past, notably in the 1980s when a number of seven-figure awards were made. The courts may take into account the damages which would be recoverable in personal injury claims when deciding what an appropriate figure to compensate a claimant is.

• *'Special' damages:* where the claimant can prove that the publication of the libel has caused him to suffer some specified loss, for example the loss of a sponsorship contract.

• *'Aggravated' damages:* where the defendant's conduct after publication has been malevolent or spiteful, and as such has 'rubbed salt in the wound', for example by repeating the libel or attacking the claimant in some other way.

• *'Exemplary' or 'punitive' damages:* where there is evidence that the defendant has calculated that any libel damages awarded against it will be outweighed by the boost that the publication will give to its sales revenues.

4.2. Injunctions

A claimant who wins at trial will normally be entitled to an injunction restraining repetition of the libel. A claimant may also seek an injunction before trial, most commonly to prevent the threatened publication of defamatory material. Such interim injunctions are rare. Section 12 of the Human Rights Act 1998 requires the courts to balance the competing rights to private life and freedom of expression under ECHR Article 10 and ECHR Article 8. There is a long-standing common law rule against 'prior restraint' and discretion will be exercised in favour of freedom of expression if the publisher (intended defendant) indicates that s/he will defend any claim on the grounds of Truth.

4.3 Publication of summary of court's judgement

Section 12 of the 2013 Act creates a power for the court to order a defendant to publish a summary of its judgement where the claimant has been successful, although the wording itself and the timing and placement of the summary are for the parties to agree themselves unless they cannot agree, in which case the court will step in.

5. Settlement and summary disposal

Most claims settle before trial. Matters likely to be dealt with in any settlement agreement include the terms of any apology to be published by the defendant, undertakings by the defendant not to repeat the libel, the making of a statement in open court (in which the defendant formally retracts the allegation), whether any damages are to be paid, and who is to bear the legal costs on each side. The Defamation Act 1996 introduced a 'fast-track' or 'summary disposal' procedure, providing a simplified mechanism for dealing with less serious complaints. This recognised the costly and time-consuming nature of libel litigation. Sections 8, 9 and 10 of the 1996 Act enable a judge alone to dismiss unrealistic claims at the outset; and s/he will also be able to dispose 'summarily' of relatively minor, but well-founded, claims, on the basis of an award of up to £10,000, a declaration that the publication was libellous, an order for the publication of an apology and an order forbidding repetition.

6. Malicious falsehood

Where a false statement is published which is not defamatory, a claimant may still be able to bring a claim under the separate (but related) tort of malicious falsehood. Claims for defamation and malicious falsehood are not mutually exclusive and may be brought together in respect of the same statement. In a claim for malicious falsehood, the claimant needs to prove that the statement:

- has been published to a third party;
- is false;
- was published maliciously, i.e. knowing it to be untrue or careless as to whether it is true; and
- is likely to cause (or has caused) the claimant to suffer financial loss (however, there are exceptions so this final requirement will not always be present).

An example is a false statement by the proprietor of a business to a member of the public that a rival proprietor has closed his business, thereby deliberately diverting the person away from his rival. The statement is not defamatory, but it is false and is calculated to cause the rival loss.

7. Scotland and Northern Ireland

The Scottish law of defamation is similar to the law in England and Wales as it stood before the 2013 Act came into force. The majority of the 2013 Act does not apply in Scotland (one notable exception being the new section 6 defence for peer-reviewed journals). In addition, under Scots law, there is no distinction between libel and slander; no requirement that the publication be made to a third party; and no summary disposal procedure. The limitation period is three years, not one. So a claimant who is too late to bring a claim in England and Wales may still be able to do so in Scotland.

In particular, the old common law defences of justification and honest comment continue to be available in Scotland, instead (respectively) of Truth and honest opinion. Justification and Truth are substantially similar, but the statutory requirement to demonstrate serious harm does not apply in Scotland (although earlier case law which would have the effect of screening out some trivial claims would apply). The requirement that companies trading for profit must show that an allegation has caused or is likely to cause serious financial loss also does not apply in Scotland.

There are some differences between honest comment and honest opinion. Most importantly, for honest comment to be available, the statement must be on a matter of public interest. The conduct of national and local government, international affairs, the administration of justice, etc are all matters of public interest, whereas other people's private affairs may very well not be, although they undoubtedly interest the public, or provoke curiosity. Second, the defence will fail if the claimant can show that the defendant was motivated by malice, the test for which reflects the requirement under the new defence that the maker of the statement genuinely holds the opinion expressed.

The defence under section 5 of the 2013 Act for 'operators of websites' does not apply in Scotland. Nor does the section 4 defence (publication on a matter of public interest). But the common law Reynolds defence, now abolished in England & Wales, continues to apply.

The 2013 Act does not apply in Northern Ireland.

8. Insurance

For any author, it is advisable to check (at the earliest possible stage prior to publication) what libel insurance a publisher carries, and whether it also covers the author. The author should always alert the publisher to any potential libel risk s/he is aware of, in order to ensure that they retain the benefit of any cover provided by the publisher. Insurance must be obtained through an insurance broker or company registered with the Financial Conduct Authority. Insurers may require authors to obtain (at their own expense) a legal opinion before they will provide cover.

Alex de Jongh is a commercial litigation solicitor at Bates Wells Braithwaite (www.bwbllp.com). He frequently advises claimants and defendants in defamation and other media-related disputes.

See also...

- *Copyright questions*, page 667
- *UK copyright law*, page 672
- *The laws of Privacy, Confidentiality and Data Protection*, page 691

Finance for writers and artists

FAQs for writers

Peter Vaines, a chartered accountant and barrister, addresses some frequently asked questions.

What can a working writer claim against tax?

A working writer is carrying on a business and can therefore claim all the expenses which are incurred wholly and exclusively for the purposes of that business. A list showing most of the usual expenses can be found in the article on *Income tax* (see page 709) but there will be other expenses that can be allowed in special circumstances.

Strictly, only expenses which are incurred for the sole purpose of the business can be claimed; there must be no 'duality of purpose' so an item of expenditure cannot be divided into private and business parts. However, HM Revenue & Customs are now able to allow all reasonable expenses (including apportioned sums) where the amounts can be commercially justified.

Allowances can also be claimed for the cost of business assets such as a car, personal computers, fax, copying machines and all other equipment (including books) which may be used by the writer. An allowance of 100% of the cost can now be claimed for most assets except cars, for which a lower allowance can be claimed. See the article on *Income tax* for further details of the deductions available in respect of capital expenditure.

Can I request interest on fees owed to me beyond 30 days of my invoice?

Yes. A writer is like any other person carrying on a business and is entitled to charge interest at a rate of 8% over bank base rate on any debt outstanding for more than 30 days – although the period of credit can be varied by agreement between the parties. It is not compulsory to claim the interest; it is your decision whether to enforce the right.

What can I do about bad debts?

A writer is in exactly the same position as anybody else carrying on a business over the payment of his or her invoices. It is generally not commercially sensible to insist on payment in advance but where the work involved is substantial (e.g. a book), it is usual to receive one third of the fee on signature, one third on delivery of the manuscript and the remaining one third on publication. On other assignments, perhaps not as substantial as a book, it could be worthwhile seeking 50% of the fee on signature and the other 50% on delivery. This would provide a degree of protection in case of cancellation of the assignment because of changes of policy or personnel at the publisher.

What financial disputes can I take to the Small Claims Court?

If somebody owes you money you can take them to the Small Claims section of your local County Court, which deals with financial disputes up to £10,000. The procedure is much less formal than normal court proceedings and involves little expense. It is not necessary to have a solicitor. You fill in a number of forms, turn up on the day and explain the background to why you are owed the money (see www.gov.uk/make-court-claim-for-money/overview).

If I receive an advance, can I divide it between two tax years?

Yes. There is a system known as 'averaging'. This enables writers (and others engaged in the creation of literary or dramatic works or designs) to average the profits of two or more consecutive years if the profits for one year are less than 75% of the profits for the highest year. This relief can apply even if the work takes less than 12 months to create and it allows the writer to avoid the higher rates of tax which might arise if the income in respect of a number of years' work were all to be concentrated in a single year.

How do I make sure I am taxed as a self-employed person so that tax and National Insurance contributions are not deducted at source?

To be taxed as a self-employed person you have to make sure that the contract for the writing cannot be regarded as a contract of employment. This is unlikely to be the case with a professional author. The subject is highly complex but one of the most important features is that the publisher must not be in a position to direct or control the author's work. Where any doubt exists, the author might find the publisher deducting tax and National Insurance contributions as a precaution and that would clearly be highly disadvantageous. The author would be well advised to discuss the position with the publisher before the contract is signed to agree that he or she should be treated as self-employed and that no tax or National Insurance contributions will be deducted from any payments. If such agreement cannot be reached, professional advice should immediately be sought so that the detailed technical position can be explained to the publisher.

Is it a good idea to operate through a limited company?

It can be a good idea for a self-employed writer to operate through a company but generally only where the income is quite large. The costs of operating a company can outweigh any benefit if the writer is paying tax only at the basic rate. Where the writer is paying tax at the higher rate of 40% (or 45%), being able to retain some of the income in a company at a tax rate of only 20% is obviously attractive. However, this will be entirely ineffective if the writer's contract with the publisher would otherwise be an employment. The whole subject of operating through a company is complex and professional advice is essential.

When does it become necessary to register for VAT?

Where the writer's self-employed income (from all sources, not only writing) exceeds £82,000 in the previous 12 months or is expected to do so in the next 30 days, he or she must register for VAT and add VAT to all his/her fees. The publisher will pay the VAT to the writer, who must pay the VAT over to HM Revenue & Customs each quarter. Any VAT the writer has paid on business expenses and on the purchase of business assets can be deducted. It is possible for some authors to take advantage of the simplified system for VAT payments which applies to small businesses. This involves a flat rate payment of VAT without any need to keep records of VAT on expenses.

If I make a loss from my writing can I get any tax back?

Where a writer makes a loss, HM Revenue & Customs may suggest that the writing is only a hobby and not a professional activity, thereby denying any relief or tax deduction for the loss. However, providing the writing is carried out on a sensible commercial basis with an expectation of profits, any resulting loss can be offset against any other income the writer may have for the same or the previous year.

Income tax

Despite attempts by successive governments to simplify our taxation system, the subject has become increasingly complicated. Peter Vaines, a chartered accountant and barrister, gives a broad outline of taxation from the point of view of writers and other creative professionals. The proposals in the March 2015 Budget are broadly reflected in this article.

How income is taxed

Generally

Authors are usually treated for tax purposes as carrying on a profession and are taxed in a similar fashion to other self-employed professionals. This article is directed to self-employed persons only, because if a writer is employed he or she will be subject to the much less advantageous rules which apply to employment income.

Employed persons may try to shake off the status of 'employee' to attain 'freelance' status so as to qualify for the tax advantages, but such attempts meet with varying degrees of success. The problems involved in making this transition are considerable and space does not permit a detailed explanation to be made here – individual advice is necessary if difficulties are to be avoided.

Particular attention has been paid by HM Revenue & Customs (HMRC) to journalists and to those engaged in the entertainment industry with a view to reclassifying them as employees so that PAYE is deducted from their earnings. This blanket treatment has been extended to other areas and, although it is obviously open to challenge by individual taxpayers, it is always difficult to persuade HMRC to change its views.

There is no reason why employed people cannot carry on a freelance business in their spare time. Indeed, aspiring authors, artists, musicians, etc often derive so little income from their craft that the financial security of an employment, perhaps in a different sphere of activity, is necessary. The existence of the employment is irrelevant to the taxation of the freelance earnings, although it is most important not to confuse the income or expenditure of the employment with that of the self-employed activity. HMRC is aware of the advantages which can be derived by an individual having 'freelance' income from an organisation of which he or she is also an employee, and where such circumstances are contrived, it can be extremely difficult to convince an Inspector of Taxes that a genuine freelance activity is being carried on. Where the individual operates through a company or partnership providing services personally to a particular client, and would be regarded as an employee if the services were supplied directly by the individual, additional problems arise from the notorious IR35 legislation and professional advice is essential.

For those starting in business or commencing work on a freelance basis HMRC produces the very useful factsheet called 'Working for yourself', which is available on its website (www.gov.uk/working-for-yourself/overview).

Income

For income to be taxable it need not be substantial, nor even the author's only source of income; earnings from casual writing are also taxable but this can be an advantage because occasional writers do not often make a profit from their writing. The expenses incurred in connection with writing may well exceed any income receivable and the resultant loss may then be used to reclaim tax paid on other income. Certain allowable expenses and capital allowances may be deducted from the income, and these are set out in more detail below. The possibility of a loss being used as a basis for a tax repayment is fully appreciated by HMRC, which sometimes attempts to treat casual writing as a hobby so that any losses incurred cannot be used to reclaim tax; of course by the same token any income receivable would not be chargeable to tax. This treatment may sound attractive but it should be resisted vigorously because HMRC does not hesitate to change its mind when profits begin to arise. In the case of exceptional or non-recurring writing, such as the autobiography of a sports personality or the memoirs of a politician, it could be better to be treated as pursuing a hobby and not as a professional author. Sales of copyright cannot be charged to income tax unless the recipient is a professional author. However, the proceeds of sale of copyright may be charged to capital gains tax, even by an individual who is not a professional author.

Royalties

Where the recipient is a professional author, the proceeds of sale of copyright are taxable as income and not as capital receipts. Similarly, lump sums on account of, or in advance of royalties are also taxable as income in the year of receipt, subject to a claim for averaging relief (see below).

Copyright royalties are generally paid without deduction of income tax. However, if royalties are paid to a person who normally lives abroad, tax must be deducted by the

Arts Council awards

Arts Council category A awards

- Direct or indirect musical, design or choreographic commissions and direct or indirect commission of sculpture and paintings for public sites.
- The Royalty Supplement Guarantee Scheme.
- The Contract Writers' Scheme.
- Jazz bursaries.
- Translators' grants.
- Photographic awards and bursaries.
- Film and video awards and bursaries.
- Performance Art Awards.
- Art Publishing Grants.
- Grants to assist with a specific project or projects (such as the writing of a book) or to meet specific professional expenses such as a contribution towards copying expenses made to a composer or to an artist's studio expenses.

Arts Council category B awards

- Bursaries to trainee directors.
- Bursaries for associate directors.
- Bursaries to people attending full-time courses in arts administration (the practical training course).
- In-service bursaries to theatre designers and bursaries to trainees on the theatre designers' scheme.
- In-service bursaries for administrators.
- Bursaries for actors and actresses.
- Bursaries for technicians and stage managers.
- Bursaries made to students attending the City University Arts Administration courses.
- Awards, known as the Buying Time Awards, made not to assist with a specific project or professional expenses but to maintain the recipient to enable him or her to take time off to develop his or her personal talents. These include the awards and bursaries known as the Theatre Writing Bursaries, awards and bursaries to composers, awards and bursaries to painters, sculptors and print makers, literature awards and bursaries.

payer or his agent at the time the payment is made unless arrangements are made with HMRC for payments to be made gross under the terms of a Double Taxation Agreement with the other country.

Grants, prizes and awards

Persons in receipt of grants from the Arts Council or similar bodies will be concerned whether or not such grants are liable to income tax. Many years ago HMRC issued a Statement of Practice after detailed discussions with the Arts Council regarding the tax treatment of the awards. Grants and other receipts of a similar nature were divided into two categories (see box) – those which were to be treated by HMRC as chargeable to tax and those which were not. Category A awards were considered to be taxable; awards made under category B were not chargeable to tax.

The Statement of Practice has not been withdrawn but it is no longer publicly available – although there is nothing to suggest that the treatment of awards in these categories will not continue to be treated in this way. In any event, the statement had no legal force and was merely and expression of the view of HMRC. It remains open to anybody in receipt of a grant or award to challenge the HMRC view on the merits of their own case.

The tax position of persons in receipt of literary prizes will generally follow a decision by the Special Commissioners in connection with the Whitbread Book Awards (now called the Costa Book Awards). In that case it was decided that the prize was not part of the author's professional income and accordingly not chargeable to tax. The precise details are not available because decisions of the Special Commissioners were not, at that time, reported unless an appeal was made to the High Court; HMRC chose not to appeal against this decision. Details of the many literary awards that are given each year start on page 534, and this decision is of considerable significance to the winners of these prizes. It would be unwise to assume that all such awards will be free of tax as the precise facts which were present in the case of the Whitbread awards may not be repeated in another case; however, it is clear that an author winning a prize has some very powerful arguments in his or her favour, should HMRC seek to charge tax on the award.

Allowable expenses

To qualify as an allowable business expense, expenditure has to be laid out wholly and exclusively for business purposes. Strictly there must be no 'duality of purpose', which means that expenditure cannot be apportioned to reflect private and business usage, for example food, clothing, telephone, travelling expenses, etc. However, HMRC will usually allow all reasonable expenses (including apportioned sums) where the amounts can be commercially justified.

It should be noted carefully that the expenditure does not have to be 'necessary', it merely has to be incurred 'wholly and exclusively' for business purposes. Naturally, however, expenditure of an outrageous and wholly unnecessary character might well give rise to a presumption that it was not really for business purposes. As with all things, some expenses are unquestionably allowable and some expenses are equally unquestionably not allowable – it is the grey area in between which gives rise to all the difficulties and the outcome invariably depends on negotiation with HMRC.

Great care should be taken when claiming a deduction for items where there may be a duality of purpose and negotiations should be conducted with more than usual care and courtesy – if provoked, the Inspector of Taxes may well choose to allow nothing. An appeal is always possible although unlikely to succeed as a string of cases in the Courts has clearly demonstrated. An example is the case of *Caillebotte* v. *Quinn* where the taxpayer (who normally had lunch at home) sought to claim the excess cost of meals incurred because he was working a long way from his home. The taxpayer's arguments failed because he did not eat only in order to work, one of the reasons for his eating was in order to sustain his life; a duality of purpose therefore existed and no tax relief was due.

Other cases have shown that expenditure on clothing can also be disallowed if it is the kind of clothing which is in everyday use, because clothing is worn not only to assist the pursuit of one's profession but also to accord with public decency. This duality of purpose may be sufficient to deny relief – even where the particular type of clothing is of a kind not otherwise worn by the taxpayer. In the case of *Mallalieu* v. *Drummond* a barrister failed to obtain a tax deduction for items of sombre clothing that she purchased specifically for wearing in Court. The House of Lords decided that a duality of purpose existed because clothing represented part of her needs as a human being.

Allowances

Despite the above, Inspectors of Taxes are not usually inflexible and the following list of expenses are among those generally allowed.

(a) Cost of all materials used up in the course of the work's preparation.

(b) Cost of typewriting and secretarial assistance, etc; if this or other help is obtained from one's spouse then it is entirely proper for a deduction to be claimed for the amounts paid for the work. The amounts claimed must actually be paid to the spouse and should be at the market rate, although some uplift can be made for unsocial hours, etc. Payments to a spouse are of course taxable in their hands and should therefore be most carefully considered. The spouse's earnings may also be liable for National Insurance contributions and it is important to take care because otherwise you may find that these contributions outweigh the tax savings. The impact of the National Minimum Wage should also be considered.

(c) All expenditure on normal business items such as postage, stationery, telephone, email, fax and answering machines, agent's fees, accountancy charges, photography, subscriptions, periodicals, magazines, etc may be claimed. The cost of daily papers should not be overlooked if these form part of research material. Visits to theatres, cinemas, etc for research purposes may also be permissible (but not the costs relating to guests). Unfortunately, expenditure on all types of business entertaining is specifically denied tax relief.

(d) If work is conducted at home, a deduction for 'use of home' is usually allowed providing the amount claimed is reasonable. If the claim is based on an appropriate proportion of the total costs of rent, light and heat, cleaning and maintenance, insurance, etc (but not the Council Tax), care should be taken to ensure that no single room is used 'exclusively' for business purposes, because this may result in the Capital Gains Tax exemption on the house as the only or main residence being partially forfeited. However, it would be a strange household where one room was in fact used exclusively for business purposes and for no other purpose whatsoever (e.g. storing personal bank statements and other private papers); the usual formula is to claim a deduction on the basis that most or all of the rooms in the house are used at one time or another for business purposes, thereby avoiding any suggestion that any part was used exclusively for business purposes.

(e) The appropriate business proportion of motor running expenses may also be claimed although what is the appropriate proportion will naturally depend on the particular circumstances of each case. It should be appreciated that the well-known scale of benefits, whereby employees are taxed according to the size of the car's CO_2 emissions, do not apply to self-employed persons.
(f) It has been long established that the cost of travelling from home to work (whether employed or self-employed) is not an allowable expense. However, if home is one's place of work then no expenditure under this heading is likely to be incurred and difficulties are unlikely to arise.
(g) Travelling and hotel expenses incurred for business purposes will normally be allowed but if any part could be construed as disguised holiday or pleasure expenditure, considerable thought would need to be given to the commercial reasons for the journey in order to justify the claim. The principle of 'duality of purpose' will always be a difficult hurdle in this connection – although not insurmountable.
(h) If a separate business bank account is maintained, any overdraft interest thereon will be an allowable expense. This is the only circumstance in which overdraft interest is allowed for tax purposes.
(i) Where capital allowances (see below) are claimed for a personal computer, laptop, iPad, fax machine, mobile phone, television, CD or DVD player, etc used for business purposes, the costs of maintenance and repair of the equipment may also be claimed.

Clearly many other allowable items may be claimed in addition to those listed. Wherever there is any reasonable business motive for some expenditure it should be claimed as a deduction although it is necessary to preserve all records relating to the expense. It is sensible to avoid an excess of imagination as this would naturally cause the Inspector of Taxes to doubt the genuineness of other expenses claimed.

The question is often raised whether the whole amount of an expense may be deducted or whether the VAT content must be excluded. Where VAT is reclaimed from HMRC by someone who is registered for VAT, the VAT element of the expense cannot be treated as an allowable deduction. Where the VAT is not reclaimed, the whole expense (inclusive of VAT) is allowable for income tax purposes.

Capital allowances

Where expenditure of a capital nature is incurred, it cannot be deducted from income as an expense – a separate and sometimes more valuable capital allowance being available instead. Capital allowances are given for many different types of expenditure, but authors and similar professional people are likely to claim only for 'plant and machinery'; this is a very wide expression which may include cars, personal computers, laptops, iPads, fax machines, televisions, CD and DVD players used for business purposes. Plant and machinery will normally qualify for an allowance of 100%.

The reason capital allowances can be more valuable than allowable expenses is that they may be wholly or partly disclaimed in any year that full benefit cannot be obtained – ordinary business expenses cannot be similarly disclaimed. Where, for example, the income of an author is not large enough to bring him above the tax threshold, he would not be liable to tax and a claim for capital allowances would be wasted. If the capital allowances were to be disclaimed their benefit would be carried forward for use in subsequent years. This would also be advantageous where the income is likely to be taxable at the higher rate of 40% (or the 45% rate) in a subsequent year. Careful planning with claims for capital allowances is therefore essential if maximum benefit is to be obtained.

As an alternative to capital allowances, claims can be made on the 'renewals' basis whereby all renewals are treated as allowable deductions in the year; no allowance is obtained for the initial purchase, but the cost of replacement (excluding any improvement element) is allowed in full. This basis is no longer widely used, as it is considerably less advantageous than claiming capital allowances as described above.

Leasing is a popular method of acquiring fixed assets, and where cash is not available to enable an outright purchase to be made, assets may be leased over a period of time. Whilst leasing may have financial benefits in certain circumstances, in normal cases there is likely to be no tax advantage in leasing an asset where the alternative of outright purchase is available.

Books

The question of whether the cost of books is eligible for tax relief has long been a source of difficulty. The annual cost of replacing books used for the purposes of one's professional activities (e.g. the cost of a new *Writers' & Artists' Yearbook* each year) has always been an allowable expense; the difficulty arose because the initial cost of reference books, etc (e.g. when commencing one's profession) was treated as capital expenditure but no allowances were due as the books were not considered to be 'plant'. However, the matter was clarified by the case of *Munby* v. *Furlong* in which the Court of Appeal decided that the initial cost of law books purchased by a barrister was expenditure on 'plant' and eligible for capital allowances. This is clearly a most important decision, particularly relevant to any person who uses expensive books in the course of exercising his or her profession.

Pension contributions

Where a self-employed person makes contributions to a pension scheme, those contributions are usually deductible.

These arrangements are generally advantageous in providing for a pension as contributions are usually paid when the income is high (and the tax relief is also high) and the pension (taxed as earned income when received) usually arises when the income is low and a lower rate of tax may be payable. There is also the opportunity to take part of the pension entitlement as a tax-free lump sum. It is necessary to take into account the possibility that the tax advantages could go into reverse. When the pension is paid it could, if rates rise again, be taxed at a higher rate than the rate of tax relief at the moment.

Each individual has a lifetime allowance (reduced this year to £1 million and when benefits crystallise, which will generally be when a pension begins to be paid, this is measured against the individual's lifetime allowance; any excess will be taxed at the individual's marginal rate.

Each individual also has an annual allowance for contributions to the pension fund, which was £40,000 for 2014/15 but may change in later years. If the annual increase in an individual's rights under all registered schemes of which he is a member exceeds the annual allowance, the excess is chargeable to tax.

For many writers and artists this means that they can contribute a large part of their earnings to a pension scheme (if they can afford to do so) without any of the previous complications. It is still necessary to be careful where there is other income giving rise to a pension because the whole of the pension entitlement has to be taken into account.

Flexible retirement is possible allowing members of occupational pension schemes to continue working while also drawing retirement benefits.

Class 4 National Insurance contributions

Allied to pensions is the payment of Class 4 National Insurance contributions, although no pension or other benefit is obtained by the contributions; the Class 4 contributions are designed solely to extract additional amounts from self-employed persons and are payable in addition to the normal Class 2 (self-employed) contributions. The rates are changed each year and for 2015/16 self-employed persons will be obliged to contribute 9% of their profits between the range £8,060–£42,385 per annum plus 2% on earnings above £42,385. This amount is collected in conjunction with the annual income tax liability.

Averaging relief

Relief for copyright payments

Professional authors and artists engaged in the creation of literary or dramatic works or designs may claim to average the profits of two or more consecutive years if the profits for one year are less than 75% of the profits for the highest year. This relief can apply even if the work took less than 12 months to create and is available to people who create works in partnership with others. It enables the creative artist to utilise their allowances fully and to avoid the higher rates of tax which might apply if all the income were to arise in a single year.

Collection of tax: self-assessment

Under 'self-assessment' you submit your tax return and work out your tax liability for yourself. If you get it wrong, or if you are late with your tax return or the payment of tax, interest and penalties will be charged. Completing a tax return is a daunting task but the term 'self-assessment' is not intended to imply that individuals have to do it themselves; they can (and often will) engage professional help. The term is only intended to convey that it is the taxpayer, and not HMRC, who is responsible for getting the tax liability right and for it to be paid on time.

The deadline for filing your tax return is 31 January following the end of the tax year. You must now file online; a paper tax return cannot be filed in most cases.

Income tax on self-employed earnings remains payable in two instalments on 31 January and 31 July each year. Because the accurate figures may not necessarily be known, these payments in January and July will therefore be only payments on account based on the previous year's liability. The final balancing figure will be paid the following 31 January together with the first instalment of the liability for the following year.

When HMRC receives the self-assessment tax return, it is checked to see if there is anything obviously wrong; if there is, a letter will be sent to you immediately. Otherwise, HMRC has 12 months from the filing date in which to make further enquiries; if it doesn't, it will have no further opportunity to do so and your tax liabilities are final – unless there is an error or an omission. In that event, HMRC can raise an assessment later to collect any extra tax together with appropriate penalties. It is essential that all records relevant to your tax return are retained for at least 12 months after the filing date in case they are needed by HMRC. For the self-employed, the record-keeping requirement is much more onerous because the records need to be kept for nearly six years. If you claim a tax deduction for an expense, it will be necessary to have a receipt or other document proving that the expenditure has been made. Because the existence of the underlying records is so important to the operation of self-assessment, HMRC will treat them very seriously and there are penalties for a failure to keep adequate records.

Interest

Interest is chargeable on overdue tax at a variable rate, which is presently 3% per annum. It does not rank for any tax relief, which can make HMRC an expensive source of credit.

However, HMRC can also be obliged to pay interest (known as repayment supplement) tax-free where repayments are delayed. The rules relating to repayment supplement are less beneficial and even more complicated than the rules for interest payable but they do exist and can be very welcome if a large repayment has been delayed for a long time. Unfortunately, the rate of repayment supplement is only 0.5% and is always less than the rate charged by HMRC on overdue tax.

Value added tax

The activities of writers, painters, composers, etc are all 'taxable supplies' within the scope of VAT and chargeable at the standard rate. (Zero rating which applies to publishers, booksellers, etc on the supply of books does not extend to the work performed by writers.) Accordingly, authors are obliged to register for VAT if their income for the past 12 months exceeds £82,000 or if their income for the coming month will exceed that figure.

Delay in registering can be a most serious matter because if registration is not effected at the proper time, HMRC can (and invariably do) claim VAT from all the income received since the date on which registration should have been made. As no VAT would have been included in the amounts received during this period the amount claimed by HMRC must inevitably come straight from the pocket of the author.

The author may be entitled to seek reimbursement of the VAT from those whom he or she ought to have charged VAT but this is obviously a matter of some difficulty and may indeed damage his or her commercial relationships. Apart from these disadvantages there is also a penalty for late registration. The rules are extremely harsh and are imposed automatically even in cases of innocent error. It is therefore extremely important to monitor the income very carefully because if in any period of 12 months the income exceeds the £82,000 limit, the Customs and Excise must be notified within 30 days of the end of the period. Failure to do so will give rise to an automatic penalty. It should be emphasised that this is a penalty for failing to submit a form and has nothing to do with any real or potential loss of tax. Furthermore, whether the failure was innocent or deliberate will not matter. Only the existence of a 'reasonable excuse' will be a defence to the penalty. However, a reasonable excuse does not include ignorance, error, a lack of funds or reliance on any third party.

However, it is possible to regard VAT registration as a privilege and not a penalty, because only VAT registered persons can reclaim VAT paid on their expenses such as stationery, telephone, professional fees, etc and even computers and other plant and machinery (excluding cars). However, many find that the administrative inconvenience – the cost of maintaining the necessary records and completing the necessary forms – more than outweighs the benefits to be gained from registration and prefer to stay outside the scope of VAT for as long as possible.

Overseas matters

The general observation may be made that self-employed persons resident and domiciled in the UK are not well treated with regard to their overseas work, being taxable on their worldwide income. It is important to emphasise that if fees are earned abroad, no tax saving can be achieved merely by keeping the money outside the country. Although exchange control regulations no longer exist to require repatriation of foreign earnings, such income remains taxable in the UK and must be disclosed to HMRC; the same applies to interest or other income arising on any investment of these earnings overseas. Accordingly, whenever foreign earnings are likely to become substantial, prompt and effective action is required to limit the impact of UK and foreign taxation. In the case of non-resident authors it is important that arrangements concerning writing for publication in the UK, for example in newspapers, are undertaken with great care. A case concerning the wife of one of the great train robbers who provided detailed information for a series of articles published in a Sunday newspaper is most instructive. Although she was acknowledged to be resident in Canada for all the relevant years, the income from the articles was treated as arising in this country and fully chargeable to UK tax.

The UK has double taxation agreements with many other countries and these agreements are designed to ensure that income arising in a foreign country is taxed either in that country or in the UK. Where a withholding tax is deducted from payments received from another country (or where tax is paid in full in the absence of a double taxation agreement), the amount of foreign tax paid can usually be set off against the related UK tax liability.

Many successful authors can be found living in Eire because of the complete exemption from tax which attaches to works of cultural or artistic merit by persons who are resident there. However, such a step should only be contemplated having careful regard to all the other domestic and commercial considerations and specialist advice is essential if the exemption is to be obtained and kept; a careless breach of the conditions could cause the exemption to be withdrawn with catastrophic consequences. Consult the Revenue Commissioners in Dublin (www.revenue.ie) for further information concerning the precise conditions to be satisfied for exemption from tax in the Republic of Ireland.

Companies

When authors become successful the prospect of paying tax at high rates may drive them to take hasty action, such as the formation of a company, which may not always be to their advantage. Indeed some authors seeing the exodus into tax exile of their more successful colleagues even form companies in low tax areas in the hope of saving large amounts of tax. HMRC is fully aware of these possibilities and has extensive powers to charge tax and combat avoidance. Accordingly, such action is just as likely to increase tax liabilities and generate other costs and should never be contemplated without expert advice; some very expensive mistakes are often made in this area which are not always able to be remedied.

To conduct one's business through the medium of a company can be a very effective method of mitigating tax liabilities, and providing it is done at the right time and under the right circumstances very substantial advantages can be derived. However, if done without due care and attention the intended advantages will simply evaporate. At the very least it is essential to ensure that the company's business is genuine and conducted properly with regard to the realities of the situation. If the author continues his/her activities unchanged, simply paying all the receipts from his/her work into a company's bank account, he/she cannot expect to persuade HMRC that it is the company and not himself who is entitled to, and should be assessed to tax on, that income.

It must be strongly emphasised that many pitfalls exist which can easily eliminate all the tax benefits expected to arise by the formation of the company. For example, company directors are employees of the company and will be liable to pay much higher National Insurance contributions; the company must also pay the employer's proportion of the contribution and a total liability of nearly 26% of gross salary may arise. This compares most unfavourably with the position of a self-employed person. Moreover, on the commencement of the company's business the individual's profession will cease and the possibility of revisions being made by HMRC to earlier tax liabilities means that the timing of a change has to be considered very carefully.

The tax return

No mention has been made above of personal reliefs and allowances; this is because these allowances and the rates of tax are subject to constant change and are always set out in detail in the explanatory notes which accompany the tax return. The annual tax return is an important document and should be completed promptly with extreme care. If filling in the tax return is a source of difficulty or anxiety, *Money Which? – Tax Saving Guide* (Consumer Association, annual, March) is very helpful.

Peter Vaines FCA, CTA, barrister, is a partner in the international law firm of Squire Patton Boggs (UK) LLP and writes and speaks widely on tax matters. He is on the Editorial Board of *Personal Tax Planning Review*, tax columnist of the *New Law Journal* and author of a number of books on taxation.

See also...

- *FAQs for writers*, page 707
- *National Insurance contributions and social security benefits*, page 719

National Insurance contributions and social security benefits

Most people who work in Great Britain either as an employee or as a self-employed person are liable to pay National Insurance contributions. The law governing this subject is complex and Peter Arrowsmith FCA (with updates by Sarah Bradford) has summarised it here for the benefit of writers and artists. This article also contains an outline of the benefits system and should be regarded as a general guide only.

All contributions are payable in respect of years ending on 5 April. See box (below) for the classes of contributions.

Employed or self-employed?

Employed earners pay Class 1 contributions and self-employed earners pay Class 2 and Class 4 contributions. It is therefore essential to know the status of a worker to ensure that the correct class of contribution is paid. The question as to whether a person is employed under a contract *of* service and is thereby an employee liable to Class 1 contributions, or performs services (either solely or in partnership) under a contract *for* service and is thereby self-employed and liable to Class 2 and Class 4 contributions, often has to be decided in practice. One of the best guides can be found in the case of *Market Investigations Ltd* v. *Minister of Social Security* (1969 2 WLR 1) when Cooke J. remarked:

Classes of contributions

Class 1 Payable by employees (primary contributions) and their employers (secondary contributions), based on earnings.

Class 1A Payable only by employers in respect of all taxable benefits in kind.

Class 1B Payable only by employers in respect of PAYE Settlement Agreements entered into by them.

Class 2 Weekly flat rate contributions payable by the self-employed.

Class 3 Weekly flat rate contributions, payable on a voluntary basis in order to provide, or make up entitlement to, certain social security benefits.

Class 3A Voluntary contributions payable from 12 October 2015 by those reaching state pension age before 6 April 2016. Amount depends on age.

Class 4 Payable by the self-employed in respect of their trading or professional income, based on earnings.

'…the fundamental test to be applied is this: "Is the person who has engaged himself to perform these services performing them as a person in business on his own account?" If the answer to that question is "yes", then the contract is a contract for services. If the answer is "no", then the contract is a contract of service. No exhaustive list has been compiled and perhaps no exhaustive list can be compiled of the considerations which are relevant in determining that question, nor can strict rules be laid down as to the relative weight which the various considerations should carry in particular cases. The most that can be said is that control will no doubt always have to be considered, although it can no longer be regarded as the sole determining factor; and that factors which may be of importance are such matters as:

- whether the man performing the services provides his own equipment,
- whether he hires his own helpers,
- what degree of financial risk he takes,
- what degree of responsibility for investment and management he has, and

• whether and how far he has an opportunity of profiting from sound management in the performance of his task.'

The above case has often been considered subsequently in Tribunal cases, but there are many factors to take into account. An indication of employment status can be obtained on the GOV.UK website (www.gov.uk/employment-status).

Exceptions

There are exceptions to the above rules, those most relevant to artists and writers being:

• The employment of a wife by her husband, or vice versa, is disregarded for National Insurance purposes unless it is for the purposes of a trade or profession (e.g. the employment of his wife by an author would not be disregarded and would result in a liability for contributions if her salary reached the minimum levels). The same provisions also apply to civil partners from 5 December 2005.

• The employment of certain relatives in a private dwelling house in which both employee and employer reside is disregarded for social security purposes provided the employment is not for the purposes of a trade or business carried out at those premises by the employer. This would cover the employment of a relative (as defined) as a housekeeper in a private residence.

Personal service companies

Since 6 April 2000, those who have control of their own 'one-man service companies' are subject to special rules (commonly referred to as IR35). If the work carried out by the owner of the company for the company's customers would be – but for the one-man company – considered as an employment of that individual (i.e. rather than self-employment), a deemed salary may arise. If it does, then some or all of the company's income will be treated as salary liable to PAYE and National Insurance contributions (NICs). This will be the case whether or not such salary is actually paid by the company. The same situation may arise where the worker owns as little as 5% of a company's share capital.

The calculations required by HMRC are complicated and have to be done very quickly at the end of each tax year (even if the company's year-end does not coincide). It is essential that affected businesses seek detailed professional advice about these rules which may also, in certain circumstances, apply to partnerships.

The rules have attracted much criticism. In April 2014 the House of Lords Select Committee published the findings of their review into the personal service company rules and made a number of recommendations. Although various changes were made to the rules, the Government is committed to retaining IR35.

In order to escape the application of the IR35 rules, a number of workers have arranged their engagements through 'managed service companies', etc where the promoter is heavily involved in all the company management to the exclusion of the workers themselves. Such companies are now subject to similar, but different, rules, which apply from 6 April 2007 for tax and 6 August 2007 for NICs.

For further information, see www.gov.uk/business-tax/ir35.

State pension age

Workers, both employed and self-employed, stop paying NICs once they reach state pension age. However, employers must continue to pay secondary Class 1 contributions in respect of earnings paid to employees who have reached state pension age.

The current state pension age for men is 65. The state pension age for women is gradually being increased so as to equalise it with that for men. The state pension age for women is being increased gradually from 6 April 2010 and will reach age 65 on 6 November 2018. From that date, the state pension age for both men and women will rise to 66 to achieve a state pension age of 66 on 6 September 2020. The state pension age will be further increased from 66 to 67 between 2026 and 2028 and will rise from 67 to 68 between 2044 and 2046. Provisions included in the Pensions Act 2014 provide for the state pension age to be reviewed every 5 years.

In 2015/16 women will reach state pension age on the following dates depending on their date of birth. Men will reach state pension age at age 65.

Date of birth	Date state pension age reached
6 October 1952 to 5 November 1952	6 May 2015
6 November 1952 to 5 December 1952	6 July 2015
6 December 1952 to 5 January 1953	6 September 2015
6 January 1953 to 5 February 1953	6 November 2015
6 February 1953 to 5 March 1953	6 January 2016
6 March 1953 to 5 April 1953	6 March 2016

Class 1 contributions

Primary Class 1 contributions are payable by employed earners and secondary Class 1 contributions are payable by self-employed workers by reference to their earnings. Where an employee contracts out of the second state pension (S2P), a rebate is payable in respect of both employee and employer contributions, which effectively reduces the contributions rate on earnings within a certain band. Since 6 April 2012, it is only possible to contract-out by means of a defined benefit (salary-related) scheme. Contracting out for money purchase schemes (COMPS) came to an end on 5 April 2012. Contracting out for salary-related schemes will come to an end on 5 April 2016 consequent on the introduction of the single-tier state pension payable to those who reach state pension age on or after that date.

Contributions are payable by employees on earnings that exceed the primary threshold (£155 per week for 2015/16) and by employers on earnings that exceed the secondary threshold (£156 per week for 2015/16). However, where the employee is under the age of 21, employer contributions are only payable on earnings that exceed the upper secondary threshold for under 21s. For 2015/16 this is set at £815 per week (the same as the upper earnings limit). Contributions are normally collected via the PAYE tax deduction machinery, and there are penalties for late submission of returns and for errors therein and also for PAYE and NICs paid late on more than one occasion in the tax year. Interest is charged automatically on PAYE and social security contributions paid late.

Employees' liability to pay

Contributions are payable by any employee who is aged 16 years and over (even though they may still be at school) and who is paid an amount equal to, or exceeding, the primary earnings threshold (£155 per week for 2015/16). Where the employee has earnings between the lower earnings limit and the primary threshold, contributions are payable at a notional zero rate. This preserves the employee's contributions record and entitlement to the state pension and contributory benefits. Nationality is irrelevant for contribution purposes and, subject to special rules covering employees not normally resident in Great Britain, Northern Ireland or the Isle of Man, or resident in EEA countries or those with which there are reciprocal agreements, contributions must be paid whether the employee concerned is a British subject or not provided he/she is gainfully employed in Great Britain.

Persons over state pension age are exempt from liability to pay primary contributions, even if they have not retired. However, the fact that an employee may be exempt from liability does not relieve an employer from liability to pay secondary contributions in respect of that employee.

Employees' (primary) contributions

From 6 April 2015, the rate of employees' contributions on earnings from the employee earnings threshold (£155 per week) to the upper earnings limit (£815 per week) is 12%. Contributions are payable at a rate of 2% on earnings above the upper earnings limit. A rebate of 1.4% is payable to contracted-out employees on earnings between the lower earnings limit and the upper accruals point (£770 per week) (meaning that the effective rate between the primary earnings threshold and upper accruals point is 10.6% rather than 12%). Certain married women who made appropriate elections before 12 May 1977 may be entitled to pay a reduced rate of 5.85%. However, they have no entitlement to benefits in respect of these contributions.

Employers' (secondary) contributions

All employers are liable to pay contributions on the gross earnings of employees above the age of 16 where their earnings exceed the secondary earnings threshold (£156 per week for 2015/16). However, from 6 April 2015 where the employee is under 21, employer contributions are only payable on earnings in excess of the upper secondary threshold for under 21s (£815 per week for 2015/16). As mentioned above, an employer's liability is not reduced as a result of employees being exempted from contributions, or being liable to pay only the reduced rate (5.85%) of contributions.

For earnings paid on or after 6 April 2015, employers are liable at a rate of 13.8% on earnings paid above the secondary earnings threshold (or, where the employee is under 21). Where the employee is in a contracted-out employment, the employer receives a rebate of 3.4% on earnings between the lower earnings limit and the upper accruals point. Most employers are entitled to an annual employment allowance of £2,000, which is offset against their secondary Class 1 liability. The allowance is claimed through the employer's real time information (RTI) software.

The employer is responsible for the payment of both employees' and employer's contributions, but is entitled to deduct the employees' contributions from the earnings on which they are calculated. Effectively, therefore, the employee suffers a deduction in respect of his or her social security contributions in arriving at his weekly or monthly wage or salary. Special rules apply to company directors and persons employed through agencies.

Items included in, or excluded from, earnings

Contributions are calculated on the basis of a person's gross earnings from their employment. This will normally be the figure shown on the deduction working sheet or computer equivalent record, except where the employee pays superannuation contributions and, from 6 April 1987, charitable gifts under payroll giving – these must be added back for the purposes of calculating Class 1 liability.

Earnings include salary, wages, overtime pay, commissions, bonuses, holiday pay, payments made while the employee is sick or absent from work, payments to cover travel between home and office, and payments under the statutory sick pay, statutory maternity pay, statutory paternity pay and statutory adoption pay schemes.

However, certain payments, some of which may be regarded as taxable income for income tax purposes, are ignored for Class 1 purposes. These include:

- certain gratuities paid other than by the employer;
- redundancy payments and some payments in lieu of notice;
- certain payments in kind;
- reimbursement of specific expenses incurred in the carrying out of the employment;
- benefits given on an individual basis for personal reasons (e.g. birthday presents);
- compensation for loss of office.

Booklet CWG 2 (2015 edition) gives a list of items to include in or exclude from earnings for Class 1 contribution purposes (available from www.gov.uk). Some such items may, however, be liable to Class 1A (employer-only) contributions.

Class 1A and Class 1B contributions

Class 1A contributions are employer-only contributions payable in respect of most taxable benefits provided to employees earning at a rate of at least £8,500 a year and to directors, as reported on form P11D. Class 1A contributions are payable at a rate of 13.8%.

Class 1B contributions are payable by employers using PAYE Settlement Agreements in respect of small and/or irregular expense payments and benefits, etc. This rate is also 13.8%.

Upper accrual point

The upper accrual point (UAP) was introduced from 6 April 2009 and is the rate from which entitlement to benefit (principally earnings-related state pension) ceases, even though main rate Class 1 contributions continue to be due. This impacts on contracted-out employees in particular. The UAP is fixed at a constant cash amount of £770 per week, the original intention being that it would gradually erode the earnings related element of

Rates of Class 1 contributions and earnings limits from 6 April 2015

Earnings per week	*Rates payable on earnings in each band*			
	Not contracted out		*Contracted out*	
	Employee	*Employer*	*Employee*	*Employer*
£	*%*	*%*	*%*	*%*
Below 112.00	–	–	–	–
112.00–154.99	0**	–	-1.4%*	-3.4%*
155.00–155.99	12	–	10.6	-3.4%*
156.00–769.99	12	13.8***	10.6	10.4***
770.00–810.00	12	13.8***	12	13.8***
Over 810.00	2	13.8	2	13.8

* Special rebates deductible in respect of this band of earnings (contracted-out salary-related schemes only).

** Contributions payable at a notional zero rate.

*** No employer contributions where employee is under 21.

Finance for writers and artists

the state pension. However, the current two-tier state pension is being replaced by a single-tier state pension for those who reach state pension age on or after 6 April 2016. Contracting out will come to an end as a result.

Class 2 contributions

Class 2 contributions are payable at the weekly rate of £2.80 as from 6 April 2015. Certain persons are exempt from Class 2 liability as follows:

- A person over state pension age.
- A person who has not attained the age of 16.
- A married woman or, in certain cases, a widow, either of whom elected prior to 12 May 1977 not to pay Class 2 contributions.
- Persons with small earnings (see below).
- Persons not ordinarily self-employed (see below).

Small profits threshold

From 6 April 2015 no liability to Class 2 contributions arises unless earnings from self-employment exceed the small profits threshold, which is set at £5,965 for 2015/16. The small profits threshold replaced the small earnings exception which applied for 2014/15 and earlier years.

- for the year of application are expected to be less than a specified limit (£5,885 in the 2014/15 tax year); or
- for the year preceding the application were less than the limit specified for that year (£5,725 for 2013/14) and there has been no material change of circumstances.

Certificates of exception must be renewed in accordance with the instructions stated thereon. At the discretion of HMRC, the certificate may commence up to 13 weeks before the date on which the application is made. Despite a certificate of exception being in force, a person who is self-employed is still entitled to pay Class 2 contributions if they wish, in order to maintain entitlement to social security benefits.

Persons not ordinarily self-employed

Part-time self-employed activities (including as a writer or artist) are disregarded for contribution purposes if the person concerned is not ordinarily employed in such activities and has a full-time job as an employee. There is no definition of 'ordinarily employed' for this purpose. Persons qualifying for this relief do not require certificates of exception but are well advised to apply for one nonetheless.

Payment of contributions

For 2015/16 onwards, Class 2 contributions are payable via the self-assessment system with income tax and Class 4 contributions. Class 2 contributions for 2015/16 are due by 31 January 2017.

Class 3 and Class 3A contributions

Class 3 contributions are payable voluntarily, at the weekly rate of £14.40 per week from 6 April 2015, by persons aged 16 or over with a view to enabling them to qualify for a limited range of benefits if their contribution record is not otherwise sufficient. In general, Class 3 contributions can be paid by employees, the self-employed and the non-employed.

Broadly speaking, no more than 52 Class 3 contributions are payable for any one tax year, and contributions cannot be paid in respect of tax years after the one in which the individual concerned reaches state pension age. Class 3 contributions may be paid by monthly direct debit, quarterly bill or by annual cheque in arrears.

A new class of voluntary contribution, Class 3A, is to be introduced from October 2015 to provide those who reach state pension age before 6 April 2016 with an opportunity to top up their state pension. The amount of the Class 3A contribution will depend on the contributor's age.

Class 4 contributions

In addition to Class 2 contributions, self-employed persons are liable to pay Class 4 contributions. These are calculated at the rate of 9% on the amount of profits or gains chargeable to income tax which exceed the lower profits limit (£8,060 per annum for 2015/16) but which do not exceed the upper profits limit (£42,385 per annum for 2015/16). Profits above the upper limit of £42,385 (2015/16) attract a Class 4 charge at the rate of 2%. The income tax profit on which Class 4 contributions are calculated is after deducting capital allowances and losses, but before deducting personal tax allowances or retirement annuity or personal pension or stakeholder pension plan premiums.

Class 4 contributions produce no additional benefits, but were introduced to ensure that self-employed persons as a whole pay a fair share of the cost of pensions and other social security benefits, yet without those who make only small profits having to pay excessively high flat rate contributions.

Payment of contributions

In general, Class 4 contributions are self-assessed and paid to HMRC together with the income tax as a result of the self-assessment income tax return, and accordingly the contributions are due and payable at the same time as the income tax liability on the relevant profits. Under self-assessment, payments on account of Class 4 contributions are payable at the same time as interim payments of tax.

Class 4 exemptions

The following persons are exempt from Class 4 contributions:

- Persons over state pension age at the commencement of the year of assessment (i.e. on 6 April).
- An individual not resident in the UK for income tax purposes in the year of assessment.
- Persons whose earnings are not 'immediately derived' from carrying on a trade, profession or vocation.
- A person under 16 years old on 6 April of the year of assessment.
- Persons not ordinarily self-employed.

Married persons and partnerships

Under independent taxation, each spouse is responsible for his or her own Class 4 liability.

In partnerships, each partner's liability is calculated separately. If a partner also carries on another trade or profession, the profits of all such businesses are aggregated for the purposes of calculating their Class 4 liability.

When an assessment has become final and conclusive for the purposes of income tax, it is also final and conclusive for the purposes of calculating Class 4 liability.

Maximum contributions

There is a form of limit to the total liability for social security contributions payable by a person who is employed in more than one employment, or is also self-employed or a partner. Where a person would otherwise pay more than the permitted maximum it may be possible to defer some contributions. The calculations are complex and guidance on the permitted maximum and deferment can be found on the GOV.UK website (see www.gov.uk/defer-self-employed-national-insurance).

Social security benefits

Benefits may be contributory (i.e. dependent upon set levels of social security contributions and/or NIC-able earnings arising in all or part of one or more tax years) or means-tested (i.e. subject to a full assessment of the income and capital of the claimant and their partner). Child benefit is one of a handful falling outside either category being neither contributory nor means-tested, although the high income child benefit tax charge claws back child benefit where anyone in the household has taxable income over £50,000 per annum. The benefit is clawed back at a rate of 1% for each £100 of income over £50,000 such that the tax is equal to the child benefit received where income is £60,000 or above.

Most benefits are administered by the Department for Work and Pensions and its agencies (such as Jobcentre Plus and The Pension Service). Some are administered wholly or partly by HMRC and the latter are marked with an asterisk in the following lists.

Universal Credit is replacing a number of benefits and is in the process of being phased in.

Universal benefits

- Child Benefit*
- Carer's Allowance (for those looking after a severely disabled person)
- Disability Living Allowance (DLA) – progressively being replaced by Personal Independence Payment (PIP) during 2013
- Personal Independence Payment (PIP) (help with some of the extra costs caused by long-term ill-health or disability for those aged 16–64)

Contributory benefits

- State Pension – basic and earnings-related
- Bereavement benefits
- Contribution-based Jobseeker's Allowance (JSA) (time limited, i.e. unemployment)
- Contribution-based Employment and Support Allowance (ESA) (time limited for some, i.e. sickness and incapacity)
- Statutory Sick Pay* (SSP) (for employees only, paid by the employer)
- Statutory Maternity Pay* (SMP) (for employees only, paid by the employer)
- Maternity Allowance (for self-employed and others meeting the conditions)
- Statutory Paternity Pay* (SPP) (for employees only, paid by the employer)

Further information

GOV.UK
website www.gov.uk/national-insurance
For guidance on National Insurance.

DWP benefits
website www.gov.uk/government/organisations/department-for-work-pensions

Tax Credits
website www.gov.uk/benefits-credits/tax-credits

Child benefit
website www.gov.uk/browse/benefits/child

Statutory payments
For SSP, SMP, SPP and SAP contact your employer in the first instance.

National Insurance Contributions & Employer Office, International Caseworker
Newcastle upon Tyne NE98 1ZZ
tel 0300 200 3506
For enquiries for individuals resident abroad.

- Shared Parental Pay* (ShPP) (for employees only, paid by the employer)
- Statutory Adoption Pay* (SAP) (for employees only, paid by the employer)
- Guardian's Allowance*

Means-tested benefits

- Income-based Jobseeker's Allowance (JSA) (i.e. unemployment)
- Income-based Employment and Support Allowance (ESA) (i.e. sickness and incapacity)
- Income Support (low-income top up for those of working age, not working but neither unemployed nor sick/incapacitated)
- Working Tax Credits* (WTC) (low-income top up for those of working age)
- Child Tax Credit* (low-income top up for those of working age with children, in addition to Working Tax Credit if applicable)
- Disabled Person's Tax Credits* (DPTC) (low-income top up for disabled people)
- Pension Credit (low-income top up for those of pension age)
- Social Fund grants (one-off assistance for low-income household with unexpected, emergency expenditure)

In addition, help with rent and rates is available on a means-tested basis from local authorities.

Many of the working age benefits are in the process of being replaced with 'Universal Credit', starting with new claimants. Universal Credit will eventually replace Income-based Jobseeker's Allowance, Income-related Employment and Support Allowance, Income Support, Working Tax Credit, Child Tax Credit and Housing Benefit.

Peter Arrowsmith FCA is a sole practitioner specialising in National Insurance matters. He is a member and former chairman of the Employment Taxes and National Insurance Committee of the Institute of Chartered Accountants in England and Wales. **Sarah Bradford** BA (Hons), ACA CTA (Fellow) is the director of Writetax Ltd and the author of *National Insurance Contributions 2015/16* (and earlier editions) published by Bloomsbury Professional. She writes widely on tax and National Insurance contributions and provides tax consultancy services.

Subject indexes
Magazines by subject area

These lists provide a broad classification and pointer to possible markets. Listings for magazines start on page 35.

Fiction

Food and drink

Puzzles and quizzes

The following take puzzles and/or quizzes on an occasional or, in some cases, regular basis. Ideas must be tailored to suit each publication: approach in writing in the first instance.

Magazines aimed at women

Magazines aimed at men

Subject articles

Advertising, design, printing and publishing

Agriculture, farming and horticulture

Architecture and building

Art and collecting

Aviation

Business, industry and management

Cinema and films

Computers

Economics, accountancy and finance

Education

Engineering and mechanics

Gardening

Health and home

History and archaeology

Hotel, catering and leisure

Humour and satire

Legal and police

Leisure interests, pets

Literary (see also Poetry)

Local government and civil service

Marketing and retailing

Medicine and nursing

Military

Motor transport and cycling

Music and recording

Natural history

Nautical and marine

Photography

Poetry

Some magazines only take the occasional poem. Check with the Editor before submitting.

Politics

Radio, TV and DVD

Religion, philosophy and New Age

Rural life and country

Sciences

Sports and games

Theatre, drama and dancing (see also Cinema and films, Music and recording)

Travel and geography

Publishers of fiction (UK)

Contact details for *Book publishers UK and Ireland* start on page 148.

Adventure/thrillers

Comedy/humour

Crime/detective/mystery

Erotica

Ethnic

Gay/lesbian

General

Graphic/cartoons

Historical

Horror

Literary

New/experimental

Romantic/chick-lit/women's

Sci-fi/fantasy

Short stories

Teen/YA

Translation/international

War

Westerns

Publishers of non-fiction (UK)

Contact details for *Book publishers UK and Ireland* start on page 148.

Academic and professional

Agriculture, farming and horticulture

Animals and birds

Archaeology

Architecture and building

Art and craft

Astronomy

Aviation

Bibliography

Biography, autobiography and memoir

Business, industry and management

Cartography/maps

Comedy, humour

Computers and computing

Cookery, food and drink

Crime

Cultural studies

Current affairs

Design

Economics, accountancy and finance

Education

Engineering and mechanics

Environment and development

Fashion

Film and cinema

Fine art and antiques

Gardening

Gender studies and gay and lesbian

General non-fiction

Health

Heritage

History

Hotel, catering and leisure

Illustrated books

International issues

Irish interest

Languages and ELT

Law

Leisure interests and hobbies

Lifestyle, home and DIY

Literary criticism and essays

Subject indexes

Local government and civil service

Local interest

Medicine and nursing

Military

Mind, body & spirit (MBS)

Music

Natural history

Nautical and marine

Novelty, gift books

Parenting, relationships and self-help

Performing arts

Photography

Politics

Popular culture

Popular reference

Puzzles and crosswords

Reference

Religion, philosophy and New Age

Rural life and country

Science

Scottish interest

Social sciences

Sports and games

The media

Transport, including cycling

Travel and geography

TV, TV tie-ins and radio

Welsh interest

Writers' guides

Children's book publishers and packagers (UK)

Listings for *Book publishers UK and Ireland* start on page 148 and listings for *Book packagers* start on page 236.

Children's fiction

Book publishers

Book packagers

Children's non-fiction

Book publishers

Book packagers

Picture books

Book publishers

Book packagers

Other

Activity and novelty

Book publishers

Book packagers

Audiobooks

Book publishers

Book packagers

Multimedia

Book publishers

Book packagers

Poetry

Book publishers

Book packagers

Religion

Book publishers

Book packagers

Publishers of plays (UK)

Playwrights are reminded that it is unusual for a publisher of trade editions of plays to publish plays which have not had at least reasonably successful, usually professional, productions on stage first. See listings beginning on page 148 for contact details.

Publishers of poetry (UK)

Addresses for *Book publishers UK and Ireland* start on page 148.

Literary agents for children's books

The following literary agents will consider work suitable for children's books, from both authors and illustrators. Listings start on page 411. See also *Art agents and commercial art studios* on page 472.

Literary agents for television, film, radio and theatre

Listings for these and other literary agents start on page 411.

Newspapers and magazines that accept cartoons

Listed below are newspapers and magazines which take cartoons – either occasionally, or on a regular basis. Approach in writing in the first instance (for contacts see listings starting on page 16 for newspapers and page 35 for magazines) to ascertain the Editor's requirements.

Consumer and special interest magazines

Business and professional magazines

Prizes and awards by subject area

This index gives the major subject area(s) only of each entry in the main listing which begins on page 534.

Biography

Children

Drama – theatre, TV and radio

Essays

Fiction

Grants, bursaries and fellowships

Illustration

Journalism

Non-fiction

Photography

Poetry

Short stories

Translation

Specialist

General index

Key topics and terms that appear in the articles within this *Yearbook* are listed here.

Listings index

All companies, public and commercial organisations, societies, festivals and prize-giving bodies that have a listing in the *Yearbook* are included in this index.